D0087036

IMPORTANT

HERE IS YOUR REGISTRATION CODE TO ACCESS MCGRAW-HILL
PREMIUM CONTENT AND MCGRAW-HILL ONLINE RESOURCES

For key premium online resources you need THIS CODE to
gain access. Once the code is entered, you will be able to
use the web resources for the length of your course.

Access is provided only if you have purchased a new book.

If the registration code is missing from this book, the registration screen on our
website, and within your WebCT or Blackboard course will tell you how to obtain
your new code. Your registration code can be used only once to establish access.
It is not transferable.

To gain access to these online resources

1. USE your web browser to go to: **www.mhhe.com/kiefer9e**

2. CLICK on "First Time User"

3. ENTER the Registration Code printed on the tear-off bookmark on the right

4. After you have entered your registration code, click on "Register"

5. FOLLOW the instructions to setup your personal UserID and Password

6. WRITE your UserID and Password down for future reference. Keep it in a safe place.

If your course is using WebCT or Blackboard, you'll be able to use this code to
access the McGraw-Hill content within your instructor's online course.

To gain access to the McGraw-Hill content in your instructor's WebCT or
Blackboard course simply log into the course with the user ID and Password provided by your instructor. Enter the registration code exactly as it appears to the
right when prompted by the system. You will only need to use this code the first
time you click on McGraw-Hill content.

These instructions are specifically for student access. Instructors are not required
to register via the above instructions.

REGISTRATION CODE
REGISTRATION CODE

The McGraw-Hill Companies

Mc Graw Hill Higher Education

Thank you, and welcome to your
McGraw-Hill Online Resources.

ISBN 13: 978-0-07-325350-3
ISBN 10: 0-07-325350-2 t/a
Kiefer: Charlotte Huck's
Children's Literature, 9/e

The McGraw-Hill Companies

Mc Graw Hill Higher Education

Higher Education

This book is printed on acid-free paper.

3 4 5 6 7 8 9 0 WCK/WCK 0 9 8

ISBN: 978-0-07-312298-4
MHID: 0-07-312298-X

Vice President and Editor-in-Chief: Emily Barrosse
Publisher: Beth Mejia
Executive Editor: David Patterson
Freelance Developmental Editor: Vicki Malinee, Van Brien & Associates
Marketing Manager: Melissa Caughlin
Media Producer: Jocelyn Arsht
Media Project Manager: Stacy Dorgan
Production Editor: Leslie LaDow
Manuscript Editor: Beverley DeWitt

Cover Designer: Preston Thomas
Interior Designer: Amanda Kavanagh & Preston Thomas
Photo Research Coordinator: Alexandra Ambrose
Photo Researcher: Christine Pullo
Art Editor: Ayelet Arbel
Print Supplement Producer: Louis Swaim
Production Supervisor: Tandra Jorgensen
Composition: 9.5/12 Palatino by Thompson Type
Printing: 45# Pub Matte by Quebecor World, Inc.

Text Credits: Chapter 1, p. 10: From *Millions of Cats* by Wanda Gág, copyright ©1928 by Wanda Gág, renewed © 1956 by Robert Janssen. Used by permission of Coward-McCann, an Imprint of Penguin Young Readers Group, a member of Penguin Group (USA), Inc. All rights reserved; **Chapter 1, p. 16:** From *Out of the Dust* by Karen Hesse. Copyright © 1997 by Karen Hesse. Reprinted by permission of Scholastic, Inc; **Chapter 4, p. 151:** Charlotte Pomerantz. *The Piggy in the Puddle and Here Comes Henny* by Charlotte Pomerantz, illustrated by Nancy Winslow. Text copyright ©1994 by Charlotte Pomerantz. Used by permission of HarperCollins Publishers; **Chapter 8, p. 359:** Poetry originally appeared in *Sing For Your Supper*. Copyright ©1938 by Eleanor Farjeon; renewed 1966 by Gervase Farjeon. Reprinted by permission of Harold Ober Associates, Inc.

Library of Congress Cataloging-in-Publication Data

Charlotte Huck's children's literature in the elementary school / Barbara Z. Kiefer ... [et al.].–9th ed. / revised by
    Barbara Z. Kiefer.
      p. cm.
      Rev. ed. of: Children's literature in the elementary school, © 2004.
      Includes bibliographical references and indexes.
      ISBN: 978-0-07-312298-4 (alk. paper)
      MHID: 0-07-312298-X (alk. paper)
      1. Literature—Study and teaching (Elementary)—United States. 2. Children's
literature—Study and teaching (Higher)—United States. 3. Literature teachers—Training
of—United States. I. Huck, Charlotte S. II. Kiefer, Barbara Zulandt, 1944– III. Children's
literature in the elementary school.

LB1575.5.U5H79 2006
372.64–dc22

2005044801

www.mhhe.com

Charlotte Huck's

Children's Literature

Ninth Edition

Barbara Z. Kiefer
The Ohio State University

with

Susan Hepler
Children's Literature Specialist
Alexandria, Virginia

Janet Hickman
The Ohio State University

Boston   Burr Ridge, IL   Dubuque, IA   Madison, WI   New York
San Francisco   St. Louis   Bangkok   Bogotá   Caracas   Kuala Lumpur
Lisbon   London   Madrid   Mexico City   Milan   Montreal   New Delhi
Santiago   Seoul   Singapore   Sydney   Taipei   Toronto

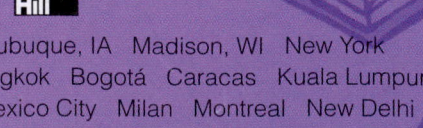

Rose, Deborah Lee. *Ocean Babies*. National Geographic, 2005.

Rosen, Michael. *We're Going on a Bear Hunt*. Illustrated by Helen Oxenbury. Macmillan, 1989.

Shannon, David. *No, David!* Scholastic, 1998.

Taback, Simms. *Joseph Had a Little Overcoat*. Viking, 1999.

Takabayashi, Mari. *I Live in Tokyo*. Houghton, 2001.

Waddell, Martin. *Snow Bears*. Illustrated by Sarah Fox-Davies. Candlewick, 2002.

Wells, Rosemary. *Edward Unready for School*. Dial, 1995.

Wood, Audrey. *The Napping House*. Illustrated by Don Wood. Harcourt, 1984.

Yolen, Jane. *How Do Dinosaurs Get Well Soon?* Illustrated by Mark Teague. Scholastic, 2003.

Zimmerman, Andrea. *Trashy Town*. Illustrated by Dan Yaccarino. HarperCollins, 1999.

Grades K–2

Aardema, Verna. *Borreguita and the Coyote*. Illustrated by Petra Mathers. Knopf, 1991.

Bang, Molly. *When Sophie Gets Angry—Really, Really Angry. . . .* Scholastic, 1999.

Chen, Chih-Yuan. *Guji Guji*. Kane/Miller, 2004.

Cooney, Barbara. *Miss Rumphius*. Viking, 1982.

Cronin, Doreen. *Diary of a Spider*. Illustrated by Harry Bliss. HarperCollins, 2005.

Curlee, Lunn. *Capital*. Atheneum, 2003.

Daly, Niki. *Jamela's Dress*. Farrar, 1999.

DePaola, Tomie. *Strega Nona*. Prentice-Hall, 1975.

Diakité, Baba Wagué. *The Hatseller and the Monkeys: A West African Folktale*. Scholastic, 1999.

Eriksson, Eva. *A Crash Course for Molly*. Translated by Elisabeth Kallick Dyssegaard. Farrar, 2005.

Gibbons, Gail. *Chickens!* Holiday, 2003.

Grey, Mini. *Traction Man Is Here!* Knopf, 2005.

Henkes, Kevin. *Lilly's Big Day*. Greenwillow, 2006.

Hesse, Karen. *Come On, Rain!* Illustrated by Jon J. Muth. Scholastic, 1999.

Hubbard, Crystal. *Catching the Moon*. Illustrated by Randy DeBurke. Lee, 2005.

Huck, Charlotte. *Princess Furball*. Illustrated by Anita Lobel. Greenwillow, 1989.

Hutchins, Pat. *There's Only One of Me*. Greenwillow, 2003.

Hyman, Trina Schart. *Little Red Riding Hood*. Holiday, 1983.

Johnson, D. B. *Henry Builds a Cabin*. Houghton, 2002.

Keller, Holly. *Sophie's Window*. Greenwillow, 2005.

Lillegard, Dee. *Wake Up House: Rooms Full of Poems*. Illustrated by Don Carter. Knopf, 2000.

Lobel, Arnold. *Frog and Toad Are Friends*. Harper, 1970.

McKissack, Patricia, and Onawumi Jena Moss. *Precious and the Boo Hag*. Illustrated by Krysten Brooker. Atheneum, 2005.

McNulty, Faith. *If You Decide to Go to the Moon*. Illustrated by Steven Kellogg. Scholastic, 2005.

Mora, Pat. *Doña Flor: A Tall Tale about a Woman with a Big Heart*. Illustrated by Raul Colón. Knopf, 2005.

Muth, Jon J. *Stone Soup*. Scholastic, 2003.

Ormerod, Jan . *When an Elephant Goes to School*. Orchard, 2005.

Park, Linda Sue. *Bee-bim Bop!* Illustrated by Ho Baek Lee. Clarion, 2005.

Pomerantz, Charlotte. *Here Comes Henny*. Illustrated by Nancy Winslow Parker. Greenwillow, 1994.

Prelutsky, Jack, ed. *The Random House Book of Poetry for Children*. Illustrated by Arnold Lobel. Random, 1983.

Rosen, Michael. *Michael Rosen's Sad Book*. Candlewick, 2005.

Rosoff, Meg. *Meet Wild Boars*. Illustrated by Sophie Blackall. Holt, 2005.

Sendak, Maurice. *Where the Wild Things Are*. Harper, 1963.

Silverman, Erica. *Don't Fidget a Feather*. Illustrated by S. D. Schindler. Macmillan, 1994.

Steig, William. *Doctor De Soto*. Farrar, 1982.

Steptoe, John. *Mufaro's Beautiful Daughter: An African Tale*. Lothrop, 1987.

Stevens, Janet. *Tops and Bottoms*. Harcourt, 1995.

Williams, Sue. *Dinnertime!* Illustrated by Kerry Argent. Harcourt, 2002.

Williams, Vera. *A Chair for My Mother*. Greenwillow, 1982.

Yolen, Jane. *Owl Moon*. Illustrated by John Schoenherr. Philomel, 1987.

To all those students and teachers whom we have taught and from whom we have learned . . .

Brief Contents

Contents

Chapter 3

The Changing World of Children's Books and the Development of Multicultural Literature   70

PART TWO Exploring Children's Literature

Chapter 4

Books to Begin On 140

Chapter 5

Picture Books 198

Chapter 6

Traditional Literature   274

Chapter 7

Modern Fantasy   348

Chapter 8

Poetry   408

Chapter 9

Contemporary Realistic Fiction   468

Chapter 10

Historical Fiction   540

Chapter 11

Nonfiction Books   586

PART THREE Developing a Literature Program

Features Guide

Wonderfully Exciting Books

Into the Classroom

Profiles in Literature

Talking Points

Literature in Action

In 1978 I had returned to college to obtain a master's degree in Reading. A course in children's literature was required, and my instructor had ordered Charlotte Huck's *Children's Literature in the Elementary School,* the third edition, as the course text. It had a silver cover, black and white photographs, and was 781 pages long. That book opened up a new world to me. I had always been an enthusiastic reader and teacher who loved reading to my first, fourth, and fifth graders, but I had no idea of the thousands of wonderful books that were written for children. Nor had I known how to choose the right book for the right child, nor how to develop a reading program that placed real books in the center.

When I completed my degree and received my certification as a reading specialist, I returned to the classroom and a wonderful group of second graders. The silver edition of Charlotte's book became my "bible," as I struggled to implement a book-centered program in the face of my school's required mastery learning curriculum, an approach called ECRI (similar to the DISTAR program). Concerned with the rigidity of this approach, I began looking for a doctoral program that would provide a child-centered alternative and that would value my love of books and my background in art. Knowing that Charlotte Huck would be speaking at a regional IRA conference, I wrote to her and asked if she could spare a few minutes to speak with me about Ohio State's doctoral program. She not only replied with a lovely note, but she invited me to lunch. We talked for two hours, and at the end I knew I had found a mentor in Charlotte and an intellectual home at Ohio State's doctoral program in Language, Literature, and Reading. Charlotte became my advisor, and I spent three wonderful years of study. It was an exciting time to be a doctoral student as research in psycholinguistics and sociolinguistics and in reading and writing processes was beginning to change the way we saw the teaching of literacy. Moreover, Charlotte played a major role in the field as one of the first and foremost scholars to understand that children's literature was central to children's literacy.

Also at Ohio State at the time were two women who became wonderful friends. Janet Hickman had just finished her own doctoral work and taught several of my classes. Susan Hepler, then a fellow doctoral student, provided me with critical understandings about literature and introduced me to classrooms where teachers were doing all that I had wanted to do with literature-based teaching. Charlotte, Janet, and Susan continued to guide me personally as I finished my degree and moved on to my own professional work. Their voices were also present in each subsequent edition of *Children's Literature in the Elementary School.* When they each decided to "retire" from active involvement with the book, I was thrilled to be asked to take it over. Their profound ideas and their passion for books and children have continued to resonate for me in this ninth edition of the text, and I hope will continue to guide me in the future.

Audience

The ninth edition of *Charlotte Huck's Children's Literature* is written, as it has always been, for all adults with an interest in providing good literature for children. It also provides a rationale and suggestions to teachers for planning and evaluating a literature-based curriculum. The text is designed for classes in children's literature at the pre-service and graduate levels in education or English departments and in library schools in colleges and universities. It is also meant to serve as a resource for classroom teachers and librarians.

Purposes

Because of the immediacy of modern communication, we seem to find ourselves dealing with tragedies of immense scope. In the face of natural or human-caused disaster, it is often difficult to find words to describe our fears and feelings. Instead, many of us turn to literature, to great works of fiction and poetry, to help us comprehend the tragedy we have witnessed and to guide us through our darkest days. Our own experiences help us understand that children, even more than adults, need their own works of literature to make sense of their fears and their sorrows as well as their joys and delights.

The primary purpose in writing this textbook is the same as in the previous eight editions—to share knowledge and enthusiasm for the literature of childhood with students, teachers, and librarians in the hope that they, in turn, will communicate their excitement about books to the children they teach.

As a nation, we have become so concerned with teaching the skills of reading that we have often neglected to help children discover the joys of reading. We have always recognized the importance of story and real books in developing readers who not only know how to read but also do read. I believe that children become readers only by reading many books of their own choosing and by hearing high-quality literature read aloud with obvious delight and enthusiasm. It is my hope that the students, teachers, and librarians who own this book will have the information and the resources to be able to create in children a love of good books and a joy in reading them.

The growth of the field of children's literature has been phenomenal since the first edition of this text was published in 1961. With more than ninety thousand children's books in print, prospective and in-service teachers and librarians need a guide, based on a knowledge of book-selection criteria and an understanding of children's responses to literature, for selecting the best ones. In addition, educators are using children's literature across the curriculum. They need a book that will enable them to plan and develop programs for their classrooms and libraries.

Organization

The three-part organization of *Charlotte Huck's Children's Literature* emphasizes the triple focus of this text: the reader, the book, and teaching. Part One focuses on the values and criteria for choosing and using literature with children at various stages in their development. It also includes an historical overview of the ways in which children's literature has changed over the years, including the important impact of children's literature from different cultures. Part Two provides an in-depth look at the various genres of children's literature and establishes evaluative criteria for each genre. Each of these chapters has been written with children at the center and includes references and resources for involving children in exploring books across the curriculum. Part Three explores this curricular strand in depth by focusing on the teaching, planning, and evaluating of literature-based programs.

New to This Edition

For this edition I have considered the changes that have occurred in approaches to teaching and in the publishing and marketing of children's books over the last forty years. During this time, the research base supporting the centrality of good literature has grown, more teachers have been putting this research into practice in literature-based classrooms, and more and more books have been published for children. At the same time, as a result of state requirements in teacher preparation and licensing, courses in children's literature have often been merged into courses in Language Arts or are offered only as electives. I continue to believe, therefore, that there is a critical need for an in-depth text on children's literature, one that will provide support for teachers and librarians beyond the confines of a single college course. In the ninth

edition I have carefully considered what has always been the central purpose of this text—the sharing of knowledge and enthusiasm for the literature of childhood. I am pleased that the widespread use of the Internet makes it possible to provide additional supporting materials and information, including an extended database and a Web site.

The text has been updated to reflect new trends in children's literature. The book lists and examples have been revised to include children's literature that has been printed since the eighth edition was published. I would particularly like to call your attention to the following new features and content included in this new edition:

New Title The title of the ninth and future editions reflects and honors Charlotte Huck, the original author of this classic text and a pioneer in the field of children's literature. Sadly, Charlotte passed away during the development of this edition, but the hallmarks of this text and her vision and enthusiasm for instilling a passion of reading and literature in our children will continue to be at the core of this text. (Please see page xxvi for a tribute to Charlotte Huck.)

 **Expanded and Highlighted Multicultural and Diversity Topics Coverage** New Chapter 3: The Changing World of Children's Books and the Development of Multicultural Literature combines the essentials of the history of children's literature with the important foundations of multicultural literature. Then, throughout the textbook, I have discussed multicultural literature as part of each genre or subject area. Students are introduced to picture books and biographies about people of all races and all cultural backgrounds. Watch for the diversity icon in the headings that highlight this content and look at the Features Guide (p. xiii) for a listing of multicultural topics. I believe that this approach ensures that the literature and accomplishments of all groups will be part of every subject taught.

New Appendix D: Hot Off the Press Each edition involves painstaking efforts to include the very latest publications in children's literature. With new titles constantly publishing, it's impossible to include everything we would like to, as well as titles due to come out after this text has gone to press. Thus, this new appendix not only points out the many new titles that are pictured in this edition, but it also includes a list of titles to watch for.

Streamlined Resources Many of the various boxed features and resources offered in the text have been revised to provide more detail and have been refined and renamed to more succinctly reflect their purpose. All have been updated to include the very latest information and resources. See the individual features described under "Special Features."

Updated Research and More Than 1,000 New Titles Added Throughout the book I have attempted to include titles that reflect the interests and developmental needs of children from birth through middle school. Children, perhaps more than ever before, need to experience the world beyond their own communities and national borders. The text has always included discussion of books from around the world. In this edition I have made an effort to include many more books published in other countries, particularly in Canada and Australia. Careful attention was given to identifying out-of-print books, and most of these were removed from the discussion. Each chapter has been rewritten to include the latest research and latest books in an effort to keep this edition as up-to-date as possible. More than 1,000 new titles have been added to the edition, and more than 100 new color pictures have been used throughout the text—including illustrations from some of the most promising recently published children's books.

Cover Illustration by Anita Lobel The ninth edition's cover was created specifically for this text by children's book illustrator Anita Lobel. For more information about the cover illustration, see About the Illustrator on page xxv.

Beautiful New Design The text's interior has been redesigned to be as much a piece of art as the children's literature illustrations it holds. The design is meant to encourage students as they journey through the world of children's literature. Anita Lobel provided the illustrations for the part openers and the icons used in the feature boxes.

As children's literature becomes more central to the curriculum, teachers and librarians need a book that will serve for many years as a reference as well as provide thorough coverage of the issues and genres in children's literature. I have hoped to produce, from endpaper to endpaper, a practical textbook that will serve as a resource both for students who are just beginning their teaching and for teachers and librarians already in the field. I believe teachers and librarians are professional people who want a book of substance, documented with pertinent research and based on real practice in the classroom. This is the kind of book I have tried to write.

Special Features

Charlotte Huck's Children's Literature has long been regarded as the source for comprehensive information about children's literature and how to use children's literature in the classroom. The text's special features exemplify why this text holds an important spot on teachers' bookshelves:

200 Books to Read Aloud The endpapers serve as an introduction to the field of children's literature by providing a quick list of 200 books to read aloud to different age groups.

Media Resources Each chapter begins with a new Media Resources box that includes a list of the many activities, features, and resources that are further explored and developed on the text's Online Learning Center Web site and Resources CD-ROM.

 Teaching Resources—**Booklists** This feature lists numerous books based on different characteristics related to the chapter topics.

Talking Points—**Issues Feature** Children's literature prompts wonderful discussions among students, teachers, and professionals. This feature asks a question meant to spark discussion, and then points the reader to the Online Learning Center to learn more about it.

Profile in Literature—**Profile Feature** Each chapter includes a profile of a notable person—author, illustrator, editor, or teacher—who works with literature. In this edition, we've included more background information that introduces the individual and why his or her contribution is noteworthy. The readers are then pointed to the Online Learning Center to learn more about this important person.

 Literature in Action—**Teachers Using Literature** This retitled feature provides brief examples—

through descriptions and children's work—of how teachers use children's literature in their classrooms.

 Evaluation Criteria—**Book Selection** This feature provides the reader with basic questions to ask when evaluating children's books.

Webs Each genre chapter includes an updated "WEB" that pictures the possibilities for exploring "Wonderfully Exciting Books." These Webs are especially designed to provide students with a picture of classroom literature exploration. The Webs present suggestions for discussion and activities that are meant to lead children back into books in order to increase their understanding and appreciation of literature and the wider world.

 Into the Classroom—**Activities to Do with Children** This feature includes an overview of general methods to use to teach the particular genre. The activity/lesson suggestions have been updated, and additional activities available on the Online Learning Center are listed.

Explorations—**Activities for Learning and Reflection** These chapter-ending activities provide the reader with opportunities to interact with the literature they are learning about.

Web Links To extend the reader's learning, Web Links related to the chapter's content are posted on the Online Learning Center. A listing of these Web Links is provided at the end of each chapter so that readers will be aware of the resources available to them.

Related Readings For readers who want to learn more about a topic discussed in the chapter, the Related Readings provides a place for them to start. This listing includes classic as well as current books and resources.

Children's Literature—**Booklist** This chapter-ending, comprehensive booklist includes hundreds of children's books related to the topics in each chapter.

Practical Appendixes The book's appendixes—Children's Book Awards, Book Selection Aids, Publishers' Addresses, and the new Hot Off the Press—are valuable, practical resources that will be used and referred to again and again.

Online Learning Center Web site Visit the book's website at **www.mhhe.com/kiefer9e** to find many valuable resources, such as quizzes with feedback, practice with key term activities, chapter objectives and summaries, annotated and updated *Web Links*, expanded *Talking Points* and *Profile in Literature* articles, expanded *Into the Classroom* activities, and downloadable lists and resources. Use of the Online Learning Center is integrated throughout the text, including the Media Resources box and the OLC icon appearing next to material that is further explored online.

Resources CD-ROM with Children's Literature Database This includes an extensive, updated Children's Literature electronic database of more than 5,500 titles that can be searched in a number of ways. The books listed have been carefully evaluated and selected as excellent books for children, including the award winners listed in Appendix A. The CD-ROM also links to numerous resources also available on the Online Learning Center, including quizzes, printable versions of the Teaching Resources and other extensive lists in the text, and features and articles for further exploration. Links to information on the CD-ROM are indicated by the CD-ROM icon found throughout the text.

Teaching and Learning Resources

This edition of *Charlotte Huck's Children's Literature* is accompanied by an expanded number of supplemental resources and learning aids for instructors and students.

For the Instructor

Instructor's Resource CD-ROM (ISBN 0-07-312299-8) All the core supplements are conveniently provided on this CD. Included are the computerized test bank, the Instructor's Manual, and PowerPoint presentations. These materials are valuable resources for teaching and evaluating students' understanding of literature.

Online Learning Center at www.mhhe.com/ kiefer9e The instructor's area of the Online Learning Center houses resources for teaching.

PageOut PageOut allows the instructor to create a course Web site. This course management tool allows you to create an interactive course syllabus that lets you post content and links, an online gradebook, lecture notes, bookmarks, and even a discussion board where students can discuss course-related topics.

See descriptions of the new **Award Winners' Classroom Response Guide**, *Litlinks* (a children's literature activity book) and *Folio*Live (an electronic portfolio tool) below. Ask your local sales representative for information on how you can package these at a reduced cost to your students.

For the Student

Resources CD-ROM (ISBN 0-07-312302-1) Free with new copies of the text, this CD-ROM includes links to resources from the text and additional activities, and the searchable **Children's Literature Database** with over 5,500 carefully selected children's literature titles.

Online Learning Center at www.mhhe.com/kiefer9e *Charlotte Huck's Children's Literature* is accompanied by a comprehensive Web site that includes quizzes, Web Links, and additional resources and activities.

New! Award Winners' Classroom Response Guide by Erika Thulin-Dawes (2006 ISBN 0-07-326789-9; 2007 ISBN 0-07-330085-3) Published annually, this innovative guide provides materials for incorporating the latest award winners into the classroom. Instructional plans are included for the following awards: Newbery, Caldecott, Coretta Scott King, Orbis Pictus, and Sibert.

LitLinks Second Edition Activities for Connected Learning in Elementary Classrooms **by Dena Beeghly (ISBN 0-07-327569-7)** This book contains guidelines and guidance for creating literature-centered lessons across the curriculum and sample lesson plans.

*Folio*Live *Folio*Live is an online portfolio tool you can use to create an electronic portfolio in three easy steps. 1. Use a template to create a homepage, 2. Choose to create a custom framework, or Framework to structure your portfolio, and 3. Add the artifacts to build your portfolio by uploading existing files (from Word to PowerPoint to Video), linking to artifacts posted elsewhere on the Web, or creating an artifact through *Folio*Live embedded forms. Go to **www.foliolive.com** to learn more about this product or to purchase a one-year account.

Acknowledgments

No one writes a book of this magnitude without the help of friends. I am deeply indebted to many people: the teachers, librarians, and children in the schools where I have always been welcomed; to students at The Ohio State University, Teachers College, and elsewhere, both undergraduates and graduate students, who have shared their insights into children's responses and interpretations of literature; and those teachers who have sent pictures of, and allowed me to take pictures in, their classrooms. I thank them all and hope they continue to share their classroom experiences and enthusiasm for children's literature.

Specifically, I wish to express our appreciation to the following teachers and schools who shared their teaching ideas, children's work, and classroom photos with us in this and past editions: Professor Cynthia A. Tyson for her careful reading of and suggestions for the revision of Chapter 3; Professor Stephen J. Thornton of Teachers College for his advice on historical and geographical accuracy in Chapters 6 and 10; Jean M. Norman, Jennifer Madden O'Hear, and Alison Coviello for creating the Webs in Chapters 5, 7, and 10; Isaac Brooks, The Manhattan School for Children and The Horace Mann School in New York City; Jennifer Taet and Brooke Young of Teachers College; Carmen Gordillo, The Beginning with Children School in Brooklyn, New York; Mary Sullivan Gallivan, PS 124 and Ilana Dubin-Spiegel, PS 116 in New York City; Faye Freeman of William B. Ward Elementary School in New Rochelle, New York; Jean M. Norman of Anna Maria College, Paxton, Massachusetts; Marlene Harbert and other faculty members at Barrington Road School, Upper Arlington, Ohio; Diane Driessen, librarian, and Jean Sperling, Peggy Harrison, Sheryl Reed, and other faculty members at Wickliffe Alternative School, Upper Arlington, Ohio; Kristen Kerstetter and the staff at Highland Park School, Grove City, Ohio; Marilyn Parker at Columbus School for Girls; Arleen Stuck, Richard Roth, and Melissa Wilson at Columbus Public Schools; Lisa Dapoz and Joan Fusco at Emerson Elementary School, Westerville, Ohio; Linda Woolard at Miller Elementary School, Newark, Ohio; Rebecca Thomas, Shaker Heights Public Schools, Ohio; Barbara Friedberg and other faculty members at the Martin Luther King, Jr., Laboratory School, Evanston Public Schools, Illinois; Joan Manzione, librarian, and Susan Steinberg, Marci El-Baba, and other staff members at George Mason Elementary School, Alexandria City Public

Schools, Virginia; Shirley Bealor at Fairfax County Public Schools, Virginia; Nancy Anderson and Joan Schleicher at Mission School, Redlands Public Schools, California; Sharon Schmidt and other faculty members at Idyllwild Elementary School, Idyllwild, California; Janine Batzle at Esther L. Watson School, Anaheim, California; Joan Nassam and other faculty members at Mt. Eden Normal School in Auckland, New Zealand; Colleen Fleming at Mangere Bridge School, Auckland, New Zealand; and Roy Wilson, formerly at Dhahran Hills Elementary School, Dhahran, Saudi Arabia. I am also grateful to Valerie and Lars Bang-Jensen and their daughter Bree, Dawn Person-Hampton, Harold Hampton, and their son Bryson, and Lisa Wright and Joe Luciani and their twins Alexandra and Matthew for their contributions. I am grateful to The Ohio State University photography department, to photographers Linda Rozenfeld, of Images Marmor Rozenfeld, and Larry Rose, of Redlands, California, for their careful work in creating many of the photographs used in this edition. I also wish to thank Connie Compton and Regina Weilbacher for special photographs.

I express gratitude to the following reviewers whose comments and suggestions were most helpful:

Susan Argyle, Slippery Rock University
Ruth Biro, Duquesne University
Judy Bivens, Trevecca Nazarene University
Alice Blake-Stalker, Niagara University
Sharon Crisman, Gannon University
Karen Donnelly, Louisiana State University
Karen Dunnagan, Spalding University
Mary Kay Farrow, University of Missouri–Kansas City

Sue Gleghorn, Texas A&M University
Yvonne Hanley, University of North Dakota
Dianne Koehnecke, Wester University
Jeraldine Kraver, University of Northern Colorado
Krista Kustra, University of South Carolina
Margaret Lehner, Moraine Valley Community College
Virginia Matthews, University of Saint Francis
John McCracken, Indiana Wesleyan University
Rebecca Pennington, Covenant College
Theresa Schoen, Coe College
Deborah Setliffe, Tennessee Tech University
Michael Shaw, St. Thomas Aquinas College
Beverly Six, Sul Ross State University
Charlotte Skinner, Arkansas State University
Helen Speed, Penn Valley Community College
Susan Swords Steffen, Elmhurst College
Julie Stepp, Tennessee Tech University
Tim Toops, Florida Southern University
Beth Ann Watson, Harding University

I give special thanks to our friends at McGraw-Hill, including David Patterson and Leslie LaDow, and Vicki Malinee of Van Brien & Associates.

Finally, I want to thank Charlotte, Janet, and Susan for their faith and trust in me. There is no adequate way to thank these three and my other friends and family except to wonder at the glory of having had their company and support in creating this text.

Barbara Z. Kiefer
Charlotte S. Huck Professor
The Ohio State University

A Guided Tour of Children's Literature

To the Student

Welcome to the ninth edition of *Charlotte Huck's Children's Literature*. This text has served as both the introduction to children's literature and a permanent resource for countless teachers, librarians, and general lovers of children's literature.

Join us for a walk through the features of the ninth edition.

Media Resources

 The Online Learning Center icon indicates that additional materials are located at www.mhhe.com/kiefer9e. For more about the Online Learning Center, see the *Student Supplements* later in this section.

 The Resources CD-ROM icon indicates that additional materials are available on the CD-ROM. For more about the Resources CD-ROM, see the *Student Supplements.*

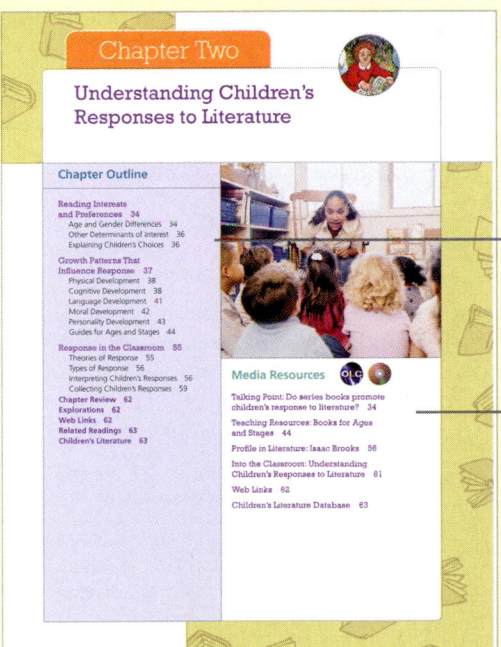

The Text

Chapter Outline

The chapter outline lists the chapter's topics and includes page numbers for easy reference.

Media Resources

This feature lists the many activities, features, and resources that are further explored on the Online Learning Center Web site and Resources CD-ROM.

Recent Publications

More than 100 new children's books are shown throughout the text.

Coverage of Diversity

The history of multicultural books and diversity issues is now introduced in Chapter 3, and numerous resources and references are integrated throughout the text. A diversity icon highlights main topic coverage. A full listing of these topics is included in the *Features Guide* on page xiii.

Evaluation Criteria

This feature provides evaluation criteria and questions to help you choose books.

Teaching Resources

This feature lists resources for the teacher based on chapter topics.

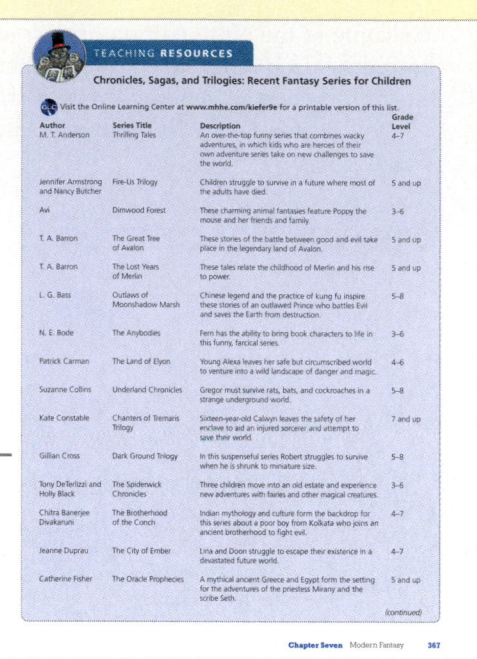

Wonderfully Exciting Books (Webs)

Each genre chapter (and the picture book chapter) includes a Web that provides an example of classroom literature exploration.

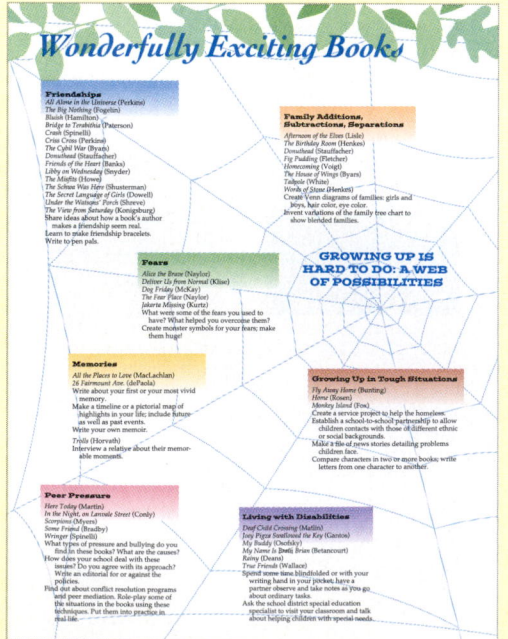

Literature in Action

The *Literature in Action* article provides examples of how children's literature is used in real classrooms—from teachers' stories to students' work.

Profile in Literature

The *Profile in Literature* feature highlights an important person in children's literature. Link to the Online Learning Center to read the profile.

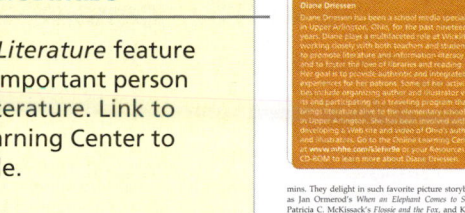

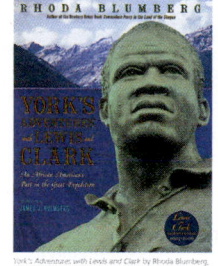

Talking Points

The *Talking Points* feature presents a controversial or thought-provoking question related to each chapter. More information about the question is available on the Online Learning Center.

End-of-Chapter Resources

Each chapter ends with a *Chapter Review* which points to the study materials housed on the Online Learning Center and Resources CD-ROM, *Explorations* with activities designed to help you interact with the chapter's content, and a listing of the *Web Links* housed on the Online Learning Center.

Into the Classroom

The *Into the Classroom* feature presents activities using children's books that can be done with children. Additional *Into the Classroom* activities are available on the Online Learning Center.

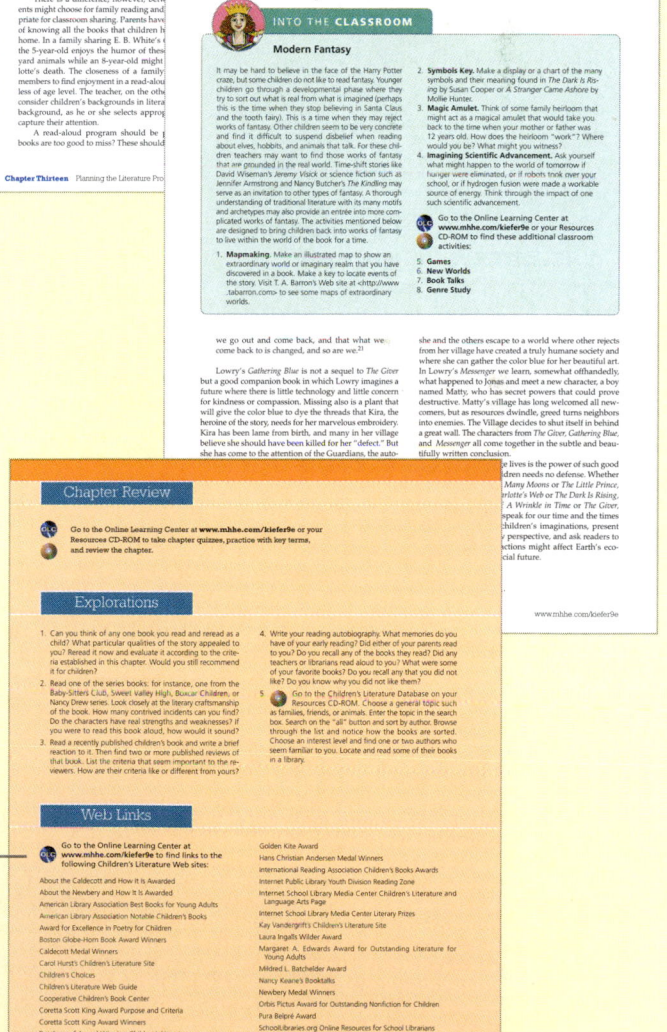

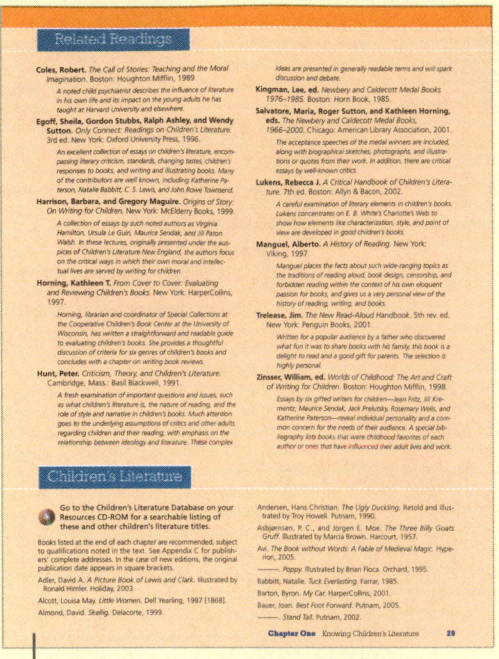

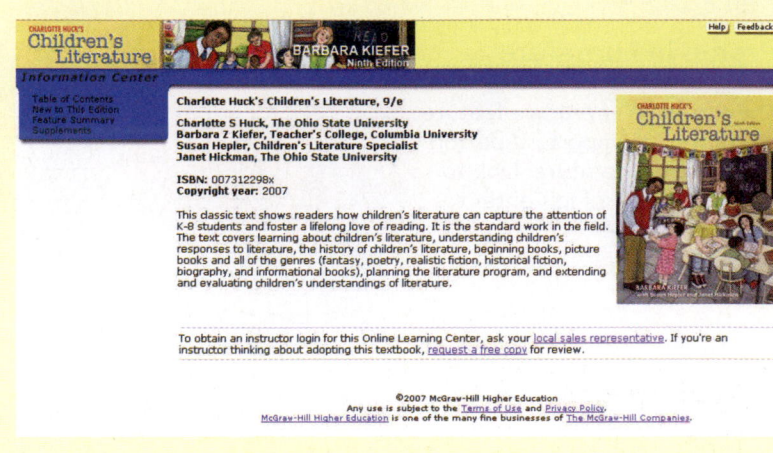

Related Readings and Children's Literature

There are two book lists available at the end of each chapter—*Related Readings,* which lists resources and books for your development, and *Children's Literature,* which lists children's books related to the chapter.

Student Supplements

Online Learning Center

The **Online Learning Center** located at **www.mhhe.com/kiefer9e** includes study and practice tools such as

- Chapter Outline
- Chapter Objectives
- Chapter Summary
- Key Terms and Practice Activity
- Multiple Choice Quizzes with feedback
- Additional *Into the Classroom* Activities
- Printable versions of the Teaching Resources boxes
- Web Links—both chapter-specific and general resource
- *Profiles in Literature*
- *Talking Points*

Resources CD-ROM*

The **Resources CD-ROM** includes the **Children's Literature Database:** a searchable database listing over 5,500 carefully selected children's books. The CD links to the numerous resources available on the Online Learning Center Web site.

*If you purchased a used copy of this text, and would like to purchase the Resources CD-ROM, call McGraw-Hill Customer Service at 1-800-338-3987.

Anita Lobel was born in Kracòw, Poland, just before World War II. In the proper Jewish household in which she lived, there was a nanny for the children. It was this strong-willed Catholic peasant who saved the lives of Anita and her brother during the war, passing them off as her own children.

They spent five years on the run from one town to another until the Nazis discovered them on Christmas Day hiding out in a convent. Anita and her brother moved through Monelupi Prison, Plaszów, and Auschwitz, ending up in Ravensbrück concentration camp. Somehow, they survived until liberation and were brought to Sweden.

Eventually, Anita's parents were located and they were reunited in Stockholm. There, Anita went to high school and began taking art lessons. When the family emigrated to New York, Anita won a scholarship to Pratt Institute.

Anita's interests in theater and music and foreign languages have served her well in her work as both an author and an illustrator. She has been an actress and a singer. "It is the 'drama' in a picture-book that interests me most," she has said. "I stage the story the way a director might work on a theater piece."

Anita's accomplishments include many of her own books as well as illustrations for texts by various writers. She collaborated with husband Arnold Lobel on *The Rose in My Garden* and *On Market Street* (for which she was awarded the Caldecott Honor in 1982). Her own adaptations from Scandinavian folk stories include *King Rooster, Queen Hen; The Pancake;* and *The Straw Maid.*

Anita had a special friendship with Charlotte Huck whom she collaborated with for *Princess Furball, Toads and Diamonds,* and *The Black Bull of Norroway.* Some of Anita's other favorites include *This Quiet Lady* by Charlotte Zolotow; and *The Cat and the Cook* retold by Ethel Heins; as well as her own alphabet books *Alison's Zinnia, Away from Home,* and *Animal Antics.* In *The Dwarf Giant,* Anita was inspired by the art of Japanese theater. She also wrote a memoir of her childhood in war-torn Poland called *No Pretty Pictures: A Child of War.*

To learn more about Anita Lobel and her many contributions to children's literature, visit **www.anitalobel.com.**

I believe that if you present the right books to children, they will read and enjoy them. So, bringing children and books together really means getting them excited about reading.

—*Charlotte S. Huck*

Charlotte S. Huck 1923–2005

Born in Evanston, Illinois, Charlotte Huck attended Wellesley College in Massachusetts, then graduated from Northwestern University, where she also earned master's and doctoral degrees. After teaching in elementary schools in Missouri and Illinois, she returned to Northwestern, this time as faculty.

Dr. Huck joined the faculty of The Ohio State University in 1955, where she created and led the first-ever graduate program in children's literature for thirty years. A national authority on this subject, she believed that stories are what motivate children to want to read, and she encouraged teachers to use children's literature in reading lessons. Her concept of "webbing," in which every subject taught to a child is supported by reading, has inspired many of her students to go on to launch children's literature programs across the country.

Charlotte Huck established an annual OSU children's literature conference that attracted thousands of teachers, librarians, and book enthusiasts from throughout Ohio to Columbus from 1982 to 2004. After she retired and moved to California, she started a similar conference at the University of Redlands. She continued to write professionally and remained active in community and school-based literacy programs.

Besides authoring the classic *Children's Literature in the Elementary School* (originally published in 1961), she also wrote books for children. With Anita Lobel, she published *Princess Furball* (1994), *Toads and Diamonds* (1995), and *The Black Bull of Norroway* (2001). Those and her other books, *Secret Places* (1993) and *A Creepy Countdown* (1999), are published by Greenwillow Books.

Dr. Huck served on the Newbery and Caldecott medal committees and was a president of the National Council of Teachers of English. The numerous awards and honors she received included The Ohio State University's Distinguished Teaching Award, the Landau Award for Distinguished Service in Teaching Children's Literature, and the Arbuthnot Award, given annually by the International Reading Association to an outstanding professor of children's literature. In 1997, she was presented with the Outstanding Educator in the English Language Arts Award by the NCTE Elementary Section.

Charlotte Huck was honored in 1987 with the NCTE Distinguished Service Award for her service to the English teaching profession and to NCTE. The 1988 NCTE President Julie Jensen made the award presentation, commending Huck for her service "to The Ohio State University, to the state of Ohio, and most of all, to language learners and teachers everywhere. They are the beneficiaries of her knowledge and enthusiasm for the literature of childhood, and of her unyielding conviction that readers are made by those who have themselves discovered the joys of reading."

Charlotte Huck was considered to be one of the foremost experts on children's literature and its uses. In 1996, Ohio State University established in her name the first endowed professorship in children's literature in the United States. In her career at OSU, she mentored Ph.D. students, teachers, and library media specialists who continue her beliefs and enthusiasm as new programs in children's literature are launched in schools and universities across the country.

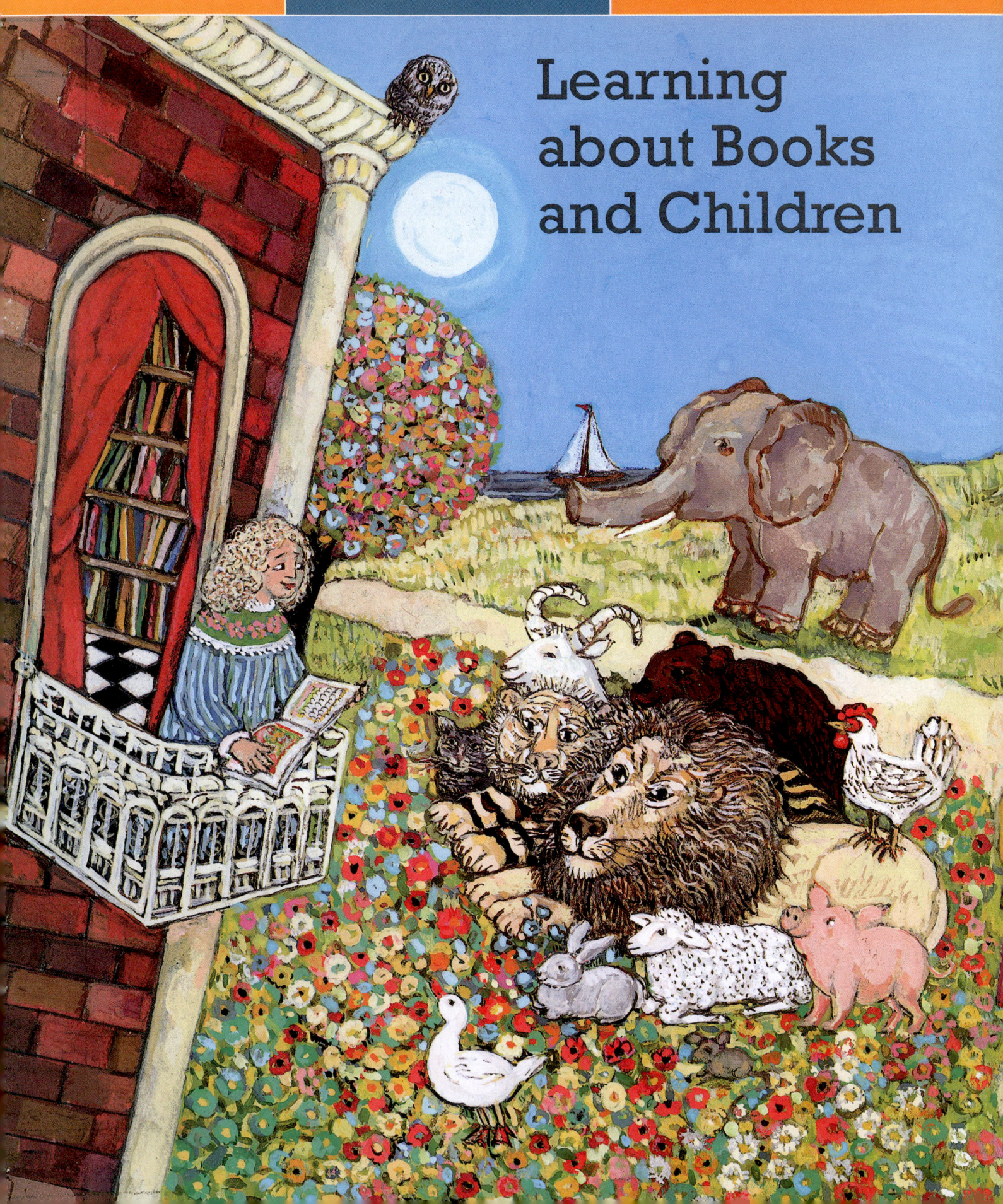

Part One

Learning about Books and Children

Chapter One

Knowing Children's Literature

Media Resources

Was there ever a baby who didn't giggle with delight when her toes were touched to the accompaniment of "This little pig went to market"? Children's introduction to literature comes in the crib as babies listen to Mother Goose rhymes and nursery songs. It continues with the toddler's discovery of Eric Carle's *The Very Hungry Caterpillar* or Byron Barton's *My Car.* Later, children beg to hear Margaret Wise Brown's *Goodnight Moon* or Beatrix Potter's *The Tale of Peter Rabbit* just one more time.

If he is fortunate in his teachers, the primary-age child will hear stories two and three times a day. He will see his own reaction to a new baby in the family mirrored in *Julius, Baby of the World* by Kevin Henkes. He will identify with the feelings of Max, who, when scolded, takes off in his imagination in *Where the Wild Things Are* by Maurice Sendak. And somewhere in those early years he will discover that he can read, and the magical world of literature will open before him.

The growing child experiences loneliness and fear as she imagines what it would be like to survive alone on an island for eighteen years as Karana did in *Island of the Blue Dolphins* by Scott O'Dell. She encounters personal toughness and resiliency as she lives the life of Gilly in Katherine Paterson's *The Great Gilly Hopkins,* the story of a foster child. She can taste the bitterness of racial prejudice in Gary D. Schmidt's *Lizzie Bright and the Buckminster Boy,* and she can share in the courage and determination of young people who helped others escape the Holocaust in *Number the Stars* by Lois Lowry.

A vast treasure of thoughts, deeds, and dreams lies waiting to be discovered in books. Literature begins with Mother Goose. It includes Sendak as well as Shakespeare, Milne as much as Milton, and Carroll before Camus. Children's literature is a part of the mainstream of all literature, whose source is life itself.

CHILDREN'S LITERATURE DEFINED

In the introduction to his book *The Call of Stories*, noted child psychiatrist Robert Coles tells how, during his childhood, his mother and father would read aloud to each other every evening. They were convinced that the great novels of Dickens, Tolstoy, and others held "reservoirs of wisdom." "Your mother and I feel rescued by these books," his father told him. "We read them gratefully."[1]

What is it about literature that can inspire such passionate attention? What is literature? And with more than ninety thousand titles for girls and boys now in print, how can we choose the books that will bring the full rewards and pleasures of literature to children?

There are many ways of defining literature. Our ideas about what should be included have changed over time; definitions vary a bit from culture to culture, from critic to critic, and from reader to reader. In this book we think of literature as the imaginative shaping of life and thought into the forms and structures of language. Where appropriate, we consider fiction as well as nonfiction, pictures as well as words, asking how different genres or sets of symbols work to produce an aesthetic experience. How do they help the reader perceive pattern, relationships, and feelings that produce an inner experience of art? This aesthetic experience might be a vivid reconstruction of past experience, an extension of experience, or the creation of a new experience.

We all have, in our experience, memories of certain books that changed us in some way—by disturbing us, by gloriously affirming some emotion we knew but could never shape in words, or by revealing to us something about human nature. Virginia Woolf calls

[1] Robert Coles, *The Call of Stories: Teaching and the Moral Imagination* (Boston: Houghton Mifflin, 1989), p. xii.

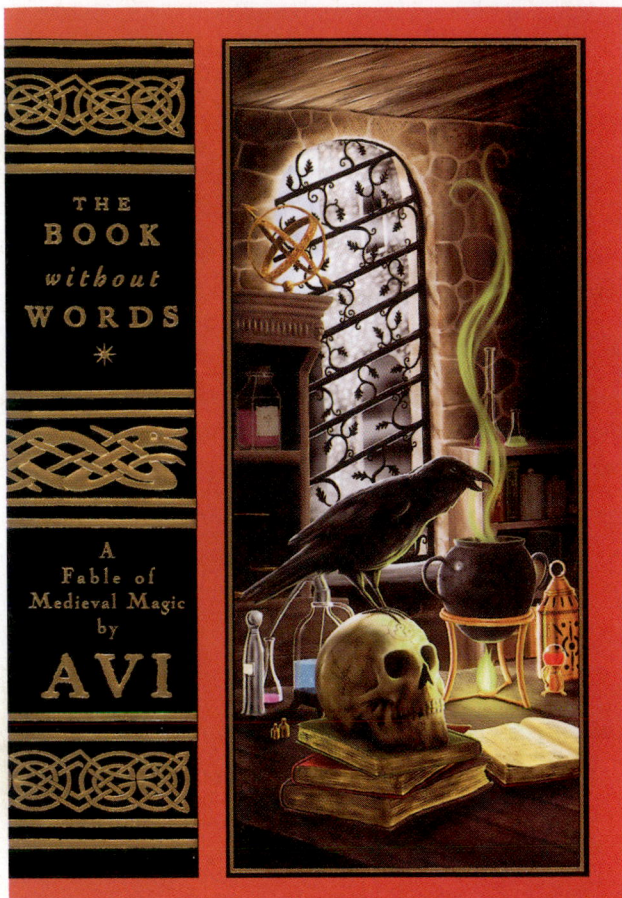

Children's enthusiasm for fantasies such as Avi's *The Book without Words* reflects a universal need for story. Cover of *The Book without Words: A Fable of Medieval Magic* by Avi. Copyright © 2005 by Avi. Reprinted by permission of Hyperion Books for Children.

such times "moments of being," and James Joyce titles them "epiphanies."[2]

The province of literature is the human condition. Literature illuminates life by shaping our insights. W. H. Auden differentiated between first-rate literature and second-rate literature, writing that the reader responds to second-rate literature by saying, "That's just the way I always felt." But first-rate literature makes one say: "Until now, I never knew how I felt. Thanks to this experience, I shall never feel the same way again."[3]

The experience of literature always involves both the book and the reader. Try as we might to set objective criteria, judgments about the quality of literature must always be tempered by an awareness of its audience. Some critics consider Lewis Carroll's *Alice's Adventures in Wonderland* the greatest book ever written for children. However, if the child has no background in fantasy, cannot comprehend the complexity of the plot, nor tolerate

the logic of its illogic, *Alice's Adventures in Wonderland* will not be the greatest book for that child.

What Is Children's Literature?

It might be said that a child's book is a book a child is reading, and an adult book is a book occupying the attention of an adult. Before the nineteenth century only a few books were written specifically for the enjoyment of children. Children read books written for adults, taking from them what they could understand. Today, children continue to read some books intended for adults, such as the works of Stephen King and Mary Higgins Clark. And yet some books first written for children—such as Margery Williams's *The Velveteen Rabbit*, A. A. Milne's *Winnie the Pooh*, J. R. R. Tolkien's *The Hobbit,* and J. K. Rowling's *Harry Potter* stories—have been claimed as their own by adults.

Books about children might not necessarily be for them. Richard Hughes's adult classic *A High Wind in Jamaica* shows the "innocent" depravity of children in contrast to the group of pirates who had captured them. Yet in Harper Lee's novel *To Kill a Mockingbird,* also written for adults, 8-year-old Scout Finch reveals a more finely developed conscience than is common in the small southern town in which she is raised. The presence of a child protagonist, then, does not ensure that the book is for children. Obviously, the line between children's literature and adult literature is blurred.

Children today appear to be more sophisticated and knowledgeable about certain life experiences than children of any previous generation were. They spend a great deal of time within view of an operating television or other electronic media. According to studies by the Kaiser Family Foundation, 30 percent of children ages 0 to 3 years have a television in their rooms, and that number zooms to 68 percent for 8- to 18-year-olds. On average children in the 8- to 18-year-old age range watch more than three hours of live television a day.[4] News broadcasts show them scenes of war or natural disasters while they eat their dinners. They have witnessed acts of terror, air strikes, assassinations, and starvation. Although many modern children are separated from firsthand knowledge of birth, death, and aging, the mass media bring vicarious and daily experiences of crime, poverty, war, and depravity into the living rooms of virtually all American homes. In addition, today's children are exposed to violence purely in the name of entertainment.

Such exposure has forced adults to reconsider what seems appropriate for children's literature. It seems unbelievable that Madeleine L'Engle's *Meet the Austins* was rejected by several publishers because it began with a death, or that some reviewers were shocked by a mild

[2]Frances Clarke Sayers, *Summoned by Books* (New York: Viking, 1965), p. 16.

[3]W. H. Auden, as quoted by Robert B. Heilman in "Literature and Growing Up," *English Journal* 45 (September 1956): 307.

[4]Kaiser Family Foundation, "The Effects of Electronic Media on Children Ages Zero to Six: A History of Research," Issue brief (January 31, 2005). March 9, 2005 <http://www.kff.org/entmedia/7239.cfm>.

"damn" in *Harriet the Spy* by Louise Fitzhugh. Such publishing taboos have long since disappeared. Children's books are generally less frank than adult books, but contemporary children's literature does reflect the problems of today, the ones children read about in the newspapers, see on television and in the movies, and experience at home.

However, the content of children's literature is limited by children's experience and understanding. Certain emotional and psychological responses seem outside the realms of childhood. For example, nostalgia is an adult emotion that is foreign to most boys and girls. Children seldom look back on their childhood, but always forward. Stories that portray children as "sweet" or that romanticize childhood, like the Holly Hobbie books that go with cards and gift products, have more appeal for adults than for children. Likewise, a sentimental book like *Love You Forever* by Robert Munsch, despite its popularity with teachers, is really not for children. Its themes of the passing of childhood and the assumption of responsibility for an aging parent both reflect adult experiences. The late Dr. Seuss (Theodor S. Geisel) also took an adult perspective in his later books such as *Oh, the Places You'll Go.* His enduring place in children's literature rests on earlier titles such as *And to Think That I Saw It on Mulberry Street* and *The Cat in the Hat,* books that are filled with childlike imagination and joyful exuberance.

Cynicism and despair are not childlike emotions and should not figure prominently in a child's book. Even though children are quick to pick up a veneer of sophistication, of disillusionment with adults and authority, they still expect good things to happen in life. And although many children do live in desperate circumstances, few react to these with real despair. They may have endured pain, sorrow, or horror; they may be in what we would consider hopeless situations; but they are not without hope. The truth of the Russian folktale by Becky Reyher, *My Mother Is the Most Beautiful Woman in the World,* shines clear. Children see beauty where there is ugliness; they are hopeful when adults have given up. This is not to suggest that all stories for children must have happy endings; many today do not. It is only to say that when you close the door on hope, you have left the realm of childhood. The only limitations, then, that seem binding on literature for children are those that appropriately reflect the emotions and experiences of children today. Children's books are books that have the child's eye at the center.

Writing for Children

Editor William Zinsser says:

> No kind of writing lodges itself so deeply in our memory, echoing there for the rest of our lives, as the books that we met in our childhood. . . . To enter and hold the mind of a child or a young person is one of the hardest of all writers' tasks.[5]

The skilled author does not write differently or less carefully for children just because she thinks they will not be aware of style or language. E. B. White asserts:

> Anyone who writes down to children is simply wasting his time. You have to write up, not down. . . . Some writers for children deliberately avoid using words they think a child doesn't know. This emasculates the prose and . . . bores the reader. . . . Children love words that give them a hard time, provided they are in a context that absorbs their attention.[6]

Authors of children's literature and those who write for adults should receive equal approbation. C. S. Lewis maintained that he wrote a children's story because a children's story was the best art form for what he had to say.[7] Lewis wrote for both adults and children, as have Rumer Godden, Madeleine L'Engle, Paula Fox, E. B. White, Isaac Bashevis Singer, Jill Patton Walsh, and many other well-known authors.

The uniqueness of children's literature, then, lies in the audience that it addresses. Authors of children's books are circumscribed only by the experiences of childhood, but these are vast and complex. Children think and feel; they wonder and they dream. Much is known, but little is explained.

Children are curious about life and adult activities. They live in the midst of tensions, of balances of love and hate within the family and the neighborhood. The author who can bring these experiences imagination and insight, give them literary shape and structure, and communicate them to children is writing children's literature.

VALUING LITERATURE FOR CHILDREN

Because children naturally take such delight in books, we sometimes need to remind ourselves that books can do more for children than entertain them. Values inherent in sharing literature with children include personal qualities that might be difficult to measure as well as qualities that result in important educational understandings.

Personal Values

Literature should be valued in our homes and schools for the enrichment it gives to the personal lives of children, as well as for its proven educational contributions.

---

[5]William Zinsser, ed., *Worlds of Childhood: The Art and Craft of Writing for Children* (Boston: Houghton Mifflin, 1990), p. 3.

[6]E. B. White, "On Writing for Children," quoted in *Children and Literature: Views and Reviews,* ed. Virginia Haviland (Glenview, Ill.: Scott, Foresman, 1973), p. 140.

[7]C. S. Lewis, "On Three Ways of Writing for Children," *Horn Book Magazine* 39 (October 1963): 460.

We will consider these affective values of literature before we discuss the more obvious educational ones.

Enjoyment

First and foremost, literature provides delight and enjoyment. Much of what is taught in school is not particularly enjoyable. Our Puritan backgrounds have made literature somewhat suspect. If children enjoy it, we reason, it can't be very good for them. Yet literature can educate at the same time as it entertains.

Children need to discover delight in books before they are asked to master the skills of reading. Then learning to read makes as much sense as learning to ride a bike; they know that eventually it will be fun. Four- and 5-year-olds who have laughed out loud at Jules Feiffer's *Bark, George!* can hardly wait to read it themselves. After hearing the ugly troll's cry of "Who's that tripping over my bridge?" children are eager to take parts in playing out *The Three Billy Goats Gruff* by P. C. Asbjørnsen and Jorgen Moe. They respond to the distinctive rhythm of the poem or to the sound of David McCord's "The Pickety Fence." Six- and 7-year-olds giggle at the silly antics in Arnold Lobel's *Frog and Toad* books, and they laugh uproariously when Ramona, in Beverly Cleary's *Ramona Quimby, Age 8,* mistakenly cracks a raw egg on her head thinking it is hard-boiled. Later they empathize with her when she overhears her teacher calling her a nuisance and a show-off.

Middle graders can identify with the characters in Andrew Clements's *Lunch Money* and his many other school stories. An older audience enjoys the trials and tribulations of the characters in *Best Foot Forward* or *Stand Tall* by Joan Bauer. Sad books also bring a kind of enjoyment, as children who have read *Bridge to Terabithia* by Katherine Paterson or *Stone Fox* by John Gardiner will tell you. Most children love being frightened by a story. Watch 6- and 7-year-olds respond to a scary sharing of Patricia McKissack's *Precious and the Boo Hag* or Charlotte Huck's *A Creepy Countdown* and you will have no doubt of their shivery delight. Many older children revel in tales of mystery and suspense such as Eva Ibbotson's *The Star of Kazan* or Joseph Bruchac's *Whisper in the Dark.*

The list of books that children enjoy can go on and on. There are so many fine ones—and so many that children won't find unless teachers, librarians, and parents share them with children. A love of reading and a taste for literature are the finest gifts we can give to our children, for we will have started them on the path of a lifetime of pleasure with books.

Narrative as a Way of Thinking

Storytelling is as old as human history and as new as today's gossip. Ask any of your friends about their week-

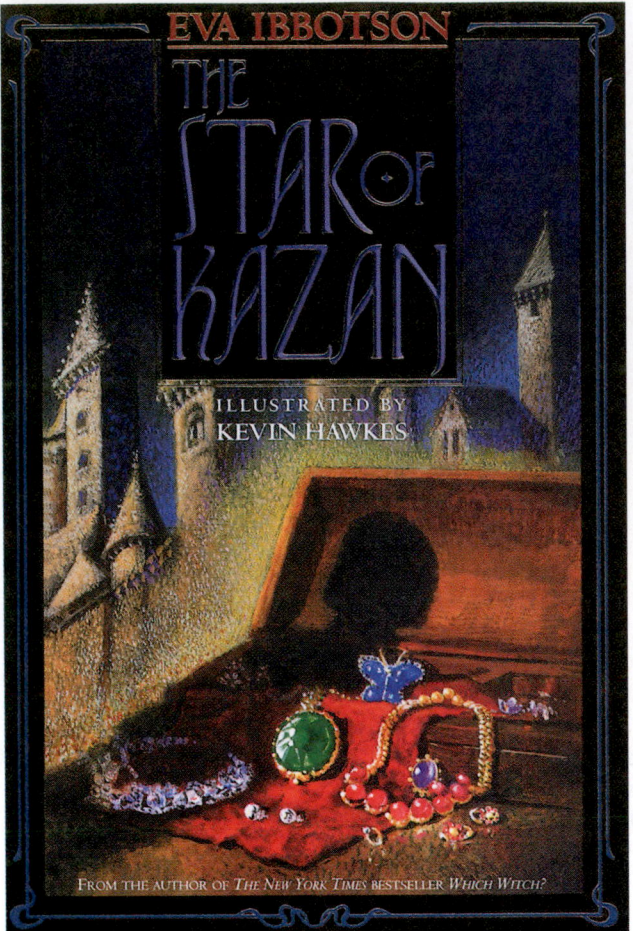

Older children are drawn to complicated stores of mystery and suspense such as Eva Ibbotson's *The Star of Kazan*. From *The Star of Kazan* by Eva Ibbotson, illustrated by Kevin Hawkes, copyright © 2004 by Kevin Hawkes, illustrations. Used by permission of Dutton Children's Books, a division of Penguin Putnam, Inc.

ends or last vacations, and they will organize their remarks in narratives about when their car stalled in the middle of a freeway or their child broke his leg or the marvelous places they stayed at by the ocean. Barbara Hardy of the University of London suggests that all our constructs of reality are in fact stories we tell ourselves about how the world works. She maintains that the narrative is the most common and effective way of ordering our world today:

> We dream in narrative, day-dream in narrative, remember, anticipate, hope, despair, believe, doubt, plan, revise, criticize, construct, gossip, learn, hate, love by narrative. In order really to live, we make up stories about ourselves and others, about the personal as well as the social past and future.[8]

---

[8]Barbara Hardy, "Narrative as a Primary Act of the Mind," in *The Cool Web: The Pattern of Children's Reading,* eds. Margaret Meek, Aidan Warlow, and Griselda Barton (New York: Atheneum, 1978), p. 13.

If thinking in narrative form is characteristic of adult thought, it is even more typical of children's thinking. Watch young children and observe all the stories they are playing out in their lives. When they are naughty and sent to their rooms, they tell themselves a story about how they will run away—and then won't their parents be sorry? Does this plot sound familiar? Of course, for it is the basis for Maurice Sendak's modern classic *Where the Wild Things Are.* Part of this book's tremendous popularity no doubt rests on the fact that it taps the wellsprings of the stories children have been telling themselves for years. Because it is literature, however, this story brings order and structure to the imagined events. Max returns to his room after his fantastic dream, "where he finds his supper waiting for him—and it was still hot."[9] Ask 5- or 6-year-olds who brought Max his supper and they will reply, "His mother." Then ask them what this ending means, and they will answer, "That she's not mad at him anymore." Critics will call the hot meal a symbol of love and reconciliation, but children are simply satisfied that all is well. The book narrative has provided a reassuring ending for the inner story that they have told themselves.

Imagination

Literature develops children's imagination and helps them consider people, experiences, or ideas in new ways. David Wiesner's wordless picture storybooks present unique and surprising views of the world and invite children to participate by constructing their own stories. Books like Paul Fleischman's *Weslandia* or Elisa Kleven's *The Puddle Pail* celebrate characters who see the world differently and make the most of their imagination. Children love to discover secrets hidden in certain illustrations: the many visual stories in Kathy Jakobsen's illustrations for Woody Guthrie's *This Land Is Your Land* or the subplots and other small details in the borders of Jan Brett's *The Mitten.*

Good writing can pique the child's curiosity just as much as intriguing art can. Literature helps children entertain ideas they never considered before—"to dwell in possibility," as one of Emily Dickinson's poems suggests. Literature frequently asks "What if?" questions. What if an Arab American girl returned to live with her father's family in Palestine and became friends with a Jewish boy? Naomi Shihab Nye explores that possibility in *Habibi* and helps us to imagine how two young people might begin to overcome hatreds of the past. Madeleine L'Engle explores the idea of changing the past in *A Swiftly Tilting Planet.* What if we could enter history? Could we change certain major decisions? Charles Wallace has to find that out, and so does the reader. Literature explores possibility.

One of the values of fairy tales and myths is that they stretch the child's imagination. How many children would imagine creating a coach out of a pumpkin, horses from mice, and coachmen from lizards? Yet they readily accept it all in the well-loved tale of Cinderella. Bruno Bettelheim maintains: "Fairy tales have unequaled value, because they offer new dimensions to the child's imagination which would be impossible for him to discover as truly on his own."[10]

Today television has made everything so explicit that children are not developing their power to visualize. Teachers need to help them see with their inner eye to develop a country of the mind. Mollie Hunter, whose

---

[9]Maurice Sendak, *Where the Wild Things Are* (New York: Harper & Row, 1963), unpaged.

[10]Bruno Bettelheim, *The Uses of Enchantment: The Meaning and Importance of Fairy Tales* (New York: Knopf, 1976), p. 7.

books such as *A Stranger Came Ashore* and *Mermaid Summer* have this power to create the visual image in the mind of the reader and to stretch the imagination, says that the whole reward of reading is

> to have one's imagination carried soaring on the wings of another's imagination, to be made more aware of the possibilities of one's mind . . . ; to be thrilled, amazed, amused, awed, enchanted in worlds unknown until discovered through the medium of language, and to find in those worlds one's own petty horizons growing ever wider, ever higher.[11]

Vicarious Experience

Their experiences with literature give children new perspectives on the world. Good writing can transport readers to other places and other times and expand their life space. Readers feel connected to the lives of others as they enter an imagined situation with their emotions tuned to those of the story. One 10-year-old boy, sharing his love of Jean George's survival story *My Side of the Mountain*, said, "You know, I've always secretly felt I could do it myself." This boy had vicariously shared Sam Gribley's adventure of "living off the land" in his tree home in the Catskill Mountains. Sam's experiment in self-sufficiency had strengthened the conviction of a 10-year-old that he, too, could take care of himself. James Britton points out that "we never cease to long for more lives than the one we have . . . [and a reader can] participate in an infinite number."[12]

How better can we feel and experience history than through a well-told story of the lives of its people and times? Readers of Lois Lowry's *Number the Stars* hold their breath as Nazi soldiers ask questions about 10-year-old Annemarie's dark-haired "sister." The girl is really Annemarie's Jewish friend Ellen, whose Star of David necklace is at that moment hidden in Annemarie's hand. Fear and courage become very real to the reader in this story of the Danish Resistance in World War II. A social studies textbook might simply list dates and facts related to this episode in history; a quality piece of imaginative writing has the power to make the reader feel, to transport her to Ellen's hiding place and allow her to feel the terror of Nazi persecution.

Literature provides vicarious experiences of adventure, excitement, and sometimes struggle. In fantasy, Will Stanton, seventh son of a seventh son, must do battle against the forces of evil, the power of the dark, and the unbelievably intense cold before he can complete his quest. The strength of this fantasy, *The Dark Is Rising* by Susan Cooper, is the degree to which the author involves the reader in Will's struggle.

Insight into Human Behavior

Literature reflects life, yet no book can contain all of living. By its very organizing properties, literature has the power to shape and give coherence to human experience. It might focus on one aspect of life, one period of time in an individual's life, and so enable a reader to see and understand relationships that he had never considered. In *The Friends* by Kazumi Yumoto, three boys feed their morbid curiosity by spying on an old man, hoping to see him die. As the boys begin to know the old man, they become more and more involved in his life and put aside their misconception of the aged to find a real, vital human being. Eventually, through their intergenerational friendship, the boys discover important qualities in themselves as well as in the old man.

So much of what we teach in school is concerned with facts. Literature is concerned with feelings, the quality of life. It can educate the heart as well as the mind. Kornei Chukovsky, the Russian poet, says:

> The goal of every storyteller consists of fostering in the child, at whatever cost, compassion and humanness, this miraculous ability of man to be disturbed by another being's misfortune, to feel joy about another being's happiness, to experience another's fate as your own.[13]

Literature can show children how others have lived and "become," no matter what the time or place. As children gain increased awareness of the lives of others, as they vicariously try out other roles, they may develop a better understanding of themselves and those around them. Through wide reading as well as living, they acquire their perceptions of literature and life.

Universality of Experience

Literature continues to ask universal questions about the meaning of life and our relationships with nature and other people. Every story provides a point of comparison for our own lives. Are we as courageous as the tiny mouse who must take responsibility for her family in Avi's *Poppy*? as conflicted by peer pressure as Palmer in Jerry Spinelli's *Wringer*? Would we have the tenacity and resilience of Angel Morgan in Katherine Paterson's *The Same Stuff as Stars*? Would we be as loyal to a friend as Ian is to Stol in *Up On Cloud Nine* by Ann Fine?

---

[11]Mollie Hunter, *The Pied Piper Syndrome* (New York: HarperCollins, 1992), p. 92.

[12]James Britton, *The Dartmouth Seminar Papers: Response to Literature,* ed. James R. Squire (Champaign, Ill.: National Council of Teachers of English, 1968), p. 10.

[13]Kornei Chukovsky, *From Two to Five,* trans. Miriam Morton (Berkeley: University of California Press, 1963), p. 138.

We also learn to understand the common bonds of humanity by comparing one story with another. Pride of accomplishment is strong for Ahmed when he learns to write his name in *The Day of Ahmed's Secret* by Florence Parry Heide and Judith Gilliland, just as it is for the Haitian children who travel miles to get to school in Denize Lauture's *Running the Road to ABC*.

The story of Max leaving home to go to the island in Sendak's *Where the Wild Things Are* follows the ancient pattern of Homer's *Iliad* and *Odyssey*. This pattern is repeated again and again in myth and legend and seen in such widely divergent stories as *Tiny's Big Adventure* by Martin Waddell, *Homecoming* by Cynthia Voigt, *A Wrinkle in Time* by Madeleine L'Engle, and *Holes* by Louis Sachar. These are all stories of a journey through trials and hardship and the eventual return home. The pattern reflects everyone's journey through life.

War stories frequently portray acts of compassion in the midst of inhumanity. *Number the Stars* by Lois Lowry and *Greater Than Angels* by Carol Matas both tell of the uncommon bravery of common people to do what they can to right a wrong. Children's literature is replete with stories of true friendships, as seen in Katherine Paterson's *Bridge to Terabithia* and E. B. White's *Charlotte's Web*, and picture books such as James Marshall's *George and Martha* and Holly Keller's *Sophie's Window*. Other stories reflect the terrible renunciation of friendship, as found in *Daniel Half Human: And the Good Nazi* by David Chotjewitz or *The Friendship* by Mildred Taylor. Literature illumines all of life; it casts its light on all that is good, but it can also spotlight what is dark and debasing in the human experience. Literature enables us to live many lives, good and bad, and to begin to see the universality of human experience.

Educational Values

The intrinsic values of literature should be sufficient to give it a major place in the curriculum. Unfortunately, our society assigns a low priority to such aesthetic experiences. Only when literature is shown to be basic to the development of measurable skills does it receive attention in the elementary schools. Fortunately, research has proven the essential value of literature in helping children learn to read and write. A wide body of evidence supports the importance of literary experiences both before and after children come to school.

Literature in the Home

Characteristic of the development of all children is the phenomenal growth of language during the preschool years. Chukovsky refers to the tremendous "speech-giftedness of the pre-school child" and maintains that "beginning with the age of two, every child becomes for a short period of time a linguistic genius."[14]

Literature clearly plays an important role in all aspects of oral language development. Reading aloud in the home has also been shown to be powerfully connected to later success in learning to read and in attitude toward reading. In study after study, researchers have confirmed the value of being read aloud to at an early age. Moreover, children in these studies did not necessarily come from wealthy homes, but they all came from homes that valued books. The families made good use of the local library and valued storytelling.[15]

Gordon Wells's longitudinal study of language and literacy development serves as a touchstone of these research studies. Wells showed that the amount of experience 5-year-old children in this study had had with books was directly related to their reading comprehension at age 7 and, even later, at age 11. Wells concluded, "Of all the activities that had been considered as possibly helpful preparation for the acquisition of literacy only one was significantly associated with later test scores. . . . That activity was listening to stories."[16]

Literature in the School

It is clear that experiences with literature at an early age can benefit children in many ways. Once children enter school, they also benefit when literature is placed at the center of the curriculum.

Reading Aloud and Learning to Read The powerful influence of books on children's language and literacy continues once they enter school. Studies with school-age children show that reading to children and giving them a chance to work with real books helps them learn to read. Reading aloud can also result in significant increases in their own reading achievement.[17] Accounts published in professional journals and books are replete with stories of teachers' successes with using children's trade books in their reading programs. These reports confirm the research that links literature with success in learning to read. They also stress that increased enjoyment and

---

[14]Ibid., pp. 7, 9.

[15]See Margaret Clark, *Young Fluent Readers* (London: Heinemann Educational Books, 1976).

[16]Gordon Wells, *The Meaning Makers* (Portsmouth, N.H.: Heinemann, 1986), p. 151.

[17]See, for example, Elizabeth Sulzby and William H. Teale, "The Development of the Young Child and Emergent Literacy," in *Handbook of Research on Teaching the English Language Arts*, ed. J. Flood, J. Jensen, D. Lapp, and J. Squire (New York: Erlbaum, 2003), pp. 300–13, and Susan L. Hall and Louisa C. Moats, "Why Reading to Children Is Important," *American Educator* (spring, 2000), pp. 26–33.

Reading aloud to older children gives the teacher a chance to introduce and discuss more complex stories than the ones children choose themselves.

interest in reading are important outcomes of regularly reading aloud to children.[18]

Developing a Sense of Book Language   Hearing books read aloud is a powerful motivation for the child to begin to learn to read. Children learn that reading provides enjoyment, and they want to learn to read themselves. They also see someone important in their lives valuing books. Too frequently we tell children that reading is important, but we show by our actions that we really value other activities more.

Listening to stories introduces children to patterns of language and extends vocabulary and meaning. Young children love to repeat such refrains as "Not by the hair on my chinny chin chin" from Paul Galdone's *The Three Little Pigs* or the well-loved rhyme from Wanda Gág's *Millions of Cats*:

> Cats here, cats there,
> Cats and kittens everywhere,
> Hundreds of cats,
> Thousands of cats,
> Millions and billions and trillions of cats.[19]

Knowing the structure of a story and being able to anticipate what a particular character will do helps young children predict the action and determine the meaning of the story they are reading. For example, children quickly learn the rule of three that prevails in most folktales. They know that if the first Billy Goat Gruff goes trip-trapping over the bridge, the second Billy Goat Gruff will go trip-trapping after him, and so will the third. In reading or listening to the story of the Gingerbread Boy, the child who has had a rich exposure to literature can anticipate the ending on the basis of what he knows about the character of foxes in stories. As one little boy said, "Foxes are clever. He won't be able to get away from him!"

This understanding of literary patterns extends to expository text as well as to narrative. In her studies of kindergartners' pretend reading of nonfiction books and storybooks, Christine Pappas found that young children are equally successful in taking on textual properties of both narrative and expository texts.[20] Furthermore, she found that the kindergartners often preferred nonfiction books to storybooks. She suggests that

to become literate the young child has to come to terms with certain important characteristics of written language that are different from spoken language—its sustained organization, its disembedded quality. And children need to understand that different conventions, rhythms, and structures are expressed in different written genres to meet various social purposes in our culture.[21]

---

[18]See, for example, Susan I. McMahon and Taffy E. Raphael, *The Book Club Connections: Literacy and Learning and Classroom Talk* (New York: Teachers College Press, 1997).

[19]Wanda Gág, *Millions of Cats* (New York: Coward-McCann, 1928), unpaged.

[20]Christine C. Pappas, "Is Narrative 'Primary'? Some Insights from Kindergartners' Pretend Readings of Stories and Information Books," *Journal of Reading Behavior* 25 (1993): 97–129.

[21]Ibid., p. 126.

The more experience children have with literature—with fiction, folktales, poetry, biography, and nonfiction books—the greater their ability will be to grasp the meaning of the text and understand the way the author tells it. This helps them become successful readers.

Developing Fluency and Understanding   The reading of many books is essential to the development of expert readers. This was the kind of reading, even rereading, of favorite stories that Margaret Clark found to be characteristic of avid readers.[22] Such reading is characteristic of middle-grade students who get "hooked" on a particular author or series of books. Frequently, a sign of a good reader is the rereading of favorite books.

In a year-long study of children's reading behavior in a literature-based program in a fifth- and sixth-grade class, Susan Hepler found that these children read an average of 45 books apiece for the year, with the range being 25 to 122 books.[23] Compare this record with the usual two basal texts read in a year by children in the typical basal reading programs. Only wide reading will develop fluency.

Such assumptions are supported by studies that link diverse reading experiences to reading proficiency and comprehension.[24] Many researchers have concluded that the extent to which children read is a significant contributor to their developed reading ability. The National Assessment of Educational Progress (NAEP) found a clear relationship between wide reading experiences and reading ability, and suggested that reading self-selected books in school and reading outside of school for enjoyment—including information books as well as stories—were important to growth in reading.[25]

With all the many demands on their time outside of school, we cannot always be sure that children will read at home. It is even more important, then, for teachers at every grade level—from preschool on up—to enable children to spend time with books every day. If they do not have the opportunity to read widely at school, children probably will not become fluent readers.

Literature and Writing   Teachers have always believed that there is a relationship between reading and writing—that the good writers are avid readers, and that good readers often are the best writers. Walter Loban conducted one of the most extensive studies of the relationship between reading achievement as measured by reading scores and the ratings of writing quality. He discovered a high correlation, particularly in the upper elementary grades, and concluded: "Those who read well also write well; those who read poorly also write poorly."[26]

If reading provides models for children's writing, then the kinds of reading children are exposed to become even more important. Exposure to much good literature appears to make a difference in children's writing abilities, just as it does in their linguistic abilities. Sharon Fox and Virginia Allen maintain: "The language children use in writing is unlikely to be more sophisticated in either vocabulary or syntax than the language they read or have had someone else read to them."[27]

The content of children's writing also reflects the literature they have heard. Whether consciously or unconsciously, children pick up words, phrases, textual structure, even intonation patterns from books they know.

A second grader wrote the following when a researcher asked him to "write a story." No other directions were given. Notice the number of stories that he "borrows" from in telling his own. The titles of his probable sources are given at right.

The Lonesome Egg

Once there lived a Lonesome Egg	*The Golden Egg Book* (Brown)
And nobody liked him because he was ugly. And there was an Ugly duck too but they didn't know each other.	*The Ugly Duckling* (Andersen)
One day while the Lonesome Egg was walking, he met the Ugly duck. And the Egg said to the Duck,	*Do You Want to Be My Friend?* (Carle)
"Will you be my friend?" "Well, O.K." "Oh, thank you."	
"Now let's go to your house, Duck."	Dialogue from the *Frog and Toad* series
"No, let's go to your house." "No, we'll go to your house first and my house too." "O.K."	

---

[22]Clark, *Young Fluent Readers*, p. 103.

[23]Susan Hepler, "Patterns of Response to Literature: A One-Year Study of a Fifth- and Sixth-Grade Classroom" (Ph.D. dissertation, Ohio State University, 1982).

[24]Jim Cipielewski and Keith E. Stanovich, "Predicting Growth in Reading Ability from Children's Exposure to Print," *Journal of Experimental Child Psychology* 54 (1992): 74–89.

[25]P. L. Donahue, R. J. Finnegan, A. D. Lutkus, N. L. Allen, and J. R. Campbell, *The Nation's Report Card: Fourth Grade Reading–2000* (Washington, D.C.: National Center for Education Statistics, April 2001), p. 216.

[26]Walter Loban, *The Language of Elementary School Children*, Research Report No. 1 (Urbana, Ill.: National Council of Teachers of English, 1963), p. 75.

[27]Sharon Fox and Virginia Allen, *The Language Arts: An Integrated Approach* (New York: Holt, Rinehart & Winston, 1983), p. 206.

And while they were walking they met a Panda Bear and they picked it up and took it to Duck's house. And then the baby Panda Bear said: "I'm tired of walking." So they rested. And soon came a tiger. And the tiger ate them up except for Duck. And right as he saw that he ran as fast as he could until he saw a woodcutter and he told the woodcutter to come very quickly. And when they got there the tiger was asleep. So the woodcutter cut open the tiger and out came Egg and Baby Panda Bear. And they ate the tiger and lived happily ever after.[28]

The Fat Cat (Kent)

The Gingerbread Boy (Galdone)

Little Red Riding Hood (Grimm brothers)

Not only the content of this writing but also certain conventions of the text reflect previous exposure to literature. The conventional beginning, "Once there lived," and the traditional ending, "lived happily ever after," are obvious examples. Phrases such as "and soon came a tiger" and "out came Egg and Baby Panda Bear" have a literary ring to them. Discussion of whose house they will go to echoes the many conversations in the *Frog and Toad* series by Arnold Lobel. There can be little doubt about the influence of other stories on the shape and content of this 7-year-old's writing. The role of literature, then, is significant to the development of writing. For as Frank Smith writes,

> the development of composition in writing cannot reside in writing alone, but requires reading and being read to. Only from the written language of others can children observe and understand convention and idea together.[29]

Literature and Critical Thinking   Calls for reform in education have stressed the need for children to become better critical thinkers and problem solvers. Many schools have set goals for developing these abilities, resulting in the publication of special practice materials and packaged programs as well as tests to measure specific skills. One of the benefits of using literature in the elementary school is that it encourages critical and creative thinking in a more natural way than worksheet exercises in logic do.

Making inferences, comparing, summarizing, and finding the main idea are generally recognized as components of critical thinking. These are also built-in features of good book discussions and other literature activities. Young children, for instance, will have many opportuni-

ties to make predictions as they follow Joseph's rapidly diminishing wardrobe through the pages of Simms Taback's *Joseph Had a Little Overcoat*. As they compare many variants of the Cinderella story, children will identify similarities and differences and weigh the comparative merits of each. Talking about the moral of a fable or the theme of a story, such as what lesson the animals learned in the tale "The Little Red Hen," is a way of exploring a story's main idea. Children might also consider which of two biographies of Christopher Columbus presents the more balanced view of the famous explorer or which of several books about the Civil War presents the most complete picture of the issues behind the conflict. Because of its variety in content and the availability of many books on one topic, literature provides great opportunity for thinking critically and making judgments.

Literature across the Curriculum   The widely read person is usually the well-informed person. The content of literature educates while it entertains. Fiction includes a great deal of information about the real world, present and past.

A 10-year-old reading *Julie of the Wolves, Julie,* or *Julie's Wolf Pack* by Jean George learns much that is authentic and true about wolf behavior. Written by a naturalist who has studied animal behavior, these stories include information about wolf communication, the hierarchy of the pack, and the division of labor within the pack. More important than the factual information, however, is each story's theme of the significance of choice and growing up.

My Brother Sam Is Dead by the Colliers gives authentic information about one part of the American Revolution while it contrasts different points of view held by the various characters toward the war itself. This story helps the reader imagine what it was like to live in a family torn

---

[28]"Study of Cohesion Elements on Three Modes of Discourse," NIE Research project, Martha L. King and Victor Rentel, co-researchers, Ohio State University, 1983.

[29]Frank Smith, *Writing and the Writer* (New York: Holt, Rinehart & Winston, 1982).

apart by divided loyalties. And it raises the larger political question concerning the role of neutrality in a revolution.

Nonfiction books can also add both facts and human perspective to the curriculum. In *Breaking Ground, Breaking Silence,* Joyce Hansen and Gary McGowan tell the story of the recent discovery of an African American burial ground in New York City. They skillfully weave together information about several periods in American history with accounts of the activities and contributions of African Americans.

Picture books, too, offer important understandings across subject areas and grade levels. Children can benefit from the questions and concepts raised in Paul Giganti Jr.'s *How Many Blue Birds Flew Away?* or Lola Schaefer's *Pick, Pull, Snap! Where Once a Flower Bloomed.* They can find inspiration in biographies such as David Adler's *A Picture Book of Lewis and Clark* illustrated by Ronald Himler or Nikki Giovanni's *Rosa.* They can study American history through Sam Fink's *The Declaration of Independence* and Woody Guthrie's *This Land Is Your Land* or cement understandings about geography with Laurie Keller's *The Scrambled States of America.*

All areas of the curriculum can be enriched through literature. Children might start with a story and research the facts, or they might start with the facts and find the true meanings in the stories surrounding those facts. Literature has the power to educate both the heart and the mind.

Introducing Our Literary Heritage   In general, the educational values of literature described here center on learning through literature. We must never forget, however, that as children have experiences with books, they are also learning about literature. As they enjoy nursery rhymes, traditional literature, and well-loved classics, they build a background for understanding genre, story structure, and many literary allusions.

Through in-depth discussions of such books as *The View from Saturday* by E. L. Konigsburg, *Lizzie Bright and the Buckminster Boy* by Gary D. Schmidt, and *Tuck Everlasting* by Natalie Babbitt, children become aware of what constitutes fine writing. Although children usually will focus on plot or story, teachers can help them see the layers of interconnections among characters in Konigsburg's complex book. They can learn to appreciate the author's skill with language as they follow Turner and Lizzie's story in *Lizzie Bright and the Buckminster Boy.* Children can be led to discover the recurring references to the wheel, the toad, and the music box in *Tuck Everlasting* as a way of shedding light on their understanding of this lovely fantasy. Children's appreciation for literature and knowledge of their literary heritage should be developed gradually in the elementary school as a way to add to the enjoyment of literature rather than as an end in itself.

EVALUATING CHILDREN'S FICTION

What makes a good children's book? Who will read it? Why? Whose purposes will it serve? All of these are important considerations to be taken up in later sections of this chapter and throughout the book. The primary concern of evaluation, however, is a book's literary and aesthetic qualities. Children show what they think of books through their responses, but they are not born critics in the conventional sense. Teachers and librarians need to value children's own interpretations and judgments. At the same time, they need to help children discover what practiced readers look for in a well-written book.

The traditional criteria by which we evaluate a work of fiction look at such elements as plot, setting, theme, characterization, style, point of view, and format. Special criteria need to be applied to different types of literature, such as picture storybooks, biographies, and nonfiction books. For example, in picture books it is important that the verbal text and illustrations interact harmoniously.

EVALUATION CRITERIA

Evaluating Children's Fiction

BEFORE READING

What kind of book is this?
What does the reader anticipate from the
  Title?
  Dust jacket illustration?
  Size of print?
  Illustrations?
  Chapter headings?
  Opening page?
For what age range is this book intended?

PLOT

Does the book tell a good story?
Will children enjoy it?
Is there action? Does the story move?
Is the plot original and fresh?
Is it plausible and credible?
  Is there preparation for the events?
  Is there a logical series of happenings?
Is there a basis of cause and effect in the happenings?
Is there an identifiable climax?
How do events build to a climax?
Is the plot well constructed?

SETTING

Where does the story take place?
How does the author indicate the time?
How does the setting affect the action, characters, or theme?
Does the story transcend the setting and have universal implications?

THEME

Does the story have a theme?
Is the theme worth imparting to children?
Does the theme emerge naturally from the story, or is it stated too obviously?
Does the theme overpower the story?
Does it avoid moralizing?
How does the author use motifs or symbols to intensify meaning?

CHARACTERIZATION

How does the author reveal characters?
  Through narration?

  In conversation?
  By thoughts of others?
  By thoughts of the character?
  Through action?
Are the characters convincing and credible?
Do we see their strengths and their weaknesses?
Does the author avoid stereotyping?
Is the behavior of the characters consistent with their ages and background?
Is there any character development or growth?
Has the author shown the causes of character behavior or development?

STYLE

Is the style of writing appropriate to the subject?
Is the style straightforward or figurative?
Is the dialogue natural and suited to the characters?
How did the author create a mood? Is the overall impression one of mystery? gloom? evil? joy? security?

POINT OF VIEW

Is the point of view from which the story is told appropriate to the purpose of the book?
Does the point of view change?
Does the point of view limit the reader's horizon, or enlarge it?
Why did the author choose this particular point of view?
What is the author's personal and cultural point of view?

ADDITIONAL CONSIDERATIONS

Do the illustrations enhance or extend the story?
Are the pictures aesthetically satisfying?
How well designed is the book?
Is the format of the book related to the text?
What is the quality of the paper?
How sturdy is the binding?
How does the book compare with other books on the same subject?
How does the book compare with other books written by the same author?
How have other reviewers evaluated this book?
What age range would most appreciate this story?

Modern fantasy has to establish believability in a way that realistic fiction does not. Historical fiction requires added criteria for authenticity of setting. Nonfiction books should be accurate and unbiased. Perhaps the most important task for critics of any age is to identify the kind of book they are reading in order to apply the appropriate criteria for evaluation. In general, though, the following elements are crucial to good works of fiction. The Evaluation Criteria for "Evaluating Children's Fiction" on page 14 summarize the criteria discussed below and may help the reader look at a book more carefully. However, not all questions will be appropriate for each book.

Plot

Of prime importance in any work of fiction for children is the plot. Children ask first, "What happens? Is it a good story?" The plot is the plan of action; it tells what the characters do and what happens to them. It is the thread that holds the fabric of the story together and makes the reader want to continue reading.

A well-constructed plot is organic and interrelated. It grows logically and naturally from the action and the decisions of the characters in given situations. The plot should be credible and ring true rather than depend on coincidence and contrivance. It should be original and fresh rather than trite, tired, and predictable.

In books that have substance, obstacles are not easily overcome and choices are not always clear-cut. When Damien, in Frank Cottrell Boyce's *Millions,* discovers a bag of money thrown from a passing train straight into his secret hideout, the pace of the story takes off. But the compelling plot is enhanced by the ethical dilemmas he wrestles with in dealing with this windfall and by our growing awareness of Damien's grief at his mother's death.

Plot is the chief element of appeal in stories of mystery and suspense. In series mysteries, the action is frequently predictable—Nancy Drew never fails, and the Hardy Boys move smoothly from one major feat to the next. The action is usually beyond the capabilities of the characters and becomes contrived and sensational. In contrast, *Shakespeare's Secret* by Elise Broach contains all the elements of mystery that appeal to middle-grade readers—a missing jewel, an unsolved crime, and an historical puzzle. However, Broach's characters are multidimensional and her writing skillful. She also develops a fascinating subplot about the authorship of William Shakespeare's plays. As in other well-plotted books, the climax of *Shakespeare's Secret* develops naturally from the interaction of characters and events.

Most plots in children's literature are presented in linear fashion. Frequently children find it confusing to follow several plot lines or to deal with flashbacks in time and place. However, several excellent books for middle graders do make use of these devices. Multiple stories are interwoven in the Newbery Medal book *Walk Two Moons* by Sharon Creech. On a cross-country trip with her grandparents, Salamanca Tree Hiddle regales them with the

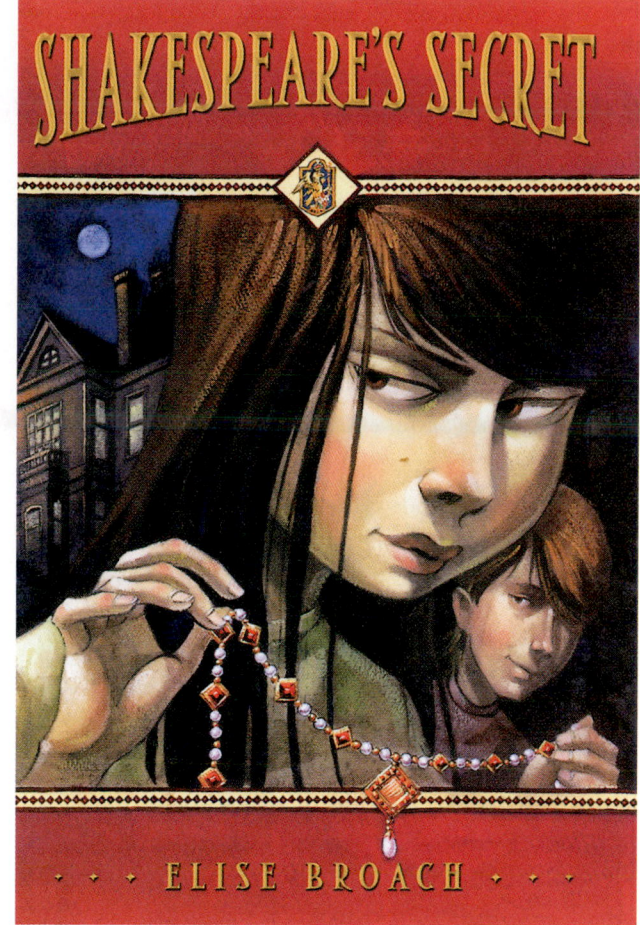

A fast-moving plot combines with depth of theme and characterization in Elise Broach's *Shakespeare's Secret.* From *Shakespeare's Secret* by Elise Broach. Copyright © 2005 by Elise Broach. Reprinted by permission of Henry Holt and Company, LLC.

somewhat wacky adventures of her friend Phoebe. As the narrative moves back and forth between the car journey and Phoebe's adventures, however, Sal's own story is revealed. These different plots represent the layers of self-understanding that Salamanca must uncover in order to accept the major changes that have occurred in her life.

In *Cousins,* Virginia Hamilton dramatically portrays the grief and guilt young Cammy feels when her cousin, spoiled Patty Ann, is drowned on a day-camp excursion. Although the book is short, it has multiple plot lines. The reader's attention is also drawn to Cammy's concern over the time her brother spends with troublesome cousin Richie and to her own attempts to brighten the life of Gram Tut, who is in the Care Home. The author uses remembered and imagined events, making part of the "action" take place in Cammy's head. This gives the story a wonderfully rich texture but makes it more challenging. The effectiveness of structure in stories like these depends on the clarity of the author's presentation and the child's ability to comprehend complexity.

Plot is but one element of good writing. If a book does not have a substantial plot, it will not hold children's interest long. But well-loved books are memorable for more than plot alone.

Setting

The structure of a story includes both the construction of the plot and its setting. The setting may be in the past, the present, or the future. The story may take place in a specific locale, or the setting may be deliberately vague to convey the universal feeling of all suburbs, all large cities, or all rural communities.

The setting for Karen Hesse's *Out of the Dust* is so well developed that readers can almost feel the grit of dirt between their teeth. Hesse's use of free verse conveys the essence of Billie Jo's terrible experiences during the Oklahoma dustbowl.

> On Sunday winds came,
> Bringing a red dust
> Like prairie fire,
> Hot and peppery,
> searing the inside of my nose,
> and the whites of my eyes.[30]

Just as the wind tore away layers of sod to lay bare the land, Hesse dispenses with flowery rhetoric for words and rhythms that reveal the depths of human courage and the heart of human love.

Both the time and the place of the story should affect the action, the characters, and the theme. Place, time, and people are inextricably bound together in Elisa Carbonne's *Stealing Freedom.* The setting that the author constructs includes geography, weather, and the details of everyday life that surrounded Ann Maria Weems, a young girl born into slavery in 1840s Maryland. Carbonne drew exhaustively from primary sources to follow Ann's journey on the Underground Railroad to Canada.

Stories of the present often seem to occur in homogenized settings that have little impact on character and action. There are notable exceptions, of course. When Brian's plane crashes at the edge of a wilderness lake in Gary Paulsen's *Hatchet,* the rigors of that setting dictate the terms of the tense survival story that follows. Jazmin and her sister CeCe in *Jazmin's Notebook* by Nikki Grimes lead lives circumscribed by their urban ghetto environment, but the physical presence of New York City provides Jazmin with metaphors for her inner strength. As she writes in her notebook, "though six-storied buildings crowd this sky, The sun scissors through and shines—and so will I."[31] Books that provide a unique sense of place are more memorable than those that do not.

The imaginary settings of fantasy must be carefully detailed in order to create a believable story. In *Charlotte's Web,* E. B. White has made us see and smell Wilbur's barnyard home so clearly that it takes little stretch of the imagination to listen in on the animals' conversations. In *A Wizard of Earthsea,* a more serious fantasy by Ursula Le Guin, the tale of wizards, dragons, and shadows is played out in an archipelago of imagined islands. Ruth Robbins has provided a map of Earthsea, for its geography is as exact as the laws and limits of magic used by the wizards of the isles. The setting of a story, then, is important in creating mood, authenticity, and credibility. The accident of place and time in a person's life might be as significant as the accident of birth, for places can have tremendous significance in our life stories.

Theme

A third point in the evaluation of any story is its overarching theme, or themes, the larger meanings that lie beneath the story's surface. Most well-written books can be read for several layers of meaning—plot, theme, or metaphor. On one level the story of *Charlotte's Web* by E. B. White is simply an absurd but amusing tale of how a spider saves the life of a pig; on another level, it reveals the meaning of loneliness and the obligations of friendship. A third layer of significance can be seen in the acceptance of death as a natural part of the cycle of life. Finally, E. B. White himself wrote that it was "an appreciative story. . . . It celebrates life, the seasons, the goodness of the barn, the beauty of the world, the glory of everything."[32]

The theme of a book reveals something of the author's purpose in writing the story. Katherine Paterson eloquently states how authors and readers are partners in calling up true meaning:

> We are trying to communicate that which lies in our deepest heart, which has no words, which can only be hinted at through the means of a story. And somehow, miraculously, a story that comes from deep in my heart calls from a reader that which is deepest in his or her heart, and together from our secret hidden selves we create a story that neither of us could have told alone.[33]

Theme provides a dimension to the story that goes beyond the action of the plot. The theme of a book might be the acceptance of self or others, growing up, the overcoming of fear or prejudice. This theme should be worth imparting to young people and be based on justice and integrity. Sound moral and ethical principles should pre-

---

[30]Karen Hesse, *Out of the Dust* (New York: Scholastic, 1997), p. 46.

[31]Nikki Grimes, *Jazmin's Notebook* (New York: Dial, 1998), p. 8.

[32]Dorothy L. Guth, ed., *Letters of E. B. White* (New York: Harper & Row, 1976), p. 613.

[33]Katherine Paterson, "Hearts in Hiding," in *Worlds of Childhood: The Art and Craft of Writing for Children,* ed. William Zinsser (Boston: Houghton Mifflin, 1990), p. 153.

vail. However, one danger in writing books for children is that the theme will override the plot. Authors might be so intent on conveying a message that they neglect story or characterization. Didacticism is still alive and well in the twenty-first century. It might hide behind the facade of ecology, drug abuse, or alienation, but it destroys fine writing.

Well-written books can make their themes fairly explicit without becoming preachy. In Natalie Babbitt's *Tuck Everlasting*, three motifs provide meaningful threads that keep reappearing: a toad, a music box, and the concept of a wheel. The wheel represents the theme of this gentle fantasy, the cycle of life and death that the Tuck family can never experience because they have drunk by accident from a spring that has frozen them in time, to live forever. As Angus Tuck tries to persuade young Winnie Foster not to drink from this water, he uses the example of a wheel to carry his message about life:

> It's a wheel, Winnie. Everything is a wheel, turning and turning, never stopping. The frog is part of it, and the bugs, and the fish and the wood thrush, too. And people. But never the same ones. Always coming in new, always growing and changing, and always moving on. That's the way it's supposed to be. That's the way it is.[34]

Children in the middle grades can comprehend symbolic meaning and recurring motifs that are woven so beautifully into the fabric of the theme.

Characterization

True characterization is another hallmark of fine writing. The people portrayed in children's books should be as convincingly real and lifelike as our next-door neighbors. Many of the animal characters in modern fantasy also have human personalities. The credibility of characters depends on the author's ability to show their true natures, their strengths, and their weaknesses.

Just as it takes time to know a new friend in all her various dimensions, so, too, does an author try to present many facets of a character bit by bit. In revealing character, an author might tell about the person through narration, record the character's conversation with others, describe the thoughts of the character, show the thoughts of others about the character, or show the character in action. A character who is revealed in only one way is apt to lack depth. If a single dimension of character is presented, or one trait overemphasized, the result is likely to be stereotyped and wooden. One-dimensional characters are the norm in folk and fairy tales, where witches are prototypes of evil and youngest children are deserving and good. However, modern fiction requires multidimensional characters whose actions and feelings grow out of the circumstances of the story. Books are usually

Arnold Lobel created two memorable animal characters in the *Frog and Toad* series. Illustration from *Frog and Toad* by Arnold Lobel. Illustrations copyright © 1970 by Arnold Lobel. Used by permission of HarperCollins Publishers.

more satisfying when readers feel they are discovering the character through the story rather than relying on authors' labels, like *jealous, troublesome,* or *shy*. Children do not need to be told that Leon Tillage is courageous for having survived years of segregation and humiliation. His own words in his *Leon's Story* reveal his resilience, his bravery, and his human dignity.

In *The View from Saturday,* E. L. Konigsburg constructs personalities for her five characters that are as complex as the pieces of jigsaw puzzles they assemble at their Saturday teas at Sillington House. Even more delightful for the reader, these characters are revealed slowly as Mrs. Olinski, Noah, Julian, Nadia, and Ethan present their views of events. Ethan reflects on discoveries he has made about himself as a result of his friendships.

> Something in Sillington House gave me permission to do things I had never done before. . . .

---

[34]Natalie Babbitt, *Tuck Everlasting* (New York: Farrar, Straus & Giroux, 1975), p. 62.

Something there had triggered the unfolding of those parts that had been incubating. Things that had lain inside me, curled up like the turtle hatchlings newly emerged from their eggs, taking time in the dark of their nest to unfurl themselves.[35]

Konigsburg unfolds her characters in just such a way, adding subtle details and connections among the five that invite the reader to take part in a contest of wits similar to the one that serves as the centerpiece of the plot.

In addition to depth in characterization, there should be consistency in character portrayal. Everything characters do, think, and say should seem natural and inevitable. We can expect them to act and speak in accordance with their age, culture, and educational background. Stanley Yelnats, the unprepossessing delinquent of Louis Sachar's *Holes,* is so credible an antihero that he lends believability to a plot that is filled with quirks and coincidences.

Another aspect of sound characterization is growth and development. Do the characters change in the course of the story, or are they untouched by the events in which they have a part? In picture books and short tales, we might expect characters to be fully described but not to change much. In longer fiction, however, characters have time to learn and grow. Many characters are best remembered for the turnarounds they have made or the way they have matured. Readers do not quickly forget the struggle of headstrong, self-centered Jo of Louisa May Alcott's *Little Women* in taming her rebellious ways. Another character who grows before the reader's eyes in a gradual and convincing manner is the title character of Katherine Paterson's *Lyddie.* A nineteenth-century New England girl who becomes a mill worker in an effort to save the family farm, Lyddie is courageous and determined throughout the story. The change comes in her ability to see the options of her life realistically and in her growing sense of the possibilities of her future as she sets off to attend the first women's college in the nation.

Not all characters change, though. A character might be well developed, multidimensional, and interesting and yet seem to remain frozen in that particular time of her or his life. Such characters are common in humorous stories. In Robert McCloskey's *Homer Price* and Astrid Lindgren's *Pippi Longstocking,* the title characters remain consistent in nature through all their adventures. Some stories, then, might be notable for character delineation rather than character development.

Long after we have forgotten their stories, we can recall some of the personalities of children's literature. We recognize them as they turn the corner of our memories, and we are glad for their friendship. The line is long; it includes animals and people. It is hard to tell

Beverly Cleary's Ramona has come alive for millions of children in books like *Ramona's World. Cover from Ramona's World* by Beverly Cleary, illustrated by Alan Tiegreen. Jacket illustration copyright © 1999 by Alan Tiegreen. Used by permission of Morrow Junior Books, a division of William Morrow Company, an imprint of HarperCollins Publishers, Inc.

where it begins, and we are happy that it has no end. In our mind's eye we see the three loyal friends Mole, Toad, and Rat returning from their adventures on the open road; Mary Poppins flies by holding tightly to her large black umbrella with one hand and carrying her carpetbag in the other; she passes right over those comic friends Frog and Toad, who are out looking for the corner that spring is just around. In the barnyard Wilbur has just discovered a wonderful new friend, Charlotte A. Cavatica, much to the amusement of the wise geese and the sly rat, Templeton. If we look closely, we can see tiny Arrietty and Pod, out for a Borrower's holiday; Stuart Little paddles his souvenir canoe along the drainage ditch; and our favorite Hobbit, Bilbo Baggins, outwits the terrifying Gollum. Gathered in the schoolyard are the Great Gilly Hopkins and her tag-along friend, Agnes Stokes; Meg Murry is consulting with the principal, Mr. Jenkins, about her little brother, Charles Wallace. Ramona comes by wearing the crown of burrs she had made so she can star in a TV commercial; Harriet, with flashlight

---

[35]E. L. Konigsburg, *A View from Saturday* (New York: Atheneum, 1996), p. 93.

and notebook, is just beginning her spy route; and Jeffrey "Maniac" Magee comes loping along with his sneaker soles slapping.

The line is long in this procession of real personages in children's literature. It reaches back in our memories to include Beth, Jo, Amy, and Meg; it stands outside the Secret Garden and listens to the laughing voices of Mary, Colin, and Dickon; and, with Laura, it delights in the warm coziness of the fire and the sound of Pa's fiddling in Laura Ingalls Wilder's *Little House in the Big Woods.* We know all these characters well because their authors blew the breath of life into each one of them. They have come alive in the pages of books, and they will live forever in our memories.

Style

An author's style of writing is simply selection and arrangement of words in presenting the story. Good writing style is appropriate to the plot, theme, and characters, both creating and reflecting the mood of the story. In Kerry Madden's *Gentle's Holler,* 12-year-old Livy Two, the book's narrator, is one of nine children in a loving family that is nonetheless scrabbling to survive in their remote North Carolina mountain community. Livy's Daddy is a talented musician, but his dreams of stardom in Nashville don't always put enough food on the table. Mama is more practical, and although she clearly loves her husband, she frets about keeping the family going and especially about 3-year-old Gentle. Gentle is blind; she "peeks at life with her ears and fingers." But neither parent is able to admit their worries and they won't discuss them with their children. In this passage Livy overhears her artistic sister Louise describing the woods near their cabin for Gentle.

> "Now Gentle, eat this blueberry and you'll understand the color blue. Azure, sapphire, navy, and indigo. That's other names for blue." I get real quiet so they don't know I'm nearby. I just want to hear Louise talk to Gentle. Next, she matter-of-factly lists all the shades of green: "Green means emerald, olive, aqua, and forest. Feel these leaves. Smell the pine and the moss. You smell all that? That's green, little gal."
>
> "Green, Louise?" Gentle repeats.
>
> Then Louise says, "Red: cardinal, crimson, russet, and scarlet. Think of the oven in the kitchen when the blast of hot air hits you in the face."
>
> "Mama's biscuits?"
>
> Louise says, "That's right. Okay, next is yellow: golden, honey, canary yellow, amber, and saffron. Think of sun on your face and honey on your bread and that's yellow. Purple: lilac, lavender, orchid, plum, and violet. Remember

In *Gentle's Holler* Kerry Madden successfully weaves visual and verbal images throughout a moving story about family connections. Jacket illustration from *Gentle's Holler: A Novel* by Kerry Madden, copyright © 2005. Used by permission of Viking Penguin, a division of Penguin Young Readers Group, a member of Penguin Group (USA) Inc., 345 Hudson Street, New York.

> the coolness in the air before it rains. Remember, Gentle?"
>
> I close my eyes and drift into Louise's words, and soon I am inside one of my sister's paintings, part of the color, light, and shadow. Another song eases into my head as I listen to my sisters talking colors.[36]

Madden's vivid lyrical style serves to reinforce the musical and artistic motifs that fill the book. Here the writer's style also underscores the basic refrains of family love and family conflict and celebrates the family bonds that can transcend tragedy.

Although some authors develop a style so distinctive that it is easily recognizable, their work might show variation from book to book. Gary Paulsen's *Hatchet* is a survival story told as a continuous record of the thoughts and actions of Brian, the survivor. The brief sentences

---

[36]Kerry Madden, *Gentle's Holler* (New York: Viking, 2005), pp. 88–89.

arranged as individual paragraphs are choppy, breathless, tense:

> I was flying to visit my father and the plane crashed and sank in a lake.
>> There, keep it that way. Short thoughts.
>> I do not know where I am.
>> Which doesn't mean much. More to the point, they do not know where I am.[37]

Paulsen's *The Winter Room* is a more lyrical story that takes as its backdrop the changing seasons of a northern Minnesota farm. Carefully placed sentence fragments punctuate this narrative also, but here they are contrasted with long chains of sensory details. The following is only a part of a sentence:

> . . . [when] Rex moves into the barn to sleep and Father drains all the water out of all the radiators in the tractors and the old town truck and sometimes you suck a quick breath in the early morning that is so cold it makes your front teeth ache; when the chickens are walking around all fluffed up like white balls and the pigs burrow into the straw to sleep in the corner of their pen, and Mother goes to Hemings for the quilting bee they do each year that lasts a full day—when all that happens, fall is over.
>> But it still isn't winter.[38]

Most children do not enjoy a story that is too descriptive, but they can appreciate figurative language, especially when the comparisons are within their background of understanding. Natalie Babbitt's vivid prologue to *Tuck Everlasting* invites children to visualize the intense images by describing the month of August as curiously silent "with blank white dawns and glaring noons and sunsets smeared with too much color."[39]

Patricia MacLachlan's style effectively mirrors the setting of the story and the background of its characters in *Sarah, Plain and Tall*. The writing reflects the prairie setting and the straightforward manner of Sarah, a mail-order bride from Maine. The tension of the story lies in its themes of longing and belonging—Sarah's understated longing for the sea and the children's longing for a mother. The beauty of the sea is contrasted with that of the prairie; the light after a prairie storm reminds Sarah of a sea squall. At the end of the story, when Sarah has decided to stay, the child-narrator, Anna, reflects on the future:

> Autumn will come, then winter, cold with a wind that blows like the wind off the sea in Maine. . . .
> There will be Sarah's sea, blue and gray and green, hanging on the wall. And songs old and new. And Seal with yellow eyes. And there will be Sarah, plain and tall.[40]

The repeated phrases in this passage have a rhythm like music, a cadence that is very satisfying, especially when the book is read aloud.

There is no one style or set of language patterns that is more appropriate than others for a children's book. Yet children's tastes do place some demands on the writer. Because young readers tend to prefer action over description or introspection, those elements must be handled with special skill. Children crave dialogue, like readers of all ages. They feel as Alice in Wonderland did when she looked into her sister's book and said, "What's the use of a book without pictures or conversation?" Masters at writing dialogue that sounds natural and amusing include Lois Lowry in *Gooney Bird and the Room Mother* and Cynthia Rylant in *Henry and Mudge and the Tumbling Trip*. Writing the dialogue for a book of contemporary realistic fiction is particularly difficult because slang and popular expressions are quickly dated. Paula Danzinger is one writer who skillfully captures the sound of today's idiom in her stories. Ralph Fletcher's sixth graders in *Flying Solo* sound convincingly real, and Christopher Paul Curtis captures African American cultural nuances in books like *Bucking the Sarge*.

The best test of an author's style is probably oral reading. Does the story read smoothly? Does the conversation flow naturally? Does the author provide variety in sentence patterns, vocabulary, and use of stylistic devices?

Although it is difficult for children to analyze a particular author's style, they do react to it. Children are quick to detect the patronizing air of an author who talks down to them in little asides, for example. They dislike a story that is too sentimental, and they see through the disguise of the too-moralistic tales of the past. Adults are more responsive than children to the clever, the slyly written, and the sarcastic. Frequently children are better able to identify what they dislike about an author's style than to identify what they like. Obviously, the matter of style is important when adults evaluate books for children.

Point of View

The term *point of view* is often used to indicate the author's choice of narrator(s) and the way the narrator reveals the story. Whose story is it? Who tells it? In folk and fairy tales, for instance, the storyteller tells the tale, and the storyteller knows the thoughts and actions of all the characters. The storyteller's voice is also used in modern fiction, for books in which the author reports the comings

---

[37]Gary Paulsen, *Hatchet* (New York: Bradbury, 1987), p. 47.

[38]Gary Paulsen, *The Winter Room* (New York: Orchard, 1989), p. 62.

[39]Natalie Babbitt, *Tuck Everlasting* (New York: Farrar, Straus & Giroux, 1985), p. 3.

[40]Patricia MacLachlan, *Sarah, Plain and Tall* (New York: Harper & Row, 1985), p. 58.

and goings, the conversations, and the feelings of all the characters, villains as well as heroes. We say that such stories have an omniscient, or all-knowing, narrator. C. S. Lewis presents his Narnia series in this way. In *The Lion, the Witch, and the Wardrobe,* we are sometimes with Lucy, sometimes with Edmund, sometimes with all four of the adventuring children, and occasionally in places where they can never go. With the use of the third person, the omniscient point of view allows the author complete freedom to crawl inside the skins of each of the characters, thinking their thoughts, speaking their words, and observing the action of the story. It also allows the author to speak directly to the reader, if she or he chooses, just as a storyteller would in a face-to-face situation. C. S. Lewis comments to his readers in parentheses, a practice that some children and adults find detracts from their enjoyment of the story.

Many children's books take a point of view that also uses the third person but gives the author less freedom. This limited-omniscient, or concealed, narrator view does, however, provide closer identification with a single character. The author chooses to stand behind one character, so to speak, and tell the story from over his or her shoulder. The story is then limited to what that character can see, hear, believe, feel, and understand. Katherine Paterson has told the story *The Great Gilly Hopkins* from this perspective. Gilly is "on stage" throughout, and we see the world as Gilly sees it. We know what others think about her through their reactions to her and her interpretations of their thoughts. For example, Gilly is having her first dinner at the home of Trotter, her latest foster mother:

> The meal proceeded without incident. Gilly was hungry but thought it better not to seem to enjoy her supper too much. William Ernest ate silently and steadily with only an occasional glance at Gilly. She could tell that the child was scared silly of her. It was about the only thing in the last two hours that had given her any real satisfaction. Power over the boy was sure to be power over Trotter in the long run.[41]

The more direct narrative voice of the first person, once considered unusual in children's books, is quite common today. In contemporary realism it is almost the norm. Judy Blume helped popularize this kind of storytelling with books like *Are You There, God? It's Me, Margaret* and *Blubber.* Blume's stories are not known for strong characterization, but they do reveal the author's ability to recreate the everyday language of children.

The advantage of using first-person narrative is that it can make for easy reading. It attempts to invite its audience by taking a stance that says, "Look—we speak the same language." In many cases this sort of writing does not stretch the reader's vocabulary or imagination. The short, choppy sentences simply reflect a 10-year-old's idioms and grammatical errors. Moreover, children's perspectives on the world are limited by their lack of experience, just as their vocabulary is. This is an added challenge for an author writing in the first person; for although it might be easy to present the narrator's thoughts and feelings in an appealing way, it will be more difficult to show that the narrator's view might be narrow, misguided, or simply immature when seen from a broader perspective.

Stories told by older characters, or those who are especially intelligent or sensitive, usually do a better job of dealing with complex issues. In books such as *Missing May* by Cynthia Rylant or David Almond's *Skellig,* the authors have created believable characters and lent power to the story through the use of first-person narration.

Almond's young protagonist, Michael, begins his deeply moving story with this description of Skellig:

> I found him in the garage on a Sunday afternoon. . . . He was lying there in the darkness behind the tea chests, in the dust and dirt. It was as if he'd been there forever. He was filthy and pale and dried out and I thought he was dead. I couldn't have been more wrong. I'd soon begin to see the truth about him, that there'd never been another creature like him in the world.[42]

Without the immediacy of Michael's narration, the reader might dismiss this book as make believe and Skellig as a magical creature such as a unicorn or hobbit. The book's strength derives from our irrational hope that creatures like Skellig do exist. Michael's voice helps us accept the events that take place and heightens the emotional power of the story.

At times authors counter the limitations of a single point of view by alternating the presentation of several views within the same story or changing points of view. Konigsburg's multiple narratives in *The View from Saturday* add great richness to the textual tapestry. Author Linda Sue Park provides an innovative twist on this technique in *Project Mulberry,* when she intersects the first-person narrative of her main character, Julia Song, with a dialogue between herself as author and Julia as a product of her imagination. This trend for authors to be more visible to readers can be found in such other books as Polly Horvath's *The Pepins and Their Problems,* but it is also a technique found in Victorian literature, as reflected by the tone of Kate DiCamillo's *The Tale of Despereaux.*

The author's personal and cultural experience is reflected in more subtle ways in every book's point of view.

---

[41]Katherine Paterson, *The Great Gilly Hopkins* (New York: Harper & Row, 1978), p. 14.

[42]David Almond, *Skellig* (New York: Delacorte, 1999), p. 1.

a novel by
Linda Sue Park

The first-person narrative of character seventh grader Julia Song is interspersed with her conversations with the author in Linda Sue Park's thought-provoking and delightful *Project Mulberry*. Cover from *Project Mulberry* by Linda Sue Park. Jacket illustrations copyright © 2005 by Debora Smith. Reprinted by permission of Clarion Books, an imprint of Houghton Mifflin Company. All rights reserved.

An author of color has a unique opportunity to illuminate those nuances of culture that outsiders can never capture. To be sure, there are writers who create fine literature from sustained contact with a culture other than their own. But their points of view are no substitute for those of an author who has lived those cultural experiences from birth.

All readers should be able to find themselves reflected in the literature they read. In the past forty years, literature by and about members of parallel cultures has increased (see Chapter 3 for a full discussion of multicultural literature), and so has recognition of these books. The gay and lesbian experience is presented to young adults by award-winning authors like Nancy Garden and Francesca Lia Block. Quality picture books like Linda de Haan and Stern Nijland's *King and King and Family* and Justin Richardson and Peter Parnell's *And Tango Makes Three* present younger children with a positive, if subtle, look at same-sex parents. Positive portrayals of children with disabilities can be found in books like Jack Gantos's *What Would Joey Do?* about a likable boy with attention deficit hyperactivity disorder. Joey has appeared in three books and is a protagonist whose struggles with teachers and family are more important to the story than his struggles with his disability. In *Deaf Child Crossing*, Marlee Matlin has written a story of two friends, one of whom happens to be deaf. About the ups and downs of friendship, the story realistically depicts the problems encountered by deaf children in a hearing world but is not driven by them.

However, there still are not enough quality books that focus on our beautiful and diverse world. In evaluating books, we need to ask not just who is telling the story but how this influences the story. What perspective does the narrator bring to events, and what vision of the world does that offer to children? It is necessary, then, to evaluate literature not only for its literary value but also for the image of the group presented by the text and illustrations— and we have attempted to do so throughout this book. [45]

Additional Considerations

The books we think of as truly excellent have significant content and, if illustrated, fine illustrations. Their total design, from the front cover to the final end paper, creates a unified look that seems in character with the content and invites the reader to proceed. Today we have so many picture storybooks and so many beautifully illustrated books of poetry, nonfiction, and other genres that any attempt to evaluate children's literature should consider both the role of illustration and the format of the book. We will discuss these criteria in greater depth in the chapters in Part 2 of this book. In general, however, we should consider what function the art in a book is intended to have. Are the pictures meant to be decorations? Were they designed to complement or clarify the text? Are they so much a part of the story that you cannot imagine the book without them?

The format of a book includes its size, shape, page design, illustrations, typography, paper quality, and binding. Frequently, some small aspect of the format, such as the book jacket, will be an important factor in a child's decision to read a story.

All types of books—novels, picture books, poetry, biography, informational books—should be well designed and well made. Many factors other than illustration are

---

[45]See Zhihui Fang, Danling Fang, and Linda L. Lamme, "Rethinking the Role of Multicultural Literature in Literacy Instruction: Problems, Paradoxes, and Possibilities," *The New Advocate*, 12(3) (summer, 1999), pp. 259–76.

important. The type should be large enough for easy reading by children at the age level for which the book is intended. At the same time, if the type is too large, children might see the book as "babyish." Space between the lines (leading) should be sufficient to make the text clear. The paper should be of high quality, heavy enough to prevent any penetration of ink. In longer works written for older children, this means off-white with a dull finish to prevent glare, although other surfaces are used for special purposes. The binding should be durable and practical, able to withstand hard use. Publishers produce many books in alternate bindings, one for the trade (bookstore sales) and an extra-sturdy version for library use. Some of these publishers even go to the trouble of including a cloth cover, often embossed, under the dust jacket as in David Wiesner's *The Three Pigs.* Rhoda Blumberg's *Shipwrecked! The True Adventures of a Japanese Boy* may not have a cloth cover but its overall design, from the elegant cover to the placement of photographs and the bordered detailing on each page, is a fine example of book design. It is important to notice that books reprinted in paperback by many book clubs may not include details from the hardcover edition such as end papers. Thus,

Rhoda Blumberg's *Shipwrecked!: The True Adventures of a Japanese Boy* is a fine example of book design with its elegant cover, patterned page borders, and pleasing layout.
Jacket illustration of *Shipwrecked!* by Rhoda Blumberg © 2001. Cover design copyright © 2001 HarperCollins. Used by permission of HarperCollins Publishers, Inc. Illustrations copyright © 2001 by Sergio Ruzzier.

while teachers may want to have inexpensive paperback copies of a picture book for their classroom libraries, it is important to make the hardcover edition available to children as well. Of course, a book should never be selected on the basis of format alone. No book is better than its content.

Comparison with Other Books

A book should be considered not in isolation but as a part of the larger body of literature. Individual books need to be compared with others on the same subject or theme. Is this just another horse story, or like Jessie Haas's *Unbroken* does it make a contribution to our understanding about human motives and desires? Every teacher and librarian should know some books well enough to develop a personal list of books of excellence that can serve as models for comparison. How does this adventure story compare with Armstrong Sperry's *Call It Courage,* or this fantasy with *A Wrinkle in Time* by Madeleine L'Engle, or this historical fiction with Mildred Taylor's *Roll of Thunder, Hear My Cry*? These reference points of outstanding books help to sharpen evaluations.

An author's new book should be compared with her or his previous works. Contributions by the same author might be inconsistent in quality. What is the best book Jean George has written? Is *On the Far Side of the Mountain* as good as *My Side of the Mountain*? How does *Water Sky* compare with *Julie of the Wolves*? Too frequently, books are evaluated on the basis of the author's reputation rather than for their inherent worth.

Many informational and biographical series are written by different authors. The quality of the book varies with the ability of the writer, despite similarities in approach and format. Rather than condemning or approving an entire series, evaluate a book on its own merits.

A book needs to be compared with outstanding prototypes, with other books written by the same author, and with other books in the same series. It can also be helpful to become familiar with some of the review journals in the field of children's literature and to compare reviews of a given book. What have reputable reviewers said about this book? Where have they placed it in relation to others of its type? Have they singled it out for special notice by starring it or providing a special focus? A comparison of reviews of one book usually reveals more similarities than differences, although reviewers have personal preferences just as other readers do. Appendixes A and B provide sources that will be helpful in evaluating and selecting children's books.

In summary, the basic considerations for the evaluation of fiction for children are a well-constructed and well-paced plot, a significant theme, an authentic setting, a credible point of view, convincing characterization, appropriate style, and an attractive format. Not all books achieve excellence in each of these areas. Some books are remembered for their fine characterizations, others for their exciting plots, and others for the evocation of the setting.

CLASSICS IN CHILDREN'S LITERATURE

Knowledge of children's classics—those books that have stood the test of time—can provide further guidance for evaluating children's books. What makes a book endure from one generation to another? Alice Jordan states: "Until a book has weathered at least one generation and is accepted in the next, it can hardly be given the rank of a classic."[46]

Many books and poems have achieved an honored position in children's literature through a combination of adult adoration, parent perpetuation, and teacher assignments. Most adults remember with nostalgia the books they read as children. They tend to think that what they read was best and ignore the possibility that any better books might be produced. It is easy to forget that every "classic" was once a new book, that some of today's new books will be tomorrow's classics. Teachers and librarians should begin with modern children and their interests, not adults' interests when they were children.

Certain books became classics when there were very few books from which children could choose. In fact, many classics were not children's books at all, but were written for adults. In their desire to read, children claimed these adult books, struggled through the difficult parts, and disregarded what they did not understand. They had no other choice. Today's children are not so persevering, because they see no reason to be. The introductory sentence of *Robinson Crusoe* runs the length of the entire first page and contains difficult vocabulary and syntax. Defoe wrote the story in 1719 for adult readers, but children quickly discovered this story of shipwreck and adventure and plunged into it. However, they can find the same tingling excitement and more readable prose in survival stories like Henning Mankell's *Secrets in the Fire*, Graham Salisbury's *Eyes of the Emperor*, or Donna Jo Napoli's *Three Days*.

The classics should not be exempted from reevaluation by virtue of their past veneration. They should be able to compete favorably with contemporary books. Unimpressed by vintage or lineage, children seldom read a book because they think they should. They read more for enjoyment than for edification. Some books have been kept alive from one generation to the next by the common consent of critics and children; these are the true classics of children's literature. No teacher or parent has to cajole a child into enjoying the adventure and suspense in Robert Louis Stevenson's *Treasure Island*, the mystery and excitement of *The Secret Garden* by Frances Hodgson Burnett, or the memorable characters in Alcott's *Little Women* or A. A. Milne's *Winnie the Pooh*. These books can hold their own amid today's ever-increasing number of new and beautiful books.

THE BOOK AWARDS

Teachers and librarians will find it helpful to be familiar with books that have won awards.[47] These awards, which have been established for various purposes, provide criteria for what experts consider to be the best in children's literature. Such awards have helped counteract the judgment of the marketplace by focusing attention on beautiful and worthwhile books. In an age of mass production, they have stimulated artists, authors, and publishers to produce books of distinction and have helped children's literature achieve a worthy status.

The award books are not always popular with children. However, most of the awards are based not on popularity but on recognized excellence. They were never intended to rubber-stamp the tastes of children; they were intended to raise them. Children's reactions to books are significant, and many awards, particularly state awards, are voted on by children. However, popularity of a book, whether for children or for adults, is not necessarily a mark of distinctive writing or artistic achievement. How many best-sellers win a Pulitzer Prize for literature? Because there are now so many awards in so many categories of children's literature, only the best-known ones will be discussed here.

The Newbery and Caldecott Medals

Two of the most coveted awards in children's literature are the Newbery and Caldecott medals. Winners are chosen every year by two committees of the Association for Library Service to Children, a division of the American Library Association. A candidate for either of the awards must be a citizen or resident of the United States.

The John Newbery Medal, established in 1922, is the oldest award for children's books. It is named for John Newbery, a British publisher and bookseller of the eighteenth century. Appropriately called the "father of children's literature," he was the first to publish books expressly for children. The Newbery Medal is awarded to the author of the most distinguished contribution to American literature for children published in the preceding year. Although the award is occasionally given to a book with outstanding illustrations, such as Nancy Wil-

---

[46]Alice M. Jordan, *Children's Classics* (Boston: Horn Book, 1974), p. 4.

[47]See Appendix A for various book awards, criteria, and winners. Information also appears in *Children's Books in Print* (New York: R. R. Bowker).

In this Caldecott Medal–winning book, *Ox-Cart Man* by Donald Hall, the father loads up his ox-cart with the many things his family has been making and growing all year to take to market. Barbara Cooney's paintings accurately reflect the New England landscapes and Early American primitive art. From *Ox-Cart Man* by Donald Hall, illustrated by Barbara Cooney, copyright © 1997 by Barbara Cooney Porter, illustrations. Used by permission of Viking Penguin, a division of Penguin Putnam.

lard's *A Visit to William Blake's Inn*, with pictures by Alice and Martin Provensen, the Newbery Medal honors the quality of the writing. Many age ranges are represented, but most of the Newbery Medal books are for able, mature readers. Frequently children need to hear these books read aloud and discuss them with an adult before they develop a taste for their excellence.

The Randolph J. Caldecott Medal is named in honor of a great English illustrator of the nineteenth century, Randolph Caldecott. Caldecott was well known for his sprightly picture books depicting the country life of England. The Caldecott Medal, established in 1938, is awarded to the most distinguished American picture book for children chosen from those first published in the United States during the previous year. The text should be worthy of the illustrations, but the award is made primarily for the artwork.

Students of children's literature would do well to acquaint themselves with some of these medal-winning books and their authors and illustrators. The Honor Books for each award are also worth knowing. Because the selection for the awards must be limited to books published during one year, the quality of the award books varies; certain years produce a richer harvest than others. The passage of time has shown most choices to have been wise ones, but there have been a few surprises. In 1953, for instance, the highly praised *Charlotte's Web* was a Newbery Honor Book, edged out in the medal competition by Ann Nolan Clark's *Secret of the Andes*, a

Talking Point

Do award-winning books neglect girls?

Go to the Online Learning Center at **www.mhhe .com/kiefer9e** or your Resources CD-ROM to learn more.

beautifully written but far less popular story. Books by Laura Ingalls Wilder were in the Honor Book category five different years, but never received the medal. Final restitution was made, perhaps, by the establishment of the Laura Ingalls Wilder Award, which serves a different purpose.

The list of Caldecott Medal winners shows great variety as to type of artwork, media used, age appeal, and subject matter. The range of artwork includes the lovely winterscapes by Mary Azarian for Jacqueline Briggs Martin's *Snowflake Bentley*; the comic, almost cartoon, style of William Steig's *Sylvester and the Magic Pebble*; the surrealism of Chris Van Allsburg's *Jumanji*; and the elegant simplicity of Kevin Henkes's *Kitten's First Full Moon*. Various media are represented among the medal winners, including woodcut, watercolor, opaque paint, collage, and various combinations of pen and ink and paint. Marcia Brown has won the Caldecott Medal three times; David Wiesner, Chris Van Allsburg, Robert McCloskey, Nonny Hogrogian, Leo and Diane Dillon, and Barbara Cooney have been honored twice. Joseph Krumgold, Elizabeth Speare, Katherine Paterson, E. L. Konigsburg, and Lois Lowry have each received two Newbery Medals; Robert Lawson continues to be the only person who has won both a Newbery and a Caldecott Medal.

International Book Awards

 The Hans Christian Andersen Medal was established in 1956 as the first international children's book award. It is given by the International Board on Books for Young People every two years to a living author and (since 1966) an illustrator, in recognition of his or her entire body of work. Meindert DeJong, Maurice Sendak, Scott O'Dell, Paula Fox, Virginia Hamilton, and Katherine Paterson are the only Americans to have received this medal so far.

The Mildred L. Batchelder Award was established to honor the U.S. publication of the year's most outstanding translated book for children. Like the Newbery and Caldecott medals, this award is given by the Association for Library Service to Children of the American Library Association. Appropriately, it is always presented on International Children's Book Day, 2 April, which was Hans Christian Andersen's birthday.

Lifetime Contribution Awards

The Laura Ingalls Wilder Award honors an author or illustrator for a substantial and lasting contribution to children's literature. It was established in 1954 by the Association for Library Service to Children and was presented first to Laura Ingalls Wilder herself, for her *Little House* books. First presented every five years, and now every three, the award makes no requirement concerning the number of books that must be produced, but a body of work is implied and the books must be published in the United States. The recipients of the award, including Milton Meltzer, Beverly Cleary, Theodor S. Geisel (Dr. Seuss), Maurice Sendak, Jean Fritz, Virginia Hamilton, Marcia Brown, Laurence Yep, and Russell Freedman, all are creators who have made an indelible mark on American children's literature.

Some of the other awards presented for a body of work are the Catholic Library Association's Regina Medal and the University of Mississippi's Children's Collection Medallion. The Kerlan Award, which honors "singular attainments" in children's literature, also recognizes the donation of original manuscripts, as resource material, to the Kerlan Collection at the University of Minnesota.

There was no major award for children's poetry until 1977, when the National Council of Teachers of English established the Award for Excellence in Poetry for Children, to be given to a living American poet. This award recognizes the writer's entire body of work. Octogenarian David McCord was the first recipient; others have included Aileen Fisher, Karla Kuskin, Myra Cohn Livingston, Eve Merriam, John Ciardi, Lillian Moore, Arnold Adoff, Valerie Worth, Barbara Esbensen, Eloise Green-

INTO THE CLASSROOM

Knowing Children's Literature

1. **Newbery Award Committee.** Form a mock Newbery award committee and review the medal winners and Honor Books for one year. Do the children agree with the opinions of the judges? Have the children state their reasons for the choices they have made.
2. **The Influence of Literature.** Ask children to interview two or three classmates or family members about the influence of literature in their lives. In what ways have books been important to them? What titles are most memorable? Why?

 Go to the Online Learning Center at **www.mhhe.com/kiefer9e** or your Resources CD-ROM to find these additional activities:

3. **Create Book Awards**
4. **Book Recommendations**
5. **Survey of Reading Habits**
6. **What Makes a Classic a Classic?**
7. **Books Reflect Their Time**

field, Mary Ann Hoberman, Nikki Grimes, and X. J. Kennedy.

Several other awards, like the Scott O'Dell Award for Historical Fiction and the Edgar Allan Poe Award of the Mystery Writers of America, honor particular kinds of writing. These prizes are given for individual books rather than for a body of work, however.

No one but the most interested follower of children's literature would want to remember all the awards that are given for children's books. And certainly no one should assume that the award winners are the only children's books worth reading. Like the coveted Oscars of the motion picture industry and the Emmys of television, the awards in children's literature focus attention not only on the winners of the year but also on the entire field of endeavor. They recognize and honor excellence and also point the way to improved writing, illustrating, and producing of worthwhile and attractive books for children.

Chapter Review

Go to the Online Learning Center at **www.mhhe.com/kiefer9e** or your Resources CD-ROM to take chapter quizzes, practice with key terms, and review the chapter.

Explorations

1. Can you think of any one book you read and reread as a child? What particular qualities of the story appealed to you? Reread it now and evaluate it according to the criteria established in this chapter. Would you still recommend it for children?

2. Read one of the series books: for instance, one from the Baby-Sitters Club, Sweet Valley High, Boxcar Children, or Nancy Drew series. Look closely at the literary craftsmanship of the book. How many contrived incidents can you find? Do the characters have real strengths and weaknesses? If you were to read this book aloud, how would it sound?

3. Read a recently published children's book and write a brief reaction to it. Then find two or more published reviews of that book. List the criteria that seem important to the reviewers. How are their criteria like or different from yours?

4. Write your reading autobiography. What memories do you have of your early reading? Did either of your parents read to you? Do you recall any of the books they read? Did any teachers or librarians read aloud to you? What were some of your favorite books? Do you recall any that you did not like? Do you know why you did not like them?

5. Go to the Children's Literature Database on your Resources CD-ROM. Choose a general topic such as families, friends, or animals. Enter the topic in the search box. Search on the "all" button and sort by author. Browse through the list and notice how the books are sorted. Choose an interest level and find one or two authors who seem familiar to you. Locate and read some of their books in a library.

Web Links

Go to the Online Learning Center at **www.mhhe.com/kiefer9e** to find links to the following Children's Literature Web sites:

About the Caldecott and How It Is Awarded

About the Newbery and How It Is Awarded

American Library Association Best Books for Young Adults

American Library Association Notable Children's Books

Award for Excellence in Poetry for Children

Boston Globe-Horn Book Award Winners

Caldecott Medal Winners

Carol Hurst's Children's Literature Site

Children's Choices

Children's Literature Web Guide

Cooperative Children's Book Center

Coretta Scott King Award Purpose and Criteria

Coretta Scott King Award Winners

Database of Award-Winning Children's Literature

Edgar Allan Poe Awards

Fairrosa Cyber Library for Children's Literature

Golden Kite Award

Hans Christian Andersen Medal Winners

International Reading Association Children's Books Awards

Internet Public Library Youth Division Reading Zone

Internet School Library Media Center Children's Literature and Language Arts Page

Internet School Library Media Center Literary Prizes

Kay Vandergrift's Children's Literature Site

Laura Ingalls Wilder Award

Margaret A. Edwards Award for Outstanding Literature for Young Adults

Mildred L. Batchelder Award

Nancy Keane's Booktalks

Newbery Medal Winners

Orbis Pictus Award for Outstanding Nonfiction for Children

Pura Belpré Award

SchoolLibraries.org Online Resources for School Librarians

The Scoop

Scott O'Dell Historical Fiction Award

Young Reader's Choice Award Winners

Related Readings

Coles, Robert. *The Call of Stories: Teaching and the Moral Imagination.* Boston: Houghton Mifflin, 1989.

> A noted child psychiatrist describes the influence of literature in his own life and its impact on the young adults he has taught at Harvard University and elsewhere.

Egoff, Sheila, Gordon Stubbs, Ralph Ashley, and Wendy Sutton. *Only Connect: Readings on Children's Literature.* 3rd ed. New York: Oxford University Press, 1996.

> An excellent collection of essays on children's literature, encompassing literary criticism, standards, changing tastes, children's responses to books, and writing and illustrating books. Many of the contributors are well known, including Katherine Paterson, Natalie Babbitt, C. S. Lewis, and John Rowe Townsend.

Harrison, Barbara, and Gregory Maguire. *Origins of Story: On Writing for Children.* New York: McElderry Books, 1999.

> A collection of essays by such noted authors as Virginia Hamilton, Ursula Le Guin, Maurice Sendak, and Jill Paton Walsh. In these lectures, originally presented under the auspices of Children's Literature New England, the authors focus on the critical ways in which their own moral and intellectual lives are served by writing for children.

Horning, Kathleen T. *From Cover to Cover: Evaluating and Reviewing Children's Books.* New York: HarperCollins, 1997.

> Horning, librarian and coordinator of Special Collections at the Cooperative Children's Book Center at the University of Wisconsin, has written a straightforward and readable guide to evaluating children's books. She provides a thoughtful discussion of criteria for six genres of children's books and concludes with a chapter on writing book reviews.

Hunt, Peter. *Criticism, Theory, and Children's Literature.* Cambridge, Mass.: Basil Blackwell, 1991.

> A fresh examination of important questions and issues, such as what children's literature is, the nature of reading, and the role of style and narrative in children's books. Much attention goes to the underlying assumptions of critics and other adults regarding children and their reading, with emphasis on the relationship between ideology and literature. These complex ideas are presented in generally readable terms and will spark discussion and debate.

Kingman, Lee, ed. *Newbery and Caldecott Medal Books 1976–1985.* Boston: Horn Book, 1985.

Salvatore, Maria, Roger Sutton, and Kathleen Horning, eds. *The Newbery and Caldecott Medal Books, 1966–2000.* Chicago: American Library Association, 2001.

> The acceptance speeches of the medal winners are included, along with biographical sketches, photographs, and illustrations or quotes from their work. In addition, there are critical essays by well-known critics.

Lukens, Rebecca J. *A Critical Handbook of Children's Literature.* 7th ed. Boston: Allyn & Bacon, 2002.

> A careful examination of literary elements in children's books. Lukens concentrates on E. B. White's *Charlotte's Web* to show how elements like characterization, style, and point of view are developed in good children's books.

Manguel, Alberto. *A History of Reading.* New York: Viking, 1997.

> Manguel places the facts about such wide-ranging topics as the traditions of reading aloud, book design, censorship, and forbidden reading within the context of his own eloquent passion for books, and gives us a very personal view of the history of reading, writing, and books.

Trelease, Jim. *The New Read-Aloud Handbook.* 5th rev. ed. New York: Penguin Books, 2001.

> Written for a popular audience by a father who discovered what fun it was to share books with his family, this book is a delight to read and a good gift for parents. The selection is highly personal.

Zinsser, William, ed. *Worlds of Childhood: The Art and Craft of Writing for Children.* Boston: Houghton Mifflin, 1998.

> Essays by six gifted writers for children—Jean Fritz, Jill Krementz, Maurice Sendak, Jack Prelutsky, Rosemary Wells, and Katherine Paterson—reveal individual personality and a common concern for the needs of their audience. A special bibliography lists books that were childhood favorites of each author or ones that have influenced their adult lives and work.

Children's Literature

 Go to the Children's Literature Database on your Resources CD-ROM for a searchable listing of these and other children's literature titles.

Books listed at the end of each chapter are recommended, subject to qualifications noted in the text. See Appendix C for publishers' complete addresses. In the case of new editions, the original publication date appears in square brackets.

Adler, David A. *A Picture Book of Lewis and Clark.* Illustrated by Ronald Himler. Holiday, 2003.

Alcott, Louisa May. *Little Women.* Dell Yearling, 1987 [1868].

Almond, David. *Skellig.* Delacorte, 1999.

Andersen, Hans Christian. *The Ugly Duckling.* Retold and illustrated by Troy Howell. Putnam, 1990.

Asbjørnsen, P. C., and Jorgen E. Moe. *The Three Billy Goats Gruff.* Illustrated by Marcia Brown. Harcourt, 1957.

Avi. *The Book without Words: A Fable of Medieval Magic.* Hyperion, 2005.

———. *Poppy.* Illustrated by Brian Floca. Orchard, 1995.

Babbitt, Natalie. *Tuck Everlasting.* Farrar, 1985.

Barton, Byron. *My Car.* HarperCollins, 2001.

Bauer, Joan. *Best Foot Forward.* Putnam, 2005.

———. *Stand Tall.* Putnam, 2002.

Blumberg, Rhoda. *Shipwrecked!: The True Adventures of a Japanese Boy.* HarperCollins, 2001.

Blume, Judy. *Are You There, God? It's Me, Margaret.* Bradbury, 1970.

———. *Blubber.* Bradbury, 1974.

Boyce, Frank Cottrell. *Millions.* HarperCollins, 2004.

Brett, Jan. *The Mitten.* Putnam, 1989.

Broach, Elise. *Shakespeare's Secret.* Holt, 2005.

Brown, Margaret Wise. *The Golden Egg Book.* Illustrated by Leonard Weisgard. Golden, 1976.

———. *Goodnight Moon.* Illustrated by Clement Hurd. Harper, 1947.

Bruchac, Joseph. *Whisper in the Dark.* Harper, 2005.

Burnett, Frances Hodgson. *The Secret Garden.* Illustrated by Shirley Hughes. Viking, 1989 [1910].

Carbonne, Elisa. *Stealing Freedom.* Knopf, 1998.

Carle, Eric. *Do You Want to Be My Friend?* Crowell, 1971.

———. *The Very Hungry Caterpillar.* Philomel, 1969.

Carroll, Lewis. *Alice's Adventures in Wonderland* and *Through the Looking Glass.* Illustrated by John Tenniel. Macmillan, 1963 [First published separately, 1866 and 1872].

Chotjewitz, David. *Daniel Half Human: And the Good Nazi.* Translated by Doris Orgel. Atheneum, 2004.

Clark, Ann Nolan. *Secret of the Andes.* Illustrated by Jean Charlot. Viking, 1952.

Cleary, Beverly. *Ramona Quimby, Age 8.* Illustrated by Alan Tiegreen. Morrow, 1981.

———. *Ramona's World.* Illustrated by Alan Tiegreen. Morrow, 1999.

Clements, Andrew. *Lunch Money.* Simon, 2005.

Collier, James Lincoln, and Christopher Collier. *My Brother Sam Is Dead.* Four Winds, 1974.

Cooper, Susan. *The Dark Is Rising.* Illustrated by Alan Cober. Macmillan, 1973.

Creech, Sharon. *Walk Two Moons.* HarperCollins, 1994.

Curtis, Christopher Paul. *Bucking the Sarge.* Random, 2004.

———. *Bud, Not Buddy.* Random, 1999.

Danzinger, Paula. *Amber Brown Is Feeling Blue.* Putnam, 1998.

Defoe, Daniel. *Robinson Crusoe.* Houghton, 1972 [1719].

DiCamillo, Kate. *The Tale of Despereaux: Being the Story of a Mouse, a Princess, Some Soup, and a Spool of Thread.* Candlewick, 2003.

Doyle, Brian. *Mary Ann Alice.* Groundwood, 2002.

Feiffer, Jules. *Bark, George!* HarperCollins, 1999.

Fine, Ann. *Up on Cloud Nine.* Delacorte, 2002.

Fink, Sam. *The Declaration of Independence.* Scholastic, 2002.

Fitzhugh, Louise. *Harriet the Spy.* Harper, 1964.

Fleischman, Paul. *Weslandia.* Illustrated by Kevin Hawkes. Candlewick, 1999.

Fletcher, Ralph. *Flying Solo.* Clarion, 1998.

Gág, Wanda. *Millions of Cats.* Putnam, 1977 [1928].

Galdone, Paul. *The Gingerbread Boy.* Clarion, 1983.

———. *The Three Little Pigs.* Clarion, 1979.

Gantos, Jack. *Jack on the Tracks: Four Seasons of Fifth Grade.* Farrar, 1999.

———. *What Would Joey Do?* Farrar, 2002.

Gardiner, John. *Stone Fox.* Illustrated by Marcia Sewall. Crowell, 1980.

George, Jean. *Julie.* Illustrated by Wendell Minor. HarperCollins, 1994.

———. *Julie of the Wolves.* Illustrated by John Schoenherr. Harper, 1972.

———. *Julie's Wolf Pack.* Illustrated by Wendell Minor. HarperCollins, 1997.

———. *My Side of the Mountain.* Dutton, 1988 [1959].

———. *On the Far Side of the Mountain.* Dutton, 1990.

———. *Water Sky.* Harper, 1987.

Giganti, Paul, Jr. *How Many Blue Birds Flew Away?* Illustrated by Donald Crews. Greenwillow, 2005.

Giovanni, Nikki. *Rosa.* Illustrated by Bryan Collier. Holt, 2005.

Grimes, Nikki. *Jazmin's Notebook.* Dial, 1998.

Grimm, Jacob, and Wilhelm Grimm. *Little Red Riding Hood.* Illustrated by Trina Schart Hyman. Holiday, 1983.

Guthrie, Woody. *This Land Is Your Land.* Illustrated by Kathy Jakobsen. Little, 1998.

Haan, Linda de, and Stern Nijland. *King and King and Family.* Tricycle, 2004.

Haas, Jessie. *Unbroken.* Greenwillow, 1999.

Hall, Donald. *Ox-Cart Man.* Illustrated by Barbara Cooney. Viking, 1979.

Hamilton, Virginia. *Cousins.* Philomel, 1990.

Hansen, Joyce, and Gary McGowan. *Breaking Ground, Breaking Silence.* Holt, 1998.

Heide, Florence Parry, and Judith Heide Gilliland. *The Day of Ahmed's Secret.* Illustrated by Ted Lewin. Lothrop, 1990.

Henkes, Kevin. *Julius, the Baby of the World.* Greenwillow, 1990.

———. *Kitten's First Full Moon.* Greenwillow, 2004.

Hesse, Karen. *Out of the Dust.* Scholastic, 1997.

Horvath, Polly. *The Pepins and Their Problems.* Farrar, 2004.

Huck, Charlotte. *A Creepy Countdown.* Illustrated by Jos A. Smith. Greenwillow, 1998.

Hughes, Richard. *A High Wind in Jamaica.* Harper, 1989 [1929].

Hunter, Mollie. *Mermaid Summer.* Harper, 1988.

———. *A Stranger Came Ashore.* Harper, 1974.

Ibbotson, Eva. *The Star of Kazan.* Illustrated by Kevin Hawkes. Dutton, 2004.

Keller, Holly. *Sophie's Window.* Greenwillow, 2005.

Keller, Laurie. *The Scrambled States of America.* Holt, 1998.

Kent, Jack. *The Fat Cat: A Danish Folktale.* Parents Magazine Press, 1971.

Kleven, Elisa. *The Puddle Pail.* Dutton, 1997.

Konigsburg, E. L. *The View from Saturday.* Atheneum, 1996.

Lauture, Denize. *Running the Road to ABC.* Illustrated by Reynold Ruffins. Simon, 1996.

Lee, Harper. *To Kill a Mockingbird.* HarperCollins, 1995 [1960].

Le Guin, Ursula K. *A Wizard of Earthsea.* Illustrated by Ruth Robbins. Parnassus, 1968.

L'Engle, Madeleine. *Meet the Austins*. Vanguard, 1960.

———. *A Swiftly Tilting Planet*. Farrar, 1978.

———. *A Wrinkle in Time*. Farrar, 1962.

Lewis, C. S. *The Lion, the Witch, and the Wardrobe*. Illustrated by Pauline Baynes. Macmillan, 1986 [1961].

Lewis, J. Patrick. *A World of Wonders: Geographic Travels in Verse and Rhyme*. Illustrated by Alison Jay. Dial, 2002.

Lindgren, Astrid. *Pippi Longstocking*. Translated by Florence Lamborn. Illustrated by Louis Glanzman. Viking Penguin, 1950.

Lobel, Arnold. *Days with Frog and Toad*. Harper, 1976.

———. *Frog and Toad All Year*. Harper, 1976.

———. *Frog and Toad Are Friends*. Harper, 1972.

———. *Frog and Toad Together*. Harper, 1972.

Locker, Thomas. *Mountain Dance*. Harcourt, 2001.

Lowry, Lois. *Gooney Bird and the Room Mother*. Illustrated by Middy Thomas. Houghton, 2005.

———. *Number the Stars*. Houghton, 1989.

MacLachlan, Patricia. *Sarah, Plain and Tall*. Harper, 1985.

Madden, Kerry. *Gentle's Holler*. Viking, 2005.

Mankell, Henning. *Secrets in the Fire*. Annick, 2003.

Marshall, James. *George and Martha: The Complete Stories of Two Best Friends*. Houghton, 1997 [1972].

Martin, Jacqueline Briggs. *Snowflake Bentley*. Illustrated by Mary Azarian. Houghton, 1998.

Matas, Carol. *Greater Than Angels*. Simon, 1998.

Matlin, Marlee. *Deaf Child Crossing*. Simon, 2002.

McCaughrean, Geraldine. *The Pirate's Son*. Scholastic, 1998.

McCloskey, Robert. *Homer Price*. Viking, 1943.

McCord, David. "The Pickety Fence." In *One at a Time*. Illustrated by Henry B. Kane. Little, 1977.

McKissack, Patricia C. *Precious and the Boo Hag*. Illustrated by Kyrsten Brooker. Atheneum, 2005.

Milne, A. A. *Winnie the Pooh*. Illustrated by Ernest H. Shepard. Dutton, 1988 [1926].

Munsch, Robert. *Love You Forever*. Illustrated by Sheila McGraw. Firefly, 1986.

Napoli, Donna Jo. *Three Days*. Dutton, 2001.

Nye, Naomi Shihab. *Habibi*. Simon, 1997.

O'Dell, Scott. *Island of the Blue Dolphins*. Illustrated by Ted Lewin. Houghton, 1990 [1960].

Park, Linda Sue. *Project Mulberry*. Clarion, 2005.

———. *A Single Shard*. Clarion, 2001.

Paterson, Katherine. *Bridge to Terabithia*. Illustrated by Donna Diamond. Crowell, 1977.

———. *The Great Gilly Hopkins*. Crowell, 1978.

———. *Lyddie*. Lodestar, 1991.

———. *The Same Stuff as Stars*. Clarion, 2002.

Paulsen, Gary. *Hatchet*. Bradbury, 1987.

———. *The Winter Room*. Orchard, 1989.

Potter, Beatrix. *The Tale of Peter Rabbit*. Warne, 1902.

Reyher, Becky. *My Mother Is the Most Beautiful Woman in the World*. Illustrated by Ruth Gannett. Lothrop, 1945.

Richardson, Justin, and Peter Parnell. *And Tango Makes Three*. Illustrated by Henry Cole. Simon, 2005.

Rylant, Cynthia. *Henry and Mudge and the Tumbling Trip*. Illustrated by Carolyn Bracken in the style of Suçie Stevenson. Simon, 2005.

———. *Missing May*. Orchard, 1992.

Sachar, Louis. *Holes*. Farrar, 1998.

Salisbury, Graham. *Eyes of the Emperor*. Random, 2005.

Schaefer, Lola. *Pick, Pull, Snap! Where Once a Flower Bloomed*. Illustrated by Lindsay Barrett George. Greenwillow, 2003.

Schmidt, Gary D. *Lizzie Bright and the Buckminster Boy*. Clarion, 2004.

Sciezska, Jon. *Math Curse*. Illustrated by Lane Smith. Viking, 1995.

Sendak, Maurice. *Where the Wild Things Are*. Harper, 1988 [1963].

Seuss, Dr. [Theodor S. Geisel]. *And to Think That I Saw It on Mulberry Street*. Random, 1989 [1937].

———. *The Cat in the Hat*. Random, 1966 [1957].

———. *Oh, the Places You'll Go*. Random, 1990.

Shannon, David. *No David!* Scholastic, 1998.

Speare, Elizabeth George. *The Sign of the Beaver*. Houghton, 1983.

Sperry, Armstrong. *Call It Courage*. Macmillan, 1940.

Spinelli, Jerry. *Wringer*. HarperCollins, 1997.

Steig, William. *Sylvester and the Magic Pebble*. Simon, 1969.

Stevenson, Robert Louis. *Treasure Island*. Illustrated by N. C. Wyeth. Scribner's, 1981 [1883].

Taback, Simms. *Joseph Had a Little Overcoat*. Viking, 1999.

Taylor, Mildred. *The Friendship*. Illustrated by Max Ginsburg. Dial, 1987.

———. *Roll of Thunder, Hear My Cry*. Illustrated by Jerry Pinkney. Dial, 1976.

Tillage, Leon Walter. *Leon's Story*. Illustrated by Susan L. Roth. Farrar, 1997.

Tolkien, J. R. R. *The Hobbit*. Houghton, 1938.

Van Allsburg, Chris. *Jumanji*. Houghton, 1981.

Van Leeuwen, Jean. *Amanda Pig and Her Best Friend Lollipop*. Illustrated by Ann Schweninger. Dial, 1998.

Voigt, Cynthia. *Homecoming*. Atheneum, 1981.

Waddell, Martin. *Tiny's Big Adventure*. Illustrated by John Lawrence. Candlewick, 2004.

Wells, Rosemary. *Yoko*. Hyperion, 1998.

White, E. B. *Charlotte's Web*. Illustrated by Garth Williams. Harper, 1952.

Wiesner, David. *Sector 7*. Clarion, 1999.

———. *The Three Pigs*. Clarion, 2001.

Wilder, Laura Ingalls. *Little House in the Big Woods*. Harper, 1953.

Willard, Nancy. *A Visit to William Blake's Inn*. Illustrated by Alice and Martin Provensen. Harcourt, 1981.

Williams, Margery. *The Velveteen Rabbit*. Illustrated by William Nicholson. Doubleday, 1969 [1922].

Wynne-Jones, Tim. *The Boy in the Burning House*. Farrar/Kroupa, 2001.

Yumoto, Kazumi. *The Friends*. Translated by Cathy Hirano. Farrar, 1996.

Chapter Two

Understanding Children's Responses to Literature

Media Resources

Five-year-old Michael hurried to the block corner from the story circle, where his teacher had just told "Little Red Riding Hood." He whispered parts of the story under his breath as he worked to build a low enclosure around himself. When an aide walked by, Michael stood and made a growling noise. "I'm the big bad wolf!" he announced.

One rainy noon hour Sean and Dan, both 7, found a quiet corner of the bookcase and read to each other from Shel Silverstein's book of verse *Where the Sidewalk Ends.* "Listen to this one!" (Giggles.) "I can read this one!" (More giggles.) Two other children discovered the fun and joined them. All four were soon arguing heatedly about which poem was "the best one."

A small group of 9- and 10-year-olds searched the well-stocked library corner of their own classroom for something to read at sustained silent-reading time. Jason picked a book, glanced at the cover, and quickly reshelved it. "Who would want to read a book like *that*?" he muttered. Emily whispered to Julie that she had found another Lois Lowry book about Anastasia Krupnik. "I get it next," the friend said, and went on looking for a book about horses.

At regular silent-reading time, 10-year-old Evie curled up in her class's reading-and-rocking chair to finish Katherine Paterson's book *The Great Gilly Hopkins.* "The way it ended wasn't fair," Evie later protested to her teacher. "Gilly should have gone back to Trotter. This way just isn't right!"

A teacher asked her sixth graders to explain why they thought Jean George had written *Cry of the Crow.* Katie wrote: "I think what the author was trying to tell you is that once something has lived in the wild, it should stay there even if it's just like your brother or sister. . . . When you catch a bird and try to make it do something, it is like being in prison for the bird."

These glimpses of children responding to literature show some of the many different ways in which they might express their preferences, thoughts, and feelings. Although each of these responses is personal and unique, each also reflects the child's age and experience. Young children like Michael are often so totally involved in a story that they relive it through dramatic play. Those like Dan and Sean, who are developing independent reading skills, seem particularly eager to demonstrate that ability and to share newly discovered favorites. Middle graders choosing books, like Jason, Emily, and Julie, show definite preferences. Both Evie's expectation of a happy ending and her concern with injustice in a character's life are typical of middle childhood. Katie's success in generalizing a theme about all wild things from the story of one crow and her fluency in discussing the author's purpose are representative of older children's growing ability to deal with abstract ideas about a story.

To have a successful literature program, teachers and librarians must know books well, but that is only half the task. It is also necessary to understand children and the changing patterns of their responses to literature.

READING INTERESTS AND PREFERENCES

The phrase *response to literature* is used in a variety of ways. Theoretically, *response* refers to any outward sign of that inner activity, something said or done that reveals a reader's thoughts and feelings about literature. A 6-year-old's drawing of a favorite character and a book review in the *New York Times* are both responses in this sense. Teachers or librarians who predict that a book will bring "a good response" use the term in a different way, focusing on the likelihood that children will find a book appealing and will be eager to read and talk about it.

Most of the early research on children and literature focused on this third area of response to discover what reading material children like or dislike. Children's interests and preferences are still a major concern for teachers, librarians, parents, publishers, and booksellers. Everyone who selects children's books can make better choices by knowing which books are likely to have immediate appeal for many children and which ones might require introduction or encouragement along the way.

Studies of reading interests over the years have consistently identified certain topics and elements of content that have wide appeal.[1] Researchers have found that *animals* and *humor,* for instance, are generally popular across age levels. Among other elements that are frequently mentioned for reader appeal are *action, suspense,* and *surprise.* Sales figures, too, can reflect children's reading interests. Surveys by *Publisher's Weekly* magazine show that tie-ins to popular movies or television shows and series books were among the best-selling children's books. The surveys show that teenagers (12- to 17-year-olds) buy fiction slightly more often than nonfiction, a figure that does not vary much with gender. Favorite topics include mysteries, science fiction/fantasy, books about celebrities and athletes, and how-to books.[2]

Even though we can identify commonly chosen topics and story features that have wide general appeal, it is still impossible to concoct a formula for books that would have unfailing popularity with *all* children. Teachers and librarians need to be sensitive to children's individual tastes, which often are unique and very particular. Nevertheless, the variations in interests among different *groups* of children seem to be linked to age, gender, and certain other influences.

Talking Point

Do series books promote children's response to literature?

Dav Pilkey's "Captain Underpants," R. L. Stine's "Goosebumps," and K. A. Applegate's "Animorphs" and "Remnants" series are highly popular with many children. What is the role of books like these in developing and deepening children's response to literature?

Go to the Online Learning Center at **www.mhhe.com/kiefer9e** or your Resources CD-ROM to learn more.

Age and Gender Differences

The most obvious change in children's interest patterns occurs with age, as children take on more complex material and new areas of concern. Good book choices for first and sixth graders seldom overlap, even when the general topic is the same. Robert McCloskey's picture book *Make Way for Ducklings* is a favorite animal story among 4- and 5-year-olds; 12-year-olds prefer their animal characters to be part of something more dramatic, as in Ann Martin's *A Dog's Life: The Autobiography of a Stray.* Seven-year-olds laugh at Peggy Parish's *Amelia Bedelia* and her literal interpretation of instructions like "Draw the drapes" and "Dress the chicken." Eleven-year-olds like "funny" books, too, but prefer a different brand of humor—the comic situations in Roald Dahl's *The BFG* or the deadpan humor of Louis Sachar's *Holes.* Older adolescents prefer the irreverent tone and the wisecracking dialogue in Louise Rennison's . . . *And Then He Ate My Boy Entrancers* or *Me, Dead Dad, and Alcatraz* by Chris Lynch.

Some of the broader shifts in preference that mark the elementary school years include a move away from a preference for folk tales toward more interest in realistic subject matter. According to many studies, children of all ages like animal stories and fantasy/science fiction. Research continues to confirm older children's liking for adventure, mystery, and series books.[3]

The influence of gender differences on reading interests is not entirely clear. Previous studies found that interests of children vary according to age and grade level and that girls read more than boys but boys had a

---

[1]Angela M. Broening, "Factors Influencing Pupils' Reading of Library Books," *Elementary English Review* 11 (1934): 155–58; Fannie Wyche Dunn, *Interest Factors in Reading Materials* (New York: Teachers College, Columbia University, 1921); Jeanie Goodhope, "Into the Eighties: BAYA's Fourth Reading Interest Survey," *School Library Journal* 29 (December 1982): 33; Mary-Jo Fresch, "Self-Selection Strategies of Early Literacy Learners," *Reading Teacher* 49 (November 1995): 220–27; Alan Purves and Richard Beach, *Literature and the Reader: Research in Response to Literature, Reading Interests, and the Teaching of Literature* (Urbana, Ill.: National Council of Teachers of English, 1972), pp. 69–71.

[2]Amanda Ferguson, "Reading Is Cool," *Publisher's Weekly* 245 (October 12, 1998): 28–31.

[3]J. W. Coomer and K. M. Tessmer, "1986 Books for Young Adults Poll," *English Journal* 75 (November 1986): 58–66; M. A. Harkrader and R. Moore, "Literature Preferences of Fourth Graders," *Reading Research and Instruction* 36 (1997): 325–39.

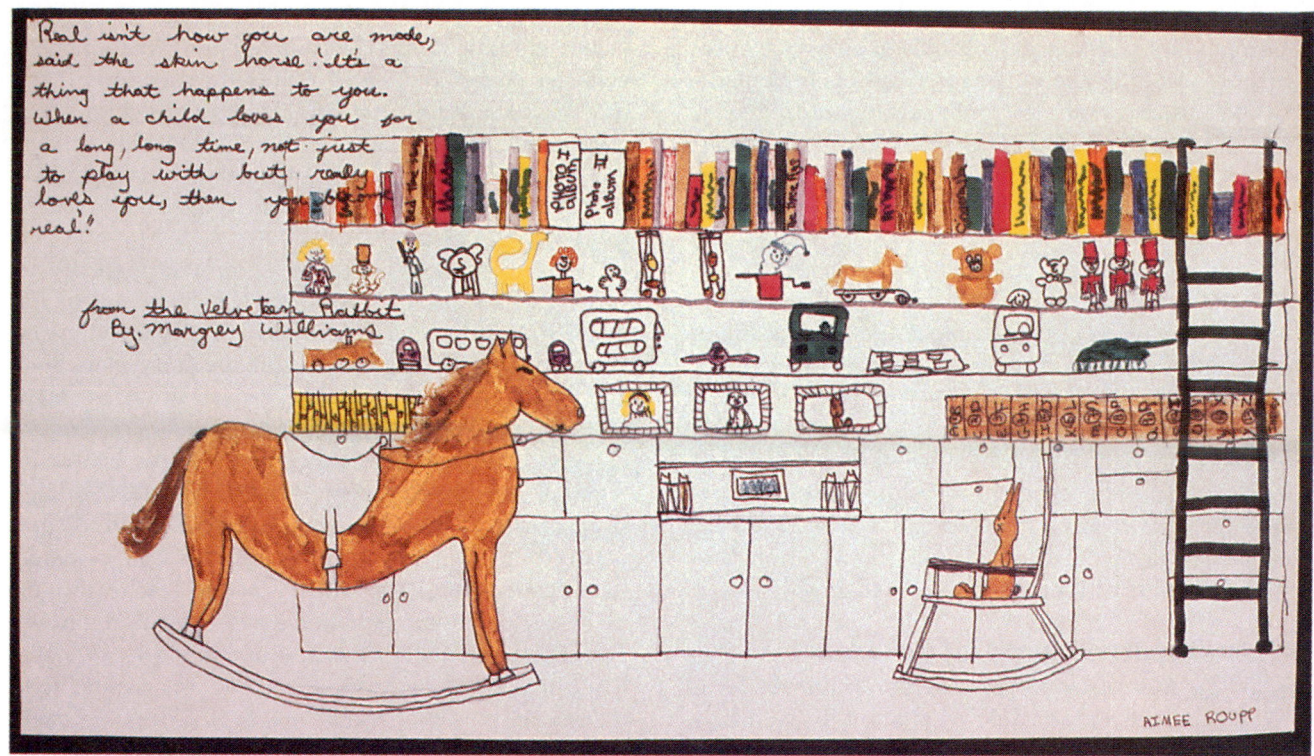

Real isn't how you are made,
said the skin horse. It's a
thing that happens to you.
When a child loves you for
a long, long time, not just
to play with but really
loves you, then you become
real.

from the Velveteen Rabbit
By Margery Williams

AIMEE ROUPP

Choosing favorites and interpreting them are both a part of response to literature. Notice how the details of the modern playroom setting in this child's illustration *The Velveteen Rabbit* provide a glimpse of her unique personal perspective on the book. Martin Luther King, Jr., Laboratory School, Evanston Public Schools, Evanston, Illinois.

wider interest range and read a greater variety. Girls showed an earlier interest in adult romantic fiction than boys, whereas boys tended to prefer nonfiction from an early age. Boys seldom showed preference for a "girl's" book, but girls read a "boy's" book more often. [4] A 1995 study done in England with close to eight thousand 10-, 12-, and 14-year-olds found a swing away from book reading as children grow older, particularly among 14-year-old boys. The survey found that although "boys' predilection for non-narrative remains, . . . its significance in boys' reading diet is somewhat overstated." There was strong evidence of the "overwhelming importance of narrative in children's reading choices," but the authors rejoiced in the enormous diversity of types of literature chosen by both sexes. [5] In a more recent study reported in 2003, Brian Sturm surveyed children enrolled in a state reading enrichment program in North Carolina. [6] Although the findings should not be generalized to the whole country, they contradict some of the previously held understandings about preferences

and gender differences. In this study Sturm analyzed a random sample of two thousand children, ages 7–13, who were asked to provide written answers to four questions (for example "What would you like to know more about?"). The answers were than categorized into thirty-six topics, the most popular of which were *animals, biographies, history, science, sports,* and *literature.* (The literature category was assigned when children mentioned authors, genres, or specific book titles.)

Sturm found that, across genders and ages, children preferred animals, science, sports, and literature. Within these categories mammals and pets, geography and astronomy, basketball and football, and specific authors and series books were most often cited as topics of interest. Surprisingly, poetry was listed third within the literature category, and the same percentage of girls (15%) preferred science topics as boys.

The influence of gender on reading interests is thus not entirely clear. What we do not know about gender differences in children's choices is whether they reflect a

[4]Glenda Childress, "Gender Gap in the Library: Different Choices for Boys and Girls," *Top of the News* 42 (fall, 1985): 69–73; Helen Huus, "Interpreting Research in Children's Literature," in *Children, Books and Reading* (Newark, Del.: International Association, 1964), p. 125.

[5]Christine Hall and Martin Coles, *Children's Reading Choices* (London: Routledge, 1999), p. 136.

[6]Brian W. Sturm, "The Information and Reading Preferences of North Carolina Children," *School Library Media Research* 6 (2003). April 25, 2005 <http://www.ala.org/ala/aasl/aaslpubsandjournals/slmrb/slmrcontents/volume62003/readingpreferences.htm>.

"natural" interest or conformity to cultural expectations. Classroom observations and a survey of library borrowing records among ninety 10- to 11-year-olds in England in 2001–02 found that classroom cultures can have an important impact on reading choices. The authors concluded that "what teachers do can have a real impact but [the study] also demonstrates the strength of children's own reading networks."[7]

Research that further updates these preference studies in our postmodern age is certainly important. We can assume, however, that in school and home settings where traditional sexual stereotypes are downplayed, boys and girls share enthusiasm for many common favorites. It is important to give children many options for book choice so that girls and boys can have a chance to explore each other's perspectives. It is just as unfortunate for girls to miss the excellent nonfiction being published today as it is for boys to turn away from fine fiction that offers insight into human relationships.

Other Determinants of Interest

 Many factors other than age and gender have been investigated in relation to children's reading interests. At one time the influence of mental age as measured by standardized tests received considerable attention. Now, however, we believe that children of varying academic abilities still are more alike than different in the character of their reading interests. It is more likely that the quantity of books involved and the rate at which interests develop will vary widely.

Illustrations, color, format, length, and type of print can also influence children's choices. It would be unwise to oversimplify the effect of these factors on children's book choices, especially because so much of the research has been done outside the context of normal reading and choosing situations. When children choose and use books in their own classrooms, their reactions to books are more complex than controlled experiments or surveys could reveal.[8]

Social and environmental influences also affect children's book choices and reading interests. Many teachers and librarians feel that cultural and ethnic factors are related to reading interests. One of the arguments for providing culturally authentic picture books and novels about Asian, Hispanic, African American, and Native American children is that readers from a particular culture will find material drawn from their own culture

more interesting. One study of African American and Hispanic American fifth graders found that African American children preferred to read culturally conscious literature. Hispanic American children were less enthusiastic about multicultural titles.[9] The relationship between interests and culture does not seem to be simple, and unfortunately there is not yet much research to clarify this point.

Although interests do not seem to vary greatly according to geographical location, the impact of the immediate environment—particularly the availability and accessibility of reading materials in the home, classroom, and public and school libraries—can be very strong. Children in classrooms where books are regularly discussed, enjoyed, and given high value tend to show livelier interest in a wider range of literature than do children from situations where books are given less attention. It is hard to tell how much of this effect is due to contact with the books and how much is social. Teachers' favorite books are often mentioned by children as their own favorites, perhaps because these are the stories closest at hand or perhaps because of positive associations with the teacher.

Children frequently influence each other in their choice of books. In the culture of the classroom, a title or an author or a topic may rise to celebrity status for a time. Shel Silverstein's *Runny Babbit* might be "the book" to read in one group of third graders, or children might make their own sign-up sheets to read the classroom's only copy of the latest *Dear America* book. Younger children might spend time on a study of bears and long afterward point out "bear stories" to each other. Media presentations like the *Reading Rainbow* series from the Public Broadcasting System create demand for specific books.

Peer recommendations are especially important to middle graders in choosing what to read. Some fifth and sixth graders are very candid: "'Everyone else in the class read it, so I figured I ought to, too.' . . . 'I usually read what Tammy reads.' '. . . most of my friends just like the same type of book I like. So, if they find a book, I'll believe them and I'll try it.'"[10]

Explaining Children's Choices

How can children influence each other's book choices so readily? Part of the answer may be simply that age-mates are likely to enjoy the same kinds of stories because they

[7]Gemma Moss and John W. MacDonald, "The Borrowers: Library Records as Unobtrusive Measure of Children's Reading Preferences," *Journal of Research in Reading* 27.34 (2004): 410.

[8]Barbara Z. Kiefer, *The Potential of Picture Books from Visual Literacy to Aesthetic Understanding* (Columbus, Ohio: Merrill/Prentice Hall, 1995).

[9]Gail Singleton Taylor, "Multicultural Literature Preferences of Low-Ability African American and Hispanic American Fifth-Graders," *Reading Improvement* 34 (spring, 1997): 37–48.

[10]Susan I. Hepler and Janet Hickman, "'The Book Was Okay. I Love You'—Social Aspects of Response to Literature," *Theory into Practice* 21 (autumn, 1982): 279. Also see Moss and MacDonald, "The Borrowers." pp. 401–12.

Asking Children to Tell about Themselves as Readers

Fourth-grade teacher Roberto Sbordone asks his students to write a "Reader's Portrait" each year to help them reflect on themselves as readers. As Bree, one of his students, reveals her journey to becoming a book lover, she shows how personal each child's responses to books can be.

A Reader's Portrait by Bree Bang-Jensen

I guess I've always loved stories because long before I knew how to read I would listen to a story tape over and over and over again for hours.

My parents used to read to me from a very early age. When I was three my parents read Laura Ingalls books to me.

Years passed, and I had no desire to learn to read. I hated those books called "Easy Readers," because to me they had no point.

In first grade it made no sense to me that I had to learn this bizarre system called reading. Then, in the Thanksgiving vacation of second grade, suddenly it all clicked in place.

I was reading the first Boxcar Children Book. I was IN the book! From then on, I spent all my time reading.

For a while, my mother had to make me go outside for half an hour everyday.

My favorite book author is Jean Little, and my favorite book is *Mine for Keeps.* My ninth birthday party was a "Book Party" where we had a book obstacle course, played charades from books, made bookmarks and used books with "treasure" in the title for a treasure hunt. There were even books in the goody bags.

You know what I like about reading? You can take a vacation almost anywhere for a dollar or two—you buy a book and read it. In reading you can be anyone, anywhere, in any situation!

Bree Bang-Jensen, Age 9
Roberto Cecere Sbordone, Teacher
Springhurst School, Dobbs Ferry, New York

---

share many developmental characteristics. As children grow and learn, their levels of understanding change, and so do their favorites in literature. A few thought-provoking studies have suggested that children prefer those stories that best represent their own way of looking at the world—stories that mirror their experiences, needs, fears, and desires at a given age.[11]

There are many things to consider in explaining children's book choices. One of the most important is prior experiences with literature. Some children have heard many stories read aloud at home or have been introduced by their teachers to many different authors and genres. These children are likely to have tastes and preferences that seem advanced compared with those of children their age who have had less exposure to books. Children's personal experiences influence their interests in ways that teachers and librarians might never be able to discover. And sometimes apparent interests are only the product of which books are available and which are not. Literature in Action: "Asking Children to Tell about Themselves as Readers" shows how one teacher managed to survey his students' feelings about books.

We must be careful not to oversimplify the reasons for children's book choices. Even so, it is important not to underestimate a developmental perspective that takes into account both experience and growth. This is a powerful tool for predicting reading interests and for understanding other ways in which children respond.

GROWTH PATTERNS THAT INFLUENCE RESPONSE

 The child-development point of view begins with recognizing and accepting the uniqueness of childhood. Children are not miniature adults but individuals with their own needs, interests, and capabilities—all of which change over time and at varying rates.

In the early decades of child study, emphasis was placed on discovery of so-called normal behavior patterns for each age. Growth studies revealed similarities in patterns of physical, mental, and emotional growth. Later, longitudinal studies showed wide variations in individual rates of growth. One child's growth might be uneven, and a spurt in one aspect of development might precede a spurt in another. Age trends continue to be useful in understanding the child, but by the 1960s, research began to be concerned with the interaction of biological, cultural, and life-experience forces. Researchers recognized that development is not simply the result of the maturation of neural cells but evolves as new experience reshapes existing structures. The interaction of

---

[11]See Andre Favat, *Child and Tale: The Origins of Interest* (Urbana, Ill.: National Council of Teachers of English, 1977), and Norma Marian Schlager, "Developmental Factors Influencing Children's Responses to Literature" (Ph.D. dissertation, Claremont Graduate School, 1974).

the individual with his or her environment, especially the social and cultural aspects of that environment, has become increasingly important to researchers. This experience affects the age at which development appears.

Studies in children's cognitive and language growth, as well as in other areas of human development, can be very helpful in the choice of appropriate books and the understanding of children's responses. Although this text can highlight only a few findings, it can serve to alert the student of children's literature to the importance of such information.

Physical Development

Children's experiences with literature can begin at a very early age. Studies of infant perception show that even tiny babies hear and see better than was thought possible a few decades ago. For instance, newborns show more response to patterned, rhythmic sounds than to continuous tones. They also show preferences for the sound frequencies of the human voice.[12] This supports the intuition of parents who chant nursery rhymes or sing lullabies that the sound of songs and rhymes provides satisfaction even for the youngest.

Infants gain visual perception very rapidly within their range of focus. Babies in their first months of life see lines, angles, and adjacent areas of high contrast and prefer black and white to muted colors up to about 2 months of age.[13] They progress to seeing simple dimensions such as forms or colors, and before 6 months are perceiving more complex patterns (faces or colored shapes) as whole units. Books designed for babies and toddlers, like Roger Priddy's *Bright Baby: First Words,* often acknowledge this developmental pattern by featuring simple, clearly defined pictures with firm outlines, uncluttered backgrounds, and bright colors.

As visual perception develops, children begin to show fascination with details and often enjoy searching for specific objects in illustrations. One 18-month-old boy spotted a clock in Margaret Wise Brown's *Goodnight Moon* and subsequently pointed out clocks in other books when he discovered them. Older preschoolers make a game of finding "hidden" things in pictures, like the Mother Goose and fairy tale characters tucked into each illustration of Janet Ahlberg and Allan Ahlberg's *Each Peach Pear Plum.*

Children's attention spans generally increase with age as well as interest. In their first school experiences, some young children have trouble sitting quietly for even a 20-minute story. It is better to have several short story times for these children than to demand their attention for longer periods and so lose their interest. Some kindergarten and primary teachers provide many opportunities for children to listen to stories in small groups of two or three by using the listening center or asking parent aides or student teachers to read to as few as one or two children.

Physical development influences children's interests as well as their attention span. Growth in size, muscularity, and coordination is often reflected in children's choice of a book in which characters share their own newly acquired traits or abilities. *Whistling* by Elizabeth Partridge, for example, seems most rewarding for young children who have just learned to whistle. The demand for sports books increases as girls and boys gain the skills necessary for successful participation.

American children are growing up faster, both physically and psychologically, than they ever have before. By sixth grade almost all girls have reached puberty, although very few boys have.[14] The age of onset of puberty figures prominently in early adolescents' self-concept and influences book choices. Girls are still reading Judy Blume's *Are You There, God? It's Me, Margaret* (1970) because it reflects their own concerns about menstruation. Margaret has frequent chats with God, which include pleas like this: "Are you there, God? It's me, Margaret. I just told my mother I want a bra. Please help me grow, God. You know where."[15]

Both physical maturity and social forces have led to the development of sexual interests at a younger age. Sophisticated 7-year-olds are teased about their "boyfriends" or "girlfriends." According to 2003 data, 47 percent of high school students have had sexual intercourse.[16] It is somehow as if childhood were something to be transcended rather than enjoyed. One result of this shortened childhood is a decrease in the length of time in which boys and girls are interested in reading children's literature. Many of them turn to reading teenage novels or adult fiction before they have read such fine books as *Secret Heart* by David Almond, *Mary Ann Alice* by Brian Doyle, or *Treasure at the Heart of Tanglewood* by Meredith Ann Pierce, all well-written, complex stories about young adolescents.

Cognitive Development

The work of the great Swiss psychologist Jean Piaget has had a great influence on educators' understanding of

---

[12]Aidan Macfarlane, *The Psychology of Childbirth* (Cambridge, Mass.: Harvard University Press, 1977).

[13]Leslie B. Cohen, "Our Developing Knowledge of Infant Perception and Cognition," *American Psychologist* 34 (1979): 894–99.

[14]Frederick C. Howe, "The Child in the Elementary School: Developmental Trends," *Child Study Journal* 23 (1993): 327–46.

[15]Judy Blume, *Are You There, God? It's Me, Margaret* (Englewood Cliffs, N.J.: Bradbury Press, 1970), p. 37.

[16]Jo Anne Grunbaum et al., *Youth Risk Behavior Surveillance—United States, 2003, Morbidity and Mortality Weekly Report* Surveillance Summary 53.SS02 (Atlanta: Centers for Disease Control and Prevention, May 21, 2004): 1–96. April 25, 2005 <http://www.cdc .gov/mmwr/PDF/SS/SS5302.pdf>.

children's intellectual development.[17] Piaget proposed that intelligence develops as a result of the interaction of environment and the maturation of the child. In his view, children are active participants in their own learning.

Piaget's observations led him to conclude that there are distinct stages in the development of logical thinking. According to his theory, all children go through these stages in the same progression, but not necessarily at the same age. He identified these stages as the *sensory-motor period*, from infancy to about 2 years of age; the *preoperational period*, from approximately 2 to 7 years; the *concrete operational period*, from about 7 to 11; and a two-phase development of *formal operations*, which begins around age 11 and continues throughout adult life.

In recent years the validity of this stage theory has been called into question by many researchers who express many concerns about the interpretation of Piaget's theory. Researchers have suggested that children's social and cultural backgrounds and their familiarity with a task or situation might influence their thinking.[18] The whole idea of stages, in fact, suggests a progression of development that might be far more orderly than what occurs in real life. Some psychologists feel that stage theory fails to describe the intricacy and complexity of children's thinking and might lead adults to focus on what children are supposedly not able to do, thus falsely lowering expectations. We need to keep these cautions in mind if we look to Piagetian theory for guidance in selecting books for children and planning literature experiences.

Piaget's main contribution to our understanding of cognitive development was his recognition of the child as a meaning maker, "his rediscovery of the child's mind."[19] Piaget's work and the work of cognitive psychologists since mid century have helped us view children as individuals. We can expect them to think about their experiences differently as they develop, and we can expect that thinking to change as they move toward adulthood. Thus, it is still useful for us to look at some of the characteristics of children's thinking described by Piaget and to compare them with those of the children we work with. Then we can consider how children's thinking patterns are related to the books they like and to their responses to literature.

In the first several years of life, infants and toddlers learn through coordinating their sensory perceptions and their motor activity. By the end of their first year, most children enjoy the action or game rhymes of Mother Goose. They delight in the rhythm of "Pat-a-Cake, Pat-

a-Cake" and anticipate the pinching and patting that accompanies the rhyme. Tactile books such as *Pat the Bunny* by Dorothy Kunhardt appeal to their sensory perceptions by encouraging them to touch special materials pasted on the page. Such an introduction to books incorporates what the young child responds to best—sensory-motor play and participation with a loving adult.

During the preschool and kindergarten years, children learn to represent the world symbolically through language, play, and drawing. Thinking seems to be based on direct experience and perception of the present moment. Many of the particular features ascribed to this stage of thought seem to be reflected in young children's response to literature. During these years, children have a hard time holding an image in mind as it changes form or shape. They enjoy predictable stories like "The Gingerbread Boy" or *It's Quacking Time!* by Martin Waddell. The built-in repetition in these stories carries the sequence of the action along from page to page. Older children who are able to follow the more complex logic of stories can remember the events without aid and often say that the repetitious language is boring.

Most children of elementary-school age would be described as being in the concrete operational stage according to Piaget's theory. Classifying and arranging objects in series are important abilities within children's command during this period, making them more systematic and orderly thinkers. Their thought also becomes flexible and reversible, allowing them to unravel and rearrange a sequence of events. It is no surprise, then, that elementary-age children begin to like mysteries and to understand stories with more complex plot features such as flashbacks or a story within a story. Older elementary-age children also seem to identify more spontaneously with different points of view. Books like *The Wolf's Story* by Toby Forward or *Red Ridin' in the Hood* by Patricia Santos Marcantonio suit this developmental level well because readers understand what the author has done with the structure of a familiar tale and can also begin to see the events through the eyes of a new narrator or a new culture.

One interesting aspect of concrete operational children's thinking is described by psychologist David Elkind as "cognitive conceit."[20] As children begin to have some success in reasoning and problem solving, they tend to get the idea that they must be as able as adults, or even smarter. They enjoy besting an older child, parent, or teacher. Although children's visions of superiority may seldom come true in real experience, books for

---

[17]Barbel Inhelder and Jean Piaget, *The Growth of Logical Thinking* (New York: Basic Books, 1962); Barry J. Wadsworth, *Piaget's Theory of Cognitive and Affective Development* (Reading, Mass.: Addison-Wesley, 1996).

[18]Margaret Donaldson, *Children's Minds* (New York: Norton, 1979), chap. 2.

[19]Deanna Kuhn, "Cognitive Development," in *Developmental Psychology: An Advanced Textbook*, 3rd ed. (Hillsdale, N.J.: Erlbaum, 1992).

[20]David Elkind, *Children and Adolescents: Interpretive Essays on Jean Piaget*, 3rd ed. (New York: Oxford University Press, 1981).

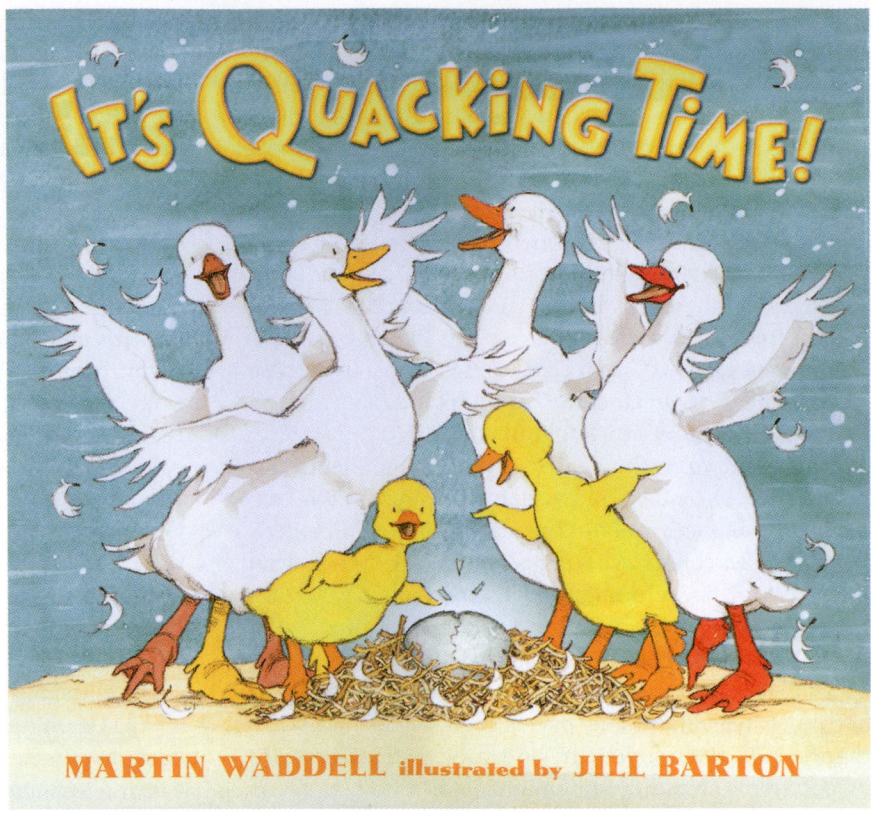

Author Martin Waddell is a master at telling engaging, predictable stories for toddlers, such as *It's Quacking Time!*.
It's Quacking Time! Written by Martin Waddell. Illustrations copyright © 2005 by Jill Barton. Reproduced by permission of the publisher, Candlewick Press, Inc., Cambridge, MA, on behalf of Walker Books Ltd., London.

middle graders often feature young protagonists on their own who manage just as well as, or better than, their elders. In E. L. Konigsburg's *From the Mixed-Up Files of Mrs. Basil E. Frankweiler*, for instance, young Claudia is clever enough to outwit adults by living undetected in New York's Metropolitan Museum of Art and shrewd enough to make an important discovery about one of the statues there.

As students begin the transitional period that corresponds roughly to the middle-school years, they begin to develop abstract theoretical thought; they are no longer dependent on concrete evidence but can reason from hypotheses to logical conclusions. This allows them to think of possibilities for their lives that are contrary to their prior experience and enables them to see the future in new ways. Complex novels and science fiction in particular begin to have appeal for students at this level. Also, students gain understanding of the use of symbols, such as letters for numbers in algebra or symbolic meanings in literature. While they have understood the use of obvious symbols like the fish in L. S. Matthews's *Fish*, they can now deal with the layers of meaning found in some poetry and complex stories like Lois Lowry's *The Giver*.

This would appear to be the time, then, when literary criticism would be most appropriately introduced. Although teachers at every grade level would have been steadily building some knowledge and appreciation of literature, detailed analysis of a work would probably not be undertaken before this period of intellectual development. Even then, teachers would want such a discussion to arise from the child's personal response to the book.

It is important to remember that not all young people entering middle schools or junior high schools have reached the level of formal operations.[21] At the same time, some young children demonstrate considerable analytical competence as they talk about books that are familiar and meaningful to them.

Other views of cognitive development can help us broaden our base for understanding children and their response to literature. Russian psychologist Lev Semenovich Vygotsky, for instance, stresses the ties between development of thought and language, the social aspect of learning, and the importance of adult-child interaction.[22] One crucial idea is that children grow in their thinking abilities within a "zone of proximal development," an

---

[21]David Elkind, "Investigating Intelligence in Early Adolescence," in *Toward Adolescence: The Middle School Years*, ed. Mauritz Johnson and Kenneth J. Rehage, Seventy-Ninth Yearbook of the National Society for the Study of Education (Chicago: University of Chicago Press, 1985), pp. 282–94.

[22]L. S. Vygotsky, *Thought and Language* (Cambridge, Mass.: MIT Press, 1962); Vygotsky, *Mind in Society: The Development of Higher Psychological Processes* (Cambridge, Mass.: Harvard University Press, 1978).

area in which they are asked to stretch their ability, but not too far. For example, if students can identify the similarities in two versions of a familiar folktale like "Little Red Riding Hood," they might also be able to see how these stories are related to Ed Young's *Lon Po Po: A Red Riding Hood Tale from China*. However, they might not yet be ready to connect these tales to the modern spoof *Ruby*, by Michael Emberley, which draws its humor from sly references to "Little Red Riding Hood" and an altered urban setting.

American psychologist Howard Gardner has proposed that there is no single "intelligence," but a cluster of at least eight intellectual abilities, or "multiple intelligences": linguistic, musical, spatial, natural, logical-mathematical, bodily, knowledge of self, and understanding of others.[23] The stages of development he sees for each of these are different. Appreciation of literature falls into the category of linguistic intelligence. Increasing sensitivity to balance, composition, style, and sound of language characterize growth within this domain. The idea of multiple intelligences would help to explain why some children breeze through math but blank out during discussions of literature, and vice versa.

However we look at cognitive development, we need to remember that it is only one part of a much larger picture of growth patterns that influence interests and responses.

Language Development

The pattern of early language learning moves from infant babbling and cooing to the use of single words, frequently ones that name familiar people or things, like *Mama* or *kitty*. Next, somewhere around 2 years, children begin to use two-word utterances. They develop the ability to change inflection, intonation, or word order to expand their range of meaning ("Daddy go?" "*Bad kitty!*"). Theorists disagree on just how children are able to acquire a functional command of such a complex system as language so early in life. There is strong evidence, however, that the child is more than just an imitator. Children seem to construct on their own the system for making themselves understood; M. A. K. Halliday calls this "learning how to mean."[24] To do so they must *use* language—talk as well as listen.

Verbal participation with an adult is an important element in young children's experience with literature. ABC or picture identification books like Margaret Miller's *Guess Who?* provide special opportunities if they are "talked through" rather than simply read as a string of nouns. Toddlers learn more than vocabulary from such encounters. Very early experiences with books encourage many aspects of language development. (See Chapters 1 and 4 for more on this point.)

Language development proceeds at a phenomenal pace during the preschool years. By the end of that time, children will have learned to express their thoughts in longer sentences that combine ideas or embed one idea within another. In short, they will have gained access to the basic structure of grammar—all this by about age 4, whatever their native language.[25]

Children improvise and explore words as they learn, chanting and playing with language as they gain confidence.[26] Rhythmic rhymes and nonsense verses are natural choices for preschoolers because they fit this pattern so well. However, children's fun in playing with language as various forms are mastered is not limited to the very young. Middle-grade children, with their wider range of language competence, are fascinated by the variety of jokes, riddles, tongue twisters, and folklore miscellany offered by Alvin Schwartz in collections like *Whoopers: Tall Tales and Other Lies*. They are also intrigued by ingenious uses of language in a story context, as in Pamela Edwards's *Some Smug Slug*, Norton Juster's *The Phantom Tollbooth*, or Christopher Paul Curtis's *Mr. Chickee's Funny Money*.

We know that children's language growth continues through the elementary grades and beyond, although the rate is never again as dramatic as during the preschool years. The average length and complexity of their statements, both oral and written, increase as children progress through school.[27] We also know, however, that children's capacity to produce language consistently lags behind their ability to understand it. This suggests that we owe students of all ages the opportunity to read and hear good writing that is beyond the level of their own conversation. Seven-year-olds, for instance, cannot speak with the eloquence and humor that characterize William Steig's picture books, such as *Zeke Pippin* or *Doctor De Soto*. Still, they can understand the language in its story context, and hearing it will add to their knowledge of how language sounds and works. Books by Virginia Hamilton or Natalie Babbitt might serve the same function for older students. Unlike novels that do little more than mirror contemporary speech, the work of these and other fine writers can give children a chance to consider the power of language used with precision and imagination.

---

[23]Howard Gardner, *Intelligence Reframed: Multiple Intelligences for the 21st Century* (New York: Basic Books, 1999).

[24]M. A. K. Halliday, *Learning How to Mean: Explorations in the Functions of Language* (New York: Elsevier, 1974).

[25]Dan I. Sobin, "Children and Language: They Learn the Same Way All Around the World," in *Contemporary Readings in Child Psychology*, 2nd ed., ed. E. Mavis Hetherington and Ross D. Parke (New York: McGraw-Hill, 1981), pp. 122–26.

[26]Ruth Weir, *Language in the Crib* (The Hague: Mouton, 1970).

[27]Walter Loban, *Language Development: Kindergarten through Grade Twelve* (Urbana, Ill.: National Council of Teachers of English, 1976).

David McPhail's *The Teddy Bear* presents young children with a little boy's moral dilemma and helps them contemplate their own response. From *The Teddy Bear* by David McPhail. Copyright © 2002 by David McPhail. Reprinted by permission of Henry Holt and Company, LLC.

Moral Development

Piaget's extensive studies of children included special attention to their developing ideas about fairness and justice. According to Piaget, the difference between younger and older children's concepts is so pronounced that there are really "two moralities" in childhood.[28] Other researchers such as Lawrence Kohlberg[29] and Carol Gilligan have contributed to our understanding of moral development in children.

According to both Piaget's and Kohlberg's descriptions of the general direction of elementary children's development, as children grow in intellect and experience, they move away from ideas of morality based on authority and adult constraint and toward morality based on the influence of group cooperation and independent thinking. To the later stages of this development Gilligan adds a dimension based on gender.[30] She suggests that as girls mature, their sense of their identity is influenced by interconnections with others to a greater degree than for boys. Consequently, their moral judgment develops along lines of an enhanced sense of responsibility and caring for others. Girls might seem less decisive than boys in discussing moral dilemmas because they are trying to take into account a whole network of people who could be affected by a choice. This concern for others is present in boys' thinking as well, but seldom takes precedence over their ideas about what is "fair."

Some of the contrasts between the moral judgment of younger and older children are as follows:

- Young children judge the goodness or badness of an act according to its likelihood of bringing punishment or reward from adults; in other words, they are constrained by the rules that adults have made. Older elementary-age children usually understand that there are group standards for judging what is good or bad and by then are very conscious of situations where they can make their own rules.

- In a young child's eyes, behavior is totally right or totally wrong, with no allowance for an alternate point of view. More-mature children are willing to consider the possibility that circumstances and situations make for legitimate differences of opinion.

- Young children tend to judge an act by its consequences, regardless of the actor's intent. By third or fourth grade, most children have switched to considering motivation rather than consequences alone in deciding what degree of guilt is appropriate.

- Young children believe that bad behavior and punishment go together; the more serious the deed, the more severe the punishment they would prescribe. Its form would not necessarily be related to the offense, but it would automatically erase the offender's guilt. Older children are not so quick to suggest all-

---

[28]Jean Piaget, *The Moral Judgment of the Child*, trans. M. Gabain (New York: Free Press, 1965).

[29]Lawrence Kohlberg, *The Meaning and Measurement of Moral Development* (Worcester, Mass.: Clark University Heinz Wemer Institute, 1981).

[30]Carol Gilligan, *In a Different Voice: Psychological Theory and Women's Development* (Cambridge, Mass.: Harvard University Press, 1982).

purpose pain. They are more interested in finding a "fair" punishment, one that somehow fits the crime and will help bring the wrongdoer back within the rules of the group.

These developmental differences are apparent in the responses of two groups of children to Taro Yashima's *Crow Boy.* When asked what the teacher in the story should do about shy Chibi, who hid under the schoolhouse on the first day, many first graders said "Spank him!" Nine- and 10-year-olds, however, suggested explaining to him that there was nothing to be afraid of or introducing him to classmates so he wouldn't be shy.

Many stories for children present different levels of moral complexity that have the potential for stimulating rich discussions among children. In *The Teddy Bear,* David McPhail provides younger children with a chance to consider the impulse to help others over their own wants and desires. *On My Honor* by Marion Dane Bauer and *Millions* by Frank Cottrell Boyce provide older readers with a chance to discuss the complexities of a tragic personal experience.

Working through dilemmas, the experts suggest, allows us to move from one level of moral judgment toward another. Literature provides a means by which children can rehearse and negotiate situations of conflict without risk, trying out alternative stances to problems as they step into the lives and thoughts of different characters.

Phyllis Root's *Oliver Finds His Way* speaks to young children's fear of separation as well as their need for initiative. From *Oliver Finds His Way,* written by Phyllis Root. Illustrations copyright © 2002 by Christopher Denise. Reproduced by permission of the publisher, Candlewick Press, Inc., Cambridge, MA.

Personality Development

Every aspect of a child's growth is intertwined with every other. All learning is a meshing of cognitive dimensions, affective or emotional responses, social relationships, and value orientation. This is the matrix in which personality develops. The process of "becoming" is a highly complex one indeed. For children to become "fully functioning" persons, their basic needs must be met. They need to feel they are loved and understood; they must feel they are members of a group significant to them; they must feel they are achieving and growing toward independence. Psychologist Abraham Maslow's research suggests that a person develops through a "hierarchy of needs" from basic animal-survival necessities to the "higher" needs that are more uniquely human and spiritual.[31] Self-actualization might take a lifetime, or it might never be achieved. But the concept that the individual is continually "becoming" is a more positive view than the notion that little change can take place in personality. Literature can provide opportunities for people of all ages to satisfy higher-level needs, but it is important to remember that books alone cannot meet children's basic needs.

Psychologist Erik Erikson sees human emotional and social development as a passage through a series of stages.[32] Each stage centers around the individual's meeting a particular goal or concern associated with that stage. Erikson theorized that accomplishments at later stages depend on how well the individual was able to meet the goals of preceding stages. According to this theory, a sense of *trust* must be gained during the first year; a sense of *autonomy* should be realized by age 3; between 3 and 6 years the sense of *initiative* is developed; and a sense of duty and *accomplishment* or *industry* occupies the period of childhood from 6 to 12 years. In adolescence a sense of *identity* is built; a sense of *intimacy,* a parental sense of *productivity,* and a sense of *integrity* are among the tasks of adulthood.

The audience for children's books can be grouped according to their orientations toward achieving *initiative, accomplishment,* and *identity.* Preschool and early primary children can be described as preoccupied with first ventures outside the circle of familiar authority. Most elementary children are caught up in the period of industry, or "task orientation," proud of their ability to use skills and tools, to plan projects, and to work toward finished products. Middle-school students are more concerned with defining values and personal roles.

---

[31]Abraham H. Maslow, *Motivation and Personality,* rev. ed. (Reading, Mass.: Addison-Wesley, 1987).

[32]Erik H. Erikson, *Childhood and Society,* rev. ed. (New York: Norton, 1993).

Writers of children's books sometimes suggest a natural audience for their work by bringing one of these orientations into the foreground. In Beatrix Potter's *The Tale of Peter Rabbit,* Peter's adventures demonstrate a developing sense of initiative like that of the preschoolers listening to the story. The fearsome aspects of taking those first steps away from Mother are reflected in Phyllis Root's *Oliver Finds His Way. Bucking the Sarge* by Christopher Paul Curtis speaks to the adolescent's struggle for identity and independence.

In considering any theory of development, we need to remember that children's prior experiences with books and their individual backgrounds can have an impact on their responses to literature. For instance, a child who has read stories of King Arthur and Lloyd Alexander's *Prydain* series will have a different understanding of what constitutes a hero in literature than someone who has not read beyond the Hardy Boys. Every child brings to literature a different lifetime of experiences and a set of constructs that is not quite the same as any other's. Whenever we consider the broad outlines of similarity that mark developmental levels, we have to remember that each reader is also one of a kind.

Guides for Ages and Stages

Adults who are responsible for children's reading need to be aware of child development and learning theory and of children's interests. They must keep in mind characteristics and needs of children at different ages and stages of development. At the same time, it is important to remember that each child has a unique pattern of growth. Teaching Resources: "Books for Ages and Stages," on pages 44–55, summarizes some characteristic growth patterns, suggests implications for selection and use of books, and provides examples of suitable books for a particular stage of development. Remember that the age levels indicated are only approximate. Also, books sug-

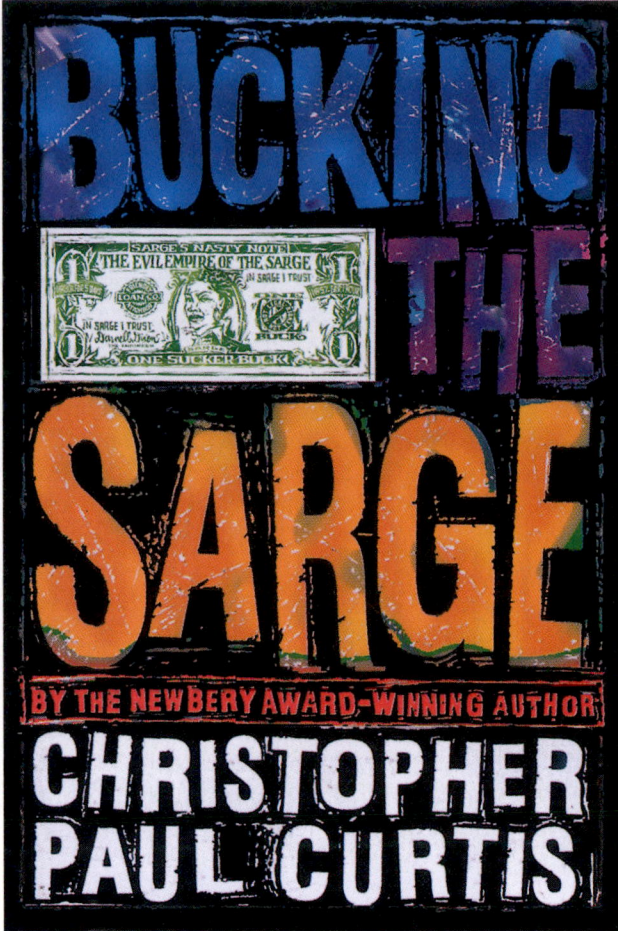

In *Bucking the Sarge,* Christopher Paul Curtis's hero mirrors the adolescent desire for control and autonomy. Cover from *Bucking the Sarge* by Christopher Paul Curtis. Used by permission of Random House Children's Books, a division of Random House, Inc.

gested as appropriate for one category might fit several other categories as well.

TEACHING **RESOURCES**

Books for Ages and Stages

 Visit the Online Learning Center at **www.mhhe.com/kiefer9e** for a printable version of this list.

BEFORE SCHOOL—INFANCY

Characteristics	Implications	Examples
Rapid development of senses. Responds to sound of human voice, especially rhythmic patterns. Vision stimulated by areas of color and sharp contrast; increasingly able to see detail.	Enjoys rhymes, songs, and lullabies. Likes simple, bright illustrations. Looks for familiar objects.	*And if the Moon Could Talk* (Banks) *Hooray for Fish!* (Cousins) *Kitten's First Full Moon* (Henkes) *My Very First Mother Goose* (Opie)

Books for Ages and Stages (*continued*)

BEFORE SCHOOL—INFANCY (*continued*)

Characteristics	Implications	Examples
Uses all senses to explore the world immediately at hand; learns through activity and participation.	Gets maximum use from sturdy books with washable pages. Needs to participate by touching, pointing, peeking, moving.	*Inside Freight Train* (Crews) *Pat the Bunny* (Kunhardt) *Sweet, Sweet Baby* (Steptoe) *Where's Spot?* (Hill)
Very limited attention span; averts eyes or turns away when bored.	Needs books that can be shared a few pages at a time or in a brief sitting; many short story times are better than one long one.	*1, 2, 3* (T. Hoban) *Baby Danced the Polka* (Beaumont) *Max's Ride* (Wells) *Mrs. McNosh Hangs Up Her Wash* (Weeks) *Rain* (Stojic)
Building foundations of language; plays with sounds, learns basic vocabulary along with concepts, begins to learn implicit "rules" that govern speech and conversation.	Needs to hear many rhymes and simple stories. Needs encouragement to use language in labeling pictures and in sharing dialogue with adults as they read aloud.	*Cow Moo Me* (Losordo) *Everywhere Babies* (Meyers) *I Swapped My Dog* (Zeifert) *Inside Mouse, Outside Mouse* (George) *Little Clam* (Reiser)
Building basic trust in human relationships.	Needs love and affection from caregivers, in stories as well as in life. Thrives on dependable routines and rituals such as bedtime stories.	*Goodnight Moon* (M. W. Brown) *Hushabye* (Burningham) *The Moon Came Down on Night Street* (Gralley) *Papa, Do You Love Me?* (Joosse) *You Are My Perfect Baby* (Thomas)
Limited mobility and experience; interests centered in self and the familiar.	Needs books that reflect self and people and activities in the immediate environment.	*Baby High, Baby Low* (Blackstone) *Boo Hoo Boo-Boo* (Singer) *Tom & Pippo's Day* (Oxenbury) *What's in Baby's Morning?* (Hindley)
Learning autonomy in basic self-help skills.	Enjoys stories of typical toddler accomplishments such as feeding self or getting dressed	*Bing: Get Dressed* (Dewan) *I Can* (Oxenbury) *On My Own* (Ford) *Potty Time* (Van Genechten)

PRESCHOOL AND KINDERGARTEN—AGES 3, 4, AND 5

Characteristics	Implications	Examples
Rapid development of language.	Interest in words; enjoyment of rhymes, nonsense, and repetition and cumulative tales. Enjoys retelling simple folktale and "reading" stories from books without words.	*Bears* (Kraus) *The Bus for Us* (Bloom) *Dinnertime* (Williams) *Millions of Cats* (Gág) *Talking Like the Rain* (Kennedy) *The Three Bears* (Rockwell) *Where Is the Green Sheep?* (Fox)
Very active, short attention span.	Requires books that can be completed in one sitting. Enjoys participation such as naming, pointing,	*Backyard Detective* (Bishop) *Each Peach Pear Plum* (Ahlberg and Ahlberg)

(continued)

Books for Ages and Stages *(continued)*

PRESCHOOL AND KINDERGARTEN—AGES 3, 4, AND 5 *(continued)*

Characteristics	Implications	Examples
Very active, short attention span. *(continued)*	singing, and identifying hidden pictures. Should have a chance to hear stories several times each day.	*The Noisy Way to Bed* (Whybrow) *Trashy Town* (Zimmerman) *The Very Hungry Caterpillar* (Carle) *Wheels on the Bus* (Raffi) *The Wheels on the Race Car* (Zane)
Child is center of own world. Interest, behavior, and thinking are egocentric.	Likes characters that are easy to identify with. Normally sees only one point of view.	*A Baby Sister for Frances* (R. Hoban) *Bunny Cakes* (Wells) *Leonardo, the Terrible Monster* (Willems) *No, David!* (Shannon) *What Shall We Do with a Boo-Hoo Baby?* (Cowell)
Curious about own world.	Enjoys stories about everyday experiences, pets, playthings, home, people in the immediate environment.	*Cowboy Baby* (Heap) *Feast for Ten* (Falwell) *Let's Get a Pup!* (Graham) *My Mom's Having a Baby!* (Butler) *When You Were Born* (Aston)
Beginning interest in how things work and the wider world.	Books feed curiosity and introduce new topics.	*Bashi, Elephant Baby* (Radcliffe) *My Pet Hamster* (Rockwell) *One Little Lamb* (Greenstein) *A Truck Goes Rattley-Bumpa* (London) *What Is a Scientist?* (Lehn)
Building concepts through many firsthand experiences.	Books extend and reinforce child's developing concepts.	*Eating the Alphabet* (Ehlert) *My Car* (Barton) *Ten Puppies* (Reiser) *This is Me and Where I Am* (Fitzgerald) *Trucks Trucks Trucks* (Sis)
Has little sense of time. Time is "before now," "now," and "not yet."	Books can help children begin to understand the sequence of time.	*Clocks and More Clocks* (Hutchins) *Cluck O'Clock* (Gray) *The Little House* (Burton) *Telling Time with Mama Cat* (Harper)
Learns through imaginative play; make-believe world of talking animals and magic seems very real.	Enjoys stories that involve imaginative play. Likes personification of toys and animals.	*10 Minutes Till Bedtime* (Rathman) *Corduroy* (Freeman) *Dog Blue* (Dunbar) *May I Bring a Friend?* (DeRegniers) *We're Going on a Bear Hunt* (Rosen) *When an Elephant Comes to School* (Ormerod)
Seeks warmth and security in relationships with family and others.	Likes to hear stories that provide reassurance. Bedtime stories and other read-aloud rituals provide positive literature experiences.	*Edward, Unready for School* (Wells) *How Do Dinosaurs Eat Their Food?* (Yolen) *Little Bear* (Minarik)

Books for Ages and Stages (continued)

PRESCHOOL AND KINDERGARTEN—AGES 3, 4, AND 5 (continued)

Characteristics	Implications	Examples
		The Runaway Bunny (M. W. Brown) *Shhhh! Everyone Is Sleeping* (Markes) *Ten, Nine, Eight* (Bang)
Beginning to assert independence. Takes delight in own accomplishments.	Books can reflect emotions. Enjoys stories where small characters show initiative.	*Alfie Gets in First* (Hughes) *The Littlest Wolf* (Brimmer) *Myrtle* (Pearson) *Will I Have a Friend?* (M. Cohen)
Makes absolute judgments about right and wrong.	Expects bad behavior to be punished and good behavior to be rewarded. Requires poetic justice and happy endings.	*The Gingerbread Man* (Aylesworth) *The Little Red Hen* (Barton) *Superdog* (Buehner) *The Tale of Peter Rabbit* (Potter) *The Three Billy Goats Gruff* (Asbjørnsen and Moe)

PRIMARY—AGES 6 AND 7

Characteristics	Implications	Examples
Continued development and expansion of language.	Frequent story times during the day provide opportunity to hear the rich and varied language of literature. Wordless books and simple tales encourage storytelling.	*Four Hungry Kittens* (McCully) *The Red Book* (Lehman) *Sylvester and the Magic Pebble* (Steig) *We're Going On a Picnic* (Hutchins)
Attention span increasing.	Prefers short stories; may enjoy a continued story provided each chapter is a complete episode.	*Frog and Toad Together* (Lobel) *It's My Birthday, Too!* (Jonell) *The Stories Julian Tells* (Cameron) *Tales from the Waterhole* (Graham)
Striving to accomplish skills expected by adults.	Proud of accomplishments in reading and writing. Needs reassurance that everyone progresses at own rate. First reading experiences should be enjoyable, using familiar or predictable stories.	*Brown Bear, Brown Bear, What Do You See?* (B. Martin) *The Day of Ahmed's Secret* (Heide and Gilliland) *Duck, Duck, Goose!* (Beaumont) *A Splendid Friend, Indeed* (Bloom) *You Read to Me, I'll Read to You* (Hoberman)
Learning still based on immediate perception and direct experiences.	Uses information books to verify as well as extend experience. Much value in watching guinea pigs or tadpoles before using a book.	*Actual Size* (Jenkins) *All about Frogs* (Arnosky) *My Puppy Is Born* (J. Cole) *On the Way to the Beach* (H. Cole)
Continued interest in own world; more curious about a wider range of things.	Needs wide variety of books. Television has expanded interests beyond home and neighborhood.	*Bee-bim Bop!* (Park) *Chameleon, Chameleon* (Cowley)

(continued)

Books for Ages and Stages *(continued)*

PRIMARY—AGES 6 AND 7 *(continued)*

Characteristics	Implications	Examples
Still sees world from an egocentric point of view.		*Here Is the Coral Reef* (Dunphy) *I Live in Tokyo* (Takabayashi) *Kumak's Fish* (Bania) *The Librarian of Basra* (Winter) *Little Shark* (Rockwell) *Red-Eyed Tree Frog* (Cowley)
Vague concepts of time.	Needs to learn basics of telling time and the calendar. Simple biographies and historical fiction may give a feeling for the past, but accurate understanding of chronology is beyond this age group.	*Grandmother Bryant's Pocket* (J. B. Martin) *The House on Maple Street* (Pryor) *Mimmy and Sophie All Around the Town* (Cohen) *Ox-Cart Man* (D. Hall) *When I Was Young in the Mountains* (Rylant)
More able to separate fantasy from reality; more aware of own imagination.	Enjoys fantasy. Likes to dramatize simple stories or use feltboard, puppets.	*I Know an Old Lady* (Taback) *I Stink!* (McMullan) *Ker-splash!* (O'Connor) *Traction Man Is Here!* (Grey) *Where the Wild Things Are* (Sendak)
Beginning to develop empathy for others.	Adults can ask such questions as "What would you have done?" "How would you have felt?"	*Crow Boy* (Yashima) *Don't Fidget a Feather* (Silverman) *Fly Away Home* (Bunting) *Rickie and Henri* (Goodall) *The Teddy Bear* (McPhail)
Has a growing sense of justice. Demands application of rules, regardless of circumstances.	Expects poetic justice in books.	*Flossie and the Fox* (McKissack) *Guji Guji* (Chen) *Once a Mouse* (M. Brown) *The Tale of Tricky Fox* (Aylesworth) *Too Many Tamales* (Soto)
Humor is developing.	Needs to hear many books read aloud for pure fun. Enjoys books and poems that have surprise endings, plays on words, incongruous situations, and slapstick comedy. Likes to be in on the joke.	*Bear Wants More* (K. Wilson) *Broom Mates* (Palatini) *Dragon's Fat Cat* (Pilkey) *Hooway for Wodney Wat* (Lester) *Meet Wild Boars* (Rosoff) *Mr. Maxwell's Mouse* (Asch) *My Little Sister Hugged an Ape* (Grossman) *Zoo's Who* (Florian)
Shows curiosity about gender differences and reproduction.	Teachers need to accept and be ready to answer children's questions about sex.	*How I Was Born* (Wabbes) *How You Were Born* (J. Cole) *Making Animal Babies* (Collard) *The New Baby at Our House* (J. Cole)

Books for Ages and Stages *(continued)*

PRIMARY—AGES 6 AND 7 *(continued)*

Characteristics	Implications	Examples
Physical contour of the body is changing; permanent teeth appear; learning to whistle and developing other fine motor skills.	Books can help the child accept physical changes in self and differences in others.	*Hue Boy* (Phillips) *One Morning in Maine* (McCloskey) *Tabitha's Terrifically Tough Tooth* (Middleton) *Whistle for Willie* (Keats) *Whistling* (Partridge) *You'll Soon Grow into Them, Titch* (Hutchins)
Continues to seek independence from adults and to develop initiative.	Needs opportunities to select own books and activities. Enjoys stories of responsibility and successful ventures.	*Elena's Serenade* (Campbell) *Galimoto* (K. Williams) *Ira Sleeps Over* (Waber) *My Rows and Piles of Coins* (Mollel) *Stella: Fairy of the Forest* (Gay)
Continues to need warmth and security in family relationships.	Books may emphasize universal human characteristics in a variety of lifestyles.	*A Bear for Miguel* (Alphin) *The Biggest Soap* (Schaefer) *A Chair for My Mother* (V. Williams) *Elizabeti's Doll* (Stuve-Bodeen) *Henry's First Moon Birthday* (Look) *What's Cooking, Jamela?* (Daly)

MIDDLE ELEMENTARY—AGES 8 AND 9

Characteristics	Implications	Examples
Attaining independence in reading skills. May read with complete absorption, or may still be having difficulty learning to read. Wide variation in ability and interest.	Discovers reading as an enjoyable activity. Prefers an uninterrupted block of time for independent reading. During this period, many children become avid readers.	*Judy Moody Declares Independence* (McDonald) *Martin Bridge: Ready for Takeoff* (Kerrin) *Ramona's World* (Cleary) *Ruby Lu, Brave and True* (Look) *Shredderman: Enemy Spy* (Van Draanen) *Suitcase* (M. P. Walter) *What You Never Know about Tubs, Toilets, and Showers* (Lauber)
Reading level may still be below appreciation level.	Essential to read aloud to children each day in order to extend interests, develop appreciation, and provide balance.	*The Fish in Room 11* (Dyer) *If Dogs Were Dinosaurs* (Schwartz) *The Penderwicks* (Birdsall) *The Pepins and Their Problems* (Horvath) *Sarah, Plain and Tall* (MacLachlan)
Peer group acceptance becomes increasingly important.	Children need opportunities to recommend and discuss books.	*Ever-Clever Elisa* (Hurwitz) *The Gold Threaded Dress* (Marsden)

(continued)

Books for Ages and Stages *(continued)*

MIDDLE ELEMENTARY—AGES 8 AND 9 *(continued)*

Characteristics	Implications	Examples
	Sharing favorites builds sense that reading is fun, has group approval. Popular books may provide status, be much in demand.	*Lucy Rose: Big on Plans* (Kelly) *Mercy Goes for a Ride* (DiCamillo) *Owen Foote, Super Spy* (Greene)
Developing standards of right and wrong. Begins to see viewpoints of others.	Books provide opportunities to relate to several points of view.	*Alec's Primer* (Walter) *Freedom on the Menu* (Weatherford) *Honeysuckle House* (Cheng) *The Journey* (Stewart) *The Other Side* (Woodson) *Through My Eyes* (Bridges)
Less egocentric, developing empathy for others. Questioning death.	Accepts some books with a less than happy ending. Discussion helps children explore their feelings for others.	*Each Little Bird That Sings* (Wiles) *Love, Ruby Lavender* (Wiles) *Michael Rosen's Sad Book* (M. Rosen) *The Quicksand Pony* (Lester) *Stone Fox* (Gardiner)
Time concepts and spatial relationships developing. This age level is characterized by thought that is flexible and reversible.	Interested in biographies, life in the past, in other lands, and the future. Prefers fast-moving, exciting stories.	*Brave Harriet* (Moss) *Freedom on the Menu* (Weatherford) *The Green Book* (Walsh) *Keeper of the Doves* (Byars) *Maritcha: A Nineteenth Century American Girl* (Bolden) *Pirate Diary* (Platt) *Sequoyah* (Rumford)
Enjoys tall tales, slapstick humor in everyday situations. Appreciates imaginary adventure.	Teachers need to recognize the importance of literature for laughter, releasing tension, and providing enjoyment.	*The Golden Goose* (King-Smith) *Grandy Thaxter's Helper* (Rees) *Hey Kids, Want to Buy a Bridge?* (Scieszka) *I Was a Rat* (Pullman) *Oh, No! Where Are My Pants?* (Hopkins) *Skinnybones* (Park) *Wake the Dead* (Harris)
Cognitive growth and language development increase capacity for problem solving and word play.	Likes the challenge of solving puzzles and mysteries. High interest in twists of plot, secret codes, riddles, and other language play.	*The Amber Cat* (McKay) *Can You See What I See?* (Wick) *A Ghost in the Family* (Wright) *Math Potatoes* (Tang) *Timothy Tunny Swallowed a Bunny* (Grossman) *Young Cam Jansen and the New Girl Mystery* (Adler)
Improved coordination makes proficiency in sports and games possible and encourages interest in crafts and hobbies.	Interest in sports books; wants specific knowledge about sports. Enjoys how-to-do-it books.	*In the Paint* (Ewing and Louis) *The Jumbo Book of Needlecrafts* (Sadler) *National Geographic Photography Guide for Kids* (N. Johnson)

Books for Ages and Stages *(continued)*

MIDDLE ELEMENTARY—AGES 8 AND 9 *(continued)*

Characteristics	Implications	Examples
		The Visual Dictionary of Baseball (Buckley Jr.)
Sees categories and classifications with new clarity; interest in collecting is high.	Likes to collect and trade paperback books. Begins to look for books of one author, series books.	*Carnival at Candlelight* (Osborne) *The Extreme Team: Wild Ride* (M. Christopher) *Horrible Harry and the Goog* (Kline) *Meet Addy* (The American Girl Collection) (Porter)
Seeks specific information to answer questions; may go to books beyond own reading ability to search out answers.	Enjoys books that collect facts, nonfiction, identification books. Requires guidance in locating information within a book and in using the library.	*The Cod's Tale* (Kurlansky) *Insectology* (Blobaum) *The International Space Station* (Branley) *Ms. Frizzle's Adventures: Ancient Egypt* (J. Cole) *New Beginnings: Jamestown and the Virginia Colony* (D. Rosen) *The Tomb of the Boy King* (Frank) *Where Did the Butterfly Get Its Name?* (Berger and Berger)

LATER ELEMENTARY—AGES 10 AND 11

Characteristics	Implications	Examples
Rate of physical development varies widely. Rapid growth precedes beginning of puberty. Girls are about two years ahead of boys in development; both increasingly curious about all aspects of sex.	Guide understanding of growth process and help children meet personal problems. Continued differentiation in reading preferences of boys and girls.	*Are You There, God? It's Me, Margaret* (Blume) *Asking About Sex and Growing Up* (J. Cole) *Llama in the Library* (Hurwitz) *What's the Big Secret? Talking about Sex with Girls and Boys* (L. Brown and M. Brown)
Understanding of gender is developing; boys and girls form ideas about their own and each other's identity.	Books may provide identification with gender roles and impetus for discussion of stereotypes.	*Girls: A History of Growing Up Female in America* (Colman) *Guys Write for Guys Read* (Scieszka) *The Loser* (J. Spinelli) *Project Mulberry* (Park) *Stanford Wong Flunks Big-Time* (Yee) *Under the Watsons' Porch* (Shreve) *When Zachary Beaver Came to Town* (Holt)
Increased emphasis on peer group and sense of belonging.	Book choices often influenced by peer group; books can highlight problems with peer pressure.	*All Alone in the Universe* (Perkins) *Lunch Money* (Clements) *Moon Runner* (Marsden) *Notes from a Liar and Her Dog* (Choldenko)

(continued)

Books for Ages and Stages *(continued)*

LATER ELEMENTARY—AGES 10 AND 11 *(continued)*

Characteristics	Implications	Examples
		Some Friend (Bradby)
		The Tulip Touch (Fine)
		Wringers (J. Spinelli)
Deliberate exclusion of others; some expressions of prejudice.	Books can emphasize unique contributions of all. Discussion can be used to clarify values.	*The Crow-Girl* (Bredsdorff)
		Days of Tears (Lester)
		Leon's Story (Tillage)
		Lizzie Bright and the Buckminster Boy (Schmidt)
		Roll of Thunder, Hear My Cry (M. Taylor)
		Yankee Girl (Rodman)
Family patterns changing; may challenge parents' authority. Highly critical of siblings.	Books may provide some insight into these changing relationships.	*Al Capone Does My Shirts* (Choldenko)
		The Birthday Room (Henkes)
		Dicey's Song (Voigt)
		Heaven (Johnson)
		Junebug in Trouble (Mead)
		Millions (Boyce)
		The Vacation (Horvath)
Begins to have models other than parents drawn from television, movies, sports figures, books. Beginning interest in future vocation.	Biographies may provide models. Career books broaden interests and provide useful information.	*Don't Tell the Girls: A Family Memoir* (Giff)
		Knots in My Yo-yo String: The Autobiography of a Kid (J. Spinelli)
		Nelson Mandela (Kramer)
		Tomboy of the Air (Cummins)
		The Voice That Challenged a Nation (Freedman)
Sustained, intense interest in specific activities.	Seeks book about hobbies and other interests.	*Berry Smudges and Leaf Prints* (Senisi)
		Bodies from the Ash (Deem)
		Galileo for Kids (Panchyk)
		The Mystery of the Mammoth Bones: And How It Was Solved (Giblin)
		Out Standing in My Field (Jennings)
A peak time for voluntary reading.	Avid readers welcome challenges, repeated contact with authors and genres.	*The Book without Words* (Avi)
		Darnell Rock Reporting (Myers)
		Harry Potter and the Half Blood Prince (Rowling)
		Permanent Rose (McKay)
		The Same Stuff as Stars (Paterson)
		The Search for Belle Prater (White)
Seeks to test own skills and abilities; looks ahead to a time of complete independence.	Enjoys stories of survival and "going it alone."	*Fish* (Matthews)
		Gnat Stokes and the Foggy Bottom Swamp Queen (Keehn)
		Hatchet (Paulsen)
		A Single Shard (Park)

Books for Ages and Stages (continued)

LATER ELEMENTARY—AGES 10 AND 11 (continued)

Characteristics	Implications	Examples
		Three Days (Napoli) *We Were There Too!: Young People in U.S. History* (Hoose)
Increased cognitive skill can be used to serve the imagination.	Tackles complex and puzzling plots in mysteries, science fiction, fantasy. Can appreciate more subtlety in humor.	*The Big House* (Coman) *The Clue of the Linoleum Lederhosen* (Anderson) *The Dark Is Rising* (Cooper) *Dust* (Slade) *The Golden Compass* (Pullman) *Holes* (Sachar) *A Thief in the House of Memory* (Wynne-Jones) *Wright 3* (Balliett)
Increased understanding of the chronology of past events; developing sense of own place in time. Begins to see many dimensions of a problem.	Literature provides opportunities to examine issues from different viewpoints. Guidance needed for recognizing biased presentations.	*Adam Canfield of the Slash* (Winerip) *A Dream of Freedom* (McWhorter) *The Friends* (Yumoto) *The Heart of a Chief* (Bruchac) *Jip: His Story* (Paterson) *Morning Girl* (Dorris) *Shades of Gray* (Reeder)
Highly developed sense of justice and concern for others.	Willing to discuss many aspects of right and wrong; likes "sad stories," shows empathy for victims of suffering and injustice.	*Bud, Not Buddy* (Curtis) *Gentle's Holler* (Madden) *Hush* (Woodson) *Missing May* (Rylant) *Number the Stars* (Lowry) *Out of the Dust* (Hesse) *The Search for Belle Prater* (White) *Shiloh* (Naylor) *Tending to Grace* (Fusco) *Up On Cloud Nine* (Fine)
Searching for values; interested in problems of the world. Can deal with abstract relationships; becoming more analytical.	Valuable discussions may grow out of teacher's reading aloud prose and poetry to this age group. Questions may help students gain insight into both the content and the literary structure of a book.	*19 Varieties of Gazelle* (Nye) *The Other Side of Truth* (Naidoo) *Shadow of Ghadames* (Stolz) *Skellig* (Almond) *Tuck Everlasting* (Babbitt) *Under the Persimmon Tree* (Staples) *The View from Saturday* (Konigsburg)

MIDDLE SCHOOL—AGES 12, 13, AND 14

Characteristics	Implications	Examples
Wide variation in physical development; both boys and girls reach puberty by age 14. Developing sex drive; intense interest in sexuality and world of older teens.	Books provide insight into feelings, concerns. Guidance needed to balance students' desire for frank content with lack of life experience.	*Blushing: Expressions of Love in Poetry and Letters* (Janeczko) *Boy2Girl* (Blacker) *The Boyfriend List* (Lockhart) *Candy* (Brooks)

(continued)

Books for Ages and Stages *(continued)*

MIDDLE SCHOOL—AGES 12, 13, AND 14 *(continued)*

Characteristics	Implications	Examples
		How I Live Now (Rosoff) *It's Perfectly Normal* (Harris) *The Key to the Golden Firebird* (Johnson)
Self-concept continues to grow. Developing a sense of identity is important.	Books help students explore roles, rehearse journey to identity. Many stories based on myth of the hero.	*Gifts* (Le Guin) *A Girl Named Disaster* (Farmer) *The Great Tree of Avalon: Shadows on the Stars* (Barron) *The Hero and the Crown* (McKinley) *The Hunter's Moon* (Melling) *The Ropemaker* (Dickinson) *Treasure at the Heart of Tanglewood* (Pierce) *A Wizard of Earthsea* (Le Guin)
Peer group becomes increasingly influential; relationships with family are changing.	Concerns about friends and families reflected in books. School should provide chance to share books and responses with peer group.	*Breaking Through* (Jiménez) *Criss Cross* (Perkins) *In Spite of Killer Bees* (Johnston) *Saving Francesca* (Marchetta) *A Step from Heaven* (Na) *Where I Want to Be* (Griffin) *Worlds Apart* (Soto)
New aspects of egocentrism lead to imagining self as center of others' attention and feeling one's own problems are unique.	Students begin to enjoy introspection; may identify with characters who are intense or self-absorbed.	*Best Foot forward* (Bauer) *Heck, Superhero* (Leavitt) *Jacob Have I Loved* (Paterson) *Jazmin's Notebook* (Grimes) *Shakespeare's Secret* (Broach) *White Girl* (Olsen)
Cognitive abilities are increasingly abstract and flexible, but not consistently so. New capacity to reason from imaginary premises, manipulate symbolic language, and make hypothetical judgments.	Students read more complex stories, mysteries, and high fantasy that call for complex logic; enjoy science fiction and high adventure. Metaphor, symbols, and imagery are understood at a different level.	*Feed* (Anderson) *The Fire-Eaters* (Almond) *Kit's Wilderness* (Almond) *Montmorency on the Rocks* (Updale) *Sea of Trolls* (Farmer) *Shade's Children* (Nix) *Skybreaker* (Oppel) *The Star of Kazan* (Ibbotson)
Able to apply ideas of relativity to questions of value; girls might see moral issues differently than boys do.	Students need discussion time to negotiate meanings in stories that pose moral dilemmas.	*The Cannibals* (Lawrence) *The Diary of Pelly D* (Adlington) *The Giver* (Lowry) *Habibi* (Nye) *Homeless Bird* (Whelan) *The Legend of Buddy Bush* (Moses) *Shabanu* (Staples)
Sensitive to great complexity in human feelings and relationships.	Students seek richer and more complex stories.	*The Glory Field* (Myers) *Go and Come Back* (Abelove)

Books for Ages and Stages (continued)

MIDDLE SCHOOL—AGES 12, 13, AND 14 (continued)

Characteristics	Implications	Examples
		Like Sisters on the Home Front (Williams-Garcia) *A Northern Light* (Donnelly) *Sonny's House of Spies* (Lyon) *Toning the Sweep* (Johnson) *A Wreath for Emmett Till* (Nelson)
Cumulative effects of development and life experience produce wide variation among individuals in abilities and interests.	Reading ability and interests in one class may range from early elementary to adult.	*Countdown* (Johannsen) *The Hobbit* (Tolkien) *Operation Red Jericho* (Mowll) *Out from Boneville* (J. Smith) *Scrib* (Ives) *The Secret under My Skin* (McNaughton)

RESPONSE IN THE CLASSROOM

Understanding children's responses to literature would be much easier if it were possible to peer inside children's heads. Then we might see firsthand what concept of story guides progress through a book or just what children are thinking as a story unfolds. Instead, teachers must be satisfied with secondary evidence. Children's perceptions and understandings are revealed in many different ways—as the children choose and talk about books, and as they write, paint, play, or take part in other classroom activities.

Classroom responses can be obvious and direct (primary children have been known to kiss a favorite book) or hidden within a situation that appears to have little to do with literature (such as block corner play). Many responses are verbal, many come without words. Some are spontaneous, bubbling up out of children too delighted to be still, or shyly offered in confidence. Other responses would not be expressed at all without the direct invitation of teachers who plan extension activities or discussions (see Chapter 13) to generate thoughtful reaction to literature. To understand any of these observed responses, it is helpful to be acquainted with a few basic theoretical perspectives.

Theories of Response

What really goes on between a reader and a story or poem is a complex question with many answers. Theories about reader response draw from many disciplines, including psychology, linguistics, aesthetics, and, of course, literature and education.

Some theories focus on what is read; others focus on the reader. For instance, some researchers have examined in careful detail the structure of stories, noting the precise arrangement of words and sequence of ideas. These patterns are called "story grammars," and studies indicate that they can affect the way readers understand and recall a story.[33] Other theorists are more concerned with individual readers and how their personalities can influence their ideas about what they read.[34] Still other researchers emphasize the cultural or social aspects of response. According to Richard Beach, "While all these theoretical perspectives rest on different assumptions about meaning, they ultimately intersect and overlap. The local—the focus on readers' textual knowledge and experience—is embedded within the global, larger social and cultural contexts." All categories of reader response research focus on the reader's textual knowledge and experience, but they are embedded within larger social and cultural contexts.[35]

---

[33]Dorothy S. Strickland and Joan Feeley, "Development in the Elementary School Years," *Handbook of Research on Teaching the English Language Arts,* eds. James Flood, Julie Jensen, Diane Lapp, and James Squire (New York: Macmillan, 1991), pp. 386–402.

[34]Norman H. Holland, *Five Readers Reading* (New Haven, Conn.: Yale University Press, 1975).

[35]Richard Beach, *A Teacher's Introduction to Reader-Response Theories* (Urbana, Ill.: National Council of Teachers of English, 1993), p. 9.

One important point on which scholars agree is that the process of reading and responding is active rather than passive. The words and ideas in the book are not transferred automatically from the page to the reader. Rather, as Louise Rosenblatt has argued,

> The literary work exists in the live circuit set up between reader and text: the reader infuses intellectual and emotional meanings into the pattern of verbal symbols, and those symbols channel his thoughts and feelings.[36]

Response is dynamic and open to continuous change as readers anticipate, infer, remember, reflect, interpret, and connect. The "meaning" and significance of stories like David Almond's *Skellig* or *The Fire-Eaters* will vary from reader to reader, depending on age and personal experience as well as experience with literature. However, each reader's response will also change, given time for reflection, discussion, or repeated readings.

Reader response theory also points out that readers approach works of literature in special ways. James Britton proposes that in all our uses of language we can be either *participants* or *spectators*.[37] In the participant role we read in order to accomplish something in the real world, as in following a recipe. In the spectator role we focus on what the language says as an end in itself, attending to its forms and patterns, as we do in enjoying poetry.

Rosenblatt suggests that reading usually involves two roles, or stances, and that we shift our emphasis from one to the other according to the material and our purposes for reading it.[38] In the *efferent* stance we are most concerned with what information can be learned from the reading. In the *aesthetic* stance our concern is for the experience of the reading itself, the feelings and images that come and go with the flow of the words. Most readers, of course, find themselves switching back and forth from one of these stances to the other as they read. One thing teachers can do to help children share the world the author has created is to help them find an appropriate stance as they begin to read.

Types of Response

Teachers who are familiar with reader response theories and who study children's responses to literature will discover that they provide a basis for deepening children's satisfaction with books and for supporting children's growth in interpretation.

The most common expressions of response to literature are statements, oral or written. In their most pol-

Profile in Literature

Teacher Isaac Brooks

As teachers gain experience in the classroom and as they continue their professional development, they learn to apply theories about reading and literature to the needs of their particular students. Isaac Brooks, a nine-year veteran, has taught grades 2 through 9, and children's literature has come to play an increasingly central role in his teaching. Go to the Online Learning Center at **www.mhhe.com/kiefer9e** or your Resources CD-ROM to learn about Isaac Brooks's approach to integrating literature with literacy.

ished form such responses are known as literary criticism, and for many years research in literature involved measuring young people's statements against a standard of mature critical ability.

Where children are concerned, it is important to remember that direct comment is only one of many ways of revealing what goes on between the book and its audience. Language used in other ways—to tell or write stories based on other stories, for instance—often provides good clues about a child's feelings and understandings about the original. Parents and teachers of young children also recognize nonverbal behaviors as signs of response. For instance, young listeners almost always show their involvement, or lack of it, in body postures and facial expressions. Children's artwork, informal drama, and other book extension activities (see Chapter 13) also provide windows on response.

Interpreting Children's Responses

Previous research in response to literature provides teachers and librarians with a framework for interpreting their students' reactions to books. This classroom-based research can give us a deeper understanding of children's responses.

Recognizing Patterns of Change

Teachers and researchers alike have observed that when children at different grade levels read and respond in ways that are comfortable for them, their responses will be alike in some ways and different in others. What might teachers expect to see in a fourth-grade classroom? What are typical first-grade responses? No one can answer these questions with exactness, for every child is a unique

---

[36]Louise M. Rosenblatt, *Literature as Exploration,* 5th ed. (New York: Modern Language Association, 1996), p. 25.

[37]James Britton et al., *The Development of Writing Abilities (11–18),* Schools Council Research Studies (London: Macmillan Education Limited, 1975).

[38]Louise M. Rosenblatt, *The Reader, the Text, the Poem: The Transactional Theory of the Literary Work* (Carbondale: Southern Illinois University Press, 1994).

"William Ernest lay a bolster pillow behind Mrs Trotter's back like

reader and every classroom represents a different composite of experiences with literature and with the world. Even so, it is helpful to know what researchers and teachers have discovered about the responses of their students at various grade levels. This section outlines some of these findings to provide information on the patterns of change in responses that usually take place as children have experiences with literature in the elementary school.[39] Although these findings are presented in an age-level sequence, keep in mind that any of these characteristics can be seen at other ages, depending on the child, the situation, and the challenge presented by the material. Like the Teaching Resources chart (pp. 44–55), this guide is more useful for making predictions about a class than for making predictions about an individual child.

Younger Children (Preschool to Primary)

Younger children are *motor oriented.* As listeners, they respond with their whole selves, chiming in on refrains or talking back to the story. They lean closer to the book, point at pictures, clap their hands. They use body movements to try out some of the story's action, "hammering" along with *John Henry* by Julius Lester or making wild faces to match the illustrations in Maurice Sendak's *Where the Wild Things Are.* Actions to demonstrate meaning ("Like this") might be given as answers to a teacher's

questions. These easily observable responses go undercover as children mature; older children reveal feelings through subtle changes of expression and posture.

At this age, children spontaneously act out stories or bits of stories using actions, roles, and conventions of literature in their *dramatic play.* Witches, kings, "wild things," and other well-defined character types appear naturally, showing how well children have assimilated elements of favorite tales. Examples of story language ("We lived happily ever after") are sometimes incorporated. Spontaneous dramatic play disappears from the classroom early in the primary years (although it persists out of school with some children) and is replaced by more structured drama of various kinds. Older children are usually much more conscious of their own references to literature.

These children respond to stories piecemeal. Their responses deal with *parts rather than wholes.* A detail of text or illustration might prompt more comment than the story itself, as children make quick associations with their own experience: "I saw a bird like that once" or "My sister has bunk beds just like those." This part-by-part organization can also be seen in very young children's art, where the pictures show individual story items without any indication of relationship ("This is the baby bear's chair, and this is Goldilocks, and this is the house the bears lived in, and here is the bed . . ."). This is the same sort of itemization or cataloging of characters,

---

[39]This section is based on observations with reference to the work of Arthur Applebee, *The Child's Concept of Story* (Chicago, Ill.: University of Chicago Press, 1978), pp. 123–25; Janet Hickman, "A New Perspective on Response to Literature," *Research in the Teaching of English* 15 (1981): 343–54; and others.

objects, and events that children sometimes use when asked to tell something about a story. Young children are more likely to respond to the story as a whole if they have heard it many times or if an adult provides that focus by asking good questions.

Children at this age use *embedded language* in answering direct questions about stories. Because young children see the world in literal, concrete terms, their answers are likely to be couched in terms of the characters, events, and objects found in the story. One first grader made a good attempt to generalize the lesson of "The Little Red Hen," but couldn't manage without some reference to the tale: "When someone already baked the cake and you haven't helped, they're probably just gonna say 'No'!" A teacher or other adult who shares the child's context—who knows the story, has heard or read it with the child, and knows what other comments have been made—will understand the intent of such a statement more readily than a casual observer will.

Children in Transition (Primary to Middle Grades)

Children in transition from the primary to the middle grades develop from being listeners to becoming readers. They go through a period of focus on the *accomplishment of independent reading*. They make many comments about quantity—number of pages read, the length of a book, or the number of books read. Conventions of print and of bookmaking might draw their attention. One third grader refused to read any of the poems from Shel Silverstein's *Where the Sidewalk Ends* without locating them in the index first; a classmate was fascinated with the book's variety of word and line arrangements for poetry. Another child studied the front matter of a picture book and pronounced it "a dedicated book." So-called independent reading may be more sociable than it sounds, since many children like to have a listener or reading partner and begin to rely on peers as sounding boards for their response.

At this age, children become more adept at *summarizing* in place of straight retelling when asked to talk about stories. This is a skill that facilitates discussion and becomes more useful as it is developed. Summarizing is one of the techniques that undergirds critical commentary, but adults use it more deliberately and precisely than children do.

These children classify or *categorize* stories in some of the same ways that adults do. Middle graders who are asked to sort out a random pile of books use categories like "mysteries," "humorous books," "make-believe," and "fantasy." If you ask kindergartners to do the same, they are more likely to classify the books by their physical properties ("fat books," "books with pretty covers," "red books") than by content.

Children at this age *attribute personal reactions to the story* itself. A book that bores an 8-year-old will be thought of as a "boring book," as if "boring" were as much a prop-

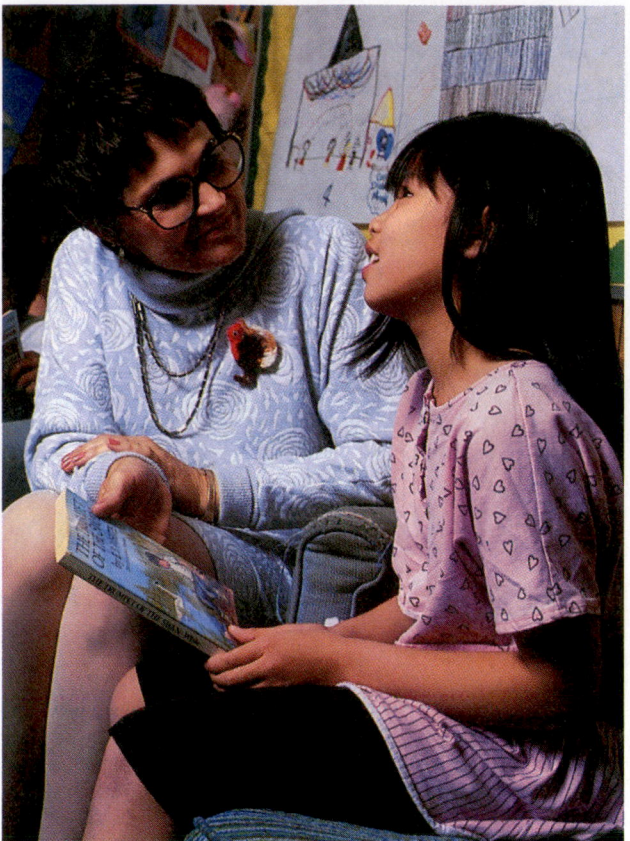

Teachers need to listen carefully to children's responses to literature in order to discover their thinking strategies. Mission School, Redlands Public Schools, Redlands, California. Joan Schleicher, teacher. Photo by Larry Rose.

erty of the story as its number of pages or its first-person point of view. Children judge a story on the basis of their response to it, regardless of its qualities as literature or its appeal to anyone else. This is a very persistent element in response; it affects the judgment of students of children's literature and of professional book reviewers as well as children in elementary school. Personal response can never be totally eliminated from critical evaluation; but with experience, readers can develop more objectivity in separating a book's literary characteristics from its personal appeal.

These children also *use borrowed characters, events, themes, and patterns from literature in their writing*, just as younger children do in dramatic play. In the earliest stages, much of this is unconscious and spontaneous. One example is a 7-year-old who was convinced that her story about a fish with paint-splashed insides was "made up out of my own head," even when reminded that the class had just heard Robert McCloskey's *Burt Dow, Deep Water Man*. A 9-year-old spontaneously combined a favorite character with a field-trip experience in his story "Paddington Bear Goes to Franklin Park Conservatory," but he was aware of his idea sources. Other children produce their own examples of patterns, forms, or genres.

The direction of growth is toward more conscious realization of the uses of literature in writing (see Chapter 13).

Older Children (Middle Grades to Middle School)

Older children express *stronger preferences*, especially for personal reading. Younger children seem to enjoy almost everything that is reasonably appropriate, but older ones do not hesitate to reject books they do not like. Some children show particular devotion to certain authors or genres or series at this time. Some children also become more intense and protective about some of their reactions, and they should not be pressed to share those feelings that demand privacy.

At this age, children are more skillful with language and more able to deal with abstractions. They can *disembed ideas* from a story and put them in more generalized terms, as in stating a universal moral for a particular fable.

These children also begin to *see* (but not consistently) *that their feelings about a book are related to identifiable aspects of the writing.* Responses like "I love this book because it's great" develop into "I love this book because the characters say such funny things" or "*Strider* [by Cleary] is my favorite because Leigh is a lot like me."

Older children go beyond categorizing stories *toward a more analytical perception* of why characters behave as they do, how the story is put together, or what the author is trying to say. They begin to test fiction against real life and understand it better through the comparison. They use some critical terminology, although their understanding of terms may be incomplete. In talk and writing, children who are encouraged to express ideas freely begin to stand back from their own involvement and take an evaluative look at literature. One sixth grader had this to say about *A Taste of Blackberries* by Doris Buchanan Smith:

> I thought the author could have put more into it. I really didn't know much about the kid who died. I mean, it really happened fast in the book. It started out pretty soon and told about how sad he was and what they used to do. All the fun things they used to do together. I wished at the beginning they would have had all the things that he talked about and then have him thinking about what a good friend he is and then all of a sudden he dies—a little closer to the end. Because when he died, you didn't much care 'cause you didn't really know him. But I guess the author wanted to talk about how it would be, or how people feel, or maybe what happened to her—how it felt when one of her friends died like that.[40]

In general, children's responses move toward this sort of conscious comment. Young children sometimes make stunningly perceptive observations about stories, but they are not usually able to step back and see the importance of what they have said. Older children begin to know what they know, and can then take command of it. This allows them to layer mature appreciation on top of the beginner's natural delight.

However, older children's increasing capacity for abstraction, generalization, and analysis should *not* be interpreted as a need for programs of formal literary analysis or highly structured study procedures. Opportunities to read, hear, and talk about well-chosen books under the guidance of an interested and informed teacher will allow elementary school children to develop their responses to their full potential.

Children, no matter what their age, will respond to a story on their own terms of understanding. It does little good (and can be destructive to the enjoyment of literature) if younger children are pushed to try to formulate the abstractions achieved by more mature children. However, James Britton maintains that teachers may refine and develop the responses that children are already making by gradually exposing them to stories with increasingly complex patterns of events.[41]

Collecting Children's Responses

Finding out how children understand literature and which books they like is such basic information for elementary teachers and librarians that it should not be left to chance. Techniques for discovering responses that are simple and fit naturally into the ongoing business of classrooms and library media centers are discussed in the context of planning the school literature program in Chapter 13. Some suggestions for observing and studying responses are presented in the Into the Classroom box on page 61.

As elementary teachers become aware of the way they can tune in to children's responses to literature, they will see the value of examining the nature of children's thinking about it. We all believe that literature is important for children, but we do not truly know what difference it makes in a child's life, if any. An in-depth study of children's responses to books is just as important as, if not more important than, the studies of children's interests in books. We should explore the developmental nature of response and conduct longitudinal studies of a child's responses over the years. As teachers and librarians, we need to be still and listen to what the children are telling us about their involvement with books and what it means to them.

---

[40]Recorded in the classroom of Lois Monaghan, teacher, Barrington School, Upper Arlington, Ohio.

[41]James Britton, in *Response to Literature*, ed. James R. Squire (Champaign, Ill.: National Council of Teachers of English, 1968), p. 4.

When asked to replicate Leo Lionni's story of *The Biggest House in the World* using a new main character, these two children demonstrated different levels in their understanding of the theme. The 8-year-old (top picture) showed a bird growing more elaborate; the 10-year-old (bottom picture) portrayed a change leading to the bird's self-destruction. Tremont Elementary School, Upper Arlington Public Schools, Upper Arlington, Ohio. Jill Boyd, teacher.

Understanding Children's Responses to Literature

1. **Create a Game Board.** Ask children to make a gameboard that traces the adventures of characters in a book like Sheila Burnford's *The Incredible Journey.* Make note of which events are important enough to represent. Do the children remember the sequence of events or refer back to the book to check?

2. **Translate through Art.** Ask children to translate meaning from a story like *The Biggest House in the World* by Leo Lionni through artwork. Ask children to choose any animal and grant it the same wish as the little snail had—namely, that it could change itself in any way.

3. **Create a Cycle of Life.** After older students have read *Tuck Everlasting* by Natalie Babbitt, ask them to chart out, with words and pictures, the cycle of their own lives, including what they know of their past and what they predict for the future. Make note of the children who transfer the ideas about life and death from the book to their own speculations and those that might reveal a deeper connection with the book. Use these charts to begin a discussion relating the book to the students' own lives.

4. **Update Neil Waldman's *Masada.*** Ask a middle grader to write an updated folktale or a story based on the information in Neil Waldman's nonfiction book *Masada.* What does the writing show about the child's knowledge of genre and the general concept of story?

5. **Response-to-Literature Case Study.** Conduct a case study of one child's response to literature, keeping track of a broad range of data like the child's contacts with literature, responses, and developing skills in reading and writing.

6. **Baby Bear's Version of "Goldilocks and the Three Bears."** Ask three children of various ages (e.g., 5, 7, 9) to retell the story "Goldilocks and the Three Bears" from the point of view of Baby Bear. Who is able to begin the story as Baby Bear? Who can maintain the role change? What problems do 5-year-olds have with language that 9-year-olds seem to solve easily?

7. **Categorize Books.** In a middle-grade classroom, assemble twenty to thirty books that are mostly familiar to the children. Ask a small group to categorize and label these for a tabletop display. Tape their comments as they work. What do you notice about their categories? About the process? If possible, repeat the activity with younger children and books that they have heard read aloud. What differences do you notice?

8. **Imaginative Play Area.** Set up a play corner in a primary classroom, including props from stories, such as a magic wand, a witch's hat, a cardboard crown. What happens over time? What seem to be the sources for the children's imaginative play?

 Go to the Online Learning Center at **www.mhhe.com/kiefer9e** or your Resources CD-ROM to find these additional classroom activities:

9. **Conduct a Reading Interview**
10. **Exploring Literature through Art**
11. **Displays, Dioramas, and Museums**
12. **Responding Dramatically**

Chapter Review

Go to the Online Learning Center at **www.mhhe.com/kiefer9e** or your Resources CD-ROM to take chapter quizzes, practice with key terms, and review the chapter.

Explorations

1. If there is a young child in your household, keep a log for four to five weeks of her or his interaction with literature. What do the child's choices, reactions, comments, and questions reveal about cognitive skills or moral judgment? Do you see any changes that reflect experiences with books?

2. Observe young children as a parent or teacher reads to them. Note as many behaviors (verbal, nonverbal, or artistic/creative) as you can. What clues do you get about the value of reading aloud and about means of effective presentation?

3. If you can meet with a class of children, ask them to submit the names of their ten favorite books. How do their choices seem to reflect their particular ages and stages of development?

4. Visit the children's room of a public or school library or the children's section of a bookstore to watch children in the process of choosing books. Keep a list, if you can, of the books examined and rejected, as well as those finally chosen. What factors seem to influence the children's choices?

5. With a small group of fellow students or teachers, read and discuss an award-winning children's book. Working together, plan two sets of questions that could be used with children, one to discover children's initial response to the story, the other to direct their thinking toward the characters' motivations and decisions, the author's effective use of language, or other noteworthy features of the writing.

6. Arrange to talk or visit a chat room with one or more readers in the 11-to-13 age range about a book that you and the child or children have read individually—for example, Jerry Spinelli's *Maniac Magee*. Plan questions and comments that will encourage the students to share their own interpretations of characters and events. How are their ideas about the book similar to or different from your own? How could you use this information in planning for teaching?

7. Go to the Children's Literature Database on your Resources CD-ROM. Search the database under the term *language*. Find five books that you think might support children's language development.

Web Links

Go to the Online Learning Center at **www.mhhe.com/kiefer9e** to find links to the following Children's Literature Web sites:

Book Links

Booklist Online

Boston Book Review

Bulletin of the Center for Children's Books

Charlotte's Web

Children's Bookwatch

Children's Literature

Choosing a Children's Book

Doucette Index K–12 Literature-Based Teaching Ideas: An Index to Books and Websites

Horn Book

Jean Piaget Society

Kirkus Reviews

Looking Glass

New York Times Books

Notes from the Windowsill

Publishers Weekly Children's Bestseller List

Publishers Weekly Online

School Library Journal Online

Voice of Youth Advocates

Vygotsky Resources

Applebee, Arthur. *The Child's Concept of Story: Ages Two to Seventeen.* Chicago: University of Chicago Press, 1978.

> A report of systematic research on children's developing perceptions of stories. Applebee provides fresh insight on the child's sense of story and response to literature. Among the contributions of this important work are a description of organization and complexity in the structure of stories children tell and a model of developmental stages in the formulation of children's responses.

Elkind, David. *The Hurried Child: Growing Up Too Fast Too Soon.* Reading, Mass.: Addison-Wesley, 1989.

> In a book addressed mainly to parents, a noted psychologist argues that contemporary children are under too much pressure. They are rushed toward adulthood both at home and at school without regard for normal patterns of development or individual differences. Chapters 5 and 6 present a very readable overview of intellectual, emotional, and social development, with particular reference to Piaget. Chapter 4, which deals with the influence of books and media in "hurrying" children, provides good discussion material for adults considering selection policies.

Holland, Kathleen E., Rachael A. Hungerford, and Shirley B. Ernst, eds. *Journeying: Children Responding to Literature.* Portsmouth, N.H.: Heinemann, 1993.

> This collection provides a comprehensive view of recent research in children's response to literature. Chapters in four sections deal with responses of children in grades K through 8 in a variety of settings. Authors describe children's responses to different literary genres and show how variables such as age, culture, and mode shape children's understanding.

Lehr, Susan, ed. *Beauty, Brains, and Brawn: The Construction of Gender in Children's Literature.* Portsmouth, N.H.: Heinemann, 2001.

> Lehr's introductory chapter details current research and understandings about gender, focusing particularly on how curriculum may reinforce traditional roles for girls. In subsequent chapters, scholars and authors offer broad perspectives on the issue of gender in children's literature.

Lehr, Susan. *The Child's Developing Sense of Theme: Responses to Literature.* New York: Teachers College Press, 1991.

> The author provides a background of discussion and research as well as a report of her own work in discovering the interpretations of story meaning held by preschool and elementary children. Her findings suggest that adults need to be very good listeners when talking to children about literature. Many examples of children's talk and an engaging, conversational tone make this scholarly work particularly readable.

Martinez, Miriam, and Nancy Roser. "Children's Responses to Literature." In *Handbook of Research on Teaching the English Language Arts,* ed. James Flood et al. New York: Macmillan, 1991.

> This comprehensive review of research since the 1960s is organized around three major categories of factors that affect children's response—characteristics of the reader, context factors, and the nature of the text. Included among the many other sections of this reference volume are the essays "Response to Literature" by Robert Probst and "Reading Preferences" by Dianne Monson and Sam Sebesta, and articles on child development in the preschool, elementary, and middle school years.

Paley, Vivian Gussin. *The Girl with the Brown Crayon.* Cambridge, Mass.: Harvard University Press, 1997.

> A well-known kindergarten teacher and recipient of a MacArthur award, Paley chronicles a school year that centered upon the works of author-illustrator Leo Lionni. The children's responses to Lionni's books illustrate the power of literature in children's lives. Paley's willingness to learn from and reflect upon their explorations provides a model for a response-centered classroom.

Purves, Alan C., Theresa Rogers, and Anna O. Soter. *How Porcupines Make Love III: Teaching a Response-Centered Literature Curriculum.* New York: Longman, 1995.

> This lively book for teachers is designed to explain the implications of reader response theory for literature instruction. Although this book deals with the adolescent years, teachers of older elementary students find many of the ideas and principles discussed here to be useful.

Rosenblatt, Louise M. *The Reader, the Text, the Poem: The Transactional Theory of the Literary Work.* Carbondale: Southern Illinois University Press, 1994.

> A scholarly discussion of the reader's role in evoking a literary work from an author's text. The distinction between aesthetic and efferent reading stances is clearly explained. Although elementary children are seldom mentioned, the book gives a valuable basis for understanding the responses of readers at any age.

Children's Literature

 Go to the Children's Literature Database on your Resources CD-ROM for a searchable listing of these and other children's literature titles.

Abelove, Joan. *Go and Come Back.* DK, 1998.

Adler, David A. *Young Cam Jansen and the New Girl Mystery.* Viking, 2004.

Adlington, L. J. *The Diary of Pelly D.* Greenwillow, 2005.

Ahlberg, Janet, and Allan Ahlberg. *Each Peach Pear Plum.* Viking, 1978.

Almond, David. *The Fire-Eaters.* Delacorte, 2004.

———. *Kit's Wilderness.* Delacorte, 2000.

———. *Skellig.* Delacorte, 1999.

Alphin, Elaine Marie. *A Bear for Miguel*. Illustrated by Joan Sanders. HarperCollins, 1996.

Anderson, M. T. *The Clue of the Linoleum Lederhosen*. Harcourt, 2006.

———. *Feed*. Candlewick, 2002.

Arnosky, Jim. *All about Frogs*. Scholastic, 2002.

Asbjørnsen P. C., and Jorgen E. Moe. *The Three Billy Goats Gruff*. Illustrated by Marcia Brown. Harcourt, 1957.

Asch, Frank. *Mr. Maxwell's Mouse*. Illustrated by Devin Asch. Kids Can, 2004.

Aston, Dianna Hutts. *When You Were Born*. Illustrated by E. B. Lewis. Candlewick, 2004.

Avi. *The Book without Words: A Fable of Medieval Magic*. Hyperion, 2005.

Aylesworth, Jim. *The Gingerbread Man*. Illustrated by Barbara McClintock. Scholastic, 1998.

———. *The Tale of Tricky Fox: A New England Trickster Tale*. Illustrated by Barbara McClintock. Scholastic, 2001.

Babbitt, Natalie. *Tuck Everlasting*. Farrar, 1975.

Balliett, Blue. *Wright 3*. Scholastic, 2006.

Bang, Molly. *Ten, Nine, Eight*. Greenwillow, 1983.

———. *When Sophie Gets Angry—Really Angry*. Scholastic, 1999.

Bania, Michael. *Kumak's Fish: A Tall Tale from the Far North*. Alaska Northwest, 2004.

Banks, Kate. *And If the Moon Could Talk*. Illustrated by Georg Hallensleben. Farrar, 1998.

Barron, T. A. *The Great Tree of Avalon: Shadows on the Stars*. Philomel, 2005.

Barton, Byron. *The Little Red Hen*. HarperCollins, 1993.

———. *My Car*. HarperCollins, 2001.

Bauer, Joan. *Best Foot Forward*. Putnam, 2005.

Bauer, Marion Dane. *On My Honor*. Clarion, 1986.

Beaumont, Karen. *Baby Danced the Polka*. Illustrated by Jennifer Plecas. Dial, 2004.

———. *Duck, Duck, Goose!* Illustrated by Jose Aruego and Ariane Dewey. HarperCollins, 2004.

Berger, Barbara. *A Lot of Otters*. Philomel, 1997.

Berger, Melvin, and Gilda Berger. *Where Did the Butterfly Get Its Name? Questions and Answers about Butterflies and Moths*. Scholastic, 2003.

Birdsall, Jeanne. *The Penderwicks: A Summer Tale of Four Sisters, Two Rabbits, and a Very Interesting Boy*. Knopf, 2005.

Bishop, Nic. *Backyard Detective*. Scholastic, 2002.

Blacker, Terence. *Boy2Girl*. Farrar, 2005.

Blackstone, Stella. *Baby High, Baby Low*. Illustrated by Denise Fraifield and Fernando Azevedo. Holiday, 1997.

Blobaum, Cindy. *Insectology: 40 Hands-on Activities to Explore the Insect World*. Chicago Review, 2005.

Bloom, Suzanne. *The Bus for Us*. Boyds Mills, 2001.

———. *A Splendid Friend, Indeed*. Boyds Mills, 2005.

Blume, Judy. *Are You There, God? It's Me, Margaret*. Bradbury, 1970.

Bolden, Tonya. *Maritcha: A Nineteenth Century American Girl*. Abrams, 2005.

Boyce, Frank Cottrell. *Millions*. HarperCollins, 2004.

Bradby, Marie. *Some Friend*. Atheneum, 2004.

Branley, Franklyn M. *The International Space Station*. Illustrated by True Kelley. HarperCollins, 2000.

Bredsdorff, Bodil. *The Crow-Girl: The Children of Crow Cove*. Farrar, 2004.

Bridges, Ruby. *Through My Eyes*. Scholastic, 1999.

Brimner, Larry Dane. *The Littlest Wolf*. Illustrated by Jose Aruego and Ariane Dewey. HarperCollins, 2002.

Broach, Elise. *Shakespeare's Secret*. Holt, 2005.

Brooks, Kevin. *Candy*. Scholastic, 2005.

Brown, Laurene Krasny, and Marc Brown. *What's the Big Secret? Talking About Sex with Girls and Boys*. Little, 1997.

Brown, Marcia. *Once a Mouse*. Scribner's, 1961.

Brown, Margaret Wise. *Goodnight Moon*. Illustrated by Clement Hurd. Harper, 1947.

———. *The Runaway Bunny*. Illustrated by Clement Hurd. Harper, 1942.

Bruchac, Joseph. *The Heart of a Chief*. Dial, 1998.

Buckley Jr., James. *The Visual Dictionary of Baseball*. DK, 2001.

Buehner, Caralyn. *Superdog: The Heart of a Hero*. Illustrated by Mark Buehner. HarperCollins, 2004.

Bunting, Eve. *Fly Away Home*. Illustrated by Ron Himler. Clarion, 1991.

Burnford, Sheila. *The Incredible Journey*. Illustrated by Carl Burger. Bantam, 1990.

Burningham, John. *Hushabye*. Knopf, 2001.

Burton, Virginia Lee. *The Little House*. Houghton, 1942.

Butler, Dori Hillestad. *My Mom's Having a Baby!* Illustrated by Carol Thompson. Whitman, 2005.

Cameron, Ann. *The Stories Julian Tells*. Illustrated by Ann Strugnell. Knopf, 1987.

Campbell, Geeslin. *Elena's Serenade*. Illustrated by Ana Juan. Atheneum, 2004.

Campbell, Rod. *Dear Zoo*. Four Winds, 1983.

Carle, Eric. *The Very Hungry Caterpillar*. Philomel, 1969.

Chen, Chih-Yuan. *Guji Guji*. Kane/Miller, 2004.

Cheng, Andrea. *Honeysuckle House*. Front St., 2004.

Choldenko, Gennifer. *Al Capone Does My Shirts*. Putnam, 2004.

———. *Notes from a Liar and Her Dog*. Putnam, 2001.

Christopher, Matt. *The Extreme Team: Wild Ride*. Illustrated by Michael Koelsch. Little, 2005.

Cleary, Beverly. *Ramona's World*. Illustrated by Alan Tiegreen. Morrow, 1999.

———. *Strider*. Illustrated by Paul O. Zelinsky. Morrow, 1991.

Clements, Andrew. *Lunch Money*. Simon, 2005.

Cohen, Miriam. *Mimmy and Sophie All Around the Town*. Illustrated by Thomas F. Yezerski. Farrar, 2004.

———. *Will I Have a Friend?* Illustrated by Lillian Hoban. Macmillan, 1971.

Cole, Henry. *I Took a Walk*. Greenwillow, 1998.

———. *On the Way to the Beach*. Greenwillow, 2003.

Cole, Joanna. *Asking About Sex and Growing Up: A Question and Answer Book for Boys and Girls.* Illustrated by Alan Tiegreen. Morrow, 1988.

———. *How You Were Born.* Morrow, 1984.

———. *Ms. Frizzle's Adventures: Ancient Egypt.* Illustrated by Bruce Degen. Scholastic, 2001.

———. *My Puppy Is Born.* Photographs by Margaret Miller. Morrow, 1990.

———. *The New Baby at Our House.* Photographs by Margaret Miller. Mulberry, 1998.

Collard III, Sneed B. *Making Animal Babies.* Illustrated by Steve Jenkins. Houghton, 2000.

Colman, Penny. *Girls: A History of Growing Up Female in America.* Scholastic, 2000.

Coman, Carolyn. *The Big House.* Boyds Mills, 2004.

Cooper, Susan. *The Dark Is Rising.* Illustrated by Alan Cober. Atheneum, 1973.

Cousins, Lucy. *Hooray for Fish!* Candlewick, 2005.

Cowell, Cressida. *What Shall We Do with a Boo-Hoo Baby?* Illustrated by Ingrid Gordon. Scholastic, 2001.

Cowley, Joy. *Chameleon, Chameleon.* Photographs by Nic Bishop. Scholastic, 2005.

———. *Red-Eyed Tree Frog.* Photographs by Nic Bishop. Scholastic, 1999.

Crews, Donald. *Freight Train.* Greenwillow, 1978.

———. *Inside Freight Train.* HarperCollins, 2001.

Cummins, Julie. *Tomboy of the Air: Daredevil Blanche Stuart Scott.* HarperCollins, 2001.

Curtis, Christopher Paul. *Bucking the Sarge.* Lamb/Random, 2004.

———. *Bud, Not Buddy.* Delacorte, 1999.

———. *Mr. Chickee's Funny Money.* Lamb/Random, 2005.

Dahl, Roald. *The BFG.* Illustrated by Quentin Blake. Farrar, 1982.

Daly, Nikki. *What's Cooking, Jamela?* Farrar, 2001.

Dane, Larry. *The Littlest Wolf.* Illustrated by Jose Aruego and Ariane Dewey. HarperCollins, 2000.

Deem, James. *Bodies from the Ash: Life and Death in Ancient Pompeii.* Houghton, 2005.

DeJong, Meindert. *Hurry Home, Candy.* Illustrated by Maurice Sendak. Harper, 1953.

DeRegniers, Beatrice Schenk. *May I Bring a Friend?* Illustrated by Beni Montesor. Atheneum, 1964.

Dewan, Ted. *Bing: Get Dressed.* Random, 2004.

DiCamillo, Kate. *Mercy Watson Goes for a Ride.* Candlewick, 2006.

Dickinson, Peter. *The Ropemaker.* Delacorte, 2001.

Donnelly, Jennifer. *A Northern Light.* Harcourt, 2003.

Dorris, Michael. *Guests.* Hyperion, 1994.

———. *Morning Girl.* Hyperion, 1992.

Doyle, Brian. *Mary Ann Alice.* Groundwood, 2002.

Dunbar, Polly. *Dog Blue.* Candlewick, 2004.

Dunphy, Madeline. *Here Is the Coral Reef.* Illustrated by Tom Leonard. Hyperion, 1998.

Dyer, Heather. *The Fish in Room 11.* Scholastic, 2004.

Edwards, Pamela Duncan. *Some Smug Slug.* Illustrated by Henry Cole. HarperCollins, 1996.

Ehlert, Lois. *Eating the Alphabet.* Harper, 1989.

Emberley, Michael. *Ruby.* Little, 1990.

Ewing, Patrick, and Linda L. Louis. *In the Paint.* Abbeville, 1999.

Falwell, Cathryn. *Feast for Ten.* Clarion, 1993.

Farmer, Nancy. *A Girl Named Disaster.* Orchard, 1997.

———. *Sea of Trolls.* Atheneum, 2004.

Feiffer, Jules. *Bark, George.* HarperCollins, 1999.

Fine, Anne. *The Tulip Touch.* Little, 1997.

———. *Up On Cloud Nine.* Delacorte, 2002.

Fitzgerald, Joanna. *This Is Me and Where I Am.* Fitzhenry and Whiteside, 2004.

Florian, Douglas, *Insectlopedia.* Harcourt, 1998.

———. *zoo's who.* Harcourt, 2005.

Ford, Meila. *On My Own.* Greenwillow, 1999.

Forward, Toby. *The Wolf's Story: What Really Happened to Little Red Riding Hood.* Illustrated by Izhar Cohen. Candlewick, 2005.

Fox, Mem. *Where Is the Green Sheep?* Illustrated by Judy Horacek. Harcourt, 2004.

Frank, John. *The Tomb of the Boy King.* Illustrated by Tom Pohrt. Farrar, 2001.

Freedman, Russell. *The Voice That Challenged a Nation: Marian Anderson and the Struggle for Civil Rights.* Clarion, 2004.

Freeman, Don. *Corduroy.* Viking, 1968.

Fusco, Kimberly Newton. *Tending to Grace.* Knopf, 2004.

Gág, Wanda. *Millions of Cats.* Coward, 1956 [1928].

Gantos, Jack. *Joey Pigza Swallowed the Key.* Farrar, 1998.

Gardiner, John. *Stone Fox.* Illustrated by Marcia Sewall. Harper, 1980.

Gay, Marie-Louise. *Stella: Fairy of the Forest.* Groundwood, 2002.

George, Jean. *Cry of the Crow.* HarperCollins, 1980.

———. *Julie's Wolfpack.* Illustrated by Wendell Minor. HarperCollins, 1997.

George, Lindsay Barrett. *Inside Mouse, Outside Mouse.* Greenwillow, 2004.

Giblin, James Cross. *The Mystery of the Mammoth Bones: And How It Was Solved.* HarperCollins, 1999.

Giff, Patricia Riley. *Don't Tell the Girls: A Family Memoir.* Holiday, 2005.

Goodall, Jane. *Rickie and Henri.* Illustrated by Alan Marks. Putnam, 2004.

Graham, Bob. *"Let's Get a Pup!" said Kate.* Candlewick, 2001.

———. *Tales from the Waterhole.* Candlewick, 2004.

Gralley, Jean. *The Moon Came Down on Night Street.* Holt, 2004.

Gray, Kes. *Cluck O'Clock.* Illustrated by Mary McQuillan. Holiday, 2004.

Greene, Stephanie. *Owen Foote, Super Spy.* Clarion, 2005.

Greenstein, Elaine. *One Little Lamb.* Viking, 2004.

Grey, Mini. *Traction Man Is Here!* Knopf, 2005.

Griffin, Adele. *Amandine.* Hyperion, 2001.

Griffin, Adele. *Where I Want to Be.* Putnam, 2005.

Grimes, Nikki. *Jazmin's Notebook.* Dial, 1998.

Grossman, Bill. *My Little Sister Hugged an Ape.* Illustrated by Kevin Hawkes. Knopf, 2004.

———. *Timothy Tunny Swallowed a Bunny.* Illustrated by Kevin Hawkes. Geringer/HarperCollins, 2001.

Hall, Donald. *Ox-Cart Man.* Illustrated by Barbara Cooney. Viking, 1979.

Hamilton, Virginia. *Cousins.* Philomel, 1990.

Harper, Dan. *Telling Time with Mama Cat.* Harcourt, 1998.

Harris, Monica A. *Wake the Dead.* Illustrated by Susan Estelle Kwas. Walker, 2004.

Harris, Robie H. *It's Perfectly Normal: A Book About Changing Bodies, Growing Up, Sex, and Sexual Health.* Illustrated by Michael Emberley. Candlewick, 1994.

———. *It's So Amazing: A Book About Eggs, Sperm, Birth, Babies and Families.* Illustrated by Michael Emberley. Candlewick, 1999.

Heap, Sue. *Cowboy Baby.* Candlewick, 1998.

Heide, Florence Parry, and Judith Heide Gilliland. *The Day of Ahmed's Secret.* Illustrated by Ted Lewin. Lothrop, 1990.

Henkes, Kevin. *The Birthday Room.* Greenwillow, 1999.

———. *Kitten's First Full Moon.* Greenwillow, 2004.

Herbert, Janice. *Marco Polo for Kids: His Marvelous Journey to China.* Chicago Review, 2001.

Hesse, Karen. *Out of the Dust.* Scholastic, 1997.

Hill, Eric. *Where's Spot?* Putnam, 1980.

Hindley, Judy. *What's in Baby's Morning?* Illustrated by Jo Burroughes. Candlewick, 2004.

Hoban, Russell. *A Baby Sister for Frances.* Illustrated by Lillian Hoban. Harper, 1964.

Hoban, Tana. *1, 2, 3.* Greenwillow, 1985.

Hoberman, Mary Ann. *You Read to Me, I'll Read to You. Very Short Stories to Read Together.* Illustrated by Michael Emberley. Little, 2001.

Holt, Kimberly. *My Louisiana Sky.* Holt, 1998.

Holt, Kimberly Willis. *When Zachary Beaver Came to Town.* Holt, 1999.

Hoose, Phillip. *We Were There Too! Young People in U.S. History.* Farrar/Kroupa, 2001.

Hopkins, Lee Bennett. *Oh, No! Where Are My Pants? and Other Disasters: Poems.* Illustrated by Wolf Erlbruch. HarperCollins, 2005.

Horvath, Polly. *Everything on a Waffle.* Farrar, 2001.

———. *The Pepins and Their Problems.* Farrar, 2004.

———. *The Vacation.* Farrar, 2005.

Hughes, Shirley. *Alfie Gets in First.* Lothrop, 1981.

Hurwitz, Joanna. *Llama in the Library.* Morrow, 1999.

Hutchins, Pat. *Clocks and More Clocks.* Macmillan, 1994 [1970].

———. *We're Going On a Picnic.* Greenwillow, 2002.

———. *You'll Soon Grow into Them, Titch.* Greenwillow, 1983.

Ibbotson, Eva. *The Star of Kazan.* Illustrated by Kevin Hawkes. Dutton, 2004.

Ives, David. *Scrib.* HarperCollins, 2005.

Janeczko, Paul. *Blushing: Expressions of Love in Poetry and Letters.* Orchard, 2003.

Jenkins, Steve. *Actual Size.* Houghton, 2004.

Jennings, Patrick. *Out Standing in My Field.* Scholastic, 2005.

Jiménez, Francisco. *Breaking Through.* Houghton, 2001.

Johannsen, Iris. *Countdown.* Bantam, 2005.

Johnson, Angela. *Heaven.* Simon, 1998.

———. *Toning the Sweep.* Orchard/Jackson, 1993.

Johnson, Maureen. *The Key to the Golden Firebird.* HarperCollins, 2004.

Johnson, Neil. *National Geographic Photography Guide For Kids.* National Geographic, 2001.

Johnston, Julie. *In Spite of Killer Bees.* Tundra, 2001.

Jonell, Lynne. *It's My Birthday Too!* Illustrated by Petra Mathers. Putnam, 1999.

Joosse, Barbara. *Ghost Trap: A Wild Willie Mystery.* Clarion, 1998.

———. *Papa, Do you Love Me?* Illustrated by Barbara Lavallee. Chronicle, 2005.

Juster, Norton. *The Phantom Tollbooth.* Random, 1961.

Keats, Ezra Jack. *Whistle for Willie.* Viking, 1964.

Keehn, Sally. *Gnat Stokes and the Foggy Bottom Swamp Queen.* Philomel, 2005.

Kelly, Katy. *Lucy Rose: Big on Plans.* Illustrated by Adam Rex. Delacorte, 2005.

Kennedy, X. J. *Talking Like the Rain.* Illustrated by Jane Dyer. Little, 1992.

Kerrin, Jessica Scott. *Martin Bridge: Ready for Takeoff!* Illustrated by Joseph Kelly. Kids Can, 2005.

King-Smith. Dick. *The Golden Goose.* Illustrated by Ann Kronheimer. Knopf, 2005.

Kline, Suzy. *Horrible Harry and the Goog.* Illustrated by Frank Remkiewicz. Viking, 2005.

Konigsburg, E. L. *From the Mixed-Up Files of Mrs. Basil E. Frankweiler.* Atheneum, 1967.

———. *The View from Saturday.* Atheneum, 1996.

Kramer, Ann. *Nelson Mandela: The Tribal Prince Who Grew Up to Be President.* National Geographic, 2005.

Krauss, Ruth. *Bears.* Illustrated by Maurice Sendak. HarperCollins, 2005.

Kunhardt, Dorothy. *Pat the Bunny.* Golden, 1962 [1940].

Kurlansky, Mark. *The Cod's Tale.* Illustrated by S. D. Schindler. Penguin Putnam, 2001.

Lauber, Patricia. *What You Never Knew about Tubs, Toilets, and Showers.* Illustrated by John Manders. Simon, 2001.

Lawrence, Iain. *The Cannibals.* Delacorte, 2005.

Leavitt, Martine. *Heck, Superhero.* Front St., 2004.

Le Guin, Ursula K. *Gifts.* Harcourt, 2004.

———. *A Wizard of Earthsea.* Illustrated by Ruth Robbins. Parnassus, 1968.

Lehman, Barbara. *The Red Book.* Houghton, 2004.

Lehn, Barbara. *What Is a Scientist?* Illustrated by Carol Krauss. Millbrook, 1998.

L'Engle, Madeleine. *A Swiftly Tilting Planet*. Farrar, 1978.

Lester, Allison. *The Quicksand Pony*. Houghton, 1998.

Lester, Helen. *Hooway for Wodney Wat*. Illustrated by Lynn Munsinger. Houghton, 1999.

Lester, Julius. *Days of Tears: A Novel in Dialogue*. Hyperion, 2005.

———. *John Henry*. Illustrated by Brian Pinkney. Dial, 1994.

Levy, Constance. *Splash!: Poems of Our World*. Illustrated by David Soman. Scholastic, 2002.

Lionni, Leo. *The Biggest House in the World*. Pantheon, 1968.

———. *Fish Is Fish*. Pantheon, 1970.

Lisle, Janet Taylor. *The Lost Flower Children*. Philomel, 1999.

Livingston, Star. *Harley*. Illustrated by Molly Bang. Sea Star, 2001.

Lobel, Arnold. *Frog and Toad Together*. Harper, 1972.

Lockhart, E. *The Boyfriend List*. Delacorte, 2005.

London, Jonathan. *A Truck Goes Rattley-Bumpa*. Illustrated by Denis Roche. Holt, 2005.

Look, Lenore. *Henry's First Moon Birthday*. Illustrated by Yumi Heo. Atheneum, 2001.

———. *Ruby Lu, Brave and True*. Illustrated by Ann Wilsdorf. Simon, 2004.

Losordo, Stephen. *Cow Moo Me*. Illustrated by Jan Conteh-Morgan. HarperCollins, 1998.

Lowry, Lois. *The Giver*. Houghton, 1993.

———. *Number the Stars*. Houghton, 1989.

Lynch, Chris. *Me, Dead Dad, and Alcatraz*. HarperCollins, 2005.

Lyon, George Ella. *Sonny's House of Spies*. Simon, 2004.

MacLachlan, Patricia. *Sarah, Plain and Tall*. Harper, 1985.

Madden, Kerry. *Gentle's Holler*. Viking, 2005.

Marcantonio, Patricia Santos. *Red Ridin' in the Hood and Other Cuentos*. Illustrated by Ranato Alarcão. Farrar, 2005.

Marchetta, Melina. *Saving Francesca*. Knopf, 2004.

Markes, Julie. *Shhhhh! Everybody's Sleeping*. Illustrated by David Parkins. HarperCollins, 2005.

Marsden, Carolyn. *The Gold Threaded Dress*. Candlewick, 2002.

———. *Moon Runner*. Candlewick, 2005.

Martin, Ann. *A Dog's Life; The Autobiography of a Stray*. Scholastic, 2005.

Martin, Bill, Jr. *Brown Bear, Brown Bear, What Do You See?* Illustrated by Eric Carle. Holt, 1983.

Matthews, L. S. *Fish*. Delacorte, 2004.

McCloskey, Robert. *Burt Dow, Deep Water Man*. Viking, 1963.

———. *Make Way for Ducklings*. Viking, 1941.

———. *One Morning in Maine*. Viking, 1952.

McCully, Emily. *Four Hungry Kittens*. Dial, 2001.

McDonald, Megan. *Judy Moody Declares Independence*. Candlewick, 2005.

McKay, Hilary. *The Amber Cat*. McElderry, 1997.

———. *Permanent Rose*. Simon, 2005.

McKenna, Colleen O'Shaughnessy. *Doggone . . . Third Grade*. Illustrated by Stephanie Roth. Holiday, 2002.

McKinley, Robin. *The Hero and the Crown*. Greenwillow, 1984.

McKissack, Patricia C. *Flossie and the Fox*. Illustrated by Rachel Isadora. Dial, 1986.

McMullan, Kate. *I Stink!* Illustrated by Jim McMullan. Cotler/HarperCollins, 2002.

McNaughton, Janet. *The Secret under My Skin*. HarperCollins, 2005.

McPhail, David. *The Teddy Bear*. Holt, 2002.

McWhorter, Diane. *A Dream of Freedom: The Civil Rights Movement from 1954–1968*. Scholastic, 2004.

Mead, Alice. *Junebug in Trouble*. Farrar, 2002.

Melling, O. R. *The Hunter's Moon (The Chronicles of Faerie)*. Abrams, 2005.

Merriam, Eve. *What in the World?* Illustrated by Barbara J. Phillips-Duke. HarperCollins, 1998.

Meyers, Susan. *Everywhere Babies*. Illustrated by Marla Frazee. Harcourt, 2001.

Middleton, Charlotte. *Tabitha's Terrifically Tough Tooth*. Fogelman, 2001.

Miller, Margaret. *Guess Who?* Greenwillow, 1994.

———. *What's on My Head?* Little Simon, 1999.

Minarik, Else Holmelund. *Little Bear*. Illustrated by Maurice Sendak. Harper, 1957.

Mollel, Tolowa. *My Rows and Piles of Coins*. Illustrated by E. B. Lewis. Clarion, 1999.

Moses, Shelia P. *The Legend of Buddy Bush*. McElderry, 2004.

Mosher, Richard. *Zazoo*. Clarion, 2001.

Moss, Marissa. *Brave Harriet*. Illustrated by C. F. Payne. Harcourt/Silver Whistle, 2001.

Mowll, Joshua. *Operation Red Jericho*. Candlewick, 2005.

Myers, Walter Dean. *Darnell Rock Reporting*. HarperCollins, 1994.

———. *The Glory Field*. Scholastic, 1994.

Na, An. *A Step from Heaven*. Front St., 2001.

Naidoo, Beverley. *The Other Side of Truth*. HarperCollins, 2001.

Napoli, Donna Jo. *Three Days*. Dutton, 2001.

Naylor, Phyllis Reynolds. *Shiloh*. Atheneum, 1991.

Nelson, Marilyn. *A Wreath for Emmett Till*. Houghton, 2005.

Nix, Garth. *Shade's Children*. HarperCollins, 1997.

Nye, Naomi Shihab. *Habibi*. Simon, 1997.

———. *19 Varieties of Gazelle: Poems of the Middle East*. Greenwillow, 2002.

O'Connor, George. *Ker-splash!* Simon, 2005.

Olsen, Sylvia. *White Girl*. Sono NIS, 2005.

Opie, Iona. *My Very First Mother Goose*. Illustrated by Rosemary Wells. Candlewick, 1996.

Oppel, Kenneth. *Skybreaker*. HarperCollins, 2006.

Ormerod, Jan. *When an Elephant Comes to School*. Orchard, 2005.

Osborne, Mary Pope. *Carnival at Candlelight*. Illustrated by Sal Murdocca. Random, 2005.

Oxenbury, Helen. *I Can*. Candlewick, 1995.

———. *Tom & Pippo's Day*. Macmillan, 1989.

Palatini, Marge. *Broom Mates*. Illustrated by Howard Fine. Hyperion, 2002.

Panchyk, Richard. *Galileo for Kids: His Life, Ideas and 25 Activities.* Chicago Review, 2005.

Parish, Peggy. *Amelia Bedelia.* Illustrated by Fritz Siebel. Harper, 1963.

Park, Barbara. *Skinnybones.* Knopf, 1982.

Park, Linda Sue. *Bee-bim Bop!* Illustrated by Ho Baek Lee. Clarion, 2005.

———. *Project Mulberry.* Clarion, 2005.

———. *A Single Shard.* Clarion, 2001.

———. *When My Name Was Keoko.* Clarion, 2002.

Partridge, Elizabeth. *Whistling.* Illustrated by Anna Grossnickle Hines. Greenwillow, 2003.

Paterson, Katherine. *The Great Gilly Hopkins.* Crowell, 1978.

———. *Jacob Have I Loved.* Crowell, 1980.

———. *The Same Stuff as Stars.* Clarion, 2002.

Paulsen, Gary. *Hatchet.* Bradbury, 1987.

Payne, Nina. *Four in All.* Illustrated by Adam Payne. Front St., 2001.

Pearson, Tracy Campbell. *Myrtle.* Farrar, 2004.

Perkins, Lynne Rae. *All Alone in the Universe.* Greenwillow, 1999.

———. *Criss Cross.* Greenwillow, 2005.

Phillips, Rita Mitchell. *Hue Boy.* Illustrated by Caroline Binch. Dial, 1993.

Pierce, Meredith Ann. *Treasure at the Heart of Tanglewood.* Viking, 2001.

———. *Dragon's Fat Cat.* Orchard, 1992.

Platt, Richard. *Pirate Diary: The Journal of Jake Carpenter.* Illustrated by Chris Riddell. Candlewick, 2001.

Porter, Connie. *Meet Addy* (the American Girl collection). Illustrated by Nancy Niles. Pleasant, 1990.

Potter, Beatrix. *The Tale of Peter Rabbit.* Warne, 1902.

Priddy, Roger. *Bright Baby: First Words.* Priddy, 2004.

Pryor, Bonnie. *The House on Maple Street.* Illustrated by Beth Peck. Morrow, 1987.

Pullman, Philip. *The Golden Compass.* Knopf, 1996.

———. *I Was a Rat.* Knopf, 2000.

Radcliffe, Theresa. *Bashi, Baby Elephant.* Illustrated by John Butler. Viking, 1998.

Raffi. *Wheels on the Bus.* Random, 1998.

Rathman, Peggy. *10 Minutes Till Bedtime.* Putnam, 1998.

Reeder, Carolyn. *Shades of Gray.* Macmillan, 1989.

Rees, Douglas. *Grandy Thaxter's Helper.* Illustrated by S. D. Schindler. Atheneum, 2004.

Reiser, Lynn. *Little Clam.* Greenwillow, 1998.

———. *Ten Puppies.* Greenwillow, 2003.

Rennison, Louise. *Then He Ate My Boy Entrancers: More Mad, Marvy Confessions of Georgia Nicholson.* HarperCollins, 2005.

Rockwell, Anne. *Little Shark.* Illustrated by Megan Halsey. Walker, 2005.

———. *My Pet Hamster.* Illustrated by Bernice Lum. HarperCollins, 2002.

———. *The Three Bears and Fifteen Other Stories.* Crowell, 1975.

Rodman, Mary Ann. *Yankee Girl.* Farrar, 2004.

Rogers, Fred. *Going to the Potty.* Illustrated by Jim Judkis. Putnam, 1986.

Root, Phyllis. *Oliver Finds His Way.* Illustrated by Christopher Denise. Candlewick, 2002.

———. *What Baby Wants.* Illustrated by Jill Barton. Candlewick, 1998.

Rosen, Daniel. *New Beginnings: Jamestown and the Virginia Colony, 1607–1699.* National Geographic, 2005.

Rosen, Michael. *Michael Rosen's Sad Book.* Candlewick, 2005.

———. *We're Going on a Bear Hunt.* Illustrated by Helen Oxenbury. McElderry, 1989.

Rosoff, Meg. *How I Live Now.* Lamb/Random, 2004.

———. *Meet Wild Boars.* Illustrated by Sophie Blackall. Holt, 2005.

Rowling, J. K. *Harry Potter and the Half-Blood Prince.* Scholastic, 2005.

Rumford, James. *Sequoyah. The Cherokee Man Who Gave His People Writing.* Translated by Anna Sixkiller Huckaby. Houghton, 2004.

Ryder, Joann. *Little Panda: The World Welcomes Hua Mei at the San Diego Zoo.* Simon, 2001.

Rylant, Cynthia. *Missing May.* Orchard, 1992.

———. *When I Was Young in the Mountains.* Illustrated by Diane Goode. Dutton, 1982.

Sachar, Louis. *Holes.* Farrar, 1998.

Sadler, Judy Ann. *The Jumbo Book of Needlecrafts.* Kids Can, 2005.

Schaefer, Carole Lexa, *The Biggest Soap.* Illustrated by Stacy Dressen-McQueen. Farrar, 2004.

Schmidt, Gary D. *Lizzie Bright and the Buckminster Boy.* Clarion, 2004.

Schwartz, Alvin. *Whoppers: Tall Tales and Other Lies.* Illustrated by Glen Rounds. HarperCollins, 1975.

Schwartz, David. *If Dogs Were Dinosaurs.* Illustrated by James Warhola. Scholastic, 2005.

Scieszka, John. *Hey Kid, Want to Buy a Bridge?* Illustrated by Adam McCauley. Viking, 2002.

Scieszka, Jon, ed. *Guys Write for Guys Read: Boys' Favorite Authors Write About Being Boys.* Viking, 2005.

Sendak, Maurice. *Where the Wild Things Are.* Harper, 1963.

Senisi, Ellen B. *Berry Smudges and Leaf Prints. Finding and Making Colors from Nature.* Dutton, 2001.

Shannon, David. *No David!* Scholastic, 1998.

Shreve, Susan. *Under the Watsons' Porch.* Knopf, 2004.

Silverman, Erica. *Don't Fidget a Feather.* Illustrated by S. D. Schindler. Macmillan, 1994.

Silverstein, Shel. *Runny Babbit: A Billy Sook.* HarperCollins, 2005.

———. *Where the Sidewalk Ends.* Harper & Row, 1963.

Singer, Marilyn. *Boo Hoo Boo-Boo.* Illustrated by Elivia Savadier. Harper, 2002.

Sis, Peter. *Trucks Trucks Trucks.* Greenwillow, 1999.

Slade, Arthur. *Dust.* Delacorte, 2003.

Smith, Doris Buchanan. *A Taste of Blackberries.* Illustrated by Charles Robinson. Crowell, 1973.

Smith, Jeff. *Out from Boneville*. Scholastic, 2005.

Sones, Sonya. *What My Mother Doesn't Know*. Simon, 2001.

Soto, Gary. *Too Many Tamales*. Illustrated by Ed Martinez. Putnam, 1993.

———. *Worlds Apart: Traveling with Fernie and Me*. Putnam, 2005.

Spinelli, Jerry. *Knots in a Yo-Yo String: The Autobiography of a Kid*. Knopf, 1998.

———. *The Loser*. HarperCollins, 2002.

———. *Maniac Magee*. Little, 1990.

———. *Wringers*. HarperCollins, 1997.

Staples, Suzanne Fisher. *Shabanu: Daughter of the Wind*. Knopf, 1989.

———. *Under the Persimmon Tree*. Farrar, 2005.

Steig, William. *Doctor De Soto*. Farrar, 1982.

———. *Sylvester and the Magic Pebble*. Simon, 1969.

———. *Zeke Pippin*. HarperCollins, 1994.

Steptoe, Javaka. *Sweet, Sweet Baby!* Scholastic, 2005.

Stewart, Sarah. *The Journey*. Illustrated by David Small. Farrar, 2001.

Stojic, Manya. *Rain*. Crown, 2000.

Stolz, Joëlle. *The Shadows of Ghadames*. Delacorte, 2004.

Stuve-Bodeen, Stephanie. *Elizabeti's Doll*. Illustrated by Christy Hale. Lee, 1998.

Taback, Sims. *I Know an Old Lady*. Dial, 1997.

Takabayashi, Mari. *I Live in Tokyo*. Houghton, 2001.

Tang, Greg. *Math Potatoes*. Illustrated by Harry Briggs. Scholastic, 2005.

Taylor, Ann. *Baby Dance*. Illustrated by Marjorie Van Heerden. HarperCollins, 1999.

Taylor, Mildred. *Roll of Thunder, Hear My Cry*. Dial, 1976.

Thomas, Joyce Carol. *You Are My Perfect Baby*. Illustrated by Nneka Bennett. HarperCollins, 1999.

Tillage, Leon. *Leon's Story*. Illustrated by Barbara Roth. Farrar, 1997.

Tolkien, J. R. R. *The Hobbit*. Illustrated by Michael Hague. Houghton, 1989 [1938].

Updale, Eleanor. *Montmorency on the Rocks*. Scholastic, 2005.

Van Draanen, Wendelin. *Shredderman: Enemy Spy*. Knopf, 2005.

Van Genechten, Guido. *Potty Time*. Simon, 2001.

Voigt, Cynthia. *Dicey's Song*. Atheneum, 1982.

Wabbes, Marie. *How I Was Born*. Tambourine, 1991.

Waber, Bernard. *Ira Sleeps Over*. Houghton, 1973.

Waddell, Martin. *It's Quacking Time*. Illustrated by Jill Barton. Candlewick, 2005.

Waldman, Neil. *Masada*. Morrow, 1998.

Walsh, Jill Paton. *The Green Book*. Illustrated by Lloyd Bloom. Farrar, 1982.

Walter, Mildred Pitts. *Alec's Primer*. Illustrated by Larry Johnson. Vermont Folklife Center, 2004.

———. *Suitcase*. Illustrated by Theresa Flavin. Lothrop, 1999.

Walter, Virginia. *Making Up Megaboy*. Illustrated by M. Katrina Roeckelein. Dorling Kindersley, 1998.

Weatherford, Carole Boston. *Freedom on the Menu: The Greensboro Sit-Ins*. Illustrated by Jerome Lagarrigue. Dial, 2005.

Weeks, Sarah. *Mrs. McNosh Hangs Up Her Wash*. Illustrated by Nadine Bernard Westcott. HarperCollins, 1998.

Wells, Rosemary. *Bunny Cakes*. Dial, 1998.

———. *Edward, Unready for School*. Dial, 1995.

———. *Max's Ride*. Dial, 1979.

Whelan, Gloria. *Homeless Bird*. HarperCollins, 2000.

White, Ruth. *Belle Prater's Boy*. Farrar, 1996.

———. *The Search for Belle Prater*. Farrar, 2005.

———. *Tadpole*. Farrar, 2003.

Whybrow, Ian. *The Noisy Way to Bed*. Illustrated by Tiphanie Beeke. Scholastic, 2004.

Wick, Walter. *Can You See What I See? Picture Puzzles to Search and Solve*. Scholastic, 2002.

Wier, Joan. *The Mysterious Visitor*. Raincoast, 2002.

Wiles, Deborah. *Each Little Bird That Sings*. Harcourt, 2005.

———. *Love, Ruby Lavender*. Harcourt, 2001.

Willems, Mo. *Leonardo, the Terrible Monster*. Hyperion, 2004.

Williams, Karen. *Galimoto*. Illustrated by Catherine Stock. Lothrop, 1990.

Williams, Sue. *Dinnertime!* Kerry Argent. Harcourt, 2002.

Williams, Vera B. *A Chair for My Mother*. Greenwillow, 1982.

Wilson, Karma. *Bear Wants More*. Illustrated by Jane Chapman. McElderry, 2003.

Winerip, Michael. *Adam Canfield of the Slash*. Candlewick, 2005.

Winter, Jeanette. *The Librarian of Basra: A True Story from Iraq*. Harcourt, 2005.

Woodson, Jacqueline. *Hush*. Putnam, 2002.

———. *The Other Side*. Illustrated by E. B. Lewis. Putnam, 2001.

Wright, Betty Ren. *A Ghost in the Family*. Scholastic, 1998.

Wynne-Jones, Tim. *A Thief in the House of Memory*. Farrar, 2005.

Yashima, Taro. *Crow Boy*. Viking, 1955.

Yee, Lisa. *Stanford Wong Flunks Big-Time*. Scholastic, 2005.

Yolen, Jane. *How Do Dinosaurs Eat Their Food?* Illustrated by Mark Teague. Scholastic, 2005.

Young, Ed. *Lon Po Po: A Red Riding Hood Story from China*. Philomel, 1989.

Yumoto, Kazumi. *The Friends*. Illustrated by Cathy Hirano. Farrar, 1996.

Zane, Alexander. *The Wheels on the Race Car*. Illustrated by James Warhola. Orchard, 2005.

Zeifert, Harriet. *I Swapped My Dog*. Illustrated by Emily Bolam. Houghton, 1998.

Zimmerman, Andrea, and David Clemesha. *Trashy Town*. Illustrated by Dan Yaccarino. HarperCollins, 1999.

Chapter Three

The Changing World of Children's Books and the Development of Multicultural Literature

Chapter Outline

Media Resources

Stories have probably been told for as long as humans have had language. As we study the changing history of children's literature, we find that social, cultural, and political norms have had an impact on the content of those stories. What seems to have remained constant over the years are the broad themes of the stories and the enjoyment of the audience. Themes center around human relationships, love, and conflicts. The illustrations on pages 71–73 show how one of these themes—friendship—has been treated differently over the past two hundred years.

"Cruel Boys" is taken from a collection of moralistic stories printed in 1863. It tells of two friends (pictured as Caucasian boys) who have wickedly robbed several birds' nests, hurting the fledglings in the process. The purpose of the story, however, was not to tell about the adventures of two friends but to instruct the young by first describing a horrible example of misbehavior and then warning of its dire consequences. The story is told in the third person from the point of view of an adult admonishing all children. The moral of the story is explicitly stated.

> And this isn't the whole story about these wicked boys. Don't you see they are in a *quarrel,* how they shall divide what they have so cruelly stolen from the birds? Ah, that is the way in doing wrong—one wrong step leads on to another; and robbing birds' nests does not usually go alone—a quarrel, or some other wickedness, usually follows it. Beware, then, of the *beginnings* of cruelty and wickedness.[1]

Let's Be Enemies, published in 1961, also centers on the relationship of two friends (also pictured as Caucasian). In this case John is angry at his friend James's behavior and decides to pick a quarrel. Janice Udry's text directly captures the experience, the feelings, and the language of the young child:

> "I came to tell you that I'm not your friend any more."
> "Well then, I'm not your friend either."
> "We're enemies."
> "All right!"
> "GOOD-BYE!"
> "GOOD-BYE!"[2]

CRUEL BOYS.

"Cruel Boys" from *Sunnybank Stories: My Teacher's Gem.*
"Cruel Boys" from *Sunnybank Stories: My Teacher's Gem* by
Asa Bullard. Boston: Lee & Shepard, 1863. © James L. Shaffer

The story is told in the first person from the point of view of the child protagonist, making it easier for the reader to identify with John's growing anger at the offenses committed by his friend. But 5-year-olds'

---

[1]Asa Bullard, *Sunnybank Stories: My Teacher's Gem* (Boston: Lee & Shepard, 1863), pp. 22–24.
[2]Janice May Udry, *Let's Be Enemies,* illus. Maurice Sendak (New York: Harper & Row, 1961), unpaged.

"GOOD-BYE!"
"GOOD-BYE!"

Let's Be Enemies by Janice May Udry, with illustrations by Maurice Sendak. Illustration from *Let's Be Enemies* by Janice May Udry. Illustrations by Maurice Sendak. Illustrations © by Maurice Sendak. Used by permission of HarperCollins Publishers, Inc.

quarrels are as fleeting as the brief showers that Maurice Sendak includes in his childlike illustrations. In this story the sun soon comes out; and true to the nature of young children, John and James are fast friends by the end of the story.

Yo! Yes? by Chris Raschka was published in 1993. It also centers on the developing friendship between two

boys, one black, one white. As the story unfolds the boys engage in a terse conversation:

Yo?
    Yes?
    Hey!
    Who?
    You!
    Me?[3]

Raschka makes clear through this minimalist dialogue and the lively illustrations that the boys' developing friendship moves from doubt to confidence and from wariness to openness. By the end of the book the two move off together, presumably to the basketball court to shoot a few hoops.

Hot Day on Abbott Avenue by Karen English returns to the theme of friends divided by a quarrel. On a hot summer day two girls nurture a squabble that began when Kishi bought the last blue ice pop from the ice cream truck even though she knew blue was Renée's favorite. Despite the intervention of an elderly neighbor, both girls insist that it is a "never-going-to-be-friends-again-day."[4] Eventually they are both distracted from their anger by a neighborhood game of double-dutch. When the ice cream truck comes around, Kishi buys the last blue ice pop. But this time she breaks it in two to share with Renée. The ice pop is now divided, and the friendship is rejoined.

The contrast in these four stories mirrors the changes in literature for children that have occurred over the past two centuries. When we compare the language, the content, and the illustrations in the books, the ways in which society has changed its cultural values and its attitude toward children become strikingly apparent.

Yo! Yes? By Chris Raschka. From *Yo! Yes?* by Chris Raschka. Published by Orchard Books/Scholastic, Inc. Copyright © 1993 by Christopher Raschka. Reprinted by permission.

---

[3]Chris Raschka, *Yo! Yes?* (New York: Orchard, 1993), unpaged.
[4]Karen English, *Hot Day on Abbott Avenue*, illus. Javaka Steptoe (New York: Clarion, 2004), unpaged.

Much later, when the fat sun hides its chin behind the tall stand of pine, Kishi sits on her front porch playing with the cat. Renée sits in the tree pretending to be the queen of Abbott Avenue.

"Come on and help me make a pitcher of ice-cold lemonade," Miss Johnson says, coming out of her house holding a wooden spoon. "It's too hot to stay mad."

12

Hot Day on Abbott Avenue by Karen English, illustrated by Javaka Steptoe. From *Hot Day on Abbott Avenue* by Karen English, illustrated by Javaka Steptoe. Illustrations copyright © 2004 by Javaka Steptoe. Reprinted by Clarion Books, an imprint of Houghton Mifflin Company. All rights reserved.

"Cruel Boys" lectures to its child audience, and the boys' friendship is seen almost as a deterrent to moral behavior. The animal protection movement in vogue at the time has also got in the way of good storytelling. A wringingly soppy plea for the poor birds all but buries any possibility of an entertaining story: "How unhappy must all these birds now be! and how wicked it is to give needless pain to any of God's creatures!" The book contains only one print, in black and white, the one pictured here. This same illustration was used in many different books at that time. The "pirating" of pictures and stories from other books was a common practice.

Centered on the relationship of two friends, *Let's Be Enemies* allows children their childhood; they can be their 5-year-old selves. Their private feelings, thoughts, and language are considered worthy of attention. As much care has gone into conveying the meaning of the story through the pictures as through the text.

Yo! Yes? is also respectful of its child audience as it explores the uncertainty of the unknown as well as the need for friendship. But by this time the almost all-white world of children's books that defined book publishing in English for so many years has disappeared. We finally see children as they exist in the world of today with all its cultural differences. The concise dialogue celebrates linguistic differences in the manner of rap or hip-hop and the call-and-response style most often attributed to African American language variations. The full-color illustrations carry the burden of the storytelling, just as visual images predominate in the child's world. They are also indicative of the changed methods of art reproduction over the centuries.

In *Hot Day on Abbott Avenue* all children are likely to find a familiar experience, but African American girls are especially likely to recognize themselves. As with the other books represented here, the theme of ups and downs of friendship is one that children are likely to have experienced—but how the essence of the story has changed from the other books! Now the main protagonists are girls, both African-Americans. Author Karen English and illustrator Javaka Steptoe are also African American, and the story and pictures reflect the reality of African American culture. Named a Notable Book of the Year by the Association of Library Services to Children, *Hot Day on Abbott Avenue* represents a triumph of the direction of children's literature that began in the late 1960s, a path to literature that represents all children and at the same time reflects a unique experience that only members of a particular culture can provide.

It has taken a very long time for children's books to move from the didactic and moralistic to the delightful and entertaining, from a chauvinistic view of ethnicity and culture to a view that embraces difference. But just as the treatment of the theme of friendship in books for children has changed over time, views of the culture of childhood have changed as well. Indeed, the idea of childhood as a separate culture may be a fairly recent one. Before the seventeenth century, evidence of childhood as a distinct and separate culture is hard to find. Children dressed like adults, played the same games, and were entertained by the same arts that interested adults, as is shown by written and artistic records that existed prior to the 1600s.[5] A man or woman from the sixteenth century would be astonished to visit the twenty-first century and see the huge range of products, stores, and entertainments created especially for children. In fact, scholars such as Philippe Ariès and Steven Mintz contend that the idea of childhood itself was a seventeenth-century invention that has been transformed and reconstituted in every subsequent historical period.[6] Books for children provide a fascinating record of society and the cultural values it has wished to inculcate in its youth.

[5]See Peter Bruegel's "Children's Games," painted in 1560, as an example. <http://www.artchive.com/artchive/B/bruegel/bruegel_games.jpg.htm>.

[6]See Philippe Ariès, *Centuries of Childhood: A Social History of Family Life,* trans. Robert Baldick (New York: Knopf, 1962), and Steven Mintz, *Huck's Raft: A History of American Childhood* (Cambridge, Mass.: Belknap Press, 2004).

Children's literature has a relatively brief history. Nevertheless, it has evolved from a rich and interesting background. Literature reflects not only the values of society but also the books that have preceded it—the literature of one generation builds on the literature of the past generation. An understanding of the family stories of today is enriched by an acquaintance with the family stories of the past. How, for example, do the novels of Angela Johnson (*A Cool Moonlight,* 2003) or Hilary McKay (*Permanent Rose,* 2005) compare with Beverly Cleary's stories of the Quimby family (such as *Ramona and Her Father,* 1977) or Cynthia Voigt's descriptions of the Tillermans in *Homecoming* (1981)? How do the relations in Virginia Hamilton's *Time Pieces* (2002) compare with *The Moffats* (1941) by Eleanor Estes or Edith Nesbit's Bastable children in *The Story of the Treasure-Seekers* (1899) or even that earliest of well-loved family stories, *Little Women* (1868), by Louisa May Alcott?

One difficulty in evaluating stories of the past is the tendency to use present-day criteria rather than to apply a broader historical review. We should remember that books for children are products of their times and need to be evaluated in relation to the other books of the day. An understanding of the struggle over social and political issues over time is needed as well. Some modern-day critics see *Little Women* as being antifeminist, but at the time of its publication in 1868 its main character was considered much too independent and tomboyish. If we consider Jo March's quest for independence in the light of women's continuing struggle for expression in many parts of the world today, then Jo still serves as a role model, and *Little Women* deserves its status as a classic. Such an understanding can help us identify other significant books and events in the changing culture of childhood.

Teaching Resources: "Landmarks in the Development of Books for Children" lists significant books and other events in the development of children's literature that will be discussed in this chapter.

TEACHING **RESOURCES**

Landmarks in the Development of Books for Children

 Visit the Online Learning Center at **www.mhhe.com/kiefer9e** for a printable version of this list.

BEFORE 1700

Oral stories told by minstrels—Beowulf, King Arthur, ballads, etc.

c.	700	Question-and-answer form of instruction—Aldhelm		1481	*Historye of Reynart the Foxe,* published by Caxton
c.	1200	*Elucidarium,* Anselm		1484	*Aesop's Fables,* published by Caxton
c.	1290	*Gesta Romanorum* (Deeds of the Romans)		1485	*Le Morte d'Arthur* (The Death of King Arthur), Malory
	1387	*Canterbury Tales,* Geoffrey Chaucer		1548	*King Henry's Primer*
c.	1440	Hornbooks developed	c.	1580s	Beginnings of chapbooks
	1477	*A Book of Curteseye,* published by Caxton			

SEVENTEENTH CENTURY

1646	*Spiritual Milk for Boston Babes . . . ,* John Cotton		1677	*The New England Primer*
			1678	*The Pilgrim's Progress,* John Bunyan
1659	*Orbis Pictus* (The World Illustrated), Johann Amos Comenius		1697	*Histoires ou Contes du Temps Passé* (Stories of Times Past), Charles Perrault

Landmarks in the Development of Books for Children (*continued*)

EIGHTEENTH CENTURY

c. 1706 *The Arabian Nights,* translated into English

1715 *Divine and Moral Songs,* Isaac Watts

1719 *Robinson Crusoe,* Daniel Defoe

1726 *Gulliver's Travels,* Jonathan Swift

1729 Perrault's *Fairy Tales,* translated into English

1744 *A Little Pretty Pocket-Book,* John Newbery

1765 *The History of Little Goody Two Shoes,* published by John Newbery

1771 *The New Lottery Book of Birds and Beasts,* Thomas Bewick

c. 1780 *Mother Goose's Melody* (may have been Newbery)

c. 1786 *Mother Goose's Melody,* Isaiah Thomas, American publisher

1789 *Songs of Innocence,* William Blake

NINETEENTH CENTURY

1804 *Original Poems for Infant Minds,* Ann and Jane Taylor

1807 *The Butterfly's Ball,* William Roscoe

1814 *Swiss Family Robinson,* Johann David Wyss

1818 *The Fairchild Family,* Martha Sherwood

1823 *Grimm's Popular Stories,* translated by Edgar Taylor, illustrated by George Cruikshank

1823 *A Visit from St. Nicholas,* Clement C. Moore

1846 *Book of Nonsense,* Edward Lear

1846 *Fairy Tales of Hans Christian Andersen,* translated by Mary Howitt

1848 *Struwwelpeter* (Shock-Headed Peter), Heinrich Hoffman (English translation)

1851 *King of the Golden River,* John Ruskin

1861 *Seven Little Sisters Who Live on the Big Round Ball That Floats in the Air,* Jane Andrews

1865 *The House That Jack Built, Sing a Song of Sixpence,* illustrated by Walter Crane

1865 *Hans Brinker, or the Silver Skates,* Mary Mapes Dodge

1865 *Alice's Adventures in Wonderland,* Lewis Carroll, illustrated by John Tenniel

1868 *Little Women,* Louisa May Alcott

1869 *Twenty Thousand Leagues Under the Sea,* Jules Verne

1871 *At the Back of the North Wind,* George MacDonald

1872 *Sing Song,* Christina Rossetti

1873 *St. Nicholas Magazine* begun, Mary Mapes Dodge, editor

1876 *The Adventures of Tom Sawyer,* Mark Twain

1877 *Black Beauty,* Anna Sewell

1878 *The Diverting History of John Gilpin,* illustrated by Randolph Caldecott

1878 *Under the Window,* Kate Greenaway

1880 *The Peterkin Papers,* Lucretia Hale

1881 *Uncle Remus Stories,* Joel Chandler Harris

1883 *The Merry Adventures of Robin Hood,* adapted and illustrated by Howard Pyle

1883 *Treasure Island,* Robert Louis Stevenson

(continued)

Landmarks in the Development of Books for Children (*continued*)

NINETEENTH CENTURY (*continued*)

1884	*The Adventures of Huckleberry Finn,* Mark Twain	1889	*La Edad de Oro* (The Golden Age), José Martí
1884	*Heidi,* Johanna Spyri, translated by Louise Brooks	1892	*The Adventures of Pinocchio,* Carlo Collodi (English translation)
1885	*A Child's Garden of Verses,* Robert Louis Stevenson	1894	*The Jungle Book,* Rudyard Kipling
1886	*Little Lord Fauntleroy,* Frances Hodgson Burnett	1897	*Jeanne d'Arc* (Joan of Arc), Maurice Boutet de Monvel (English translation)
1889	*The Blue Fairy Book,* Andrew Lang	1898	*Wild Animals I Have Known,* Ernest Thompson Seton

FIRST HALF OF THE TWENTIETH CENTURY

1900	*The Wizard of Oz,* L. Frank Baum	1922	Newbery Medal established for most distinguished book for children
1902	*Just So Stories,* Rudyard Kipling	1924	*When We Were Very Young,* A. A. Milne, illustrated by Ernest H. Shepard
1902	*Songs of Childhood,* Walter de la Mare		
1902	*The Tale of Peter Rabbit,* Beatrix Potter	1926	*Winnie the Pooh,* A. A. Milne, illustrated by Ernest H. Shepard
1903	*The Call of the Wild,* Jack London	1928	*Millions of Cats,* Wanda Gág
1903	*Johnny Crow's Garden,* L. Leslie Brooke	1932	*The Dream Keeper,* Langston Hughes
1903	*Rebecca of Sunnybrook Farm,* Kate Douglas Wiggin	1932	*Little House in the Big Woods,* Laura Ingalls Wilder
1906	*Peter Pan in Kensington Gardens,* J. M. Barrie, illustrated by Arthur Rackham	1932	*Perez and Martina,* Pura Belpré
		1934	*The Little Auto,* Lois Lenski
1908	*Anne of Green Gables,* Lucy Montgomery	1934	*Mary Poppins,* Pamela Travers
1908	*The Wind in the Willows,* Kenneth Grahame, illustrated by Ernest H. Shepard	1935	*Araminta,* Eva Knox Evans
		1935	*Caddie Woodlawn,* Carol Ryrie Brink
1910	*The Farm Book* and *Chicken World,* E. Boyd Smith	1936	*Roller Skates,* Ruth Sawyer
1910	*The Secret Garden,* Frances Hodgson Burnett	1936	*The Story of Ferdinand,* Munro Leaf, illustrated by Robert Lawson
1920	*The Brownies' Book,* W. E. B. DuBois	1937	*And to Think That I Saw It on Mulberry Street,* Dr. Seuss
1921	*Here and Now Story Book,* Lucy Sprague Mitchell	1937	*The Hobbit,* J. R. R. Tolkien

Landmarks in the Development of Books for Children (*continued*)

FIRST HALF OF THE TWENTIETH CENTURY (*continued*)

1938	Caldecott Medal established for most distinguished picture book for children	1941	*Paddle to the Sea,* Holling C. Holling
1939	*I Am a Pueblo Indian Girl,* E-Yeh-Shuré	1942	*The Little House,* Virginia Lee Burton
1939	*Madeline,* Ludwig Bemelmans	1943	*Homer Price,* Robert McCloskey
1939	*Mike Mulligan and His Steam Shovel,* Virginia Lee Burton	1943	*Johnny Tremain,* Esther Forbes
1939	*The Noisy Book,* Margaret Wise Brown, illustrated by Leonard Weisgard	1944	*Folktales of China,* Lim Sian-tek
		1944	*The Hundred Dresses,* Eleanor Estes, illustrated by Louis Slobodkin
1939	*Tobe,* Stella Gentry Sharp	1945	*Call Me Charley,* Jesse Jackson
1939	*You Can't Pet a Possum,* Arna Bontemps	1946	*Bright April,* Marguerite de Angeli
1940	*Blue Willow,* Doris Gates	1947	*Judy's Journey,* Lois Lenski
1941	*Curious George,* H. A. Rey	1947	*Stone Soup,* Marcia Brown
1941	*In My Mother's House,* Ann Nolan Clark	1947	*Terrapin's Pot of Sense,* Harold Courlander
1941	*Make Way for Ducklings,* Robert McCloskey	1947	*White Snow, Bright Snow,* Alvin Tresselt, illustrated by Roger Duvoisin
1941	*The Moffats,* Eleanor Estes		

SECOND HALF OF THE TWENTIETH CENTURY

1950	*Pippi Longstocking,* Astrid Lindgren	1962	*A Wrinkle in Time,* Madeleine L'Engle
1951	*Chariot in the Sky,* Arna Bontemps	1963	*Where the Wild Things Are,* Maurice Sendak
1952	*Anne Frank: The Diary of a Young Girl,* Anne Frank	1964	*Harriet the Spy,* Louise Fitzhugh
1952	*Charlotte's Web,* E. B. White, illustrated by Garth Williams	1965	"The All White World of Children's Books," Nancy Larrick
1953	International Board on Books for Young People founded	1966	Mildred L. Batchelder Award established for most outstanding translated book
1956	*Bronzeville Boys and Girls,* Gwendolyn Brooks	1967	*Zeely,* Virginia Hamilton
1957	*The Cat in the Hat,* Dr. Seuss	1969	Coretta Scott King Award established for best African American children's literature
1959	*Tom's Midnight Garden,* Philippa Pearce		
1962	*The Snowy Day,* Ezra Jack Keats		*(continued)*

Landmarks in the Development of Books for Children (*continued*)

SECOND HALF OF THE TWENTIETH CENTURY (*continued*)

1969	*Stevie*, John Steptoe
1969	*Where the Lilies Bloom*, Vera and Bill Cleaver
1970	*Are You There God? It's Me, Margaret*, Judy Blume
1970	*In the Night Kitchen*, Maurice Sendak
1971	*Journey to Topaz*, Yoshiko Uchida, illustrated by Donald Carrick
1972	*Jimmy Yellow Hawk*, Virginia Driving Hawk Sneve
1974	*M. C. Higgins the Great*, Virginia Hamilton
1974	*My Brother Sam Is Dead*, James and Christopher Collier
1974	*Where the Sidewalk Ends*, Shel Silverstein
1975	*Why Mosquitoes Buzz in People's Ears*, retold by Verna Aardema, illustrated by Leo and Diane Dillon
1977	Excellence in Poetry for Children Award established by the National Council of Teachers of English
1980	*Hiroshima No Pika* (The Flash of Hiroshima), Toshi Maruki
1981	*A Visit to William Blake's Inn*, Nancy Willard, illustrated by Alice and Martin Provensen
1986	*The Magic School Bus at the Waterworks*, Joanna Cole, illustrated by Bruce Degan
1987	*Lincoln: A Photobiography*, Russell Freedman
1987	*Mufaro's Beautiful Daughters: An African Tale*, John Steptoe
1990	*Baseball in April and Other Stories*, Gary Soto
1990	*Black and White*, David Macaulay
1990	Orbis Pictus Award for outstanding children's nonfiction established by the National Council of Teachers of English
1991	*Maniac Magee*, Jerry Spinelli
1994	*Christmas in the Big House, Christmas in the Quarters*, Patricia and Fredrick McKissack
1994	*Earthshine*, Theresa Nelson
1995	*Catherine Called Birdy*, Karen Cushman
1996	*The Friends*, Kazumi Yumoto
1996	Pura Belpré Award established for excellence in Latino literature
1997	*Forged by Fire*, Sharon Draper
1997	*Out of the Dust*, Karen Hesse
1998	*Harry Potter and the Sorcerer's Stone*, J. K. Rowling
1999	*The Birchbark House*, Louise Erdrich
2000	Robert F. Sibert Informational Book Award established for a distinguished work of nonfiction for children

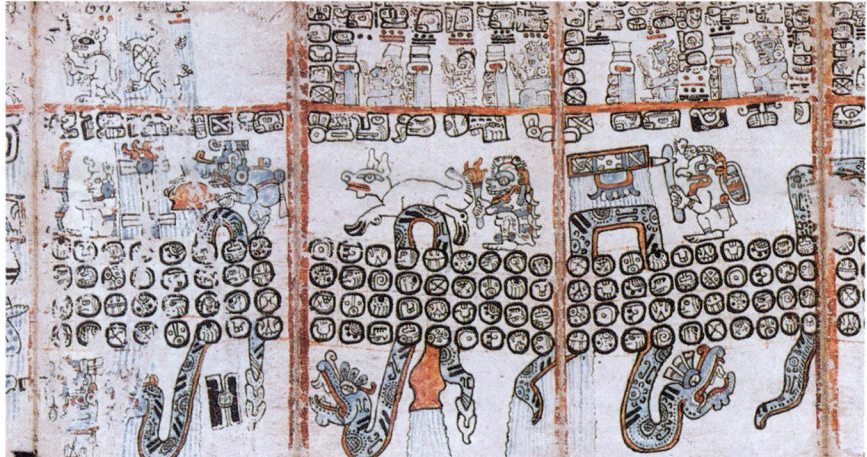

The Egyptian scroll and the Mayan codex show that images and words have been integrated in books for thousands of years. Egyptian scroll copyright © the Trustees of The British Museum. Codex used by permission of Akademischen Druck und Verlagsanstalt Grasz-Austria (ADEVA).

A WORLDWIDE TRADITION OF STORY

Before there were books, there were stories. Today's literature for children has grown out of oral traditions that exist in every society. Suzanne Langer has argued that "imaging is the mode of our untutored thinking and stories their earliest product."[7] We can assume, then, that in all human societies, stories and poems that were passed on by revered storytellers or griots and retold by the common people were likely enjoyed by a wide audience of adults and children.

Eventually, in many cultures, these oral stories came to be preserved in more permanent forms—on cave walls, sculptures, and carvings, as well as in objects that more closely resemble today's books. The *Epic of Gilgamesh* was recorded on clay tablets as early as 2100 B.C. China has a 3,000-year history of literature written in a single language, a literature that is as much visual as verbal. An African (Egyptian) papyrus that dates from approximately 1295 B.C. depicts a humorous tale that includes an antelope and a lion seated on chairs engaged in a game of senet. The Mayan codices (which used a combination of glyphs and pictures) that survived the Spanish invasion suggest a written literary tradition has long existed in the Western Hemisphere. Although we have no evidence that any of this literature was written for a child audience, we can assume that some children were entertained by the same literature that adults in various societies enjoyed.[8]

EARLY BEGINNINGS OF WESTERN CHILDREN'S LITERATURE

In medieval Europe—from the fifth to the fifteenth century—stories were told around the fires in cottages or sung in the great halls of castles. Young and old alike listened, with no distinction made between stories for children and stories for adults, just as there was little difference in the work they did, the food they ate, or the clothes they wore. All gathered to listen, to be entertained after a hard day's labor.

The Oral Tradition

In the Middle Ages, there were differences between the kinds of stories told in the cottages and the kinds told in the castles, and in the ways they were told. In the castles and great manor houses, wandering minstrels or bards told the heroic tales of Beowulf or King Arthur or the ballad of Fair Isabella, whose stepmother had her cooked and served in a pie. By contrast, the tales told around the peat fires in the cottages or at the medieval fairs were about simple folk—farmers, woodcutters, and millers—or were beast tales about wolves, foxes, and hens. Frequently, the stories portrayed the poor peasant outwitting the lord of the manor or winning the hand of

---

[7]Suzanne Langer, *Philosophy in a New Key* (Cambridge, Mass.: Harvard University Press, 1942), p. 145.

[8]The scope of this chapter does not permit us to trace the history of world children's literature. However, we encourage students to search out research on the history of children's literature in other languages and cultures.

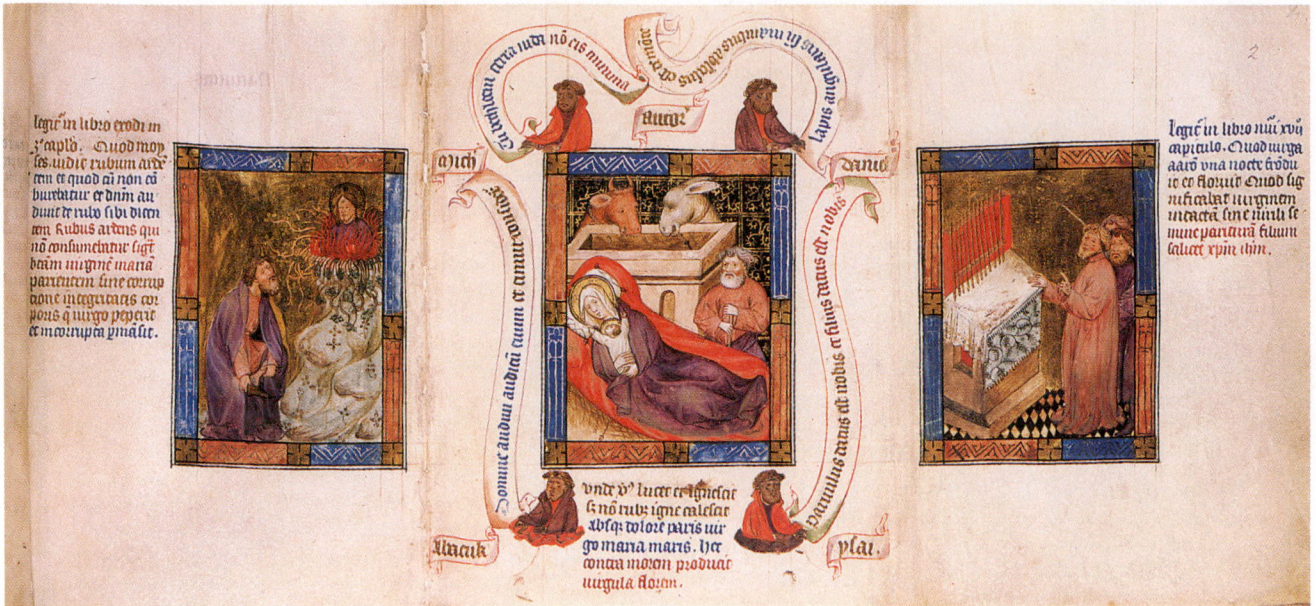

The layout of this picture bible or Biblia Pauperum is strikingly similar to today's picture book. It may have been used for religious instruction of the illiterate poor or for instruction of the young children of the nobility. King's 5 manuscript, British Library "Moses and the Burning Bush," King's 5 fol 2 (1010335.011). By permission of the British Library, Special Collections.

the princess by a daring deed. These tales were told over and over for generations until they were finally collected by scholars and thus passed into recorded literature.

The Earliest Manuscripts

Before the invention of movable type, the first books that European children might have read were picture Bibles or lesson books. Picture Bibles included such types as the Bible Moralisée, Biblia Pauperum, and Bible Historiale and were remarkably similar to modern picture books in their page design and balance of image and word. Mostly religious or instructional, these were intended only for the wealthy or for use by teachers in monastery schools. Such handwritten books were extremely valuable; houses and lands were often exchanged for a single volume.[9]

Most early lesson books followed one of two forms, which continued in popularity up to the early twentieth century: (1) a dialogue between the pupil and teacher, usually in the form of questions and answers, or (2) rhymed couplets, which made for easy memorization. Aldhelm, abbot of Malmesbury during the seventh century, is credited with introducing the question-and-answer approach. Also during this century, the Venerable Bede translated and wrote some forty-five books for his students at the monastery at Jarrow in England.

Another type of book, the Elucidarium, or book of general information for young students, was developed by Anselm, archbishop of Canterbury during the

twelfth century. This type of book, a forerunner of the encyclopedia, treated such topics as manners, children's duties, the properties of animals and plants, and religious precepts.

These early books are important to the history of children's literature only in that they represent some concession to developing specific books for the instruction of children. Another six centuries would pass before John Newbery would add the word *amusement* to the word *instruction.*

However, it is likely that many children were entertained by stories that were written for adults. The *Gesta Romanorum* (Deeds of the Romans), compiled in Latin in the early fourteenth century, served as a sourcebook for stories for the clergy for instruction and for enlivening sermons. This compilation of stories included many myths, fables, and tales from as far away as India. These tales were often dressed up with suitable morals and then told to children.

Only one well-known work remains from medieval manuscripts, Chaucer's *Canterbury Tales.* Although written for adults in 1387, the tales are full of legendary stories and folktales that were known to children as well as adults of the period.

The Printed Book

The earliest printed books originated in China as early as A.D. 175 and were printed from stone rubbings. China also preceded the West in the development of wood

---

[9]Louise Frances Story Field [Mrs. E. M. Field], *The Child and His Book,* 2nd ed. (London: Wells Gardner, 1892; reprint: Detroit: Singing Tree Press, 1968), p. 13.

block printing in the eighth century and movable type in the eleventh century.[10] Some historians maintain that Western printing first began in Holland sometime between 1380 and 1420.[11] However, in the 1450s, Gutenberg in Germany devised a practical method for using movable metal type, far superior in quality to the Dutch type. William Caxton, an English businessman, went to Cologne, Germany, to learn the printing trade. Returning to England, he set up a printing press in Westminster about 1476. Among the first books he published were *A Book of Curteseye* (1477), the *Historye of Reynart the Foxe* (1481), and *Aesop's Fables* (1484). Malory's *Le Morte d'Arthur* first appeared in printed form in 1485. Caxton is credited with publishing some 106 books, including traditional romance literature, ballads, texts, and religious books. His books were of high quality and expensive, which made them available only to wealthy adults, not children. The impact of the printing press can be seen, however, in the number of books owned by some individuals. Before the invention of the press in the 1450s, even scholars and physicians possessed only a few books. A century later, to give one example, Columbus of Seville (the son of Christopher Columbus) owned a library of more than fifteen thousand titles.

Hornbooks, ABCs, and Primers

The first children's books to be influenced by the invention of printing were then the only children's books: lesson books or textbooks. In the mid fifteenth century, young children learned to read from "hornbooks." A hornbook was really a little wooden paddle to which was pasted a sheet of parchment printed with the alphabet, the vowels, and the Lord's Prayer. A thin sheet of transparent protective horn bound with strips of brass covered the text. Most hornbooks were tiny, measuring two by five inches. Sometimes a hole in the handle made it possible for the child to carry the book on a cord around his or her neck or waist. This also lent them their nickname *battledore,* for they were often used to bat around a shuttlecock in a game of badminton. What made these little "books" unique was that now the child could handle them and see the print close up, rather than merely look at a manuscript held by the teacher.

Children advanced from hornbooks to ABC books and primers. These had more text than hornbooks but were still of a religious nature. The first primers developed from the books of hours, which were intended as private devotionals for laypeople, with prayers for eight specified times of the day. In 1514 an alphabet was added to a book of hours for use by children. When Henry VIII came to the throne, he authorized printing a set of English primers for children that presented his

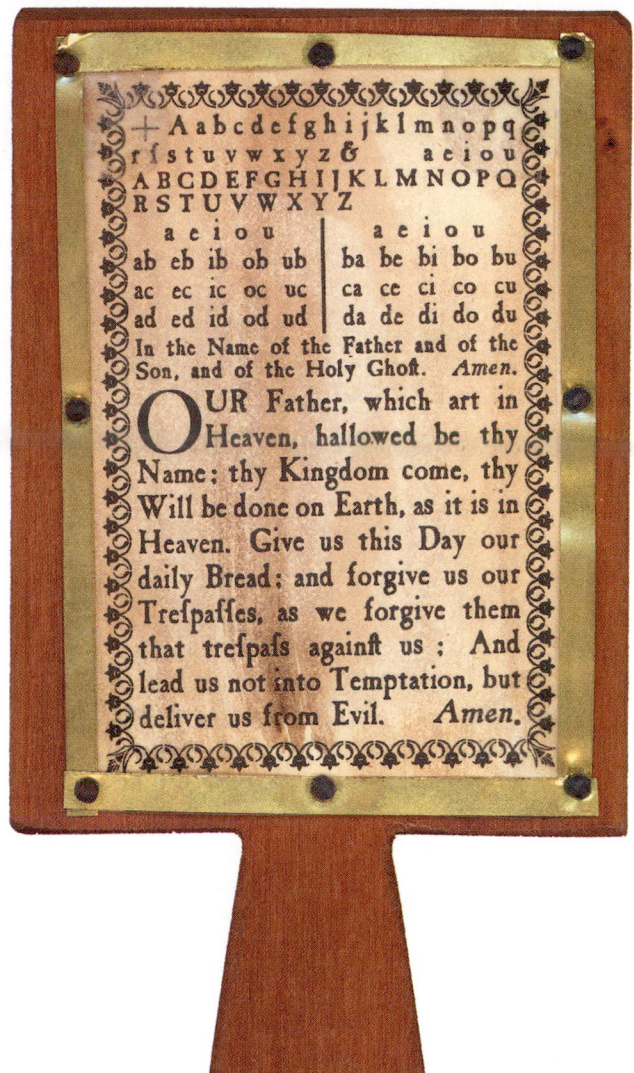

This facsimile of a colonial hornbook was ordered from The Horn Book, Inc. *The Horn Book Replica*, reprinted by permission of The Horn Book, Inc. 56 Roland St., Suite 200, Boston, MA 02129, 617–625–0225.

religious beliefs. These little books, appropriately called *King Henry's Primer,* appeared about 1548.

Lasting Contributions of the Period

Children were not much better off after the invention of printing than before. They still derived their enjoyment from the told story. True, some concession had been made to their youth in devising special books of instruction for them. But only crudely written and printed chapbooks provided a kind of underground literature of enjoyment for both adults and children. The two lasting

---

[10]See Michael Olmert, *The Smithsonian Book of Books* (Washington, D.C.: Smithsonian Books, 1992).

[11]Elva S. Smith, *Elva S. Smith's History of Children's Literature,* rev. by Margaret Hodges and Susan Steinfirst (Chicago: American Library Association, 1980), p. 38.

books of this period are Chaucer's *Canterbury Tales* and Thomas Malory's collection of Arthurian legends, later published in 1485 by Caxton under the title *Le Morte d'Arthur.* Neither of these books was written for children, but children probably knew the stories from hearing them told by bards and minstrels.

What strikes a twenty-first-century reader as remarkable about this period is how few books there were and how long they stayed in print. Many of the books published by Caxton in the 1470s were still in print in the late 1600s, more than two hundred years later. This seems almost unbelievable when compared with today's publishing world, where some books go out of print in less than a year.

CHILDREN'S BOOKS: THE SEVENTEENTH AND EIGHTEENTH CENTURIES

In the seventeenth and eighteenth centuries, many books for children in the Western world were meant to be educational rather than entertaining. Over time, however, authors, illustrators, and publishers began to present children with books that were meant to delight as well as to inform. It should be noted, nonetheless, that the children who were soon to be delighted by books written for their enjoyment came mainly from the white middle and upper classes. A literature for all the world's children was still many years in the future.

The "Goodly Godly" Books of the Puritans

Books of the seventeenth century were dominated by the stern spiritual beliefs of Puritanism. The Puritans considered children to be miniature adults, and thus equally subject to sin and eternal damnation. Concern for the salvation of children's souls became the central goal of their parents and teachers. Given the high mortality rate of infants and young children (more than half did not live to reach the age of 10), instruction in the fear of God began early. John Cotton's catechism, *Spiritual Milk for Boston Babes in Either England, Drawn from the Breasts of Both Testaments for Their Souls' Nourishment,* was originally published in England in 1646, and revised for American children in 1656, the first book written and printed for children in the American colonies.

Even alphabet rhymes for the youngest emphasized the sinful nature of humans. *The New England Primer,* first advertised in 1677, includes "In Adam's fall / We sinned all." This primer also provided a catechism, the Ten Commandments, verses about death, and a woodcut of Martyr John Foxe burning at the stake, watched by his wife

and nine children. This primer was in print for more than a century and sold about three million copies.

In England in 1671, James Janeway published his book of gloomy joy titled *A Token for Children, Being an Exact Account of the Conversions, Holy and Exemplary Lives and Joyful Deaths of Several Young Children.* In his preface to Part 1, Janeway reminds his readers that they are "by Nature, Children of Wrath." Cotton Mather added the life histories of several New England children and published an American edition of Janeway's book in Boston in 1700 under the title *A Token for Children of New England, or Some Examples of Children in Whom the Fear of God Was Remarkably Budding Before They Died.*

Religious leaders also could give approval to the moral and spiritual instruction in John Bunyan's *Pilgrim's Progress,* first printed in 1678. No doubt children skipped the long theological dialogues as they found adventure by traveling with the clearly defined characters.

Primers and instructional books continued to be popular during this time. Edward Topsell's *Historie of Four-Footed Beasts,* published in 1607, was perhaps the first work of nonfiction written for children.[12] Many of these educational books were emblem books. They followed a pictorial format developed in Germany and the Netherlands in which each verse or couplet was illustrated with a small picture. Johann Amos Comenius's *Orbis Pictus* (The World in Pictures) was influenced by this style. It was translated into English in 1659 and published with many woodcuts illustrating everyday objects. *Orbis Pictus* is often referred to as the first picture book for children.

Lighter Fare

Luckily, there was some relief from the doom and gloom of the religion-oriented books of the Puritans. Chapbooks—small, inexpensive, folded-paper booklets sold by peddlers, or chapmen—first appeared in the late 1500s, but they achieved real popularity in the seventeenth and eighteenth centuries. Sold for a few pennies, these crudely printed little books brought excitement and pleasure into the lives of both children and adults with tales about Dick Whittington, Sir Guy of Warwick, Robin Hood, and other heroes. A ballad of a "most strange wedding of the froggee and the mouse" was licensed as early as 1580. Other chapbooks gave accounts of crimes and executions, descriptions of the art of making love, and riddles. Although these books were decried by the Puritans, they were read and reread by the common people of England and America. Their popularity with children is said to have influenced John Newbery's decision to publish a book solely for children. The chapbooks' greatly abbreviated texts and crude woodcut illustrations suggest that they were fore-

---

[12]Mary V. Jackson, *Engines of Instruction, Mischief, and Magic: Children's Literature in England from Its Beginnings to 1839* (Lincoln: University of Nebraska Press, 1990), p. 36.

runners of today's comic strips, still read by both adults and children.

Another source of enjoyment for children came in the form of fairy tales; the first was printed in France in 1697 by Charles Perrault. Titled *Histoires ou contes du temps passé, avec des moralités* (Stories or Tales of Times Past, with Morals), the collection included "The Sleeping Beauty," "Cinderella or the Glass Slipper," "Red Riding Hood," "Puss-in-Boots," and "Blue Beard." These tales were in fashion at the French court of the Sun King, Louis XIV, where they were told to adults. The frontispiece of Perrault's book, however, showed an old woman spinning and telling stories to children. The caption read *Contes de ma Mère l'Oye* (Tales of Mother Goose); this was the first reference to Mother Goose in children's literature. Translated into English in 1729, these fairy tales have remained France's gift to the children of the world. Following the success of Perrault, other French authors, including Mme. d'Aulnoy, created original fairy tales. Only one remains well known today and that is "Beauty and the Beast," rewritten from a longer version by Mme. de Beaumont.

The Arabian Nights is a collection of old tales from India, Persia, and North Africa. Galland published these tales in French in 1558, but not until about 1706 were they available in English. Intended for adults, such stories as "Aladdin," "Ali Baba," and "Sinbad the Sailor" were quickly appropriated by children.

Children of the seventeenth and eighteenth centuries would also have enjoyed nursery rhymes, those that have traditionally been called Mother Goose rhymes and that included counting-out rhymes, finger plays, and alphabet verses. No one knows for sure the exact origin of these rhymes, but they are likely to have originated in the spoken language of both common folk and royalty. Some have been traced as far back as the pre-Christian era. The association of these traditional rhymes with a character called Mother Goose is unclear. The oldest surviving nursery rhyme book was published by Mary Cooper in 1744 in two or perhaps three little volumes under the title *Tommy Thumb's Pretty Song Book;* a single copy of volume 2 is a treasured possession of the British Museum. John Newbery is supposed to have published *Mother Goose's Melody or Sonnets for the Cradle* about 1765, although the book was not ad-

Chapbooks have entertained children and adults for centuries. *From The Treasures of Childhood: Books, Toys, and Games from the Opie Collection by Iona and Robert Opie and Brian Anderson. Copyright © 1989 by Iona Opie. Used by permission of Pavilion Books Limited in association with Michael Joseph Limited, an imprint of Penguin Books, a Member of Putnam Group (USA), Inc., 345 Hudson St., New York, NY 10014. All rights reserved.*

vertised until 1780, which is the more likely date of its publication. No copy of this edition exists. However, Isaiah Thomas of Worcester, Massachusetts, produced a second edition of *Mother Goose's Melody* in 1794.

John Newbery's first publications, *A Little Pretty Pocket-Book* and *Little Goody Two Shoes,* reflected a new interest in providing enjoyable books for children. *A Little Pretty Pocket-Book . . . Worchester, Mass.,* printed for John Newbery, London, 1767, title page. Rare Books Division, The New York Public Library, Astor, Lenox and Tilden Foundations. *Little Goody Two Shoes* by John Newbery [Liverpool?, 1878?], title character. Rare Books Division, The New York Public Library, Astor, Lenox and Tilden Foundations.

Books written for adults during this time were often adopted by child readers. Daniel Defoe did not write his account of the eighteenth-century hero Robinson Crusoe for them, but children made his story part of their literature. *The Life and Strange and Surprising Adventures of Robinson Crusoe* (1719) was later printed in an abridged and pocket-sized volume that became a "classic" of children's literature. Children, no doubt, did not understand the scathing satire about high society in Swift's *Gulliver's Travels,* but they did find enjoyment in the hero's adventures with the huge and tiny folk and the talking horses. Thus young and old alike enjoyed this tale of adventure, first published in 1726.

Newbery Publishes for Children

In the mid-eighteenth century strict religious beliefs about child rearing began to give way to ideas influenced by such thinkers as John Locke, Jean Jacques Rousseau, and David Hume. With the rise of the Enlightenment, a literature for childhood emerged. This transformation usu-

ally dates from 1744, the year the English publisher John Newbery printed *A Little Pretty Pocket-Book.* Newbery was influenced by John Locke's *Thoughts Concerning Education* (1693) in which Locke maintained that as soon as children know their alphabet they should be led to read for pleasure. Locke advocated the use of pictures in books and deplored the lack of easy, pleasant books for children to read, except for *Aesop's Fables* and *Reynard the Fox,* both dating back to Caxton's times. In *A Little Pretty Pocket-Book* Newbery included John Locke's advice that children should enjoy reading. The book itself attempted to teach the alphabet "by Way of Diversion," including games, fables, and little rhymes about the letters of the alphabet. What was significant about the book was that Newbery deliberately and openly set out to provide amusement for children, something no other publisher had had the courage or insight to do.

Newbery's books were all illustrated with pictures based on the text, rather than just any woodcuts available, as was the custom of other printers of the day. Many of his books were bound with Dutch gilt paper covers, which made for a gay appearance. Even though moral lessons were clearly there for young readers, Newbery's stories did emphasize love and play rather than the wrath and punishment of God. Newbery is also responsible for *Little Goody Two Shoes,* "the first piece of original English fiction deliberately written for children."[13] Except for *Little Goody Two Shoes,* none of his work has lasted, but we honor the man who was the first to recognize that children deserve a literature of their own.

Didactic Literature

A body of literature that resembles modern children's literature did not emerge overnight. During the last half of the eighteenth century, women writers entered the field of juvenile literature, determined to influence the moral development of children. In 1749, Mrs. Sarah Fielding published *The Governess,* which included character-building stories about Mrs. Teachum's School for Girls. Mrs. Sarah Trimmer published a magazine titled *Guardian of Education,* which contained articles on moral subjects and book reviews. Mrs. Trimmer did not approve of fairy tales or Mother Goose. "All Mother Goose tales . . . were only fit to fill the heads of children with confused notions of wonderful and supernatural events brought about by the agency of imaginary beings."[14]

Other didactic writers of this period maintained that they followed Rousseau's theory of education by accompanying children in their natural search for knowledge. These stories frequently contained lengthy "conversations" that tried to conceal moral lessons under the guise of an exciting adventure. The children found in these books served as models of behavior for nearly a hundred years.

In this period, poetry for children also emphasized religion and instruction. However, John Newbery printed *Pretty Poems for Children Three Feet High* and added this inscription: "To all those who are good this book is dedicated by their best friend." Although Isaac Watts spent most of his time writing hymns, he did write some poetry for children. In the preface to *Divine and Moral Songs Attempted in Easy Language for Use of Children* (1715), Watts wrote that his songs were to be memorized, which was how children were to be given "a relish for virtue and religion." Though written by a Puritan, these hymns such as "Joy to the World" and the lovely "Cradle Hymn," were kind and loving, and the collection made up a real child's book. The engraver and artist William Blake wrote poetry that children enjoyed, but the poems constituting *Songs of Innocence* (1789) were not specifically written for children. Blake's poetry was filled with imagination and joy and made the reader aware of beauty without preaching. Children still respond to his happy poem that begins "Piping down the valleys wild, / Piping songs of pleasant glee."

As the eighteenth century neared its end, most of the stories for children were about how to live the "good life." Information about the natural world was peddled in didactic lectures sugarcoated with conversational style. Exceptionally well-behaved children were models for young people to follow. However, there was now a literature directed to a child audience, even if that audience was exclusively Caucasian and predominantly middle and upper class. Authors and publishers were aware of a new market for books. Parents and teachers were beginning to recognize the importance of literature for children.

CHILDREN'S LITERATURE: THE NINETEENTH CENTURY

In the nineteenth century, the genres written for children expanded greatly. Children could choose to read about a wide variety of topics. Books and magazines sought to present children with works of literature that celebrated their unique enthusiasms and explored their special worlds. Children's literature in the nineteenth century, however, still represented an "Anglo world."

Books of Instruction and Information

In the seventeenth and eighteenth centuries, most of the books published for children in English were produced in England. Following the American Revolution, however, there was a rush to publish textbooks that reflected the changing social purposes and interests of the new nation. Noah Webster's *Blue Backed Speller, Simplified and Standardized,* first published in 1783, was widely used. Revised many times, the third part of the series contained stories and became America's first secular reader. It sold more than eighty million copies during the nineteenth century. Reading for patriotism, good citizenship, and industry was the purpose of the well-loved *Eclectic Readers* by William H. McGuffey. They were used so widely from 1834 to 1900 that one could almost say these readers constituted the elementary curriculum in literature.

In the early nineteenth century, Samuel Goodrich was responsible for eliminating the British background in books for American children. Influenced by both the English and the American Sunday school movements, which produced moral tales for the uneducated masses of children who could attend school only on Sunday,

---

[13]F. J. Harvey Darton, *Children's Books in England,* 3rd ed., rev. by Brian Alderson (Cambridge: Cambridge University Press, 1932, 1982), p. 128.

[14]Ibid, p. 97.

Goodrich wrote more than a hundred books for children. He created the venerable Peter Parley, an elderly gentleman who told stories to children based on his travels and personal experiences. History, geography, and science were included in his *Tales of Peter Parley about America* (1827). The Little Rollo series by Jacob Abbott became as popular as the Peter Parley books. Abbott wrote about Little Rollo learning to talk, Rollo learning to read, and Rollo's travels to Europe. In the first books of the series, published in 1834, Rollo was a natural little boy, but as he became older and traveled about the world, he became somewhat stuffy.

Family Stories

In the first half of the nineteenth century the didactic school of writing continued to flourish, with perhaps one exception. In 1839, Catherine Sinclair, whose many other books were highly moral and sedate, published *Holiday House,* "certainly the best original children's book written up to that time and one of the jolliest and most hilarious of any period."[15] Her characters were children who got into mischief, and they were sometimes aided in this by an adult—their irreverent and fun-loving Uncle David.

For the most part, however, women writers in the early nineteenth century wielded influential pens, condemned fairy stories, and relentlessly dispensed information in lengthy dialogues between parent and child. Mrs. Martha Sherwood, a prolific writer, produced more than 350 moralizing books and religious tracts. Sherwood is remembered best for a series of stories including *The Fairchild Family,* the first part of which was published in 1818, the third and last in 1847. Considered one of the first "family" stories, it contained some frighteningly realistic passages. In one scene, to teach his quarreling children a lesson, Mr. Fairchild takes them to see something "very dreadful, . . . a gibbet on which the decomposed body of a man still hangs in irons. The face of the corpse was so shocking the children could not look at it."

In contrast to the religious severity of *The Fairchild Family,* Charlotte Yonge described the milder Victorian experiences of the eleven motherless children of the May family in *The Daisy Chain* (1856). Women were always portrayed in the Victorian novel as inferior to men. This attitude is reflected in *The Daisy Chain* when Ethel May is advised not to try to keep up with her brother Norman in his university studies because "a woman cannot hope to equal a man in scholarship." Yonge had an ear for dialogue and was a superb storyteller who wrote more than 120 books.

American children wept pools of tears over the pious, sentimental Elsie Dinsmore. Writing under her maiden name, Martha Farquharson, Martha Finley initiated the Elsie Dinsmore series in 1867. The series contains eighteen books, published from 1867 to 1905, that follow Elsie,

Jessie Wilcox Smith created eight full-color illustrations painted in oils for the popular 1915 edition of *Little Women.* Alcott, Louisa May, *Little Women,* with illustrations by Jessie Wilcox Smith, Boston, 1922. Special Collections, The New York Public Library.

at all times righteous and good, from girlhood through motherhood and widowhood and into grandmotherhood. Unbelievable as the stories seem to us today, the Elsie Dinsmore books were tremendously popular.

The next year saw the publication of *Little Women* (1868) by Louisa May Alcott. This story must have blown like a fresh breeze through the stifling atmosphere of pious religiosity created by books like those in the Elsie Dinsmore series. As described by the irrepressible Jo (who was Louisa May Alcott herself), the March family were real people who faced genteel poverty with humor and fortitude. Louisa May Alcott didn't preach moral platitudes but described the joys, the trials, and the fun of growing up in a loving family. Jo, one of the first tomboys in children's literature, hates the false Victorian standards of the day and sets out to earn a living as a writer. Still loved today, *Little Women* has been transformed into many languages, including Russian, Arabic, Bengali, and Urdu.

---

[15]Darton, *Children's Books in England,* p. 220.

Another vivacious heroine appeared in the celebrated Katy stories written by Susan Coolidge (pseudonym of Sarah Chauncey Woolsey). This series included such titles as *What Katy Did* (1872), *What Katy Did at School* (1873), and *What Katy Did Next* (1886). Harriet Lathrop, under the pseudonym Margaret Sidney, presented a lively family story about a widowed mother and her five children in a series starting in 1881 with *Five Little Peppers* and concluding in 1916 with *Our Davie Pepper*. Other authors wrote dramatic family stories with foreign settings. In *Hans Brinker, or the Silver Skates*, Mary Mapes Dodge gave accurate glimpses of Dutch life in 1865. Johanna Spyri's well-loved *Heidi* was translated from the German by Louise Brooks and published in this country in 1884. Not only did readers share the joys and sorrows of Heidi's life with her grandfather, they "breathed" the clear mountain air and "lived" in Switzerland. Frances Hodgson Burnett described family conflict within the English aristocracy in *Little Lord Fauntleroy* (1886). Although born in England, Mrs. Burnett was an American citizen. Burnett's second book, *Sara Crewe* (1888), told of the pitiful plight of a wealthy pupil who is orphaned and reduced to servitude in a boarding school. Mrs. Burnett's best-written and most popular book is *The Secret Garden* (1910), which presents an exciting plot in a mysterious setting. This story depicts the gradual change wrought in two lonely and selfish children by a hidden garden. It is still read and loved by children today.

Tales of Adventure

The rise of family stories and series books for girls prompted more attention to tales of adventures and the development of so-called boys' series. *The Swiss Family Robinson* was written by Johann David Wyss, a Swiss pastor, and translated into English in 1814. Inaccurate in its description of flora and fauna (almost everything grew on that tropical island), it still delighted children's imaginations. Sir Walter Scott's novels *Rob Roy* (1818) and *Ivanhoe* (1820), while intended for adults, were frequently appropriated by young people. James Fenimore Cooper's Leatherstocking novels of tales of Indians and pioneers in North America were avidly read by young and old alike. Richard Henry Dana's *Two Years Before the Mast* (1840) describes the author's own adventures as a young seaman sailing around Cape Horn to California. Also written for adults, it provided adventure for children. British writers such as Captain Frederick Marryat and George A. Henty wrote books based on military histories and adventures that were read with enthusiasm by American children. At the same time, the American names Horatio Alger, Jr., Oliver Optic, and Harry Castlemon were well known to English readers. The emphasis in American series was more on individual achievement, usually against unbelievable odds. The stories by Horatio Alger epitomized this rags-to-riches theme. In fact, because his first successful novel, *Ragged Dick* (1868), was based on this formula, he saw no reason to change it in the more than a hundred books that followed.

Although most of these series books provided plenty of adventure, the characters and plots tended to be superficial and predictable. However, there was one superb adventure story written during the last half of the nineteenth century that included not only a bloody, exciting, and tightly drawn plot but also well-depicted characters. Serialized in an English magazine called *Young Folks* in 1881 and 1882, Robert Louis Stevenson's *Treasure Island* was published in book form in 1883. For the first time, adults were drawn to a children's book for adventure, a reverse of the pattern of children reading adults' books. *Treasure Island* was an immediate success.

Gradually books written for boys changed in their portrayal of childhood, and obedient and dutiful characters became real live boys. Thomas Bailey Aldrich's *The Story of a Bad Boy* (1870) was based on his own life in Portsmouth, New Hampshire. The tale of this Tom's pranks and good times paved the way for another story of a real boy's adventures in Hannibal, Missouri. *The Adventures of Tom Sawyer* was published in 1876 by Mark Twain (pseudonym of Samuel Clemens). This book was soon followed by *The Adventures of Huckleberry Finn* (1884). Mark Twain combined realism, humor, and adventure in these realistic portrayals of growing up in a small town near the end of the nineteenth century.

Animal Stories

In *A Dog of Flanders and Other Stories* (1872), Louise de la Ramée presented a collection of stories that included the sad tale of a Belgian work dog and his friend, a boy artist. It has been considered the first modern dog story. Anna Sewell's *Black Beauty* appeared in 1877 as a protest against cruel treatment of horses. Children skipped the lectures calling for more humane treatment of animals and read the compelling first-person story of the life of Black Beauty. Some children today continue to enjoy Sewell's rather overdrawn and sentimental tale. Rudyard Kipling's *The Jungle Books* (1894–1895) were exciting animal stories. Many children today know the story of Mowgli, a child raised by a wolf family, a bear, and a panther, although they might be more familiar with the animated movie than with the original book.

The Rise of Folktale Collections and Fantasy

Early in the nineteenth century two German brothers went about asking servants and peasants to recall stories they had heard. In 1812 Jacob and Wilhelm Grimm published the first volume of *Kinder und Hausmärchen* (Household Stories). These serious scholars tried to preserve the form as well as the content of the old tales, which were translated and published in England by Edgar Taylor from 1823 to 1826. "The Elves and the Shoemaker," "Rumpelstiltskin," and "Snow White," in addition to many others, became part of the literature of childhood.

In 1846 Mary Howitt translated Hans Christian Andersen's tales under the title *Wonderful Stories for Children.* Now both English and American children could enjoy "The Princess and the Pea," "Thumbelina," and "The Emperor's New Clothes." In these stories, inanimate objects and animals like the heroic Tin Soldier and the Ugly Duckling come to life. The values and foibles of human life are presented in the stories with action and rich language.

Not until the last half of the nineteenth century were folktales and fantasy completely accepted for children. John Ruskin was influenced by the Grimm tales as he wrote his *King of the Golden River* (1851). Charles Dickens's *The Magic Fishbone* appeared first as a serial in 1868. *The Wonder Book for Boys and Girls* was published by Nathaniel Hawthorne in 1852, followed by *Tanglewood Tales* in 1853. Sir George Dasent translated *Popular Tales from the North* in 1859, making it possible for children to enjoy more tales from Scandinavia. Andrew Lang's famous series of collections of folktales began with *The Blue Fairy Book.* The *Red, Green,* and *Yellow* fairy books followed the 1889 publication of the first volume of folklore. Joseph Jacobs was also interested in retelling folktales especially for children. *English Fairy Tales, Volumes I and II* were published between 1890 and 1894. Joel Chandler Harris collected stories from the South for *Uncle Remus, His Songs and Savings.* Although the character of Uncle Remus later became a stereotype of the "happy slave," the stories themselves are vibrant reminders of our African American literary heritage.

The first stirrings of modern fantasy can be seen in a tale written by an English clergyman and scientist in 1863. *The Water Babies* by Charles Kingsley is a strange mixture of the fanciful overlaid with heavy doses of morality. Hidden within this little tale was Kingsley's social concern for the plight of the chimney sweeps, plus his attempt to reconcile the new science (Darwin's *The Origin of Species* had been published in 1859) with his religious beliefs. On a summer day in 1862 an Oxford professor of mathematics, Charles Dodgson, told a story to three little girls on a picnic. At the children's request, Dodgson wrote down that story (as "Alice's Adventures Underground") and presented it to his young friends as a Christmas gift in 1864. At the insistence of others, he decided to have it published. By 1865 the artist John Tenniel had completed the drawings, and *Alice's Adventures in Wonderland,* published under the pseudonym Lewis Carroll, was ready for the host of readers to come. What made this story unique for its time was that it contained not a trace of a lesson or a moral. It was really made purely for enjoyment, and it has delighted both children and adults ever since.

The beginnings of science-fiction adventure stories came to us from France in the translations of Jules Verne's *Journey to the Center of the Earth* (1864), *Twenty Thousand Leagues Under the Sea* (1869), and *Around the World in Eighty Days* (1872). Modern readers might be surprised

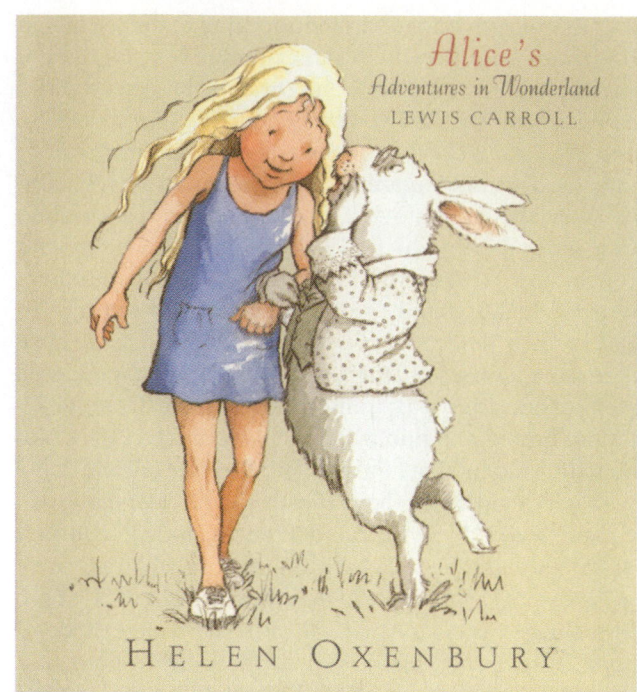

Helen Oxenbury is one of many artists (including Lewis Carroll himself) who have illustrated *Alice's Adventures in Wonderland. Alice's Adventures in Wonderland.* Written by Lewis Carroll. Illustrations copyright © 2003 by Helen Oxenbury. Reproduced by permission of the publisher Candlewick Press, Inc., Cambridge, MA, on behalf of Walker Books Ltd., London.

to note the early dates of these books. Other well-known fantasies were published near the end of the nineteenth century. George MacDonald was a friend of Lewis Carroll's; in fact, he was one of the persons who had urged the publication of *Alice.* However, his own "invented fairy-tale," *At the Back of the North Wind* (1871), has much more of the sad spiritual quality found in many of Hans Christian Andersen's fairy tales than the mad inconsistencies of the world of Lewis Carroll.

Even though many of the early books for children included the word *amusing* in their titles, their main purpose was to instruct or moralize. Undoubtedly, children enjoyed the broad humor in some of the folktales and the nonsense in Mother Goose, but few books used humor or nonsense as a central theme before the middle of the nineteenth century.

The Adventures of Pinocchio by Carlo Collodi first appeared in a children's newspaper in Rome in 1881; it was translated into English in 1892 under the title *The Story of a Puppet.* Children still enjoy this story of the mischievous puppet whose nose grew longer with each lie he told the Blue Fairy. Collodi's real name was Carlos Lorenzini.

The prototype for Amelia Bedelia, Miss Pickerell, Mary Poppins, and all the other eccentric women characters in children's literature can be found in the nonsensical antics of Mrs. Peterkin and her family. Published in 1880 by Lucretia Hale, *The Peterkin Papers* provided chil-

Ernest Nester's bicycling bears are on their way to *The Animals' Picnic* in one of today's numerous reissues of Victorian pop-up books. From *The Animals' Picnic*, by Ernest Nester. Copyright © 1988 by The Putnam & Grosset Group, New York, NY. Reprinted by permission.

dren with real humor. In one story, "The Lady Who Put Salt in Her Coffee," Mrs. Peterkin mistakenly substitutes salt for sugar in her coffee. The whole family troops to the chemist and the herb lady to find out what to do. Finally "the lady from Philadelphia" provides the answer—make another cup of coffee!

Also in the category of books for fun may be included the many books with movable parts. Harlequinades, or turn-ups, first appeared in 1766. They consisted of pages of pictures that could be raised or lowered to create other scenes. Later (from the 1840s through the 1890s), pictures were made like Venetian blinds to create another scene. Circular wheels could be turned to provide more action, and whole pop-up scenes created miniature stages.

Poetry

Poetry for children began to flourish in the nineteenth century. In the first part of the century, poetry, like prose, still reflected the influence of religion and moral didacticism. The Taylor sisters, Ann and Jane, emphasized polite behavior, morals, and death in the poetry for their first book, *Original Poems for Infant Minds* (1804). While Jane Taylor wrote the often-parodied "Twinkle Twinkle Little Star" for this collection and Ann provided the lovely "Welcome, welcome little stranger, to this busy world of care," the book also included some fairly morbid poems.

However, William Roscoe's *The Butterfly's Ball and the Grasshopper's Feast* (1807) provided pure nonsense, rhyme, and rhythm that delighted children. There were no moral lessons here, just an invitation: "Come take up your hats and away let us haste / To the Butterfly's Ball and the Grasshopper's Feast." Roscoe, an historian and botanist, wrote the book for the pleasure of his own child. It was so fresh and different that it generated many imitations.

Clement Moore, a professor who also wrote to please his own children, gave the world the Christmas classic *A Visit from St. Nicholas*. One of the first American contributions to a joyous literature for children, the book was published under that title in 1823, but it is now known by the title *The Night Before Christmas*. *Mary Had a Little Lamb*, first written by Sarah Josepha Hale in 1830, was included in *McGuffey's Reader* in 1837 and has since been recited by generations of American schoolchildren.

Dr. Heinrich Hoffman's *Struwwelpeter* (Shock-Headed Peter) was translated from the German in about 1848. His subjects included "Shock-Headed Peter," who wouldn't comb his hair or cut his nails, and Harriet, who played with fire. These cautionary tales in verse were meant to frighten children into good behavior. Instead, children loved the pictures and gruesome verse. Surely these poems are the forerunners of some of the modern verse by Shel Silverstein and Jack Prelutsky.

The century's greatest contribution to lasting children's poetry was the nonsense verse of Edward Lear, a poet who, like Lewis Carroll, wrote only to entertain. Lear was by profession a landscape painter and illustrator. He wrote his first book, *A Book of Nonsense,* in 1846 for his child friends; *More Nonsense* (1877) appeared more than thiry years later. Generations have delighted in "Quangle Wangle" and "The Owl and the Pussycat." Lear did not invent the limerick, but he certainly became master of the form. His black-line illustrations are as clever as his poetry.

Some of Christina Rossetti's poetry is reminiscent of Mother Goose, such as the well-loved "Mix a Pancake." Other selections, such as "Who has seen the wind?" gave children vivid descriptions of the world around them. Many poems from Rossetti's book *Sing Song* (1872) are found in anthologies today.

The century ended with a unique volume of poetry that celebrated the everyday life and thought of the child. *A Child's Garden of Verses* (1885) by Robert Louis Stevenson was first published under the title *Penny Whistles.* Stevenson was a poet who could discover joy in child's play and enter the child's imaginings in such well-loved poems as "My Shadow," "Bed in Summer," "The Swing," "Windy Nights," and "My Bed Is a Boat."

Two notable American poets were writing for children at the close of the nineteenth century. Eugene Field's *Poems of Childhood* (1896) included "The Sugar Plum Tree" and "The Duel." James Whitcomb Riley employed dialect as he described local incidents and Indiana farm life. This Hoosier dialect has made most of his poems seem obsolete, except for "Little Orphant Annie" and "The Raggedy Man," which continue to give children pleasure.

Magazines

Magazines formed a significant part of the literature for children in the last half of the nineteenth century. The first magazines, which grew out of the Sunday school movement, were pious in their outlook.

The first true children's magazine for English children appeared in 1853 under the title *Charm.* Stating that there would always be room for stories of the little people or fairies on its pages, it was ahead of its time and lasted only two years. The first magazine planned for children in America was published in 1826. *The Juvenile Miscellany* was edited by Lydia Maria Child, a former teacher who wanted to provide enjoyable material for children to read. The magazine was very successful until Child, an ardent abolitionist, spoke out against slavery. Sales dropped immediately, and the magazine stopped

Edward Lear's laughable limericks and illustrations are more than a hundred years old, but they are still enjoyed today.
From The Complete Verse and Other Nonsense by Edward Lear. Copyright © 2002. Used by permission of Penguin Books, published by the Penguin Group, a division of Penguin Putnam, Inc.

publication in 1834. *The Youth's Companion* survived the longest of all the children's magazines in America, beginning in 1827 and merging with *The American Boy* in 1929, which in turn ceased publication in 1941. It published such well-known writers as Kipling, Oliver Wendell Holmes, Jack London, Mark Twain, and Theodore Roosevelt, among others.

In 1873 Mary Mapes Dodge, author of *Hans Brinker, or the Silver Skates,* became editor of the most famous magazine for children, *St. Nicholas Magazine.* The publisher announced that in this magazine "there must be entertainment, no less than information; the spirit of laughter would be evoked; there would be 'no sermonizing, no wearisome spinning out of facts, no rattling of dry bones of history,' while all priggishness was condemned."[16] The magazine attracted well-known artists and writers such as Arthur Rackham, Reginald Birch, Howard Pyle, Frances Hodgson Burnett, Rudyard Kipling, Robert Louis Stevenson, and Louisa May Alcott. Many of the novels that were first serialized in *St. Nicholas Magazine* were published as books and became classics of their day. These included Louisa May Alcott's *An Old-Fashioned Girl* (1870) and Frances Hodgson Burnett's *Little Lord Fauntleroy* (1886). This magazine guided children's reading for more than three-quarters of a century and set standards of excellence for the whole publishing field.

---

[16]Alice M. Jordan, *From Rollo to Tom Sawyer* (Boston: Horn Book, 1948), p. 134.

Illustrators of the Nineteenth Century

Until the late eighteenth century illustrations had been, for the most part, crude woodcuts, due in great part to the lack of sophisticated color reproduction techniques. Illustrators were not identified, and pictures were frequently interchanged among books. During the nineteenth century, however, as engraving processes were refined and lithographic techniques developed, the quality of illustrations improved and the great book artists actually preferred to work in black and white. Illustrators of children's books began to achieve as much recognition as the authors. Several outstanding artists emerged as illustrators of children's books during this time. The engraver George Cruikshank illustrated the English edition of *Grimm's Fairy Tales* in 1823. His tiny, detailed etchings portrayed much action and humor, real characters, and spritely elves and fairies. His interpretations were so appropriate and seemed so much a part of these tales that they were republished in Germany with the original text.

The growth in popularity of the illustrated weekly newspaper attracted many artists to the field of illustration. Charles Bennett, a caricaturist for *Punch* magazine, lent his talents to some surprisingly lively illustrations in books for children from 1857 until his death in 1867. His *Nine Lives of a Cat* has a quality of page design and playfulness that are common in picture books of today. Richard ("Dicky") Doyle designed the original cover of *Punch* and later did the illustrations for John Ruskin's *King of the Golden River* (1851). *In Fairyland* (1870) is "considered to be among the finest picturebooks printed in color during the nineteenth century."[17]

Both Bennett and Doyle worked with printer Edmund Evans. Evans's extraordinary talent as an engraver and his important improvements in color printing techniques were responsible for dramatic changes in picture books for children in the last half of the nineteenth century. In addition to artists such as Doyle and Bennett, Evans recruited artists who would become the best known illustrators of the nineteenth century—Walter Crane, Randolph Caldecott, and Kate Greenaway.

Walter Crane, the son of a portrait painter, knew that Evans wanted to print some quality illustrated books for children, something that interested Crane also. Crane created beautifully designed pictures for four nursery-rhyme books: *Sing a Song of Sixpence, The House That Jack Built, Dame Trot and Her Comical Cat,* and *The History of Cock Robin and Jenny Wren.* Evans and Crane convinced Warne to publish these high-quality "toy books" during the years 1865 and 1866. They were very successful, and Crane went on to design some thirty-five other picture books, including two well-known nursery-rhyme col-

Walter Crane's decorative borders and fine sense of design are seen in this frontispiece for *The Baby's Own Aesop*.
Crane, Walter, *The Baby's Own Aesop*, Frederick Warne, London, 1887, frontispiece. Wallach Division of Arts, Prints, and Photographs, The New York Public Library, Astor, Lenox and Tilden Foundations.

lections with music and illustrations, *The Baby's Opera* (1877) and *The Baby's Bouquet* (1878). Crane had a strong sense of design and paid particular attention to the total format of the book, including the placement of the text, the quality of the paper, and even the design at the beginning and end of the chapters. He characteristically used flat colors with a firm black outline, and his pages usually were decorated with elaborate borders.

The picture books by Randolph Caldecott established new standards of illustration for children's books. Caldecott filled his drawings with action, the joy of living, and good fun. His love of animals and the English countryside is reflected in his illustrations, which seem to convey much meaning through a few lines. Although Caldecott, like Crane, illustrated many books, he is best remembered for his series of picture books, also called toy books. These included *The House That Jack Built* (1878), *The Diverting History of John Gilpin* (1878), *Sing a Song of Sixpence* (1880), and *Hey Diddle Diddle Picture Book* (1883). On the Caldecott Medal for distinguished illustrations there is a reproduction of one of his pictures showing John Gilpin's ride, a reminder of this famous illustrator of the nineteenth century.

Kate Greenaway's name brings visions of English gardens, delicate prim figures, and the special style of costume worn by her rather fragile children. Her art

---

[17]Joyce Irene Whalley and Tessa Rose Chester, *A History of Children's Book Illustration* (London: John Murray with the Victoria and Albert Museum, 1997), p. 68.

Randolph Caldecott was one of the first illustrators for children to show action in his pictures. The design for the Caldecott Medal is taken from this scene in *The Diverting History of John Gilpin*. Cowper, William, *The Diverting History of John Gilpin* with drawings by Randolph Caldecott, London, 1878, illustration (Caldecott Medal scene).

defined the fanciful world of Victorian sentimentality. After the publication of her first book, *Under the Window* (1878), it became the fashion to dress children in Greenaway costumes with large floppy hats. Greeting cards, wallpaper, and even china were made with designs copied after Greenaway. Her best-known works include *Marigold Garden* (1885), *A Apple Pie* (1886), and *The Pied Piper of Hamelin* (1888). The Kate Greenaway Medal, similar to our Caldecott Medal, is given each year to the most distinguished British picture book.

In America, Howard Pyle was writing and illustrating his versions of *The Merry Adventures of Robin Hood of Great Renown* (1883), *Pepper and Salt* (1886), and *The Wonder Clock* (1888). He created real people in his illustrations for these collections of folktales and legends. His characters from the Middle Ages were strong; the life of the times was portrayed with interesting, clear detail. Another of his important contributions was establishing classes for illustrators of children's books. Pyle's students included N. C. Wyeth, Maxfield Parrish, and Jessie Wilcox Smith, all of whom became well-known illustrators in the twentieth century.

By the close of the nineteenth century, children's literature was alive and flourishing in America and England. Pious, moralistic, didactic books were no longer being written. Gone were the make-believe accounts of impossible children. In their place were real live persons living in fun-loving families. Pure nonsense and the fanciful were welcomed in both poetry and fantasy. The old folktales and the fairies were accepted once again. Children's books were more beautiful, with illustrations by recognized artists and pictures playing an increasingly important role. A few magazines had given consideration to the place of literary criticism.

A literature for children, designed to bring them joy and happiness, had begun. However, this body of work was limited to books written for and reflective of the white mainstream culture. The idea that race, ethnicity, gender, or class should be reflected in the authorship or subject matter of children's books was unthinkable. Not until the latter part of the next century would books for children begin to reflect the reality of a multicultural world.

CHILDREN'S LITERATURE: THE TWENTIETH CENTURY

The nineteenth century saw the firm establishment of a literature for children, although the implied readers of that literature were white middle and upper class. The twentieth century saw the recognition of literary and artistic quality in children's books, the growth of children's book departments in publishing houses, and the expansion of both public and school library service to all children. In the twentieth century technological improvements made it possible to create beautifully illustrated, well-bound books for children and just as easy to mass-produce shoddy, cheap editions. The picture book as we know it today was created early in the twentieth century, as were fine nonfiction books for all ages. Most important, in the twentieth century, publishers, authors, and illustrators finally recognized that children's literature needed to reflect the many faces and cultures of American society. As the century ended, the concept of multicultural literature was firmly established in the world of children's books.

Recognition of Children's Literature

Disturbed by the influence of the cheaply produced fifty-cent books for juveniles, Franklin K. Mathiews, chief librarian for the Boy Scouts, sought to raise the level of reading for children. His suggestion to establish Children's Book Week was promoted in 1919 by Frederick Melcher as a project of the American Booksellers Association. Schools, libraries, newspapers, and bookstores supported the event, which became a significant stimulant to the development of children's literature. In 1945 the Children's Book Council was established to promote Children's Book Week and to distribute information on children's books throughout the year.

Melcher also promoted another event that has encouraged the development of children's literature: He proposed the presentation of an annual award for the most distinguished book for children. Initiated in 1922, the Newbery Medal was the first award in the world to be given for "distinguished contribution to literature for children." The Caldecott Medal for the most distinguished illustration of the year was first given in 1938. Both of these awards have had great influence in raising the standards of writing and illustrating in children's books. They also gave prestige to the idea of creating books for children.

The addition of children's departments to publishing firms indicated the growing importance of literature for the young. In 1919 Macmillan made Louise Seaman its children's editor, and other companies were quick to follow this innovation. May Massee became editor of children's books at Doubleday in 1922. The first critical reviews of children's books appeared in *The Bookman* in 1918. Anne Carroll Moore continued this influential work in her *New York Herald Tribune* column, "The Three Owls." *The Horn Book Magazine,* a publication devoted solely to children's literature, was first published in 1924 under the editorship of Bertha Mahony.

Public libraries instituted children's rooms, and many elementary schools had libraries. By 1915 the American Library Association had established a School Library division. The enactment of the Elementary and Secondary Education Act of 1965 made the concept of school library media centers for every elementary school a viable possibility.

The Junior Literary Guild was established in 1929 and was the first organization to send children selected books each month. In the late 1950s, paperback book clubs made it possible for more children to own books and increased their enthusiasm for reading.

The Rise of the Picture Storybook

Improvements in printing processes begun in the nineteenth century continued to attract artists to the world of children's books in the twentieth. Best known and still loved of these illustrators was Beatrix Potter, whose *Tale of Peter Rabbit* appeared at the turn of the twentieth century. Potter later introduced stories of many other animals, such as Jemima Puddle-Duck, Benjamin Bunny, and Mrs. Tittlemouse, but Peter Rabbit's family is the best known and best loved. At the same time as Potter was writing and illustrating, Leslie Brooke was creating wonderfully humorous pictures for his nursery-rhyme picture books. His whimsical details and costumed and personified animals delighted children in books such as *Johnny Crow's Garden* (1903). The other well-known English illustrator of this period was Arthur Rackham. He is recognized for the imaginative detail of his pictures, which frequently portrayed grotesque people and humanlike trees, evoking an eerie atmosphere. He illustrated many books, including *Cinderella,* J. M. Barrie's *Peter Pan in Kensington Gardens, Aesop's Fables,* and Hans Christian Andersen's *Fairy Tales.*

A trusting fowl listens to a "foxy-whiskered gentleman" in this scene from *Jemima Puddle-Duck.* Beatrix Potter created real personalities in both the text and the pictures of her many books. Potter, Beatrix, *The Tale of Jemima Puddle-Duck,* New York, 1910. The New York Public Library, Astor, Lenox and Tilden Foundations.

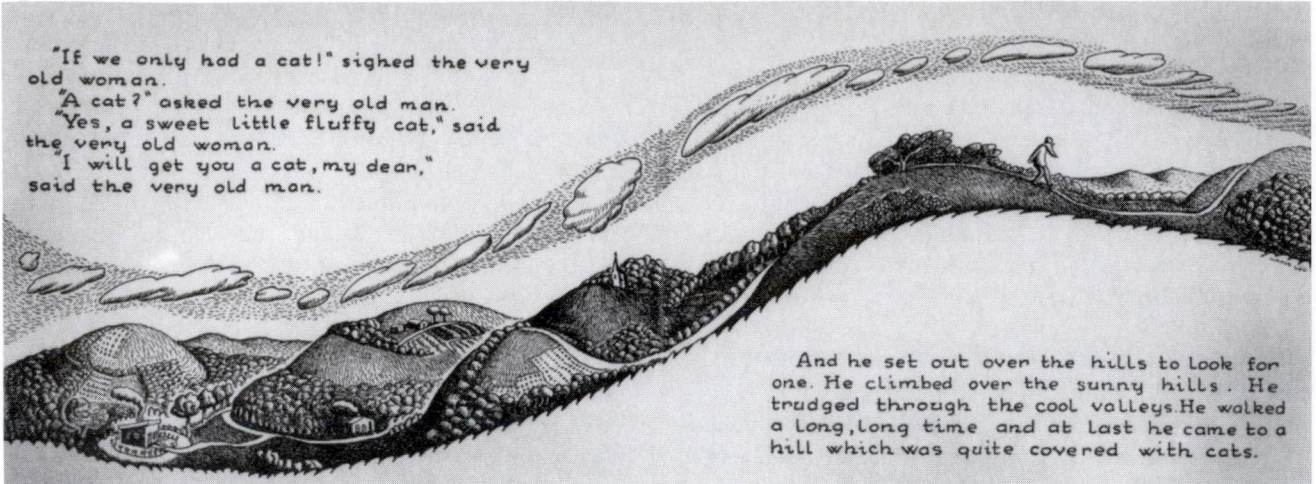

"If we only had a cat!" sighed the very old woman.

"A cat?" asked the very old man.

"Yes, a sweet little fluffy cat," said the very old woman.

"I will get you a cat, my dear," said the very old man.

And he set out over the hills to look for one. He climbed over the sunny hills. He trudged through the cool valleys.He walked a long, long time and at last he came to a hill which was quite covered with cats.

Wanda Gág's delightful tale *Millions of Cats,* published in 1928, has been called the first American picture storybook. From *Millions of Cats* by Wanda Gág, copyright © 1928 by Wanda Gág, renewed © 1956 by Robert Janssen. Used by permission of Coward-McCann, Inc., a division of Penguin Putnam Inc.

For many years these English books, along with those of Caldecott, Crane, and Greenaway, supplied the American picture-book market. British illustrator William Nicholson is credited with creating the first true picture storybook, *Clever Bill,* published in England in 1926 and in New York in 1927. The original story about a little girl and her toy soldier contained minimal text—two long run-on sentences—and it relied heavily on the pictures to tell the story.

Wanda Gág's delightful tale *Millions of Cats,* published in 1928, has been called the first American picture storybook. This is an outstanding example of how text and pictures work together. Like a folktale with its repetition and refrain of "hundreds of cats, thousands of cats, millions and billions and trillions of cats," the story is still popular with children today. It opened the door to what was to become a treasure house of beauty and enjoyment for children, the modern picture storybook.

Progressive education and the growth of the nursery school movement made an impact on the development of books for the preschool child. Lucy Sprague Mitchell of the Bank Street School published her *Here and Now Story Book* in 1921. She pointed out the young child's preoccupation with self and interest in daily experiences. Mitchell conducted classes on writing for children and introduced one of her students, Margaret Wise Brown, to publisher William Scott and his partner, who had decided to start a new firm to publish books just for the very young child. The success of Brown's first effort, *The Noisy Book* (1939), opened the door to the publication of nearly a hundred books by Brown, and to the nurturing of many wonderful book illustrators such as Clement Hurd, Jean Charlot, and Garth Williams. Brown's most frequent illustrator was Leonard Weisgard, who won the Caldecott Medal for their book *The Little Island* (1947). Many of Brown's books are still popular today, including *Goodnight Moon* (1947), perhaps still the favorite bedtime story of all.

Other author-illustrators of this period include Marjorie Flack, who, like Margaret Wise Brown, knew how to tell a good story for preschoolers. Her *Angus and the Ducks* (1930) and *Ask Mr. Bear* (1932) are still shared with youngsters. Lois Lenski began creating her picture storybooks *The Little Family* (1932) and *The Little Auto* (1934) at about this time. These pictured 5-year-olds as little adults doing what young children wished they could do, such as drive a car, sail a boat, or be a firefighter. Machines became popular characters in such books as Watty Piper's *The Little Engine That Could* (1929), Hardie Gramatky's *Little Toot* (1930), and Virginia Lee Burton's *Mike Mulligan and His Steam Shovel* (1939). In *The Little House* (1942), Burton personified a house, which was first built in the country, then engulfed by the city, and finally rescued and returned to the country again. This story, which won the Caldecott Medal, has been called a child's first sociology book.

Dr. Seuss wrote and illustrated the first of many hilarious rhymed stories for children, *And to Think That I Saw It on Mulberry Street,* in 1937. That delightful daredevil Madeline appeared on the Paris streets in 1939. Though *Madeline* was not Ludwig Bemelmans's first book, it is certainly his best known. Robert McCloskey's ducklings made their difficult journey across Boston streets in 1941. *Make Way for Ducklings* richly deserved the Caldecott Medal it received. In the same year, H. A. Rey introduced the antics of everyone's favorite monkey in *Curious George.*

During the late 1930s and early 1940s the United States benefited from the influx of many fine European artists seeking political refuge in this country. These artists found a legitimate outlet for their creative talents in the field of children's literature. Their unique contributions greatly enriched the world of picture storybooks. A glance at a roster of some of the names of well-known illustrators indicates the international flavor of their backgrounds: d'Aulaire, Duvoisin, Eichenberg, Mordvinoff, Petersham, Rojankovsky, Simont, Shulevitz, Slobodkin, and many more. Certainly the variety of their national backgrounds has added a flavor to our picture books that is unprecedented in both time and place.

Unfortunately, until the late 1960s, picture books and their creators still reflected a white Anglo-Saxon world, with a few exceptions. *I Am a Pueblo Indian Girl,* written by E-Yeh-Shuré and illustrated by several Native American artists, was published in 1939 and is perhaps the first book to be both written and illustrated by Native Americans. Although not strictly a picture book as we would define the genre today, this book was marked by especially fine illustrations and book design. Ann Nolan Clark's *In My Mother's House,* illustrated by Velino Herrera and published in 1941, is one of the few picture books from that time that remains in print to this day. *Tobe* (1939) by Stella Gentry Sharpe is a first-person narrative of incidents from the life of a six-year-old African American boy from North Carolina. Illustrated with beautiful photographs by Charles Farrell, the book represents African American life in the rural South, but many of the scenes depicted are common to children of many races.

Before the 1950s however, most books that portrayed people of color showed overgeneralized cultural details or depicted outright racist stereotypes. The bandanna-wearing fat mammy and the kinky-haired, thick-lipped "funny" boy were epitomized in the Nicodemus series written by Inez Hogan in the late 1930s with such titles as *Nicodemus and the Gang* (1939). Asian stereotypes such as slanted eyes, yellow skin, and outdated clothing appeared in books about Asian characters such as *The Five Chinese Brothers* (1938) by Claire Bishop.[18] Even as late as 1973 a Caldecott Medal was awarded Blair Lent for Arlene Mosel's *The Funny Little Woman,* a picture book that objectifies and trivializes Japanese culture. The use of stereotypes extended to Latino cultures, which often found themselves depicted as sombrero wearing, lazy, or fiesta loving. Books such as Leo Politi's *Three Stalks of Corn* (1976) brimmed with idealized Mexican images. Native Americans were misrepresented in many books by illustrators who routinely depicted them as vicious

E-Yeh-Shuré's *I Am a Pueblo Indian Girl* is generally considered the first picture book to be authored and illustrated by Native Americans. Illustration from *I Am a Pueblo Indian Girl* by E-Yeh-Shuré (Blue Corn). Copyright William Morrow and Company, © 1939. Used by permission of HarperCollins Publishers.

savages or as animals or objects. In Maurice Sendak's illustrations for *Alligators All Around: An Alphabet* (1962), the letter *I* page shows dancing alligators dressed as Indians and brandishing tomahawks. In fact, the "*I* is for Indian" stereotype was common in alphabet books.

Even in the 1960s, when illustrations portrayed fewer stereotypical characters, race was not mentioned in the text. Examples include *Whistle for Willie* by Ezra Jack Keats and *Mississippi Possum* (1965) by Miska Miles. In the 1970s such books were criticized for "whitewashing" African-Americans and attempting to make everyone the same. It was not until African American author and illustrator John Steptoe created *Stevie* (1969) that a more authentic African American character was presented to mainstream audiences. Nancy D. Tolson writes that in *Stevie* "Steptoe was able to capture the voice and imagery that many Black children know, bringing a valid representation of Black identity to the picturebook format."[19]

By the end of the twentieth century, more and more cultures would come to be accurately and authentically represented in picture books for children. Even today, however, teachers and librarians need to read and evaluate books in ways that are reflective of sensibilities

---

[18]See Weimin Mo and Wenju Shen, "Accuracy Is Not Enough: The Role of Cultural Values in the Authenticity of Picture Books," in *Stories Matter: The Complexity of Cultural Authenticity in Children's Literature,* ed. Dana L. Fox and Kathy G. Short (Urbana, Ill.: NCTE, 2003), pp. 198–221 for suggestions on criteria for representations of Asian cultures.

[19]Nancy D. Tolson, "The Black Aesthetic in Children's Books," in *Exploring Culturally Diverse Literature for Children and Adolescents: Learning to Listen in New Ways,* ed. Darwin L. Henderson and Jill P. May (Boston: Allyn & Bacon, 2005), p. 71.

Stella Gentry Sharp's *Tobe*, illustrated with Charles Farrell's photographs, is one of the few picture storybooks to offer a positive look at rural African American life in the first half of the twentieth century. From *Tobe* by Stella Gentry Sharpe. Copyright © 1939 by the University of North Carolina Press. Used by permission of the publisher.

John Steptoe's *Stevie* was one of the first picture books to present an African American family through an insider's eyes. It was published before this gifted author/illustrator was 20 years old. Illustration from *Stevie* by John L. Steptoe. Copyright © 1969 by John L. Steptoe. Used by permission of HarperCollins Publishers, Inc.

toward many diverse lived experiences. To be sensitive to matters that are offensive or hurtful to different cultural groups is not enough. It is imperative that we understand how a text and/or illustrations can lead to the creation of reinforcement of stereotypes and how those stereotypes then become fodder for personal and institutional manifestations of racism, sexism, classism, heterosexism, ableism, or anti-Semitism. Children, especially very young children, often approach the world with the view that a stranger is a friend they have not yet met.[20] Individuals are not genetically predisposed to prejudice, bias, discrimination, or hate. These are learned behaviors. For example, in Carolina Binch's illustrations

for Mary Hoffman's *Amazing Grace* (1996), an otherwise uplifting story about an Afro-Caribbean girl, Grace is shown "dressed up" as Hiawatha, with a full headdress, braids, and war paint on her face, a long-held stereotype of Native cultures. Often, illustrators do not do careful research on details of a culture, or they may generalize facts about several unique cultures to one particular group. In *Knots on a Counting Rope* (1990), written by Bill Martin and John Archambault, the story suggests that it takes place in a Navajo community. However, the illustrations mix details from several tribes and include erroneous information about dress and ceremonial occasions. In other cases, illustrators and authors have appropriated and/or rewritten tales that are sacred and secret to a tribe. Gerald McDermott's *Arrow to the Sun* has been criticized for just such irreverence.[21]

---

[20]See Cynthia A. Tyson, "'Shut My Mouth Wide Open': Realistic Fiction and Social Action," *Theory into Practice* 38.3 (summer, 1999): 155–59.

[21]See Laura B. Smolkin and Joseph H. Suina, "Artistic Triumph or Multicultural Failure: Perspectives on a 'Multicultural' Award Winning Book," in *Stories Matter: The Complexity of Cultural Authenticity in Children's Literature,* ed. Dana L. Fox and Kathy G. Short (Urbana, Ill.: NCTE, 2003), pp. 213–30.

E. Boyd Smith was one of the first Americans to produce artistic and accurate informational picture books. *The Railroad Book* was first published in 1913. Smith, E. Boyd, *The Railroad Book,* 1913. The New York Public Library, Astor, Lenox and Tilden Foundations.

The Growth of Nonfiction Books

Increased understanding of human development brought the recognition that children are naturally curious and actively seek information. No longer did a discussion of nature have to be disguised as "an exciting walk with Uncle Fred," who lectured on the flowers and trees. Children enjoy facts, and they eagerly accept information given to them in a straightforward manner. E. Boyd Smith created some of the earliest nonfiction picture books—*Chicken World* (1910), *The Seashore Book* (1912), and *The Railroad Book* (1913). The illustrations for these books were large, colored, double-page spreads filled with fascinating detail. From Sweden came a translation of *Pelle's New Suit* (1929) by Elsa Beskow. Large colored pictures illustrate the process of making clothes, beginning with the shearing of Pelle's lamb, carding the wool, spinning it, dyeing it, weaving the cloth, and making the suit, and ending with a bright Sunday morning when Pelle wears his new suit.

Maud and Miska Petersham used rich, vivid colors on every page of their nonfiction books, which frequently described processes. Their books, such as *The Story Book of Things We Use* (1933), and *The Story Book of Wheels, Trains,*

and Aircraft (1935), spawned some fifteen smaller books and were the predecessors of Holling C. Holling's beautifully illustrated story of the travels of a little carved canoe, *Paddle-to-the-Sea* (1941). W. Maxwell Reed, a former professor at Harvard, started to answer his nephew's questions in a series of letters that resulted in two books, *The Earth for Sam* (1932) and the popular *Stars for Sam* (1931). These books exemplify the beginnings of accurate nonfiction books written by recognized authorities in the field.

As a result of the preschool movement with its emphasis on the "here and now," very young children also had their nonfiction or concept books. Mary Steichen Martin produced *The First Picture Book: Everyday Things for Babies* (1930), while her photographer father, Edward Steichen, provided the pictures of such common objects as a cup of milk with a slice of bread and butter, a faucet with a bar of soap, a glass holding a toothbrush, and a brush and comb set. No text accompanied these pictures, which were clear enough to provoke recognition and discussion for the child. Their books paved the way for other photographic information books, such as Lewis W. Hine's *Men at Work* (1932), which pictured train engineers, workers on a skyscraper, and cowboys. *My Dog*

Rinty, published in 1946, was written by Ellen Tarry and Marie Hall Ets, and illustrated with photographs by Alexander Alland. It was one of the first photo-essay books to present a realistic and nonstereotypical view of a young African American boy, his dog, and his day-to-day adventures in New York City.

Biographies appeared to satisfy children's interest in national heroes. For many years these biographies portrayed only the positive facts about their subjects. Ingri and Edgar Parin d'Aulaire presented somewhat idealized images in their large picture-book biographies *George Washington* (1930), *Abraham Lincoln* (1939), *Pocahontas* (1949), and many more. James Daugherty portrayed many American pioneers with strong, vibrant pictures and ringing epic prose. His *Daniel Boone* (1939) was awarded the Newbery Medal. More biographies for young children became available, including such lively and authentic books as Jean Fritz's *And Then What Happened, Paul Revere?* (1973) and *Poor Richard in France* (1973) by F. N. Monjo. Fritz's books were notable not only for their accessibility for younger children but also for Fritz's meticulously presented research.

Biography was one of the first genres to represent people of color to children. The 1940s saw biographies of such international figures as Nehru and Sun Yat Sen. In 1951 Catherine Owen Peare's *Mary McLeod Bethune* was published. That same year, Arna Bontemps published *Chariot in the Sky: A Novel of the Jubilee Singers*, a fictionalized biography of one of the members of the internationally recognized choral group made up of former slaves. Bontemps's fictional character, named Caleb Willow, was based on the life of chorus member Benjamin J. Holmes, and the book gave readers important understandings about the lives of slaves and their struggles after the Civil War.

By the 1960s social attitudes began to be reflected in nonfiction about historical events and biography. New books for social studies included *America: Adventures in Eyewitness History* (1962) and *Africa: Adventures in Eyewitness History* (1963), both by Rhonda Hoff. These books, based on original sources, recognized children's ability to read complex materials and draw their own conclusions about history. Alex Bealer's *Only the Names Remain: The Cherokees and the Trail of Tears* (1972) was representative of a new emphasis on readable, carefully documented history that attempted to balance recorded history by presenting a Native American point of view.

There is no accurate accounting of the number of nonfiction children's titles that are published, in contrast to fiction titles, but a survey of the new titles would suggest that most of the children's books published today (including series books) could be classified as nonfiction. Many of the top trade nonfiction titles now focus on the stories of people of color that were suppressed for so many years. In addition, nonfiction books by and about members of parallel cultures regularly appear on notable book award lists. By the end of the twentieth century

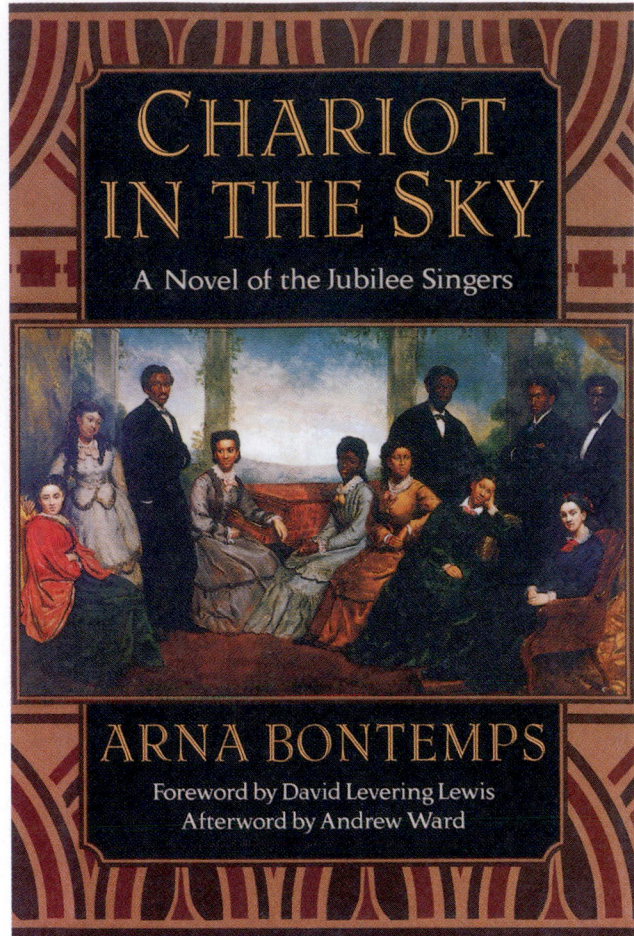

Arna Bontemps's *Chariot in the Sky* is a fictionalized biography based on the Jubilee Singers, a group of African Americans who became known around the world in the late nineteenth century. Illustration used with the permission of Fisk University Library's Special Collections. Copyright © 2002. Used by permission of Oxford University Press.

there was a healthy demand for nonfiction books for all children.

Folktales of the World

The publication of Grimm's *Household Stories* in the early part of the nineteenth century represented only the beginning of interest in recording the told tale. Not until the twentieth century would children have access to the folktales of almost the entire world. However, this genre was probably the first to represent all cultures for all children. A famous storyteller, Gudrun Thorne-Thomsen, recorded stories from Norway in *East o' the Sun and West o' the Moon* in 1912. Kate Douglas Wiggin edited *Tales from the Arabian Nights* in 1909, and Ellen Babbitt brought forth *Jataka Tales*, a collection of tales from India, in 1912. Constance Smedley provided children with stories from Africa and Asia in her *Tales from Timbuktu* (1923). The next year, Charles Finger published stories that he had collected from indigenous people of South America in his Newbery Medal book *Tales from Silver Lands* (1924).

Pura Belpré grew up in Puerto Rico in a family of storytellers and later became the first Puerto Rican librarian in the New York Public Library system. She told many of her favorite childhood stories to American children in library story hours and published a shortened version of a world-renowned tale called *Perez and Martina* in 1932. In 1946 a collection of her favorite stories was published as *The Tiger and the Rabbit*. Harold Courlander, a folklorist and musicologist, gathered many fine collections of stories in West Africa, Ethiopia, Indonesia, Asia, and the islands of the Pacific. Courlander worked like the Grimm brothers, collecting his stories from the native storytellers of the country. The tales in *The Terrapin's Pot of Sense* (1947) were collected from African American storytellers in Alabama, New Jersey, and Michigan. Courlander related these stories to their origins in Africa in his interesting notes at the back of the book.

Lim Sian-tek, a Chinese writer, spent ten years gathering many different Chinese myths, legends, and folktales from her country. These were introduced to American children in *Folk Tales from China* (1944). *The Dancing Kettle and Other Japanese Folk Tales* (1949) contains the favorite stories from Yoshiko Uchida's childhood. She also adapted old Japanese tales for children in her popular *Magic Listening Cap* (1955) and *The Sea of Gold* ([1965] 1985).

Many other collections continue to be published, presenting children with the folklore of the world. They also served as source material for the many individual folktale picture storybooks that became so popular in the second half of the century. Marcia Brown developed this trend of illustrating single folktales in a picture-book format with her publication of the French tale of

trickery *Stone Soup* (1947). Her *Cinderella* (1954) and *Once a Mouse* (1961) won Caldecott medals; her other fairy tales, *Puss in Boots* and *Dick Whittington and His Cat*, were Caldecott Honor books. Other illustrators who have brought children richly illustrated picture-book fairy tales include Paul Galdone, Nonny Hogrogian, and Margot Zemach.

Greater emphasis was placed on individual African folktales, Jewish folktales, and legends of Native Americans during the decades of the 1960s and 1970s. Gail Haley won the Caldecott Medal in 1971 for *A Story, a Story, an African Tale of Anansi; Anansi the Spider* by Gerald McDermott won an Honor Medal in 1973. Leo Dillon and Diane Dillon were Caldecott Medal winners for *Why Mosquitoes Buzz in People's Ears* (1975), an African tale retold by Verna Aardema. Two Jewish tales, *The Golem* (1976) by Beverly Brodsky McDermott and *It Could Always Be Worse* (1977) by Margot Zemach, were Honor books.

A Native American tale, *The Story of Jumping Mouse*, retold by African American writer and illustrator John Steptoe, won the Caldecott Honor Medal in 1984. Asian Americans were finally represented in the medal lists when Alan Say won an Honor Medal for *The Boy of the Three Year Nap* (a Japanese tale retold by Diane Stanley) in 1989. The following year Ed Young won the Caldecott Medal for his retelling of the Chinese tale *Lon Po Po*. Issues regarding faithfulness of translation and accurate representation of cultural details still exist, but folktales

Pura Belpré's *Perez y Martina* was one of the first Latino folktales to be published for children. From the cover of *Perez y Martina* by Pura Belpré White, illustrated by Carlos Sanchez, copyright © 1966 by Carlos Sanchez, illustrations. Used by permission of Viking Penguin, a division of Penguin Putnam, Inc.

Noted collector Harold Courlander traveled the world to compile stories such as those from Ethiopia and Eritrea found in *The Fire on the Mountain*. *The Fire on the Mountain and Other Stories from Ethiopia and Eritrea* by Harold Courlander and Wolf Leslau, illustrations by Robert Kane. Illustrations copyright © 1950, 1978 by Robert Kane. Reprinted by permission of Henry Holt and Company, LLC.

Traditional Chinese stories were retold for children by Lim Sian-tek in *Folk Tales from China,* first published in 1944. Reprinted by permission of the John Day Company.

from around the world are not only an established part of children's literature but also a frequently honored genre.

Fantasy

Fantasy for children in the first half of the twentieth century seemed to come mainly from the pens of English writers. Rudyard Kipling stimulated the child's imagination with his *Just So Stories* (1902), humorous accounts of the origins of animal characteristics—how the elephant got a trunk or the camel a hump. Much of the delight of these stories is in Kipling's use of rich language like "great grey-green, greasy Limpopo River all set about with fever-trees."

Another English storyteller, Kenneth Grahame, brought to life for his son the adventures of a water rat, a mole, a toad, and a badger. *The Wind in the Willows* was published in 1908 with pictures by Ernest Shepard. This story of four loyal friends became a children's classic and has been reissued in a variety of editions. The boy who refused to grow up and lose the beauties of Never Never Land, Peter Pan, first appeared in a London play by J. M. Barrie in 1904. Later the play was made into a book

titled *Peter Pan in Kensington Gardens* (1906), with elaborate illustrations by Arthur Rackham.

The Wizard of Oz, by L. Frank Baum, has been called the first American fantasy. Published in 1900, this highly inventive story of the Cowardly Lion, the Tin Woodsman, the Scarecrow, and Dorothy in the Land of Oz has been enjoyed by countless children.

Talking animals have always appealed to children. Hugh Lofting created the eccentric Dr. Dolittle, who could talk to animals as well as understand their languages. There were ten books in this series; the second one, *The Voyages of Doctor Dolittle* (1922), won the Newbery Medal. Later readings would reveal racial stereotypes in these books, but as with other fantasies, such as P. L. Travers's *Mary Poppins,* readers in the 1920s were not sensitive to such flaws in writing.

Remembering her love of toys, Margery Williams wrote *The Velveteen Rabbit* (1922) while living in England. This story, with its moving description of what it means to be real, has delighted children and adults. One of the most endearing stories of well-loved toys is A. A. Milne's *Winnie the Pooh,* which he wrote for his son in 1926. Eeyore, Piglet, and Pooh may be stuffed animals, but they have real, believable personalities. Ernest Shepard created unsurpassed illustrations of these lovable toys. These stories paved the way for the most loved animal fantasy to be written by an American, E. B. White's *Charlotte's Web* (1952). This book, with its multiple themes of friendship, loyalty, and the celebration of life, is now delighting new generations of children.

Other significant fantasy appearing in the twentieth century certainly must include J. R. R. Tolkien's *The Hobbit* (1937), first discovered by college students and only recently shared with children, and *The Little Prince* by Antoine de Saint-Exupéry, which also appealed primarily to adults. Translated in 1943 from the French, this tale of a pilot's encounter with a Little Prince, who lives alone on a tiny planet no larger than a house, is really a story of the importance of uniqueness and love.

Fantasy in the second half of the century emphasized serious themes. C. S. Lewis's *The Lion, the Witch, and the Wardrobe* (1950) was the first of seven books about the imaginary kingdom of Narnia. These popular fantasy adventure tales reflect the author's background as a theologian and carry strong messages about right and wrong. The term *high fantasy* came into use during the 1960s to describe books that took as their themes the battle between good and evil and other cosmic issues. Some of the most memorable works of high fantasy in the United States were written by Madeleine L'Engle, Lloyd Alexander, Susan Cooper, and Ursula K. Le Guin (see Chapter 7 for further discussion of their work).

In the 1980s authors such as Virginia Hamilton and Laurence Yep succeeded in creating outstanding fantasies, rich with accoutrements of their respective cultures. Hamilton's *The Magical Adventures of Pretty Pearl* (1983) wove motifs and characters from African folklore together with the history of slavery in America. Later Hamilton would delve into other types of fantasy such as "The Justice Cycle" and *Sweet Whispers, Brother Rush.* Lawrence Yep's *Dragon of the Lost Sea* (1982) and others in this series and subsequently his Tiger's Apprentice series were just as richly based in Chinese folklore as Hamilton's books were in African American forms.

As the twentieth century ended, fantasy maintained a strong hold on children's imaginations. Teachers still do not find it difficult to tempt 10- and 11-year-olds into reading J. K. Rowling's *Harry Potter* or Brian Jacques's *Redwall* series, even though the books have hundreds of pages. It is likely that these popular books inspired the many other fantasy titles that burgeoned as the twenty-first century began.

Poetry

The beginning of the twentieth century saw the publication of the first work by a rare children's poet, Walter de la Mare's *Songs of Childhood* (1902). This was a poet who understood the importance and meaning of early childhood experiences. Eleanor Farjeon, also English, was writing merry imaginative verse for children at the same time as Walter de la Mare was creating his poetry. Many of her poems later appeared in a collection titled *Eleanor Farjeon's Poems for Children* ([1931, 1951] 1984). A. A. Milne brought joy and fun into the nursery with *When We Were Very Young* (1924) and *Now We Are Six* (1927).

In the United States, Rachel Field, Dorothy Aldis, and Aileen Fisher were interpreting the delight of the child's everyday world. Frances Frost and Elizabeth Coatsworth were writing lyrical poems about nature. The transition in children's poetry from the didactic to the descriptive, from moralizing to poems of fun and nonsense, had at last been achieved. No longer were poems *about* children; they were *for* children.

The 1930s and 1940s saw many collections of poetry selected especially for children from the works of well-known contemporary poets. These included Edna St. Vincent Millay's *Poems Selected for Young People* (1917), Vachel Lindsay's *Johnny Appleseed and Other Poems* (1928), Carl Sandburg's *Early Moon* (1930), Sara Teasdale's *Stars Tonight* (1930), Emily Dickinson's *Poems for Youth* (1934), Robert Frost's *Come In and Other Poems* (1943), and later his *You Come Too* (1959).

Two fine poets for children, Harry Behn and David McCord, emerged during the early 1950s. Harry Behn's books—among them, *The Little Hill* (1949)—ranged from pure nonsense to childhood memories to lyrical poems about nature. David McCord's poetry is more playful and humorous. His first book of poetry was *Far and Few: Rhymes of Never Was and Always Is* (1952).

African American authors were more prominent in the world of poetry for children than in other mainstream genres. Selected works by the noted African American poet Langston Hughes were published for young readers in *The Dream Keeper* as early as 1932, and Countee Cullen's

The Lost Zoo was published in 1940. Hildegarde Hoyt Swift gave a poetic interpretation of African American experience in her book *North Star Shining* (1947), illustrated with powerful pictures by Lynd Ward. The Pulitzer Prize–winning African American poet Gwendolyn Brooks presented the poignant poems of *Bronzeville Boys and Girls* in 1956. Each of these poems carries a child's name as its title and is written in the voice of that child.

Specialized collections of poetry celebrating the uniqueness of African Americans, Native Americans, and others were published in the 1960s and 1970s. These included Arnold Adoff's collection *I Am the Darker Brother: An Anthology of Modern Poems by Negro Americans* (1968); Hettie Jones's *The Trees Stand Shining* (1971), a collection of Papago Indian poems; and Knud Rasmussen's recordings of virile Inuit poetry in his *Beyond the High Hills: A Book of Eskimo Poems* in 1961. Such specialized collections continue to surface, although they do not seem to stay in print very long. (See Chapter 8 for more information on multicultural poets and poetry.)

Two books about the uniqueness of girls marked a new awareness of feminist perspectives in the 1970s. *Girls Can Too* (1972) was edited by Lee Bennett Hopkins; *Amelia*

First published in 1932, Langston Hughes's *The Dream Keeper* was reissued with illustrations by Brian Pinkney in 1992. *The Dreamkeeper and Other Poems* by Langston Hughes. Illustrated by Brian Pinkney. Reprinted and used by permission of Alfred A. Knopf, a division of Random House, Inc.

Mixed the Mustard and Other Poems (1975) was selected and edited by Evaline Ness.

With such increased interest in poetry for children, it seems particularly fitting that the National Council of Teachers of English established the Excellence in Poetry for Children Award in 1977.

Historical Fiction

Early in the twentieth century, authors employed the genre of historical fiction to give children details about the past. Laura Richards quoted from diaries and letters as she wrote *Abigail Adams and Her Times* (1909). A historical overview was provided in Hendrik Van Loon's *The Story of Mankind* (1921), the first Newbery Medal winner. Starting with *Little House in the Big Woods* (1932), Laura Ingalls Wilder gave children detailed descriptions of life on the midwestern frontier in her series of *Little House* books. Carol Ryrie Brink wrote of a vivacious tomboy in *Caddie Woodlawn* the following year. As with titles in other genres, however, these books reflected the views of the time, one in which white males believed in the doctrine of manifest destiny that justified their claims of superiority over other races and their lands. Although books like *Little House in the Big Woods* are still immensely popular today, it is important for teachers and children to read them critically and to ask questions of texts that see Native American and other races as less than human.

By the 1970s most historical fiction was concerned with social conscience than with personal issues. In 1970 *Sounder* by William H. Armstrong won the Newbery award. This book was a well-meaning if misguided attempt to provide mainstream children with a view of the suffering of African Americans. Armstrong managed to perpetuate stereotypes by portraying the African American family as nameless figures with little energy or inclination to resist their circumstances. In 1974 the Newbery Medal went to *The Slave Dancer* by Paula Fox, who tried realistically to face up to the wrongs of the past. Told from a white boy's perspective, however, the book did little to inform readers about the cultural identities or personalities of Africans kidnapped into the slave trade. Yet only four years later Mildred Taylor, an African American, won the Newbery award for *Roll of Thunder, Hear My Cry,* (Virginia Hamilton had been the first African American to win the Newbery Medal, in 1975). Taylor was finally able to present readers with a profoundly moving and culturally accurate account of the African American experience in the Jim Crow South. The publication in 1999 of *The Birchbark House,* Louise Erdrich's Ojibwa view of the times and places depicted in Laura Ingalls Wilder's *Little House* books, seemed an appropriate way to bring a century of historical fiction to a close.

Contemporary Realistic Fiction

In the beginning of the twentieth century, children continued to derive pleasure from fictional works written in a contemporary setting—such as *Little Women* (1868) and the other Alcott books, and the Frances Hodgson Burnett books, including *A Little Princess* (1905) and *The Secret Garden* (1910). These books continue to bring pleasure to children today—although they read them as historical fiction rather than contemporary realistic fiction. Teachers will want to ask children reading anything from earlier eras to do so through a critical lens. In the case of *Little Women,* they may want to raise questions about gender roles in Alcott's time. Racial stereotypes are not immediately apparent in *The Secret Garden* and *A Little Princess,* but class and social issues do deserve a critical look.

Perhaps the success of the orphaned *Little Princess* accounted for the number of realistic stories about orphans that were written in the early twentieth century. L. M. Montgomery wrote the very popular story *Anne of Green Gables* (1908) about a young orphan girl living on Prince Edward Island in Canada. Seven sequels covered Anne's growing up, her adulthood, and her children. *Pollyanna* (1913) by Eleanor H. Porter was another popular story of an orphan, in this case one who was unfailingly optimistic despite any hardships. Although the child in Dorothy Canfield's *Understood Betsy* (1917) was not an orphan, she was a sickly city child sent to live with relatives on a Vermont farm in order to regain her health. Lucinda of Ruth Sawyer's *Roller Skates* (1936) was not an orphan either but was left with her teacher and sister while her father and mother went abroad.

Kate Douglas Wiggin's *Rebecca of Sunnybrook Farm* (1903) epitomizes the happy family stories that were characteristic of the first half of the twentieth century. Carolyn Haywood began her many *Betsy and Eddie* stories, for younger children, in 1939 with *B Is for Betsy;* these stories tell of simple everyday doings of children at school and home. In *Thimble Summer* (1938) Elizabeth Enright told an entertaining family story set on a Wisconsin farm. In three books, *The Moffats* (1941), *The Middle Moffats* (1942), and *Rufus M* (1943), Eleanor Estes detailed the delights of growing up in West Haven, Connecticut. For the most part, these books featured generic white Anglo-Saxon Protestant families, but in 1951 Sydney Taylor's *All-of-a-Kind Family* and its sequels presented the adventures of five Jewish girls growing up on New York's Lower East Side.

As we have seen with other genres, very few books of contemporary fiction before the 1950s and 1960s portrayed people of color with fidelity or respect. As early as 1934, however, African American poet Arna Bontemps drew on authentic language patterns of the rural South in *You Can't Pet a Possum* and later in *Sad-Faced Boy* (1937). His work, largely forgotten for many years,[22] has seen

---

[22]See Violet J. Harris, "From *Little Black Sambo* to *Popo and Fifina:* Arna Bontemps and the Creation of African-American Children's Literature," *The Lion and the Unicorn* 14 (June 1990): 108–27.

Realistic fiction about African American characters, such as *Sad-Faced Boy* by Arna Bontemps, was published in the 1930s but reached a small audience. Cover from *Sad-Faced Boy* by Arna Bontemps. Copyright © 1938, and renewed 1965 by Arna Bontemps. Reprinted by permission of Houghton Mifflin Company. All rights reserved.

renewed interest with the publication of *Popo and Fifina* (1993) and *Bubber Goes to Heaven* (1998).

The segregation of blacks was clearly shown in *Araminta* (1935) by Eva Knox Evans, but it was not until nearly ten years later that prejudice was openly discussed for the first time in Jesse Jackson's *Call Me Charley* (1945) and Marguerite de Angeli's *Bright April* (1946). *Mary Jane* (1959) by Dorothy Sterling, *The Empty Schoolhouse* (1956) by Natalie Carlson, and *Patricia Crosses Town* (1965) by Betty Baum discussed the new social problems caused by school integration.

Two humorous stories appeared at this time: Robert McCloskey's classic tale *Homer Price* (1943) about Homer's amusing adventures in Centerburg and Beverly Cleary's *Henry Huggins* (1950). Both centered around all-American boys growing up in small towns, and they have remained popular with children for more than half a century.

In the twentieth century, "fiction factories" were developed by Edward Stratemeyer, who manufactured the plots for literally hundreds of books, including *The Bobb-*

sey *Twins* (1904–) and *The Hardy Boys* (1927–), to name just a few. Using a variety of pseudonyms, Stratemeyer would give hack writers a three-page outline of characters and plot to complete. His daughter, Harriet Stratemeyer Adams, continued his work after his death, writing nearly two hundred children's books, including the well-known Nancy Drew series (1930–), until her death at 89 in 1982. Although modern versions of the series books deal with nuclear war, space flights, and submarines, the plots and characters are much the same. The hero or heroine is always a child or adolescent acting with adult wisdom and triumphing over all obstacles—unaided, undaunted, undefeated. The books have found their modern-day counterparts in many other popular series.

Not all realistic fiction told happy or humorous tales of growing up in mainstream America. As the century progressed, realistic fiction often reflected war, depression, and contemporary social problems. As authors for adults began to write more about the various ethnic and regional groups in our nation, children's books also reflected this interest. Lois Lenski pioneered in presenting authentic, detailed descriptions of life in specific regions of the United States. By living in the communities, observing the customs of the people, and listening to their stories, she was able to produce a significant record of American life from the 1940s into the 1960s. *Strawberry Girl* (1945), which won the Newbery Medal, told of life among descendants of Florida's "crackers." *Judy's Journey* (1947), Lenski's most forceful book, concerned the plight of migrant workers. Doris Gates also dramatized the problems of migrant workers in her classic story *Blue Willow* (1940), named after the family's one prized possession, a blue willow plate. Eleanor Estes was one of the first to write about poverty and children's interrelationships in that closed society. Her book *The Hundred Dresses* (1944) enabled teachers to undertake and guide frank discussions of the problem of being "different."

The "new freedoms" of the 1960s were reflected in both adult and children's books. The so-called new realism in children's literature can probably be dated from the publication of *Harriet the Spy* (1964) by Louise Fitzhugh. Harriet is an 11-year-old antiheroine who keeps a notebook in which she records with brutal honesty her impressions of her family and friends and characters in her New York neighborhood. Unlike Lucinda, who made friends with the people she met in Ruth Sawyer's *Roller Skates*, Harriet spies on others. Harriet's parents are psychologically absent, being too engrossed in their own affairs to be overly concerned about their daughter's activities. Children readily identified with Harriet, for she had the courage to think and say the things they didn't dare to say, including swearing. Following the breakthrough made by *Harriet the Spy*, many long-standing taboos in children's literature came tumbling down.

Vera Cleaver and Bill Cleaver wrote about death and suicide in *Where the Lilies Bloom* (1969) and *Grover* (1970); alcoholism and homosexuality are described in *I'll Get*

There, It Better Be Worth the Trip (1969) by John Donovan; and *George* (1970) by E. L. Konigsburg includes divorced parents, a psychologically disturbed child, and LSD. In Judy Blume's popular novel *Are You There, God? It's Me, Margaret* (1970), Margaret's vague interest in religion is overshadowed by the more immediate concern of when she will start menstruating. Blume's *Deenie* (1973) is primarily the story of a beautiful girl who discovers she must wear a back brace for four years. This story contains several references to masturbation.

By the mid-1960s, a few works of realistic fiction such as Louisa Shotwell's *Roosevelt Grady* (1963) showed African American characters in the illustrations, but as with the picture books of the time, they did not mention race in the text. In other cases, books about people of color were written by white authors who had no understanding of cultural nuances. The result was often a book like Theodore Taylor's *The Cay* (1969), which garnered praise and awards from mainstream audiences but deeply offended African Americans for its "racist stereotypes and anti humane values."[23]

In 1967 *Zeely* by Virginia Hamilton, an African American writer, finally captured something of the special pride and beauty of the African American experience in realistic fiction. This story about two city-dwelling siblings who spend their summer at their Uncle Ross's farm provides an authentic and positive look at black history and culture. In 1972 Virginia Driving Hawk Sneve's *Jimmy Yellow Hawk*, a story that focuses on the difficulty that many Native American children find in trying to live in two worlds, became the first novel by a Native American for children. *M. C. Higgins the Great* by Virginia Hamilton won the Newbery Medal for distinguished writing in 1975. This award followed Newbery Honor medals to Hamilton for fantasy, *The Planet of Junior Brown* (1972), and to Julius Lester for *To Be a Slave* (1969), a work of nonfiction. Books by and about people of color that represented authenticity of cultural experience had at long last received recognition. However, even today the number of authors from parallel cultures is small compared with their representation in the overall population.

The literature published for the child's expanding world reflected the changes and challenges of life in the mid to late twentieth century. Just as adult literature mirrored the disillusionment of depression, wars, and materialism by becoming more sordid, sensationalist, and psychological, children's literature became more frank and honest, portraying situations like war, drugs, divorce, abortion, sex, and homosexuality. No longer were children protected by stories of happy families. Rather, it was felt that children would develop coping behaviors as they read about others who had survived problems similar to theirs. Legitimate concerns of childhood, all these

Virginia Hamilton's *Zeely* is considered the first book of modern realism to present an authentic look at African American culture. Reprinted with permission of Aladdin Paperbacks, an imprint of Simon & Schuster Children's Publishing Division from *Zeely* by Virginia Hamilton. Illustration © 1967 by Macmillan Publishing Company.

problems have always existed, but only in the past forty years have they been openly and honestly written about in books for children.

Most significantly, in the latter part of the twentieth century the need for children to see their own experiences, as well as those of other races and cultures, reflected in books was widely recognized and accepted by editors, publishers, teachers, and librarians. The "all-white world of children's books" that had been in place for almost two hundred years had given way to a colorful mosaic.

THE MULTICULTURAL WORLD OF CHILDREN'S BOOKS

As we have seen, very few books published for the mainstream audience before the 1970s accurately portrayed people of African descent or those of any other parallel culture. "Overall, the lives and works of people

---

[23]Beryle Banfield, "Commitment to Change: The Council on Interracial Books for Children and the World of Children's Books," *African American Review* (spring, 1998): 19.

LITERATURE IN **ACTION**

Studying Books of the Past

Children in the fourth grade at the Martin Luther King, Jr., Laboratory School in Evanston, Illinois, were studying the past through the history of their families. Their teacher, Barbara Friedberg, shared with them books like *Miss Rumphius* by Barbara Cooney, *When I Was Young in the Mountains* by Cynthia Rylant, *Three Names* and *Sarah, Plain and Tall*, both by Patricia MacLachlan, and *The Night Journey* by Kathryn Lasky.

Together the teacher and children developed questions they could ask their parents or grandparents in an interview or letter. Here are some of the questions they included on their lists:

What were their favorite foods as children?
What did they do on their birthdays or special days?
What did they remember about their schools?
What were their favorite books to read?
What historic days do they remember?

The students made graphs and charts to depict what they found out. Some children, remembering the story of the samovar that the family saved in *The Night Journey,* asked their parents what was the oldest thing they had in their homes that had belonged to the family.

Frequently, the oldest things were books. Several children brought in the favorite children's books of both their parents and their grandparents. They were excited to find out that their grandparents had read and enjoyed *The Secret Garden* by Frances Hodgson Burnett and *Little Women* by Louisa May Alcott. The children made a display of the old editions and compared them with their new editions. They also exhibited some of the textbooks that were used for reading instruction, including an old McGuffey Reader belonging to a great-grandparent, several Elson Readers that a grandmother had in her basement, and their parents' *Dick and Jane* readers.

Dating and labeling these books for display helped the students see how books had changed over the years. They became aware of how many more books they had than their grandparents had had, for example. But probably the greatest value of this focus unit lay in the discussions that took place between family members recounting the traditions and excitement of the "olden days."

Barbara Friedberg
Martin Luther King, Jr., Laboratory School, Evanston, Illinois

---

of color continued to be either misrepresented or omitted entirely from the literature published for children in the early and mid twentieth century."[24] This does not mean, however, that the voices of people of color were silenced completely. On the contrary, beginning in the late nineteenth century Latinos, African Americans, and Native Americans in particular were working to produce books that spoke directly to children from parallel cultures. The growing movement for social justice and civil rights that began in the early twentieth century and the growing strength of the civil rights movement that followed *Brown vs. Board of Education* in 1954 would eventually open up the world of children's literature to peoples of all cultures.

The Rise of Multicultural Literature

At the same time that mainstream white America largely ignored issues of race or culture, the Latino and the African American communities recognized the need for children to see themselves reflected in their books and stories. As early as 1889 Cuban writer and statesman José Martí addressed the Spanish-speaking children of the Americas in a journal called *La Edad de Oro* (The Golden Age). Published in New York, the four issues were distributed throughout the Americas. The journal's stories, poems, biographies, and essays were surprisingly modern in their content, their literary tone, and their intent to delight children. In addition, Martí saw the need to address social issues without the usual preaching of the time. One story, "La muñeca negra" (The Black Doll) has a young protagonist who prefers her old black doll to the blond white one she has received. Martí also felt that people of the Americas had a rich indigenous heritage as well as a European one and urged children to recognize their indigenous roots, regardless of their ethnicity. Although the publication was short-lived, much of the material still exists in various forms. *La Edad de Oro* certainly laid the groundwork for Latino children's literature. Unfortunately it would take almost a hundred years for a body of Latino children's literature to take root.[25]

In the early part of the twentieth century children's literature published in English for children of color may not have had broad national distribution, but works for children often flourished at small community presses,

---

[24] Kathleen T. Horning and Ginny Moore Kruse, "Looking in the Mirror: Considerations behind the Reflections," in *The Multicultural Mirror: Cultural Substance for Children and Young Adults,* ed. Merri V. Lindgren (Fort Atkinson, Wisc.: Highsmith, 1991), p. 1.

[25] See Alma Flor Ada, "Words of Jade and Coral," in *A Magical Encounter: Latino Literature in the Classroom* (Boston: Allyn & Bacon, 2003).

community centers, and churches. In 1909, the National Association for the Advancement of Colored People (NAACP) was founded by a multiracial group that included W.E.B. DuBois and Ida Wells Barnett. DuBois, who edited the group's magazine, *The Crisis*, included a "children's corner" in each issue and once a year devoted an issue primarily to children.

By the 1920s and 1930s the rich flowering of social thought and the arts that had emerged in New York City's African American community gave rise to an attempt to provide authentic literature for African American children. Called the Harlem Renaissance, this movement introduced the wider world to poets such as Langston Hughes, Arna Bontemps, Zora Neale Hurston, Countee Cullen, Ann Petry, and artists such as William H. Johnson and, later, Romare Beardon and Jacob Lawrence.

The artistic flowering of the Harlem Renaissance led W.E.B. DuBois to turn his attention to the arts for African American children. In 1920 DuBois published the first issue of *The Brownies' Book,* a magazine intended to help colored children realize that being "colored is a normal thing."[26] Considered to mark the beginning of African American literature for children, this magazine published stories, poetry, songs, and pictures to entertain African American children. In addition, the publishers and editors of the magazine attempted "to abolish the stigma of alleged inferiority borne by current and succeeding generations of Black children.[27]

In 1933 Sterling A. Brown took on the racist images of African-Americans as portrayed by so many white writers. His book, *Negro Character As Seen by White Authors,* categorized seven major stereotypes in literature: "(1) The Contented Slave, (2) The Wretched Freeman, (3) The Comic Negro, (4) The Brute Negro, (5) The Tragic Mulatto, (6) The Local Color Negro, (7) The Exotic Primitive."[28] These categories would help future critics from other parallel cultures to further define stereotypes and to articulate criteria for evaluating books about people of color.

In the 1940s African American librarians such as Augusta Baker of the New York Public Library and Charlemae Hill Rollins of the Chicago Public Library began to draw attention to the dearth of literature representing a realistic picture of African American life. In 1939 Baker began putting together a collection of well-written books that presented authentic pictures of African American culture. Published in book form in 1946 as *Books about Negro Life for Children,* in 1971 the title of the collection

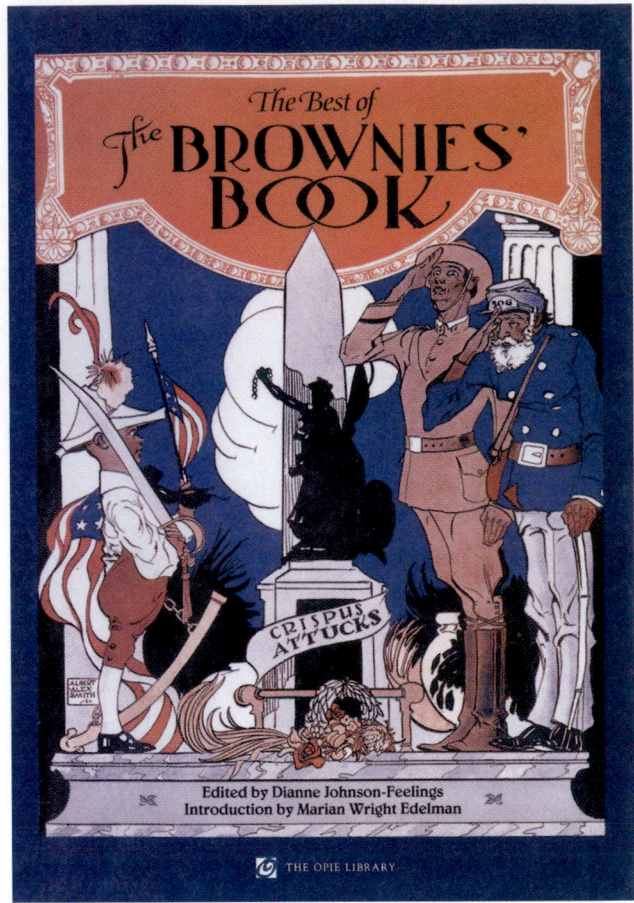

W.E.B. DuBois, concerned that African American children have positive role models as well as well-written stories, began the magazine *The Brownies' Book* in 1920. Used by permission of Oxford University Press. Copyright © 1996 by Oxford University Press, Inc.

was changed to *The Black Experience in Children's Books.* Rollins's *We Build Together* (1948) also established criteria for books about the African American experience and provided a list of recommended titles.

The effort to create Native American picture books that accurately reflected Native cultures started not long after W.E.B. DuBois began publishing *The Brownies' Book.* During the 1920s and into the 1930s, mainstream educators and administrators began to question the treatment of Native American children in the Bureau of Indian Affairs (BIA) boarding schools and to call for a return to the teaching of Native customs and languages. In 1922, Elizabeth DeHuff, wife of the superintendent of the Santa Fe Indian School, enlisted the Hopi artist Fred Kabotie

---

[26]W.E.B. DuBois, "The True Brownies," *The Crisis* 18 (1919): 285, and Rudine Sims Bishop, "Reframing the Debate about Cultural Authenticity," in *Stories Matter: The Complexity of Cultural Authenticity in Children's Literature,* ed. Dana L. Fox and Kathy G. Short (Urbana, Ill.: NCTE, 2003), pp. 25–40.

[27]Violet J. Harris, *"The Brownies' Book": Challenge to the Selective Tradition in Children's Literature* (Ph.D. dissertation, University of Georgia, 1986), p. 58.

[28]Sterling A. Brown, *The Negro in American Fiction* (Washington, D.C.: Associates in Negro Folk Education, 1937), p. 167.

to contribute the illustrations for a collection of Pueblo folktales titled *Taytay's (Grandfather) Tales*. In 1936 Willard Walcott Beatty, director of Indian education for the BIA, who was influenced by other progressive educators such as John Dewey, was determined to create bilingual books for Native American children and to have Native American artists illustrate them. As a result of Beatty's influence, writers such as Ann Nolan Clark followed in DeHuff's footsteps throughout the Depression, collecting Native stories and folktales and enlisting Native artists to illustrate them.[29]

In 1954 the U.S. Supreme Court's *Brown vs. Board of Education* decision set the stage for the civil rights movement and the ensuing rise of multicultural literature. In 1965 the Council on Interracial Books for Children (CIBC) was founded to find ways to encourage authors and illustrators from minority cultures to enter the field. Board members included Scholastic Book Club editor Lillian Moore, civil rights lawyer Stanley Faulkner, and political activist Franklin Folsom. That same year an article by Nancy Larrick in the *Saturday Review* titled "The All-White World of Children's Books" surveyed children's books published by members of the Children's Book Council, a mainstream organization of children's book publishers, and found that of five thousand books published between 1962 and 1964 only four-fifths of one percent (forty books) included mention of contemporary African Americans in either text or pictures. This article, along with other factors at the height of the civil rights movement, seems to have energized editors and other professionals in children's literature to call for a change. At almost the same time, the federal government enacted the Elementary and Secondary Education Act of 1965, a component of Lyndon Johnson's War on Poverty, to provide funds for educational services to low-income children. Among the beneficiaries of those funds were school libraries. As a result, library media directors who were calling for more books about children of color also had the money to purchase them. Initially, many of these books "contained the same myths, stereotypes and distortions previously found offensive but in subtler and more sophisticated forms, which made them more difficult to detect."[30] It would be some years before a more widespread appreciation of cultural nuances took hold among the children's literature community.

With the publication of Virginia Hamilton's *Zeely* in 1967 and John Steptoe's *Stevie* in 1969, a new phase marked by the publication of authentic and accurate books about people of color began. In 1969 the CIBC established contests for unpublished writers and illus-

trators of color and encouraged mainstream publishers and editors to take note. The CIBC's criteria called for high literary quality in manuscripts that were "culturally authentic, and free of race and gender bias."[31] These contests attracted more authors of color to write for children. Walter Dean Myers, Sharon Bell Mathis, and Mildred Taylor are among those whose careers began under the auspices of the CIBC awards.

Over the course of the next thirty years, many awards for books by and about people of color were established. The Coretta Scott King Award (eventually administered by the American Library Association) was set up in 1969 by African American librarians. There followed other awards, including the Pura Belpré and the Américas awards for Latino writers and illustrators, and the Asian Pacific Award for Literature. In addition, the number of presses owned by people of color or created especially to promote multicultural publishing has grown. In 2001, the Cooperative Children's Book Center at the University of Wisconsin listed fifty-nine of these publishers, including Children's Book Press, a nonprofit publisher of multicultural and bilingual books; Black Butterfly Press and Just Us Books (African American books); Arte Público (Latino); Greenfield Review Press (Native American); Polychrome Publishing Corporation (Asian); and Lee & Low (multiple cultures). Mainstream publishers also began to pay more attention to multicultural literature and to recruit authors and illustrators of color. In 1998 Hyperion Books for Children and editor Andrea Davis Pinkney created Jump at the Sun, the first African American imprint from a major publisher. HarperCollins soon followed Hyperion's lead with its Amistad imprint.

Furthermore, although there was a dip in the publishing of multicultural literature after federal support for school libraries dropped off in the latter part of the twentieth century, the number of books written by or about people of color has remained fairly steady in the new century, and a higher proportion of these books seem to be written by people of color. In addition, the number of award-winning multicultural books remains high. In the first six years of this century, three Newbery awards went to books by and about people of color. Some have suggested that this strong showing could be due to the difficulty people of color have in breaking into publishing—only the very best manuscripts by people of color are accepted. However, awards do draw the attention of mainstream audiences to books about parallel cultures, and even though the number of books written by authors of color still does not match their proportions in the general population, there is reason to be hopeful that

---

[29]Rebecca C. Benes, *Native American Picturebooks of Change: The Art of Historic Children's Editions* (Santa Fe, N.M.: Museum of New Mexico Press, 2004).

[30]Banfield, "Commitment to Change," p. 18.

[31]Ibid.

children will continue to have the opportunity to experience many cultures in the literature of childhood.

Defining Multicultural Literature

As authentic literature by and about people of color began to gain wider acceptance in the mainstream world, teachers, librarians, and publishers sought to define this emerging body of work and to develop criteria for judging it.

The term *multicultural literature* grew out of the field of multicultural education, a movement that resulted from the changes wrought by *Brown vs. Board of Education* and the civil rights movement, which called for societal and educational reform. Led by such notable African American scholars as James A. Banks, Geneva Gay, and Carl Grant, the movement was soon joined by people of other races. Eventually other groups such as women, the elderly, people with disabilities, and gay men and lesbians would join the call for justice and equity in education. Their goals included the belief that all students should be helped to acquire "the competencies and commitments to participate" in creating a just and equitable society.[32]

Initially, the term *multicultural literature* referred less to literature itself than to how such books might be used in the schools. Books about different cultures were touted for their ability to promote diversity rather than for their literary excellence and were often reviewed in terms of their minimally additive value to the curriculum. Early on, *any* book about people of color seemed to be celebrated, even when it contained flaws that were abhorrent to members of the culture. Terms to describe literature about different cultures varied, as did definitions. Author Ruth Carlson stated that "multiethnic literature is the literature about a racial or minority ethnic group that is culturally and socially different from the white Anglo Saxon majority in the United States."[33] Merri Lindgren of the Cooperative Children's Book Center (CCBC) defines the term *multicultural* as "referring to people of color."[34] Other authors have defined "multicultural" literature by the topics of discussion and the organization of their books. *Our Family, Our Friends, Our World,* edited by Lyn Miller-Lachman, organizes titles by world geographical areas. In *Multicultural Children's Literature* Donna Norton groups topics into sections: African American, Native American, Latino, Asian, Jewish, and Middle Eastern literature.[35]

Mingshui Cai and Rudine Sims Bishop have suggested that today we might consider *multicultural literature* as an umbrella term that includes at least three kinds of literature: world literature (literature from non-Western countries), cross-cultural literature (literature about relations between cultural groups or by authors writing about a cultural group other than their own), and minority literature or literature from parallel cultures (literature written by members of a parallel culture that represents their unique experiences as members of that culture).[36] We would add a fourth category that we call "intersecting cultures" that represents mixed-race or biracial individuals who desire to be identified by their own unique cultural and racial heritage rather than by a label that implies only one race or ethnicity. Indeed, an alternative to all of these terms or to the term *multicultural literature* might be *literature of diversity.* Such a term allows us to broaden our understanding of the term *culture* to include people with disabilities or with same-sex attraction.

As definitions of multicultural literature were refined during the latter years of the twentieth century another question arose among professionals of children's literature: Who owns the experiences of people of color? The raw feelings held over from the earlier decades when the only published books about children of color seemed to be written by white authors led to lively and thoughtful debates in the pages of professional journals like *Multicultural Review* and *The Horn Book.* The argument about whether only the people of a given culture could write about that culture was a common and often passionate one.[37] Thelma Seto declared that it was simply wrong for Caucasians to write about parallel cultures. She earnestly stated that "when Euro-Americans take on one of

[32]James A. Banks, *Teaching Strategies for Ethnic Studies* (Needham Heights, Mass.: Allyn & Bacon, 1991), p. 28. Also see Geneva Gay, *Culturally Responsive Teaching: Theory, Research and Practice* (New York: Teachers College Press, 2000), and Carl Grant, *Making Choices for Multicultural Education: Five Approaches to Race, Class, and Gender* (San Francisco: Wiley/Jossey-Bass, 2002).

[33]Ruth Kearney Carlson, *Emerging Humanity: Multiethnic Literature for Children and Adolescents* (Dubuque, Iowa: Brown, 1972), p. 503.

[34]Merri V. Lindgren, "Preface," in *The Multicultural Mirror: Cultural Substance for Children and Young Adults* (Fort Atkinson, Wisc.: Highsmith, 1991), p. viii.

[35]Lyn Miller-Lachman, *Our Family, Our Friends, Our World: A Multicultural Guide to Significant Multicultural Books for Children and Teenagers* (New Providence, N.J.: Bowker, 1992), and Donna E. Norton, *Multicultural Children's Literature: Through the Eyes of Many Children* (Upper Saddle River, N.J.: Merrill Prentice-Hall, 2001).

[36]Mingshui Cai and Rudine Sims Bishop, "Multicultural Children's Literature: Towards a Clarification of Concept," in *The Need for Story: Cultural Diversity in Classroom and Community,* eds. Anne Haas Dyson and Celia Genishi (Urbana, Ill.: English, 1994), p. 62.

[37]See Dana L. Fox and Kathy G. Short, *Stories Matter: The Complexity of Cultural Authenticity in Children's Literature* (Urbana, Ill.: NCTE, 2003).

my cultures I feel quite violated. It is a form of cultural imperialism—that euphemism for cultural rape."[38] Others argued that writing was an act of the imagination in which any author could and should engage. Kathryn Lasky contended that the quality of its writing is the only factor on which a book should succeed or fail. "It seems to me that the new insistence on certain rules for authorship and provenance of story (or who writes what and where) is indeed threatening the very fabric of literature and literary criticism," she argued.[39]

Cai, in an overview concerning the ownership arguments, concluded that both imagination and authenticity were not mutually exclusive but that "when imagination departs from the reality of ethnic culture, it leads to misrepresentation or distortion of reality. . . . No matter how imaginative and well written a story is, it should be rejected if it seriously violates the integrity of a culture."[40] Today there seems to be widespread understanding that authenticity is as important as accuracy in writing about parallel and intersecting cultures. We would hope that an author writes out of the emotional and cultural roots to which he or she was born. The only way readers can genuinely explore cultures other than their own is first and foremost through the eyes of insiders. If attempts are made to portray people outside one's own culture, they need to be grounded not only in research but also in close proximity to, and long interaction with, that culture. According to Cynthia Tyson of the Ohio State University, "An outsider to any culture will always be an outsider. I may walk a mile in your shoes, but will always have the option to take them off at the end of the journey."[41] In the end, therefore, we must seek out and encourage the voices of many cultures if we are to provide children with an honest picture of the world.

To fully evaluate works of literature for children, then, we must consider the cultural perspective of the writer—her or his personal point of view—in addition to traditional aspects of criticism such as characterization and theme (discussed in Chapter 1). The Evaluation Criteria box "Evaluating Literature through a Multicultural Lens" (page 110) introduces some of the general criteria that teachers and librarians should keep in mind when reading literature written about other cultures. Evaluation checklists developed by the Council on Interracial Books for Children can be found on the Web at <http://www.always-whitewolf.com/articles/article1.htm> and <http://www.birchlane.davis.ca.us/10quick.htm>. Other sources useful in evaluating literature about diversity can be found in Appendix B. Although the emphasis should be placed on selecting high-quality literature, the Evaluation Criteria may be useful in evaluating literature that depicts individuals or members of a particular culture.

An International Literature for Children

At the same time that the need for books about multicultural experience became more widespread, an interest in international children's books was on the rise. This was indicated by an increased flow of children's books between countries. In 1950 *Pippi Longstocking*, by the Swedish author Astrid Lindgren, arrived in the United States and was an immediate success. This was the beginning of many such exchanges.

The Mildred L. Batchelder Award, for the most outstanding translated children's book originally published abroad and then published in the United States, was established in 1966 by the Association for Library Service to Children of the American Library Association. It honored the organization's retiring executive secretary, who had worked tirelessly for the exchange of books. This award has served as an impetus in promoting the translation of fine children's books from abroad. Such excellent books as *Friedrich* (1970) by Hans Richter of Germany and *Shadow of Ghadames* by Joelle Stolz of France (2004) have been the recipients of this award.

Another indicator of the growing internationalism of children's literature during the 1950s was the number of congresses, book fairs, and exhibitions of children's books that were held around the world. The first general assembly of the International Board on Books for Young People (IBBY) was held in 1953. Jella Lepman, founder of the IBBY, maintained that the organization should serve as a world conscience for international children's books and call attention to the best in the field by awarding international prizes. Consequently, the IBBY awarded its first Hans Christian Andersen Medal to Eleanor Farjeon in 1956. In 1966 the IBBY decided to extend the award to include a medal for the most outstanding artist as well as author of children's books. Alois Carigiet was the first artist to receive this award. Then, in 1967, Jella Lepman created the annual International Children's Book Day, which was appropriately established on April 2, Hans Christian Andersen's birthday. In 2004 IBBY published *Under the Spell of the Moon* (Aldana), a collection of art by award-winning illustrators from around the world.

---

[38]Thelma Seto, "Multiculturalism Is Not Halloween," in *Stories Matter: The Complexity of Cultural Authenticity in Children's Literature,* ed. Dana L. Fox and Kathy G. Short (Urbana, Ill.: NCTE, 2003), p. 95.

[39]Kathryn Lasky, "To Stingo with Love: An Outsider's Perspective on Writing outside One's Culture," *The New Advocate* 9 (winter, 1996): 7.

[40]Mingshui Cai, "Can We Fly across Cultural Gaps on the Wings of Imagination?" in *Stories Matter: The Complexity of Cultural Authenticity in Children's Literature,* ed. Dana L. Fox and Kathy G. Short (Urbana, Ill.: NCTE, 2003), pp. 167–81.

[41]Cynthia A. Tyson, e-mail message, March 2, 2005, 4:34 P.M.

Evaluating Literature through a Multicultural Lens

First and foremost, it is important that any book chosen for use with children be of high literary quality. Given the limited quantity of multicultural literature, this basic requirement may be even more important to remember because "there may be a greater tendency to accept poor literary quality just to have something in the classroom or library."[1] Coupled with an emphasis on quality, the following guidelines may be useful in evaluating literature that depicts individuals or members of a particular culture and may move readers beyond only a superficial approach to diversity and difference.

1. **Diversity and range of representation.** In portraying any cultural group, a collection of books should show a wide range of representation of that particular race or ethnic group. Some African-Americans live in urban settings; others, in rural areas. Some live in upper-class areas; others, in middle-class suburbs or small towns. Some Hispanic Americans make a living in migrant camps; most hold jobs that have nothing to do with seasonal crops. Only when a collection of books about a particular group offers a wide spectrum of occupations, educational backgrounds, living conditions, and lifestyles will we honestly be moving away from stereotyping in books and offering positive images about minorities.

2. **Avoidance of stereotyping.** Literature must depict the varieties of a particular culture or ethnic group. Illustrations should portray the distinctive yet varied characteristics of a group or race so that readers know they are looking at a people of, for example, Sioux, Jamaican, or Vietnamese descent. The portrayal of stereotypical articles should be avoided, such as the sombrero and poncho, feathered headdress and moccasins, or "pickaninny with a watermelon" so often pictured in children's books from earlier decades. Literature should avoid implying that specific occupations (such as computer expert), recreational pastimes (such as soccer), family organizational structure, or values are descriptive of any particular race or ethnic group. (For further discussion of stereotypes, see the sections in Chapter 5: "Picture Books," Chapter 9: "Contemporary Realistic Fiction," and Chapter 11: "Nonfiction Books.")

3. **Language considerations.** Historical or contemporary terms that can be interpreted as derogatory to particular racial groups should not be used in stories about minorities unless these are essential to a conflict or used in historical context. Even then, it should be made clear that the use of these unacceptable terms casts aspersion on the speaker, not on the one spoken about or to. The characters' use of language should accurately reflect their historical and contemporary speech patterns. Some recent books about African-Americans make a conscious effort to reproduce the cadence and syntax of certain language patterns without resorting to phonetically written spellings or stereotypical dialect. Books that incorporate the language of a minority group, such as Spanish, do not need to translate a word if context defines it. Children need to understand that all languages adequately serve their speakers and that no one language is better than another.

4. **The perspective of the book.** In evaluating a book about a particular culture, we need to ask if it truly represents that group's experience. This is a difficult guideline to define because we don't want to suggest there is only one sort of African American experience, for example. Who solves the problems in the story? Does an African American or a person with a disability take the initiative in problem solving, or are solutions provided by paternalistic adults? Are racial pride and positive self-image apparent in the story? Do the details of the story authentically portray the experience of the represented minority? Is the experience of the protagonist interpreted by someone from the dominant culture?

No one is free from his or her particular bias or background. Teachers or librarians in specific school settings might want to add other criteria to this list as they select books for children. It is essential to provide books about many cultures for all children and to choose variety, not merely to reflect the population served by the specific school. Books can help develop children's appreciation for and strategies for critiquing our ever-changing pluralistic society. Tyson notes: "A factor often overlooked in all the discussion of literacy instruction for children has been using the social realities of children's lives as strategies to facilitate vision and develop a critical framework for personal, communal, and civic social action."[2] More detailed criteria for specific cultures can be found in books listed in the Related Readings section at the end of this chapter.

---

[1]Rudine Sims Bishop, "Evaluating Books by and about African-Americans," in *The Multicolored Mirror,* ed. M. V. Lindgren (Fort Atkinson, Wisc.: Highsmith, 1992), p. 48.

[2]Cynthia A. Tyson, e-mail message, March 2, 2005, 4:34 P.M.

In 1967 the Biennale of Illustrations in Bratislava, Czechoslovakia (BIB), supported with funds from UNESCO, held its first exhibition. It is now scheduled to meet in the odd-numbered years, alternating with the IBBY congress. Other international displays include the annual Frankfurt Book Fair in September of each year and the Bologna Children's Book Fair in April.

In 2002 the International Children's Digital Library (ICDL) was created by the University of Maryland with a grant from the National Science Foundation. One of the goals of the five-year project is to create a digital collection of more than ten thousand children's books in at least one hundred languages that is freely available on the Internet. The ICDL is also collaborating with a team of children to create computer interface technologies that support children's sharing of books in electronic forms.[42]

The field of multicultural literature is dynamic and ever-changing. We can (and must) expect many races, many cultures, and many languages to appear in our schools and communities. As professionals we should make every attempt to learn from these groups and to continue to call for their representation in books for children "because of demographic shifts in the nation's schools and communities but most importantly because of a sense of shared democratic ideals for life, liberty and social justice for all."[43] None of us can ever know all the cultural nuances of all the cultural groups in the world. But we can try to be knowledgeable about problems of the past and sensitive to issues that may occur in the future. We should, as Dan Hade reminds us, read *all* books multiculturally. This means, according to Hade, that as we read we must ask some of the following questions of the text: How does the author use race, class and gender to "mean"? What assumptions does the author make about race, class, and gender? What assumptions do each of us bring to the text?[44] No matter what our own cultural background, we need to challenge assumptions about race, class, and gender in all the books we read. Furthermore, we need to teach our students how to do the same.

Today, children from many cultures can see themselves reflected in the pages of the books they read. Perhaps even more important, children can discover other worlds than their own. Books can be the avenues to travel the globe as well as the neighborhood, to find the glorious diversity that exists in human culture as well as the unifying commonalities. More than 250 years from the time Newbery first conceived of it, literature especially for children's enjoyment—children from many cultures—has achieved worldwide recognition. Literature for all children has indeed come of age.

Under the Spell of the Moon, a collection of art by illustrators from around the world, is the result of efforts by the International Board on Books for Young People. Cover illustration from *Under the Spell of the Moon.* Collection © 2004 by Manuel Monroy. First published in Canada by Groundwood Books Ltd. Reprinted by permission of the publisher.

See Teaching Resources: "A Sampling of Notable Authors and Illustrators from Parallel Cultures" for a list that highlights the reach of cultural roots in children's books. Additional multicultural coverage can be found in the chapters in Part 2: "Exploring Children's Literature"; it is identified by the multicultural icon.

RECENT TRENDS IN CHILDREN'S BOOKS

As the twenty-first century began, several trends seemed poised to affect the future direction of children's books. Changes in the ways books are marketed, produced, and used by children are likely to influence the types of literature that children will enjoy in the new century.

Children's Books: Big Business

The publication and distribution of children's books is now big business. Enormous growth in children's book publishing occurred in the late 1980s; children's book sales skyrocketed to $1 billion in 1990. The number of hardcover juveniles published in 2000 was more than twenty times the number published in 1880. In 2004 the

---

[42]Visit the International Children's Digital Library at <http://www.icdlbooks.org/>.

[43]Tyson, e-mail.

[44]Daniel D. Hade, "Reading Multiculturally," in *Using Multiethnic Literature in the K–8 Classroom,* ed. Violet J. Harris (Norwood, Mass.: Christopher Gordon, 1997), pp. 233–56.

A Sampling of Notable Authors and Illustrators from Parallel Cultures

Note: In column 1, A = author; I = illustrator; A-I = author-illustrator. For illustrators, the author's name follows the title of the illustrated book, in parentheses, in column 3.

AFRICAN ROOTS

Author/Illustrator	Culture Represented	Selected Titles
Benny Andrews (I)	African American	*The Hickory Chair* (Fraustino) *Pictures for Miss Josie* (Belton)
Sandra Belton (A)	African American	*Beauty, Her Basket* *Ernestine and Amanda*
James Berry (A)	Jamaican	*Ajeemah and His Son* *Everywhere Faces Everywhere*
Tonya Bolden (A)	African American	*Maritcha: A Nineteenth Century American Girl* *Wake Up Our Souls*
Ashley Bryan (A-I)	African American	*Beautiful Blackbird* *The Cat's Purr*
Alice Childress (A)	African American	*A Hero Ain't Nothin' but a Sandwich* *Rainbow Jordan*
R. Gregory Christie (I)	African American	*DeShawn Days* (Medina) *Love to Langston* (Medina)
Bryan Collier (A-I, I)	African American	*Uptown* *Martin's Big Words* (Rappaport)
Floyd Cooper (A-I, I)	African American/ Native American	*Jump!* *Freedom School, Yes!* (Littlesugar)
Donald Crews (A-I)	African American	*Bigmama's* *Freight Train*
Pat Cummings (A-I, I)	African American	*Harvey Moon, Museum Boy* *Squashed in the Middle* (Winthrop)
Christopher Paul Curtis (A)	African American	*Bucking the Sarge* *Bud, Not Buddy*
Edwidge Danticat (A)	Haitian	*Anacona, Golden Flower* *Behind the Mountains*
Baba Wagué Diakité (A-I, I)	Mali, West Africa	*The Hatseller and the Monkeys* *Jamari's Drum* (Bynum)
Sharon Draper	African American	*Forged by Fire* *Darkness before Dawn*
Karen English (A)	African American	*Francie* *Hot Day on Abbott Avenue*
Sharon Flake (A)	African American	*Bang* *Begging for Change*

A Sampling of Notable Authors and Illustrators from Parallel Cultures (continued)

AFRICAN ROOTS (continued)

Author/Illustrator	Culture Represented	Selected Titles
Valery Flournoy (A)	African American	*Celie and the Harvest Fiddler* *The Patchwork Quilt*
Jan Spivey Gilchrist (I)	African American	*For the Love of the Game* (Greenfield) *How They Got Over* (Greenfield)
Nikki Giovanni (A)	African American	*The Genie in the Jar* *The Sun Is So Quiet*
Eloise Greenfield (A)	African American	*Honey, I Love* *In the Land of Words*
Nikki Grimes (A)	African American	*Bronx Masquerade* *Danitra Brown, Class Clown*
Monica Gunning (A)	Jamaican	*Not a Copper Penny in Me House* *Under the Breadfruit Tree*
Rosa Guy (A)	African American	*The Disappearance* *The Friends*
Virginia Hamilton (A)	African American	*M. C. Higgins, the Great* *Time Pieces*
Joyce Hansen (A)	African American	*The Captive* *One True Friend*
bell hooks (A)	African American	*Be Boy Buzz* *Happy to Be Nappy*
Elizabeth Fitzgerald Howard (A)	African American	*Aunt Flossie's Hats* *Virgie Goes to School with Us Boys*
Angela Johnson (A)	African American	*A Cool Moonlight* *Heaven*
Lynn Joseph (A)	Trinidadian	*The Mermaid's Twin Sister* *A Wave in Her Pocket*
Julius Lester (A)	African American	*Day of Tears* *Why Heaven Is Far Away*
E. B. Lewis (I)	African American	*My Rows and Piles of Coins* (Mollel) *This Little Light of Mine* (Sandland)
Sharon Bell Mathis (A)	African American	*The Hundred Penny Box* *Listen for the Fig Tree*
Alice McGill (A)	African American	*Miles's Song* *Sure as Sunrise*

(continued)

A Sampling of Notable Authors and Illustrators from Parallel Cultures (*continued*)

AFRICAN ROOTS (*continued*)

Author/Illustrator	Culture Represented	Selected Titles
Patricia McKissack and Fredrick McKissack (A)	African American	*Madame C. J. Walker* *The Royal Kingdoms of Ghana, Mali, and Songhay*
Angela Shelf Medearis (A)	African American	*Rum-a-Tum-Tum* *Singing for Dr. King*
Tony Medina (A)	African American	*DeShawn Days* *Love to Langston*
Tololwa M. Mollel (A)	Tanzanian	*My Rows and Piles of Coins* *The Orphan Boy*
Christopher Myers (I)	African American	*Harlem* (Myers) *Lies and Other Tall Tales* (Hurston)
Walter Dean Myers (A)	African American	*Here in Harlem* *Monster*
Beverly Naidoo (A)	South African	*Journey to Jo'burg* *The Other Side of Truth*
Kadir A. Nelson (I)	African American	*Big Jabe* (Nolen) *Ellington Was Not a Street* (Shange)
Marilyn Nelson (A)	African American	*Fortune's Bones* *A Wreath for Emmett Till*
Jerdine Nolen (A)	African American	*Big Jabe* *Raising Dragons*
Ifeoma Onyefulu (A)	Nigerian	*A Is for Africa* *Emeka's Gift*
Andrea Davis Pinkney (A)	African American	*Bill Pickett, Rodeo-Ridin' Cowboy* *Let It Shine*
Brian Pinkney (A-I, I)	African American	*The Adventures of Sparrowboy* *Alvin Ailey* (A. Pinkney)
Jerry Pinkney (A-I, I)	African American	*Noah's Ark* *Mirandy and Brother Wind* (P. McKissack)
James Ransome (I)	African American	*Uncle Jed's Barbershop* (Mitchell) *Under the Quilt of Night* (Hopkinson)
Faith Ringgold (A-I)	African American	*If a Bus Could Talk* *Tar Beach*
Reynold Ruffins (I)	African American	*The Gift of the Crocodile* (Sierra) *Running the Road to ABC* (Lauture)
Charles R. Smith, Jr. (A-I)	African American	*Hoop Queens* *Rim Shots*

A Sampling of Notable Authors and Illustrators from Parallel Cultures (*continued*)

AFRICAN ROOTS (*continued*)

Author/Illustrator	Culture Represented	Selected Titles
Hope Anita Smith (A)	African American	*The Way a Door Closes*
Javaka Steptoe (A-I, I)	African American	*In Daddy's Arms I Am Tall* *Hot Day on Abbott Avenue* (English)
Mildred Taylor (A)	African American	*The Land* *Roll of Thunder, Hear My Cry*
Eric Velasquez (I)	African American	*The Piano Man* (Chocolate) *A Season for Mangoes* (Hanson)
Mildred Pitts Walter (A)	African American	*Justin and the Best Biscuits in the World* *Suitcase*
Carole B. Weatherford (A)	African American	*Freedom on the Menu* *Remember the Bridge*
Jacqueline Woodson (A)	African American	*Locomotion* *Maizon at Blue Hill*

ASIAN PACIFIC ROOTS

Author/Illustrator	Culture Represented	Selected Titles
An Na (A)	Korean American	*A Step from Heaven*
Jose Aruego (I)	Filipino	*Duck, Duck, Goose!* (Beaumont) *Turtle's Race with Beaver* (Bruchac)
Sook Nyul Choi (A)	Korean	*Halmoni and the Picnic* *Year of Impossible Goodbyes*
Yangsook Choi (A-I)	Korean	*The Name Jar* *Peach Heaven*
Narinda Dahmi (A)	Indian, British	*Bend It Like Beckham* *Bindi Babies*
Sheila Hamanaka (A)	Japanese	*All the Colors of the Earth* *Grandparents' Song*
Oki S. Han (I)	Korean	*Basho and the River Stones* (Myers) *Kongi and Potgi* (Plunkett)
Yumi Heo (A-I, I)	Korean	*The Green Frogs* *Uncle Peter's Amazing Chinese Wedding* (Look)
Tanuja Desai Hidier (A)	Indian, British	*Born Confused*
Minfong Ho (A)	Chinese American	*The Clay Marble* *The Stone Goddess*

(continued)

A Sampling of Notable Authors and Illustrators from Parallel Cultures *(continued)*

ASIAN PACIFIC ROOTS *(continued)*

Author/Illustrator	Culture Represented	Selected Titles
Uma Krishnaswami (A)	Indian	*Chachaji's Cup* *Naming Maya*
Dom Lee (I)	Korean	*Passage to Freedom* (Mochizuki) *Sixteen Seconds in Sixteen Years* (Yoo)
Ho Baek Lee (A-I, I)	Korean	*While We Were Out* *Bee-bim Bop!* (Park)
Huy Voun Lee (A-I)	Chinese	*In the Leaves* *1, 2, 3, Go!*
Jeanne M. Lee (A-I)	Chinese, Vietnamese	*Bitter Dumplings* *The Song of Mu Lan*
Marie Lee (A)	Korean American	*Finding My Voice* *If It Hadn't Been for Yoon Jun*
Grace Lin (A-I)	Chinese American	*Dim Sung for Everyone!* *The Year of the Dog*
Lenore Look (A)	Chinese American	*Henry's First Moon Birthday* *Ruby Lu, Brave and True*
Bette Bao Lord (A)	Chinese-born American	*In the Year of the Boar and Jackie Robinson* *Middle Heart*
Ken Mochizuki (A)	Japanese American	*Heroes* *Passage to Freedom*
Kyoko Mori (A)	Japanese-born American	*One Bird* *Shizuko's Daughter*
Lensey Namioka (A)	Chinese-born American	*Half and Half* *Yang the Youngest and His Terrible Ear*
Takayo Noda (A-I)	Japanese	*Dear World* *Song of the Flowers*
Soyung Pak (A)	Korean American	*Dear Juno* *Sumi's First Day of School Ever*
Linda Sue Park (A)	Korean American	*Project Mulberry* *A Single Shard*
Mitali Perkins (A)	Indian American	*Monsoon Summer* *The Sunita Experiment*
LeUyen Pham (A-I, I)	Vietnamese-born American	*Big Sister, Little Sister* *Sing-Along Song* (Macken)

A Sampling of Notable Authors and Illustrators from Parallel Cultures (continued)

ASIAN PACIFIC ROOTS (continued)

Author/Illustrator	Culture Represented	Selected Titles
Allen Say (A-I)	Japanese American	*Grandfather's Journey* *Kamishibai Man*
Kashmira Sheth (A)	Indian American	*Blue Jasmine*
Chris K. Soentpiet (I)	Korean American	*Coolies* (Yin) *Jin Woo* (Bunting)
Aki Sogabe (A-I, I)	Japanese	*Aesop's Fox* *The Loyal Cat* (Namioka)
John Son (A)	Korean American	*Finding My Hat*
Mari Takabayashi (A-I)	Japanese	*I Live in Brooklyn* *I Live in Tokyo*
Yoshiko Uchida (A)	Japanese American	*Journey to Topaz* *The Magic Purse*
Lynette Dyer Vuong (A)	Vietnamese	*The Brocaded Slipper*
Yoko Kawashima Watkins (A)	Japanese	*My Brother, My Sister, and I* *So Far from the Bamboo Grove*
Janet Wong (A)	Korean/Chinese American	*Apple Pie Fourth of July* *A Suitcase of Seaweed*
Sandra Yamate (A)	Asian American	*The Best of Intentions* *Char Siu Bao Boy*
Belle Yang (A-I)	Taiwanese American	*Baba* *Hannah Is My Name*
Lisa Yee (A)	Chinese American	*Millicent Min: Girl Genius* *Stanford Wong Flunks Big-Time*
Paul Yee (A)	Chinese Canadian	*The Bone Collector's Son* *Tales from Gold Mountain*
Laurence Yep (A)	Chinese American	*Dragon's Gate* *Thief of Hearts*
Ed Young (A)	Chinese American	*I Doko: The Tale of a Basket* *The Sons of the Dragon King*
Kazumi Yumoto (A)	Japanese	*The Friends* *The Letters*
Ange Zhang (A)	Chinese Canadian	*Grandfather Counts* *Red Land, Yellow River*

(continued)

A Sampling of Notable Authors and Illustrators from Parallel Cultures *(continued)*

LATINO ROOTS

Author/Illustrator	Culture Represented	Selected Titles
Alma Flor Ada (A)	Cuban	*I Love Saturdays y Domingos* *My Name Is María Isabel*
Francisco X. Alarcón (A)	Peruvian American	*Angels Ride Bikes/Los Ángeles Andan En Bicicleta* *Laughing Tomatoes: Jitomates Risueños*
Julia Alvarez (A)	Dominican American	*Before We Were Free* *How Tia Lola Came to (Visit) Stay*
Rudolfo Anaya (A)	Mexican American	*Farolitos for Abuelo* *Roadrunner's Dance*
George Ancona (A)	Mexican American	*Charro: The Mexican Cowboy* *Mi Casa: My House*
Jorge Argueta (A)	Salvadoran	*A Movie in My Pillow/Una Película en Mi Almohada* *Xochitl and the Flowers/Xóchitl, la Niña de las Flores*
Paula Barragán (I)	Ecuadorian American	*Poems to Dream Together/Poemas Para Soñar Juntos* (Alarcón) *Spicy Hot Colors/Colores Piquantes* (Shahan)
Carmen T. Bernier-Grand (A)	Puerto Rican	*César: ¡Si, Se Puede!* *In the Shade of the Nispero Tree*
Cozbi A. Cabrera (I)	Honduran American	*Beauty, Her Basket* (Belton)
Joe Cepeda (I)	Mexican American	*Juan Bobo Goes to Work* (Montes) *Mice and Beans* (Ryan)
Raúl Colón (I)	Puerto Rican	*Doña Flor* (Mora) *Thomas and the Library Lady* (Mora)
Lulu Delacre (A)	Puerto Rican	*Golden Tales* *Salsa Stories*
David Diaz (I)	Mexican American	*Going Home* (Bunting) *The Pot That Juan Built* (Andrews-Goebel)
Carmen Lomas Garza (A-I)	Mexican American	*In My Family/En Mi Familia* *Magic Windows*
Elizabeth Gómez (I)	Mexican	*A Movie in My Pillow/Una Película en Mi Almohada* (Argueta) *The Upside Down Boy/El Niño de Cabeza* (Herrera)
Susan Guevara (I)	Puerto Rican/ Argentinian	*Chato Goes Cruisin'* (Soto) *Chato and the Party Animals* (Soto)
Francisco Jiménez (A)	Mexican American	*Breaking Through* *The Circuit*

A Sampling of Notable Authors and Illustrators from Parallel Cultures (continued)

LATINO ROOTS (continued)

Author/Illustrator	Culture Represented	Selected Titles
Ana Juan (I)	Spanish	*Elena's Serenade* (Geeslin) *The Night Eater* (Geeslin)
Victor Martinez (A)	Mexican American	*Parrot in the Oven, Mi Vida*
Nicholasa Mohr (A)	Puerto Rican	*Felita* *The Song of el Coqui*
Marisa Montes (A)	Puerto Rican	*Juan Bobo Goes to Work* *Mystery Neighbors*
Pat Mora (A)	Mexican American	*Confetti* *Pablo's Tree*
Yuyi Morales (A-I, I)	Mexican	*Just a Minute* *Harvesting Hope* (Krull)
Judith Ortiz (Cofer) (A)	Puerto Rican	*An Island Like You* *The Hunger of Birds*
Nancy Osa (A)	Cuban	*Cuba 15*
Pam Muñoz Ryan (A)	Mexican American	*Becoming Naomi Leon* *Experanza Rising*
Enrique O. Sanchez (I)	Dominican	*Abuela's Weave* (Castañeda) *Amelia's Road* (Altman)
Simón Silva (I)	Mexican American	*Gather the Sun* (Ada) *La Mariposa* (Jiménez)
Gary Soto (A)	Mexican American	*Help Wanted* *Worlds Apart: Traveling with Fernie and Me*
Ana Veciana-Suarez (A)	Cuban	*Flight to Freedom*

NATIVE AMERICAN ROOTS

Author/Illustrator	Culture Represented	Selected Titles
Shonto Begay (I)	Navajo/Diné	*Alie Yazzie's Year* (Maher) *The Mud Pony* (Cohen)
Joseph Bruchac (A)	Abenaki	*The Arrow over the Door* *Code Talker*
Michael Dorris (A)	Modoc	*Guests* *Morning Girl*
Louise Erdrich (A)	Ojibwe	*The Birchbark House* *The Game of Silence*

(continued)

A Sampling of Notable Authors and Illustrators from Parallel Cultures (continued)

NATIVE AMERICAN ROOTS (continued)

Author/Illustrator	Culture Represented	Selected Titles
Joy Harjo (A)	Muskogee-Creek	*The Good Luck Cat*
Sally M. Hunter (A)	Winnebago	*Four Seasons of Corn*
Michael Arvaarluck Kusugak (A, I)	Innuit	*Baseball Bats for Christmas* *A Promise Is a Promise* (Munsch)
Michael Lacapa (A-I)	Apache, Hopi, Tewa	*Antelope Woman* *Less Than Half, More Than Whole*
George Littlechild (A-I, I)	Cree	*This Land Is My Land* *A Man Called Raven* (Van Camp)
Lawrence Loyie (A)	Cree	*As Long as the Rivers Flow*
S. D. Nelson (A-I, I)	Lakota Sioux	*Gift Horse* *Jim Thorpe's Bright Path* (Bruchac)
Simon Ortiz (A)	Acoma	*The Good Rainbow Road* *The People Shall Continue*
Cynthia Leitich Smith (A)	Muscogee	*Jingle Dancer* *Rain Is Not My Name*
Virginia Driving Hawk Sneve (A)	Lakota Sioux	*Bad River Boys* *The Sioux*
Virginia Stroud (A-I, I)	Cherokee	*Doesn't Fall Off His Horse* *The Story of the Milky Way* (Bruchac)
Luci Tapahonso (A)	Navajo/Diné	*A Breeze Swept Through* *Songs of Shiprock Fair*
Richard Van Camp (A)	Dogrib (Northwest Territories, Canada)	*What's the Most Beautiful Thing You Know About Horses?* *A Man Called Raven*
Bernelda Weaver (A)	Cree	*Where Did You Get Your Moccasins?*

MIDDLE EASTERN ROOTS

Author/Illustrator	Culture Represented	Selected Titles
Daniella Carmi (A)	Jewish Israeli	*Samir and Yonaton*
Naomi Shihab Nye (A)	Palestinian American	*Habibi* *19 Varieties of Gazelle*
Uri Orlev (A)	Polish/Israeli	*Lydia, Queen of Palestine* *Run Boy, Run*
Rafik Schami (A)	Syrian	*Damascus Nights* *A Handful of Stars*

number of juvenile hardcover books published was an astonishing 13,522.

The following statistics on the number of juveniles published in the given years show the increased rate of growth in the publication of juveniles for more than a century.[45]

Year	Number of Books Published
1880	270
1890	408
1900	527
1910	1,010
1920	477
1930	933
1940	984
1950	1,059
1960	1,725
1970	2,640
1980	2,895
1990	5,000
2000	5,119
2004	13,522

A factor not revealed by the statistics is the large number of titles that go out of print each year. Although it appears that many more books are being published, title turnover is far greater today than in the early years of children's books. The life of a modern book is seldom more than 5 years, in contrast to the 10- to 20-year life span of books in the mid twentieth century or, in the case of the very early books, the 200-year life span. However, certain books do stay in print and continue to sell and sell. In 2001, *Publisher's Weekly* listed 189 hardcover children's books that had sold more than 750,000 copies since they were published. Among the top five sellers of all time were *The Poky Little Puppy* by Janette Sebring Lowrey (14,898,341), Beatrix Potter's *Tale of Peter Rabbit* (9,380,274), J. K. Rowling's *Harry Potter and the Goblet of Fire* (7,913,765), *Tootle* by Gertrude Crampton (8,560,277), and *Green Eggs and Ham* by Dr. Seuss (8,143,088). Heading the list of best-selling paperback titles were E. B. White's *Charlotte's Web* (9,899,696), S. E. Hinton's *The Outsiders* (9,695,159), and Judy Blume's *Tales of a Fourth Grade Nothing* (7,131,648).[46]

Series books for children have remained popular in the new century. Of books published in 2003, seven hardcover series titles each sold more than 200,000 copies.

Many of these books are reminiscent of those churned out by the syndicates that produced Nancy Drew and the Hardy Boys. Written to formula and requiring little mental energy from child readers, series such as Barbara Park's Junie B. Jones, Lemony Snicket's Series of Unfortunate Events, and Tony diTerlizzi's Spiderwick Chronicles brought in millions.[47] Movie tie-ins such as *Finding Nemo* and *The Cat in the Hat* account for more than a million copies sold.

Recent years have also seen the rise of celebrity authors on the best-seller list. Madonna, Katie Couric, Jerry Seinfeld, and Jay Leno have all tried their hand at writing children's books. The present climate of celebrity worship has ensured that their books sell well despite the fact that they are not always well written. In 2004 Madonna's two picture books, *The English Roses* (Penguin) and *Mr. Peabody's Apples,* sold more than one million copies.

The negative side of these sales figures is that *none* of the eighty-eight front-list best-selling titles listed by *Publisher's Weekly* was by or about a person of color. In 2004, the Cooperative Children's Book Center looked at 3,200 titles sent to it by publishers the previous year and found that only 407 of those titles were by or about people of color. Clearly, although books about parallel cultures are holding their own in the children's book market, they do not count for much of the profits. Librarians and educators must continue to demand books about people of color for all children. We must also continue to educate the book-buying public about the importance of multicultural literature as well as its quality.

Although children's book publishing has remained strong in the new century, the marketing of books has changed in recent years. Commercial booksellers have joined libraries and schools as major buyers, and although independent children's bookstores and children's book fairs still exist, an increasing market share has been captured by large chain stores. Chain stores have the advantage over independents in that they can buy the cheaper books produced for mass marketing. This also applies to the jobbers, whose entire business is supplying book fairs. Generally, book fairs sponsored by independent stores are more responsive to the schools' needs and provide better-quality books.

Another trend in publishing is the increased number of mergers between publishing houses and large conglomerates. Few independently owned publishing companies are left today. A publishing company owned by a large conglomerate must show a profit; it is measured against the success of other companies in the corporation, most of which have nothing to do with publishing. Many of these changes began in the late 1970s, when the cutback in federal assistance to education was

[45]*Bowker Annual of Library and Book Trade Information,* 50th ed. (New York: Bowker, 2005), p. 522.

[46]Diane Roback and Jason Britton, "All-Time Best Selling Children's Books," *Publisher's Weekly* 248.51 (December 17, 2001): 24–32.

[47]Diane Roback, "Big Year for *Harry, Lemony, Cat in the Hat*," *Publisher's Weekly* 21.12 (March 12, 2004): 35–43.

felt in schools throughout the United States. To counteract the loss of school sales, publishers increased their emphasis on the trade book market. In spite of the mergers and company changes in response to the economic pressures of recent years, however, children's hardcover book sales in 2004 were $581.4 million.[48]

Shifts in Publishing Emphases

Picture storybooks and picture-book formats have dominated the market over the past twenty-five years, but that trend may now be at an end. Many publishers' catalogs still highlight their hardcover picture storybooks or profusely illustrated books, but hardcover fiction, especially fantasy, has blossomed in the early years of the twenty-first century. Publishers find this trend encouraging, not least because fiction is more economical to print. At the same time, the extreme profits from the Harry Potter series have led to an increase in bidding wars for new series titles among publishers. These auctions, as well as generous author advances and high-profile agents, had been characteristic of the adult-trade rather than the children's book market. We could see a reversal of this trend toward fantasy series if the market becomes saturated. Indeed, this may have happened with hardcover picture books. With a dropping birth rate and a decrease in library funding, the huge number of picture books published each year through the 1990s could not be sustained in a milieu that increasingly became dominated by bookstore sales. This could mean that authors of best-selling picture books (more than 100,00 copies sold) may win out over new and untried talent as the market for picture books shrinks.[49]

If many of the current works of fantasy are formulaic series, there are also many well-written works of fantasy available to children. Experienced writers such as Tamora Pierce, Diana Wynne Jones, and Terry Pratchet

have been joined by newcomers such as Catherine Fisher, Cornelia Funke, Suzanne Collins, and Philip Reeve in providing high-quality, exciting works of fantasy for children and young adults.

In general, the content of realistic fiction has moved away from the narrowly focused "problem novel" of the 1960s and 1970s. Serious fiction is more realistically balanced, with characters less prone to despair than in the books of a decade or two ago. Many sober themes remain, of course. Published in the early twenty-first century, *Speak* by Laurie Halse Anderson (1999) deals with date rape, and *No Laughter Here* by Rita Williams-Garcia (2004) deals with genital mutilation.

If the picture book is in a slump at the moment, there seems to be an increased emphasis on the visual, especially in the rise of graphic novels and interactive picture books for children and young adults. The international phenomenon of Japanese anime (animated films) and manga (graphic novels) has resulted in a flood of publications in English. Of questionable quality, these comic book adventure stories are tremendously popular, particularly with adolescents, and they have inspired clubs, conventions, and role-playing all over the world. The comic book format has also given rise to some serious exploration in books for older readers and adults. Art Spiegelman's *Maus: A Survivor's Tale*, an account of the Holocaust first published in 1986, is considered one of the touchstones of excellence in graphic novels. Spiegelman's *In the Shadow of No Towers* (2004) is an equally chilling account of the World Trade Center disaster and its aftermath. Iranian-born Marjane Satrapi has also used the graphic format in *Persépolis: A Story of a Childhood* and its sequel. Her first book won the American Library Association's Alex Award (for adult books that appeal to teenagers). On a lighter note, Avi and Brian Flocca explored the graphic novel format in *City of Light, City of Dark* in 1991 and Orchard Books reissued it with a new cover in 2004. Andy Runton's *Owly* (2004), Jef Czekaj's *Grampa and Julie: Shark Hunters* (2004), and Mark Alan Stamaty's *Alia's Mission* are among the best graphic novels for middle-grade readers.

Toy books have risen to new heights with Robert Sabuda and Matthew Reinhart's *Encyclopedia Prehistorica: Dinosaurs* (2005). This wonder of paper engineering presents multiple pop-ups of dinosaurs on each double-page spread and will delight readers of all ages. This type of multimodal interweaving of image and word can be found in other formats for older readers. In *Monster* (1999) Walter Dean Myers mixes handwritten journal entries, a film script, and black-and-white photographs to relate the story of a 16-year-old on trial for murder. Paula Danzinger's funny *The United Tates of America* (2002) includes main character Skate Tate's scrapbook as a 32-

[48]*Bowker Annual*, 2005, p. 527.

[49]Diane Roback, "The Kids Are Alright, But . . . ," *Publisher's Weekly* 252.8 (February 21, 2005): 75–81.

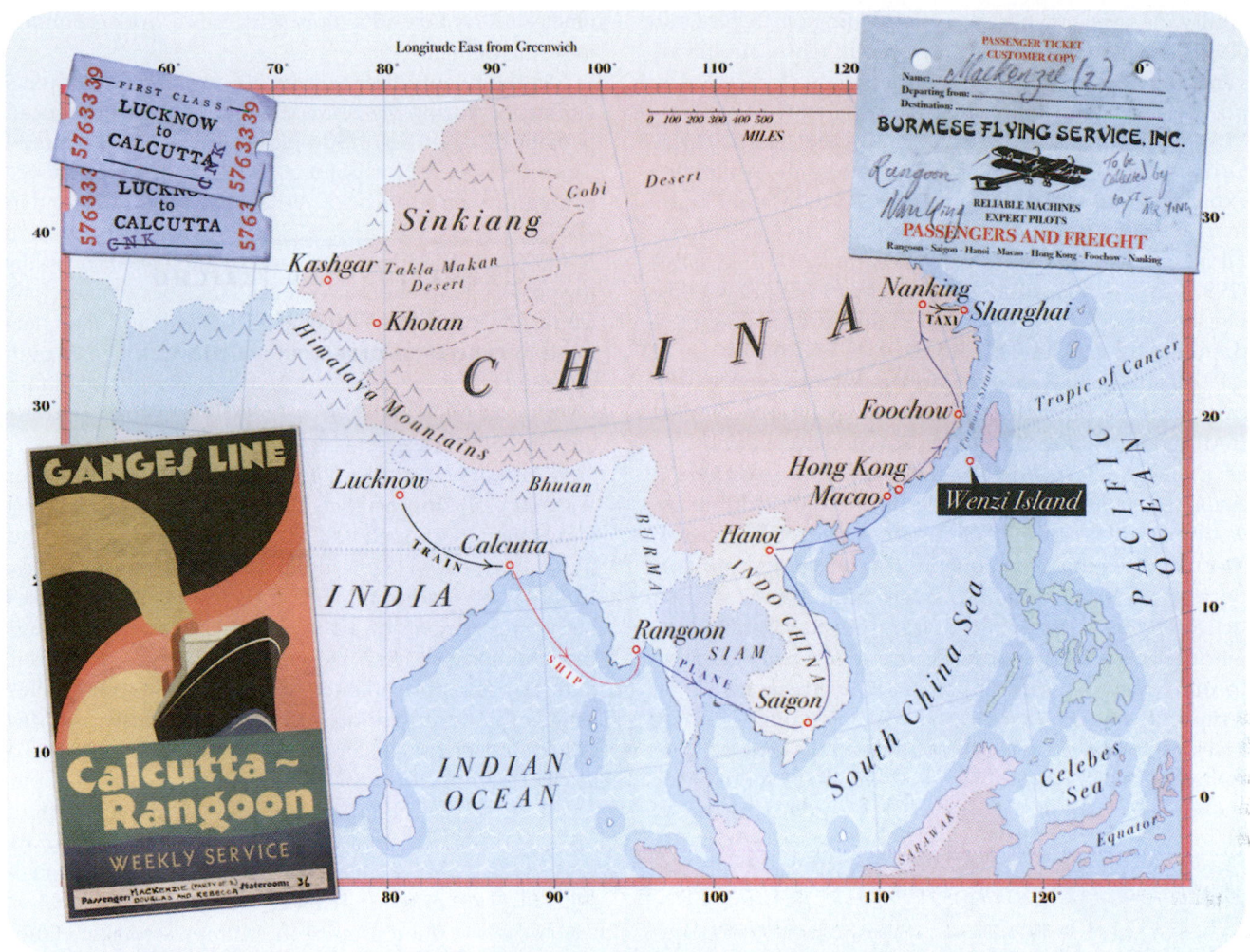

Joshua Mowll's *Operation Red Jericho* is a traditional adventure story made multimodal with diagrams, maps, photos of artifacts, and other visual information. *Operation Red Jericho: The Guild of Specialists: Book 1.* Written by Joshua Mowll. Map illustration copyright © 2005 Joshua Mowll. Reproduced by permission of the publisher, Candlewick Press, Inc., Cambridge, MA, on behalf of Walker Books, Ltd., London.

page, full-color insert. Dr. Ernest Drake's *Dragonology* (2003), *Egyptology* by Emily Sands (2004), and *Wizardology by Master Merlin* (Anne Yvonne Gilbert, 2005) are multimodal texts that includes pull-outs, pop-ups, maps, and other visuals, as well as novelty items like dragon skin, phoenix feathers, and jewels embedded in the pages. *Operation Red Jericho* (2005) by Joshua Mowll is an adventure novel bound like a personal diary and including maps, diagrams, and other documents. Books such as Vera B. Williams's *Amber Was Brave, Essie Was Smart* (2001) and Dav Pilkey's popular Captain Underpants series seem to reflect the increasingly visual interests of twenty-first-century children by including a variety of images within the context of the traditional novel.

Changes in Writing and Illustration

Today writers and illustrators have great freedom to experiment with style and format. For years it was assumed that all books for children should be told in the third person, past tense; children were not supposed to like introspective first-person accounts. The recognition and popularity of such books as *Meet the Austins* (1960) by Madeleine L'Engle and Judy Blume's *Are You There, God? It's Me, Margaret* (1970) certainly put an end to this myth. Even historical fiction and biography have assumed the first-person point of view in such books as *My Brother Sam Is Dead* (1974). Linda Sue Park's *My Name Was Keoko* (2002) and Brian Doyle's *Mary Ann Alice* (2002) demonstrate how this device gives readers a sense of immediacy and intimate participation in the character's experience.

Another trend in writing can be seen in books told from various points of view. The use of shifting points of view, which can heighten the suspense of a story, serves the same purposes as flashbacks, cut-ins, and other devices on television and in films. There also seems to be an increasing interest in experimenting with language styles and structures. In *Music of Dolphins* (1996), Karen Hesse changes grammatical structures from simple to highly complex to indicate the difference between the character's inner mental speech and her spoken-language ability. Hesse's Newbery award–winning *Out of the Dust* (1997) is told in the first person, present tense, but in free verse rather than prose. This emphasis on stories told in poetry can be seen in the huge increase in novels in verse. Virginia Euwer Wolfe, Sharon Creech, Mel Glenn, Nikki Grimes, and Angela Johnson are among those authors experimenting with novels in verse. Author Paul Fleishman displays innovative writing styles in *Joyful Noise: Poems for Two Voices* (1988), *Bull Run* (1993), *Seedfolks* (1997), *Seek* (2001), and *Zap* (2005). With each new book Fleishman seems to be pushing literary forms for children into the postmodern world.

As authors tell stories in intriguing new ways, they can create books that are hard to classify according to traditional definitions of genre. For instance, books such as *The Root Cellar* (1983) by Janet Lunn and *The Devil's Arithmetic* (1988) by Jane Yolen have combined fantasy with historical fiction. African American writer Walter Moseley uses this technique in *47*, a vivid and moving portrait of slavery in 1832, intermingled with science fiction/fantasy involving mythical African and otherworldly characters. These books use an element of fantasy to unite the past with the present and to capture contemporary children's interest in an earlier time. In other cases, historical fiction such as Elizabeth Updale's *Montmorency: Doctor, Thief, Murderer* (2005) reads more like a nineteenth-century adventure story than a work grounded in historical fact.

In the twenty-first century, we find more children's authors exploring the genre of magic realism, influenced perhaps by noted South American writers such as Gabriel García Márquez. This point of view accepts the presence of magic in the real world. Writers like David Almond in *The Fire-Eaters* (2004) and Adele Griffin in *Where I Want to Be* (2005) ask their readers to accept (or at least consider) the possibility of alternative, even fantastic, explanations for real events. Chris Crutcher's *The Sledding Hill* is narrated by a dead character and includes Crutcher's own appearance in the book, to testify before a censorship hearing on his book *Warren Peese*. Books such as these are difficult to classify as traditional fantasy.

Current books cross conventional genre lines in other ways as well. For instance, the boundaries between fact and fiction are crossed and recrossed by Joanna Cole and illustrator Bruce Degen in the Magic School Bus series. In these best-selling nonfiction books, Ms. Frizzle takes her young students on a fantasy field trip and then brings them home again to an everyday world of group projects and science reports. Blends of story and information for younger children are offered in Lois Ehlert's *Leaf Man* (2005) and other concept books. Books like this use a playful approach to draw readers into a content topic.

Illustrators have also departed from old notions about what is appropriate for a children's book. Earlier in this century, for instance, experts advised against photography in children's books, claiming that photos were not clear enough or appealing enough for a young audience. Now, thanks to improved quality of reproduction and rising standards of artistry, nonfiction books such as Alexandra Siy's *Mosquito Bite* and Stephen Kramer's *Hidden Worlds* can show micrographs of insects, algae, or dust mites.

Technology advances have also lifted restrictions and encouraged experimentation with new tools for picture making. Daniel Pinkwater illustrated his story *The Muffin Fiend* (1986) on his Macintosh computer. Now computer-generated art is regularly seen in picture books such as David Kirk's Little Robot series. Cameras, scanners, and other equipment can now efficiently reproduce illustrations created in any medium, from the plasticine creations in Barbara Reid's *The Subway Mouse* (2005) to the natural and man-made materials in Jeannie Baker's intricate collage illustrations for *Home* (2004). Although new uses of media might be the most noticeable change in illustrations, artists have also established a more important role for the

Advances in modern printing techniques have made possible reproduction of three-dimensional art in such books as Barbara Reid's *Subway Mouse*. *The Subway Mouse* copyright © 2003 by Barbara Reid. All rights reserved. Reprinted by permission of Scholastic Canada Ltd.

visual elements in books. In picture storybooks, some artists are creating more and more complex interactions between pictures and print, as David Wiesner does in his Caldecott Medal winner, *The Three Pigs* (2001). Nonfiction has benefited from improved printing techniques as well. Tanya Bolden's *Maritcha: A Nineteenth Century American Girl* and Steve Jenkins's beautiful collage illustrations in *Prehistoric Actual Size* are as well designed and artistically pleasing as any good picture storybook.

Children's Literature in the School and Community

The last several decades of the twentieth century saw the growing use of children's trade books in classrooms—for reading instruction, integrated language arts programs, and a variety of uses across the curriculum. Research conducted in the last third of the twentieth century led to new understandings about children's literacy learning and brought the use of real literature to the classrooms of many schools. Unlike the 1960s, this was not a trend nurtured by government funds; it was fostered by the grassroots interest of teachers and the encouragement of professional associations.

The emphasis on standards and testing has been a phenomenon in predominately English-speaking countries such as Canada, the United Kingdom, and Australia. In the United States in the early twenty-first century, with the advent of the "No Child Left Behind" measure and an increased emphasis on testing, the extent of the use of children's books in instructional programs across the country is difficult to estimate. A renewed emphasis on the systematic teaching of phonics has also had a negative impact on the trend to use real literature rather than textbooks. Another complicating factor is that teachers and supervisors often use the same terminology to describe widely different practices.

The disturbing aspect of this trend is that some instructional programs use literature without regard for its imaginative and aesthetic characteristics. In other instances, students read "real" books, but still use the same skill-and-drill activities that teachers were trying to avoid by switching from the basal textbooks. In both cases, the move toward more standardized measures of assessment and the skill-and-drill of phonics instruction have created a context of "forced choice" for many teachers who want to keep good literary works written for children and young adults at the core of their literacy instruction. Uses of literature that ruin children's enjoyment of good books are a real disservice to children, teachers, and literature.

Children's books have long been part of many community literacy programs. One such program that gained national prominence early on was the Citizenship Schools. Created in 1957 by Septima Poinsette Clark, an African American educator and activist, the schools provided valuable training to adults throughout the eleven states of the Deep South. Based on older models of literacy schools, such as Cora Wilson Stewart's Moonlight Schools begun in 1911, the Citizenship Schools used books written for children and young adults when Clark discovered that parents' motivation to read to and with their children was a hook.

By the 1980s, problems of illiteracy in the United States were widely acknowledged. Government agencies with an eye to tight budgets worked to involve corporations and private foundations in assisting community and school efforts, particularly among the poor. An Internet search using the term *community literacy programs* turned up more than eight million entries. In addition, corporations and national education organizations sponsor literacy projects such as the National Education Association's Read across America initiative. First Lady Laura Bush, a former elementary teacher and librarian, has sponsored many literacy and library-related projects, including the Ready to Read, Ready to Learn initiative. Another important national project is the Reach Out and Read Program begun at the Boston Medical Center, which includes information about books and literacy as part of well-baby checkups.

Recognition of children's literature has also spread worldwide through many international and national programs. The International Board on Books for Young People has moved beyond recognition of quality literature worldwide to providing books and publishing opportunities to developing countries. In South Africa, the Centre for the Book has developed a program that seeks to reach young children and their caregivers with good books that promote a culture of reading. Called First Words in Print, the program has donated sets of four books printed in one of the eleven official South African languages to more than 25,000 poor children.

The Development of a Multiliterate Society

Dire predictions have been made about the death of the book as we know it today; our society has been called a postliterate society. Modern technology has certainly affected literature and the arts, with developments like interactive fiction, where the "reader" responds to and creates plot variations for the story appearing on her computer screen. Computers can be programmed to generate poetry, pictures, and music. Some of these works meet high standards of artistry and receive appropriate critical recognition. With the rise of CD-ROMs, more publishers are putting popular books on discs or making them available for downloading onto personal digital players like Apple's iPod.

The Internet and the World Wide Web have had an incredible impact on the world of children's books in the past few years. Through the International Children's Digital Library <http://www.icdlbooks.org>, children from all over the world have access to books if they can access a computer. Many authors have their own Web sites, and some will interact with their readers. Even more exciting

INTO THE CLASSROOM

The Changing World of Children's Books

Before encouraging children to study literary classics, we need to provide them with some background about how our society's attitudes, mores, and points of view have changed over the years. Many of the excellent works of literature from centuries past were not written with the understandings we now have about equal rights, diverse cultures, or people with disabilities. At the same time, authors like Harriet Beecher Stowe, Charles Kingsley, and Anna Sewell had some power to influence changes in social customs and attitudes. By integrating the reading of classics into historical studies of the Industrial Revolution, women's and children's rights, slavery and the civil rights movement, and human rights issues, today's teachers can help children develop a keener awareness of the author's point of view. In addition, such studies can deepen their understanding of how literature and the arts contribute to our ever-changing social and political climate.

1. **Comparison of Caldecott Medal Books.** Ask children to compare Caldecott Medal books over the past fifty years. How have the illustrations changed? What changes do they notice in the stories?
2. **The History of Books.** Conduct a classroom study on the history of books. What factors have caused changes in books' appearance? How has the audience for books changed?

3. **Comparison of Classic and Contemporary Characters.** Read a classic and a contemporary story that have similar characters and problems—for example, *Anne of Green Gables* (Montgomery, 1908) and *The Great Gilly Hopkins* (Paterson, 1978). Create a Venn diagram to show how the characters are alike and different. How do each of the books reflect the author's view of childhood for that period?
4. **Timeline Activity.** Create a timeline showing important milestones in the history of books.
5. **The History of Writing and Printing.** Study the history of writing and printing. How has this factor affected the history of books? Visit Web sites of important libraries and museums, such as the British Library <http://www.bl.uk> or the Getty Museum <www.getty.edu/art/exhibitions/making> to see more about the history of books.

 Go to the Online Learning Center at **www.mhhe.com/kiefer9e** or your Resources CD-ROM to find these additional classroom activities:

6. **Printmaking**
7. **Bookmaking**
8. **Online publishing**

---

are the chat rooms where children can discuss books with other readers from around the world. Online bookstores welcome reader reviews, and a book search will reveal that children are responding with enthusiastic and often insightful commentary. Furthermore, Web sites of groups that provide information on and criteria for evaluating multicultural books and the Web sites of multicultural publishers give us access to multicultural titles that in the past would have been hard to find.[50]

It seems likely, then, that today's youth will become multiliterate, using the new technologies for the rapid retrieval of information of all kinds, for writing and editing their thoughts, for communicating about books with children in distant places, and for creating original programs of their own. Just as many youth today are multilingual,

so the youth of the future will become multiliterate and multimodal, reading a wide variety of formats. They will still need reading for a wide range of skills, and they will need books for pleasure. Perhaps, most importantly, they will still need to touch the pages of books and be able to hug books close to their hearts.

As we move further into the new century, the future of the book is uncertain. Computers, videotapes, cassettes, films, cable television—all have the potential to give us instant information in many forms. Will the book be as important in the twenty-first century as it was in the twentieth? Those of us who love literature and have witnessed its positive influence on children's lives can only hope that it will be—that it will continue to live and flourish.

---

[50]See, for example, Oyate <www.oyate.org>, the Cooperative Children's Book Center <http://www.soemadison.wisc.edu/ccbc>, Children's Book Press <http://www.childrensbookpress.org/>, Lee & Low <http://www.leeandlow.com>, and Groundwood Books <http://www.groundwoodbooks.com>.

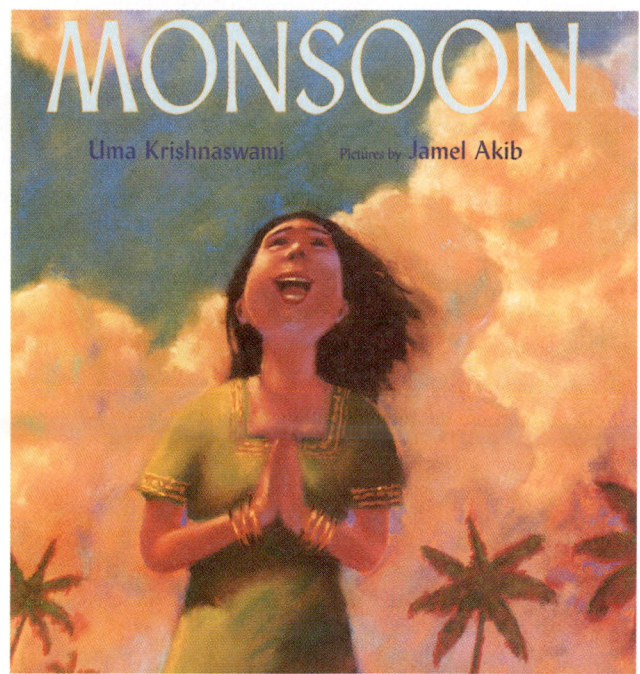

The advocacy of educators and other professionals has helped to encourage the publication of books such as these about many parallel cultures. Cover illustration from *Jamari's Drum*. Text © 2004 by Eboni Bynum and Roland Jackson. Illustrations © 2004 by Baba Wagué Diakité. First published in Canada by Groundwood Books Ltd. Reprinted by permission of publisher; *Poems to Dream Together, Poemas para Soñar Juntos* by Francisco X. Alarcón. Illustrated by Paula Barragán. Copyright © 2005. Used by permission of Lee & Low Books, Inc.; Cover of *Monsoon* by Uma Krishnaswami. Jacket art © 2003 by Jamel Akib. Reprinted by permission of Farrar, Strauss, & Giroux, LLC; Reprinted with permission of the publisher, Children's Book Press, San Francisco, CA, www.childrensbookpress.org. *What's the Most Beautiful Thing You Know About Horses?* Illustration copyright © 1998 by George Littlechild.

Chapter Review

Go to the Online Learning Center at **www.mhhe.com/kiefer9e** or your Resources CD-ROM to take chapter quizzes, practice with key terms, and review the chapter.

Explorations

1. Interview five adults of different ages and ask about their favorite childhood books and reading interests. How similar are their responses? How much overlapping of titles is there?

2. Conduct a survey of your literature class to find out how many students have read *Little Women, Alice's Adventures in Wonderland, The Wind in the Willows, Charlotte's Web,* or one of Judy Blume's books. Make a chart of your findings.

3. Prepare a display of early children's books; note the printing and binding, the illustrations, the subject matter. Display a varied selection of recent books as well. What contrasts do you see, and what similarities?

4. Read one of the new original paperbacks produced for a series. Compare it with a Nancy Drew book or a Sue Barton book. What similarities and differences do you see? Another person could compare it with a modern realistic story for children like those by Cynthia Voigt or Katherine Paterson. Again, how do they compare?

5. Plan a panel discussion on the role of the book in the future. What would you lose if you didn't have books?

6. Go to the Children's Literature Database on your Resources CD-ROM. Search the database under the term *classics* and find a modern-day retelling of a children's classic. How does the new edition represent modern points of view? If possible, compare your version to the original.

Web Links

Go to the Online Learning Center at **www.mhhe.com/kiefer9e** to find links to the following children's literature Web sites:

Baldwin Library of Historical Children's Literature

The Beatrix Potter Society

Children's Books On-Line: The Rosetta Project

Cotsen Children's Library

Eric Carle Museum of Picture Book Art

de Grummond Children's Literature Collection

How a Book Is Made

J. Paul Getty Collection of Illuminated Manuscripts

Landmarks in the History of Children's Literature

Picturing Childhood

Social History of Children's Literature

Related Readings

Ada, Alma Flor. *A Magical Encounter: Latino Children's Literature in the Classroom,* 2nd ed. Boston: Allyn & Bacon, 2003.

> This book, by a scholar and writer of Latino children's literature, is a thorough and practical guide to choosing and using books about Latinos. The book includes a history of the field and provides recommended book lists as well as classroom activities.

Ariès, Philippe. *Centuries of Childhood: A Social History of Family Life.* Translated from the French by Robert Baldick. New York: Knopf, 1962.

> In this definitive study of the development of the concept of childhood, Ariès maintains that childhood was not discovered until the seventeenth century. Although some have disputed this claim, Ariès's book has formed the basis of most historical studies of childhood.

Benes, Rebecca C. *Native American Picture Books of Change: The Art of Historic Children's Editions.* Sante Fe: Museum of New Mexico Press, 2004.

> Benes provides a valuable look at the development of Native American picture books over much of the twentieth century. The movement to create books written about Native culture enlisted Native American artists and allowed for the development of standardized alphabets for many tribal languages.

Fox, Dana L., and Kathy G. Short. *Stories Matter: The Complexity of Cultural Authenticity in Children's Literature.* Urbana, Ill.: NCTE, 2003.

> This book brings together some of the most important articles on multicultural literature published during the 1990s, along with new chapters that frame the dialogue about teaching, writing, and reading multicultural literature.

Harris, Violet J., ed. *Using Multicultural Literature in the K–8 Classroom.* Norwood, Mass.: Christopher Gordon, 1997.

> This book is an indispensable guide to the issues surrounding the teaching of multicultural literature. Various chapters provide criteria for choosing African American, Asian Pacific, Native American, Puerto Rican, Mexican American, and Caribbean children's books, as well as suggested titles.

Henderson, Darwin L., and Jill P. May, eds. *Exploring Culturally Diverse Literature for Children and Adolescents: Learning to Listen in New Ways.* Boston: Allyn & Bacon, 2005.

> This book is an excellent and thoughtful addition to the ongoing dialogue about the teaching and evaluation of multicultural literature. It expands the field to include articles on religion and gender.

Lurie, Alison. *Don't Tell the Grown-Ups: Subversive Children's Literature.* Boston: Little, Brown, 1990.

> In a collection of essays from the 1980s, this well-known scholar and novelist demonstrates that the enduring works of children's literature did not conform to the ideal values of their own times. She points to characters from folklore and fairy tales to the middle of the twentieth century who are disobedient and who mock adult hypocrisy.

Marcus, Leonard S., ed. *Dear Genius: The Letters of Ursula Nordstrom.* New York: HarperCollins, 1998.

> Nordstrom was one of the legendary children's book editors of the twentieth century, and this collection of her letters to such authors and illustrators as Laura Ingalls Wilder, Maurice Sendak, E. B. White, and John Steptoe reveals a witty, wise, and very independent woman. Marcus's introduction provides a context for understanding children's book publishing during what has been called its golden age.

———. *Margaret Wise Brown: Awakened by the Moon.* Boston: Morrow, 1999 [1992].

> Marcus's exhaustive, well-written, and engaging biography details not only a writer's life but also a much broader por-trait—of the progressive education movement and the major figures who created, influenced, and guided children's books during a most fertile period.

Mintz, Steve. *Huck's Raft: A History of American Childhood.* Cambridge, Mass.: Belknap Press, 2004.

> Mintz examines the past three hundred years of childhood in America, from the Puritan era to the present day. He shows that despite our rosy memories of an idealistic past for children, childhood has been a difficult rite of passage in every era.

Silvey, Anita, ed. *Children's Books and Their Creators.* Boston: Houghton Mifflin, 1995.

> This beautiful book focuses on twentieth-century American children's books. It includes overviews of the types of books written for various ages; essays on issues, history, and genres; biographical information on important authors and illustrators; and essays by creators of children's books.

———, ed. *The Essential Guide to Children's Books and Their Creators.* Boston: Mariner Books/Houghton Mifflin, 2002.

> This book summarizes information about books for children in a comprehensive first-edition paperback directed toward parents, educators, and students.

Townsend, John Rowe, ed. *John Newbery and His Books.* Metuchen, N.J.: Scarecrow Press, 1994.

> This collection of essays includes background and commentary on John Newbery by Townsend, edited chapters of Charles Welsh's 1885 biography of Newbery, and selections by Newbery contemporaries Samuel Johnson and George Coleman that give glimpses of this important figure in children's literature.

———. *Written for Children: An Outline of English Children's Literature,* 4th ed., rev. New York: HarperCollins, 1992.

> Townsend supplies a readable overview of the development of children's books in England and America, with a brief nod to Canada and Australia. His critical comments add interest to the text and help put the books in perspective. The survey ranges from before 1840 into the 1980s.

Whalley, Joyce Irene, and Tessa Rose Chester. *A History of Children's Book Illustration.* London: John Murray, 1997.

> Although the authors' focus is on mainstream British publishing, their coverage of book illustration is well written and thorough. Reproductions in both color and black and white add to our understanding of the field.

Children's Literature

 We have tried to limit the references for this chapter to books still in print. Dates in square brackets refer to the original publication of the text portion of the book.

Aardema, Verna. *Why Mosquitoes Buzz in People's Ears.* Illustrated by Leo Dillon and Diane Dillon. Dial, 1975.

Ada, Alma Flor. *Gathering the Sun: An Alphabet in Spanish and English.* Translated by Rosa Zubizarreta. Illustrated by Simón Silva. Lothrop, 1997.

———. *I Love Saturdays y Domingos.* Illustrated by Elivia Savadier. Atheneum, 2002.

———. *My Name is María Isabel.* Atheneum, 1993.

Adoff, Arnold. *I Am the Darker Brother: An Anthology of Modern Poems by Negro Americans.* Macmillan, 1968.

Alarcón, Francisco X. *Angels Ride Bikes/Los Ángeles Andan En Bicicleta.* Illustrated by Maya Christina Gonzalez. Children's, 1999.

———. *Poems to Dream Together / Poemas Para Soñar Juntos.* Illustrated by Paula Barragán. Lee, 2005.

———. *Laughing Tomatoes; Jitomates Risueños,* Illustrated by Maya Christina Gonzalez. Children's, 1997.

Alcott, Louisa May. *Little Women.* Illustrated by James Prunier. Viking, 1997 [1868].

———. *An Old-Fashioned Girl.* Dell Yearling, 1987 [1870].

Aldana, Patricia, ed. *Under the Spell of the Moon: Art for Children from the World's Great Illustrators.* Groundwood, 2004.

Alger, Horatio, Jr. *Struggling Upward.* Galloway, 1971 [n.d.].

Almond, David. *The Fire-Eaters.* Delacorte, 2004.

———. *Skellig.* Delacorte, 1999.

Altman, Linda Jacobs. *Amelia's Road.* Illustrated by Enrique O. Sanchez. Lee, 1995.

Alvarez, Julia. *Before We Were Free.* Scholastic, 2003.

———. *How Tia Lola Came to (Visit) Stay.* Knopf, 2001.

An, Na. *A Step from Heaven.* Front St., 2001.

Anaya, Rudolfo. *Farolitos for Abuelo.* Illustrated by Edward Gonzales. Hyperion, 1999.

———. *Roadrunner's Dance.* Illustrated by David Diaz. Hyperion, 2000.

Ancona, George. *Charro: The Mexican Cowboy.* Harcourt, 1999.

———. *Mi Casa: My House.* Scholastic, 2004.

Anderson, Laurie Halse. *Speak.* Farrar, 1999.

Andrews-Goebel, Nancy. *The Pot That Juan Built.* Illustrated by David Diaz. Lee, 2002.

Argueta, Jorge. *A Movie in My Pillow/Una Película en Mi Almohada.* Illustrated by Elizabeth Gómez, Children's, 2001.

———. *Xochitl and the Flowers/Xóchitl, la Niña de las Flores.* Illustrated by Carl Angel, Children's, 2003.

Armstrong, William H. *Sounder.* HarperCollins, 1969.

Avi. *City of Light, City of Dark.* Illustrated by Brian Flocca. Orchard, 2004 [1993].

Baker, Jeannie. *Home.* Greenwillow, 2004.

Barrie, J. M. *Peter Pan in Kensington Gardens.* Illustrated by Arthur Rackham. Buccaneer, 1980 [1906].

Baum, L. Frank. *The Wizard of Oz.* Illustrated by Michael Hague. Holt, 1982 [1900].

Bealer, Alex. *Only the Names Remain: The Cherokees and the Trail of Tears.* Illustrated by William S. Bock. Little, 1972.

Beaumont, Karen. *Duck, Duck, Goose!* Illustrated by Jose Aruego and Ariane Dewey. HarperCollins, 2004.

Belpré, Pura. *Perez and Martina: A Puerto Rican Folk Tale.* Illustrated by Carlos Sánchez. Viking, 1991 [1932].

Belton, Sandra. *Beauty, Her Basket.* Illustrated by Cozbi A. Cabrera. Amistad, 2004.

———. *Ernestine and Amanda.* Simon, 1996.

———. *Pictures for Miss Josie.* Illustrated by Benny Andrews. Amistad, 2003.

Bemelmans, Ludwig. *Madeline.* Viking Penguin, 1958 [1939].

Bernier-Grand, Carmen T. *César: ¡Si, Se Puede! Yes, We Can!* Illustrated by David Diaz. Cavendish, 2005.

———. *In the Shade of the Nispero Tree.* Illustrated by David Diaz. Scholastic, 1999.

Berry, James. *Ajeemah and His Son.* HarperCollins, 1992.

———. *Everywhere Faces Everywhere.* Illustrated by Reynold Ruffins. Simon, 1997.

Beskow, Elsa. *Pelle's New Suit.* Harper, 1929.

Bishop, Clair Huchet. *The Five Chinese Brothers.* Illustrated by Kurt Wiese. Coward, 1938.

Blume, Judy. *Are You There, God? It's Me, Margaret.* Bradbury, 1970.

———. *Blubber.* Bradbury, 1974.

———. *Deenie.* Bradbury, 1973.

———. *Tales of a Fourth Grade Nothing.* Dell, 1973.

Bolden, Tonya. *Maritcha: A Nineteenth Century American Girl.* Abrams, 2005.

———. *Wake Up Our Souls: A Celebration of Black American Artists.* Abrams, 2004.

Bontemps, Arna. *Bubber Goes to Heaven.* Illustrated by Daniel Minter. Oxford, 1998.

———. *Popo and Fifina.* Illustrated by E. Simms Campbell. Oxford, 1993 [1932].

Bontemps, Arna, and Langston Hughes. *The Pasteboard Bandit.* Illustrated by Peggy Turley. Oxford, 1997.

Brink, Carol Ryrie. *Caddie Woodlawn.* Macmillan, 1970 [1935].

Brooke, L. Leslie. *Johnny Crow's Garden.* Warne, 1986 [1903].

Brooks, Gwendolyn. *Bronzeville Boys and Girls.* Illustrated by Ronni Solbert. Harper, 1956.

Brown, Marcia. *Cinderella.* Macmillan, 1954.

———. *Dick Whittington and His Cat.* Macmillan, 1988 [1950].

———. *Once a Mouse.* Macmillan, 1961.

———. *Puss in Boots.* Scribner's, 1952.

———. *Stone Soup.* Macmillan, 1947.

Brown, Margaret Wise. *Goodnight Moon.* Illustrated by Clement Hurd. Harper, 1947.

———. *The Noisy Book.* Illustrated by Leonard Weisgard. Harper, 1939.

Bruchac, Joseph. *The Arrow over the Door.* Dial, 1998.

———. *Code Talker.* Dial, 2005.

———. *Jim Thorpe's Bright Path.* Illustrated by S. D. Nelson. Lee, 2004.

———. *The Journal of Jesse Smoke—A Cherokee Boy: Trail of Tears, 1838.* Scholastic, 2001.

———. *The Story of the Milky Way: A Cherokee Tale.* Illustrated by Virginia Stroud. Dial, 1995.

———. *Turtle's Race with Beaver: A Traditional Seneca Story.* Illustrated by Jose Aruego and Ariane Dewey. Penguin, 2003.

Bryan, Ashley. *Beautiful Blackbird.* Atheneum, 2003.

———. *The Cat's Purr.* Atheneum, 1985.

Bullard, Asa. *Sunnybank Stories: My Teacher's Gem.* Lee & Shepard, 1863.

Bunting, Eve. *Going Home.* Illustrated by David Diaz. Harper-Collins, 1996.

———. *Jin Woo.* Illustrated by Chris Soentpiet. Houghton, 2001.

Burnett, Frances Hodgson. *Little Lord Fauntleroy.* Godine, 1993 [1886].

———. *A Little Princess.* Illustrated by Jamichael Henterly. Grossett, 1995 [1905].

———. *Sara Crewe.* Scholastic, 1986 [1888].

———. *The Secret Garden.* Illustrated by Tasha Tudor. Harper, 1987 [1910].

Burton, Virginia Lee. *The Little House.* Houghton, 1978 [1942].

———. *Mike Mulligan and His Steam Shovel.* Houghton, 1939.

Bynum, Eboni, and Roland Jackson. *Jamari's Drum.* Illustrated by Baba Wagué Diakité. Groundwood, 2004.

Caldecott, Randolph. *Sing a Song of Sixpence.* Barron, 1988 [1880].

Canfield, Dorothy. *Understood Betsy.* Buccaneer, 1981 [1917].

Carlson, Natalie. *The Empty Schoolhouse.* Illustrated by John Kaufman. Harper, 1965.

Carmi, Daniella. *Samir and Yonaton.* Levine/Scholastic, 2000.

Carroll, Lewis [Charles Dodgson]. *Alice's Adventures in Wonderland.* Illustrated by Helen Oxenbury. Candlewick, 1999 [1865].

———. *Alice's Adventures in Wonderland.* Illustrated by Anthony Browne. Knopf, 1988 [1865].

———. *Through the Looking-Glass.* Illustrated by John Tenniel. St. Martin's, 1977 [1871].

Castaneda, Omar. *Abuela's Weave.* Illustrated by Enrique O. Sanchez. Lee, 1995.

Childress, Alice. *A Hero Ain't Nothin' but a Sandwich.* Putnam, 2000.

———. *Rainbow Jordan.* Morrow, 1982.

Chocolate, Debbi. *The Piano Man.* Illustrated by Eric Velasquez. Walker, 1999.

Choi, Sook Nyul. *Halmoni and the Picnic.* Illustrated by Daren Dugan. Houghton, 1993.

———. *Year of Impossible Goodbyes.* Houghton, 1991.

Choi, Yangsook. *The Name Jar.* Knopf, 2003.

———. *Peach Heaven.* Farrar, 2005.

Cleary, Beverly. *Henry Huggins.* Illustrated by Louis Darling. Morrow, 1950.

———. *Ramona and Her Father.* Illustrated by Alan Tiegreen. Morrow, 1977.

Cleaver, Vera, and Bill Cleaver. *Grover.* Illustrated by Frederic Marvin. Harper, 1970.

———. *Where the Lilies Bloom.* Lippincott, 1970.

Cofer, Judith Ortiz. *See* Ortiz Cofer, Judith.

Cohen Caron Lee. *The Mud Pony.* Illustrated by Shonto Begay. Scholastic, 1988.

Cole, Joanna. *The Magic School Bus Explores the Senses.* Illustrated by Bruce Degen. Scholastic, 1999.

Collier, Bryan. *Uptown.* Holt, 2000.

Collier, James L., and Christopher Collier. *My Brother Sam Is Dead.* Macmillan, 1974.

Collodi, Carlo. *The Adventures of Pinocchio.* Illustrated by Roberto Innocenti. Knopf, 1988 [1891].

Cooper, Floyd. *Jump! From the Life of Michael Jordan.* Philomel, 2004.

Cooper, James Fenimore. *The Last of the Mohicans.* Illustrated by N. C. Wyeth. Scribner's, 1986 [1826].

Cormier, Robert. *The Chocolate War.* Knopf, 1994 [1974].

Courlander, Harold, and Wolf Leslau. *The Fire on the Mountain: Stories from Ethiopia and Eritrea.* Illustrated by Robert Kane. Holt, 1995 [1950].

Crampton, Gertrude. *Tootle.* Golden, 1945.

Creech, Sharon. *Love That Dog.* HarperCollins, 2001.

Crews, Donald. *Bigmama's.* Greenwillow, 1991.

———. *Freight Train.* Greenwillow, 1978.

Crutcher, Chris. *The Sledding Hill.* Greenwillow, 2005.

Cummings, Pat. *Harvey Moon, Museum Boy.* HarperCollins, 2006.

Curtis, Christopher Paul. *Bucking the Sarge.* Lamb/Random, 2004.

———. *Bud, Not Buddy.* Delacorte, 1999.

Czekaj, Jef. *Grampa and Julie: Shark Hunters.* Top Shelf, 2004.

D'Aulaire, Ingri, and Edgar Parin d'Aulaire. *Abraham Lincoln.* Doubleday, 1957 [1939].

Dana, Richard Henry. *Two Years Before the Mast.* Airmont, 1985 [1840].

Danticat, Edwidge. *Anacona, Golden Flower.* Scholastic, 2005.

———. *Behind the Mountains.* Orchard, 2002.

Danzinger, Paula. *The United Tates of America.* Scholastic, 2002.

Delacre, Lulu. *Golden Tales: Myths, Legends, and Folklore from Latin America.* Scholastic, 1995.

———. *Salsa Stories.* Scholastic, 2000.

de la Mare, Walter. *Peacock Pie.* Illustrated by Edward Ardizzone. Faber, 1988 [1913].

———. *Songs of Childhood.* Dover, n.d. [1902].

dePaola, Tomie. *Charlie Needs a Cloak.* Simon, 1974.

de Saint-Exupéry, Antoine. *The Little Prince.* Harcourt, 1943.

Dhami, Narinder. *Bend It Like Beckham.* Delacorte, 2004.

———. *Bindi Babes.* Delacorte, 2004.

Diakité, Baba Wagué. *The Hatseller and the Monkeys: A West African Folktale.* Scholastic, 1999.

———. *The Hunterman and the Crocodile: A West African Folktale.* Scholastic, 1997.

———. *The Magic Gourd.* Scholastic, 2003.

Dickinson, Emily. *Poems for Youth.* Illustrated by Doris Hauman and George Hauman. Little, 1934.

DiTerlizzi, Tony, and Holly Black. *The Wrath of Mulgarath: The Spiderwick Chronicles, Book 5.* Simon, 2004.

Divakaruni, Chitra Banerjee. *The Conch Bearer.* Simon, 2003.

———. *Neela: Victory Song.* American Girl, 2002.

Dixon, Franklin W. *Absolute Zero (The Hardy Boy Casefiles, No. 121).* Archway, 1997.

Dodge, Mary M. *Hans Brinker, or the Silver Skates.* Scholastic, 1988 [1865].

Donovan, John. *I'll Get There, It Better Be Worth the Trip.* Harper, 1969.

Dorris, Michael. *Guests.* Hyperion, 1994.

———. *Morning Girl.* Hyperion, 1992.

Dowdy, Linda Cress. *Barney Goes to the Zoo.* Illustrated by Karen Malzeke-McDonald. Scholastic, 1993.

Doyle, Brian. *Mary Ann Alice.* Groundwood, 2002.

Drake, Earnest. *Dragonology.* Candlewick, 2003.

Draper, Sharon. *Darkness before Dawn.* Simon, 2002.

———. *Forged by Fire.* Simon, 1997.

English, Karen. *Francie.* Farrar, 1999.

———. *Hot Day on Abbott Avenue.* Illustrated by Javaka Steptoe. Clarion, 2004.

Enright, Elizabeth. *Thimble Summer.* Holt, 1938.

Erdrich, Louise. *The Birchbark House.* Hyperion, 1999.

———. *The Game of Silence.* Hyperion, 2005.

Estes, Eleanor. *The Hundred Dresses.* Illustrated by Louis Slobodkin. Harcourt, 1974 [1944].

———. *The Middle Moffats.* Dell, 1989 [1942].

———. *The Moffats.* Illustrated by Louis Slobodkin. Harcourt, 1941.

———. *Rufus M.* Illustrated by Louis Slobodkin. Harcourt, 1943.

Farjeon, Eleanor. *Eleanor Farjeon's Poems for Children.* Harper, 1984 [1931, 1951].

Field, Eugene. *Poems of Childhood.* Armont, 1969 [1896].

Fitzhugh, Louise. *Harriet the Spy.* Harper, 1964.

Flack, Marjorie. *Angus and the Ducks.* Macmillan, 1989 [1930].

———. *Ask Mr. Bear.* Macmillan, 1986 [1932].

Flake, Sharon. *Bang.* Hyperion, 2005.

———. *Begging for Change.* Hyperion, 2003.

———. *The Skin I'm In.* Hyperion, 1998.

Fleischman, Paul. *A Joyful Noise: Poems for Two Voices.* HarperCollins, 1988.

———. *Seedfolks.* HarperCollins, 1997.

———. *Seek.* Cricket/Marcato, 2001.

———. *Zap.* Candlewick, 2005.

Flournoy, Valerie. *The Patchwork Quilt.* Illustrated by Jerry Pinkney. Dial, 1985.

Flournoy, Vanessa, and Valerie Flournoy. *Celie and the Harvest Fiddler.* Illustrated by James E. Ransome. Morrow, 1995.

Forbes, Esther. *Johnny Tremain.* Illustrated by Lynd Ward. Houghton, 1943.

Fox, Paula. *The Slave Dancer.* Illustrated by Eros Keith. Bradbury, 1973.

Fraustino, Lisa Rowe. *The Hickory Chair.* Illustrated by Benny Andrews. Scholastic, 2001.

Fritz, Jean. *And Then What Happened, Paul Revere?* Illustrated by Margot Tomes. Putnam, 1973.

Frost, Robert. *You Come Too.* Illustrated by Thomas W. Nason. Holt, 1959.

Gág, Wanda. *Millions of Cats.* Putnam, 1928.

Garza, Carmen Lomas. *Family Pictures/Cuadros de Familia.* Children's, 1990.

———. *In My Family/En Mi Familia.* Sagebrush, 2000.

———. *Magic Windows/Ventanas Magicás.* Illustrated by Francisco X. Alarcón. Children's, 2003.

Gates, Doris. *Blue Willow.* Viking Penguin, 1940.

Geeslin, Campbell. *Elena's Serenade.* Illustrated by Ana Juan. Atheneum, 2004.

———. *The Night Eater.* Illustrated by Ana Juan. Atheneum, 2004.

Gilbert, Anne Yvonne, et al. *Wizardology: The Book of the Secrets of Merlin* (as Told by Master Merlin). Candlewick, 2005.

Giovanni, Nikki. *The Genie in the Jar.* Illustrated by Chris Raschka. Holt, 1996.

———. *The Sun Is So Quiet.* Illustrated by Ashley Bryan. Holt, 1996.

Grahame, Kenneth. *The Wind in the Willows.* Illustrated by Ernest H. Shepard. Scribner's, 1983 [1908].

Gramatky, Hardie. *Little Toot.* Putnam, 1978 [1930].

Greenfield, Eloise. *For the Love of the Game: Michael Jordan and Me.* Illustrated by Jan Spivey Gilchrist. HarperCollins, 1998.

———. *Honey, I Love: And Other Poems.* Illustrated by Leo Dillon and Diane Dillon. Harper, 1978.

———. *How They Got Over: African Americans and the Call of the Sea.* Illustrated by Jan Spivey Gilchrist. HarperCollins, 2003.

———. *In the Land of Words.* Illustrated by Jan Spivey Gilchrist. HarperCollins, 2004.

Grimes, Nikki. *Bronx Masquerade.* Putnam, 2002.

———. *Danitra Brown, Class Clown.* Illustrated by Floyd Cooper. HarperCollins, 2005.

Grimm, Jacob, and Wilhelm Grimm. *Grimm's Fairy Tales.* Illustrated by George Cruikshank. Dover, n.d. [1823].

Gunning, Monica. *Not a Copper Penny in Me House: Poems from the Caribbean.* Wordsong, 2003.

———. *Under the Breadfruit Tree: Island Poems.* Wordsong, 1998.

Guy, Rosa. *The Disappearance.* Sagebrush, 1980.

———. *The Friends.* Doubleday, 1992.

Hale, Lucretia P. *The Peterkin Papers.* Sharon, 1981 [1880].

Hale, Sarah Josepha. *Mary Had a Little Lamb.* Illustrated by Tomie dePaola. Holiday, 1984 [1830].

Haley, Gail. *A Story, a Story.* Atheneum, 1970.

Hamanaka, Sheila. *All the Colors of the Earth.* HarperCollins, 1994.

———. *Grandparents' Song.* HarperCollins, 2003.

Hamilton, Virginia. *The Magical Adventures of Pretty Pearl.* HarperCollins, 1974.

———. *M. C. Higgins, the Great.* Macmillan, 1974.

———. *The Planet of Junior Brown.* Simon, 1991.

———. *Sweet Whispers Brother Rush.* Philomel, 1982.

———. *Time Pieces: The Book of Times.* Scholastic, 2002.

———. *Zeely.* Illustrated by Symeon Shimin. Macmillan, 1967.

Hansen, Joyce. *The Captive.* Scholastic, 1994.

———. *One True Friend.* Clarion, 2005.

Hanson Regina. *A Season for Mangoes.* Illustrated by Eric Velasquez. Clarion, 2005.

Harjo, Joy. *The Good Luck Cat.* Illustrated by Paul Lee. Harcourt, 2000.

Harris, Joel Chandler. *Uncle Remus.* Illustrated by A. B. Frost. Schocken, 1987 [1881].

Hawthorne, Nathaniel. *Tanglewood Tales.* Sharon, 1981 [1853].

———. *The Wonder Book for Boys and Girls.* White Rose, 1987 [1852].

Haywood, Carolyn. *B Is for Betsy.* Harcourt, 1987 [1939].

Heo, Yumi. *The Green Frogs: A Korean Folktale.* Houghton, 1996.

Herrera, Juan Felipe. *The Upside Down Boy/El Niño de Cabeza.* Illustrated by Elizabeth Gómez. Children's, 2000.

Hesse, Karen. *The Music of Dolphins.* Scholastic, 1996.

———. *Out of the Dust.* Scholastic, 1997.

Hidier, Tanuja Desai. *Born Confused.* Scholastic, 2002.

Hinton, S. E. *The Outsiders.* Viking, 1967.

Ho, Minfong. *The Clay Marble.* Farrar, 1991.

———. *The Stone Goddess.* Orchard, 2003.

Hoffman, Mary. *Amazing Grace.* Illustrated by Caroline Binch. Dial, 1991.

Holling, Holling C. *Paddle-to-the-Sea.* Houghton, 1980 [1941].

hooks, bell. *Be Boy Buzz.* Illustrated by Chris Raschka. Hyperion, 2002.

———. *Happy to Be Nappy.* Illustrated by Chris Raschka. Hyperion, 1999.

Hope, Laura L. *The Bobbsey Twins.* Simon, 1990.

Hopkinson, Deborah. *Under the Quilt of Night.* Illustrated by James E. Ransome. Simon, 2001.

Howard, Elizabeth Fitzgerald. *Aunt Flossie's Hats (and Crab Cakes Later).* Illustrated by James Ransome. Houghton, 1991.

———. *Virgie Goes to School with Us Boys.* Illustrated by E. B. Lewis. Simon, 2000.

Hughes, Langston. *The Dream Keeper and Other Poems.* Illustrated by Brian Pinkney. Knopf, 1994 [1932].

Hunter, Sally M. *Four Seasons of Corn: A Winnebago Tradition.* Lerner, 1996.

Hurston, Zora Neale. *Lies and Other Tall Tales.* Illustrated by Christopher Myers. HarperCollins, 2005.

Jackson, Jesse. *Call Me Charley.* Illustrated by Doris Speigel. Harper, 1945.

Jacobs, Joseph. *English Fairy Tales.* Dover, 1967 [Roth, 1890].

Jenkins, Steve. *Prehistoric Actual Size.* Houghton, 2005.

Jiménez, Francisco. *Breaking Through.* Houghton, 2001.

———. *The Circuit: Stories from the Life of a Migrant Child.* Houghton, 1999.

———. *La Mariposa.* Illustrated by Simón Silva. Houghton, 2000.

Johnson, Angela. *A Cool Moonlight.* Dutton, 2003.

———. *Heaven.* Simon, 1998.

Jones, Hettie. *The Trees Stand Shining: Poetry of the North American Indians.* Illustrated by Robert A. Parker. Dial, 1993 [1971].

Joseph, Lynn. *The Mermaid's Twin Sister: More Stories from Trinidad.* Illustrated by Donna Perrone. Clarion, 1994.

———. *A Wave in Her Pocket: Stories from Trinidad.* Illustrated by Brian Pinkney. Clarion, 1991.

Keats, Ezra Jack. *Whistle for Willie.* Viking, 1964.

Kingsley, Charles. *The Water Babies.* Penguin, 1986 [1863].

Kipling, Rudyard. *The Jungle Books.* Illustrated by Fritz Eichenberg. Grosset, 1950 [1894–95].

———. *Just So Stories.* Woodcuts by David Frampton. HarperCollins, 1991 [1902].

Kirk, David. *Nova's Ark.* Calloway/Scholastic, 1999.

Konigsburg, E. L. *George.* Dell, 1985 [1970].

Kramer, Steven. *Hidden Worlds: Looking through a Scientist's Microscope.* Houghton, 2001.

Krishnaswami, Uma. *Chachaji's Cup.* Illustrated by Souyama Sitaraman. Children's, 2003.

———. *Monsoon.* Illustrated by Jamel Akib. Farrar, 2003.

———. *Naming Maya.* Farrar, 2004.

Krull, Kathleen. *Harvesting Hope: The Story of Cesar Chavez.* Illustrated by Yuyi Morales. Harcourt, 2003.

Kusugak, Michael. *Baseball Bats for Christmas.* Illustrated by Vladyana Krykorka. Annick, 1993.

Lacapa, Kathleen, and Michael Lacapa. *Less Than Half, More Than Whole.* Northland, 1994.

Lacapa, Michael. *Antelope Woman.* Northland, 1992.

Lang, Andrew, ed. *The Blue Fairy Book.* Airmont, 1969 [1889].

Lauture, Denizé. *Running the Road to ABC.* Illustrated by Reynold Ruffins. Simon, 1996.

Lear, Edward. *Nonsense Poems of Edward Lear.* Illustrated by Leslie Brook. Clarion, 1991.

Lee, Ho Baek. *While We Were Out.* Kane/Miller, 2003.

Lee, Huy Voun. *In the Leaves.* Holt, 2005.

———. *1,2,3, Go!* Holt, 2001.

Lee, Jeanne M. *Bitter Dumplings.* Farrar, 2002.

———. *The Song of Mu Lan.* Front St., 1991.

Lee, Marie G. *Finding My Voice.* Houghton, 1992.

———. *If It Hadn't Been for Yoon Jun.* HarperCollins, 1995.

L'Engle, Madeleine. *Meet the Austins.* Dell, 1981 [1960].

Lenski, Lois. *Judy's Journey.* Harper, 1947.

———. *The Little Auto.* McKay, 1980 [1934].

———. *Strawberry Girl.* Harper, 1988 [1945].

Leslie, Brooke. *A Nursery Rhyme Book.* Clarion, 1992 [1922].

Lester, Julius. *Day of Tears: A Novel in Dialogue.* Hyperion, 2005.

———. *To Be A Slave.* Illustrated by Tom Feelings. Dial, 1968.

———. *Why Heaven Is Far Away.* Illustrated by Joe Cepeda. Scholastic, 2002.

Leverich, Kathleen. *Best Enemies.* Illustrated by Walter Lorraine. Morrow, 1989.

Lewis, C. S. *The Lion, the Witch, and the Wardrobe.* Illustrated by Pauline Baynes. Macmillan, 1988 [1950].

Lin, Grace. *Dim Sum for Everyone!* Random, 2003.

Lin, Grace. *The Year of the Dog*. Little, 2006.

Lindgren, Astrid. *Pippi Longstocking*. Illustrated by Louis S. Glanzman. Translated by Florence Lambron. Viking Penguin, 1950.

Lindsay, Vachel. *Johnny Appleseed and Other Poems*. Buccaneer, 1981 [1928].

Littlechild, George. *This Land Is My Land*. Children's, 2003.

Littlesugar, Amy. *Freedom School, Yes!* Illustrated by Floyd Cooper. Philomel, 2001.

Lofting, Hugh. *The Voyages of Dr. Dolittle*. Delacorte, 1988 [1922].

London, Jack. *The Call of the Wild*. Macmillan, 1963 [1903].

Look, Lenore. *Henry's First Moon Birthday*. Illustrated by Yumi Heo. Atheneum, 2001.

———. *Ruby Lu, Brave and True*. Illustrated by Ann Wilsdorf. Simon, 2004.

———. *Uncle Peter's Amazing Chinese Wedding*. Illustrated by Yumi Heo. Atheneum, 2004.

Lord, Bette Bao. *In the Year of the Boar and Jackie Robinson*. HarperCollins, 1994.

———. *Middle Heart*. Sagebrush, 1997.

Lowrey, Janette Sebring. *The Poky Little Puppy*. Illustrated by Gustaf Tenggren. Golden, 1942.

Loyie, Lawrence. *As Long as the Rivers Flow*. Illustrated by Heather Holmlund. Groundwood, 2002.

MacDonald, George. *At the Back of the North Wind*. Illustrated by Lauren Mills. Godine, 1988 [1871].

Macken, JoAnn Early. *Sing-Along Song*. Illustrated by LeUyen Pham. Viking, 2004.

Madonna. *The English Roses*. Illustrated by Jeffrey Fulvimari. Calloway, 2003.

———. *Mr. Peabody's Apples*. Illustrated by Loren Long. Calloway, 2003.

Maher, Ramona. *Alice Yazzie's Year*. Illustrated by Shonto Begay. Tricycle, 2003.

Martin, Bill, Jr., and John Archambault. *Knots on a Counting Rope*. Illustrated by Ted Rand. Holt, 1987.

Martinez, Victor. *Parrot in the Oven: Mi Vida*. HarperCollins, 1996.

Mathis, Sharon Bell. *The Hundred Penny Box*. Illustrated by Leo Dillon and Diane Dillon. Viking, 1975.

———. *Listen for the Fig Tree*. Viking, 1975.

McCloskey, Robert. *Homer Price*. Viking Penguin, 1943.

———. *Make Way for Ducklings*. Viking Penguin, 1941.

McDermott, Beverly Brodsky. *The Golem*. Lippincott, 1976.

McDermott, Gerald. *Anansi the Spider*. Holt, 1972.

———. *Arrow to the Sun*. Viking, 1974.

McGill, Alice. *Miles's Song*. Scholastic, 2002.

———. *Sure as Sunrise, Bruh Rabbitt and His Walkin', Talkin' Friends*. Houghton, 2004.

McKay, Hilary. *Permanent Rose*. McElderry, 2005.

McKissack, Patricia. *Mirandy and Brother Wind*. Illustrated by Jerry Pinkney. Knopf, 1988.

McKissack, Patricia, and Fredrick McKissack. *Madame C. J. Walker: Self-Made Millionaire*. Enslow, 2001.

———. *The Royal Kingdoms of Ghana, Mali, and Songhay*. Sagebrush, 1995.

Medearis, Angela Shelf. *Rum-a-Tum-Tum*. Illustrated by James Ransome. Holiday, 1997.

———. *Singing for Dr. King*. Illustrated by Cornelius van Wright. Scholastic, 2004.

Medina, Tony. *DeShawn Days*. Illustrated by R. Gregory Christie. Lee, 2001.

———. *Love to Langston*. Illustrated by R. Gregory Christie. Lee, 2002.

Millay, Edna St. Vincent. *Edna St. Vincent Millay's Poems Selected for Young People*. Illustrated by Ronald Keller. Harper, 1979 [1917].

Milne, A. A. *Now We Are Six*. Illustrated by Ernest H. Shepard. Dutton, 1988 [1927].

———. *When We Were Very Young*. Illustrated by Ernest H. Shepard. Dutton, 1988 [1924].

———. *Winnie the Pooh*. Illustrated by Ernest H. Shepard. Dutton, 1988 [1926].

Mitchell, Margaree King. *Uncle Jed's Barbershop*. Illustrated by James Ransome. Simon, 1993.

Mochizuki, Ken. *Heroes*. Illustrated by Dom Lee. Lee, 1995.

———. *Passage to Freedom: The Sugihara Story*. Illustrated by Dom Lee, 1997.

Mohr, Nicholasa. *Felita*. Bantam, 1979.

———. *The Song of el Coqui and Other Tales of Puerto Rico*. Illustrated by Antonio Martorell. Viking, 1995.

Mollel, Tololwa. *My Rows and Piles of Coins*. Illustrated by E. B. Lewis. Clarion, 1999.

———. *The Orphan Boy*. Illustrated by Paul Morin. Clarion, 1991.

Monjo, F. N. *Poor Richard in France*. Dell, 1990 [1973].

Montes, Marisa. *Juan Bobo Goes to Work: A Puerto Rican Folktale*. Illustrated by Joe Cepeda. HarperCollins, 2000.

———. *Mystery Neighbors: Get Ready for Gabí*. Scholastic, 2003.

Montgomery, L. M. *Anne of Green Gables*. Bantam, 1976 [1908].

Moore, Clement. *The Night Before Christmas*. Illustrated by Jan Brett. Putnam, 1998 [1823].

———. *The Night Before Christmas*. Illustrated by Robert Sabuda. Simon, 2002.

Mora, Pat. *Confetti: Poems for Children*. Illustrated by Enrique O. Sanchez. Lee, 1996.

———. *Doña Flor; A Tall Tale about a Giant Woman with a Great Big Heart*. Illustrated by Raúl Colón. Knopf, 2005.

———. *Pablo's Tree*. Illustrated by Cecily Lang. Macmillan, 1994.

———. *Thomas and the Library Lady*. Illustrated by Raúl Colón. Dragonfly, 2000.

Morales, Yuyi. *Just a Minute: A Trickster Tale and Counting Book*. Chronicle, 2003.

Mori, Kyoko. *One Bird*. Holt, 1995.

Mosel, Arlene. *The Funny Little Woman*. Illustrated by Blair Lent. Dutton, 1972.

Mosley, Walter. *47*. Little, 2005.

Munsch, Robert. *A Promise Is a Promise*. Illustrated by Michael Arvaaluk Kusugak. Annick, 1992.

Myers, Tim. *Basho and the River Stones.* Illustrated by Oki S. Han. Cavendish, 2004.

Myers, Walter Dean. *Harlem.* Illustrated by Christopher Myers. Scholastic, 1997.

———. *Here in Harlem: Poems in Many Voices.* Holiday, 2004.

———. *Monster.* Illustrated by Christopher Myers. Scholastic, 1999.

———. *My Name Is America: The Journal of Joshua Loper, a Black Cowboy.* Scholastic, 1998.

Naidoo, Beverley. *Journey to Jo'burg.* Illustrated by Eric Velasquez. Harper, 1986.

———. *The Other Side of Truth.* HarperCollins, 2001.

Namioka, Lensey. *Half and Half.* Delacorte, 2003.

———. *The Loyal Cat.* Illustrated by Aki Sogabe. Browndeer, 1995.

———. *Yang the Youngest and His Terrible Ear.* Illustrated by Kees de Kiefte. Little, 1992.

Naylor, Phyllis Reynolds. *Achingly Alice.* Atheneum, 1999.

Nelson, Marilyn. *Carver, A Life in Poems.* Front St., 2001.

———. *A Wreath for Emmett Till.* Houghton, 2005.

———. *Fortune's Bones: The Manumission Requiem.* Houghton, 2004.

Nelson, S. D. *Gift Horse: A Lakota Story.* Abrams, 1999.

Nesbit, E. *The Enchanted Castle.* Illustrated by Paul O. Zelinsky. Morrow, 1992 [1907].

Nister, Ernest. *The Animals' Picnic.* Putnam, 1988 [reissue].

Noda, Takayo. *Dear World.* Dial, 2003.

———. *Song of the Flowers.* Dial, 2006.

Nolen, Jerdine. *Big Jabe.* Illustrated by Kadir A. Nelson. HarperCollins, 2000.

———. *Raising Dragons.* Illustrated by Elise Primavera. Harcourt, 1998.

Nye, Naomi Shihab. *Habibi.* Simon, 1997.

———. *19 Varieties of Gazelle: Poems of the Middle East.* Greenwillow, 2002.

O'Neill, Alexis. *Estela's Swap.* Illustrated by Enrique O. Sanchez. Lee, 2002.

Onyefulu, Ifeoma. *A Is for Africa.* Cobblehill, 1993.

———. *Emeka's Gift: An African Counting Story.* Cobblehill, 1995.

Orlev, Uri. *Lydia, Queen of Palestine.* Translated from the Hebrew by Hillel Halkin. Houghton, 1993.

———. *Run Boy, Run.* Translated from the Hebrew by Hillel Halkin. Houghton, 2003.

Ortiz Cofer, Judith. *The Hunger of Birds.* Farrar, 2005

———. *An Island Like You: Stories of the Barrio.* Orchard, 1995.

Ortiz, Simon. *The Good Rainbow Road.* Illustrated by Michael Lacapa. U Arizona P, 2004.

———. *The People Shall Continue.* Illustrated by Sharol Graves. Children's, 1988.

Osa, Nancy. *Cuba 15.* Delacorte, 2003.

Pak, Soyung. *Dear Juno.* Illustrated by Susan Kathleen Hartung. Viking, 2003.

———. *Sumi's First Day of School Ever.* Illustrated by Joung Un Kim. Viking, 1999.

Park, Barbara. *Junie B., First Grader (At Last).* Random, 2001.

Park, Linda Sue. *Bee-bim Bop!* Illustrated by Ho Baek Lee. Clarion, 2005.

———. *My Name Was Keoko.* Clarion, 2002.

———. *Project Mulberry.* Clarion, 2005.

———. *A Single Shard.* Clarion, 2001.

Pearce, Philippa. *Tom's Midnight Garden.* Harper, 1984 [1959].

Perkins, Mitali. *Monsoon Summer.* Delacourt, 2004.

———. *The Sunita Experiment.* Hyperion, 1994.

Pham, LeUyen. *Big Sister, Little Sister.* Hyperion, 2005.

Pilkey, Dav. *Captain Underpants and the Wrath of the Wicked Wedgie Woman.* Blue Sky/Scholastic, 2001.

Pinkney, Andrea Davis. *Alvin Ailey.* Illustrated by Brian Pinkney. Hyperion, 1993.

———. *Bill Picket, Rodeo-Ridin' Cowboy.* Illustrated by Brian Pinkney. Hyperion, 1996.

———. *Let It Shine: Stories of Black Women Freedom Fighters.* Illustrated by Stephen Alcorn. Harcourt/Gulliver, 2000.

Pinkney, Brian. *The Adventures of Sparrowboy.* Simon, 2000.

Pinkney, Jerry. *Noah's Ark.* Chronicle, 2002.

Pinkwater, Daniel. *The Muffin Fiend.* Lothrop, 1986.

Piper, Watty. *The Little Engine That Could.* Putnam, 1990 [1929].

Plunkett, Stephanie. *Kongi and Potgi: A Korean Cinderella.* Illustrated by Oki S. Han. Dial, 1996.

Politi, Leo. *Three Stalks of Corn.* Scribner's, 1947.

Porte, Barbara Ann. *Something Terrible Happened.* Orchard, 1994.

Porter, Eleanor H. *Pollyanna.* Yearling Classics, 1987 [1913].

Potter, Beatrix. *Jemima Puddle-Duck.* Warne, 1994 [1908].

———. *The Tale of Peter Rabbit.* Warne, 1972 [1902].

Pyle, Howard. *The Merry Adventures of Robin Hood of Great Renown.* Dover, 1968 [1883].

———. *The Story of King Arthur and His Knights.* Scribner's, 1984 [1903].

———. *The Wonder Clock.* Dover, n.d. [1888].

Rappaport, Doreen. *Martin's Big Words.* Illustrated by Bryan Collier. Hyperion/Jump at the Sun, 2001.

Raschka, Chris. *Yo! Yes?* Orchard, 1993.

Reid, Barbara. *The Party.* Scholastic, 1999.

———. *The Subway Mouse.* Scholastic, 2005.

Rey, H. A. *Curious George.* Houghton, 1973 [1941].

Richter, Hans. *Friedrich.* Penguin, 1987 [1970].

Ringgold, Faith. *If a Bus Could Talk: The Story of Rosa Parks.* Simon, 1999.

———. *Tar Beach.* Random, 1991.

Rossetti, Christina. *Sing Song.* Illustrated by Arthur Hughes. Dover, 1969 [1872].

Rowling, J. K. *Harry Potter and the Goblet of Fire.* Scholastic, 2002.

———. *Harry Potter and the Sorcerer's Stone.* Scholastic, 1998.

Runton, Andy. *Owly: The Way Home and the Bittersweet Summer.* Top Shelf, 2004.

Ruskin, John. *King of the Golden River.* Illustrated by Richard Doyle. Dover, 1974 [1851].

Ryan, Pam Muñoz. *Becoming Naomi Leon.* Scholastic, 2004.

———. *Esperanza Rising.* Scholastic, 2000.

———. *Mice and Beans.* Illustrated by Joe Cepeda. Scholastic, 2001.

Sabuda, Robert, and Matthew Reinhart. *Encyclopedia Prehistorica: Dinosaurs.* Candlewick, 2005.

Sandburg, Carl. *Early Moon.* Illustrated by James Daugherty. Harcourt, 1978 [1930].

Sandburg, Reg. *This Little Light of Mine.* Illustrated by E. B. Lewis. Random, 2005.

Sands, Emily. *Egyptology.* Candlewick, 2004.

Satrapi, Marjane. *Persépolis.* Translated by Anjali Singh. Pantheon, 2003.

Sawyer, Ruth. *Roller Skates.* Illustrated by Valenti Angelo. Penguin, 1986 [1936].

Say, Allen. *Grandfather's Journey.* Houghton, 1993.

———. *Kamishibai Man.* Houghton, 2005.

Schami, Rafik. *Damascus Nights.* Touchstone, 1995.

———. *A Handful of Stars.* Dutton, 1990.

Scott, Walter. *Ivanhoe.* Airmont, 1964 [1820].

Sebring, Janette. *See* Lowrey, Janette Sebring.

Sendak, Maurice. *Alligators All Around.* HarperCollins, 1962.

———. *In the Night Kitchen.* Harper, 1970.

———. *Where the Wild Things Are.* Harper, 1988 [1963].

Seton, Ernest Thompson. *Wild Animals I Have Known.* Creative Arts, 1987 [1898].

Seuss, Dr. [Theodor S. Geisel]. *And to Think That I Saw It on Mulberry Street.* Random, 1989 [1937].

———. *The Cat in the Hat.* Random, 1957.

———. *Green Eggs and Ham.* Random, 1960.

Sewell, Anna. *Black Beauty.* Grosset, 1945 [1877].

Shahan, Sherri. *Spicy Hot Colors/Colores piquantes.* Illustrated by Paula Barragán. August, 2004.

Shange, Ntozake. *Ellington Was Not a Street.* Illustrated by Kadir A. Nelson. Simon, 2004.

Sherlock, Philip. *Anansi: The Spider Man.* Illustrated by Marcia Brown. Harper, 1954.

Sheth, Kashira. *Blue Jasmine.* Hyperion, 2004.

Shotwell, Louisa R. *Roosevelt Grady.* Putnam, 1963.

Sidney, Margaret. *Five Little Peppers and How They Grew.* Puffin, 1990 [1881].

Sierra, Judy. *The Gift of the Crocodile: A Cinderella Story.* Illustrated by Reynold Ruffins. Simon, 2000.

Siy, Alexandra, and Dennis Kunkle. *Mosquito Bite.* Charlesbridge, 2005.

Smith, Charles R., Jr. *Hoop Queens.* Candlewick, 2003.

———. *Rim Shots: Basketball Pix, Rolls, and Rhythms.* Dutton, 1999.

Smith, Cynthia Leitich. *Jingle Dancer.* Illustrated by Cornelius Van Wright. HarperCollins, 2000.

———. *Rain Is Not My Name.* HarperCollins, 2001.

Smith, E. Boyd. *The Railroad Book.* Houghton, 1983 [1913].

———. *The Seashore Book.* Houghton, 1985 [1912].

Smith, Hope Anita. *The Way a Door Closes.* Illustrated by Shane Evans. Holt, 2003.

Sneve, Virgina Driving Hawk. *Bad River Boys: A Meeting of the Lakota Sioux with Lewis and Clark.* Illustrated by Bill Farnsworth. Holiday, 2005.

———. *The Sioux.* Illustrated by Ron Himler. Holiday, 1993.

Snicket, Lemony. *The Hostile Hospital, A Series of Unfortunate Events, No. 8.* HarperCollins, 2001.

Sogabe, Aki. *Aesop's Fox.* Browndeer, 1999.

Son, John. *Finding My Hat.* Orchard, 2003.

Soto, Gary. *Chato and the Party Animals.* Illustrated by Susan Guevara. Putnam, 2000.

———. *Chato Goes Cruisin'.* Illustrated by Susan Guevara. Putnam, 2005.

———. *Help Wanted.* Harcourt, 2005.

———. *Worlds Apart: Traveling with Fernie and Me.* Putnam, 2005.

Spiegelman, Art. *In the Shadow of No Towers.* Pantheon, 2004.

———. *Maus: A Survivor's Tale.* Pantheon, 1986.

Spyri, Johanna. *Heidi.* Illustrated by Troy Howell. Messner, 1982 [1884].

Stamaty, Mark Alan. *Alia's Mission: Saving the Books of Iraq.* Knopf, 2004.

Steptoe, Javaka. *In Daddy's Arms I Am Tall: African Americans Celebrating Fathers.* Lee, 1997.

Steptoe, John. *Stevie.* Harper, 1969.

———. *The Story of Jumping Mouse.* HarperCollins, 1984.

Stere, Dugald, ed. *Dragonology.* Candlewick, 2003.

Stevenson, Robert Louis. *A Child's Garden of Verses.* Illustrated by Michael Foreman. Delacorte, 1985 [1885].

———. *Treasure Island.* Illustrated by N. C. Wyeth. Scribner's, 1981 [1883].

Stolz, Joelle. *Shadow Ghadames.* Farrar, 2004.

Stroud, Virginia. *Doesn't Fall Off His Horse.* Dial, 1994.

Takabayashi, Mari. *I Live in Brooklyn.* Houghton, 2004.

———. *I Live in Tokyo.* Houghton, 2001.

Tapahonso, Luci. *A Breeze Swept Through.* U New Mexico P, 1987.

———. *Songs of Shiprock Fair.* Illustrated by Anthony Chee Emerson. Kiva, 1999.

Taylor, Mildred. *The Land.* Dial, 2001.

———. *Roll of Thunder, Hear My Cry.* Illustrated by Jerry Pinkney. Dell, 1976.

Taylor, Sydney. *All-of-a-Kind Family.* Illustrated by John Helen. Dell, 1980 [1951].

Taylor, Theodore. *The Cay.* Delacorte, 1969.

Tolkien, J. R. R. *The Hobbit.* Illustrated by Michael Hague. Houghton, 1989 [1937].

Tran, Truong. *Going Home, Coming Home.* Illustrated by Ann Phong. Children's, 2003.

Travers, P. L. *Mary Poppins*. Harcourt, 1934.

Tresselt, Alvin. *White Snow, Bright Snow*. Illustrated by Roger Duvoisin. Lothrop, 1989 [1947].

Twain, Mark [Samuel Clemens]. *The Adventures of Huckleberry Finn*. Scholastic, 1982 [1884].

———. *The Adventures of Tom Sawyer*. Illustrated by Barry Moser. Morrow, 1989 [1876].

Uchida, Yoshiko. *The Dancing Kettle and Other Japanese Folk Tales*. Creative Arts, 1986 [1949].

———. *Journey to Topaz*. Illustrated by Donald Carrick. Scribner's, 1971.

———. *The Magic Listening Cap*. Creative Arts, 1987 [1955].

———. *The Magic Purse*. Illustrated by Keiko Narahasi. McElderry, 1993.

Udry, Janice May. *Let's Be Enemies*. Illustrated by Maurice Sendak. Harper, 1961.

Updale, Eleanor. *Montmorency: Doctor, Thief, Murderer*. Scholastic, 2005.

Van Camp, Richard. *A Man Called Raven*. Illustrated by George Littlechild. Children's, 1997.

———. *What Is the Most Beautiful Thing You Know about Horses?* Illustrated by George Littlechild. Children's, 2003.

Van Loon, Hendrik. *The Story of Mankind*. Updated in a new version for the 1980s. Liveright, 1985 [1921].

Veciana-Suarez, Ana. *Flight to Freedom*. Scholastic, 2002.

Verne, Jules. *Around the World in Eighty Days*. Illustrated by Barry Moser. Morrow, 1988 [1872].

———. *Journey to the Center of the Earth*. Penguin, 1986 [1864].

———. *Twenty Thousand Leagues Under the Sea*. Airmont, 1964 [1869].

Voigt, Cynthia. *Homecoming*. Atheneum, 1981.

Vuong, Lynette Dyer. *The Brocaded Slipper and Other Vietnamese Tales*. Illustrated by Vo-Dinh Mai. HarperCollins, 1991.

Walter, Mildred Pitts. *Justin and the Best Biscuits in the World*. Illustrated by Catherine Stock. Knopf, 1986.

———. *Suitcase*. Lothrop, 1999.

Watkins, Yoko Kawashima. *My Brother, My Sister, and I*. Bradbury, 1994.

———. *So Far from the Bamboo Grove*. Lothrop, 1986.

Weatherford, Carole Boston. *Freedom on the Menu: The Greensboro Sit-Ins*. Illustrated by Jerome Lagarrigue. Dial, 2005.

———. *Remember the Bridge: Poems of a People*. Philomel, 2002.

Wheeler, Bernelda. *Where Did You Get Your Moccasins?* Illustrated by Herman Bekkering. Peguis, 1995.

White, E. B. *Charlotte's Web*. Illustrated by Garth Williams. Harper, 1952.

Wiesner, David. *The Three Pigs*. Clarion, 2001.

———. *Tuesday*. Clarion, 1991.

Wiggin, Kate Douglas. *Rebecca of Sunnybrook Farm*. Penguin, 1986 [1903].

Wilder, Laura Ingalls. *Little House in the Big Woods*. Illustrated by Garth Williams. Harper, 1953 [1932].

Williams, Margery. *The Velveteen Rabbit*. Illustrated by William Nicholson. Doubleday, 1969 [1922].

Williams, Vera B. *Amber Was Brave, Essie Was Smart*. Greenwillow, 2001.

Williams-Garcia, Rita. *No Laughter Here*. Amistad/HarperCollins, 2004.

Winthrop, Elizabeth. *Squashed in the Middle*. Illustrated by Pat Cummings. Holt, 2005.

Wong, Janet S. *Apple Pie Fourth of July*. Illustrated by Margaret Chodos-Irvine. Harcourt, 2002.

———. *A Suitcase of Seaweed and Other Poems*. McElderry, 1996.

Woodson, Jacqueline. *Locomotion*. Putnam, 2003.

———. *Maison at Blue Hill*. Delacourt, 1992.

Wyss, Johann. *The Swiss Family Robinson*. Sharon, 1981 [1814].

Yamate, Sandra. *The Best of Intentions*. Illustrated by Wendy K. Lee. Polychrome, 1993.

———. *Char Siu Bao Boy*. Illustrated by Carolina Yao. Polychrome, 2004.

Yang, Belle. *Baba: A Return to China on My Father's Shoulders*. Harcourt, 1994.

———. *Hannah Is My Name*. Candlewick, 2004.

Yee, Lisa. *Millicent Min, Girl Genius*. Scholastic, 2003.

———. *Stanford Wong Flunks Big-Time*. Scholastic, 2005.

Yee, Paul. *The Bone Collector's Son*. Cavendish, 2005.

———. *Tales from Gold Mountain*. Illustrated by Simon Ng. Macmillan, 1990.

Yep, Laurence. *The Dragon of the Lost Sea*. HarperCollins, 1988.

———. *Dragon's Gate*. HarperCollins, 1993.

———. *Thief of Hearts*. HarperCollins, 1995.

Yin. *Coolies*. Illustrated by Chris Soentpiet. Philomel, 2001.

Yolen, Jane. *The Devil's Arithmetic*. Viking, 1988.

Yoo, Paula. *Sixteen Seconds in Sixteen Years: The Sammy Lee Story*. Illustrated by Dom Lee. Lee, 2005.

Young, Ed. *I Doko: The Tale of a Basket*. Philomel, 2004.

———. *Lon Po Po: A Red Riding Hood Tale from China*. Philomel, 1989.

———. *The Sons of the Dragon King: A Chinese Legend*. Simon, 2004.

Yumoto, Kazumi. *The Friends*. Translated by Cathy Hirano. Farrar, 1996.

———. *The Letters*. Translated by Cathy Hirano. Farrar, 2002.

Zemach, Margot. *It Could Always Be Worse*. Farrar, 1990 [1977].

Zhang, Ange. *Grandfather Counts*. Lee, 2003.

———. *Red Land, Yellow River*. Groundwood, 2004.

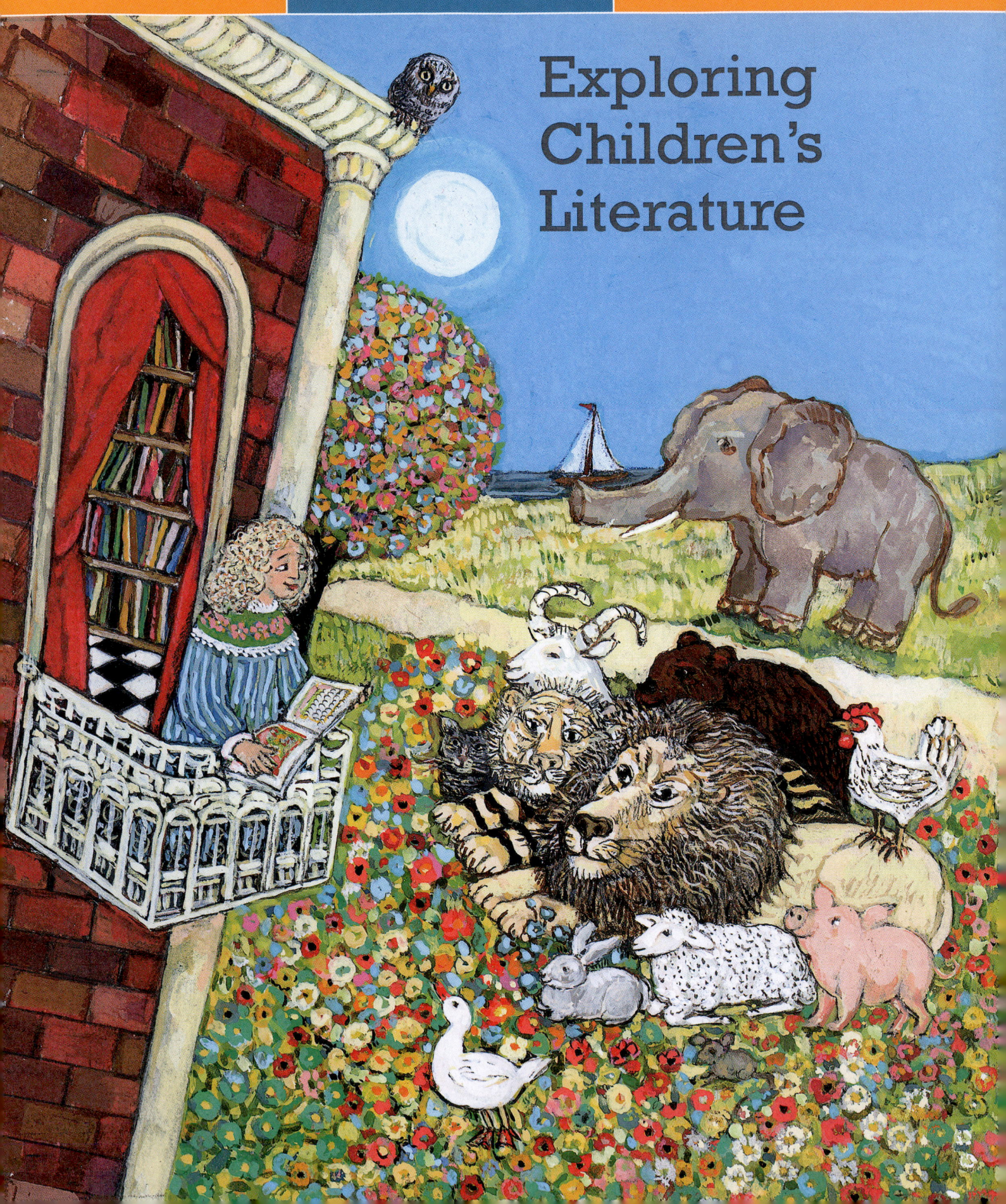

Part Two

Exploring Children's Literature

Chapter Four

Books to Begin On

Chapter Outline

Media Resources

One

One of our colleagues is a proud new grandfather. Every time we meet him, he regales us with tales of his granddaughter's progress in "reading"—Laura is 18 months old. However, he is determined that Laura will grow into reading as naturally as she is learning to speak.

So he floods her house with books; he mixes books with her blocks so she will think of them as toys; he built her a special bookshelf for her books; he bought a miniature supermarket basket that he filled with books so she can have books available in every room in the house; he takes her to the library frequently. Of course, whenever he visits he is greeted with the welcome words, "Grandpapa, read!" And he always does. Laura's mother and father read to her also, so it is not unusual for Laura to hear six to ten stories a day.

Laura has favorite books, which she can readily find, and she asks to hear them over and over again. She relates books to her own life. Each night when she hears *Goodnight Moon* by Margaret Wise Brown, she softly whispers, "Night night, chair, night night, Bear." Laura's grandfather is achieving his purpose. Laura is learning to love books and learning to read naturally in the process.

DEVELOPING INITIAL LITERACY

What a lot Laura already knows about books and reading at 18 months! First, she knows books are enjoyable, and she even has particular favorites. She also knows that adults hold the key to reading and can give meaning to the text. She herself knows how to hold a book and that it has to be right-side-up to read the print. She is beginning to relate books to her own life. If at 18 months she knows this much about how to read a book, think what she will know when she enters school.

At a year and a half, Laura already has entered the world of literature. She is learning to love books as she has many opportunities to snuggle up close to her mother, father, and grandfather for story time. She is also increasing her vocabulary as she points to pictures and names them or hears new words used in the context of the story. The language development of children at this age is phenomenal; preoccupation with words and the sounds of language is characteristic of the very young child. Books help to fulfill this insatiable desire to hear and learn new words. Hearing literature of good quality helps children to develop to their full language potential.

Children cannot be introduced to books too soon. The human baby is attuned to various sound patterns almost from the moment of birth. She will be startled by a cross word or a loud noise, soothed by a gentle, loving voice or a softly sung lullaby. Gradually the baby

Research suggests that one of the most important gifts a family can give to children is an early love of books. Photo © Brand X Pictures/Punchstock.

A toddler shares his interest in *Machines at Work* by Byron Barton with his Raggedy Andy. Photo by Susan Fertig.

A toddler enjoys the wonder of reading. Photo © Brand X Pictures/Punchstock.

begins to develop comprehension skills as she attaches meaning to the sounds around her. Talk is essential at this time, and the special language of books is especially important. One parent read a best-selling novel to her infant son just so he could hear the sound of her voice. Primarily, however, the very young child listens for the "quack quack" of a duck in a picture book or the "roar" of a lion. Singing simple nursery rhymes or playing such finger rhymes as "This little pig went to market" makes babies giggle with delight. Increasingly, publishers are producing books for babies' enjoyment, for, in Dorothy Butler's words, "Babies need books."[1]

The young child who has the opportunity to hear and enjoy many stories is also beginning to learn to read. No one taught Laura how to hold a book or where to begin to read the text. Through constant exposure to stories, Laura is learning about book handling and developing some beginning concepts about the print.[2] She is spontaneously learning some of the attitudes, concepts, and

skills needed to become literate, including a positive attitude toward books, an understanding about the sense-making aspect of stories, the stability of print to tell the same story each time, and the form and structure of written language itself. All of this learning occurs at the prereading stage and seems to be essential for later success in reading.[3]

We have previously discussed, in Chapter 1, the research that shows the importance of books in the young child's life. It is clear that hearing many stories in the preschool years can have lasting benefit for children. Boys and girls who enter school having had many experiences with books are well prepared to acquire literacy,[4] and these children are more likely to remain active readers well into late elementary and middle school.

During the times in which they share books with their young children, parents appear to use consistent language patterns when labeling objects in a picture book. Even before the baby can talk, the child and mother (or father) take turns engaging in a dialogue and collaboratively make meaning out of the text. As they read Margaret Wise Brown's *Goodnight Moon* over the course of many bedtimes, the mother points to a picture and says, "Can you find the red balloon? Where's the mouse?" and the baby delightedly points to these tiny objects. As the child acquires a simple vocabulary, the parent might ask, "What's this?" or respond to the same query from the

[1]Dorothy Butler, *Babies Need Books: Sharing the Joy of Books with Children from Birth to Six* (Portsmouth, N.H.: Heinemann, 1998).

[2]See Marie Clay, *An Observation Survey of Early Literacy* (Portsmouth, N.H.: Heinemann, 2002) for a description of her Concepts about Print test.

[3]Don Holdaway, *The Foundations of Literacy* (Sydney: Ashton Scholastic, 1979).

[4]Gordon Wells, *The Meaning Makers: Children Learning Language and Using Language to Learn* (Portsmouth, N.H.: Heinemann Educational Books, 1986), p. 151.

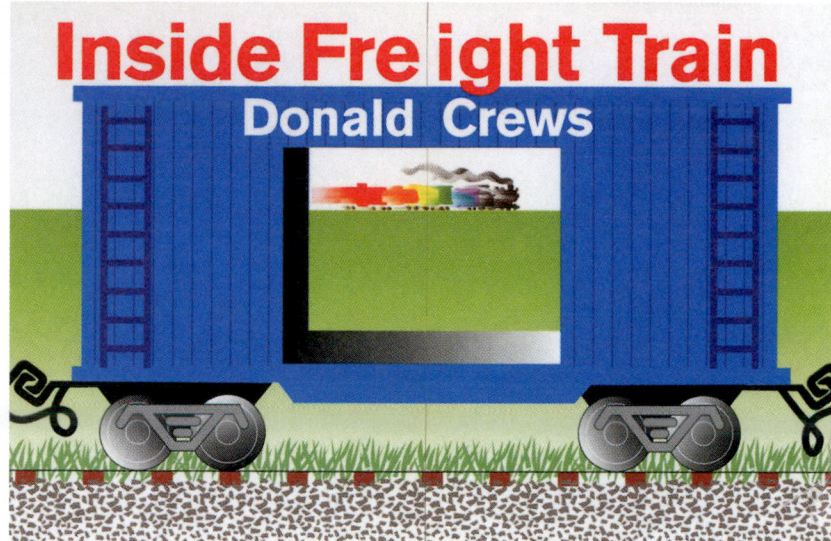

Donald Crews's *Inside Freight Train* is a sturdy board book that slides open to reveal the contents of each car. Cover of *Inside Freight Train* by Donald Crews. Copyright © 1978 by Donald Crews. Used by permission of HarperCollins Publishers.

child with the name of the object. This book-reading context is unique because the attention of both participants is focused on pictures and words that stay the same for each rereading. Thus the child can predict the story and build up vocabulary over numerous readings.

Early exposure to books and plenty of time for talk and enjoyment of the story appear, then, to be key factors in the child's acquisition of literacy.[5] One father whose child has been exposed to books from infancy said, "You know, I haven't the slightest doubt that David will learn to read, any more than I was concerned that he would talk." The illustration, "Learning to Read Naturally" on pages 144–45 provides a picture of the types of experiences with books that can naturally lead young children to literacy.

BABIES' FIRST BOOKS

First books for young children are frequently identification books, "naming books," or books with simple narrative lines that allow the child to point to one picture after another, demanding to know "wha dat?" It is probably this give-and-take of language between the adult and the child that makes sharing books at this age so important. Recognizing the need for the young child to identify and name objects, publishers have produced many of these simple, sturdy "first books."

The growth of good books for babies and toddlers was a publishing phenomenon of the 1980s and 1990s. As part of the interest in books for babies, publishers reissued well-known nursery classics or enlisted well-known illustrators or writers in creating series of baby books. Donald Crews has created *Inside Freight Train*,

a board-book version of his perennial favorite *Freight Train*. Kevin Henkes's popular characters Lilly, Wemberly, Julius, Owen, and Sheila Rae now all appear in their own board-book stories. Ian Falconer's irrepressible pig, Olivia, appears in *Olivia Counts* and *Olivia's Opposites*.

British illustrators Helen Oxenbury and Jan Ormerod were among the first illustrators to routinely show children of many cultures in board books such as *Dressing* and *Young Joe*. More recently Andrea Davis Pinkney and Brian Pinkney have created a set of books about toddler experiences that includes *Pretty Brown Face* and *Watch Me Dance*. Eloise Greenfield's *Water, Water* illustrated by Jan Spivey Gilchrist and Pat Cumming's *Purrrrr* are other well-written texts with lively illustrations. Javaka Steptoe has produced *Sweet, Sweet Baby!*, a cloth book with mirror and rattle that can be hung on a crib.

Books for this age group need to be well constructed, with heavy laminated cardboard, cloth, or plastic pages that will withstand teeth or sticky fingers. Illustrations should be simple, uncluttered, and easily identifiable. Tana Hoban's photographic concept books such as *What Is That?* and *Red, Blue, Yellow Shoe* present clear, colored photographs of familiar objects like a sock, a shoe, a bib, a cup, and a spoon. Only one object is pictured on a page, shown against a plain white background, in these sturdy first books. Rosemary Wells's little board books about Max, a lovable rabbity creature, are labeled "Very First Books." However, the humor is for slightly older toddlers. In *Max's First Word*, Max's sister tries to get him to talk. She names everything she shows him, and Max always responds with "Bang." Giving him an apple, Ruby suggests he say "Yum, yum," but Max surprises her with "Delicious."

---

[5]See Susan B. Newman, "Books Make a Difference: A Study of Access to Literacy," *Reading Research Quarterly* 34, no. 3 (July–September, 1999): 286–311.

Wonderfully Exciting Books

Playing with Sounds
Beginning readers need many opportunities to play with the sounds of language.

Buzz, Buzz, Buzz (Barton)
A Truck Goes Rattley-Bumpa (London)
The Cow That Went Oink (Most)
Here Comes Henny (Pomerantz)
The Piggy in a Puddle (Pomerantz)

Linking Experiences to Books
Beginning readers need books that match their own experiences.

Being Little
The Littlest Wolf (Brimmer)
The Biggest Boy (Henkes)
Titch (Hutchins)

Changes
Will I Have a Friend? (Cohen)
Pablo's Tree (Mora)

New Babies
When the New Baby Comes I'm Moving Out (Alexander)
She Come Bringing Me That Little Baby Girl (Greenfield)

Losing Control
When Sophie Gets Angry Really, Really Angry (Bang)
No, David! (Shannon)

Reading to Find Out
Beginning readers need experiences with nonfiction.

My Five Senses (Aliki)
Flash, Crash, Rumble and Roll (Branley)
Zipping, Zapping, Zooming Bats (Earle)
All Pigs Are Beautiful (King-Smith)

LEARNING TO READ NATURALLY: A WEB OF POSSIBILITIES

Celebrating Being a Reader
Beginning readers need to be part of a reading and writing community.

Share a favorite book with a reading partner.
Have a book character parade.
Prepare a literary lunch.

Stone Soup (Brown)
Pancakes, Pancakes! (Carle)
Chicken Soup with Rice (Sendak)
The Little Red Hen (Makes a Pizza) (Sturges)

Having Fun with Pictures
Beginning readers can apply reading strategies to pictures before they are able to read words.

Find the hidden clues that artists include in their pictures.

Each Peach, Pear, Plum (Ahlberg and Ahlberg)
We Hide, You Seek (Aruego)
The Alphabet Tale (Garten)

Read stories in wordless books.
Dictate or rewrite the story in your own words.

Truck (Crews)
Pancakes for Breakfast (dePaola)
The Red Book (Lehman)
A Boy, a Dog, and a Frog (Meyer)
School (McCully)

"Reading" Familiar Texts
Beginning readers can gain confidence by reading books that they already know well.

Favorite Songs
Fiddle-I-Fee (Hillenbrand)
Over in the Meadow (Langstaff)
There Was an Old Lady Who Swallowed a Fly (Taback)
The Farmer in the Dell (Wallner)
The Wheels on the Bus (Zelinsky)

Memorable Stories
Duck, Duck, Goose! (Beaumont)
Good Night Moon (Brown)
The Very Hungry Caterpillar (Carle)
Under My Hood I Have a Hat (Kuskin)
Where the Wild Things Are (Sendak)
Owl Babies (Waddell)

Books to Begin Reading

Beginning readers can practice reading in books with limited vocabulary.

Freight Train (Crews)
Titch (Hutchins)
Brown Bear, Brown Bear, What Do You See? (Martin)
Marvin One Too Many (Paterson)
Sheep in a Jeep (Shaw)

Playing with Patterns

Beginning readers need support from predictable patterns in texts.

Cumulative Tales
One Fine Day (Hogrogian)
The Cake That Mack Ate (Robart)
The Napping House (Wood)

Refrains and Repetition
Teeny Tiny (Bennett)
The Bus for Us (Bloom)
A Dark, Dark Tale (Brown)
Chicken Soup with Rice (Sendak)

ABCs and 1,2,3s
Big Fat Hen (Baker)
Alligator Arrived with Apples (Dragonwagon)
Feast for Ten (Falwell)
On Market Street (Lobel)
Chicka Chicka Boom Boom (Martin)

Verbalizing Stories

Beginning readers need many opportunities to develop their abilities to communicate orally.

Dramatizing Stories

Act out favorite stories.
Make costumes or masks.

Drummer Hoff (Emberley)
Where the Wild Things Are (Sendak)
Caps for Sale (Slobodkina)

Telling Stories

Tell stories using props and costumes.

The Little Red Hen (Galdone)
The Turnip (Morgan)
The Little Old Lady Who Was Not Afraid of Anything (Williams)

Tell stories with a flannel board.

The Gingerbread Baby (Brett)
The Mitten (Brett)
It Could Always Be Worse (Zemach)

Calling Attention to Print

Beginning readers need to develop concepts about letters, letter sounds, and words.

Look at Letters and Words
Meow! (Arnold)
A, B, See! (Hoban)
Alphabet City (Johnson)
Yuck! (Manning)
Car Wash (Steen and Steen)

Use Labels and Signs
I Read Signs (Hoban)
I Read Symbols (Hoban)

Collect Words on a Word Wall
Scary words
Noisy words
Holiday words

Sort Words That Look Alike
Add your own labels in your classroom.

Making Books

Beginning readers need many opportunities to write.

Make big books from favorite class books.
Draw pictures to match the printed words.
Collaborate on the writing of a book about a class trip or a special holiday.
Collect a personal library of photocopied books of favorite nursery rhymes.
Collect wallpaper and make books for dictated writing.
Create shape books for special writing (trucks, giraffes).

Building a Sense of Story

Beginning readers need to build an experiential background for understanding stories.

Predictable Endings
The Seven Silly Eaters (Hoberman)
Rosie's Walk (Hutchins)
Joseph Had a Little Overcoat (Taback)

Predictable Characters
The silly chicken (*Chicken Little* by Kellogg)
The clever fox (*Aesop's Fox* by Sogabe)
The wicked witch (*Heckedy Peg* by Wood)

Stories on One Theme
Colors
Animals
One author

Stories of 3s
The Three Bears (Galdone)
The Three Billy Goats Gruff (Galdone)
The Three Little Pigs (Galdone)

Variations on a Theme

Make comparison charts.

Goldilocks and the Three Bears (Brett)
Deep in the Forest (Turkle)

The Three Little Pigs (Galdone)
The Three Little Pigs and the Fox (Hooks)

The Little Red Hen (Galdone)
Cook-a-Doodle-Doo! (Stevens and Stevens)
The Little Red Hen (Makes a Pizza) (Sturges)

There are many fine picture books that appeal to babies and toddlers and that introduce them to the rhythms and forms of literature from an early age. These are often the books that, like Margaret Wise Brown's *Goodnight Moon*, become bedtime classics although they don't have to be about going to sleep. Favorites with toddlers include Robert Kraus's *Whose Mouse Are You?*; Vera Williams's *"More More More," Said the Baby*; Nina Payne's *Summertime Waltz*; and Olivier Dunrea's series of little books about Gossie, Ollie, and their gosling friends. These are books that often invite babies' participation in the form of finding objects in the pictures, repeating simple refrains like "more, more, more" or "so much," or getting tummy tickles and hugs and kisses.

TOY BOOKS

Young children can respond to a book by pointing or labeling, but some books have a kind of "built-in participation" as part of their design. These books have flaps to lift up and peek under, soft flannel to touch, or holes to poke fingers through. Such books can serve as the transition between toys and real books. *Pat the Bunny* by Dorothy Kunhardt has been a best-seller for very young children for more than sixty years. In this little book the child is invited to use senses other than sight and sound. A "pattable" bunny made of flannel is on one page, and Daddy's unshaven face, represented by rough sandpaper, is on another. Young children literally wear out this tactile book.

An increasing number of sophisticated cutout books and lift-the-flap stories are appearing on the market. Lucy

Profile in Literature

Author Rosemary Wells

Rosemary Wells is a well-known and well-loved author of books for younger children. Her books, including *Shy Charles* and *Bunny Cakes*, capture the essence of the preschool psyche and delight parents as well. Wells has contributed board books, song books, and Mother Goose collections (with Iona Opie) as well as many wonderful stories. Her *Emily's First 100 Days of School* could serve as a curriculum guide for early-childhood programs. She is also passionately committed to the cause of reading to children as a stepping stone to literacy. Go to the Online Learning Center at **www.mhhe.com/kiefer9e** or your Resources CD-ROM to learn more about Rosemary Wells.

Cousins has created appealing series of lift-the-flap books, one starring Maisy the Mouse and another with Jazzy the Giraffe. In *Maisy Goes to Bed*, Maisy goes to a potty that "flushes," puts on her pajamas, and ends up in bed reading a bedtime book. Eric Hill's lift-the-flap stories about the dog Spot never fail to intrigue young children. These books are sturdily made, the pictures are bright and clear, and the stories are imaginative. Titles in the series include *Where's Spot?*, *Good Night Spot*, and *Spot Goes to School*. Roxie Munro's *Doors* and Jez Alborough's *Duck's Key, Where Can It Be?* follow a similar "What's hiding here?" format. Karen Beaumont's *Baby Danced the Polka* takes a more inventive path. In this rollicking story, Baby refuses to go to sleep so that his (her?) parents can

Karen Beaumont's *Baby Danced the Polka* invites toddler participation in lifting flaps and in guessing each of the stuffed animals that Baby is dancing with. *From Baby Danced the Polka* by Karen Beaumont. Illustrations copyright © 2004 by Jennifer Plecas. Used by permission of Dial Books for Young Readers, a division of Penguin Young Readers Group, a Member of Penguin Group (USA) Inc., 345 Hudson St., NY.

Evaluating Books for the Very Young Child

THE BEST BOOKS FOR BABIES AND TODDLERS SHOULD:

- Relate to familiar life experiences
- Provide clear, uncluttered illustrations with little or no distracting background
- Be well constructed with sturdy, durable pages

- Use clear, natural language
- Have predictable stories
- Provide some humor, especially so the child will feel superior
- Offer opportunities for participation and interaction
- Hold the child's attention

finish their chores on the farm. Jennifer Plecas's charming illustrations show Baby polka-ing, boogie-woogie-ing, cha-cha-ing, and shoobie-doobie-ing with one stuffed animal after another. Finally, Papa and Mama give up and hold a polka-fest under the summer moon until everyone is tuckered out enough to get to sleep.

Eric Carle's story *The Very Hungry Caterpillar* is a favorite with children ages 3 through 6. This imaginative tale describes the life cycle of a ravenous caterpillar who leaves behind a trail of holes in all the food that he eats. Children love to stick their fingers through the holes and count them. In Carle's multisensory story *The Very Busy Spider,* children are invited to feel the pictures as well as see them. Brilliant collages depict familiar animals whose questions are never answered by the spider, who is too busy spinning her tactile web. Carle's *The Very Quiet Cricket, The Very Clumsy Click Beetle,* and *The Very Lonely Firefly* have technological support that brings each tale to its conclusion. The sound of the cricket and the click beetle coming from a computer chip imbedded in the pages of the cricket and beetle books and tiny blinking lights in the fireflies' bodies surprise and delight children in these multisensory books.

Books like Margaret Mayo's *Choo Choo Clickety-Clack!* that describe different kinds of sounds invite their own special kind of noisy participation. *Early Morning in the Barn* by Nancy Tafuri begins with a large double-page spread picturing a rooster waking the barnyard with his "cock-a-doodle-doo," which awakens his brother and sister. All three run out of the hen house into the barnyard, where they are greeted by an array of animals each making their familiar noise. Kevin Lewis's *Chugga-Chugga Choo-Choo,* illustrated by Daniel Kirk, incorporates the rhythm and pacing of an exciting train ride with plenty of opportunity for toddlers to join in on the "Whoo-whoo" of the whistle. Bright, sunny pictures add to the fun of these noisy books.

If a book does not provide for participation, the adult reader can stimulate it by the kinds of questions he or she asks. For example, when sharing the old favorite *Caps for Sale* by Esphyr Slobodkina, the parent might say to the child, "Find the monkey—not the one in the red hat, not the one in the blue hat, but the one in the green

hat!" Such participation will help children develop visual discrimination and introduce the child to important aspects of conversational patterns. More importantly, it will add to the fun of the story time. The Evaluation Criteria box "Evaluating Books for the Very Young Child" lists criteria for the best books for infants and toddlers.

FINGER RHYMES AND NURSERY SONGS

Finger rhymes are one traditional way to provide for young children's participation as they play "Five Little Pigs" or sing "Where Is Thumbkin?" and the ever popular "Eensy, Weensy Spider." Finger plays date back to the time of Friedrich Froebel, the so-called father of the kindergarten movement, who collected the finger plays and games that the peasant mothers in the German countryside were using with their children. Jane Yolen's *Trot, Trot to Boston* includes lap songs, finger plays, clapping games, and pantomime rhymes. Will Hillenbrand's delightfully detailed illustrations add to the appeal of this lively book. Judy Sierra has collected games for older children in *Schoolyard Rhymes: Kids' Own Rhymes of Rope-skipping, Hand Clapping, Ball Bouncing and Just Plain Fun.* Priscilla Lamont's *Playtime Rhymes* has amusing illustrations to accompany the twenty-two finger plays and includes photos of children of different ages and races engaged in the action. In Zita Newcome's *Head, Shoulders, Knees, and Toes and Other Action Rhymes,* buoyant and bouncing toddlers invite youngsters to act out "Pat-a-Cake," "Ten in the Bed," and more. Elisa Kleven has illustrated several books of songs and play rhymes collected by José-Luis Orozco, among them, *Diez Deditos and Other Play Rhymes and Action Songs from Latin America.*

Babies and toddlers often first respond to the sounds of music and singing. Many authors and illustrators have created new and innovative interpretations for familiar songs. Mary Ann Hoberman and Nadine Bernard Wescott have teamed up to interpret several old-favorite songs such as *Miss Mary Mack* and *Bill Grogan's Goat.* Philemon Sturges's retelling of *She'll Be Comin' 'Round the Mountain* takes note of the song's origin in the African American spiritual "When the Chariot Comes." However,

Sturges and illustrator Ashley Wolff give the song a lively Southwestern setting, where one desert creature after another gathers for a party at the local town center. The lively ending reveals that the "she" they have been so eagerly anticipating is the librarian, driving the mobile book van.

Marla Frazee has created a highly imaginative realization of a familiar Appalachian lullaby in *Hush, Little Baby*. Pencil and ink illustrations evoke a pioneer setting and spirit as two frantic parents try to calm a squalling baby. An older sister, who is at first jealous of the attention, grows into a caring sibling as she enlists an old peddler in finding just the right object to quiet the child. The printed text and background color alternate to highlight the repeated refrain, a nice touch that draws the young child's attention to words. Frazee has also created an old-fashioned prairie setting for Woody Guthrie's *New Baby Train*.

Santiago Cohen, Jakki Wood, Melissa Sweet, and Will Hillenbrand have all illustrated *Fiddle-I-Fee*, an American folk song with a cumulative pattern that children enjoy. Cohen's board-book version shows each animal against a brightly colored page facing the cumulative pattern, with each animal's sound ("neigh-neigh," "chimmy-chuck," and so on) written in a different font beside its picture. Sweet's version shows a little boy trying to feed the animals on his farm. As each animal is fed, it joins an ever-longer parade through the countryside. When the boy's bucket is empty, his parents appear on a tractor and drive everyone back to the farmhouse for a final feast. Wood's version has less narrative and focuses on close-ups of a blonde-haired child and the animals. It also ends with an owl rather than a cow. In Hillenbrand's delightful version we follow farm animals and a farm wife through the course of several seasons. In the last several pages we discover the wife is pregnant, and a new baby appears with Mom and Dad at the end of the book! Hillenbrand has also created the imaginative illustrations for *Down By the Station*. Here baby animals climb aboard a train headed for the children's zoo and arrive just in time to greet the school bus full of children who have come to visit.

Children love to make up additional verses to the rollicking old folk song adapted by John Langstaff in *Oh, A-Hunting We Will Go*. Nancy Winslow Parker's childlike illustrations are carefully arranged so as not to give away the last lines of each verse. Once children have determined the pattern of the song, they can guess what they will see in the next picture. They easily predict that the goat will end up "in a boat," but they laugh at the bear who gets put "in underwear." Langstaff and Feodor Rojankovsky collaborated on another old song, *Over in the Meadow*. Other versions of this counting song have been created by Louise Voce, Ezra Jack Keats, and Paul Galdone.

Children have their choice of many editions of *Old MacDonald Had a Farm*. Rosemary Wells has created a board-book version for younger readers that invites toddlers to suggest more animal noises to put in the song. By way of contrast, Glen Rounds uses bold primitive drawings to depict his bowlegged farmer and angular animals, including a skunk! Amy Schwartz has a modern-day, young farmer MacDonald and his extended family with animal sounds written in colors to call attention to the print. Carol Jones creates a peephole on each page of her engaging version. The first peephole view shows just a part of a chicken. Turn the page and you see the whole chicken in the hen house. Frances Cony's version of *Old MacDonald Had a Farm* has pull tabs and lift flaps. In *Old MacDonald Had a Woodshop* by Lisa Shulman and illustrated by Ashley Wolff, Old MacDonald and his crew of animals go to work building a toy farm for all the baby animals.

In *I Know an Old Lady Who Swallowed a Fly*, Nadine Westcott illustrates the traditional version of the popular song. After using seven cans of bug spray to kill the fly she swallowed, the old lady reels from one epicurean delight to another. Devouring the horse, she dies of course! Colin and Jacqui Hawkins have the old lady sneeze after swallowing the horse and up come all the animals. By lifting up the old lady's apron, the reader can see all the

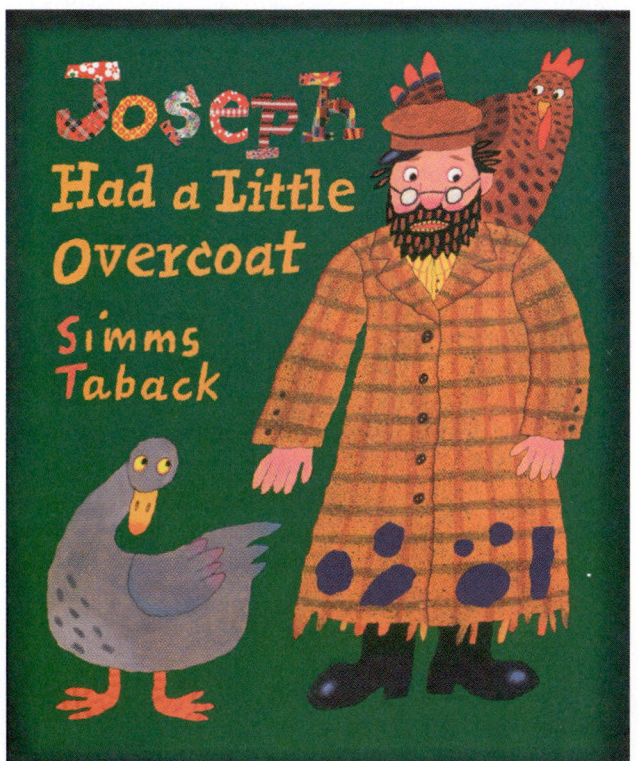

Simms Taback's Caldecott Medal–winning *Joseph Had a Little Overcoat* invites young children to participate in "reading" a folksong. From *Joseph Had a Little Overcoat* by Simms Taback, copyright © 1999 by Simms Taback, illustrations. First published 1977 by Random House, Inc. Used by permission of Viking Penguin, a division of Penguin Putnam Inc.

animals in her stomach. This would make an excellent model for an enlarged old lady that children could then insert their drawn animals into. A sealed sandwich bag stapled behind her apron would make a good imitation stomach. Open the bag and you could remove the animals. Also, the speech balloons in the Hawkinses' tale encourage children's own original writing. Simms Taback's hilarious *There Was an Old Lady Who Swallowed a Fly* has die-cut holes in the old lady's stomach. These grow increasingly larger as each animal is swallowed. His Caldecott Medal–winning *Joseph Had a Little Overcoat* is a retelling of an old folk song that evokes the lively dances and patterns of an old-world Yiddish village. In both books Taback's amusing visual asides encourage children to look carefully at the illustrations so as not to miss the fun.

One of primary children's favorite songs is "The Wheels on the Bus," and they can choose from several wonderful versions in picture-book format. Lenny Hort delivers a delicious variant in *The Seals on the Bus.* Here, instead of wheels going round and round the seals go errp, errp, errp. Other animals riding the bus add silly sounds. In *The Wheels on the Bus,* Maryann Kovalski provides a London setting for her picture story of Jenny and Joanna and their grandma, who sing this song as they wait for their bus. They become so involved with their actions and singing, they miss their bus and have to take a taxi. Alexander Zane's *Wheels on the Race Car* will certainly appeal to all the NASCAR fans and every other child who loves to chant "vroom-vroom." James Warhola's amusing illustrations depict a zoo-ful of animals who have taken the day off to go to the race track and try their paws at the wheel of a racing car. The horizontal format of the book lends it a rollicking sense of speed. Paul O. Zelinsky's interpretation of this song features paper engineering—wheels spin, the windshield wipers go "swish, swish, swish," and flaps and pullouts provide other items to manipulate. Well constructed, this movable version captivates children. In *Knick-Knack Paddywhack!,* another movable-parts book by Zelinsky, a boy and his dog visit a succession of different old men and their dogs with delightful results.

In *We're Going on a Bear Hunt,* Michael Rosen recounts a popular action rhyme as an exciting adventure tale. Pictures by Helen Oxenbury portray a father and his four children (including the baby) crossing a field of waving grass ("Swishy, swashy"), wading in the mud ("Squelch, squerch"), and braving a snowstorm ("Hoooo, woooo") until they reach a gloomy cave and see a bear! Oxenbury alternates black-and-white pictures with sweeping landscapes in full color. Children will relish the sound effects, the humor, and the drama of this tale.

All children need to hear songs, from the time they are babies right through school. Many emergent readers' first books are shared nursery rhymes and songs or chants. Children "read" the familiar words as they sing

By illustrating this chart about various cumulative stories and songs, children learned to retell the stories in proper sequence. Highland Park Elementary School, South-Western City Schools, Grove City, Ohio. Kristen Kerstetter, teacher.

the songs. Just as families have favorite songs that they sing in the bath or in the car, classes should have favorite songs to start the day or to sing while they are waiting to go to lunch or outside to play. A class without favorite songs is as sad as a class without favorite books.

MOTHER GOOSE

For many children, Mother Goose is their first introduction to the world of literature. These folk rhymes are passed down from generation to generation and are found across many cultures. The character of Mother Goose, discussed in Chapter 3, has come to represent this type of speech play.

Even a 1-year-old child will respond with delight to the language games of "Pat-a-Cake! Pat-a-Cake!" or "This Little Pig Went to Market." Many of the Mother Goose rhymes and jingles continue to be favorites of children 4 and 5 years old. What is the attraction of Mother Goose that makes her so appealing to these young children? What accounts for her survival through these many years? Much of the language in these rhymes is obscure;

for example, modern-day children have no idea what curds and whey are, yet they delight in Little Miss Muffet. Nothing in current literature has replaced the venerable Mother Goose for the nursery-school age.

The Appeal of Mother Goose

Much of the appeal of Mother Goose lies in the musical quality of the varied language patterns, the rhythm and rhyme of the verses, the alliteration of such lines as "Wee Willie Winkie runs through the town" or "Deedle, deedle, dumpling, my son John."

Researchers have now linked children's experience with nursery rhymes and speech play to the development of sensitivity to the sounds within words, an ability they call "phonemic awareness." Children's ability to manipulate the sounds of words as they sing and chant nursery rhymes is a necessary foundation for understanding relationships between letters and sounds and contributes to their emergent literacy development.[6]

More importantly, however, children love the sounds of the words, for they are experimenting with language in this period of their lives. The child learns new words every day; he likes to try them out, to chant them while playing. Mother Goose rhymes help the young child satisfy this preoccupation with language patterns and stimulate further language development.

Mother Goose rhymes also offer young children many opportunities for active participation and response. The young child loves to get bounced on Daddy's knee to the rhythm of "Ride a Cock Horse" or to clap hands to the sound of "Pat-a-cake, pat-a-cake, baker's man." Some of the rhymes—such as "Pease Porridge Hot," "London Bridge," or "Ring a Ring o' Roses"—are games that involve direct action from the child. Other verses include counting rhymes—as in "1, 2, buckle my shoe, 3, 4, shut the door." Slightly older children enjoy answering the riddles in some of the Mother Goose verses or attempting to say their favorite tongue twisters. Every child likes to fool someone with the well-known riddle: "As I was going to St. Ives, I met a man with seven wives." And they never fail to delight in successful recitation of the entire verse of "Peter Piper picked a peck of pickled peppers."

Another attraction of many of the Mother Goose rhymes is their narrative quality; they tell a good story with quick action. In just six lines "Little Miss Muffet" proves to be an exciting tale with action, a climax, and a satisfying conclusion. This is also true of "Simple Simon," "Sing a Song of Sixpence," "The Old Woman in the Shoe," and "Three Blind Mice." Preschool and kindergarten children enjoy pantomiming or dramatizing these well-known verse stories.

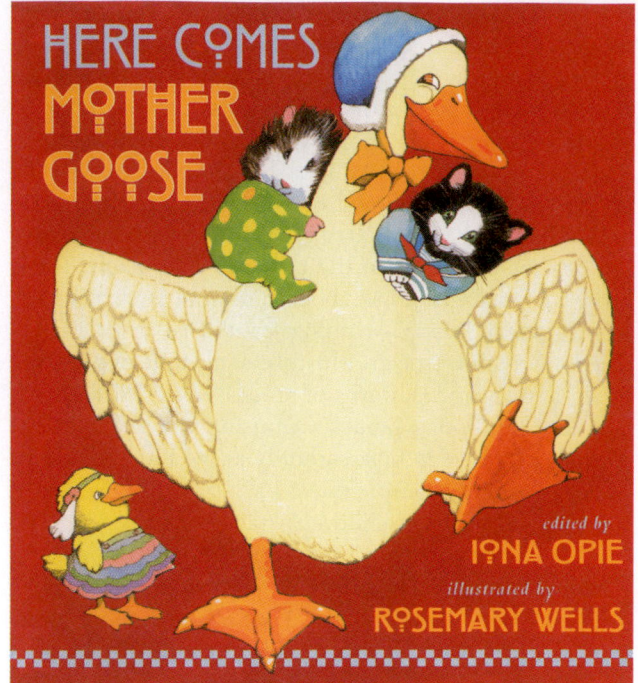

Young children and parents can take delight in repeated visits to *Here Comes Mother Goose* in a superb collection by Iona Opie with vividly appealing illustrations by Rosemary Wells. *Here Comes Mother Goose.* Illustrations © 1999 Rosemary Wells; selection © 1999 Iona Opie. Reproduced by permission of the publisher Candlewick Press, Inc., Cambridge, MA.

Many of the characters in Mother Goose have interesting, likable personalities: Old King Cole *is* a merry old soul; Old Mother Hubbard not only tries to find her poor dog a bone but she runs all over town at his special bidding; and although Tommy Lynn puts the pussy in the well, Johnny Stout pulls her out! Unpleasant but intriguing character traits are suggested by "Crosspatch," "Tom, the Piper's Son," and "Lazy Elsie Marley."

The content of the verses reflects the interests of young children. Many favorites are rhymes about animals—"The Three Little Kittens," "The Cat and the Fiddle," and the story of the mouse that ran up the clock in "Hickory Dickory Dock." Some of the verses are about simple everyday experiences and include such incidents as Lucy Locket losing her pocket, the Three Little Kittens losing their mittens, and Little Bo Peep losing her sheep. Children's pranks are enacted in "Ding, Dong, Bell!" and "Georgie Porgie." Peter, Peter, Pumpkin-Eater has a housing problem, as does the Old Woman in the Shoe. There are many verses about seasons and the weather, a concern of both young and old. The pleading request of one child in "Rain, Rain, Go Away" reflects the universal feelings of children.

---

[6]Morag Maclean, Peter Bryant, and Lynette Bradley, "Rhymes, Nursery Rhymes, and Reading in Early Childhood," *Merrill-Palmer Quarterly, Journal of Developmental Psychology* 33 (July 1987): 255–81.

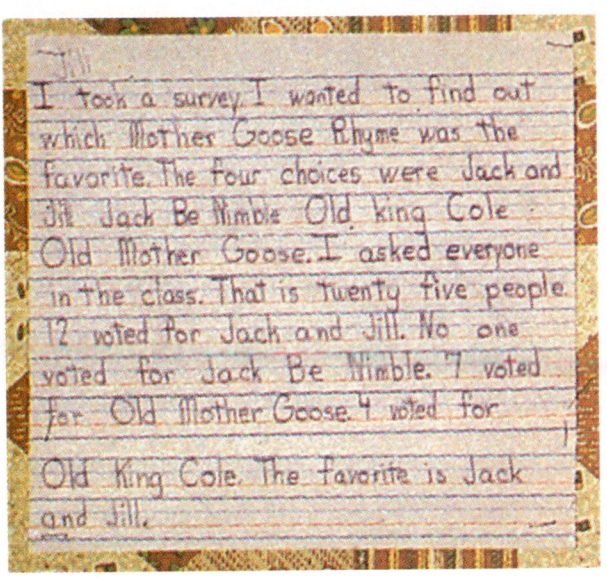

Third graders conducted a survey of the children's favorite Mother Goose rhymes. They then wrote about how they had made the survey and graphed the results. Columbus Public Schools, Columbus, Ohio. Arleen Stuck, teacher.

A major appeal of Mother Goose is the varied humor. There is the jolly good fun of a ridiculous situation:

One misty, moisty morning
When cloudy was the weather,
I chanced to meet an old man
Clothed all in leather;
He began to compliment
And I began to grin—
"How do you do" and "How do you do"
And "How do you do" again!

Two 6-year-olds interpreted this verse in action by pretending to pass each other; as one moved to the left, the other moved in the same direction. Their movements were perfect for this amusing and familiar situation.

The young child's rather primitive sense of humor, which delights in other persons' misfortune, is satisfied by the verses in "Jack and Jill" and "Dr. Foster":

Doctor Foster went to Gloucester
In a shower of rain;
He stepped in a puddle up to his middle
And never went there again.

The pure nonsense in Mother Goose tickles children's funny bones. Kornei Chukovsky, a Russian poet, reminds us that there is sense in nonsense; a child has to know reality to appreciate the juxtaposition of the strawberries and the herrings in this verse:[7]

The man in the wilderness asked me
How many strawberries grow in the sea.
I answered him as I thought good,
As many as red herrings grow in the wood.

Different Editions of Mother Goose

Today's children are fortunate in being able to choose among many beautifully illustrated Mother Goose editions. There is no *one* best Mother Goose book, for this is a matter for individual preference. Some Mother Goose books seem to stay in print indefinitely. Each generation may have its favorite edition, yet older versions remain popular. The children in every family deserve at least one of the better editions, however. Preschool and primary teachers will also want to have one that can be shared with small groups of children who might not have been fortunate enough ever to have seen a really beautiful Mother Goose.

Collections

One of the most glorious nursery-rhyme collections is *Tomie dePaola's Mother Goose.* Each of the more than two hundred verses is illustrated with brilliant jewel tones

---

[7]Kornei Chukovsky, *From Two to Five,* trans. Miriam Morton (Berkeley: University of California Press, 1963), p. 95.

against a clear white background. Characters of many races are included quite naturally. Pictures are large enough to be shared with a large group of children. Several include a full-page spread; many show a sequence of action. Careful placement of the rhymes provides interesting artistic contrasts, such as the jagged lines of the crooked man's house next to the rounded haystack of Little Boy Blue. The total format of this comprehensive Mother Goose is pleasing to the eye.

The Arnold Lobel Book of Mother Goose, edited and illustrated by Arnold Lobel, was one of the last books published before his death in 1987. Originally published as *The Random House Book of Mother Goose,* it was reissued with the new title in 2003, a fitting honor for the well-loved author and artist. Lobel illustrated over three hundred rhymes in this lively collection. Filled with fresh images and spontaneity, Lobel's Mother Goose book is a lasting contribution to children from this talented and well-loved illustrator. *Whiskers and Rhymes,* also by Lobel, is a lively collection of rhymes about cats. Although it features only several dozen rhymes, *James Marshall's Mother Goose* provides young children with a fresh and funny look at the venerable Old Goose. Most of the rhymes included in this collection are humorous, with hilarious illustrations to match. Children clever enough to spy the knife slipping through the pumpkin shell will realize that Peter is not going to be able to keep his wife forever, despite the last line of the rhyme. Sharing Marshall's funny parody on "Hey Diddle Diddle" might inspire older children to create their own original Mother Goose rhymes.

A collection by Zena Sutherland consists of some seventy-five verses under the title *The Orchard Book of Nursery Rhymes.* Brilliant detailed illustrations by Faith Jaques depict an eighteenth-century setting of rural England, the source of many of these verses. A few, such as "How much wood would a woodchuck chuck," reveal their American origin. Adding to the authenticity of this edition are the carefully researched notes on the sources and variants of these verses by both author and illustrator.

Scholars of nursery rhymes are all indebted to Iona and Peter Opie for their definitive work *The Oxford Dictionary of Nursery Rhymes,* in which they assembled almost everything known about these verses. Maurice Sendak illustrated a new version of the Opies' first collection, *I Saw Esau,* which includes 170 rhymes, tongue twisters, jeers, and jump-rope rhymes. The many small pictures are just as sly and naughty as the children's rhymes. Only 7 by 5 inches, this "Schoolchild's Pocket Book" is a superb example of fine bookmaking. Iona Opie and illustrator Rosemary Wells have collaborated on two beautiful collections, *My Very First Mother Goose* and *Here Comes Mother Goose.* The rhymes are attractively placed on each page and nicely paced throughout the book so as not to overwhelm parents and babies with too many images and too much black type. The layout gives young children time to make eye contact with the engaging illus-

trations and to wander around the page looking at all the little visual details, while Mother or Dad reads the rhyme. There are many full-page illustrations facing a rhyme to attract baby's attention and keep her visually stimulated. In these cases the text is always accompanied by smaller pictures which elaborate on the visual narrative opposite.

With such a proliferation of nursery-rhyme books, parents, teachers, and librarians will want to examine a variety of collections before sharing them with their children. Even though you might have a favorite collection, try new ones with fresh images and unfamiliar rhymes after you have read the more traditional ones. Mother Goose should never be enjoyed only once, but read over and over again. See the Evaluation Criteria box "Evaluating Mother Goose Books" for some considerations to take into account when selecting Mother Goose editions.

Single-Verse Editions

A recent publishing trend has been the production of picture books portraying only one Mother Goose rhyme or a limited number of rhymes around a single theme, often in board-book format.

Maurice Sendak was one of the first to extend the text of two single verses with illustrations in his *Hector Protector and As I Went Over the Water.* The rhyme about Hector Protector is only five lines in length, but twenty-four action-filled pictures expand the story behind this five-line verse.

Mary Had a Little Lamb was first written by Sarah Josepha Hale in 1830 and then appeared in a McGuffey Reader. Since that time, however, it has been included in many Mother Goose collections. Bruce McMillan uses full-color photos of an African American child who poses for a rural Mary in his artfully crafted version of Hale's verse. Sally Mavor has used all kinds of fabrics and stitchery to construct the pictures for her version of Mary's tale. The old-fashioned costumes and setting and the subtle links to woolly fibers and American folk art add surprising depth to the familiar rhyme. Equally faithful, in very different ways, to the historical context of this verse, both of these books would be good choices for sharing with children.

Several authors and illustrators have found ingenious ways to play with traditional nursery rhymes. *Each Peach Pear Plum* by Janet Ahlberg and Allan Ahlberg pulls together characters from Mother Goose and traditional folktales in a kind of "I Spy" game. Starting with Little Tom Thumb, each successive picture hides a new character somewhere in its design. Thus the picture of Baby Bunting carries the text "Baby Bunting fast asleep, I spy Bo-Peep," while the next picture of Bo-Peep challenges the viewer to find Jack and Jill. Young children delight in playing this game, and they particularly love the ending. In *Hey, Mama Goose* Jane Breskin Zalben and illustrator Emilie Chollat send Mother Goose to help the Old Woman in the Shoe find better housing for her growing

Evaluating Mother Goose Books

With so many editions of Mother Goose, what factors should be considered when evaluating them? The following points might be useful in studying various editions:

COVERAGE

How many verses are included? Are they well-known rhymes, or are there some fresh and unusual ones?

ILLUSTRATIONS

What medium has been used? What colors? Are the illustrations realistic, stylized, or varied? Are the illustrations consistent with the text? Do they elaborate the text? What is the mood of the illustrations (humorous, sedate, high-spirited)? Has the illustrator created a fresh approach, avoiding cliché-ridden images?

TEXT

Does the text read smoothly, or have verses been altered? Is the text all on the same page, or fragmented by the need to turn the page?

SETTING

What background is presented—rural or urban? Does the book take place in any particular country? Is the setting modern or in the past? What does the setting add to the collection?

CHARACTERS

Do the characters come from a variety of ethnic backgrounds? Do the characters have distinct personalities? Are adults and children featured? Only children? How are animals presented—as humans or realistically?

ARRANGEMENT

Is there a thematic arrangement of the verses? Is there a feeling of unity to the whole book, rather than just separate verses? Are pictures and verses well spaced or crowded? Is it clear which picture illustrates which verse?

FORMAT

What is the quality of the paper and the binding? Is the title page well designed? Is there an index or table of contents? Is there harmony among endpapers, cover, and jacket?

No matter what edition is selected, children should be exposed to the rhythm and rhyme of Mother Goose. It is part of their literary heritage and might be their first introduction to the realm of literature.

---

brood. Unfortunately, her new house turns out to be Snow White's cottage. Snow White moves in with Rapunzel, while Rumplestiltskin takes over the Gingerbread House and the Three Little Pigs move into Sleeping Beauty's castle. By the end of the story, the Old Woman and her children are lonely for their familiar shoe, and everyone else is happy to return home, too. Pamela Duncan Edwards provides some aid to ailing nursery-rhyme characters in *The Neat Line: Scribbling through Mother Goose*, illustrated by Diana Cain Bluthenthal. Edwards and Bluthenthal tell a delightful story of a little scribble who grows up to draw solutions to many characters' problems. The line creates a horn for Little Boy Blue to call the cows and sheep home, a set of steps so that Jack and Jill can make it up the hill, and a big bird to scare away Miss Muffet's Spider. Children will delight in proposing solutions that the line might offer other nursery-rhyme characters.

The cumulative format of "This Is the House That Jack Built" has inspired many interpretations over the years, including a version by Randolph Caldecott. Recently the rhyme has inspired *This Is the House That Was Tidy and Neat* by Teri Sloat, and *This Is the Van That Dad Cleaned* by Lisa Campbell Ernst. Simms Taback's *This Is the House That Jack Built* stays close to the original rhyme, but his illustrations provide a lively look at modern real estate as one character after another almost thwarts the sale of Jack's home.

Nursery-Rhyme Collections from Other Lands

Although nursery rhymes are difficult to translate because they are based on sound and nonsense, several collections capture the elements of rhythm and sound that are so appealing to young children, and several bilingual collections are available. Illustrator Barbara Cooney creates authentic settings for her pictures of Latin American rhymes collected from Spanish-speaking communities in the Americas. Each rhyme in *Tortillitas Para Mama* by Margot Griego and others is written in both Spanish and English. The English verses do not rhyme, but the Spanish ones do. *Arroz Con Leche: Popular Songs and Rhymes from Latin America* and *Arrorró, Mi Niño. Latino Lullabies and Gentle Games*, both collected by Lulu Delacre, are other sources of rhymes of Spanish origin. Alma Flor Ada and F. Isabel Campoy's *Mamá Goose* is a treasury of Latino folklore that includes lullabies, jump-rope songs, riddles, and song games.

Alma Flor Ada collects all manner of Latino speech play and nursery rhymes in *Mamá Goose*, illustrated by F. Isabel Campoy. From *Mamá Goose: A Latino Nursery Treasury* by Alma Flor Ada and F. Isabel Campoy. Illustration copyright © 2004 by Maribel Suarez. Reprinted by permission of Hyperion Books for Children.

Sharing rhymes from other countries lets children of many cultures tap into their parents' memories to find rhymes in a variety of languages. The creation of nursery rhymes for the young child is a universal activity.

Young children enjoy all kinds of poetry besides nursery rhymes. See Chapter 8 for more about poetry. For a comparison of the unique features of various Mother Goose editions, see Teaching Resources: "Mother Goose Books."

ALPHABET BOOKS

In colonial days, children were first taught their ABCs from cautionary rhymes like "In Adam's Fall/we sinned all," which combined early literacy and religion. Later, pictures of animals beginning with certain letters were added to hornbooks and early primers for younger children. Alphabet books today can be equally deceptive. Many of them have moved beyond teaching children their alphabet to serving as a format to present detailed information about a particular subject for older boys and girls, to showcase an art book, or to create complicated puzzles. Most of the alphabet books and criteria for their evaluation discussed in this chapter are directed at ABC books for the young child, however. Ages are given when an older audience is implied.

Besides teaching the names and shapes of the letters, ABC books can also be used for identification or naming, as they provide the young child with large, bright pictures of animals or single objects to look at and talk about. One of the liveliest and jazziest alphabet books is Bill Martin, Jr., and John Archambault's *Chicka Chicka Boom Boom*, illustrated with vibrant colors by Lois Ehlert. An alphabet chant, this book helps children memorize the letters and identify them. It does not provide an object or animal that goes with a beginning sound as most alphabet books do, but it does provide for much fun and merriment as children chant these active letters.

Certain factors need to be considered in selecting alphabet books for the youngest child. Objects should be clearly presented on the page, and these should be easily identifiable and meaningful for the intended age level. Only one or two objects should be shown for the very young child, and it is best to avoid portraying anything that might have several correct names. For example, if a rabbit is presented for *R*, the very young child might refer to it as a "bunny." Since text is necessarily limited, the pictures usually "carry" the story. For this reason they should be both clear and consistent with the text, reflecting and creating the mood of the book.

Alphabet books vary, in both their texts and their pictorial presentation, from very simple to intricate levels of abstraction. Authors and illustrators use a variety of organizing structures to create ABC texts. Four types of ABC books are discussed here (some books incorporate several types): (1) word-picture formats, (2) simple narratives, (3) riddles or puzzles, and (4) topical themes. Today there are so many alphabet books that only outstanding examples of each type are described here.

Striking pictures of realistic animals climb, poke through, or push large black block letters in *Animal Alphabet* by Bert Kitchen. A giraffe chins himself on the huge *G*, while a small snail climbs up the *S*. Each page contains only the letter and the picture of the animal. Names of animals are given on a page at the end of this handsome book.

David Frampton employs an entirely different style to depict his animals in *My Beastie Book of ABC*. His sharp-edged shapes and bold colors are the perfect accompaniment to his silly alphabet verses. His A is for an alligator reads, "Her teeth are quite awesome. Yours will be too if you just brush and floss 'em" (p. 4).

Arnold Lobel and Anita Lobel combined their many talents to create a handsome and unique alphabet book. Starting with the picture of a small Victorian boy determinedly lacing up his high shoes, sailor hat ready to go and purse fat with change, we follow him on his journey to the page displaying the title, *On Market Street*. Then he proceeds on his way through the shops from A to Z. He returns home in the evening exhausted, with an empty purse but a gorgeous array of gifts, each purchased from a different shop. Rather than portray all the stores, Anita Lobel creates tradespeople and shopkeepers out of their

Mother Goose Books

 Visit the Online Learning Center at **www.mhhe.com/kiefer9e** for a printable version of this list.

TRADITIONAL COLLECTIONS

Author, Illustrator	Title	Unique Features
Leslie Brooke	*Ring o'Roses*	Published in 1923, this was the first collection to include humorous animals.
Kate Greenaway	*Mother Goose, or the Old Nursery Rhymes*	This has been a treasured classic since 1901. Tiny format and precise old-fashioned pictures of proper children.
Arthur Rackham	*Mother Goose, or the Old Nursery Rhymes*	Small, eerie pictures of pointed-eared elves and personified trees.
Feodor Rojankovsky	*The Tall Book of Mother Goose*	The illustrations depict natural-looking children showing real emotions. Humpty Dumpty is portrayed as Hitler, appropriate to the time of this book's publication in 1942.
Blanche Fisher Wright	*The Real Mother Goose*	With pale, flat, traditional pictures, this book has been divided into four narrow-sized board books with checkered covers.

CONTEMPORARY COLLECTIONS

Author, Illustrator	Title	Unique Features
Nina Crews	*The Neighborhood Mother Goose*	Crews's photo-collage interpretations set familiar nursery rhymes within a multicultural city neighborhood.
Marguerite de Angeli	*The Book of Nursery and Mother Goose Rhymes*	Some 250 soft watercolor illustrations portray the English countryside and show the author's love for and knowledge of children.
Tomie dePaola	*Tomie dePaola's Mother Goose*	See text.
Michael Foreman	*Playtime Rhymes*	Foreman lends his distinctive artistic style to a lively collection of rhymes.
Mary Ann Hoberman, Michael Emberley	*You Read to Me, I'll Read to You*	Mother Goose rhymes arranged for two voices.
Arnold Lobel	*The Arnold Lobel Book of Mother Goose*	See text.
James Marshall	*James Marshall's Mother Goose*	See text.
Iona Opie and Peter Opie, Maurice Sendak	*I Saw Esau*	See text.
Iona Opie, Rosemary Wells	*Here Comes Mother Goose* and *My Very First Mother Goose*	See text.

(continued)

Mother Goose Books (*continued*)

CONTEMPORARY COLLECTIONS (*continued*)

Author, Illustrator	Title	Unique Features
Maud Petersham and Miska Petersham	*The Rooster Crows*	Includes many well-known American rhymes and jingles, such as "A bear went over the mountain" and "How much wood would a woodchuck chuck."
Robert Sabuda	*A Movable Mother Goose*	This glorious pop-up with modernized visuals of traditional rhymes will fascinate older readers.
Zena Sutherland, Faith Jaques	*The Orchard Book of Nursery Rhymes*	See text.
Tasha Tudor	*Mother Goose*	Small, soft pastel pictures are quaint and charmingly reminiscent of the work of Kate Greenaway.

SINGLE-VERSE EDITIONS

Author, Illustrator	Title	Unique Features
Lorinda Bryan Cauley	*The Three Little Kittens*	Appealing kittens that delight very young children.
Tomie dePaola	*The Comic Adventures of Old Mother Hubbard and Her Dog*	Comedy set behind a proscenium arch invites dramatic play.
Sarah Josepha Hale, Bruce McMillan	*Mary Had a Little Lamb*	See text.
Sarah Josepha Hale, Salley Mavor	*Mary Had a Little Lamb*	See text.
Susan Jeffers	*Three Jovial Huntsmen*	Three bumbling hunters search and search for their quarry and never see the many hidden animals watching them.
Salley Mavor	*Hey, Diddle, Diddle!*	A board book featuring Mavor's distinctive needlework compositions.
Tracey Campbell Pearson	*Diddle, Diddle, Dumpling*	One of a series of board books that feature individual nursery rhymes.
Maurice Sendak	*Hector Protector and As I Went Over the Water*	See text.

own wares, making intriguing characters from books, clocks, eggs, quilts, toys, and zippers.

In brilliant watercolor collages, Lois Ehlert introduces children to a wide variety of fruits and vegetables in her book *Eating the Alphabet*. Sometimes as many as four vegetables appear on a single page, but they are clearly depicted. Children might not know all the items pictured, but it would extend their knowledge and be an excellent book to use prior to a trip to the grocery store.

Children can continue to eat their way through the alphabet in two other delicious books. Crescent Dragonwagon's *Alligator Arrived with Apples* is an alliterative tale that can serve as a model for children's own alphabet books. Older children will enjoy Mike Lester's *A Is for Salad*—for the Alligator pictured eating the salad, of course. For each letter, children are asked to look at the picture rather than the word to match beginning letters.

Mm   m is for **moon**   Nn   n is for **nest**

Alison Jay's folktale-style illustrations of familiar objects in *ABC: A Child's First Alphabet Book* are just right for the youngest child. From *ABC: A Child's First Alphabet Book* by Alison Jay, copyright © 1994 by Alison Jay, illustrations. Used by permission of Dutton, a division of Penguin Putnam, Inc.

Anita Lobel's *Alison's Zinnia* is a brilliant alphabet book glowing with flower paintings. Listen to the carefully planned sentences in this book:

Alison acquired an Amaryllis for Beryl
Beryl bought a Begonia for Crystal

and so it goes until

Yolanda yanked a Yucca for Zena
Zena zeroed in on a Zinnia for Alison.

Topical themes are frequently used to tie the alphabet together. For example, *V for Vanishing: An Alphabet of Endangered Animals* by Patricia Mullins, Ann Jonas's *Aardvarks Disembark!*, and *Gone Forever! An Alphabet of Extinct Animals* by Sandra Markle and William Markle provide information on endangered or extinct animals. In *A Caribou Alphabet*, Mary Beth Owens portrays the world of the caribou, from "A for Antlers" to "Z for Below Zero Weather." A compendium at the end gives even more information about this endangered species.

Children can explore the world around them or beyond their borders through alphabet books like Alma Flor Ada's *Gathering the Sun*, illustrated by Simón Silva, or Nikki Grimes's *C Is for City*, illustrated by Pat Cummings. Ada's bilingual poems introduce readers to the lives of field workers like Cesar Chavez. Silva's warm, richly textured paintings convey the quiet beauty of life on farms and the dignity of field workers. On the other hand, Grimes and Cummings show the lively multicultural world of a big city through rhyming text and detailed paintings. In this urban setting, for example, *H* is for handball, hopscotch, hot dogs, and Hasidim. Older children might enjoy creating their own alphabet book

based on a chosen subject, using these two books as models. Such theme books suggest ways for older students to organize material they might be presenting for a particular study. Children could make their own ABC books of "Life at the Seashore," "Pioneer Life," or their favorite books. For a description of the unique features of many ABC books, see Teaching Resources: "ABC Books."

COUNTING BOOKS

Ideally, girls and boys should learn to count by playing with real objects like blocks, boxes, bottle caps, or model cars. They can manipulate and group these as they wish, actually seeing what happens when you add one more block to nine or divide six blocks into two groups. Since time immemorial, however, we have been providing children with counting books, substituting pictures for real objects. Young children can make this transition from the concrete to its visual representation if they first experience the real objects and the visual illustrations are clearly presented.

In evaluating counting books, then, we look to see if the objects to be counted stand out clearly on the page. Groupings of objects should not look cluttered or confusing. Illustrations and page design are most important in evaluating counting books. Accuracy is essential.

Counting books, too, vary from the very simple to the more complex. For the purposes of this text they are discussed under three categories: (1) one-to-one correspondence, (2) other simple mathematical concepts, and (3) number stories and puzzles. Examples of each category are given; Teaching Resources: "Counting Books" lists other titles by structure.

ABC Books

 Visit the Online Learning Center at **www.mhhe.com/kiefer9e** for a printable version of this list.

WORD/PICTURE IDENTIFICATION

Author, Illustrator	Title	Age Level	Unique Features
John Burningham	*John Burningham's ABC*	2–4	One clear picture for each letter. Unusual choices: *T* is for tractor; *V* shows a volcano.
C. B. Falls	*ABC Book*	2–4	A reissue of a classic originally published in 1923.
Tana Hoban	*A, B, See!*	2–4	Black-and-white photograms illustrate familiar objects.
Bert Kitchen	*Animal Alphabet*	2–5	See text.
Edward Lear, Suse MacDonald	*A Was Once an Apple Pie*	3–7	Lear's silly alphabet verses are brought to life by MacDonald's illustrations.
Suse MacDonald	*Alphabatics*	5–12	Each letter grows or tilts to become part of a beautifully clear graphic picture on the next page.
Helen Oxenbury	*Helen Oxenbury's ABC of Things*	3–6	Provides a small vignette for each letter. *H* is represented by a very funny picture of a hare and a hippopotamus lying in bed in a hospital.

SIMPLE NARRATIVE

Author, Illustrator	Title	Age Level	Unique Features
Deborah Chandra, Keiko Narahashi	*A Is for Amos*	4–7	Poetic text and lovely watercolors show a little girl taking an imaginary ride on her rocking horse.
Michael Chesworth	*Alphaboat*	7–9	A rhyming story of an ocean voyage told with letters that stand in for words.
Doreen Cronin, Betsy Lewin	*Click, Clack, Quackity-Quack*	3–7	The indomitable duck of Cronin and Lewin's many books decides to teach the farm animals the alphabet.
Crescent Dragonwagon, Jose Aruego and Ariane Dewey	*Alligator Arrived with Apples*	6–10	See text.
Denise Fleming	*Alphabet Under Construction*	3–7	An intrepid mouse goes about building the alphabet.
Wanda Gág	*The ABC Bunny*	2–4	A little rabbit provides the story line for each letter.
Piet Gobler	*Little Bird's ABC*	4–8	Whimsical birds create sounds to match each letter of the alphabet.

ABC Books (continued)

SIMPLE NARRATIVE (continued)

Author, Illustrator	Title	Age Level	Unique Features
Maira Kalman	*What Pete Ate from A–Z (Really!)*	3–9	Pete the Dog travels through the neighborhood eating everything in sight.
Arnold Lobel, Anita Lobel	*On Market Street*	5–7	See text.
Joseph Slate, Ashley Wolff	*Miss Bindergarten Takes a Field Trip with Kindergarten*	3–7	Further adventures of Miss Bindergarten and her kindergartners, a class of 26 children, named from A to Z.
June Sobol, Melissa Iwai	*B Is for Bulldozer: A Construction ABC*	3–7	The story of constructing an amusement park.
Clyde Watson, Wendy Watson	*Applebet*	5–7	A farmer and her daughter take a cart full of apples to the county fair. The accompanying verse asks the child to find the apple hidden in each picture.
Ken Wilson-Max, Manya Stojic	*A Book of Letters*	3–7	A lift-the-flap alphabet story told through the mail.

RIDDLES OR PUZZLES

Author, Illustrator	Title	Age Level	Unique Features
Jennifer Belle, David McPhail	*Animal Stackers*	6–10	Each letter begins a word that forms an acrostic story.
Lisa Campbell Ernst	*The Turn-Around Upside-Down Alphabet Book*	6–10	Inventive visual play is suggested for each graphic letter form.
Jan Garten	*The Alphabet Tale*	5–7	Each letter is introduced on the preceding page by showing just the tail of an animal; turn the page and you see the whole animal.
Mike Lester	*A Is for Salad*	4–7	See text.
Lucy Mickelwait	*I Spy: An Alphabet in Art*	5–10	Children are invited to play "I Spy" and find objects in famous paintings.
David Pellitier	*The Graphic Alphabet*	7–14	Letters turn into art in stunning visual designs.
Steve Schnur, Leslie Evans	*Autumn: An Alphabet Acrostic and other seasons*	7–12	The word representing each alphabet letter becomes an acrostic poem about each of the seasons and invites children to try their own versions.
Chris Van Allsburg	*The Z Was Zapped*	6–10	A drama presented on stage in 26 acts.

(continued)

ABC Books (continued)

TOPICAL THEMES

Author, Illustrator	Title	Age Level	Unique Features
Alma Flor Ada, Simón Silva	*Gathering the Sun: An Alphabet in Spanish and English*	6–10	See text.
Jim Aylesworth, Stephen Gammell	*Old Black Fly*	6–10	Marvelously funny illustrations portray this tiresome fly as he buzzes around the alphabet.
Mary Azarian	*A Farmer's Alphabet*	5–12	A handsome book that celebrates rural life in Vermont. Striking black-and-white woodcuts portray a barn, a quilt, and a wood stove, for example.
Jo Bannatyne-Cugnet, Yvette Moore	*A Prairie Alphabet*	6–14	Highly detailed paintings provide a tour of the seasons and people of the northern prairie.
Betsy Bowen	*Antler, Bear, Canoe*	6–10	Hand-colored woodcuts show the four seasons in the North woods. Compare to Azarian's Vermont woodcuts.
Eve Bunting, Suzanne Bloom	*Girls A to Z*	5–12	A lively celebration of being a girl.
Ying Chang Compestine, YongSheng Xuan	*D Is for Dragon Dance*	4–8	An ABC takes readers through a Chinese New Year's celebration.
Chris Demarest	*Firefighters from A to Z*	3–9	Paintings depict a firefighter's world.
Joanne Dugan	*ABC NYC*	6–10	Dugan provides a graphically exciting look at New York City.
Lois Ehlert	*Eating the Alphabet*	4–7	See text.
Muriel Feelings, Tom Feelings	*Jambo Means Hello*	6–14	Muriel Feelings gives children a simple lesson in Swahili while introducing some important aspects of the geography and culture of East Africa.
David Frampton	*My Beastie Book of ABC*	3–7	See text.
Nikki Grimes, Pat Cummings	*C Is for City*	K–4	See text.
Elissa Grodin, Victor Jahsz	*D Is for Democracy*	7–12	One of a series of alphabet books that focus on the world, the United States, and its states.
Ted Harrison	*A Northern Alphabet*	7–14	This striking book about northern Canada and Alaska describes people, places, animals, and objects for each letter.

ABC Books *(continued)*

TOPICAL THEMES *(continued)*

Author, Illustrator	Title	Age Level	Unique Features
Lee Bennett Hopkins, Barry Root	*April, Bubbles, Chocolate*	6–10	Favorite poems to highlight the alphabet. Selections include "Foghorns" by Lilian Moore and Richard Brautigan's "Xerox Candy Bar."
Peter Hunt	*Illuminations*	8–14	An illuminated alphabet of the Middle Ages.
Rachel Isadora	*City Seen from A to Z*	6–9	This book captures the action of the city through body postures and storytelling vignettes.
———.	*On Your Toes: A Ballet ABC*	3–10	Elegant paintings of the ballet world.
Martin Jarrie	*ABC USA*	4–7	A lively, folk-art look at aspects of the United States.
Stephen Johnson	*Alphabet City*	6–10	Photo-realistic paintings capture the lines, shapes, and textures of the city.
Ann Jonas	*Aardvarks Disembark!*	7–12	See text.
Anita Lobel	*Alison's Zinnia*	7–12	See text.
———.	*Animal Antics A–Z*	3–7	Animals play with the letters from A to Z, while acrobats form them with their bodies.
———.	*Away from Home*	7–12	Children travel to the far corners of the earth, beginning with Adam, who "arrived in Amsterdam," and ending with Zachary, who "zigzagged in Zaandam."
Celeste Davidson Mannis, Bagram Ibatoulline	*The Queen's Progress*	7–12	Elizabeth I takes an alphabet journey through the English countryside.
Sandra and William Markle, Felipe Dávalos	*Gone Forever: An Alphabet of Extinct Animals*	K–4	See text.
Wynton Marsalis, Paul Rogers	*Jazz ABZ*	7–12	Biographies of jazz greats are presented through vivid Art Deco illustrations.
Michael McCurdy	*The Sailor's Alphabet*	7–12	This text is based on a sea chantey and introduces readers to the world of eighteenth-century sailing vessels.
Patricia Mullins	*V for Vanishing*	7–14	See text.
Margaret Musgrove, Leo Dillon and Diane Dillon	*Ashanti to Zulu: African Traditions*	7–14	This is the only alphabet book to have won the Caldecott Medal. The illustrations picture the people, their homes, and an artifact and animal for each of 26 African tribes.

(continued)

ABC Books (*continued*)

TOPICAL THEMES (*continued*)

Author, Illustrator	Title	Age Level	Unique Features
Ifeoma Onyefulu	A Is for Africa	6–12	Striking photographs and pleasing page design introduce African cultures and customs.
Mary Beth Owens	A Caribou Alphabet	7–14	See text.
Jerry Pallotta	The Beetle Alphabet Book	6–10	One of a series of alphabet books that focus on science topics.
Diana Pomeroy	Wildflower ABC	6–12	Pomeroy has created illustrations for each wildflower using potato prints and inviting similar efforts by children.
Alice Provensen, Martin Provensen	A Peaceable Kingdom: The Shaker Abecedarius	6–12	The Provensens illustrated this old 1882 alphabet verse of the Shakers in a way that depicts the rhyme of the animals but also provides much information about the way the Shakers lived.
Marilyn Sanders, Eve Sanders	What's Your Name? From Ariel to Zoe	6–10	Twenty-six children from a variety of cultures talk about their names. Each class will want to create their own name alphabet book.
Luci Tapahonso, Eleanor Schick	Navajo ABC	7–14	Beginning with "A for Arroyo," lovely realistic illustrations give information about the Navajo, or Diné, culture.
Tobi Tobias	A World of Words	7–14	A beautifully illustrated collection of quotations accompany each letter.
Tasha Tudor	A Is for Annabelle	5–7	Delicate watercolors portray an old-fashioned doll with her different belongings representing different letters.
Richard Wilbur, David Diaz	The Disappearing Alphabet	7–14	Poems about how our language would be different if a letter disappeared.

Tana Hoban's *1, 2, 3* is a sturdy, well-designed first counting book that presents simple one-to-one correspondence. Colored photographs picture well-known objects like two shoes, five small fingers, six eggs, seven animal crackers, and ten toes. Numbers and names of the numerals are given in this first board book for very young children. Such a beginning counting book might serve more for identification of the object than for actual counting. Certainly it requires a lower level of associative thinking for the very young child.

A watery theme can be found in Lois Ehlert's *Fish Eyes: A Book You Can Count On*, illustrated with brilliant colored graphics. A little black fish takes the reader on a journey through the ocean to discover "one green fish, two jumping fish, three smiling fish." Always the black fish adds himself to the group: "Three smiling fish plus me makes 4." Children delight in the spots and stripes of these gleaming fish with die-cut eyes.

Captivating language characterizes Charlotte Huck's *A Creepy Countdown,* illustrated by Jos. A. Smith. The tension mounts deliciously as Huck's fearsome creatures—scarecrows, toads, jack o'lanterns, owls, bats, witches, ghosts, cats, skeletons, and mice—gather together, say "boo to you!" and then disperse again until only "two lumpy toads hid beneath a stone, one tall scarecrow stood all alone." Smith's black-and-white scratchboard

Counting Books

 Visit the Online Learning Center at **www.mhhe.com/kiefer9e** for a printable version of this list.

ONE-TO-ONE CORRESPONDENCE

Author, Illustrator	Title	Age Level	Unique Features
Arlene Alda	Arlene Alda's 123: What Do You See?	3–6	Photos of everyday objects invite child's participation in finding hidden numerals.
Kathi Appelt, Emilie Chollat	Rain Dance	3–7	Living things in a rainstorm.
Keith Baker	Big Fat Hen	4–6	Count eggs and chicks to the rhyme "1, 2, buckle my shoe."
Molly Bang	Ten, Nine, Eight	4–6	Starting with his daughter's ten toes, a father begins a countdown until she is in bed.
Eric Carle	1, 2, 3, to the Zoo	4–6	A circus train serves as the vehicle for this counting book as each passing car contains an increasing number of animals.
Philippe Dupasquier	1 2 3 Follow Me!	2–6	Board book has cutout shapes of numbers on each page, as first one chick, then other animals assemble.
Cathryn Falwell	Feast for Ten	4–7	Beginning with one grocery cart, these bold, textured collages show an African American family shopping for, preparing, and eating a feast for ten.
———.	Turtle Splash: Countdown at the Farm	3–7	In a reverse count from ten, turtles share their home with other creatures.
Muriel Feelings, Tom Feelings	Moja Means One	7–12	This is as much an informational book on East Africa and the Swahili language as a counting book.
Arthur Geisert	Pigs from 1 to 10	5–9	Detailed etchings hide pigs to count and adventures to follow.
Tana Hoban	Let's Count	1–6	Clear bright pictures of everyday objects from 1 to 20, 50 and 100 are accompanied by large numerals and schematics.
———.	1, 2, 3	1–3	See text.
Rachel Isadora	1 2 3 Pop!	5–9	Isadora uses Pop Art images to illustrate numbers from 1 to 20.
Bert Kitchen	Animal Numbers	5–9	A stunning counting book that begins with one baby kangaroo in its mother's pouch and ends with a hundred baby tadpoles and frog eggs.

(continued)

Counting Books (continued)

ONE-TO-ONE CORRESPONDENCE (*continued*)

Author, Illustrator	Title	Age Level	Unique Features
Kim Parker	*Counting in the Garden*	3–6	Brightly colored paintings of flowers hide animals in the garden.
Diana Pomeroy	*One Potato: A Book of Potato Prints*	4–7	Objects from the garden are created through lovely potato prints. Directions for making prints are included.
Lynn Reiser	*Ten Puppies*	3–7	Lively puppies from 1 to 10.
Phyllis Root, Susan Gaber	*Ten Sleepy Sheep*	3–6	One by one, ten sheep reluctantly go to sleep.
Peter Sis	*Waving: A Counting Book*	5–7	Mary's mother waved to a taxi. Two bicyclists waved back to her while three boys waved to the bicyclists. A city background provides even more things to count.
Jessica Spanyol	*Carlo Likes Counting*	3–6	Giraffe counts around the city.

OTHER MATHEMATICAL CONCEPTS

Author, Illustrator	Title	Age Level	Unique Features
Mitsumasa Anno	*Anno's Counting Book*	4–7	See text.
Donald Crews	*Ten Black Dots*	4–8	A graphic counting book that shows what you can do with ten black dots. One can make a sun, two become fox's eyes, or eight the wheels of a train.
Lois Ehlert	*Fish Eyes: A Book You Can Count On*	6–8	See text.
Paul Giganti, Jr., Donald Crews	*How Many Blue Birds Flew Away?*	6–8	Crews's bright illustrations help depict the concept of subtraction.
———.	*How Many Snails?*	4–8	A counting book that asks increasingly difficult questions: not only how many snails, but how many snails with stripes? how many striped snails with their head stuck out?
Tana Hoban	*26 Letters and 99 Cents*	6–8	Letters are matched with toys or objects beginning with that letter. Turn the book around for all the possible sets of coins to make up each number.
Emily Jenkins, Tomek Bogacki	*Five Creatures*	4–9	Three humans and two cats show many ways to achieve a set of five.
Ann Jonas	*Splash!*	6–9	See text.
Bruce McMillan	*Eating Fractions*	6–10	Photographs show food divided into parts, and children are having a wonderful time eating up the parts.

Counting Books (continued)

OTHER MATHEMATICAL CONCEPTS (continued)

Author, Illustrator	Title	Age Level	Unique Features
Eve Merriam, Bernie Karlin	*12 Ways to Get to 11*	5–7	In an imaginative introduction to sets, eleven different combinations of things add up to twelve.
Lloyd Moss, Marjorie Priceman	*Zin! Zin! Zin! A Violin*	6–10	Musical instruments come together to count to ten through musical groups, from solo to nonet to a chamber group that performs a stellar concert.
Pam Muñoz Ryan, Benrei Huang	*One Hundred Is a Family*	5–8	The rhyming text first counts to ten, illustrated with pictures of families from many cultures. Then counting by tens shows families as larger communities working together for a better world.

NUMBER STORIES AND PUZZLES

Author, Illustrator	Title	Age Level	Unique Features
Ruth Brown	*Ten Seeds*	4–8	The life cycle of a sunflower from single seed to plant and back to seed.
Eric Carle	*10 Little Rubber Ducks*	3–6	Rubber ducks fall off a container ship and head in different directions.
———.	*The Very Hungry Caterpillar*	5–7	See text.
Kathryn Cave, Gisele Wulfson	*One Child, One Seed*	5–10	This counting book provides information about South Africa.
Cynthia Cotton	*At the Edge of the Woods*	3–7	Similar to the familiar "Over in the Meadow."
Michael Dahl, Todd Ouren	*One Big Building: A Counting Book about Construction*	3–6	Counting through the construction of twelve buildings.
Sarah Hayes	*Nine Ducks Nine*	5–7	Nine ducks go for a walk, followed by a fox. One by one, the ducks take off for the rickety bridge where Mr. Fox receives his come-uppance. A wonderful story that helps children count down.
Charlotte Huck, Jos. A. Smith	*A Creepy Countdown*	5–7	See text.
Pat Hutchins	*1 Hunter*	5–7	An account of a hunter's humorous walk through a jungle filled with hidden animals.
———.	*The Doorbell Rang*	5–7	See text.

(continued)

Counting Books *(continued)*

NUMBER STORIES AND PUZZLES *(continued)*

Author, Illustrator	Title	Age Level	Unique Features
Stephen T. Johnson	*City by Numbers*	5–10	Johnson's painterly eye finds numbers in common city objects.
Anita Lobel	*One Lighthouse, One Moon*	4–8	A year with Nini the cat.
George Ella Lyon, Ann W. Olson	*Counting on the Woods*	6–10	A lovely poem illustrated with vivid photographs celebrates the woods.
Celeste Davidson Mannis, Susan Kathleen Hartung	*One Leaf Rides the Wind: Counting in a Japanese Garden*	3–7	A girl makes her way through a lovely Japanese garden, counting each object with a haiku verse.
Bill Martin, Jr. and Michael Sampson, Heather Cahoon	*Rock It, Sock It, Number Line*	4–8	Numbers round up vegetables to make soup for the king and queen.
Zoran Milich	*City 1 2 3*	4–8	Vivid photographs depict city objects and show numerals to match them.
Ifeoma Onyefulu	*Emeka's Gift*	6–10	Beautiful photographs celebrate family and community in a Nigerian village.
Charlotte Pomerantz, Jose Aruego and Ariane Dewey	*One Duck, Another Duck*	5–7	A grandmother owl teaches her grandson to count to ten. Easy and entertaining story.
Laura Rankin	*Swan Harbor*	5–12	Detailed paintings picture a harbor and its denizens through the seasons.
Christopher Wormell	*Teeth, Tails, and Tentacles*	4–8	Prints depict each numeral and match it to body parts of animals (e.g., eight octopus tentacles).

illustrations are wonderfully spooky, with touches of yellow and red that add to the supernatural atmosphere.

Many mathematical concepts are developed in one of the most inventive and perfect counting books of late, *Anno's Counting Book* by Mitsumasa Anno. Delicate watercolors portray a landscape changing with the various times of day, seasons, and year. The clock in the church steeple tells the time of day while adults, children, and animals go about their daily activities. As the buildings in the village increase, so do the groups and sets of children, adults, trees, trains, boats, and so on. This is one of the few counting books to begin with zero—a cold winter landscape showing only the river and the sky, no village. It ends with a picture of the twelfth month, a snowy Christmas scene and twelve reindeer in the sky.

Anno's Counting Book requires real exploration to find the sets of children, adults, buildings, and animals, generating a higher level of thought and discussion about numerical concepts than a simple one-to-one counting book.

Pat Hutchins's well-loved story *The Doorbell Rang* could also be used for its math concepts. Victoria and Sam's mother makes them a dozen cookies just like Grandmother's to share (six each). The doorbell rings and two friends are welcomed in to share the cookies (three each). The doorbell rings twice more until there are a dozen children and a dozen cookies. The doorbell rings again. Should they answer it? They do, and it is their grandmother with an enormous tray of cookies!

Ann Jonas's *Splash!* will challenge primary children learning about adding and subtracting. The book begins

In *Anno's Counting Book*, Mitsumasa Anno's delicate watercolors portray a landscape changing with the various times of day, seasons, and year. The clock in the church steeple tells the time of day while sets of adults, children, and animals go about their daily activities. How many sets of nine can you discover on this page? *Illustration from* Anno's Counting Book *by Mitsumasa Anno. Copyright © 1975 by Kodansha (Tokyo). Used by permission of HarperCollins Publishers.*

on a lazy summer day at a backyard pond where two catfish and four goldfish swim lazily. On the bank three frogs, one turtle, and one dog are napping while one robin rests on a bird house. When one cat comes home, she startles the turtle, who jumps in the water. "How many are in my pond?" becomes the refrain that carries through the rest of the book as animals, amphibians, fish, birds, and insects get in and out of the pond.

Certainly there is no dearth of counting books and books that can be used for the development of math concepts. Because the Evaluation Criteria for counting books are similar to those for alphabet books, we have combined the criteria for both in "Evaluating ABC and Counting Books."

CONCEPT BOOKS

ABC books and counting books are really concept books; so, too, are the books that help children learn spatial relations and patterns and to identify and discriminate colors. Some books combine multiple concepts in an ABC or counting format. Laurie Kreb's *We All Went on*

EVALUATION CRITERIA

Evaluating ABC and Counting Books

ABC BOOKS

- The objects or animals should be presented clearly.
- For very young children, only one or two objects should be pictured on a page.
- Common objects or animals that are easily identifiable are best for the young child.
- ABC books should avoid the use of objects that might be known by several names.
- The author/illustrator's purpose for the book should be clear.
- The illustrations should be consistent with the text and reflect the mood of the book.
- The organizing principle of the presentations should be clear.

- The intended age level should be considered in both pictures and text.

COUNTING BOOKS

- Objects to be counted should stand out clearly.
- Accuracy is essential.
- Common objects that children know, such as fingers, toes, and eggs, are usually best for the young child.
- Groupings or sets should be clearly differentiated.
- Number concepts should not be lost in the story.
- The level of thinking required should be challenging for appropriate ages.

We're Sailing to Galapagos incorporates concepts about days of the week with facts about the flora and fauna of the Galapagos Islands. First published in 2005 by Barefoot Books, Inc. Text copyright © 2005 by Laurie Krebs. Illustrations copyright © 2005 by Grazia Restelli.

Safari, illustrated by Julie Cairns, provides numbers from one to ten in both English and Swahili and gives children an introduction to Tanzanian culture as well. Krebs's *We're Sailing to Galapagos*, illustrated by Grazia Restelli, takes children on a journey through each day of the week around the islands of the Galapagos. The book provides fascinating facts about the fauna of the islands and simple endnotes that include information about Charles Darwin.

Photographer Tana Hoban has created a number of exceptional concept books such as *Is It Larger? Is It Smaller?* and *Shapes, Shapes, Shapes*. In *Colors Everywhere* Hoban places photographs of a basket of buttons, a pea-

Vividly colored photographs portray a full spectrum of color in Tana Hoban's *Colors Everywhere*. Copyright © 1995 by Tana Hoban. Used by permission of HarperCollins Publishers.

cock in a field of daffodils, a carnival, and a pile of autumn leaves next to separate bands of color that a child can name and match in each picture. In *Exactly the Opposite*, Hoban uses a variety of situations to show open and shut, front and back, empty and full, and far and near.

In addition to Hoban, photographers Bruce McMillan, Ann Morris, and Margaret Miller can be relied on to provide attractive and informative photo-essays for young children. In his earlier books McMillan explored concepts such as counting and colors. In more recent titles he visits the natural world and shows children engaged in fascinating activities. In *Days of the Ducklings* and *Night of the Pufflings* he follows the growth of eider ducks and puffins on an Icelandic island. He returns to Iceland in *Going Fishing* to follow a young boy as he goes to work with his father. Morris brings an international focus to the concepts of family, food, transportation, and the like in *Loving; Bread, Bread, Bread;* and *Houses and Homes.* In each of her books she provides photographs of children from a multitude of cultures. Simple text accompanies the picture, and a simple glossary at the end matches photo to country with a brief fact. Miller explores professions and trades in two well-conceived concept books, *Whose Hat?* and *Who Uses This?* A clear colored picture shows just a chef's hat. Turn the page and there is a picture of a chef in his kitchen. The opposite page pictures white and African American girls stirring a big pot, each wearing chef's hats. Miller has developed a similar question-and-answer format in *Can You Guess?* ("What do you comb in the morning?"), *Guess Who?* ("Who flies an airplane?"), and *Where Does It Go?* ("Where does a sock go?"). Photographs of four silly answers follow each question; turning the page reveals the correct response.

Lois Ehlert, whose *Fish Eyes* and *Eating the Alphabet* we discussed earlier in this chapter, has created a number of beautiful concept books. Her distinctive *In My World, Color Zoo,* and *Color Farm* use sophisticated die-cut graphics to create stylized creatures. In *Red Leaf, Yellow Leaf* Ehlert uses collage to tell the story of her favorite maple tree. *Waiting for Wings* illustrates the life cycle of butterflies, beginning with very small pages as caterpillars lay eggs and increasing to full size as the butterflies emerge in their glory. Some of Lois Ehlert's books convey concepts for primary children as well as tell little stories. *Feathers for Lunch,* written with a rhyming text, tells about a little cat who would like to catch all the different birds that he sees, but luckily his bell frightens them away. The birds are pictured with life-size brilliant collages, and plants and trees are labeled.

Many of Donald Crews's books, such as *Freight Train, Truck, School Bus,* and *Harbor,* can be classified as concept books or easy informational books. Certainly all of them explore the various dimensions of their subject. In *Freight Train,* Crews pictures an empty track, then each of the different cars: red caboose, orange tank car, yellow hopper car, green cattle car, blue gondola, purple box car, and finally the black steam engine. Both colors and specific

After exploring Lois Ehlert's style, children choose similar shapes and colors to respond to *Color Zoo*. Emerson and Central College Elementary Schools, Westerville, Ohio. Lisa Dapoz, Joan Fusco, and Jean Sperling, teachers. Photo by Connie Compton.

names for the cars provide real information for young children. In *Truck,* using bold graphics, Crews swings a big red truck across the country from east to west through cities, small towns, night and day, rain and shine. No text appears in this concept book except for all the environmental print one naturally encounters on a trip.

Many publishers have found the preschool audience a strong market for simple books of nonfiction as well as concepts. HarperCollins has focused on nonfiction for the very young in its Let's-Read-and-Find-Out Science Books series. *Wiggling Worms at Work* by Wendy Pfeffer with collage illustrations by Steve Jenkins is a fascinating look at the life and life cycle of earthworms. This excellent series also includes Carolyn Otto's *What Color Is Camouflage?* and Franklin Branley's *Air Is All Around You.*

Artist Steve Jenkins has created award-winning nonfiction for the youngest children in books such as *What*

Do You Do with a Tail Like This? and *I See a Kookaburra!*, co-authored by Robin Page. Children are fascinated with *Actual Size* and *Prehistoric Actual Size*, which provide them with an understanding of how big an animal is or a dinosaur would be relative to their own size. Even the large trim size of the book (12 by 20 inches in a double-page spread) can only show the eye of a giant squid or the foot of an African elephant!

Dick King-Smith's *I Love Guinea Pigs* and *All Pigs Are Beautiful* are a particularly delightful pair from the Read and Wonder series published by Candlewick. They are books that convey simple concepts about the natural world in the context of stories or poems. King-Smith's chatty format and his enthusiasm for his subjects provide just enough information for young children. For example, he explains immediately that guinea pigs aren't pigs, but rodents. In smaller, hand-printed captions he provides information about a major characteristic of rodents such as that guinea pigs and pigs have in common the fact that males and females are called "boars" and "sows." Children will also be fascinated by other books in this fine series, including *One Tiny Turtle* by Nicola Davies and *Gentle Giant Octopus* by Karen Wallace.

Other notable nonfiction for young children includes books about ocean life such as Anne Rockwell's *Little Shark*, Eric Carle's *Mister Seahorse*, and Sylvia Earle's *Hello Fish! Visiting the Coral Reef*. Young children can learn about the animal world in Lindsay Barrett George's *Inside Mouse, Outside Mouse* or Betty Tatham's *Baby Sea Otter*. They can discover where wool comes from in Elaine Greenstein's *One Little Lamb* or learn how gravity works in Vicki Cobb's *I Fall Down*.

These excellent concept and nonfiction books help the youngest child see relationships between objects, develop awareness of similarities and differences, and grasp the various dimensions of an abstract idea. Information for the younger child should be presented in a clear, unconfusing manner, with one or more examples given. Where appropriate, the functions of objects should be made clear. Concepts should be within the developmental scope of the child. These books can be used to enrich or reinforce an experience, not substitute for it. Young children enjoy hearing these books read aloud along with fictional stories, for young children are curious and seek information. They want to know the names of things, how they work, and why this is so. See Chapter 11 for more on choosing and evaluating nonfiction for children.

WORDLESS BOOKS

Wordless books are picture books in which the story line is told entirely through pictures. They are increasingly popular with today's TV-oriented child. Many of them are laid out in the same sequential manner as comic books and have wide appeal to different age levels.

Textless books are surprisingly helpful in developing some of the skills necessary for reading. Handling the book, turning the pages, beginning at the left-hand side and moving to the right are all skills that give the young child a sense of directionality and the experience of acting like a reader. These books are particularly useful in stimulating language development through encouraging children to take an active part in storytelling. As the child relates the story, she will become aware of beginnings, endings, the sequence of the story, the climax, the actions of the characters—all necessary for learning how a story works and for developing a sense of story. "Reading," or telling what is happening in the pictures in a wordless book, also requires specific comprehension skills. Teachers may want to record children's stories in language experience booklets. Older children might want to write their own creative stories to accompany the illustrations. To help the child tell the story, pictures must show action and sequence clearly so children will not be confused in their tellings. Also, children should be given an opportunity to examine the book and look through it completely before they try to tell the story orally. Otherwise, they will describe the action on each page but not understand the sequential relationship of the events.

Mercer Mayer was one of the first illustrators to create wordless books. His series that includes *A Boy, a Dog, and a Frog* is very popular with children ages 5 and up. Simple line drawings in green and black portray the friendship between a boy, his dog, his frog, and a turtle. The stories are amusing and full of slapstick fun, particularly *Frog Goes to Dinner*, in which frog hides in the boy's pocket and goes to the restaurant with the family.

In *Do You Want to Be My Friend?* Eric Carle gives the child latitude to create her own story about a little mouse who, in seeking a friend, follows the lead of one tail after another, only to be very surprised at what is at the other end! The brilliant collage pictures will delight children and provide the opportunity for them to tell their own versions of this story.

Alexandra Day tells a series of humorous stories about an almost human rottweiler dog named Carl. In each wordless story, when Carl is left to mind the baby, he gives the child a marvelous time and manages to keep the grown-ups ignorant of their escapades. Carl's adventures can be found in *Good Dog, Carl; Carl Goes Shopping; Carl's Sleepy Afternoon;* and others. It is hard to tell who is the more lovable and dependable—Carl or the delightful child.

Pat Hutchins has created two innovative books that invite children's retelling. *Changes, Changes* features two resourceful wooden dolls who save their burning block house by dismantling it and building a fire engine. In *Rosie's Walk*, Hutchins has written and illustrated a story with the use of only one sentence. In this book Rosie—a very determined, flat-footed hen—goes for a walk, un-

mindful of the fact that she is being stalked by a hungry fox. At every turn of *Rosie's Walk,* the hen unwittingly foils the fox in his plans to catch her. The brightly colored comic illustrations help youngsters tell Rosie's story.

Another book that is a favorite with young children is *Deep in the Forest* by Brinton Turkle. This book is really a variant of "Goldilocks and the Three Bears," with the unique twist that a baby bear wreaks havoc in a pioneer cabin. Usually when the children see baby bear eating porridge from three different-size bowls, they recall having "heard" something like this before. Barbara Lehman's *The Red Book* is also a twist on a familiar tale, that of "Town Mouse, Country Mouse." As two children, a city girl and an island boy, both find the same red book and imagine themselves in the story, we discover that this charming text is really a book about the power of books and the imagination.

Emily McCully tells delightful stories of a large mouse family and their seasonal fun in *Picnic, First Snow,* and *School.* In *Picnic* a little mouse falls out of the truck as it is going down a bumpy road. Her absence is not discovered until all eight of her brothers and sisters are ready to eat. Then the whole family piles into the truck to go find her. McCully's style of painting changes in *Four Hungry Kittens* but not her ability to develop a great story with visuals alone. In a barnyard setting a mother cat takes great care to feed her four kittens until she is accidentally locked in a storage room. The farm's dog is

obviously worried by her absence, and he tries his best to find food for the kittens, with amusing results. Mother cat is finally found and the kittens fed, to the obvious relief of the dog.

The story of *Noah's Ark* has been translated from the Dutch by Peter Spier in *Noah's Ark* and appears in verse form on the first page. What follows, however, is the virtually wordless story of all that transpires both inside and outside the ark for forty days and forty nights. Various-size pictures portray Noah's many activities on the ark and capture his every mood, from deep concern to jubilant rejoicing over the dove's return with the olive branch. Mrs. Noah's washline of clothes contrasts sharply with the dirty, messy interior of the ark at the end of its long voyage. Humorous touches run throughout this book, including the number of rabbits that leave the ark and the slow final departure of the snails and tortoise. Each viewing of the book reveals more of Spier's wit and artistic talent. This book richly deserved the Caldecott Medal it received. Spier's *Rain* is also a wordless book about rain but one that is set in the modern world.

Another beautiful wordless book is Raymond Briggs's *The Snowman.* Using soft colored pencils in a comic-strip format, Briggs tells the story of a small boy and his snowman who comes to life one night. The boy and the snowman share a meal and a fantastic predawn flight before returning home and the sad reality of the next morning's sunny dawn. Many wordless books like *The*

Snowman appeal to children of all ages. David Wiesner's fascinating book *Tuesday* is the second almost-wordless book to receive the Caldecott Medal. On "Tuesday evening, around eight," all the frogs take off from their lily pads. Brilliant watercolors portray their joyous flight as they zoom through a house, chase birds and a dog, and return home at dawn. The next Tuesday evening, the pigs fly! Wiesner's other wordless books, such as *Free Fall* and *Sector 7,* are of equally inventive artistic imagination. Gregory Rogers's equally imaginative *The Boy, the Bear, the Baron, and the Bard* is a rollicking farce that follows a young boy into a decrepit theater and back to Shakespeare's time, where he mixes it up with Elizabeth I, a dancing bear, an angry playwright, and a fugitive baron.

Jeannie Baker's wordless books, such as *Home* and *Where the Forest Meets the Sea,* have an environmental message that appeals to older children. Baker's collages, constructed with many natural materials, subtly reflect the care for the environment that the books inspire. Mitsumasa Anno's wordless books, including *Anno's Journey, Anno's USA,* and *Anno's Spain,* reflect the cultural world of particular places. Children enjoy pouring through the pages to find characters, natural monuments, and historical references that pertain to each particular journey. Whatever age the audience, the illustrator intends for wordless books to give readers the power to enter into the book and tell their own story.

BOOKS ABOUT THE COMMON EXPERIENCES OF YOUNG CHILDREN

Increasingly, publishers are producing books that mirror the common everyday experiences and feelings of preschoolers across cultures. In these books for 2- through 5-year-olds the illustrations are simple and clear. The young child's activities and concerns are at the center of the action, but frequently the humor is directed at the parent reader.

David Shannon's *No, David!* and Molly Bang's *When Sophie Gets Angry—Really, Really Angry* both do a superb job of capturing the terrible toddler in action. Shannon's lively illustrations show a preschooler doing his worst—stealing cookies from the cookie jar, playing with food, and running naked down the street. His antics are accompanied by a brief text, from an obviously harassed adult, which consists mostly of the words "No, David!" David is finally sent for a time-out but in the end receives a hug and the words "I love you!" David's misadventures continue in *David Goes to School* and *David Gets in Trouble.* Bang's Sophie is put upon by an older sister who grabs her favorite toy. Sophie gets so angry, "she kicks, she screams she wants to smash the world to smithereens." Bang's intensely colored illustrations represent Sophie's rage perfectly, following her outside as she runs away from her anger and then back home to the embrace of her now peaceful family. Both books acknowledge the mercurial emotions and sometimes difficult-to-

In Molly Bang's *When Sophie Gets Angry—Really, Really Angry . . .* a young child finds space for a tantrum and room to calm down again. From *When Sophie Gets Angry—Really, Really Angry . . .* by Molly Bang. Published by the Blue Sky Press/Scholastic Inc. Copyright © 1999 by Molly Bang. Reprinted by permission.

control actions that characterize the preschooler yet provide a reassuring message of acceptance and love.

The impulsiveness of the young child is typified by the character of Jamela in Niki Daly's *Jamela's Dress* and *What's Cooking Jamela?*, warmhearted family stories set in South Africa. In *Jamela's Dress*, Jamela's mother has bought some beautiful fabric to make herself a dress, and Jamela is so enamoured of it that she wraps herself up in the cloth and parades around town without considering the consequences. When she arrives home, Jamela is horrified to find that she has gotten the fabric stained and torn. Luckily, a photographer who has captured her picture wins a prize and gives Jamela some of the prize money. There is enough for her mother to make her own dress and one for Jamela as well. Any child who has ever acted without thinking will identify with Jamela's predicament and find comfort in the happy outcome. In *What's Cooking, Jamela?* Jamela's pet chicken is about to be served up for Christmas dinner until Jamela lets her escape.

The youngest child frequently feels left out, the tag end of the family. Pat Hutchins captures these feelings in her well-loved books *Titch; You'll Soon Grow into Them, Titch;* and *Tidy Titch.* In the first book Titch is too small to ride a two-wheel bicycle, fly a kite, or use a hammer. But he is not too small to plant a seed, and Titch's plant grows and grows. The ending of the story is a classic example of poetic justice for the youngest and smallest of a family. The classic story *The Carrot Seed* by Ruth Krauss has a theme similar to that in *Titch.* Here, the smallest in the family triumphs over all the doubts raised by his family. Little children need to feel big, if only through their stories.

In books for the very young, animal characters often stand in for human children. Amy Hest's Baby Duck is the epitome of the difficult child. When she's unhappy or fearful, she pouts. Despite the reassurances of her parents, she has a difficult time adjusting to new experiences. In *Baby Duck Goes to School, In the Rain with Baby Duck,* and *Guess Who, Baby Duck?* it takes Grampa Duck's coaxing of the reluctant Baby to get her past her fears so that she can enjoy an adventure.

Separation anxiety is a normal part of development in young children, and books can help reassure children that they are not being abandoned when their loved ones are absent. Jane Simmons's *Come Along Daisy!* offers important reassurance to children who fear becoming lost. Despite Mama Duck's admonitions to "come along," Daisy is distracted while out for a swim and loses track of her mother. Simmons's thickly textured paintings portray Daisy's sudden panic, showing a very, very small duck in the middle of a suddenly frightening world. Daisy's face, peeking out from behind a bunch of water reeds as she hears a rustling along the river bank, is priceless. Happily, the rustling is Mama Duck, who calls out "Daisy, Come Along!" Reunited with her mother, Daisy vows to stay close to Mama.

Martin Waddell's *Owl Babies* might be the perfect book to reassure a toddler who fears the nighttime separation from mother. In this charming, predictable book, three little owl siblings find themselves alone on their leafy branch. "Where's Mommy?" asks Sarah; "Oh my goodness!" explains Percy; and "I want my mommy!" wails Bill, the smallest. Patrick Benson's expressive illustrations lend just the right amount of suspense to the story, in which the night seems to get darker and darker.

Young Jamela's impulsive behavior gets her into trouble in Niki Daly's heart-warming *Jamela's Dress.* Illustration from *Jamela's Dress* by Niki Daly. Copyright © 1999 by Niki Daly. Farrar, Straus and Giroux, LLC by arrangement with The Inkman, Cape Town, S.A. Hand lettering by Andrew van der Merwe, Frances Lincoln, Ltd., Great Britain.

Sarah and Percy try to reassure each other that Mom will be back, while Bill continues to cry for Mother until she swoops "soft and silent" through the trees and home to her children. Bill's plaintive wail will resonate with every child who is frightened of the dark, and the message that mother is never far away is a reassuring finale that will linger in sleepy memories.

Oliver Finds His Way by Phyllis Root follows a small bear who chases a leaf into the woods as his parents do chores in their yard. When Oliver suddenly realizes he doesn't know the way home, he starts to cry despondently. But then Oliver stops a moment "to think, and think and think." Then "Oliver has an idea." "Roar!," Oliver repeats, louder and louder. When Mama and Papa roar back, Oliver finds his way safely home.

The Littlest Wolf by Larry Dane Brimmer is about an insecure preschooler in the guise of a little wolf. Teased by his bigger brother and sister wolves, he is moping behind a tree when his father, Big Gray, finds him. Big Gray asks him to demonstrate his perceived inadequacies. The little wolf complains that he can't roll like the wind, he can't pounce as high as the clouds, he can't run like the wind, and his sister told him he was a slowpoke. With each complaint Big Gray asks for a demonstration and then finds something to admire in the little wolf's clumsy efforts. "It is true that Ana runs like the wind and you run like a soft breeze," he said. "That is just as it should be." "Are you sure?" the little wolf asked. "I am

sure, said Big Gray. "Running like the wind comes later." Jose Aruego and Ariane Dewey's wonderfully expressive illustrations are perfect for relating this warmhearted and reassuring story.

Young children also need much love and reassurance that they will always be needed and belong to their family. This is the theme of the favorite story *The Runaway Bunny* by Margaret Wise Brown. A little bunny announces that he is going to run away, and his mother tells him that she will run after him. The little bunny thinks of all the things he will become—a fish in a stream, a crocus, a sailboat. His mother in turn says she will become a fisherman, a gardener, the wind—and come after him. The little rabbit decides to stay and just be her little bunny, after all. This story might seem suffocating for older children, but it is just what the preschool child wants to hear.

Bedtime stories provide the comfort and reassurance that children need to face the dark alone. There are several recent bedtime books that have the potential to become modern-day classics, although probably no book for the very young child will ever replace Margaret Wise Brown's *Goodnight Moon*, first published in 1947. Kevin Henkes's Caldecott Medal-winning *Kitten's First Full Moon* is a perfect story for the youngest child. The subdued illustrations and patterned text follow the adventures of a little kitten who thinks the moon is a bowl of milk. Kitten's journey almost ends in disaster, but like

Kindergarten children enjoy reading their alternative version of *Goodnight Moon* by Margaret Wise Brown. Mission School, Redlands Public School, Redlands, California. Nancy Anderson, teacher and photographer.

Max in Maurice Sendak's *Where the Wild Things Are*, Kitten returns home to find dinner, a big bowl of milk, waiting.

Kate Banks has written several lovely bedtime books such as *The Great Blue House* and *Close Your Eyes*. Her *And If the Moon Could Talk*, with illustrations by Georg Hallensleben, is reminiscent of *Goodnight Moon* in its lyrical text and vivid primary colors. A little girl is in her room getting ready for bed, "and if the moon could talk it would tell of evening stealing through the woods and a lizard scurrying home to supper." As each part of the child's nighttime ritual is completed, the refrain "and if the moon could talk" is repeated and we see people and animals around the world settling in for the night. Finally, as the little girl sleeps safely in her bed, the moon peeks in her window and whispers "good night."

Barbara Berger's *A Lot of Otters* features Mother Moon, who has misplaced her little baby. There is no reason to worry, however, for the baby is safe with a loving family of otters who care for him until Mother returns. The exquisitely beautiful illustrations and gentle story will be enjoyed reading after reading and generation after generation. The musical text of Mem Fox's *Time For Bed* with Jane Dyer's lovely watercolor illustrations will no doubt have a similar soothing effect on toddlers. Beginning with a tiny mouse, animal and insect families get ready for sleep. Finally, a human mother wishes her baby sweet dreams against the background of a starry pillow and a starry sky: "The stars on high are shining bright—/Sweet Dreams, my darling, sleep well . . . good night!" Molly Bang has written and illustrated both a counting book and a loving bedtime story in *Ten, Nine, Eight*. Starting with his daughter's ten toes, a daddy

counts backward until she is ready for bed. This is a warm, reassuring story of an African American father and his daughter.

Good Night, Gorilla by Peggy Rathmann is an almost wordless book that is sure to delight toddlers. A sleepy zookeeper is locking up for the night when a gorilla baby takes his keys. As the keeper says good night to the animals, one by one, the gorilla opens their cages and the animals all follow the keeper home and bed down in his room. His sleepy wife suddenly realizes what has happened and takes all the animals back to their cages— except for the little gorilla and a tiny mouse, who manage to follow her back to bed and slide in under the covers.

Stories that have no relationship to bedtime make fine reading at this time, too, of course. Teaching Resources: "A Sampling of Stories for the Youngest Child" lists some of our favorite books for the young child. Young children should also see many of the appropriate picture storybooks described in Chapter 5 and hear the well-loved traditional tales of "The Three Bears," "The Three Billy Goats Gruff," and "The Gingerbread Man" discussed in Chapter 6. For although young children need books that mirror their own feelings and experiences, they also need books to take them beyond those experiences and to help their imaginations soar.

BOOKS FOR THE BEGINNING READER

Learning to read begins at home with children hearing stories on their parents' laps and seeing loved persons in their lives valuing books. The child lucky enough to have had such a wide exposure to books will usually

TEACHING **RESOURCES**

A Sampling of Stories for the Youngest Child

EVERYDAY EXPERIENCES AND CONCERNS

Author, Illustrator	Title	Description
Suzanne Bloom	*A Splendid Friend, Indeed*	A *very* annoying duck finally charms a polar bear after many aborted attempts at friendship.
Emma Chichester Clark	*Up in Heaven*	This gentle book about the death of a pet suits the youngest child.
Carol Foskett Cordsen, Douglas B. Jones	*The Milkman*	A milkman makes his rounds through the town in the early morning doing small favors and kindnesses for the inhabitants.
Olivier Dunrea	*Ollie's Eggs*	One of a series of small books and simple stories about a group of goslings.
Karen English, Sean Qualls	*The Baby on the Way*	A grandmother tells her grandson about her own childhood.

(continued)

A Sampling of Stories for the Youngest Child *(continued)*

EVERYDAY EXPERIENCES AND CONCERNS *(continued)*

Author, Illustrator	Title	Description
Heather Henson, Susan Gaber	*Angel Coming*	A little girl anticipates the arrival of a new sibling who will be brought by an angel on horseback, a reference to the nurse-midwives who traveled the Appalachian Mountains in the 1920s.
Clare Jarret	*The Best Picnic Ever*	A young boy has imaginative adventures while Mom sets out on a picnic in the park.
Emily Jenkins, Pierre Pratt	*That New Animal*	Two dogs have to deal with a newcomer in this charming book about sibling rivalry.
Norton Juster, Chris Raschka	*The Hello Goodbye Window*	A little girl's visit to her grandparents' house is lovingly detailed.
Holly Keller	*Sophie's Window*	Keller's uncanny understanding of preschoolers is exhibited in this story about a little fledgling and her unlikely friend.
Ho Baek Lee	*While We Were Out*	A little pet rabbit has adventures when he sneaks inside after his family has left for the day. Set in Korea.
Cathryn Valckx	*Lizette's Green Sock*	Lizette finds a single green sock and discovers an ingenious use for it.
Martin Waddell, John Lawrence	*Tiny's Big Adventure*	Tiny the mouse accompanies his big sister on an adventure in the wild.
Mo Willems	*Knuffle Bunny*	A toddler's stuffed bunny disappears on an outing with her father, and she desperately tries to communicate her loss.

BEDTIME STORIES

Author, Illustrator	Title	Description
Dianna Hutts Aston	*When You Were Born*	Lilting text and warm pictures describe a family's reactions to a new baby.
Scott Beck	*Little House, Little Town*	A trip through a baby's day and back to sleep again.
Carolyn Curtis, Alison Jay	*I Took the Moon for a Walk*	The poetic text reflects young children's belief that the moon can follow them.
Thatcher Hurd	*Sleepy Cadillac: A Bedtime Drive*	Impressionistic paintings invite readers aboard a magic Cadillac as it journeys through the night.
Ana Juan	*The Night Eater*	Chagall-like illustrations accompany this fanciful look at how night becomes day.
Nina Payne, Gabi Swiatkowska	*Summertime Waltz*	Poetic language and fanciful illustrations capture the simple joys of a summer evening.
Lauren Thompson, Stephen Savage	*Polar Bear Night*	Lino-cuts on special papers evoke a magical polar night during which a small polar bear sets off to explore before coming home to sleep.

Thatcher Hurd's *Sleepy Cadillac* is a good-night book that lures children on a lyrical journey into slumber. Illustration from *Sleepy Cadillac: A Bedtime Drive* by Thatcher Hurd © 2005. Used by permission of HarperCollins Publishers, Inc. HarperCollins Children's Books, a division of HarperCollins Publishers.

learn to read easily and fluently. The importance of reading aloud to young children, if they are to be successful in learning to read, has been consistently proven by researchers in this country and abroad.[8]

The books for the very young child that have been discussed in this chapter can be read again when children of 5 or 6 start to become readers. Increasingly, theories of reading emphasize the importance of reading for meaning and enjoyment from the very start of learning to read. Many preprimers and primers that are part of reading textbook series have stilted, unnatural language and pointless plots that thwart the child's spontaneous attempts to read; in contrast, stories that children love and have heard over and over again have natural language and satisfying plots that encourage reading. Many of these books utilize repetitious language and story pat-

Talking Point

Reading levels and children's choices
Many early reading programs assign children to books by reading level. What are the pros and cons of such programs?

Go to the Online Learning Center at **www.mhhe.com/kiefer9e** or your Resources CD-ROM to learn more.

terns that help children learn to read naturally as they join in on the refrains or predict the action of the story.

Jerome Bruner was the first to use the term *scaffold* to characterize adult assistance to children's language development.[9] Some books can also be an instructional

---

[8]See Margaret Clark, *Young Fluent Readers* (London: Heinemann Educational Books, 1976); Dorothy Cohen, "The Effect of Literature on Vocabulary and Reading Achievement," *Elementary English* 45 (February 1968): 209–13; Dolores Durkin, *Children Who Read Early* (New York: Columbia Teachers College Press, 1966); Robert Ladd Thorndike, *Reading Comprehension, Education in 15 Countries: An Empirical Study*, vol. 3, International Studies in Education (New York: Holstead Wiley, 1973); Gordon Wells, *The Meaning Makers* (Portsmouth, N.H.: Heinemann, 1986).

[9]Identified by C. B. Cazden, "Adult Assistance to Language Development: Scaffolds, Models, and Direct Instruction," in *Developing Literacy: Young Children's Use of Language*, ed. R. P. Parker and F. A. Davis (Newark, Del.: International Reading Association, 1983), pp. 3–18.

Teacher and children share the reading of the alternative text they created, "Greedy Kid," following the pattern of *Greedy Cat* by Joy Cowley. Mission School, Redlands Public Schools, Redlands, California. Nancy Anderson, teacher. Photo by Larry Rose.

scaffold or a temporary help in the child's first attempts to read. Such books include familiar texts like Mother Goose rhymes or songs that children know by heart and can easily "read"; or they might be books with repetitive language or story patterns that help children remember or predict the story easily. Margaret Meek points out that as children explore a variety of texts, they learn how books work.[10] She also emphasizes the importance of repeated readings, maintaining that each time a book is revisited, new understandings are gained.[11]

Teachers and librarians are sometimes confused about which books are suitable for beginning readers. Barbara Peterson studied a wide range of books for beginning readers and categorized multiple sources of support on a continuum from easier to more complex. These sources included the predictability of the language in the book; the support for meaning given by illustrations; the linguistic patterns; the complexity of the narrative structure; the layout of the text; and the overall length of the text.[12] After testing many of the books with children,

Peterson concluded that "beginning readers are able to read and learn from challenging, difficult texts. It is unnecessary to provide specialized texts with severely limited controlled vocabulary for beginning readers." Three categories of books that support children in gaining reading fluency are discussed in the next sections.

Predictable Books

Books that can help emergent readers can be identified by such characteristics as repetitive language patterns or story patterns or the use of familiar sequences like numbers, the days of the week, or hierarchical patterns. Frequently, texts combine several of these characteristics in a single story.

Many stories include repetitive words, phrases, or questions that invite children to share in the reading. Children quickly learn the language pattern of Eric Hill's *Where's Spot?* and chime in as the word *no* is revealed under each lifted flap. They will want to join in and repeat the word *suddenly!* in Colin McNaughton's delightful

---

[10]Margaret Meek, *How Texts Teach What Readers Learn* (London: Thimble Press, 1988).

[11]See also Miriam Martinez and Nancy Roser, "Read It Again: The Value of Repeated Readings during Storytime," *Reading Teacher* 38 (1985): 782–86.

[12]Barbara Leach Peterson, *Characteristics of Texts That Support Beginning Readers,* Ph.D. dissertation, Ohio State University, 1988. Abstract from Digital Dissertations. 29 June 2005 <http://www.lib.umi.com/dissertations/fullcit/8820339>.

We looked at the trees and what did we find?

Trees with branches, Trees with trunks

book entitled *Suddenly!* They will also be tickled by the suspenseful plot as an ingenuous pig is set upon by a nasty wolf on his way home from school. Preston the pig escapes from each increasingly bizarre assault, seemingly unaware that the wolf is after him. Preston's further adventures can be followed in *Boo!, Yum!,* and *Preston's Goal!* The illustrations in these books, like those in Pat Hutchins's *Rosie's Walk,* give the real story away.

Denise Fleming's books, such as *In the Tall Tall Grass,* have predictable refrains that also convey simple concepts about animal behavior and habitats. In *In the Small Small Pond,* "wiggle, jiggle, tadpoles wriggle," and in *Barnyard Banter* "pigs in the wallow, muck muck muck." These visually appealing books also offer children interesting vocabulary within the context of the predictable text.

A well-liked patterned question-and-answer book is *Brown Bear, Brown Bear, What Do You See?* by Bill Martin, Jr. The question in the title is put to a large brown bear, who replies that he sees a redbird looking at him. The question is then directed at the redbird: "Redbird, redbird, what do you see?" He sees a yellow duck, who in turn sees a blue horse, and so on. Identification of animal and color on the picture allows the child to chime in on the answer for each page. The large, bold collage pictures by Eric Carle are a perfect match for the text and support the child's reading of the story.

In Pat Hutchins's *We're Going on a Picnic!* three birds set off to find a picnic spot one beautiful day. Hen brings berries ("because Hen liked berries best"), Goose brings apples ("because Goose liked apples best"), and Duck brings pears ("because Duck liked pears best"). They are just as finicky about the best picnic spot. One spot is too shady for Duck, another is too windy for Goose, and a third is too hot for Hen. While they continue to argue about a place to eat, first a mouse, then a squirrel, and finally a rabbit, raid their picnic basket. Repeated words and phrases and the predictable plot will have young readers joining in. As in Hutchins's *Rosie's Walk,* many of the surprises are hidden in the pictures.

Rather than simply repeat words and phrases, some books play with the sounds of language in a more complex way. Alliteration is a hallmark of many of Pamela Duncan Edwards and Henry Cole's picture books. In *Clara Caterpillar,* Clara and Catisha clash over their coloring, but Clara's friend Cornelius assures her that "Catisha is conceited." In *Rosie's Roses* Rosie Racoon and her brother Robert prepare a rose bouquet for Aunt Ruth. Charlotte Pomerantz's *The Piggy in a Puddle* and *Here Comes Henny* also have irresistible refrains that will have children chanting along with enthusiasm. Piggy is in the middle of a "muddy little puddle" and dawdles and diddles there while daddy, mommy, and brother try to convince her to come out. In a rollicking ending they all dive in and join her in the "squishy-squashy, mooshy-squooshy, oofy-poofy" mud. Henny is a mother chicken who plans a picnic for her chickies and packs it in her backpack,

> which she carries
> pickabacky
> back and forth
> and forth and backy.[13]

These are picky chickies, however, and they will only eat snacky snickies, not the snicky snackies that Henny has packed. In the end the chicks collect their own pack of

---

[13]Charlotte Pomerantz, *Here Comes Henny,* illus. Nancy Winslow Parker (New York: Greenwillow, 1994), p. 5. Reprinted by permission of HarperCollins Publishers.

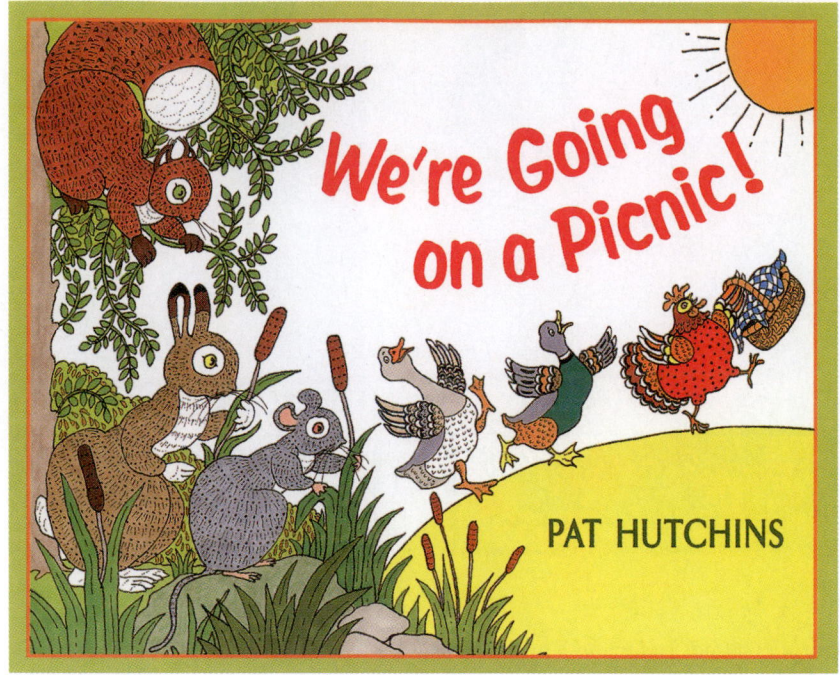

snackies and have a happy picnic-nicky. In addition to being irresistible fun for children, this type of sound play helps make them more aware of the internal sounds of words and the fact that language is made up of individual sounds. This understanding—phonemic awareness— seems to be crucial to emergent reading strategies. Hallie Kay Yopp and other researchers suggest that a certain level of phonemic awareness is necessary for children to benefit from more-formal reading instruction.[14]

Building on children's knowledge of numbers and the days of the week provides a kind of scaffold for reading. Clear pictures by Tomie dePaola illustrate the predictable book *Cookie's Week* by Cindy Ward. If a child knows the days of the week, she can easily read the description of everything a mischievous little black-and-white cat does each day. Much to children's delight, the book begins with "On Monday . . . Cookie fell in the toilet." The next page sets the pattern of the book: "And there was water everywhere." Knowledge of the days of the week and numbers helps children read *The Very Hungry Caterpillar* by Eric Carle. They particularly enjoy reciting the part where the caterpillar eats through *one* apple on Monday, *two* pears on Tuesday, *three* plums on Wednesday, until he has a huge feast on Sunday. In Maurice Sendak's rhyming *Chicken Soup with Rice*, each verse begins with the month and ends with doing something to the soup, such as blowing on it or sipping it. Some groups have made up their own verses for the months, using Sendak's pattern and repeated phrases. Hierarchies based

on such concepts as size can also help children to read stories. With one reading, children easily discern the pattern of being the littlest in Pat Hutchins's story *Titch*. They know that if Titch's brother has a *great big bike* and his sister a *big bike,* then Titch will have a *tricycle.*

Repetitive story patterns also help the child predict the action in the story. The easy folktales with their patterns of three, such as *The Three Billy Goats Gruff* by Glen Rounds, *The Three Little Pigs* and *The Three Bears* by Paul Galdone, and *The Little Red Hen* by Byron Barton, support the child's reading. For once children recognize the story structure, they know that if the great big bear says, "Someone has been tasting my porridge," then the middle-size bear and the baby bear will both say the same thing.

Cumulative tales have repeated patterns and phrases that become longer and longer with each incident. In Mem Fox's *Shoes from Grandpa* a simple gift for Jessie turns into a whole wardrobe as different members of her family decide to buy her an article of clothing "to go with the shoes from grandpa." There are lots of rhyming pairs here, such as "mittens soft as kittens" and a "skirt that won't show the dirt," that will invite children to make up their own special wardrobes. Patricia Mullins's lively collages include bits of fabric that reflect the theme and add to the humor of the story.

The familiar patterns of cumulative nursery rhymes such as "This Is the House That Jack Built" support children's reading and invite them to compose their own versions. Children love Audrey Wood and Don Wood's

---

[14]Hallie Kay Yopp, "Developing Phonemic Awareness in Young Children," *Reading Teacher* 45 (May 1992): 696–703; Steven A. Stahl, Ann M. Duffy-Hester, and Katherine Anne Doughty Stahl, "Everything You Wanted to Know About Phonics (But Were Afraid to Ask)," *Reading Research Quarterly* 33. 3 (1998): 338–55.

variation on the traditional rhyme, *The Napping House,* in which an old lady, a boy, a dog, a cat, and a mouse are sleeping until a flea "bites the mouse who scares the cat," and so on, until everyone wakes to a glorious day. Rose Robart creates a rollicking cumulative tale in *The Cake That Mack Ate.* Even though every verse ends in the title phrase, it is only in the last few pictures that children discover the identity of Mack, a huge dog.

The popular song reprised in *Mary Wore Her Red Dress* by Merle Peek or familiar Mother Goose rhymes such as "Little Miss Muffet" or "Old Mother Hubbard" all enable the child to assume the role of reader. Children can hold the books or point to a large chart and "read the words" because they know the song or the verse. As they match sentences and phrase cards or point to individual words in the text, they begin to read the story. In the meantime, they are learning that those symbols stand for the words they already know. This enables them to behave like readers.

Some concept books, like *Truck* by Donald Crews, give children an opportunity to read environmental print. Tana Hoban's books *I Read Signs* and *I Read Symbols* provide excellent photographs of the signs in their environmental context. Other books use print as an important part of the visual art and thus draw children's attention to letters and words. In Pat Hutchins's predictable *Little Pink Pig,* Mother Pig searches for her baby pig at bedtime. As she asks each animal for help, their animal responses are printed in a more decorative, larger, colored type. Suse MacDonald's *Here a Chick, Where a Chick?* is a lift-the-flap book similar to Eric Hill's *Where's Spot?* As young children look under each of the flaps to help

Mother Hen find her chicks, they discover a colorfully written animal sound—"meow," "honk," and finally "cheep!"—that draws their eyes and invites their participation. Mick Manning's *Yuck!* is a nonfiction book about what baby animals eat, and to human children those meals sound pretty yucky. Each animal swallows or gobbles or gulps something unappetizing (a crunchy spider, a furry rat). "That's not our baby's supper," the text declares. Then a giant "YUCK!" is displayed in prominent black letters, just begging children to join in. In addition to being wonderful literature, books like these strengthen children's concepts about print, and they can also help teachers see how aware of print children are becoming.

Easy-Reading Books

Most basal reading series control the number of words, the sounds of the words, and the length of the stories for beginning readers. This often results in the stilted and unnatural language found in the well-known Dick and Jane series. Until the advent of books for babies and preschoolers, most picture storybooks were written to be read *to* children and thus were at a reading level of at least third grade. They were geared to the young child's interest appreciation level, not reading-ability level. That left very little for the beginning reader to read, except for preprimers and primers. This is no longer true with the number of easy, predictable picture books available today.

A new genre of books was created when Dr. Seuss published *The Cat in the Hat* in 1957. This book was written with a controlled vocabulary (derived from the Dolch vocabulary list of 220 words) for the young child

The lively illustrations and colorful text draw emergent readers' attention to print in *Here a Chick, Where a Chick?* From *Here a Chick, Where a Chick?* by Suse MacDonald. Published by Cartwheel Books/Scholastic, Inc. Copyright © 2004 by Suse MacDonald. Reprinted by permission. No part of this material may be reproduced in whole or in part without the express written permission of the author or her agent, Rosenstone/Wender.

to read independently. Since then many publishers have developed "easy-reading" books. Some of these books, such as *Little Bear* by Else Minarik and illustrated by Maurice Sendak, and the superb Frog and Toad series by Arnold Lobel, are easy-reading books that can take their rightful place in children's literature. In fact, *Frog and Toad Are Friends* was a Caldecott Honor Book, and *Frog and Toad Together* was a Newbery Honor Book two years later, suggesting that quality writing can be achieved with a limited vocabulary.

Cynthia Rylant's Henry and Mudge series features Henry and his lovable 180-pound dog, Mudge. In Henry and Mudge, short episodes about these two inseparable friends are divided into chapters, just right for the newly independent readers who love them. The language is simple but it has an almost poetic quality. Some of the well-loved Mudge stories include *Henry and Mudge and the Great Grandpas, Henry and Mudge and the Starry Night,* and *Henry and Mudge and the Tall Tree House.* Rylant's knack for writing these controlled-vocabulary books has led to several other excellent series including The High Rise Private Eyes (*The Case of the Fidgety Fox*), Mr. Putter and Tabby (*Mr. Putter and Tabby Catch the Cold*), and Poppleton the Pig (*Poppleton in Winter*).

Today there are literally hundreds of these easy-reading books. Some, like Claudia Mills's *Gus and Grandpa and the Piano Lesson*, Elissa Haden Guest's *Iris and Walter and the Field Trip,* and Shelley Moore Thomas's *Get Well, Good Knight,* are good stories. Others, such as Joan Holub's *The Garden That We Grew,* or Emily Arnold McCully's *The Battle for St. Michaels,* appeal to special interests such as science, sports, mysteries, or history. Not all achieve the literary excellence of the Little Bear, Frog and Toad, or Henry and Mudge series. Some appear contrived and restricted by the controlled vocabulary. Research has shown that the meaning of the story is far more important for ease of reading than limiting vocabulary. We should not accept a book just because it has a beginning-to-read label. Each book must be evaluated for literary qualities, child appeal, and difficulty of reading.

Helping children choose the right book at the right time is an important aspect of literacy instruction.[15] We note with alarm the growing trend to sort trade books by levels of difficulty and then assign children to read through these levels. Sometimes children need to pick a book that is easy to read, just for the fun of it. At other times children have a fascination with a long book in which they search for familiar words and teach themselves to read. We need not limit the emergent reader's book exposure to just predictable books. Gerald, with whom one of the authors read in England, had taught himself to read with the Frances stories by Russell Hoban. He had learned to read *Bread and Jam for Frances* and

Beginning readers are supported and entertained by such "easy-reading" books as Cynthia Rylant's *The Case of the Fidgety Fox,* one of the titles in The High Rise Private Eyes series illustrated by G. Brian Karas. Cover of *The High-Rise Private Eyes: The Case of the Fidgety Fox* by Cynthia Rylant. Jacket illustration copyright © 2003 by G. Brian Karas. Used by permission of HarperCollins Publishers.

was working on *A Baby Sister for Frances.* These are difficult books, but Gerald wanted to read them, and that is the key to helping children learn to read.

As more and more primary teachers begin to use real books for teaching children to read, textbook publishers are beginning to produce made-to-order books and books written to a formula. These books frequently lack the imaginative quality of true literature. They might use repetitive phrases or questions, but they have deadly dull plots and the unnatural language of primers. Look rather for imaginative trade books with natural language, a creative plot, and real child appeal. Look, too, for fine artwork such as that found in the books by Eric Carle, Denise Fleming, Pat Hutchins, Marisabina Russo, and many more outstanding author-illustrators.

---

[15]For insights on helping children choose their own books, see Marilyn Olhausen and Mary Jepson, "Lessons from Goldilocks: 'Somebody's Been Choosing My Books But I Can Make My Own Choices Now,'" *New Advocate* 5 (winter, 1992): 31–46.

The titles we have discussed here are all trade books that meet the criteria we have suggested. They help the emergent reader learn to read naturally and with real delight. For a list of books for young readers grouped by their characteristics, see Teaching Resources: "Books for Beginning Readers."

TEACHING RESOURCES

Books for Beginning Readers

 Visit the Online Learning Center at **www.mhhe.com/kiefer9e** for a printable version of this list.

LANGUAGE PATTERNS: REPETITIVE WORDS, PHRASES, QUESTIONS

Jill Bennett, *Teeny Tiny*
Suzanne Bloom, *The Bus for Us*
Ruth Brown, *A Dark, Dark Tale*
Rod Campbell, *Dear Zoo*
Eric Carle, *Do You Want to Be My Friend?*
————, *Have You Seen My Cat?*
————, *"Slowly, Slowly, Slowly," Said the Sloth*
————, *The Very Busy Spider*
————, *The Very Lonely Firefly*
————, *The Very Quiet Cricket*
Pamela Duncan Edwards, *Clara Caterpillar*
————, *Rosie's Roses*
Denise Fleming, *Barnyard Banter*
————, *In the Small Small Pond*
————, *In the Tall Tall Grass*
————, *Mama Cat Has Three Kittens*
Douglas Florian, *A Pig Is Big*
Rita Gelman, *Doodler Doodling*
Phillis Gershator, *Greetings Sun*
Mirra Ginsburg, *The Chick and the Duckling*

————, *Good Morning, Chick*
Laura Godwin, *Little White Dog*
Eric Hill, *Where's Spot?*
Robert Kraus, *Where Are You Going, Little Mouse?*
————, *Whose Mouse Are You?*
Ruth Krauss, *Bears*
Kim Lewis, *My Truck Is Stuck*
Bill Martin, Jr., *Brown Bear, Brown Bear, What Do You See?*
Bernard Most, *Z-Z-Zoink!*
Nina Payne, *Four in All*
Charlotte Pomerantz, *Here Comes Henny*
————, *The Piggy in a Puddle*
Nancy Shaw, *Sheep in a Jeep*
Nancy Tafuri, *Have You Seen My Duckling?*
————, *Silly Little Goose!*
Martin Waddell, *Farmer Duck*
Sue Williams, *I Went Walking*
————, *Let's Go Visiting*

FAMILIAR SEQUENCES: NUMBERS, DAYS OF WEEK, MONTHS, HIERARCHIES

Eric Carle, *The Very Hungry Caterpillar*
Eileen Christelow, *Five Little Monkeys Jumping on the Bed*
Paul Galdone, *The Three Bears*
————, *The Three Billy Goats Gruff*
Pat Hutchins, *Titch*

Eve Merriam, *Ten Rosy Roses*
Phyllis Root, *One Duck Stuck*
Maurice Sendak, *Chicken Soup with Rice*
Uri Shulevitz, *One Monday Morning*
Cindy Ward, *Cookie's Week*

REPETITIVE STORY PATTERNS AND PREDICTABLE PLOTS

Karen Beaumont Alarcón, *Louella Mae, She's Run Away!*
Byron Barton, *Buzz Buzz Buzz*
Ken Brown, *The Scarecrow's Hat*
Margaret Wise Brown, *Goodnight Moon*
————, *Four Fur Feet*
John Burningham, *Mr. Gumpy's Outing*
Stephanie Calmenson, *The Teeny Tiny Teacher: A Teeny Tiny Ghost Story, Adapted a Teeny Tiny Bit*
Paul Galdone, *The Three Bears*
————, *The Little Red Hen*
————, *The Three Little Pigs*
Deborah Guarino, *Is Your Mama a Llama?*
Pat Hutchins, *Good-Night, Owl!*

————, *Happy Birthday, Sam*
————, *Little Pink Pig*
————, *Rosie's Walk*
————, *We're Going on a Picnic*
————, *You'll Soon Grow Into Them, Titch*
Ruth Krauss, *The Carrot Seed*
Eve Rice, *Sam Who Never Forgets*
Phyllis Root, *What Baby Wants*
Carol Roth, *The Little School Bus*
Glen Rounds, *The Three Billy Goats Gruff*
Jeff Sheppard, *Splash Splash*
Martin Waddel, *Webster J. Duck*
Sue Williams, *Dinnertime!*

(continued)

Books for Beginning Readers (*continued*)

CUMULATIVE TALES

Jane Cabrera, *If You're Happy and You Know It!*
Alyssa Satin Capucilli, *Inside a House That Is Haunted*
———, *Inside a Zoo in the City; A Rebus Read-Aloud*
Rebecca Platt Davidson, *The Boy Who Writes Poems and Plays*
Barbara Emberley, *Drummer Hoff*
Lisa Campbell Ernst, *This Is the Van That Dad Cleaned*
Candace Fleming, *This Is the Baby*
Paul Galdone, *The Gingerbread Boy*
Sarah Hayes, *This Is the Bear*
Christopher Manson, *The Tree in the Wood*

Shirley Neitzel, *Our Class Took a Trip to the Zoo*
Patricia Polacco, *In Enzo's Splendid Garden*
Rose Robart, *The Cake That Mack Ate*
Lola M. Schaefer, *This Is the Sunflower*
Teri Sloat, *This Is the House That Was Tidy and Neat*
Cyndy Szekeres, *The Mouse That Jack Built*
Simms Taback, *This Is the House That Jack Built*
Linda Williams, *The Little Old Lady Who Was Not Afraid of Anything*
Audrey Wood, *The Napping House*
Ed Young, *What About Me?*

FAMILIAR SONGS AND RHYMES

Allan Ahlberg, *Mockingbird*
Pamela Duncan Edwards, *Miss Polly Has a Dolly*
Denise Fleming, *The First Day of Winter*
Marla Frazee, *Hush, Little Baby*
Colin Hawkins and Jacqui Hawkins, *I Know an Old Lady Who Swallowed a Fly*
Will Hillenbrand, *Fiddle-I-Fee*
Mary Ann Hoberman, *Bill Grogan's Goat*
———, *The Eensy Weensy Spider*

———, *Miss Mary Mack*
Lenny Hort, *The Seals on the Bus*
Carol Jones, *Old MacDonald Had a Farm*
———, *This Old Man*
Merle Peek, *Mary Wore Her Red Dress and Henry Wore His Green Sneakers*
Paul Zelinsky, *Knick-Knack Paddywhack! A Moving Parts Book*

ARTISTIC USE OF PRINT

Katya Arnold, *Meow!*
Molly Bang, *When Sophie Gets Angry—Really, Really Angry . . .*
Donald Crews, *Night at the Fair*
———, *School Bus*
———, *Truck*
Tana Hoban, *I Read Signs*
———, *I Read Symbols*
Pat Hutchins, *Little Pink Pig*

Gail Jorgensen, *Crocodile Beat*
Karla Kuskin, *Roar and More*
Jonathon London, *Wiggle Waggle*
Suse MacDonald, *Here a Chick, Where a Chick?*
Jan Ormerod, *When an Elephant Comes to School*
Phyllis Root, *One Windy Wednesday*
Sandra Steen and Susan Steen, *Car Wash*
Ken Wilson-Max, *A Book of Letters*

CONTROLLED-VOCABULARY BOOKS

Alma Flor Ada, *Daniel's Pet*
Monika Bang-Campbell, *Little Rat Rides*
Betsy Byars, *Little Horse*
Denys Cazet, *Minnie and Moo: The Meet Frankenswine*
Joy Cowley, *Agapanthus Hum and the Angel Hoot*
Doug Cushman, *Inspector Hopper*
Jack Gantos, *Rotten Ralph Helps Out*
Elissa Haden Guest, *Iris and Walter and the School Play*
Joan Holub, *The Garden That We Grew*
Ruth Horowitz, *Breakout at the Bug Lab*
Daniel Laurence, *Captain and Matey Set Sail*

Jean Little, *Emma's Yucky Brother*
Barbara Maitland, *The Bookstore Valentine*
Emily Arnold McCully, *The Battle for St. Michaels*
Kate McMullan, *Pearl and Wagner: Three Secrets*
Claudia Mills, *Gus and Grandpa and the Piano Lesson*
Katherine Paterson, *Marvin One Too Many*
Cynthia Rylant, *The Case of the Desperate Duck*
———, *Mr. Putter and Tabby Catch the Cold*
Lisa Thiesing, *The Viper*
Shelley Moore Thomas, *Get Well, Good Knight*
Jean Van Leeuwen, *Oliver and Albert, Friends Forever*

Big Books

As primary teachers begin to use real books to teach emergent readers, some of them put favorite stories and poems on large charts so that everyone in the class can see them. During shared reading time, the children read them together as someone points to the words.

Frequently, children illustrate these homemade charts with their own drawings, and then the teacher puts them together as a big book. Teachers might chat about the words and ask a child to point to a particular word that they are certain the child knows or to find all the words that begin with the same letter as their name. At other times, children might create their own original version of a favorite story. One group transposed the popular tale *Five Minutes' Peace* by Jill Murphy, which tells of a harassed mother elephant who could not get away from her family, to a schoolroom setting and a teacher's need for five minutes' peace.

First graders show much interest in reading the big book they have created. Idyllwild Elementary School, Idyllwild, California. Sharon Schmidt, teacher. Photo by Larry Rose.

LITERATURE IN **ACTION**

Creating Big Books with Emergent Readers

At the end of the year, Nancy Anderson's group of kindergartners/first graders at Mission School in Redlands, California, did a unit on insects. They read informational books on insects and Eric Carle's stories about insects, including *The Very Hungry Caterpillar, The Very Busy Spider,* and *The Very Quiet Cricket.*

Using the structure of *Brown Bear, Brown Bear, What Do You See?* by Bill Martin, Jr., they wrote and illustrated their own big book with insects as their main characters. They read this together in shared reading time.

(continued)

The cover and one page from the story created by kindergartners and first graders about "Ladybug Saves the Day." Notice their use of fingerpaint paper in their collage pictures, which they tried to do in the same way Eric Carle makes his. Mission School, Redlands Public Schools, Redlands, California. Nancy Anderson, teacher. Photo by Larry Rose.

Creating Big Books with Emergent Readers *(continued)*

Later they decided to write their own story about a ladybug and illustrate it the way Eric Carle illustrated his stories. Using their fingerpaint pictures, they cut out butterflies, ladybugs, and bumblebees to illustrate their story:

Ladybug Saves the Day

Once there was a red shiny spotted ladybug. She lived in the forest. She kept busy eating aphids off the flowers and bushes.

Along came a black and orange butterfly who was being chased by a fierce mean bumblebee. The ladybug heard a terrible buzzing sound. The butterfly cried, "Help Help!" The ladybug waved and whispered, "Come over here, hide with me. Come in my house, it's safe."

The butterfly followed the ladybug to her house. She said, "Thank you for saving my life."

Both big books reflect what the children learned about insects. The first one shows how a book helped to provide structure to their story; the second one gave them an opportunity to illustrate like Eric Carle, their favorite illustrator.

Nancy Anderson
Mission School, Redlands, California

Using the structure of *Brown Bear, Brown Bear, What Do You See?* first graders created their own story about insects.

Mission School, Redlands, California. Nancy Anderson, teacher. Photo by Larry Rose.

Ladybug, ladybug, What do you see? I see an aphid looking at me. Aphid, aphid, What do you see? I see a red ant looking at me. Red ant, red ant, What do you see? I see a bumblebee looking at me. Bumblebee, bumblebee, What do you see? I see a dragonfly looking at me.

Children love these alternative stories that they have a part in producing either by illustrating or by writing. They take ownership of them and read them to each other over and over again. In two trips we made to New Zealand to visit schools, these homemade big books were the only ones we saw.

Publishers have recognized a need for commercial big books and predictable books and created their own. Commercial big books are necessarily expensive and do not provide the same sense of ownership that comes with the class-made books. This cost needs to be balanced against the number of trade books that can be purchased with the money. Some of the commercial big books use the same illustrations as the trade books; others have new illustrations. Almost all of the traditional tales, such as "The Three Bears," are available in big books. Teachers need to ask if this is the version they want to share with their class or if they would prefer a different one. Also, they must evaluate the text for ease of reading. Is this a version that helps students read the text? Does the placement of the text show the repetitious phrases, for example? Do the illustrations help the children read the story? Big books need to be evaluated before their purchase. The best of the commercial ones are those that replicate good, predictable trade books exactly; examples are *The Chick and the Duckling* by Mirra Ginsburg and *Rosie's Walk* by Pat Hutchins.

Today, with the number of fine trade books available in a variety of formats, it is quite possible to find books that children want to read and that they find pleasure in learning to read. There can be no better way for children to begin with books.

Books to Begin On

Books for young children present special challenges to adults who share them with children. As we pointed out in Chapter 2, children ages birth to 7 are very different developmentally than school-age children and adolescents. We have seen some of our students, new to working with this age group, dismiss a book like Martin Waddell's *Owl Babies* because of its brevity and simplicity. But this brevity and simplicity is often what makes a book so appealing to this age group. Preschool teachers who have shared *Owl Babies* with their 3- and 4-year-olds unanimously agree that the book is one of their students' favorites. It speaks directly to their fears of separation from mother as they set off for school each day or go off to sleep at night. In selecting Books to Begin On, consider these developmental guidelines and try the books mentioned here with young children. Below are some ideas to take into the home and classroom.

1. **Student Retelling of a Story.** Select a wordless picture book to use with children of various ages. Record the retelling of the story by each child, noting differences in language development, sense of story, descriptive phrases, and complexity of plot. Be sure to let the child look through the book once before beginning to tell the story.

2. **Predictable-Book Activity.** Select what you consider to be a predictable book. Share it with 5- and 6-year-olds, then reread it, waiting for them to join in at various places. What did you learn about your selection?

3. **Student Retelling Using Illustrations.** Read a story and an information book to a 5- or 6-year-old child.

Ask that child to retell each book to you using only the pictures. What important ideas and vocabulary does the child remember? What additional details does the child give from the illustrations? What questions does the child ask about the book?

4. **Making a Big Book.** Make a big book with young children. Choose a favorite predictable book and ask 4-, 5-, or 6-year-olds to rewrite the story changing some aspect of the text to personalize it to their own experience. Record their words on large pieces of paper and ask the children to illustrate their book. How does this activity invite children to inspect written language? What aspects of the illustrator's work do the children incorporate into their book?

5. **Mother Goose Web Site Activity.** Visit the Mother Goose Web site at <http://www.librarysupport.net/mothergoosesociety>. Learn more about Mother Goose and practice one of the finger plays. Can the children learn the finger plays? What is difficult for them? Have them interview family members and make a class collection of favorite nursery rhymes and finger plays.

 Go to the Online Learning Center at **www.mhhe.com/kiefer9e** or your Resources CD-ROM to find these additional classroom activities:

6. **Picture-Book Editions of Single Songs**
7. **Movement and Literature**
8. **A Survey of Alphabet Books**

Chapter Review

Go to the Online Learning Center at **www.mhhe.com/kiefer9e** or your Resources CD-ROM to take chapter quizzes, practice with key terms, and review the chapter.

Explorations

1. Share several stories with a child under 1 year of age. What appears to capture her or his attention? How many different ways can you provide for the child's active participation in the story?

2. Assume you are going to compile a small Mother Goose book of twenty to twenty-five rhymes. Which ones would you choose? How would you arrange them in your book?

3. Find a concept book about one particular subject. *Before* you read it, list all the possible dimensions of that concept. Then compare your list with what the author/artist chose to include.

4. Read three or four bedtime stories to one child or several children. Which ones do they ask to hear repeatedly? Can you find any patterns among their favorites?

5. Compare several preprimers and primers with the books for the beginning reader described in this text. What do you notice as being different or significant for an emerging reader?

6. Go to the Children's Literature Database on your Resources CD-ROM. Choose a topic such as bugs, small worlds, or weather that could form the basis of a classroom study for younger children. Search the database and check the titles by interest level. Make a list of at least ten books for the younger child in as many different genres as you can. Try several of these titles with younger children. What are their reactions?

Web Links

Go to the Online Learning Center at **www.mhhe.com/kiefer9e** to find links to the following children's literature Web sites:

Between the Lions

Born to Read

Mem Fox: Teaching, Learning, Living

Mother Goose Pages: Mother Goose, Nursery Rhymes, and Children's Songs

Mother Goose Society

National Association for the Education of Young Children

National Center for Family Literacy

Official Eric Carle Website

Reading Is Fundamental

Reading Rockets: Launching Young Readers

The World of Rosemary Wells

Related Readings

Barton, Bob, and David Booth. *Mother Goose Goes to School.* York, Maine: Stenhouse, 1995.

A collection of more than a hundred nursery rhymes with ideas for teachers to extend the rhymes through creative drama, art activities, and examples of children's work.

Butler, Dorothy. *Babies Need Books.* New York: Atheneum.

A firm believer in the importance of books for the young child, this New Zealander writes from her experience as a mother, grandmother, and children's bookseller. She not only recommends books for ages 1 through 5, but she gives

practical suggestions about when and how to read to wiggly children.

Fisher, Bobbi. *Joyful Learning.* Portsmouth, N.H.: Heinemann Educational Books, 1998.

————. *Thinking and Learning Together.* Portsmouth, N.H.: Heinemann Educational Books, 1995.

Written by an experienced primary-grade teacher, these two books describe a rich literature-based environment for children's literacy development. Practical suggestions are offered about organizing the day, developing emergent reading and writing activities, carrying out evaluation and portfolio assessment, and communicating with parents.

Hart-Hewins, Linda, and Jan Wells. *Real Books for Reading: Learning to Read with Children's Literature.* Portsmouth, N.H.: Heinemann Educational Books, 1990.

> The subtitle of this book evolved from the extensive experience of two former teachers in Canada using children's literature as the core of their classroom reading program. Practical suggestions for reading aloud, buddy reading, conferencing with children, and writing opportunities are all given. An extensive bibliography of books for children is also included.

McConaghy, June. *Children Learning through Literature.* Portsmouth, N.H.: Heinemann Educational Books, 1990.

> A Canadian describes her experience of teaching first graders to read by using literature. She emphasizes discussing children's responses to books rather than quizzing them with questions. She describes literature's influence on children's

writing and gives examples of children's stories. She also provides samples from her own journal entries to show her growth as a teacher.

Taylor, Denny, and Dorothy S. Strickland. *Family Storybook Reading.* Portsmouth, N.H.: Heinemann Educational Books, 1998 [1986].

> These authors provide real-life experiences and photographs of the various ways parents share books in the home. Astute observers, the authors focus on the natural ways parents lead children to develop literacy.

Wells, Gordon. *The Meaning Makers: Children Learning Language and Using Language to Learn.* Portsmouth, N.H.: Heinemann Educational Books, 1986.

> Wells reports on the importance of story and reading aloud to preschoolers for their later educational attainment. Based on fifteen years of longitudinal research, this is a significant book.

Children's Literature

 Go to the Children's Literature Database on your Resources CD-ROM for a searchable listing of children's literature titles.

Ada, Alma Flor. *Daniel's Pet.* Illustrated by G. Brian Karas. Harcourt, 2002.

———. *Gathering the Sun: An Alphabet in Spanish and English.* Translated by Rosa Zubizarreta. Illustrated by Simón Silva. Lothrop, 1997.

Ada, Alma Flor, and F. Isabel Campoy. *Mamá Goose: A Latino Nursery Treasury.* Illustrated by Maribel Suárez. Hyperion, 2005.

Ahlberg, Allan. *Mockingbird.* Illustrated by Paul Howard. Candlewick, 1998.

Ahlberg, Janet, and Allan Ahlberg. *Each Peach Pear Plum.* Viking, 1979.

Alarcón, Karen Beaumont. *Louella Mae, She's Run Away!* Illustrated by Rosanne Litzinger. Holt, 1998.

Alborough, Jez. *Duck's Key, Where Can It Be?* Kane/Miller, 2005.

Alda, Arlene. *Arlene Alda's 1 2 3: What Do You See?* Tricycle, 1998.

Alexander, Martha. *When the New Baby Comes I'm Moving Out.* Dial, 1992.

Aliki [Aliki Brandenburg]. *My Five Senses.* HarperCollins, 1990.

Anno, Mitsumasa. *Anno's Counting Book.* Crowell, 1977.

———. *Anno's Journey.* Philomel, 1997 [1977].

———. *Anno's Spain.* Philomel, 2004.

———. *Anno's USA.* Philomel, 1983.

Appelt, Kathi. *Rain Dance.* Illustrated by Emilie Chollat. HarperCollins, 2001.

Arnold, Katya. *Meow!* Holiday, 1998.

Aruego, Jose. *We Hide. You Seek.* Illustrated by Ariane Dewey. Greenwillow, 1979.

Aston, Dianna Hutts. *When You Were Born.* Candlewick, 2004.

Aylesworth, Jim. *Old Black Fly.* Illustrated by Stephen Gammell. Holt, 1992.

Azarian, Mary. *A Farmer's Alphabet.* Godine, 1981.

Baker, Jeannie. *Home.* Greenwillow, 2004.

———. *Where the Forest Meets the Sea.* Greenwillow, 2000.

Baker, Keith. *Big Fat Hen.* Harcourt, 1994.

Bang, Molly. *Ten, Nine, Eight.* Greenwillow, 1983.

———. *When Sophie Gets Angry—Really, Really Angry. . . .* Scholastic, 1999.

Bang-Campbell, Monika. *Little Rat Rides.* Illustrated by Molly Bang. Harcourt, 2004.

Banks, Kate. *And If the Moon Could Talk.* Illustrated by Georg Hallensleben. Foster, 1998.

———. *Close Your Eyes.* Illustrated by Georg Hallensleben. Farrar, 2002.

———. *The Great Blue House.* Illustrated by George Hallensleben. Farrar, 2005.

Bannatyne-Cugnet, Jo. *A Prairie Alphabet.* Illustrated by Yvette Moore. Tundra, 1992.

Barton, Byron. *Buzz Buzz Buzz.* Macmillan, 1973.

———. *The Little Red Hen.* HarperCollins, 1994.

———. *Machines at Work.* Crowell, 1987.

Beaumont, Karen. *Baby Danced the Polka.* Illustrated by Jennifer Plecas. Dial, 2004.

———. *Duck, Duck, Goose!* Illustrated by Jose Aruego and Ariane Dewey. HarperCollins, 2004.

Beck, Scott. *Little House, Little Town.* Abrams, 2004.

Belle, Jennifer. *Animal Stackers.* Illustrated by David McPhail. Hyperion, 2005.

Bennett, Jill. *Teeny Tiny.* Illustrated by Tomie dePaola. Putnam, 1986.

Berger, Barbara. *A Lot of Otters.* Philomel, 1997.

Bloom, Suzanne. *The Bus for Us*. Boyds Mills, 2001.

———. *A Splendid Friend, Indeed*. Boyds Mills, 2005.

Bowen, Betsy. *Antler, Bear, Canoe: A Northwoods Alphabet Year*. Little, 1991.

Branley, Franklin. *Air Is All Around You*. Illustrated by Holly Keller. HarperCollins, 2000.

———. *Flash, Crash, Rumble, and Roll*. Illustrated by True Kelley. HarperCollins, 1999.

Brett, Jan. *The Gingerbread Baby*. Putnam, 1999.

———. *Goldilocks and the Three Bears*. Dodd-Mead, 1992.

———. *The Mitten: A Ukrainian Folktale*. Putnam, 1999.

Briggs, Raymond. *The Snowman*. Random, 1978.

Brimmer, Larry Dane. *The Littlest Wolf*. Illustrated by Jose Aruego and Ariane Dewey. HarperCollins, 2002.

Brown, Ken. *The Scarecrow's Hat*. Peachtree, 2001.

Brown, Marcia. *Stone Soup*. Scribner's, 1947.

Brown, Margaret Wise. *Four Fur Feet*. Watermark, 1989 [William R. Scott (Hopscotch Books), 1961].

———. *Goodnight Moon*. Illustrated by Clement Hurd. Harper, 1947.

———. *The Runaway Bunny*. Illustrated by Clement Hurd. Harper, 1972 [1942].

Brown, Ruth. *A Dark, Dark Tale*. Dial, 1981.

———. *Ten Seeds*. Knopf, 2001.

Bunting, Eve. *Girls A to Z*. Illustrated by Suzanne Bloom. Boyds Mills, 2002.

Burningham, John. *John Burningham's ABC*. Crown, 1993 [1986].

———. *Mr. Gumpy's Outing*. Holt, 1971.

Byars, Betsy. *Little Horse*. Illustrated by David McPhail. Holt, 2002.

Cabrera, Jane. *If You're Happy and You Know It!* Holiday, 2003.

Calmenson, Stephanie. *The Teeny Tiny Teacher: A Teeny Tiny Ghost Story, Adapted a Teeny Tiny Bit*. Scholastic, 1998.

Campbell, Rod. *Dear Zoo*. Four Winds, 1983.

Capucilli, Alyssa Satin. *Inside a House That Is Haunted: A Rebus Read-Along Story*. Illustrated by Tedd Arnold. Scholastic, 1998.

———. *Inside a Zoo in the City: A Rebus Read-Aloud*. Illustrated by Tedd Arnold. Scholastic, 2001.

Carle, Eric. *1, 2, 3, to the Zoo*. Philomel, 1968.

———. *10 Little Rubber Ducks*. HarperCollins, 2005.

———. *Do You Want to Be My Friend?* Harper, 1971.

———. *Have You Seen My Cat?* Picture Book Studio, 1987.

———. *Mister Seahorse*. Philomel, 2004.

———. *Pancakes, Pancakes!* Simon, 1990.

———. *"Slowly, Slowly, Slowly," said the Sloth*. Philomel, 2002.

———. *The Very Busy Spider*. Philomel, 1984.

———. *The Very Clumsy Click Beetle*. Philomel, 1999.

———. *The Very Hungry Caterpillar*. Philomel, 1969.

———. *The Very Lonely Firefly*. Philomel, 1995.

———. *The Very Quiet Cricket*. Philomel, 1990.

Cauley, Lorinda Bryan. *The Three Little Kittens*. Putnam, 1982.

Cave, Kathryn. *One Child, One Seed; A South African Counting Book*. Photographs by Gisele Wulfson. Holt, 2002.

Cazet, Denys. *Minnie and Moo: The Meet Frankenswine*. HarperCollins, 2002.

Chandra, Deborah. *A Is for Amos*. Illustrated by Keiko Narahashi. Farrar, 1999.

Chesworth, Michael. *Alphaboat*. Farrar, 2002.

Christelow, Eileen. *Five Little Monkeys Jumping on the Bed*. Clarion, 1989.

Clark, Emma Chichester. *Up in Heaven*. Random, 2004.

Cobb, Vicki. *I Fall Down*. Illustrated by Julia Gorton. HarperCollins, 2004.

Cohen, Miriam. *Will I Have a Friend?* Illustrated by Lillian Hoban. Macmillan, 1967.

Cohen, Santiago. *Fiddle-I-Fee*. Blue Apple, 2003.

Compestine, Ying Chang. *D Is for Dragon Dance*. Illustrated by YongSheng Zuan. Holiday, 2005.

Cony, Frances. *Old MacDonald Had a Farm*. Illustrated by Iain Smyth. Scholastic, 2002.

Cordsen, Carol Foskett. *The Milkman*. Illustrated by Douglas B. Jones. Dutton, 2005.

Cotton, Cynthia. *At the Edge of the Woods*. Illustrated by Reg Cartwright. Holt, 2002.

Cousins, Lucy. *Maisy Goes to Bed*. Little, 1990.

Cowell, Cressida. *What Shall We Do With a Boo-Hoo Baby?* Illustrated by Ingrid Gordon. Scholastic, 2001.

Cowley, Joy. *Agapanthus Hum and the Angel Hoot*. Illustrated by Jennifer Plecas. Philomel, 2003.

———. *Greedy Cat*. Owens, 1988.

Crews, Donald. *Flying*. Greenwillow, 1986.

———. *Freight Train*. Greenwillow, 1978.

———. *Harbor*. Greenwillow, 1982.

———. *Inside Freight Train*. Greenwillow, 2001.

———. *Night at the Fair*. Greenwillow, 1998.

———. *Sail Away*. Greenwillow, 1995.

———. *School Bus*. Greenwillow, 1984.

———. *Ten Black Dots*. Greenwillow, 1986 [1968].

———. *Truck*. Greenwillow, 1980.

Crews, Nina. *The Neighborhood Mother Goose*. Greenwillow, 2004.

Cronin, Doreen. *Click, Clack, Quackity-Quack: An Alphabetical Adventure*. Atheneum, 2005.

Crowther, Robert. *Shapes*. Candlewick, 2002.

Cummings, Pat. *Purrrrr*. HarperCollins, 1999.

Curtis, Carolyn. *I Took the Moon for a Walk*. Illustrated by Alison J. Barefoot, 2004.

Cushman, Doug. *Inspector Hopper*. HarperCollins, 2000.

Dahl, Michael. *One Big Building: A Counting Book about Construction*. Illustrated by Todd Ouren. Picture Window, 2004.

Daly, Niki. *Jamela's Dress*. Farrar, 1999.

———. *What's Cooking, Jamela?* Farrar, 2001.

Davidson, Rebecca Platt. *The Boy Who Writes Poems and Plays.* Illustrated by Anita Lobel. Greenwillow, 2003.

Davies, Nicola. *Big Blue Whale.* Illustrated by Nick Maitland. Candlewick, 2001.

———. *One Tiny Turtle.* Chapman, 2004.

Day, Alexandra. *Carl Goes Shopping.* Farrar, 1989.

———. *Carl's Sleepy Afternoon.* Farrar, 2005.

———. *Good Dog, Carl.* Green Tiger, 1985.

de Angeli, Marguerite. *The Book of Nursery and Mother Goose Rhymes.* Doubleday, 1954.

Delacre, Lulu, ed. *Arrorró, Mi Niño. Latino Lullabies and Gentle Games.* Lee, 2004.

———, ed. *Arroz Con Leche: Popular Songs and Rhymes from Latin America.* Scholastic, 1989.

Demarest, Chris L. *Firefighters from A to Z.* McElderry, 2000.

dePaola, Tomie. *The Comic Adventures of Old Mother Hubbard and Her Dog.* Harcourt, 1981.

———. *Pancakes for Breakfast.* Harcourt, 1978.

———. *Tomie de Paola's Mother Goose.* Putnam, 1985.

Dragonwagon, Crescent. *Alligator Arrived with Apples.* Illustrated by Jose Aruego and Ariane Dewey. Macmillan, 1987.

Dugan, Joanne. *ABC NYC: A Book about Seeing New York.* Abrams, 2005.

Dunrea, Olivier. *Ollie's Eggs.* Houghton, 2006.

Dupasquier, Philippe. *1 2 3 Follow Me!* Candlewick, 2002.

Earle, Ann. *Zipping, Zapping, Zooming Bats.* Illustrated by Henry Cole. HarperCollins, 1995.

Earle, Sylvia. *Hello Fish! Visiting the Coral Reef.* Photographs by Wolcott Henry. National Geographic, 1999.

Edwards, Pamela Duncan. *Clara Caterpillar.* Illustrated by Henry Cole. HarperCollins, 2004.

———. *The Neat Line: Scribbling through Mother Goose.* Illustrated by Diana Cain Bluthenthal. HarperCollins, 2005.

———. *Miss Polly Has a Dolly.* Illustrated by Elicia Castell. Putnam, 2003.

———. *Rosie's Roses.* Illustrated by Henry Cole. HarperCollins, 2003.

Ehlert, Lois. *Color Farm.* Lippincott, 1990.

———. *Color Zoo.* Lippincott, 1990.

———. *Eating the Alphabet.* Harcourt, 1989.

———. *Feathers for Lunch.* Harcourt, 1990.

———. *Fish Eyes: A Book You Can Count On.* Harcourt, 1990.

———. *In My World.* Harcourt, 2002.

———. *Red Leaf, Yellow Leaf.* Harcourt, 1991.

———. *Waiting for Wings.* Harcourt, 2001.

Emberley, Barbara. *Drummer Hoff.* Illustrated by Ed Emberley. Prentice-Hall, 1967.

English, Karen. *The Baby on the Way.* Illustrated by Sean Qualls. Farrar, 2005.

Ernst, Lisa Campbell. *The Turn-Around Upside-Down Alphabet Book.* Simon, 2004.

———. *This Is the Van That Dad Cleaned.* Simon, 2005.

Falconer, Ian. *Olivia Counts.* Simon/Schwartz, 2002.

———. *Olivia's Opposites.* Simon/Schwartz, 2002.

Falls, C. B. *ABC Book.* Morrow, 1998.

Falwell, Cathryn. *Feast for Ten.* Clarion, 1993.

———. *Turtle Splash: Countdown at the Farm.* Greenwillow, 2001.

Feelings, Muriel. *Jambo Means Hello: Swahili Alphabet Book.* Illustrated by Tom Feelings. Dial, 1974.

———. *Moja Means One: Swahili Counting Book.* Illustrated by Tom Feelings. Dial, 1971.

Fleming, Candace. *This Is the Baby.* Illustrated by Maggie Smith. Farrar, 2004.

Fleming, Denise. *Alphabet Under Construction.* Holt, 2002.

———. *Barnyard Banter.* Holt, 1993.

———. *The First Day of Winter.* Holt, 2005.

———. *In the Small Small Pond.* Holt, 1993.

———. *In the Tall Tall Grass.* Holt, 1991.

———. *Mama Cat Has Three Kittens.* Holt, 1998.

Florian, Douglas. *A Pig Is Big.* Greenwillow, 2000.

Foreman, Michael. *Playtime Rhymes.* Candlewick, 2002.

Fox, Mem. *Shoes from Grandpa.* Illustrated by Patricia Mullins. Orchard, 1990.

———. *Time for Bed.* Illustrated by Jane Dyer. Harcourt, 1993.

Frampton, David. *My Beastie Book of ABC.* HarperCollins, 2002.

Frazee, Marla. *Hush, Little Baby: A Folk Song with Pictures.* Harcourt, 1999.

Gág, Wanda. *The ABC Bunny.* Coward-McCann, 1933.

Galdone, Paul. *The Gingerbread Boy.* Clarion, 1975.

———. *The Little Red Hen.* Clarion, 1973.

———. *Over in the Meadow.* Prentice-Hall, 1986.

———. *The Three Bears.* Clarion, 1972.

———. *The Three Billy Goats Gruff.* Clarion, 1981.

———. *The Three Little Pigs.* Clarion, 1970.

Gantos, Jack. *Rotten Ralph Helps Out.* Farrar, 2001.

Garten, Jan. *The Alphabet Tale.* Illustrated by Muriel Batherman. Greenwillow, 1994 [1964].

Geisert, Arthur. *Pigs from 1 to 10.* Houghton, 1992.

Gelman, Rita. *Doodler Doodling.* Illustrated by Paul O. Zelinsky. Greenwillow, 2003.

George, Lindsay Barrett. *Inside Mouse, Outside Mouse.* Greenwillow, 2004.

Gershator, Phillis. *Greetings Sun.* Illustrated by Synthia St. James. DK Ink, 1998.

Giganti, Paul, Jr. *How Many Blue Birds Flew Away? A Counting Book with a Difference.* Illustrated by Donald Crews. Greenwillow, 2005.

———. *How Many Snails?* Illustrated by Donald Crews. Greenwillow, 1988.

———. *The Chick and the Duckling.* Illustrated by Jose Aruego and Ariane Dewey. Macmillan, 1972.

———. *Good Morning, Chick.* Illustrated by Byron Barton. Greenwillow, 1980.

Gobler, Piet. *Little Bird's ABC.* Front St., 2005.

Godwin, Laura. *Little White Dog.* Illustrated by Dan Yaccarino. Hyperion, 1998.

Greenaway, Kate. *Mother Goose, or the Old Nursery Rhymes.* Warne, n.d.

Greenfield, Eloise. *She Come Bringing Me That Little Baby Girl.* Illustrated by John Steptoe. Lippincott, 1974.

———. *Water, Water.* Illustrated by Jan Spivey Gilchrist. HarperCollins, 1999.

Greenstein, Elaine. *One Little Lamb.* Viking, 2004.

Griego, Margot C., et al. *Tortillitas Para Mama and Other Nursery Rhymes/Spanish and English.* Illustrated by Barbara Cooney. Holt, 1981.

Grimes, Nikki. *C Is for City.* Illustrated by Pat Cummings. Boyds Mills, 2002.

Grodin, Elissa. *D Is for Democracy: A Citizen's Alphabet Book.* Illustrated by Victor Jahsz. Sleeping Bear, 2004.

Guarino, Deborah. *Is Your Mama a Llama?* Illustrated by Steven Kellogg. Scholastic, 1989.

Guest, Elissa Haden. *Iris and Walter and the Field Trip.* HarperCollins, 2005.

———. *Iris and Walter and the School Play.* Illustrated by Christine Davenier. Harcourt, 2003.

Guthrie, Woody. *New Baby Train.* Illustrated by Marla Frazee. Little, 2004.

Hale, Sarah Josepha. *Mary Had a Little Lamb.* Photo-illustrated by Bruce McMillan. Scholastic, 1990.

———. *Mary Had a Little Lamb.* Illustrated by Salley Mavor. Orchard, 1995.

Harrison, Ted. *A Northern Alphabet.* Tundra, 1982.

Hawkins, Colin, and Jacqui Hawkins. *I Know an Old Lady Who Swallowed a Fly.* Putnam, 1987.

Hayes, Sarah. *Nine Ducks Nine.* Lothrop, 1990.

———. *This Is the Bear.* Illustrated by Helen Craig. Lippincott, 1986.

Henkes, Kevin. *The Biggest Boy.* Illustrated by Nancy Tafuri. Greenwillow, 1995.

———. *Julius's Candy Corn.* Greenwillow, 2003.

———. *Kitten's First Full Moon.* Greenwillow, 2004.

———. *Lilly's Chocolate Heart.* Greenwillow, 2004.

———. *Owen's Marshmallow Chick.* Greenwillow, 2002.

———. *Sheila Rae's Peppermint Stick.* Greenwillow, 2001.

———. *Wemberly's Ice-Cream Star.* Greenwillow, 2003.

Henson, Heather. *Angel Coming.* Illustrated by Susan Gaber. Atheneum, 2005.

Hest, Amy. *Baby Duck Goes to School.* Illustrated by Jill Barton. Candlewick, 1999.

———. *Guess Who, Baby Duck?* Illustrated by Jill Barton. Little, 2004.

———. *In the Rain with Baby Duck.* Illustrated by Jill Barton. Candlewick, 1996.

———. *Make the Team, Baby Duck.* Illustrated by Jill Barton. Candlewick, 2002.

———. *Off to School, Baby Duck!* Illustrated by Jill Barton. Candlewick, 1999.

Hill, Eric. *Good Night Spot.* Putnam, 1999.

———. *Spot Goes to School.* Putnam, 1994.

———. *Where's Spot?* Putnam, 1980.

Hillenbrand, Will. *Down By the Station.* Harcourt, 1999.

———. *Fiddle-I-Fee.* Harcourt, 2002.

Hoban, Russell. *A Baby Sister for Frances.* Illustrated by Lillian Hoban. Harper, 1964.

———. *Bread and Jam for Frances.* Illustrated by Lillian Hoban. Harper, 1964.

Hoban, Tana. *1, 2, 3.* Greenwillow, 1985.

———. *26 Letters and 99 Cents.* Greenwillow, 1987.

———. *A, B, See!* Greenwillow, 1982.

———. *Colors Everywhere.* Greenwillow, 1995.

———. *Exactly the Opposite.* Greenwillow, 1983.

———. *I Read Signs.* Greenwillow, 1983.

———. *I Read Symbols.* Greenwillow, 1983.

———. *Is It Larger? Is It Smaller?* Greenwillow, 1985.

———. *Let's Count.* Greenwillow, 1999.

———. *Red, Blue, Yellow Shoe.* Greenwillow, 1986.

———. *Shapes, Shapes, Shapes.* HarperCollins, 1986.

———. *So Many Circles, So Many Squares.* Greenwillow, 1998.

———. *What Is That?* Greenwillow, 1994.

Hoberman, Mary Ann. *Bill Grogan's Goat.* Illustrated by Nadine Bernard Westcott. Little, 2002.

———. *The Eensy Weensy Spider.* Illustrated by Nadine Bernard Westcott. Little, 2000.

———. *Miss Mary Mack.* Illustrated by Nadine Bernard Westcott. Little, 1998.

———. *The Seven Silly Eaters.* Illustrated by Marla Frazee. Browndeer, 1997.

———. *You Read to Me, I'll Read to You: Very Short Mother Goose Tales to Read Together.* Illustrated by Michael Emberley. Little, 2005.

Hogrogian, Nonny. *One Fine Day.* Macmillan, 1971.

Holub, Joan. *The Garden That We Grew.* Illustrated by Hiroe Nakata. Viking, 2001.

Hooks, William H. *Three Little Pigs and the Fox.* Illustrated by S. D. Schindler. Simon, 1997.

Hopkins, Lee Bennett. *April, Bubbles, Chocolate: An ABC of Poetry.* Illustrated by Barry Root. Simon, 1994.

Horowitz, Ruth. *Breakout at the Bug Lab.* Illustrated by Joan Holub. Dial, 2001.

Hort, Lenny. *The Seals on the Bus.* Illustrated by G. Brian Karas. Holt, 2000.

Huck, Charlotte. *A Creepy Countdown.* Illustrated by Jos. A. Smith. Greenwillow, 1998.

Hughes, Shirley. *The Big Alfie and Annie Rose Storybook.* Lothrop, 1989.

Hunt, Peter. *Illuminations.* Bradbury, 1989.

Hurd, Thatcher. *Sleepy Cadillac: A Bedtime Drive.* HarperCollins, 2005.

Hutchins, Pat. *1 Hunter*. Greenwillow, 1982.

———. *Changes, Changes*. Macmillan, 1971.

———. *The Doorbell Rang*. Greenwillow, 1986.

———. *Good-Night, Owl!* Macmillan (Penguin), 1972.

———. *Happy Birthday, Sam*. Penguin, 1981.

———. *Little Pink Pig*. Greenwillow, 1994.

———. *Rosie's Walk*. Macmillan, 1968.

———. *Tidy Titch*. Greenwillow, 1991.

———. *Titch*. Macmillan, 1971.

———. *We're Going on a Picnic!* Greenwillow, 2002.

———. *You'll Soon Grow into Them, Titch*. Greenwillow, 1983.

Isadora, Rachel. *1 2 3 Pop!* Viking, 2000.

———. *City Seen from A to Z*. Greenwillow, 1983.

———. *On Your Toes: A Ballet ABC*. Greenwillow, 2003.

Jarret, Clare. *The Best Picnic Ever*. Candlewick, 2005.

Jarrie, Martin. *ABC USA*. Sterling, 2005.

Jay, Alison. *ABC: A Child's First Alphabet Book*. Dutton, 2005.

Jeffers, Susan. *Three Jovial Huntsmen*. Macmillan, 1989.

Jenkins, Emily. *Daffodil*. Illustrated by Tomek Bogacki. Farrar, 2004.

———. *Five Creatures*. Illustrated by Tomek Bogacki. Farrar, 2001.

———. *That New Animal*. Illustrated by Pierre Pratt. Farrar, 2005.

Jenkins, Steve. *Actual Size*. Houghton, 2005.

———. *Prehistoric Actual Size*. Houghton, 2005.

Jenkins, Steve, and Robin Page. *I See a Kookaburra!* Houghton, 2005.

———. *What Do You Do with a Tail Like This?* Houghton, 2003.

Johnson, Stephen T. *Alphabet City*. Viking, 1995.

———. *City by Numbers*. Viking, 1998.

Jonas, Ann. *Aardvarks Disembark!* Greenwillow, 1989.

———. *Splash!* Greenwillow, 1995.

Jones, Carol. *Old MacDonald Had a Farm*. Houghton, 1989.

———. *This Old Man*. Houghton, 1990.

Jorgensen, Gail. *Crocodile Beat*. Illustrated by Patricia Mullins. Simon, 1989.

Juan, Ana. *The Night Eater*. Scholastic, 2004.

Juster, Norton. *The Hello Goodbye Window*. Illustrated by Chris Raschka. Hyperion, 2005.

Kalman, Maira. *What Pete Ate from A–Z (Really!)*. Putnam, 2001.

Keats, Ezra Jack. *Over in the Meadow*. Four Winds, 1971.

Keller, Holly. *Sophie's Window*. Greenwillow, 2005.

Kellogg, Steven. *Chicken Little*. Morrow, 1987.

King-Smith, Dick. *All Pigs Are Beautiful*. Illustrated by Anita Jeram. Candlewick, 1993.

———. *I Love Guinea Pigs*. Illustrated by Anita Jeram. Candlewick, 1995.

Kirk, Daniel. *Go!* Hyperion, 2001.

Kitchen, Bert. *Animal Alphabet*. Dial, 1984.

———. *Animal Numbers*. Dial, 1987.

Kovalski, Maryann. *The Wheels on the Bus*. Little, 1987.

Kraus, Robert. *Where Are You Going, Little Mouse?* Illustrated by Jose Aruego and Ariane Dewey. Greenwillow, 1986.

———. *Whose Mouse Are You?* Illustrated by Jose Aruego and Ariane Dewey. Macmillan, 1970.

Krauss, Ruth. *Bears*. Illustrated by Maurice Sendak. HarperCollins, 2005.

———. *The Carrot Seed*. Illustrated by Crockett Johnson. Harper, 1945.

Krebs, Laurie. *We All Went on Safari: A Counting Journey through Tanzania*. Illustrated by Julia Cairns. Barefoot, 2004.

———. *We're Sailing to Galapagos: A Week in the Pacific*. Illustrated by Grazia Restelli. Barefoot, 2005.

Kunhardt, Dorothy. *Pat the Bunny*. Golden, 1962 [1940].

Kunhardt, Edith. *Pat the Puppy*. Golden, 1993.

Kuskin, Karla. *Roar and More*. HarperCollins, 1990.

———. *Under My Hood I Have a Hat*. Illustrated by Fumi Kosaka. HarperCollins, 2004.

Lamont, Priscilla. *Playtime Rhymes*. Kindersley, 1998.

Langstaff, John. *Oh, A-Hunting We Will Go*. Illustrated by Nancy Winslow Parker. Atheneum, 1974.

———. *Over in the Meadow*. Illustrated by Feodor Rojankovsky. Harcourt, 1967.

Laurence, Daniel. *Captain and Matey Set Sail*. Illustrated by Claudio Munoz. HarperCollins, 2001.

Lear, Edward. *A Was Once an Apple Pie*. Illustrated by Suse MacDonald. Scholastic, 2005.

Lee, Ho Baek. *While We Were Out*. Kane/Miller, 2003.

Lehman, Barbara. *The Red Book*. Houghton, 2004.

Leopold, Niki Clark. *K Is for Kitten*. Illustrated by Susan Jeffers. Putnam, 2002.

Lester, Mike. *A Is for Salad*. Putnam, 2000.

Lewis, Kevin. *Chugga-Chugga Choo-Choo*. Illustrated by Daniel Kirk. Hyperion, 1999.

Lewis, Kim. *My Truck Is Stuck*. Illustrated by Daniel Kirk. Hyperion, 2005.

Little, Jean. *Emma's Yucky Brother*. Illustrated by Jennifer Plecas. HarperCollins, 2001.

Lobel, Anita. *Alison's Zinnia*. Greenwillow, 1990.

———. *Animal Antics A–Z*. Greenwillow, 2005.

———. *Away from Home*. Greenwillow, 1994.

———. *One Lighthouse, One Moon*. Greenwillow, 2000.

Lobel, Arnold. *Days with Frog and Toad*. Harper, 1979.

———. *Frog and Toad All Year*. Harper, 1976.

———. *Frog and Toad Are Friends*. Harper, 1970.

———. *Frog and Toad Together*. Harper, 1972.

———. *On Market Street*. Illustrated by Anita Lobel. Greenwillow, 1981.

———. *Whiskers and Rhymes*. Greenwillow, 1985.

———, ed. and illus. *The Arnold Lobel Book of Mother Goose*. Knopf, 2003 [Random, 1986].

London, Jonathan. *A Truck Goes Rattley-Bumpa*. Illustrated by Denis Roche. Holt, 2005.

London, Jonathan. *Wiggle Waggle*. Illustrated by Michael Rex. Harcourt, 1999.

Lyon, George Ella. *Counting on the Woods*. Photographs by Ann W. Olson. DK Ink, 1998.

MacDonald, Flora. *Flora MacDonald's ABC*. Candlewick, 1997.

MacDonald, Suse. *Alphabatics*. Bradbury, 1986.

———. *Here a Chick, Where a Chick?* Scholastic, 2004.

Maitland, Barbara. *The Bookstore Valentine*. Illustrated by David LaRochelle. Dutton, 2002.

Manning, Mick. *Yuck!* Illustrated by Brita Granström. Lincoln, 2005.

Mannis, Celeste Davidson. *One Leaf Rides the Wind: Counting in a Japanese Garden*. Illustrated by Susan Kathleen Hartung. Viking, 2002.

———. *The Queen's Progress: An Elizabethan Alphabet*. Illustrated by Bagram Ibatoulline. Viking, 2003.

Manson, Christopher. *The Tree in the Wood: An Old Nursery Song*. North-South, 1993.

Markle, Sandra, and William Markle. *Gone Forever! An Alphabet of Extinct Animals*. Illustrated by Felipe Dávalos. Atheneum, 1998.

Marsalis, Wynton. *Jazz ABZ: A Collection of Jazz Portraits from A to Z*. Illustrated by Paul Rogers. Candlewick, 2005.

Marshall, James. *James Marshall's Mother Goose*. Farrar, 1979.

Martin, Bill, Jr. *Brown Bear, Brown Bear, What Do You See?* Illustrated by Eric Carle. Holt, 1983.

———. *Polar Bear, Polar Bear, What Do You Hear?* Illustrated by Eric Carle. Holt, 1991.

Martin, Bill, Jr., and John Archambault. *Chicka Chicka Boom Boom*. Illustrated by Lois Ehlert. Simon, 1989.

Martin, Bill, Jr., and Michael Sampson. *Rock It, Sock It, Number Line*. Illustrated by Heather Cahoon. Holt, 2001.

Mavor, Salley. *Hey, Diddle, Diddle!* Houghton, 2005.

Mayer, Mercer. *A Boy, a Dog, and a Frog*. Dial, 1967.

———. *Frog Goes to Dinner*. Dial, 1974.

———. *One Frog Too Many*. Dial, 1975.

Mayo, Margaret. *Choo Choo Clickety-Clack!* Carolrhoda, 2005.

McCully, Emily Arnold. *The Battle for St. Michaels*. HarperCollins, 2002.

———. *First Snow*. HarperCollins, 2004 [1985].

———. *Picnic*. Harper, 1984.

———. *School*. Harper, 1987.

———. *Four Hungry Kittens*. Dial, 2001.

McCurdy, Michael. *The Sailor's Alphabet*. Houghton, 1998.

McMillan, Bruce. *Days of the Ducklings*. Houghton, 2001.

———. *Eating Fractions*. Scholastic, 1991.

———. *Going Fishing*. Houghton, 2005.

———. *Night of the Pufflings*. Houghton, 1997.

McMullan, Kate. *Peal and Wagner: Three Secrets*. Illustrated by R. W. Alley. Dial, 2004.

McNaughton, Colin. *Boo!* Harcourt, 1996.

———. *Preston's Goal*. Harcourt, 1998.

———. *Suddenly!* Harcourt, 1994.

———. *Yum!* Harcourt, 1999.

Merriam, Eve. *12 Ways to Get to 11*. Illustrated by Bernie Karlin. Simon, 1993.

———. *Ten Rosy Roses*. Illustrated by Julia Gorton. HarperCollins, 1999.

———. *What in the World?* Illustrated by Barbara J. Phillips-Duke. HarperCollins, 1998.

Mickelwait, Lucy. *I Spy: An Alphabet in Art*. Greenwillow, 1992.

Milich, Zoran. *City 1 2 3*. Kids Can, 2005.

Miller, Margaret. *Can You Guess?* Greenwillow, 1993.

———. *Guess Who?* Greenwillow, 1994.

———. *Where Does It Go?* Greenwillow, 1992.

———. *Who Uses This?* Greenwillow, 1990.

———. *Whose Hat?* Greenwillow, 1988.

Mills, Claudia. *Gus and Grandpa and the Piano Lesson*. Illustrated by Catherine Stock. Farrar, 2005.

Minarik, Else Holmelund. *Little Bear*. Illustrated by Maurice Sendak. Harper, 1957.

Moak, Allan. *Big City ABC*. Tundra, 2002.

Mora, Pat. *Pablo's Tree*. Illustrated by Cecily Lang. Macmillan, 1994.

Morgan, Pierr. *The Turnip: An Old Russian Folktale*. Paper Star, 1996.

Morris, Ann. *Bread, Bread, Bread*. Photographs by Ken Heyman. Lothrop, 1989.

———. *Houses and Homes*. Photographs by Ken Heyman. Lothrop, 1992.

———. *Loving*. Photographs by Ken Heyman. Lothrop, 1990.

———. *Play*. Lothrop, 1998.

———. *Work*. Lothrop, 1998.

Moss, Lloyd. *Zin! Zin! Zin! A Violin*. Illustrated by Marjorie Priceman. Simon, 1995.

Most, Bernard. *The Cow That Went Oink*. Harcourt, 1990.

———. *Z-Z-Zoink!* Harcourt, 1999.

Mullins, Patricia. *V for Vanishing: An Alphabet of Endangered Animals*. HarperCollins, 1993.

Munro, Roxie. *Doors*. Chronicle, 2004.

Murphy, Jill. *Five Minutes' Peace*. Putnam, 1986.

Musgrove, Margaret. *Ashanti to Zulu: African Traditions*. Illustrated by Leo Dillon and Diane Dillon. Dial, 1976.

Neitzel, Shirley. *The House I'll Build for the Wrens*. Greenwillow, 1997.

———. *Our Class Took a Trip to the Zoo*. Illustrated by Nancy Winslow Parker. Greenwillow, 2002.

Newcome, Zita. *Head, Shoulders, Knees, and Toes and Other Action Rhymes*. Candlewick, 2002.

Onyefulu, Ifeoma. *A Is for Africa*. Cobblehill, 1993.

———. *Emeka's Gift: An African Counting Story*. Cobblestone, 1995.

Opie, Iona. *Here Comes Mother Goose*. Illustrated by Rosemary Wells. Candlewick, 1999.

———. *My Very First Mother Goose*. Illustrated by Rosemary Wells. Candlewick, 1996.

Opie, Iona, and Peter Opie. *I Saw Esau*. Illustrated by Maurice Sendak. Candlewick, 1992.

———. *The Oxford Dictionary of Nursery Rhymes*. Oxford, 1951.

Ormerod, Jan. *When an Elephant Comes to School*. Orchard, 2005.

———. *Young Joe*. Morrow, 1986.

Orozco, José-Luis. *Diez Deditos and Other Play Rhymes and Action Songs from Latin America*. Illustrated by Elisa Kleven. Dutton, 2002.

Otto, Carolyn. *What Color Is Camouflage?* Illustrated by Megan Lloyd. HarperCollins, 2000.

Owens, Mary Beth. *A Caribou Alphabet*. Illustrated by Mark McCollough. Tilbury, 1988.

Oxenbury, Helen. Baby Board Books. *Dressing. Family. Friends. Playing. Working*. All Simon, 1995 [1981].

———. *Helen Oxenbury's ABC of Things*. Watts, 1972.

Pallotta, Jerry. *The Beetle Alphabet Book*. Charlesbridge, 2004.

Parker, Kim. *Counting in the Garden*. Orchard, 2005.

Paterson, Katherine. *Marvin One Too Many*. Illustrated by Jane Clark Brown. HarperCollins, 2001.

Payne, Nina. *Four in All*. Illustrated by Adam Payne. Front St., 2001.

———. *Summertime Waltz*. Illustrated by Gabi Swiatkowska. Farrar, 2005.

Pearson, Tracey Campbell. *Diddle, Diddle, Dumpling*. Farrar, 2005.

Peek, Merle. *Mary Wore Her Red Dress and Henry Wore His Green Sneakers*. Clarion, 1985.

Pellitier, David. *The Graphic Alphabet*. Orchard, 1996.

Petersham, Maud, and Miska Petersham. *The Rooster Crows*. Macmillan, 1945.

Pfeffer, Wendy. *Wiggling Worms at Work*. Illustrated by Steve Jenkins. HarperCollins, 2004.

Pinkney, Andrea. *Pretty Brown Face*. Illustrated by Brian Pinkney. Harcourt, 1997.

———. *Watch Me Dance*. Illustrated by Brian Pinkney. Harcourt, 1997.

Polacco, Patricia. *In Enzo's Splendid Gardens*. Philomel, 1997.

Pomerantz, Charlotte. *Here Comes Henny*. Illustrated by Nancy Winslow Parker. Greenwillow, 1994.

———. *One Duck, Another Duck*. Illustrated by Jose Aruego and Ariane Dewey. Greenwillow, 1984.

———. *The Piggy in a Puddle*. Illustrated by James Marshall. Macmillan, 1974.

Pomeroy, Diana. *One Potato: A Counting Book of Potato Prints*. Harcourt, 1996.

———. *Wildflower ABC*. Harcourt, 1997.

Provensen, Alice, and Martin Provensen. *A Peaceable Kingdom: The Shaker Abecedarius*. Viking, 1978.

Rackham, Arthur. *Mother Goose, or the Old Nursery Rhymes*. Appleton, 1913.

Raffi. *Down By the Bay: Songs to Read*. Illustrated by Nadine Bernard Westcott. Crown, 1987.

———. *Five Little Ducks*. Illustrated by Jose Aruego and Ariane Dewey. Crown, 1989.

Rankin, Laura. *Swan Harbor: A Nature Counting Book*. Dial, 2003.

Rathmann, Peggy. *10 Minutes Till Bedtime*. Putnam, 1999.

———. *Good Night, Gorilla*. Putnam, 1994.

Reiser, Lynn. *Ten Puppies*. Greenwillow, 2003.

Rice, Eve. *Sam Who Never Forgets*. Mulberry. 1987.

Robart, Rose. *The Cake That Mack Ate*. Illustrated by Maryann Kovalski. Joy Street/Little, 1986.

Rockwell, Anne. *Little Shark*. Illustrated by Megan Halsey. Walker, 2005.

Rogers, Gregory. *The Boy, the Bear, the Baron, and the Bard*. Roaring Brook, 2004.

Rojankovsky, Feodor. *The Tall Book of Mother Goose*. Harper, 1942.

Root, Phyllis. *Oliver Finds His Way*. Illustrated by Christopher Denise. Candlewick, 2002.

———. *One Duck Stuck*. Illustrated by Jane Chapman. Candlewick, 1998.

———. *One Windy Wednesday*. Illustrated by Helen Craig. Candlewick, 1996.

———. *Ten Sleepy Sheep*. Illustrated by Susan Gaber. Candlewick, 2004.

———. *What Baby Wants*. Illustrated by Jill Barton. Candlewick, 1998.

Rose, Deborah Lee. *Ocean Babies*. National Geographic, 2005.

Rosen, Michael. *We're Going on a Bear Hunt*. Illustrated by Helen Oxenbury. Macmillan, 1989.

Roth, Carol. *The Little School Bus*. Illustrated by Pamela Paarone. North-South, 2002.

Rounds, Glen. *Old MacDonald Had a Farm*. Holiday, 1981.

———. *The Three Billy Goats Gruff*. Holiday, 1993.

Ryan, Pam Munoz. *One Hundred Is a Family*. Illustrated by Benrei Huang. Hyperion, 1994.

Rylant, Cynthia. *The Case of the Fidgety Fox (High Rise Private Eyes)*. Illustrated by G. Brian Karas. Greenwillow, 2003.

———. *Henry and Mudge*. Illustrated by Suçie Stevenson. Bradbury, 1987.

———. *Henry and Mudge and the Great Grandpas*. Illustrated by Suçie Stevenson. Simon, 2005.

———. *Henry and Mudge and the Starry Night*. Illustrated by Suçie Stevenson. Simon, 1998.

———. *Henry and Mudge and the Tall Tree House*. Illustrated by Carolyn Bracken. Simon, 2002.

———. *The High Rise Private Eyes: The Case of the Desperate Duck*. Illustrated by G. Brian Karas. Greenwillow, 2005.

———. *Mr. Putter and Tabby Catch the Cold*. Illustrated by Arthur Howard. Harcourt, 2002.

———. *Poppleton in Winter*. Illustrated by Mark Teague. Scholastic, 2001.

Sabuda, Robert. *The Movable Mother Goose*. Simon, 1999.

Sanders, Marilyn. *What's Your Name? From Ariel to Zoe*. Photographs by Eve Sanders. Holiday, 1995.

Schaefer, Lola M. *This Is the Rain*. Illustrated by Jane Wattenburg. Greenwillow, 2001.

———. *This Is the Sunflower*. Illustrated by Donald Crews. Greenwillow, 2000.

Schnur, Steven. *Autumn: An Alphabet Acrostic.* Illustrated by Leslie Evans. Clarion, 1997.

———. *Spring: An Alphabet Acrostic.* Illustrated by Leslie Evans. Clarion, 1999.

———. *Summer: An Acrostic Alphabet.* Illustrated by Leslie Evans. Clarion, 2001.

———. *Winter: An Acrostic Alphabet.* Illustrated by Leslie Evans. Clarion, 2002.

Schwartz, Amy. *Old MacDonald.* Scholastic, 1999.

Sendak, Maurice. *Chicken Soup with Rice.* HarperCollins, 1962.

———. *Hector Protector and As I Went Over the Water.* HarperCollins, 1990 [1965].

———. *Where the Wild Things Are.* HarperCollins, 1963.

Seuss, Dr. [Theodor S. Geisel]. *The Cat in the Hat.* Beginner Books, 1957.

Shannon, David. *David Goes to School.* Scholastic, 2001.

———. *David Gets in Trouble.* Scholastic, 2002.

———. *No, David!* Scholastic, 1998.

Shaw, Nancy. *Sheep in a Jeep.* Illustrated by Margot Shaw. Houghton, 1986.

Sheppard, Jeff. *Splash, Splash.* Illustrated by Dennis Panek. Macmillan, 1994.

Shulevitz, Uri. *One Monday Morning.* Scribner's, 1967.

Shulman, Lisa. *Old Macdonald Had a Woodshop.* Illustrated by Ashley Wolff. Putnam, 2002.

Sierra, Judy. *Schoolyard Rhymes: Kids' Own Rhymes for Rope-Skipping, Hand Clapping, Ball Bouncing and Just Plain Fun.* Illustrated by Melissa Sweet. Knopf, 2005.

Simmons, Jane. *Come Along Daisy!* Little, 1998.

———. *Daisy Says, "Here We Go 'Round the Mulberry Bush."* Little, 2002.

———. *Quack, Daisy, Quack.* Little, 2002.

Sis, Peter. *Waving: A Counting Book.* Greenwillow, 1988.

Slate, Joseph. *Miss Bindergarten Takes a Field Trip with Kindergarten.* Illustrated by Ashley Wolff. Dutton, 2001.

Sloat, Teri. *This Is the House That Was Tidy and Neat.* Illustrated by R. W. Alley. Holt, 2005.

Slobodkina, Esphyr. *Caps for Sale.* Addison, 1947.

Sobel, June. *B Is for Bulldozer: A Construction ABC.* Illustrated by Melissa Iwai. Harcourt, 2003.

Sogabe, Aki. *Aesop's Fox.* Browndeer, 1999.

Spanyol, Jessica. *Carlo Likes Counting.* Candlewick, 2002.

Spier, Peter. *Noah's Ark.* Doubleday, 1977.

———. *Peter Spier's Rain.* Doubleday, 1982.

Steen, Sandra, and Susan Steen. *Car Wash.* Illustrated by G. Brian Karas. Putnam, 2001.

Steptoe, Javaka. *Sweet, Sweet Baby!* Scholastic, 2005 (cloth).

Steptoe, John. *Baby Says.* Lothrop, 1988.

Stevens, Janet. *The House That Jack Built.* Greenwillow, 1983.

Stevens, Janet, and Susan Crummel Stevens. *Cook-a-Doodle-Doo!* Harcourt, 1999.

Sturges, Philemon. *The Little Red Hen (Makes a Pizza).* Illustrated by Amy Walrod. Dutton, 1999.

———. *She'll Be Comin' 'Round the Mountain.* Illustrated by Ashley Wolff. Little, 2004.

Sutherland, Zena. *The Orchard Book of Nursery Rhymes.* Illustrated by Faith Jaques. Orchard, 1990.

Sweet, Melissa. *Fiddle-I-Fee.* Little, 1992.

Szerkeres, Cyndy. *The Mouse That Jack Built.* Scholastic, 1997.

Taback, Simms. *Joseph Had a Little Overcoat.* Viking, 1999.

———. *There Was an Old Lady Who Swallowed a Fly.* Viking, 1997.

———. *This Is the House That Jack Built.* Putnam, 2002.

Tafuri, Nancy. *Early Morning in the Barn.* Greenwillow, 1983.

———. *Follow Me!* Greenwillow, 1990.

———. *Have You Seen My Duckling?* Greenwillow, 1984.

———. *Junglewalk.* Greenwillow, 1988.

———. *Silly Little Goose!* Scholastic, 2001.

Tapahonso, Luci, and Eleanor Schick. *Navajo ABC: A Diné Alphabet Book.* Illustrated by Eleanor Schick. Little, 1995.

Tatham, Betty. *Baby Sea Otter.* Illustrated by Joan Paley. Holt, 2005.

Thiesing, Lisa. *The Viper.* Dutton, 2002.

Thomas, Shelley Moore. *Get Well, Good Knight.* Illustrated by Jennifer Plecas. Dutton, 2002.

———. *Good Night, Good Knight.* Illustrated by Jennifer Plecas. Dutton, 2000.

Thompson, Lauren. *Polar Bear Night.* Illustrated by Stephen Savage. Scholastic, 2004.

Tobias, Tobi. *A World of Words: An ABC of Quotations.* Illustrated by Peter Malone. Lothrop, 1998.

Tudor, Tasha. *A Is for Annabelle.* Walck, 1954.

———. *Mother Goose.* Walck, 1944.

Turkle, Brinton. *Deep in the Forest.* Dutton, 1976.

Valckx, Cathryn. *Lizette's Green Sock.* Clarion, 2005.

Van Allsburg, Chris. *The Z Was Zapped: A Play in Twenty-Six Acts.* Houghton, 1987.

Van Leeuwen, Jean. *Oliver and Albert, Friends Forever.* Illustrated by Ann Schweninger. Dial, 2000.

Voce, Louise. *Over in the Meadow.* Candlewick, 1999.

Waddell, Martin. *Can't You Sleep, Little Bear?* Illustrated by Barbara Firth. Candlewick, 1996.

———. *Farmer Duck.* Illustrated by Helen Oxenbury. Candlewick, 1993.

———. *Owl Babies.* Illustrated by Patrick Benson. Candlewick, 1992.

———. *Snow Bears.* Illustrated by Sarah Fox-Davies. Candlewick, 2002.

———. *Tiny's Big Adventure.* Illustrated by John Lawrence. Candlewick, 2004.

———. *Webster J. Duck.* Illustrated by David Parkins. Candlewick, 2001.

Wallace, Karen. *Gentle Giant Octopus.* Illustrated by Mike Bostock. Candlewick, 1998.

Wallner, Alexandra. *The Farmer in the Dell.* Holiday, 1998.

Ward, Cindy. *Cookie's Week.* Illustrated by Tomie dePaola. Putnam, 1988.

Watson, Clyde. *Applebet.* Illustrated by Wendy Watson. Farrar, 1982.

Wells, Rosemary, *Bunny Cakes.* Puffin, 2001.

———. *Emily's First 100 Days of School.* Hyperion, 2000.

———. *Old Macdonald.* Scholastic, 1998.

———. *Shy Charles.* Viking, 2001.

———. *Very First Books. Max's Bath,* 1985. *Max's Bedtime,* 1985. *Max's Birthday,* 1985. *Max's Breakfast,* 1985. *Max's First Word,* 1979. *Max's Ride,* 1979. *Max's Toys,* 1979. All Dial.

Westcott, Nadine Bernard. *I Know an Old Lady Who Swallowed a Fly.* Little, 1980.

———. *Peanut Butter and Jelly: A Play Rhyme.* Dutton, 1987.

Wiesner, David. *Free Fall.* Lothrop, 1988.

———. *Sector 7.* Clarion, 1999.

———. *Tuesday.* Clarion, 1991.

Wilbur, Richard. *The Disappearing Alphabet.* Illustrated by David Diaz. Harcourt, 1999.

Wildsmith, Brian. *Brian Wildsmith's Mother Goose.* Watts, 1963.

Willems, Mo. *Knuffle Bunny.* Hyperion, 2001.

Williams, Linda. *The Little Old Lady Who Was Not Afraid of Anything.* Illustrated by Megan Lloyd. Harper, 1986.

Williams, Sue. *Dinnertime!* Illustrated by Kerry Argent. Harcourt, 2002.

———. *I Went Walking.* Illustrated by Julie Vivas. Harcourt, 1990.

———. *Let's Go Visiting.* Illustrated by Julie Vivas. Harcourt, 1998.

Williams, Vera B. *"More More More," Said the Baby.* Greenwillow, 1990.

Wilson-Max, Ken. *A Book of Letters.* Illustrated by Manya Stojic. Scholastic, 2002.

Wood, Audrey. *Heckedy Peg.* Illustrated by Don Wood. Harcourt, 1987.

———. *The Napping House.* Illustrated by Don Wood. Harcourt, 1984.

Wood, Jakki. *Fiddle-I-Fee.* Bradbury, 1994.

Wormell, Christopher. *Teeth, Tails, and Tentacles: An Animal Counting Book.* Running Press, 2004.

Wright, Blanche Fisher. *The Real Mother Goose.* Running Press, 1992 [1916].

Yolen, Jane. *Trot, Trot to Boston: Lap Songs, Finger Plays, Clapping Games and Pantomime Rhymes.* Illustrated by Will Hilenbrand. Candlewick, 2005.

Young, Ed. *What About Me?* Philomel, 2002.

Zalben, Jane Breskin. *Hey, Mama Goose.* Illustrated by Emilie Chollat. Dutton, 2005.

Zane, Alexander. *The Wheels on the Race Car.* Illustrated by James Warhola. Orchard, 2005.

Zelinsky, Paul O. *Knick-Knack Paddywhack! A Moving Parts Book.* Dutton, 2002.

———. *The Wheels on the Bus.* Dutton, 1990.

Zemach, Margot. *It Could Always Be Worse: A Yiddish Folktale.* Farrar, 1990.

Chapter Five

Picture Books

Photo © O'Brien Productions/CORBIS

Vivian

Gussin Paley is a master teacher and recipient of a John D. and Catherine T. MacArthur "genius grant." She has described the complex lives of her kindergartners in books like *Wally's Stories* and *Kwanzaa and Me.*[1] In her delightful *The Girl with the Brown Crayon,* Paley details a year-long odyssey that began when she read Leo Lionni's *Frederick* to her 5- and 6-year-olds. In *Frederick* Lionni creates his own version of the fable of the ant and the grasshopper, only this tale celebrates the contribution of Frederick, a mouse poet. The other mice bring in the harvest for the long winter, but Frederick does not work. He is gathering a harvest of sights and feelings. When the wind is cold and there is no food, Frederick shares his contribution of words and colors with his friends. He makes up poetry about the sun and the flowers and warms their souls.

Paley describes the responses of a little 5-year-old girl following the first reading of the book.

> Reeny, a five-year-old, has fallen in love with Leo Lionni's Frederick, "because that brown mouse seem to be just like me! . . . Because I'm always thinking 'bout colors and words the same like him."

Paley reports that having identified with Frederick, Reeny is compelled to investigate further.

> She takes the book to a table and turns the pages, slowly tracing the mice with her finger. "They so . . . ," she sighs, unable to complete the sentence. But she puts her brown crayon to the task. The first picture Reeny copies is of Frederick sitting with his eyes closed under a warm yellow sun, while the other mice struggle to carry ears of corn to their hideout in the stones. "He is so quiet." In his stillness Reeny finds her word.
>
> "Frederick's not as nice as them," Cory argues, puzzled at her new friend's interest. "He's being mean."
>
> Reeny touches Cory's arm. "That's not the same as mean. He's thinking. Anyway, those others is nicer but I still like Frederick. Look how his tail is, Cory, don't you love his tail the way it goes?"
>
> "Can you do the eyes for me?" Cory asks, pushing her paper in front of Reeny.

Leo Lionni's *Frederick* provided the motivation for a study of Lionni's books by Vivian Gussin Paley's kindergarten class. From *Frederick* by Leo Lionni, copyright © 1967 by Leo Lionni. Copyright renewed 1995 by Leo Lionni. Used by permission of Alfred A. Knopf, an imprint of Random House Children's Books, a division of Random House, Inc.

When Paley looks again, five more children are drawing mice. "By some unspoken agreement they [the children] are following a new curriculum."[2]

---

[1]Vivian Gussin Paley, *Wally's Stories: Conversations in Kindergarten* (Cambridge, Mass.: Harvard University Press, 1987), and *Kwanzaa and Me: A Teacher's Story* (Cambridge, Mass.: Harvard University Press, 1995).
[2]Vivian Gussin Paley, *The Girl with the Brown Crayon* (Cambridge, Mass.: Harvard University Press, 1997).

This sensitively written book shows how an artist and one little girl transformed a whole classroom community. Lionni's books inspired the children's visual, mental, and verbal imaginations, and this wonderful teacher related his books to their life experiences, and life experiences back to the books! Repeated readings heightened the children's appreciation for the language and art of the story. Their experiences with art helped them see what they could do with media, and talking and writing about their own pictures enhanced their vocabularies.

In the process of looking at one illustrator in depth, children learned much about the way text and illustrations work together to create a story. Even more important, they learned so much about life. A picture book had provided for the development of these students' visual, mental, and verbal imaginations. Moreover, in following the curriculum that the children created, their teacher discovered critical life lessons about race, identity, gender, and human needs.

THE PICTURE BOOK DEFINED

Although we discuss picture books in Chapters 4, 6, and 11, this chapter is primarily concerned with picture books as art objects. These are books in which images and ideas join to form a unique whole. In the best picture books, the illustrations extend and enhance the written text, providing the reader with an aesthetic experience that is more than the sum of the book's parts.

Barbara Bader maintains:

As an art form [the picture book] hinges on the interdependence of picture and words, on the simultaneous display of two facing pages, and on the drama of the turning of the page.[3]

In discussing the art of children's picture books, Perry Nodelman states:

We perceive new experiences in terms of the experiences preceding them. . . . Each picture in a picture book establishes a context for the picture that follows—it becomes a schema that determines how we will perceive the next picture.[4]

Any book with a picture-book format can be included under the umbrella term *picture book*. A picture book might be an alphabet book, a counting book, a first book, or a concept book (the books discussed in Chapter 4). In these the pictures must be accurate and synchronized with the text; however, it is not essential that they provide the continuity required by a story line. The illustrations for a concept book or an alphabet book can depict a different object or an animal on each page, providing

for much variety in the pictures. Examples would be Bert Kitchen's *Animal Alphabet,* which shows large individual pictures for each letter, or Tana Hoban's *Shadows and Reflections,* which explores various dimensions of a concept with stunning photographs. In a nonfiction book (discussed in Chapter 11) the illustrations can help support important concepts and clarify ideas.

In a picture book that tells a story, the message is conveyed equally through two media—picture and word. In a well-designed book in which the total format reflects the meaning of the story, both the illustrations and the text must bear the burden of narration. The pictures help tell the story, showing the action and expressions of the characters, the changing settings, and the development of the plot.

Paul O. Zelinsky's illustrations for *Swamp Angel* by Anne Isaacs are a fine example of the integral partnership between pictures and text. This original story is based on a particularly American folktale form, the tall tale. In a tall tale, heroes and heroines are larger than life and perform impossible feats, all in a spirit of comic horseplay that children love. For his illustrations, Zelinsky has looked to another American folk art that has been identified with America's past, the landscapes and portraits done during the colonial period by mostly untrained painters called limners. Inspired by their style, Zelinsky chose to work in oils on wood veneers that subtly recall the tall forests of the Appalachian Mountains of Tennessee, where the story takes place. On these warm and glowing woods, he paints the story of Angelica Longrider, who is "born scarcely taller than her mother" but grows up to save the people of Tennessee

---

[3]Barbara Bader, *American Picturebooks from Noah's Ark to the Beast Within* (New York: Macmillan, 1976), introduction.
[4]Perry Nodelman, *Words about Pictures* (Athens: University of Georgia Press, 1988), p. 176.

from Thundering Tarnation, a bear so big that his pelt covered the entire state of Montana and his bear soul became the Big Dipper. The portrait of Angelica opposite the title page introduces the wide-eyed heroine, and the look of unassuming innocence on her face sets the tone of the story: what is to come is good fun and not to be taken seriously. Throughout the book Zelinsky adds a wealth of visual detail to Isaacs's story. On the first double-page spread, for example, he shows Angelica stopping a flash flood with her apron, harnessing a rain cloud to put out a cabin fire, and knitting herself striped pantaloons with two tree trunks. His choice of color scheme creates a sense of lively action throughout the book. To heighten the excitement, aqua blue skies and soft gray-green mountains are set against the warm reds and oranges of his figures and the oak, ash, and cherry veneers of the background. In addition, the page design also has great energy. Zelinsky varies the frame for each picture from oval to semicircle to rectangle. On some double-page spreads he shows multiple scenes; on others he highlights the action in single frames. He also moves the story along by varying the point of view from a close-up to a distant shot and from looking straight at the scene to looking down from a bird's-eye view. Zelinsky's artistic choices add to the delight of the story, so that the reader closes the book with an experience that is more than the sum of its parts. This book represents the type of real marriage between pictures and text that we hope to find in good picture books.

An illustrated book is different from a picture book. In an illustrated book, only particular incidents in the story might be illustrated to create interest. Leo Dillon and Diane Dillon, noted for their fine picture books, provided full-color plates for Virginia Hamilton's *Her Stories.* This book is a beautiful example of fine bookmaking, but it is not a picture book.

THE ART AND ARTISTS OF PICTURE BOOKS

A picture book, then, must be a seamless whole conveying meaning in both the art and the text. Moreover, in a picture book that tells a story the illustration does not merely reflect the idea or action on a single page but shares in moving the story forward and in engaging the reader with the narrative on both an intellectual and an emotional level. Throughout the narration the pictures should convey and enhance the meaning behind the story. Artists create meaning in picture books in a variety of subtle and interesting ways. In Chapter 4 we described how the illustrations contributed to the meaning of various picture-book formats for very young children.

Paul O. Zelinsky's richly layered paintings extend and enhance the written text of Anne Isaacs's *Swamp Angel.*
From *Swamp Angel* by Anne Isaacs. Illustrations copyright © 1994 by Paul O. Zelinsky. Used by permission of Dutton Children's Books, a division of Penguin Putnam, Inc.

In this chapter we will extend understandings of artistic meaning-making in picture books.

Illustration and Plot Development

An outstanding example of illustrations that help move the plot can be found in the classic *Blueberries for Sal* by Robert McCloskey. This is a story that children can tell by themselves just by looking at the clear blue-and-white pictures. The illustrations help the reader anticipate both the action and the climax, as Sal and her mother are seen going berry picking up one side of Blueberry Hill, and Little Bear and his mother are seen coming up the other side. McCloskey uses a false climax, a good storytelling technique. Sal hears a noise and starts to peer behind an ominously dark rock; the reader expects her to meet the bears, but instead she sees a mother crow and her children. On the next page Sal calmly meets Mother Bear and tramps along behind her. A parallel plot gives Little Bear a similar experience, but Sal's mother is not so calm about meeting him! The human expressions of surprise, fear, and consternation on the faces of both mothers express emotion as well as action.

Artwork might show mounting tension by increasing the size of the pictures. One of the best-known examples of this is in Maurice Sendak's fine story *Where the Wild Things Are*. The pictures in this book become larger and larger as Max's dream becomes more and more fantastic. Following the climactic wild rumpus, which is portrayed on three full-sized spreads with no text whatsoever, Max returns home. The pictures decrease in size, although never down to their original size—just as, symbolically, Max will never be quite the same again after his dream experience.

Picture-book artists also provide clues to the future action of a story. A close look at the first and second pages of *Where the Wild Things Are* shows the mischievous Max dressed in his wild-thing suit and stringing up a home-made tent. A plush toy looking vaguely like a wild thing hangs nearby. Later the tent and wild things appear in Max's dream trip to the far-off land of the wild things. His drawing of a wild thing on page 2 shows his preoccupation with creating these creatures that later inhabit his dreams.

Some picture-book illustrations use visual metaphors in the same way that poets add to the image-making qualities of their poems. In *Once a Mouse*, Marcia Brown reinforces the drama of the little mouse who is about to be snatched up in the beak of a crow by making the shape of a hill in the background look like an open beak. Again, as Brown creates shadows of the animals, the reader can see that the shadow of the tiger is that of a dog, his former self before the hermit transformed him.

Illustration and Mood

Pictures not only should reflect the action and climax of the plot, they also should help create the basic mood of the story. Uri Shulevitz used increasing light and color in *Dawn* to portray his quietly beautiful story of a man and his grandson rowing out on a lake to see the dawn break. The book begins before dawn and the colors are monochromatic, shades and tints of deepest blue that convey the cool, quiet beauty of the lake. As living creatures awake and enter the landscape, the color scheme

The changes in colors in the paintings in *Michael Rosen's Sad Book* are a direct reflection of the narrator's mood.
Michael Rosen's Sad Book. Written by Michael Rosen. Illustrations © 2004 by Quentin Blake. Reproduced by permission of the publisher Candlewick Press, Inc., Cambridge, MA, on behalf of Walker Books, Ltd., London.

begins to broaden until finally the sun rises to reveal a full-color vista. Don Wood used a similar technique in illustrations for *The Napping House* by Audrey Wood. When everyone in the house is sleeping, the overall color is a restful blue-grey. As the house's inhabitants wake up, the illustrations move to all the bright colors of the rainbow that appear on the final page.

Michael Rosen's Sad Book is a moving and honest book about the death of the author's son and the author's process of grieving. Rosen makes powerful use of watercolor washes over sketchy line drawings to provide filtered images that help children accept this sad story. In addition, Rosen moves back and forth from dark gray tones to brighter hues as the book progresses. This technique in no way diminishes Rosen's grief but offers a realistic picture of his slow and tentative recovery from terrible loss.

Illustration and Character Development

Besides creating the basic mood of a story, illustrations help create convincing character delineation and development. Characters like Kevin Henkes's Lilly, Ezra Jack Keats's Peter, Rosemary Wells's Max, and Arnold Lobel's Frog and Toad become real and remain memorable to us because of the illustrations' power rather than the strength of the words.

The characterization in the pictures must correspond to that in the story. There is no doubt that David Shannon's antihero in *No, David!*, *David Goes to School*, and *David Gets in Trouble* is a holy terror. Yet David's vulnerable side is revealed in Shannon's spare line drawings that add just the right dimension of complexity to David's character.

Expression and gesture can also reveal character and move the action forward. In *Just Plain Fancy*, Patricia Polacco tells the story of Naomi, an Amish girl, and her little sister, who hatch a peacock from a fancy egg they find. Frightened that their bird is too fancy for Amish ways, they decide to hide it. The expression of awe and amazement on their faces when they first see Fancy raise his peacock feathers provides the emotional climax of this delightful story. Peggy Rathmann's comical drawings carry the weight of the narrative in *Officer Buckle and Gloria*, the Newbery Medal–winning story of two friends who learn the value of partnership. The expressions on the faces of these characters convey a range of emotions and help the reader empathize with the predicament of Officer Buckle. Bob Graham uses line and space to create original characters and to add tension and emotion to his story, *"Let's Get a Pup!" said Kate.* When Kate and her Mom and Dad decide to get a puppy, they know just the qualities they are looking for. They head to the dog pound and find just the perfect dog—Dave. He's small, he's cute, and he's brand new! On their way out, however, they spy Rosy, who is too big, too old, and too smelly. The looks exchanged across the empty space of the double-page spread are priceless. The family heads home, but Graham's skilled depiction of their body language and facial expressions is a sure plot giveaway. After a sleepless night they return to take Rosy home, too. The book's last page showing Kate, Rosy, and Dave curled up on the bed together is a deeply satisfying ending.

One of the few picture books to portray character development is the Japanese story *Crow Boy* by Taro

Bob Graham provides a moment of visual drama in *"Let's Get a Pup!" said Kate. "Let's Get a Pup!" said Kate.* Copyright © 2001 Bob Graham. Reproduced by permission of the publisher Candlewick Press Inc., Cambridge, MA, on behalf of Walker Books, Ltd., London.

Learning about the Art of Picture Books

During Book Week in the fall, teachers in the Highland Park School in Grove City, Ohio, presented several minicourses on the making of books. One minicourse gave an overview of all the kinds of books a child might want to write. The teacher showed the children various kinds of ABC books and counting books. They looked at concept books for the young child, collections of poetry, and many informational books, from Aliki's simple books *My Feet* and *My Hands* to more complicated books such as Patricia Lauber's *The News about Dinosaurs*. Special books that are takeoffs on fairy tales, such as *The Principal's New Clothes* by Stephanie Calmenson, were discussed. Children then started to write their own stories in their classrooms.

Another minicourse emphasized the use of art media, introducing children to the collages of Eric Carle, Ezra Jack Keats, and Jeannie Baker. The teachers had cloth and newspapers available as they discussed the material Keats used in *The Snowy Day* or *Whistle for Willie*. They had fingerpaint paper to make large animals like those in Eric Carle's stories, and natural materials like the grasses, sponges, and mosses that Jeannie Baker uses.

Another teacher had collected books with interesting endpapers, like *The Great White Man-Eating Shark* by Margaret Mahy, *At Grammy's House* by Eve Rice, and *Henny Penny* by Stephen Butler. Then children made stamps from inner tubes, vegetables, or plastic foam meat trays to create their own endpapers. This same teacher had a collection of books with interesting title pages. In all instances, the teacher talked about the ways the artwork strengthened the theme of the book.

Another minicourse emphasized different ways to bind books with cloth or wallpaper covers.

At the end of the week, the children had all created their own books. More important, they had learned about the ways text and art work together to create a unified impression. They had developed a greater appreciation for picture storybooks and the amount of work involved in creating fine books, and they looked at books differently after this experience.

Faculty of Highland Park School
Kristen Kerstetter, project coordinator
Grove City, Ohio

Yashima. In the very first picture of this wonderfully sensitive story, Chibi is shown hidden away in the dark space underneath the schoolhouse, afraid of the schoolmaster, afraid of the other children. Once Chibi is inside the school, he and his desk are pictured as being far removed from all the other children. The artist's use of space helps emphasize Chibi's isolation and intensifies the representation of his feelings of loneliness. In subsequent pictures Chibi is always alone, while the other children come to school in twos and threes. With the arrival of the friendly schoolmaster and his discovery of Chibi's ability to imitate crows, we see Chibi grow in stature and courage.

In illustrating Paul Heins's version of the Grimm brothers' *Snow White*, Trina Schart Hyman shows the gradual deterioration of the stepmother until, in the last picture, she has the stare of a mad woman as she stands in front of a mirror framed with skulls and jeering faces. Nancy Burkert, on the other hand, in her interpretation of Randall Jarrell's translation of the Grimm brothers' *Snow White*, never shows the evil queen's face, only her back. But on the queen's workbench is every conceivable symbol of evil and death, including deadly nightshade, the thirteenth tarot card, a skull, spiders, bats, mushrooms, and an open book of formulas for poisonous concoctions. These symbols of evil are as eloquent as the mad queen's face. Each illustrator manages to bring a very personal interpretation to this old tale.

Illustration and Fidelity to the Text

Another requirement of an excellent picture book is that the art be accurate and consistent with the text. If the story states, as in Ludwig Bemelmans's *Madeline*, "In an old house in Paris that was covered with vines lived twelve little girls in two straight lines," children are going to look for the vines, they are going to count the little girls, and they are going to check to see that the lines are straight. Bemelmans was painstakingly careful to include just eleven little girls in his picture after Madeline goes to the hospital. Six-year-olds are quick to point out his one failure in a small picture that shows twelve girls breaking their bread, even though Madeline was still hospitalized. Accuracy is a requirement of all types of picture books.

THE MATTER OF STYLE

Style is an elusive quality of an artist's work based on the arrangement of line, color, and mass into a visual image. It is possible to define style as

> as a "manner of expressing." The meaning of the word *express*—to make known, reveal, show—is in keeping with the dual nature of style. The word *manner* can encompass all the conscious as well as unconscious choices the artist embraces to "make known." Aspects of style such as formal elements, techniques, and pictorial

conventions, then, are among the choices the artist makes to accomplish the primary purpose of expressing meaning.[5]

An illustrator's style will be influenced by her or his own skill as an artist and the vision of the story that is being interpreted. The primary decision for the artist to make is how to create visual images that will harmonize with and enhance the meaning of the text. The illustrator also needs to consider how the art might extend or add a new dimension to the message of the story.

Elements of Design

Crucial to the visual meaning in a picture book are the choices artists make about certain elements of design, particularly the use of line, shape, color, and space, as they decide what to illustrate in the story and how best to do it.

Line and Shape

Line is so inevitably a part of every illustration that we forget that this element, too, can convey meaning. A horizontal line suggests repose and peace, a vertical line gives stability, and a diagonal line suggests action and movement. Line is the very essence of story and theme in Peter Holwitz's *Scribbleville,* an allegory about a town where there are no straight lines until someone new moves into the neighborhood—someone straight as a "stick." The townspeople are horrified at first. But barriers gradually break down as a romance between a Scribbleville woman and the stick man leads to a much richer picture of community. In *Stevie,* John Steptoe uses a heavy black outline for his figures to emphasize Robert's resentment of Stevie, the little boy Robert's mother takes care of during the day. The tiny, sketchy lines in Marcia Brown's version of Perrault's *Cinderella* suggest the somewhat fussy elegance of the story's setting at the sixteenth-century French court. Chris Raschka uses the element of line to great effect in books like *Yo! Yes?, Like Likes Like,* and *Skin Again* by bell hooks. His lines predominate the otherwise empty space, defining the characters and moving the plot forward. The simplicity of line underscores Raschka's fundamental themes: our fears of our isolation and the unknown, and our overwhelming need for human companionship.

A line that encloses space creates shape, and this element is equally evocative of meaning. Susanna Gretz uses lines and shapes as a metaphor for the power of the imagination in the delightful *Riley and Rose in the Picture.* Here two friends, a dog and a cat, are trapped inside on a rainy day and decide to draw some pictures. Riley the dog is a realist and insists on drawing dots, lines, and geometric shapes. Rose the cat sees other forms—raindrops, bugs, and lollipops. The two bicker until Rose adds a boat to Riley's zigzag lines. Since Riley loves to sail, he adds a red sail and the two take off on a mad adventure. Dan Yaccarino is another illustrator who uses the element of shape to great effect, in *Circle Dogs* by Kevin Henkes and *Little White Dog* by Laura Godwin. In all these books the reliance on shape rather than on realistic depiction of objects creates pleasing pictorial designs that subtly evoke themes for the intended audience of young children.

Shapes with sharp edges and corners can evoke tension and movement, as they do in Christopher Meyers's *Black Cat.* On the other hand, when shapes have the nongeometric curving forms found in nature, they can breathe a sense of life into illustrations. Suzanne Bloom's naturalistic shapes in *A Splendid Friend, Indeed* move the story along visually and provide a pleasing contrast between characters. They also echo the pesky questions of the bothersome duck, who just won't leave the bear alone with his book. Bloom's organic forms indicate that ultimately, of course, these two will become the best of friends.

Use of Color

Many classic picture books did not use color in the illustrations—the sepia pictures of Robert McCloskey's *Make Way for Ducklings,* the black-and-white humorous illustrations by Robert Lawson for *The Story of Ferdinand* by Munro Leaf, and the well-loved black-and-white illustrations for *Millions of Cats* by Wanda Gág.

Modern publishing techniques make it much easier and less expensive to publish full-color books, but many illustrators are still using black-and-white graphics to create fine picture books. Kevin Henkes, who usually works in full color, chose black and white for his Caldecott Medal–winning *Kitten's First Full Moon,* and these tones seem perfect for this simple story about a white cat, a moon, and a bowl of milk. Interestingly, the art for the book was separated into four colors normally used for a full-color book (magenta, cyan, blue, and black). The book was then printed in color, which gave the black-and-white images an unusual warmth. This process captures the nuances of Henkes's fluid lines and penciled backgrounds. The unique story *Round Trip* by Ann Jonas describes a trip to the city past farms, silos, and steel highway wires, to ride on the subway; turn the book around and the reader returns in the dark. The farm and silos become factories, the highway poles support the freeway, and the subway becomes a parking garage. Black and white are the appropriate colors for this triumph of design. Ian Falconer's use of black, tints, and shades of red is a perfect accompaniment to his stories of Olivia, the iconoclastic piglet. In *Olivia* and *Olivia Saves*

[5]Barbara Z. Kiefer, *The Potential of Picturebooks: From Visual Literacy to Aesthetic Understanding* (Columbus, Ohio: Merrill/Prentice-Hall, 1995), p. 120.

What are you doing?
Are you reading?

the Circus, one might expect to find a little pig who is colored pink as in most children's stories. But Olivia defies convention in action as well as in actuality. She is depicted in black and white while the accoutrements of her world hold the touches of pink. Chris Van Allsburg's black-and-white illustrations help create an eerie otherworldly cast in *Zathura, The Widow's Broom, The Garden of Abdul Gasazi, Jumanji,* and *The Mysteries of Harris Burdick.*

The choice of colors depends on the theme of the book. Certainly, the choice of blue for both pictures and text in *Blueberries for Sal* by McCloskey was appropriate. Tawny yellow and black were the natural choices for Don Freeman's wonderfully funny *Dandelion,* the story of Dandelion the lion who suddenly decides to live up

to the double meaning of his name. Uri Shulevitz's *Snow,* a quiet, nostalgic story, demands soft tones that suggest the breathless anticipation of the first snowfall of winter. By way of contrast, Joe Cepeda's intense colors are an appropriate choice for Julius Lester's *What a Truly Cool World* and *Why Heaven Is Far Away,* lively and energetic creation tales. Choice of color, then, can set the mood of the story.

Pierr Morgan's illustrations for *Cool Time Song* by Carole Lexa Schaefer make use of thick acrylic paint and brilliant orange and red hues to convey the parched landscape of the African savannah and the slow movement of the animals through the heat of the day. Eventually the "earth turns" and evening approaches. The setting

But Earth turns.
Dusk comes.
And even Sun's fierce power
fades.

In that hour,
before lions begin to prowl,
or hyenas to follow their trail,

The colors and thickly painted images of Pierr Morgan's illustrations for Carole Lexa Schaefer's *Cool Time Song* seem to burn with the heat of the African day. From *Cool Time Song* by Carole Lexa Schaefer, illustrations by Pierr Morgan, copyright © 1995 by Pierr Morgan, illustrations. Used by permission of Penguin Young Readers Group, a division of Penguin Putnam, Inc.

sun gives way to cool blues and greens as animals arrive at the water hole to slack their thirst. Marcia Brown uses red to signify danger in her illustrations for *Once a Mouse.* Starting with cool forest green, mustard yellow, and a trace of red, the red builds up in increasing amounts until the climax is reached and the tiger is changed back to a mouse. Only cool green and yellow are seen in the last picture as the hermit is once again "thinking about big— and little." Australian artist Shaun Tan makes powerful use of color in *The Red Tree.* This book is an emotionally powerful exploration of the isolation and hopelessness that can sometimes seem to overwhelm us. For most of the book a young girl is pictured in various scenes, painted in tones of brown and gray, that symbolize these moments of despair. At the end of the book, however, a brilliant red tree appears in the girl's room, providing a surge of hope that the future will be better than the past. This is not a book for the very young, but Tan's complexly executed images and his compelling use of color may prove cathartic to older children.

Value

If we were to make a black-and-white photocopy of a full-color page of a book like *Luke's Way of Looking* or *What Faust Saw,* we would see how illustrator Matt Ottley considered the element of value, the amount of lightness or darkness in a picture. There is great contrast in the values on each page, and this lends extra energy and zing to the books. In fact, readers are always astonished to find out that Matt Ottley is color blind, because his colors are so intense and true. Ottley reports that his color blindness has taught him to pay critical attention to the value relationships he sees as he paints. Illustrator Chris

Van Allsburg uses the element of value to create a dramatic three-dimensional effect for all his books. His masterful depiction of light and dark in books like *The Polar Express* and *Jumanji* suggests that the figures and objects might leap off the page at any moment. On the other hand, the uniform values in Jon Muth's watercolors for Karen Hesse's *Come On, Rain!* give the book the lazy, hazy feel of a hot summer day.

Space

The creative use of space can produce a feeling of isolation, as we have seen in Taro Yashima's *Crow Boy,* or the blurred line between reality and legend, as in the illustrations by Stephen Gammell for *Where the Buffaloes Begin* by Olaf Baker. In *Come Along Daisy!*—Jane Simmons's story about a wayward duck who becomes separated from her mother—we see a tiny Daisy almost invisible in the expanse of a huge blue-green world. Simmons's use of space effectively emphasizes Daisy's fright at being separated from her mother.

Molly Bang makes use of negative space in her surrealistic wordless book *The Grey Lady and the Strawberry Snatcher.* The gray lady appears to fade into the background of trees as she runs away from the strawberry snatcher. Part of the fun of David Macaulay's experimental book *Black and White* is his use of negative space to hide an escaping convict in a herd of Holstein cows. In a similar fashion David Wiesner's illustrations for *The Three Pigs* violate our expectations of traditional picture-book space by turning a double-page spread into multiple layers of story and style. In *Little White Dog* by Laura Godwin, Dan Yaccarino provides preschoolers with a visual riddle by hiding the colored shapes of various animals

David Wiesner's *The Three Pigs* breaks picture-book traditions when the pigs break out of their traditional story to write a new ending. Illustration from *The Three Pigs* by David Wiesner. Copyright © 2001 by David Wiesner. Reprinted by permission of Clarion Books/Houghton Mifflin Company. All rights reserved.

against the same colored background. The white dog, for example, is hidden against a white snowbank and only his black eyes and nose can be seen.

The decision to use borders also reflects the artist's use of space. The borders in Vera Williams's *A Chair for My Mother* or Trina Hyman's interpretation of *Little Red Riding Hood* provide a kind of coziness to these stories and help create a unified whole out of each double-page spread.

In inexpensive mass-marketed books or in basal reading textbooks, which frequently must conform to one size for all, artists cannot afford the creative use of space. In a well-designed picture book, however, the illustrators can use space to enhance the meaning of the story.

Point of View, or Perspective

Just as an author decides what would be the best point of view from which to tell a story, so too does an artist think about perspective. One way to convey action in what might otherwise be a static series of pictures is to change the focus, just as a movie camera changes perspective or shows close-ups and then moves back to pan the whole scene. In *The Napping House* by Audrey Wood, for example, the scene is almost always in the bedroom, where the granny, the dog, the cat, the mouse, and the flea are seen in various postures as they sleep during the quiet rain. Don Wood shows us a fish-eye view of the scene, with the bed growing increasingly concave until its final collapse. As the story progresses, Wood moves the point of view slowly upward until he is directly above the sleeping figures for the climax, when the flea bites the cat and wakes them and the bed falls down.

Part of the perfection of the poetic Caldecott Medal book *Owl Moon* by Jane Yolen is the way John Schoenherr uses shifting perspectives to provide the action. It is the quiet story of a father and child who go out late one snowy night to look for owls. Starting with an owl's view of the farm bathed in moonlight, the artist shifts his focus, showing the pair trudging through the snow from the side, from the front, and finally looking up in awe at the huge owl landing on the tree. This picture of the owl is the only close-up in the story, a fact that underlines the climax of the story and intensifies the excitement of finally seeing the owl.

The perspective in Chris Van Allsburg's surrealistic pictures for *Jumanji* changes from a worm's-eye point of view to a bird's-eye view, adding to the constant shifts between reality and fantasy in that story. Seen from the floor level of an ordinary living room, two charging rhinoceroses look much more frightening than in the zoo! Wade Zahares uses similar techniques of perspective to picture *Liberty Rising* by Pegi Deitz Shea. In this case the end result is not a feeling of unreality but rather of awe at the tremendous task of building the Statue of Liberty.

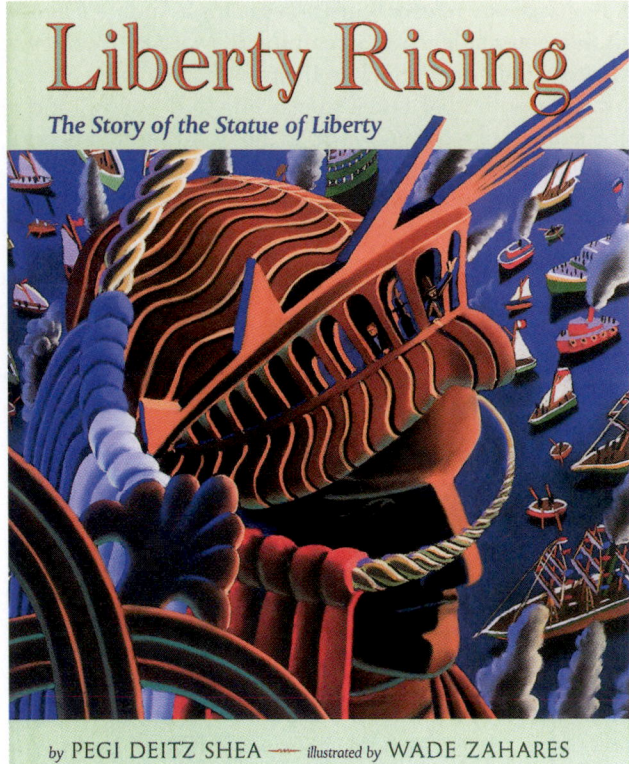

Wade Zahares's changing visual perspectives in Pegi Deitz Shea's *Liberty Rising* lend a sense of wonder to the story of the building of the Statue of Liberty. From *Liberty Rising: The Story of the Statue of Liberty* by Pegi Dietz Shea. Illustrations copyright © 2005 by Wade Zahares. Used by permission of Henry Holt & Company.

Not all artists work with changing perspectives. When they do, however, it is interesting to ask why and look to see how this adds to the meaning of the story.

The Artist's Choice of Media

Children accept and enjoy a variety of media in their picture-book illustrations. The illustrator's choice of original media can be as important to the meaning of the book as the choice of the elements of the art. Many artists today are using the picture book as a vehicle for experimentation with new and interesting media and formats. (See also Teaching Resources: "Exploring Artists' Media" in Chapter 13.) In the kind of creative experimentation that is taking place in picture books today, the medium the artist uses is not nearly as important as the appropriateness of the choice for a particular book and how effectively the artist uses it. Nevertheless, teachers and children are fascinated with the various aspects of illustrating and always ask what medium is used. This is becoming increasingly difficult to answer because artists these days use a combination of media and printing techniques to achieve a particular effect. Some publishing houses provide information on the art techniques in some of their outstanding books—in the foreword, on the copyright page, or on a jacket flap. It is a service that teachers and librarians hope more companies will offer. The following sections give a brief overview of some of the media choices available to the artist.

Woodcuts and Similar Techniques

In the beginning of the history of printing, the woodcut or wood engraving was the only means of reproducing art. These methods are still used effectively today. In the making of a woodcut, the nonprinting areas are cut away, leaving a raised surface that, when inked and pressed on paper, duplicates the original design. If color is to be used, the artist must prepare as many woodcuts as colors, or the printed picture can be painted by hand. Woodcut illustrations produce a bold simplicity and have a power not found in any other medium.

Caldecott Medal winner Mary Azarian has long been recognized as an outstanding artist in the medium of woodcut. Her illustrations are lovely hand-colored prints that convey the rough edges of life in another century. In *Snowflake Bentley*, by Jacqueline Briggs Martin, Azarian's strong black lines create pleasing patterns and echo the patterns of individual snowflakes that Bentley sought to photograph. Azarian's skill with the woodcut technique effectively imparts the New England setting and theme of the book.

Printmaker David Frampton uses woodcuts in such books as *My Son John* by Jim Aylesworth and *Riding the Tiger* by Eve Bunting. In *The Song of Frances and the Animals* by Pat Mora and *At Jerusalem's Gate* by Nikki Grimes, Frampton's use of the medium seems particularly appropriate to visualize these religious stories, recalling the woodcuts of the early printed Bibles of the fifteenth century. In *Once a Mouse*, a fable of India, Marcia Brown

takes full advantage of her medium, allowing the texture or grain of the wood to show through. This adds depth and interesting patterns to these dramatic illustrations.

Wood engravings are cut on the end grain of very hard wood (usually boxwood) rather than with the grain on the plank side of a soft wood. This process gives a delicate, finer line to the illustrations than a woodcut has. Barry Moser has used this technique to illustrate Patricia MacLachlan's *What You Know First*, an evocative memoir that examines the importance of one's roots. Rooted in this centuries-old printing method, the book's text is quietly enhanced.

Etching is another type of engraving technique. A design is drawn with a tool on a waxed metal plate, then the plate is dipped in acid, which eats thin lines into the metal. The wax is removed, and prints are then made from the inked plate. Arthur Geisert makes use of this medium in his many books including *Lights Out*. His *Pigs from A to Z* is illustrated with detailed etchings of seven little pigs constructing a tree house. Each picture shows five hidden forms of the letter and the seven pigs, and part of the fun of the book is to find them. The fine lines of these intricate etchings make superb hiding places for the letters. In *Haystack*, *Desert Town*, *Mountain Town*, *Prairie Town*, and *River Town*, written with his wife, Bonnie, Geisert hand-colors the etchings and gives a lovely timeless feeling to these stories about passing time in the heartlands of America.

Linoleum block prints also give a finer line than woodcuts. Mary Wormell uses this technique to add a lively charm to her stories of a sweet, rather egocentric hen in *Hilda Hen's Search* and *Hilda Hen's Happy Birthday*. Ashley Wolff uses linoleum block prints to illustrate

Mary Azarian's Caldecott Medal–winning woodcuts for Jacqueline Briggs Martin's *Snowflake Bentley* evoke the time and place of nineteenth-century Vermont. *Illustration from* Snowflake Bentley *by Jacqueline Briggs Martin. Text copyright © 1998 by Jacqueline Briggs Martin. Illustrations copyright © 1998 by Mary Azarian. Reprinted by permission of Houghton Mifflin Company. All rights reserved.*

many of her books, such as *Goody O'Grumpity* by Carol Ryrie Brink. The crisp black lines of the linoleum cuts seem to make the animals, birds, and people stand out in relief against brilliant skies and seasonal landscapes.

Scratchboard illustrations can be confused with wood engravings, because their appearance is similar. However, the process of making them is very different. In the making of scratchboard illustrations, a very black ink is usually painted on the smooth white surface of a drawing board or scratchboard. When the ink is thoroughly dry, the picture is made by scratching through the black-inked surface with a sharp instrument. Color can be added with a transparent overlay, painted on the white scratchboard prior to applying the black ink, or applied after the drawing is complete. Scratchboard techniques produce crisply textured illustrations. Michael McCurdy, who has been a wood engraver for many years, uses a similar painstaking technique for the scratchboard drawings in two books by Donald Hall, *Lucy's Christmas* and *Lucy's Summer.* The books about Lucy have personal connections to Hall's mother's childhood in New Hampshire, and the fine linear work that McCurdy achieves on scratchboard resembles old wood engravings and evokes a lovely sense of the past as well as the hardy nature of family connections. Brian Pinkney creates stunning effects with scratchboard in books like *Max Found Two Sticks, Cosmo and the Robot,* and Kim Siegelson's *In the Time of the Drums.* By adding color in inventive ways, Pinkney cre-

ates interesting textures that give his illustrations drama and excitement. Beth Krommes has used scratchboard to pleasing effect in Jacqueline Briggs Martin's *The Lamp, The Ice, and the Boat Called Fish* about an expedition to the Arctic that is stranded on the ice. In this book the scratchboard technique recalls the scrimshaw carving of the nineteenth-century whalers or the ivory carvings of Inuit artists. The icy landscapes of prehistoric times are captured in Kurt Cyrus's scratchboard and watercolor illustrations for Lisa Wheeler's *Mammoths on the Move.* In both books the dazzling white surface of the scratchboard captures a sense of light reflected off snowy surfaces.

Collage and Construction

The use of collage for illustrating children's books has become very popular. The effect of this medium is simple and childlike, not unlike pictures children might make themselves. The word *collage,* derived from the French verb *collar,* meaning "to paste," refers to the kind of picture that is made by cutting out a variety of different kinds of materials—newspaper clippings, patterned wallpaper, fabric, and the like—and assembling them into a unified, harmonious illustration. Ezra Jack Keats proved himself a master of this technique with his award-winning *The Snowy Day.* Using patterned and textured papers and pen and ink, Keats captured young Peter's delight in a snowy day. Leo Lionni used collage in many of his highly original books. Abstract circles of torn paper convey a satisfying story of families in *Little Blue and Little Yellow.* Lionni also uses his familiar collage techniques and brilliant colors to tell a fable of art, love, and the role of the imagination in seeing beauty in all things in *Matthew's Dream.*

Eric Carle's many books are well-loved favorites of younger children. To create his collages, Carle first paints many sheets of paper with various colors to achieve pleasing patterns and textures. Then he cuts out shapes and pastes them together to create interesting characters, as in *The Very Hungry Caterpillar* and *Mister Seahorse.* His technique invites children to try their own hands at paper painting and collage.

Lois Ehlert combines handmade papers and natural materials in highly inventive ways in her picture books. Her illustrations for books such as *Leaf Man, Cukoo=Cuco,* and *Hands* intrigue and delight children of all ages. Javaka Steptoe's collages lend a jazzy, modern tone to books such as *The Jones Family Express* and *Hot Day on Abbott Avenue* by Karen English. Other artists who make skillful use of collage include Bryan Collier, Christopher Meyers, and Susan Roth.

The oldest mother led the way across the steppes both night and day. The females followed in her tracks, majestic glaciers at their backs.

Kurt Cyrus's scratchboard illustrations bring a frigid look to the Ice Age described in Lisa Wheeler's *Mammoths on the Move.* Illustrations from *Mammoths on the Move* by Lisa Wheeler, illustration copyright © 2006 by Kurt Cyrus, reprinted with permission of Harcourt, Inc.

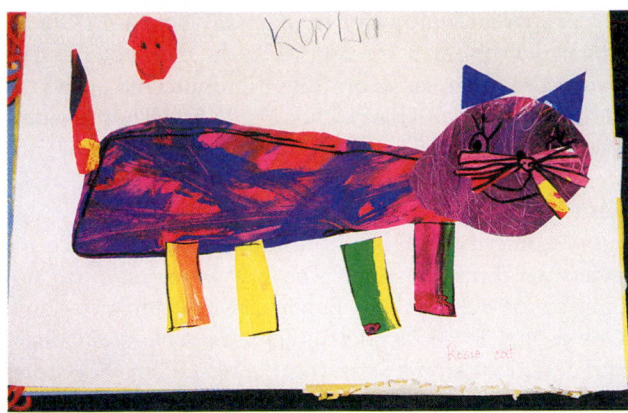

Illustrator Eric Carle's bright collages inspire a kindergartner to experiment with forms. Photograph courtesy of Nicole Boruchin.

Modern reproduction techniques have freed illustrators to go beyond collage, which is relatively flat, to work in three dimensions. Jeannie Baker makes what she calls "collage constructions" or "assemblage" to illustrate her fine books, such as *The Hidden Forest* and *Window*. Plasticine, a claylike substance, is the favored medium of Barbara Reid in *The Subway Mouse* and *The Party*. The sculptured, three-dimensional effects of her creations lend a fanciful reality to her books.

Stitchery and other fabric art can be found in Faith Ringgold's *Tar Beach* and Aminah Brenda Lynne Robinson's *To Be a Drum*, written by Evelyn Coleman. Both of these internationally known artists reach into African quilting traditions to create their work, and the storytelling quality of their fabric art is highly effective in books for children. Cultural traditions are also made the most of in *Goha, the Wise Fool* by Denys Johnson-Davies. This collection of Middle Eastern trickster stories will delight younger children with their playful humor, but even more delightful are the khiyamiya tapestries used for the illustrations. These traditional forms of stitchery were done by Egyptian tent makers and enhance the cultural authenticity of the tales. Anna Grossnickle Hines has created cloth art for Elizabeth Partridge's gentle story *Whistling*. This medium seems perfect for telling a simple family story about a boy who takes a day out with his father in great anticipation of a special event—he learns to whistle!

Other artists are working in innovative ways with paper. Robin Brickman's stunning illustrations for Sneed B. Collard III's *One Night in the Coral Sea* were created by cutting, sculpting, and gluing painted watercolor paper. The resulting pictures give the viewer a sense of intimacy with the underwater environment. *The Wave of the Sea-Wolf* is one of David Wisniewski's many stories illustrated with intricately cut paper. Placed in layers that provide a feeling of depth to the pictures and add excitement and tension, the meticulously cut shapes tell an original story of a young Tlingit princess who saves her people from natural and human threats. Wisniewski won the Caldecott Award in 1997 for his hair-raising retelling of *The Golem*.

Other artists have used the traditional Asian technique of paper cutting to create their illustrations. Ed Young's illustrations for Jane Yolen's *The Emperor and the Kite* imply a subtle relationship to the paper kite that is at the center of the story. The lacy linear design that results also gives a feeling of airy lightness that suits the book's ending. Aki Sogabe illustrated *The Loyal Cat* by Lensey Namioka and *Kogi's Mysterious Journey* by Elizabeth Partridge using single sheets of black paper that she cut freehand and then placed over hand-painted rice papers. The result is a jewellike quality well suited to these stories.

Denise Fleming works with cotton rag fibers colored with pigments to create handmade papers for the illustrations in such books as *Pumpkin Eye, Mama Cat Has Three Kittens,* and *Barnyard Banter*. Debra Frasier has experimented with paste paper cutouts in William Stafford's *The Animal That Drank Up Sound* and with collages made from tie-dyed papers for Kim Stafford's *We Got Here Together*. In all these books the abstract shapes and the textures that result from these artistic processes match the poetic texts of the printed words.

Anna Grossnickle Hines created the pictures for Elizabeth Partridge's *Whistling* by using fabric and stitchery. Illustration from *Whistling* by Elizabeth Partridge and Anna Grossnickle Hines, illustrator. Illustrations copyright © 2003 by Anna Grossnickle Hines. Used by permission of HarperCollins Publishers.

Computer-Generated Art

As technology improves, we are likely to see more picture books containing artwork that has been created on the computer. Many of these books, such as David Kirks's *Nova's Ark* and William Joyce's *Rolie Polie Olie*, recall computer-animated motion pictures and are likely to be popular with children familiar with this imagery. As applications have become more sophisticated, however, we have seen a variety of styles emerge. We can find flat, simplified colors and images in *Stanley Mows the Lawn* by Craig Frazier and in Scott Menchin's illustrations for *Wiggle* by Doreen Cronin. *Mr. Maxwell's Mouse*, by Frank Asch and Devin Asch, has a limited color palette but highly contrasting values that lend a macabre mood to this picture-book fantasy. In *The Mystery of Eatum Hall* John Kelly and Cathy Tincknell create painterly images that enhance the delicious irony of the story. We can continue to hope for other such surprises in computer-generated art in picture books.

Paints and Pen and Ink

The vast majority of illustrations for children's books are done in paint, pen and ink, or combinations of these media. The creation of materials like plastic paints, or acrylics, and new techniques frequently make it very difficult to determine what medium has been used.

Generally, paint can be divided into two kinds: paint that is translucent and has a somewhat transparent quality, such as watercolor, and paint that is opaque and impenetrable to light, such as tempera, gouache, and oils.

The transparency of watercolor can be seen in books like Uri Shulevitz's *Rain Rain Rivers*, Jon J. Muth's *Zen Shorts*, and Karen Hesse's *Come On, Rain!* illustrated by Jon Muth. For all three books, watercolor is the perfect choice of medium, for it allows the artists to convey the feeling of clouds bleeding into rainy skies and light reflected in watery puddles. Allen Say makes fine use of transparent watercolor in his many books. In *Grandfather's Journey* and *Tea with Milk*, the effect of the medium conveys a sense of quiet dignity to the stories of his grandfather and his mother. David Small's soft watercolor washes seem just right for the gently humorous stories *The Journey*, *The Library*, and *The Gardener*, books written by his wife, Sarah Stewart.

We might think of old-fashioned, delicate pictures when we think of watercolor, but watercolors do not have to look dated. Ted Lewin's rich watercolors flow with energy in books such as *Top to Bottom, Down Under* and Tony Johnston's *Sunsets of the West*. Chris Soentpiet is another fine artist who brings tremendous energy to his watercolor painting for books such as *Coolies* by Yin or *Where Is Grandpa?* by T. A. Barron.

Watercolors can provide a warm and cozy feeling, too, as we see in Vera Williams's *A Chair for My Mother*. In this story of a family's struggle to recover from a household fire, we celebrate the day they have saved enough money to buy a big, fat, comfortable chair for the little girl's mother. Watercolors create the symbolic borders of these pictures and the velvet texture of the chairs in the furniture store.

Opaque paints can give an intense, brilliant look, as in Mollie Bang's illustrations in *When Sophie Gets Angry—Really, Really Angry*, or they can produce the flatter colors of Bagram Ibatoulline's wonderfully detailed paintings for *Crossing*, written by Philip Booth. Maurice Sendak contrasted dark green and blue tempera with shades of purple to create Max's weird fantasy world in *Where the Wild Things Are*. Texture and shading are achieved with pen-and-ink crosshatch strokes.

Gouache (pronounced "gwash") paint is watercolor with the addition of chalk and has an effect similar to tempera. Marisabina Russo uses gouache to produce paintings for books like *The Trouble with Baby* and *Always Remember Me: How One Family Survived the War*. Russo's

Jon J. Muth's transparent watercolors mirror the watery puddles in Karen Hesse's *Come On, Rain!* Illustration copyright © 1999 by Jon J. Muth from *Come On, Rain!* by Karen Hesse. Published by Scholastic Press/Scholastic, Inc. Reprinted by permission.

subject matter is the world of the younger child, both past and present, and her choice of medium suits the subject matter perfectly. The use of gouache is also characteristic of the many books illustrated by Alice Provensen and Martin Provensen, including their well-known *A Visit to William Blake's Inn* by Nancy Willard and the Caldecott Medal winner *The Glorious Flight: Across the Channel with Louis Blériot.*

Acrylics (plastic paints) produce vibrant, almost glowing colors. When mixed with water, acrylics resemble transparent watercolors. More often acrylics are used straight from the tube. Like oils, they can be built up on the painting surface to give a dense texture; however, they dry faster than oils. Jerome Lagarrigue uses acrylic in paintings for *Freedom on the Menu* by Carole Boston Weatherford and *Going North* by Janice Harrington. The thick, opaque result of his technique adds emotional depth to these stories of the civil rights movement.

We can also find picture books illustrated with oil paints. Because the medium is slower drying than acrylic, it allows the artist to build up layers and to work back into the colors as well as to create thick surface textures. Floyd Cooper uses oil paint on canvas board and works back into the paint with a soft malleable eraser before the paint dries. This technique gives his paintings layers of subtle color tones that seem to glow with a rich sheen and

In books such as *Danitra Brown Leaves Town*, written by Nikki Grimes, Floyd Cooper builds up many layers of oil paint to embody his figures. Illustration from *Danitra Brown Leaves Town* by Nikki Grimes. Illustrated by Floyd Cooper © 2002. Reprinted by permission of Amistad, an imprint of HarperCollins Publishers, Inc.

that add depth and drama to his scenes. This medium is particularly suited to the warm human stories Cooper illustrates, such as *Coming Home: From the Life of Langston Hughes* and Nikki Grimes's *Danitra Brown Leaves Town.*

Thomas Locker, a well-known landscape artist, illustrates his picture books with majestic full-color oil paintings. Locker's rendering of light in such books as *Where the River Begins, The Mare on the Hill, Family Farm,* and *Sky Tree* reminds us of the early landscape painters of the Hudson River School. Locker's *The Young Artist* reflects the influence of the early Dutch masters. Oil paint is used to good effect by Mike Wimmer in Patricia MacLachlan's *All the Places to Love* and Margaret Hodges's *Moses.* These are warm, richly textured stories, and the medium of oil paint enhances the emotional mood of the books.

Crayon, Chalk, Charcoal, and Pencil

Crayon and soft-pencil illustrations are frequently employed for children's books. The subtle texture of crayon is easily discernible. In *Fish Is Fish,* Leo Lionni creates an underwater world with crayons, but he portrays the fish's conception of the frog's world with the brilliant colors of acrylics. The difference in color and media helps to separate the imagined world from the real one.

Pastels and charcoal are the most appropriate media for Thomas Allen's rich illustrations for books that have strong connections to people and places. *Climbing Kansas Mountains* by George Shannon tells of a long-ago summer on a Kansas farm where the only mountains to climb were the grain elevators. Scott Russell Sanders's *A Place Called Freedom* follows a family of former slaves as they establish an African American community in Indiana. In both books, Allen builds up the pastels on the surface of the page, and the rich textures mingle with the tinted charcoal papers like the love that surrounds these families. Ed Young also uses pastels effectively in books like *Little Plum* and Rafe Martin's *Foolish Rabbit's Big Mistake.* Here he makes full use of brilliant color applied thickly to add intensity and life to the stories. In stories that convey a quieter mood, Young chooses softer tones and applies the colors more delicately. He often keeps his edges rough and lets the texture of the paper show through. This gives his illustrations something of a dreamlike quality and is very effective for stories like *The Dreamcatcher,* written by Audrey Osafsky.

Stephen Gammell's soft-pencil drawings create a mystical mood for the legend *Where the Buffaloes Begin* by Olaf Baker and suggest the legendary nature of this Native American tale. Peter McCarty's delicate colored-pencil drawings for *Hondo and Fabian* capture the everyday adventures of a cat and dog with quiet warmth. Wendy Anderson Halperin's pencil drawings for Anne Shelby's *Homeplace* are overlaid with soft watercolor washes and convey a lovely pastoral setting for this folksy story.

Using a conté pencil, a rather hard drawing pencil, Chris Van Allsburg creates a surrealistic world for the playing of the game in *Jumanji* and its sequel, *Zathura.*

Sandpapering the conté pencil and applying the dust with cotton balls, he gives the pictures a spooky, dreamlike feeling. Van Allsburg is adept in the use of a variety of drawing materials; he used carbon pencil for his first book, *The Garden of Abdul Gasazi,* full-color pastels for *The Wreck of the Zephyr,* and oil pastels for *The Polar Express.*

Increasingly, artists are using combinations of many media. Ed Young uses a combination of inks, cut paper, and pastels in many of his more recent books, such as *I Doko: The Story of a Basket* and *The Sons of the Dragon King.* Kadir Nelson applied oil paint to photocopies of pencil drawings to create the textured illustrations for *The Village That Vanished* by Ann Grifalconi. Rosemary Wells used paint, origami, rubber stamps, and traditional Washi papers to create the mixed media collages in *Yoko's Paper Cranes.* These beautiful silk-screened papers are often decorated with gold leaf, and gold was used as an additional color when the book was printed. In addition, Wells used familiar motifs from Japanese prints and screens. Each elegant page design is a visual treat that lends authenticity to this lovely story about Yoko and the grandparents she left behind in Japan when she came to the United States.

Artistic Conventions

Style can also refer to the particular artistic properties associated with eras, like Renaissance art or Impressionism, or with cultures, such as the culture of the people of Tibet or of Northern Plains Indian tribes. Pictorial styles can be distinguished by certain constant elements or "umbrella conventions," which are widely accepted ways of depicting.[6] Illustrators often borrow these conventions to enhance or extend their visual message. Teachers might want to know these terms and conventions, just as they develop an understanding of literary terms for more careful evaluation of books for children. However, it is more important to teach children to look and really see how an illustrator creates meaning than it is to be glib with terms they might not understand. Also, these terms were developed to describe the art of single paintings hung on walls, not the cumulative effect of many images seen by turning the pages of a picture book.

Realism, or Representational Art

No designation of an art style can be precise because of the infinite variation within styles; however, realism is perhaps the easiest to recognize because it presents a picture of the world as we see it in real life. Of course, the pictures still incorporate the artist's interpretation of the story, the choice of scenes to visualize, the point of view, the expressions, and so forth. Barry Moser's realistic watercolor illustrations for Cynthia Rylant's *Appalachia: The Voices of Sleeping Birds* have the feeling of arrested motion, almost like Depression-era photographs. The beauty of the countryside contrasts sharply with the harshness of the life, as seen in the face of the

---

[6]Kiefer, *The Potential,* pp. 118–20.

exhausted coal miner. Kam Mak's photo-realistic paintings in *My Chinatown: One Year in Poems* could almost be classified as magic realism. His close-ups of everyday objects and his unusual perspectives emphasize the sense of wonder felt by a small boy who has left Hong Kong behind for a new land. The realism of Angelo Rinaldi's glowing paintings for Malachy Doyle's *Cow* raises this familiar farm animal to noble status. Unusual close-ups, lush landscapes, and vivid portraiture celebrate a day from the cow's point of view. Doyle's simple second-person narrative is a gentle accompaniment to the book and doesn't overshadow the real wonder of the artwork.

Impressionistic Art

The term *Impressionism* is associated with the French artists who worked in and around Paris in the latter part of the nineteenth century, including such well-known painters as Monet, Sisley, and Pissarro. They were concerned with observing nature as it really was and so attempted to capture their first visual impressions before intellect or emotion could define the image further.

A wonderful example of an homage to Impressionism can be found in the Monet-like paintings by Mau-

rice Sendak for *Mr. Rabbit and the Lovely Present*, written by Charlotte Zolotow. In luscious shades of blues and greens, Sendak has created a dreamlike world where a very sophisticated rabbit and a little girl wander about the countryside looking for presents of red, yellow, green, and blue (her mother's favorite colors) for the little girl's mother. The dappled endpapers for this book are examples of impressionistic techniques in themselves.

Raúl Colón's method of working paint into a textured surface provides an impressionistic atmosphere to books such as *My Mama Had a Dancing Heart* by Libba Moore Gray and *Dona Flor* by Pat Mora. The softened figures and glowing light in the paintings convey a warm emotional undertone to these stories.

G. Brian Karas uses impressionistic rendering to create a very different mood for Megan MacDonald's *The Bone Keeper*. This spooky story tells of the old Bone Woman who lives in a deep cave by night and by day "sifts and searches the sand, searches and sifts for bones, bones bleached white in the desert sun." Karas's unfinished edges, hazy images, and textured surfaces perfectly visualize MacDonald's haunting story. Karas's work does not echo the subject matter of the Impressionists, but his technique certainly recalls their methods.

Kam Mak's realistic paintings and changing points of view provide readers with an intimate glimpse of everyday life in *My Chinatown*. Illustration from *My Chinatown: One Year in Poems* by Kam Mak © 2002. Used by permission of HarperCollins Publishers, Inc.

Expressionistic Art

Aspects of expressionistic art include shocking colors, figures slightly out of proportion, and rough, rapid brushwork. The emphasis is on the artist's own inner emotions and on self-expression rather than on the reproduction of what he or she sees.

In illustrations for children's books, expressionism might take the form of brilliant blue horses or blue cats, as seen in some of Eric Carle's pictures for very young children. In *Chato's Kitchen, Chato and the Party Animals,* and *Chato Goes Cruisin'* Gary Soto introduces a low-riding Latino cat whose party spirit leads him into all kinds of trouble. In *Chato's Kitchen* Chato and his friend Novio Boy have designs on a family of mice. However, the mice find an ally in Chorizo the dog, and Chato and Novio Boy end up with a fiesta instead of a fight. Susan Guevara's expressionistic paintings add heat to the stories and visually convey the rhythms of the barrio.

David Diaz's illustrations for *Smoky Night* are aptly suited to Eve Bunting's story of a community torn apart by riots. This is a difficult subject to present to children, and Bunting's text is quietly understated. She provides a glimpse of these upheavals through the eyes of a young narrator who is puzzled, then frightened, by events but also concerned about his missing cat. Diaz's paintings, framed in collages of papers, broken glass, shoe leather, and other found objects, provide emotional punch to the story without overwhelming children with concepts that might be beyond their understanding. The faces of the people are done in vivid greens, purples, and blues that heighten the tensions yet avoid racial stereotypes. The thick paint and black lines that frame the figures add movement and texture that also increase the emotional power of the illustrations.

Perhaps no artist has captured musical expression as well as Chris Raschka does in *John Coltrane's Giant Steps* and *Mysterious Thelonious.* Raschka pays homage to these two great musicians, Coltrane and Thelonious Monk. *Mysterious Thelonius* is a prose poem in words and images that can also be viewed as a series of jazz riffs or read in chromatic scales. Raschka takes a similar tack in *John Coltrane's Giant Steps,* mixing colors and shapes that vibrate with rhythm. However one approaches the two books, the experience of seeing music and hearing art is intense and exciting.

Surrealistic Art

Surrealism is characterized more by subject matter than by technique, for the surrealist combines realistic yet incongruous images in unnatural juxtapositions. To make the viewer believe in this unreal scene, the artwork will be meticulously realistic in detail. Anthony Browne creates a surreal world in his picture books *My Dad, My Mom, Voices in the Park, Changes,* and *The Piggybook.* In

The intense colors and thick textures in Susan Guevara's paintings for Gary Soto's *Chato's Kitchen* convey the culture of East Los Angeles. From *Chato's Kitchen* by Gary Soto, illustrations by Susan Guevara, copyright © 1995 by Susan Guevara, illustrations. Used by permission of G. P. Putnam's Sons, a division of Penguin Putnam Inc.

The Tunnel, Jack and his sister Rose do not get along. She wants to read fairy tales, while he insists on exploring a tunnel. Finally, when he doesn't come back, Rose must go through the frightening tunnel and find him. Once on the other side, she enters a dark forest of trees whose roots and branches form weird, threatening shapes. Finally, in a clearing, she spies the figure of her brother Jack, turned to stone. Fearing she is too late, she throws her arms around him and he is slowly transformed back to his original self. The transformation is also apparent in their friendship. This modern fairy tale becomes very real and frightening in this surrealistic setting.

In explaining his choice of surrealism, Browne is quoted as saying:

> It's a part of not losing that visual openness that kids have . . . surrealism corresponds to a childlike view of the world, in that everything can be made new by putting unrelated objects together.[7]

Chris Van Allsburg's surrealistic world in *Jumanji* is certainly well known, since this story won a Caldecott

---

[7]In Douglas Martin's *The Telling Line* (New York: Delacorte Press, 1990), p. 283.

Medal. The fourteen pictures that make up *The Mysteries of Harris Burdick* are beautiful examples of surrealism. Houses lift off their foundations, schooners magically appear, and a nun sits in a chair suspended thirty feet above the cathedral floor! Even though the pictures have no connecting narrative, they stimulate children to tell their stories. Van Allsburg is a master of juxtaposition of the real with the unreal.

Naive or Folk Art

One form of naive art is the style often found in self-taught artists like Grandma Moses, Henri Rousseau, and the itinerant painters, or limners, of colonial America. It can be characterized by a lack of such conventions as perspective and so-called real appearances. It also suggests the art of common people and thus implies art that is centered in community.

We have seen how Paul Zelinsky used these conventions in Anne Isaacs's *Swamp Angel.* Barbara Cooney also adapted her style to imitate that of the early American limners for *Ox-Cart Man* by Donald Hall. Tomie

dePaola uses gouache paints reminiscent of the paintings on wood done by the early itinerant painters for *The Quilt Story* by Tony Johnston. His brightly colored illustrations for *Tomie dePaola's Mother Goose* echo the early folk art style.

Kathy Jakobsen's folk art paintings for Woody Guthrie's *This Land Is Your Land* and Reeve Lindbergh's narrative poem *Johnny Appleseed* seem most appropriate for celebrating America's history and heroes. Brightly colored pictures show journeys across the country and through the seasons. In *This Land Is Your Land*, originally written in the late 1940s, Jakobsen visually conveys a half century of social history in a style that seems to belong to all the people. Her *My New York* is a feast of visual details that represent a personal view of Jakobsen's years in New York City. Although set in modern times, the story is told in the form of a letter to a friend from a child who has moved from the Midwest to the city. Jakobsen's childlike paintings are appropriate to the theme and invite children everywhere to represent their own home places in art and writing.

Frané Lessac's brilliantly colored paintings represent naive art and provide a folksy tone to her visits to places such as the Caribbean (*My Little Island* and *Caribbean Canvas*) or American sites (*Monday on the Mississippi* by Marilyn Singer and *Capital! Washington D.C. from A to Z* by Laura Kraus Melmed). Lessac also illustrated *The Chalk Doll* by Charlotte Pomerantz, in which a mother tells her daughter stories of her happy childhood growing up in Jamaica. These detailed paintings are childlike and beautiful in their simplicity of style.

Cartoon Art

Many children's books are illustrated in a style that depends on a lively line to create movement and humor. The term *cartoon* was originally used to refer to the large, fully developed line drawings that artists prepared and then transferred to frescoes or easel paintings. This style has often been called comic art or comic-book style. However, the best comic art in picture books has more in common with the works of eighteenth-century artists such as painter William Hogarth or political caricaturist Thomas Rowlandson than it does with superheroes' comic books or the Sunday color comics of today.

Certainly the gross exaggerations of the zany animals of Dr. Seuss are representative of comic art. From the weird birds in *Scrambled Eggs Super!* to the mess created in *The Cat in the Hat*, Seuss utilized cartoon art to tell his far-fetched stories. Sendak used this style very effectively in some of his early art for *A Hole Is to Dig* and *A Very Special House*, both by Ruth Krauss. The little boy who swings on doors and jumps on beds in *A Very Special House* is the only one painted in color, so the reader knows that all the other goings-on in this very special house are "root in the noodle" of his "head head head."

More recently, Betsy Lewin has achieved a comic triumph in Doreen Cronin's Caldecott honor–winning *Click, Clack, Moo: Cows That Type*; *Giggle, Giggle, Quack*; and *Duck for President*. With minimal, yet assured, lines Lewin creates an exuberantly comic group of cows, ducks, and other farm animals and their nemesis, Farmer Brown. In the tradition of good comic art, Lewin's illustrations also make a subtle statement about labor, working conditions, and the heartlessness of big business.

Steven Kellogg's wonderful drawings are fine examples of the expression and humor that can be achieved with this style of art. *The Rattlebang Picnic* by Margaret Mahy is surely the silliest of summer getaways, and the McTavish family manages to escape from an erupting volcano none too soon. Kellogg's illustrations for Joanne Ryder's *Big Bear Ball* are as energetic as the dances performed at the Bear jamboree. Bursting with action and slapdash humor, Kellogg's illustrations always fill in many details that are never mentioned in the text.

Renowned *New Yorker* cartoonist William Steig created his sophisticated characters in line-and-wash drawings for his many books, including *Pete's a Pizza*, *The Amazing Bone*, and *Doctor De Soto*. Although Steig used background in many of his pictures, the flat-looking characters and clever lines carry the weight of visual storytelling. James Stevenson, a fellow cartoonist at the *New Yorker*, has also created many books utilizing the cartoon style of art. His tall-tale stories about Grandpa use cartoon balloons for speech and watercolor illustrations. Stevenson's comic illustrations for *No Laugh-*

Betsy Lewin needs only a few bold lines and a wash of color to convey the comic goings-on at Farmer Brown's place in *Giggle, Giggle, Quack* by Doreen Cronin. Reprinted with the permission of Simon & Schuster Books for Young Readers, an imprint of Simon & Schuster Children's Publishing Division from *Giggle, Giggle, Quack* by Doreen Cronin, pictures by Betsy Lewin. Illustrations copyright © 2002 Betsy Lewin.

ing, No Smiling, No Giggling encourage just the opposite, and children find them irresistible.

Several artists have made use of the visual layout and linear qualities of the art found in comic books. The flat painted figures and speech balloons that are typical of this cultural icon can be seen in Maurice Sendak's pictures for *In the Night Kitchen* and in works by British artist Raymond Briggs. Briggs's *Father Christmas* and *Ug: Boy Genius of the Stone Age* are masterpieces of visual irony that have great appeal for older children. Kevin O'Malley's *Captain Raptor and the Moon Mystery*, illustrated by Patrick O'Brien, is a wonderful tribute to superhero comic books like Captain Marvel and Superman. Captain Raptor and his compatriots are more unusual than the usual superheroes, however. Living on the Planet Jurassica, these characters bear uncanny resemblances to the dinosaurs of Earth's Jurassic era.

Cultural Conventions

 Many artists illustrating stories, folktales, or legends make use of the conventions found in art forms of their respective countries or cultures. David Diaz uses elements of Mexican folk art to tell contemporary stories set within the Mexican and Mexican/American cultures. In Eve Bunting's *Going Home*, the story of a farm family returning to Mexico for Christmas, Diaz creates endpapers that feature close-up photographs of brilliant "artesanias Mexicanas," decorative objects, figures, and other popular arts found in the marketplaces of Mexico. This "arté popular" then forms the background on which the paintings and type are placed. Folk art silhouettes outline these panels; they are also found on the title page and the final page, set against a brilliant presidential blue background.

Paul Goble's use of Plains Indian designs in his folktales, such as *Storm Maker's Tipi* and *Mystic Horses*, recalls the hide paintings of these Native Americans. Just as they made use of African motifs and art in Margaret Musgrove's *Ashanti to Zulu*, Leo Dillon and Diane Dillon have created vibrant, powerful illustrations for Leontyne Price's retelling of the opera *Aïda*, using borders and motifs from the one-dimensional Egyptian style of art. Deborah Nourse Lattimore always uses the style of art of the culture from which her tales come. For example, her Mayan tale *Why There Is No Arguing in Heaven* is illustrated with many bluish-gray figures that suggest the stone carvings of the ancient Mayas. In *The Sailor Who Captured the Sea*, she recreates the extraordinary art and design of the ancient Irish *Book of Kells* while telling its story. Chapter 6 details other works of traditional literature in which artists have used cultural conventions to enhance the meaning of the story.

David Diaz's Mexican folk art motifs provide a culturally rich visual setting for Eve Bunting's *Going Home*. Illustration from *Going Home* by Eve Bunting, illustrations by David Diaz. Illustrations copyright © 1996 by David Diaz. Photographs by Cecelia Zeiba-Diaz. Joanna Cotler Books. Used by permission of HarperCollins Publishers, Inc.

Personal Styles

Few picture-book artists use only one style of art; they adapt their work to meet the requirements of a particular story. At the same time, many of them do develop a recognizable personal style that can be identified by their preference for a particular pictorial style of art, use of medium, even choice of content. Thus we have come to associate the use of collage with Leo Lionni, Ezra Jack Keats, and Eric Carle, even though they differ in how they use the medium. The delicate, old-fashioned style of Tasha Tudor's watercolors is as easily recognizable as the flowing, massive look of Warwick Hutton's watercolors. Tomie dePaola's use of the symbols of folk art, such as hearts, doves, and rabbits, is a recognizable mark of his work. The amusing animals in the stories by Pat Hutchins are frequently stylized with patterned fur and feathers. Her birds and animals in *We're Going on a Picnic!*, *What Game Shall We Play?*, and that self-assured hen in *Rosie's Walk* are obviously vintage Hutchins. Frequently, hers are the first illustrations children can identify by the artist's name. And yet Hutchins employs a very different style in *The Very Worst Monster* and *It's My Birthday!*

Some artists continue to experiment with both style and media and seem to gather strength with each new book. Paul O. Zelinsky is a talented artist who is able to choose styles that are beautifully suited to the mood and meaning of each of his books. His two toy books, *The Wheels on the Bus* and *Knick-Knack Paddywhack!*, use softened tints and simple shapes that suit a younger audience. In *Doodler Doodling*, written by Rita Golden Gelman, Zelinsky abandons restraint and lets his pencil and brush play with images just as Gelman plays with words. His *The Maid, the Mouse and the Odd Shaped House* is equally lighthearted, and his softened tints and stylized figures evoke the decorative arts of the nineteenth century to retell an old nursery rhyme about an old woman and her pet mouse who make themselves at home in a very odd house. On the other hand, Zelinsky uses oil paints and borrows conventions from Renaissance art to retell *Rapunzel* and the Grimm brothers' *Hansel and Gretel* and *Rumpelstiltskin*. This style beautifully evokes the setting and the origin of these old tales. His illustrations for *Swamp Angel* by Anne Isaacs are more playful, and here his style makes a direct connection to early American art and folklore.

Molly Bang seems to relish the challenge of widely different types of books by experimenting with different styles and media. Bang used found-object constructions to illustrate her own original story *One Fall Day*, and paper sculpture for *The Paper Crane*. *When Sophie Gets Angry* is executed in full-color opaque paint in an expressionist style that, in the latter part of the book, recalls Vincent Van Gogh's superb patterned landscapes. In *Nobody Particular: One Woman's Fight to Save the Bays*, she combines richly painted background borders and black-and-white cartoon-style drawings (see Chapter 11). This provides an authentic feel to this newsworthy story of a woman who successfully fought the chemical companies that were polluting her Texas bay.

Maurice Sendak's style is immediately recognizable, yet each book is a unique work of art. His pastoral watercolors for Charlotte Zolotow's *Mr. Rabbit and the Lovely Present* recall the landscape paintings of Claude Monet. The trees and endpapers of *Where the Wild Things Are* have been compared to Henri Rousseau's French primitive paintings. However, Max with his roguish smile and the big, ludicrous beasts with their "terrible eyes and terrible teeth" are very much Sendak. Max reappears in lighter and livelier form in Sendak's illustrations for Ruth Krauss's *Bears*. While his illustrations for *In the Night Kitchen* reflect the influence that Disney and the comics had on Sendak in his youth, they are very definitely Sendak's own creation. Max has now become Mickey, who sheds the last of his inhibitions in a dream in which he falls out of his clothes and into the night kitchen. Comic-book characters have been refined into a work of art that captures the feelings and dream wishes of childhood. The lush paintings in *Outside Over There* and in *Brundibar* by Tony Kushner represent other directions in Sendak's work. In *Outside Over There*, Sendak seems to be reaching the child at a deeper psychological level through symbolic art. His artistic metaphors call for the same inner feelings that Ida is struggling with as she imagines in a momentary daydream what it would be like to be rid of the responsibility of her baby sister.

Brundibar, a retelling of an opera performed by the children of the Terezin concentration camp, includes visual references to Nazi horrors yet also provides readers with a sense of hope. With each of his books, Sendak's involvement with his "child within" seems to grow deeper.

Style, then, is an elusive quality. It includes signature features like the big hands and feet that Sendak always draws and the small, chunky figures in Roy Gerrard's amusing illustrations. Style can be the use of characteristic media, like Eric Carle's collages or Pat Hutchins's patterned animals and birds or Anthony Browne's surrealism. Style is an elusive quality of the artist, which changes and varies over the years and with the particular demands of the work. Today there is more freedom to experiment in illustrating children's picture books. Many of our artists are taking advantage of this new freedom and producing fresh and original art.

Exposure to a variety of art styles through fine picture books can help children develop visual maturity and appreciation. Certainly there is no *one* style that is appropriate for children or preferred by children. The major consideration in evaluating style is how well it conveys and enhances *meaning*. Exploring the work of an illustrator through an intense classroom study can give children time to articulate their responses to an artist's work and to identify some of the many components that can be part of an illustrator's style. The Web "Brian Pinkney: A Web of Possibilities" shows how teachers might plan to study the work of Brian Pinkney.

The Format of the Book

A picture book is not made up of single illustrations but conveys its message through a series of images bound together within two covers. The impact of the total format of the book is what creates the art object known as the picture book. Kevin Henkes's *Kitten's First Full Moon* is a fine example of overall book design. The simplicity of this story of a kitten who thinks the moon is a big bowl of milk is reflected in the black-and-white illustrations and organic shapes used throughout. The size of the book is large, and its square shape nicely balances the round moon and the rounded body of Kitten. The silver letters of the cover's title reflect the glow of a full moon, and the cream-colored, textured matte paper gives the book a luxurious three-dimensional feel. The visual layout is rhythmic, moving back and forth between large double-page images and smaller vignettes and balancing the patterned text. The care taken in writing, illustrating, and producing this fine book really honors the aesthetic potential of the young child.

Book size and shape are often decisions made jointly by the illustrator and the art director of the publishing house. They might search for a size that will enhance the theme of the story. *The Bear* by Raymond Briggs is almost fifteen inches tall—big enough, it seems, to contain the huge bear within. *The Biggest Boy* by Kevin Henkes is also a large book, and Nancy Tafuri's close-up pictures make the little boy character seem even bigger, in keeping with his lively imagination. *Goose* by Molly Bang tells the story of an orphaned goose. Raised by a family of woodchucks, the little goose feels different and longs desperately for something else. She sets out to find it, but finds herself instead in an overwhelmingly frightening world. When by accident she discovers that she can fly, she flies home to her loving woodchuck family. The book's small size speaks to its small preschool audience and implies the character's feeling lost out in a great big world.

The shape of some books suggests their content. The horizontal shape of Donald Hall's *Ox-Cart Man,* illustrated by Barbara Cooney, is very appropriate for portraying the long trek to the Portsmouth market to sell the family's produce in the early fall and the long walk home through leafless trees in late autumn after the father has sold everything, including the ox and his cart. The shape of *Fish Eyes* by Lois Ehlert is long and narrow like a fish or small aquarium. *Giants in the Land* by Diana Appelbaum, illustrated by Michael McCurdy, and *A Tree Is Nice* by Janice Udry, illustrated by Marc Simont, are tall and vertical in shape, much like the trees described in the books.

Both the cover and dust jacket of a book should receive careful attention. The primary purpose of the jacket is to call attention to the book. The cover of Doreen Rappaport's *Martin's Big Words* needs no words. Bryan Collier's elegant, almost life-size close-up of Martin Luther King's face is instantly recognizable. The jacket for the award-winning *Puss in Boots* illustrated by Fred Marcellino certainly calls attention to itself, for it features the huge head of a hat-bedecked puss in a ruffled collar that could only be the famous *Puss in Boots* by Charles Perrault. But the cover carries no title. Turn the book over and there is the title on the back. A dark brown cloth cover and golden brown endpapers harmonize well with the picture on the jacket.

Good cloth designs are usually small and symbolic of the content. For example, for *A Chair for My Mother,* Vera Williams uses an imprint of a chair, heart-shaped to show the family's intense desire for a beautiful, comfortable chair for their mother. Publishers are increasingly duplicating the image from the dust jacket on the book's cover rather than preparing a separate cloth cover that few people ever see. However, a peek beneath a dust jacket can still reveal pleasant surprises. David Wiesner's books, such as *Sector 7* and *The Three Pigs,* have embossed designs on their cloth covers. In *Rushmore* by Lynn Currie, the front of the dust jacket shows a close-up of artisans working on the statue of Washington, while the back shows the mountain half finished and covered by scaffolds. The cover underneath the jacket is a different picture—the finished sculptures are shown spread out over the back and front covers. The cloth cover beneath the

Profile in Literature

Illustrator Bryan Collier

Bryan Collier's work in *Martin's Big Words* by Doreen Rappaport demonstrates how illustration and book design can affect the reader's emotional experience with a book. The large trim size of the book and the close-up of Martin Luther King's face on the cover emphasize the heroic stature of the man. He was, indeed, larger than life. The fact that no title words are needed on the cover draws attention to Martin's words, words so important that they changed a nation. Go to the Online Learning Center at **www.mhhe.com/kiefer9e** or your Resources CD-ROM to learn more about Bryan Collier and his work.

lovely full-color dust jacket of George Ella Lyon's *Book,* illustrated by Peter Catalanoto, has a wide green binding and a dark blue cover vertically embossed with the letters B-O-O-K. This careful attention to detail evokes the lovingly crafted, handmade books of earlier centuries.

The endpapers of a picture book can also add to its attractiveness. These are the first and last pages of the book; one half of each is glued to the inside of the cover, while the other is not pasted down. Endpapers are usually of stronger paper than printed pages. In picture books, endpapers are often of a color that harmonizes with the cover or other pictures in the book, and frequently they are illustrated. Decorated endpapers can reflect the setting, the theme, or the content of the book and serve as a special invitation into the book. Jerry Pinkney's exquisitely painted endpapers for Hans Christian Andersen's *The Ugly Duckling* are as much a part of the storytelling as the other pages in the book. The opening endpapers show a parade of ducks swimming and diving in a pristine stream with an odd-looking bird struggling to bring up the rear. At the book's end a glorious, full-grown white swan is depicted in the same locale. In Paul Fleischman's *Weslandia,* illustrated by Kevin Hawkes, the main character is a social outcast who invents his own civilization for his summer project. Wesley's invented hieroglyphic alphabet appears on the endpapers and will have kids scrambling to figure out the code. Leo Dillon and Diane Dillon created stylized lotus blossoms and seedpods on marbleized paper for *Aïda,* retold by Leontyne Price. The endpapers of *Crow Boy* by Taro Yashima show a flower and a butterfly alone against a dark background. They seem to symbolize the metamorphosis of Crow Boy's life from dark despair to brilliant hope.

Even the title page of a picture book can be beautiful, informative, and symbolic. Marcia Brown has created a striking title page for Blaise Cendrars's *Shadow.* She portrays a young boy in silhouette anxiously looking back at his long shadow, which falls across a double-page

Wonderfully Exciting Books

Magic, Mystery, and Discovery

In the Time of the Drums (Siegelson)
The Faithful Friend (San Souci)
The Ballad of Belle Dorcas (W. Hooks)
The Dark Thirty (McKissack)
The Boy and the Ghost (San Souci)
Peggony-Po: A Whale of a Tale (A. Pinkney)

Compare southern tales with tales from
   other regions or cultures.
Have a ghost-telling celebration at a pretend
   "dark-thirty" time, one-half hour of
   supernatural stories.
List the spells and the effects of each.
Find other folktales that contain three
   characters similar to the three witches,
   spells, or transformations.

Where Does the Trail Lead? (Burton)
Take a nature walk by the seashore.
Go on a scavenger hunt looking for specific
   objects along the trails.
Follow a guidebook of trails along seashores
   and sand dunes.

All in the Family

Explore the life of the illustrator through
family members.

Father: Jerry Pinkney (illustrator)
Mother: Gloria Jean Pinkney (writer)
Wife: Andrea Davis Pinkney (writer
   and editor)

Make a comparison chart of various books
   created by each family member
   comparing story content, art techniques,
   and connection to authors.
Collect data in the library involving the
   work of the illustrator.
Write a letter to editors who publish the
   works of the Pinkney family to obtain
   background information.
Research how and why authors and
   illustrators work together on projects.

BRIAN PINKNEY: A WEB OF POSSIBILITIES

Sing and Swing to the Beat

Ella Fitzgerald: The Tale of a Vocal Virtuosa
   (A. Pinkney)
Alvin Ailey (A. Pinkney)
*Duke Ellington, The Piano Prince and His
   Orchestra* (A. Pinkney)
Visit a ballet class.
Listen to the music of jazz and blues bands.
   Create your own music and dance to
   celebrate these famous lives.

Watch Me Dance (A. Pinkney)
Shake Shake Shake (A. Pinkney)
Max Found Two Sticks (B. Pinkney)
Make a list of the sounds that are similar to
   the sounds that Max's sticks made.
Collect different natural objects to represent
   different instruments.

Celebrate Kid Power

Jojo's Flying Side Kick (B. Pinkney)
Max Found Two Sticks (B. Pinkney)
The Adventures of Sparrowboy (B. Pinkney)
Cosmo and the Robot (B. Pinkney)
Benjamin and the Shrinking Book (B. Pinkney)

How did each of these characters do
   something extraordinary?
Choose something that you like to do and
   write a story about how you became a
   superpower at it.

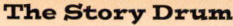

The Story Drum

Cut from the Same Cloth (San Souci)
Make a graph of the most popular
  characters/tall tales among the boys and
  girls in the class.
Label the locations of each legendary character
  on a map.
Read *Her Stories* (Hamilton). Try to find
  more female characters in other folklore,
  or create a heroine in your own tall tale.

The Elephant's Wrestling Match (Sierra)
Write your own talking drum story with animal
  characters from Africa.
Make a story drum. Try using various containers
  with string or bands wrapped from end to
  end.

Sukey and the Mermaid (San Souci)
Following Pinkney's scratchboard technique,
  create a picture of the mermaid's world.
Explore and compare other tales of mermaids.
  Find their origins.

In the Time of the Drums (Siegelson)
A Wave in Her Pocket (Joseph)
Cendrillon (San Souci)
Sleeping Cutie (A. Pinkney)
Ask a family member or relative to come into
  class to tell stories passed down from
  generation to generation.

Art Techniques

Celebrate Brian Pinkney's work. Compare
  Thumbelina (Anderson) to Pinkney's
  earlier works. How has his style changed
  over time? Set up an illustrator corner
  with books Pinkney has illustrated as
  well as work done by the children.
How does Pinkney's work convey the
  theme of each book? Affect its mood?
Display art media used in Pinkney's
  illustrations.
Create your own scratchboard pictures.
  Use oil pastel, paint, or other media to
  color the picture.
Compare Pinkney's scratchboard
  illustrations with the work of other
  illustrators such as Barbara Cooney or
  Marcia Sewall.

I Smell Honey and *Pretty Brown Face*
  (A. Pinkney)
Compare Pinkney's technique in his board
  books for young children with that in his
  books for older children.
Compare the techniques of scratchboard
  with block prints, wood engravings, and
  etchings. How are they similar/different?
  Can you tell the difference between these
  art techniques?

Discovering People in the Past

Bill Pickett: Rodeo Riding Cowboy (A. Pinkney)
Alvin Ailey (A. Pinkney) (see "Sing and
  Swing to the Beat")
Dear Benjamin Banneker (A. Pinkney)
Happy Birthday, Martin Luther King
  (Marzollo)
Harriet Tubman and Black History Month
  (Carter)
The Dreamkeeper and Other Poems (L. Hughes)

Make a timeline of African Americans who
  have contributed to American life and
  history.

Celebrate!

Seven Candles for Kwanzaa (A. Pinkney)

Discuss the seven principles of Kwanzaa,
  and discover the origins of Kwanzaa.
Weave your own straw"mkeka"(placemat).
Make some Kwanzaa gifts: a fabric doll or
  a bead necklace.

Day of Delight (Schur)
The Stone Lamp (Hesse)

Examine Jewish traditions. How are they
  alike and different from other religious
  traditions.
Discover kosher recipes.

Happy Birthday, Martin Luther King
  (Marzollo)

Plan a birthday celebration in honor of
  Martin Luther King.

Mim's Christmas Jam (A. Pinkney)

Find out more about New York City in 1915.
Plan an authentic dinner including
  Mim's jam.

Poetry

The Dream Keeper (Hughes)
I Never Told (cover art) (Livingston)
A Time to Talk (Livingston)

Find favorite poems to read aloud.
Create scratchboard pictures for
  individual poems.
Research the lives of the poets Langston
  Hughes and Myra Cohn Livingston.
  What are the similarities and differences
  between the two? Their work?

Jerry Pinkney's exquisitely painted endpapers for Hans Christian Andersen's *The Ugly Duckling* reflect thoughtful care and book design. Illustration from *The Ugly Duckling* by Hans Christian Andersen, illustrations by Jerry Pinkney. Illustrations copyright © 1999 by Jerry Pinkney. Used by permission of HarperCollins Publishers.

spread, while the spirits of his ancestors, shown as white masks, look on. This primitive fear of, and respect for, shadows permeates the book. William Steig emphasizes the friendship of a mouse and a whale at the same time as he contrasts their size with his title page for *Amos and Boris*. The title page of *Just Plain Fancy* by Patricia Polacco provides the clue to the origin of the fancy peacock egg that Naomi and Ruth found in the tall grass by the drive. In Bob Graham's *"Let's Get a Pup!" said Kate* the story actually begins before the title page. On the book's very first page, usually reserved for the title, Kate lies in bed missing her dead cat, Tiger, who died the previous winter. But Kate suddenly has a brilliant idea and is out of bed in a snap. "Let's Get a Pup!" she calls to her still-sleeping parents, and now the story can proceed. All aspects of a book can reinforce or extend the meaning of the story.

The layout of pictures and text on each double-page spread and on succeeding pages can have an important impact on the meaning and movement of a story. Full-size pictures might be interspersed with smaller ones, or a page might show a sequence of pictures. Beatriz Vidal's placement of pictures and use of shapes complement the rhythm of Verna Aardema's *Bringing the Rain to Kapiti Plain*. This African tale from the Nandi tribe is cumulative, reminiscent of the nursery rhyme "The House That Jack Built." First, Vidal shows a verdant plain mostly on the right-hand page; then she switches to the left, while the third page rests the eye with a double-page spread showing a heavy cloud mass spreading over the entire plain. Then once again Vidal places her masses on the right and then left page—readers anticipate this shift just as they anticipate the cumulative rhyme. This is not done throughout the book, however; it would be too monotonous. This is a beautiful example of how one image on a page blends into the next to create the total impact of the book.

The spacing of the text on the page, the choice of margins, and the white space within a book contribute to the making of a quality picture book. In Virginia Lee Burton's *The Little House,* the arrangement of the text on the page suggests the curve of the road in the opposite picture. In the very funny story of the dog poet in *Max Makes a Million* by Maira Kalman, Max dreams of going to Paris. These longings are printed on the paper in the shape of the Eiffel Tower.

Appropriate type design is also a matter for consideration. *Type* is the name given to all printed letters, and *typeface* refers to the thousands of letter styles available today. Before the advent of computer-created fonts, printers chose from some six thousand different styles then available. Nicolas Sidjakov describes the difficulty he and his editor had in finding a suitable typeface for Ruth Robbins's *Baboushka and the Three Kings*. When they did find one they liked, it was obsolete and not easily available. They finally located enough fonts to handset *Baboushka* a page at a time.[8]

---

[8]Nicolas Sidjakov, "Caldecott Award Acceptance," in *Newbery and Caldecott Medal Books: 1956–1965*, ed. Lee Kingman (Boston: Horn Book, 1965), pp. 223–25.

Now the computer allows artists much more freedom. David Diaz designed the fonts for Eve Bunting's *Going Home* to resemble the linear forms of the Mexican folk art that fills the book. Joe Cepeda created the display type for Julius Lester's *What a Truly Cool World* and *Why Heaven Is Far Away,* and the remainder of each book was printed in a font called "smile and party."[9]

Whether they are traditional or computer created, typefaces or fonts vary in legibility and the feeling they create. Some seem bold, others delicate and graceful, some crisp and businesslike. The type should enhance or extend the overall design of the book. It is also important that the text can be read easily and is not printed on dark paper. In Paul Goble's *The Girl Who Loved Wild Horses,* the text was changed to white when it was placed on the dark pages that represented night. The result is far more pleasing aesthetically than if the type had been printed in white rectangles and placed on the dark background.

Other factors in a picture book must be considered from a utilitarian standpoint. The paper should be dull enough so that it does not easily reflect light, opaque enough to prevent print from showing through, and strong enough to withstand heavy use. Side sewing in the binding of many picture books makes them more durable, but it might distort double-page spreads unless the artwork is prepared with the gutter separation in mind. Tall, narrow books with side sewing will not lie flat when the book is open. Many librarians complain that today's bindings are of poor quality and will not last for the life of the book. These, then, are some of the practical considerations that can affect a book's beauty and durability.

In sum, no single element creates an outstanding picture book. What does create one is all elements working together to create a cohesive whole that pleases the eye and delights the imagination.

THE LANGUAGE OF PICTURE BOOKS

The words of picture books are as important as the illustrations; they can help children develop an early sensitivity to the imaginative use of language and add to their overall experience with a picture book. Since most of these books are read to children rather than by them, there is no reason to oversimplify or write down to today's knowledgeable and sophisticated child. Beatrix Potter knew that, given the context of *The Tale of Peter Rabbit* and the picture of Peter caught in the gooseberry net, most children would comprehend the words "his sobs were overheard by some friendly sparrows, who flew to him in great excitement, and implored him to exert himself" (p. 45).

Steig's *Amos and Boris* is a comical story of the unlikely friendship between a mouse and a whale. Amos, the mouse, delighted by all things nautical, builds himself a jaunty little boat, which he names *Rodent.* Admiring the starry skies one night, he rolls overboard and is saved by a huge whale, who is amazed to find that the mouse is also a mammal. The whale gives the mouse a ride to safety, and, true to the lion and rat fable on which the story is based, Amos is able to reciprocate at a later time. Steig's luxuriant use of language and superb pictures make this an unusual picture book. The description of the whale and the mouse's trip home details their growing friendship:

> Swimming along, sometimes at great speed, sometimes slowly and leisurely, sometimes resting and exchanging ideas, sometimes stopping to sleep, it took them a week to reach Amos's home shore. During that time, they developed a deep admiration for one another. Boris admired the delicacy, the quivering daintiness, the light touch, the small voice, the gemlike radiance of the mouse. Amos admired the bulk, the grandeur, the power, the purpose, the rich voice, and the abounding friendliness of the whale. (unpaged)

These words might seem difficult words to understand, but children do make sense of the story, using the context of both the pictures and the text. They sweep back and forth from one to the other, obtaining the general feeling for this unusual friendship even if they do not know the exact meaning of every single word. This is the way children increase their vocabularies—by hearing or reading words they do not know but in a context that provides a general sense of the meaning.

In contrast to Steig's exuberant use of words in *Amos and Boris,* the well-known New England poet Donald Hall portrays the journey of *Ox-Cart Man* in cadenced language that is as slow and deliberate as the pace of the ox on the ten-day journey to Portsmouth. When the father packs the family's products, which had taken them a whole year to make, the author describes them in a kind of litany of words:

> He packed a bag of wool he sheared from the sheep in April.
> He packed a shawl his wife wove on a loom from yarn spun at the spinning wheel from sheep sheared in April.
> He packed five pairs of mittens his daughter knit from yarn spun at the spinning wheel from sheep sheared in April. (unpaged)

All children can appreciate figurative language, provided the comparisons are within the realm of their

---

[9]Kathryn Falwell's picture book *The Letter Jesters* (Boston: Ticknor and Fields, 1994) provides a sprightly overview of printing.

experience. The vivid word pictures in Alvin Tresselt's *White Snow, Bright Snow* are thoroughly enjoyed by 5- and 6-year-olds and reflect a child's point of view:

> In the morning a clear blue sky was overhead and blue shadows hid in all the corners. Automobiles looked like big fat raisins buried in snow drifts.
>
> Houses crouched together, their windows peeking out from under great white eyebrows. Even the church steeple wore a pointed cap on its top. (p. 20)

The dialogue of a story can be rich and believable or it can be stilted, as in a Dick and Jane basal reader. Arnold Lobel was a master at creating understated humor-

ous dialogue in his Frog and Toad series. Similarly, part of the charm of the Frances stories by Russell Hoban is the natural-sounding dialogue of everybody's favorite badger, Frances. The expressive pictures are as humorous as the dialogue in both of these well-written series.

In evaluating picture books, it is important to remember that a story should be told quickly because the action must be contained within a 32- to 64-page book. Even with this limitation, the criteria developed in Chapter 1 for all fiction apply equally well to picture books that tell stories. Both text and illustrations should be evaluated. The artistry of the words should be equal to the beauty of the illustrations. See Evaluation Criteria: "Evaluating Picture Books" for some questions that can help you evaluate these books.

EVALUATION **CRITERIA**

Evaluating Picture Books

The following questions are meant to help the reader determine the strengths of a picture book. Not every question is appropriate for every book.

CONTENT

- How appropriate is the content of the book for its intended age level?
- Is this a book that will appeal to children, or is it really written for adults?
- When and where does the action take place? How has the artist portrayed this?
- Are the characters well delineated and developed?
- Are race, gender, and other stereotypes avoided?
- What is the quality of the language of the text?
- How is the theme developed through text and illustrations?

ILLUSTRATIONS

- In what ways do the illustrations help create the meaning of the text?
- How are pictures made an integral part of the text?
- Do the illustrations extend the text in any way? Do they provide clues to the action of the story?
- Are the pictures accurate and consistent with the text?
- Where the setting calls for it, are the illustrations authentic in detail?

MEDIUM AND STYLE OF ILLUSTRATIONS

- What medium has the illustrator chosen to use? Is it appropriate for the mood of the story?
- How has the illustrator used line, shape, and color to extend the meaning of the story?

- How would you describe the style of the illustrations? Is the style appropriate for the story?
- How has the illustrator varied the style and technique? What techniques seem to create rhythm and movement?
- How has the illustrator created balance in composition?

FORMAT

- Does the size of the book seem appropriate to the content?
- Does the jacket design express the theme of the book?
- Do the cover design and endpapers convey the spirit of the book?
- In what way does the title page anticipate the story to come?
- Is the type design well chosen for the theme and purpose of the book?
- What is the quality of the paper?
- How durable is the binding?

OVERALL EVALUATION

- How is this work similar to or different from other works by this author and/or illustrator?
- How is this story similar to or different from other books with the same subject or theme?
- What comments have reviewers made about this book? Do you agree or disagree with them?
- What has the artist said about her or his work?
- Will this book make a contribution to the growing body of children's literature? How lasting do you think it will be?

THE CONTENT OF PICTURE BOOKS

 Several recent changes can be noted in the content of picture books. One is the increasing publication of books that are based on sharing memories of times past with children. Frequently these are told by grandparents, much as they might once have been told around the dinner table. Perhaps these books compensate for the lack of frequent contact with extended families in our fast-paced lives. These books seldom have a real plot but are based on what life was like when grandfather, or grandmother, or parents were children.

Another development in the content of picture books is a tremendous increase in books that are geared to children in the middle grades and older. This seems appropriate for today's visually minded child. As the age range for picture books increases, it becomes imperative to evaluate the appropriateness of the content for the age level of its intended audience. You do not want to share *Hiroshima No Pika* (The Flash of Hiroshima) by Toshi Maruki with young children any more than you would read *Goodnight Moon* by Margaret Wise Brown to older children.

Other considerations regarding the content of picture books need to be examined. For example, does the book avoid race, gender, and age stereotyping? Gender stereotyping begins early. Examples can be found in pictures as well as in text. In the imaginative story *Can I Keep Him?* by Steven Kellogg, Albert asks his mother if he can keep one pet after another, ranging from real to imaginary to human. His distraught mother is always pictured attending to such household chores as scrubbing, ironing, and cleaning the toilet bowl. She explains in very literal terms why Albert cannot keep his pets; for example, a snake's scales could clog the vacuum. While the contrast between Albert's highly original ideas and his mother's mundane preoccupation with household duties is funny, it is also a stereotyped image of the traditional housewife.

Books that counteract gender stereotyping are not as hard to find as they were when *William's Doll*, by Charlotte Zolotow, was published in 1972. William is a little boy who desperately wants a doll but is misunderstood by family and teased by friends. Only his grandmother understands how he feels, and so she brings him a baby doll "to hug . . . so that when he's a father . . . he'll know how to care for his baby."

More and more books portray characters who are willing to step outside of traditional roles to have fulfilling lives. In *Max* by Rachel Isadora, a young baseball player decides to take ballet lessons. He finds that it is a super way to warm up for baseball.

As we have seen in Chapter 3, we have picture books that portray the experiences of more diverse cultures than ever before, although the total number of multicultural books is still small compared with the proportion of ethnic and racial groups in the population. Many people from parallel cultures are now represented in stories about contemporary children as well as in folktales. *In My Mother's House* by Ann Nolan Clark, a poetic story of life among Pueblo Indians, has been reissued with handsome black-and-white and colored illustrations by Velino Herrera. *This House Is Made of Mud,* by Ken Buchanan, celebrates the joy of living in a Navajo hogan. The desert is its yard, the mountains its fence, and all the animals and birds are welcome visitors. Lovely clear watercolors by Libba Tracy add to the beauty of this simple story.

The past few years have seen an increase in books about Latino cultures, in bilingual books, and in translated books. *Playing Lotería/El juego de la lotería,* by René Colato Laínez, is a bilingual story about a young boy who is reluctant to spend a summer visit with his grandmother in Mexico because he doesn't speak very much Spanish and she doesn't speak much English. However, Abuela's *lotería* (a form of bingo) booth at the fair soon provides a catalyst for both of them. Abuela teaches the boy the Spanish phrases she sings out as she calls the *lotería* cards, and he teaches her the English version. Alexis O'Neill's *Estela's Swap* is a warmhearted story about a young Hispanic girl who brings her music box to the swap meet her father attends each week. She wants to earn money for folk-dance lessons and hopes to sell the box. She leaves it behind in a sudden windstorm to go help an older flower seller. When she returns, the box has been damaged, and Estela thinks she's lost the chance to earn her money. But the flower seller gives her a beautiful "falda," a special skirt for dancing in the Ballet Folklórico. The old woman, grateful for Estela's help in cleaning up her flower stall, tells her, "Since we are at a swap meet, it is only fair that we swap." Illustrator Enrique O. Sanchez created richly textured, bright paintings to convey this warmhearted story. In modern-day China, Long-Long also hopes to make money when he accompanies his grandfather to market in *Long-Long's New Year* by Catherine Gower. Long-Long's hopes to buy presents for his family seem thwarted at first until, like Estela, Long-Long's kindness to others saves the day and he returns home with many presents. He Zhihong's watercolor illustrations resemble traditional Chinese screen paintings and lend cultural authenticity to the setting.

Though there are now more books about older people than ever before, we can find stereotypes among these, too. One young-appearing grandfather went to a bookstore recently and said he wanted "a book about a grandfather in which the main character doesn't die." Many grandparents today in their sixties and seventies are vigorous and healthy; we might well ask if they are being portrayed this way.

Picture books frequently give children their first impressions of various ethnic and racial groups. Only when our books portray characters of both sexes, all ages,

The Chinese setting of Catherine Gower's *Long-Long's New Year* is visualized through He Zhihong's adaptation of traditional painting styles. From *Long-Long's New Year* by Catherine Grower and illustrated by He Zhihong, copyright © 2005. Reproduced by permission of Frances Lincoln, Ltd., 4 Torriano Mews, Torriano Avenue, London NW5 2RZ. Published in the USA by Tuttle Publishing.

and all ethnic and racial groups in a wide range of occupations and from a great variety of socioeconomic backgrounds and settings will we have moved away from stereotyping to a more honest portrayal of the world for children.

THEMES AND SUBJECTS IN PICTURE BOOKS

It is important that we, as teachers and librarians, know all the criteria by which to judge a quality picture book. Children are more interested in one criterion—does it tell a good story? They will respond most deeply to books that touch their interests and their imagination with words and pictures. In this section we briefly discuss picture books by theme for the benefit of those selecting particular books or preparing units of study.

Family Stories

Contemporary realistic family stories include single-parent families, divorced and remarried (blended) families, adoptive and foster families, and the extended family. Children always beg to hear stories about when their parents were small. The little African American girl in *Tell Me a Story, Mama* by Angela Johnson knows exactly what family stories she wants to hear, and she knows them so well that she can tell them herself, with her mother adding just the right comment. This is the story of a tender parent-child relationship.

Sibling conflict is portrayed more frequently in picture books than are love and compassion. In Elizabeth Winthrop's *Squashed in the Middle* Daisy feels that her middle-child status means that no one pays attention to her. When she takes matters into her own hands, family members gain new respect for her. Pat Cummings's wonderful illustrations emphasize Daisy's frustrations and celebrate her triumphs.

The warm, jubilant picture book *The Relatives Came*, by Cynthia Rylant, celebrates the joys of family reunions. Illustrated by Stephen Gammell, the book describes a summer when some six or seven relatives arrive, having driven up from Virginia in an old station wagon. The relatives stay for weeks and weeks, helping tend the garden and mend any broken things. Gammell used brightly colored pencil drawings for this award-winning book. Two perfect companions to Rylant's book are Jacqueline Woodson's *We had a Picnic This Sunday Past*, illustrated by Diane Greenseid, about an African American family picnic, and Sonia Manzano's *No Dogs Allowed!*, illustrated by Jon J. Muth, about an extended Latino family and their riotous trip to the beach.

Several themes can be discerned in the many stories about grandparents. One theme is the grandparent's helping the child overcome a fear or learn something new, or just enjoyment of the relationship. A second type is learning to say good-bye and adjusting to the death of a grandparent. A third is the sharing of family stories, frequently including a feeling for the culture of the country from which the grandparents emigrated. Tomie dePaola has written several stories about grandparents. *Tom* describes his relationship with his irrepressible maternal grandfather, who must have given him his sense of humor as well as his name. *Nana Upstairs and Nana Downstairs* is more serious, describing a boy's visits with his bedridden great-grandmother. *Now One Foot, Now the Other* is dePaola's story of a little boy helping his grandfather recover from a stroke and learn to walk again.

Every family makes its own history, creating its own mythology by retelling family stories that are often represented by family heirlooms. In Valerie Flournoy's *The Patchwork Quilt*, Tanya loves to hear her grandmother tell the stories of the material she is using to make a quilt. The young girl helps her cut the squares and listens to her story of the quilt of memories. Flournoy's story and the realistic pictures by Jerry Pinkney capture a young girl's love for her treasured grandmother. In *The Keeping Quilt* by Patricia Polacco, Great Gramma Anna, a Russian Jew who immigrated to this country, makes a quilt to help the family always remember their homeland.

Through four generations the quilt is a Sabbath table-cloth, a wedding canopy, and a blanket that welcomes babies warmly into the world. To this day, Patricia Polacco still treasures this family quilt. The warm sepias of the drawing set against the full color in the quilt itself visually recreate the textures of memory and the fabric of tradition.

Familiar Everyday Experiences

Everything is new to the young child the first time it happens—going to school, making friends, losing teeth, taking a trip, moving away, the death of a pet. Children soon become accustomed to familiar experiences; nevertheless, books can help keep alive the wonder and anticipation of many such experiences. They can also alleviate some of children's concerns and worries about the new and unknown.

Ezra Jack Keats used collage and bright acrylic paints for his well-loved stories of Peter and his friends. Beginning with *The Snowy Day*, *Whistle for Willie*, *Peter's Chair*, and *A Letter to Amy*, the stories deal with simple events that are central to a young child's life. As Peter grows up, he is joined by his friend Archie in *Goggles*, *Hi, Cat!*, and *Pet Show!* All these stories take place in the inner city and have exciting story lines and convincing characterization.

Birthdays are extra-special events for children, and Vera Williams's brightly colored paintings add extra warmth to her stories about Rosa and her family. In *Something Special for Me*, Williams makes very real the decision that Rosa, the little girl in *A Chair for My Mother*, must make. Soon it will be her birthday, and this time she can have the money in the large money jar that contains her mother's waitressing tips to buy anything she wants. After much soul-searching, Rosa decides to spend the money on a used accordion.

Appreciating Cultural Diversity

 American children of the twenty-first century will need to develop a worldview that appreciates the richness of other cultures while preserving and celebrating their own uniqueness. In this text we integrate multiracial and ethnic stories throughout the chapters just as we would hope they will be used in schools. A global view requires exposure to books about other cultures and countries that children might not be able to visit. Fortunately, we have an increasing number of both nonfiction and fiction titles that will introduce children to others who share this earth and who are like them in so many ways.

In *Elizabeti's Doll*, Elizabeti desperately wants a baby of her own to care for after her little sister is born. She doesn't have a doll, but she finds a special rock that she cares for just as lovingly. The story celebrates the power of a child's imagination and every child's longing for something to call her own. Set in Tanzania and illustrated by Christy Hale, Stephanie Stuve-Bodeen's delightful stories about Elizabeti include *Mama Elizabeti* and *Elizabeti's School*.

Catherine Stock has told and illustrated the story of another African child in *Where Are You Going, Manyoni?* Manyoni wakes early. After breakfast, when the sun is just rising, she sets out on a journey. She travels past the baobab tree, across a ridge, under the wild fig trees, past the malala palms, through the fever-tree pan, over the place where impala feed beside the red sandstone, above the dam, and on and on until finally, when the sun is high over the veld, she arrives at the end of her journey. She has come to school. The lovely watercolor illustrations give us an education while Manyoni travels to hers. We learn about the flora and fauna of Zimbabwe and come to appreciate the very real effort children like

Seven-year-olds create a collage mural of the book *Hi, Cat!* by Ezra Jack Keats. Barrington Road School, Upper Arlington Public Schools, Ohio. Marlene Harbert, teacher.

In Denizé Lauture's *Running the Road to ABC*, artist Reynold Ruffins's illustrations evoke Haitian children's passionate yearning for schooling.
Reprinted with the permission of Simon & Schuster Books for Young Readers, an imprint of Simon & Schuster Children's Publishing Division from *Running the Road to ABC* by Denizé Lauture, illustrated by Reynold Ruffins. Illustrations copyright © 1996 Reynold Ruffins.

Manyoni must make to get an education. Another book that demonstrates children's determination to go to school is *Running the Road to ABC* by Denizé Lauture. Although the title makes the book sound like an alphabet book, these Haitian children are running to learn. "On the white turf and roads of red clay they run. On roads of rocks and roads of mud they run." For one more letter, and one more sound, and one more word, they run. In Florence Parry Heide and Judith Gilliland's *The Day of Ahmed's Secret*, Ahmed, a young butagaz boy in Cario, Egypt, makes his daily rounds through sun-bleached streets and daily market stalls to deliver cooking oil. Ahmed hugs a special secret to his heart. Home, at last, he can finally show his newly acquired skill to his family: Ahmed has learned how to write his name.

Australian illustrator Alison Lester traveled to Gunbalanya in the Northern Territory to work with the Gunbalanya Schools as an artist in residence. The result was *Ernie Dances to the Didgeridoo*, a delightful story based on experiences. Ernie leaves his school friends behind to live in Arnhem Land, where his parents go to work in the local hospital. The book is told through Ernie's letters to each of his six friends at home. Each is written about one of the six seasons in Arnhem Land and one of the six new friends he makes. Lester's book is a fascinating introduction to Aboriginal culture and to the climate and geography of Northern Australia.

These stories about the world beyond children's own neighborhoods can lead to much discussion of the contrast between wealthy Western countries and those of the developing world. English-speaking children need to develop a world vision at an early age.

Picture Books about Older People

For many years we believed that children identified only with stories about children their own age. More recently we have given them literature that includes persons of all ages. Mem Fox's *Wilfrid Gordon McDonald Partridge* is the story of a small redheaded boy who makes friends with folks who live next door in a home for older people. He likes them all, but his particular friend is 96-year-old Miss Nancy. When he hears his parents say she has lost her memory, he decides to help her find it. Julie Vivas's exuberant pictures provide unique characterizations that are painted almost larger than life and seen from unusual perspectives. Vivas teams up with Margaret Wild for the loving and wonderfully funny *Our Granny.* Grandmothers are also seen in active, positive roles in Janet Lord's *Here Comes Grandma!* illustrated by Julie Paschkis. Both of these books are as much a positive look at older women as they are a celebration of one grandmother.

Barbara Cooney illustrated two popular stories about older people, *Emma* and *Miss Rumphius.* Emma, written by Wendy Kesselman, is about a woman the author knew who didn't start painting until she was in her late eighties. In this story Barbara Cooney depicts her as a kind of Grandma Moses character who creates many primitive paintings based on her memories of her town. Cooney's *Miss Rumphius* is a fine model of an independent older person. As a youngster the girl told her grandfather that she, too, wished to travel to faraway places as he had and to live by the sea. He told her there was a third thing she must do—make the world more beautiful. And so, years later, she planted lupine all over her little seacoast village. The story line repeats itself as a very elderly Miss Rumphius passes along her grandfather's advice to her grandniece. The many objects that we first see in the grandfather's house or on Miss Rumphius's travels, and that now comfortably reside in Miss Rumphius's home by the sea, nicely reinforce the continuity of life.

In *Ernie Dances to the Didgeridoo,* Alison Lester introduces readers to the places, climate, and culture of Australia's Northern Territory. Illustration from *Ernie Dances to the Didgeridoo* by Alison Lester. Copyright © 2000 by Alison Lester. Hodder Headline Australia/Reprinted by permission of Houghton Mifflin Company. All rights reserved.

The Child's World of Nature

Sometimes young children seem more at-tuned to the world about them than adults do. Watch children on the first day of snow, for example, and see the excitement in their eyes and their eagerness to go out-side. Adults might complain about hav-ing to shovel the snow or the car's getting stuck, but for children a snowstorm is pure joy. It is this very contrast between adults' and children's reactions to snow that formed the basis for Alvin Tresselt's well-loved book *White Snow, Bright Snow,* illustrated with Roger Duvoisin's spark-ling pictures. Henry Cole invites young children to tune in to the natural world in several delightful books. In *Jack's Garden,* Jack builds a garden in his back yard to the refrain from "This Is the House That Jack Built." The book shows a young child diligently caring for the seeds he has planted and gives detail of the important

Julie Paschkis's energetic senior citizen is anything but stereotypical in *Here Comes Grandma!* From *Here Comes Grandma!* by Julie Paschkis. Illustrations © 2005 by Julie Paschkis. Reprinted by permission of Henry Holt and Company, LLC.

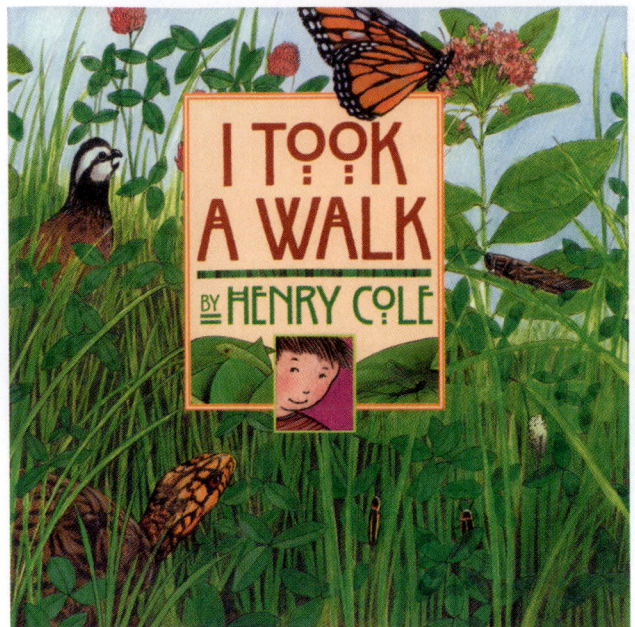

The illustrations in Henry Cole's *I Took a Walk* call attention to the simple beauty of the natural world. From *I Took a Walk* by Henry Cole. Copyright © 1998 by Henry Cole. Used by permission of Greenwillow Books.

ecosystem that supports his garden. In *I Took a Walk* and *On the Way to the Beach* Jack moves out of the garden and investigates the ecology of the beaches, forest, meadow, stream, and pond. In *Atlantic* and *On Earth* G. Brian Karas presents children with a broad perspective of the earth's

ecology and its intricate cycles. Karas's evocative illustrations provide a visual sense of immense space and wonder. Books like Cole's and Karas's and those by Byrd Baylor, such as *Your Own Best Secret Place* and *I'm in Charge of Celebrations*, help children appreciate and value the thousands of natural treasures that make up their world.

Rachel Carson tells us in the sensitive essay that she wrote about her grandnephew Roger just a few years before her death: "If a child is to keep alive his inborn sense of wonder . . . he needs the companionship of at least one adult who can share it, rediscovering with him the joy, excitement and mystery of the world we live in."[9] Books are not a substitute for real experiences, but through the sharing of beautiful picture books, teachers can enhance a real experience and keep the wonder of it alive with their own enthusiasm and appreciation for nature. See Teaching Resources: "Picture Books about the Child's Everyday World" for a list of many picture books about children's everyday experiences.

Animals as People

Ever since the day Peter Rabbit disobeyed his mother and squeezed through Mr. MacGregor's garden fence, children have enjoyed stories in which animals act like people, frequently like small children. In fact, many of these stories would be listed as family stories if you read just the text, since only in the pictures are the characters revealed as animals. Usually the animals are dressed and live in cozily furnished homes, hollow trees, or burrows and face the same problems as their child readers, whose lives are mirrored in these stories.

---

[9]Rachel Carson, *The Sense of Wonder,* photographs by Charles Pratt and others (New York: Harper & Row, 1956, 1965), p. 45.

TEACHING **RESOURCES**

Picture Books about the Child's Everyday World

 Visit the Online Learning Center at **www.mhhe.com/kiefer9e** for a printable version of this list.

FAMILY STORIES

Author, Illustrator	Title	Description
Alma Flor Ada, Elivia Savadier	*I Love Saturdays y Domingos*	A young child looks forward to weekends, Saturdays with her English-speaking grandparents and Sundays with her Spanish-speaking Abuelita and Abuelito.
Cari Best, Dale Gottlieb	*Taxi Taxi*	A story of the loving relationship between a little girl, a child of divorced parents, and her Papi, who comes to pick her up every Sunday in his yellow taxi.

Picture Books about the Child's Everyday World (continued)

FAMILY STORIES (continued)

Author, Illustrator	Title	Description
Cari Best, G. Brian Karas	*Are You Going to Be Good?*	Robert attends his great-grandmother's hundredth birthday party and tries to be good.
Anthony Browne	*My Dad*	In Browne's distinctive surrealist style, a young child celebrates what he loves about his father.
	My Mom	A child offers a loving tribute to a mother in Browne's unique surrealist style.
Judith Caseley	*Mama Coming and Going*	Mama is distracted by a new baby and doesn't know if she's coming or going. A warm and funny story about imperfections and affections.
Karen English, Sean Qualls	*The Baby on the Way*	Grandmother tells her grandson about her own childhood.
Carmen Lomas Garza	*Family Pictures: Cuadros de Familia*	A family album of all the special events the author remembers from her childhood days of growing up in Kingsville, Texas.
Bob Graham	*Oscar's Half Birthday*	An assortment of family members and neighbors celebrate a baby's first half-birthday.
Pat Hutchins	*There's Only One of Me*	As they prepare for a feast, a young girl names her relationships to members of her large extended family.
Angela Johnson, David Soman	*Tell Me a Story, Mama*	See text.
Mavis Jukes, Lloyd Bloom	*Like Jake and Me*	Bloom's bold illustrations capture the strong personalities in a sensitive story about stepfather and son.
Patricia MacLachlan, Ruth Lercher Bornstein	*Mama One, Mama Two*	A foster child is reassured that she will be loved and cared for until her real mother recovers from her mental depression and the two of them can be together again.
Donna Jo Napoli, Cathie Felsted	*Flamingo Dream*	A girl makes a scrapbook to remember her last year with her father.
Jan Ormerod	*Who's Whose?*	A delightful look at three families whose close friendship has intertwined them into one huge extended family.
Linda Sue Park, Ho Baek Lee	*Bee-bim Bop!*	A Korean American girl looks forward to eating "mix, mix rice" with her family.
Eileen Roe, Robert Casilla	*Con Mi Hermano: With My Brother*	Joyous times that a little boy spends with his older brother—playing ball, helping him deliver newspapers, and sharing picture books together.
Gary Soto, Terry Widener	*If the Shoe Fits*	Rigo, the youngest in his family, always seems to be the one to get hand-me-downs.

(continued)

Picture Books about the Child's Everyday World (continued)

FAMILY STORIES (continued)

Author, Illustrator	Title	Description
Ann Turner, James-Graham Hale	*Through Moon and Stars and Night Skies*	Lovely, tender, but not sentimental watercolor pictures illustrate this story of a brave little boy coming to a strange land to his adoptive parents.
Belle Yang	*Hannah Is My Name*	A Chinese American girl describes her family's emigration from Taiwan.

SIBLING RIVALRY

Author, Illustrator	Title	Description
Eloise Greenfield, John Steptoe	*She Come Bringing Me That Little Baby Girl*	Kevin dislikes all the attention given to his new sister until his uncle tells him how he used to take care of his baby sister, Kevin's mother.
Elizabeth Starr Hill, Sandra Speidel	*Evan's Corner*	Evan takes a corner of his family's two-room apartment for his special place and then decides to help his brother fix up his own place.
Ezra Jack Keats	*Peter's Chair*	Peter decides to run away before all of his possessions are painted pink for his new baby sister. However, when he discovers that he no longer fits in his chair, he decides that maybe it would be fun to paint it pink himself.
LeUyen Pham	*Big Sister, Little Sister*	Little sister is tired of getting all the hand-me-downs.
Jeanne Titherington	*A Place for Ben*	Ben invites his baby brother to come and play in his special place.
Mildred Pitts Walter, Pat Cummings	*My Mama Needs Me*	Bright illustrations show an African American older child's desire to be of help, as well as his resentment, when a baby sister arrives.
Vera B. Williams	*Amber Was Brave, Essie Was Smart*	Two sisters share the ups and downs of their life together.
Elizabeth Winthrop, Pat Cummings	*Squashed in the Middle*	See text.

RELATIVES

Author, Illustrator	Title	Description
Eve Bunting, Donald Carrick	*The Wednesday Surprise*	For Dad's birthday surprise Anna teaches her grandmother to read by sharing books every Wednesday night when her grandma comes to babysit.
Jeannette Caines, Pat Cummings	*Just Us Women*	Realistic illustrations detail the fun that African American women plan to have on their special trip to North Carolina in Aunt Martha's new car.
Judith Caseley	*Dear Annie*	Annie's grandfather celebrates his love for her through his many letters and postcards.

Picture Books about the Child's Everyday World *(continued)*

RELATIVES *(continued)*

Author, Illustrator	Title	Description
Andrea Cheng, Ange Zhang	*Grandfather Counts*	Helen and her Chinese grandfather learn to speak each other's language.
Jane Cutler, Hiroe Nakata	*The Birthday Doll*	A grandmother helps her granddaughter to appreciate the gift of a rag doll.
Tomie dePaola	*Watch Out for the Chicken Feet in Your Soup*	Joey and his friend Eugene visit Joey's Italian grandmother.
	Nana Upstairs and Nana Downstairs	See text.
	Now One Foot, Now the Other	See text.
	Tom	See text.
Elizabeth Fitzgerald Howard, James Ransome	*Aunt Flossie's Hats (and Crab Cakes Later)*	Two sisters listen to the stories of their great-great aunt's many hats.
René Colato Laínez, Jill Arena	*Playing Lotería/El juego deloa lotería*	See text.
Patricia MacLachlan, Deborah Ray	*Through Grandpa's Eyes*	A tender story in which the grandson realizes that his blind grandfather has many ways of seeing.
Sonia Manzano, Jon Muth	*No Dogs Allowed*	Members of an extended Latino family trek off to the beach with the pet dog only to find that no dogs are allowed.
Margaree King Mitchell, James Ransome	*Uncle Jed's Barbershop*	Uncle Jed puts off his dreams to help others during the Depression.
Pat Mora, Cecily Lang	*Pablo's Tree*	Pablo's grandfather planted a tree when Pablo was born, and each year he decorates it as Pablo's special birthday surprise.
Patricia Polacco	*Thunder Cake*	A little girl is terrified of thunder until her Russian grandmother teaches her to make a special Thunder Cake.
Jama Kim Rattigan, Lillian Hsu-Flanders	*Dumpling Soup*	Marisa is finally old enough to contribute to her family's New Year festival in Hawaii.
Cynthia Rylant, Stephen Gammell	*The Relatives Came*	See text.
Mary Stolz, Pat Cummings	*Storm in the Night*	A grandfather and grandson sit together in the dark and enjoy the sounds and smells of the rain.

(continued)

Picture Books about the Child's Everyday World (*continued*)

RELATIVES (*continued*)

Author, Illustrator	Title	Description
Jacqueline Woodson, Diane Greenseid	*We Had a Picnic This Sunday Past*	See text.
Jacqueline Woodson, Jon J. Muth	*Our Gracie Aunt*	Abandoned by their sick mother, a brother and sister find love in the home of an aunt.

FAMILY HISTORY

Author, Illustrator	Title	Description
Lynne Barasch	*Radio Rescue*	A young ham radio operator, the author's father, helps out in a hurricane in the 1920s.
Sandra Belton, Cozbi A. Cabrera	*Beauty, Her Basket*	Grandmother shares the history of the Sea Islands baskets with her granddaughter.
Maire Bradby, Ted Rand	*Once Upon a Farm*	A young boy recalls the halcyon days on his farm.
Barbara Cooney	*Island Boy*	Stunning pictures portray seascapes and the family members who make up four generations of a New England family who settled on Tibbett's Island.
	Hattie and the Wild Waves	Cooney describes the affluent life of her mother growing up in Brooklyn and then Long Island while searching for her life's work.
Valerie Flournoy, Jerry Pinkney	*The Patchwork Quilt*	See text.
Janice N. Harrington, Jerome Lagarrigue	*Going North*	An African American family makes the long trip North for a better life.
Claire Hartfield, Jerome Lagarrigue	*Me and Uncle Romie*	James travels to New York City to visit his uncle, the artist Romare Bearden.
Tony Johnston, Barry Moser	*That Summer*	A boy recalls a summer that changed his life.
Riki Levinson, Diane Goode	*Watch the Stars Come Out*	Impressionistic watercolors detail the journey two young children make alone on a ship from Europe to their strange new home in America.
Patricia C. McKissack, Jerry Pinkney	*Goin' Someplace Special*	Tricia Ann takes a bus trip in the segregated South of the 1950s.
Margaree King Mitchell, James Ransome	*Uncle Jed's Barbershop*	See text.
Willie Perdomo, Bryan Collier	*Visiting Langston*	An aspiring writer visits Langston Hughes in Harlem.

Picture Books about the Child's Everyday World (continued)

FAMILY HISTORY

Author, Illustrator	Title	Description
Patricia Polacco	*The Keeping Quilt*	See text.
Allen Say	*Grandfather's Journey*	See text.
	Tea with Milk	See text.
Jacqueline Woodson, E. B. Lewis	*Coming On Home Soon*	A young girl and her grandmother are separated from Mama when she moves North to work during World War II.

FAMILIAR EXPERIENCES

Author, Illustrator	Title	Description
Cari Best, Holly Meade	*Goose's Story*	A young girl finds an injured Canada goose and learns a lesson about disabilities.
Carol Carrick, Donald Carrick	*The Accident*	This story describes Christopher's dismay when his dog, Bodger, is run over by a truck and killed. Children facing the death of a pet may find comfort in the book.
Miriam Cohen, Lillian Hoban	*Will I Have a Friend?, When Will I Read?, Best Friends,* and others	Illustrations of a multicultural first-grade classroom are as warm and reassuring as Jim's teachers and friendly classmates are as they face the everyday worries of young children.
Tomie dePaola	*Stage Struck*	Young Tommy tries to take over the class play when he doesn't get the lead role.
Patricia Lee Gauch, Satomi Ichikawa	*Presenting Tanya, Ugly Duckling,* and others	A series of warmhearted stories about Tanya, who loves to dance.
Bob Graham	*"Let's Get a Pup!" said Kate*	See text.
Juanita Havill, Anne Sibley O'Brien	*Jamaica and the Substitute Teacher,* and others	Jamaica is an irrepressible young African American girl whose experiences are warmly related. In this book a special teacher helps her to understand that copying someone else's work isn't necessary and that she doesn't have to be perfect to be special.
Florence Parry Heide, Jules Feiffer	*Some Things Are Scary*	A reassuring look at childhood anxieties.
Paul B. Johnson and Celeste Lewis	*Lost*	A child never gives up hope that her lost dog will be found.
Ezra Jack Keats	*The Snowy Day, Whistle for Willie,* and others	See text.
Antonio Hernández Madrigal, Gerrardo Suzán	*Blanca's Feather*	A little girl loses her pet hen at the blessing of the animals on St. Francis of Assisi Day.

(continued)

Picture Books about the Child's Everyday World *(continued)*

FAMILIAR EXPERIENCES *(continued)*

Author, Illustrator	Title	Description
Robert McCloskey	*One Morning in Maine*	Sal announces her loose tooth to anyone who will listen. Story and illustrations show how important such changes are to young children.
Isaac Millman	*Moses Goes to a Concert*	Moses and his other deaf classmates go to a concert where they hold balloons on their laps to feel the vibrations and are introduced to the orchestra's deaf percussionist.
Leslea Newman, Ron Himler	*The Best Cat in the World*	A young boy struggles to deal with the death of his cat and with a new kitten who is very different in nature.
Lynne Rae Perkins	*The Broken Cat*	A child waits with his injured cat and is comforted by his mother's recollections of her own broken arm.
Mary Ann Rodman, E. B. Lewis	*My Best Friend*	A young girl tries hard to make friends with an older girl at the swimming pool.
Marc Simont	*The Stray Dog: From a True Story by Reiko Sassa*	A family picnics in the park and encounters a stray dog, whom they can't forget.
John Steptoe	*Stevie*	Robert resents Stevie, who stays at Robert's house every day while Stevie's mother goes to work, but Robert realizes that he misses Stevie after he goes back to his family.
Judith Viorst, Erik Blegvad	*The Tenth Good Thing about Barney*	The little black-and-white ink sketches by Erik Blegvad underscore the sincerity of this story of a boy's first experience with death.
Judith Viorst, Ray Cruz	*Alexander and the Terrible, Horrible, No Good, Very Bad Day, and others*	Cruz's illustrations add to these wonderfully funny stories about the frustrations of being a kid.
Bernard Waber	*Ira Sleeps Over*	Illustrations reflect Ira's dilemma as he tries to decide if he will take his teddy bear to his first sleepover.
Vera B. Williams	*Something Special for Me* and *A Chair for My Mother*	See text.
	Music, Music for Everyone	Rosa uses her birthday accordion to earn money to help pay the bills.

APPRECIATING CULTURAL DIVERSITY

Author, Illustrator	Title	Description
Jan Andrews, Ian Wallace	*Very Last First Time*	In this picture of life in the Inuit village of Ungava Bay in northern Canada, an Inuit girl goes to gather mussels alone for the first time.
Barbara Helen Berger	*All the Way to Lhasa: A Tale From Tibet*	A boy and his yak overcome obstacles and travel to Lhasa, Tibet.

Picture Books about the Child's Everyday World *(continued)*

APPRECIATING CULTURAL DIVERSITY *(continued)*

Author, Illustrator	Title	Description
Eve Bunting, Beth Peck	*How Many Days to America? A Thanksgiving Story*	Bunting tells the story of a Cuban family's flight to America in a small boat.
Eve Bunting, Ted Rand	*One Green Apple*	A Middle Eastern girl finds a way to connect to her new American classmates.
Julie Cummins, Ted Rand	*Country Kid, City Kid*	A boy and a girl live in different places but are very much alike.
Ina Cumpiano, José Ramírez	*Quinto's Neighborhood/ El Vecindario de Quinto*	A young Latino boy describes his neighborhood and the people that make it a community.
Nigel Gray, Philippe Dupasquier	*A Country Far Away*	Two children—one black, one white—wake, sleep, play, eat, and share in family life on opposite sides of the globe.
Florence Parry Heide and Judith Heide Gilliland, Ted Lewin	*The Day of Ahmed's Secret*	See text.
	Sami and the Time of the Troubles	A young boy must struggle to maintain a normal life during the war in Lebanon.
Mary Hoffman, Karin Littlewood	*The Color of Home*	Hassan, a refuge from Somalia, tries to adjust to his first days of school and new home in America.
Rachel Isadora	*At the Crossroads*	After children wait all day and all night for their fathers to come home after ten months of working in the mines in South Africa, they share a joyful reunion.
Uma Krishnaswami, Shiraaz Bhabba	*The Closet Ghosts*	The Hindu Monkey God helps a young girl adjust to her new home.
Denizé Lauture, Reynold Ruffins	*Running the Road to ABC*	See text.
Grace Lin	*Kite Flying*	A family gathers supplies and makes a dragon kite.
Lenore Look, Yumi Heo	*Henry's First Moon Birthday*	A Chinese American boy prepares for the celebration of his brother's first moon or month.
Kam Mak	*My Chinatown*	See text.
Tony Medina, R. Gregory Christie	*DeShawn Days*	With pride and determination, DeShawn describes his life in the projects.
Tololwa Mollel, E. B. Lewis	*My Rows and Piles of Coins*	A young Tanzanian boy is trying to save enough money to buy a bicycle so that he can help his mother deliver her goods to market.
Naomi Shihab Nye, Nancy Carpenter	*Sitti's Secret*	A Palestinian American girl goes to visit her grandmother in Palestine.

(continued)

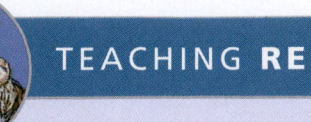
Picture Books about the Child's Everyday World (*continued*)

APPRECIATING CULTURAL DIVERSITY (*continued*)

Author, Illustrator	Title	Description
Soyung Pak and Susan Kathleen Hartung	*Dear Juno*	A young Korean American boy draws picture letters to stay in touch with his Korean grandmother.
Amada Irma Pérez, Maya Christina Gonzalez	*My Very Own Room/ Mi propio cuartito*	A young girl, with five younger brothers, longs for her own room.
Charlotte Pomerantz, Frané Lessac	*The Chalk Doll*	A mother shares stories of her growing up in Jamaica with her little daughter, Rose.
Sarah Stewart, David Small	*The Journey*	A young Amish girl travels to Chicago and compares her farm life with life in the big city.
Catherine Stock	*Gugu's House*	In Zimbabwe a young girl loves to visit her grandmother and help paint decorations on her house.
	Where Are You Going, Manyoni?	A young South African girl has a long journey to school.
Stephanie Stuve-Bodeen, Christy Hale	*Elizabeti's Doll*	See text.
	Elizabeti's School	Elizabeti goes to school for the first time.
	Mama Elizabeti	Elizabeti must care for her year-old brother when her mother has a new baby.
Mari Takabayashi	*I Live in Tokyo*	A Japanese school girl describes her life in Tokyo.
Karen Williams, Catherine Stock	*Galimoto*	A young Malawian boy succeeds in making his own toy car.
	Painted Dreams	A Haitian girl dreams of being an artist.
Janet S. Wong, Margaret Chodos-Irvine	*Apple Pie Fourth of July*	An immigrant Chinese girl worries that customers won't eat her family's chow mein on the Fourth of July.
Janet S. Wong, Yangsook Choi	*This Next New Year*	A Korean Chinese boy gets ready to celebrate Chinese New Year.

BOOKS ABOUT OLDER PEOPLE

Author, Illustrator	Title	Description
Sandra Belton, Benny Andrews	*Pictures for Miss Josie*	A grown artist recalls his inspiration, Miss Josie.
Nancy White Carlstrom, Amy Schwartz	*Blow Me a Kiss, Miss Lilly*	Small, precise illustrations add to the appeal of this story of a friendship between a young child and a very old lady. After Lilly's death, young Sara remembers her in a special way.

Picture Books about the Child's Everyday World (continued)

BOOKS ABOUT OLDER PEOPLE (continued)

Author, Illustrator	Title	Description
Mem Fox, Terry Denton	*Night Noises*	Strange noises can't wake Lily Laceby, who has drifted off to sleep. Finally the commotion wakes her, and she discovers that her family has come to wish her a happy birthday.
Mem Fox, Julie Vivas	*Wilfrid Gordon McDonald Partridge*	See text.
Lisa Rowe Fraustino, Benny Andrews	*The Hickory Chair*	A young, blind boy holds on to his memories of his Gran.
Army Hest, Jon Muth	*Mr. George Baker*	A first grader and an older man share a special bond while waiting for the school bus.
Gloria Houston, Susan Condie Lamb	*My Great-Aunt Arizona*	The story of a special teacher who taught in the mountains of Virginia for many years.
Simon James	*The Birdwatchers*	Grandfather, who loves to exaggerate, shares his love of birdwatching with his granddaughter.
Wendy Kesselman, Barbara Cooney	*Emma*	See text.
	Miss Rumphius	See text.
Janet Lord, Julie Paschkis	*Here Comes Grandma!*	See text.
Ian Wallace	*Mavis and Myrna*	A young girl and an older woman form a lifelong friendship.
Margaret Wild, Julie Vivas	*Our Granny*	See text.
	The Very Best of Friends	A poignant story of the loving friendship between James and Jessie, and James and his cat, William.

THE CHILD'S WORLD OF NATURE

Author, Illustrator	Title	Description
Byrd Baylor, Peter Parnall	*Everybody Needs a Rock; Your Own Best Secret Place; The Other Way to Listen; The Way to Start a Day*	All of Baylor's books develop sensitivity to all aspects of the natural world.
Henry Cole	*I Took a Walk; Jack's Garden; On the Way to the Beach*	See text.
Sheila Cole, Virginia Wright-Frierson	*When the Tide Is Low*	The illustrations provide watery seascapes and accurate pictures of sea animals and shells for this quiet story of a mother and daughter's delightful day.

(continued)

Picture Books about the Child's Everyday World (*continued*)

THE CHILD'S WORLD OF NATURE (*continued*)

Author, Illustrator	Title	Description
Karen Hesse, Jon Muth	*Come On, Rain!*	See text.
G. Brian Karas	*Atlantic, On Earth*	See text.
Kathryn Lasky, Mike Bostock	*Pond Year*	This story details the changes that occur in the ecology of a backyard pond and describes the rich playground it provides for two friends.
Jonathan London, Greg Couch	*Sun Dance, Water Dance*	A group of children celebrate a day and night in summer.
Joanne Ryder, Keiko Narahashi	*A Fawn in the Grass*	A young child finds treasures in the world around her.
Allen Say	*The Lost Lake*	Glowing watercolors portray the wilderness trip a Japanese American father and his son take to a lost lake.
Mary Serfozo, Keiko Narahashi	*Rain Talk*	The various sounds the rain makes are explored in the poetic picture book that portrays the child's delight in this summer rain.
Uri Shulevitz	*Rain Rain Rivers*	Watercolors in greens and blues are the appropriate medium and colors for a book that expresses the mood of a rainy day in the city and the country.
Peter Spier	*Peter Spier's Rain*	All the dimensions of a rainstorm are included here—children's and animals' reactions, indoor and outdoor fun in the rain.
Alvin Tresselt, Roger Duvoisin	*White Snow, Bright Snow*	See text.
David Wiesner	*Hurricane*	Detailed watercolors capture all of the excitement of two boys waiting out a hurricane in their snug home.
Taro Yashima	*Umbrella*	A little Japanese American girl is impatient for rain because she wants to wear her new red rubber boots and carry her new umbrella to nursery school.

Kevin Henkes is the creator of a remarkable mouse child named Lilly, who was the very best until the arrival of her baby brother in *Julius, Baby of the World*. Lilly thinks he is disgusting and hopes he will go away; she hates Julius and the way her parents fawn over him. When no one is looking, Lilly pinches his tail, teaches him his numbers backward, and tells him that "if he was a number, he would be zero." Lilly spends a great deal of time in what her parents call "the uncooperative chair." But then Cousin Garland comes to visit and

says Julius is disgusting. Suddenly Lilly has a complete change of heart. Lilly is a real character wearing her queen's crown and red cowboy boots. She was first introduced in *Chester's Way*, a story of the friendship between Chester and Wilson and, finally, Lilly. In *Lilly's Purple Plastic Purse*, Lilly is an irrepressible second grader who finds it hard to keep her zippy new plastic purse in her desk until show and tell. When Mr. Slinger, her beloved teacher, takes it away from her, she lets her anger get the best of her. It takes a patient teacher and loving parents to restore Lilly's equilibrium. In *Lilly's Big Day* Lilly is certain that she is going to be Mr. Slinger's flower girl at his wedding. This misunderstanding is also lovingly—and hysterically—resolved.

Animal characters often provide a good venue for stories about moral values. Children might recognize a familiar situation in Erica Silverman's *Don't Fidget a Feather*. Gander and Duck are so full of self-adulation that they hold contests to see who is the better swimmer and who can fly higher. When neither of these competitions has a clear winner, Duck suggests a freeze-in place contest. Through many distractions they don't "fidget a feather," even when a fox takes the two back to this stew pot. When the fox prepares to cook Gander, however, Duck decides that winning the contest is not as important as saving Gander's life. S. D. Schindler's pastel drawings manage to maintain a state of high tension and add a note of realism to this story with its underlying note of conflict. Chih-Yuan Chen's *Guji Guji* is a delightful story about a crocodile whose egg ends up in a duck's nest. Mother Duck and her chick accept the fellow as one of the family, and he is perfectly happy to act like a duck until the other crocodile kids make him question his true nature. Children can wrestle with the nature-versus-nurture argument through Chen's wise words and droll illustrations.

There may be no better example of the power of putting people in animal guise than D. B. Johnson's five books about Henry, a bear based on the character of Henry Thoreau. The books, *Henry Builds a Cabin, Henry Climbs a Mountain, Henry Takes a Trip, Henry Works,* and *Henry Hikes to Fitchburg,* based on real events in Thoreau's life, and all convey the essence of his philosophy. It's hard to imagine reading Thoreau's *Walden Pond* to grade-schoolers, but these books are wonderful introductions. In *Henry Hikes to Fitchburg* Henry decides to challenge his friend to a race to Fitchburg. His friend sells out to earn the money for train fare doing odd jobs (for Bronson Alcott, Ralph Waldo Emerson, and Nathaniel Hawthorne). Henry sets off, meandering down side roads and

In *Henry Builds a Cabin* by D. B. Johnson, a likable bear stands in for the character of Henry Thoreau. Illustration from *Henry Builds a Cabin* by D. B. Johnson. Copyright © 2002 by D. B. Johnson. Reprinted by permission of Houghton Mifflin Company. All rights reserved.

through blackberry patches. Henry loses the race, but nobody can doubt that he had the better journey. Johnson's illustrations have great child appeal, yet the subtle colors and patterns of the paintings evoke Thoreau's love of nature just as these stories do.

Modern Folktale Style

Perhaps Rudyard Kipling started the trend of writing modern folktales. The humor of his pourquoi tales, *Just So Stories*, is based on his wonderful use of words and his tongue-in-cheek asides to the reader. A favorite with children is *The Elephant's Child*, the story of how a young elephant got his trunk. Originally his nose was no bigger than a bulgy boot. His "satiable curiosity" causes him all kinds of trouble and spankings. To find out what the crocodile has for dinner, he departs for the "banks of the great grey-green, greasy Limpopo River, all set about with fever-trees." Here he meets the crocodile, who whispers in his ear that today he will start his meal with the elephant's child! Then the crocodile grabs his nose and pulls and pulls. When the poor elephant is free, he has a trunk for a nose. Some of these stories—such as *The Elephant's Child, How the Camel Got His Hump*, and *How the Leopard Got His Spots*—have been attractively illustrated in single picture-book editions by Jan Mogensen, Lorinda Cauley, Caroline Ebborn, and Quentin Blake. Children need to hear the language in these tales read aloud by an enthusiastic teacher or librarian.

Contemporary authors have also used the traditional folktale format to compose original stories. Jerdine Nolen's *Hewitt Anderson's Great Big Life*, illustrated by Kadir Nelson, is a tall tale about a normal-size boy born to giant-size parents. Despite his small size, Hewitt proves to have enormous courage, to his parents' proud satisfaction. Nelson's unusual perspectives and richly painted scenes emphasize the differences in size between the giant adults and the child. Lynne Bertrand's *Granite Baby* features five giant sisters who create a baby out of stone. The infant is very much flesh and blood, and the sisters are stumped as to how to comfort him until a young girl helps them out. Kevin Hawkes's bold figures and varying perspectives bring these unusual characters to life. Both books will be satisfying to children who often feel small and helpless among oversize adults.

Many of Leo Lionni's stories are modern folktales. In *Frederick* Lionni makes a statement about the role of the artist in society that is direct and to the point. His *Alexander and the Wind-Up Mouse* includes a purple pebble, a magic lizard, and a transformation. Alexander envies a wind-up mouse, Willie, and wants to become one himself. Fortunes change, however, and in order to save his friend, Alexander asks the magic lizard to make Willie a real mouse, just like Alexander.

Certain contemporary stories provide modern twists on well-loved tales and require previous knowledge of the folktales. Steven Kellogg's retelling of and illustrations for *Chicken Little* are very funny indeed. The story

Kadir Nelson creates exaggerated contrasts to depict the scenes in Jerdine Nolen's original tall tale, *Hewitt Anderson's Great Big Life.* Illustration copyright © 2005 by Kadir Nelson. Jacket of *Hewitt Anderson's Great Big Life* by Jerdine Nolan. Published by Simon & Schuster Books for Young Readers.

starts out with Chicken Little's famous warning that "The sky is falling" after she has been hit on the head by an acorn. Foxy Loxy hears the animals cry for the police and quickly changes his "poultry" truck sign to read "poulice." Thinking his Thanksgiving dinner is safely locked in the truck, he shows the foolish fowls the harmless acorn and tosses it up in the air. It gets caught in Sergeant Hippo Hefty's helicopter, which crashes to the earth, landing on the truck and freeing all the birds while Sergeant Hefty "flattens the fleeing fox." Foxy Loxy is sent to prison, and Chicken Little plants the acorn. It grows into a fine, tall tree by the side of her house, where her grandchildren come to hear her retell her famous story. Action-packed illustrations accompany this hilarious retelling of the Chicken Little story.

Other books take known characters or the bones of a traditional tale and flesh them out in new and intriguing ways. Author Jon Scieszka and illustrator Lane Smith have great fun playing with traditional tales in *The True Story of the Three Little Pigs* and *The Stinky Cheese Man and Other Fairly Stupid Tales*. Their hilarious version of "The Three Pigs" is told from the wolf's point of view. His explanation is that he just wanted to borrow a cup of sugar to bake a cake for his old granny when he accidentally sneezed and blew the pigs' houses down. It seems like a shame to leave a perfectly good warm dinner lying there in the straw. So he eats one pig, and the second one too. He blames the whole bad rap on the reporters and the fact that when the third pig insulted his granny, he went berserk. Older students love this retelling, which invites them to write from a different point of view. In *The Stinky Cheese Man* Scieszka and Smith turn ten familiar tales, including "The Ugly Duckling," "Chicken Little," and "Jack and the Beanstalk," inside out and upside down. They do the same thing and more with the format of the picture book, inserting the endpapers in the middle of the book, moving the table of contents to page 9, altering typeface, and changing size. Scieszka and Smith continue the silliness in *Squids Will Be Squids*.

Humor

Young children's sense of fun is simple and obvious. Illustrations in picture books often provide the humor that children might miss through words alone. Steven Kellogg is a master at drawing utter confusion and slapstick. A bored young girl gives her mother a deadpan account of the class trip to the farm in the hilarious story of *The Day Jimmy's Boa Ate the Wash* by Trinka Noble. The contrast between the girl's reporting of events and the exuberant illustrations is extreme. The same approach is used in *Jimmy's Boa and the Bungee Jump Slam Dunk* and *Jimmy's Boa Bounces Back*, written and illustrated by the same team. The low-key narration is nicely balanced by the action-packed pictures. Kellogg has also produced many equally funny books of his own. The tales of his great Dane in *A Penguin Pup for Pinkerton; Pinkerton, Behave!; A Rose for Pinkerton;* and *Prehistoric Pinkerton* provide the frame for his madcap pictures.

Martha is another indomitable dog who takes matters into her own paws in Susan Meddaugh's *Martha Speaks*. When Martha swallows a bowl of alphabet soup, letters go straight to her brain and convert Woof to English. At first her family is delighted, but soon Martha won't shut up and becomes an embarrassment. Her talents are finally appreciated when she saves the family treasures from a burglar. Martha in turn learns to appreciate the finer points of conversational etiquette. Martha's adventures are continued in *Martha and Skits, Martha Calling, Martha Walks the Dog, Martha Blah Blah,* and *Perfectly Martha*.

There have been many feisty and funny girl characters introduced to children's literature in the past few decades, beginning perhaps with Kaye Thompson's *Eloise*. None seems quite so feisty, funny, or fearless as Clarice Bean, who appears in *Clarice Bean, That's Me; Clarice Bean, Guess Who's Babysitting?;* and *What Planet*

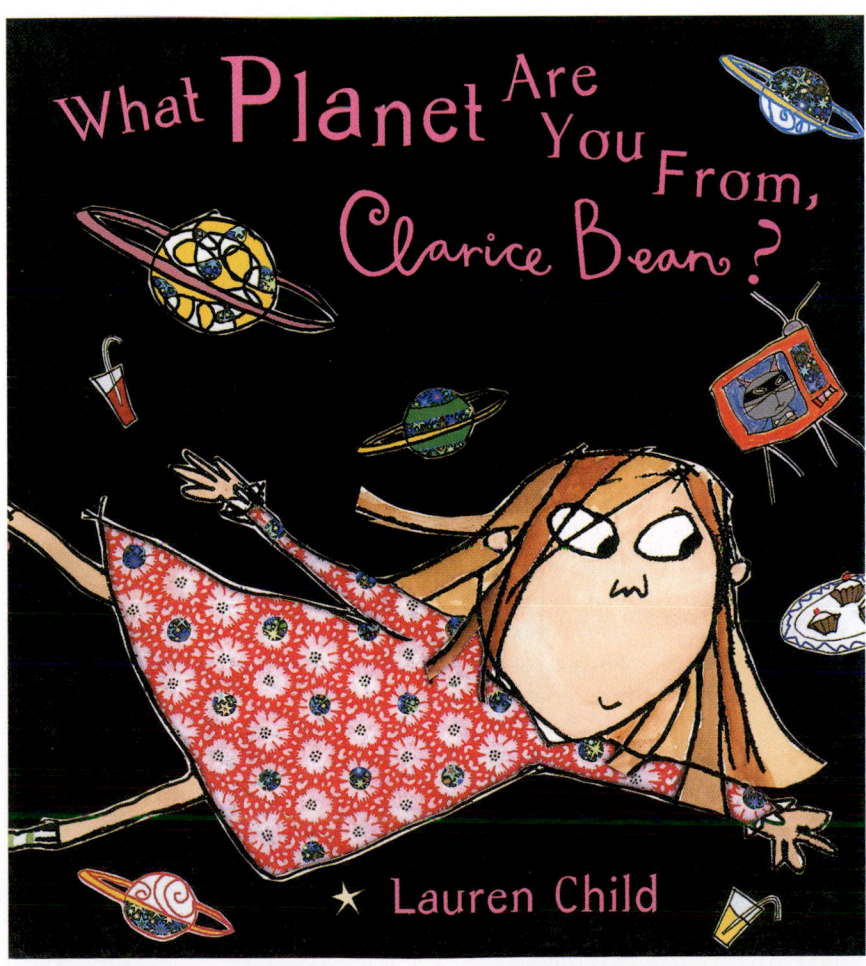

Lauren Child's exuberant illustrations for *What Planet Are You From, Clarice Bean?* convey the chaos of Clarice's comic adventures. *What Planet Are You From, Clarice Bean?* Copyright © 2002 Lauren Child. Reproduced by permission of the publisher Candlewick Press, Inc., Cambridge, MA.

Are You From, Clarice Bean? by Lauren Child. Made from the same British mold as Georgia Nicolson, heroine of *Angus, Thongs, and Full Frontal Snogging* (see Chapter 9), Clarice's narratives revolve around her everyday experiences with her extended family, her friends, and her school. Her larger-than-life escapades are anything but "everyday." Child's linear renderings recall the bold and comic brush strokes of Edward Lear. Her juxtaposition of cartoon art, realistic collage photographs, and meandering typeface adds to the atmosphere of nonsense.

Another favorite character of children is Harry Allard and James Marshall's Miss Nelson, the lovely, sweet teacher who cannot make the class behave. In *Miss Nelson Is Missing*, she is replaced by Miss Viola Swamp, who wears a dark black dress and is a witch, the children decide. After one week with Miss Swamp's rules and homework, the children are delighted to welcome Miss Nelson back. At home Miss Nelson takes off her coat and hangs it right next to an ugly black dress.

Marc Brown's Arthur stories are equally popular and include a variety of animal characters. Arthur bears the brunt of a good deal of teasing in *Arthur's Nose* and *Arthur's Eyes* (when he must wear glasses). Never very brave, Arthur is seen as very courageous when he goes into a large spooky house on Halloween to find his baby sister in *Arthur's Halloween*. In *Arthur, It's Only Rock 'n' Roll* Arthur tries out for Francine's rock 'n' roll band but doesn't make the cut. All these Arthur books satisfy 6- and 7-year-olds' sense of humor and demand for poetic justice. Brown's full-color illustrations for Judy Sierra's *Wild about Books* are very different from those in his Arthur books but perfectly suited to this rollicking story of animals hungry to read.

Mo Willems is a relative newcomer to books for children, but his lively Pigeon character has tickled funny bones with *Don't Let the Pigeon Drive the Bus!*, *The Pigeon Finds a Hot Dog*, and *Don't Let the Pigeon Stay Up Late*, three stories about a pigeon whose lack of self-control bears an uncanny resemblance to that of many preschoolers. *Leonardo the Terrible Monster* features a monster child who, try as he may, just can't be at all monstrous. In all his books Willems's spare use of line and color plays a major role in the fun.

Fantasy

The line between humorous picture stories for children and fanciful ones is blurred. Talking beasts and modern spinoffs on folktales are certainly fanciful stories, yet they can be very humorous. However, children appear to see a difference between a make-believe story and a funny one. Imaginary trips are a common theme in picture books. In Arthur Dorros's *Abuela* and *Isla*, Rosalba and her grandmother visit favorite places in the city and Abuela's island home by flying over them. In Faith Ringgold's *Tar Beach*, Cassie Louise Lightfoot dreams of being free, of going anywhere she wants. One night up on Tar Beach, the rooftop of her family's Harlem apartment building, her dream comes true. Cassie can fly over the city.

Paul Fleischman's *Weslandia* involves an entire imaginary civilization created by a boy who simply won't conform to childhood norms. When Wesley is told to work on a project over the summer, he decides to create his own civilization. He nurtures a group of seeds that have mysteriously appeared overnight in his garden patch. Once the plants mature, Wesley devises a full range of products from the plants; creates his own shelter and clothing; and establishes an economic system, a recreational system, and a language. His once-scornful classmates are intrigued and then won over by Wesley's incredible imagination.

Another form of young children's fantasy involves anthropomorphism, or the personification of inanimate objects, such as toys and machines. Most children know and love Watty Piper's story *The Little Engine That Could* with new illustrations by Loren Long, and Hardie Gramatky's story *Little Toot*. Most of the books written by Virginia Lee Burton contain personification: *Mike Mulligan and His Steam Shovel*, *Kate and the Big Snow*, and *The Little House*. The encroachment of the city on the country is portrayed in Burton's classic *The Little House*, about a house that stands on a hill and watches day and night as the seasons pass. Gradually a road is built and cars come, and soon the city grows up around the little house. Elevated cars speed by her; subway trains speed under her; and people rush to and fro in front of her. One day the great-great-granddaughter of the original owner sees the little house, buys her, and has her moved back to the country where she can once again see the stars. Several picture books personify toys and dolls.

There are many editions of Margery Williams's sentimental classic *The Velveteen Rabbit: Or How Toys Become Real*. The most attractive ones are those illustrated by Michael Hague, Ilse Plume, and David Jorgensen. Any child who has loved a stuffed animal of her own will understand the conversation between the old skin horse and the velveteen rabbit on the subject of becoming real. Barbara McClintock's *Dahlia* is a beautiful china doll who is not coddled by her young owner, Charlotte. In fact, Charlotte, who'd rather be making mud pies than playing with dolls, drags Dahlia along in all her rambunctious outdoor play. By the end of this charming story Dahlia emerges a bit the worse for wear, but Charlotte learns that loving a doll doesn't limit her to traditional female role-playing such as giving tea parties and taking sedate walks with a pram.

Today there might be more stories about monsters and superheroes than there are about toys and dolls. In the delightful *Traction Man Is Here!* by Mini Grey we manage to step into the persona of a toy action figure and accompany him on his adventures to save the world. The illustrations reveal that that world is a small one, the house and the garden of his child owner. In Kevin O'Malley's *Captain Raptor and the Moon Mystery*, Captain

Raptor is an unusual superhero who lives on the planet Jurassica and bears a strong resemblance to a tyrannosaurus rex. In true hero fashion, he saves human visitors from a dangerous monster.

Chris Van Allsburg is certainly the best-known creator of fantasy in children's picture books. *The Polar Express* is a haunting Christmas story for all children and for those who remain children at heart. *Jumanji* and its sequel, *Zathura,* relate the eerie events that occur when a game board comes to life. Van Allsburg's other books, such as *The Widow's Broom* and *The Stranger,* hold an air of mystery that will have the children guessing at their true meaning.

A similar sense of mystery can be found in two other picture-book fantasies, *The Mysterious Collection of Dr. David Harleyson* by Jean Cassels and *Mr. Maxwell's Mouse* by Frank Asch and Devin Asch. In Cassel's book visual images and written clues left by a variety of familiar fairytale characters eventually provide the answer to the disappearance of Dr. Harleyson, a world-trotting pig. Mr. Maxwell is a proud office-worker cat whose promotion leads to a dinner celebration at which the main course is live mouse on lettuce. The wily mouse has other plans, however, and tricks Mr. Maxwell into biting into his own tail. In both of these books the style of the illustrations enhances the air of mysterious fantasy. See Teaching Resources: "Picture Books about the Child's Imaginary World" for a list of other picture books exploring children's imaginary experiences.

Social and Environmental Concerns

As more and more picture books are written for older children, more are dealing with major social and environmental concerns. Eve Bunting's moving story *Fly Away Home* tells of a homeless boy and his father who live in a large airport, moving from terminal to terminal and trying never to be noticed. A trapped bird that finally manages to fly free becomes the boy's metaphor for hope. Ronald Himler's watercolors are as understated and honest as this story. In *Uncle Willie and the Soup Kitchen* by DyAnne DiSalvo-Ryan, a young boy goes with his uncle who volunteers at a soup kitchen. They stop and pick up chickens at the butcher shop. Then the boy meets the other volunteers and helps set tables for "the guests," as Uncle Willie calls them. Uncle Willie is a wonderful model as he stands at the door and greets the guests and shares his zest for living. The warm, sensitive story and pictures were inspired by the author's own experience as a soup kitchen volunteer. Books sometimes portray the wrenching changes that often occur in the name of progress.

Jean Cassels gives intriguing visual clues that lead to a solution of *The Mysterious Collection of Dr. David Harleyson. The Mysterious Collection of Dr. David Harleyson.* Written by Jean Cassels. Illustrations copyright © 2005 Jean Cassels. Reproduced by permission of Walker Books Ltd., London.

Picture Books about the Child's Imaginary World

 Visit the Online Learning Center at **www.mhhe.com/kiefer9e** for a printable version of this list.

ANIMALS AS PEOPLE

Author, Illustrator	Title	Description
Jim Aylesworth, Barbara McClintock	*The Tale of Tricky Fox*	A tricky fox tries to trick a teacher but is out-foxed.
Barbara Bottner and Gerald Kruglik, Olaf Landström	*Wallace's Lists*	Wallace the mouse is compulsive about making and following lists until a friend teaches him to loosen up.
Caralyn Buehner, Mark Buehner	*Superdog: The Heart of a Hero*	A small dachshund is determined to overcome his lowly status.
Chih-Yuan Chen	*Guji Guji*	See text.
Eileen Christelow	*The Great Pig Escape; The Great Pig Search*	Pigs escape from Bert and Ethel's farm and a culinary end to go to Florida.
Doreen Cronin, Harry Bliss	*Diary of a Spider Diary of a Worm*	The world as seen through the eyes (and words) of a young spider and worm.
Doreen Cronin, Betsy Lewin	*Click, Clack, Moo: Cows That Type*	Cows, then ducks, agitate Farmer Brown for better working conditions.
	Duck for President	Duck decides to leave Farmer Brown's farm and run for president until he finds out how much work he has to do.
	Giggle, Giggle, Quack	Farmer Brown takes a holiday and the ducks get out of hand.
Jean de Brunhoff	*The Story of Babar*	Well-loved stories about an elephant king and his friends and family. Continued in sequels by de Brunhoff's son, Laurent.
Roger Duvoisin	*Petunia*	A silly goose thinks she has acquired wisdom when she finds a book but does not know that it is important to learn to read what is in the book.
Eva Eriksson	*A Crash Course for Molly*	Molly the pig learns about bike safety the hard way.
Ian Falconer	*Olivia*	Olivia the pig sets about subduing her world.
	Olivia Saves the Circus	Outrageous Olivia tells about the time she saved the circus.
Mem Fox, Pamela Lofts	*Koala Lou*	A little koala bear feels neglected when new brothers and sisters arrive, and she tries to win her mother's attention. Her mother assures her that she always has, and always *will*, love her.
Don Freeman	*Dandelion*	The story of a lion who becomes such a "dandy" in order to go to a party that his hostess does not recognize him and shuts the door in his face.

Picture Books about the Child's Imaginary World *(continued)*

ANIMALS AS PEOPLE *(continued)*

Author, Illustrator	Title	Description
Bob Graham	*Benny*	Graham's exuberant illustrations bring this tale of a hobo dog to life and to the story's final happy conclusion.
Kevin Henkes	*Lilly's Purple Plastic Purse; Chester's Way; Julius, the Baby of the World*	See text.
	Chrysanthemum	A lively mouse thinks her name is "absolutely perfect" until she goes to school and is teased about her long flower name.
	Owen	Owen must deal with an interfering neighbor, Mrs. Tweezers, who convinces Owen's parents that he is too old for his security blanket.
Russell Hoban, Garth Williams	*Bedtime for Frances* and other Frances stories	Frances is an engaging, uproariously funny badger who mirrors the behavior of young children.
James Howe, Amy Walrod	*Horace and Morris but Mostly Dolores*	When her friends decide to form a boys-only club, Dolores has her revenge.
Pat Hutchins	*Good-Night, Owl!*	A beautifully designed book about a poor owl who is kept awake by noisy animals during the day and then gets his revenge at night.
D. B. Johnson	*Henry Builds a Cabin; Henry Climbs a Mountain; Henry Hikes to Fitchburg; Henry Takes a Trip; Henry Works*	See text.
Tony Johnston, Stacy Innert	*The Worm Family*	Worms celebrate their unique talents in this story about self-acceptance.
Holly Keller	*Farfallina and Marcel*	A charming story of friendship between a goose and a butterfly.
Robert Kraus, Jose Aruego and Ariane Dewey	*Leo the Late Bloomer*	Leo, a baby tiger, can't do anything right until he's ready to.
	Owliver Milton the Early Riser	More charming animal stories.
Petra Mathers	*Lottie's New Friend*	Herbie Duck and Lottie are best friends until Dodo arrives. Lottie is smitten with Dodo's exotic experiences, and Herbie feels left out.
David McKee	*Elmer*	A lovely story about a patchwork-colored elephant who wants to be gray like all the other elephants.

(continued)

Picture Books about the Child's Imaginary World *(continued)*

ANIMALS AS PEOPLE *(continued)*

Author, Illustrator	Title	Description
Nigel McMullen	*Not Me!*	Baby bear is blamed for his older brother's missteps.
David McPhail	*Pig Pig Grows Up*	An overprotected pig refuses to grow up and act his age until disaster occurs.
Antoine Ó. Flatharta, Meilo So	*Hurry and the Monarch*	Hurry the Tortoise observes and muses on the migrations of monarch butterflies.
H. A. Rey	*Curious George*	A comical monkey has one escapade after another, but the man in the yellow hat always manages to save him from real danger.
Pam Muñoz Ryan, Claudia Rueda	*Nacho and Lolita*	Two birds of very different feathers find happiness together.
Joanne Ryder, Steven Kellogg	*Big Bear Ball*	See text.
Dr. Seuss	*Horton Hatches the Egg; Thidwick, the Big-Hearted Moose*	These two are among the many wonderfully original stories by an author who is a favorite of young children.
George Shannon, Jose Aruego and Ariane Dewey	*Lizard's Guest*	Lizard takes in an injured friend, who stays and stays and stays.
Erica Silverman, S. D. Schindler	*Don't Fidget a Feather*	See text.
Gary Soto, Susan Guevara	*Chato and the Party Animals*	Chato the cat decides to throw a birthday party for his friend Novio Boy.
	Chato's Kitchen	See text.
Mark Teague	*Dear Mrs. Larue: Letters from Obedience School*	Ike the dog is sent to the Brotweiler Academy and tries to escape.
Bernard Waber	*The House on East 88th Street; Lyle, Lyle Crocodile*	Lyle, a performing crocodile, lives happily with the Pimm family in several comic stories.
Rosemary Wells	*Shy Charles*	A reserved mouse turns out to be a hero.
Jeanne Willis, Tony Ross	*Tadpole's Promise*	A tadpole and a caterpillar fall in love with somewhat macabre results.
Karma Wilson, Jane Chapman	*Bear Snores On*	While Bear is hibernating, other animals find his cave to their liking and throw a party.
Elizabeth Winthrop, Betsy Lewin	*Dumpy LaRue*	Dumpy is a boy pig who just wants to dance, to the dismay of his family.

Picture Books about the Child's Imaginary World *(continued)*

MODERN FOLKTALE STYLE

Author, Illustrator	Title	Description
Lynne Bertrand, Kevin Hawkes	*Granite Baby*	See text.
Raymond Briggs	*Jim and the Beanstalk*	A sequel to "Jack and the Beanstalk."
Stephanie Calmenson, Denise Brunkus	*The Frog Principal*	A funny twist on *The Frog Prince*.
	The Principal's New Clothes	Hysterically funny modern-day version of "The Emperor's New Clothes."
Randy Cech	*One Dark and Dreadful Night*	A troop of child actors interprets (and fractures) familiar fairy tales.
Eileen Christelow	*Where's the Big Bad Wolf?*	Dog detective is hot on the trail of a chicken thief.
Pamela Edwards, Henry Cole	*Dinorella*	Prehistoric fairy tale. A Stone Age version told in alliterative prose.
Mem Fox, Julie Vivas	*Possum Magic*	Grandma Poss and Hush set off on what becomes a culinary visit of the cities of Australia to find the proper magic food to turn Hush from invisible to visible.
Colin Hawkins and Jacqui Hawkins	*Fairytale News*	Mother Hubbard's son Jack delivers papers to fairy tale characters to earn money to fill the Hubbards' cupboards.
Tony Johnston, James Warhola	*Bigfoot Cinderrrrrella*	Hilarious reversal has an oversize heroine and hero and a beary godmother.
Steven Kellogg	*Chicken Little*	See text.
Rudyard Kipling, various illustrators	*How the Camel Got His Hump; The Elephant's Child; How the Leopard Got His Spots*	See text.
Kathryn Lasky, David Catrow	*The Emperor's Old Clothes*	A comical sequel in which a farmer finds the emperor's old clothes.
Leo Lionni	*Alexander and the Wind-Up Mouse; Frederick*	See text.
Arnold Lobel	*Fables*	These modern fables include a pirouetting camel in a tutu and an elephant reading the *Daily Trumpet*.
Susan Lowell, Randy Cecil	*Dusty Locks and the Three Bears*	A retelling of Goldilocks set way out west.
David Martin, Susan Meddaugh	*Five Little Piggies*	The true story of what happened to the famous five including the one who ran home crying wee wee wee.

(continued)

Picture Books about the Child's Imaginary World *(continued)*

MODERN FOLKTALE STYLE *(continued)*

Author, Illustrator	Title	Description
Patricia McKissack and Onawumi Jean Moss, Kyrsten Brooker	*Precious and the Boo Hag*	A little girl manages to trick a trickster when she is left at home alone.
Susan Meddaugh	*Cinderella's Rat*	The adventures of one of Cinderella's coach boys who finds it hard to give up his rat-like ways.
	The Witch's Walking Stick	Margaret puts her Cinderella existence behind her as she sets out on her own and finds a witch's walking stick.
Marianne Mitchell, Bryan Langdo	*Joe Cinders*	Cinderella retold in the Old West with male characters.
Pat Mora, Raúl Colón	*Dona Flor: A Tall Tale about a Woman with a Big Heart*	A kind and helpful woman rescues her village from a giant puma.
Jerdine Nolen, Kadir Nelson	*Hewitt Anderson's Great Big Life*	See text.
Mary Pope Osborne, Giselle Potter	*The Brave Little Seamstress*	A retelling of the traditional Brave Little Tailor with a female heroine.
	Kate and the Beanstalk	A retelling of "Jack and the Beanstalk" with a female heroine.
Douglas Rees, S. D. Schindler	*Grandy Thaxter's Helper*	Set in colonial New England, the tale relates how a clever old woman outwits Mister Death.
Jon Scieszka, Lane Smith	*Squids Will Be Squids; The True Story of the Three Little Pigs; The Stinky Cheese Man*	See text.
Jon Scieszka, Steve Johnson	*The Frog Prince Continued*	Shows that every marriage has its rocky places after the "They lived happily ever after" ending.
Diane Stanley	*The Giant and the Beanstalk*	"Jack and the Beanstalk" is told from the giant's point of view.
William Steig	*Sylvester and the Magic Pebble; The Amazing Bone; Doctor DeSoto; Brave Irene; Shrek!; Zeke Pippin*	Steig continues to enchant children with his superbly written stories and appealing illustrations.
Janet Stevens, Susan Stevens Crummel	*Cook-a-Doodle Do!*	A descendant of the Little Red Hen attempts to cook a strawberry cake with disastrous results.
	And the Dish Ran Away with the Spoon	Nursery-rhyme characters have a new adventure.

Picture Books about the Child's Imaginary World (continued)

MODERN FOLKTALE STYLE (continued)

Author, Illustrator	Title	Description
Philemon Sturges, Amy Walrod	The Little Red Hen (Makes a Pizza)	A traditional tale takes a playful twist with clever additions in the illustrations.
Eugene Trivias, Helen Oxenbury	The Three Little Wolves and the Big Bad Pig	Three innocent wolves play the victims of a psychotic pig.
Jane Yolen, Victoria Chess	King Longshanks	The Frog Prince meets the Emperor's New Clothes in the amusing amphibian version of an Andersen classic tale.

HUMOROUS PICTURE BOOKS

Author, Illustrator	Title	Description
Jon Agee	Terrific	Eugene Crumb, the world's most pessimistic man, meets a parrot who improves his outlook.
Allan Ahlberg, Raymond Briggs	The Adventures of Bert; A Bit More Bert	Prose that reads like a Dick and Jane primer and hilarious illustrations present the adventures of the simple-minded but lovable Bert.
Harry Allard and James Marshall	Miss Nelson Has a Field Day; Miss Nelson Is Missing	See text.
Harry Allard, James Marshall	The Stupids	Hilarious stories about the dimmest family in the world.
Judi Barrett, Ron Barrett	Animals Should Definitely Not Act Like People; Animals Should Definitely Not Wear Clothing	Children love the visual ridiculousness of animals garbed in highly inappropriate clothing.
Teresa Bateman, Nadine Bernard Westcott	April Foolishness	Two children and their Grandpa get mixed up about April Fool's Day.
Karen Beaumont, David Catrow	I Ain't Gonna Paint No More!	An out-of control artist just can't manage to put his brushes down.
Marc Brown	Arthur's Nose and other Arthur stories	See text.
Lauren Child	Clarice Bean, Guess Who's Babysitting?	Clarice is left with her favorite uncle when Mom has to go abroad.
	Clarice Bean, That's Me	Clarice seeks peace and quiet from the chaos in her family.
	Hubert Horatio Bartle Bobton-Trent	This male version of Eloise tries to curb his parents' reckless spending.
	What Planet Are You From, Clarice Bean?	Clarice is assigned a science project with unusual results.

(continued)

Picture Books about the Child's Imaginary World (*continued*)

HUMOROUS PICTURE BOOKS (*continued*)

Author, Illustrator	Title	Description
Michael Delaney	*Birdbrain Amos*	Amos, the Hippopotamus, is bugged by bugs and seeks relief with a humorous outcome.
Beatrice Schenk de Regniers, Beni Montresor	*May I Bring a Friend?*	Slapstick and nonsense are the order of the day.
Mary Ann Hoberman, Nadine Bernard Westcott	*There Once Was a Man Named Michael Finnegan*	Poor old Michael, who holds up his pants with a pin-agin, has a riotous set of adventures.
Simon James	*Baby Brains; Baby Brains Superstar*	These tongue-in-cheek spoofs on giftedness will have all children feeling bright.
Steven Kellogg	*Pinkerton, Behave!* and other stories	See text.
John Kelly and Cathy Tincknell	*The Mystery of Eatum Hall*	Mr. and Mrs. Pork-Fowler are invited to dine with Dr. Hunter, who plans to serve them as the main course.
Julius Lester, Joe Cepeda	*Why Heaven Is Far Away*	God and Irene God and their heavenly crew try to keep heaven and earth together.
Margaret Mahy, Jonathan Allen	*The Great White Man-Eating Shark*	Norvin, a boy who looks rather like a shark, takes to swimming with a dorsal fin strapped to his back. He has the beach to himself until a female shark falls in love with him.
James Marshall	*George and Martha*	This collection of brief stories about the adventures of two hippo friends is both poignant and hysterical.
Kate McMullan, Jim McMullan	*I Stink!*	A garbage truck reveals the gory details of his day.
Susan Meddaugh	*Martha Blah Blah*	See text.
	Martha Calling	Martha again takes charge, this time of the family vacation.
	Martha Speaks	See text.
	Martha Walks the Dog	Martha finds out that kind words are better than negative slurs in changing a neighborhood bully.
	Perfectly Martha	See text.
Trinka Noble, Steven Kellogg	*The Day Jimmy's Boa Ate the Wash; Jimmy's Boa Bounces Back; Jimmy's Boa and the Bungee Jump Slam Dunk*	See text.
Marge Palatini, Richard Egielski	*The Web Files*	Ducktective Web investigates crimes involving nursery-rhyme characters.

Picture Books about the Child's Imaginary World *(continued)*

HUMOROUS PICTURE BOOKS *(continued)*

Author, Illustrator	Title	Description
Margie Palatini, Richard Egielski	*Three French Hens*	Palatini uses traditional forms such as "The Twelve Days of Christmas" as the basis for this funny retelling.
Tom Paxton, Steven Kellogg	*Engelbert the Elephant*	The illustrations are as uproarious as the antics of the guests when Engelbert crashes the queen's party.
Dav Pilkey	*Dog Breath*	Hally, the pet dog of the Tosis family, has breath problems, but she conquers a bunch of crooks—not with teeth but with odors.
Meg Rosoff, Sophie Blackall	*Meet Wild Boars*	A quartet of wild boars stands in for the most ill-behaved children ever.
Pam Muñoz Ryan, Joe Cepeda	*Mice and Beans*	A forgetful grandmother prepares for her granddaughter's birthday with the help of some clever mice.
Rob Scotton	*Russell the Sheep*	A goofy sheep is afraid to go to sleep and tries counting different objects to relax himself.
James Stevenson	*Could Be Worse!; That Terrible Halloween Night*	Children appreciate the humor of Grandpa's exaggerated tall tales. Stevenson's watercolor and cartoon-style illustrations are as funny as his stories.
Nancy Van Laan, George Booth	*Possum Come A-Knockin'*	Booth's wry cartoons illustrate this silly story about a little old possum just trying to have fun.
Mo Willems	*Don't Let the Pigeon Drive the Bus; Don't Let the Pigeon Stay Up Late!; The Pigeon Finds a Hot Dog; Leonardo the Terrible Monster*	See text.

FANTASY IN PICTURE BOOKS

Author, Illustrator	Title	Description
Jon Agee	*Milo's Hat Trick*	An inept magician meets a talented bear who teaches him a lesson about stardom.
Frank Asch, Devin Asch	*Mr. Maxwell's Mouse*	See text.
Pablo Bernasconi	*Captain Arsenio: Inventions and (Mis)Adventures in Flight*	This mock biography details the history of a loopy inventor who is determined to build a flying machine.
Eve Bunting, David Christiana	*I Am the Mummy Heb-Nefert*	In a wonderfully haunting book for older readers, a mummy recalls her days of glory and muses on the brevity of life.

(continued)

Picture Books about the Child's Imaginary World *(continued)*

FANTASY IN PICTURE BOOKS *(continued)*

Author, Illustrator	Title	Description
Virginia Lee Burton	*The Little House; Mike Mulligan and His Steam Shovel; Katie and the Big Snow*	See text.
Jean Cassels	*The Mysterious Collection of Dr. David Harleyson*	See text.
Arthur Dorros, Elisa Kleven	*Abuela, Isla*	See text.
Paul Fleischman, Kevin Hawkes	*Weslandia*	See text.
Don Freeman	*Corduroy*	In this satisfying story, a plush-toy bear waits patiently in the department store for someone to buy him.
Cornelia Funke, Kerstin Meyer	*The Princess Knight*	The King's daughter is determined to be a knight, very much against her father's wishes.
Bob Graham	*Jethro Byrd, Fairy Child*	Annabelle has a visit from a fairy family but no one else seems to appreciate the magic of her encounter.
Hardie Gramatky	*Little Toot*	See text.
Mini Grey	*Traction Man Is Here!*	An action figure comes to life in this delightful fantasy.
Barbara Jean Hicks, Alexis Deacon	*Jitterbug Jam: A Monster Tale*	A young monster is scared of the boy hiding under his bed.
Arthur Howard	*Hoodwinked*	In a different take on the child-who-wants-a-pet theme, Mitzi the witch goes through one outrageous pet after another, until she finds just the right one.
William Joyce	*A Day with Wilbur Robinson*	Strange incongruities occur when Wilbur invites a friend to his house for the day.
	Dinosaur Bob and His Adventures with the Family Lazardo	Bob, discovered while the family is on a safari, scares off burglars, dances, and plays baseball.
	George Shrinks	George dreams he is small and wakes to find it is true.
Maira Kalman	*Max in Hollywood; Max Makes a Million; Ooh La La, Max in Love*	The wacky adventures of Max, a dog, a poet, and a dreamer.
David LaRochelle, Hanako Wakiyama	*The Best Pet of All*	A mother doesn't know what she's in for when she promises her son that he can keep a pet dragon (if he can find one).

Picture Books about the Child's Imaginary World (continued)

FANTASY IN PICTURE BOOKS (continued)

Author, Illustrator	Title	Description
Mercer Mayer	*There's a Nightmare in My Closet*	A small boy who is afraid of the dark ends up comforting a monster who has a nightmare.
Barbara McClintock	*Dahlia*	See text.
Jerdine Nolen, Elise Primavera	*Raising Dragons*	A daughter of farmers puts her agricultural knowledge to use raising a dragon.
George O'Connor	*Kapow!, Ker-splash!*	Two children imagine themselves as superheroes in these silly stories.
Kevin O'Malley, Patrick O'Brien	*Captain Raptor and the Moon Mystery*	See text.
Watty Piper, Loren Long	*The Little Engine That Could*	See text.
Faith Ringgold	*Tar Beach*	See text.
Peter Sis	*Madelinka's Dog*	Madelinka introduces her imaginary dog to her neighbors.
Sean Taylor, Bruce Ingman	*Boing!*	In this giddy tale, a trampoline champion turns superhero.
Chris Van Allsburg	*Jumanji; The Garden of Abdul Gasazi; The Wreck of the Zephyr; The Stranger; The Polar Express; Zathura*	See text.
	Bad Day at Riverbend	A brave sheriff rides out to find the villain when a slimy substance begins to attack people, beasts, and countryside.
	Just a Dream	This book predicts the kind of future we are going to have if we keep polluting the earth.
	The Wretched Stone	This message book suggests the evils of watching television.
	The Sweetest Fig	A little dog receives poetic justice after years of mistreatment by a despicable dentist.
	The Widow's Broom	The title character needs a little help from the Widow Shaw to overcome its tormentors.
Margery Williams; Michael Hague, David Jorgensen, Ilse Plume	*The Velveteen Rabbit*	See text.

This is the *reef*
that feeds the tide pool
that lies on the beach
that meets the mangrove
that follows the river
that weaves through the forest
that filters the air
that circles the world
that we want.

Kim Michelle Toft's gorgeous silk paintings for *The World That We Want* will help children experience the fragility of the Great Barrier Reef and fuel their desire to protect it. 2005 first U.S. edition. Copyright © 2005 by Kim Michelle Toft. Used with permission by Charlesbridge Publishing, Inc. All rights reserved.

Concern for the environment is another important theme in many picture books. The cumulative text of *The World That We Want* by Australian artist Kim Michelle Toft takes readers on a journey from the sky, to forest, to ocean, to learn about the ecology of the Australian rain forest and Great Barrier Reef. A final foldout mural summarizes the interconnectedness of the flora and fauna that survive in such delicate balance. Toft's exquisite silk paintings will have children marveling at the beauty of this world as well as appreciating the need to protect it. Jeannie Baker is another artist who champions social and environmental concerns. Her collage illustrations, made from a multitude of materials—textured items, preserved grass, leaves, feathers, hair, and paints—are fascinating creations, but more important, they subtly underscore the importance of her messages. In Baker's *Where the Forest Meets the Sea* a young boy takes delight in exploring the rain forest as shadows of dinosaurs can be seen in the trees. However, on the last page, shadows of a future Star Hotel, skyscrapers, homes, and swimming pools are superimposed on the picture of the beach and bay, foretelling the destructive cycle of urban sprawl. Baker suggests a more hopeful future in *Home*. In this book we follow the story of a baby girl who, out of the window of her new home, sees a blighted urban landscape. As she grows older, however, we see that members of the community take responsibility for their surroundings, and the scarred landscape gradually is made beautiful.

A story with a similar message depicts actual events in Lynne Cherry's *A River Ran Wild*. This stunning book details the history of the Nashua River in New Hampshire. Beginning long ago, when the river ran so clear that its pebbled bottom was visible, Cherry shows how the ecology of the river gradually changed as the land was colonized and then industrialized. Eventually the river became so badly polluted that nothing lived in it. However, a community campaign led by one determined woman reversed this terrible decline, and the river became a thriving ecosystem once again. The book is a model for action in other communities, and Cherry's illustrations, and her detailed borders showing wildlife and other artifacts from various eras, invite children to create similar social and ecological histories. Children will surely be moved to become involved in such positive action by these and other picture books that point out the interconnectedness of people and planet.

War and Its Aftermath

Art can portray the devastation of war in ways that mere words cannot. Picture books that tell of effects of the war in times past and present may help a new generation bring about a peaceful future. Patricia Polacco's *Pink and Say* is a tremendously moving book based on events that happened to her great-grandfather during the American Civil War. The story tells of Pinkus Aylee, an African American soldier, and Sheldon Russell Curtis (Say), a white soldier. The two become friends during the last stages of the Civil War as a severely wounded Say is nursed to health by Pink's mother, Moe Moe. Before they can get to safety, however, southern marauders kill Moe Moe, and on their way to rejoin their units, Pink and Say are captured by Confederate soldiers. In their last moments together, a close-up illustration shows Pink reaching out to touch Say's hand, the hand that once shook the hand of President Lincoln. An afterword relates that Say survived (barely) the terrible Andersonville prison and that Pink was hanged. Polacco meant the book to serve as a written memory because Pinkus had no descendants to preserve the story for him.

The horrors of World War II are recounted in several moving picture books. Toshi Maruki's *Hiroshima No Pika* (The Flash of Hiroshima) is a devastating account of the bombing of Hiroshima as recalled by a survivor who was a child at the time. The expressionistic pictures of the fires, the thunder and lightning, and the wounded and dying all recreate the horror of an atomic attack. Yet the book was written in the hope that such horrors would never happen again. This, of course, is the reason teachers should share this book. For somehow, when pain is particularized for a specific family, it becomes more real and immediate than when it is depersonalized into mass numbers who were killed that day.

For many years children have been moved by Eleanor Coerr's novel *Sadako and the Thousand Paper Cranes.* For her picture book *Sadako,* Coerr rewrote this story of a young girl who died of leukemia as a result of the atomic bomb. Ed Young's use of soft pastels mediates this tragic story for children but does not lessen its emotional impact. Figures are hazily drawn, particularly when the most frightening scenes are rendered. Instead of using realistic depictions, Young lets color convey the feelings that underlie the story. As Sadako gets sicker and sicker, the colors darken, until the pages on which she dies are predominantly the blue-black color of night. On the following page, however, Young changes the colors to the soft blues and peaches of a sunrise. The paper cranes that Sadako tried so hard to make have become real cranes flying toward heaven. Young's moving artwork and Sadako's statue in Hiroshima suggest that Sadako left behind a powerful legacy of peace.

The Holocaust is the subject of several moving picture books for children. In *Rose Blanche* by Christophe Gallaz and Roberto Innocenti, the kindness of one child who cared for and provided food for children in a concentration camp is related. Illustrated with paintings of almost photographic clarity, this picture book is certainly for older children. Innocenti has also created the illustrations for *Erika's Story* by Ruth Vander Zee. As a first-person narrator imagines the terrible train journey of one young Jewish couple and their infant child, Innocenti portrays the story in dull sepia tones. The exception is the yellow stars on many of the people and a pink blanket wrapped around the baby girl. As it becomes clear to the desperate parents that their journey will have a deadly end, they throw the baby into the weeds by the side of the track. On the final page we see the train pull into the yard of a concentration camp. However, the narrator's story, based on a survivor's account, ends with a full-color double-page spread reflecting the rescue of the child by a country woman and her growing up to become a mother herself.

Another true account from the Holocaust is told in *The Flag with Fifty-six Stars* by Susan Goldman Rubin. The American flag, secretly made by survivors of the Mauthausen concentration camp for their American liberators, had too many stars because the inmates did not know that there were only forty-eight states at the time. Bill Farnsworth's realistic paintings show the depravations of the camp but also illuminate the ultimate liberation of these brave survivors and so many others like them.

Sadly, the tragedy of inhumanity and war continues beyond the World War II generation into the present day. In *The Wall,* a little boy visits Washington, D.C., with his father, and they find the name of the boy's grandfather on the Vietnam Memorial. Eve Bunting tells this poignant story, and Ronald Himler creates stark watercolor pictures for it. The pain the boy's father feels at the loss of his father is contrasted with the young child's comments. His father tells the boy he is proud that the grandfather's name is on this wall. The boy replies:

> "I am, too.
> I am.
> But I'd rather have my grandpa here, taking me to the river, telling me to button up my jacket because it's cold.
> I'd rather have him here." (p. 32)

It is not hard to imagine that a few years from now someone will write a similar book about another grandfather (or grandmother) who did not survive the Iraq War.

Two picture books have managed to encapsulate the tragedy of September 11 for children. Maira Kalman's *Fireboat* is a true account of the *John J. Harvey,* a little fireboat that had been decommissioned but was on hand to lend aid to survivors of the World Trade Center attack. The story and Kalman's bright pictures focus attention on the small triumphs that occur in immense disasters and provide reassurance to small children who may feel powerless on such occasions. In *September Roses* Jeanette

Talking Point

Should children read picture books about sensitive subjects?

Are picture books about such topics as war and homelessness appropriate for children? What role do illustrations play in mediating difficult topics for children?
Go to the Online Learning Center at **www.mhhe.com/kiefer9e** or your Resources CD-ROM to learn more.

Two words on the lips of the world, talk peace.

Talk Peace by Sam Williams, with illustrations by Mique Moriuchi, is a simple yet heartfelt appeal that should encourage children's future actions. Illustration copyright © 2005 Mique Moriuchi. All rights reserved. Reprinted from *Talk Peace*, written by Sam Williams, by permission of Holiday House, Inc.

Winter focuses on two sisters who took action during the days following the attack. In this case the two women from South Africa had come to New York to display their roses at a flower show when the 9/11 attacks occurred. Stranded in the city, they are taken in by helpful New Yorkers and in gratitude they take their roses to Union Square and arrange them into two Towers in memory of the victims.

Certainly, countless generations have dreamed that the hope for the future lies in their children. Now that picture books command a world audience, those hopes might be fulfilled on a universal basis. Such books as *For Every Child* (UNICEF) and *The Rights of the Child* (Grobler and others) are based on the 1959 United Nations Declaration and will serve to remind the world's children of their connections to each other. *The Rights of the Child* was rewritten, illustrated, and printed in all the official languages of South Africa by Kwela Books, a South African publisher. Sam Williams's brief rhyming text for *Talk Peace* and Mique Moriuchi's bright abstract images of the world's children will instill in young children the desire to bring an end to these continuing conflicts.

Picture books are for all ages, and they can be about all subjects. They can enlarge children's lives, stretch their imaginations, increase their sensitivity, and enhance their living. The growth of beautiful picture books for children of all ages is an outstanding accomplishment of the past fifty years of publishing. Children do not always recognize the beauty of these books, but early impressions do influence the development of children's permanent tastes as they grow up.

INTO THE CLASSROOM

Picture Books

Picture books depend on the visual art for their meaning as much as, if not more than, the words. When reading picture books aloud to children, it is important for adults to hold the book with pages facing outward in order to give children time to peruse the pictures fully. Children will often see small details in the pictures that adults miss, so encourage children to look for the "secrets," as one teacher calls them. Questions such as "How do these pictures make you feel?" or "What are you thinking about as you look at these pictures?" should encourage children to think more deeply about their responses to the art of the picture book.

1. **Caldecott Award Committee.** Form a mock Caldecott Award committee and review the Honor Books and Medal-winning book for one specific year. What criteria do the children think are important? Would they have made the same decision as the American Library Association committee? Why or why not?
2. **Medium Experimentation.** Find three or four books that are examples of the use of one medium, such as scratchboard or collage. Invite children to experiment with the materials used in this medium to make a picture of their own.
3. **Favorite Illustrator Study.** Help children plan a study of a favorite illustrator. What resources are available to find out more about that artist? How would they categorize the artist's books? Brainstorm ways to display the artist's work and to invite other children to learn more about that illustrator.
4. **Connecting Illustrators and Museum Artists.** Enlist your art teacher to help children make connections between the historical and cultural conventions used by illustrators and works of art they might find in a museum. For example, Anthony Browne's *Voices*

in the Park pays tribute to the work of René Magritte. Have children visit the online collections of great art museums. Make a list of paintings and artists that remind them of the work of picture-book illustrators (for example, Italian Renaissance paintings and Paul O. Zelinsky's *Rapunzel*).

Art Institute of Chicago
http://www.artic.edu/aic

Metropolitan Museum in New York
http://www.metmuseum.org

Museum of Fine Arts, Boston
http://www.mfa.org

National Gallery of Art in Washington, D.C.
http://www.nga.gov

5. **The History of Bookmaking.** Study the history of bookmaking. Hold a bookmaking workshop and have children write and illustrate their own bound books.

Go to the Online Learning Center at **www.mhhe.com/kiefer9e** or your Resources CD-ROM to find these additional classroom activities:

6. **Murals**
7. **Media Exploration**
8. **Making Alphabet Books**
9. **Using the Web as a Resource for Learning about Authors and Illustrators**
10. **Exploring the Principles of Picture Book Design**

Chapter Review

Go to the Online Learning Center at **www.mhhe.com/kiefer9e** or your Resources CD-ROM to take chapter quizzes, practice with key terms, and review the chapter.

Explorations

1. Look closely at three or more picture books to discover how the illustrations extend the story's meaning beyond the words. Note the effect of the artist's choice of medium, style, and color; look for content details present in the pictures but not in the text.

2. Study the work of one Caldecott Medal–winning illustrator. What medium does this artist use? What terms would you use to describe the style? How do earlier books compare to the artist's most recent ones? Read the artist's acceptance speech for the Caldecott. How has the illustrator's style been influenced by her or his concepts of childhood?

3. Find examples of picture books that you think might increase children's sensitivity to well-used language. Look for vivid descriptions, repetition of unusual words or phrases, and figures of speech within the child's experience.

4. Select a group of stories based on a single subject or theme, such as stories about grandparents, "Be yourself" themes, or environmental concerns. Discuss which ones you would use to introduce a unit, which ones you would read aloud as a teacher, and which ones would be appropriate for children's reading.

5. Collect stories written by one author, such as Mem Fox, Eve Bunting, or Cynthia Rylant, but illustrated by different artists. How do the artists' visions affect the moods of the stories?

6. Go to the Children's Literature Database on your Resources CD-ROM. Search the database under one of the subtopics, such as grandparents or humor, discussed in Chapter 5. Cross-reference the titles by interest level and the genre of picture books. Compile a list of picture books that would make a good text set for your classroom.

Web Links

Go to the Online Learning Center at **www.mhhe.com/kiefer9e** to find links to the following children's literature Web sites:

The Art of Illustration

The Artist's Toolkit

Audrey Wood Clubhouse

Caldecott Medal Home Page

Children's Literature Navigator

Chris Van Allsburg

Eric Carle Museum of Picture Book Art

History of Paper and Bookmaking

How a Book Is Made

Molly Bang

Official Eric Carle Web Site

Purple Crayon Site

Telling Stories with Pictures: The Art of Children's Book Illustration

Related Readings

Cianciolo, Patricia. *Picture Books for Children.* 4th ed. Chicago: American Library Association, 1997.

A thorough discussion of the art of picture books, with an annotated listing of all kinds of picture books for children. Particular attention is given to the medium and style of illustrating for each entry as well as the ethnic and racial backgrounds of the characters in the stories.

Cummins, Julie. *Children's Book Illustration and Design.* PBC International, 1997.

This beautiful volume includes biographical information and personal reflections of 56 picture-book illustrators and information about their techniques. The book is a follow-up to the first volume published in 1992 (currently out of print) and includes large full-color reproductions.

Kiefer, Barbara Z. *The Potential of Picturebooks: From Visual Literacy to Aesthetic Understanding.* Columbus, Ohio: Merrill/Prentice-Hall, 1995.

> This book discusses classroom research on children's responses to picture books, provides a history of picture books, looks at some of the modern-day artists who create them, and suggests a theory for evaluating the art of the picture book. The last section provides practical suggestions for classroom activities.

Kingman, Lee, ed. *Newbery and Caldecott Medal Books: 1956–1965.* Boston: Horn Book, 1965.

———. *Newbery and Caldecott Medal Books: 1966–1975.* Boston: Horn Book, 1975.

———. *Newbery and Caldecott Medal Books: 1976–1985.* Boston: Horn Book, 1985.

> These volumes contain the acceptance speeches and biographies of the Newbery and Caldecott Medal winners, reprinted from August issues of Horn Book Magazine. In the most recent volume, Barbara Bader gives a very critical review of the committee's choices. She far prefers some of the Honor Books over the Medal winners and tells you why.

Lewis, David. *Reading Contemporary Picturebooks: Picturing Text.* New York: Routledge/Falmer, 2001.

> In a scholarly view of picture books, this British author offers such topics as how picture books come to possess meaning and a discussion of the grammar of visual design. The discussion is of British books, but most will be familiar to an international audience.

Marantz, Kenneth, and Sylvia Marantz. *Artists of the Page: Interviews with Children's Book Illustrators.* Jefferson, N.C.: McFarland, 1992.

———. *Creating Picturebooks: Interviews with Editors, Art Directors, Reviewers, Booksellers, Professors, Librarians and Showcasers.* Jefferson, N.C.: McFarland, 1997.

> These two volumes offer a complete picture of the world of picture books and those who are involved in every professional way. The Marantzes' depth of experience with libraries, art education, and picture-book criticism allows them to provide penetrating insights.

Nikolajeva, Maria, and Carole Scott. *How Picturebooks Work.* New York: Garland Publishing, 2001.

> This is a thorough and scholarly explication of the picture book from an international perspective. The authors include discussion of theoretical typologies and an analysis of the meaning-making potential of picture books from the work in multimodal literacies of Gunther Kress, Theo Van Leuwen, and others.

Nodelman, Perry. *Words about Pictures: The Narrative Art of Children's Picture Books.* Athens: University of Georgia Press, 1988.

> Nodelman explores the various means by which pictures tell stories. These elements include design, style, code, tension, action, irony, and rhythm. Nodelman draws on a number of aesthetic and literary theories in his discussions. Unfortunately, this significant book contains few pictures.

Salisbury, Martin. *Illustrating Children's Books: Creating Pictures for Publication.* Haupague, N.Y.: Barron's, 2004.

Shulevitz, Uri. *Writing with Pictures: How to Write and Illustrate Children's Books.* New York: Watson-Guptill, 1997.

> These two books by master illustrators/artists provide superb explanations of the illustrator's art. Shulevitz includes information on writing as well as illustrating books. Salisbury provides an extended discussion of types of media. Both authors talk about picture-book conventions, composition, layout, and technical information on reproduction and publishing.

Schwarcz, Joseph H., and Chava Schwarcz. *The Picture Book Comes of Age.* Chicago: American Library Association, 1991.

> This remarkable book reveals knowledge of the creative process, children, artistic and literary expertise, and books from several different countries. A professor at the University of Haifa, Joseph Schwarcz taught children's literature for many years before his death in 1988.

Children's Literature

 Go to the Children's Literature Database on your resources CD-ROM for a searchable listing of these and other children's literature titles.

Aardema, Verna. *Bringing the Rain to Kapiti Plain.* Illustrated by Beatriz Vidal. Dial, 1981.

Ada, Alma Flor. *I Love Saturdays y Domingos.* Illustrated by Elivia Savadier. Atheneum, 2002.

Agee, Jon. *Milo's Hat Trick.* Hyperion, 2001.

———. *Terrific.* Hyperion, 2005.

Ahlberg, Allan. *The Adventures of Bert.* Illustrated by Raymond Briggs. Farrar, 2001.

———. *A Bit More Bert.* Illustrated by Raymond Briggs. Farrar, 2002.

Albert, Burton. *Where Does the Trail Lead?* Illustrated by Brian Pinkney. Simon, 1993.

Aliki. *My Feet.* HarperCollins, 1992.

———. *My Hands.* HarperCollins, 1992.

Allard, Harry. *The Stupids Die.* Illustrated by James Marshall. Houghton, 1981.

———. *The Stupids Have a Ball.* Illustrated by James Marshall. Houghton, 1977.

———. *The Stupids Step Out.* Illustrated by James Marshall. Houghton, 1978.

Allard, Harry, and James Marshall. *Miss Nelson Has a Field Day.* Illustrated by James Marshall. Houghton, 1985.

———. *Miss Nelson Is Missing.* Illustrated by James Marshall. Houghton, 1977.

Altman, Linda Jacobs. *Amelia's Road.* Illustrated by Enrique O. Sanchez. Lee, 1996.

Andersen, Hans Christian. *Thumbelina.* Illustrated by Brian Pinkney. Greenwillow, 2003.

———. *The Ugly Duckling.* Illustrated by Jerry Pinkney. Morrow, 1999.

Andrews, Jan. *Very Last First Time.* Illustrated by Ian Wallace. McElderry, 1985.

Appelbaum, Diana. *Giants in the Land.* Illustrated by Michael McCurdy. Houghton, 1993.

Ardizzone, Edward. *Little Tim and the Brave Sea Captain.* Penguin, 1983.

Asch, Frank. *Mr. Maxwell's Mouse.* Illustrated by Devin Asch. Kids Can, 2004.

Aylesworth, Jim. *My Son John.* Illustrated by David Frampton. Holt, 1994.

———. *The Tale of Tricky Fox: A New England Trickster Tale.* Illustrated by Barbara McClintock. Scholastic, 2001.

Baker, Jeannie. *The Hidden Forest.* Greenwillow, 2000.

———. *Home.* Greenwillow, 2004.

———. *Where the Forest Meets the Sea.* Greenwillow, 1987.

———. *Window.* Greenwillow, 1991.

Baker, Olaf. *Where the Buffaloes Begin.* Illustrated by Stephen Gammell. Warne, 1981.

Bang, Molly. *Goose.* Scholastic, 1996.

———. *The Grey Lady and the Strawberry Snatcher.* Four Winds, 1980.

———. *Nobody Particular: One Woman's Fight to Save the Bays.* Holt, 2001.

———. *The Paper Crane.* Greenwillow, 1985.

———. *One Fall Day.* Greenwillow, 1994.

———. *When Sophie Gets Angry—Really, Really Angry. . . .* Scholastic, 1999.

Barasch, Lynne. *Radio Rescue.* Farrar, 2000.

Barrett, Judi. *Animals Should Definitely Not Act Like People.* Illustrated by Ron Barrett. Atheneum, 1980.

———. *Animals Should Definitely Not Wear Clothing.* Illustrated by Ron Barrett. Atheneum, 1970.

Barron, T. A. *Where Is Granpa?* Illustrated by Chris Soentpiet. Philomel, 2001.

Bateman, Teresa. *April Foolishness.* Illustrated by Nadine Bernard Westcott. Whitman, 2004.

Baylor, Byrd. *Everybody Needs a Rock.* Illustrated by Peter Parnall. Scribner's, 1974.

———. *I'm in Charge of Celebrations.* Illustrated by Peter Parnall. Scribner's, 1986.

———. *The Other Way to Listen.* Illustrated by Peter Parnall. Scribner's, 1978.

———. *The Way to Start a Day.* Illustrated by Peter Parnall. Scribner's, 1978.

———. *Your Own Best Secret Place.* Illustrated by Peter Parnall. Scribner's, 1979.

Beaumont, Karen. *I Ain't Gonna Paint No More.* Illustrated by David Catrow. Harcourt, 2005.

Belton, Sandra. *Beauty, Her Basket.* Illustrated by Cozbi A. Cabrera. Amistad, 2004.

———. *Pictures for Miss Josie.* Illustrated by Benny Andrews. Greenwillow, 2003.

Bemelmans, Ludwig. *Madeline.* Viking, 1962 [1939].

Berger, Barbara Helen. *All the Way to Lhasa: A Tale From Tibet.* Philomel, 2002.

Bernasconi, Pablo. *Captain Arsenio: Inventions and (Mis)Adventures in Flight.* Houghton, 2005.

Bertrand, Lynne. *Granite Baby.* Illustrated by Kevin Hawkes. Farrar, 2005.

Best, Cari. *Are You Going to Be Good?* Illustrated by G. Brian Karas. Farrar, 2005.

———. *Goose's Story.* Illustrated by Holly Meade. Farrar, 2002.

———. *Taxi Taxi.* Illustrated by Dale Gottlieb. Little, 1994.

Bloom, Suzanne. *A Splendid Friend, Indeed.* Boyds Mills, 2005.

Booth, Philip. *Crossing.* Illustrated by Bagram Ibatoulline. Candlewick, 2001.

Bottner, Barbara, and Gerald Kruglik. *Wallace's Lists.* Illustrated by Olaf Landström. HarperCollins, 2004.

Bradby, Maire. *Once Upon a Farm.* Illustrated by Ted Rand. Scholastic, 2002.

Briggs, Raymond. *The Bear.* Random, 1994.

———. *Father Christmas.* Random, 1973.

———. *Jim and the Beanstalk.* Coward-McCann, 1970.

———. *The Snowman.* Random, 1978.

———. *Ug: Boy Genius of the Stone Age.* Knopf, 2002.

Brink, Carol R. *Goody O'Grumpity.* Illustrated by Ashley Wolff. North-South, 1994.

Brown, Marc. *Arthur, It's Only Rock 'n' Roll.* Little, 2002.

———. *Arthur's Eyes.* Little, 1979.

———. *Arthur's Halloween.* Little, 1983.

———. *Arthur's Nose.* Little, 1976.

Brown, Marcia. *Once a Mouse.* Scribner's, 1961.

Brown, Margaret Wise. *Goodnight Moon.* Illustrated by Clement Hurd. Harper, 1975 [1947].

Browne, Anthony. *Changes.* Knopf, 1986.

———. *My Dad.* Farrar, 2001.

———. *My Mom.* Farrar, 2005.

———. *The Piggybook.* Knopf, 1986.

———. *The Tunnel.* Knopf, 1990.

———. *Voices in the Park.* Knopf, 1998.

Buchanan, Ken. *This House Is Made of Mud/Esta casa esta hecha.* Illustrated by Libba Tracy. Rising Moon, 1991.

Buehner, Caralyn. *Superdog: The Heart of a Hero.* Illustrated by Mark Buehner. HarperCollins, 2004.

Bunting, Eve. *Fly Away Home*. Illustrated by Ronald Himler. Clarion, 1991.

———. *Going Home*. Illustrated by David Diaz. HarperCollins, 1996.

———. *How Many Days to America? A Thanksgiving Story*. Illustrated by Beth Peck. Houghton, 1988.

———. *I Am the Mummy Heb-Nefert*. Illustrated by David Christiana. Harcourt, 1997.

———. *One Green Apple*. Illustrated by Ted Rand. Clarion, 2006.

———. *Riding the Tiger*. Illustrated by David Frampton. Clarion, 2001.

———. *Smoky Night*. Illustrated by David Diaz. Harcourt, 1994.

———. *The Wall*. Illustrated by Ronald Himler. Clarion, 1990.

———. *The Wednesday Surprise*. Illustrated by Donald Carrick. Clarion, 1989.

Burton, Virginia Lee. *Katie and the Big Snow*. Houghton, 1943.

———. *The Little House*. Houghton, 1942.

———. *Mike Mulligan and His Steam Shovel*. Houghton, 1939.

Butler, Stephen. *Henny Penny*. Morrow, 1991.

Caines, Jeannette. *Just Us Women*. Illustrated by Pat Cummings. Harper, 1982.

Calmenson, Stephanie. *The Frog Principal*. Illustrated by Denise Brunkus. Scholastic, 2002.

———. *The Principal's New Clothes*. Illustrated by Denise Brunkus. Scholastic, 1989.

Carle, Eric. *Mister Seahorse*. Philomel, 2004.

———. *The Very Hungry Caterpillar*. World, 1968.

Carlstrom, Nancy White. *Blow Me a Kiss, Miss Lilly*. Illustrated by Amy Schwartz. HarperCollins, 1990.

Carrick, Carol. *The Accident*. Illustrated by Donald Carrick. Clarion, 1976.

Carter, Polly. *Harriet Tubman*. Illustrated by Brian Pinkney. Silver Press, 1992.

Caseley, Judith. *Dear Annie*. Greenwillow, 1991.

———. *Mama Coming and Going*. Greenwillow, 1994.

Cassels, Jean. *The Mysterious Collection of Dr. David Harleyson*. Walker, 2004.

Cech, Randy. *One Dark and Dreadful Night*. Holt, 2004.

Cendrars, Blaise. *Shadow*. Illustrated by Marcia Brown. Scribner's, 1982.

Chen, Chih-Yuan. *Guji Guji*. Kane/Miller, 2004.

Cheng, Andrea. *Grandfather Counts*. Illustrated by Ange Zhang. Lee, 2003.

Cherry, Lynne. *A River Ran Wild*. Gulliver/Harcourt, 1992.

Child, Lauren. *Clarice Bean, Guess Who's Babysitting?* Candlewick, 2001.

———. *Clarice Bean, That's Me*. Candlewick, 1999.

———. *Hubert Horatio Bartle Bobton-Trent*. Candlewick, 2005.

———. *What Planet Are You From, Clarice Bean?* Candlewick, 2002.

Christelow, Eileen. *The Great Pig Escape*. Clarion, 2001.

———. *The Great Pig Search*. Clarion, 2001.

———. *Where's the Big Bad Wolf?* Clarion, 2002.

Clark, Ann Nolan. *In My Mother's House*. Illustrated by Velino Herrera. Viking, 1991 [1941].

Coerr, Eleanor. *Sadako*. Illustrated by Ed Young. Putnam, 1993.

———. *Sadako and the Thousand Paper Cranes*. Illustrated by Ron Himler. Putnam, 1977.

Cohen, Miriam. *Best Friends*. Illustrated by Lillian Hoban. Macmillan, 1971.

———. *When Will I Read?* Illustrated by Lillian Hoban. Greenwillow, 1977.

———. *Will I Have a Friend?* Illustrated by Lillian Hoban. Macmillan, 1967.

Cole, Henry. *I Took a Walk*. Greenwillow, 1998.

———. *Jack's Garden*. Greenwillow, 1995.

———. *On the Way to the Beach*. Greenwillow, 2003.

Cole, Sheila. *When the Tide Is Low*. Illustrated by Virginia Wright-Frierson. Lothrop, 1985.

Coleman, Evelyn. *To Be a Drum*. Illustrated by Aminah Brenda Lynne Robinson. Walker, 2000.

Collard, Sneed B., III. *One Night in the Coral Sea*. Illustrated by Robin Brickman. Charlesbridge, 2005.

Cooney, Barbara. *Chanticleer and the Fox*. Crowell, 1958.

———. *Hattie and the Wild Waves*. Viking, 1990.

———. *Island Boy*. Viking, 1988.

———. *Miss Rumphius*. Viking, 1982.

Cooper, Floyd. *Coming Home: From the Life of Langston Hughes*. Philomel, 1994.

Cronin, Doreen. *Click, Clack, Moo: Cows That Type*. Illustrated by Betsy Lewin. Simon, 2000.

———. *Diary of a Spider*. Illustrated by Harry Bliss. HarperCollins, 2005.

———. *Diary of a Worm*. Illustrated by Harry Bliss. HarperCollins, 2005.

———. *Duck for President*. Illustrated by Betsy Lewin, Simon, 2004.

———. *Giggle, Giggle, Quack*. Illustrated by Betsy Lewin. Simon, 2002.

———. *Wiggle*. Illustrated by Scott Menchin. Atheneum, 2005.

Cummins, Julie. *Country Kid, City Kid*. Illustrated by Ted Rand. Holt, 2002.

Cumpiano, Ina. *Quinto's Neighborhood/El Vecindario de Quinto*. Illustrated by José Ramírez. Children's, 2005.

Currie, Lynn. *Rushmore*. Scholastic, 1999.

Cutler, Jane. *The Birthday Doll*. Illustrated by Hiroe Nakata. Farrar, 2004.

Davidson, Rebecca Platt. *The Boy Who Writes Poems and Plays*. Illustrated by Anita Lobel. Greenwillow, 2003.

de Brunhoff, Jean. *The Story of Babar*. Random, 1960.

Delaney, Michael. *Birdbrain Amos*. Putnam, 2002.

DePaola, Tomie. *First One Step, Then Another*. Putnam, 2005.

———. *Nana Upstairs and Nana Downstairs*. Penguin, 1978.

———. *Now One Foot, Now the Other*. Putnam, 1981.

———. *Stage Struck*. Putnam, 2005.

———. *Strega Nona*. Prentice-Hall, 1975.

———. *Tom*. Putnam, 1993.

———. *Tomie dePaola's Mother Goose*. Putnam, 1985.

———. *Watch Out for the Chicken Feet in Your Soup*. Prentice-Hall, 1974.

de Regniers, Beatrice Schenk. *May I Bring a Friend?* Illustrated by Beni Montresor. Atheneum, 1964.

DiSalvo-Ryan, DyAnne. *Uncle Willie and the Soup Kitchen*. Morrow, 1991.

Dorros, Arthur. *Abuela*. Illustrated by Elisa Kleven. Dutton, 1991.

———. *Isla*. Illustrated by Elisa Kleven. Dutton, 1995.

Doyle, Malachy. *Cow*. Illustrated by Angelo Rinaldi. McElderry, 2002.

Duvoisin, Roger. *Petunia*. Knopf, 1950.

Edwards, Pamela. *Dinorella: A Prehistoric Fairytale*. Illustrated by Henry Cole. Hyperion, 1997.

Ehlert, Lois. *Cukoo=Cuco: A Mexican Folktale=Un Cuento Folklorico Mexicano*. Harcourt, 1997.

———. *Fish Eyes: A Book You Can Count On*. Harcourt, 1990.

———. *Hands*. Harcourt, 1997.

———. *Leaf Man*. Harcourt, 2005.

English, Karen. *The Baby on the Way*. Illustrated by Sean Qualls. Farrar, 2005.

———. *Hot Day on Abbott Avenue*. Illustrated by Javaka Steptoe. Clarion, 2004.

Eriksson, Eva. *A Crash Course for Molly*. Translated by Elisabeth Kallick Dyssegaard. Farrar, 2005.

Falconer, Ian. *Olivia*. Atheneum, 2000.

———. *Olivia Saves the Circus*. Atheneum, 2001.

Fierstein, Harvey. *The Sissy Duckling*. Illustrated by Henry Cole. Simon, 2002.

Fleischman, Paul. *Weslandia*. Illustrated by Kevin Hawkes. Candlewick, 1999.

Fleming, Denise. *Barnyard Banter*. Holt, 1994.

———. *Mama Cat Has Three Kittens*. Holt, 1998.

———. *Pumpkin Eye*. Holt, 2001.

Flournoy, Valerie. *The Patchwork Quilt*. Illustrated by Jerry Pinkney. Dial, 1985.

Fox, Mem. *Koala Lou*. Illustrated by Pamela Lofts. Harcourt, 1989.

———. *Night Noises*. Illustrated by Terry Denton. Harcourt, 1989.

———. *Possum Magic*. Illustrated by Julie Vivas. Harcourt, 1990.

———. *Wilfrid Gordon McDonald Partridge*. Illustrated by Julie Vivas. Kane/Miller, 1985.

Fraustino, Lisa Rowe. *The Hickory Chair*. Illustrated by Benny Andrews. Scholastic, 2001.

Frazier, Craig. *Stanley Mows the Lawn*. Chronicle, 2005.

Freeman, Don. *Corduroy*. Viking, 1968.

———. *Dandelion*. Viking, 1964.

Funke, Cornelia. *The Princess Knight*. Translated by Anthea Bell. Illustrated by Kerstin Meyer. Scholastic, 2004.

Gág, Wanda. *Millions of Cats*. Coward-McCann, 1928.

Gallaz, Christophe, and Roberto Innocenti. *Rose Blanche*. Illustrated by Roberto Innocenti. Harcourt, 1996.

Garza, Carmen Lomas. *Family Pictures: Cuadros de Familia*. Children's, 1990.

Gauch, Patricia Lee. *Presenting Tanya, Ugly Duckling*. Illustrated by Satomi Ichikawa. Philomel, 1999.

Gelman, Rita Golden. *Doodler Doodling*. Illustrated by Paul O. Zelinsky. Greenwillow, 2003.

Geisert, Arthur. *Lights Out*. Houghton, 2005.

———. *Pigs from A to Z*. Houghton, 1986.

Geisert, Bonnie, and Arthur Geisert. *Desert Town*. Houghton, 2001.

———. *Haystack*. Houghton, 1998.

———. *Mountain Town*. Houghton, 2000.

———. *Prairie Town*. Houghton, 1998.

———. *River Town*. Houghton, 1998.

Gerrard, Roy. *Wagons West!* Farrar, 2001.

Goble, Paul. *The Girl Who Loved Wild Horses*. Bradbury, 1978.

———. *Mystic Horses*. HarperCollins, 2003.

———. *Storm Maker's Tipi*. Jackson/Atheneum, 2002.

Godwin, Laura. *Little White Dog*. Illustrated by Dan Yaccarino. Hyperion, 1998.

Gower, Catherine, and He Zhihong. *Long-Long's New Year*. Tuttle, 2005.

Graham, Bob. *Benny: An Adventure Story*. Candlewick, 1999.

———. *Jethro Byrd, Fairy Child*. Candlewick, 2002.

———. *"Let's Get a Pup!" said Kate*. Candlewick, 2001.

———. *Oscar's Half Birthday*. Candlewick, 2005.

Gramatky, Hardie. *Little Toot*. Putnam, 1939.

Gray, Libba Moore. *My Mama Had a Dancing Heart*. Illustrated by Raúl Colón. Orchard, 1995.

Gray, Nigel. *A Country Far Away*. Illustrated by Philippe Dupasquier. Orchard, 1989.

Greenfield, Eloise. *She Come Bringing Me That Little Baby Girl*. Illustrated by John Steptoe. Lippincott, 1974.

Gretz, Susanna. *Riley and Rose in the Picture*. Candlewick, 2005.

Grey, Mini. *Traction Man Is Here!* Knopf, 2005.

Grifalconi, Ann. *The Village That Vanished*. Illustrated by Kadir Nelson. Dial, 2002.

Grimes, Nikki. *At Jerusalem's Gate*. Illustrated by David Frampton. Eerdmans, 2005.

———. *Danitra Brown Leaves Town*. Illustrated by Floyd Cooper. HarperCollins, 2005.

Grimm brothers. *Hansel and Gretel*. Retold by Rika Lesser. Illustrated by Paul Zelinsky. Dodd, 1984.

———. *Rumpelstiltskin*. Retold and illustrated by Paul O. Zelinsky. Dutton, 1986.

———. *Snow White*. Translated by Paul Heins. Illustrated by Trina Schart Hyman. Little, 1974.

———. *Snow White and the Seven Dwarfs*. Translated by Randall Jarrell. Illustrated by Nancy Ekholm Burkert. Farrar, 1972.

Grobler, Piet, and other illustrators. *The Rights of a Child*. Kwela Books (South Africa), 2004.

Guthrie, Woody. *This Land Is Your Land*. Illustrated by Kathie Jakobsen. Little, 1998.

Hall, Donald. *Lucy's Christmas*. Illustrated by Michael McCurdy. Browndeer/Harcourt, 1994.

———. *Lucy's Summer*. Illustrated by Michael McCurdy. Browndeer/Harcourt, 1995.

———. *Ox-Cart Man*. Illustrated by Barbara Cooney. Viking, 1979.

Hamilton, Virginia. *Her Stories: African American Folktales, Fairy Tales and True Tales*. Illustrated by Leo Dillon and Diane Dillon. Scholastic, 1995.

Harrington, Janice. *Going North*. Illustrated by Jerome Lagarrigue. Farrar, 2004.

Hartfield, Claire. *Me and Uncle Romie*. Illustrated by Jerome Lagarrigue. Dial, 2002.

Havill, Juanita. *Jamaica and the Substitute Teacher*. Illustrated by Anne Sibley O'Brien. Houghton, 1999.

Hawkins, Colin, and Jacqui Hawkins. *Fairytale News*. Candlewick, 2004.

Heide, Florence Parry. *Some Things Are Scary*. Illustrated by Jules Feiffer. Candlewick, 2000.

Heide, Florence Parry, and Judith Heide Gilliland. *The Day of Ahmed's Secret*. Illustrated by Ted Lewin. Lothrop, 1990.

———. *Sami and the Time of the Troubles*. Illustrated by Ted Lewin. Clarion, 1992.

Henkes, Kevin. *The Biggest Boy*. Illustrated by Nancy Tafuri. Greenwillow, 1995.

———. *Circle Dogs*. Illustrated by Dan Yaccarino. Greenwillow, 1998.

———. *Chester's Way*. Greenwillow, 1988.

———. *Chrysanthemum*. Greenwillow, 1991.

———. *Julius, Baby of the World*. Greenwillow, 1990.

———. *Kitten's First Full Moon*. Greenwillow, 2004.

———. *Lilly's Big Day*. Greenwillow, 2006.

———. *Lilly's Purple Plastic Purse*. Greenwillow, 1996.

———. *Owen*. Greenwillow, 1993.

Hesse, Karen. *Come On, Rain!* Illustrated by Jon J. Muth. Scholastic, 1999.

———. *The Stone Lamp*. Illustrated by Brian Pinkney. Hyperion, 2003.

Hest, Amy. *Mr. George Baker*. Illustrated by Jon J. Muth. Candlewick, 2005.

Hicks, Barbara Jean. *Jitterbug Jam: A Monster Tale*. Illustrated by Alexis Deacon. Farrar, 2005.

Hill, Elizabeth Starr. *Evan's Corner*. Illustrated by Sandra Speidel. Viking, 1991 [1967].

Hoban, Russell. *Bedtime for Frances*. Illustrated by Garth Williams. Harper, 1960.

Hoban, Tana. *Shadows and Reflections*. Greenwillow, 1990.

Hoberman, Mary Ann. *There Once Was a Man Named Michael Finnegan*. Illustrated by Nadine Bernard Westcott. Little, 2001.

Hodges, Margaret. *Moses*. Illustrated by Mike Wimmer. Harcourt, 2006.

———. *Saint George and the Dragon*. Illustrated by Trina Schart Hyman. Little, 1984.

Hoffman, Mary. *The Color of Home*. Illustrated by Karin Littlewood. Fogelman, 2002.

Holwitz, Peter. *Scribbleville*. Philomel, 2005.

hooks, bell. *Skin Again*. Illustrated by Chris Raschka. Hyperion, 2004.

Hooks, William H. *The Ballad of Belle Dorcas*. Illustrated by Brian Pinkney. Knopf, 1990.

Houston, Gloria. *My Great-Aunt Arizona*. Illustrated by Susan Condie Lamb. HarperCollins, 1992.

Howard, Arthur. *Hoodwinked*. Harcourt, 2001.

Howard, Elizabeth Fitzgerald. *Aunt Flossie's Hats (and Crab Cakes Later)*. Illustrated by James Ransome. Houghton, 1991.

Howe, James. *Horace and Morris but Mostly Dolores*. Illustrated by Amy Walrod. Atheneum, 1999.

Hughes, Langston. *The Dream Keeper*. Illustrated by Brian Pinkney. Knopf, 1994.

Hutchins, Pat. *Good-Night, Owl!* Macmillan, 1972.

———. *It's My Birthday!* Greenwillow, 1999.

———. *Rosie's Walk*. Macmillan, 1968.

———. *There's Only One of Me*. Greenwillow, 2003.

———. *The Very Worst Monster*. Greenwillow, 1985.

———. *We're Going on a Picnic!* Greenwillow, 2002.

———. *What Game Shall We Play?* Greenwillow, 1990.

Hyman, Trina Schart. *Little Red Riding Hood*. Holiday, 1983.

Isaacs, Anne. *Swamp Angel*. Illustrated by Paul O. Zelinsky. Dutton, 1994.

Isadora, Rachel. *At the Crossroads*. Greenwillow, 1991.

———. *Max*. Macmillan, 1976.

Jakobsen, Kathy. *My New York*. Little, 1993.

James, Simon. *Baby Brains*. Candlewick, 2004.

———. *Baby Brains Superstar*. Candlewick, 2004.

———. *The Birdwatchers*. Candlewick, 2002.

Johnson, Angela. *Tell Me a Story, Mama*. Illustrated by David Soman. Orchard, 1989.

Johnson, D. B. *Henry Builds a Cabin*. Houghton, 2002.

———. *Henry Climbs a Mountain*. Houghton, 2003.

———. *Henry Hikes to Fitchburg*. Houghton, 2000.

———. *Henry Takes a Trip*. Houghton, 2003.

———. *Henry Works*. Houghton, 2004.

Johnson, Paul Brett, and Celeste Lewis. *Lost*. HarperCollins, 1996.

Johnson-Davies, Denys. *Goha, the Wise Fool*. Illustrated by Hany El Saed Ahmed and Hag Hamdy Mohamed Fattouh. Philomel, 2005.

Johnston, Tony. *Bigfoot Cinderrrrella*. Illustrated by James Warhola. Putnam, 1998.

———. *The Quilt Story*. Illustrated by Tomie dePaola. Putnam, 1985.

———. *Sunsets of the West*. Illustrated by Ted Lewin. Philomel, 2002.

———. *That Summer*. Illustrated by Barry Moser. Harcourt, 2002.

———. *The Worm Family*. Illustrated by Stacy Innert. Harcourt, 2004.

Jonas, Ann. *Round Trip.* Greenwillow, 1983.

Joseph, Lynn. *A Wave in Her Pocket: Stories from Trinidad.* Illustrated by Brian Pinkney. Clarion, 1991.

Joyce, William. *A Day with Wilbur Robinson.* HarperCollins, 1990.

———. *Dinosaur Bob and His Adventures with the Family Lazardo.* Harper, 1988.

———. *George Shrinks.* Harper, 1985.

———. *Rolie Polie Olie.* HarperCollins, 1999.

Jukes, Mavis. *Like Jake and Me.* Illustrated by Lloyd Bloom. Knopf, 1984.

Kalman, Maira. *Fireboat: The Heroic Adventures of the* John J. Harvey. Putnam, 2002.

———. *Max in Hollywood.* Viking, 1995.

———. *Max Makes a Million.* Viking, 1990.

———. *Ooh La La, Max in Love.* Viking, 1991.

Karas, G. Brian. *Atlantic.* Putnam, 2002.

———. *On Earth.* Putnam, 2005.

Keats, Ezra Jack. *Goggles.* Macmillan, 1969.

———. *Hi, Cat!* Macmillan, 1970.

———. *A Letter to Amy.* Harper, 1968.

———. *Pet Show!* Macmillan, 1972.

———. *Peter's Chair.* Harper, 1967.

———. *The Snowy Day.* Viking, 1962.

———. *Whistle for Willie.* Viking, 1964.

Keller, Holly. *Farfallina and Marcel.* Greenwillow, 2002.

Kellogg, Steven. *Can I Keep Him?* Dial, 1971.

———. *Chicken Little.* Morrow, 1985.

———. *A Penguin Pup for Pinkerton.* Dial, 2001.

———. *Pinkerton, Behave!* Dial, 1979.

———. *Prehistoric Pinkerton.* Dial, 1987.

———. *A Rose for Pinkerton.* Dial, 1981.

Kelly, John, and Cathy Tincknell. *The Mystery of Eatum Hall.* Candlewick, 2004.

Kesselman, Wendy. *Emma.* Illustrated by Barbara Cooney. Doubleday, 1980.

Kipling, Rudyard. *The Elephant's Child.* Illustrated by Lorinda B. Cauley. Harcourt, 1983.

———. *The Elephant's Child.* Illustrated by Jan Mogensen. Crocodile/Interlink, 1989.

———. *How the Camel Got His Hump.* Illustrated by Quentin Blake. Bedrick, 1985.

———. *How the Camel Got His Hump.* Illustrated by Krystyna Turska. Warne, 1988.

———. *How the Leopard Got His Spots.* Illustrated by Caroline Ebborn. Bedrick, 1986.

———. *Just So Stories.* Illustrated by David Frampton. HarperCollins, 1991 [1983].

Kirk, David. *Nova's Ark.* Scholastic, 1999.

Kitchen, Bert. *Animal Alphabet.* Dial, 1984.

Kraus, Robert. *Leo the Late Bloomer.* Illustrated by José Aruego. Crowell, 1971.

———. *Milton the Early Riser.* Illustrated by José Aruego and Ariane Dewey. Windmill, 1972.

———. *Owliver.* Illustrated by José Aruego and Ariane Dewey. Windmill, 1974.

Krauss, Ruth. *Bears.* Illustrated by Maurice Sendak. HarperCollins, 2005.

———. *A Hole Is to Dig.* Illustrated by Maurice Sendak. Harper, 1952.

———. *A Very Special House.* Illustrated by Maurice Sendak. Harper, 1953.

Krishnaswami, Uma. *The Closet Ghosts.* Illustrated by Shiraaz Bhabba. Children's, 2006.

Kushner, Tony. *Brundibar.* Illustrated by Maurice Sendak. Farrar, 2003.

Laínez, René Colato. *Playing Loteria/El juego deloa lotería.* Illustrated by Jill Arena. Luna Rising, 2005.

LaRochelle, David. *The Best Pet of All.* Illustrated by Hanako Wakiyama. Dutton, 2004.

Lasky, Kathryn. *The Emperor's Old Clothes.* Illustrated by David Catrow. Harcourt, 1999.

———. *Pond Year.* Illustrated by Mike Bostock. Candlewick, 1995.

Lattimore, Deborah Nourse. *The Sailor Who Captured the Sea.* HarperCollins, 1991.

———. *Why There Is No Arguing in Heaven.* Harper, 1989.

Lauber, Patricia. *The News about Dinosaurs.* Bradbury, 1989.

Lauture, Denizé. *Running the Road to ABC.* Illustrated by Reynold Ruffins. Simon, 1996.

Leaf, Munro. *The Story of Ferdinand.* Illustrated by Robert Lawson. Viking, 1936.

Lessac, Frané. *Caribbean Canvas.* Lippincott, 1989.

———. *My Little Island.* Tambourine, 1985.

Lester, Alison. *Ernie Dances to the Didgeridoo.* Houghton, 2001.

Lester, Julius. *What a Truly Cool World.* Illustrated by Joe Cepeda. Scholastic, 1999.

———. *Why Heaven Is Far Away.* Illustrated by Joe Cepeda. Scholastic, 2002.

Levinson, Riki. *Watch the Stars Come Out.* Illustrated by Diane Goode. Dutton, 1985.

Lewin, Ted, and Betsy Lewin. *Top to Bottom, Down Under.* HarperCollins, 2005.

Lin, Grace. *Kite Flying.* Knopf, 2002.

Lindbergh, Reeve. *Johnny Appleseed.* Illustrated by Kathy Jakobsen. Little, 1990.

Lionni, Leo. *Alexander and the Wind-Up Mouse.* Pantheon, 1969.

———. *An Extraordinary Egg.* Knopf, 1994.

———. *Fish Is Fish.* Pantheon, 1970.

———. *Frederick.* Pantheon, 1967.

———. *Little Blue and Little Yellow.* Astor-Honor, 1959.

———. *Matthew's Dream.* Knopf, 1991.

Livingston, Myra Cohn. *I Never Told and Other Poems.* Cover art by Brian Pinkney. McElderry, 1992.

———. *A Time to Talk: Poems of Friendship.* Illustrated by Brian Pinkney. McElderry, 1992.

Lobel, Arnold. *Days with Frog and Toad*. Harper, 1979.

———. *Fables*. Harper, 1980.

———. *Frog and Toad All Year*. Harper, 1976.

———. *Frog and Toad Are Friends*. Harper, 1970.

———. *Frog and Toad Together*. Harper, 1972.

Locker, Thomas. *Family Farm*. Dial, 1988.

———. *The Mare on the Hill*. Dial, 1985.

———. *Sky Tree*. With Candace Christiansen. HarperCollins, 1995.

———. *Where the River Begins*. Dial, 1984.

———. *The Young Artist*. Dial, 1989.

London, Jonathan. *Sun Dance, Water Dance*. Illustrated by Greg Couch. Dutton, 2001.

Look, Lenore. *Henry's First Moon Birthday*. Illustrated by Yumi Heo. Atheneum, 2001.

Lord, Janet. *Here Comes Grandma!* Illustrated by Julie Paschkis. Holt, 2005.

Lowell, Susan. *Dusty Locks and the Three Bears*. Illustrated by Randy Cecil. Holt, 2001.

Lunge-Larsen, Lise. *The Hidden Folk: Stories of Dwarves, Selkies and Other Secret Beings*. Illustrated by Beth Krommes. Houghton, 2004.

Lyon, George Ella. *Book*. Illustrated by Peter Catalanoto. DK Ink, 1999.

Macaulay, David. *Black and White*. Houghton, 1990.

MacDonald, Megan. *The Bone Keeper*. Illustrated by G. Brian Karas. DK Ink, 1999.

MacLachlan, Patricia. *All the Places to Love*. Illustrated by Mike Wimmer. HarperCollins, 1994.

———. *Mama One, Mama Two*. Illustrated by Ruth Lercher Bornstein. Harper, 1982.

———. *Through Grandpa's Eyes*. Illustrated by Deborah Ray. Harper, 1979.

———. *What You Know First*. Illustrated by Barry Moser. HarperCollins, 1995.

Madrigal, Antonio Hernández. *Blanca's Feather*. Illustrated by Gerrardo Suzán. Rising Moon/Northland, 2000.

Mahy, Margaret. *The Great White Man-Eating Shark*. Illustrated by Jonathan Allen. Dial, 1990.

———. *The Rattlebang Picnic*. Illustrated by Steven Kellogg. Dial, 1994.

Mak, Kam. *My Chinatown: One Year in Poems*. HarperCollins, 2002.

Manzano, Sonia. *No Dogs Allowed*. Illustrated by Jon J. Muth. Simon, 2005.

Marshall, James. *George and Martha: The Complete Stories of Two Best Friends*. Houghton, 1997.

Martin, Bill, Jr., and John Archambault. *Knots on a Counting Rope*. Illustrated by Ted Rand. Holt, 1987.

Martin, David. *Five Little Piggies*. Illustrated by Susan Meddaugh. Candlewick, 1998.

Martin, Jacqueline Briggs. *The Lamp, The Ice, and the Boat Called Fish: Based on a True Story*. Illustrated by Beth Krommes. Houghton, 2001.

———. *Snowflake Bentley*. Illustrated by Mary Azarian. Houghton, 1998.

Martin, Rafe. *Foolish Rabbit's Big Mistake*. Illustrated by Ed Young. Putnam, 1985.

Maruki, Toshi. *Hiroshima No Pika* (The Flash of Hiroshima). Lothrop, 1980.

Marzollo, Jean. *Happy Birthday, Martin Luther King*. Illustrated by Brian Pinkney. Scholastic, 1993.

Mathers, Petra. *Lottie's New Friend*. Simon, 1999.

Mayer, Mercer. *There's a Nightmare in My Closet*. Dial, 1968.

McCarty, Peter. *Hondo and Fabian*. Holt, 2002.

McClintock, Barbara. *Dahlia*. Farrar, 2002.

McCloskey, Robert. *Blueberries for Sal*. Viking, 1963.

———. *Make Way for Ducklings*. Viking, 1941.

———. *One Morning in Maine*. Viking, 1952.

———. *Time of Wonder*. Viking, 1957.

McCurdy, Michael. *An Algonquian Year. The Year According to the Full Moon*. Houghton, 2000.

McGaughrean, Geraldine. *My Grandmother's Clock*. Illustrated by Stephen Lambert. Clarion, 2002.

McKee, David. *Elmer*. Lothrop, 1989 [1968].

McKissack, Patricia C. *The Dark Thirty: Southern Tales of the Supernatural*. Illustrated by Brian Pinkney. Knopf, 1992.

———. *Goin' Someplace Special*. Illustrated by Jerry Pinkney. Simon, 2001.

McKissack, Patricia, and Onawumi Jean Moss. *Precious and the Boo Hag*. Illustrated by Kyrsten Brooker. Atheneum, 2005.

McMullan, Kate. *I Stink!* Illustrated by Jim McMullan. Cotler/HarperCollins, 2002.

McMullen, Nigel. *Not Me!* Dutton, 2001.

McPhail, David. *The Bear's Toothache*. Little, 1972.

———. *Pig Pig Grows Up*. Dutton, 1980.

Meddaugh, Susan. *Cinderella's Rat*. Houghton, 2002.

———. *Martha Blah Blah*. Houghton, 1998.

———. *Martha Calling*. Houghton, 1994.

———. *Martha and Skits*. Houghton, 2005.

———. *Martha Speaks*. Houghton, 1992.

———. *Martha Walks the Dog*. Houghton, 1998.

———. *Perfectly Martha*. Houghton, 2004.

———. *The Witch's Walking Stick*. Houghton, 2005.

Medina, Tony. *DeShawn Days*. Illustrated by R. Gregory Christie. Lee, 2001.

Melmed, Laura Kraus. *Capital! Washington D.C. from A to Z*. Illustrated by Frané Lessac. HarperCollins, 2003.

Meyers, Christopher. *Black Cat*. Scholastic, 1999.

Miles, Miska. *Annie and the Old One*. Illustrated by Peter Parnall. Little, 1971.

Millman, Isaac. *Moses Goes to a Concert*. Farrar, 1998.

Mitchell, Margaree King. *Uncle Jed's Barbershop*. Illustrated by James Ransome. Simon, 1993.

Mitchell, Marianne. *Joe Cinders*. Illustrated by Bryan Langdo. Holt, 2002.

Mollel, Tololwa. *My Rows and Piles of Coins*. Illustrated by E. B. Lewis. Clarion, 1999.

Mora, Pat. *Dona Flor: A Tall Tale about a Woman with a Big Heart*. Illustrated by Raúl Colón. Knopf, 2005.

———. *Pablo's Tree*. Illustrated by Cecily Lang. Macmillan, 1994.

———. *The Song of Frances and the Animals*. Illustrated by David Frampton. Eerdmans, 2005.

Musgrove, Margaret. *Ashanti to Zulu: African Traditions*. Illustrated by Leo Dillon and Diane Dillon. Dial, 1976.

Muth, Jon J. *Stone Soup*. Scholastic, 2003.

———. *Zen Shorts*. Scholastic, 2005.

Namioka, Lensey. *The Loyal Cat*. Illustrated by Aki Sogabe. Browndeer/Harcourt, 1995.

Napoli, Donna Jo. *Flamingo Dream*. Illustrated by Cathie Felsted. Greenwillow, 2002.

Newman, Leslea. *The Best Cat in the World*. Illustrated by Ron Himler. Eerdmans, 2004.

Noble, Trinka H. *The Day Jimmy's Boa Ate the Wash*. Illustrated by Steven Kellogg. Dial, 1980.

———. *Jimmy's Boa Bounces Back*. Illustrated by Steven Kellogg. Dial, 1984.

———. *Jimmy's Boa and the Bungee Jump Slam Dunk*. Illustrated by Steven Kellogg. Dial, 2003.

Nolen, Jerdine. *Hewitt Anderson's Great Big Life*. Illustrated by Kadir Nelson. Simon, 2005.

———. *Raising Dragons*. Illustrated by Elise Primavera. Harcourt, 1998.

Nye, Naomi Shihab. *Sitti's Secret*. Illustrated by Nancy Carpenter. Four Winds, 1994.

Ó. Flatharta, Antoine. *Hurry and the Monarch*. Illustrated by Meilo So. Knopf, 2005.

O'Connor, George. *Kapow!* Simon, 2004.

———. *Ker-splash!* Simon, 2005.

O'Malley, Kevin. *Captain Raptor and the Moon Mystery*. Illustrated by Patrick O'Brien. Walker, 2005.

O'Neill, Alexis. *Estela's Swap*. Illustrated by Enrique O. Sanchez. Lee, 2002.

Ormerod, Jan. *Who's Whose?* Lothrop, 1998.

Osafsky, Audrey. *The Dreamcatcher*. Illustrated by Ed Young. Orchard, 1992.

Osborne, Mary Pope. *The Brave Little Seamstress*. Illustrated by Giselle Potter. Atheneum, 2002.

———. *Kate and the Beanstalk*. Illustrated by Giselle Potter. Atheneum, 2000.

Ottley, Matt. *Luke's Way of Looking*. Kane/Miller, 2001.

———. *What Faust Saw*. Dutton, 1996.

Pak, Soyung. *Dear Juno*. Illustrated by Susan Kathleen Hartung. Viking, 1999.

Palatini, Marge. *Three French Hens*. Illustrated by Richard Egielski. Hyperion, 2005.

———. *Three Silly Billies*. Illustrated by Barry Moser. Simon, 2005.

———. *The Web Files*. Illustrated by Richard Egielski. Hyperion, 2001.

Partridge, Elizabeth. *Kogi's Mysterious Journey*. Illustrated by Aki Sogabe. Dutton, 2003.

———. *Whistling*. Illustrated by Anna Grossnickle Hines. Greenwillow, 2003.

Park, Linda Sue. *Bee-bim Bop!* Illustrated by Ho Baek Lee. Clarion, 2005.

Paxton, Tom. *Engelbert the Elephant*. Illustrated by Steven Kellogg. Morrow, 1995.

Perdomo, Willie. *Visiting Langston*. Illustrated by Bryan Collier. Holt, 2002.

Pérez, Amada Irma. *My Very Own Room/Mi Propio Cuartito*. Illustrated by Maya Christina Gonzalez. Children's, 2000.

Perkins, Lynne Rae. *The Broken Cat*. Greenwillow, 2002.

Perrault, Charles. *Cinderella*. Illustrated by Marcia Brown. Scribner's, 1954.

———. *Puss in Boots*. Illustrated by Fred Marcellino. Farrar, 1990.

Pham, LeUyen. *Big Sister, Little Sister*. Hyperion, 2005.

Pilkey, Dav. *Dog Breath: The Horrible Trouble with Hally Tosis*. Blue Sky, 1994.

Pinkney, Andrea Davis. *Alvin Ailey*. Illustrated by Brian Pinkney. Hyperion, 1993.

———. *Bill Pickett: Rodeo Riding Cowboy*. Illustrated by Brian Pinkney. Harcourt, 1996.

———. *Dear Benjamin Banneker*. Illustrated by Brian Pinkney. Harcourt, 1994.

———. *Duke Ellington, The Piano Prince and His Orchestra*. Illustrated by Brian Pinkney. Hyperion, 1998.

———. *Ella Fitzgerald*. Illustrated by Brian Pinkney. Harcourt, 2001.

———. *I Smell Honey*. Illustrated by Brian Pinkney. Harcourt, 1997.

———. *Mim's Christmas Jam*. Illustrated by Brian Pinkney. Harcourt, 2001.

———. *Peggony-Po: A Whale of a Tale*. Illustrated by Brian Pinkney. Hyperion/Jump at the Sun, 2006.

———. *Pretty Brown Face*. Illustrated by Brian Pinkney. Harcourt, 1997.

———. *Seven Candles for Kwanzaa*. Illustrated by Brian Pinkney. Dial, 1993.

———. *Shake Shake Shake*. Illustrated by Brian Pinkney. Harcourt, 1997.

———. *Sleeping Cutie*. Illustrated by Brian Pinkney. Harcourt, 2005.

———. *Watch Me Dance*. Illustrated by Brian Pinkney. Harcourt, 1997.

Pinkney, Brian. *The Adventures of Sparrowboy*. Simon, 1997.

———. *Benjamin and the Shrinking Book*. HarperCollins, 2003.

———. *Cosmo and the Robot*. Greenwillow, 2000.

———. *Jojo's Flying Side Kick*. Simon, 1995.

———. *Max Found Two Sticks*. Simon, 1994.

Piper, Watty. *The Little Engine That Could*. Illustrated by George Hauman and Doris Hauman. Platt & Munk, 1954 [1930].

———. *The Little Engine That Could*. Illustrated by Loren Long. Philomel, 2005 [1930].

Polacco, Patricia. *Just Plain Fancy*. Bantam/Doubleday, 1990.

———. *The Keeping Quilt*. Simon, 1988.

———. *Pink and Say*. Philomel, 1994.

———. *Thunder Cake*. Philomel, 1990.

Pomerantz, Charlotte. *The Chalk Doll*. Illustrated by Frané Lessac. Lippincott, 1989.

Potter, Beatrix. *The Tale of Peter Rabbit*. Warne, 1902.

Price, Leontyne. *Aïda*. Illustrated by Leo Dillon and Diane Dillon. Harcourt, 1990.

Provensen, Alice, and Martin Provensen. *The Glorious Flight: Across the Channel with Louis Blériot*. Viking, 1983.

Rappaport, Doreen. *Martin's Big Words*. Illustrated by Bryan Collier. Hyperion, 2001.

Raschka, Chris. *John Coltrane's Giant Steps*. Jackson/Atheneum, 2002.

———. *Like Likes Like*. DK Ink, 1999.

———. *Mysterious Thelonious*. Orchard, 1997.

———. *Yo! Yes?* Orchard, 1993.

Rathmann, Peggy. *Officer Buckle and Gloria*. Putnam, 1995.

Rattigan, Jama Kim. *Dumpling Soup*. Illustrated by Lillian Hsu-Flanders. Little, 1993.

Rees, Douglas. *Grandy Thaxter's Helper*. Illustrated by S. D. Schindler. Atheneum, 2004.

Reid, Barbara. *The Party*. Scholastic, 1999.

———. *The Subway Mouse*. Scholastic, 2005.

Rey, H. A. *Curious George*. Houghton, 1941.

Rice, Eve. *At Grammy's House*. Greenwillow, 1990.

Ringgold, Faith. *Cassie's Word Book*. Knopf, 2002.

———. *Tar Beach*. Crown, 1991.

Robbins, Ruth. *Baboushka and the Three Kings*. Illustrated by Nicholas Sidjakov. Parnassus, 1960.

Rodman, Mary Ann. *My Best Friend*. Illustrated by E. B. Lewis. Viking, 2005.

Roe, Eileen. *Con Mi Hermano: With My Brother*. Illustrated by Robert Casilla. Bradbury, 1991.

Rosen, Michael. *Michael Rosen's Sad Book*. Candlewick, 2005.

Rosoff, Meg. *Meet Wild Boars*. Illustrated by Sophie Blackall. Holt, 2005.

Rubin, Susan Goldman. *The Flag with Fifty-six Stars: A Gift from the Survivors of Mauthausen*. Illustrated by Bill Farnsworth. Holiday, 2005.

Russo, Marisabina. *Always Remember Me: How One Family Survived the War*. Greenwillow, 2005.

———. *Hannah's Baby Sister*. Greenwillow, 1998.

———. *I Don't Want to Go Back to School*. Greenwillow, 1994.

———. *The Trouble with Baby*. Greenwillow, 2003.

Ryan, Pam Muñoz. *Mice and Beans*. Illustrated by Joe Cepeda. Scholastic, 2001.

———. *Nacho and Lolita*. Illustrated by Claudia Rueda. Scholastic, 2005.

Ryder, Joanne. *Big Bear Ball*. Illustrated by Steven Kellogg. HarperCollins, 2001.

———. *A Fawn in the Grass*. Illustrated by Keiko Narahashi. Holt, 2001.

Rylant, Cynthia. *Appalachia: The Voices of Sleeping Birds*. Illustrated by Barry Moser. Harcourt, 1991.

———. *The Relatives Came*. Illustrated by Stephen Gammell. Bradbury, 1985.

———. *When I Was Young in the Mountains*. Illustrated by Diane Goode. Dutton, 1982.

Sanders, Scott Russell. *A Place Called Freedom*. Illustrated by Thomas B. Allen. Atheneum, 1997.

San Souci, Robert D. *The Boy and the Ghost*. Illustrated by Brian Pinkney. Simon, 1989.

———. *Cendrillon: A Caribbean Cinderella*. Illustrated by Brian Pinkney. Simon, 1998.

———. *Cut from the Same Cloth: American Women of Myth, Legend, and Tall Tale*. Illustrated by Brian Pinkney. Putnam/Philomel, 1993.

———. *The Faithful Friend*. Illustrated by Brian Pinkney. Simon, 1995.

———. *Sukey and the Mermaid*. Illustrated by Brian Pinkney. Four Winds, 1992.

Say, Allen. *Grandfather's Journey*. Houghton, 1993.

———. *The Lost Lake*. Houghton, 1989.

———. *Tea with Milk*. Houghton, 1999.

Schaefer, Carole Lexa. *Cool Time Song*. Illustrated by Pierr Morgan. Viking, 2005.

Schur, Maxine R. *Day of Delight*. Illustrated by Brian Pinkney. Dial, 1994.

———. *When I Left My Village*. Illustrated by Brian Pinkney. Dial, 1996.

Scieszka, Jon. *The Frog Prince Continued*. Illustrated by Steve Johnson. Viking, 1991.

———. *Squids Will Be Squids*. Illustrated by Lane Smith. Viking, 1998.

———. *The Stinky Cheese Man and Other Fairly Stupid Tales*. Illustrated by Lane Smith. Viking, 1992.

———. *The True Story of the Three Little Pigs*. Illustrated by Lane Smith. Viking, 1989.

Scotton, Rob. *Russell the Sheep*. HarperCollins, 2005.

Sendak, Maurice. *In the Night Kitchen*. Harper, 1970.

———. *Outside Over There*. Harper, 1981.

———. *Where the Wild Things Are*. Harper, 1963.

Serfozo, Mary. *Rain Talk*. Illustrated by Keiko Narahashi. McElderry/Macmillan, 1990.

Seuss, Dr. [Theodor S. Geisel]. *And to Think That I Saw It on Mulberry Street*. Vanguard, 1937.

———. *The Cat in the Hat*. Random, 1957.

———. *Horton Hatches the Egg*. Random, 1993 [1940].

———. *Scrambled Eggs Super!* Random, 1953.

———. *Thidwick, the Big-Hearted Moose*. Random, 1948.

Shannon, David. *David Gets in Trouble*. Scholastic, 2002.

———. *David Goes to School*. Scholastic, 1999.

———. *No, David!* Scholastic, 1998.

Shannon, George. *Climbing Kansas Mountains*. Illustrated by Thomas B. Allen. Bradbury, 1993.

———. *Lizard's Guest*. Illustrated by Jose Aruego and Ariane Dewey. Greenwillow, 2003.

Shea, Pegi Deitz. *Liberty Rising: The Story of the Statue of Liberty*. Illustrated by Wade Zahares. Holt, 2005.

Shelby, Anne. *Homeplace*. Illustrated by Wendy Anderson Halperin. Orchard, 1995.

Shulevitz, Uri. *Dawn*. Farrar, 1974.

———. *Rain Rain Rivers*. Farrar, 1969.

———. *Snow*. Farrar, 1998.

Siegelson, Kim L. *In the Time of the Drums*. Illustrated by Brian Pinkney. Hyperion, 1999.

Sierra, Judy. *The Elephant's Wrestling Match*. Illustrated by Brian Pinkney. Lodestar/Dutton, 1992.

———. *Wild about Books*. Illustrated by Marc Brown. Knopf, 2004.

Silverman, Erica. *Don't Fidget a Feather*. Illustrated by S. D. Schindler. Macmillan, 1994.

Simmons, Jane. *Come Along Daisy!* Little, 1998.

Simont, Marc. *The Stray Dog: From a True Story by Reiko Sassa*. HarperCollins, 2001.

Singer, Marilyn. *Monday on the Mississippi*. Illustrated by Frané Lessac. Holt, 2005.

Sis, Peter. *Madelinka's Dog*. Farrar, 2002.

Sklansky, Amy. *From the Doghouse: Poems to Chew On*. Illustrated by Karla Firehammer et al. Holt, 2002.

Sogabe, Aki. *Aesop's Fox*. Browndeer, 1999.

Soto, Gary. *Chato and the Party Animals*. Illustrated by Susan Guevara. Putnam, 2000.

———. *Chato Goes Cruisin'*. Illustrated by Susan Guevara. Putnam, 2005.

———. *Chato's Kitchen*. Illustrated by Susan Guevara. Putnam, 1995.

———. *If the Shoe Fits*. Illustrated by Terry Widener. Putnam, 2002.

Spier, Peter. *Peter Spier's Rain*. Doubleday, 1982.

Stafford, Kim. *We Got Here Together*. Illustrated by Debra Frasier. Harcourt, 1992.

Stafford, William. *The Animal That Drank Up Sound*. Illustrated by Debra Frasier. Harcourt, 1992.

Stanley, Diane. *The Giant and the Beanstalk*. HarperCollins, 2004.

Steig, William. *The Amazing Bone*. Farrar, 1976.

———. *Amos and Boris*. Farrar, 1971.

———. *Brave Irene*. Farrar, 1986.

———. *Doctor DeSoto*. Farrar, 1982.

———. *Pete's a Pizza*. HarperCollins, 1998.

———. *Shrek!* Farrar, 1990.

———. *Sylvester and the Magic Pebble*. Windmill, 1979.

———. *Zeke Pippin*. HarperCollins, 1994.

Steptoe, Javaka. *The Jones Family Express*. Lee, 2003.

Steptoe, John. *Stevie*. Harper, 1969.

Stevens, Janet, and Susan Crummel Stevens. *Cook-a-Doodle-Doo!* Harcourt, 1999.

Stevenson, James. *Could Be Worse!* Greenwillow, 1977.

———. *No Laughing, No Smiling, No Giggling*. Farrar, 2004.

———. *That Terrible Halloween Night*. Greenwillow, 1983.

Stewart, Sarah. *The Gardener*. Illustrated by David Small. Farrar, 1997.

———. *The Journey*. Illustrated by David Small. Farrar, 2001.

———. *The Library*. Illustrated by David Small. Farrar, 1995.

Stock, Catherine. *Gugu's House*. Clarion, 2001.

———. *Where Are You Going, Manyoni?* Morrow, 1993.

Stolz, Mary. *Storm in the Night*. Illustrated by Pat Cummings. Harper, 1988.

Sturges, Philemon. *The Little Red Hen (Makes a Pizza)*. Illustrated by Amy Walrod. Dutton, 1999.

Stuve-Bodeen, Stephanie. *Elizabeti's Doll*. Illustrated by Christy Hale. Lee, 1998.

———. *Elizabeti's School*. Illustrated by Christy Hale. Lee, 2002.

———. *Mama Elizabeti*. Illustrated by Christy Hale. Lee, 2000.

Takabayashi, Mari. *I Live in Tokyo*. Houghton, 2001.

Tan, Shaun. *The Red Tree*. Lothian, 2002.

Taylor, Sean. *Boing!* Illustrated by Bruce Ingman. Candlewick, 2005.

Teague, Mark. *Dear Mrs. Larue: Letters from Obedience School*. Scholastic, 2002.

Thompson, Kay. *Eloise*. Illustrated by Hilary Knight. Simon, 1969.

Titherington, Jeanne. *A Place for Ben*. Greenwillow, 1987.

Toft, Kim Michelle. *The World That We Want*. Charlesbridge, 2005.

Tresselt, Alvin. *White Snow, Bright Snow*. Illustrated by Roger Duvoisin. Lothrop, 1988 [1947].

Trivias, Eugene. *The Three Little Wolves and the Big Bad Pig*. Illustrated by Helen Oxenbury. McElderry, 1993.

Turner, Ann. *Through Moon and Stars and Night Skies*. Illustrated by James-Graham Hale. HarperCollins, 1990.

Udry, Janice May. *A Tree Is Nice*. Illustrated by Marc Simont. Harper, 1956.

UNICEF. *For Every Child: The Rights of the Child in Words and Pictures*. Text adapted by Caroline Castle. Illustrated by John Burningham and others. Fogelman, 2001.

Van Allsburg, Chris. *Bad Day at Riverbend*. Houghton, 1995.

———. *The Garden of Abdul Gasazi*. Houghton, 1979.

———. *Jumanji*. Houghton, 1981.

———. *Just a Dream*. Houghton, 1990.

———. *The Mysteries of Harris Burdick*. Houghton, 1984.

———. *The Polar Express*. Houghton, 1985.

———. *The Stranger*. Houghton, 1986.

———. *The Sweetest Fig*. Houghton, 1993.

———. *The Widow's Broom*. Houghton, 1992.

———. *The Wreck of the Zephyr*. Houghton, 1983.

———. *The Wretched Stone*. Houghton, 1991.

———. *Zathura*. Houghton, 2002.

Vander Zee, Ruth. *Erika's Story*. Illustrated by Roberto Innocenti. Creative Editions, 2003.

Van Laan, Nancy. *Possum Come A-Knockin'*. Illustrated by George Booth. Knopf, 1990.

Viorst, Judith. *Alexander and the Terrible, Horrible, No Good, Very Bad Day*. Illustrated by Ray Cruz. Atheneum, 1972.

———. *The Tenth Good Thing about Barney*. Illustrated by Erik Blegvad. Atheneum, 1971.

Waber, Bernard. *The House on East 88th Street*. Houghton, 1962.

———. *Ira Sleeps Over*. Houghton, 1972.

———. *Lyle, Lyle Crocodile*. Houghton, 1965.

Waddell, Martin. *Tiny's Big Adventure*. Illustrated by John Lawrence. Candlewick, 2004.

Wallace, Ian. *Mavis and Myrna*. Groundwood, 2005.

Walter, Mildred Pitts. *My Mama Needs Me*. Illustrated by Pat Cummings. Lothrop, 1983.

Weatherford, Carole Boston. *Freedom on the Menu: The Greensboro Sit-Ins*. Illustrated by Jerome Lagarrigue. Dial, 2005.

Wells, Rosemary. *Noisy Nora*. Dial, 1973.

———. *Shy Charles*. Dial, 1988.

———. *Yoko's Paper Cranes*. Hyperion, 2001.

Wheeler, Lisa. *Mammoths on the Move*. Illustrated by Kurt Cyrus. Harcourt, 2006.

Wiesner, David. *Hurricane*. Clarion, 1990.

———. *Sector 7*. Houghton, 1999.

———. *The Three Pigs*. Clarion, 2001.

Wild, Margaret. *Our Granny*. Illustrated by Julie Vivas. Ticknor, 1994.

———. *The Very Best of Friends*. Illustrated by Julie Vivas. Harcourt, 1990.

Willard, Nancy. *A Visit to William Blake's Inn*. Illustrated by Alice Provensen and Martin Provensen. Harcourt, 1981.

Willems, Mo. *Don't Let the Pigeon Drive the Bus*. Hyperion, 2003.

———. *Don't Let the Pigeon Stay Up Late!* Hyperion, 2006.

———. *Leonardo the Terrible Monster*. Hyperion, 2005.

———. *The Pigeon Finds a Hot Dog*. Hyperion, 2004.

Williams, Karen Lynn. *Galimoto*. Illustrated by Catherine Stock. Lothrop, 1990.

———. *Painted Dreams*. Illustrated by Catherine Stock. Lothrop, 1998.

Williams, Margery. *The Velveteen Rabbit: Or How Toys Become Real*. Illustrated by Michael Hague. Holt, 1983.

———. *The Velveteen Rabbit: Or How Toys Become Real*. Illustrated by David Jorgensen. Knopf, 1985.

———. *The Velveteen Rabbit: Or How Toys Become Real*. Illustrated by Ilse Plume. Harcourt, 1987.

Williams, Sam. *Talk Peace*. Illustrated by Mique Moriuchi. Holiday, 2005.

Williams, Vera B. *Amber Was Brave, Essie Was Smart*. Greenwillow, 2001.

———. *Music, Music for Everyone*. Greenwillow, 1984.

———. *Something Special for Me*. Greenwillow, 1983.

———. *A Chair for My Mother*. Greenwillow, 1982.

Willis, Jeanne. *Tadpole's Promise*. Illustrated by Tony Ross. Atheneum, 2005.

Wilson, Karma. *Bear Snores On*. Illustrated by Jane Chapman. McElderry, 2001.

Winter, Jeanette. *September Roses*. Farrar, 2004.

Winthrop, Elizabeth. *Dumpy LaRue*. Illustrated by Betsy Lewin. Holt, 2001.

———. *Squashed in the Middle*. Illustrated by Pat Cummings. Holt, 2005.

Wisniewski, David. *The Golem*. Clarion, 1996.

———. *The Wave of the Sea-Wolf*. Clarion, 1994.

Wong, Janet S. *Apple Pie Fourth of July*. Illustrated by Margaret Chodos-Irvine. Harcourt, 2002.

———. *This Next New Year*. Illustrated by Yangsook Choi. Farrar, 2000.

Wood, Audrey. *The Napping House*. Illustrated by Don Wood. Harcourt, 1984.

Woodson, Jacqueline. *Coming On Home Soon*. Illustrated by E. B. Lewis. Putnam, 2004.

———. *Our Gracie Aunt*. Illustrated by Jon J. Muth. Hyperion, 2002.

———. *We Had a Picnic This Sunday Past*. Illustrated by Diane Greenseid. Hyperion, 1998.

Wormell, Mary. *Hilda Hen's Happy Birthday*. Harcourt, 1995.

———. *Hilda Hen's Search*. Harcourt, 1994.

Yang, Belle. *Hannah Is My Name*. Candlewick, 2004.

Yashima, Taro [Jun Iwamatsu]. *Crow Boy*. Viking, 1955.

———. *Umbrella*. Viking Penguin, 1958.

Yin. *Coolies*. Illustrated by Chris Soentpiet. Philomel, 2001.

Yolen, Jane. *The Emperor and the Kite*. Illustrated by Ed Young. Philomel, 1988 [1967].

———. *King Langshanks*. Illustrated by Victoria Chess. Harcourt, 1998.

———. *Owl Moon*. Illustrated by John Schoenherr. Philomel, 1987.

Young, Ed. *I Doko: The Story of a Basket*. Philomel, 2004.

———. *Little Plum*. Philomel, 1994.

———. *The Sons of the Dragon King*. Atheneum, 2004.

Zelinsky, Paul O. *Knick-Knack Paddywhack! A Moving Parts Book*. Dutton, 2002.

———. *The Maid, the Mouse and the Odd Shaped House*. Dodd, 1981.

———. *Rapunzel*. Dutton, 1997.

———. *The Wheels on the Bus! A Moving Parts Book*. Dutton, 1990.

Zolotow, Charlotte. *Mr. Rabbit and the Lovely Present*. Illustrated by Maurice Sendak. Harper, 1962.

———. *William's Doll*. Illustrated by William Pène Du Bois. Harper, 1972.

Traditional Literature

Chapter Outline

Media Resources

Photo © David Pollack/CORBIS

Ever since human beings realized they were unique among animals in that they could think and talk, they have tried to explain themselves and their world. Who were the first humans? How did they come to be? What made the sun and the moon and the stars? Why are the animals made the way they are? What caused night and day, the seasons, the cycle of life itself? Why are some people greedy and some unselfish, some ugly and some handsome, some dull and some clever?

As people pondered these questions and many more, they created stories that helped explain the world to their primitive minds. The storytellers told these tales again and again around the fires of the early tribes, by the hearths of humble cottages, before the great fire in the king's hall; they told them as they sat in the grass huts of the jungle, the hogans of the southern plains, and the igloos of the northern tundra. Their children told them, and their children's children, until the stories were as smooth and polished as the roundest stones in a stream. And so people created their myths and their folktales, their legends and epics—the literature of the fireside, the poetry of the people, and the memory of humankind.

A PERSPECTIVE ON TRADITIONAL LITERATURE

Traditional literature can provide a window on cultural beliefs and on the spiritual and psychological qualities that are part of our human nature. These stories also form the basis for many works of more-modern literature, drama, and other art forms. It is important to help children become familiar with the rich heritage of stories that have come down to us from cultures around the world.

The Origin of Folk Literature

We have no one word that encompasses all of the stories born of the oral tradition. The stories most often are labeled "folklore," "folk literature," or "mythology." Generally we say that myths are about gods and the creation of things; legends are about heroes and their mighty deeds before the time of recorded history; and folktales, fairy tales, and fables are simple stories about talking beasts, woodcutters, and princesses who reveal human behavior and beliefs while playing out their roles in a world of wonder and magic.

Children sometimes identify these stories as "make-believe," as contrasted with "true" or "stories that could really happen." Unfortunately, the word *myth* has sometimes been defined as "imagined event" or "pagan falsehood" and contrasted with "historical fact" or "religious truth." In literary study, however, a myth is not "untrue"; rather, it is a story with a generalized meaning, or a universal idea, that expresses a significant truth about humans and their lives. A single myth is a narrative that tells of origins,[1] explains natural or social phenomena, or suggests the destiny of humans through the interaction of people and supernatural beings. A *mythology* is a group of myths of a particular culture. Myth making is continuous and still in process today.[2] Usually myth is a product of a society rather than of a single author.

The origin of the myths has fascinated and puzzled folklorists, anthropologists, and psychologists. How, they wonder, can we account for the similarities among these stories that grew out of ancient cultures widely separated from each other? The Greek myth Cupid and Psyche retold by M. Charlotte Craft is very much like the Norwegian tale told in George Dasent's *East o'the Sun and West o'the Moon*. The Chinese "Cinderella" story recounted in Ai-Ling Louie's *Yeh-Shen* is similar to Perrault's French *Cinderella* except that a fish acts on the poor girl's behalf. And the Cinderella story is found throughout the world, with nearly five hundred variants in Europe alone.

[1] X. J. Kennedy, *Literature: An Introduction to Fiction, Poetry and Drama* (Boston: Little, Brown, 1983), p. 610.
[2] Joseph Campbell, with Bill Moyers, *The Power of Myth* (New York: Doubleday, 1988).

Children will recognize many aspects of the Western Cinderella story in *The Gift of the Crocodile,* a tale from Indonesia retold by Judy Sierra and Reynold Ruffins. Reprinted with the permission of Simon & Schuster Books for Young Readers, an imprint of Simon & Schuster Children's Publishing Division. Illustration © 2000 by Reynold Ruffins.

In trying to explain this phenomenon, one group of early mythologists proposed the notion of *monogenesis,* or inheritance from a single culture. The Grimm brothers, who were among the first nineteenth-century scholars of folklore, theorized that all folktales originated from one prehistoric group called Aryans, later identified as Indo-Europeans by modern linguists. As this group migrated to other countries, the scholars reasoned, they took their folklore with them; such reasoning led scholars to the theory of *diffusion.*

Another approach to folklore involves the theory of *polygenesis,* or multiple origins. It is argued that each story could have been an independent invention growing out of universal human desires and needs. Early anthropologists viewed myth as the religion of the people derived from rituals that were recounted in drama and narratives. They identified recurrent themes in myths of different cultures. Clyde Kluckhohn's study of the myths of fifty cultures revealed recurring themes like the flood, the slaying of monsters, incest, sibling rivalry, and castration.[3] Kluckhohn also found several patterns repeated in the myth of the hero. Sir James Frazer's twelve-volume analysis of ritual, taboos, and myths, *The Golden Bough,*[4]

was of major importance. This anthropological study ascribed sexual symbolic meaning to primitive myths and greatly influenced modern literature.

Sigmund Freud's analysis of myth as dream, or disguised wish fulfillment, was the beginning of psychological literary criticism.[5] Freud held the view that all myths expressed the Oedipus theme with its incest motive, guilt, and punishment. Another psychological viewpoint was that of Carl Jung, a contemporary of Freud, who thought that a "collective unconscious" is "inherited in the structure of the brain."[6] These unconscious, recurring images created the primitive mythic heroes and still exist as individual fantasies for the civilized person as a kind of "race memory," according to Jung. The folklorist, however, might disagree with such psychological interpretations. Richard Dorson argues that "folk literature cannot all be prettily channeled into the universal monomyth" and that "the folklorist looks with jaundiced eye at the excessive straining of mythologists to extort symbols from folk tales."[7]

Folktales are also of special interest to scholars of narrative theory. Because of the way the tales are honed by many generations of telling, only the most important

---

[3]Clyde Kluckhohn, "Recurrent Themes in Myth and Mythmaking," in *The Making of Myth,* ed. Richard M. Ohrmann (New York: Putnam, 1962), pp. 52–65.

[4]Sir James Frazer, *The Golden Bough,* 3rd ed. (London: Macmillan, 1911–1915).

[5]Stanley E. Hyman, *The Armed Vision,* rev. ed. (New York: Vintage, 1955).

[6]Carl C. Jung, "On the Relation of Analytic Psychology to Poetic Art," in *Modern Continental Literary Criticism,* ed. O. B. Hardison, Jr. (New York: Appleton, 1962), pp. 267–88.

[7]Richard Dorson, "Theories of Myth and the Folklorist," in *The Making of Myth,* ed. Richard M. Ohrmann (New York: Putnam, 1962), p. 45.

Talking Point

Is there too much violence in traditional literature?

Go to the Online Learning Center at
www.mhhe.com/kiefer9e or your Resources
CD-ROM to learn more.

elements of the story survive. Close study of the patterns of action and character relationships shows how language shapes a form we recognize as a story. Vladimir Propp, for instance, analyzed Russian tales and identified a set sequence of thirty-one "functions" that might occur in a tale, such as these: The hero leaves home (departure); one member of a family lacks or desires something (lack); or a villain attempts to deceive his victim (trickery).[8] Other researchers have used simplified folktale structures to develop models of children's story comprehension. Although looking at tales in such a technical way is definitely an adult perspective, children who have heard and enjoyed many traditional stories begin to discover for themselves that folktales seem to follow certain structural rules. One 10-year-old girl who wrote instructions for "making a fairy story" summed up by saying, "Fairy tales have to have a sort of pattern or they would just be regular stories."

However scholars choose to look at them, folktales and myths are literature derived from human imagination to explain the human condition. Literature today continues to express our concern about human strengths and weaknesses and the individual's relationships to the world and to other people. Traditional literature forms the foundation of understandings of life as expressed in modern literature.

The Value of Folk Literature for Children

When Jacob and Wilhelm Grimm published the first volume of their *Household Stories* in 1812, they did not intend it for children. These early philologists were studying the language and grammar of such traditional tales. In recent years, as we have seen, anthropologists study folklore in order to understand the inherent values and beliefs of a culture. Psychologists look at folktales and myths and discover something of human motivation and feelings. Folklorists collect and categorize various stories, types, and motifs from around the world. These are all adult scholars of folk literature, which itself was first created by adults and usually told to an adult community. How, then, did folk literature become associated with children's literature, and what value does this kind of literature have for children?

Originally folklore was the literature of the people; stories were told to young and old alike. Families or tribes or the king's court would gather to hear a famous storyteller in much the same way that an entire family today will watch their favorite television program together. With the age of scientific enlightenment, these stories were relegated to the nursery, often kept alive by resourceful nursemaids or grandmothers, much to the delight of children.

Children today still enjoy these tales because they are good stories. Born of the oral tradition, these stories usually are short and have fast-moving plots. They frequently are humorous and almost always end happily. Poetic justice prevails; the good and the just are eventually rewarded; the evil are punished. This appeals to children's sense of justice and their moral judgment. Wishes come true, but usually not without the fulfillment of a task or trial. The littlest child, the youngest child, or the smallest animal succeeds; the oldest or the largest is frequently defeated. Youngsters, who are the little people of their world, thrive on such turns of events.

Beyond the function of pure entertainment, folktales can kindle the child's imagination. Behind every great author, poet, architect, mathematician, or diplomat are that person's dreams of what she or he hopes to achieve. These dreams or ideals have been created by the power of imagination. If we always give children stories of "what is," stories that only mirror the living of today, then we have not helped them to imagine "what might have been" or "what might be."

Bruno Bettelheim, in his remarkable book *The Uses of Enchantment*, maintains that fairy tales help children cope with their dreams and inner turmoil. "Each fairy tale," he says, "is a magic mirror which reflects some aspects of our inner world and of the steps required by our evolution from immaturity to maturity."[9]

Kornei Chukovsky, the Russian poet, tells of a time when it was proposed that all folktales and fairy tales be eliminated from the education of the Russian child in favor of simple realistic stories. Then one of the major Russian educators began keeping a diary of her child's development. She found that her child, as if to compensate for the loss of the fairy tales he had been denied, began to make up his own. He had never heard a folktale, but his world became peopled with talking tigers, birds, and bugs. Chukovsky concludes: "Fantasy is the most valuable attribute of the human mind and should be diligently nurtured from earliest childhood."[10]

Our speech and vocabulary reflect many contributions from traditional literature. Think of the figures of

---

[8]Vladimir Propp, *The Morphology of the Folktale* (Austin: University of Texas Press, 1968).

[9]Bruno Bettelheim, *The Uses of Enchantment* (New York: Knopf, 1976), p. 309.

[10]Kornei Chukovsky, *From Two to Five*, trans. and ed. Miriam Morton (Berkeley: University of California Press, 1963), p. 119.

speech that come from Aesop's fables: "sour grapes," "dog in the manger," "boy who cried wolf." Our language is replete with words and phrases from the myths—*narcissistic, cereal, labyrinth, siren,* and many more.

Traditional literature is a rightful part of a child's literary heritage and lays the groundwork for understanding all literature. Poetry and modern stories allude to traditional literature, particularly the Greek myths, Aesop's fables, and Bible stories. Northrop Frye maintains that "all themes and characters and stories that you encounter in literature belong to one big interlocking family."[11] As you meet recurring patterns or symbols in mythlike floods, savior heroes, cruel stepmothers, the seasonal cycle of the year, the cycle of a human life, you begin to build a framework for literature. Poetry, prose, and drama become more emotionally significant as you respond to these recurring archetypes.

FOLKTALES

Folktales have been defined as "all forms of narrative, written or oral, which have come to be handed down through the years."[12] This definition would include epics, ballads, legends, and folk songs, as well as myths and fables. In using folk literature in the elementary school, we have tended to confine the rather simple folktales—such as the popular "Three Billy Goats Gruff," "Little Red Riding Hood," and "Rumpelstiltskin"—to the primary grades; we recommend the so-called fairy tales or wonder tales—such as "Snow White" and "Cinderella"—for slightly older children, because these tales are longer and contain romantic elements. Such a division appears arbitrary; it is based more on use than on any real difference in the stories. To complicate matters even further, modern fanciful stories created by known authors are often also referred to as fairy tales. Hans Christian Andersen's stories are becoming part of the heritage that might be described as folktales, but *many originated in written rather than oral form.* Thus they are distinguished from the stories told by the common folk that were finally collected and recorded. Stories that are written in a folktale style but originated in an author's imagination are often referred to as "literary folktales" (see "Modern Folktale Style" in Chapter 5 and "Modern Fairy Tales" in Chapter 7).

Questions often arise about which of the available print versions of a tale is the "correct" or authentic text. From a folklorist's point of view, a tale is recreated every time it is told, and therefore *every* telling is correct in its own way. A great deal of variation is also acceptable in print versions, where literary style carries the same uniqueness as the teller's voice. Authors and illustrators

Children in kindergarten/first grade create their interpretations of "Little Red Riding Hood," a favorite folktale. Highland Park Elementary School, South-Western City Schools, Grove City, Ohio. Kristen Kerstetter, teacher.

may also add original twists, customize their stories for a chosen audience, or adapt a familiar tale to an unfamiliar setting, as oral storytellers do. There might be a problem, however, when a print version suggests by its title, or lack of an author's note, that it represents a tale derived directly from a previously printed source. Readers of a story identified as recorded and published by the Grimm brothers, for instance, have a right to find that this tale has been subsequently published without major additions, omissions, or distortions.

This chapter discusses folktales in children's literature that come from the oral tradition. It also includes a description of epics, myths, and stories from the Bible,

---

[11]Northrop Frye, *The Educated Imagination* (Bloomington: Indiana University Press, 1964), p. 48.

[12]Ibid.

which are all a part of traditional literature. Modern fanciful stories written by known authors are discussed in Chapter 7.

Types of Folktales

The many folktales that have found their way into the hands and hearts of children come from many cultures. There will be features of these stories that are unique to each culture, but children will also find particular aspects of plot or characterization that occur across cultures. Recognizable literary patterns can be found in cumulative tales, pourquoi tales, beast tales, wonder tales, and realistic tales.

Cumulative Tales

Very young children are fascinated by such cumulative stories as "The Old Woman and Her Pig" with its "Rat! rat! gnaw rope; rope won't hang butcher; butcher won't kill ox; ox won't drink water; water won't quench fire; fire won't burn stick; stick won't beat dog; dog won't bite pig; piggy won't get over the stile; and I shan't get home tonight." (See versions by Eric Kimmel and Roseanne Litzinger.) The story itself is not as important as the increasing repetition of the details building up to a quick climax. The story of the gingerbread boy who ran away from the old woman, defiantly crying "Catch me if you can!" as in Paul Galdone's *The Gingerbread Boy,* has been told in many different versions, including Jim Ayles-worth's *The Gingerbread Man* and Ruth Sawyer's Appalachian version, *Journey Cake, Ho!* Richard Egielski has created an entirely modern setting for the traditional tale in his *The Gingerbread Boy.* Construction workers, street musicians, and other urban mainstays chase the mischievous cookie through the streets of New York City instead of the countryside.

In another familiar cumulative tale, one day an acorn falls on Henny Penny (see Steven Kellogg's *Chicken Little*). Thinking the sky is falling down, she persuades Cocky-Locky, Ducky-Daddles, Goosey-Poosey, and Turkey-Lurkey to go along with her to tell the king. Children delight in the sound of the rhyming double names, which are repeated over and over. Young children, especially, enjoy extending and personalizing these cumulative tales through dramatic play. You will find repetitive stories in practically all folklore.

Pourquoi Tales

Some folktales are "why," or *pourquoi,* stories that explain certain animal traits or characteristics or human customs. In "How the Animals Got Their Tails" in *Beat the Story-Drum, Pum-Pum,* Ashley Bryan tells an African tale of a time when all animals were vegetarians. Then Raluvhimba created a mistake, the flies who were flesh eaters and bloodsuckers. "I can't take back what I've done. After all, that's life," the god said. But he did give the rest of the animals tails with which to swish away the flies.

LITERATURE IN **ACTION**

Creating Pourquoi Stories with Fifth Graders

A fifth-grade teacher assembled many African *pourquoi* stories and led her class in reading and discussing the patterns. Children noted that most explained animal characteristics or habits and natural phenomena. Children also discussed the illustrations and were particularly impressed with the clear colors and white-outlined shapes that Leo Dillon and Diane Dillon used for the Caldecott Medal–winning pictures in Verna Aardema's *Why Mosquitoes Buzz in People's Ears.* When the teacher asked children to produce their own "how" or "why" stories and illustrate them, here is what one child created:

Why Flies Eat Rotten Food

A long time ago, in a jungle, Fly was very hot. So he flew to the river and rolled around in the mud. After that Fly was very hungry so he flew home. On the way he looked down and saw a big juicy steak lying on the ground.

Now fly was *very* hungry so he flew down and started eating it. But he was so dirty that when he landed he got mud on the steak and as he walked around eating it he got even more mud on it.

By the time Fly was done eating, the whole steak was covered with mud. Just then King Lion (the owner of the steak who had been taking a nap) walked into the clearing. "What have you done to my steak you stupid fly?" roared his majesty.

"Oh," said Fly, "I was just—." Then he looked at the steak. "Oh your majesty! I am very sorry. So very sorry," apologized Fly.

Then the King said, "As a punishment you can never eat fresh food again. You must always eat things like this steak."

Fly was so ashamed that he flew off with his head down but because he does not dare oppose King Lion he has eaten dirty and rotten food ever since.

Allison Fraser, fifth grade
Susan Steinberg, teacher
George Mason Elementary School, Alexandria, Virginia

Many Native American stories are "why" stories that explain animal features, the origin of certain natural features, or how humans and their customs came to be. Paul Goble's retelling of a Cheyenne myth in *Her Seven Brothers* explains the origins of the Big Dipper. The Cherokee *Story of the Milky Way* has been retold by Joseph Bruchac and Gayle Ross. Kristina Rodanas's *Follow the Stars* is an Ojibwa story that tells how the North Star was placed in the sky.[13]

Beast Tales

Probably the favorite folktales of young children are beast tales in which animals act and talk like human beings. The best known of these frequently appear in newly illustrated versions. In his version of *The Three Little Pigs,* Paul Galdone portrays the wolf as a ferocious doggy creature. James Marshall's red-capped wolf looks like a thug in his red-striped polo shirt. Barry Moser's version has a particularly detestable wolf and an ultra-hip third little pig. Other beast tales found in several versions include Asbjørnsen and Moe's *The Three Billy Goats Gruff* (versions illustrated by Marcia Brown and Glen Rounds), *The Little Red Hen* (Paul Galdone, Margot Zemach), and *Puss in Boots* (Galdone, Perrault).

Many African stories are "wise beast/foolish beast" tales of how one animal, such as a spider or rabbit, outwits a lion, hyena, leopard, or other foe. In Verna Aardema's *Rabbit Makes a Monkey of Lion*, Rabbit and Turtle steal Lion's honey and continually trick him into letting them go. So Lion hides in Rabbit's house in hopes of eating him for supper. But Rabbit notices the beast's footprints and calls out, "How-de-do, Little House." When the house doesn't reply, Rabbit pretends to be puzzled. "Little House, you always tell me *how-de-do.* Is something wrong today?" Of course, the confused Lion answers for the house, reveals his presence, and is tricked once again. In Margaret Read MacDonald's Limba tale, *Mabela the Clever,* a wonderfully wicked cat convinces a group of mice to join his secret Cat Society. He marches them in single file and has them sing the society song, "When we are marching,/We never look back!/The Cat is at the end,/Fo Feng! Fo Feng!" With each "Fo Feng!" the cat gobbles up another mouse. Fortunately, Clever Mabela, whose father taught her to use all her senses, becomes suspicious, traps the cat, and saves the mice. Many beast tales that traveled to the United States with enslaved Africans were collected by Joel Chandler Harris in the late 1800s. These have been retold in two series, one by Julius Lester that begins with *The Tales of Uncle Remus: The Adventures of Brer Rabbit,* and the other by Van Dyke Parks, beginning with *Jump: The Adventures of Brer Rabbit.*

Talking animals appear in folktales of all cultures. Fish are often in English, Scandinavian, German, and

Rapunzel, retold and illustrated by Paul O. Zelinsky, is a wonder tale, a story that involves romance, magic, and difficult tasks. From *Rapunzel* by Paul O. Zelinsky, copyright © 1997 by Paul O. Zelinsky. Used by permission of Dutton Children's Books, a division of Penguin Putnam Inc.

South Seas stories. Tales of bears, wolves, and the firebird are found in Russian folklore. Spiders, rabbits, tortoises, crocodiles, monkeys, and lions are very much a part of African tales; rabbits, badgers, monkeys, and even bees are represented in Japanese stories. A study of just the animals in folklore would be fascinating.

Wonder Tales

Children call wonder tales about magic and the supernatural "fairy tales." Very few tales have fairies or even a fairy godmother in them, but the name persists. Wicked witches, Baba Yaga in Russian folklore, demons such as the *oni* of Japanese tales, or monsters and dragons abound in these stories. Traditionally we have thought of the fairy tale as involving romance and adventure. "Cinderella," "Snow White and the Seven Dwarfs," and "Beauty and the Beast" all have elements of both. The long quest tales—such as the Norwegian tale told in George Dasent's *East o' the Sun and West o' the Moon*—are complex wonder tales in which the hero, or heroine, triumphs against all odds to win the beautiful princess, or handsome prince, and makes a fortune. Children know that these tales will end with ". . . and they lived happily

---

[13]For modern pourquoi tales, see the section on Rudyard Kipling's *Just So Stories* in Chapter 5.

ever after." In fact, part of the appeal of the fairy tale is the secure knowledge that no matter what happens, love, kindness, and truth will prevail—and hate, wickedness, and evil will be punished. Wonder tales have always represented the glorious fulfillment of human desires.

Realistic Tales

Surprisingly, there are a few realistic tales included in folklore. The story in Marcia Brown's *Dick Whittington and His Cat* could have happened; in fact, there is evidence that a Richard Whittington did indeed live and was mayor of London. Like the American story in Reeve Lindbergh's *Johnny Appleseed,* the tale began with a real person but has become so embroidered through various tellings that it takes its place in the folklore of its culture.

"Zlateh the Goat," the title story in a collection of Jewish tales by Isaac Bashevis Singer, is a survival story. The son of a poor peasant family is sent off to the butcher to sell Zlateh, the family goat. On the way, he and the goat are caught in a fierce snowstorm. They take refuge in a haystack, where they stay for three days. Zlateh eats the hay while the boy survives on Zlateh's milk and warmth. When the storm is over, they return home to a grateful family. No one ever again mentions selling Zlateh.

Teaching Resources: "A Cross-Cultural Study of Folktale Types" is the first of three boxes in this chapter that group folktales from various countries in specific ways to help teachers more easily plan curricula. This box groups together titles that tell similar tales. The other two boxes group tales by motif and by variants.

Characteristics of Folktales

Because folktales have been told and retold from generation to generation within a particular culture, we may ask how they reflect the country of their origin and its oral tradition. An authentic tale from Africa will include references to the flora and fauna of Africa and to the tribespeople's food, huts, customs, foibles, and beliefs. It will sound like it is being *told.* Although folktales have many elements in common, it should not be possible to confuse a folktale from Japan with a folktale from the fjords of Norway. What then are the characteristics common to all folktales? What are some of the things to look for when reading folktales? The Evaluation Criteria box "Evaluating Folktales" summarizes the criteria that need to be considered when evaluating this genre for children.

Plot Structures

Of the folktales best known in children's literature, even the longer stories are usually simple and direct. A series of episodes maintains a quick flow of action. If it is a "wise beast/foolish beast" story, the characters are quickly delineated, the action shows the inevitable conflict and resolution, and the ending is usually brief. If the tale is a romance, the hero or heroine sets forth on a journey, often helps the poor on the way, frequently receives magical power, overcomes obstacles, and returns to safety. The plot that involves a weak or innocent child going forth to meet the monsters of the world is another form of the "journey-novel." In the Grimm brothers' *Hansel and Gretel* the children go out into a dark world and meet the witch, but goodness and purity triumph. Almost all folktale plots are success stories of one kind or another (unlike many myths, in which characters meet a sad end through their own human failings).

Repetition is a basic element in many folktale plots. Frequently three is the magic number. There are three little pigs whose three houses face the puffing of the wolf. The wolf gives three challenges to the pig in the brick house—to get turnips, to get apples, and to go to the fair. In the longer tales, each of the three tasks becomes increasingly more difficult, and the intensity of the wonders becomes progressively more marvelous. This repetition satisfies listeners or readers with its orderliness.

The repetition of responses, chants, or poems is frequently a part of the structure of a tale. "Mirror, mirror on the wall, who is fairest of them all?" and "Fee, fi, fo, fum" are repetitive verses familiar to all. Some versions of *Hansel and Gretel* end with a storyteller's coda, such as Elizabeth Crawford's: "My tale is done, and there a mouse does run. Whoever catches it can make a big fur

EVALUATION **CRITERIA**

Evaluating Folktales

The following might guide the evaluation of folktales for children:

- Is there some mention or citation of the original source for this tale?
- Is the plot simple and direct?
- Is the language lively and engaging and in keeping with the oral tradition?

- Does a theme emerge from the telling of the tale? If so, what is the story's message or moral?
- Do illustrations add to and extend the story? Are illustrations and details true to the culture represented?
- Does the story represent cultural norms, or is it rewritten to conform to Western mores?

A Cross-Cultural Study of Folktale Types

 Visit the Online Learning Center at **www.mhhe.com/kiefer9e** for a printable version of this list.

CUMULATIVE TALES

Tale (Author)	Culture
Chicken Little (Kellogg)	England
The Gingerbread Man (Aylesworth)	England
One Fine Day (Hogrogian)	Armenia
Only One Cowry (Gershator)	Dahomey
The Rooster Who Went to His Uncle's Wedding (Ada)	Cuba
What about Me? (Young)	Sufi (Middle East)

POURQUOI TALES

Tale (Author)	Culture
The Cat's Purr (Bryan)	West Indian
The Day Ocean Came to Visit (Wolkstein)	Nigeria
The Golden Flower (Jaffee)	Puerto Rico
"How Animals Got Their Tails," in *Beat the Story-Drum, Pum-Pum* (Bryan)	Africa
How Chipmunk Got His Stripes (Bruchac and Bruchac)	Native American
"Jack and the Devil," in *The People Could Fly* (Hamilton)	African American
"Tia Miseria's Pear Tree," in *The Magic Orange Tree* (Wolkstein)	Haiti
Why Lapin's Ears Are So Long (Doucet)	Cajun
Why the Sun and the Moon Live in the Sky (Dayrell)	Africa

BEAST TALES

Tale (Author)	Culture
Beat the Story-Drum, Pum-Pum (Bryan)	Africa
The Bremen-Town Musicians (Grimm brothers, Orgel)	Germany
"Brer Terrapin," in *Jump!* (Parks and Jones)	African American
Foolish Rabbit's Big Mistake (Martin)	India
Rabbit Makes a Monkey of Lion (Aardema)	Africa (Tanzania)
The Rabbit's Tail (Han)	Korea
Rockaby Crocodile (Aruego and Dewey)	Philippines
The Three Billy Goats Gruff (Absjørnsen and Moe)	Norway

A Cross-Cultural Study of Folktale Types *(continued)*

BEAST TALES *(continued)*

Tale (Author)	Culture
Three Little Pigs and the Big Bad Wolf (Rounds)	England
Three Samurai Cats (Kimmel)	Japan

WONDER TALES

Tale (Author)	Culture
Ali Baba and the Forty Thieves (Early)	Middle East
Beauty and the Beast (de Beaumont)	France
The Black Bull of Norroway (Huck)	Scotland
The Castle of Cats (Kimmel)	Latvia
Jack and the Beanstalk (Kellogg)	England
Snow White (Grimm brothers)	Germany
The Son of the Sun and the Daughter of the Moon (Huth)	Scandinavia
Tam Lin (Cooper)	Scotland
Vasilissa the Beautiful (Winthrop)	Russia
A Weave of Words (San Souci)	Armenia

REALISTIC TALES

Tale (Author)	Culture
The Boy of the Three-Year Nap (Snyder)	Japan
"The Case of the Uncooked Eggs," in *The Magic Orange Tree* (Wolkstein)	Haiti
Dick Whittington and His Cat (Brown)	England
The Empty Pot (Demi)	China
Fire on the Mountain (Kurtz)	Ethiopia
The Hungry Coat (Demi)	Turkey
Juan Verdades: The Man Who Couldn't Tell a Lie (Hayes)	U.S. Southwest
My Mother Is the Most Beautiful Woman in the World (Reyher)	Russia
The Race of the Birkebeiners (Lunge-Larsen)	Norway
Something from Nothing (Gilman)	Jewish
Two Brothers (Waldman)	Jewish
Zlateh the Goat (Singer)	Jewish

cap of it." These serve both the storyteller and the listener as memory aids and familiar markers of the unfolding plot.

Time and place are established quickly in the folktale. Margaret Hodges's *The Boy Who Drew Cats* begins, "In a small country village in Japan, there once lived a poor farmer and his wife, who were very good people." Virginia Hamilton opens *The Girl Who Spun Gold* with "There be this tale told about a tiny fellow who could hide in a foot of shade amid old trees." Time is always past, and frequently described by such conventions as "Once upon a time" or "In olden times when wishing still helped. Time also passes quickly in the folktale. In Trina Schart Hyman's version of the Grimms' *The Sleeping Beauty*, the woods and brambles encircled Sleeping Beauty's palace in a quarter of an hour, and "when a hundred years were gone and passed," the prince appeared at the moment the enchantment ended. The setting of the folktale is not specific, but in some faraway land, in a cottage in the woods, in a beautiful palace.

The introduction to the folktale usually presents the conflict, characters, and setting in a few sentences. In "Anansi and Nothing Go Hunting for Wives" (in Harold Courlander and George Herzog's *The Cow-Tail Switch*) the problem is established in the first two sentences:

> It came to Anansi one time, as he sat in his little hut, that he needed a wife. For most men this would have been a simple affair, but Anansi's bad name had spread throughout the country and he knew that he wouldn't be likely to have much luck finding a wife in near-by villages. (p. 95)

With little description, the storyteller goes to the heart of his story, capturing the interest of his audience.

The conclusion of the story follows the climax very quickly and includes few details. In the Grimm brothers' *The Seven Ravens*, after the small sister finds her brothers who have been bewitched as ravens, she leaves her tiny ring in the cup belonging to one of the ravens. He sees it and makes a wish:

> "Would God that our own little sister were here, for then we should be free . . . !"
>
> When the maiden, who was standing behind the door listening, heard the wish, she came out, and then all the ravens regained human forms again. And they embraced and kissed one another and went joyfully home. (unpaged)

Even this is a long ending compared with "And so they were married and lived happily ever after."

The structure of the folktale, with its quick introduction, economy of incident, and logical and brief conclusion, maintains interest through suspense and repetition. Because the storyteller has to keep the attention of the audience, each episode must contribute to the theme of the story. Written versions, then, should follow the oral tradition, adding little description and avoiding lengthy asides or admonitions.

Characterization

Characters in folktales are shown in flat dimensions, symbolic of the completely good or entirely evil. Character development is seldom depicted. The beautiful girl is usually virtuous, humble, patient, and loving. Stepmothers are ugly, cross, and mean. The hero, usually fair-haired or curly-haired, is strong, virile, brave, kind, and sympathetic. The poor are often kind, generous, and long-suffering; the rich are imperious, hardhearted, and often conniving, if not actually dishonest. Physical characteristics may be described briefly, but readers form their own pictures as they read. In describing the daughter of the Dragon King, the Chinese grandmother says: "Now this young woman was poorly dressed, but her face was as fair as a plum blossom in spring, and her body was as slender as a willow branch."[14]

Qualities of character or special strengths or weaknesses of the characters are revealed quickly, because this factor will be the cause of conflict or lead to resolution of the plot. The trickster character of Brer Rabbit in Van Dyke Parks's *Jump Again!* is established in a few swift phrases: "Brer Rabbit could cut more capers than a hive has bumbly-bees. Under his hat, Brer Rabbit had a mighty quick thinking apparatus" (p. 2).

Seeing folktale characters as symbols of good, evil, power, trickery, wisdom, and other traits, children begin to understand the basis of literature that distills the essences of human experience.

Style

Folktales offer children many opportunities to hear rich qualitative language and a wide variety of language patterns. Story introductions may range from the familiar "Once upon a time" to the Persian "There was a time and there wasn't a time"; and then there is the African tale that starts: "We do not mean, we do not really mean that what we are going to say is true."

The introductions and language of the folktale should maintain the "flavor" of the country but still be understood by its present audience. Folktales should not be "written down" to children, but they might need to be simplified. Wanda Gág described her method of simplification in adapting folktales for children:

> By simplification I mean:
> (a) freeing hybrid stories of confusing passages

---

[14]Frances Carpenter, *Tales of a Chinese Grandmother*, illustrated by Malthe Hasselriis (New York: Doubleday, 1949), p. 75.

(b) using repetition for clarity where a mature style does not include it

(c) employing actual dialogue to sustain or revive interest in places where the narrative is too condensed for children.

However, I do not mean writing in words of one or two syllables. True, the careless use of large words is confusing to children; but long, even unfamiliar words are relished and easily absorbed by them, provided they have enough color and sound value.[15]

Some folktales include proverbs of the country. For example, in Diane Wolkstein's *The Magic Orange Tree* a king says to his followers after hearing the story of a man whose second wife murdered his son: "Choose whom you want to marry, but if you choose a tree that has fruit, you must care for the fruit as much as for the tree" (p. 97). In Elizabeth Winthrop's Russian story *Vasilissa the Beautiful,* a small doll counsels the sorrowful Vasilissa to shut her eyes and sleep, for "The morning is wiser than the evening."

Although there is a minimum of description in the folktale, figurative language and imagery are employed by effective narrators. In *Mazel and Shlimazel,* Isaac Singer uses delightful prose to introduce the Jewish tale about the wager between the spirits of good luck and bad luck:

In a faraway land, on a sunny spring day, the sky was as blue as the sea, and the sea was as blue as the sky, and the earth was green and in love with them both. (p. 1)

In Verna Aardema's East African story *Bimwili and the Zimwi,* a little girl, Bimwili, was playing by the ocean, and "something that looked like a daytime moon came rolling in with a wave, and it tumbled at Bimwili's feet." The daytime moon, a simile for a seashell, begins all of Bimwili's many nights of troubles.

Frequently storytellers imitate the sounds of the story. In Verna Aardema's retelling of a West African tale in *Why Mosquitoes Buzz in People's Ears,* a python slithers into a rabbit's hole *wasawusu, wasawusu, wasawusu,* and the terrified rabbit scurries away *krik, krik, krik.* In Isaac Olaleye's Nigerian tale *In the Rainfield: Who Is the Greatest,* a feat of wills takes place among Fire, Wind, and Water. Wind whistles furiously, "fuuu, fuuu." Fire eats "everything in its way, weere, weere," but gentle Rain, singing "wini-wini, wini-wini," puts out Fire and cannot be doused by Wind. These onomatopoeic words help listeners hear the story and are wonderful additions for those who tell and read stories to children.

When the tales are written as though the storyteller is speaking directly to the reader, the oral tradition is more clearly communicated. Joyce Arkhurst uses this style effectively in *The Adventures of Spider:*

I have already told you, and you have already seen for yourselves, that Spider was very full of mischief. He was often naughty and always greedy. But sometimes, in his little heart, he wanted very much to be good. . . . He tried hard, but his appetite almost always got in the way. In fact, that is why Spider has a bald head to this day. Would you like to hear how it got that way? (p. 21)

Dialect enhances a story, but it is difficult for children to read. The teacher will need to practice reading or telling a story with dialect, but it is worth the effort if it is done well. Julius Lester, in his retellings of the Uncle Remus stories collected by Joel Chandler Harris, tried to do what Harris had done: namely, to write tales "so that the reader (listener) would feel as if he or she were being called into a relationship of warmth and intimacy with another human body."[16] His contemporary storyteller communicates through asides, imagery, and allusions. For instance, in "Brer Rabbit Gets Even," in Julius Lester's *The Tales of Uncle Remus,* Brer Rabbit decides to visit with Miz Meadows and the girls:

"Don't come asking me who Miz Meadows and her girls were. I don't know, but then again, ain't no reason I got to know. Miz Meadows and the girls were in the tale when it was handed to me, and they gon' be in it when I hand it to you. And that's the way the rain falls on that one. . . ." (p. 16)

The major criteria for style in the written folktale, then, are that it maintain the atmosphere of the country and culture from which it originated and that it sound like a tale *told* by a storyteller.

Themes

The basic purpose of the folktale is to tell an entertaining story, yet these stories do present important themes. Some tales might be merely humorous accounts of foolish people who are so ridiculous that the listeners see their own foolish ways exaggerated in them. Many of the stories once provided an outlet for feelings against the kings and nobles who oppressed the poor. Values of the culture are expressed in folklore. Humility, kindness, patience, sympathy, hard work, and courage are invariably rewarded. These rewards reflect the goals of people—long life, a good spouse, beautiful homes and fine clothing, plenty of food, freedom from fear of the ogre or giant. Sometimes these themes are stated explicitly at the end of the book as in Ed Young's *What about Me?* This Sufi tale recalls the

---

[15]Wanda Gág, *Tales from Grimm* (New York: Coward-McCann, 1936), p. ix.

[16]Julius Lester, "The Storyteller's Voice: Reflections on the Rewriting of Uncle Remus," *New Advocate* 1, no. 3 (summer 1988): 144.

The theme of giving and receiving is clearly stated in Ed Young's cumulative story *What about Me?* From *What about Me?* by Ed Young, copyright © 2002 by Ed Young. Used by permission of Philomel Books, a division of Penguin Young Readers Group, a division of Putnam Group (USA), Inc., 345 Hudson St., New York, NY 10014. All rights reserved.

cumulative pattern of Nonny Hogrogian's *One Fine Day.* In both of these stories a character must accomplish one difficult task after another to reach a goal. In Hogrogian's tale a naughty fox's goal is the restoration of his tail. In Young's story the young hero desires knowledge. When he approaches the Grand Master, he is sent out to get a small carpet for the Master's work. This, of course, is not as simple a task as it sounds. After many arduous trials the boy finds that the knowledge he sought was already his. The Grand Master cautions, "Some of the most precious gifts that we receive are those we receive when we are giving," and "Often, knowledge comes to us when we least expect it" (p. 32). In Verna Aardema's *Koi and the Kola Nuts: A Tale from Liberia,* a young man who has inherited a seemingly useless nut tree packs up some of the nuts and sets off on a journey. To his surprise, Koi encounters three people who desperately need the very nuts he carries. Koi shares them willingly and is, of course, justly rewarded. The power of love, mercy, and kindness is one of the major themes of folktales. The thematic wisdom of Mme. de Beaumont's *Beauty and the Beast* and Charlotte Huck's *Black Bull of Norroway* is that we should not trust too much to appearances. The valuing of the inner qualities of kindness and a loving heart above outward appearance is dramatically presented.

Many folktales feature the small and powerless achieving good ends by perseverance and patience. In Gail Haley's African tale *A Story, a Story,* Anansi the spider man wins stories for his people by outsmarting a leopard, the hornets, and a fairy and presenting them all to the Sky God. Both Marina, the good child in Eric Kimmel's *Baba Yaga,* and Sasha, the kind girl in Joanna Cole's *Bony-Legs,* have good luck when they are kind to objects and animals. Thus they are able to outwit the formidable old Russian witch, Baba Yaga.

Feminists have expressed concern that folktale themes most often favor courageous, independent boy adventurers and leave girl characters languishing at home. Though it is true that it is easier to find tales that feature plucky boys, there are folktales that portray resourceful, courageous, clever, and independent girls. In Susan Cooper's *Tam Lin,* an outspoken heroine perseveres in saving a young man bewitched by the fairies even though they change him into many fearsome animals. In the Grimm brothers' *Princess Furball,* the heroine doesn't need a fairy godmother; she wins a prince because of her own cleverness. In Harve Zemach's *Duffy and the Devil,* the heroine makes a pact with the devil, but she finally outwits him—and manages to get out of spinning and knitting for the rest of her days. Anait in Robert D. San Souci's *A Weave of Words* is independent and goal directed. She rejects the pretty prince until he learns to read and write and learn a skill, then she is the one to save him from a three-headed ogre. In Anthony Manna's *Mr. Semolina-Semolinus: A Greek Folktale,* the heroine is so dissatisfied with her suitors that she creates the perfect mate out of almonds, sugar, and semolina. Other tales do not involve romance at all but show a heroine who, though small and young, outwits the large and powerful. In Margaret Willey's *Clever Beatrice* the main character sets out to replenish the family coffers by outwitting a giant. In Katrin Tchana's *Sense Pass King* the heroine receives that name because she is smarter than the ruler. Because of her sense and great courage, she outsmarts the king. She becomes the ruler in his stead and gains a new name, Queen Ma'antah. Tales that feature spirited and courageous heroines have been gathered in several collections. Robert D. San Souci's *Cut from the Same Cloth: American Women of Myth, Legend and Tall Tale,* Virginia Hamilton's *Her Stories: African American Folktales,* Ethel Johnston Phelps's *The Maid of the North,* Katrin Tchana's *The Serpent Slayer and Other Tales of Strong Women,* and editor Rosemary Minard's *Womenfolk and Fairy Tales* are examples of collections from the world over that preserve and honor stories of strong, clever, and often brave women. Jane Yolen has provided boys with nontraditional role models in *Mightier Than the Sword,* illustrated by Raul Colón. In these stories "brain trumps brawn almost every time," unlike the heroes boys encounter in the popular media.

Parents, teachers, and some psychologists have expressed concern about themes of cruelty and horror in folktales. "Little Red Riding Hood," for example, has been rewritten so that the wolf eats neither the grandmother nor the heroine. Goals are not accomplished easily in folktales; they frequently require sacrifice. But usually harsh acts occur very quickly with no sense of pain and no details. In the Grimm brothers' *Seven Ravens*, no blood drips from the sister's hand when she cuts off a finger; not an "ouch" escapes her lips. Children accept these stories as they are—symbolic interpretations of life in an imaginary land of another time.

Motifs

Folklorists analyze folktales according to motifs or patterns, numbering each tale and labeling its episodes.[17] *Motif* has been defined as the smallest part of a tale that can exist independently. Motifs can be seen in the recurring parade of characters in folktales—the younger brother, the wicked stepmother, the abused child, the clever trickster—or in supernatural beings like the fairy godmother, the evil witch, and the terrifying giant. The use of magical objects (a slipper, a doll, a ring, a tablecloth) is another pattern found in many folktales. Stories of enchantment, long sleeps, or marvelous transformations are typical motifs. Some motifs have been repeated so frequently that they have been identified as a type of folk story. Thus we have beast tales about talking animals and wonder tales about supernatural beings.

Even the story plots have recurring patterns—three tasks to be performed, three wishes that are granted, three trials to be endured. A simple tale will have several motifs; a complex one will have many. Recognizing some of the most common motifs in folklore will help a teacher to suggest points of comparison and contrast in a cross-cultural approach to folk literature.

Magical Powers Magical powers are frequently given to persons or animals in folktales. A common motif in folklore is the presence of "helpful companions" who all have magical talents. In Arthur Ransome's *The Fool of the World and the Flying Ship*, the fool sails away with eight companions who can eat huge quantities, hear long distances, and drink whole lakes. Later these talents help them overcome trials the czar imposes on the fool. In William Hooks's *Moss Gown*, the gris-gris woman can make a girl fly as well as create a gown for her out of moss, in which she is able to attend the Carolina plantation owner's ball. Of course, the Grimms' *Rumpelstiltskin* can spin straw into gold. The possessors of magical powers always aid heroes and heroines in obtaining their goals.

Transformations The transformation of an animal into a person, or the reverse, is a part of many folktales. *Beauty and the Beast* by Mme. de Beaumont and *The Lady and the Lion* by Laurel Long and Jacqueline K. Ogburn are

Laurel Long's illustrations for *The Lady and the Lion*, retold with Jacqueline K. Ogburn, provide a medieval setting for this tale of transformation. *From The Lady and the Lion: A Brothers Grimm Tale. Illustrated by Laurel Long, © 2003 by Laurel Long, illustrations. Used by permission of Dial Books for Young Readers, a division of Penguin Putnam, Inc.*

two versions of the familiar tale of a bewitched animal transformed by love. A crane turns into a woman and back into a crane when her spouse is disloyal in the Japanese tale recounted in Odds Bodkin's *The Crane Wife*. "Selkies" are seals that have shed their skins and assumed human form in Susan Cooper's *The Selkie Girl*. Children who feel caught between two cultures or between the world of childhood and the world of adolescence might see themselves reflected in such stories. In fact, in *The Star Fisher*, a work of historical fiction, Laurence Yep uses a tale similar to *The Crane Wife* to represent the conflict felt by a young Chinese girl whose family moves to West Virginia from China.

Magical Objects Magical objects are essential aspects of many tales that also reflect other themes or motifs. Both a ring and a lamp play essential parts in the story recounted in Eric Kimmel's *The Tale of Aladdin and the*

---

[17]Stith Thompson, *Motif Index of Folk Literature* (Bloomington: Indiana University Press, 1955–1958), 6 vols.

Wonderful Lamp. In Elizabeth Winthrop's *Vasilissa the Beautiful,* the heroine is able to outwit Baba Yaga's demands with the help of a magical little doll given to her by her mother. In Tomie dePaola's *Strega Nona,* the title character owns a magical cooking pot that can be started by saying "Bubble, bubble, pasta pot" to make all the pasta anyone needs. But Big Anthony, a true noodlehead, starts the pot without observing Strega Nona's method of getting it to stop: blowing three kisses. The title character of Arlene Mosel's *The Funny Little Woman* has a magical rice paddle that she uses to good advantage both underground and above. Other magical objects that figure in folktales are purses, harps, hens that lay golden eggs, tables, sticks, and tinderboxes. A magical object often heightens a good character's courage and cleverness, whereas in other stories the misuse of a magical object can cause disaster for a bad character.

Wishes Many stories are told of wishes that are granted and then used foolishly or in anger or greed. In *The Three Wishes* Margot Zemach recounts the tale of the woodsman who was so hungry that he wished for a sausage; his wife was so angry at this wish that she wished the food would stick to his nose; then, of course, they have to use the third wish to get it off. In Gerald McDermott's *The Stonecutter,* a character wishes to have more power but ends up in a position of powerlessness. In the Grimm brothers' *The Fisherman and His Wife,* as in these other stories, greed destroys any gains a character might make.

In a Native American tale, *Gluskabe and the Four Wishes,* retold by Joseph Bruchac, Gluskabe gives four men wishing pouches but warns them not to look inside until they get home. Three men cannot resist and are justly punished. The fourth man is rewarded for his patience in an unusual way.

Trickery Both animals and people trick their friends and neighbors in folk literature. The wolf tricks Little Red Riding Hood into believing he is her grandmother; Hansel and Gretel trick the mean old witch into crawling into the oven.

Almost every culture has an animal trickster in its folklore. In European folktales it is usually a wolf or a fox; in Japan it is a badger or a hare; Indonesia has Kantjil, a tiny mouse deer; Africa has three well-known tricksters—Anansi the spider, Zomo the rabbit, and Ijapa the tortoise. Coyote and Raven play this role in Native American tales.

Three realistic tales feature humans tricking others. In the familiar tale in Marcia Brown's *Stone Soup,* three poor soldiers dupe greedy peasants into contributing all of the ingredients for a pot of soup, save one—a stone, with which they generously start off the pot. In Diane Snyder's *The Boy of the Three-Year Nap,* the lazy boy tricks a rich merchant, but then is tricked into a lifetime occupation by his wise old mother. In Demi's *One Grain of Rice: A Mathematical Tale,* a village girl tricks a raja into giving up a billion grains of rice.

Magical powers, transformations, the use of magical objects, wishes, and trickery are just a few of the motifs that run through the folklore of all countries, as we have seen. Others might include the power of naming, as in Paul Galdone's *Rumpelstiltskin;* the ability to make yourself invisible, as the man did in Marianna Mayer's *The Twelve Dancing Princesses;* becoming stuck to a person or object, as in the African American tale "The Wonderful Tar-Baby Story" in Van Dyke Parks's *Jump Again;* or an enchanted or lengthy sleep, as in "Urashimo Taro and the Princess of the Sea," in Yoshiko Uchida's *The Dancing Kettle;* or in the Grimms' *Snow White.* One way to understand the common elements of all folklore is to make your own lists of motifs or have the children in your classroom do so.

Teaching Resources: "A Cross-Cultural Study of Folktale Motifs" mentions both well-known and lesser-known tales as a beginning for those wishing to pursue a study of motifs. There are many other titles that could be listed for these five motifs, and, of course, there are many more motifs around which to group folklore.

Variants

The number of variants of a single folktale can fascinate beginning students of folklore. Each variant has basically the same story or plot as another, but it might have different characters and a different setting or it might use different motifs. For example, in Robert D. San Souci's retelling of an African American story in *The Talking Eggs,* a poor girl is kind to an old woman and in return is given some plain eggs that become riches when tossed behind her. Later her greedy stepsister is critical and unhelpful to the old woman. She chooses to take fancy eggs instead of plain ones, but when these are tossed, out come stinging insects. In the Philippine tale retold by Jose Aruego and Ariane Dewey in *Rockabye Crocodile,* a kind boar and a greedy one end up in similar situations when one rocks a cranky baby crocodile while the other ignores it. In John Steptoe's *Mufaro's Beautiful Daughters,* the sister who takes time to stop and help people is the one who wins the prince's love. The theme of rewards for a generous and willing person and punishment for a greedy and disobedient one seems to be universal.

A comparison of the variants of the Cinderella story illustrates differences in theme and motif. Scholars have found versions of this story in ancient Egypt, in ninth-century China, and in tenth-century Iceland. Cinderella receives her magical gifts in many different ways. In the French and most familiar version (see Charles Perrault's), a fairy godmother gives them to her; in the Grimms' version, a dove appears on the tree that grew from the tears she had shed on her mother's grave; in the Chinese version in Ai-Ling Louie's *Yeh-Shen,* magical fish bones bestow gifts on her. She attends three balls in some stories, and her treatment of the stepsisters varies from blinding them to inviting them to live at the palace. The

A Cross-Cultural Study of Folktale Motifs

 Visit the Online Learning Center at **www.mhhe.com/kiefer9e** for a printable version of this list.

MAGICAL POWERS

Tale (Author)	Culture
The Fool of the World and the Flying Ship (Ransome)	Russia
Moss Gown (Hooks)	United States
Rumpelstiltskin (Galdone)	Germany
The Seven Chinese Brothers (Mahy)	China
Yeh-Shen (Louie)	China

TRANSFORMATIONS

Tale (Author)	Culture
Beauty and the Beast (de Beaumont)	France
Cinderella (Perrault)	France
The Crane Wife (Bodkin)	Japan
The Frog Prince or Iron Henry (Grimm brothers)	Germany
The Lady and the Lion (Long and Ogburn)	Germany
The Loathsome Dragon (Wiesner)	Britain
The Orphan Boy (Mollel)	Africa (Kenya)
The Story of Jumping Mouse (Steptoe)	Native American
Tam Lin (Cooper)	Scotland

MAGICAL OBJECTS

Tale (Author)	Culture
The Magic Purse (Uchida)	Japan
The Patient Stone (Wolfson)	Persia
The Tale of Aladdin and the Wonderful Lamp (Kimmel)	Middle East
The Talking Eggs (San Souci)	African American
The Three Princes (Kimmel)	Middle East
The Twelve Dancing Princesses (Mayer)	France
Two of Everything (Hong)	China
Vasilissa the Beautiful (Winthrop)	Russia

(continued)

A Cross-Cultural Study of Folktale Motifs *(continued)*

WISHES

Tale (Author)	Culture
The Fisherman and His Wife (Grimm brothers)	Germany
Gluskabe and the Four Wishes (Bruchac)	Native American
The Seven Ravens (Grimm brothers)	Germany
The Stonecutter (McDermott)	Japan
The Three Wishes (M. Zemach)	Germany

TRICKERY

Tale (Author)	Culture
The Boy of the Three-Year Nap (Snyder)	Japan
Finn MacCoul and His Fearless Wife (Byrd)	Ireland
"Firefly and the Apes," in *More Stories to Solve* (Shannon)	Philippines
Goha, the Wise Fool (Johnson-Davies)	Egypt
Jabuti the Tortoise (McDermott)	Amazon River region
Just a Minute (Morales)	Mexico
Lapin Plays Possum (Doucet)	Louisiana
Lon Po Po (Young)	China
Love and Roast Chicken (Knutson)	Andes Mountains
The Man Who Tricked a Ghost (Yep)	China
Mrs. Chicken and the Hungry Crocodile (Paye and Lippert)	Liberia
Please, Malese! (A. MacDonald)	Haiti
Rabbit Makes a Monkey of Lion (Aardema)	Africa (Tanzania)
"Shrewd Todie and Lyzer, and Mizer," in *When Shlemiel Went to Warsaw* (Singer)	Jewish
Stone Soup (Brown)	France
The Tale of Rabbit and Coyote (Johnston)	Mexico
Three Sacks of Truth (Kimmel)	France

Vietnamese version, "The Brocaded Slipper," recounted by Lynette Dyer Vuong, is made longer by the narrative of the stepsister's finally meeting her own death after "killing" her Cinderella sister, Tam, three times. In Rafe Martin's *The Rough-Face Girl,* an Algonquin story, the daughter of a poor man is made to sit by the fire by her cruel elder sisters. After a time her face and hands become horribly scarred and she is rejected by the villagers. For this reason she is often called "Little Burnt Face" in other versions of this tale.

Variants of the Rumpelstiltskin story (see the retelling by Paul Zelinsky) include the hero's need to know the antagonist's name in order to have his services or to be safe from his magical powers. A character in these stories is able to discover the name and trick an imp, dwarf, or fairy. Variations on this theme can be found in Harve Zemach's Cornish *Duffy and the Devil*, Evaline Ness's English *Tom Tit Tot*, and the Scottish *Whuppity Stoorie* by Carolyn White, all of which are discussed later in this chapter in the section titled "British Folktales."

Knowledge of the variants of a tale, common motifs, and common types of folktales enable teachers to help children see similar elements in folktales across cultures. Knowledge of the folklore of a particular country or cultural group aids in identifying the uniqueness and individuality of that group. Both approaches to a study of folklore seem essential. Teaching Resources: "A Cross-Cultural Study of Folktale Variants" can help the teacher organize tales by variants for classroom presentation.

Folktales of the World

 Every culture has produced folklore. A study of the folktales of West Africa, Russia, Japan, or North America can provide insights into the beliefs of these peoples, their values, their jokes, their lifestyles, their histories. At the same time, a cross-cultural study of folk literature can help children discover the universal qualities of humankind.

British Folktales

 The first folktales that most children in the United States hear are the English ones. This is because Joseph Jacobs, the folklorist who collected many of the English tales, deliberately adapted them for young children, writing them, he said, "as a good old nurse will speak when she tells Fairy Tales." His collection includes cumulative tales such as "The Old Woman and Her Pig" and "Henny Penny," and the much-loved talking-beast stories "The Little Red Hen," "The Three Bears," and "The Three Little Pigs."

An element of realism runs through some English folktales. The story of Dick Whittington and his cat has its basis in history. There was once a real Richard Whittington who was three times mayor of London, in 1396, 1406, and 1419. And what an exceptional mayor he must have been—enacting prison reforms, providing the first public lavatory and drinking fountain, and building a library and a wing on the hospital for unmarried mothers. It is no wonder that the common people made him the popular hero of one of their most cherished tales. The story "Dick and His Cat" was found in some of the very earliest chapbooks of the day. Marcia Brown's picture storybook *Dick Whittington and His Cat* portrays this realistic tale with handsome linoleum block prints appropriately printed in gold and black.

A Cornish variation on the German "Rumpelstiltskin" is presented in Harve Zemach's *Duffy and the Devil*. Illustrator Margot Zemach depicts the devil as a "squinny-eyed creature"; he dances and sings:

Tomorrow! Tomorrow! Tomorrow's the day!
I'll take her! I'll take her! I'll take her away!
Let her weep, let her cry, let her beg, let her pray—
She'll never guess my name is Tarraway! (unpaged)

However, Duffy's outwitting of the devil makes all of her husband's handspun clothes disappear! Both the language and the pen-and-wash illustrations retain the Cornish flavor of this folklore comedy. In the Scottish *Whuppity Stoorie* by Carolyn White, an evil fairy cures a poor woman's prize pig and demands her daughter Kate in return unless she can guess her name. The noble pig earns her keep by leading Kate deep into the forest where she overhears the fairy call herself "Whuppity Stoorie."

For his retelling of *The Well at the End of the World*, Robert D. San Souci consulted several versions of a British tale that dates back at least as far as Elizabethan times. This story is a variant of the kind-person/greedy-person theme in which Princess Rosamond undertakes a journey to obtain the magic waters that will cure her father's illness. On her trip she kindly does three favors. She is, of course, rewarded with the healing water—and with jewels, coins, and flowers that fall out of her mouth when she speaks. Her selfish stepsister is not so lucky when she undertakes the same journey out of greed. San Souci and illustrator Rebecca Walsh give the story a self-confident princess who is also an accomplished accountant and ardent reader!

Susan Cooper's *Tam Lin*, a version of the story told in the Scottish ballad "Tamlane," shows how storytellers and illustrators give new meanings to a story. Young

Rebecca Walsh's illustrations emphasize nontraditional character roles in a traditional tale, *The Well at the End of the World*, retold by Robert D. San Souci. Illustration © 2004 by Rebecca Walsh. Used by permission of Chronicle Books, LLC.

A Cross-Cultural Study of Folktale Variants

 Visit the Online Learning Center at **www.mhhe.com/kiefer9e** for a printable version of this list.

CINDERELLA

Theme	Culture
Adelita (dePaola)	Mexico
Cendrillon (R. San Souci)	Caribbean
Cinderella (Perrault)	France
The Egyptian Cinderella (Climo)	Egypt
Fair, Brown, and Trembling (Daly)	Ireland
The Gift of the Crocodile (Sierra)	Indonesia
The Golden Sandal (Hickox)	Middle East
Kongi and Potgi (Han)	Korea
The Korean Cinderella (Climo)	Korea
The Little Gold Star (R. San Souci)	Spanish American
Moss Gown (Hooks)	United States
Princess Furball (Grimm brothers)	Germany
Sootface (R. San Souci)	Native American
Vasilissa the Beautiful (Winthrop)	Russia
Yeh-Shen (Louie)	China

MAGICAL GIFTS

Theme	Culture
"The Lad Who Went to the North Wind," in *East o'the Sun and West o'the Moon* (Asbjørnsen and Moe)	Norway
The Magic Purse (Uchida)	Japan
The Table, the Donkey, and the Stick (Grimm brothers)	Germany
Willa and the Wind (Del Negro)	Scandinavia

MAGICAL POTS

Theme	Culture
The Bachelor and the Bean (Fowles)	Moroccan Jewish
The Funny Little Woman (Mosel)	Japan
The Magic Gourd (Diakité)	Mali
The Magic Porridge Pot (Galdone)	Germany
Strega Nona (dePaola)	Italy

A Cross-Cultural Study of Folktale Variants *(continued)*

GENEROUS PERSON/GREEDY PERSON

Theme	Culture
Baba Yaga (Kimmel)	Russia
The Impudent Rooster (Rascol)	Romania
The Language of Birds (Martin)	Russia
Mufaro's Beautiful Daughters (Steptoe)	Africa (Zimbabwe)
Rockaby Crocodile (Aruego and Dewey)	Philippines
The Talking Eggs (R. San Souci)	African American
Toads and Diamonds (Huck)	France
The Well at the End of the World (R. San Souci)	England

HELPFUL COMPANIONS

Theme	Culture
Anansi the Spider (McDermott)	West Africa
The Fool of the World and the Flying Ship (Ransome)	Russia
Iron John (Kimmel)	Germany
The Little Humpbacked Horse (Winthrop)	Russia
The Loyal Cat (Namioka)	Japan
Ouch! (Babbitt)	Germany
The Seven Chinese Brothers (Mahy)	China
The Shark God (Martin)	Hawaii
The Silver Charm (R. San Souci)	Japan

NAMING

Theme	Culture
Ananse and the Lizard (Cummings)	West Africa
Duffy and the Devil (H. Zemach)	England
The Girl Who Spun Gold (Hamilton)	West Indies
Rumpelstiltskin (Grimm brothers)	Germany
Tom Tit Tot (Ness)	England
Whuppity Stoorie (White)	Scotland

Margaret has a mind of her own. Rather than sit around the castle rubbing cucumber into her skin, she longs for adventure and sets out to pick roses in the haunted Carterhays wood. In the forest she meets a young man who has been claimed by the fairies over a hundred years before. He is Tam Lin, and if she cannot save him by Midsummer's Eve he will die, his soul sent to hell. The way she must save him is to pull him from his horse when the fairy procession passes and hold him no matter what shape he assumes. Margaret perseveres, outwits the fairies, and wins herself a husband. Warwick Hutton's ethereal watercolors give this version a dreamlike appearance, and his depiction of Tam Lin's transformation is dramatically rendered over three pages.

In *The Selkie Girl*, Cooper and Hutton present another legend of Scottish or Irish origin, concerning a man who takes as his wife a selkie, who is a gray seal in the water but a woman on land. He hides her sealskin and for many years the woman lives as his wife and mother to their five children. But when the youngest child finds his mother's sealskin, she confesses that she also has a family of five children in the sea, bids farewell to her landbound family, and disappears into the sea. Children familiar with Tam Lin or selkie stories can recognize the shape-changing or transformation motif, which is found in ancient mythology as well as modern fantasy (see Chapter 7). Cooper and Hutton have produced another tale of transformation in their Welsh story, *The Silver Cow*. In this story the Scottish fairies, the Fey, turn cows into waterlilies when a farmer's greed gets the better of his judgment.

British folklore includes wonderfully exotic characters that often appeared in Celtic mythology—selkies, kelpies, hobs, and, of course, giants such as the one found in Jack and the Beanstalk (see versions retold by Ann Benaduce and Steven Kellogg). The Irish folk giant Finn McCool and his wife Oona can be found in Jessica Souhami's *Mrs. McCool and the Giant Cuhullin* and Robert Byrd's *Finn MacCoul and His Fearless Wife*. This region has developed fewer of the complicated wonder tales that abound in French and Russian folklore. Its stories are often more robust and humorous than some other European tale traditions. Its greatest contribution has been made to the youngest children in providing such nursery classics as "The Three Little Pigs," "Henny Penny," "The Little Red Hen," and "Johnny-cake."

German Folktales

 Next in popularity to the English folktales are those of German origin. Jacob and Wilhelm Grimm spent more than twelve years collecting the tales they published in 1812 as the first volume of *Kinder und Hausmärchen* (Household Stories). They did not adapt their stories for children, as Joseph Jacobs did for British folktales, but were very careful to preserve (without benefit of a tape recorder) the form and content of the tales as they were told. In 1823 to 1826, these were then translated into English by Edgar Taylor.

German folklore is enlivened by elves, dwarfs, and devils, rather than the fairies of other cultures. The Grimm brothers' *The Elves and the Shoemaker* tells of a kindly but poor shoemaker who is aided in his work by elves until he and his wife return the favor by making the elves clothes. Then, off the elves scamper, never to be seen again. Natalie Babbitt has written an amusing version of the Grimms' "The Devil with the Three Golden Hairs" in her story *Ouch!* The story tells of a young man who wins the hand of the king's daughter by obtaining three hairs from the devil with the help of the devil's grandmother. Fred Marcellino creates an elaborate Renaissance setting in his sprightly illustrations.

Paul O. Zelinsky's elegant paintings for his edition of the Grimm brothers' *Rumpelstiltskin* set the tale in a medieval castle, and the gold of the spun straw shines richly from the pages. Paul Galdone's version presents a weepier daughter, a less elegant castle, and a more dwarflike little man. In comparing these versions, children would discover these subtle differences in aspects of the illustrations, as well as the demise of the little man, the verse in which he reveals his name, and the name guesses the miller's daughter offers.

Many children know a version of "Snow White" only from the cartoon story created by Walt Disney Studios. However, Nancy Ekholm Burkert's illustrations and Randall Jarrell's retelling in *Snow-White and the Seven Dwarfs* more faithfully recreate the original Grimm story. Burkert used her own 14-year-old daughter as the model for Snow White. Her drawings of dwarfs are based on weeks of medical library research studying characteristic proportions of dwarfs. And so Burkert's dwarfs are not grotesque elves, but real people who are loving and proud. The medieval cottage of the dwarfs is an authentic depiction; every architectural detail, the rich fabrics on floor and wall, the very plates and mugs on the table, were copied from museum pieces. In keeping with artistic styles of the late Middle Ages, Burkert used images symbolically: the white dog, the basket of cherries, and the lilies on the table signify virginity; the meadow rue embroidered on the girl's apron was supposed to protect the wearer against witches; a Tarot card, the red mushrooms, spiders, and other articles in the witch's workroom signify evil. Another edition of *Snow White* has been faithfully translated by Paul Heins and illustrated with robust, more romantic pictures by Trina Schart Hyman. In this version, the artist skillfully portrays the ravaging effects of the queen's jealous madness through the changing appearance of her face.

The villain in the few beast tales in German folklore is usually a wolf. Perhaps the best-known wolf appears in the Grimms' story "Little Red Cap." In the familiar story, the heroine ignores her mother's warnings, and as a result she and her grandmother are eaten. Both escape through the intervention of a passing hunter who thinks that the wolf's loud snores couldn't be coming from a healthy grandmother. After her adventure, the little girl vows always to obey her mother's advice. Lisbeth Zwerger, in *Little Red Cap*, and Trina Schart Hyman, in *Little Red Riding Hood*, have portrayed this story with striking but differing illustrations. Hyman presents a younger, more innocent child distracted by the wolf. Small vignettes depicting household details, wildflowers, and insects are enclosed in changing border frames, giving the whole book a delightfully old-fashioned look. Beautiful, spare watercolors by Zwerger portray a contrastingly older Red Cap, and only essential props are set against a soft and muted backdrop. James Marshall has illustrated his version of this tale in his characteristically humorous way.

Some of the Grimm tales can be grim, dark, and forbidding. Small children can be frightened by *Hansel and Gretel*, the somber tale of a brother and sister abandoned in the woods by their parents and nearly eaten by a horrible witch. However, justice does prevail in this wonder tale. The witch dies in the same way as she had intended to kill the children; the stepmother also dies; and the children, laden with wealth, are reunited with their joyful father. Several very different illustrated versions present this tale to children. Paul Zelinsky's oil paintings somberly recreate the forest settings and the interior of the poor woodcutter's house, and we can almost smell the witch's tasty house. Lisbeth Zwerger's illustrations portray characters against a brown wash that gives the action a dreamlike, long-ago appearance. Younger children will find Will Moses's folk art illustrations less frightening than Zelinsky's or Zwerger's.

Other Grimm stories featuring witches have been illustrated and retold. In *Rapunzel*, a witch, though never unkind to Rapunzel, nevertheless keeps her locked in a tower until a prince climbs her braids. When the witch discovers the prince, she throws him from the tower and he is blinded by the sharp thorns below. A year later, he and Rapunzel are reunited and her tears restore his sight. Paul O. Zelinsky received the Caldecott Medal for his painstakingly rendered illustrations for *Rapunzel*. As he explains in a detailed afterword, he chose to set the story in Renaissance Italy in keeping with Italian elements of the story that he included. Trina Schart Hyman's dark and mysterious illustrations for this story have a Slavic appearance and owe a debt to Russian illustrator Ivan Biliban's use of small rectangular vignettes and borders. In Alix Berenzy's version, the illustrations and page design recall the miniatures and decorations in illuminated manuscripts.

Another Grimm tale with a moral is *The Frog Prince*, which stresses the importance of keeping a promise, even if it is made by a princess to a frog. So the king makes his daughter honor her promise to welcome a frog that has retrieved her golden ball from a deep, dark pond. After the princess lets the frog sit by her side, eat from her plate, and sleep in her bed for three nights, the frog becomes a prince and the two are married. Binette Schroeder has created an eerie surrealistic version that includes the prince's faithful servant, Henry, who has bound iron rings around his heart in grief at his master's bewitchment.

Charlotte Huck's "Cinderella" variation on the Grimm story of "Many Furs" is titled *Princess Furball*. A cruel king betroths his motherless daughter to an ogre in exchange for fifty wagonloads of silver. But the princess hopes to foil his plan by first demanding that her father give her three dresses, one as golden as the sun, another as silvery as the moon, and the last as glittering as the stars, as well as a coat made of a thousand pieces of fur, one from every animal in the kingdom. When the king actually fulfills these demands, the princess runs away with her dresses and three tiny treasures that had belonged to her mother. Disguised in her fur coat, she is discovered and taken to another king's castle, where she becomes a scullery maid known as Furball. When the king gives a ball, she appears in one of her dresses and the following day leaves a token in the king's soup. At the third ball, the king slips a ring on Furball's finger and is later able to identify the scullery maid as his own true love, saying, "You are as clever as you are lovely." Practical, independent, and resourceful, Furball has capably managed to create a happy future. Anita Lobel uses opening portraits to personify Furball's dead mother, while a portrait of the ogre looks like the father-king. A series of imprisoning enclosures such as long hallways, deep forests, and windowless kitchens symbolically give way to more open scenes in lighter and brighter colors, with more windows, and finally to the fresh air of an outdoor wedding. In contrast to many other Cinderella characters, Princess Furball is a strong, responsible female who actively brings about her own happy end.

Although there is little mercy for the wicked in these German tales, there is much joy for the righteous. The plots are exciting, fast-moving, and a little frightening. Evil stepmothers, wicked witches, and an occasional mean dwarf hold princes and princesses in magical enchantments that can be broken only by kindness and love. Such were the dreams and wishes of the common folk of Germany when the Grimm brothers recorded their tales.

Scandinavian Folktales

 Most of the Scandinavian folktales are from the single Norwegian collection titled *East o'the Sun and West o'the Moon*. These stories were gathered in the early 1840s by Peter Christian Asbjørnsen and Jorgen Moe. The collection ranks in popularity with the Grimms' fairy tales for much the same reason; the stories capture the vigorous language of the storyteller. Ten years after their publication in Norway, they were ably translated by an Englishman, George Dasent, and made available to the English-speaking world.

Perhaps the best known of all of these stories is *The Three Billy Goats Gruff* (by Asbjørnsen and Moe). These billy goats "trip-trapped" across the troll's bridge to eat the green grass on the other side in a tale that is a perfect example of folktale structure: the use of three billy goats, the increasing size of each one, and the anticipated downfall of the mean old troll. Fast action and an economy of words lead directly to the storyteller's conventional ending: "Snip, snap, snout / This tale's told out." Marcia Brown's matchless illustrations for the version by Asbjørnsen and Moe is faithful to the Norwegian origin of this tale in both the setting of her lively illustrations and in the text. Paul Galdone's picture-book version, showing large close-up illustrations of the goats and the troll, will appeal particularly to the younger child. Norse writer Lise Lunge-Larsen has included the story with nine other troll tales in *The Troll with No Heart in His Body,* a wonderful collection illustrated with woodcuts by Betsy Bowen. Glen Rounds has also illustrated a version of this tale.

Eric Kimmel has placed one of Asbjørnsen's tales in a pioneer setting in *Easy Work.* A husband thinks his wife has it pretty easy staying at home each day. When he chides her, she offers to exchange jobs with him. At first he thinks it is "easy work" and devises some Rube Goldberg inventions to help him mind the baby, churn the butter, bake the biscuits, and watch the cow. When his overconfident macho attitude ends in disaster, he finally admits how hard his wife has to work. Andrew Glass's illustrations bring glorious life to this funny story. In an end note, Kimmel explains that he retold the Asbjørnsen story in honor of Oregon women's rights crusader Abigail Scott Duniway.

George Dasent's *East o'the Sun and West o'the Moon* is a complex tale in which a poor man gives his youngest daughter to a white bear, who promises to make the family rich. The white bear comes to her every night and throws off his beast shape, but he leaves before dawn so she never sees him. When her mother tells her to light a candle and look into his face, she sees a handsome prince, but three drops of hot tallow awaken him. He then tells her of his wicked enchantment in which for one year he must be a bear by day. Now that she has seen him, he must return to the castle that lies east of the sun and west of the moon and marry the princess with a long nose. So the girl seeks the castle, finally arriving there on the back of the North Wind. Before the prince will marry, he sets one condition: he will only marry the one who can wash out the tallow spots on his shirt. Neither his long-nose troll bride-to-be nor an old troll hag can do it, but the girl who has posed as a beggar can wash it white as the snow. The wicked trolls burst, and the prince and princess marry and leave the castle that lies east of the sun and west of the moon. Gillian Barlow's framed paintings in the style of folk art glow with warm colors. Children who know the Greek myth of Cupid and Psyche (see the retelling by M. Charlotte Craft) will recognize similarities in the girl's nighttime curiosity and the trouble it begets. Kathleen Hague and Michael Hague's retelling in their *East of the Sun and West of the Moon* follows the original structure of the story faithfully.

In many of the Norwegian tales, the hero is aided in the accomplishment of seemingly impossible tasks by animals or people that he has been kind to. The hero of Eric Kimmel's *Boots and His Brothers* sets out with his two brothers, Peter and Paul, to seek his fortune. They meet an old woman along the way who tells them that their fortune can be gained from an old king who needs an oak tree chopped down and a well dug. The two older boys push the old woman out of the way and hurry off. But because Boots stops and takes time to talk to her, she gives him three magical objects and some good advice. These help him chop down the enchanted oak tree, dig a well in iron rocks, and fill it with cool, clear water from a hundred leagues away. The king is so delighted with Boots, he gives him his weight in gold and half his kingdom. For the greedy brothers, the king has a job as dogkeepers.

Scandinavian tales often seem to reflect the harsh elements of the northern climate. Animal helpmates assist heroes in overcoming giants or wicked trolls. Frequently heroes are human beings who are held by an evil spell. The Scandinavian tales, characterized by many trolls, magical objects, and enchantments, often are also humorous, exciting, and fast-moving. The youngest son performs impossible tasks with ease and a kind of practical resourcefulness.

French Folktales

 French folktales were the earliest to be recorded, and they are also the most sophisticated and adult. This is probably because these tales were the rage among the court society of Louis XIV. In 1697, Charles Perrault, a distinguished member of the French Academy, published a little volume of fairy tales. The title page bore no name, and there has been some debate as to whether they were the product of Charles Perrault or his son, Pierre. Although the stories were probably very close to the ones told to Pierre by his governess, they have the consciously elegant style of the "literary tale" rather than the "told tale" of the Grimms.

The fairy godmother in *Cinderella* is Perrault's invention, as are the pumpkin coach, the six horses of dappled mouse gray, and the glass slipper. In this French version, Cinderella is kind and forgiving of her two stepsisters, inviting them to live at the palace with her. Illustrators Marcia Brown and Barbara McClintock have both been faithful to the French setting and the original text in their illustrations for Perrault's *Cinderella*. Brown's ethereal pictures in delicate blues and pinks portray the splendid palace scenes. McClintock has depicted the interiors of Versailles and the Paris Opera for the Prince's castle and pays homage to the French painters Watteau and Fragonard in her sumptuous drawings.

The sister story to "Cinderella" is the well-known "Sleeping Beauty," and Perrault's version closely parallels the one collected by the Grimms. It is interesting to

Barbara McClintock's illustrations for *Cinderella* reflect the portraits and landscapes of French painters of the Baroque era.
Cinderella by Barbara McClintock. Published by Scholastic Press/Scholastic Inc. Copyright © 2005 by Barbara McClintock. Reprinted by permission.

compare the wishes that the fairies give to the newborn baby. In the German tale they endow Briar Rose with virtue, beauty, riches, and "everything in the world she could wish for"; in the French version they bestow on her beauty, an angelic disposition, and the abilities to dance, sing, and play music. In both versions the jealous uninvited fairy predicts that the child will prick her finger on a spindle and die. This wish is softened by the last fairy, who changes it to the long sleep of a hundred years to be broken by the kiss of a prince.

On the cover of the version of Perrault's *Puss in Boots* illustrated by Fred Marcellino, a very French Puss looks out past the reader as if plotting his next moves. While he is the only inheritance of the youngest son of a poor miller, he proves his worth by fooling the king into believing the miller's son is the imaginary Marquis of Carabas. He then tricks an ogre out of his gold and proclaims the ogre's castle as his master's. The king is delighted to give his daughter in marriage to the "Marquis," and Puss retires to a life of luxury. Marcellino's illustrations and large type crowd the page as if the story would burst the confines of the book. Children famil-

iar with this version and with the one containing Alain Vaës's elegant illustrations could compare them with Paul Galdone's swashbuckler cat.

The French telling of "The Twelve Dancing Princesses" is more ornate than the German version. In this story a poor soldier discovers an underground kingdom where twelve girls dance their shoes to pieces nightly. Marianna Mayer's cumbersome retelling of the story introduces new elements as well, but Kinuko Y. Craft's luminous paintings are well suited to the spirit of the original tale.

The best-known French wonder tale, other than those by Perrault, is *Beauty and the Beast*, adapted from a long story written in 1757 by Madame de Beaumont. This story of love based on essence rather than appearance has been variously illustrated. Jan Brett's economical text and rich illustrations are framed in jeweled borders, and the elegant tapestries in the background reveal the boar-beast's true identity.

Marcia Brown's *Stone Soup* has long been staple primary-grade fare. As the French villagers clad in wooden shoes and smocks hurry their contributions to the huge soup kettle, the three soldiers maintain a subtly earnest but amused look. In John Stewig's version, Grethel is a solo hungry traveler. When villagers turn down their mouths "like unlucky horseshoes" at her request for food, the girl goes to work with her magic stone and soon has created an evening, and a soup, to remember. Margot Tomes's soft, flat tones give the Stewig story a homespun look.

The folktales of France are usually not the tales of the poor but those of the rich. Most have all the trappings of the traditional fairy tale, including fairy godmothers, stepsisters, and handsome princes. Tales of romance and sophisticated intrigue, they must surely have been the "soap operas" of their day.

Russian Folktales

 Folktales from Russia feature universal patterns of tasks and trials, tricks, and transformations. Russian folktales are often longer and more complicated than those of other countries and frequently involve several sets of tasks. Elizabeth Winthrop's retelling of the story *The Little Humpbacked Horse* is quite complex and begins with a tale of how a modest hero, Ivan, tamed a mare with a golden mane. In return for her freedom, she gives him three horses—two fit as gifts for the tsar and the other a little humpbacked horse. These gifts take Ivan to the tsar, where he becomes stablemaster, but it is the little humpbacked horse who becomes Ivan's helpful companion and helps him through many trials to his final triumph.

Russian folklore is replete with other stories of poor but lucky men. A soldier saves a helpless tsar in Uri Shulevitz's *Soldier and Tsar in the Forest*. In Arthur Ransome's *The Fool of the World and the Flying Ship,* a youngest son goes forth, accompanied by eight companions, each of whom has a magical power that helps in outwitting the treacherous tsar; the fool wins the princess and riches for them both in this Caldecott Medal book. The youngest son is also the hero in Eric Kimmel's *The Castle of Cats,* illustrated by Katya Krenina. Along with his two brothers, Ivan is asked to complete difficult tasks to see who will win the family farm. Ivan succeeds through his own naiveté. However, he decides to give up the family farm to return to the castle and become a cat.

The witch Baba Yaga is a complex character who figures in many Russian tales, including Eric Kimmel's *I-Know-Not-What, I-Know-Not-Where* and *Baba Yaga.*[18] Elizabeth Winthrop's *Vasilissa the Beautiful* is often called "the Russian Cinderella." In this tale, Vasilissa is sent by her stepmother to Baba Yaga to get a light for the cottage, with the hope that the witch will eat her up. But Vasilissa carries with her a doll that her mother gave her before she died. When Baba Yaga gives Vasilissa impos-

sible tasks to perform, the unfortunate girl is saved by the doll's magic and its advice: to go to sleep, for "the morning is wiser than the evening." The renowned Russian illustrator Alexander Koshkin richly paints the story in a seventeenth-century setting. The arrival of Baba Yaga in her mortar and pestle is boldly lit by the glowing eyes of the picketed skulls surrounding her chicken-footed house. K. Y. Craft's paintings for Marianna Mayer's *Baba Yaga and Vasilisa the Brave* are reminiscent of the miniatures found on Russian lacquer boxes.

The same characters reappear in different guises in many Russian tales, and one story often braids into another. Gennady Spirin retells an archetypal Russian story in *The Tale of the Firebird.* In this story Ivan, the youngest son of Tsar Vasilyi, is promised half of his father's kingdom if he can capture the firebird who is eating the golden apples in the royal garden. As in many tales, Ivan accomplishes part of this task, but through his own frailty must soon set upon another, more difficult trial. In this version he has the help of a wolf, the older and wiser companion who appears in many forms in folktales. In addition to performing difficult feats he also encounters traditional Russian villains, Baba Yaga and Koshchei the Immortal, before he returns home victorious.

Not all Russian folktales are dark and complex. The theme of cooperation is addressed in Aleksei Tolstoy's *The Gigantic Turnip.* An old man plants a turnip seed, which grows so big that he needs to call his wife to help by pulling him as he pulls. Eventually they are able to pull up the turnip with the help of their daughter, a dog, a cat, and finally a mouse. This humorous story would make a good primary drama.

The theme of beauty's being in the eye of the beholder is presented in another story. A child lost in the wheatfields, separated from her mother, sobs and proclaims her mother's beauty in Becky Reyher's *My Mother Is the Most Beautiful Woman in the World.* After the townsfolk assemble all of the local beauties for Varya's inspection, a large toothless woman pushes through the crowd and mother and child are reunited.

Jan Brett's *The Mitten* is a Ukrainian tale in which animals small and large accumulate in Nicki's dropped mitten. Jan Brett divides the pages with a birchbark window through which the increasingly stuffed mitten can be seen. A mitten-shaped panel on the left depicts Nicki's busy day; on the right, the next animal who will try to squeeze into the mitten is shown. Alvin Tresselt's version features different animals and reads aloud as if it were a reminiscence. Both Yaroslava, the illustrator of this version, and Jan Brett have included traditional Ukrainian details, costumes, and patterns.

A tale with a musical theme has been retold by Aaron Shepard in *The Sea King's Daughter.* Sadko, a poor mu-

---

[18]See the vivid description of one classroom's discovery of patterns when a teacher presented students with versions of "Baba Yaga" tales, in Joy F. Moss's *Focus on Literature: A Context for Literacy Learning* (Katonah, N.Y.: Richard C. Owen, 1990), pp. 49–62.

Ivan Tsarevitch and the lovely Yelena ride off on a magic horse in Gennady Spirin's *The Tale of the Firebird*. From *The Tale of the Firebird*, by Gennady Spirin, translated by Tatiana Popova, copyright © 2002 by Gennady Spirin. Used by permission of Philomel Books, a division of Penguin Young Readers Group, a Member of Putnam Group (USA), Inc., 345 Hudson St., New York, NY 10014. All rights reserved.

sician from Novgorod, chances to play his gusli while sitting on the banks of the River Volkhov. The King of the Sea is so impressed by his music that he gives him a golden fish and invites Sadko to play in his undersea palace. When Sadko arrives, he finds an amazing kingdom and, as promised, he plays for the Sea King's banquet. Eventually the King offers him one of his daughters in marriage, but Sadko is homesick for Novgorod and wishes to return. When the Sea Queen warns him that he'll never go home if he kisses his bride, he restrains himself. The next morning he finds himself back home. Gennady Spirin's exquisite paintings bring the Russian settings to life and lend sumptuous mystery to the undersea kingdom. Celia Barker Lottridge has retold the same story with a different focus in *Music for the Tsar of the Sea*. In this version there is no river Volkov when the story begins. Sadko, the poor musician, charms the Sea King and journeys to his kingdom to play for the feast. When the king offers him his choice of wife, Sadko marries

the King's daughter Volkova. Volkova realizes, however, that Sadko belongs in the bright world, not under the sea. Sadko falls asleep, and when he awakes, he is back at home with a beautiful river flowing beside him. Volkova has chosen this way to remain close to him, and thus the river Volkov was created. Harvey Chan's richly glowing pastel paintings add a warm intensity to this more emotionally satisfying version of the story.

Jewish Folktales

 Jewish tales have a poignancy, wit, and ironic humor unmatched in any other folklore. Many of them have been preserved by the masterful writing of Isaac Bashevis Singer, who has retained the flavor of both the oral tradition and the Yiddish origin. Singer's warm, humorous stories in *Zlateh the Goat* and *When Shlemiel Went to Warsaw* are based on tradition and his own childhood memories. The amiable fools of Chelm (that fabled village where only fools live), lazy shlemiels, and shrewd poor peasants who outwit rich misers are familiar characters in Singer's tales. In Chelm the wise elders are the most foolish of all, and their "solutions" to people's problems make for some hilarious stories. One night they plan to gather the pearls and diamonds of the sparkling snow so the jewels can be sold for money. Worried about how they can prevent the villagers from trampling the snow, they decide to send a messenger to each house to tell the people to stay inside. But the "wise elders" realize the messenger's feet will spoil the snow, so they have him carried on a table supported by four men so that he will not make any footprints as he goes from house to house! David Adler has readers celebrate *Chanukah in Chelm* with silly Mendel, the caretaker of Chelm's synagogue.

Shelley Fowles has retold a Jewish folktale from Morocco in *The Bachelor and the Bean*. In this amusing tale a grumpy old bachelor loses a bean in his well and complains so loudly and so bitterly that he disturbs an imp who lives there. To placate the old man, the imp gives him a magic pot that cooks whatever he desires. The old bachelor brags about his pot to his neighbors, and a jealous old woman steals it from him. When he complains to the imp, he's given another pot that produces dishes of gold. When that, too, is stolen, the old man approaches the imp for the last time. He is given a pot of water that reflects the face of the thief, the old woman. The old bachelor decides she is the perfect wife for him, just as grumpy and mean as he is!

In *It Could Always Be Worse*, Margot Zemach tells the familiar tale of the poor farmer whose house is so crowded that he seeks the rabbi's advice. Following the rabbi's wise counsel, the farmer brings one animal after another into the house, until the noise and confusion become unbearable. The rabbi then advises their removal, and the house appears to be very large and peaceful. Zemach has created a humorous version of this tale with large robust pictures that seem to swarm with

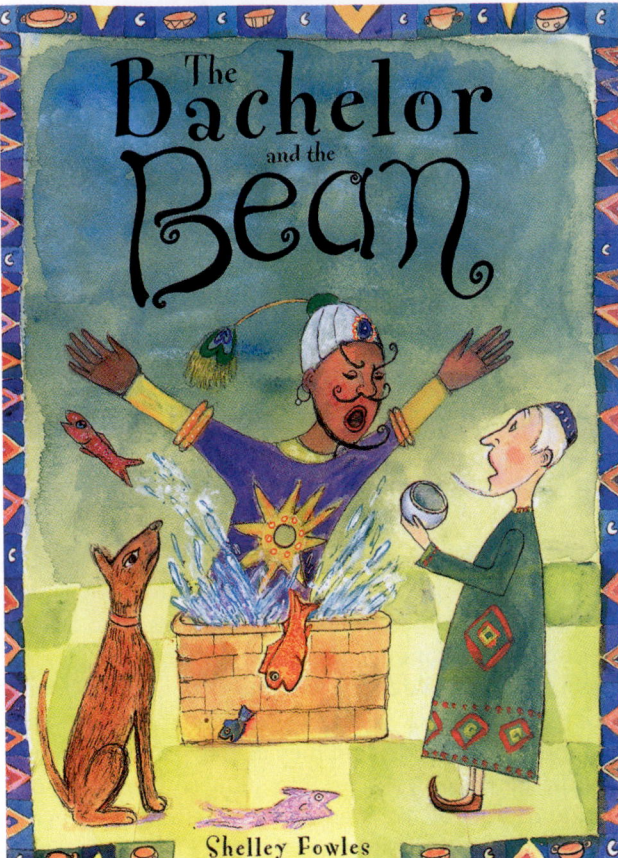

Shelley Fowles's main character gets what he deserves in the funny Moroccan Jewish tale *The Bachelor and the Bean*. From *The Bachelor and the Bean* by Shelley Fowles © 2003. Reproduced by permission of Frances Lincoln Ltd., 4 Torriano Mews, Torriano Avenue, London NW5 2RZ. Published in the USA by Farrar, Straus & Giroux.

the world. Here readers meet the giant Og, the fools of Chusham, King Solomon, and even a Jewish Thumbelina, Katanya. Uri Shulevitz illustrated most of these tales with brilliant paintings.

Folktales from the Middle East and India

 Folktales from Middle Eastern countries and from India would take several books, for these areas are the birthplace of many of our Western stories. Unfortunately, these tales are not as well known in the United States as they deserve to be. Rather than describe many unfamiliar stories available only in out-of-print collections, this section discusses only available tales or books that might serve as an introduction. Nonny Hogrogian's *One Fine Day* is an Armenian cumulative story that begins when an old woman catches a fox licking up her pail of milk and cuts off his tail. She agrees to sew it back on only when he replaces the milk, which proves to be a difficult task. The simplicity of Hogrogian's drawings is perfect for the rustic humor and setting of this circular tale. In Robert San Souci's lovely Armenian tale *A Weave of Words,* a weaver's daughter refuses the hand of a young prince because he can neither read nor write nor earn a living with his hands. He learns for her sake and weaves her a beautiful carpet. They are married and live happily for many years as king and queen. When the king is captured by a three-headed monster, the queen's skills of reading, writing, and weaving enable her to rescue her husband. Raul Colón's glowing, finely textured paintings resemble the lovely patterns and colors of the very rugs that form the basis of the story. David Kherdian and Nonny Hogrogian have retold a version of this story in *The Golden Bracelet.* Both versions offer a strong heroine who knows her own mind and sets her own course.

Scheherazade's Arabian Nights tales have provided stories for generations since they were first published in 1712. Sir Richard Burton's translation made them available to English speakers and has been used as the basis for such collections as Neil Philip's lavishly illustrated *The Arabian Nights.* Deborah Nourse Lattimore selected three of the stories to retell in *Arabian Nights:* the well-known "Aladdin," "The Queen of Serpents," and "The Lost City of Brass." In this last tale, Scheherazade describes how three men—a storyteller, a wise man, and a ruler—travel to find the lost city of Ubar in order to find the ancient brass bottles in which King Solomon imprisoned all the evil Jinn of the earth. Despite many terrible impediments along the way, the three are righteous men, praising Allah, doing good deeds, and thinking good thoughts. They reach the lost city and finally retrieve one of Solomon's bottles. In an author's note Lattimore tells that the remains of this ancient city, which was long thought to be mythical, have recently been unearthed. The city had disappeared into a sinkhole sometime between A.D. 200 and A.D. 400, and it now seems that Scheherazade's story was rooted in fact.

squalling children, rambunctious animals, and horrified adults.

Phoebe Gilman's *Something from Nothing* tells of a boy whose grandfather makes him a precious blanket. As Joseph grows older the blanket is made into smaller and smaller pieces of clothing, first a jacket, then a vest, a handkerchief, and finally a button. When he loses the button, the boy is told, "You can't make something from nothing." But Joseph does—he writes a story about his blanket. Gilman's illustrations set the story in the villages of the old country. Simms Taback's Caldecott Medal–winning *Joseph Had a Little Overcoat* is based on a musical version of the story and aimed at an audience of younger children.

Isaac Bashevis Singer retells a Hebrew legend in *Elijah the Slave,* which is magnificently illustrated by Antonio Frasconi. In this story Elijah, a messenger from God, sells himself as a slave in order to help a poor, faithful scribe. The pictures appear to be woodcut prints cut out and pasted on radiant backgrounds. The effect is breathtaking and reminiscent of medieval art.

The Diamond Tree, by Howard Schwartz and Barbara Rush, is a collection of fifteen Jewish tales from around

In an early version Andrew Lang introduced children to Burton's *Aladdin*. Eric Kimmel's *The Tale of Aladdin and the Wonderful Lamp* expands the story, and Ju-Hong Chen's warmly colored, impressionistic paintings evoke the textured surfaces of the desert landscapes and ancient cities of the story's origin. Philip Pullman's accomplished retelling of *Aladdin and the Enchanted Lamp* has been sumptuously illustrated by Sophy Williams. Both the Kimmel and Pullman versions are more inclusive than Burton's retelling, and both texts capture some of the flavor of the told tale. *Sinbad in the Land of the Giants*, retold and illustrated by Ludmila Zeman, has the flavor of Persia and the sumptuous look of Persian carpets.

John Yeoman has retold *The Seven Voyages of Sinbad* in a volume illustrated by Quentin Blake. Blake's sense of humor adds the right touch to these lighthearted adventures about a well-known hero. Sinbad is really a merchant, not a sailor, and Yeoman suggests that the tales arose out of yarns spun by real travelers. Sinbad's adventures recall the exaggerated antics of American tall-tale heroes (see "Tall Tales," p. 317).

Readers will recognize recurring folktale themes and motifs in several other tales from the Middle East. Denys Johnson-Davies has retold fifteen stories of a Middle Eastern trickster figure in *Goha, the Wise Fool*. These stories focus on humor and more serious moral lessons. The book's illustrations are by Hany El Saed Ahmed and Hag Hamdy Mohamed Fattouh, tent makers who sell their traditional khiyamiya tapestries in the markets of Cairo. In *How the Fisherman Tricked the Genie* by Kitoba Sunami, a poor fisherman casts his net out three times and on the third try lands a magical bottle. When he releases the genie inside, he is not given three wishes, but rather the promise of death. The genie has been in the bottle for many thousands of years, and his anger at the world outside has grown. The fisherman tells the genie two stories to illustrate the moral that a good deed cannot be punished with evil. When the genie is unconvinced, the fisherman relies on his wiles and tricks the genie back into his bottle. *Rimonah of the Flashing Sword*, a retelling by Eric Kimmel, has its origins in North Africa but contains many elements of "Snow White." When Rimonah's mother dies, her father is tricked into marriage by an evil sorceress. Instead of a magic mirror to answer her questions, however, Rimonah's wicked stepmother has a magic bowl. When the stepmother orders a huntsman to take Rimonah into the desert and kill her, Rimonah escapes and is taken in by a tribe of Bedouins. Later she lives with forty thieves. In this version Rimonah is not at all passive. When her prince awakens her from her enchanted sleep, she takes charge and leads her friends in battle against the wicked sorceress.

In Kimmel's *The Three Princes*, three cousins hope to win the hand of a wise and beautiful princess. Realizing that she loves Moshen, the youngest and poorest of the three, the princess sets the cousins the difficult task of finding the greatest wonder in the world. After a year's journey the three meet and compare their treasures. Prince Fahad has found a crystal ball, Prince Muhammed has obtained a magic carpet, and Prince Moshen has been given an orange. When the crystal ball tells them that the princess is dying, they climb aboard the magic carpet to return to the palace. Moshen feeds his orange to the princess and saves her life, but the princess's councilors cannot decide whose gift was the most wondrous. The princess declares that Fahad and Muhammed both still have their treasures but since Moshe gave up everything for her, he is the one she will marry. Leonard Everett Fisher's boldly colored and textured paintings add a sense of visual magic to this tender story.

Other rich sources of stories are the Hodja stories, known throughout the Mediterranean countries, Turkey, the Balkans, and Greece. Nasredden Hodja was thought to have lived several hundred years ago in Turkey, where he served as a

Sophy Williams's paintings reflect the jewels of a sultan's court in Philip Pullman's *Aladdin and the Enchanted Lamp*. Illustration © 2004 by Sophy Williams, 2004 from *Aladdin and the Enchanted Lamp* by Philip Pullman. Published by Scholastic Children's Books in the UK and by Arthur A. Levine Books, an imprint of Scholastic, Inc., in the USA. All rights reserved. Reproduced with permission of Scholastic Ltd.

religious teacher or judge when the occasion demanded. The wisdom of the Hodja is seen in the way he settles disputes. One day he watches a man cut wood while his companion rests nearby but groans helpfully each time the man swings his axe (see Barbara Walker's *Watermelons, Walnuts, and the Wisdom of Allah*). When the woodcutter finally sells his wood at the bazaar, the companion demands half the pay. The Hodja listens to both sides, takes the coins, and drops them one by one on a stone. He awards the sound to the companion and the coins to the woodcutter.

Indian folk traditions have their share of greedy characters and wise men. Meilo So's *Gobble, Gobble, Slip, Slop* tells of a cat so gluttonous that it ends up eating the entire neighborhood, including an elephant! Fortunately the crab the cat swallows has sharp claws and cuts its way out of the cat's stomach, freeing all the feline's other victims. "The Sticks of Truth" in George Shannon's collection *Stories to Solve* tells of an Indian judge asked to determine who stole a gold ring. He gives each suspect a stick and says that only the stick of the thief will grow in the night. In the morning, he is able to accuse the one with the shortest stick of the thievery. Why? In this collection of short pieces, the reader is invited to guess before turning the page to discover the answer. In this case, the girl trims her stick in an effort to hide its growth, thereby proving her guilt.

The Jataka (birth) stories found in India tell of the previous reincarnations of the Buddha and are known to have existed as early as the fifth century A.D. Many of these tales are moralistic or religious in nature. *The Brave Little Parrot*, retold by Rafe Martin, is a story of a small gray bird who desperately tries to put out a forest fire even though his fellows think the task is hopeless. His efforts elicit tears from the eagle god and these quench the flames. In return for his bravery, the parrot is rewarded with feathers in flaming colors. These stories of faith and persistence are typical of many of the early Jataka tales but have few other elements of traditional folktales. Later, beast tales were drawn from this collection to form the *Panchatantra*, stories that were used to instruct young princes in morality. When these stories are translated into English, their morals and teaching verses are usually eliminated. The resulting Indian tales sound more like folktales.

Rafe Martin retells an ancient ancestor of "Henny Penny" or "Chicken Little" in the Jataka tale *Foolish Rabbit's Big Mistake*. Rabbit hears an apple fall from a tree and wonders if the earth is breaking up. He panics and arouses a chain of animals who thoughtlessly run with him until a wise lion stops the stampede. He carries the silly rabbit back to the scene, proves it was only an apple that fell from the tree, and finally defends the rabbit from the anger of his friends by pointing out that they, too, ran without trying to find out the true cause of the alarm. Ed Young's large-scale paintings depict the action in dramatic close-ups and vibrant explosions of color.

Manu and the Talking Fish by Roberta Arenson is a story from Hindu tradition that is linked to a worldwide group of myths about a great flood. In this case, a prince named Manu, who is a great philosopher, saves a little fish from being eaten by a bigger fish. Eventually, the fish warns the prince that a great flood is coming. He tells the prince to construct a large boat and gather all the plants and animals he can find. In addition, seven wise men from the ends of the earth join him. As predicted, great rains occur and flood the earth, but the fish guides Manu's boat through the deluge and all survive. When they land on a high mountain peak, Manu plants the seed and bulbs and leaves the animals free. He and the seven wise men gather to give thanks to the gods with milk and cheese, and a woman rises out of the milk to become Manu's wife. "They had many children and so filled the earth once more with people" (p. 30).

In vigorous woodcuts, Marcia Brown illustrates the fable *Once a Mouse*, which must have warned young princes about the folly of pride in one's origins. Seeing a mouse about to be eaten by a crow, a hermit rescues it. But a cat stalks the pet, so the hermit changes the mouse into a bigger cat. Each change results in new dangers, until finally the meek mouse is transformed into a huge tiger. But he "peacocked about the forest" until the hermit reminds him that he was once a mouse. When the tiger threatens the hermit, the hermit reduces it to its original shape of a mouse.

While these tales represent but a small portion of stories from the Middle Eastern countries and India, they are indicative of a rich source on which children's literature has yet to draw fully. Perhaps the next decades will provide a greater number of single-tale editions of stories such as these so that children might become more familiar with this important literary tradition.

Folktales from Asia

 There are increasing numbers of outstanding, well-illustrated single-tale editions of folktales from Japan, China, Korea, and Southeast Asia.

Ai-Ling Louie's *Yeh-Shen* is based on one of the oldest written variants of "Cinderella," predating European versions by a thousand years. Left in the care of a stepmother and stepsister, Yeh-Shen is made to do the heaviest chores. Her only friend is a fish, which she feeds and talks with each day until the stepmother kills and eats it. However, its magical power lives on in its bones. Through it, Yeh-Shen is able to go to a festival dressed in a gown, a cloak made of kingfisher feathers, and gold slippers. There, the suspicious stepsister causes the girl to run away and lose a slipper. Immediately Yeh-Shen's fine clothes turn to rags. But the king, struck by her beauty, places the slipper in a roadside pavilion and hides to wait for the girl who will reclaim it. When Yeh-Shen creeps, under cover of darkness, to retrieve the slipper, they are united, and later they marry. As in the German version of the Cinderella story, however, the stepsister and mother are punished, "crushed to death in a shower of flying stones." Ed Young's depictions of costumes and footwear reflect his research into textiles, costuming, and festivals of the ancient Hmong people. In addition, each shimmering pastel and watercolor illustration reminds us, in shape or shadow, of the contours of the magic fish. A much longer but similar version of the tale is the title story in Lynette Dyer Vuong's *The Brocaded Slipper and Other Vietnamese Tales.*

Young's Caldecott Medal book *Lon Po Po* tells a tale that comes from an ancient oral tradition and is thought to be more than a thousand years old. Child readers will recognize similarities between this story and "Red Riding Hood." However, this wolf perishes by falling from the gingko tree as a result of three children's trickery and resourceful teamwork. Combining Chinese panel format with contemporary pastel and watercolors, Young creates a mysterious nighttime setting illuminated by candles, moonlight, and the shining eyes of the wolf.

One of the most popular stories in the Chinese storytelling tradition is recounted in Margaret Mahy's *The Seven Chinese Brothers.* Each brother looks like the others but has one unique feature, such as unusual strength, amazing eyesight, acute hearing, bones that will not break, or unhappy tears that will flood an entire village. When Third Brother is imprisoned by the Emperor, the other brothers use their talents to bring about the Emperor's downfall. The carefully researched details of Jean Tseng and Mou-Sien Tseng's watercolors reflect our contemporary concerns with authenticity in illustration as well as text. This version contrasts with Claire Huchet Bishop's simpler retelling and Kurt Wiese's black-line stereotyped illustrations from an earlier era for *The Five Chinese Brothers.*

Eric Kimmel's *Ten Suns* tells of the dilemma that arises on earth of long ago. At this time there were ten suns, and when they all decide to go walking together in the heavens at the same time they cause havoc. The earth's emperor begs the sun's father for help. When the ten suns ignore him, their father sends the heavenly archer Hu Yi to shoot them out of the sky. Nine of the suns are turned into black crows when they are pierced by the arrows. Just in time, however, the emperor realizes that if all the suns are gone the earth will die. He sends a messenger who steals Hu Yi's last arrow. The last sun is spared, and from that time crows greet their remaining brother sun each morning at dawn with loud cawing. Nine brothers are featured in Ed Young's *Sons of the Dragon King.* In this story the sons are also liable to wreak havoc, but the outcome of this story is more positive than in *Ten Suns.* Instead of shooting his wayward sons, the dragon king has the patience to help each find his niche on earth, and the nine dragons can still be found helping humans to this day.

Caring for others above oneself is also a theme of Chinese folktales. In *Lord of the Cranes* by Kerstin Chen,

Lord of the Cranes, a Chinese folktale by Kerstin Chen, tells a familiar story of kindness rewarded. From *Lord of the Cranes* by Kerstin Chen, illustrated by Jian Jiang Chen. Copyright © 2000 by Nord-Sud Verlag AG, Gossau Zurich, Switzerland. Used by permission of North-South Books, Inc., New York. All rights reserved.

Tian, an immortal being whose beloved companions are beautiful cranes, comes to earth to make sure that humans have remembered to be kind and generous. He assumes the guise of a beggar and finds little sympathy until he encounters Wang, the owner of a small inn. When Tian asks for food, Wang happily gives him succor and continues to do so each and every day that the beggar comes to the inn. The beggar rewards Wang by painting a mural of cranes on the wall of his inn. When people are happy and singing, the cranes come to life and dance. This marvelous painting becomes the talk of the city and makes Wang a rich man. When Wang learns the true identity of the beggar, Wang asks how he can repay Tian for his gift. Tian tells him to teach others to be as kind and generous as he has been to Tian. The immortal one then calls his cranes from the wall with a magic flute and they return to heaven.

Demi's *The Donkey and the Rock* is an amusing story that gently chides the human propensity to be sold a bill of goods. A merchant on the way to market rests his jar of oil on a large rock. When the donkey of another merchant accidentally smashes the jar of oil against the rock, no one can decide who is responsible. The king agrees to try the case in court, and curious people rush to witness the trial between a rock and a donkey. The king charges each of them a fee for being so silly as to believe anyone could judge a rock or a donkey. He uses the money to compensate the merchant.

Lily Toy Hong's *Two of Everything* is a lighthearted farce that contains elements of many magical-pot stories. When poor old Mr. Haktak finds a brass pot in his field, he brings it home to his wife. They discover that this pot duplicates anything that they put into it, even Mrs. Haktak, who has fallen in by accident. In his consternation over his two identical wives, the farmer trips and falls in, too. Now there are two Mr. Haktaks and two Mrs. Haktaks. The clever solution will appeal to younger children, who might also discover the concept of multiplication.

Japanese folktales contain miniature people; monsters called *oni;* and, like Chinese tales, themes of gentleness toward animals and other people, the value of hard work, and respect for the elderly.

"Momotaro, or the Story of the Son of a Peach" is said to be the most popular folktale in Japan, where Momotaro is held up to children as an example of kindness, courage, and strength. In Virginia Haviland's retelling in *Favorite Folktales Told in Japan,* a tiny boy who has stepped out of a huge split peach must fight the horned demons, who are robbing and attacking the people. With the help of three companions, Momotaro storms the stronghold of the blue-bodied monsters. He returns victorious, bringing home all the gold and silver the *oni* had stolen from the people.

The Crane Wife, retold by Odds Bodkin, is a tale of the results of succumbing to poor advice and greed. Osamu, a poor sail maker, rescues an injured crane during an autumn storm. The crane flies off, but one night Yukiko, a stunningly beautiful woman, knocks at Osamu's door. Eventually the two fall in love. However, because Osamu earns so little at his sail making trade, they soon face starvation. Yukiko offers to weave a magic sail but warns Osamu that he must never look at her as she works. After a night passes Yukiko emerges from her room exhausted, but she presents Osamu with a sail that he is able to sell in the marketplace for enough gold to last for six months. When the gold is gone and they begin to starve again, he asks Yukiko to weave another sail. She warns him that the weaving takes "all that she is," but she agrees to one more sail. This time the weaving takes her two days. The two live happily for a while, but one day a rich sea captain approaches Osamu and offers enough gold to last his lifetime for one of the magic sails. Despite Yukiko's entreaties Osamu orders her to weave the sail. When three days pass and Yukiko is still not done, Osamu becomes angry at her unwillingness to share the secret of her sail making. He rushes into her room to see a crane plucking feathers from her own breast in order to weave the beautiful cloth. No longer able to remain in human form, Yukiko, the crane, flies away. Gennady Spirin has created lovely paintings that capture the gorgeous images of medieval Japanese screens and positively glow with visual energy. It would be interesting for children to compare Molly Bang's literary use of the tale in *Dawn,* which is set in nineteenth-century New England, with Bodkin's version. The alert reader might spot clues to *Dawn's* true identity, such as pieces of eggshell under her bed when she gives birth to a daughter and the quilt pattern she is piecing, called "Wild Geese Flying."

Dianne Snyder's *The Boy of the Three-Year Nap* is a humorous realistic folktale involving trickery. A poor widow, tired of supporting her son Taro, who is "lazy as a rich man's cat," pesters him to go to work for a rich rice merchant. Declining to work, the boy tricks the merchant into betrothing him to his daughter. Taro's mother works her own ruse, however, and in the end Taro is caught in his own tricks. Allen Say's precise watercolor illustrations reflect the Japanese love of order. The expressive faces of both the tricksters and the duped make readers laugh at the humorous situations.

Katherine Paterson's *The Tale of the Mandarin Ducks* presents a Japanese tale of a greedy lord who captures a magnificently plumed drake so as to have a beautiful caged bird. Shozo, a former mighty samurai who has lost an eye in battle, warns the lord that the wild bird will surely die in captivity, but the lord shuns his advice. When Yasuko, a kitchen maid, takes pity on the bird and frees him, the lord blames Shozo, strips him of his rank, and puts him to work in the kitchen, where he falls in love with Yasuko. The jealous and vindictive lord sentences them to death by drowning for releasing the duck. On their way to be executed, the condemned couple are rescued and taken to a hut in the forest. In the morning, they wish to thank their saviors but find instead the mandarin duck and his mate, who seem to bow before flying away. Shozo and Yasuko live on for many years in their forest hut in great happiness, for they had learned that "trouble can always be borne when it is shared." Leo Dillon and Diane Dillon studied *ukiyo-e,* a Japanese art movement that depicted the everyday life of common people, before creating their lovely watercolor and pastel illustrations for the story that suggest the natural beauty of a simple life. Although the art superbly recalls this traditional form, the illustrations are less accurate. For example, women would not wear their zori, or shoes, on a tatami mat as pictured in the third double-page spread, nor would they wear their zori without the little socks called tabi.

Rabbit is a familiar character in Asian folktales and often appears in the role of a clever trickster who also might be petty and vain. In *The Rabbit's Tail,* Suzanne Crowder Han's retelling of a Korean story, a proud tiger is tricked into believing that a persimmon is more frightening than he is. He runs through the jungle and sees images of the scary persimmon monster wherever he goes. This convoluted plot involves a poor farmer who gets into the middle of the tiger's terror and a curious rabbit whose curiosity loses him his tail. In Daniel San

Trina Schart Hyman brings Vietnamese folktales to vivid life in *Children of the Dragon*, a collection of stories retold by Sherry Garland. Illustration from *Children of the Dragon: Selected Tales from Vietnam* by Sherry Garland, illustration copyright © 2001 by Trina Schart Hyman, reprinted with permission of Harcourt, Inc.

Souci's *The Rabbit and the Dragon King,* the dragon king, who lives in an underwater kingdom, is told that he needs a rabbit's heart to cure his sickness. Only after Turtle lures Rabbit to the underwater kingdom does Rabbit learn what the dragon king requires. She is able to think fast, however, and convinces the king that her heart is hidden on land. Once back on terra firma, she sends a persimmon fruit in place of her heart. The dragon king has a miraculous recovery and all involved live happily ever after.

In addition to single-edition folktales, there are several fine collections of Asian tales. These include Shelley Fu's *Ho Yi the Archer; and Other Classic Tales from China* and Lotta Carswell Hume's *Favorite Children's Stories from China and Tibet,* a reissue of a book originally published in 1962. Lynette Dyer Vuong's *The Brocaded Slipper and Other Vietnamese Tales* has among them the Vietnamese version of Cinderella in its title story, "The Brocaded Slip-

per." Sherry Garland has collected six Vietnamese tales in *Children of the Dragon*. Trina Schart Hyman's wonderful paintings illuminate these tales, which include several pourquoi stories, "How the Tiger Got His Stripes" and "The Legend of the Monsoon Rains." Garland provides copious notes about each tale and its origin in Vietnamese culture.

Folktales from Africa

 Children today are the fortunate recipients of a rich bounty of African folktales collected by folklorists such as Harold Courlander.[19] Many of these tales have been retold in single editions by authors like Verna Aardema and Ashley Bryan, and many of these stories have received Caldecott awards. The trickster tale of Anansi the spider told in *A Story, a Story* by Gail Haley won a Caldecott Medal, as did Aardema's pourquoi story *Why Mosquitoes Buzz in People's*

---

[19]See Nina Jaffe's biography *A Voice for the People: The Life and Work of Harold Courlander* (Holt, 1997).

Ears with illustrations by Leo Dillon and Diane Dillon. Caldecott Honor books have included two other African pourquoi stories, Elphinstone Dayrell's *Why the Sun and the Moon Live in the Sky* with Blair Lent's distinguished illustrations, and *The Village of Round and Square Houses* by Ann Grifalconi; a second story of the trickster, *Anansi the Spider,* illustrated by Gerald McDermott; and John Steptoe's tale of a greedy sister and a generous sister, *Mufaro's Beautiful Daughters.*

Storytelling is a highly developed art in Africa, particularly in West Africa. These tales have an aural cadence found in no other stories of the world. They come from the oral tradition and are frequently written in the storyteller's voice. Short sentences, frequent use of parallel constructions, repetition, and dialogue characterize the style of many of the African tales. In Ashley Bryan's rhythmical tale from the Antilles, *The Dancing Granny,* Granny can't resist the song of Spider Ananse, who lures her to dance far out of sight while he raids her vegetable plot. The story sings with rhythmic prose and repeated refrains. Bryan's *The Story of Lightning and Thunder,* a story from Southern Nigeria, is filled with similar word music. It begins,

> A long time ago, I mean a long, long time ago, if you wanted to pat Lightning or chat with Thunder, you could do it. Uh huh, you could! (unpaged)

This tale of how thunder and lightning went to live in the sky is accompanied by Bryan's sparkling paintings, which, with their colorful abstracted patterns, seem to flash with a special lightning all their own. Bryan's *Beautiful Blackbird* is a tale from Zambia that celebrates the unsurpassed beauty of the color black. In this and the previous story Bryan's sparkling paintings with their colorful abstract patterns glow with an African warmth.

Many similar African tales are about personified animals, including those tricksters Anansi the spider, a rabbit, and a tortoise. In Gerald McDermott's *Zomo the Rabbit,* Zomo asks the Sky God for wisdom. The Sky God agrees but sets the rabbit three difficult tasks. This speedy trickster accomplishes the tasks but wreaks havoc in the jungle, angering Big Fish, Wild Cow, and Leopard. Sky God gives him the wisdom he has asked for, but warns him that he might have a lot of courage, a little good sense, but no caution whatsoever. Therefore, warns the Sky God, he had better learn to run very, very fast. McDermott's illustrations recall the patterned designs of African textiles and bring Zomo's tricky character to life. In Tololwa Mollel's *Ananse's Feast,* Ananse the spider and the turtle Akye have a battle of wits over a meal. Ananse wins the first round but as often happens in trickster stories, the trickster spider is out-tricked by the long-suffering turtle. Verna Aardema's *Anansi Does the Impossible* is a retelling of the three impossible tasks Anansi must accomplish in order to win the Sky God's stories. Readers will recognize a similar version in Gail Haley's *A Story, a Story.*

Trickster Rabbit appears in a more helpful mood in *The Hunterman and the Crocodile,* a charming retelling of a West African tale by Baba Wagué Diakité. Diakité has also told *The Hatseller and the Monkeys,* an African tale that children will recognize as similar to the favorite *Caps for Sale* by Esphyr Slobodkina. In this version BaMusa, a hatseller on his way to market with a load of hats, falls asleep under a mango tree. When he awakens he finds that the monkeys in the tree have taken his hats. He tries everything he can think of to get his hats back, until he realizes that the monkeys are imitating his every move. When he takes off his hat and throws it at the monkeys, they take off theirs and throw them at him. Diakité's paintings are executed on ceramic tile, and the bright patterns he creates in his pictures are a fresh addition to the folktale genre.

Verna Aardema has retold a West African tale in *Why Mosquitoes Buzz in People's Ears.* In this cumulative story the mosquito tells the iguana a tall tale, setting off a chain reaction that ends in disaster for a baby owl. Until the animals can find the culprit who is responsible for the owlet's death, Mother Owl refuses to hoot and wake the sun. King Lion holds a council and listens to everyone's excuse until the blame comes to rest on the mosquito. The white outline of the stylized watercolors gives a cool but brilliant atmosphere to this story. Leo Dillon and Diane Dillon won the Caldecott Medal for their beautiful illustrations of this story and also illustrated Aardema's humorous Masai tale *Who's in Rabbit's House?* as a play featuring masked actors.

Some mischievous monkeys are tricked out of their stolen hats by the merchant BaMusa in Baba Wagué Diakité's delightful *The Hatseller and the Monkeys.* From *The Hatseller and the Monkeys* by Baba Wagué Diakité. Published by Scholastic Press/Scholastic, Inc. Copyright © 1999 by Baba Wagué Diakité. Reprinted by permission.

Verna Aardema has retold many other folktales from Africa. *Misoso*, Aardema's collection of "once upon a time tales," is a delightful literary tour of the continent. In addition to a map showing each tale's place of origin, every story is introduced with a glossary and pronunciation guide and followed with notes about the tale and its place in African folklore. Accompanied by beautiful stylized illustrations by Reynold Ruffins, this book is a superb introduction to serious study of African folklore for older children.

Many other African stories may also be described as pourquoi stories. Ashley Bryan's wonderful retelling of "How the Animals Got Their Tails" in his *Beat the Story Drum, Pum-Pum* tells of the origins of characteristic features of African animals. Raouf Mama's *Why Goats Smell Bad* is a collection of twenty traditional stories from Benin. Gail Haley's *A Story, a Story* explains the origins of a different type of tale—how humans got their stories. The way in which people came to be is told by Won-Ldy Paye and Margaret H. Lippert in *Head, Body, Legs: A Story from Liberia*, and the way in which people came to be farmers is explained in Mary-Joan Gerson's *Why the Sky Is Far Away*. *Master Man* by Aaron Shepard is a tale from the Hausa people of Nigeria, where stories of tests of strength are popular. In this tale Shadusa calls himself Master Man because he thinks he is the strongest man in the world. To his dismay he encounters a real Master Man, a man so strong and so big he eats elephants for dinner. Shadusa escapes a test of strength with his life only because this Master Man meets an even bigger Master Man. The two turn on each other and fight on and on until they rise into the air and become thunder and lightning. David Wisniewski's cut-paper illustrations lend the story a delicious edge.

A play on words is a favored form of humor in some African tales. In *The Cow-Tail Switch*, Harold Courlander and George Herzog retell the story of the very wealthy man named Time. Change of fortune reduces him to a beggar, and persons remark, "Behold, Time isn't what it used to be!" (p. 77). The same collection has a story about the young hunters who try to capture "The One You Don't See Coming," which is their name for sleep. In another Anansi story in this collection, there is a character named Nothing. Anansi kills him, and all the villagers "cry for nothing!"

Frequently an African tale will present a dilemma and then the storyteller will invite the audience to participate in suggesting the conclusion. The problem of which son should be given the cow-tail switch as a reward for finding his lost father is asked in the title story of *The Cow-Tail Switch* collection by Courlander and Herzog. The boys undertake the search only after the youngest child learns to speak and asks for his father. Each of the sons has a special talent he uses to help restore his father to life. It is then that the storyteller asks who should receive the father's cow-tail switch.

While searching for an African variant of "Cinderella," John Steptoe came upon the story he retells in *Mufaro's Beautiful Daughters*, turning it into a strikingly illustrated tale about conflict and contrast. Manyara, the bad-tempered, selfish sister, predicts that one day she will be queen and her sister will be a servant. Nyasha, the humble and hardworking sister, is happy to work in her garden and care for their father. When a message arrives from the king inviting all the worthy daughters in the land to appear before him so that he can choose a bride, Manyara hurries on ahead, thinking to beat her sister to the king's palace. Along the way she meets a hungry boy with whom she haughtily refuses to share her food, and she ignores the advice of an old woman. The next day, however, Nyasha shares her food with both people. When her sister arrives, Manyara comes running from the palace in hysterics because she has seen a five-headed serpent on the throne. But Nyasha bravely approaches and is relieved to find a little garden snake that transforms itself into the king. He reveals that he had also taken the shape of the little boy and the old woman and thus knows that she is the most beautiful daughter in the land, worthy to be his wife. Steptoe's careful research creates an accurate picture of the region. The intensely colored plants and animals living in the forest, architectural details from the actual ruined city of Zimbabwe, and a pair of crowned cranes that symbolize the royal couple all contribute authenticity to this Caldecott Honor winner.[20]

Obviously there is no dearth of folk literature from Africa, where oral tradition has been maintained. Children who hear these tales will become familiar with other cultures and the rhythmical chord of ancient African storytellers. They will learn of a land where baobab trees grow and people fear lions, leopards, droughts, and famines. More importantly, they will learn something about the wishes, dreams, hopes, humor, and despair of other peoples. They may begin to see literature as the universal story of humankind.

Folktales of Canada and the United States

 When the early settlers, immigrants, and slaves came to Canada and the United States, they brought their folktales with them from Europe, China, and West Africa. As they repeated their folktales, some of the tales took on an unmistakable flavor. Indigenous to the place are folktales told by Native Americans and tall tales that developed from the pioneer spirit of the young American country.

In a discussion of folktales from this region, it is impossible to describe any one body of folklore such as the Grimms discovered in Germany. However, the folklore

---

[20]Darcy Bradley, "John Steptoe: Retrospective of an Imagemaker," *New Advocate* 4, no. 1 (winter 1991): 21.

of Canada and the United States may be sorted into four large categories:

1. Native American, Eskimo, and Inuit tales that were originally here
2. Tales that came from other countries, primarily from West Africa, and were changed in the process to form the basis of African American folktales
3. Tales that came primarily from Europe and were modified into new variants
4. Tall tales, legends, and other Americana that developed here

Virginia Haviland's collection *North American Legends*[21] presents tales from each of these categories and gives a broad overview of folklore in the United States. *From Sea to Shining Sea,* Amy Cohn's extensively researched collection of American folklore and folk songs offers children a stirring journey into an America that consists of many cultures, many stories, and many songs. Fourteen Caldecott Medal–winning artists provide the visual map for this marvelous exploration. A glossary, extensive footnotes, and suggested readings add to the book's value as a classroom resource.

Other notable collections include Laurence Yep's *The Rainbow People* and *Tongues of Jade,* tales Chinese immigrants told not only to remind themselves of home but also to show how a wise person could survive in a strange new land. Paul Yee's *Tales from Gold Mountain* draws on the wellspring of stories told by the Chinese who settled in Vancouver's Chinatown. Eighteen stories from Americans of European descent are collected in Neil Philip's *Stockings of Buttermilk,* illustrated by Jacqueline Mair. Nancy Van Laan's *With a Whoop and a Holler* includes stories from the Deep South, and readers will find familiar characters such as Jack and Brer Rabbit as well as superstitions and riddles. African-Americans are represented in such fine collections as Virginia Hamilton's *The People Could Fly* and *Her Stories.* Both collections have been illustrated by Leo Dillon and Diane Dillon in their distinctive style. Native American tales have been assembled in thematic collections such as Joseph Bruchac and James Bruchac's *When the Chenoo Howls: Native American Tales of Terror,* and in tribal collections such as Joseph Bruchac's *The Boy Who Lived with the Bears and Other Iroquois Stories.* Increasingly, readers will find that many other well-written collections and beautifully illustrated tales represent the many colorful threads that make up America's rich tapestry of story.

 **Native American Folktales** To try to characterize all the folklore of the various Native American tribes as one cohesive whole is as unreasonable as it would be to lump all of the folklore of Europe together. Variations in Native American dwellings, such as pueblos, longhouses, and teepees, or in the symbolic artwork of totem poles, beading, story skins, and carvings are mirrored in the variations of Native American folktales. Teaching Resources: "Some Native American Folktales by Region" is a useful grouping of tales for those wishing to study Native American folktales, specifically of a particular geographical area. However, there are some common characteristics among the various tribes and between the folklore of Native Americans and that of northern Europeans.

Many Native American tales might be categorized as mythology, for they include creation myths and sacred legends. Jean Monroe and Ray Williamson's *They Dance in the Sky* is a collection of Native American star myths that includes stories of the origin of the Pleiades, the Big Dipper, and other constellations. Manitonquat's *The Children of the Morning Light* brings together creation myths and other legends from the Wampanoag people of southeastern Massachusetts. Some myths attempt to explain religious beliefs while telling people about tribal customs and how to act. Some of these tales were told as separate stories, but as with Greek or Roman mythology, they were heard by insiders who understood these tales within the context of a large interlocking set of stories.

Native American tales, when originally told, were loosely plotted rather than highly structured like European fairy tales. Thomas Leekley, who retold some of the stories of the Chippewa and Ottawa tribes in his *The World of Manobozho,* says:

> Indian folklore is a great collection of anecdotes, jokes, and fables, and storytellers constantly combined and recombined these elements in different ways. We seldom find a plotted story of the kind we know. Instead, the interest is usually in a single episode; if this is linked to another, the relationship is that of two beads on one string, seldom that of two bricks in one building. (pp. 7–8)

The very act of storytelling was considered to be of ceremonial importance in various tribal groups. Storytelling took place at night and, in certain tribes such as the Iroquois, it was permitted only in the winter. Men, women, and children listened reverently to stories, some of which were "owned" by a teller and could not be told by any other person. The sacred number four is found in all Indian tales, rather than the pattern of three common to other folktales. Four hairs might be pulled and offered to the four winds; or four quests must be made before a mission will be accomplished.

Many Native American tales are nature myths, pourquoi stories that explain how animals came to earth or why they have certain characteristics. Paul Goble tells of the origin of the first horses in *The Gift of the Sacred Dog,*

---

[21]Virginia Haviland, *North American Legends,* illustrated by Ann Strugnell (New York: Collins, 1979).

Some Native American Folktales by Region

 Visit the Online Learning Center at **www.mhhe.com/kiefer9e** for a printable version of this list.

PLAINS

Caron Lee Cohen, *The Mud Pony* (Pawnee)

Paul Goble, *Iktomi and the Berries: A Plains Indian Story* (Lakota Sioux)

———, *Mystic Horse* (Pawnee)

Joe Medicine Crow, *Brave Wolf and the Thunderbird* (Crow)

John Steptoe, *The Story of Jumping Mouse: A Native American Legend*

Douglas Wood, *Rabbit and the Moon* (Cree)

WOODLAND

John Bierhorst, ed., *The White Deer and Other Stories Told by the Lenape*

Joseph Bruchac, *Turtle's Race with Bear* (Seneca)

Joseph Bruchac and James Bruchac, *How Chipmunk Got His Stripes* (Iroquois)

———, *Raccoon's Last Race* (Abenaki)

Virginia Hamilton, "Divine Woman the Creator" (Huron), in *In The Beginning: Creation Stories from around the World*

Rafe Martin, *The Rough-Face Girl* (Algonquin)

Robert D. San Souci, *Sootface: An Ojibwa Cinderella*

Pat Sherman, *The Sun's Daughter* (Iroquois)

Nancy Van Laan, *Shingebiss, an Ojibwe Legend*

SOUTHWEST

Byrd Baylor, ed., *And It Is Still That Way*

John Bierhorst, *Doctor Coyote: A Native American Aesop's Fables*

Tomie dePaola, *The Legend of the Bluebonnet: An Old Tale of Texas* (Comanche)

Gerald McDermott, *Arrow to the Sun* (Pueblo)

———, *Coyote* (Zuni)

Kristina Rodanas, *Dragonfly's Tale* (Zuni)

Nancy Wood, *The Girl Who Loved Coyote: Stories of the Southwest*

(continued)

Some Native American Folktales by Region *(continued)*

NORTHWEST

John Bierhorst, *The People with Five Fingers* (West Coast)

Fiona French, *Lord of the Animals* (Miwok)

Gerald McDermott, *Raven: A Trickster Tale from the Pacific Northwest*

Jean Guard Monroe and Ray A. Williamson, "How Coyote Arranged the Night Stars" (Wasco), in *They Dance in the Sky*

Laura Simms, *The Bone Man* (Modoc)

Richard Lee Vaughan, *Eagle Boy* (Pacific Northwest)

SOUTHEAST

Joseph Bruchac, *The First Strawberries: A Cherokee Story*

————, *The Great Ball Game: A Muskogee Story* (Creek)

Robert Bushyhead, *Yonder Mountain* (Cherokee)

Deborah Duvall, *The Opossum's Tale* (Cherokee)

————, *Rabbit Goes Duck Hunting* (Cherokee)

Gretchen Will Mayo, "Ice Man Puts Out the Big Fire" (Cherokee), in *Earthmaker's Tales: North American Indian Stories from Earth Happenings*

Jean Guard Monroe and Ray A. Williamson, "What the Stars Are Like" (Cherokee), in *They Dance in the Sky*

FAR NORTH

John Bierhorst, *The Dancing Fox* (Arctic region)

Dale De Armond, *The Seal Oil Lamp* (Inuit)

Virginia Hamilton, "Raven the Creator," in *In the Beginning: Creation Stories from around the World* (Inuit)

James Houston, *The White Archer: An Eskimo Legend* (Inuit)

Howard Norman, *The Girl Who Dreamed Only Geese* (Inuit)

in which the gift is the Great Spirit's attempt to help the Plains tribes hunt the buffalo more efficiently.

Perhaps one of the best-known stories of explanation, which combines religious beliefs, how-and-why explanations, and references to Indian custom, is "Star Boy," which has many versions. Paul Goble retells this tale in *Star Boy* with beautiful illustrations drawn from careful references to Blackfoot artistic traditions. In this story, Star Boy, expelled from the sky world with his mother and marked with a mysterious scar because of

her disobedience, becomes known as Scarface. In order to marry, he must make a journey to the Sun, who removes the scar. To commemorate and honor the Sun's gesture, the Blackfeet have a sacred Sun Dance each summer. In Goble's version, Star Boy becomes another star and joins his father, Morning Star, and his mother, Evening Star.

The heavens hold special significance for native peoples, as can be seen in such tales as Joseph Bruchac and Gayle Ross's *The Story of the Milky Way*, a Cherokee tale; Paul Goble's *Her Seven Brothers,* a Cheyenne myth about the origin of the Big Dipper; and Goble's *The Lost Children,* a Blackfoot story about the origin of the Pleiades.

Almost all Native American folklore traditions contain a trickster figure who mediates between the sky world and earth. The Woodland tribes tell tales of Manabozho, a kind of half god, half superpower among the eastern tribes. The Great Plains trickster Coyote snatches fire from the burning mountain and to this day, says the legend, Coyote's fur is singed and yellow along his sides where the flames blew backward as he ran down the mountain carrying the burning brand.

Paul Goble has illustrated many tales from the Plains tribes, including several about the Plains trickster, Iktomi. Amusing stories that often have moral lessons within, they were to be told only after the sun had set. These stories were meant to elicit audience participation, and Goble has incorporated this in an inviting way. Asides like "It looks like the end of Iktomi, doesn't it?" and Iktomi's often self-serving remarks would make these tales very funny as a shared reading. *Iktomi and the Coyote* and *Iktomi Loses His Eyes* are two of many stories about this Plains Indian trickster. Goble's illustrations for other titles, such as his *The Great Race of the Birds and the Ani-*

Profile in Literature

Joseph Bruchac

Joseph Bruchac, of Slovac, German, and Abenaki ancestry, feels most inspired by his Native American roots and has made a career of preserving Abenaki culture. Among his many notable books are retellings of folktales of the Woodland Indians. Bruchac is a noted storyteller, and he performs traditional music with a group called the Dawnland Singers. Go to the Online Learning Center at **www.mhhe.com/kiefer9e** or your Resources CD-ROM to learn more about Joseph Bruchac.

mals, Storm Maker's Tipi, and *Buffalo Woman,* are filled with patterns of flowers, trees, birds, and other animals indigenous to the prairie. Goble received the Caldecott Medal for his stunning illustrations for *The Girl Who Loved Wild Horses.* All of Goble's work draws on Native American artistic traditions as well.

The trickster of the Pacific Northwest is Raven. While he is a wily, crafty being who loves to get the better of others, he is also a friend to humankind. Gerald McDermott's version of this story, *Raven: A Trickster Tale*

Raccoon's Last Race, retold by Native American storyteller Joseph Bruchac with James Bruchac, explains how raccoons ended up with their odd appearance and rolling gait. From *Raccoon's Last Race* by Joseph Bruchac & James Bruchac. Illustrated by Jose Aruego & Ariane Dewey, copyright © 2004 by Jose Aruego and Ariana Dewey, illustrations. Used by permission of Dial Books for Young Readers, a division of Penguin Putnam, Inc.

from the Pacific Northwest, is illustrated in watercolors, but Raven in his many guises wears the more abstract and solidly colored patterns of Northwest tribal art. In an Eskimo version, another Raven story tells how he created the first human from a peavine (Virginia Hamilton, *In the Beginning*).

The stories of many tribes often revolved around a cultural hero like the Woodland character Gluskap, Glooscap, or Gluskabe. This hero accomplished great deeds and often served as helper to the Great Spirit. In Joseph Bruchac's *Gluskabe and the Four Wishes*, Gluskabe has retired across the big water to take a rest after making the world a better place for his children. Four Abenaki men decide to undertake a difficult journey to ask Gluskabe for their hearts' desires. Impressed by the difficulties they have faced to get to him, Gluskabe gives them each a pouch but warns them not to look inside until they get home. The first three men cannot resist a peek and are justly punished. The fourth man, who only asked to be a good hunter to provide food for his people, resists temptation, but when he returns home he finds the pouch is empty. As he is about to despair, however, he hears the voices of the animals, who speak to him of the proper ways to prepare for the hunt and how to show respect for the animals. "From that day on he was the best hunter among the people. He never took more game than was needed, yet he always provided enough to feed his people."

Other, more human, heroes can be found in many Native American stories. Rafe Martin's *The Rough-Face Girl* is a retelling of an Algonquin story and has many elements of the Cinderella tales. In this version, Rough Face is the youngest of three sisters and has become scarred from sitting too close to the fire in order to feed the flames. Although her sisters both hope to be the ones to marry the Invisible Being, Rough Face is the only one who can see his face in the beauty of the world around her. When she has passed the tests set her, the Invisible Being appears and sees her true beauty. Then she is sent to bathe in the lake and her physical scars disappear, revealing her true form to all. David Shannon's carefully modeled paintings bring the characters in the story to life.

Robert San Souci's *Sootface* is an Ojibwa story that is very similar to many other Native American versions of this tale. In this variant, Sootface, the youngest sister, is only dirty with the soot from the fire rather than physically scarred. When she goes to meet the Invisible Warrior, she dresses in a gown of birch bark and wears a crown of wildflowers on her head. Daniel San Souci's realistic illustrations are based on thoroughly researched details of mid-1700s Ojibwa life.

Rafe Martin's poignant *The Boy Who Lived with the Seals* is based on a Chinook legend and tells of a boy who is torn between the world of The People and the undersea world of the seals. Although he does not transform physically into a seal as do the Selkies of North Atlantic

legend, he eventually chooses to live in their kingdom, returning only once a year to leave a beautiful carved canoe for the humans he has left behind.

The character of Mouse Woman figures prominently in Dale De Armond's *The Seal Oil Lamp*, another story about a child caught between two worlds. Because Allegua was blind and Inuit tribal law stated that no child may live if it cannot grow up to support itself, his family sadly left him behind when they moved to the summer fish camp. But the 7-year-old had fed a starving mouse that winter, so the Mouse Woman and her family take care of Allegua and he comes to know and love their world.

> They told him wonderful stories about the mouse world and about the owls and foxes and eagles who try to catch them, and how the mouse people outwit their enemies. They told him about Raven and the magic that lives under the earth and in the sky country. And the mouse people sang their songs for him and did their dances on the back of his hand so he could feel how beautiful their dances were. (p. 20)

De Armond's stylized wood engravings suggest dramatically the powerful beauty of Inuit artwork.

Although survival themes are constant in Indian tales, they are particularly strong in Inuit stories. James Houston, who spent many years among the Inuit, is especially sensitive to authentic depictions of Inuit art and culture. His illustrations often look like renderings of Inuit carvings. In his *Tikta' Liktak*, a legendary hunter is isolated when an ice pan breaks away. In a dream, he gains courage, kills a seal, and is able to find his way home. *The White Archer* is a tale of a vengeful hunter who finally succumbs to the kindness and wisdom of an Inuit couple.

Teaching Resources: "A Study of Folktales by Culture" provides a start for comparing characteristics, characters, collectors, and typical tales representative of specific areas around the world.

 **European Variants in the United States** Richard Chase collected and published *The Jack Tales* and *Grandfather Tales*, which are American variations of old stories brought to this country by English, Irish, and Scottish settlers in the seventeenth and eighteenth centuries. They are as much a part of Americana as the Brer Rabbit stories are. In some respects Jack is an equivalent to Brer Rabbit. He is a trickster hero who overcomes his opponent through quick wit and cunning, rather than through the strength that triumphs in the tall tales that originated in the United States. All of these variants come from the mountain folk of the southern Appalachians. Cut off from the mainstream of immigration and changing customs, these people preserved their stories and songs in the same way that they continue to weave the Tudor rose into their fabrics.

A Study of Folktales by Culture

 Visit the Online Learning Center at **www.mhhe.com/kiefer9e** for a printable version of this list.

BRITISH FOLKTALES

Cultures and Collectors	Typical Tales (Author)	Characters	Characteristics
Joseph Jacobs (1854–1916)	*Finn MacCoul and His Fearless Wife* (Byrd)	Lazy Jack	Cumulative tales for youngest children
		Giants	
	Jack and the Beanstalk (Kellogg, Benaduce)		Beast tales
		"Wee folk"	
			Droll humor
	The Little Red Hen (J. Pinkney, Galdone, M. Zemach)	Dick Whittington	
			Transformations
	The Loathsome Dragon (Wiesner)		
			Giant killers
	Tam Lin (Cooper)		
	The Three Little Pigs (Rounds)		

GERMAN FOLKTALES

The Grimm brothers Jacob (1785–1863) Wilhelm (1786–1859)	*The Elves and the Shoemaker* (Grimm brothers)	Tom Thumb	Somber stories
	The Frog Prince (Grimm brothers)	Rumpelstiltskin	Children as characters
		Hansel and Gretel	Harsh punishments
	Hansel and Gretel (Grimm brothers)	Red Riding Hood	Romances
	Little Red Cap (Grimm brothers)	Witches, elves, dwarfs	Transformations
	Rumpelstiltskin (Grimm brothers)	Bears, wolves	
	Snow White and the Seven Dwarfs (Grimm brothers)	Snow White	
		King Thrushbeard	

SCANDINAVIAN FOLKTALES

Peter Christian Asbjørnsen (1812–1885)	*Boots and His Brothers* (Kimmel)	Trolls, Tomte	Tongue-in-cheek humor
		Many-headed giants	Helpful animals
Jorgen E. Moe (1813–1882)	*East o'the Sun and West o'the Moon* (Dasent)	Youngest sons or "Boots"	Magical objects
Translated into English by George Webbe Dasent (1817–1896)	"The Lad Who Went to the North Wind," in *East o'the Sun and West o'the Moon* (Asbjørnsen and Moe)	North Wind	Magical enchantments
		White bears	Many trials and tasks
		Salmon	Poor boy succeeds
	The Three Billy Goats Gruff (Galdone, Rounds)	Reindeer, elk	*(continued)*

A Study of Folktales by Culture (continued)

FRENCH FOLKTALES

Cultures and Collectors	Typical Tales (Author)	Characters	Characteristics
Charles Perrault (1628–1703)	*Beauty and the Beast* (de Beaumont, Geras)	Fairy godmothers	Traditional fairy tale
	Cinderella (Perrault, McClintock)	Jealous stepsisters	Romance
	Puss in Boots (Perrault)	Royalty	Wicked enchantments
	Stone Soup (Brown)	Talking cats	Long sleep
	The White Cat (R. San Souci)	Unselfish youngest daughter	

RUSSIAN FOLKTALES

Alexander Afanasyev (1826–1871)	*Baba Yaga* (Arnold)	Vasilissa, beautiful and wise	Peasants outwit tsars
	Baba Yaga and Vasilisa the Brave (Mayer)	Ivan, youngest brother	Many tasks
	The Fool of the World and the Flying Ship (Ransome)	Baba Yaga, the witch	Quest for firebird
			Dire punishments
	The Little Humpbacked Horse (Winthrop)	Wolves, bears	Helpful animals
		Firebird	
	The Tale of the Firebird (Spirin)	Koschey the Deathless	Fool or youngest triumphs

JAPANESE FOLKTALES

	The Boy of the Three-Year Nap (Snyder)	Momotaro	Transformation to birds
	The Boy Who Drew Cats (Hodges)	Wicked *oni,* ogres	Childless couples have "different" children
		Trickster badger	Respect for elderly
	The Crane Wife (Bodkin)	Urashima Taro	Self-sacrifice
	The Farmer and the Poor God (Wells)	Poor farmers, fishermen	
	Momotaro, the Peach Boy (Shute)		
	The Wise Old Woman (Uchida)		

AFRICAN FOLKTALES

Harold Courlander and other present-day collectors	*The Cow-Tail Switch* (Courlander and Herzog)	Anansi, trickster spider	Pourquoi stories
		Zomo, trickster rabbit	Talking-beast tales
	Mufaro's Beautiful Daughters (Steptoe)	Various animals	Animal tricksters

A Study of Folktales by Culture (continued)

AFRICAN FOLKTALES (continued)

Cultures and Collectors	Typical Tales (Author)	Characters	Characteristics
	Rabbit Makes a Monkey of Lion (Aardema)		"Why" humor
	A Story, a Story (Haley)		Onomatopoeia
	Zomo the Rabbit (McDermott)		Wordplay

NATIVE AMERICAN FOLKTALES

Henry Rowe Schoolcraft (1820s–1850s)	*Gluskabe and the Four Wishes* (Bruchac)	Gluskap, Gluskabe	Nature myths
	Star Boy (Goble)	Manabozho	Tricksters
	The Gift of the Sacred Dog (Goble)	Hare	Transformation tales
		Coyote	Pattern of four
	Iktomi and the Buzzard (Goble)	Raven	Pourquoi stories
	The Dark Way (Hamilton)	Iktomi	Interaction with spirit world
	The Blind Hunter (Rodanas)	Sky People	
		Little People	
		Mouse Woman	

The Jack Tales is a cycle of stories in which Jack is always the central figure. You'd expect to find him playing this role in "Jack in the Giant's Newground" and "Jack and the Bean Tree." However, he shows up again in "Jack and the Robbers," which is a variant of "The Bremen Town Musicians." The delightful aspect of these tales is Jack's nonchalance about his exploits and the incongruous mixing of the mountaineer dialect with unicorns, kings, and swords.

In *Moss Gown,* William H. Hooks retells an old story from North Carolina that melds elements of "Cinderella" with motifs from *King Lear.* Rejected by her father and banished from home by her two sisters, Candace meets a gris-gris woman who gives her a shimmering gown that will change back into Spanish moss when the morning star sets. Candace finds work in the kitchen of a plantation where the Young Master is about to give a series of balls. Calling on the gris-gris woman for help, Candace goes to each of the three balls and falls in love with the Young Master. When Candace finally reveals herself, the Young Master has come to know her through conversation and, it is implied, to love her for more than her beauty. Although the moss gown has magic to help her, Candace is more similar in spirit to Princess Furball and The Rough-Face Girl than to the Disney and Perrault Cinderellas, for it is her own intelligence and spirit that wins her a husband, a home, and her father's love once again.

Authors continue to Americanize European folktales. Hooks has also written an Appalachian *The Three Little Pigs and the Fox* that depends on local detail, colloquial language, and mountain customs for flavor. In it, Hamlet rescues her two pig brothers from a "droolymouth fox" and comes home in time for Sunday dinner. Donald Davis's version of this story, titled *The Pig Who Went Home on Sunday,* has three grown pigs whose Mama invites them back to dinner every Sunday. She also gives them good advice about building codes that helps them to outwit a slick fox. Alan Schroeder's *Smoky Mountain Rose* is a version of Cinderella with a hog as fairy godmother and a man who has made his fortune in sowbellies and grits as her "prince."

The Pig Who Went Home on Sunday is a fresh and amusing Appalachian version of the traditional "Three Little Pigs" tale.

Illustration from *The Pig Who Went Home on Sunday: An Appalachian Folktale* by Donald Davis. Illustrated by Jennifer Mazzuco, copyright © 2004. Used by permission of August House Little Folk Publishers.

 **African American Folktales** Africans who were brought to North America as slaves continued to tell the tales they remembered, particularly the talking-beast tales. Some of these stories took on new layers of meaning about the relationship between the slaves and their masters. In the late 1800s, Joel Chandler Harris, a Georgia newspaperman, recorded these tales in a written approximation of the Gullah dialect in which the tales were told to him. In his *Uncle Remus: His Songs and His Sayings,* Harris invented Uncle Remus, an elderly plantation slave who told these talking-beast tales to a little white boy (see Harris's *The Complete Tales of Uncle Remus*). Harris was later criticized for his portrayal of the Old South, but the "Brer Rabbit" stories live on in retellings by other people.

Two excellent series have adapted these stories for today's children. In *Jump Again!* Van Dyke Parks presents "The Wonderful Tar-Baby Story," in which Brer Fox sets up a sticky contraption and then, "Brer Fox, he lay low." When Brer Rabbit is finally stuck, Brer Fox saunters forth and laughs threateningly, showing "his teeth all white and shiny, like they were brand-new." Of course, Brer Rabbit pleads with the fox to do anything but throw him into a briar patch, and the gullible fox is tricked once again into sparing the rabbit's life, for Brer Rabbit was "bred and born in a briar patch" (p. 9). In contrast, Julius Lester's "Brer Rabbit and the Tar Baby" from his *Tales of*

Uncle Remus is a more rambunctious version that sounds as if it is being told directly to the reader. Asides, contemporary allusions, creative figurative language, and interjections are characteristic of this storyteller. Lester describes Brer Rabbit as strutting "like he owned the world and was collecting rent from everybody in it" (p. 11). But by the time the poor rabbit is stuck, Brer Fox saunters out "as cool as the sweat on the side of a glass of ice tea" (p. 14). Full-color watercolors by Jerry Pinkney depict incidents in the story. Julius Lester's forewords for his Uncle Remus collections dispel many of the myths surrounding the "Brer Rabbit" stories, discuss the nature of storytelling, and reflect on the role of the trickster figure in valuing a little disorder in today's society.

Robert D. San Souci has retold a longer version of a short tale from the Sea Islands of South Carolina in *Sukey and the Mermaid.* In this story, Sukey has a mean stepfather who works her from dawn to dusk. Mama Jo, a mermaid, befriends her and gives her a gold coin whenever she calls her to the shore. Sukey's stepfather eventually discovers the mermaid's existence and tries to capture her for her gold. Sukey is led on several journeys between the world of the sea and that of her home on land, but eventually she decides to give up the mermaid's treasure for the love of a simple man.

Virginia Hamilton was responsible for several superior collections of stories representing African American folktales. In *The People Could Fly,* she collected twenty-four stories, including animal tales, stories with motifs of transformation and trickery, Jack tales and a tale of John de Conquer, and slave tales of freedom, including one handed down in the author's own family. Leo Dillon and Diane Dillon, who illustrated the original volume, created new illustrations for a single edition of the title story, *The People Could Fly,* following Hamilton's death. In *Her Stories,* Hamilton followed a similar organizational format, but these tales have their roots in the history and folklore of African American women. They include animal stories, fairy tales, stories of the supernatural, and stories about real-life heroines. Hamilton preserved the individual voices of the storytellers from whom the stories were collected. Some of the stories are in Gullah or plantation dialect, and others include African words whose meanings are lost to us today. Excellent classroom resources, these collections contain author notes and extensive bibliographies. Bold black-and-white illustrations by the Dillons evoke the humor, beauty, and liveliness of these traditional stories.

According to Steve Sanfield's introduction to his *Adventures of High John the Conqueror,* the High John stories were popular among slaves but for obvious reasons were never shared with white people. Although John was a slave, he spent his time doing as little slaving as possible, tricking the Old Master out of a roasting pig or a few hours of rest. Sanfield prefaces eight of the sixteen tales with notes explaining historical context or giving background. In "Tops and Bottoms," titled after a motif found in many tales, John asks Boss which half of the planting he wants. Thinking that High John will plant cotton, Boss chooses the top. But John has planted sweet potatoes. Each of the next three years, Boss is tricked by John. Finally, he chooses *both* tops and bottoms, which leaves High John the middle. But John, no fool, plants corn, and Boss is left with a heap of tassels and stalks while High John takes the corn. Virginia Hamilton extended the adventures of this sometimes mythical hero into a folktale-like novel, *The Magical Adventures of Pretty Pearl.*

Louisiana, with its mixed heritage of African American, Anglo, French, and Cajun peoples, has a rich vein of folktales from which to draw. Sharon Arms Doucet has collected several delightful Cajun trickster tales in *Lapin Plays Possum.* Compère Lapin and his friend Compère Bouki come from the same African roots as their cousin Brer Rabbit. Their exploits have a delightfully different Creole/Cajun flavor. *The Talking Eggs* by Robert D. San Souci is a Creole folktale that seems to have its roots in European tales like those in Charlotte Huck's *Toads and Diamonds* and in San Souci's *The Well at the End of the World.* A poor widow and her two daughters live on a farm that looks like "the tail end of bad luck." One daughter, Blanche, who has to do all the work, runs into the forest one day and meets a strange old woman who gives her the gift of special eggs. The eggs will turn into riches when she throws them over her shoulder. But she is warned to take only the ones that say "Take me." Blanche follows this advice even though the eggs she leaves are jewel-encrusted. When she arrives home with fancy clothes and a carriage, her mother plots to steal Blanche's things and send Rose for more. But Rose steals the jeweled eggs and is paid for her greediness by the release of whip snakes, wasps, and a cloud of bad things that chase her home. Jerry Pinkney's rich and colorful illustrations magically evoke the forest and swamp settings of this Louisiana "generous person/greedy person" tale.

 **Tall Tales** Ask any visitors to the United States what they have seen, and they are apt to laugh and reply that, whatever it was, it was the "biggest in the world"—the longest hot dog, the highest building, the largest store, the hottest spot. This is the land of superlatives, of "the best." Many countries have tall tales in their folklore, but only the United States has developed so many huge legendary heroes. Perhaps the vast frontier made settlers seem so puny that they felt compelled to invent stories about superheroes. Whatever the reasons, North American tall tales contain a glorious mixture of the humor, bravado, and pioneer spirit that was needed to tame a wilderness.

Paul Bunyan was a huge lumberjack who bossed a big gang of lumbermen in the North Woods of Michigan, Minnesota, and Wisconsin. Paul's light lunch one day was "three sides of barbecued beef, half a wagon load of potatoes, carrots and a few other odds and ends," Glenn Rounds reports in *Ol' Paul, the Mighty Logger*

(p. 28). Rounds asserts, as do most chroniclers of Paul's doings, that he worked for Paul and was the biggest liar ever in camp. By switching from past to present tense, Rounds gives these eleven tales special immediacy. Steven Kellogg synopsizes Paul Bunyan's life in his humorously illustrated picture-book version, *Paul Bunyan.* Tidy endpapers depict Paul's New England seacoast beginnings, and a map of the States highlights Paul's feats. This action-packed version serves as an introduction to Bunyan's exploits, but the extended text of the other versions fleshes out individual tall tales and makes them better choices for reading aloud.

Kellogg's *Pecos Bill* tells the tale of a Texan who, as a child, fell out of his parents' wagon as they moved west and was raised by coyotes. Bill's exploits include squeezing the poison from a rattler to create the first lasso, and inventing cattle roping. He also bred cattle with shorter legs on the uphill side so that they could graze steep pinnacles without falling off. His taming of a wild horse eventually won him a bride, Slue-Foot Sue. Kellogg's depiction of this exuberant tall-tale hero is full of humor, exaggeration, and boundless energy.

Of all the heroes, only Johnny Appleseed was a gentle, tame person who lived to serve others. His real name was John Chapman, and he grew up in the Connecticut Valley before setting out for Pennsylvania, Ohio, and Indiana. Kathy Jakobsen's full-page folk-art paintings for Reeve Lindbergh's *Johnny Appleseed* capture the changing face of the land as settlers moved west in this poetic retelling. Steven Kellogg's *Johnny Appleseed,* in contrast, focuses on the more rollicking incidents that grew around the tales Chapman told to settlers and their own embellishments of these stories. Both authors include notes that help readers see how storytellers select events to shape into tales.

Industry has its heroes, too. "Joe Magarac," in Adrien Stoutenberg's *American Tall Tales,* tells of a man of steel who came to Hunkietown. The word *magarac* means "jackass" (which to steelworkers was a term of admiration), and Joe Magarac worked and ate like one. He finally melted himself down to become part of a new steel mill. John Henry was a powerful African American who swung his mighty hammer in a contest with a steam drill to build the transcontinental railroad. Jerry Pinkney won a Caldecott Honor Medal for his sparkling watercolor illustrations for Julius Lester's robust retelling in *John Henry.* Steve Sanfield's illustrated short story *A Natural Man* also chronicles John Henry's life from childhood to his death after defeating the steam drill. Ezra Jack Keats created bold figures to depict this legendary hero in his picture book *John Henry.* Mary E. Lyons has adapted a tall tale retold by Zora Neale Hurston in *Roy Makes a Car,* illustrated by Terry Widener. Like Joe Magarac and John Henry, Roy Tyle is a supertalented worker, so talented that God borrows his design for an automobile. Other folklore collected by Hurston can be found in *Lies and Other Tall Tales.* This collection of short whoppers has

Jerry Pinkney portrays a magnificent American tall-tale hero in Julius Lester's retelling of *John Henry.* From *John Henry* by Julius Lester, illustrated by Jerry Pinkney, copyright © 1994 by Jerry Pinkney, illustrations. Used by permission of Dial Books for Young Readers, a division of Penguin Putnam Inc.

found the perfect complement in Christopher Myers's sharp-edged collages.

Mose Humphreys is introduced in *New York's Bravest* by Mary Pope Osborne. Mose was a real fireman in New York in 1848 whose exploits and bravery became the stuff of legend. In view of the events of September 11 it is likely that this superhero will come to represent not just one man but all firefighters. The book was researched and written before September 11 and is dedicated to the 343 firefighters who gave their lives to save others on that terrible day. Osborne has also collected the stories of nine other heroes in *American Tall Tales.* In the tradition of nineteenth-century storytellers, she uses figurative language easily and has combined, edited, and added her own touches to these stories. Michael McCurdy's watercolor-washed bold wood engravings of Pecos Bill, John Henry, and Stormalong perfectly suit the exaggerated language of the tall tale.

Andrew Glass wove history and story together in *Mountain Men: True Grit and Tall Tales.* Glass provides biographies and then the tall tales about real-life individuals such as Hugh Glass, John Colter, Mike Fink, and Kit Carson. In *Cut from the Same Cloth,* Robert D. San Souci has assembled a marvelous multicultural collection of tall tales with female heroines. Illustrated by Brian Pinkney, the stories are arranged by region and include such characters as Sal Fink, wife of the famous Mike; Annie Christmas, an African American heroine; and Otoonah, a member of the Sugpiaq people of the Aleutian Islands. Although not all of these stories can be strictly defined as tall tales, they do feature women who are tall in courage and strong in will. Picture books such as *Steamboat Annie and the Thousand Pound Catfish* by Catherine Wright and *Swamp Angel* by Anne Isaacs are surely based on these wonderful heroines.

Teaching Resources: "Some American Tall-Tale Heroes" outlines some of the characteristics of eight of these legendary heroes. Others whom children might research and add to the list include Casey Jones, Old Stormalong, Slue-Foot Sue, Febold Feboldson, Tony Beaver, and Mike Fink.

Folktales from Mexico, the Caribbean, and Central and South America

 Each year a little more of the rich story heritage of the Caribbean, Mexico, and Central and South America becomes available. These stories have their roots in the many cultures that have inhabited this vast region. Lynn Joseph's *A Wave in Her Pocket: Stories from Trinidad,* illustrated by Brian Pinkney, and *The Mermaid's Twin Sister: More Stories from Trinidad,* illustrated by Donna Perrone, present traditional Afro-Caribbean stories within modern-day narratives. Amber loves hearing her Tantie's tales about Trinidad, and both of these books place those traditional tales within stories about Amber and her island family. Lulu Delacre has retold and illustrated twelve stories with Native American and Spanish roots in *Golden Tales: Myths, Legends, and Folklore from Latin America.* She provides detailed notes about the stories' origins and about the people who told them. Mary-Joan Gerson has collected stories about Mexican heroines in *Fiesta Femina: Celebrating Women in Mexican Folktales.* Many stories appear in excellent collections of folktales, myths, or fables edited by John Bierhorst. *The Monkey's Haircut and Other Stories Told by the Maya* includes stories collected from Mayan Indians in Guatemala and southeastern Mexico since 1900. Some are obvious variations of European tales, and others are *ejemplos* (explanatory myths). Robert Andrew Parker's gray-washed drawings and Bierhorst's informative introduction both contribute appeal for middle-grade readers. (See the sections "Fables" and "Myths" in this chapter for other Bierhorst titles.) Lucia M. Gonzalez's carefully researched *Señor Cat's Romance* contains six stories from Latin America and is illustrated by Latina artist Lulu Delacre. Nicholasa Mohr's *The Song of el Coqui and Other Tales of Puerto Rico* includes stories with Taino, African, and Spanish origins and is indicative of the rich interweaving of cultures that contributed to the folklore of this vast region.

Folktales from the African Caribbean tradition have been collected in several books for children, and the islands have certainly contributed many stories to

Some American Tall-Tale Heroes

 Visit the Online Learning Center at **www.mhhe.com/kiefer9e** for a printable version of this list.

JOHNNY APPLESEED (JOHN CHAPMAN) (1774–1845)

Hero and Tales	Occupation/Locale	Characteristics
Johnny Appleseed (Kellogg, Lindbergh) "Johnny Appleseed," in *American Tall Tales* (Osborne) "Rainbow Walker," in *American Tall Tales* (Stoutenberg)	Born in Massachusetts; wanderer in Pennsylvania, Indiana, and Ohio; planter of apple trees	Selfless; friend to animals; dressed in rags with cook pot for hat

PAUL BUNYAN

Hero and Tales	Occupation/Locale	Characteristics
Ol' Paul, the Mighty Logger (Rounds) *Paul Bunyan* (Shephard, Kellogg) "Paul Bunyan," in *American Tall Tales* (Osborne) "Sky Bright Axe," in *American Tall Tales* (Stoutenberg)	Lumberjack; North American woods; created the Great Lakes, St. Lawrence Seaway, and Grand Canyon	Huge; strong even as a baby; Babe the Blue Ox was the pet; inventive problem solver

JOE MAGARAC

Hero and Tales	Occupation/Locale	Characteristics
"Steelmaker," in *American Tall Tales* (Stoutenberg)	Steelworker; Pittsburgh, or "Hunkietown"	Made of steel; works and eats like a mule; born from an ore pit; stirs steel with bare hands

PECOS BILL

Hero and Tales	Occupation/Locale	Characteristics
"Coyote Cowboy," in *American Tall Tales* (Stoutenberg) *Pecos Bill* (Kellogg) "Pecos Bill," in *American Tall Tales* (Osborne) "Slue-Foot Sue and Pecos Bill" in *Larger Than Life* (R. San Souci)	Cowboy; first rancher; Texas Panhandle and the Southwest	Raised by coyotes; Widowmaker was his horse; Slue-Foot Sue was his wife; invented lasso, six-shooter, cattle roping

(continued)

Some American Tall-Tale Heroes (continued)

SALLY ANN THUNDER ANN WHIRLWIND CROCKETT

Hero and Tales	Occupation/Locale	Characteristics
Sally Ann Thunder Ann Whirlwind Crockett (Kellogg)	Kentucky, Mississippi River	Could outwrestle, outrun, and outfish her brothers even as a child; rescued Davy Crockett, then married him

JOHN HENRY

Hero and Tales	Occupation/Locale	Characteristics
"Hammerman," in *American Tall Tales* (Stoutenberg) *John Henry* (Keats, Lester) "John Henry," in *American Tall Tales* (Osborne) "John Henry the Steel Driving Man," in *Larger Than Life* (R. San Souci) *A Natural Man* (Sanfield)	Railroad man; West Virginia west to the Mississippi	African American wanderer, exceedingly strong even as a baby; Polly Ann was his wife; companion was Little Willie.

DAVY CROCKETT (1786–1836)

Hero and Tales	Occupation/Locale	Characteristics
"Davy Crockett," in *American Tall Tales* (Osborne) *Davy Crockett Saves the World* (Schanzer) "Frontier Fighter," in *American Tall Tales* (Stoutenberg)	Frontiersman; Tennessee	Tall; good hunter and fighter; Betsy was his rifle; tamed a bear; wore coonskin cap

ALFRED BULLTOP STORMALONG

Hero and Tales	Occupation/Locale	Characteristics
"Five Fathoms Tall," in *American Tall Tales* (Stoutenberg) "Old Stormalong: The Deep Water Sailor," in *Larger Than Life* (R. San Souci) "Stormalong," in *American Tall Tales* (Osborne)	Sailor whaler, ship's captain; Massachusetts and northern coasts	Giant man, huge appetite; ship called the Tuscarora; made the White Cliffs of Dover with soap

the mainland African American tradition. Robert D. San Souci has relied on several Creole tales from the French West Indies to tell *Cendrillon: A Caribbean Cinderella.* The story is narrated by Cendrillon's godmother, a washerwoman whose only treasure is a mahogany wand that changes one thing into another. When Cendrillon wishes to go to the ball given by Monsieur Thibault for his son Paul, the godmother turns a breadfruit into a carriage, rodents into horses, and lizards into footmen. The story has its traditional happy ending. San Souci has also retold a Caribbean hero tale in *The Twins and the Bird of Darkness.* This story is a variation on the generous person/greedy person theme as two brothers set out to save a beautiful princess. Virginia Hamilton's *The Girl Who Spun Gold* is another variation on the familiar European tale *Rumpelstiltskin.* In this version a mother brags to Big King that her daughter Quashiba can spin a whole field of gold thread. After their marriage Big King (who "had to become even bigger than he needed to be") tells Quashiba that in a year and a day she'll be expected to weave three rooms of golden things. When the time arrives she is locked into a huge room and weeps in despair at her impossible task. She is overheard by Lit'mahn, a mischievous little imp who promises to fill the room with gold. In return, if she can't guess his name after three tries on three nights she'll become small like him and be carried off to live as his wife. After a second unsuccessful night of guessing, Quashiba dines with Big King and he tells her how he overheard the singing of a strange little man out hunting in the woods. The song, of course, reveals Lit'mahn's full name, and when Quashiba guesses it correctly he goes "POP-OP" and disappears. As for a "happily ever after" end, it doesn't happen just yet. Quashiba is so mad at Big King for his greed that she doesn't speak to him for three long years. When he apologizes three long fields full, she forgives him and they live "fairly" happily ever after. Hamilton retells this story with her usual flair for the cadence of West Indian dialect, and Leo Dillon and Diane Dillon's lush golden illustrations are perfectly beautiful.

Marisa Montes's Juan Bobo is a favorite folk hero in Puerto Rico and is typical of the many noodlehead characters found around the world. In *Juan Bobo Goes to Work,* Juan sets out to get a job from a farmer. The first time he is paid he forgets what his mother, Doña Juana, told him and puts the coins in his holey pocket rather than holding them in his hand. The next time he sets out, Doña Juana tells him to put his pay in the burlap

bag she gives him. This does not go well when he is paid in milk. The third day Juan goes to the grocer for work. Doña Juana instructs him to carry the pail of milk on his head. When he is paid with cheese instead of milk he puts it under his hat. Of course, the cheese melts as he walks home in the hot sun. The next week Doña Juana gives Juan Bobo a piece of string and tells him to tie up whatever the grocer gives him. He obeys, and drags a ham behind him on the string. The village dogs and cats proceed to have a feast. All is not lost because, as he walks by the window of a rich man, the man's sick daughter sees him. The daughter laughs out loud and is cured. In gratitude the rich man sends Juan and his mother a ham every Sunday.

Mexico has contributed many delightful stories to the corpus of folktales for children. In Verna Aardema's *Borreguita and the Coyote,* a crafty "little lamb" outwits a coyote. Petra Mathers's stylish watercolor paintings feature bright saturated colors and primitive figures reminiscent of Henri Rousseau. Tomie dePaola has retold several folktales from Mexico. Some, like *The Lady*

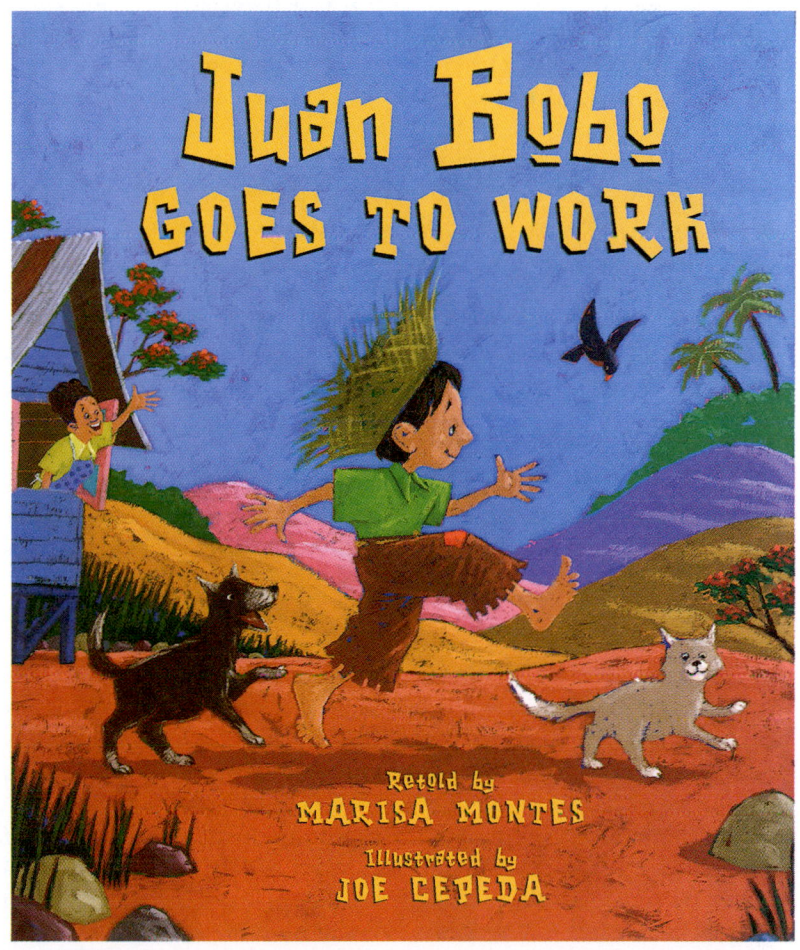

Joe Cepeda has envisaged a likable personality for a traditional Puerto Rican hero in *Juan Bobo Goes to Work,* retold by Marisa Montes. Cover of *Juan Bobo Goes to Work* retold by Marisa Montes, illustrated by Joe Cepeda. Illustration copyright © 2000 by Joe Cepeda. Used by permission of HarperCollins Publishers.

of *Guadalupe* and *The Legend of the Poinsettia*, have their connections to Catholicism. DePaola's *Adelita* is a Mexican version of the Cinderella story. Adelita, forced to work in the kitchen by her stepmother, goes to Javier's party with the help of Esperanza, an old serving woman. She wears a beautiful rebozo, or shawl, and when Javier sees it in her window the next morning, the two are happily united.

Pourquoi stories are as common in Central and South America as they are in other cultures. Lois Ehlert's *Moon Rope* is a bilingual retelling of a Peruvian tale in which Mole and Fox try to climb to the moon on a grass rope. Mole falls off the rope and is so embarrassed by the other animals' teasing that he goes to live underground. As for Fox, Lois Ehlert's illustrations, adapted from Peruvian folk arts, show his face, just visible in the silvery moon. A pourquoi story tells how birds became brightly colored. "Humming-Bird and the Flower" appears in Charles Finger's *Tales from Silver Lands*, a collection of South American stories illustrated with woodcuts. It won a Newbery Medal in 1925. The story attributes the hummingbird's colors to clay, jewels, the color of the sunset, and the greens of the forests, which Panther helped the bird to gather after it helped restore Panther's eyesight. Nancy Van Laan has retold another pourquoi tale for younger readers. *So Say the Little Monkeys* tells why black-mouth monkeys live in the trees; they mean to be industrious but end up playing all the time instead. Gerald McDermott explains how music came into the world in his *Musicians of the Sun*, a retelling of an Aztec myth.

Water seems to be a common motif in South American folktales. Caroline Pitcher's *Mariana and the Merchild: A Folktale from Chile* tells of a lonely old woman who longs for children to play with. One day after a great storm Mariana finds a baby in a crab shell. She is a merbaby, put in the shell by a Sea Spirit to protect her from the sea wolves who prowl during ocean tempests. The old woman offers the baby back to her Spirit mother, but the Spirit allows the old woman to keep the child for a time. Mariana and the Merchild live happily together, visited each day by the Sea Spirit who feeds her and teaches her how to swim. The Merchild grows strong, and her happy play attracts other children to Mariana's hut. When it is time for the child to return to the sea, Mariana is comforted by the other children. She is no longer alone. This tale has elements of the many other legends where a creature from a watery environment lives on land for some time. Children will enjoy comparing it to Susan Cooper's *The Selkie Girl* and Rafe Martin's *The Boy Who Lived with the Seals*.

Water is central to *The Great Canoe* by María Elena Maggi. In this Venezuelan story of a great flood the Kariña people are warned by Kaputano, the Sky Dweller, that the world will soon be covered by a great flood. Only four couples believe him and set about helping him build a great canoe. When they finish they gather two of

each animal and seeds from each plant. They are saved from the flood, and when the waters recede Kaputano allows them to choose the geographic features of their new world. Gloria Calderón's lovely scratchboard illustrations are perfectly suited to the story. An Argentinean tale by Nancy Van Laan also focuses on water, but here it is the lack of water, not too much, that is the problem. In *The Magic Bean Tree*, the Great Bird of the Underworld has caused a drought that is threatening all the wildlife on the Argentinean pampas. Little Topec figures out how to scare away the miserable bird with the help of the beans from a carob tree, and relieves the drought.

With the changing population in the United States and Canada, we need more editions of traditional folktales, myths, and legends that reflect the many peoples of Caribbean, Mexican, and Central and South American cultural heritage. More publishers have begun to feature folktales of the region, and teachers will need to be persistent in finding these sources.

The "Exploring Folktales" Web on page 323 suggests the rich possibilities inherent in a study of this genre of literature. It provides for a serious look at the types of folktales and certain motifs found in the tales that would appeal to younger children. A study of more-complex tales or myths or a cross-cultural study could be planned for older children.

FABLES

Fables are usually associated with Aesop, a Greek slave who is supposed to have been born in Asia Minor about 600 B.C. Some scholars doubt his actual existence and believe that his works were the product of several storytellers. We know that some of the fables appeared in Greek literature two centuries before Aesop's birth, and in India and Egypt before that. The first written fables were in Greek, translated into Latin and again into English by William Caxton, and printed in 1484.

Other sources for fables, as we have seen, were the Jataka tales—animal stories that told of the previous births of the Buddha—and the *Panchatantra*, which was written for the purpose of instructing the young princes of India. These stories, longer than Aesop's fables, have moralistic verses interspersed throughout. When these are removed, the tales are closer to folktales. (See the earlier section "Folktales.")

A third common source for fables is the work of Jean De La Fontaine, a French poet, who wrote his fables in verse form. However, he drew largely on the collections of Aesop's fables that were available in the seventeenth century.

Characteristics of Fables

Fables are brief, didactic tales in which animals, or occasionally the elements, speak as human beings. Examples of these might be the well-known race between the hare and the tortoise or the contest between the sun and the

Wonderfully Exciting Books

Beast Tales

The Bremen-Town Musicians (Grimm/Plume)
The Little Red Hen (Zemach, J. Pinkney)
Rabbit Makes a Monkey of Lion (Aardema)
The Three Bears (Marshall, Aylesworth)
The Three Billy Goats Gruff (Brown)

Make a "book of threes."
Make a story box of one tale.
Bake Red Hen's bread.
Put on a play of Tondo or Billy Goats.
Make paper-bag puppets and retell a story.

Wonder Tales

Ali Baba and the Forty Thieves (McVitty)
Baba Yaga (Kimmel)
Momotaro (Wada)
Puss in Boots (Perrault)
Snow White (Grimm)
Tam Lin (Cooper)

Make a catalog of magical objects.
Make a wanted poster for a villain.
Make a chart of transformation from/to.

Cumulative Tales

The Giant Turnip (Tolstoy)
The Gingerbread Boy (Galdone)
The Mitten (Brett)
One Fine Day (Hogrogian)

Make a chart of what accumulates.
Make a flannelboard story.
Make a circular map of the action.
Write your own version.

Porquoi, or "Why," Tales

Beginning readers can practice reading in books with limited vocabulary.

The Cat's Purr (Bryan)
First Palm Trees (Berry)

Make a collage picture.

The Great Race (Goble)
How Night Came from the Sea (Gerson)
The Villages of Round and Square Houses (Grifalconi)

Write your own nature "why" tale.

Actions

Folktale Party
Read stories about eating.
The Fat Cat (M. MacDonald)
Stone Soup (M. Brown, Muth)
Yoshi's Feast (Kajikawa)

Dress as a character from a tale. Invite others. Serve folktale fare:
Gingerbread cookies
Strega Nona's pasta (dePaola)
Stone Soup (Stewig)
Anansi's baked yams from *A Story, A Story* (Haley)
Snow White's unpoisoned apples
Conduct tours of the Folktale Museum.

Surveys
Favorite folktale character
Best-illustrated version of one story
Most disliked character
Parent's best-remembered tale
Favorite folktale food

Pulling It Together
Make a mural of houses from folktales (Gretel's witch's candy house; Baba Yaga's stilted house).
Assemble a museum of things important to folktales (Princess's pea; Hansel's chicken bone; Wiley's rope; Beauty's rose), and write labels for each one.
Make a "Photograph Album;" draw snapshots from a tale.
Locate these tales on a wall map of the world and, for each, place a label and string to the country of origin. What do you notice?

EXPLORING FOLKTALES: A WEB OF POSSIBILITIES

Comparing Versions and Variants

Little Red Hiding Hood (Grimm/Hyman)
Lon Po Po (Young)

List similarities and differences.
Compare wolf illustrations.
Write another story from the wolf's point of view.

Rockabye Crocodile (Aruego and Dewey)
The Talking Eggs (R. San Souci)
Toads and Diamonds (Huck)
The Well at the End of the World (R. San Souci)

Make a comparison chart.

Cinderella (Perrault/LeCain)
The Golden Sandal (Hickox)
Yeh-Shen (Louie)

Compare the stories.
Write a "lost and found" ad and make a picture for a girl who owns the shoe.
How many years separate these versions?
Why do you think they are so similar?
Write a modern version of Cinderella.

Motifs

Transformations

The Crane Wife (Bodkin)
The Selkie Girl (Cooper)
The Story of Jumping Mouse (Steptoe)

List real-life transformations (ice/water; gelatin; caterpillar/butterfly).
Group by what causes transformation (love, disloyalty, magic, etc.).
Retell from transformed point of view.

Trickery

The Boy of the Three-Year Nap (Snyder)
Bruh Rabbit and the Tar Baby Girl (Hamilton)
Puss in Boots (Perrault)
The Tale of Rabbit and Coyote (Johnston)

Write the tricky plans for a character.
Make a "bad guy" out of stuffed construction paper.
Interview the trickster for television.

north wind. Humans do appear in a few fables, such as "The Country Maid and the Milk Pail" or "The Boy Who Cried Wolf." The characters are impersonal, with no name other than "fox," rabbit," or "cow." They do not have the lively personalities of Anansi the spider or Raven the trickster of folktale fame. The animals merely represent aspects of human nature—the lion stands for kingliness, the fox for cunning, the sheep for innocence and simplicity, and so on. Fables seldom have more than three characters, and the plots are usually based on a single incident. Fables were primarily meant to instruct. Therefore, all of them contain either an implicit or an explicit moral.

Because of their brevity, fables appear to be simple. However, they convey an abstract idea in relatively few words, and for that very reason they are highly complex. In selecting fables, then, it is wise to look at the quality of both language and illustrations. Compare the following two beginnings for "The Town Mouse and the Country Mouse." The first is Lisbeth Zwerger's, in her *Aesop's Fables:*

> A Town Mouse went to visit his cousin in the country. This Country Mouse lived simply, and he was not rich, but he brought out all that he had to feed and entertain his honored guest. (unpaged)

Jan Brett's version, *Town Mouse, Country Mouse,* begins,

> One morning the town mouse woke up shivering from a dream about the kitchen cat who prowled the house. "I need a vacation," he said to his wife. "Let me take you to the countryside where I was born. Life is quiet and peaceful there. The sun shines brightly every day and the air is so clear that you can see the stars every night. And nothing will prepare you for the taste of wild blackberries." (unpaged)

Zwerger's illustrations feature a simple picture of two mice conversing on a hillside. Brett's highly detailed drawings have woodland borders that contain visual subplots. In addition she introduces two new characters to the traditional fable, an owl and a cat. These reflect some of the unique and various treatments given to Aesop's stories for today's readers.

Editions
Younger children might appreciate some fables, but they are not usually able to extract a moral spontaneously until about second or third grade. Fulvio Testa's *Aesop's Fables* recounts fables concisely, with morals concealed in the conversation rather than appended. Testa's use of crisp line and bright borders makes this version especially useful in reading aloud to larger groups.

In *A Sip of Aesop,* Jane Yolen has also used rhymes to retell thirteen of the fables, including "The Dog in the Manger" and "Counting Your Chickens." Her amusing introduction sets the tone for these decidedly modern retellings. Brightly colored paintings by Karen Barbour recall the work of Henri Matisse and are vivid reminders of the timeliness of the stories.

Jerry Pinkney applies his characteristic style to *Aesop's Fables* with grand results. His exquisite watercolor illustrations for sixty of Aesop's best tales make this an essential collection for classrooms and libraries. The book is meticulously designed, and Pinkney's multicultural interpretation of human and animal characters is highly original. Bert Kitchen's illustrations for Doris Orgel's *Lion and the Mouse and Other Aesop's Fables* are typical of this artist's masterful and detailed animal portraits. A re-issue of *The Caldecott Aesop* shows how Randolph Caldecott applied the moral of a fable to a contemporary (for Caldecott) setting. Each fable has two pictures—one, a literal animal scene, and the second, a human one. The title character of "The Ass in the Lion's Skin" impresses the other animals until the disguise blows off. In Caldecott's satiric second interpretation, a pompous art critic is discovered to know nothing. In *Aesop and Company,* Barbara Bader has sandwiched nineteen of Aesop's fables between an introduction to the origins of the stories and an afterword that retells the legends that surround Aesop's life. Detailed etchings by Arthur Geisert add visual complexity to the brief fables and provide a nice feel of timelessness. Noted English wood engraver Christopher Wormell has lent his unique style to a charming collection titled *Mice, Morals and Monkey Business.* Wormell's bold images are just right for a younger audience of children. Veronica Uribe expands her sights beyond Aesop to include fables from around the world in *Little Book of Fables.* Constanza Bravo's stylish illustrations complement Uribe's delightful and lively retellings.

John Bierhorst, a distinguished collector and editor of Native American literature, discovered that Aesop's fables had been recorded by the Aztecs in the sixteenth century. His *Doctor Coyote* is a collection of these stories, translated from the Aztec manuscript, in which the main character of each fable became Coyote, a Native American trickster. Bierhorst's cohesive collection of twenty fables weaves one story into the next and shows Coyote getting a little wiser with each "lesson." With ample use of blues and roses, Wendy Watson's full-color illustrations warmly depict the desert and mountain settings of New Mexico.

Other illustrators have chosen fewer tales for interpretation. Illustrator Aki Sogabe has woven several of Aesop's fox fables into a single tale in *Aesop's Fox.* Startling close-ups heighten the drama of "little and big" in Ed Young's black-and-white illustrations for *The Lion and the Mouse.* By contrast, Young's vividly colored collages for the Indian fable *Seven Blind Mice* highlight the patchwork nature of understanding that these mice bring to their definition of an elephant.

Older children might enjoy comparing treatments of several of these fables. In this way they would become familiar with the spare language, the conventional

Fine feathers don't make fine birds.

Christopher Wormell's elegant wood engravings illustrate the morals from Aesop's fables in *Mice, Morals and Monkey Business*. Illustration from *Mice, Morals and Monkey Business: Lively Lessons from Aesop's Fables* by Christopher Wormell, copyright © 2005. Used by permission of Running Press Book Publishers.

characters, and the explicit or implied morals of fables. They will appreciate Amy Lowry Poole's Chinese setting for a retelling of "The Grasshopper and the Ant," and they will enjoy reading modern writers of fables, such as Leo Lionni, whose *Frederick* is similar to Eric Carle's, or William Steig, whose *Amos and Boris* mirrors "The Lion and the Mouse." After such comparisons, discussions, and readings, they would then be well prepared to write their own fables and variations.

MYTHS

Mythology evolved as primitive peoples searched their imaginations and related events to forces, as they sought explanations of the earth, sky, and human behavior. These explanations moved slowly through the stages of a concept of one power or force in human form, who controlled the phenomena of nature; to a complex system in which the god or goddess represented such virtues as wisdom, purity, or love; to a worshipping of the gods in organized fashion. Gods took the forms of men and women, but they were immortal and possessed supernatural powers.

Myths deal with human relationships with the gods, with the relationships of the gods among themselves, with the way people accept or fulfill their destiny, and with people's struggles with good and evil forces both within themselves and outside themselves. The myths are good stories, too, for they contain action, suspense, and basic conflicts. Usually each story is short and can be enjoyed by itself, without deep knowledge of the general mythology. Geraldine McCaughrean has written several fine collections of myths and legends from around the world in *The Golden Hoard, The Silver Treasure,* and *The Bronze Cauldron.* The fine illustrations by Bee Willey and the source notes in each volume mark these volumes as essential to any study of mythology. John Bierhorst's expertise in Aztec literature is the basis for his *The Mythology of Mexico and Central America.* This book traces twenty basic myths and explains how they functioned among the ancient Aztec and Maya people and how they survive today. This volume, as well as its two companions, *The Mythology of South America* and *The Mythology of North America,* would give teachers and older students the background they need to understand these creation stories.

Children who compare myths may marvel at the human imagination and see the world in a different way. Comparing myths also often raises interesting questions for children about the similarities, connections, and migrations of early peoples.

Types of Myths

 Many myths can be characterized by the type of explanation they offer about the beginnings of the world or about some natural phenomenon. Other myths might focus on difficult tasks or obstacles to be overcome by the hero or heroine.

Creation Myths

Every culture has a story about how the world began, how people were made, how the sun and the moon got into the sky. These are called creation myths, or origin myths; they give an explanation for the beginnings of things. Diane Hofmeyr's *The Star-Bearer* is a creation myth from Egypt that dates from 3000 B.C. In this myth Atum, a child god, emerges from a lotus flower to bring light to a dark universe. Lonely, Atum creates a male god and a female god who go on to have children. These children become the earth's crust and the heaven's stars. John Bierhorst's *The Woman Who Fell from the Sky* is an Iroquois creation story in which First Woman falls from her home in the sky and lands on Turtle's back, creating the world. She soon gives birth to two boys, Sapling and Flint. Sapling busies himself creating gifts for the people who are soon to come. Flint, whose heart is hard, injects difficulties into every gift. Then Flint invents terrible troubles for people, but Sapling mediates and makes these easier to bear. Finally, Sapling takes some earth and makes human beings, teaching them to make houses and light fires. Then he and Flint return to the sky, each taking a separate path that becomes the Milky Way. A more harmonious beginning can be found in *Sun Mother Wakes the World*, an Australian creation myth retold by Diane Wolkstein. In this tale Sun Mother creates the world, its creatures, and Moon and Morning Star, who then give birth to the first woman and the first man. Sun Mother entreats these two to care for the land and all its animals before she soars back to the sky. She promises to revisit them each day if they keep that pledge. Also on a more positive note, Paul Morin has provided the luscious illustrations for a Native American creation story by Timothy Kessler titled *When God Made the Dakotas*.

Virginia Hamilton chose creation stories from around the world for her collection *In the Beginning*.

> These myths from around the world were created by people who sensed the wonder and glory of the universe. Lonely as they were, by themselves, early people looked inside themselves and expressed a longing to discover, to explain who they were, why they were, and from what and where they came. (p. xi)

Barry Moser's watercolor portraits and representations are mysterious and dramatic accompaniments to these tales. An Eskimo story tells how Raven the Creator made a pea pod from which humans sprang. A Chinese story explains how Phan Ku burst from a cosmic egg to create the world. A California Indian legend, "Turtle Dives to the Bottom of the Sea," begins with a sea turtle that dives underwater to bring up enough earth to make dry land.

Nature Myths

The nature myths include stories that explain seasonal changes, animal characteristics, earth formations, constellations, and the movements of the sun and earth. Many Native American nature myths are easier for young children to comprehend than are the creation myths. Some of these myths have been previously discussed in the section "Native American Folktales."

The Greek story of Demeter and Persephone explains the change of seasons. Hades, god of the underworld, carried Persephone off to the underworld to be his bride, and Demeter, her mother, who made plants grow, mourned so for her daughter that she asked Zeus to intercede. It was granted that the girl might return if she had eaten nothing in Hades. Because she had eaten four seeds of a pomegranate, she was compelled to return to Hades for four months each year, during which time the earth suffered and winter came. Warwick Hutton has illustrated a single picture-book edition of *Persephone*.

Hero Myths

The hero myths, found in many cultures, do not attempt to explain anything at all. These myths have some of the same qualities as wonder stories—the hero is given certain tasks or, in the case of Heracles, labors, to accomplish. Frequently the gods help (or hinder) a particular favorite (or disliked) mortal. Monsters, such as gorgons, hydras, and chimeras, are plentiful in the Greek stories, but these provide the hero with a challenge. Characteristic of the hero or heroine is that he or she accepts all

As part of a study of myths, sixth graders created stories and illustrations describing their own mythological creatures. George Mason Elementary School, Alexandria City Public Schools, Alexandria, Virginia. Susan Steinberg, teacher.

dangerous assignments and accomplishes the quest or dies in one last glorious adventure.

Greek Mythology

 The myths with which we are most familiar are those of the ancient Greeks collected by the poet Hesiod sometime during the eighth century B.C. The Roman versions of these myths were adapted by the poet Ovid during the first century B.C. in his well-known *Metamorphoses*. This has caused some confusion, in that the Roman names for the gods are better known than the Greek, even though the stories originated with the Greeks. However, the more recent versions of these myths are using Greek names. In work-

ing with children, it is best to be consistent in your choice of names, or they will become confused. You might wish to reproduce Teaching Resources: "Some Gods and Goddesses of Greek and Roman Mythology" for their reference. Geraldine McCaughrean's *Greek Gods and Goddesses* provides an introduction to the pantheon.

Greek mythology is composed of many stories of gods and goddesses, heroes, and monsters. The Greeks were the first to see their gods in their own image. As their culture became more sophisticated and complex, so too did their stories of the gods. These personified gods could do anything that humans could do, but on a much mightier scale. The gods, although immortal, freely entered into the lives of mortals, helping or hin-

TEACHING **RESOURCES**

Some Gods and Goddesses of Greek and Roman Mythology

 Visit the Online Learning Center at www.mhhe.com/kiefer9e for a printable version of this list.

Greek	Roman	Title	Relationship
Zeus	Jupiter or Jove	Supreme Ruler, Lord of the Sky	
Poseidon	Neptune	God of the Sea	Brother of Zeus
Hades or Pluto	Pluto	God of the Underworld	Brother of Zeus
Hestia	Vesta	Goddess of the Home and Hearth	Sister of Zeus
Hera	Juno	Goddess of Women and Marriage	Wife and sister of Zeus
Ares	Mars	God of War	Son of Zeus and Hera
Athena	Minerva	Goddess of Wisdom	Daughter of Zeus
Apollo	Apollo	God of Light and Truth, the Sun God	Son of Zeus and Leto
Aphrodite	Venus	Goddess of Love and Beauty	Daughter of Zeus, wife of Hephaestus
Hermes	Mercury	Messenger of the Gods	Son of Zeus and Maia
Artemis	Diana	Goddess of the Moon and Hunt	Twin sister of Apollo
Hephaestus	Vulcan	God of Fire	Son of Hera
Eros	Cupid	God of Love	Son of Aphrodite (in some accounts)
Demeter	Ceres	Goddess of Grain	Daughter of Cronus and Rhea
Dionysus or Bacchus	Bacchus	God of Wine	Son of Zeus and Semele
Persephone	Proserpine	Maiden of Spring	Daughter of Demeter

dering them, depending on their particular moods. Their strength was mighty and so was their wrath. Many of the myths are concerned with the gods' conflicts and loves. Their jealousy and their struggles for power often caused trouble for humans. (Some of the stories concerning the loves and quarrels of the immortals are inappropriate for children.)

Greek mythology includes the creation story that Earth and Sky were the first gods. Their children were the giant Cyclopes and the Titans, one of whom was Cronus, who drove his father away with a scythe (the source of the traditional picture of Father Time). Cronus swallowed his children so they would not usurp his place, but his wife gave him a stone in place of her last child, Zeus. Of course, Zeus overthrew his father and made him disgorge his brothers and sisters, who were still alive. Zeus married the jealous Hera, who caused all kinds of trouble. Prometheus was a Titan who defied the other gods in order to give fire to humankind. Zeus punished his disobedience by chaining him to Mount Caucasus, where each day his liver was devoured by an eagle but each night it was renewed. Zeus also sent Pandora and a box of trouble to punish Prometheus and humankind (see Robert Burleigh's picture-book version and "Pandora" in Virginia Hamilton's *In the Beginning*). Warned not to open the box, Pandora was so curious that she could not help herself. All the evils of the world were released, but hope remained in the box and gave humans the ability to endure.

Another story concerned Zeus's punishment of the greedy King Midas (see the versions by Demi, Alice Low, Neil Philip, and John Stewig). Midas's curse was that everything he touched, including his little daughter, turned to gold. Children who have a good background in folktales will find that many of the same elements are present in the Greek myths. In *D'Aulaires' Book of Greek Myths* the story of King Midas is economically told in two pages with a bold stone lithograph illustration. The D'Aulaires' collection presents a well-woven selection of tales ranging from the birth of Cronus's children to the stories of the mortal descendants of Zeus.

The gods could not tolerate human pride, which the Greeks called *hubris*. Bellerophon slew the monster Chimaera, defeated the Amazons, and rode Pegasus. But when he boasted that he would fly to Olympus, the offended Zeus caused a gadfly to sting Pegasus, who

Raul Colón's textured paintings heighten the tension to Robert Burleigh's retelling of the Greek myth *Pandora*.
Illustration from *Pandora* by Robert Burleigh, illustration copyright © 2002 by Raul Colón, reproduced with permission of Harcourt, Inc.

bucked and tossed Bellerophon to his death. Arachne was transformed into a spider because of her pride when she foolishly challenged the goddess Athena to a weaving contest. This story is brought to vivid life by Blair Drawson's paintings in *Arachne Speaks* by Kate Hovey. Hovey tells the story in the first person, in a form that recalls the stories of Homer and other ancient poets. Alternating with Arachne's voice is that of Athena. Printed in a deep red, the type foretells Arachne's pitiful transformation. Yet in the end, Arachne has her final triumph. She speaks to us from a web that will continue until the end of time through her descendants, while Athena now sits on her throne, forgotten by mortals.

Other stories of the disastrous results of hubris include the myths of Daedalus and Phaethon. In Jane Yolen's *Wings,* Daedalus is presented as a proud Athenian inventor who is banished for inadvertently killing a nephew. Exiled to Crete, he designs and builds a labyrinth for King Minos but years later gives the Athenian Theseus the key to its maze. In punishment for this, Daedalus and his young son, Icarus, are imprisoned in a high tower. Using candle wax, Daedalus makes a framework of wings from bird feathers. As they are about to escape, he warns his son not to fly too high or the sun will melt the wax, but Icarus does not heed his father's warning and falls to his death in the ocean. In italics, Yolen's text provides a Greek chorus, or commentary by the gods, who give approval, observe, laugh, or listen gravely. Dennis Nolan's illustrations show the faces of the gods hidden in the clouds, looking on, mourning, but doing nothing to prevent Icarus's death. The story of the winged horse Pegasus also involves a mortal whose pride gets the best of him.

Descended from the sun god, Helios, Phaethon desires to drive the sun chariot to prove his parentage to his friends. When his father is finally tricked into agreeing, Phaethon cannot control the sun chariot and nearly burns up the earth. Zeus saves humankind by killing Phaethon with a thunderbolt. Alice Low retells both of these stories and many others in *The Macmillan Book of Greek Gods and Heroes.* An excellent, insightfully illustrated collection of stories that feature more dialogue than the d'Aulaire versions, Low's book also includes hero tales of Perseus, Heracles, Jason, Theseus, and Odysseus.

Pride is also the downfall of Atalanta, a young woman who is a skillful hunter and the swiftest of runners, in Shirley Climo's *Atalanta's Race.* Reluctant to marry and give up her life of freedom, Atalanta finally agrees to wed the man who can beat her in a foot race. Melanion, a suitor whom she has admired, is given three golden apples by Aphrodite, who is angered by Atalanta's lack of reverence for the gods. As the two race side by side, Melanion throws an apple in Atalanta's path, distracting her so that he can win the race. The two marry and live relatively happily for many years, but because they have ignored the gods, Aphrodite punishes the two by changing them into lions. Alexander Koh-

skin's painted illustrations are set in Corinthian columns and resemble the murals found in Greek and Roman dwellings.

In *Cupid and Psyche* Charlotte M. Craft retells the story of Cupid, who has been sent by the jealous Aphrodite to find a horrible mate for the beautiful Psyche. Instead, he falls in love with her. Invisible, Cupid woos Psyche, and she falls in love with him sight unseen. When Psyche's sisters talk her into lighting a lamp in order to see her husband, Cupid flees. To win him back, Psyche must perform difficult tasks, and the last one kills her. Cupid carries her to Olympus, where the gods honor her for her steadfastness by making her immortal. Children will be struck by the similarity of patterns in this tale with the folktales in *East o'the Sun and West o'the Moon* (see the version by Asbjørnsen and Moe).

Older children who have been introduced to Greek mythology through the simpler stories will be ready for the longer hero tales of Perseus, the gorgon-slayer; Theseus, killer of the minotaur; Heracles and his many labors; Jason and his search for the golden fleece; and the wanderings of Odysseus.

Robert Byrd's *The Hero and the Minotaur* is a good picture-book introduction to the myth of Theseus and his battle with the monster in the labyrinth. Doris Orgel has told the Theseus myth from Ariadne's point of view in the short chapter book *Ariadne, Awake!,* illustrated by Barry Moser. The first-person narrative has an exciting immediacy as Ariadne, a sheltered teenager, tells of falling in love with the beautiful but callow Theseus. After he has used her to gain his own ends, his abandonment of her is especially heart-rending. Left alone on the island of Naxos, Ariadne is visited by the god Dionysus. He comforts her with the thought that even love that ends in pain is merely a stop along the way to greater love. His advice seems to be true, for eventually, these two are married and live a long and happy life. This powerfully romantic version will have special appeal for early adolescents.

Norse Mythology

 A mythology derives its characteristics from the land and peoples of its origin. The land of the Norse was a cold, cruel land of frost, snow, and ice. Life was a continual struggle for survival against these elements. It seems only natural that Norse mythology was filled with gods who also had to battle against huge frost giants. These were heroic gods who, unlike the immortal Greek gods safe in their home on sunny Mount Olympus, knew that they and their home on Asgard would eventually be destroyed. And in a way their prophecy was fulfilled, for Christianity all but extinguished talk of the old gods, except in Iceland. There, in the thirteenth century, Snorri Sturluson—a poet, scholar, and historian—collected many of the Norse myths and legends into a book called the *Prose Edda.* Much of his writing was based on an earlier verse collection called

the *Poetic Edda.* These two books are the primary sources for our knowledge of Norse mythology.

It is too bad that children do not know these myths as well as they know those of the Greeks. In some ways the Norse tales seem more suited to children than the highly sophisticated Greek tales. These stories appeal to the child's imagination, with their tales of giants and dwarfs, eight-legged horses and vicious wolves, magic hammers and rings. Primarily they are bold, powerful stories of the relationships among the gods and their battles against the evil frost giants. Odin is the serious protector of the humans he created, willingly sacrificing one of his eyes to obtain wisdom that would allow him to see deep into their hearts. The largest and the strongest of the gods is Thor, owner of a magic hammer that will hit its mark and then return to his hands. And Balder, the tragic god of light, is the most loved by all the other gods.

Ingri D'Aulaire and Edgar Parin D'Aulaire's *Book of Norse Myths,* out of print for some years, has been recently reissued and is a good introduction to the body of Norse myths and heroes for children of all ages. Some of the stories are amusing. Seven- and 8-year-olds would enjoy the picture-book version of the story of Thor's stolen hammer by Shirley Climo. In *Stolen Thunder* the enormous Thor, the god of Thunder, is dressed as a bride and goes with Loki, who is his "bridesmaid," to trick the giant Thrym into returning Thor's magic hammer. Loki is a mischievous sidekick in Climo's version, although in the original myths he became increasingly evil.

If children have time to become acquainted with only one mythology, they should know the Greek stories (or their Roman adaptations). No other tales have so influenced the literature and art of the Western world. Norse mythology, too, has left its marks on Western culture, as in the names *Thursday* ("Thor's day") and *Friday* ("Freya's day"). Also, these tales have a special appeal for children. However, there are many other important mythologies that might be sampled as a part of the study of a culture or simply be enjoyed as literature.

EPIC AND LEGENDARY HEROES

 An epic is a long narrative or a cycle of stories clustering around the actions of a single hero. Epics grew out of myths or along with them, since the gods still intervene in earlier epics like the *Iliad* and the *Odyssey.* Gradually, the center of action shifted from the gods to human heroes, so that in tales like "Robin Hood" the focus is completely on the daring adventures of the man himself.

The epic hero is a cultural or national hero embodying all the ideal characteristics of greatness in his time. Thus Odysseus and Penelope, his wife, represented the Greek ideals of intelligence, persistence, and resourcefulness. Odysseus survived by his wit rather than his great strength. Both King Arthur and Robin Hood appealed to the English love of justice and freedom: King Arthur and his knights represented the code of chivalry; Robin Hood was the champion of the commoner—the prototype of the "good outlaw." The epics, then, express the highest moral values of a society. A knowledge of the epics gives children an understanding of a particular culture; but more importantly, it provides them with models of greatness through the ages.

The Epic of Gilgamesh

The Epic of Gilgamesh, recorded more than four thousand years ago in Mesopotamia, is one of the oldest hero stories. The epic poem, first discovered written on clay tablets in the library of Assur-Bani-Pal, an Assyrian king who ruled from 668 to 626 B.C., is probably the compilation of many earlier myths. The original stories actually concerned three figures: Gilgamesh, a Sumerian king; Enkidu, a primitive wild man; and Utnapishtim, the man we would call Noah. Canadian author Ludmila Zeman has retold and illustrated these three episodes in a highly readable trio of picture books. In *Gilgamesh the King* we are introduced to the god-king who plays the central role in the three books. He is a bitter and cruel king because he has not experienced the power of human companionship. When his desire to build a great wall threatens his people's survival, the sun god sends Enkidu, another man as strong as Gilgamesh, to earth, where he lives in the forest and cares for the animals. When he threatens one of Gilgamesh's hunters, Gilgamesh sends the lovely singer Shamat to tempt Enkidu out of the forest. In spite of his beastly appearance, she teaches him about human love and they leave the forest to confront Gilgamesh. The two men engage in a terrible struggle on Gilgamesh's famous wall, but because their powers are equal they seem to be at an impasse. Then Gilgamesh stumbles on a stone and would fall to his death except that Enkidu reaches out a hand to help him. Gilgamesh's experience with human kindness is transforming, and the two become like brothers. In the second book, *The Revenge of Ishtar,* the two meet the goddess Ishtar, who offers to marry Gilgamesh and give him a chariot of gold. When he spurns her, he makes a great enemy who will plague him all his life and cause the deaths of Shamat and Enkidu. In *The Last Quest of Gilgamesh,* the great king is so heartbroken by the death of his friends that he sets out to find the secret of immortality. When he learns that Utnapishtim is the only human who knows that secret, Gilgamesh endures a terrible journey across the waters of death to Utnapishtim's island. Utnapishtim explains that he arrived on the island on a great ark after he had been warned of a terrible flood that would destroy the earth. Gilgamesh cannot accomplish the task that Utnapishtim sets him to become immortal, and after one more battle with Ishtar he returns home heartbroken at his failure. Enkidu is sent by the gods to show him that the immortality he craves is there in the great civilization he has created. Zeman's majestic illustrations, done in mixed media and incorporating motifs from Mesopotamian art, have a wonderful sense of timelessness. Geraldine McCaughrean has provided a superb retelling of the epic for older readers in *Gilgamesh the Hero*.

The *Iliad* and the *Odyssey*

According to tradition, a blind minstrel named Homer composed the epic poems the *Iliad* and the *Odyssey* about 850 B.C.; but scholars generally believe that parts of the stories were sung by many persons and that they were woven into one long narrative before they were written. The *Iliad* is an account of the Trojan War fought over Helen, the most beautiful woman in the world. When Helen is kidnapped by Paris, a Trojan, her Greek husband, King Menelaus, enlists the Greeks in a ten-year siege of Troy that is led by the Greek warriors Agamemnon and Achilles. The complex story is long and difficult to understand, although specific incidents, such as the final defeat of the Trojans by the cunning device of the Trojan Horse, do intrigue some children.

Ludmila Zeman's *The Revenge of Ishtar* is one of a trilogy of picture books that provide a retelling of the Gilgamesh epic for children. Taken from *The Revenge of Ishtar,* copyright © 1993 by Ludmila Zeman, published by Tundra Books.

The *Odyssey* is the story of the hazardous ten-year journey of Odysseus (called Ulysses by the Romans) from Troy to his home in Ithaca, following the end of the war. Odysseus has one terrifying experience after another, which he manages to survive by his cunning. For example, he defeats the horrible one-eyed Cyclops by blinding him and then strapping his men to the undersides of sheep, which were allowed to leave the cave. His ship safely passes between the whirlpool of Charybdis and the monster Scylla, but later is shipwrecked and delayed for seven years. A loyal servant and his son aid the returned hero in assuming his rightful throne and saving his wife; Penelope has had a difficult time discouraging the many suitors who wished to become king. While children or teachers might be acquainted with episodes from the story, it is the total force of all Odysseus's trials that presents the full dimensions of this hero. The wanderings of Odysseus have also come to provide the template for many contemporary journey stories. Author Cynthia Voigt makes many overt references to the *Odyssey* in her first book about the Tillerman family, *Homecoming* (see Chapter 9). A good introduction to the epic is the "Tales from the Odyssey" series by Mary Pope Osborne. In books such as *The One-Eyed Giant* and *Mermaids and Monsters,* illustrated by Troy Howell, Osborne retells one of the episodes from Odysseus's journey. Geraldine McCaughrean and Rosemary Sutcliff have both written versions of the *Odyssey* for middle-grade readers. Sutcliff's *Black Ships before Troy: The Story of the Iliad* is a fine companion book. Padraic Colum's *The Children's Homer*

keeps the essence of the traditional poem, and Willy Pogany's illustrations distinguish this book from others. An edition suitable for older readers is Colum's *The Trojan War and the Adventures of Odysseus,* illustrated by Barry Moser. Leonard Everett Fisher and Warwick Hutton both created picture-book retellings of Odysseus's battle with the Cyclops. Virgil's *Aeneid*, the story of Aeneas's escape from Troy, is a worthy successor to the epics of Homer.

The *Ramayana*

The *Ramayana* is the great epic tale of India that tells how the noble Rama, his devoted brother, and his beautiful, virtuous wife, Sita, manage to defeat the evil demon Ravana. Heir to the throne, Rama is banished from his home through the trickery of his stepmother. Prince Rama, his brother, and the devoted Sita spend fourteen years in wandering and adventure. One day Sita vanishes, kidnapped by Ravana. Rama searches for her unsuccessfully and then turns to a tribe of monkeys for help. Finally Sita is found, and with the help of an entire army of monkeys, Rama rescues her. To be cleansed from her association with the demon, Sita must withstand a trial by fire. Her faithfulness proved, she is united with her beloved Rama. Peace and plenty prevail during Rama's reign.

Composed in India by the sage Vlamiki during the fourth century B.C., the *Ramayana* represented some 24,000 couplets that were memorized and repeated. It constitutes part of the gospel of Hindu scripture, for Rama and his wife are held as the ideal man and woman. Rama is believed to be an incarnation of the god Vishnu come to earth in human form.

Surely Western children should know something of this epic hero who is so important to a large part of the world. Jessica Souhami's *Rama and the Demon King* is a picture-book version that focuses on Rama's exile and his battle with Ravana. Souhami's cut-paper illustrations recall Indian folk art forms and provide the story with a dramatic touch. David Weitzman pays visual homage to Indonesian stick puppets in his illustrations for *Rama and Sita: A Tale from Ancient Java*. A longer version of Rama and Sita's story can be found in *The Story of Divaali*, retold by Jatinder Verma.

Heroes of the Middle Ages

The oldest hero tale with European roots is the epic saga "Beowulf," recorded in Old English sometime after the tenth century. The poem relates the exploits of a Scandinavian warrior of the sixth century. Many of us may remember struggling through a reading of the work in the original Old English, but an accessible picture-book version exists for younger children. In *The Hero Beowulf* Eric A. Kimmel has summarized the early adventures of the mythic figure to concentrate on his battle with the monster Grendel. Leonard Everett Fisher's textured paintings capture the drama and the horror of their encounter.

Some historians believe there was a King Arthur who became famous around the sixth century. Defeated by the invading Saxons, his people fled to Wales and Brittany and told stories of his bravery and goodness. Other stories became attached to these, and the exploits of Tristram, Gawaine, and Lancelot were added to the Arthurian cycle. The religious element of the quest for the Holy Grail, the cup used by Christ at the Last Supper, was also added. Whether or not the chalice actually existed, it remains as a symbol of purity and love. In the fifteenth century, Sir Thomas Malory's *Morte d'Arthur* was one of the first books printed in England and became a major source of later versions.

In the short novel *The Dragon's Boy*, Jane Yolen tells of the boyhood of Arthur, here called Artos. Artos has been raised by Sir Ector in a small castle. One day while searching for a prized dog he discovers a cave in which a dragon dwells. Both fascinated and terrified, Artos agrees to seek wisdom from the dragon when he is not doing his work at the castle. Children will find this a compelling introduction to the Arthur legends as they sympathize with the lonely boy who confronts his fears to discover the truth about the supposed dragon, his own parentage, and his future as the great King Arthur.

Other illustrated books about Arthur and Merlin also introduce children to these stories. Hudson Talbott's *King Arthur and the Round Table* and *Excalibur* recount single episodes in Arthur's life, and Talbott's vivid watercolors reflect the romance of the tale. Margaret Hodges retells three episodes from Arthur's life in *Merlin and the Mak-*

ing of the King. Trina Schart Hyman's lovely illustrations for this small volume are embellished in gold and recall the illuminated manuscripts of the medieval period. T. H. White's *The Sword in the Stone* is an imaginative retelling of Arthur's boyhood and growth under Merlin's tutelage. Middle-school readers enjoy this novel for its humor.

Rosemary Sutcliff brings thirteen stories from the Arthurian cycle to life in *The Sword and the Circle*. Beginning with the events surrounding Arthur's accession to the throne, she weaves other stories into the text in separate chapters. "Tristan and Iseult," "Beaumains, the Kitchen Knight," "Sir Gawain and the Green Knight," and "Gawain and the Loathly Lady" are but a few of the tales included. Two other volumes, though concerning important parts of Arthurian legend, deal with less adventurous or romantic aspects of the story and might be of less interest to middle-grade readers. *The Light Beyond the Forest: The Quest for the Holy Grail* details the wanderings of Lancelot, Galahad, Percival, and others in search of the Grail but also in search of their own salvation. *The Road to Camlann* tells of the sad end of Arthur and the Round Table fellowship. Sutcliff has also retold the romantic *Tristan and Iseult* in a full-length novel by that title. The language has a lyrical quality reminiscent of the old storytellers:

> It was young summer when they came to the hidden valley; and three times the hawthorn trees were rusted with berries and the hazelnuts fell into the stream. And three times winter came and they huddled about the fire in the smoky bothie and threw on logs from the woodstore outside. (p. 90)

Sidney Lanier's *The Boy's King Arthur*, which first appeared in 1880, and Howard Pyle's *The Story of King Arthur and His Knights*, which was published as a four-volume work between 1902 and 1910, are classic works told in a stately mode.

Children who wish to learn more about the legendary King Arthur would appreciate Kevin Crossley-Holland's *The World of King Arthur and His Court*. Crossley-Holland presents the many King Arthur legends and carefully explores the historical facts behind them. In addition he provides wonderful anecdotes about daily life in the Middle Ages.

Several stories set in King Arthur's time and retold with pictorial conventions of the Middle Ages are available in picture storybook format. Margaret Hodges retells the first part of "The Tale of Sir Gareth of Orkney," taken from Malory's *Le Morte d'Arthur*, in *The Kitchen Knight*. In this story, Gareth, who is a nephew of King Arthur, wishes to earn his knighthood by deeds, not by birthright. So he becomes a kitchen lad in Arthur's castle and accepts a quest that no other knight will undertake, that of saving the beautiful Linette's sister, Linesse, from

The Lady of the Lake appears in her various guises in Kevin Crossley-Holland's *The World of King Arthur and His Court*.
From *The World of King Arthur and His Court: People, Places, Legends, and Lore* by Kevin Crossley-Holland, illustrated by Peter Malone, copyright © 1998 by Peter Malone, illustrations. Used by permission of Dutton Children's Books, a division of Penguin Putnam, Inc.

imprisonment in the castle of the Knight of the Red Plain. He vanquishes the Red Knight, but it takes extra effort to win the gratitude of Linette and the acceptance of the highly selective Lady Linesse, whom he has rescued. Trina Schart Hyman researched weaponry, enabling her to accurately depict a leather rather than metal shield and an early horned helmet that was discovered recently in the Thames River.

Hyman also conducted painstaking research to produce accurate illustrations for Hodges's *Saint George and the Dragon*, set in fourth-century England. She studied ancient lore of wildflowers and herbs in order to use them symbolically in the borders of each picture. For example, when Saint George engages the dragon in battle, agrimony, which was a charm against serpents, appears in the borders. The fourth century was a time in which Christianity and ancient beliefs competed, so red-winged angels and pale fairies are both part of the borders. A pre-Norman sailing vessel appears in small pictures as a symbol of the hero's progress. Children are appropriately awed and thrilled by the truly terrible dragon, which Hyman drew after a long siege she had with a snapping turtle in her New Hampshire pond. While the story of St. George has little to do with King Arthur, it shares similar time, theme, and conventions with other tales told in the Middle Ages.

All of these books contribute to a child's knowledge of the mystique that surrounds the story of King Arthur. Students seldom discover these tales on their own, but once introduced to them, they delight in taking their place at that round table of adventure.

Another legendary hero who captures children's imagination is Robin Hood. Scholars have been unable to agree on whether there was indeed a medieval outlaw by the name of Robin Hood or whether he was really a mythical character derived from festival plays that took place in France at Whitsuntide. But by the fifteenth century, May Day celebrations in England were called "Robin Hood's Festivals," and the story of Robin Hood had become a legend for all time.

Children love this brave hero who lived in Sherwood Forest, outwitted the Sheriff of Nottingham, and shared his stolen goods with the poor. Others in the band included the huge Little John, Friar Tuck, the minstrel Alan-a-Dale, and Robin's sweetheart, Maid Marian. These characters can be found in Howard Pyle's classic, *The Merry Adventures of Robin Hood*. Ann McGovern retells this familiar legend in clear, direct language; a few words, such as *perchance* and *thou*, retain the spirit of the medieval language without making her *Robin Hood of Sherwood Forest* too difficult to read.

Robin McKinley's *The Outlaws of Sherwood* presents a Robin Hood for modern times. Robin is not much of a shot, but others in his band do the hunting while Robin broods over how to manage, shelter, and feed his ever-growing group. McKinley fleshes out the emotions of Little John, Robin Hood, Maid Marian, and others while exploring various dimensions of heroism. Theresa Tomlinson tells Marian's story in *The Forestwife*. In this version Marian runs away to the forest with her nurse, Agnes, in order to escape an unwanted marriage. As she and Agnes provide aid to other poor refugees, Marian meets Agnes's son Robert, who, falsely accused of murder, has also made the forest his home. The story continues in *Child of May*. Older readers who understand loyalty and appreciate the romance of a good tale will find these stories rewarding and compelling.

THE BIBLE AS LITERATURE

All children deserve to know the spiritual and religious beliefs that have shaped the world in which they live. This religious heritage is often conveyed in the form of stories. As we have seen in this chapter many peoples around the world have their creation stories, and there are numerous recountings of a great flood. In particular, many Native American stories reflect the religious beliefs of their tellers. We have discussed the Jataka and Panchatantra stories from Buddhist traditions and the *Ramayana* from Hindu scriptures. The Bible has an important and rightful place in any comprehensive discussion of traditional literature because it is a written record of people's continuing search to understand themselves and their relationships with others and their creator. It makes little sense to tell children the story of Jack the Giant Killer but to deny them the stories about David and Goliath or Samson. They read of the wanderings of Odysseus, but not those of Moses. They learn in Gilgamesh that Utnapishtim built an ark and survived a flood, but do not know the story of Noah. Our fear should not be that children will know the Bible; rather, it should be that they will not know it. Whatever our religious persuasion or non-persuasion, children should not be denied their right to knowledge of the traditional literature of the Bible. Children cannot fully understand other literature unless they are familiar with the outstanding characters, incidents, poems, proverbs, and parables of this literature of the Western world of thought.

We must clarify the difference between the practice of religious customs and indoctrination in one viewpoint and the study of the Bible as a great work of literature. In 1963 the Supreme Court asserted that "religious exercises" violated the First Amendment, but the Court also encouraged study of the Bible as literature:

> In addition, it might well be said that one's education is not complete without a study of comparative religion or the history of religion and its relationship to the advancement of Civilization. It certainly may be said that the Bible is worthy of study for its literary and historic qualities.[22]

The literary scholar Northrop Frye believes it is essential to teach the Bible, for it presents humans in all their history. "It's the *myth* of the Bible that should be the basis of literary training, its imaginative survey of the human situation which is so broad and comprehensive that everything else finds its place inside it."[23] Some critics will be disturbed by the use of the term *myth* unless they understand its larger literary context as the human search for and expression of truth and meaning.

Collections of Bible Stories

When a school staff agrees that children should have an opportunity to hear or read some of the great stories from the Bible, it faces the task of selecting material. Walter de la Mare provides an excellent background for understanding the problems of translation. He compares versions of the story of Ruth in the Geneva Bible (1560), the Douai Bible (1609), and the Authorized Version (1611). The old form of spelling is used in his quotations from Wycliffe of 1382, John Purvey of 1386, and Miles Coverdale of 1536. He clearly explains the differences between the literal, allegorical, oral, and analogical meanings of given words and phrases. This book presents the Creation, the Flood, and the stories of Moses, Joseph, Samson, Samuel, Saul, and David. The text combines modern descriptive imagery with a biblical style of narration. For example: "As Joseph grew older, and in all that he was and did showed himself more and more unlike themselves, jealousy gnawed in their hearts like the fretting of a cankerworm."[24]

Walter Dean Meyers and his son Christopher have collaborated on *A Time to Love: Stories from the Old Testament*. Told through the eyes of young people, these six stories make a fine introduction to the Bible for children. Christopher Meyers's wonderful illustrations bring a unique point of view to each of the tales. In *Does God Have a Big Toe?* Marc Gellman, a rabbi, follows a long-held Jewish tradition of telling midrashim, stories about stories in the Bible. These involve readers with their often humorous, contemporary tellings. For instance, Noah doesn't have the heart to tell his friends what God has told him, so he hints: "You know, Jabal, this might be a very good time for you to take those swimming lessons you have been talking about for so long" (p. 31). Miriam Chaikin's *Clouds of Glory* and *Angels Sweep the Desert Floor* and Jan Mark's *God's Story* are three other beautifully designed and written collections informed by the Midrash. In *When the Beginning Began: Stories about God, the Creatures, and Us*, Julius Lester retells tales from Genesis and includes other creation stories from Jewish and other traditions. Lester's unique wit and special storytelling voice bring these stories to marvelous life.

A more complete undertaking is *The Bible Story*, written by Philip Turner and illustrated by Brian Wildsmith. Presented in chronological order, stories from both the Old Testament and the New Testament are told with dignity and illustrated with colorful flair.

Several books of collected stories focus on important people of the Old Testament. Barbara Diamond Goldin has gathered eight stories about the Old Testament prophet Elijah in *Journeys with Elijah*. Goldin points out that Elijah is an important figure in Christian and Islamic teaching as well as in Jewish traditions. She sets her stories in various places and times where Jews have lived

---

[22]Quoted by Betty D. Mayo, "The Bible in the Classroom," *Christian Science Monitor,* 30 (September 1966): 9.

[23]Northrop Frye, *The Educated Imagination* (Bloomington: Indiana University Press, 1964), p. 111.

[24]Walter de la Mare, *Stories from the Bible,* illustrated by Edward Ardizzone (New York: Knopf, 1961), p. 62.

rather than adhere to the Biblical time period, thus giving the stories a wonderful universality. Jerry Pinkney's illustrations are a wonderful addition. Fran Manushkin's *Daughters of Fire* focuses on heroic women from the Old Testament including Eve, Sarah, Ruth, Esther, and many others. Uri Shulevitz contributed the mixed-media illustrations that lend the book a rich and velvety depth.

Single Bible Stories

Many individual picture books based on individual stories from the Bible are especially useful to introduce children to this literature. The story of the creation in Genesis has inspired several wonderful editions for children. *Light* by Sarah Waldman is a simple retelling of the story of creation brought vividly to life through Neil Waldman's glowing impressionistic paintings. The story of the first humans is retold by Jane Ray in *Adam and Eve and the Garden of Eden*. Ray's patterned, folk art paintings evoke the original purity of Adam and Eve and provide for their future as mortal beings. Jerry Pinkney brings his accomplished watercolor and pencil illustrations to tell the story of *Noah's Ark* and creates a detailed and majestic visual interpretation of the story. Children will enjoy comparing this version to Peter Spier's Caldecott Medal–winning book. Tomie dePaola has also contributed beautiful editions of single stories from the Bible such as *The Miracles of*

Jesus. DePaola's muted watercolor paintings and posed figures appropriately recall the medieval Italian frescoes of Giotto and Fra Angelico. British illustrator Brian Wildsmith has created several retellings of Bible stories, including *Joseph, Jesus,* and *Exodus.* The books sparkle and glow with Wildsmith's wonderfully rich colors and patterns and are printed using gold as a fifth color.

Leo Dillon and Diane Dillon have illustrated a full-length picture book around the well-known Bible verses from Ecclesiastes in *To Everything There Is a Season.* Each double-page spread presents the viewpoint of a different cultural and historical period to emphasize the meaning of the verses, and the Dillons' pictorial style changes to further enhance the passage. An afterword gives information about the pictorial style chosen to represent each culture.

The Christmas story has been retold in words and pictures many times. Brian Wildsmith tells *A Christmas Story* through the eyes of naive onlookers, heightening the wonder of the story for children. Wildsmith's glorious gold-edged paintings are purely marvelous. Julie Vivas uses the King James text for her exuberantly childlike vision of the Christmas story, *The Nativity.* Mary is shown in a cozy tête-à-tête with the angel Gabriel, and her look of surprise and delight as she tells Joseph his news is priceless. After she gives birth, Mary leans

In the bare earth beyond Eden, Adam and Eve planted a new garden for their family.

Jane Ray's lush landscapes for *Adam and Eve and the Garden of Eden* bring this Old Testament story vividly to life. From *Adam and Eve and the Garden of Eden* by Jane Ray, copyright © 2005. Used by permission of Random House Children's Books, a division of Random House, Inc.

exhaustedly against Joseph, who lovingly cradles the baby Jesus. These glowing pictures must surely present the story as seen through the innocent eyes of a child. John Bierhorst recounts an Aztec version in *Spirit Child;* Barbara Cooney's beautiful paintings portray the story against a background of Central American mountains abloom with yucca and poinsettia.

Many legends are associated with the Christmas story as well. Ruth Robbins's *Baboushka and the Three Kings* presents the Russian story of the old woman who was too busy sweeping to follow the three wise men and so is destined to wander the world forever. Tomie dePaola's Italian version is *The Legend of Old Befana.* His

The Story of the Three Wise Kings begins with an historical note about how this story has developed over the centuries. It would make a good companion to either of the previous stories. The stories concerning Befana would be ripe for reading on 6 January, or Twelfth Night, the traditional Feast of the Three Kings.

The Bible, myths and legends, fables, and folktales represent literature of people through the ages. Folk literature has deep roots in basic human feelings. Through this literature, children can form a link with the common bonds of humanity from the beginnings of recorded time, as well as form a foundation for much of their future reading.

INTO THE **CLASSROOM**

Traditional Literature

In this chapter we have defined traditional literature as all forms of narrative, written or oral, which have come to be handed down through the years. These stories are generally seen to come from the people of a culture rather than from a specific person (excepting of course, Aesop, Homer, and other ancient tellers or writers of tales). As with the other types of literature we discuss in this book, the definitions are not always simple, and boundaries are not set in stone. We have covered the modern folktale style in Chapter 5 and will discuss literary folktales in Chapter 7. We have tried to limit the books in this chapter to those that have some documented connection to the oral and written traditions long past. In addition to sharing traditional literature for the many aesthetic and emotional reasons we set forth here, teachers often find that traditional literature is a valuable source for introducing world cultures and geographical regions. As you do so, it is important to remember that these stories represent a culture in general but not in specifics. If your purpose is to exemplify a culture, you will need to be critical about the original source of the story, the type of retelling or translation, and the details provided in both story and illustrations. The following activities are ways to begin studying traditional literature with children.

1. **Folktale Comparison Charts.** The variants on a folktale make excellent comparison material, and elementary children enjoy discovering the similarities and differences. Classroom-made charts, with the tale titles going down the left margin and topics listed across the top, allow children to compare aspects like these:
   - Opening and ending conventions
   - Origin of the tale
   - Clues to the country or region of origin
   - Talents of the characters

   - Tasks to be done
   - Verses, refrains, chants, and their outcomes
   - Illustrations
   - Special or unique vocabulary

   Each group of variants will have other categories to compare as well. For example, categories might be "Instructions for Stopping a Pot from Cooking," "How Rumpelstiltskin's Name Is Discovered," or "Greedy Person's Reward." Children should be encouraged to develop their own category titles whenever possible.

2. **Learning about Cultures from Folktales and Myths.** Read folktales and myths from one country or one geographical or cultural region. Assume that these stories provide your only basis for understanding the country. Chart what you might derive from these tales, using categories like climate, food, animals, typical occupations, customs, geography, values, expressions, and story conventions.

3. **Editions Comparison.** Find as many different editions as you can of well-known stories like "Cinderella," "Hansel and Gretel," "Sleeping Beauty," "Noah's Ark," or "Puss in Boots." Chart or compare both the language of the retellings and the illustrations.

4. **Writing a Fable or Myth.** Study fables or myths and then encourage children to write their own versions.

Go to the Online Learning Center at **www.mhhe.com/kiefer9e** or your Resources CD-ROM to find these additional classroom activities:

5. **Story-Retelling Aids**
6. **Fooling with Folktales, Fables, and Myths**
7. **Heroes**

Chapter Review

Go to the Online Learning Center at **www.mhhe.com/kiefer9e** or your Resources CD-ROM to take chapter quizzes, practice with key terms, and review the chapter.

Explorations

1. Select one folktale that you think you would like to learn to tell. Prepare it and tell it to four or five members of your class or to a group of children. What suggestions do they or you have for improving your presentation?

2. Beginning with a moral chosen from one of the fable collections, write a modern fable. Use present-day animals, people, or objects.

3. Collect advertisements and references that show our use of words from the myths: for example, *Ajax* cleanser, *Mercury* as a floral delivery symbol, or *Atlas* tires. Using a collection of myths, determine the story behind the reference and decide why the advertiser might wish consumers to connect this reference with its product.

4. On the basis of your knowledge of the characteristics of an epic, what do you think the hero of a North American epic might be like? Consider personal qualities, obstacles, achievements, and so forth.

5. Develop a simple inventory of names from folktales, myths, legends, and the Bible. Give it to a group of children to determine which names are familiar to them. How well known is traditional literature today?

6. Choose one motif, such as transformations or wishes, or one topic, such as siblings or stars. Search the Children's Literature database, and see how many different tales you can find with this motif and how many different cultures or countries your collection represents.

Web Links

Go to the Online Learning Center at **www.mhhe.com/kiefer9e** to find links to the following children's literature Web sites:

Aesop's Fables
Arabian Nights
Center for Children's Books: Storytelling
Encyclopedia Mythica
"How the Leopard Got His Spots"
Moonlit Road

Mother Goose Pages: Mother Goose, Nursery Rhymes, and Children's Songs
Native American Lore Index
Readers' Theater
Rumpelstiltskin
Snow White
Sur La Lune Fairy Tale Pages
Tales of Wonder
Traditional Literature: Lesson Plans

Related Readings

Bettelheim, Bruno. *The Uses of Enchantment.* New York: Knopf, 1976.

This noted child psychologist maintains that fairy tales have a unique place in children's development, satisfying many of their deepest emotional needs. He offers detailed analysis of several individual tales to show how they enable children to cope with their emotions and their world.

Bosma, Betty. *Fairy Tales, Fables, Legends, and Myths: Using Folk Literature in Your Classroom.* 2nd ed. New York: Teachers College Press, 1992.

This practical handbook provides a brief overview and rationale for using folktales, then lists classroom activities for exploring this genre with children. The emphasis is on reading, writing, and oral language activities, but suggestions also include responding to these stories with puppetry, art, drama, and music. An annotated bibliography is included.

Caduto, Michael J., and Joseph Bruchac. *Keepers of the Earth: Native American Stories and Environmental Activities for Children.* Foreword by N. Scott Momaday. Illustrated by John Kahionhes and Carl Wood. Golden, Col.: Fulcrum, 1989.

> *This is a collection of Native American folktales grouped under such headings as Creation, Fire, Earth, and Life/Death/Spirit, retold and illustrated with black-line drawings. Stories are followed by discussion and many far-ranging activities for the elementary-age child. The map of Native American tribes and cultural boundaries is a helpful organizer for teachers. See also, by the same authors,* Keepers of the Animals, *illustrated by John K. Fadden (Fulcrum, 1991);* Keepers of Life, *illustrated by John K. Fadden (Fulcrum, 1994); and* Keepers of the Night, *illustrated by John K. Fadden (Fulcrum, 1994).*

Campbell, Joseph, and Bill Moyers. *The Power of Myth.* New York: Doubleday, 1988.

> *Campbell, a preeminent teacher and scholar of mythology, converses with Moyers about myth in the modern world, the first storytellers, the power of myth in our lives, and mythical themes across cultures.*

Dundes, Alan, ed. *Cinderella: A Casebook.* New York: Wildman Press, 1989.

> *This is a collection of scholarly essays spanning the history of folklore research on the Cinderella theme. Of special interest to teachers and librarians are the essay "Cinderella in Africa," the Jungian approach in the essay "The Beautiful Wassilissa," and Jane Yolen's look at Cinderella in the mass market in "America's Cinderella."*

Frye, Northrop. *The Great Code: The Bible in Literature.* San Diego: Harcourt Brace Jovanovich, 1982.

> *The eminent literary critic develops a theory of literature based on patterns found in the Bible.*

Hamilton, Edith. *Mythology.* New York: New American Library, 1953.

> *The introduction to this literary standard summarizes the emergence of Greek ideas, followed by a readable presentation of Creation, Stories of Love and Adventure, and Heroes of the Trojan War. Genealogical tables are helpful inclusions.*

Moss, Joy F. *Focus on Literature: A Context for Literacy Learning.* Katonah, N.Y.: Richard C. Owen, 1990.

> *With classroom examples, Moss presents ten "focus units" developed around such themes as "Baba Yaga Tales," "Cat Tales," "Magic Object Tales," and "Bird Tales." Units involve traditional and other genres of literature, thoughtful discussions of children's learning and curriculum development, and excellent bibliographies. This is a valuable teacher resource and a companion volume to Moss's* Focus Units in Literature *(Urbana, Ill.: National Council of Teachers of English, 1984).*

Opie, Iona, and Peter Opie. *The Classic Fairy Tales.* New York: Oxford University Press, 1974.

> *This volume presents twenty-four of the best-known fairy tales as they first appeared in print in English. Pictures are gleaned from two centuries of illustrators. Invaluable sources of information on primary sources are the Opies' introductory essays for the tales.*

Schmidt, Gary D., and Donald R. Hettinga, eds. *Sitting at the Feet of the Past: Retelling the North American Folktale for Children.* Westport, Conn.: Greenwood Press, 1992.

> *This collection of essays focuses on tales told in the context of a North American setting and raises issues of concern to authors, illustrators, critics, and teachers. Authors of selections include Paul Goble, Patricia McKissack, William H. Hooks, and Steven Kellogg.*

Thompson, Stith. *The Folktale.* Berkeley: University of California Press, 1978.

> *Various theories of the origins of folktales and folktale themes are presented in a thorough manner in this book.*

Children's Literature

 Go to the Children's Literature Database on your Resources CD-ROM for a searchable listing of these and other children's literature titles.

Except where obvious from the title, the country or culture of origin follows each entry in parentheses. Modern stories with strong folktale roots are referred to as "Modern Literary." The notation (S) stands for single-tale edition. Dates in square brackets are original publication dates.

Folktales

Aardema, Verna. *Anansi Does the Impossible: An Ashanti Tale.* Illustrated by Lisa Desimini. Atheneum, 1997. (S)

———. *Bimwili and the Zimwi.* Illustrated by Susan Meddaugh. Dial, 1985. (S)(Africa, Zanzibar)

———. *Borreguita and the Coyote.* Illustrated by Petra Mathers. Knopf, 1991. (S)(Mexico)

———. *Koi and the Kola Nuts: A Tale from Liberia.* Illustrated by Joe Cepeda. Atheneum, 1999. (S)

———. *Misoso: Once Upon a Time Tales from Africa.* Illustrated by Reynold Ruffins. Applesoup/Knopf, 1994.

———. *Rabbit Makes a Monkey of Lion.* Illustrated by Jerry Pinkney. Dial, 1989. (S)(Africa, Tanzania)

———. *Who's in Rabbit's House?* Illustrated by Leo Dillon and Diane Dillon. Dial, 1977. (S)(West Africa)

———. *Why Mosquitoes Buzz in People's Ears.* Illustrated by Leo Dillon and Diane Dillon. Dial, 1975.

Ada, Alma Flor. *The Rooster Who Went to His Uncle's Wedding.* Illustrated by Kathleen Kuchera. Putnam, 1993. (S)(Cuba)

Adler, David. *Chanukah in Chelm.* Illustrated by Kevin O'Malley. Lothrop, 1997. (S)(Jewish)

Alvarez, Julia. *A Gift of Gracias: The Legend of Altagracia.* Illustrated by Beatriz Vidal. Knopf, 2005. (S)(Dominican Republic)

Arenson, Roberta. *Manu and the Talking Fish.* Barefoot, 2000. (S)(India)

Arkhurst, Joyce Cooper. *The Adventures of Spider: West African Folk Tales.* Illustrated by Jerry Pinkney. Little, 1964.

Arnold, Katya. *Baba Yaga: A Russian Folktale.* North-South, 1996. (S)

———. *Knock, Knock, Teremok!* North-South, 1994. (S)(Russia)

Aruego, Jose, and Ariane Dewey. *Rockabye Crocodile.* Greenwillow, 1988. (S)(Philippines)

Asbjørnsen, Peter Christian, and Jorgen E. Moe. *East o'the Sun and West o'the Moon.* Translated by George Webbe Dasent. Dover, 1970 [1842–1843]. (Norway)

———. *The Three Billy Goats Gruff.* Illustrated by Marcia Brown. Harcourt, 1957. (S)(Norway)

———. *The Three Billy Goats Gruff.* Illustrated by Glen Rounds. Holiday, 1993. (S)(Norway)

Aylesworth, Jim. *The Gingerbread Man.* Illustrated by Barbara McClintock. Scholastic, 1998. (S)(English)

———. *Goldilocks and the Three Bears.* Illustrated by Barbara McClintock. Scholastic, 2003. (S)

Babbitt, Natalie. *Ouch!* Illustrated by Fred Marcellino. HarperCollins, 1998. (S)(Germany)

Bang, Molly. *Dawn.* Morrow, 1983. (S)(United States)

Baylor, Byrd. *And It Is Still That Way: Legends Told by Arizona Indian Children.* Scribner's, 1976. (Native American)

Benaduce, Ann Keay. *Jack and the Beanstalk.* Illustrated by Gennady Spirin. Philomel, 1999. (S)(English)

Berenzy, Aliz. *Rapunzel.* Holt, 1995. (S)(Germany)

Berry, James. *First Palm Trees: An Anancy Spiderman Story.* Illustrated by Greg Couch. Simon, 1997. (S)(West Indies)

Bierhorst, John. *The Dancing Fox: Arctic Folktales.* Illustrated by Mary K. Okheena. Morrow, 1997.

———. *Dr. Coyote: A Native American Aesop's Fables.* Illustrated by Wendy Watson. Simon, 1987.

———, ed. *The Monkey's Haircut and Other Stories Told by the Maya.* Illustrated by Robert Andrew Parker. Morrow, 1986. (Central American)

———. *The People with Five Fingers. A Native Californian Creation Tale.* Illustrated by Robert Andrew Parker. Cavendish, 2000.

———, ed. *The White Deer and Other Stories Told by the Lenape.* Morrow, 1995.

Bishop, Claire Huchet. *The Five Chinese Brothers.* Illustrated by Kurt Wiese. Coward-McCann, 1938. (S)

Bodkin, Odds. *The Crane Wife.* Illustrated by Gennady Spirin. Harcourt, 1998. (S)(Japan)

Brett, Jan. *The Mitten.* Putnam, 1989. (S)(Ukrainian)

Brown, Marcia. *Dick Whittington and His Cat.* Scribner's, 1950. (S)(England)

———. *Once a Mouse.* Scribner's, 1961. (S)(India)

———. *Stone Soup.* Scribner's, 1947. (S)(France)

Bruchac, Joseph. *The Boy Who Lived with the Bears and Other Iroquois Stories.* Illustrated by Murv Jacob. HarperCollins, 1995.

———. *The First Strawberries: A Cherokee Story.* Illustrated by Anna Vojtech. Dial, 1993. (S)

———. *Gluskabe and the Four Wishes.* Illustrated by Christine Nyburg Shrader. Cobblehill, 1995. (S)(Native American)

———. *The Great Ball Game: A Muskogee Story.* Illustrated by Susan L. Roth. Dial, 1994. (S)(Native American)

———. *Turtle's Race with Bear: A Traditional Seneca Story.* Illustrated by Jose Aruego and Ariane Dewey. Penguin, 2005. (S)

Bruchac, Joseph, and James Bruchac. *How Chipmunk Got His Stripes: A Tale of Bragging and Teasing.* Illustrated by Jose Aruego and Ariane Dewey. Dial, 2001. (S)

———. *Raccoon's Last Race: A Traditional Abenaki Story.* Illustrated by Jose Aruego and Ariane Dewey. Dial, 2004. (S)

———. *When the Chenoo Howls: Native American Tales of Terror.* Illustrated by Netamuxwe and William Bock. Walker, 1998.

Bruchac, Joseph, and Gayle Ross. *The Story of the Milky Way.* Illustrated by Virginia Stroud. Dial, 1995. (S)(Cherokee)

Bryan, Ashley. *Beat the Story-Drum, Pum-Pum.* Atheneum, 1980. (Africa)

———. *Beautiful Blackbird.* Simon, 2003. (S)(Zambia)

———. *The Cat's Purr.* Atheneum, 1985. (S)(West Indies)

———. *The Dancing Granny.* Atheneum, 1977. (S)(Antilles)

———. *The Story of Lightning and Thunder.* Atheneum, 1993. (S)(West Africa)

Bushyhead, Robert H. *Yonder Mountain: A Cherokee Legend.* Written by Kay Thorpe Bannon. Illustrated by Kristina Rodanas. Cavendish, 2002. (S)

Byrd, Robert. *Finn MacCoul and His Fearless Wife: A Giant of a Tale from Ireland.* Dutton, 1999.

Chase, Richard. *Grandfather Tales.* Houghton, 1973 [1948]. (United States)

———. *The Jack Tales.* Illustrated by Berkeley Williams, Jr. Houghton, 1993 [1943]. (United States)

Chen, Kerstin. *Lord of the Cranes.* Illustrated by Jian Jiang Chen. North-South, 2000. (S)(China)

Climo, Shirley. *The Egyptian Cinderella.* Illustrated by Ruth Heller. Crowell/Harper, 1989. (S)

———. *The Korean Cinderella.* Illustrated by Ruth Heller. HarperCollins, 1993. (S)

Cohen, Caron Lee. *The Mud Pony.* Illustrated by Shonto Begay. Scholastic, 1988. (S)(Native American)

Cohn, Amy. *From Sea to Shining Sea.* Illustrated by various artists. Scholastic, 1993.

Cole, Joanna. *Bony-Legs.* Illustrated by Dirk Zimmer. Four Winds, 1983. (S)(Russia)

Cooper, Susan. *The Selkie Girl.* Illustrated by Warwick Hutton. McElderry, 1986. (S)(Scotland)

———. *The Silver Cow: A Welsh Tale.* Illustrated by Warwick Hutton. McElderry, 1983. (S)

———. *Tam Lin.* Illustrated by Warwick Hutton. McElderry, 1991. (S)(Scotland)

Courlander, Harold, and George Herzog. *The Cow-Tail Switch and Other West African Stories.* Illustrated by Madye Lee Chastian. Holt, 1947.

Cummings, Pat. *Ananse and the Lizard. A West African Tale.* Holt, 2002. (S)

Dabovich, Lydia. *The Polar Bear Son: An Innuit Tale.* Clarion, 1997. (S)

Daly, Jude. *Fair, Brown and Trembling: An Irish Cinderella Story.* Farrar, 2001. (S)

Dasent, George. *East o'the Sun and West o'the Moon.* Illustrated by Gillian Barlow. Philomel, 1988. (S)(Norway)

Davis, Donald. *The Pig Who Went Home on Sunday: An Appalachian Folktale.* Illustrated by Jennifer Mazzucco. August, 2004.

Dayrell, Elphinstone. *Why the Sun and the Moon Live in the Sky.* Illustrated by Blair Lent. Houghton, 1968. (S)(Africa)

De Armond, Dale. *The Seal Oil Lamp.* Sierra Club/Little, 1988. (S)(Inuit)

de Beaumont, Mme. *Beauty and the Beast.* Illustrated by Jan Brett. Houghton, 1989. (S)(France)

De Felice, Cynthia. *Cold Feet.* Illustrated by Robert Andrew Parker. DK Ink, 2001. (Scotland)

De Felice, Cynthia, and Mary DeMarsh. *Three Perfect Peaches.* Illustrated by Irene Trias. Orchard, 1995. (S)(France)

Delacre, Lulu. *Golden Tales: Myths, Legends, and Folklore from Latin America.* Scholastic, 1995.

Del Negro, Janice. *Willa and the Wind.* Illustrated by Heather Solomon. Cavendish, 2005. (S)(Scandinavia)

dePaola, Tomie. *Adelita: A Mexican Cinderella Story.* Putnam, 2002. (S)

———. *The Lady of Guadelupe.* Holiday, 1980. (S)(Mexico)

———. *The Legend of the Bluebonnet: An Old Tale of Texas.* Putnam, 1983. (S)(Comanche)

———. *The Legend of the Poinsettia.* Putnam, 1994. (S)(Mexico)

———. *Strega Nona.* Prentice-Hall, 1975. (S)(Italy)

Demi. *The Donkey and the Rock.* Holt, 1999. (S)(China)

———. *The Empty Pot.* Holt, 1990. (S)(China)

———. *The Hungry Coat: A Tale from Turkey.* Simon, 2004.(S)

———. *King Midas: The Golden Touch.* McElderry, 2002.

———. *One Grain of Rice: A Mathematical Tale.* Scholastic, 1997. (S)(India)

Diakité, Baba Wagué. *The Hatseller and the Monkeys: A West African Folktale.* Scholastic, 1999. (S)

———. *The Hunterman and the Crocodile: A West African Folktale.* Scholastic, 1997. (S)

———. *The Magic Gourd.* Scholastic, 2003. (S)(Mali)

Doherty, Berlie. *The Famous Adventures of Jack.* Illustrated by Sonja Lamut. Greenwillow, 2001.

Doucet, Sharon Arms. *Lapin Plays Possum. Trickster Tales from the Louisiana Bayou.* Illustrated by Scott Cook. Farrar, 2002. (S)(United States)

———. *Why Lapin's Ears Are So Long: And Other Tales from the Louisiana Bayou.* Orchard, 1997. (S)

Duvall, Deborah. *The Opossum's Tale.* Illustrated by Murv Jacob. U New Mexico P, 2005. (S)(Cherokee)

———. *Rabbit Goes Duck Hunting. A Traditional Cherokee Legend.* Illustrated by Murv Jacob. U New Mexico P, 2005. (S)

Early, Margaret. *Ali Baba and the Forty Thieves.* Abrams, 1989.

Egielski, Richard. *The Gingerbread Boy.* HarperCollins, 1997. (S)(English)

Ehlert, Lois. *Moon Rope/Un Lazo de la Luna.* Harcourt, 1992. (S)(South America)

Finger, Charles. *Tales from Silver Lands.* Illustrated by Paul Honore. Doubleday, 1924. (Central and South America)

Fowles, Shelley. *The Bachelor and the Bean.* Farrar, 2004. (S)(Moroccan Jewish)

French, Fiona. *Lord of the Animals: A Miwok Indian Creation Myth.* Millbrook, 1997. (S)

Fu, Shelley. *Ho Yi the Archer; and Other Classic Tales from China.* Illustrated by Joseph F. Abboreno. Linnet, 2001.

Galdone, Paul. *The Gingerbread Boy.* Clarion, 1984 [1968]. (S)(England)

———. *The Little Red Hen.* Clarion, 1979 [1974]. (S)(England)

———. *The Magic Porridge Pot.* Clarion, 1979 [1976]. (S)(Germany)

———. *Puss in Boots.* Clarion, 1979 [1976]. (S)(France)

———. *Rumpelstiltskin.* Houghton, 1985. (S)(Germany)

———. *The Three Billy Goats Gruff.* Clarion, 1979 [1970]. (S)(Norway)

———. *The Three Little Pigs.* Clarion, 1981 [1973]. (S)(Norway)

Garland, Sherry. *Children of the Dragon: Selected Tales from Vietnam.* Illustrated by Trina Schart Hyman. Harcourt, 2001.

Geras, Adele. *Sleeping Beauty.* Illustrated by Christian Birmingham. Orchard, 2004. (S)(France)

Gershator, Phillis. *Only One Cowry: A Dahomean Tale.* Illustrated by David Soman. Orchard, 2000. (S)

Gerson, Mary-Joan. *Fiesta Femina: Celebrating Women in Mexican Folktales.* Barefoot, 2001.

———. *How Night Came from the Sea.* Illustrated by Carla Golembe. Little, 1994. (S)(Brazil)

———. *Why the Sky Is Far Away.* Illustrated by Carla Golembe. Joy St., 1992. (S)(Nigeria)

Gilman, Phoebe. *Something from Nothing.* Scholastic, 1992. (S)(Jewish)

Glass, Andrew. *Mountain Men: True Grit and Tall Tales.* Doubleday, 2001.

Goble, Paul. *Buffalo Woman.* Bradbury, 1984. (S)(Plains Indian)

———. *The Gift of the Sacred Dog.* Bradbury, 1980. (S)(Plains Indian)

———. *The Girl Who Loved Wild Horses.* Bradbury, 1978. (S)(Plains Indian)

———. *The Great Race of the Birds and the Animals.* Bradbury, 1985. (Plains Indian)

———. *Her Seven Brothers.* Bradbury, 1988. (S)(Native American)

———. *Iktomi and the Berries: A Plains Indian Story.* Orchard, 1989. (S)

———. *Iktomi and the Buzzard.* Scholastic, 1994.

———. *Iktomi and the Coyote.* Orchard, 1998. (S)(Plains Indian)

———. *Iktomi Loses His Eyes.* Orchard, 1999. (S)(Plains Indian)

————. *The Lost Children.* Bradbury, 1993. (S)(Blackfoot)

————. *Mystic Horse.* HarperCollins, 2003. (S)(Pawnee)

————. *Star Boy.* Bradbury, 1983. (S)(Plains Indian)

————. *Storm Maker's Tipi.* Atheneum, 2001. (S)(Sisiska)

Gonzalez, Lucia M. *Señor Cat's Romance: And Other Favorite Stories from Latin America.* Illustrated by Lulu Delacre. Scholastic, 1997.

Grifalconi, Ann. *The Village of Round and Square Houses.* Little, 1986. (S)(West Africa, Cameroon)

Grimm brothers. *The Bremen-Town Musicians.* Retold and illustrated by Ilse Plume. Doubleday, 1980. (S)(Germany)

————. *The Elves and the Shoemaker.* Illustrated by Bernadette Watts. North-South, 1986. (S)(Germany)

————. *The Fisherman and His Wife.* Retold by John Warren Stewig. Illustrated by Margot Tomes. Holiday, 1988. (S)(Germany)

————. *The Frog Prince or Iron Henry.* Translated by Naomi Lewis. Illustrated by Binette Schroeder. North-South, 1998. (S)(Germany)

————. *Hansel and Gretel.* Illustrated by Paul Galdone. McGraw-Hill, 1982. (S)(Germany)

————. *Hansel and Gretel.* Retold by Rika Lesser. Illustrated by Paul O. Zelinsky. Dodd, 1984. (S)(Germany)

————. *Hansel and Gretel.* Translated by Elizabeth D. Crawford. Illustrated by Lisbeth Zwerger. Morrow, 1979. (S)(Germany)

————. *Household Stories of the Brothers Grimm.* Translated by Lucy Crane. Illustrated by Walter Crane. Dover, n.d. [1886].

————. *Little Red Cap.* Translated by Elizabeth D. Crawford. Illustrated by Lisbeth Zwerger. Morrow, 1983. (S)(Germany)

————. *Little Red Riding Hood.* Illustrated by Trina Schart Hyman. Holiday, 1983. (S)(Germany)

————. *Princess Furball.* Retold by Charlotte Huck. Illustrated by Anita Lobel. Greenwillow, 1989. (S)(Germany)

————. *Rapunzel.* Retold by Barbara Rogasky. Illustrated by Trina Schart Hyman. Holiday, 1982. (S)(Germany)

————. *Rumpelstiltskin.* Illustrated by Paul Galdone. Clarion, 1985. (S)(Germany)

————. *Rumpelstiltskin.* Retold and illustrated by Paul O. Zelinksy. Dutton, 1986. (S)(Germany)

————. *The Seven Ravens.* Translated by Elizabeth D. Crawford. Illustrated by Lisbeth Zwerger. Morrow, 1981. (S)(Germany)

————. *The Sleeping Beauty.* Retold and illustrated by Trina Schart Hyman. Little, 1974. (S)(Germany)

————. *Snow White and the Seven Dwarfs.* Translated by Randall Jarrell. Illustrated by Nancy Ekholm Burkert. Farrar, 1972. (S)(Germany)

————. *Snow White.* Translated by Paul Heins. Illustrated by Trina Schart Hyman. Little, 1974. (S)(Germany)

————. *The Table, the Donkey, and the Stick.* Illustrated by Paul Galdone. McGraw-Hill, 1976.

Hague, Kathleen, and Michael Hague. *East of the Sun and West of the Moon.* Illustrated by Michael Hague. Harcourt, 1980. (S)(Norway)

Haley, Gail E. *A Story, a Story.* Atheneum, 1970. (S)(Africa)

Hamilton, Virginia. *Bruh Rabbit and the Tar Baby Girl.* Illustrated by James E. Ransome. Scholastic, 2003. (S)(African American)

————. *The Dark Way: Stories from the Spirit World.* Illustrated by Lambert Davis. Harcourt, 1990. (Native American)

————. *The Girl Who Spun Gold.* Illustrated by Leo Dillon and Diane Dillon. Scholastic, 2000. (S)(West Indies)

————. *Her Stories: African American Folktales.* Illustrated by Leo Dillon and Diane Dillon. Blue Sky, 1995. (S)(African American)

————. *In the Beginning: Creation Stories from around the World.* Illustrated by Barry Moser. Harcourt, 1988.

————. *The Magical Adventures of Pretty Pearl.* Harper, 1983. (African American)

————. *The People Could Fly.* Illustrated by Leo Dillon and Diane Dillon. Knopf, 1985. (African American)

————. *The People Could Fly.* Illustrated by Leo Dillon and Diane Dillon. Knopf, 2004. (S)(African American)

Han, Oki S. *Kongi and Potgi.* Dial, 1996. (S)(Korea)

Han, Suzanne Crowder. *The Rabbit's Tail: A Tale from Korea.* Illustrated by Richard Wehrman. Holt, 1999. (S)

Harris, Joel Chandler. *The Complete Tales of Uncle Remus.* Compiled by Richard Chase. Illustrated by Arthur Frost and others. Houghton, 1955. (African American)

Haviland, Virginia. *Favorite Folktales Told in Japan.* Morrow, 1996.

Hayes, Joe. *Juan Verdades: The Man Who Couldn't Tell a Lie.* Illustrated by Joseph Daniel Fiedler. Orchard, 2002.

Hickox, Rebecca. *The Golden Sandal: A Middle Eastern Cinderella.* Illustrated by Will Hillenbrand. Holiday, 1998.

Ho, Minfong. *Brother Rabbit: A Cambodian Tale.* Illustrated by Jennifer Hewiston and Jou-Sien Tseng. Lothrop, 1997. (S)

Hodges, Margaret. *The Boy Who Drew Cats.* Illustrated by Aki Sogabe. Holiday, 2002. (S)(Japan)

Hogrogian, Nonny. *One Fine Day.* Macmillan, 1971. (S)(Armenia)

Hong, Lily Toy. *Two of Everything.* Whitman, 1993. (S)(China)

Hooks, William. *Moss Gown.* Illustrated by Donald Carrick. Clarion, 1987. (United States)

————. *The Three Little Pigs and the Fox.* Illustrated by S. D. Schindler. Macmillan, 1989. (S)(United States)

Houston, James. *Tikta' Liktak: An Eskimo Legend.* Harcourt, 1965. (S)

————. *The White Archer: An Eskimo Legend.* Harcourt, 1967. (S)

Huck, Charlotte. *The Black Bull of Norroway: A Scottish Tale.* Illustrated by Anita Lobel. Greenwillow, 2001. (S)

————. *Toads and Diamonds.* Illustrated by Anita Lobel. Greenwillow, 1996. (S)(French)

Hume, Lotta Carswell. *Favorite Children's Stories from China and Tibet.* Illustrated by Lo Koon-chiu. Tuttle, 2001 [1962].

Hurston, Zora Neale. *Lies and Other Tall Tales.* Illustrated by Christopher Myers. HarperCollins, 2005. (S)(African American)

Huth, Holly. *The Son of the Sun and the Daughter of the Moon: A Sammi Folktale.* Illustrated by Anna Votech. Atheneum, 2000. (S)(Scandinavia)

Isaacs, Anne. *Swamp Angel.* Illustrated by Paul O. Zindel. Dutton, 1994. (Modern Literary)

Jaffe, Nina. *The Golden Flower: A Taino Myth from Puerto Rico.* Illustrated by Eric O. Saná. Piñata, 2005. (S)

————. *A Voice for the People: The Life and Work of Howard Courlander.* Holt, 1997.

Johnson-Davies, Denys. *Goha, the Wise Fool*. Illustrated by Hany El Saed Ahmed and Hag Hamdy Mohamed Fattough. Philomel, 2005. (Egypt)

Johnston, Tony. *The Tale of Rabbit and Coyote*. Illustrated by Tomie dePaola. Putnam, 1994. (S)(Mexico)

Joseph, Lynn. *The Mermaid's Twin Sister: More Stories from Trinidad*. Illustrated by Donna Perrone. Clarion, 1994.

————. *A Wave in Her Pocket: Stories from Trinidad*. Illustrated by Brian Pinkney. Clarion, 1991.

Kajikawa, Kimiko. *Yoshi's Feast*. Illustrated by Yumi Heo. DK, 2000. (S)(Japan)

Karlin, Barbara. *Cinderella*. Illustrated by James Marshall. Little, 1989. (S)(France)

Keats, Ezra Jack. *John Henry: An American Legend*. Pantheon, 1965. (S)(African American)

Kellogg, Steven. *Chicken Little*. Morrow, 1988. (S)(United States)

————. *Jack and the Beanstalk*. Morrow, 1991. (S)(England)

————. *Johnny Appleseed*. Morrow, 1988. (S)(United States)

————. *Paul Bunyan*. Morrow, 1986. (S)(United States)

————. *Pecos Bill*. Morrow, 1986. (S)(United States)

————. *Sally Ann Thunder Ann Whirlwind Crockett*. Morrow, 1995. (S)(United States)

Kherdian, David. *The Golden Bracelet*. Illustrated by Nonny Hogrogian. Holiday, 1998. (S)(Armenian)

Kimmel, Eric A. *Baba Yaga: A Russian Folktale*. Illustrated by Megan Lloyd. Holiday, 1991. (S)

————. *Boots and His Brothers*. Illustrated by Kimberly Bulken Root. Holiday, 1992. (S)(Norway)

————. *The Castle of Cats*. Illustrated by Katya Krenina. Holiday, 2004. (S)(Ukraine)

————. *Easy Work: An Old Tale*. Illustrated by Andrew Glass. Holiday, 1998. (S)(Norway)

————. *I-Know-Not-What, I-Know-Not-Where: A Russian Tale*. Illustrated by Robert G. Sauber. Holiday, 1994. (S)

————. *Iron John*. Illustrated by Trina Schart Hyman. Holiday, 1994. (S)(German)

————. *The Old Woman and Her Pig*. Illustrated by Giora Carmi. Holiday, 1993. (S)(English)

————. *Rimonah of the Flashing Sword*. Illustrated by Omar Rayyan. Holiday, 1995. (S)(Middle East)

————. *The Tale of Aladdin and the Wonderful Lamp*. Illustrated by Ju-Hong Chen. Holiday, 1992. (S)(Middle East)

————. *Ten Suns: A Chinese Legend*. Illustrated by Yongsheng Xuan. Holiday, 1998. (S)

————. *The Three Princes*. Illustrated by Leonard Everett Fisher. Holiday, 1995. (S)(Middle East)

————. *Three Sacks of Truth: A Story from France*. Illustrated by Robert Rayevsky. Holiday, 1993. (S)(France)

————. *Three Samurai Cats*. Illustrated by Mordecai Gerstein. Holiday, 2003. (S)(Japan)

Knutson, Barbara. *Love and Roast Chicken: A Trickster Tale from the Andes Mountains*. Carolrhoda, 2004. (S)

Kurtz, Jane. *Fire on the Mountain*. Illustrated by E. B. Lewis. Simon, 1994. (S)(Ethiopia)

Lang, Andrew. *The Arabian Nights Entertainments: Aladdin, Sinbad, and 24 Other Favorite Stories*. Dover, 1969.

Lattimore, Deborah Nourse. *Arabian Nights: Three Tales*. HarperCollins, 1995. (S)(Middle East)

Lester, Julius. *How Many Spots Does a Leopard Have? and Other Tales*. Illustrated by David Shannon. Scholastic, 1989. (Africa)

————. *John Henry*. Illustrated by Jerry Pinkney. Dial, 1994. (S) (African American)

————. *The Knee-High Man and Other Tales*. Illustrated by Ralph Pinto. Dial, 1972. (African American)

————. *The Last Tales of Uncle Remus*. Illustrated by Jerry Pinkney. Dial, 1994. (African American)

————. *More Tales of Uncle Remus: Further Adventures of Brer Rabbit, His Friends, Enemies, and Others*. Illustrated by Jerry Pinkney. Dial, 1988. (African American)

————. *The Tales of Uncle Remus: The Adventures of Brer Rabbit*. Illustrated by Jerry Pinkney. Dial, 1987. (African American)

————. *Uncle Remus: The Complete Tales*. Illustrated by Jerry Pinkney. Dial, 1999.

Lindbergh, Reeve. *Johnny Appleseed*. Illustrated by Kathy Jakobsen. Little, 1990. (S)(United States)

Litzinger, Roseanne. *The Old Woman and Her Pig: An Old English Tale*. Harcourt, 1992. (S)

Lottridge, Celia Baker. *Music for the Tsar of the Sea*. Illustrated by Harvey Chan. Groundwood, 1998. (S)(Russia)

Long, Laurel, and Jacqueline K. Ogburn. *The Lady and the Lion*. Illustrated by Laurel Long. Dial, 2003. (S)(Germany)

Louie, Ai-Ling. *Yeh-Shen: A Cinderella Story from China*. Illustrated by Ed Young. Philomel, 1982. (S)

Lunge-Larsen, Lise. *The Hidden Folk: Stories of Fairies, Dwarves, Selkies, and Other Secret Beings*. Illustrated by Beth Krommes. Houghton, 2004.

————. *The Race of the Birkebeiners*. Illustrated by Mary Azarian. Houghton, 2001. (S)(Norway)

————. *The Troll with No Heart in His Body*. Illustrated by Betsy Bowen. Houghton, 1999.

Lyons, Mary. *Roy Makes a Car: Based on a Story Collected by Zora Neale Hurston*. Illustrated by Terry Widener. Atheneum, 2005. (S)(African American)

MacDonald, Amy. *Please, Malese! A Trickster Tale from Haiti*. Illustrated by Emily Lisker. Farrar, 2002. (S)

MacDonald, Margaret Read. *The Fat Cat: A Danish Folktale*. Illustrated by Julie Paschkis. Whitman, 2001. (S)(Denmark)

————. *Mabela the Clever*. Illustrated by Tim Coffey. Whitman, 2001. (S)(Limba/Africa)

Maggi, María Elena. *The Great Canoe: A Kariña Legend*. Translated by Elisa Amado. Illustrated by Gloria Calderón. Groundwood, 2001. (S)(Venezuela).

Mahy, Margaret. *The Seven Chinese Brothers*. Illustrated by Jean Tseng and Mou-Sien Tseng. Scholastic, 1990. (S)

Mama, Raouf. *Why Goats Smell Bad and Other Stories from Benin*. Illustrated by Imna Arroyo. Linnet, 1998.

Manitonquat. *The Children of the Morning Light: Wampanoag Tales*. Illustrated by Mary F. Arguette. Macmillan, 1994. (Native American)

Manna, Athony. *Mr. Semolina-Semolinus: A Greek Folktale.* Illustrated by Giselle Potter. Atheneum, 1997. (S)

Marshall, James. *Goldilocks and the Three Bears.* Dial, 1988. (S) (England)

———. *Red Riding Hood.* Dial, 1987. (S)(Germany)

———. *The Three Little Pigs.* Dial, 1989. (S)(England)

Martin, Rafe. *The Boy Who Lived with the Seals.* Illustrated by David Shannon. Putnam, 1993. (S)(Native American)

———. *The Brave Little Parrot.* Illustrated by Susan Gaber. Putnam, 1998. (S)(India)

———. *Foolish Rabbit's Big Mistake.* Illustrated by Ed Young. Putnam, 1985. (S)(India)

———. *The Language of Birds.* Illustrated by Susan Gaber. Putnam, 2000. (S)(Russia)

———. *The Rough-Face Girl.* Illustrated by David Shannon. Putnam, 1992. (S)(Native American)

——— *The Shark God.* Illustrated by David Shannon. Levine, Scholastic, 2001. (S)(Hawaii)

Mayer, Marianna. *Baba Yaga and Vasilisa the Brave.* Illustrated by Kinuko Y. Craft. Morrow, 1994. (S)(Russia)

———. *The Twelve Dancing Princesses.* Illustrated by Kinuko Y. Craft. Morrow, 1989. (S)(France)

Mayo, Gretchen Will. *Earthmaker's Tales: North American Indian Stories from Earth Happenings.* Walker, 1989.

McClintock, Barbara. *Cinderella.* Scholastic, 2005. (S)(France)

McDermott, Gerald. *Anansi the Spider.* Holt, 1972. (S)(Africa)

———. *Arrow to the Sun.* Viking, 1974. (S)(Native American)

———. *Coyote: A Trickster Tale from the American Southwest.* Harcourt, 1994. (S)(Native American)

———. *Jabuti, the Tortoise: A Trickster Tale from the Amazon.* Harcourt, 2001. (S)

———. *Musicians of the Sun.* Simon, 1997. (S)(Mexico)

———. *Raven: A Trickster Tale from the Pacific Northwest.* Harcourt, 1993. (S)(Native American)

———. *The Stonecutter: A Japanese Folk Tale.* Penguin, 1975. (S)

———. *Zomo the Rabbit: A Trickster Tale from West Africa.* Harcourt, 1992. (S)

McVitty, Walter. *Ali Baba and the Forty Thieves.* Illustrated by Margaret Early. Abrams, 1989. (S)(Middle East)

Medicine Crow, Joe. *Brave Wolf and the Thunderbird.* Illustrated by Linda R. Martin. Abbeville, 1998. (S)(Native American, Crow)

Minard, Rosemary, ed. *Womenfolk and Fairy Tales.* Illustrated by Suzanne Klelin. Houghton, 1975.

Mohr, Nicholasa. *The Song of el Coqui and Other Tales of Puerto Rico.* Illustrated by Antonio Martorell. Viking, 1995.

Mollel, Tololwa M. *Ananse's Feast: An Ashanti Tale.* Illustrated by Andrew Glass. Clarion, 1997. (S)

———. *The Orphan Boy: A Maasai Story.* Illustrated by Paul Morin. Clarion, 1991. (S)(Africa)

Monroe, Jean Guard, and Ray A. Williamson. *They Dance in the Sky: Native American Star Myths.* Illustrated by Edgar Stewart. Houghton, 1987. (Native American)

Montes, Marisa. *Juan Bobo Goes to Work: A Puerto Rican Folktale.* Illustrated by Joe Cepeda. HarperCollins, 2000. (S)

Morales, Yuyi. *Just a Minute: A Trickster Tale and Counting Book.* Chronicle, 2003. (S)(Mexico)

Mosel, Arlene. *The Funny Little Woman.* Illustrated by Blair Lent. Dutton, 1972. (S)(Japan)

Moser, Barry. *The Three Little Pigs.* Little, 2001. (S)(England)

Moses, Will. *Hansel and Gretel.* Philomel, 2006.

Muth, Jon J. *Stone Soup.* Scholastic, 2003.

Namioka, Lensey. *The Loyal Cat.* Illustrated by Aki Sogabe. Browndeer, 1995. (S)(Japan)

Ness, Evaline. *Tom Tit Tot.* Scribner's, 1965. (S)(England)

Norman, Howard. *The Girl Who Dreamed Only Geese: And Other Tales of the Far North.* Illustrated by Leo Dillon and Diane Dillon. Harcourt, 1997.

Olaleye, Isaac. *In the Rainfield: Who Is the Greatest.* Illustrated by Ann Grifalconi. Blue Sky/Scholastic, 2002. (S)(Nigeria)

Orgel, Doris. *The Bremen Town Musicians: And Other Animal Tales from Grimm.* Illustrated by Bert Kitchen. Roaring Brook, 2004. (Germany)

Osborne, Mary Pope. *American Tall Tales.* Illustrated by Michael McCurdy. Knopf, 1991.

———. *New York's Bravest.* Illustrated by Steve Johnson and Lou Fancher. Knopf, 2002. (S)(United States)

Parks, Van Dyke. *Jump Again! More Adventures of Brer Rabbit.* Illustrated by Barry Moser. Harcourt, 1987. (African American)

———. *Jump on Over! The Adventures of Brer Rabbit and His Family.* Illustrated by Barry Moser. Harcourt, 1989. (African American)

Parks, Van Dyke, and Malcolm Jones. *Jump! The Adventures of Brer Rabbit.* Illustrated by Barry Moser. Harcourt, 1986. (African American)

Paterson, Katherine. *The Tale of the Mandarin Ducks.* Illustrated by Leo Dillon and Diane Dillon. Lodestar, 1990. (S)(Japan)

Paye, Won-Ldy, and Margaret H. Lippert. *Head, Body, Legs: A Story from Liberia.* Illustrated by Julie Paschkis. Holt, 2002. (S)

———. *Mrs. Chicken and the Hungry Crocodile.* Illustrated by Julie Paschkis. Holt, 2003. (S)(Liberia)

Perrault, Charles. *Cinderella.* Illustrated by Marcia Brown. Scribner's, 1954. (S)(France)

———. *Cinderella, or the Little Glass Slipper.* Illustrated by Errol Le Cain. Bradbury, 1973. (S)(France)

———. *Puss in Boots.* Retold by Lincoln Kirstein. Illustrated by Alain Vaës. Little, 1992. (S)(France)

———. *Puss in Boots.* Translated by Malcolm Arthur. Illustrated by Fred Marcellino. Farrar, 1990, 1993. (S)(France)

———. "Sleeping Beauty" in *The Complete Fairy Tales of Charles Perrault.* Clarion, 1993.

Phelps, Ethel Johnston. *The Maid of the North: Feminist Folk Tales from Around the World.* Illustrated by Lloyd Bloom. Holt, 1981.

Philip, Neil. *The Arabian Nights.* Illustrated by Sheila Moxley. Orchard, 1994. (S)(Middle East)

———. *Stockings of Buttermilk: American Folktales.* Illustrated by Jacqueline Mair. Clarion, 1999.

Pinkney, Jerry. *The Little Red Hen.* Dial, 2006. (S)(England)

Pitcher, Caroline. *Mariana and the Merchild: A Folktale from Chile.* Illustrated by Jackie Morris. Eerdmans, 2000. (S)

Polette, Nancy. *The Little Old Woman and the Hungry Cat*. Illustrated by Frank Modell. Greenwillow, 1989. (S)(Norway)

Pullman, Philip. *Aladdin and the Enchanted Lamp*. Illustrated by Sophy Williams. Scholastic, 2005. (S)(Middle Eastern)

Ransome, Arthur. *The Fool of the World and the Flying Ship*. Illustrated by Uri Shulevitz. Farrar, 1968. (S)(Russia)

Rascol, Sabin I. *The Impudent Rooster*. Illustrated by Holly Berry. Orchard, 2004. (S)(Romania)

Reneaux, J. J. *How Animals Saved the People: Animal Tales From the South*. Illustrated by James Ransome. HarperCollins, 2001.

Reyher, Becky. *My Mother Is the Most Beautiful Woman in the World*. Illustrated by Ruth Gannett. Lothrop, 1945. (S)(Russia)

Rodanas, Kristina. *The Blind Hunter*. Cavendish, 2003. (S)(Native American)

———. *Dragonfly's Tale*. Clarion, 1991. (Zuni/Native American)

———. *Follow the Stars: A Native American Woodlands Tale*. Cavendish, 1998. (S)

Rohmer, Harriet. *The Invisible Hunters*. Illustrated by Joe Sam. Children's, 1987. (S)(Nicaragua)

Rounds, Glen. *Ol' Paul, the Mighty Logger*. Holiday, 1949. (S)(United States)

———. *Three Little Pigs and the Big Bad Wolf*. Holiday, 1992. (S)(England)

Rubalcaba, Jill. *Uncegila's Seventh Spot: A Lakota Legend*. Illustrated by Irving Toddy. Clarion, 1995. (S)

San Souci, Daniel. *The Rabbit and the Dragon King*. Illustrated by Eujin Kim Neilan. Boyds Mills, 2002. (S)(Korea)

San Souci, Robert D. *Cendrillon, a Caribbean Cinderella*. Illustrated by Brian Pinkney. Simon, 1998. (S)

———. *Cut from the Same Cloth: American Women of Myth, Legend and Tall Tale*. Illustrated by Brian Pinkney. Philomel, 1993. (United States)

———. *Larger Than Life: The Adventures of American Legendary Heroes*. Illustrated by Andrew Glass. Doubleday, 1991. (United States)

———. *The Little Gold Star. A Spanish American Cinderella Story*. Illustrated by Sergio Martinez. HarperCollins, 2000. (S)

———. *The Silver Charm: A Folktale from Japan*. Illustrated by Yoriko Ito. Doubleday, 2002. (S)

———. *Six Foolish Fishermen*. Illustrated by Douglas Kennedy. Dial, 2000. (S)(United States)

———. *Sootface: An Ojibwa Cinderella*. Illustrated by Daniel San Souci. Doubleday, 1994. (S)

———. *Sukey and the Mermaid*. Illustrated by Brian Pinkney. Four Winds, 1992. (S)(African American)

———. *The Talking Eggs*. Illustrated by Jerry Pinkney. Dial, 1989. (S)(African American)

———. *The Twins and the Bird of Darkness: A Hero Tale from the Caribbean*. Illustrated by Terry Widener. Simon, 2002. (S)

———. *A Weave of Words: An Armenian Tale*. Illustrated by Raul Colón. Orchard, 1998.

———. *The Well at the End of the World*. Illustrated by Rebecca Walsh. Chronicle, 2004. (S)(England)

———. *The White Cat*. Illustrated by Gennady Spirin. Orchard, 1990. (S)(France)

Sanfield, Steve. *The Adventures of High John the Conqueror*. Illustrated by John Ward. Orchard, 1989. (African American)

———. *A Natural Man*. Illustrated by Peter J. Thornton. Godine, 1986. (S)(African American)

Sawyer, Ruth. *Journey Cake, Ho!* Illustrated by Robert McCloskey. Viking, 1953. (S)(United States)

Schanzer, Rosalyn. *Davy Crockett Saves the World*. HarperCollins, 2001. (S)(United States)

Scholey, Arthur. *Baboushka*. Illustrated by Helen Cann. Candlewick, 2001. (S)(Russia)

Schroeder, Alan. *Smoky Mountain Rose: An Appalachian Cinderella*. Illustrated by Brad Sneed. Dial, 1997. (S)(American)

Schwartz, Howard, and Barbara Rush. *The Diamond Tree: Jewish Tales from around the World*. Illustrated by Uri Shulevitz. HarperCollins, 1991.

Shannon, George. *More Stories to Solve: Fifteen Folktales from around the World*. Illustrated by Peter Sis. Greenwillow, 1990.

———. *Stories to Solve: Folktales from around the World*. Illustrated by Peter Sis. Greenwillow, 1985.

Shepard, Aaron. *Master Maid: A Tale from Norway*. Illustrated by Pauline Ellison. Dial, 1997.

———. *Master Man: A Tale of Nigeria*. Illustrated by David Wisniewski. HarperCollins, 2001. (S)

———. *The Sea King's Daughter*. Illustrated by Gennady Spirin. Atheneum, 1997. (S)(Russia)

Shephard, Esther. *Paul Bunyan*. Harcourt, 1985. (S)(North America)

Sherlock, Philip M. *West Indian Folktales*. Illustrated by Joan Kindell-Monroe. Oxford UP, 1988.

Sherman, Pat. *The Sun's Daughter*. Illustrated by R. Gregorie Christie. Clarion, 2005. (S)(Iroquois)

Shulevitz, Uri. *Soldier and Tsar in the Forest: A Russian Tale*. Translated by Richard Lourie. Farrar, 1972. (S)

Shute, Linda. *Momotaro, the Peach Boy*. Lothrop, 1986. (S)(Japan)

Sierra, Judy. *The Gift of the Crocodile: A Cinderella Story*. Illustrated by Reynold Ruffins. Simon, 2000. (S)(Indonesia)

Simms, Laura. *The Bone Man: A Native American Modoc Tale*. Illustrated by Michael McCurdy. Hyperion, 1997. (S)

Singer, Isaac Bashevis. *Elijah the Slave*. Translated by the author and Elizabeth Shub. Illustrated by Antonio Frasconi. Farrar, 1970. (S)(Jewish)

———. *Mazel and Shlimazel, or the Milk of a Lioness*. Illustrated by Margot Zemach. Farrar, 1967. (S)(Jewish)

———. *When Shlemiel Went to Warsaw and Other Stories*. Translated by the author and Elizabeth Shub. Illustrated by Margot Zemach. Farrar, 1968. (Jewish)

———. *Zlateh the Goat, and Other Stories*. Translated by the author and Elizabeth Shub. Illustrated by Maurice Sendak. Harper, 1966. (Jewish)

Slobodkina, Esphyr. *Caps for Sale*. HarperCollins, 1987.

Snyder, Dianne. *The Boy of the Three-Year Nap*. Illustrated by Allen Say. Houghton, 1988. (S)(Japan)

So, Meilo. *Gobble, Gobble, Slip Slop: A Tale of a Very Greedy Cat*. Knopf, 2004. (S)(India)

Souhami, Jessica. *Mrs. McCool and the Giant Cuhullin: An Irish Tale*. Holt, 2002. (S)

————. *No Dinner! The Story of the Old Woman and the Pumpkin*. Cavendish, 2000. (S)(South Asia)

Speare, Elizabeth George. *The Sign of the Beaver*. Houghton, 1983.

Spirin, Gennady. *The Tale of the Firebird*. Philomel, 2002.

Steptoe, John. *Mufaro's Beautiful Daughters: An African Tale*. Lothrop, 1987. (S)(Zimbabwe)

————. *The Story of Jumping Mouse: A Native American Legend*. Morrow, 1984. (S)

Stewig, John Warren. *Stone Soup*. Illustrated by Margot Tomes. Holiday, 1991. (S)(France)

Stoutenberg, Adrien. *American Tall Tales*. Illustrated by Richard M. Powers. Penguin, 1976.

Sunami, Kitoba. *How the Fisherman Tricked the Genie: A Tale within a Tale within a Tale*. Illustrated by Amiko Hirao. Atheneum, 2002. (S)(Middle East)

Taback, Simms. *Joseph Had a Little Overcoat*. Viking, 1999.

Tchana, Katrin. *Sense Pass King: A Story from Cameroon*. Illustrated by Trina Schart Hyman. Holiday, 2002. (S)

————. *The Serpent Slayer: And Other Tales of Strong Women*. Illustrated by Trina Schart Hyman. Little, 2002.

Tolstoy, Aleksei. *The Gigantic Turnip*. Illustrated by Niamh Sharkey. Barefoot, 1999. (S)(Russia)

Tresselt, Alvin. *The Mitten*. Illustrated by Yaroslava. Lothrop, 1964. (S)(Ukrainian)

Uchida, Yoshiko. *The Dancing Kettle and Other Japanese Folk Tales*. Illustrated by Richard C. Jones. Harcourt, 1949.

————. *The Magic Purse*. Illustrated by Keiko Narahasi. McElderry, 1993. (S)(Japan)

————. *The Wise Old Woman*. Illustrated by Martin Springetti. McElderry, 1994. (S)(Japan)

Van Laan, Nancy. *The Magic Bean Tree: A Legend from Argentina*. Illustrated by Beatriz Vidal. Houghton, 1998. (S)

————. *Shingebiss: An Ojibwe Legend*. Illustrated by Betsy Bowen. Houghton, 1997. (S)

————. *So Say the Little Monkeys*. Illustrated by Umi Heo. Atheneum, 1998. (S)(Brazil)

————. *With a Whoop and a Holler: A Bushel of Lore from Way Down South*. Illustrated by Scott Cook. Atheneum, 1998.

Vaughan, Richard Lee. *Eagle Boy: A Pacific Northwest Native Tale*. Illustrated by Lee Christiansen. Sasquatch, 2001. (S)

Vuong, Lynette Dyer. *The Brocaded Slipper and Other Vietnamese Tales*. Illustrated by Vo-Dinh Mai. HarperCollins, 1991.

Wada, Stephanie. *Momotaro and the Island of Ogres: A Japanese Folktale*. Illustrated by Kano Naganobu. Braziller, 2005.

Waldman, Neil. *Two Brothers; A Legend of Jerusalem*. Atheneum, 1997. (S)

Walker, Barbara. *Watermelons, Walnuts, and the Wisdom of Allah and Other Tales of the Hoca*. Illustrated by Harold Berson. Texas Tech UP, 1991 [1967]. (Middle East)

Wattenberg, Jane. *Henny Penny*. Scholastic, 2000.

Wells, Ruth. *The Farmer and the Poor God*. Illustrated by Yoshi. Simon, 1996. (S)(Japan)

White, Carolyn. *Whuppity Stoorie*. Illustrated by S. D. Schindler. Putnam, 1997. (S)(Scotland)

Wiesner, David, and Kim Kahng. *The Loathsome Dragon*. Illustrated by David Wiesner. Clarion, 2005 [1987]. (S)(England).

Willey, Margaret. *Clever Beatrice*. Illustrated by Heather Solomon. Atheneum, 2001. (S)(Canada)

Winthrop, Elizabeth. *The Little Humpbacked Horse*. Illustrated by Alexander Koshkin. Clarion, 1997. (S)(Russia)

————. *Vasilissa the Beautiful*. Illustrated by Alexander Koshkin. HarperCollins, 1991. (S)(Russia)

Wolfson, Margaret Olivia. *The Patient Stone: A Persian Love Story*. Juan Canéba Clavero. Barefoot, 2001. (S)

Wolkstein, Diane. *The Day Ocean Came to Visit*. Illlustrated by Steve Johnson and Lou Fancher. Harcourt/Gulliver, 2001. (S) (Nigeria)

————. *The Magic Orange Tree and Other Haitian Folktales*. Illustrated by Elsa Henriquez. Knopf, 1978.

Wood, Douglas. *Rabbit and the Moon*. Illustrated by Leslie Baker. Simon, 1998. (S)(Cree)

Wood, Nancy. *The Girl Who Loved Coyote: Stories of the Southwest*. Illustrated by Diana Bryer. Morrow, 1995.

Wright, Katherine. *Steamboat Annie and the Thousand Pound Catfish*. Illustrated by Howard Fine. Philomel, 2001. (S)(United States)

Yee, Paul. *Tales from Gold Mountain*. Illustrated by Simon Ng. Macmillan, 1990. (Chinese American)

Yeoman, John. *The Seven Voyages of Sinbad*. Illustrated by Quentin Blake. McElderry, 1997. (Middle East)

Yep, Laurence. *The Man Who Tricked a Ghost*. Illustrated by Isadore Seltzer. Bridgewater, 1993. (S)(China)

————. *The Rainbow People*. Illustrated by David Wiesner. Harper, 1989. (Chinese American)

————. *The Star Fisher*. Morrow, 1991.

————. *Tongues of Jade*. Illustrated by David Wiesner. HarperCollins, 1991. (Chinese American)

Yolen, Jane. *Mightier than the Sword: World Folklore for Boys*. Illustrated by Raul Colón. Harcourt, 2003.

Young, Ed. *Lon Po Po: A Red Riding Hood Story from China*. Philomel, 1989. (S)

————. *The Sons of the Dragon King*. Atheneum, 2004. (S)(China)

————. *What about Me?* Philomel, 2002. (S)(Sufi)

Zelinsky, Paul O. *Rapunzel*. Dutton, 1997. (S)(Italian)

Zemach, Harve. *Duffy and the Devil*. Illustrated by Margot Zemach. Farrar, 1973. (S)(England)

Zemach, Margot. *It Could Always Be Worse*. Farrar, 1977. (S) (Jewish)

————. *The Little Red Hen*. Farrar, 1983. (S)(England)

————. *The Three Wishes: An Old Story*. Farrar, 1986. (S)(England)

Zeman, Ludmila. *Sinbad in the Land of the Giants*. Tundra, 2001. (S)(Middle East)

Fables

Bader, Barbara. *Aesop and Company*. Illustrated by Arthur Geisert. Houghton, 1991.

Bierhorst, John. *Doctor Coyote: A Native American Aesop's Fables*. Illustrated by Wendy Watson. Macmillan, 1987.

Brett, Jan. *Town Mouse, Country Mouse*. Putnam, 1994. (S)

Brown, Marcia. *Once a Mouse*. Scribner's, 1961. (S)

Caldecott, Randolph. *The Caldecott Aesop*. Doubleday, 1978 [1883].

Galdone, Paul. *The Monkey and the Crocodile*. Seabury, 1969. (S)

Lionni, Leo. *Frederick*. Pantheon, 1967. (S)(Modern Literary)

Orgel, Doris. *The Lion and the Mouse: And Other Aesop's Fables*. Illustrated by Bert Kitchen. DK, 2001.

Pinkney, Jerry. *Aesop's Fables*. North-South, 2000.

Poole, Amy Lowry, reteller. *The Ant and the Grasshopper*. Holiday, 2000.

Sogabe, Aki. *Aesop's Fox*. Browndeer, 1999.

Steig, William. *Amos and Boris*. Farrar, 1971. (S)(Modern Literary)

Testa, Fulvio. *Aesop's Fables*. Barron's, 1989.

Uribe, Veronica, reteller. *Little Book of Fables*. Translated by Susan Ouriou. Illustrated by Constanza Bravo. Groundwood, 2004.

Wormell, Christopher. *Mice, Morals and Monkey Business*. Running Press, 2005.

Yolen, Jane. *A Sip of Aesop*. Illustrated by Karen Barbour. Blue Sky, 1995.

Young, Ed. *The Lion and the Mouse*. Doubleday, 1980. (S)

———. *Seven Blind Mice*. Philomel, 1992. (S)

Zwerger, Lisbeth. *Aesop's Fables*. Picture Book Studios, 1989.

Myths and Legends

Bierhorst, John. *The Mythology of Mexico and Central America*. Morrow, 1990.

———. *The Mythology of North America*. Morrow, 1985.

———. *The Mythology of South America*. Morrow, 1988.

———. *The Woman Who Fell from the Sky*. Illustrated by Robert Andrew Parker. Morrow, 1993. (S)

Burleigh, Robert. *Pandora*. Illustrated by Raul Colón. Harcourt, 2002.

Byrd, Robert. *The Hero and the Minotaur*. Dutton, 2005.

Climo, Shirley. *Atalanta's Race*. Illustrated by Alexander Koshkin. Clarion, 1995. (S)

———. *Stolen Thunder*. Illustrated by Alexander Koshkin. Clarion, 1994. (S)

Colum, Padraic. *The Children's Homer: The Adventures of Odysseus and the Tale of Troy*. Illustrated by Willy Pogany. Macmillan, 1962.

———. *The Trojan War and the Adventures of Odysseus*. Illustrated by Barry Moser. Morrow, 1997.

Craft, M. Charlotte. *Cupid and Psyche*. Illustrated by Kinuko Craft. Morrow, 1996. (S)

Crossley-Holland, Kevin. *The World of King Arthur and His Court: People, Places, Legends, and Lore*. Illustrated by Peter Malone. Dutton, 1999.

D'Aulaire, Ingri, and Edgar Parin D'Aulaire. *D'Aulaires' Book of Greek Myths*. Doubleday, 1962.

———. *D'Aulaires' Book of Norse Myths*. New York Review of Books, 2005 [1967].

Demi. *King Midas: The Golden Touch*. McElderry, 2002.

Evslin, Bernard. *Hercules*. Illustrated by Joseph A. Smith. Morrow, 1984. (S)

———. *Jason and the Argonauts*. Illustrated by Bert Dodson. Morrow, 1986.

Evslin, Bernard, Dorothy Evslin, and Ned Hoopes. *Heroes and Monsters of Greek Myth*. Illustrated by William Hunter. Scholastic, 1970.

Fisher, Leonard Everett. *Jason and the Golden Fleece*. Holiday, 1990. (S)

———. *The Olympians*. Holiday, 1984.

———. *Theseus and Minotaur*. Holiday, 1988. (S)

Gaer, Joseph. *The Adventures of Rama*. Illustrated by Randy Monk. Little, 1954.

Graves, Robert. *Greek Gods and Heroes*. Laurel Leaf, 1995 [1960].

Green, Roger Lancelyn. *Tales of the Greek Heroes*. Penguin, 1958.

Hamilton, Virginia. *In the Beginning: Creation Stories from around the World*. Illustrated by Barry Moser. Harcourt, 1988.

Hodges, Margaret. *The Kitchen Knight: A Tale of King Arthur*. Illustrated by Trina Schart Hyman. Holiday, 1990. (S)

———. *Merlin and the Making of the King*. Illustrated by Trina Schart Hyman. Holiday, 2004.

———. *Saint George and the Dragon*. Illustrated by Trina Schart Hyman. Little, 1984. (S)

Hofmeyr, Dianne. *The Star-Bearer: A Creation Tale from Ancient Egypt*. Illustrated by Jude Daly. Farrar, 2001.

Hovey, Kate. *Arachne Speaks*. Illustrated by Blair Drawson. McElderry, 2001.

Hutton, Warwick. *Odysseus and Cyclops*. McElderry, 1994. (S)

———. *Persephone*. McElderry, 1994.

———. *Perseus*. McElderry, 1994. (S)

———. *Theseus and the Minotaur*. McElderry, 1989. (S)

Kessler, Timothy. *When God Made the Dakotas*. Illustrated by Paul Morin. Eerdmans, 2006.

Kimmel, Eric A. *The Hero Beowulf*. Illustrated by Leonard Everett Fisher. Farrar, 2005.

Lanier, Sidney. *The Boy's King Arthur*. Illustrated by N. C. Wyeth. Scribner's, 1989 [1917].

Low, Alice. *The Macmillan Book of Greek Gods and Heroes*. Illustrated by Arvis Stewart. Macmillan, 1985.

Lunge-Larsen, Lise. *The Troll with No Heart in His Body: And Other Tales of Trolls from Norway*. Illustrated by Betsy Bowen. Houghton, 1999.

McCaughrean, Geraldine. *The Bronze Cauldron: Myths and Legends of the World*. Illustrated by Bee Willey. McElderry, 1998.

———. *Gilgamesh the Hero*. Illustrated by David Parkins. Eerdmans, 2004.

———. *The Golden Hoard: Myths and Legends of the World*. Illustrated by Bee Willey. McElderry, 1995.

———. *Greek Gods and Goddesses*. Illustrated by Emma Chichester Clark. McElderry, 1998.

———. *Odysseus*. Illustrated by David Parkins. Cricket, 2004.

———. *The Odyssey*. Illustrated by Victor Ambrus. Oxford UP, 1997.

————, reteller. *Roman Myths.* Illustrated by Emma Chichester Clark. McElderry, 2001.

————. *The Silver Treasure: Myths and Legends of the World.* Illustrated by Bee Willey. McElderry, 1996.

McGovern, Ann. *Robin Hood of Sherwood Forest.* Illustrated by Tracy Sugarman. Scholastic, 1970.

McKinley, Robin. *The Outlaws of Sherwood.* Greenwillow, 1988.

Orgel, Doris. *Ariadne, Awake!* Illustrated by Barry Moser. Viking, 1994. (S)

Osborne, Mary Pope. *Mermaids and Monsters.* Illustrated by Troy Howell. Hyperion, 2003.

————. *The One-Eyed Giant.* Illustrated by Troy Howell. Hyperion, 2003.

Philip, Neil. *King Midas.* Illustrated by Isabelle Brent. Little, 1994. (S)

Pyle, Howard. *The Merry Adventures of Robin Hood.* Scribner's, 1946 [1888].

————. *The Story of King Arthur and His Knights.* Scribner's, 1954.

Souhami, Jessica. *Rama and the Demon King: An Ancient Tale from India.* DK, 1997. (S)

Stewig, John. *King Midas.* Illustrated by Omar Rayyan. Holiday, 1999. (S)

Sutcliff, Rosemary. *Black Ships before Troy: The Story of the Iliad.* Illustrated by Alan Lee. Delacorte, 1993.

————. *The Road to Camlann.* Dutton, 1982.

————. *The Sword and the Circle.* Dutton, 1981.

————. *Tristan and Iseult.* Dutton, 1981.

————. *The Light Beyond the Forest: The Quest for the Holy Grail.* Dutton, 1980.

————. *The Wanderings of Odysseus: The Story of the Odyssey.* Illustrated by Alan Lee. Delacorte, 1996.

Talbott, Hudson. *Excalibur.* Illustrated by Peter Glassman. Morrow, 1996.

————. *King Arthur and the Round Table.* Illustrated by Peter Glassman. Morrow, 1995.

Tomlinson, Theresa. *Child of May.* Orchard, 1998.

————. *The Forestwife.* Orchard, 1995.

Verma, Jatinder. *The Story of Divaali.* Illustrated by Nilesh Mistry. Barefoot, 2002.

Weitzman, David. *Rama and Sita: A Tale from Ancient Java.* Godine, 2003.

White, T. H. *The Sword in the Stone.* Putnam, 1939.

Wolkstein, Diane. *Sun Mother Wakes the World: An Australian Creation Story.* Illustrated by Bronwyn Bancroft. HarperCollins, 2004.

Yolen, Jane. *The Dragon's Boy.* HarperCollins, 1990. (S)

————. *Wings.* Illustrated by Dennis Nolan. Harcourt, 1991. (S)

Zeman, Ludmila. *Gilgamesh the King.* Tundra, 1995. (S)

————. *The Last Quest of Gilgamesh.* Tundra, 1995. (S)

————. *The Revenge of Ishtar.* Tundra, 1995. (S)

Bible

Bierhorst, John, trans. *Spirit Child: A Story of the Nativity.* Illustrated by Barbara Cooney. Morrow, 1984. (S)(Mexico)

Chaikin, Miriam. *Angels Sweep the Desert Floor: Legends about Moses in the Wilderness.* Illustrated by Alexander Koshen. Clarion, 2002.

————. *Clouds of Glory: Jewish Stories and Legends about Bible Times.* Illustrated by David Frampton. Clarion, 1998.

dePaola, Tomie. *The Lady of Guadalupe.* Holiday, 1980. (S)(Mexico)

————. *The Legend of Old Befana.* Harcourt, 1980. (S)

————. *The Miracles of Jesus.* Holiday, 1987.

————. *The Parables of Jesus.* Holiday, 1987.

————. *The Story of the Three Wise Kings.* Putnam, 1983. (S)

Dillon, Leo, and Diane Dillon. *To Everything There Is a Season.* Scholastic, 1998.

Gellman, Marc. *Does God Have a Big Toe? Stories about Stories in the Bible.* Illustrated by Oscar de Mejo. Harper, 1989.

Goldin, Barbara Diamond. *Journeys with Elijah: Eight Tales of the Prophet.* Illustrated by Jerry Pinkney. Gulliver/Harcourt, 1999.

Lester, Julius. *When the Beginning Began: Stories about God, the Creatures, and Us.* Harcourt, 1999.

Manushkin, Fran. *Daughters of Fire: Heroines of the Bible.* Illustrated by Uri Shulevitz. Silver Whistle/Harcourt, 2001.

Mark, Jan. *God's Story.* Illustrated by David Parkins. Candlewick, 1998.

McCaughrean, Geraldine. *God's People: Stories from the Old Testament.* McElderry, 1998.

Meyer, Marianna. *The Prophets. Stories and Quotes from Prophets of the Bible.* Illustrated by various artists. Fogelman, 2003.

Myers, Walter Dean. *A Time to Love: Stories from the Old Testament.* Illustrated by Christopher Myers. Scholastic, 2003.

Petersham, Maud, and Miska Petersham. *The Christ Child.* Doubleday, 1931. (S)

Pinkney, Jerry. *Noah's Ark.* Sea Star, 2002.

Ray, Jane. *Adam and Eve and the Garden of Eden.* Eerdmans, 2005.

Robbins, Ruth. *Baboushka and the Three Kings.* Illustrated by Nicolas Sidjakov. Parnassus, 1960. (S)

Spier, Peter. *Noah's Ark.* Doubleday, 1978.

Turner, Philip. *The Bible Story.* Illustrated by Brian Wildsmith. Oxford UP, 1987.

Vivas, Julie. *The Nativity.* Harcourt, 1986. (S)

Waldman, Sarah. *Light.* Illustrated by Neil Waldman. Harcourt, 1993. (S)

Wildsmith, Brian. *A Christmas Story.* Eerdmans, 1998.

————. *The Easter Story.* Eerdmans, 1999.

————. *Exodus.* Eerdmans, 1998.

————. *Jesus.* Eerdmans, 2000.

————. *Joseph.* Eerdmans, 1997.

Chapter Seven

Modern Fantasy

Chapter Outline

Photo © Andrew Fox/CORBIS

Media Resources

...ve teacher maintained a diary in which she recorded sig-
...teaching day. These excerpts reveal her students' responses
... the well-known fantasy *Charlotte's Web* by E. B. White:

...aming eyes,
...*Charlotte's*
...e of an irre-
...ond that, if
children aren't read to, how will they see the
purpose of such a difficult skill?

February 6
Judy came in glowing.

"We've bought a baby pig. Mother took me
to a nearby farm."

"How marvelous. What's his name?"

"Wilbur," she said, in a matter-of-fact voice—
as if the name of the pig in *Charlotte's Web*
was the only one possible. "He's quite cuddly
for a pig. We bathe him every day."

February 20
When I'm alone with Judy, I ask about Wilbur.

"Oh, he's getting along just fine. We bought
him a large pink ribbon and only take it off
when he goes to bed."

"Where does he sleep?"

"In my bed," said Judy, as if I ought to know.

March 2
Everyone was silent at the end of *Charlotte's
Web*. David wept when Charlotte died. Later
he asked to borrow the book. It'll be interesting to see how he maneuvers such difficult
reading. But there's the motivation they talk
about.

April 3
Judy's mother hurried over to me at the P.T.A.
meeting.

"What's all this about your pig?" she queried.

"My pig?" I answered incredulously. "You
mean your pig; the one you and Judy bought
at the farm."

"Come now," said Mrs. F. "This is ridiculous.
Judy's been telling me for weeks about the
class pig. The one you named for Wilbur in
Charlotte's Web."

We looked at each other, puzzled, and suddenly the truth dawned upon us.

Wilbur, that immaculately clean pig in his dazzling pink ribbon, belonged to neither Mrs. F.
nor me. He was born in dreams—a creature of
Judy's wonderful imagination.[1]

A book of fantasy had seemed so real to these children that 7-year-old David had cried at its end, and
Judy had continued the story in her imagination, convincing both her teacher and her mother that Wilbur
did indeed exist.

FANTASY FOR TODAY'S CHILD

Some educators and parents question the value of fantasy for today's child. They argue that children want
contemporary stories that are relevant and speak to
the problems of daily living—"now" books about the
real world, not fantasies about unreal worlds. Others
object to any fantasy at all for children, afraid that reading about goblins, trolls, and witches will lead children to practices of satanism or belief in the occult.[2]

But good fantasy might be critical to children's
understanding of themselves and of the struggles they

---

[1]Jean Katzenberg, "More Leaves from a Teacher's Diary: On Reading," *Outlook* issue 2 (spring 1974): 28–29. Published by
the Mountain View Center for Environmental Education, University of Colorado.

[2]According to the *Newsletter on Intellectual Freedom* (March 1994, p. 54), for example, a group who objected to Lloyd
Alexander's classic *Prydain Chronicles* said that the series "contained religious themes that are pagan in nature and young
minds would be drawn to the allure of witchcraft and black magic that runs through the books."

will face as human beings. Lloyd Alexander argues that fantasy is of the utmost value for children.

> We call our individual fantasies dreams, but when we dream as a society, or as a human race, it becomes the sum total of all our hopes. Fantasy touches our deepest feelings and in so doing, it speaks to the best and most hopeful parts of ourselves. It can help us learn the most fundamental skill of all—how to be human.[3]

The great fantasies frequently reveal new insights into the world of reality. Both *Charlotte's Web* and Kenneth Grahame's *The Wind in the Willows* detail the responsibilities and loyalties required of true friendship. The fundamental truth underlying Ursula Le Guin's story *A Wizard of Earthsea* is that each of us is responsible for the wrong that we do and that we are free of it only when we face it directly. In a book of realism, such a theme might appear to be a thinly disguised religious lesson; in fantasy it becomes an exciting quest for identity and self-knowledge. Fantasy consistently asks the universal questions concerning the struggle of good versus evil, the humanity of humankind, and the meaning of life and death.

A modern realistic fiction novel can be out of date in five years, but well-written fantasy endures. Hans Christian Andersen's *The Nightingale* speaks directly to this century's adoration of mechanical gadgetry to the neglect of what is simple and real. Lois Lowry's *The Giver* asks how the freedom of an individual can be weighed against the needs of the group. Natalie Babbitt's *Tuck Everlasting* questions whether anything or anyone would wish to live forever.

More important, however, fantasy helps the child develop imagination. To be able to imagine, to conceive of alternative ways of life, to entertain new ideas, to create strange new worlds, to dream dreams—these are all skills vital to human survival. Maxine Greene argues that "of all our cognitive capacities, imagination is the one that permits us to give credence to alternative realities."[4]

> It is imagination—with its capacity to both make order out of chaos and open experience to the mysterious and the strange—that moves us to go in quest, to journey where we have never been.[5]

Susan Cooper suggests that because of the heterogeneous mix of cultures in the United States, children here have no shared myths to inherit as children in more homogeneous cultures do. She believes that the role of fantasy, with its heroes, struggles, and allegories, becomes

Natalie Babbitt's *Tuck Everlasting* asks children to consider what it means to be mortal. Reprinted by permission of Farrar, Straus & Giroux, LLC: Jacket design from *Tuck Everlasting* by Natalie Babbitt. Copyright © 1975 by Natalie Babbitt.

even more important because it satisfies our modern-day hunger for myth.[6]

These arguments aside, children themselves have shown that they continue to want books that satisfy this hunger. J. K. Rowling's Harry Potter books are undoubtedly the most popular children's books to be published in the past fifty years. E. B. White's *Charlotte's Web*, Brian Jacques's Redwall series, C. S. Lewis's Narnia series, and Madeleine L'Engle's *A Wrinkle in Time* are all fantasies that rank among children's favorite books. And many of the classics, books that have endured through generations—such as Lewis Carroll's *Alice in Wonderland*, A. A. Milne's *Winnie the Pooh*, Kenneth Grahame's *The Wind in the Willows*, and J. M. Barrie's *Peter Pan*—are also fantasies. These books have inspired contemporary contributions such as *Peter and the Shadow Thieves* and *Peter*

---

[3]Lloyd Alexander, "Fantasy and the Human Condition," *New Advocate* 1.2 (spring 1983): 83.

[4]Maxine Greene, *Releasing the Imagination: Essays on Education, the Arts, and Social Change* (San Francisco: Jossey-Bass, 1995), p. 3.

[5]Ibid., p. 23.

[6]Susan Cooper, "Fantasy in the Real World," *Dreams and Wishes: Essays on Writing for Children* (New York: Simon & Schuster, 1996), pp. 57–71.

and the Star Catchers by Dave Barry and Ridley Pearson. As Mollie Hunter suggests, children (and writers of fantasy) are the ones who "never pass a secret place in the woods without a stare of curiosity for the mystery implied . . . who still turn corners with a lift of expectation at the heart."[7] And who still open a book of fantasy with that same sense of anticipation.

The modern literature of fantasy is diverse. We have contemporary fairy tales; stories of magic, talking toys, and other wonders; quests for truth in lands that never were; and narratives that speculate on the future. Though these types of stories might seem very different, they do have something in common: they have roots in earlier sources—in folktales, legends, myths, and the oldest dreams of humankind.

All literature borrows from itself, but the fantastic genre is particularly dependent. The motifs, plots, characters, settings, and themes of new fantasy books often seem familiar. And well they should, for we have met them before, in other, older stories.

Jane Yolen, in an essay on the importance of traditional literature, says:

> Stories lean on stories, art on art. This familiarity with the treasure-house of ancient story is necessary for any true appreciation of today's literature. A child who has never met Merlin—how can he or she really recognize the wizards in Earthsea? The child who has never heard of Arthur—how can he or she totally appreciate Susan Cooper's *The Grey King*?[8]

Many authors borrow directly from the characters and motifs of folklore. The African American folk heroes John de Conquer and John Henry Roustabout enliven the unusual fantasy *The Magical Adventures of Pretty Pearl* by Virginia Hamilton. John de Conquer, or High John, also forms the basis of the otherworldly magical helper in Walter Mosley's *47*, the first book in a series about African American history. Mollie Hunter's fantasy books are filled with the magic folk of her native Scotland. There are, among others, worrisome trows; water sprites called kelpies, often seen as horses; and the selkies, who are seals capable of taking human form on land.[9]

Such shape shifting often occurs in folk and fairy tales, and similar transformations are frequently arranged by authors of modern fantasy. In *The Cat Who Wished to Be a Man*, Lloyd Alexander's wizard transforms his cat Lionel into a young man whose catlike ways wear off only gradually. The wizard himself, of course, is a char-

acter drawn from the magician figures of old tales. In the same book, a good-hearted rogue named Tudbelly invites inhospitable townspeople to a feast, promising them a special stew, and then tricks them into furnishing the ingredients themselves. Readers who have had prior experience with folktales may recognize that Alexander's "delicious Pro Bono Publico" stew is made from the same basic recipe as *Stone Soup* in the retelling by Marcia Brown.

In the case of Robin McKinley's *Beauty* and Donna Jo Napoli's *Beast*, the debt to Mme. de Beaumont's *Beauty and the Beast* is immediately clear. McKinley recasts the tale in the form of a novel by exploring character, motive, and the everyday details that do not fit within the frame of a conventional fairy tale. The result is a rich and satisfying book that manages to sustain a sense of anticipation even in readers who know the outcome. In addition to de Beaumont's version, Napoli acknowledges Charles Lamb's poetry version written in 1811, in which he names the beast Orasmyn and gives his origin as Persia. Indeed, Napoli tells the tale from Orasmyn's point of view and begins the story in Persia where Orasmyn's violation of a religious custom causes him to be turned into a lion. In this and her other books such as *Zel* and *Spinners*, all for mature readers, Napoli excels at mining the psychological heart of the wonder tale, often from the point of view of the antagonist. In *The Magic Circle*, another powerful story for older readers, Napoli's healer gives a gripping yet sensitive account of how she came to be bewitched, and why she fled deep into a magic forest so that she might do no harm to humans. Here she lives for years until one day two children named Hansel and Gretel stumble upon her cottage. Although they will prove to be her undoing, they will also be her salvation from the evil powers that have held her in their grip for so many years. In this book, and in others, Napoli explores the complex nuances of human relationships within the framework of traditional tales.

Some bodies of traditional lore have proven to be more popular than others as sources of new stories. Echoes of King Arthur—both the Arthur of the medieval romances (as in Malory's *Le Morte d'Arthur*) and his historic precursor Arthur, the tribal chieftain of early Britain—are found in a great many modern fantasies. William Mayne's *Earthfasts*; Nancy Springer's *I Am Morgan le Fay* and *I Am Mordred*; Kevin Crossley-Holland's Arthur series, which includes *The Seeing Stone, At the Crossing Place,* and *King of the Middle March*; and Gerald Morris's *The Squire's Tale* and its sequels, *The Squire, His*

---

[7]Mollie Hunter, "One World," in *Talent Is Not Enough* (New York: Harper & Row, 1976), p. 77.

[8]Jane Yolen, "How Basic Is Shazam?" in *Touch Magic: Fantasy, Faerie and Folklore in the Literature of Childhood* (New York: Philomel Books, 1981), p. 15.

[9]See Barbara Z. Kiefer, "Exploring the Roots of Fantasy with Mollie Hunter's *Stranger Came Ashore*." In *Children's Literature in the Classroom: Extending Charlotte's Web*, eds. Janet Hickman, Bernice E. Cullinan, and Susan Hepler (Norwood, Mass.: Christopher Gordon, 1994), pp. 103–22.

Knight, and His Lady, Parsifal's Page, The Savage Damsel and the Dwarf, The Ballad of Sir Dinadin, and *The Lioness and Her Knight* are books much in Arthur's debt. Susan Cooper's five books that make up the Dark Is Rising sequence weave together elements of the Arthurian legends and broader themes from Celtic mythology, with an emphasis on ancient powers. Lloyd Alexander's Prydain Chronicles and T. A. Barron's The Lost Years of Merlin and The Great Tree of Avalon series borrow extensively from the Welsh stories known as the "Mabinogion."

A study of traditional tales can provide children with the framework for reading these more complex works of fantasy. Teaching Resources: "Connecting Traditional Tales and Fantasy Novels" lists some of the stories, motifs, and themes in some of the novels discussed in this chapter.

Many fantasies incorporate motifs and elements from multiple sources. Perhaps it is this striking of several familiar notes at once that brings them such enduring popularity. *The Hobbit,* by J. R. R. Tolkien, places the archetypal hero of mythology against a smaller-scale setting more common in folktales. C. S. Lewis's Narnia series puts centaurs and fauns from classical myths in company with modern children fighting medieval battles parallel to those recounted in Christian theology. Madeleine L'Engle draws on a similar array of referents. The volumes of her Time Trilogy (*A Wrinkle in Time, A Wind in the Door, A Swiftly Tilting Planet*) explore intriguing possibilities of astrophysics and cellular biology, as befits science fiction, but the books also reflect her knowledge of theology, classical literature, myths, legends, and history.

The ultimate taproot of all fantasy is the human psyche. Like the ancient tale-tellers and the medieval bards, modern fantasy writers speak to our deepest needs, our darkest fears, and our highest hopes. Maurice Sendak, for instance, relies on such themes in his picture storybooks and in the singular small volume titled *Higglety, Pigglety, Pop!* In this book a dog named Jennie sets out on an unspecified quest because "There must be more to life than having everything."[10] Her experiences are childlike and highly symbolic: the comforts of eating, and the fear of being eaten in turn by a lion; the importance of one's own real name; the significance of dreams. Jennie's quest, as it turns out, may be read as the search for maturity and personal identity.

Ursula K. Le Guin conducts a similar psychic adventure for an older audience in *A Wizard of Earthsea,* where a young magician must learn the power of naming and recognize the Shadow that pursues him as part of himself. Adults might find, in these and similar stories, many of the collective images or shared symbols called archetypes by the great psychologist Carl Jung. Children will simply recognize that such a fantasy is "true." All our best fantasies, from the briefest modern fairy tale to the most complex novel of high adventure, share this quality of truth.

MODERN FAIRY TALES

The traditional folklore or fairy tale had no identifiable author but was passed on by retellings by one generation to the next. Even though the names Grimm and Jacobs have become associated with some of these tales, they did not *write* the stories; they compiled and edited the folktales of Germany and England. The modern literary fairy tale utilizes the form of the old but has an identifiable author.

Hans Christian Andersen is generally credited with being the first *author* of modern fairy tales, although some of his stories, such as *The Wild Swans,* are definite adaptations of the old folktales. (Compare Andersen's *The Wild Swans* with the Grimm brothers' "The Six Swans," for example.) Many of Andersen's stories bear his unmistakable stamp of gentleness, melancholy, and faith in God. Often even his retellings of old tales are embellished with deeper meanings, making them very much his creations.

Some of Andersen's tales are really commentaries on what he saw as the false standards of society. In *The Emperor's New Clothes,* farce is disclosed by a child who tells the truth—that the Emperor indeed has no clothes. *The Nightingale* warns of the perils of coveting material objects instead of appreciating the beauties of the natural world. Others of Andersen's tales are thought to be autobiographical commentaries. In *The Ugly Duckling* the jest of the poultry yard became a beautiful swan, just as the gawky Andersen suffered in his youth but was later honored by the Danish king and the world. *The Steadfast Tin Soldier* was rejected by his ballerina love just as Andersen was rejected by the woman he loved.

Andersen was not afraid to show children cruelty, morbidity, sorrow, and even death in his stories. *The Little Match Girl* freezes to death on Christmas Eve while seeing a vision of her grandmother, the only person who truly loved her, in the flames of her unsold matches. The grandmother carries the girl to heaven. In the long tale of *The Snow Queen,* a glass splinter enters Kai's (or Kay's) eye and stabs his heart. He becomes spiteful and angry with his friend Gerda, who is hurt by the change in his behavior. When he disappears with the Snow Queen, Gerda searches for and finds him, and her tears melt the splinter and dissolve his icy demeanor.

Other early authors of the modern literary fairy tale are Oscar Wilde and George MacDonald. Wilde's *The Happy Prince* is the sentimental story of a bejeweled statue who little by little gives his valuable decorations to the poor. His emissary and friend is a swallow who

---

[10]Maurice Sendak, *Higglety, Pigglety, Pop!* (New York: Harper & Row, 1967), p. 5.

Connecting Traditional Tales and Fantasy Novels

OLC Visit the Online Learning Center at **www.mhhe.com/kiefer9e** for a printable version of this list.

Book (Author)	Motif, Theme, or Topic	Fantasy Novel (Author)
East o'the Sun and West o'the Moon (Asbjørnsen and Moe)	Shape changing	*East* (Pattou)
		Gnat Stokes and the Foggy Bottom Swamp Queen (Keehn)
The Frog Prince (Grimm)		
Tam Lin (Cooper)		*I Was a Rat* (Pullman)
		The Moorchild (McGraw)
		Owl in Love (Kindl)
Beauty and the Beast (de Beaumont)	Transformation by love	*Beast* (Napoli)
The Snow Queen (Andersen)		*The Golden Compass* (Pullman)
The Tunnel (Browne)		*Kit's Wilderness* (Almond)
		The Lion, the Witch, and the Wardrobe (Lewis)
		Skellig (Almond)
		A Wrinkle in Time (L'Engle)
Selkie (McClure)	Selkie legend	*The Folk Keeper* (Billingsley)
The Selkie Girl (Cooper)		*A Stranger Came Ashore* (Hunter)
Duffy and the Devil (Zemach)	Power of naming	*Straw into Gold* (Schmidt)
The Girl Who Spun Gold (Hamilton)		*The Wings of Merlin* (Barron)
Rumpelstiltskin (Grimm brothers)		*A Wizard of Earthsea* (Le Guin)
Dove Isabeau (Yolen)	Nature of dragons	*Dealing with Dragons* (Wrede)
The Egg (Robertson)		*The Dragon of the Lost Sea* (Yep)
St. George and the Dragon (Hodges)		*Dragon Rider* (Funke)
		Dragon's Blood (Yolen)
		Eragon (Paolini)
		The Hobbit (Tolkien)
		The Hunting of the Last Dragon (Jordan)

faithfully postpones his winter migration to Egypt to do the prince's bidding, only to succumb to the cold at the statue's feet. When the town councillors melt down the now shabby statue for its lead, all burns except the heart, which is cast on the same ash heap as the body of the dead bird. Together, the two are received in Heaven as the most precious things in the city. Wilde's *The Selfish Giant* has even more religious symbolism.

Many of MacDonald's fairy tales are also religious in nature, including *The Golden Key*, which has been sensitively illustrated by Maurice Sendak. Sendak also illustrated MacDonald's *The Light Princess*, the story of a princess deprived of gravity by an aunt who was angry at not being invited to her christening. MacDonald is also remembered for *At the Back of the North Wind*, pub-

lished in 1871 and one of the foundation stories of modern fantasy.

Other well-known authors have been captivated by the possibilities of the literary fairy tale. Kenneth Grahame's *The Reluctant Dragon* is the droll tale of a peace-loving dragon who is forced to fight Saint George. The dragon's friend, called simply "Boy," arranges a meeting between Saint George and the dragon, and a mock fight is planned. Saint George is the hero of the day, the dragon is highly entertained at a banquet, and Boy is pleased to have saved both the dragon and Saint George. Black-line drawings by Ernest Shepard add to the subtle humor of this book. James Thurber's *Many Moons* is the story of a petulant princess who desires the moon. The characterizations of the frustrated king, the perplexed wise men, and the understanding jester are well realized. Princess Lenore solves the problem of obtaining the moon in a completely satisfying and childlike manner. A popular fairy tale of our time for adults and children is the haunting story *The Little Prince* by Antoine de Saint-Exupéry. Written in the first person, the story tells of the author's encounter with the Little Prince in the Sahara Desert, where he has made a forced landing with his disabled plane. Bit by bit, the author learns the strange history of the Little Prince, who lives all alone on a tiny planet no larger than a house. He possesses three volcanoes, two active and one extinct, and one flower unlike any other flower in all the galaxy. However, when he sees a garden of roses, he doubts the uniqueness of his flower until a fox shows him that what we love is always unique to us. This gentle story means many things to different people, but its wisdom and beauty are for all.

MODERN FANTASY

Fantasy, like poetry, means more than it says. Underlying most of the great books of fantasy is metaphorical commentary on society today. Some children will find deeper meanings in a tale like *The Little Prince,* others will simply read it as a good story, and still others will be put off from reading it altogether because it isn't "real." Children vary in their capacity for imaginative thinking. The literal-minded child finds the suspension of reality a barrier to the enjoyment of fantasy; other children relish the opportunity to enter the world of enchantment. Frequently, teachers can help children develop a taste for fantasy by reading aloud books such as Beverly Cleary's *Ralph S. Mouse,* Kenneth Oppel's *Silverwing,* Avi's *Poppy,* or Sid Fleischman's *The Whipping Boy.*

Evaluating Modern Fantasy

Well-written fantasy, like other fiction, has a well-constructed plot, convincing characterization, a worthwhile theme, and an appropriate style. However, additional considerations must guide the evaluation of fantasy. The primary concern is the way the author makes the fantasy believable. A variety of techniques can be used to create belief in the unbelievable. Many authors firmly ground a story in reality before gradually moving into fantasy. Not until Chapter 3 in *Charlotte's Web* does author E. B. White suggest that Fern can understand the farm animals as they talk. And even then, Fern never talks to the animals; she only listens to them. By the end of the story Fern is growing up and really is more interested in listening to Henry Fussy than to the animals. White's description of the sounds and smells of the barnyard allows readers to experience the setting as well.

Creating belief by careful attention to the detail of the setting is a technique also used by Mary Norton in *The Borrowers.* Norton's graphic description of the Borrowers' home beneath the clock enables the reader to visualize this domestic background and to feel what it

would be like to be as small as the Borrowers. J. K. Rowling has created such wonderfully detailed settings for her Harry Potter series that children have no trouble accepting the magical creatures and the fantastic events that occur at Hogwarts School of Witchcraft and Wizardry.

Having one of the characters mirror the disbelief of the reader is another device for creating convincing fantasy. In *Jeremy Visick,* David Wiseman has portrayed his protagonist, Matthew, as a boy who thinks history is rubbish. Therefore, when even he is persuaded that the past lives again, the reader shares Matthew's terror as he descends to sure disaster within the depths of the Wheal Maid mine.

The use of appropriate language adds a kind of authenticity to fantasy. Underground for nearly two hundred years, the drummer uses such obsolete words as *arfish* for "afraid" in *Earthfasts,* by William Mayne, and his lack of understanding of modern words like *breakfast* seems very authentic indeed. In *The Fox Busters,* a clever story full of wordplay and puns, Dick King-Smith creates languages for a farm community in which chickens speak Hennish while the foxes speak Volpine. When one of the hens curses, using "fowl language," she tells a fox, "Go fricassee yourself," and calls a human a "stupid scrambled boy." The hens are named after famous farm-implement companies like Massey-Harris or Allis-Chalmers, which adds further authenticity to this delightful fantasy.

The proof of real objects gives an added dimension of truth in books. How can we explain the origin of Greta's kitten or her father's penknife if not from Blue Cove in Julia Sauer's story *Fog Magic*? In *Tom's Midnight Garden* by Philippa Pearce, it is the discovery of a pair of ice skates that confirms the reader's belief in Tom's adventures.

Another point to be considered when evaluating fantasy is the consistency of the story. Each fantasy should have a logical framework and an internal consistency in the world set forth by the author. For instance, characters should not become invisible whenever they face difficulty unless invisibility is a well-established part of their natures. The laws of fantasy may be strange indeed, but they must be obeyed.

Lloyd Alexander, master of the craft of writing fantasy, explains the importance of internal consistency within the well-written fantasy:

> Once committed to his imaginary kingdom, the writer is not a monarch but a subject. Characters must appear plausible in their own setting, and the writer must go along with the inner logic. Happenings should have logical implications. Details should be tested for consistency. Shall animals speak? If so, do *all* animals speak? If not, then which—and how? Above all, why? Is it essential to the story, or lamely cute? Are there enchantments? How powerful? If an

Evaluating Modern Fantasy

The following specific questions might guide an evaluation of modern fantasy.

What are the fantasy elements of the story?
How has the author made the story believable?
Is the story logical and consistent within the framework established by the author?

Is the plot original and ingenious?
Is there a universal truth underlying the metaphor of the fantasy?
How does the story compare with other books of the same kind or by the same author?

enchanter can perform such-and-such, can he not also do so-and-so?[11]

Finally, while all plots should be original, the plots of fantasy must be ingenious and creative. A contrived or trite plot seems more obvious in a fanciful tale than in a realistic story.

Modern fantasy makes special demands on authors. The Evaluation Criteria box "Evaluating Modern Fantasy" summarizes the criteria that need to be considered when evaluating this genre for children.

Animal Fantasy

Children might first be introduced to fantasy through tales of talking animals, toys, and dolls. The young child frequently ascribes powers of thought and speech to pets or toys and might already be acquainted with some of the Beatrix Potter stories or the more sophisticated tales of William Steig.

A humorous introduction to animal fantasy is *Bunnicula* by Deborah Howe and James Howe. When the Monroe family returns from seeing the movie *Dracula* with a small rabbit they found on a theater seat, the family cat, Chester, is immediately suspicious. Evidence mounts up: A note written in an obscure Transylvanian dialect is tied around the rabbit's neck; in the kitchen a white tomato and other vegetables appear drained of their juices; and the rabbit can go in and out of his locked cage. Is Bunnicula a vampire? Chester is convinced of it, and his efforts to protect the Monroes are laconically observed and recounted by Harold, the family dog. Older children can appreciate Harold's clever observations and his very dog-like concern for food. There are several pun-filled sequels in this series, including *The Celery Stalks at Midnight, Howliday Inn,* and *Bunnicula Strikes Again!*

Other introductions to animal fantasy are Beverly Cleary's *The Mouse and the Motorcycle, Runaway Ralph,* and *Ralph S. Mouse.* In the first story, Ralph makes friends with a boy who gives him a small toy motorcycle. *Run-*

Talking Point

Does fantasy and fantasizing harm children?

Go to the Online Learning Center at **www.mhhe.com/kiefer9e** or the Resources CD-ROM to learn more.

away Ralph continues Ralph's adventures with the motorcycle. In the third story, to escape his jealous mouse relatives, Ralph goes to school in the pocket of his friend Ryan, becomes a class project, and loses his precious motorcycle but gains a sports car. Cleary's excursions into the world of fantasy are as well accepted by children as are her realistic humorous stories of Henry Huggins and Ramona Quimby.

Michael Bond's Paddington series continues to please children who are just discovering the pleasures of being able to read longer books. Bond's first book, *A Bear Called Paddington,* introduces readers to the bear found in a London railway station and taken home by the Brown family. Paddington earnestly tries to help the Browns, but invariably ends up in difficulty. There are many other books in the series, and the numerous commercial spinoffs from this popular series have made Paddington a household word.

British writer Dick King-Smith introduces Thomas, Richard, and Henry Gray, three intrepid mouse brothers, in *Three Terrible Trins.* Their mother is determined that the boys will not meet the same unhappy fate as their father, who was killed at the paws of Bertha the cat. She undertakes a rigorous training schedule, the outcome of which is to produce three guerrilla fighters in the cause of mousedom. In a hilarious sequence of events the trins not only rid the house of cats but also convince Farmer and Mrs. Budge, the human owners, that mice are pretty good companions to have around. The title character of Avi's *Poppy* is an equally fearless mouse heroine who is willing to brave the terrible Mr. Oxcax, an owl bully who

---

[11]Lloyd Alexander, "The Flat-Heeled Muse," in *Children and Literature,* ed. Virginia Haviland (Glenview, Ill.: Scott, Foresman, 1973), p. 243.

has run a protection racket in Dimwood Forest for years. Poppy defeats the owl bully with the help of a grumpy porcupine and finds a desperately needed new home for her large mouse family.

In another mouse story, poet Lilian Moore gives younger readers a chance to think about the art of poetry. In *I'll Meet You at the Cucumbers*, Adam, a country mouse, shares his love for his natural surroundings with his mouse pen-pal friend, Amanda, who lives in the city. When he finally visits Amanda, Adam is nearly overwhelmed by all that the city has to offer. But his best discovery is the library, where Amanda tells him about human story hour and all the wonderful stories humans have written about mice. Amanda finally shows Adam that the thoughts he has written to her are really poems when she reads aloud poetry by Judith Thurman and Valerie Worth. In this gentle and humorous book, Moore skirts the "city mouse/country mouse" issue of which place is best in order to deal with larger themes. She helps readers think about the value of new experiences and new friendships, and the way poetry helps us see the world from a fresh perspective.

The same qualities of wonder and tenderness are found in the story of a small brown bat who becomes a poet in Randall Jarrell's *The Bat-Poet*. A perfect story and a commentary on the writing of poetry itself, it features a bat who cannot sleep during the day and makes up poems. The other bats aren't interested, and the mockingbird comments only on the form of his poem. The chipmunk, however, is delighted with his poems and believes them. The fine pen-and-ink drawings by Maurice Sendak are as faithful to the world of nature as are the animals and the poetry in this story.

Poetry is not foremost in the mind of Shade, another bat, but he is kin to the Bat-Poet in his longing for something different, something more beautiful, than the life he knows. Kenneth Oppel has created a captivating trilogy about Shade in *Silverwing*, *Sunwing*, and *Firewing*. As his story begins, Shade, a fatherless runt, is desperately trying to grow strong in order to accompany his colony on their migration to their winter hibernating ground. Shade is a weakling who, according to some in his colony, should have been killed at birth. Even worse, he is curious and a dreamer. When he violates animal law in order to see the sun rise, he sets in motion terrible consequences for himself and his colony. He also opens possibilities for a new and better way of life for them all. On his adventures he encounters fearsome owls and pigeons, traditional bat enemies. Even more loathsome is Goth, a huge vampire bat, and his sidekick, Throbb. As with all heroes, however, Shade has the support of helpful companions—Ariel, his loving mother; Frieda, the venerable head of the council of Silverwing elders; and Marina, a Brightwing bat. Marina is another bat outsider, expelled from her colony because she has a silver band on her wing. Ultimately, this sign of human contact drives the continuing mystery and adventure in the trilogy. Oppel weaves his

thrilling stories around bat lore and builds a believable fantasy world that will entrance middle graders.

Clem Martini has developed a similarly believable world of crows in *The Mob*. As in the Silverwing series, the plot develops when a young outsider, Kyp ru Kurea, breaks the rules and is evicted from the flock. Ultimately, it is Kyp whose defiant behavior saves the group. Martini's characters are developed out of an extensive understanding of crow behavior. It is that very behavior, however, that lends itself to this sensitive examination of the conflict between generations, and between new ideas and old traditions, that affects human communities.

Unquestionably the most beloved animal fantasy of our time is E. B. White's delightful tale *Charlotte's Web*. While much of our fantasy is of English origin, *Charlotte's Web* is as American as the Fourth of July and just as much a part of our children's heritage. Eight-year-old Fern can understand all of the animals in the barnyard—the geese who always speak in triplicate ("certainly-ertainly-ertainly"), the wise old sheep, and Templeton, the crafty rat—yet she cannot communicate with them. The true heroine of the story is Charlotte A. Cavatica—a beautiful large gray spider who befriends Wilbur, a humble little pig. When the kindly old sheep inadvertently drops the news that as soon as Wilbur is nice and fat he will be butchered, Charlotte promises to save the hysterical pig. By miraculously spinning words into her web that describe the pig as "radiant," "terrific," and "humble," she

A loyal Charlotte spins out her opinion of her friend Wilbur in Garth Williams's illustration for E. B. White's *Charlotte's Web*. Illustration from *Charlotte's Web* by E. B. White, illustrations by Garth Williams. Illustrations copyright renewed © 1980 by the Estate of Garth Williams. Used by permission of HarperCollins Publishers.

makes Wilbur famous. The pig is saved, but Charlotte dies alone at the fairgrounds. Wilbur manages to bring Charlotte's egg sac back to the farm so that the continuity of life in the barnyard is maintained. Wilbur never forgets his friend Charlotte, though he loves her children and grandchildren dearly. Because of her, Wilbur may look forward to a secure and pleasant old age:

> Life in the barn was very good—night and day, winter and summer, spring and fall, dull days and bright days. It was the best place to be, thought Wilbur, this warm delicious cellar, with the garrulous geese, the changing seasons, the heat of the sun, the passage of swallows, the nearness of rats, the sameness of sheep, the love of spiders, the smell of manure, and the glory of everything.[12]

This story has humor, pathos, wisdom, and beauty. Its major themes speak of the web of true friendship and the cycle of life and death. All ages find meaning in this most popular fantasy.

Children also enjoy two other animal fantasies by White, *Stuart Little* and *The Trumpet of the Swan*. Neither book has all the strengths of *Charlotte's Web*, but both appeal to children for their curious blend of fantasy and reality.

Alan Armstrong's *Whittington* will remind children of *Charlotte's Web* with its strong rural setting, memorable cast of characters, and poignant stories. At the beginning of the story Whittington the cat, somewhat the worse for wear, arrives at Bernie's barn and politely requests admittance to the animal community. Lady, a duck that was "lopsided and lurched," consults the other animals, among them a pair of horses rescued from the knacker's yard and Corragio, the bombastic rooster, and his harem of bantam hens. Whittington is invited to stay and proves to be a needed addition to the community. A gifted storyteller and skillful conflict negotiator, Whittington is descended from the cat who helped Dick Whittington make his fortune in London in the late fourteenth century. There are three interwoven stories here: that of the original Dick Whittington and his cat; the story of Ben and Abby, two orphaned children who are struggling with learning disabilities; and the ongoing events of the seasons on the farm. Armstrong does a skillful job of telling these tales, and children are sure to find satisfaction and enjoyment in *Whittington*.

The English counterpart of Wilbur the pig is Daggie Dogfoot, the runt hero of Dick King-Smith's *Pigs Might Fly*. Saved from the Pigman's club by luck and his own determination, Daggie watches birds and aspires to fly. He discovers instead a talent for swimming that allows him to help rescue all the pigs from a flood. Like E. B. White's barn, the pigyard and pastures here are described

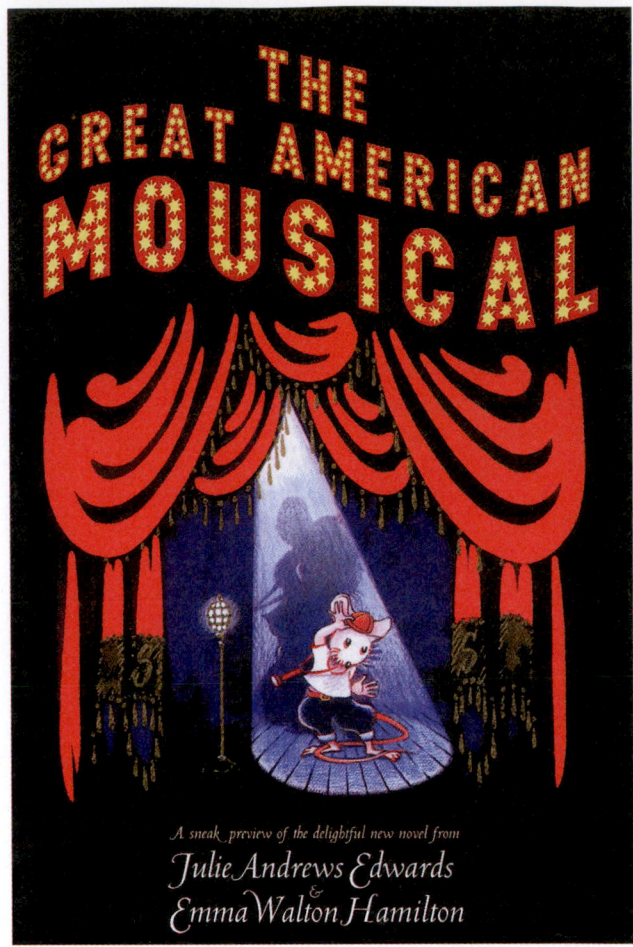

Julie Andrews Edwards and Emma Walton Hamilton use their knowledge of musical theater to give life to the delightful animal fantasy *The Great American Mousical*. Jacket from *The Great American Mousical* by Andrews and Emma Walton Hamilton. Jacket illustration copyright © 2006 by Tony Walton. Used by permission of HarperColllins Publishers.

in sharp, sensory detail, and the animals' conversations reflect the author's shrewd perceptions about human as well as animal nature. Another pig hero is King-Smith's *Babe: The Gallant Pig*, whose remarkable ability to speak politely to sheep gains him a stunning victory in a sheep-dog trial meet. In *Ace: The Very Important Pig*, Babe's great-grandson even manages to communicate with his owner in this joyful and absurd continuation of a barnyard saga.

In *Rabbit Hill*, Robert Lawson has written a satisfying and tender story about all the little animals who live on Rabbit Hill. When they discover that new folks are moving into the big house on the hill, the animals are worried: Will they be planting folks who like small animals, or shiftless, mean people? Although on probation for several days after their arrival, the new folks win approval by putting up a large sign that says: "Please Drive Carefully on Account of Small Animals."

---

[12]E. B. White, *Charlotte's Web*, illustrated by Garth Williams (New York: Harper & Row, 1952), p. 183.

Urban counterparts of *Charlotte's Web* and *Rabbit Hill* can be found in two charming animal fantasies. In *The Cricket in Times Square* by George Selden, a fast-talking Broadway mouse named Tucker and his pal, Harry the Cat, initiate a small country cricket called Chester into the vagaries of city living. Chester spends the summer in New York City, having been transported there in someone's picnic basket. The climax of Chester's summer adventures comes when the cricket begins giving nightly concerts from the Bellinis' newsstand, saving his benefactors from bankruptcy. A Broadway benefit is also the aim in *The Great American Mousical* by Julie Andrews Edwards and Emma Walton Hamilton. This performance is planned by a colony of mice and headlined by Adelaide, the greatest mouse Broadway has ever seen. The mice have been living for generations in a subbasement of a venerable Broadway theater, where they use the architectural model of the theater as their stage. They are getting ready to put on the performance of their lives when Adelaide goes missing; she has wandered into a mouse trap and is (humanely) dumped out in the country by a kindly truck driver. Adelaide's struggle to make the performance and the mice's preparations for the great moment add up to a madcap story that will surely entice young thespians into putting on their own shows.

In chronicling the year-long survival of a mouse on an island, William Steig firmly establishes himself as a superb author as well as illustrator. *Abel's Island* details the survival of Abel, a very Victorian mouse, who is trapped on an island after being caught in a torrential rainstorm. Left on his own, this rodent Crusoe finds a hollow log and learns to feed off the land. In addition to battling physical elements, he overcomes the psychological fears of loneliness and overwhelming despair. Finally, after almost a year of foraging for himself, Abel is able, and easily swims the distance to shore. Creating more than a mouse melodrama, Steig shows us what qualities help a mouse or person survive. Abel relies on his resourcefulness, but he is kept alive by his love for his wife, Amanda, his art, his friendship with a forgetful frog, and his joy of life.

Tor Seidler has created a memorable cast of animal and human characters in *Mean Margaret*. The story begins when Fred, a fastidious bachelor woodchuck, finally gives in to matrimonial urges and marries the lovely Phoebe. Soon a little one arrives in the burrow. Unfortunately for Fred, the newcomer is not a baby woodchuck but an utterly terrible 2-year-old human child who has been abandoned in a ditch by her older siblings. Kindhearted Phoebe cannot bear to leave the helpless child out in the cold, and Margaret (whom they name for Phoebe's mother) is brought home to the burrow, where she wreaks havoc and turns Fred's cozy life upside down. When Margaret is finally returned to her rightful human family, she has been oddly humanized by her stay with the animals. In addition, the lives of her animal guardians, particularly Fred's, have been changed,

Abel contemplates his fate from the sheltered branch of his home away from home in William Steig's *Abel's Island*.
Reprinted by permission of Farrar, Straus & Giroux, LLC: Jacket design from *Abel's Island* by William Steig. Copyright © 1976 by William Steig.

one might even say humanized, by the sacrifices they had to make for her.

What E. B. White did to popularize and humanize spiders, Robert C. O'Brien has accomplished for rats in *Mrs. Frisby and the Rats of NIMH*. Part of the story, which could be categorized either as animal fantasy or as science fiction, concerns the widowed mouse Mrs. Frisby and her efforts to save her family and their cement-block house in the garden from the spring plowing. The other part gradually reveals the history of a remarkable band of rats who—along with Mrs. Frisby's late husband—were trained to read and write in a laboratory at NIMH (National Institute for Mental Health—although it is never so identified in the story). When Mrs. Frisby meets the rats of NIMH, they are just completing a plan to move to a wilderness preserve where they can establish a self-sufficient community. The rats agree to help move the cement block, thus saving Mrs. Frisby's family, and she returns the favor by warning them about government exterminators who are coming with cyanide gas. Jane Conly, O'Brien's daughter, has written two sequels. In *Racso and the Rats of NIMH*, Mrs. Frisby's son Timothy meets

Racso, a cocky and streetwise rat from the city, locates the rat preserve, and cooperates with the rats to thwart the building of a dam that would flood their home. Short chapters, fast-moving plots advanced frequently by conversation, and memorable characters help make this longer book accessible and exciting to readers. The Literature in Action box on keeping journals shows how journals helped sixth graders respond to *Mrs. Frisby and the Rats of NIMH.*

The well-loved *The Wind in the Willows* by Kenneth Grahame endures even though it is slow-paced, idyllic, and more sentimental than more-modern animal fantasy. It is the story of four friends: kindly and gruff old Badger; practical and good-natured Ratty; gullible Mole; and boisterous, expansive, and easily misled Toad. Toad gets into one scrape after another, and the other three loyally rescue their errant friend and finally save his elegant mansion from a band of wicked weasels and stoats. The themes of friendship, the importance of a home place, and love of nature pervade this pastoral fantasy. Not all children have the experience or patience with words

to appreciate this book, but generations of parents have read it aloud a chapter at a time, which is perhaps the best way to introduce the book.

The villainous animals threatening Toad Hall in *The Wind in the Willows* are the same sorts who threaten Redwall Abbey in Brian Jacques's Redwall books. But this series is swiftly told, complexly plotted, and action-packed by comparison. Redwall tells of Matthias, a clumsy, young, and peace-loving mouse, who galvanizes himself to defeat the evil rat, Cluny the Scourge. Aided by Cornflower the Fieldmouse, Constance the Badger, and Brother Methuselah, Matthias's efforts to fortify the Abbey alternate with chapters of the terrible Cluny subduing woodland creatures to his will. The sinister names of Cluny's band (Fangborn, Cheesethief, Ragear, Mangefur) alert young readers to the evil characters. In fact, one of the major appeals of the Redwall stories is that one never doubts that good will triumph. The series resembles high fantasy (discussed later in this section), in that good and evil battle for possession of the Redwall Abbey world; quests are undertaken; the heroes are small, un-

LITERATURE IN **ACTION**

Journals Help Children Understand Fantasy

In September, a sixth-grade language arts teacher asked her students to keep a journal and react to Robert C. O'Brien's *Mrs. Frisby and the Rats of NIMH.* She divided the book into about ten parts, and children responded in their journals after reading each assignment. The diversity of the children's responses shows how differently individual readers engage with a story.

One girl challenged the believability of this fantasy: "I wonder where Mr. Ages gets the paper for the bags for medicine? . . . I wonder how Mrs. Frisby can hold on to Jeremy's back. She's too small to wrap her 'arms' around it. I also wonder how mice can understand people talk." The teacher acknowledged her concerns and invited her to try to find some answers. She also reminded her that this was an animal fantasy that had its own rules.

Another girl sympathized with Mrs. Frisby's very modern predicament and mused about the humor of the story: "Mrs. Frisby has a lot on her mind being a single parent with four children and one sick in bed with pneumonia. I would feel really pressured like that and Moving Day coming. . . . I like the crow Jeremy. He's funny and stupid. He picked up the string because it was *sparkly.* (That's cute.)" The teacher called attention to the way an author creates believability when she wrote back, "O'Brien has given the crow some human characteristics but has kept the animal habits faithful to the species."

Children asked questions: "I don't understand what the Boniface Estate is," said one. "I still have a question. What does *NIMH* stand for?" asked another. A third lamented,

"All my questions aren't answered yet. I may seem like a bottomless pit of questions." The teacher reassured them that it is fine to have questions, clarified meanings, or referred a child to a classmate or back to a page in the book.

Some children worried about the morality of experimenting on animals: "I am very very very very very mad that they give those poor rats shocks plus giving the rats injections. I think it is very mean." "It made me wonder if given injections, animals are in as much pain as they look." The teacher asked children to talk about the animal experimentation in this story and scientific experimentation in general.

In their final journal entries, some children were dissatisfied with the ending. "I think he should have put more pictures in and made the story a couple of chapters longer. He should have said something about like how Jeremy had a family." "Who died in the rat hole?" Others found the sequels and filled themselves in on what happened next.

Writing journals allowed the children to work out the meaning of the story for themselves. They also revealed themselves to the teacher in ways that would help her plan discussions, choose books, select writing topics, and diversify instruction for the rest of the school year.

Based on journals selected from the sixth-grade language arts class taught by Susan Steinberg
George Mason Elementary School, Alexandria, Virginia

prepared, and sometimes unwilling; and courage, truth, wisdom, and goodness are finally rewarded. Even though these books are long, they provide satisfaction to readers who enjoy adventurous quests, humor, and intrigue but are not yet ready for the deeper themes, ambiguous characters, or created worlds of high fantasy.

In works of animal fantasy such as the Redwall series, the animal characters are really humans in disguise. Other authors like David Clement-Davies, Richard Adams, and Soinbhe Lally have attempted to stay closer to the animal natures of their characters. Although Clement-Davies has woven traditional elements of mythology into *The Sight*, about a herd of deer, and *Fire Bringer*, about a Transylvanian wolf clan, his animals have the characteristics of their kind. They are not deer and wolves dressed up in medieval clothing. Older readers will be spellbound by these stories of the battle of good and evil set within believably authentic animal worlds.

Richard Adams's *Watership Down*, published as adult fiction in the United States, is the remarkable story of a rabbit band who cherish their freedom enough to fight for it. The book is lengthy and complex, but many older children have found it compelling. Adams has created a complete rabbit civilization, including a history, a religion, a mythology, and even a lapine language with a partial set of accompanying linguistic rules. The central character is Hazel, a young buck who leads a little band of bucks away from their old warren, which is doomed by a new housing tract. He does so reluctantly but at the urging of his younger, weaker brother, Fiver, who has a form of extrasensory perception. The slow, steady growth of Hazel as a leader is told in this surprisingly unsentimental, even tough, story. It is more realistic than most "realism," because the story is firmly rooted in a world we feel we know: Rabbits mate, make droppings, and talk and joke about both, very much as humans do. They get hurt, bleed, and suffer; they grow ugly with age, and they die. During the band's storytelling sessions, readers learn of El-ahrairah, the great chief rabbit and trickster. In a remarkable creation legend and a deeply moving story, a rabbit redeemer braves the palace of death to offer his own life for his people. And at the end of the book, when one of the does tells her little one a new story of El-ahrairah, we know that she is telling a garbled version of the story of the establishment of Watership Down and adding Hazel's accomplishments to those of the legendary rabbit—a comment on the entire process of mythmaking. When *Watership Down* was first published in England, one reviewer maintained that the "story is what one might expect had *The Wind in the Willows* been written after two world wars, various marks of nuclear bomb, the Korean and Vietnam obscenities and half a dozen other hells created by the inexhaustibly evil powers of man."[13]

A Hive for the Honeybee by Soinbhe Lally is an unusual animal fantasy that begins as an aged queen bee and many of her attendants leave their hive to find another home. The bees left behind await the arrival of a new queen and carry on with the life of the hive. We meet Thora, a young worker bee who dares to imagine a life of contemplation; Mo, a drone who is a political radical; and Alfred, another drone who composes poems and ponders the meaning of life. Each of them reacts in different ways to the demands of their position within the hive, but like the rabbits in *Watership Down* these bees cannot escape the limitations of their nature. At the close of the book with winter approaching, Mo, Alfred, and the other drones are refused entrance to the hive and fly off to their predetermined end. Thora too, now old and tired, makes her last flight in the dying rays of the autumn sun. This allegory demands sophisticated readers, but it is richly imagined and raises intriguing questions about human behavior that could evoke thoughtful discussion among such children.

The World of Toys and Dolls

As authors have endowed animals with human characteristics, so, too, have they personified toys and dolls. Young children enjoy stories that bring inanimate objects such as a tugboat or a steam shovel to life. Seven-, 8-, and 9-year-olds still like to imagine that their favorite playthings have a life of their own. Hans Christian Andersen appealed to this desire in "The Steadfast Tin Soldier," "The Fir Tree," and many other stories.

Probably no one has made toys seem quite so much like people as has A. A. Milne in his well-loved Pooh stories. Each chapter contains a separate adventure about the favorite stuffed toys of Milne's son, Christopher Robin. The good companions introduced in *Winnie the Pooh* include Winnie-the-Pooh, "a bear of little brain"; Eeyore, the doleful donkey; Piglet, the happy follower and devoted friend of Pooh; and Rabbit, Owl, Kanga, and little Roo. A bouncy new friend, Tigger, joins the group in Milne's second book, *The House at Pooh Corner*. They all live in the "100 Aker Wood" and spend most of their time getting into—and out of—exciting and amusing situations. Eight- and 9-year-olds thoroughly enjoy the humor of the Heffalump story, the self-pity of gloomy Eeyore on his birthday, and kindly but forgetful Pooh, who knocks at his own door and then wonders why no one answers. The humor in these stories is not hilarious but quiet, whimsical, and subtle. Such humor is usually lost on young children but greatly appreciated by third graders. However, younger children might enjoy the Pooh stories when they are read within a family circle. Parents' chuckles are contagious, and soon everyone in the family becomes a Pooh admirer.

---

[13]Aidan Chambers, "Letter from England: Great Leaping Lapins!" *Horn Book Magazine*, June 1973, p. 255.

Kate DiCamillo has created a memorable rabbit doll in *The Miraculous Journey of Edward Tulane*. Edward is a very handsome, very narcissistic doll made almost entirely of china—with real rabbit-hair ears and tail and a wardrobe of elegant costumes. He is passionately loved by his mistress, Abilene, but he is coldly immune to her affections. It is only when he falls overboard on an ocean voyage that his travail and his humanization begin. Passed over the years from one human to another, Edward gradually comes to open his heart to his need for love. Although the book is sure to remind readers of Margery Williams's *The Velveteen Rabbit* (see Chapter 3), DiCamillo has created a fresh and moving examination of the relationship between children and their beloved toys.

Miss Hickory by Carolyn Bailey is the story of a unique country doll whose body is an applewood twig and whose head is a hickory nut. Miss Hickory has all the common sense and forthright qualities that her name implies. She survives a severe New Hampshire winter in the company of her friends—Crow, Bull Frog, Ground Hog, and Squirrel.

Annabelle Doll is 8 years old going on 108 in Ann Martin and Laura Godwin's *The Doll People* and *The Meanest Doll in the World*. In *The Doll People* Annabelle and her family live in a lovely Victorian dollhouse that was imported from England to America in 1898 for a little girl named Gertrude Cox. The dollhouse and the porcelain dolls have been handed down to succeeding generations of girls and to their present owner, Kate Palmer. The members of the Doll family have been fairly content with their lives. However, Annabelle begins to feel restless and bored. When she finds the diary of her long-lost Auntie Sarah, Annabelle vows to solve the mystery of Sarah's disappearance. Breaking a long-held Doll taboo, Annabelle leaves the dollhouse one night, searching for answers. Instead of Auntie Sarah, however, she discovers the Funcraft family in their plastic dollhouse, a modern set bought for Nora, Kate's devilish younger sister. Life for Annabelle and the Doll family becomes much more adventuresome with these new neighbors, and eventually they all band together to find Auntie Sarah. In *The Meanest Doll in the World* Annabelle and her best friend, Tiffany Funcraft, wind up in a house terrorized by Mimi, a princess doll who thinks she rules the world. These two books are charming stories and will resonate with every child who has wondered if her dolls might come to life at night after she has gone to sleep.

In her books about the Mennyms, Sylvia Waugh has created a family of three generations of dolls who have survived after the death of the old woman who made them.

> They were not human you see—at least not in the normal sense of the word. They were not made of flesh and blood. They were just a whole lovely family of life-size ragdolls. They were living and walking and talking and breathing,

Kate DiCamillo's *The Miraculous Journey of Edward Tulane* centers on a child's doll whose cold heart is finally awakened to love. *The Miraculous Journey of Edward Tulane*. Written by Kate DiCamillo. Illustration copyright © 2006 Bargram Ibatoulline. Reproduced by permission of the publisher Candlewick Press, Inc., Cambridge, MA.

> but they were made of cloth and kapok. They each had a little voicebox, like the sort they put in teddy bears to make them growl realistically. Their frameworks were strong but pliable. Their respiration kept their bodies supplied with oxygen that was life to the kapok and sound to the voices. (p. 17)

These are fully realized characters, doll-like only in that they are made of cloth and stuffing. Otherwise, they have the same idiosyncrasies, quarrels, and desires as any other family, and these conflicts are played out in all five tautly paced stories. In *The Mennyms* the dolls are faced with the threat of discovery after successfully hiding their secret for forty years. In trying to avoid this disaster, they discover a new sister hidden in an old trunk in the attic. In *The Mennyms in the Wilderness*, Brocklehurst Grove, the only home they have ever known, is threatened by a superhighway. In *The Mennyms under Siege*, the family secret is in danger of being revealed by an impetuous Mennym and a nosy neighbor. *The Mennyms Alone* and *The Mennyms Alive* complete this unusual series. The Mennym family members are so beautifully realized that children will be reluctant to close the covers of these imaginative books.

In *The Indian in the Cupboard* by Lynne Reid Banks, a toy plastic Indian comes to life when Omri puts it inside a cupboard, locks it, and then unlocks it with a special key. Nine-year-old Omri feels pride and responsibility in caring for "his" Indian, Little Bear, and is quickly involved in providing for his needs. But trouble begins when Omri's friend Patrick places a cowboy in the cupboard. The British author uses stereotypical language in this and the other books in the series ("Little Bear fight like mountain lion. Take many scalps!"), but the characters transcend this in their growing concern for each other's welfare. Banks suggests once again to readers that we are responsible for what we have tamed or brought to life.

Elizabeth Winthrop's *The Castle in the Attic* also examines responsibility for one's own actions. Although an accomplished gymnast, 10-year-old William lacks confidence in himself. When he hears that Mrs. Phillips, his lifelong friend and live-in baby-sitter, is returning to her native England, he is crushed but determined to find a way to make her stay. Inside her parting gift to him, a huge model of a castle that has been in her family for generations, William discovers a tiny lead knight that comes to life at his touch. The knight shows William a charm that can be used to miniaturize objects or people, and William uses it to reduce his baby-sitter to toy size and keep her in the castle. Regretting this hasty act, he submits himself to the charm, travels back in time with the knight, and recovers the amulet that will reverse the spell. On this quest William discovers unexpected strengths in himself. He returns victorious, prepared to wish Mrs. Phillips farewell. In *The Battle for the Castle* Mrs. Phillips sends William a magic token for his twelfth birthday; twelve was the age at which a young man could be trained as a squire in the Middle Ages. The token allows William to return to the land of the castle, where further adventures teach him about love, courage, and loyalty. The strong grounding in reality and the elaborately described castle give these fantasies special appeal for upper-elementary students.

Another strangely cruel yet tender tale by Russell Hoban, *The Mouse and His Child,* tells of two windup toys and their efforts to become "self-winding." New and shiny in the toy shop the day before Christmas, the naive little toys end up on the rubbish heap in the cruel clutches of Manny Rat. In their long and tedious journey, they search for a home, a family, and "their territory." The story is not a gentle one. It is filled with images of death and decay, violence and vengeance, tears, and laughter. Like Carroll's *Alice's Adventures in Wonderland,* the complex ideas, satire, and symbolism might appeal more to mature readers than to young children. Yet it is a fantasy that is not easily forgotten.

Eccentric Characters and Preposterous Situations

Many fantasies for children are based on eccentric characters or preposterous situations. Cars or people might fly, eggs might hatch into dinosaurs or dragons, ancient magical beings might come up against modern technology. Often these characters and situations occur in otherwise very normal settings—which allows readers to believe more readily.

Pippi Longstocking, a notoriously funny character created by Astrid Lindgren, has delighted children for more than fifty years. Pippi is an orphan who lives alone with her monkey and her horse in a child's utopian world where she tells herself when to go to bed and when to get up! Although she is only 9 years old, Pippi can hold her own with anyone, for she is so strong that she can pick up a horse or a man and throw him into the air. Children love this amazing character who always has the integrity to say what she thinks, even if she shocks adults. Seven-, 8-, and 9-year-olds enjoy her madcap adventures in *Pippi Longstocking* and in the sequels, *Pippi Goes on Board, Pippi in the South Seas,* and *Pippi on the Run.*

When the east wind blew the title character of P. L. Travers's *Mary Poppins* into the Bankses' house in London to care for Michael and Jane, it blew her into the hearts of many thousands of readers. Wearing her shapeless hat and white gloves and carrying her parrot-handled umbrella and a large carpetbag, this nursemaid with strange magical powers is beloved by children all over the world. Nothing seems impossible for this prim autocrat of the nursery, as she goes serenely on her way through other funny adventures in *Mary Poppins Comes Back, Mary Poppins Opens the Door,* and *Mary Poppins in the Park.* In 1981 Travers revised *Mary Poppins,* originally published in 1934, in response to criticism of racial stereotypes in the first edition.

A nursemaid for the twenty-first century can be found in Debi Gliori's hilarious Pure Dead series. Mrs. Flora MacLachlan is hired to look after the Strega-Borgia children: Titus, Pandora, and Damp, the baby, so named for obvious reasons. Mrs. MacLachlan takes the castle of StregaSchloss ("three miles from the little Highland town of Auchenlochtercuhty") in stride. Wielding a handheld computer rather than an umbrella to make her magic, Mrs. MacLachlan deals efficiently with a cast of eccentric human characters that includes Great-great-great-great great-great-grandmother Strega Nona, who is cryogenically preserved in the basement freezer. She also deftly juggles the needs of the "wee pets," among them Sab, the griffin; Ffup, the dragon; and Kot, the yeti. These are madcap stories whose wordplay older children will particularly enjoy.

Mr. Popper's Penguins by Richard Atwater and Florence Atwater has long been the favorite funny story of many primary-grade children. Mr. Popper is a mild little house painter whose major interest in life is the study of the Antarctic. When an explorer presents Mr. Popper with a penguin, he promptly names him Captain Cook, and he obtains Greta from the zoo to keep Captain Cook company. After the arrival of ten baby penguins, Mr. Popper puts a freezing plant in the basement of his house and moves his furnace upstairs to the living room. The Atwaters' serious account of a highly implausible situation adds to the humor of this truly funny story.

One of the most popular fantasies for children is Roald Dahl's tongue-in-cheek morality tale *Charlie and the Chocolate Factory*. Mr. Willie Wonka suddenly announces that the five children who find the gold seal on their chocolate bars will be allowed to visit his fabulous factory. One by one the children disobey Willie and meet with horrible accidents in the chocolate factory, except of course for the virtuous and humble Charlie, who by the story's conclusion has brought his poor family to live in the chocolate factory and is learning the business from his benefactor.

In Dahl's *James and the Giant Peach,* James, one of the saddest and loneliest boys in the world, lives with his wicked aunts in an old, ramshackle house on a high hill in the south of England. Given a bag of green crystals by an old man, James hurries home with them, but he trips and falls, and all of the magic crystals disappear into the ground under an old peach tree. In the enormous peach that grows on the tree, James discovers six amazing creatures who have been waiting for him. When one of them, a centipede, gnaws off the stem, the huge peach rolls down the hill, incidentally crushing the aunts, and the marvelous adventure begins. This book is popular with children of all ages. Its short chapters make it a good read-aloud selection for first and second graders, as well as for older children.

Allan Ahlberg's *The Giant Baby* is another book that will delight 7- to 9-year-olds. Alice Hicks desperately wants a baby brother, but her parents insist there's no room in their little house. When late one night thunderous footsteps approach the Hicks house and then fade off into silence, Alice is delighted to discover a big bundle left on the doorstep. Inside is an amazingly large baby. The Hicksses are flabbergasted. Feeding the baby is a bit of a problem, and changing diapers is an even bigger difficulty. Pretty soon the giant baby is no secret in the neighborhood. The press gets wind of the story, and this brings onto the scene the Grubbling Brothers, circus people who are down on their luck, and other villains. The giant baby keeps falling into the wrong hands, but Alice and her friends keep rescuing him. Finally, the biggest rescue of all occurs when the giant baby's giant mother returns for her "little baby." Alice, who "had wanted a baby brother, got one and lost him," is inconsolable. But happily after all, Mr. and Mrs. Hicks had gotten quite attached to the big baby, so at the very end Alice is invited to the hospital to meet her new and "proper size" baby brother. This is a delightful story told with wit and warm good humor that is given added zest by Fritz Wegner's pen-and-ink illustrations.

Like the giant baby, Gnat Stokes is a larger-than-life character, but her encounters with strange situations are somewhat more sinister in *Gnat Stokes and the Foggy Bottom Swamp Queen* by Sally M. Keehn. Gnat is a mother-less child who is an outcast in her Appalachian community. When she sets out to battle the evil Swamp Queen to rescue a young man who has gone missing, she finds danger, adventure, and her own identity, not to mention a wonderful cat named Eat-More-Beans. Based on the "Tam Lin" folktale, Keehn's version is both funny and suspenseful. Gnat's colloquial, first-person narrative makes this a natural story to read aloud.

Philip Pullman, best known for the His Dark Materials trilogy, has written several lighthearted fantasies for younger readers with plenty of eccentric characters and outlandish situations. *I Was A Rat* is Pullman's hilarious spoof of old-fashioned fairy tales and modern tabloid publishing. Old Bob, a cobbler, and his wife, Joan, are a loving couple who have always missed having a child of their own. When they answer a knock at their door one evening, they find a little boy dressed in a tattered page's uniform. The child is confused about his origins and can only tell them, "I was a rat." The kindhearted couple take in the child, whom they name Roger, and they try to do their best by him. But rat nature and human nature soon complicate the plot. Roger can't seem to stop chewing things up, eating curtain tassels, pencils, and other strange fare. His odd behavior is spotted by a carnival shyster who kidnaps him and exhibits him as a half-human/half-rat monster. Bob and Joan are hot on his trail, however, and after a few more mishaps and some help from a newly married princess, Roger finds a happy home. The book makes the most of Cinderella and other traditional tales, and pokes fun at the media feeding frenzies that seem to accompany almost every aspect of modern life. Pullman's *The Scarecrow and His Servant* relates the strange adventures of a scarecrow who comes to life after he is struck by lightning. He enlists the help of young Jack, and they set off on a madcap journey to discover the scarecrow's identity. Little do the two realize that they are being pursued by the evil Buffalonis. *The Firework-Maker's Daughter* revolves around Lila, a girl whose temperament somewhat resembles the fireworks her father manufactures. Thwarted in her attempts to join the family business, Lila also undertakes a journey and faces a villain, Razvani the Firefiend. All these stories are, of course, happily resolved.

N. E. Bode's characters in *The Anybodies* are eccentric and preposterous. A family of shape-shifters, they have been separated from young Fern since she was switched at birth with the poor Howard Drudger. When the mistake is finally discovered, Fern goes to spend the summer with her father and discovers her own ability to make story characters come to life. After a close encounter with the evil Miser, Fern helps her father regain his lost shape-shifting abilities. In *The Nobodies*, the hilarious sequel, Fern and Howard go to a summer camp called Camp Happy Sunshine Good Times, which is, of course, anything but happy, sunshiney, and full of good times.

M. T. Anderson's *Whales on Stilts* is preposterous in a totally different vein. This uproariously silly takeoff of comic books and pulp fiction involves clueless adults and an evil villain. Larry, a half-human, half-whale (and Lily Gelfelty's father's boss), intends to take over the world by implanting whales with mind-controlling lasers. Only shy young Lily and her two intrepid friends, both heroes of their own adventure series, can save the day. In the end, Larry is defeated; the whales are returned to their natural habitat; and Lily, who has long underestimated her talents, is given her own adventure series.

Fish of a different sort figure in Heather Dyer's *The Fish in Room 11*. The Flots, a family of mer-people who live in a cave near the Grand Hotel, are at risk of exploitation by Mr. Harris, the greedy hotel manager, until young Toby steps in to stop him. Mr. Harris has grudgingly allowed Toby, found abandoned in one of the hotel rooms as an infant, to live in the Grand, in exchange for doing odd jobs. Toby encounters Eliza under the pier near the hotel one day and realizes that she is a mermaid. They soon become friends, and Eliza invites Toby back to the cave to meet her parents. When he leaves, the Flots give him a precious ring as a keepsake. Mr. Harris discovers the ring and is convinced it is part of a lost treasure. His get-rich-quick schemes soon threaten the existence of the Flots. Toby decides to hide them in plain sight in Room 11 of the Grand Hotel with the help of Mr. Harris's reclusive Aunt Margot and an old sea captain. Eventually, in this tale filled with comic coincidences, villainy is thwarted, treasure is recovered, and the mer-people are saved.

Older readers will find similar enjoyment in Patricia Kindl's *Owl in Love*. Owl Tycho is an unusual 14-year-old who belongs to a family of shape-shifters, and she has the ability to change into an owl. This causes great distress for her as she tries to fit into the teenage world. She can't eat in the cafeteria because her diet consists of grasshoppers and mice. She can't participate in the science class experiment on blood types because her blood is black. And worst of all she is madly in love with her science teacher, and state law says they cannot marry for several more years. This hilarious story finds Owl as troubled and torn as any other youngster trying to deal with the changing body and shifting emotions of adolescence, and her journey to self-understanding is no less poignant because it takes place in a tree in the cool night air as often as at a desk in a brightly lit classroom. Kindl's characterization is flawless and her sense of humor right on target for middle-school readers.

Golden and Grey by Louise Arnold involves a friendship between two highly eccentric characters. Tom Golden is a misfit at his new school who is made miserable by the taunts and tricks of his new classmates. His misery is so great that he cries out in the night, and his cry resonates with another misfit, Grey Authur, who can't seem to find a niche for himself in the world of ghosts. Grey Arthur instantly decides that his purpose in life is to be an invisible friend to Tom. Tom, of course, has no idea that Arthur is there until a group of bullies pushes him into the path of an oncoming car. The result of the

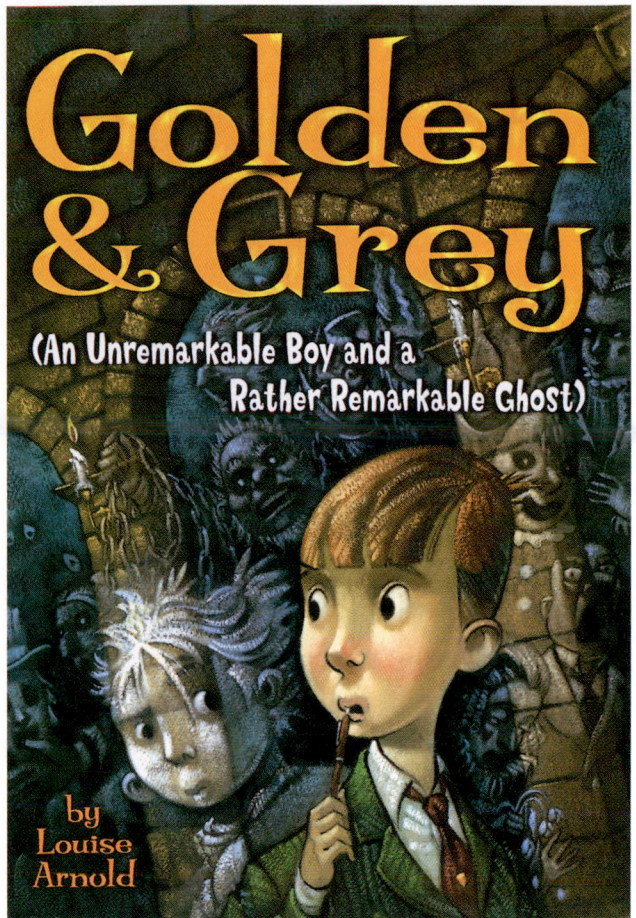

Two lonely outcasts, one human and one spectral, team up in Louise Arnold's enchanting *Golden and Grey*. Reprinted with permission of Margaret K. McElderry Books, an imprint of Simon & Schuster Children's Publishing Division from *Golden & Grey: An Unremarkable Boy and a Rather Remarkable Ghost* by Louise Arnold. Copyright © 2002 Louise Arnold.

knock on the head he receives is that Grey Arthur and all the other strange beings who live in the world of ghosts become visible to Tom. *Golden and Grey* is a charming story about friendship and identity that is fresh and funny, a welcome counterpoint to the many derivative books that have followed in Harry Potter's wake.

The title character of Susan Cooper's *The Boggart* is an ancient sort who must wrestle with the modern world. When a Canadian family inherits an old Scottish castle, they do not realize that the property includes the Boggart, an ancient and mischievous spirit. Trapped in a desk that the family ships back to Canada, the Boggart discovers a new world of technological wonders. His pranks, however, wreak havoc on the Volnik family, who blame each other for the Boggart's tricks. A solution is found only when the Volnik children and the Boggart enter the world of computer "magic" and the Boggart is returned to his familiar world. There he continues to play his tricks on the new owner of his castle home in *The Boggart and the Monster*. The beauty of Cooper's stories lies as much in the Boggart's thoroughly developed character as in the stories' well-paced plots. The Boggart is not simply a naughty spirit but one who has feelings and needs friends and companionship as much as any human child does.

Technology of a different sort is encountered in *The Twenty-One Balloons* by William Pène DuBois. Professor Sherman leaves San Francisco on 15 August 1883 in a hot-air balloon, telling reporters that he hopes to be the first person to fly across the Pacific Ocean. He is picked up three weeks later in the Atlantic Ocean clinging to the wreckage of a platform that has been flown through the air by twenty-one balloons. The story, told as the professor's speech to the Explorers' Club, recounts his forced landing on the volcanic island of Krakatoa, where he discovers twenty families who live over the most fabulous diamond mine in the world. The professor describes in graphic detail the inventions and customs of Krakatoans and their escape when the volcano erupts. As usual, DuBois's minute descriptions are matched only by the meticulous perfection of his pen-and-ink drawings.

It seems preposterous to try to raise a dinosaur in a small New Hampshire town. However, that is precisely what Nate Twitchell does in Oliver Butterworth's *The Enormous Egg* when the egg he is taking care of hatches into a baby triceratops. Consulted about the problem, members of Congress attempt to have "Uncle Beazley" (the dinosaur) destroyed, since he is extinct and probably un-American! This satire on U.S. politics is a delightful mixture of humor and truth.

A preposterous situation is presented in one of the few satires really enjoyed by children, Jean Merrill's *The Pushcart War*. The story is presented as a "documented report" of the famous Pushcart War of 1996 (more than thirty years in the future when the book was first published). Believing that we cannot have peace in the world unless people understand how wars start, the "author-historian" proceeds to describe the beginning of the war, between the giant trucks of New York City and the pushcarts, that began when Mack, driver of the Mighty Mammoth, rode down the cart of Morris the Florist. The straight-faced account of the progress of the war and the eventual triumph of the pushcart peddlers provides a funny and pathetic commentary on life today. Children thoroughly enjoy this satire; in fact, when one fifth-grade class returned for report cards on the last day of school, they stayed an extra hour to hear their teacher finish reading the book. Few books can claim such devotion!

Extraordinary Worlds

When Alice followed the White Rabbit down his rabbit hole and entered a world that grew "curiouser and curiouser," she established a pattern for many modern books of fantasy. Often starting in the world of reality, they move quickly into a world where the everyday becomes extraordinary, yet still believable. The plausible impossibilities of Lewis Carroll's *Alice's Adventures in Wonderland* include potions and edibles that make poor Alice grow up

and down like an elevator. Always the proper Victorian young lady, however, Alice maintains her own personality despite her bizarre surroundings, and her acceptance of this nonsense makes it all seem believable. She is the one link with reality in this amazingly fantastic world.

The British landscape where Alice's adventures began has formed the setting for many other fine works of fantasy. *Harry Potter and the Sorcerer's Stone,* the first book in J. K. Rowling's phenomenally popular series, begins in what seems to be a run-of-the-mill middle-class neighborhood as Mr. Dursley picks up his briefcase, bids his wife and son goodbye, and heads off to work. As he drives off, however, he fails to notice a cat sitting on the street reading a map. Mr. Dursley might be clueless, but readers know immediately that this is no ordinary work of realism. They are soon immersed in the magical world of Harry Potter, his awful Dursley relatives, and a host of magical and muggical characters (*muggle* being the term for people who have no magical powers). Rowling has adapted the familiar characters of school stories—a well-meaning and earnest hero and his likable friends, a school bully, an acerbic teacher and a kindhearted one, and finally a wise if uneducated janitor to whom the kids go for advice and comfort. Her plots are fast moving and straightforward. The hero is confronted with a serious problem that, in spite of many obstacles, is eventually solved. What make these books so enjoyable are the good humor and obvious zest with which Rowling writes and the wonderful details of Harry's extraordinary world. Harry's required school equipment includes such textbooks as "A Beginner's Guide to Transfiguration" by Emeric Switch, "a cauldron (pewter, standard size 2)," and "one pointed hat (black) for day wear." He arrives at school, not in a yellow bus, but on a train that departs King's Cross Station from platform nine and three quarters or in a flying car. His homework assignments include a three-foot-long composition on "The Medieval Assembly of European Wizards" for a History of Magic course. His mail is delivered by owls, his dorm is haunted by a ghost fondly known as Nearly Headless Nick, and he plays the intricate sport of Quidditch, on a Nimbus Two Thousand broomstick (later replaced by an awesome Firebolt). In addition to all these elements, the very real dangers that confront Harry and his own sense of vulnerability are likely reasons for the sustained popularity of the series—and for the huge increase in fantasy series in general. Teaching Resources: "Chronicles, Sagas, and Trilogies: Recent Fantasy Series for Children" lists some of the newer crop of continued stories.

Eva Ibbotson's *The Secret of Platform 13*, published in the same year as *Harry Potter and the Sorcerer's Stone,* is equal to the Harry Potter books in its richly imagined world. Platform 13 is located in an abandoned railway station under the River Thames. It is a "gump," a magical place where every nine years for nine days a door opens into another world inhabited by ogres, wizards, fairies, and other creatures. The delightful tale centers on

Chronicles, Sagas, and Trilogies: Recent Fantasy Series for Children

OLC Visit the Online Learning Center at **www.mhhe.com/kiefer9e** for a printable version of this list.

Author	Series Title	Description	Grade Level
M. T. Anderson	Thrilling Tales	An over-the-top funny series that combines wacky adventures, in which kids who are heroes of their own adventure series take on new challenges to save the world.	4–7
Jennifer Armstrong and Nancy Butcher	Fire-Us Trilogy	Children struggle to survive in a future where most of the adults have died.	5 and up
Avi	Dimwood Forest	These charming animal fantasies feature Poppy the mouse and her friends and family.	3–6
T. A. Barron	The Great Tree of Avalon	These stories of the battle between good and evil take place in the legendary land of Avalon.	5 and up
T. A. Barron	The Lost Years of Merlin	These tales relate the childhood of Merlin and his rise to power.	5 and up
L. G. Bass	Outlaws of Moonshadow Marsh	Chinese legend and the practice of kung fu inspire these stories of an outlawed Prince who battles Evil and saves the Earth from destruction.	5–8
N. E. Bode	The Anybodies	Fern has the ability to bring book characters to life in this funny, farcical series.	3–6
Patrick Carman	The Land of Elyon	Young Alexa leaves her safe but circumscribed world to venture into a wild landscape of danger and magic.	4–6
Suzanne Collins	Underland Chronicles	Gregor must survive rats, bats, and cockroaches in a strange underground world.	5–8
Kate Constable	Chanters of Tremaris Trilogy	Sixteen-year-old Calwyn leaves the safety of her enclave to aid an injured sorcerer and attempt to save their world.	7 and up
Gillian Cross	Dark Ground Trilogy	In this suspenseful series Robert struggles to survive when he is shrunk to miniature size.	5–8
Tony DeTerlizzi and Holly Black	The Spiderwick Chronicles	Three children move into an old estate and experience new adventures with fairies and other magical creatures.	3–6
Chitra Banerjee Divakaruni	The Brotherhood of the Conch	Indian mythology and culture form the backdrop for this series about a poor boy from Kolkata who joins an ancient brotherhood to fight evil.	4–7
Jeanne Duprau	The City of Ember	Lina and Doon struggle to escape their existence in a devastated future world.	4–7
Catherine Fisher	The Oracle Prophecies	A mythical ancient Greece and Egypt form the setting for the adventures of the priestess Mirany and the scribe Seth.	5 and up

(continued)

Chronicles, Sagas, and Trilogies (*continued*)

Author	Series Title	Description	Grade Level
John Flanagan	The Ruins of Gorlan	An orphan is enlisted into the mysterious Ranger Corps to fight an evil ruler.	5 and up
Dennis Foon	The Longlight Legacy	Roon must save himself and his sister in a dystopian future.	5 and up
Cornelia Funke	Inkheart	Meggie and her father can live in two worlds, their own and the world of the book *Inkheart*.	4–7
Debi Gliori	Pure Dead	An over-the-top comedy series featuring the Strega-Borgia clan.	4–7
Margaret Haddix	Shadow Children	Third children are illegal in a future world and thus exist in great peril.	4–7
Charlotte Haptie	The Books of Karmidee	Otto struggles for his identity in a world of "normals" and magical beings.	4–7
Mary Hoffman	Stravaganza	Teens are transported between modern-day London and medieval Italy.	7 and up
Brian Jacques	Redwall	A large cast of animal characters fight for right in the mythical medieval kingdom of Redwall.	4–7
Lene Kaaberbol	The Shamer Chronicles	Mother and daughter can detect evil in others.	5 and up
Justine Larbalestier	Magic or Madness Trilogy	Teenagers seek their identities in a world where reason is pitted against magic.	7 and up
Michael Lawrence	Wivern Rise	Teens living in very different circumstances exchange realities.	7 and up
Clem Martini	Feather and Bone: The Crow Chronicles	Crows are the central characters in these animal fantasies.	5 and up
O. R. Melling	The Chronicles of Faerie	Teens enamored of ancient Irish lore become involved in the world of fairies.	7 and up
Gerald Morris	The Squire's Tales	A witty and adventurous series that focuses on characters at King Arthur's court.	4–7
William Nicholson	The Noble Warriors	Sixteen-year-old Seeker undertakes a quest to restore his brother's honor and save his people.	5 and up
William Nicholson	The Wind on Fire Trilogy	Twins Bowman and Kestral lead their people on a journey to their ancestral home.	5 and up
Garth Nix	The Abhorsen Trilogy	A haunting series in which characters from two worlds, the living and the dead, do battle for supremacy.	7 and up
Kenneth Oppel	Silverwing Trilogy	A young bat ventures out into the wide world to save his colony and find his identity.	3–6

Chronicles, Sagas, and Trilogies (*continued*)

Author	Series Title	Description	Grade Level
Christopher Paolini	Inheritance	A boy bonds with a dragon to fight evil in his kingdom.	5 and up
Michelle Paver	The Chronicles of Ancient Darkness	A boy bonds with a wolf to fight evil in a prehistoric world.	5 and up
Tamora Pierce	Circle of Magic, The Circle Opens The Circle Reforged	These series follow the adventures of four mages from their training to the major roles they play in their society.	4–7
Tamora Pierce	The Provost's Dog	This new series takes place 200 years before the Song of the Lioness series and features a girl raised to be a manhunter.	4–7
Terry Pratchett	The Bromeliad Trilogy	This hilarious series features miniature people who live in Harrod's department store and use the store's marketing slogans as their philosophy for life.	7 and up
Terry Pratchett	The Wee Free Men	A young-old witch must save her brother from the Queene of Faerie and begin her apprenticeship in magic.	4–7
Philip Reeve	The Hungry City Chronicles	In a future world, mechanized cities travel around the globe trying to destroy each other.	5 and up
Rick Riordan	Percy Jackson and the Olympians	A boy with attention-deficit/hyperactivity disorder finds out he is the half-human son of a Greek god. His quest is to restore order in the supernatural realm and discover his true identity.	5–9
Gloria Skurzynski	The Virtual War Chronologs	Teens of a future world battle with evil in cyberspace.	5 and up
Lemony Snicket	A Series of Unfortunate Events	The three Baudelaire orphans encounter one horribly funny adventure after another.	3–7
Paul Stewart and Chris Riddell	The Edge Chronicles	Young Twig has adventures in a world filled with magical beings, sky pirates, and evil villains.	3–6
Jeff Stone	The Five Ancestors	Five young apprentices to a kung fu grand master must battle against one of their own in an epic power struggle.	4–7
Jonathan Stroud	The Bartimaeus Trilogy	Bartimaeus, the djinni, an ambitious young magician, and a young resistance fighter struggle for power in an alternate Victorian universe.	5 and up
Patricia Wrede	Enchanted Forest Chronicles	The unconventional Princess Cimorene befriends dragons, battles wizards, and rescues princesses in this lighthearted series.	4–7
Laurence Yep	The Tiger's Apprentice	A young Chinese boy is trained in magic by a shape-changing tiger.	4–7

a unique band of monsters, led by the young hag Odge Gribble, who decides to travel to London and rescue a young prince who had disappeared there nine years before. Ibbotson's *Which Witch?* has an equally weird group of characters who are all witches pitted against one another in a contest to win the hand of Arriman the Awful, Loather of Light and Wizard of the North. In *Island of the Aunts, Dial a Ghost,* and *The Great Ghost Rescue* Ibbotson comes up with more wonderfully eccentric characters, both living and dead. The unearthly personalities, the ghoulish magic, and the mistaken identities in Ibbotson's books will be hard for children to resist.

The city of London has proved to be a particularly popular stepping-off place in fantasy for children, and London trains seem to hold a particular fascination for authors such as J. K. Rowling and Eva Ibbotson. In *Whispering to Witches* Anna Dale makes use of the train from London when 12-year-old Joe Binks, on his way to Canterbury to spend Christmas with his mother and stepfather, gets off at the wrong stop and enters the Dread-nettle Coven and a world filled with witches. Joe is caught up in a plot to steal a page from an ancient spell book, but with the help of his witch friend Twiggy, he manages to thwart the plot and rescue his little sister Esme from the clutches of a rival coven.

In the Bartimaeus Trilogy, Jonathan Stroud has imagined an alternate history for the city in which a group of magicians have taken over Parliament. They are engaged in a struggle for power with the Resistance, a band of commoners that includes young Kitty Jones. In the first book, *The Amulet of Samarkand,* Nathaniel, a headstrong young magician, summons Bartimaeus, a five-thousand-year-old djinn. Bartimaeus, who narrates parts of the story with great wit and tongue firmly in cheek, has his own take on unfolding events, and he proves to be a reluctant and very funny assistant for Nathaniel. In the second book, *The Golem's Eye,* Nathaniel has been promoted to a job in the Department of Human Affairs, and he summons a reluctant Bartimaeus to help defeat a golem that is stalking London. Kitty Jones plays a bigger role in this book and, in her desire to defeat the powerful magicians, emerges as the most sympathetic of the three main characters. *Ptolemy's Gate* sees the conflict between humans and djinns, magicians and commoners escalate until eventually, Nathaniel, Kitty, and Bartimaeus find a way to resolve their differences.

Joan Aiken also sets her stories within an alternate England with a nod to history as well. *The Wolves of Willoughby Chase* has all the ingredients of a nineteenth-century chiller, including wicked wolves without and an outrageously wicked governess within. The story takes place in a period of history that never existed—the Stuarts, in the person of good King James III, are on the throne in the nineteenth century. Readers will applaud Aiken's resourceful heroines and hiss the evil villains in all the Wolves Chronicles. Eleven-year-old Dido is the resourceful heroine of *The Wolves of Willoughby Chase,*

Black Hearts in Battersea, Nightbirds on Nantucket, Dangerous Games, and *Midwinter Nightingale,* In *The Witch of Clatteringshaws,* Dido sets out to save her friend Simon from having to reign as King of England. She must fend off giant otterworms and invading Wends before the happy resolution. Dido's distant relative, "Is" Twite, has her own hair-raising adventures in *Is Underground* and *Cold Shoulder Road.* As with all these titles, children will find the books hard to put down.

Extraordinary worlds have been created both above and below ground by several authors. Jeanne DuPrau's *The City of Ember* takes place in a future world where humans have spent the past 250 years living underground. The main characters in Suzanne Collins's *Gregor the Overlander,* the first in her Underland Chronicles series, find themselves suddenly plunged into a world where people exist entirely under the surface of the earth. The setting of Kenneth Oppel's *Airborn* bears a strong resemblance to the Victorian world, although the story takes place thousands of feet above the earth in a marvelous airship,

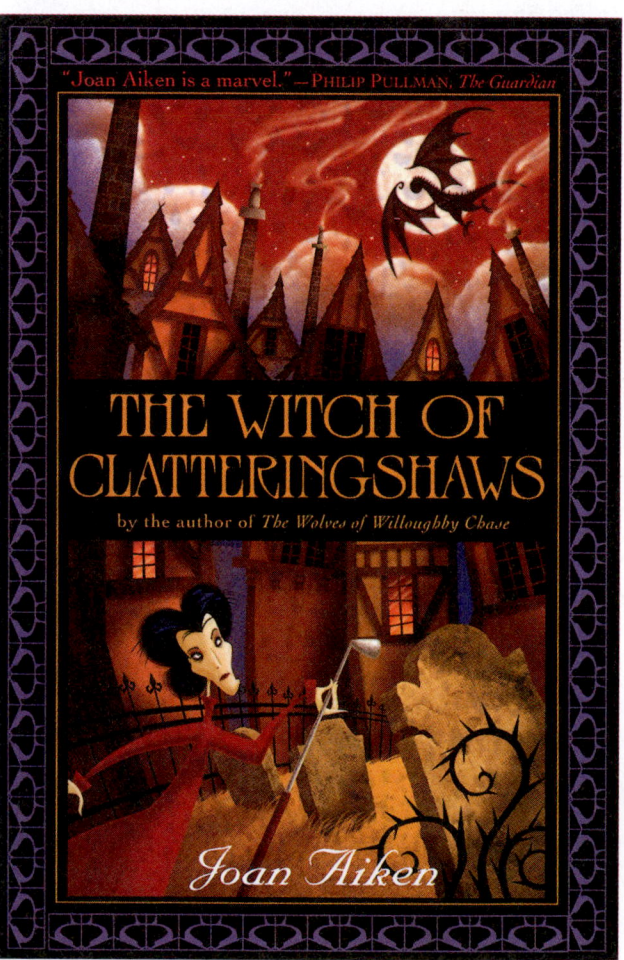

Joan Aiken's many books about the indefatigable Dido Twite culminate with *The Witch of Clatteringshaws.* From *The Witch of Clatteringshaws* by Joan Aiken. Jacket illustration © 2005 by Jimmy Pickering. Used by permission of Random House Children's Books, a division of Random House, Inc., NY.

the Aurora. Matt Cruse is a cabin boy who dreams of becoming a captain someday. Kate de Vries is a young passenger who has come aboard to try and solve the mystery of her grandfather's death, the grandfather that Matt tried to rescue the year before. The two become friends and allies as they are plunged into an adventure filled with pirates and magical beings called cloud cats. Oppel's setting, complete with blueprints for the Airborn, is strongly developed and lends credence to events that surround the coming of age of both main characters. In *Skybreaker,* the sequel, Matt and Kate climb aboard the Sagarmatha to search for the Hyperion, marooned at altitudes beyond the reach of most airships and rumored to contain a fabulous treasure.

Miniature worlds have always fascinated children, and Mary Norton's Borrowers series tells a fascinating story about tiny people who try to coexist with normal-size humans. The Borrowers derive their names from their occupation, which is "borrowing" from human "beans," those "great slaves put there for them to use." "Borrowing" is a dangerous trade, for if one is seen by human beings, disastrous things may happen. Therefore, in *The Borrowers* Pod and Homily Clock are understandably alarmed when they learn of their daughter Arrietty's desire to explore the world upstairs. Finally, Pod allows Arrietty to go on an expedition with him. While Pod is borrowing fibers from the hall doormat to make a new brush for Homily, Arrietty wanders outside, where she meets a boy. Arrietty's disbelief about the number of people in the world who are the boy's size, compared with those of her size, is most convincing:

> "Honestly—" began Arrietty helplessly and laughed again. "Do you really think—I mean, whatever sort of world would it be? Those great chairs . . . I've seen them. Fancy if you had to make chairs that size for everyone? And the stuff for their clothes . . . miles and miles of it . . . tents of it . . . and the sewing! And their great houses, reaching up so you can hardly see the ceilings . . . their great beds . . . the food they eat . . . great smoking mountains of it, huge bags of stew and soup and stuff." (p. 78)

In the end, the Borrowers are "discovered" and flee for their lives. This surprise ending leads directly to the sequel, *The Borrowers Afield.* Strong characterizations, apt descriptions of setting, and detailed illustrations by Beth Krush and Joe Krush make the small-scale world of the Borrowers come alive. Other titles continue the series.

The Kansas prairie has certainly ushered in a venerable series in L. Frank Baum's *The Wizard of Oz.* The cyclone that blew Dorothy into the Land of Oz continues to blow swirling controversies around this series of books by Baum and others. Some maintain that *The Wizard of Oz* is a skillfully written fantasy, a classic in its own right. Others condemn the first book because some of the forty-plus volumes that followed are poorly written. Dorothy

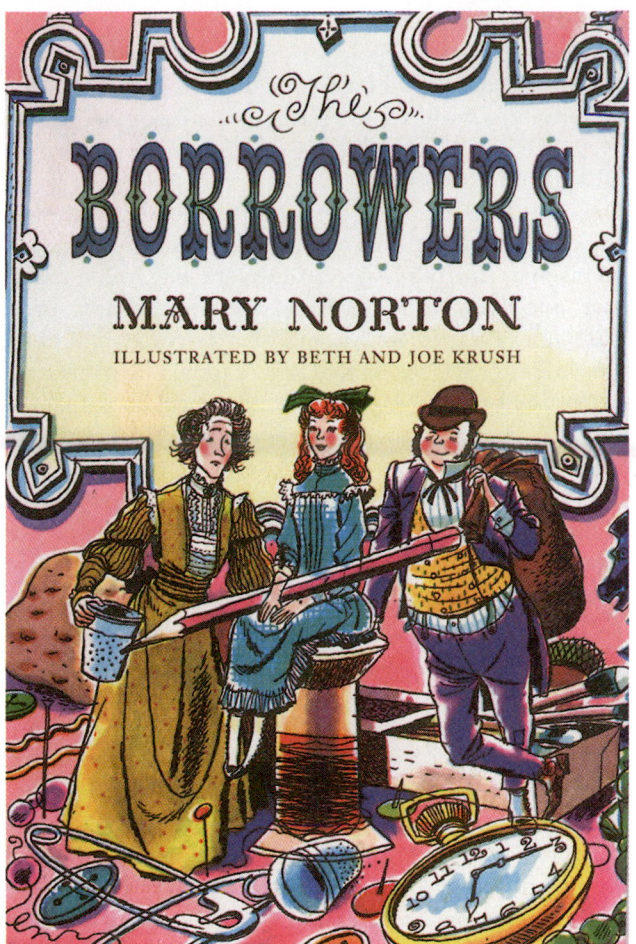

Mary Norton creates a memorable miniature world in *The Borrowers.* Cover art from *The Borrowers,* copyright © 1953, 1952 by Mary Norton and renewed 1981, 1980 by Mary Norton, Beth Krush and Joe Krush, reprinted with permission of Harcourt, Inc.

and her companions eventually achieve their particular wishes, but the wizardry is what they do for themselves, rather than anything that the Wizard does for them. For the most part this fantasy depends on the strange situations and creatures that Dorothy and her companions meet. Readers never doubt that the four will overcome all odds and achieve their wishes. Even the Wizard holds no terror for practical, matter-of-fact Dorothy. This lack of wonder and awe—the basic ingredients of most fantasy—makes *The Wizard of Oz* seem somewhat pedestrian when compared with other stories of its kind.

A landscape of numbers greets Milo in Norton Juster's *The Phantom Tollbooth,* when he goes through a peculiar tollbooth and discovers a strange and curious world indeed: "The Lands Beyond," which include the Foothills of Confusion, the Mountains of Ignorance, and the Sea of Knowledge. Here Milo meets King Azaz the Unabridged, the unhappy ruler of Dictionopolis, the Mathemagician who serves them subtraction stew and increases their hunger, and the watchdog Tock, who keeps on ticking throughout their adventures. The substance of this fantasy is in its play on words rather than its characters or situations. Its appreciation is dependent on the reader's knowledge of the definitions of various words, phrases, and allusions. For this reason children with mature vocabularies particularly enjoy its humor.

Magical Powers

The children in books of fantasy often possess a magical object, know a magical saying, or have magical powers themselves. In *Half Magic* by Edward Eager, the nickel that Jane finds turns out to be a magical charm, or at least half of a magical charm, for it provides half of all the children's wishes, so that half of them will come true. Eager's *Seven-Day Magic* tells of a magical book that the children borrow from the library. When they open the book, they find it is about themselves. Everything they did that morning is in the book, and the rest of the book is shut tight waiting for them to create it. Logic and humor are characteristic of the many books of fantasy that were Eager's legacy of modern magic to today's children.

Frequently, less demanding fantasy relies on magical powers, slight characterization, and fast-moving plots to interest less-able readers. Scott Corbett's "trick" books, such as *The Lemonade Trick,* rely on Kirby Maxwell's use of a magic chemistry set belonging to Mrs. Greymalkin, a neighborhood witch. Greedy John Midas suffers the consequences of his newly acquired magical power, *The Chocolate Touch*, in Patrick Skene Catling's new twist on an old story. Many children come to discover the pleasures of wide reading and build skills for more complex stories through books such as these.

Eleven-year-old Louise, Betsy Hearne's heroine in *Wishes, Kisses, and Pigs,* loves to make a wish on the first star each night. One evening as she chants the familiar "star light, star bright" to herself, she is unmercifully teased by her older brother, Willie, who is on his way to feed the pigs. Enraged, Louise tells him that *he* is a pig. Willie disappears (as their father did seven years before) and a new pig shows up in the farmyard. Louise figures out that Willie is the new pig and confides in her mother, who matter-of-factly accepts the news. The two set about making plans to change Willie back into human form, but they find that wishes are complicated things. After some setbacks, Louise finds the patterns that she needs to set things right. In the end she finds more than the brother she wished for. This is a charming and satisfying story that weaves familiar motifs from folktales together with highly original characters and plot.

Several authors have shown how books can prove to be magic in more ways than one. Jon Scieszka's Time Warp Trio—*Tut Tut*; *Oh Say, I Can't See*; and *Da Wild, Da Crazy, Da Vinci*—features "The Book," a birthday present from Joe's magician uncle, which whisks Joe and his friends, Fred and Sam, back into other eras. Short chapters, broad humor, and gross characters; the quirky line illustrations; a fast-moving plot; and contemporary-sounding dialogue appeal especially to boys in the second to fifth grades. A book is also the catalyst for adventure in Nina Bernstein's *Magic by the Book*. Her three children—Anne, Emily, and Will—find a dusty old volume among the pile of books they've brought home from the library for their summer reading. The two girls first discover its magic when they open it and find themselves transported to Sherwood Forest. Will, the youngest, discovers it later and finds himself in his own world, only in miniature. Finally, the three find themselves in a scene from *War and Peace*. With each adventure the children rely on the knowledge they've gained as readers to solve the problems of the imaginary characters they interact with. A magical volume, indeed, is Avi's *The Book without Words*. This book has the recipe for eternal life but can be read only by a person with green eyes. One such person is the despicable Thorston, who stole the book years before and plans to use it to return to his youth. Another is Brother Wilfred, from whom the book was stolen and who wishes nothing but to return it to its rightful owner. A third is young Alfric, a homeless orphan who finds himself caught up in a convoluted set of farcical circumstances that involve the book, hidden gold, and buried

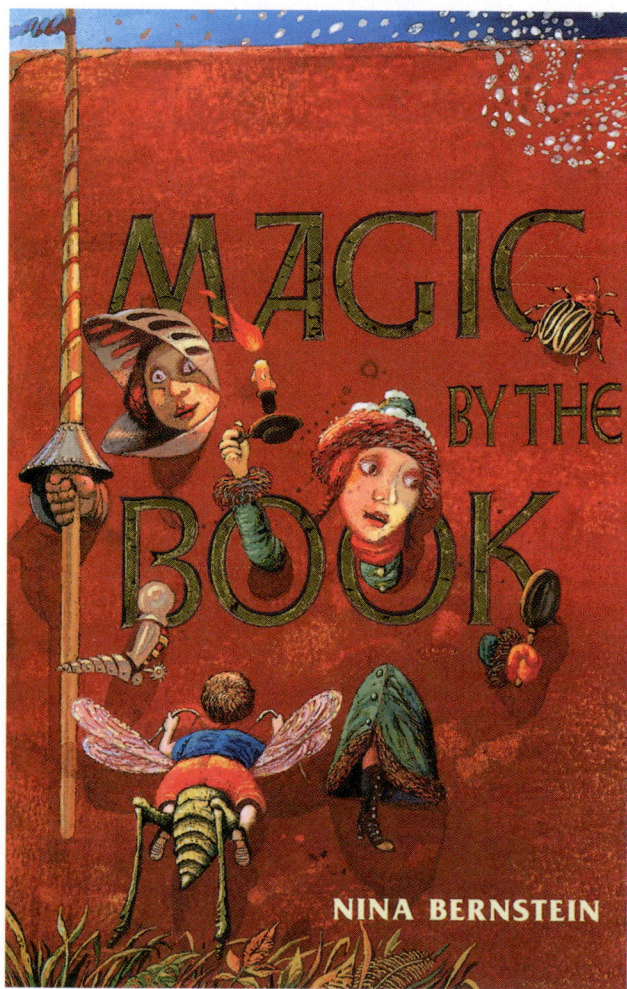

Nina Bernstein uses a book to transport her characters into unusual adventures in *Magic by the Book*. Jacket art © 2005 by Boris Kulikov. Reprinted by permission of Farrar, Straus and Giroux, LLC.

bodies. In Cornelia Funke's *Inkspell* and *Inkheart,* Meggie and her bookbinder father seem to live ordinary lives until a mysterious stranger arrives with warnings about the sinister Capricorn. Meggie suddenly discovers that her father is anything but ordinary. He has the magical power to make characters in books come alive when he reads about them. Now it seems that Capricorn, one of those characters, is after him. Meggie suddenly finds herself caught in the middle of a dangerous intrigue as she fights to save her father and return Capricorn to his book. In both of these stories Funke has developed fresh and suspenseful plots and complex characters. Older readers are sure to find them compelling.

Jane Langton has created several stories of mystery and magical powers surrounding the Halls, who live in a strange old turreted house in Concord, Massachusetts. In *The Diamond in the Window,* Uncle Freddy had been a world-renowned authority on Emerson and Thoreau until the mysterious disappearance of his younger brother and sister left him slightly deranged. In the tower room two beds are made up in a vain hope for the return of the two children. Edward and Eleanor move to the tower room and search in their dreams for the two missing members of the family. Another story of the Hall family, *The Fledgling,* centers upon 8-year-old Georgie's desire, and eventual ability, to fly. She is befriended by the Goose Prince, who takes her on his back and teaches her to glide in the air by herself. Although Georgie outgrows her gift and the goose falls prey to a gun, he leaves her with a magical present—a ball that projects an image of the whole world, and the admonition "Take good care of it." Langton's descriptions give the story a warm and comfortable tone; her evocation of flying might make earthbound readers' spirits soar.

In a much lighter vein, Sid Fleischman sets his fantasy *The Midnight Horse* near the New England town of Cricklewood, New Hampshire: "Population 217. 216 Fine Folks & 1 Infernal Grouch." An orphan comes to claim his inheritance from the infernal grouch, a shady judge who is his great-uncle. Fleischman, in setting the scene, minces no words:

> It was raining bullfrogs. The coach lurched and swayed along the river road like a ship in rough seas. Inside clung three passengers like unlashed cargo.
>
> One was a blacksmith, another was a thief, and the third was an orphan boy named Touch. (p. 1)

When Touch arrives in Cricklewood, Judge Wigglesforth tries to force him to sign for his inheritance, thirty-seven cents. No fool, Touch refuses to sign and escapes to a ram-shackle inn. In fast-paced, humorous, short chapters, Touch discovers his real inheritance, saves the inn, and unmasks both the thief and the judge. Fleischman's ear for comic dialogue, his inspired similes, and his ability to strip a tale to its essentials make this a lively story in the same vein as his *The Whipping Boy.*

Like the characters in "The Fisherman and His Wife" and other traditional tales, the characters in Franny Billingsley's *Well Wished* don't always use their wishes wisely. Due to one of these misguided wishes, made on a magic wishing well, the townspeople of Bishop Mayne have lost all their children, except for Catty, a young girl in a wheelchair. When Nuria arrives to live with her grandfather, she and Catty soon become friends. Catty, who wants desperately to walk again, convinces Nuria that she can outsmart the wishing well, and despite her grandfather's repeated warnings, Nuria makes a wish. However, she is soon trapped by the terrible consequences that are the result of that wish, and Nuria must put a devilishly complex scheme into play in order to make things right. The magic in *Well Wished* is dark magic, and the story has overtones of the supernatural, but the important themes such as the power of love and the sacrifices made for friendship will also appeal to children.

Older readers with a tolerance for invented worlds and the ability to follow a large cast of characters will enjoy the many books by Diana Wynne Jones. *Howl's Moving Castle* features Sophie Hatter, an adolescent who is turned into an old woman by the Wicked Witch of the Waste. In *Charmed Life* the magician Chrestomanci must help young Eric Chant (called "Cat" for short) to discover his own powers while he preserves his household against the evil that assails it from outside the castle walls. *The Lives of Christopher Chant,* a prequel, is about the boyhood of Chrestomanci, who is able to dream himself into strange worlds and bring back from these places what others cannot. Like Eric, he is naive about adult motives, an unwitting accomplice to his uncle's wicked plans, and an unwilling heir to the previous Chrestomanci's power. These imaginatively plotted stories reveal the author's wry humor, her love of language, and her ability to balance aspects of time and space in impossible but believable ways.

Suspense and the Supernatural

Interest in the occult and the supernatural, always an adult preoccupation, also captures the imagination of children. They enjoy spooky, scary stories, just as they like being frightened by TV or theater horror stories.[14] This may in part explain the popularity of authors like John Bellairs, whose mysteries, such as *The House with a*

[14]See Carl M. Tomlinson and Michael O. Tunnell, "Children's Supernatural Stories: Popular but Persecuted," in *Censorship: A Threat to Reading, Thinking and Learning,* ed. John S. Simmons (Newark, Del.: International Reading Association, 1994), pp. 107–13; and Jodi Wilgoren, "'Don't Give Us Little Wizards,' The Anti-Potter Parents Cry," *New York Times,* 1 November 1999.

Clock in Its Walls, are full of spooky old houses, scary characters, fast-moving plots, and plenty of dialogue. Increasingly, publishers issue finely crafted suspense fantasies that are often superior to the usual ghost story or mystery tale. These well-written tales of suspense and the supernatural deserve attention.

Diane Stanley's *The Mysterious Matter of I. M. Fine* is a funny send-up of written-to-formula horror fiction. Fifth-grader Franny and her family move every year for her father's job as a consultant. She has a hard time fitting in, unlike her popular younger sister, Zöe, and her easygoing brother, J. D. Franny tends to retreat into books and is an avid reader, but she prefers more challenging books like *David Copperfield* to the Chillers series that all her classmates are reading. When she's paired up with Beamer for a school project, the two find they have much in common. When increasingly malevolent things start happening to the kids who are reading the Chillers books, Franny and Beamer set about finding the author and putting things right. Stanley provides many plot twists before bringing the story to a happy conclusion. She also offers some gentle messages about friendship, families, and the joys of reading.

Paul Fleischman's *The Half-a-Moon Inn* has the tone of a folktale and a setting to match. Born mute, 12-year-old Aaron sets off to find his mother when she becomes lost in a great snowstorm. He accidentally stumbles into the Half-a-Moon Inn, where he is imprisoned by the evil Miss Grackle, who needs a boy to tend the bewitched fires that none but honest folk can kindle. Aaron's escape, his reunion with his mother, and the folktale-like demise of the witch (she freezes to death beside her unlit fireplace) provide a satisfying conclusion. The narration is lighter than the content, and the well-wrought dialogue makes this a challenging and entertaining choice for reading aloud to 9- and 10-year-olds.

Arthur Slade builds the suspense to an almost unbearable pitch in the eerie *Dust,* set in Canada during the drought of the Depression years. The book begins with the mysterious disappearance of 7-year-old Matthew, younger brother of Robert Steelgate, the book's protagonist. Not long after this event a mysterious stranger, Abram Harisch, arrives in town with promises of a miraculous rainmaking machine, a magical mirror show that seems to have a hypnotic effect on the people in the area. Robert seems to be the only one who sees the evil in Harisch. When Robert begins to suspect Harisch may be behind the disappearance of Matthew and other area children, he sets out to expose the man and find Matthew. Slade constructs a vivid setting and creates a complex character in Robert, but his greatest feat is the development of a tense and suspenseful plot that will have readers on the edge of their seats.

Eloise McGraw's *The Moorchild* is a haunting story that relies on elements from traditional folktales such as "Tam Lin" and other Celtic lore. Saaski is half fairy and half human, born to a fairy mother and fathered by a young man lured into their caverns by fairy magic. Because Saaski does not have the right fairy skills, she is banished from their kingdom and exchanged for a human baby. Here she grows up as an outsider, little understood by her perplexed parents and miserable at her failure to fit in. As the townspeople become more and more hostile and fearful of her strangeness, Saaski pieces together her origins and makes a courageous attempt to return her changling counterpart to her real home, knowing that she herself belongs in neither world.

O. R. Melling, Elizabeth Marie Pope, and Sally Gardner also explore mythic faerie lore in books for older readers. In Melling's *The Hunter's Moon* two cousins who are fans of Celtic culture set off on a journey through rural Ireland, where they toy with rituals that open up the world of Faerie with serious consequences. When Findabhair is kidnapped by the King of Faeries, Gwen feels she must rescue her cousin and bring her back to the present-day world. Pope's *The Perilous Gard* is set in Elizabethan England and involves Kate Sutton, a young woman exiled to a remote castle by Queen Mary. Kate becomes involved in a series of mysteries that eventu-

O. R. Melling weaves Irish faerie lore into the romantic yet chilling *The Hunter's Moon. Cover of The Hunter's Moon: The Chronicles of Faerie* by O. R. Melling, copyright © 2005. Reprinted by permission of Harry N. Abrams, Inc.

ally lead her into the supernatural and frightening world of Faerie. In *I, Coriander* Gardner's heroine moves in and out of the world of Faerie and a vividly described world of seventeenth-century London. In all three books the realm of Faerie is both attractive and menacing, and the characters wrestle with real longings to be part of that magical world. The characters and their dilemmas will resonate with adolescents caught between the worlds of childhood and adulthood.

Michael Gruber's *The Witch's Boy* is a superb fantasy infused with the tales of the Grimm brothers and Hans Christian Andersen, although not in the way that we have traditionally known them. The witch of the title is able to work magic, but her role is keeping the balance of the earth, adjusting "the pattern of things so that life flowed smoothly through time" (p. 10). Change comes to her remote forest as men and women move out from the towns and encroach on the natural balance that has existed in the witch's domain. An even more portentous event occurs when a small baby is left by the witch's cottage, a baby so misshapen and ugly the witch calls him Lump. Lump is nursed by a bear and tutored by an afreet, or demon, while the witch, who means better, neglects him for her own work. Having been told all his young life that he is beautiful, Lump doesn't expect the horror with which he is greeted when he tries to play with the two children who have moved nearby. In a rage Lump releases the afreet from the witch's chains. When the afreet takes a horrible vengeance and utterly destroys the family and their property, he upsets the balance of nature in the magic wood, and the witch is punished by the loss of her powers. She, Lump, and Falance, who was once a cat but has now taken the form of a man, set out for faraway places to try to earn an honest living. Bitter and angry, Lump takes his unhappiness out on his mother. He takes to wearing a mask to hide his features and escapes to lose himself in the realms of the faerie kingdom. His redemption comes when he discovers his talents as a stonemason and his broken heart is mended by the love of Nuala, a young blind girl.

In *The Mermaid Summer,* Mollie Hunter explores the ancient legend of a mermaid who was thought to live near the "Drongs" and could lure poor fishermen to their deaths on these rocks. Eric Anderson refuses to believe in the legend until he nearly loses his entire fishing crew to her singing. No one will sail with Eric after that, and he is forced to leave his wife, son, and two grandchildren, named Jon and Anna, and find a place on a large ship leaving for faraway ports. When Anna and Jon trick the vain and deadly mermaid into removing the curse from their grandfather, he is able to return home. Filled with the cadenced language of the storyteller, this tale evokes the rich heritage of Scottish folklore.

Mollie Hunter has based another eerie tale, *A Stranger Came Ashore,* on the old legends of the Shetland Islands that tell of the Selkie Folk, seals who can take on human form. Only young Robbie Henderson and his grandfather are suspicious of the handsome stranger who appears in their midst on the stormy night of a shipwreck. After Old Da dies, Robbie must put together the clues that reveal the real identity of Finn Learson and the sinister nature of his interest in the golden-haired Elspeth, Robbie's sister. Events build to a fearsome climax on a night of ancient magic, when the dark powers of the sea are pitted against the common folk dressed as earth spirits and celebrating the last of the yule festival. Teachers who read aloud *A Stranger Came Ashore* find Susan Cooper's picture book *The Selkie Girl* a good prior introduction to selkie lore. Children familiar with the story are much more sensitive to Hunter's use of foreshadowing, folk beliefs, mood, and setting in this finely crafted novel.

Selkies appear in two other fine works of fantasy for older readers, but in these books the selkies are not villains but victims. In *Daughter of the Sea* author Berlie Doherty uses a vivid storyteller's voice to reveal her story. Munroe, a young fisherman, finds a baby floating near his boat one night in a storm, and he brings the child home to his wife, Jannet. They name the baby Giogga, and they love her as their own. Although they try to ignore the fact that this child is different, eventually there is a price that must be paid for their happiness and for their refusal to accept the fact that Giogga is a child of the sea. In a moving climax, the sacrifices made by both human and selkie allow Giogga to follow her true nature and return to her real home.

In Franny Billingsley's *The Folk Keeper* the main character is Corinna, a sullen orphan with strange abilities to tame the Folk, malevolent creatures who haunt the caves and tunnels beneath the surface. Summoned from her orphanage to be the folk keeper at a great estate near the sea, Corinna finds a friend in the young stepson of the mansion's master. Plunged into dangerous intrigues and a battle of wits with both human and nonhuman opponents, Corinna comes to accept the qualities that have set her apart from other children. When she realizes her true heritage, she understands her strange and terrible longing for the sea. Told through the pages of Corinna's diary, *The Folk Keeper* is a complex and eerie interweaving of folklore and selkie legend that will demand the careful attention of older readers but reward them with an exciting and imaginative tale.

Several recent books don't pull any stops when it comes to horror. Both involve resourceful heroines who are forced to act in the face of their terror when their parents disappear. Neil Gaiman's *Coraline* is an only child, as out of sorts with the world as Corinna in *The Folk Keeper.* Left to fend for herself by her preoccupied parents, Coraline explores the house they have just moved into, an old mansion that has been converted into flats. One rainy day she finds a door blocked up with bricks. A mysterious warning not to go through the door only encourages Coraline, and when Mother and Daddy are out, she takes the old key to the door and opens it. The bricks are gone and the door leads to a dark hallway—and to a terrifying alternative universe. This other world is a nightmare reflection of her own, and Coraline has let loose events that she cannot control. Gaiman masterfully builds the tension as the true horror of this other world is revealed. Coraline realizes that she must somehow undo the wrong she has committed and restore normalcy. *Coraline* is horror writing at its best, with intriguing characters, a well-constructed and eerie setting, and a thrilling and suspenseful plot. Joseph Bruchac's *The Dark Pond, Whisper in the Dark,* and *Skeleton Man,* although set in the present, are based on traditional Native American tales. In *Skeleton Man* the heroine, Molly, relates this traditional Abenaki tale at the beginning of her own narrative story. As her story proceeds, Molly becomes involved with a mysterious great-uncle who turns up when her parents disappear. Locked in her room each night, Molly suspects that the uncle may be Skeleton Man, a legendary creature who devoured himself and then, still hungry, ate everyone around him. Molly realizes that, like the young girls in the original tale, she is the only one who can defeat him. These novels are flat-out terrifying through their final pages. Readers who find they have the nerve for *Coraline* and Bruchac's books will also relish Garth Nix's *Sabriel, Lirael,* and *Abhorsen.* In these books Australian writer Nix creates a frightening world full of necromancy, ghouls, and the undead.

Stories about ghosts and spirits who haunt the real world are more likely to attract readers who don't have the attention span or the background knowledge for complex stories like *The Folk Keeper* or *Coraline.* Barbara Brooks Wallace's *Ghosts in the Gallery* is more of an old-fashioned Victorian Gothic novel than it is a frightening ghost story, but it is a good introduction to the genre for readers who might not be ready for the terrifying horror in *Coraline.* When first 11-year-old Jenny's father and then her mother die, she must return to the New England home of a long-lost grandfather. Here she is met with disbelief and villainy, put to work as a scullery maid by the evil Madame Dupray. *Ghosts in the Gallery* is as spellbinding in its fast-moving plot and evil characters as any ghost story, if a bit less frightening.

On the other hand, Mary Downing Hahn's *Wait Till Helen Comes* and *The Old Willis Place: A Ghost Story* are not for the fainthearted. In *Wait Till Helen Comes* a ghost child named Helen has perished in a fire and now waits by a pond to drag children to their deaths as play companions. When Molly and Michael's mother remarries, their new father's child joins the family, but Heather is a brat who forever whines about imagined injustices. Nobody believes Heather's stories of the ghostly Helen until Molly begins to develop some sympathy for her stepsister's point of view. In a chilling ending, Molly pieces together the mystery, saves Heather from a sure death, and forges a hopeful beginning of a loving family. Hahn's *The Old Willis Place: A Ghost Story* explores the theme of friendship in a supernatural setting. Hahn's fast-paced stories consistently win young-readers awards presented by

various states, showing how much children appreciate a good, scary ghost story.

Betty Ren Wright is another writer who can spin a good ghost story. In *The Ghost Comes Calling,* a ghost comes to call on 9-year-old Chad Weldon, who is a reluctant camper at an old cottage his father is trying to restore. The ghost is old Tim Tapper, who years earlier was wrongly accused of misconduct by the townspeople and went to live in the old cabin as a recluse. When Chad proposes a solution that restores the old man's good name, the ghost can finally rest in peace. In Wright's *Out of the Dark,* a ghost appears to 12-year-old Jessica in a nightmare just after she and her family move in to house-sit for her grandmother. Jessie is even more terrified to find that the setting of her nightmare, an old one-room schoolhouse, exists in the middle of a nearby nature preserve and that her grandmother had attended the school as a young girl. The ghost of her dreams begins to appear in various places in and around Gran's house and is obviously trying to harm her. This apparition in white almost succeeds in locking her and a neighbor girl in a metal storage room in the floor of the old school. The mystery of the ghost's identity and Gran's role in a long-ago incident is finally resolved in a riveting conclusion.

Friendship binds a child from the present with a child from the past in Pam Conrad's *Stonewords.* Zoe, who lives with her grandparents in an old farmhouse while her flighty mother "shows up when she shows up," makes friends with a strange, transparent girl from the past named Zoe Louise, whom only she can see. The ghost girl appears, plays with Zoe, and enigmatically states that she is looking in Zoe's eyes for "the truth." On a rare visit, Zoe's mother points out the memory roses planted for a child who died on the property. When Zoe realizes that her ghost friend is that child, she must find out how her death occurs in order to prevent it from happening. A stack of old newspapers moldering away in the basement provides a clue, and the real Zoe is able to go up the back stairs into the past and change history and the present as well.

Margaret Mahy is a masterful writer of all genres, and in *The Haunting* she turns her talents to the supernatural. *The Haunting* blends a ghost story with careful observations of family interactions. Shy Barney Palmer is receiving unwanted messages from a ghostly relative but is afraid to tell anyone, especially his beloved new stepmother, who is about to have a baby. At a family gathering, writing appears on the page of a book Barney is looking at. Barney soon discovers that on his real mother's side of the family, there is in each generation a magician or psychic. His black-sheep Uncle Cole, holder of the magical power for his generation, is lonesome for other psychics and is trying to possess Barney's mind. In an effort to remain normal, Barney struggles against his uncle's mounting frustration and anger. When the malevolent Uncle Cole finally arrives in Barney's house, different family members come to Barney's aid, revealing individual strengths with surprising results. Mahy's trenchant observations of family communications, her deft and often humorous turns of phrase, and a riveting plot make this an excellent choice for reading aloud to older elementary school children.

The opening paragraph of *Sweet Whispers, Brother Rush* by Virginia Hamilton quickly draws the reader into a remarkable story:

> The first time Teresa saw Brother was the way she would think of him ever after. Tree fell head over heels for him. It was love at first sight in a wild beating of her heart that took her breath. But it was a dark Friday three weeks later when it rained, hard and wicked, before she knew Brother Rush was a ghost. (p. 9)

Fourteen-year-old Tree takes care of her older brother Dab while her mother, Viola, works in another city as a practical nurse. Tree painfully accepts her mother's ab-

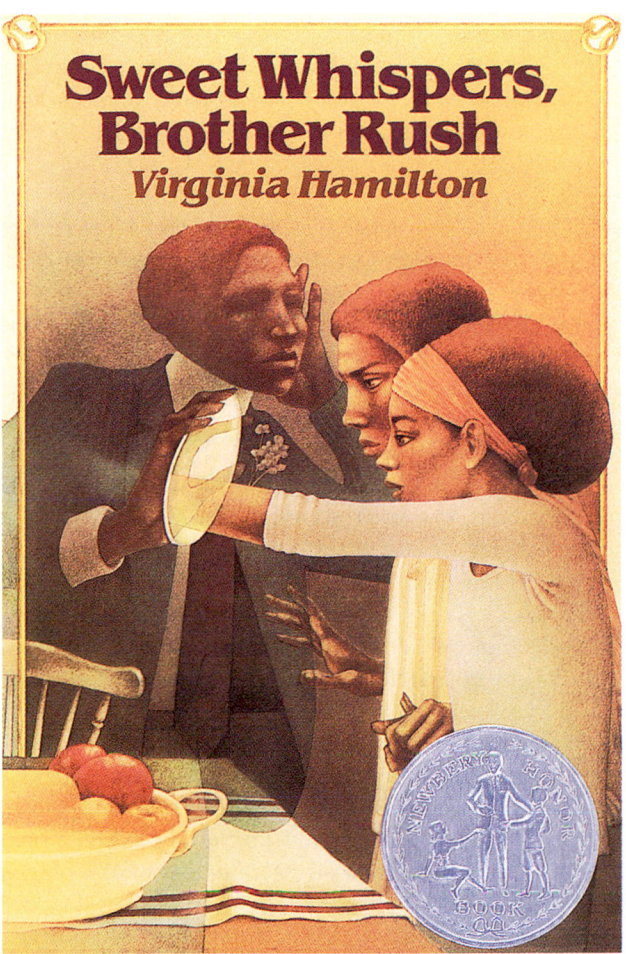

Teresa reaches for images in the mirror held by her uncle's ghost to try to grasp what she has seen but has yet to understand in Leo Dillon and Diane Dillon's painting for the jacket of Virginia Hamilton's story *Sweet Whispers, Brother Rush.* Jacket art from *Sweet Whispers, Brother Rush* by Virginia Hamilton. Copyright © 1982 by Leo & Diane Dillon. Used by permission of Penguin Putnam, Inc.

sences and devotes her time to schoolwork and caring for her brother. As Dab's occasional bouts of sickness suddenly become more frequent, Brother Rush appears to Tree and shows her her family's recent past, which until now she has not questioned. Through Brother Rush, Tree begins to understand why her mother has always avoided Dab, the hereditary nature of Dab's sickness, and something about her father. When Dab succumbs to the disease, Tree's experiences with Brother Rush enable her to understand what has happened. But it is her mother's love and the gentle strength of her companion Silversmith that pull Tree through her anger and despair toward an acceptance of her brother's death and the promise of new extended-family relationships. Making use of African American cadences and inflections, Hamilton moves surely from narration to dialogue and into Tree's thoughts. She has created complex characters whose steady or fumbling reachings for each other may linger with middle-school readers long past the end of this story.

David Almond's *Skellig* is a quietly beautiful story of faith, hope, and friendship. Michael, the protagonist and storyteller, has just moved into a new home with his mother and father and his prematurely-born baby sister. The book begins as Michael finds an odd creature in the garage of his new home, a bag of bones "sitting with his legs stretched out and his head tipped back against the wall. He was covered with dust and webs like everything else and his face was thin and pale. Dead bluebottles were scattered on his hair and shoulders" (p. 8). Michael's encounters with this mysterious creature, named Skellig, are interwoven with his interactions with his mother and father, who are distracted by their concern for the baby. His growing friendship with Mina, an oddly eccentric neighbor girl who is fond of quoting William Blake, provides relief from the tensions at home. As his baby sister, still unnamed, fights for her life amid the tubes and machines of modern medicine, Michael and Mina care for Skellig, slowly bringing him back to health. The questions of Skellig's identity and the role he is meant to play in healing Michael's sister must ultimately be decided by the reader. Quoting William Blake ("Love is the child that breathes our breath / Love is the child that scatters death"), Almond makes the profound suggestion that love can heal when it is aided by the power of the imagination. This strangely moving story is a testament to the power of that belief. Almond's *Secret Heart, Kit's Wilderness,* and *The Fire Eaters* are frightening and complex stories of the supernatural for older readers.

Time-Shift Fantasy

Probably everyone at one time or another has wondered what it would be like to visit the past. We have looked at old houses and wished they could tell us of their previous occupants; we have held antique jewelry in our hands and wondered about its former owners. Our curiosity has usually been more than just historical interest;

we have wished to communicate, to enter into the lives of the past without somehow losing our own particular place in time.

Recognizing this, authors of books for children have written many fantasies that are based on characters who appear to shift easily from their particular moment in the present to a long-lost point in someone else's past. Usually these time leaps are linked to a tangible object or place that is common to both periods. In *Tom's Midnight Garden* by Philippa Pearce, for example, the old grandfather clock that strikes thirteen hours serves as the fixed point of entry for the fantasy.

Julia Sauer's *Fog Magic* is the tender, moving story of Greta Addington, a young girl of Nova Scotia. One day while walking in the fog, Greta discovers a secret world, Blue Cove, a fishing village that is present only in the fog. Here Greta forms a friendship with a girl her own age, whose mother senses that Greta is from "over the mountain" and quietly reminds her each time the fog is lifting that it is time to go home. On the foggy evening of her twelfth birthday, Greta enters Blue Cove, where her friend's mother gives her a soft gray kitten and quietly wishes her "safe passage for all the years ahead." Greta senses that this will be the last time that she will be able to visit Blue Cove. She walks slowly down the hill to find her father waiting. As she shows him her kitten, he reaches into his pocket and pulls out an odd little knife that he had received on his twelfth birthday at Blue Cove. This is a hauntingly beautiful story, memorable for its mood and setting. Part of its appeal may come from the underlying view, common in mystical fantasy, that childhood confers special sensibilities that adults can no longer share.

No one is more skillful in fusing the past with the present than L. M. Boston in her stories of Green Knowe, that mysterious old English house in which the author lived. In *The Children of Green Knowe,* the first in this series, Boston tells the story of Tolly, who is sent to live with his great-grandmother. Over the large fireplace in the drawing room hangs a picture of three children who grew up at Green Knowe in the seventeenth century. When Tolly's great-grandmother tells him stories about the children, they seem so real that Tolly is convinced they often play hide-and-seek with him. His great-grandmother believes him, and soon the reader does too. Each story of Green Knowe blends a child of the present with characters and situations from previous centuries while creating for the reader a marvelous sense of place.

One of the finest time fantasies ever written is the mysterious and exciting *Tom's Midnight Garden* by Philippa Pearce. Forced to spend part of a summer with a rather boring aunt and uncle, Tom finds his visit quite dull until he hears the grandfather clock in the hall strike thirteen. Then he is able to slip into the garden and play with Hatty, a child of the past. Tom becomes so absorbed in his midnight visits, when "there is time no longer," that he does not wish to return home. One fateful night Tom opens the back door and sees only the paving and the fences that stand there in daylight—Hatty and her garden have vanished. When Tom meets the real Hatty Bartholomew, a little old lady, he understands why the weather in the garden has always been perfect, why some nights it has been one season and the next night a different one, why Hatty was sometimes young and sometimes older; it all depended on what old Mrs. Bartholomew had been dreaming. Lonely and bored, Tom joined her in her dreams. This is a fascinating story that should please both boys and girls in the middle grades.

While the characters in most time fantasies slip in and out of the past, the problem in *Tuck Everlasting* is that the Tuck family is trapped forever in the present. Natalie Babbitt's elegant prose leads the reader to expect a quiet Victorian fantasy, but the book holds many surprises— including a kidnapping, a murder, and a jailbreak. The story opens with Winnie Foster, an overprotected 10-year-old, sitting in front of her family's prim touch-me-not cottage on a hot August day talking to a large, plump toad. She informs the toad that she wants to do something interesting, something that will make a difference to the world. The very next morning Winnie "runs away" to the nearby woods owned by her parents and sees a young man of 17 (although he first says he is 104 years old) drinking from a spring. When Winnie asks for a drink, Jesse Tuck warns her not to take one. Just at that moment his mother, Mae Tuck, and brother Miles arrive. With all due apologies to Winnie, they bundle her onto their horse to go back to their home to have a talk with Mae's husband, Angus Tuck. On the way, Mae tells Winnie that drinking the spring water has given them everlasting life. Back at the shabby three-room cottage of the Tucks, they gently try to persuade Winnie to guard their secret. In the morning Angus Tuck takes Winnie rowing on the lake and explains to her what it is like to live forever. He longs for a natural conclusion to his life. "I want to grow again, . . . and change. And if that means I got to move on at the end of it, then I want that, too" (p. 63). Although the Tucks intend to let Winnie make her own decision, they do not know that a man in a yellow suit, who has been searching for them for years, has overheard Mae Tuck reveal their secret to Winnie. Caught in the melodrama of the Tucks' lives, Winnie decides to protect and help them, a decision that does indeed change her life. The simplicity of the Tucks and their story belies the depth of the theme of *Tuck Everlasting*. With its prologue and epilogue, the story is reminiscent of a play, a kind of *Our Town* for children.

Mystery is also an important part of the complex fantasy by Eleanor Cameron titled *The Court of the Stone Children*. The story of modern-day Nina, who has a "Museum Feeling" and thinks she would like to be a curator, is intertwined with the story of Dominique, a young noblewoman of nineteenth-century France whose father was executed by Napoleon's regime and whose family possessions are now housed in a French museum in San

Francisco. Domi enlists Nina's help in the task of clearing her father's name of the charge of murder. A suspenseful mystery, with telling clues foreshadowed in one of Nina's "real-life" dreams, leads to a painting that serves as evidence of the count's innocence. A Chagall painting, *Time Is a River without Banks,* which also hangs in the museum, is used throughout the story as a symbol of Nina's unusual interest in the abstract nature of time. This is a profound theme explored by a truly accomplished writer. However, young readers will more likely value the book for its exciting events and for the haunting presence of Domi in her museum domain than for its eloquent abstractions.

Like L. M. Boston's Green Knowe stories, *A String in the Harp* gains strength from its setting and also from its connection to legend. Nancy Bond tells of an American family's adjustment to living in Wales when their newly widowed father accepts a university post. It is a particularly difficult time for 12-year-old Peter, who is stubborn, lonely, and hateful until he finds a strange object later identified as the harp key of Taliesin, the great sixth-century bard who lived in this part of Wales. When the key draws Peter back in time, his present-day life is adversely affected. Eventually he is able to return the key to its proper place and assume a responsible place in his family. This strongly characterized but lengthy story mingles past and present time in a believable and involving way.

In *Earthfasts* William Mayne also draws on legendary characters to tell his story of three interwoven times. When two boys meet at a swelling in the earth, the ground begins to vibrate with the sound of drumming. Out of the earth emerges a stranger who is beating a drum and clutching a steady, cold white flame. It is Nellie Jack John, who according to local legend went underground two hundred years ago to seek the treasure of King Arthur. Nellie Jack John's disturbance of time causes many bizarre events: ancient stones called "earthfasts" work up in a farmer's field; a family's poltergeist returns after a long absence; and one boy vanishes in what looks like a flash of lightning. Only by restoring the candle to its proper place because "King Arthur's time has not yet come" can the boys right the imbalance of time. This unforgettable book owes much of its impact to Mayne's use of language and his finely realized setting.

Mary Downing Hahn's *Time for Andrew* is a gripping time-shift mystery. Staying at his great-grandfather's old house for the summer while his parents travel abroad, Drew is a nervous 12-year-old, afraid of bullies, bad storms, and bogeymen. Exploring the attic one day, he finds a bag of marbles that had belonged to Andrew, a distant relative who died of diphtheria at the age of 12. Disturbing the marbles has also disrupted time, however, and as the hour of Andrew's death approaches, he is transported to Drew's bedroom. Andrew begs Drew to change places with him and give him a chance to live. Reluctantly Drew does so, going back to the early 1900s to live as Andrew. Here he must face bullies and frightening situations similar to those he feared in his own time. Most frightening of all, however, is Andrew's growing reluctance to trade places and allow Drew back into his own time. The longer Drew stays in Andrew's time, the more he begins to forget his own. Yet he also finds some of the courage he lacked in the modern world and grows to appreciate the close family life he has never had. Hahn is a master at building tension as the story approaches its resolution, and the question of Drew's and Andrew's futures is brought to a satisfying and wholly believable conclusion.

Self-understanding and better family relationships are also the outcomes for characters in a time-shift fantasy by Canadian author Kit Pearson. In *A Handful of Time* a 12-year-old girl is sent to her cousins' camp on a lake near Edmonton while her parents' divorce becomes final. Patricia is definitely the "city cousin" who knows little about boating or horseback riding and is the constant butt of her cousins' jokes. When she discovers an old watch hidden under the floor of a guest house, she finds herself taken back in time to the same summer cabin when her mother was 12 and equally miserable. In her frequent trips to view the past, Patricia learns much about her short-tempered grandmother and her beautiful but reserved mother. By coming to understand her mother, Patricia moves toward understanding herself.

In some books where characters are shifted from modern times into specific periods of history, the concern with social and political issues of the past is very strong. Several notable examples serve the purposes of historical fiction as well as fantasy. In *A Chance Child* by Jill Paton Walsh, Creep, a present-day English boy who has been abused and kept locked in a closet, gets out by chance and follows a canal that takes him back to the Industrial Revolution. As a child laborer, he travels from one exhausting and dangerous job to another, eventually losing his grip on the present altogether. His half-brother, the only person with any clue to his disappearance, searches historical documents from the early 1800s and is at last satisfied that Creep has escaped into the past and lived out his life there. The amount of technological information about work in the coal mines, the nailer's forge, the pottery, and the textile mill attests to the research necessary for recreating these settings. Walsh's juxtaposition of the abusive treatment of children in the nineteenth century and Creep's contemporary plight makes a strong statement about children and society. Equally compelling is David Wiseman's *Jeremy Visick.* This book explores the conditions of child laborers in England's nineteenth-century copper mines when the hero's school assignment leads him into a mine disaster of a previous century.

Welwyn Wilton Katz, a Canadian author, imagines a disastrous future for Earth in *Time Ghost.* In the year 2044, the natural world is far removed from most people, who live in large block buildings in crowded cities and rarely venture outdoors for fear of air pollution and ultraviolet radiation. Sara's grandmother is an environmental lawyer determined to protect the last remaining wild areas of the Arctic from oil industry tycoons, and Sarah joins her on a trip to the North Pole. Through a botched experiment, Sara is sent back in time to central Canada of 1993. Struggling to figure out a way to return to her own time, Sara comes to new understandings about the beautiful natural world she has lost. The story ends with real growth for Sara and other characters and real hope for the little natural wilderness they have left.

Janet Lunn, American born but now living in Canada, weaves together a haunting tale of a contemporary child, an old Canadian farmhouse, and the American Civil War in her book *The Root Cellar*. When her grandmother dies, Rose is sent to live with her Aunt Nan's family in their country home on the northern shore of Lake Ontario. A shy child who has lived only with adults in New York City, 12-year-old Rose feels desperately lonely in the midst of Aunt Nan and Uncle Bob's lively family. When she discovers an old root cellar door covered with vines and grass, she opens it and finds herself in a world more than a hundred years past. She is more comfortable in this world and easily makes friends with Susan and Will. When Will runs off to fight in the Civil War and does not return, Rose and Susan set out on a hazardous journey that eventually takes them to an army hospital in Washington, D.C. On the journey Rose discovers a strength and determination she did not know she had that helps her when she returns to her own time.

Susan Cooper has created a richly detailed time-travel story in *King of Shadows*. Nat Field is a passionate actor and a member of a group of boys who have been chosen to perform William Shakespeare's *A Midsummer Night's Dream* at the recently opened replica of the Globe Theatre in London. Nat keeps himself busy with rehearsals and throws himself into his part of Puck, partly out of love for acting and partly to block out thoughts about his father's suicide. Soon after his arrival in London, Nat becomes ill and wakes from his fever to find himself in sixteenth-century London. There he is still called Nat Field and he is still an actor. But now he finds he is to play the part of Puck alongside Will Shakespeare on the boards of the original Globe. Cooper manages to fill the story with information about Shakespeare, his time, and the craft of acting, but the story is not driven by these details. Instead, Nat's personal pain and his developing insight into himself as well as the elements of suspense and mystery in the plot remain central. Children should enjoy the well-told story and come to share Nat's affectionate attachment to Shakespeare and his passion for the man's beautiful plays.

Readers captivated by the world of the Elizabethan theater in *King of Shadows* will enjoy Jane Louise Curry's *The Black Canary*. In this time-shift fantasy 13-year-old James, a biracial child, has rejected the musical world of

In Susan Cooper's *King of Shadows* Nat Field, an aspiring young actor, is transported to Elizabethan London and finds work with Will Shakespeare's troop. Illustrations copyright © 1999 by John Clapp. Jacket of *King of Shadows* by Susan Cooper. Published by Simon & Schuster Books for Young Readers. November 1999.

his career-oriented parents. When he accompanies them to London, he finds a mysterious door in the cellar of their borrowed flat. Stepping through, James is plunged into Elizabethan times, where he is forced to join the Queen's performers. In addition to dealing with issues of race, Curry tells a gripping coming-of-age story in *The Black Canary*. Both *The Black Canary* and *King of Shadows* introduce themes of interest to early adolescents. In addition, they present readers with the historical background of a vivid age.

Imaginary Realms

Many authors of fantasy create believability by setting their stories in an imaginary society where kings and queens rule feudal societies that resemble the Middle Ages. Often lighter in tone than high fantasy, these stories might nonetheless feature some of its attributes—such as a human character's search for identity, a quest, or the struggle against evil—and are good introductions to the more complex and more serious works of high fantasy. Children are often drawn to this kind of fantasy, as it seems so closely related in many ways to folktales and traditional literature.

Two of Natalie Babbitt's stories, *The Search for Delicious* and *Kneeknock Rise,* are set in an imaginary medieval kingdom. In the first story, young Gaylen is sent out as the king's messenger to poll the kingdom as to which food should stand for the word *delicious* in the dictionary the prime minister is compiling. Before he finishes, Gaylen uncovers Hemlock's plot to overthrow the king. With the help of supposedly fictitious creatures such as woldwellers, dwarfs, and Ardis the mermaid, Gaylen is able to foil Hemlock and save his king. In *Kneeknock Rise,* Egan climbs the mountain and finds a perfectly rational explanation for the groaning noises of the mythical Megrimum. When he eagerly relates his findings to the villagers, they refuse to listen to him, and Egan discovers that people do not relinquish their myths easily; harmless monsters may be preferable to facts.

Authors have long enjoyed playing with the characters and elements of traditional tales. Gail Carson Levine, Diane Stanley, and Patricia Wrede are three writers who have relied on familiar fairy tales to create humorous, highly readable fantasies. In *Ella Enchanted* Levine has taken the Cinderella story and provided a reasonable interpretation for Cinderella's subservience to her stepmother and stepsisters. A well-meaning fairy has given her the gift of obedience, but the gift turns into a curse when her stepfamily starts ordering her around. This wily heroine eventually breaks the wish through willing self-sacrifice and wins the Prince through her own devices. Levine's *The Two Princesses of Bamarre* is an original fairy tale but just as charming. In *Bella at Midnight* Diane Stanley serves up a delightful twist on the Cinderella story, with a bit of the Joan of Arc legend thrown in. Bella, whose mother dies as a result of her birth, is rejected by her mean-spirited father. His mother's sister (and Bella's godmother) takes her to a Beatrice Smith, a wet nurse on Sir Edward's country estate, where she is raised as a daughter by the Smiths alongside their own children and Beatrice's other nursling, Prince Julian. In her adolescence Bella's father remarries a disgraced widow with two daughters and demands that Bella be sent home to act as companion to the girls. Shocked to learn of her real parentage, Bella is more comfortable in the kitchen than the drawing room. The story of how she saves her kingdom and finds her prince will delight readers. Patricia Wrede's Enchanted Forest Chronicles feature the unconventional Princess Cimorene. In *Dealing with Dragons,* Cimorene runs off to be librarian and cook for the dragon Kazul rather than stay in the palace, sew, and wait for a suitor. Cimorene organizes the dragon's hoard, reads ancient books, and makes friends with neighboring princesses captured by dragons and awaiting rescue. Cimorene's gradual mastery of rudimentary magic and her friendship with the witch Morwen allow her to defeat an evil band of wizards who are trying to influence the choice of the new dragon ruler.

Cimorene's further adventures are told in *Searching for Dragons* and *Calling on Dragons. Talking to Dragons* finds Cimorene's son Daystar and a feisty fire-witch named Shiara ready for their own adventure with Kazul. All the books make many sly references to folktale and fantasy conventions. Children who enjoy Wrede's unconventional feminine adventurer would appreciate being guided to *The Dragonriders of Pern* and the Dragonsinger stories of Anne McCaffrey, as well as to many of the works of Robin McKinley and Lloyd Alexander, whose heroines appeal to slightly older readers.

This same audience will appreciate the books of Tamora Pierce, who has developed several series that feature characters who will not stay put in the roles their societies have dictated for them. Pierce's Lioness Quartet is especially popular with early adolescents and follows the career of Alanna, a young girl whose dearest wish is to train as a warrior maiden. In the books, Alanna faces many trials and tribulations as she attempts to restore the Dominion Jewel to the King of Tortall and a just peace to the kingdom. *Wild Magic, Wolf Speaker, The Realms of the Gods,* and *Emperor Mage* are set in the same imaginary land of Tortall and feature Daine, a heroine whose magical talent is the ability to communicate with animals. *First Test* features Keladry, a 10-year-old heroine who meets many obstacles in her quest to become a knight. These books feature fast-paced adventures with strong females. Pierce has also written several other series including Circle of Magic, The Circle Opens, The Circle Reforged, and Protector of the Small. Circle of Magic, which begins with *Sandry's Book,* is told with the same attention to storytelling but with different characters—male and female outcasts who discover their special talents and inner strengths during their training at the Winding Circle Temple, a school of magic in the kingdom of Tortall. Series written in a similar vein include Katherine Roberts's Echorium Sequence, which begins with *Song Quest,* and for older readers, Tanith Lee's Claidi Journals, which begins with *Wolf Tower.*

Sid Fleischman sets *The Whipping Boy,* his humorous variation on the-prince-and-the-pauper theme, in a time of velvet britches, princely tutors, and robber brigands. Jemmy, the whipping boy for Prince Brat, has taken all the abuse for the prince that he can stand. Each time the bored prince makes mischief and is caught, Jemmy must receive the twenty whacks. But before Jemmy can leave, the prince commands the former street urchin to sneak away from the dull palace with him to see what the world holds. When the boys are kidnapped by two notorious outlaws, Hold-Your-Nose-Billy and Cutwater, one of the boys' identities is given away: Prince Brat had thoughtfully stowed his crown in his picnic basket. But which one is the prince? Because Jemmy had learned to read and write as a tutor futilely labored to teach the prince, the cutthroats consider the whipping boy the one to be ransomed. The exaggerated characters in humorous situations are balanced by the prince's gradual transition into a decent person when he finds that none of his future subjects think much of him. Fleischman's appealing use of colorful figurative language, witty repartee, broadly drawn characters, and clever chapter titles makes this a good shared-reading choice for fourth or fifth graders. Peter Sis's quirky drawings and small chapter openings are perfectly suited to this spoof.

If Fleischman has woven his story around a nebulous medieval setting, Kevin Crossley-Holland, Gerald Morris, and Nancy Springer have placed their fantasies squarely within the tradition of Arthurian legend. Crossley-Holland's trilogy, which includes *The Seeing Stone*, *At the Crossing Place*, and *King of the Middle March*, takes place in the latter part of the twelfth century in England. This England is not a mythical place but a carefully researched historical setting. It is a time when the English face great danger as the villainous King John assumes the throne after King Richard's death. Thirteen-year-old Arthur, the series's protagonist, is named after the legendary king and he will play a special role in the coming events. Given a special stone by his father's friend Merlin, Arthur begins to see back into the past to the original Arthur's story. In both books, young Arthur is guided through his thrilling adventures by what he sees in the stone. Morris's stories are clearly set into mythical Arthur's time period. *The Squire's Tale* and *The Squire, His Knight and His Lady* are the somewhat lighthearted stories of 14-year-old Terence Springer's apprenticeship to Sir Gawain and his adventures at King Arthur's court. Other titles in the series include *Parsifal's Page*, *The Savage Damsel and the Dwarf*, and *The Lioness and Her Knight*. Springer's *I Am Mordred* and *I Am Morgan le Fay* are more somber but ultimately uplifting stories of the traditional villains in King Arthur's tale.

The land and lore of Scandinavia have inspired several fine fantasies. Edith Pattou's *East* draws from the Norwegian myth "East of the Sun, West of the Moon" and features trolls, an enchanted prince, and the icy landscapes of northern climes. *Troll Fell* by Katherine Langrish involves two human children with the kingdom of Trolls. When Peer's father dies, he is claimed by his two brutish half-uncles, Baldur and Grim. He soon discovers that they have plans to trade him to the King of Troll Fell, as a human servant for his soon-to-be-married daughter. This fast-paced story is rich with references to stories and characters from Scandinavian legend, including Granny Greenteeth, a water sprite; Nis, a magical house slave; and two dogs named Loki and Grendel. Nancy Farmer has incorporated Scandinavian motifs and characters into *The Sea of Trolls*, an exciting tale of adventure and a boy's search for identity. When Jack and his sister Lucy are kidnapped by Viking raiders, they are plunged into the often-brutal world of Viking culture and characters. King Ivar the Boneless wears a cloak made from the beards of his defeated enemies, and his wife, Queen Firth, is a half-human, half-troll who threatens Lucy's life. Fortunately, Jack has the gift of magic and the gift of

In *Troll Fell* by Katherine Langrish a young boy finds adventure among the characters and landscapes of Scandinavian folklore. Jacket from *Troll Fell* by Katherine Langrish. Copyright © 2004. Used by permission of HarperCollins Children's Books, a division of HarperCollins Publishers, Inc.

song and soon finds allies who help him on his quest to find Mimir's well and save his sister.

Readers will find a different mythical kingdom realistically portrayed in Susan Fletcher's *Shadow Spinner*. The setting here is ancient Persia, where Marjan, a young girl with a talent for storytelling, finds herself dragged from her home to the sultan's palace. Her storytelling talents are badly needed by a young princess named Sharazad, who must entertain the sultan with a new tale every night in order to prolong her life. Marjan's role in bringing about the famous Arabian Nights tales is richly imagined and deftly woven into a suspenseful story that will engage middle-grade readers and send them off in search of all thousand and one tales.

Peter Dickinson's *The Ropemaker* also has a Middle-Eastern flavor, although the setting is purely imaginary. Tilja, her grandmother Meena, Tahl, and his grandfather Alnor undertake a perilous journey to find the magician Faheel, who wove the spell that has, until now, protected their valley from its enemies. The four are good foils for one another, in both their talents and their personalities.

They endure one difficult task after another as they journey through an empire devastated by evil magicians who want to claim power. Both Tilja and Tahl discover their own hidden strengths as they finally find Faheel's successor, the Ropemaker. William Nicholson has sent his characters on a similar set of thrilling adventures in his Wind on Fire Trilogy, which includes *The Wind Singer, Slaves of Mastery,* and *Firesong.* In this imaginary kingdom, the citizens of Aramath are carefully separated into classes in which they must dress and live in a particular color. When three children rebel against the system, their parents are exiled to the Gray tenements. The children—Kestral, her brother, Bowman, and their friend, Mumpo—leave the city to search for the Wind Singer, an instrument that holds the key to freedom. They succeed, but in the continuing books they face more trials and tribulations until they ultimately succeed in finding a homeland.

Writers from Australia and New Zealand have contributed many fine works of fantasy to the body of children's literature. Australian writer Emily Rodda has created a delightful series of books for middle-grade readers in the Rowan series. In *Rowan of Rin* we meet a young boy who was traumatized as a toddler when his father died rescuing him from a fire. Rowan is afraid of everything and is limited to performing only the easiest task in the village, caring for the gentle Buckshahs on whose milk the villagers depend for their living and their lives. When the only stream that the Buckshahs can drink from dries up, the villagers are terrified of starving. They seek the wisdom of a mad hermit woman who mocks them with a mysterious message and a map she throws at Rowan. It turns out that Rowan is the only one who can read the map, so he must accompany the six adults chosen to climb up the mountain to find the source of the stream. Old Sheba's prediction that the mountain will break the seven hearts that make the journey is fulfilled as the individual failings of one adult after another cause them to leave the quest. Soon only Rowan and Strong Jonn, his dead father's friend, are left to face the greatest peril, a wounded dragon who guards the stream. Rowan, despite his fear, must carry out the final task, believing he is sacrificing his life. Old Sheba's prediction comes true—Rowan's heart seems to break when he thinks he will never see his home again. This is a lovely story about what courage and strength of will really mean. *Rowan of Rin* won the Children's Book Council of Australia's book of the year award for younger readers. The Rowan series continues in *Rowan and the Keeper of the Crystal, Rowan and the Travelers, Rowan and the Zebak,* and *Rowan and the Ice Creepers.*

New Zealander Sherryl Jordan is also an accomplished writer of high fantasy. In *The Raging Quiet* and *Secret Sacrament,* both written for mature readers, she sets characters on quests where they must discover their true nature as well as sacrifice something for the greater good of others. *The Hunting of the Last Dragon,* set in a mythical medieval world, is a superb story of two orphans, Jude and Jing-Wei (or Lizzie), who are total op-

Rowan and the Ice Creepers by Emily Rodda is one of a series of tales about an unlikely hero and his courageous deeds in the imaginary realm of Rin. Jacket from *Rowan and the Ice Creepers* by Emily Rodda. Copyright © 2003. Used by permission of Greenwillow Books, an imprint of HarperCollins Publishers, Inc. by arrangement with Scholastic Australia Pty. Ltd.

posites in their backgrounds and characters. Jude is an illiterate peasant whose village and family are wiped out in a terrible fire when he is away at a fair. Many believe the fire was caused by marauding Scots, but some report seeing a flying shadow near other burned-out villages. Jude is totally traumatized by the tragedy and wanders off with the members of a traveling fair. Here he meets Lizzie, who is kept in a cage and displayed to the public as a freak. In truth Lizzie is Chinese, orphaned while on a trip with her upper-class family. She has been put on display because of her exotic looks and her bound feet. Jude soon befriends her, and the two escape the traveling sideshow to find sanctuary with Old Lan, also Chinese. She is the area wise-woman, a healer and seer who helps reset Jing-Wei's crippled feet. She also insists that Jing-Wei and Jude are the only ones who can slay the last dragon, the one who is laying waste to the countryside. This is a task that Jude is terrified to undertake. The story of Jude and Jing-Wei's journey and their ultimate encounter with the last dragon is told by Jude to Brother Benedict in a flashback after the two have taken refuge in a monastery. This device is an added delight to a well-written tale, because Brother Benedict writes down *every* word that Jude utters, including the asides as he enters and leaves the scriptorium each day. Thus, in addition to the story of the last dragon, we get glimpses of life in the monastery and ultimately discover the outcome of Jude and Jing-Wei's relationship.

Lloyd Alexander has a gift for portraying comic adventures in which serious themes lie under a surface of fast action and polished wit. *The Gorgon and the Boy, Gypsy Rizka, The Cat Who Wished to Be a Man, The Marvelous Misadventures of Sebastian,* and *The Wizard in the Tree* are books of this sort. *The Arkadians* is equally light-hearted, with all the trappings of madcap adventure, but it also includes some serious ideas about the craft of story-telling. Lucian is a young accountant in the court of King Bomios who finds his life threatened when he discovers that Calchas, the king's royal soothsayer, is fiddling with the royal books. Lucian must flee for his life, and his journey to restore his good name takes him throughout the hills and dales of Arkadia. In the company of Fronto, a poet who has been turned into a donkey, he encounters all manner of refugees from Greek myths as well as a charming but spirited young woman named Joy-in-the-Dance. The three sometimes-reluctant companions have wonderful adventures before all wrongs are righted and all characters are restored to their original forms. Alexander's *The Iron Ring* and *The Remarkable Journey of Prince Jen* are adventures interwoven with the mythologies of India and China. Alexander's books share certain common elements: rich use of language, comic tone, usually a strong-willed female foil to the likable, all-too-human hero, and a setting in an imaginary kingdom. Filled with humor, excitement, and wisdom, any of these books would make a superb story to read aloud to middle-grade students.

Older readers find satisfaction in two series by Lloyd Alexander, both of which take place in unmagical but imagined settings. *Westmark* is the story of Theo, a printer's apprentice, who pursues questions of honor, justice, and freedom of the press as he tries to avoid the villainous chief minister of the realm. Theo helps restore his street-urchin friend Mickle to her rightful place as princess, but he also questions the concept of a monarchy: Does anyone have a rightful place on a throne? *The Kestrel* and *The Beggar Queen* are sequels in which Theo and Mickle, now the "Beggar Queen," prove their worth in battle but learn the cost of personal victory. In a lighter vein, Vesper Holly is the intrepid young woman who, with her guardian Brinnie, embarks on adventures in *The Illyrian Adventure, The El Dorado Adventure, The Drack-enburg Adventure, The Jedera Adventure, The Philadelphia Adventure,* and *The Xanadu Adventure.* The high-minded heroine and her guardian journey to imaginary places in Europe, Africa, and Central America where they discover treasure, recover important antiquities, foil villains, and narrowly escape all dangers. Lidi, a new but no less intrepid heroine, is introduced in *The Rope Trick.* Told with Alexander's usual wit, these stories invite middle-grade readers to create their own adventure "movies of the mind."

High Fantasy

Many readers who learn to enjoy popular stories of magic, ghosts, time travel, and the like go on to become fans of a more serious and demanding type of story called high fantasy. These complex narratives, which often extend into sequels, are characterized by certain recurring themes and motifs. For instance, the stories frequently take place in created worlds or imaginary realms. Characters might call on ancient and fundamental powers, for good or ill. The conflict between these opposing forces becomes the focus of many stories. Frequently the protagonists of high fantasy have a quest to fulfill. Finally, although there may be touches of humor, the overall tone of high fantasy is serious, because its purpose is serious. High fantasy concerns itself with cosmic questions and ultimate values: goodness, truth, courage, wisdom.

In accepting the National Book Award for *The Farthest Shore,* Ursula K. Le Guin spoke about the intent of fantasy at this level:

> The fantasist, whether he uses the ancient archetypes of myth and legend or the younger ones of science and technology, may be talking as seriously as any sociologist—and a good deal more directly—about human life as it is lived, and as it might be lived, and as it ought to be lived. For after all, as great scientists have said and as all children know, it is above all by the imagination that we achieve perception, and compassion, and hope.[15]

High fantasy's best audience stretches over a wide age range, from preadolescents to adults. Some of its most enthusiastic readers are the same young people who are devoted to video games of imagined adventures. Many older readers simply call themselves science fiction fans and make little distinction between the two types of books. In fact, much science fiction is also high fantasy; Madeleine L'Engle's *A Wrinkle in Time* is one familiar example. Some stories, like Anne McCaffrey's *Dragonsong,* appear to be science fiction with their extra-terrestrial settings and use of precepts of science (in this case, the bonding of a newborn animal and a mother fig-

---

[15]Ursula K. Le Guin, "National Book Award Acceptance Speech," in *The Language of the Night: Essays on Fantasy and Science Fiction,* ed. Susan Wood (New York: Putnam, 1979), p. 58.

ure). But *Dragonsong* seems more fantasy than science because the newborns are traditional dragons and "fire lizards."

Not all critics will agree about the proper categorization of books like these. But it is the book itself, not its label, that matters to the reader. However it might be identified, well-written high fantasy rewards its audience with new understandings as well as a good read.

The Struggle between Good and Evil

The age-old conflicts between good and evil, light and darkness, life and death are recurring themes in modern fantasy as well as in traditional literature. The setting for the struggle might be the world as we know it, or an invented land like Narnia, which some children know as well as their own backyards or city blocks. C. S. Lewis, a well-known English scholar and theologian, created seven fantasies about the country of Narnia. The best of the series is the first one published, *The Lion, the Witch, and the Wardrobe,* although it was the second in the sequence according to the history of Narnia. Beginning quite realistically in our time and world, four children find their way into the land of Narnia through the back of a huge wardrobe (or closet) in one of the large rooms of an old English house. The land, blanketed in snow and ice, is under the wicked Snow Queen's spell, which controls the weather so that it is "always winter and never Christmas." The children and the Narnians pit themselves against the evil witch and her motley assortment of ghouls, boggles, minotaurs, and hags. With the coming, sacrifice, and resurrection of the great Aslan the Lion, signs of spring are seen in the land. The children successfully aid the lion king in destroying the evil forces, and he crowns them Kings and Queens of Narnia. Narnia has its own history and time, and in *The Magician's Nephew* the reader is told of the beginnings of Narnia.[16] In the last of the books of Narnia, *The Last Battle,* King Tirian calls on the Earth Children to come to his aid. Narnia is destroyed; yet the real Narnia, the inner Narnia, is not. The children learn that no good thing is ever lost, and the real identity of Aslan is finally revealed to them. These stories are mysterious, intriguing, and beautifully written. Even if children do not always understand their religious allegory, they can appreciate them as wondrous adventures that somehow reveal more than they say.

Susan Cooper has written a series of five books about the cosmic struggle between good and evil. *Over Sea, Under Stone* introduces the three Drew children, who, on holiday in Cornwall, find an ancient treasure map linked to King Arthur. The third book in the series, *Greenwitch,* continues this quest story. Both stories are less complex than the remarkable second book, *The Dark Is Rising.* On Midwinter Day, his eleventh birthday, Will Stanton discovers that he is the last of the Old Ones, immortals dedicated throughout the ages to keeping the world from the forces of evil, the Dark. Will must find the six Signs of Life in order to complete his power and defeat, even temporarily, the rising of the Dark. Strange powers enable him to move in and out of time, where he meets Merriman Lyon, the first of the Old Ones, who becomes his teacher and mentor. While rich in symbolism and allegory, the story is grounded in reality so that both Will's "real" life and his quest in suspended time are distinct, yet interwoven. In the fourth book of the series, *The Grey King,* Will once again must prepare for the coming battle between the Dark and the Light. Special help comes from Bran, a strange albino boy, and his dog, Cafall. Set in Wales, the story works on many levels— with the feud over a sheep-killing dog taking on more significance when Bran's mysterious background is revealed. *Silver on the Tree* draws together characters from the previous four novels for a final assault on the Dark. Much that was hidden in the other tales is made explicit here, and knowledge of the major threads of the first four books is necessary to understand this exciting and fulfilling climax to the saga.

T. A. Barron has also drawn on myths surrounding King Arthur in his five-book The Lost Years of Merlin series. This saga begins with a young boy who finds himself lying on a rocky shore robbed of his memory and his identity. Over the course of the series this child will uncover his past and his magical gifts. More important, however, as he faces increasingly difficult trials, he will learn to control his marvelous talents and to accept the responsibilities that come with power. Barron has developed a multifaceted character in this young wizard, who grows from an impulsive and irresponsible child to a young person who accepts his dark side along with his great gifts. Only through such understandings can this young boy become Merlin, the mage who will guide King

Profile in Literature

T. A. Barron

Author T. A. Barron grew up in Colorado and, after graduating from Yale, traveled the world as a Rhodes scholar. After managing a venture capital firm in New York City, he gave up his lucrative career to move his family back to Colorado and become a writer of books for children and young adults. His concern for the environment and belief in the power of the human spirit are evident in all his books. Go to the Online Learning Center at **www.mhhe.com/kiefer9e** or your Resources CD-ROM to learn more about T. A. Barron.

---

[16]See Brian Sibley's *The Land of Narnia,* with illustrations by Pauline Baynes (New York: HarperCollins, 1990), for help in sorting out the chronology of Narnia, notes on the creation of the series, and a simplified biography of C. S. Lewis.

Arthur. Barron sees the story of Merlin's coming of age as a metaphor for the human spiritual journey. "Like the boy who washed ashore with no clue whatsoever about his wondrous future, each of us harbors hidden capacities, hidden possibilities. Though they may be undiscovered they are nonetheless there."[17] The revelation of these fundamental human needs interwoven with tests of courage and set in a mythical land peopled with marvelous characters typifies the genre of high fantasy.

Barron's Great Tree of Avalon series continues his exploration of Celtic lore and the myth of Merlin. The land of Avalon is a great tree among whose roots live many magical creatures. Now a thousand years after Avalon grew from a seed planted by Merlin, a dark and evil presence threatens the very existence of this enchanted world. Tamwyn, Elli, and Scree are the three main characters engaged in a battle with the evil Rhita Gawr, who is determined to destroy this beautiful land. One of the three may prove to be Avalon's savior, whereas another may bring about its end. As with *The Wings of Merlin* and earlier titles in the Lost Years of Merlin series, Barron develops a rich setting and cast of characters. His story and themes about identity and the fragility of our world have much to say to adolescents of today.

Philip Pullman, whose skillful writing has given us such fine books as the suspenseful *The Ruby in the Smoke,* the supernatural *Clockwork,* and the farcical *The Firework-Maker's Daughter* and *I Was a Rat,* has created high fantasy of matchless proportion in his His Dark Materials series. The trilogy, which includes *The Golden Compass, The Subtle Knife,* and *The Amber Spyglass,* is a richly complex work of the imagination. Inspired by a phrase from Milton's *Paradise Lost,* Pullman wrestles with profound issues of innocence, individuality, and spirituality. Lyra, the central character in *The Golden Compass,* is a young waif who has been raised amid the corridors of intellectual power at a university that seems to be Oxford in a country that closely resembles England. We quickly surmise that there is something off-kilter here. For one thing, Lyra is accompanied everywhere by a daemon, a shapeshifting creature that is her soul's companion. For another thing, Lyra's world has strange devices such as anbaric lamps and alethiometers. There are only five planets revolving around this world's sun. Most important, there is something mysterious and powerful called Dust. Lyra's burning desire to discover the importance of Dust propels her on a journey into the far North where she meets a complement of astounding characters. The most important of these is Iorek Brynison, outcast member of the panserbjørne, a race of armored bears. Iorek becomes an important companion for Lyra and a father figure who counters the evil actions of her parents. In *The Subtle Knife* Lyra is introduced to Will Parry, son of an adventurer who, like Lyra's father, has learned to travel

In his Great Tree of Avalon series, T. A. Barron has created complex works of high fantasy based in ancient legends and myths. From *The Great Tree of Avalon: The Eternal Flame, Book III* by T. A. Barron, copyright © 2002 by T. A. Barron. Used by permission of Philomel Books, a division of Penguin Young Readers Group, a Member of Putnam Group (USA), Inc., 345 Hudson St., New York, NY 10014.

between universes. Will's search for his father is intertwined with Lyra's quest for Dust as both seek understanding of the evil mysteries that bind their worlds. In *The Amber Spyglass* these characters' unequaled adventures see them travel between parallel worlds for a confrontation between the forces of good and evil. These compelling books, with their connections to Judeo-Christian traditions, their underpinnings in literary classics, and their references to theories of quantum physics, demand much of readers, but those willing to accept the challenging puzzles will be rewarded with an exceptionally satisfying experience. Literature in Action: "The Lure of *The Golden Compass*" exemplifies the rich responses that arise from Pullman's wonderful works of high fantasy.

Quests and Adventures

High fantasy is almost always the story of a search—for treasure, justice, identity, understanding—and of a hero

---

[17]T. A. Barron, "The Remarkable Metaphor of Merlin," *Book Links* 7.3 (January 1998): 40–44.

The Lure of *The Golden Compass*

Bree and Madeline are best friends and best book buddies. When Philip Pullman's *The Golden Compass* was first published, they were in fifth grade and their reaction to the book was passionate and heartfelt. They both felt it was "stupendous." As ninth graders, the two reflected on their experiences with the book.

> Our first encounters with *The Golden Compass* began a continuing dialogue about daemons, pronunciations, and auroras. One year, in September, we both had the same idea—to dress up as *Golden Compass* characters for Halloween. Bree ended up being Lyra, and Madeline went as a girl we imagined Lyra would meet on the other side of the Aurora. (The sequels, *The Subtle Knife* and *The Amber Spyglass*, weren't out yet.) Of course, the people giving away candy didn't guess what we were, but we didn't really expect them to. Since reading the book, we have both been "lured" by hopes of seeing the Aurora Borealis. Bree looked for it at camp in Quebec, and Madeline on her trip to Norway. We are both members of a mother-daughter book group, which read this book over one summer. During our meeting, we assigned daemons to each other, then created our adopted daemon out of socks and fabric markers. Madeline was a type of monkey, and Bree a griffin. During sleep-overs, while we were about to drift off to sleep, we would begin assigning each person we knew their *true* type of daemon. Factors to be considered: outer and inner personalities, interests, level of personal hypocrisy, animal stereotypes, and whether it *just seemed right*. We have yet to figure out what our own daemons really are, but it is a relief to realize that we are not quite grown up yet anyhow, and our daemons have not yet chosen their permanent form.
>
> *The Golden Compass* is our measuring stick when comparing the caliber of other books. We ask each other, "But is it as good as *The Golden Compass*"? Are the characters as realistic? Is the setting as vivid? Is the plot as compelling? The currently popular *Harry Potter* books, while very good, don't meet our *Golden Compass* standards, and the main problem is that nothing ever does.

Bree Bang-Jensen, age 14, ninth grade
Dobbs Ferry High School, Dobbs Ferry, New York

Madeline Kerner, age 14, ninth grade
Dobbs Ferry High School, Dobbs Ferry, New York

figure who learns important lessons in the adventuring. One of the most famous seekers in all fantasy is J. R. R. Tolkien's Bilbo Baggins in *The Hobbit*. Generally hobbits are very respectable creatures who never have any adventures or do anything unexpected. Bilbo Baggins, however, has an adventure and finds himself doing and saying altogether unexpected things. He is tricked by the dwarfs and the elves into going on a quest for treasure when he would much rather stay at home where he could be sure of six solid meals a day rather than be off fighting dragons. On the way, he becomes lost in a tunnel and is nearly consumed by a ghoulish creature called Gollum, who is "dark as darkness except for his two big round pale eyes." Gradually the hobbit's inner courage emerges, as he struggles on through terrifying woods, encounters with huge hairy spiders, and battles with goblins to a somewhat enigmatic victory over the dragon (a more heroic figure is allowed to slay it). *The Hobbit* gives children an introduction to Middle Earth and its creatures. Later they may pursue this interest in Tolkien's vastly expanded view of Middle Earth in The Lord of the Rings, a 1,300-page trilogy that again draws on the author's scholarly knowledge of the myth and folklore of northwestern Europe.

Welsh legends and mythology are the inspiration for the intriguing chronicles of the imaginary land of Prydain as told by Lloyd Alexander. In *The Book of Three* the reader is introduced to Taran, an assistant pigkeeper who dreams of becoming a hero. With a strange assortment of companions he pursues Hen Wen, the oracular pig, and struggles to save Prydain from the forces of evil. The chronicles are continued in the most exciting of all of the books, *The Black Cauldron*. Once again the faithful companions fight evil as they seek to find and destroy the great cauldron in which the dread Cauldron-Born are created, "mute and deathless warriors" made from the stolen bodies of those slain in battle. Taran is proud to be chosen to fight for Lord Gwydion, for he believes he will have more opportunity to win honor than when washing pigs or weeding a garden. His wise and sensitive companion Adaon tells him:

> I have marched in many a battle host . . . but I have also planted seeds and reaped the harvest with my own hands. And I have learned there is greater honor in a field well plowed than in a field steeped in blood. (p. 43)

Gradually, Taran learns what it means to become a man among men—the sacrifice of his gentle Adaon, the final courage of the proud Ellidyr, and the faithfulness of his companions. He experiences treachery, tragedy, and triumph; yet a thread of humor runs throughout to lighten the tension. Good does prevail, and Taran has matured and is ready for his next adventure. *The High King,* the masterful conclusion to this cycle of stories about the kingdom of Prydain, received the Newbery Medal. However, the recognition carried praise for all five of these chronicles. Each can be read independently, but together they present an exciting adventure in some of the best-written fantasy of our time.

In Robin McKinley's *The Blue Sword,* a book with closer ties to the world as we know it, a young woman called Harry discovers that her heritage has destined her to be a "Lady Hero." A ward of her brother, Harry feels vaguely out of place in the military outpost where he has brought her to live and is strangely drawn by the mountains where Free Hillfolk live. When Corlath the Hill-King comes to ask the Homelanders' cooperation in turning back the Northerners, who have demonic powers in battle, he is rebuffed. But his visionary gift of *kelar* drives him to kidnap Harry. She is treated as an honored captive and is destined to play a part in the Hillfolk's efforts against the hordes of the North. More and more at ease with her abductors, Harry trains for battle and earns the right to be a King's Rider and to bear the treasured Blue Sword, whose special power in her hand must finally stand between the Hillfolk and their enemies. The girl's poignant relationship with Corlath and his people is put in new perspective by her defiant courage and by her discovery of an ancestral link that proves she is in truth one of them. The story is rich with details of horsemanship, combat, and the romance of a nomadic life. It also speaks directly about women's roles and responsibilities, a message all the more intriguing for being set in a frame of military and desert life, where traditional roles for women are often rigid. *The Hero and the Crown* happens in time before *The Blue Sword* and features many of the same themes. It chronicles the coming of the king's only child, Aerin, into her powers, while leaving the reader with the desire to know more of what Aerin's future will bring.

Meredith Pierce, author of the Firebringer and Dark Angel trilogies, has written a remarkable quest story in *Treasure at the Heart of the Tanglewood.* Hannah is a young woman who lives at the edge of Tanglewood forest. Called Brown Hannah because of the plain brown garb she wears, she is unusual for the flowers that grow out of her hair. Each month she must pluck the flowers to make a brew for the wizard who lives in Tanglewood. She cannot remember her past, nor does she realize that she is being kept captive there by this man, who sucks her very life force to maintain his evil power. She provides charms and healing remedies to the local villagers brave enough to approach her, but she is shunned by them and has only the company of talking animals—a badger, a magpie, and three fox cubs. She is shaken out of her complacence with the arrival of a young knight, one of many who travel into Tanglewood to slay the golden boar who guards its treasure. When she finds him near death from an encounter with the boar, she nurses him back to health and falls in love. As she gains confidence from her relationship, she also begins to challenge the wizard's hold over her. Furious at her rebellion, the wizard turns her knight into a mute fox. When Hannah

Treasure at the Heart of the Tanglewood revolves around a quest but also speaks about a journey to self-understanding. "Jacket illustration" copyright © 2001 by Rafael Olbinski, jacket illustration, from *Treasure at the Heart of the Tanglewood* by Meredith Ann Pierce. Used by permission of Viking Books, a division of Penguin Young Readers Group, a Member of Penguin Group (USA) Inc., 345 Hudson St., New York, NY 10014, All rights reserved.

sets out to find the means to change him back into human form, she also discovers her true nature. As in all good quest stories, she also finds that the treasure at the heart of Tanglewood was not gold and precious jewels, but herself. Pierce has created an imaginative and romantic allegory that will captivate older readers.

A superior tale against which other novels of high fantasy may be judged is *A Wizard of Earthsea* by Ursula K. Le Guin. Studying at the School for Wizards, Sparrowhawk is taunted by a jealous classmate to use his powers before he is ready. Pride and arrogance drive him to call up a dreadful malignant shadow that threatens his life and all of Earthsea. Thus begins a chase and the hunt between the young wizard and the shadowbeast across the mountains and the waters of this world. Sparrowhawk, or Ged, his true name known only by his most trusted friends, is a well-developed character who transforms from an intelligent, impatient adolescent into a wise and grateful mage, or wizard. A major theme of the story is the responsibility that each choice carries with it. When Ged asks one of his teachers at the school how transformation of objects can be made permanent, he is answered:

> . . . you will learn it, when you are ready to learn it. But you must not change one thing, one pebble, one grain of sand, until you know what good and evil will follow the act. The world is in Equilibrium. A wizard's power of Changing and of Summoning can change the balance of the world. It is dangerous, that power. It is most perilous. It must follow knowledge, and serve need. To light a candle is to cast a shadow. (p. 57)

The word *shadow* is one of the recurring motifs of the story: Ged's boat bears this name; the evil he releases into the world is called a shadow; and in the end, Ged recognizes this evil as a shadow of himself and his hasty deed. The power of knowing the true name of someone or something, a common motif in traditional literature, is of central importance to this story. So, too, is the value of self-knowledge:

> Ged's ultimate quest . . . had made him whole: a man who knowing his whole true self, cannot be used or possessed by another power other than by himself, and whose life therefore is lived for life's sake and never in the service of ruin, or pain, or hatred, or the dark. (p. 203)

The next story in this Earthsea quartet is *The Tombs of Atuan,* the sinister tale of Tenar, a child priestess given at the age of 5 to a cult of darkness and evil. This more somber story provides important insights into trust and

the price of freedom. *The Farthest Shore* in a sense completes the mighty deeds of Ged, as the wizard must use all of his wisdom to defeat evil forces threatening to overcome Earthsea. *Tehanu* returns to Tenar and her attempts to save a child who has been abused both physically and sexually. Ged returns to these hills entirely spent of his powers and humiliated, but it is his human act, rather than his powers of wizardry, that saves Tenar and the child. This volume explores the many sources of a woman's strength—hearth, heart, and humanity—that she draws upon to arrive at mature and vital love. In *Gifts* Le Guin returns, not to Earthsea, but to the themes of identity and power that she has explored throughout her career. The metaphors in all her books speak clearly and profoundly to today's world.

SCIENCE FICTION

The line between fantasy and science fiction has always been difficult to draw, particularly in children's literature. Children are likely to use the label *science fiction* for any book that includes the paraphernalia of science, although critics make finer distinctions. It has been suggested that fantasy (even "science fantasy") presents a world that never was and never could be, whereas science fiction speculates on a world that, given what we now know of science, might just one day be possible. Sylvia Engdahl suggests that "science fiction differs from fantasy not in subject matter but in aim, and its unique aim is to suggest real hypotheses about mankind's future or about the nature of the universe."[18] Of course, the difficulty comes in deciding what constitutes a "real hypothesis." Are talking cats possible? Plants with a crystalline structure? Spaceships that think and are self-repairing? All these ideas have been put forth by science fiction writers asking themselves "What if . . . ?"

Science fiction is relevant for today's rapidly changing world. Writers must speculate about future technology and how new discoveries will affect our daily lives and thoughts. To do this, they must construct a world in which scientific frontiers of genetic engineering, artificial intelligence, space exploration, or robotics have advanced beyond our present knowledge. As in modern fantasy, detailed descriptions of these "scientific principles" and the characters' acceptance of them make the story believable. H. M. Hoover speaks about the author's responsibility to be consistent with "facts":

> If the story takes place on an alien world, the reader must be able to believe humans can walk there. Everything, from gravity and atmosphere, geology and life forms, must fit and be a part of that world if it is to ring true. . . . If not, somewhere a bright child will say "baloney" or

[18]Sylvia Louise Engdahl, "The Changing Role of Science Fiction in Children's Literature," *Horn Book Magazine* (October 1971): 450.

a less polite equivalent, and toss the book aside. Children may be gullible from lack of time to learn, but they're not stupid, and they remember details.[19]

In addition, authors who speak to today's reader about the future must consider the ethical or social implications inherent in the scientific issues they raise.

One of the values of science fiction is its ability to develop children's imagination and intuition as well as exercise their speculative and improvisational abilities. Most literature offers a view of society as it is; science fiction assumes a vastly different society. Madeleine L'Engle suggests that children enter this world of speculation more easily than adults do: "Children have always been interested in these cosmic questions and riddles that adults often attempt to tame by placing into categories fit only for scientists or adults or theologians."[20]

Much science fiction that considers cosmic questions falls within the realm of young-adult novels. For instance, in *The Diary of Pelly D*, L. J. Adlington imagines a seemingly utopian world where growing prejudice about genetic ancestry leads society to a futuristic holocaust. In *Eva* Peter Dickinson considers the consequences when the mind of a human girl is transferred from her ruined body to that of a healthy chimpanzee. M. T. Anderson's *Feed* contemplates a frightening future where at birth almost everyone is wired to the Internet through brain implants. *The Duplicate* by William Sleator gives a teenage boy the power to be in two places at once, with chilling results. Occasionally, however, older-elementary and middle-school readers, drawn by a love of science, might read well above what adults consider their usual reading levels. Because newer science fiction tends to emphasize a concern with the complex emotional and physical consequences of technological breakthroughs to the future of humankind rather than the dangers posed by aliens or intergalactic warfare, perhaps science fiction readers will be more compassionate and informed in choosing the future. The Web *"The Giver"* on pages 392–93 shows how such concerns might be explored.

Through the Door

Many children come easily to science fiction by way of books that might not fit a purist's definition of the genre but that incorporate some of its trappings, such as robots, spaceships, futuristic settings, or scientific terminology. Eleanor Cameron's *The Wonderful Flight to the Mushroom Planet* begins a series of stories about Mr. Bass, who lives on the planet Basidium. Alfred Slote has written a popular series that begins with *My Robot Buddy*, in which Jack Jameson and his robot Danny One switch places to foil robotnappers. Few of these books tackle

In *The Diary of Pelly D* by L. J. Adlington a young man discovers an old diary that suggests an explanation for the chaos of his own era. Copyright © 2005. Used by permission of Greenwillow Books, an imprint of HarperCollins Publishers, Inc.

weighty themes, but they provide satisfaction to readers who can follow the characters through a series of adventures or who relish the ultimately happy conclusions in a science fiction setting.

An exceptional book that presents a hopeful view of the future is Jill Paton Walsh's *The Green Book*. A family escapes Earth with others in a preprogrammed spacecraft before the "Disaster." Father tells Joe, Sarah, and Pattie that they can take very little with them but that this includes "one book per voyager." Pattie is ridiculed for wasting her choice on a blank green-covered book. When they arrive at their destination planet, Pattie, as the youngest, has the privilege of naming their new home, a place of red foliage and shimmering silver plains. "We are at Shine, on the first day," says Pattie. Ironically, this shine is produced by the crystalline structure of the plant life on the planet. When the wheat seeds brought from Earth produce a crop of grains like "hexagonal yellow

[19]H. M. Hoover, "Where Do You Get Your Ideas?" *Top of the News* 39 (fall 1982): 61.

[20]Madeleine L'Engle, "Childlike Wonder and the Truths of Science Fiction," *Children's Literature* 10 (1982): 102.

beads, shining like golden glass," it appears that the colony will face starvation. The children secretly grind the glasslike beads, mix and bake the dough, and eat the bread without harm. It is then that Pattie's blank book is needed to keep records, and the story-starved people discover that the green book is now full of the most satisfying story of all—their own. An excellent choice for reading aloud and discussing with third and fourth graders, this brief, high-quality book raises thought-provoking speculations about life and survival on another planet. The writing is vivid and tight, evocative without being obscure, and an interesting twist in the narrative voice neatly brings together the opening and closing sentences. Illustrations by Lloyd Bloom match the solemn tone of the text and are memorable for their rounded shapes softened by the light on Shine.

Visitors to Earth

Television and motion pictures have eased our acceptance of the possibility of visitors from other parts of the universe. Whether the visitor arrives purposefully or inadvertently, young readers today are willing to suspend disbelief and are usually prepared to consider the dilemmas that interactions between visitors and humans present.

Alexander Key presents a visitor to Earth in *The Forgotten Door,* which explores the rights of individuals and challenges readers' assumptions about the nature of human society. Little Jon awakens cold and bruised in a mossy cave and cannot remember who he is or where he came from. He is found by the kindly Bean family, who gradually discover that he is not from this world. Rumors about his strange powers spread, however, and soon the federal government demands custody of Little Jon. Other political groups would like to use Jon's powers, and the Beans are desperate for help. Finally, Jon is able to hear his parents calling him, and he communicates his concern for his friends, the Beans. As various forces close in on their tiny cabin, Jon and the Beans disappear through the Forgotten Door to the world Jon has described to them—a world so simple as to need no laws, leaders, or money, and where intelligent people work together. The fast pace of the story and its substantial characters and challenging themes have made this a good discussion choice for small groups of fourth and fifth graders.

The title character in Dick King-Smith's *Harriet's Hare* is really a visitor from the planet Pars who has been dropped off on Earth for a brief vacation. He assumes the shape of a hare and is discovered by Harriet in the middle of a flattened circle in her father's wheat field. Harriet, a lonely child since her mother's death, is thrilled to have a new friend, whom she names Wiz. The two have a wonderful time exploring the countryside together. Wiz is certainly an extraordinary friend, and because he can communicate with animals he shows Harriet the natural world in a new and magical way. Dreading the

end of his vacation, Harriet implores him to stay longer, but he reminds her that he misses his home and must return. He leaves behind several wonderful gifts, however—three little hare offspring and a new mother for Harriet. Although this is a lovely surprise to Harriet, it is no wonder at all to readers who have watched the romance grow between Harriet's father and a children's book author who has moved in nearby. King-Smith spins a warm and gentle tale for younger readers, filled with the wonders of the English countryside and brimming with likable and amusing characters.

Sylvia Waugh's *Space Race, Earth Born,* and *Who Goes Home?* are charming stories that will be enjoyed by the same middle-grade audience that reads *Harriet's Hare.* In Waugh's books the visitors to Earth are from the Planet Ormingat. The families in these books have assumed human form in order to study life on our planet. The problems occur because the protagonists in each story have been raised as human children and know nothing of their origins. All three children must make difficult choices when they find that they must leave Earth to return to their home planet. Interestingly, each character makes a different choice, and each decision has unexpected consequences for family and friends. In these well-told stories Waugh raises important questions about identity, family loyalty, and individual needs that will invite much discussion from middle-grade readers.

In Kate Gilmore's *The Exchange Student,* Fen, a seven-foot alien from the planet Chela, comes to Earth as an exchange student. When he arrives at his host family's abode, he is delighted to discover that 16-year-old Daria Wells, the Wells's youngest daughter, is in charge of a breeding zoo for endangered Earth animals. Fen's unusual interest in her animals does not surprise Daria, who feels such passion herself. But readers will soon suspect something more sinister. As Fen secretly communicates with his fellow exchange students, a plot to steal animal DNA from Earth's breeding center is revealed. The Chelan people, it turns out, have destroyed their own animals in an ecological disaster, and the planet is overrun with insect pests who are uncontrolled by natural predators. Fen's attempted theft and his strong love for Earth animals is a response to that disaster. There is a strong environmental message in *The Exchange Student,* but it does not overwhelm a good story or overshadow the likable characters, both human and alien.

Outer Space and Cyberspace

The technology of the early twenty-first century makes visits beyond Earth's surface much more plausible to today's child, and many writers have tapped into the premise that interstellar travel is just around the corner. *Enchantress from the Stars* by Sylvia Louise Engdahl centers on the mission of Elana to save the Adrecians from the Imperialists. Elana belongs to an anthropological service of the future that represents the most advanced humanity in the universe. By contrast, the Andrecians are

Wonderfully Exciting Books

Names

How are names used in the community? How does that compare with the way we use names in our society today? Why do you think that all the "new children" are assigned numbers at birth, but not given names until the Ceremony of One? Why does Jonas's father think that calling Gabriel by his name might help him?

Research the meanings of characters' names. Read the biblical stories of the archangel Gabriel and Jonah. How do these stories change or add to your understanding of the novel?

Is there any significance to the fact that the Giver's daughter's name, Rosemary, has been associated with "remembrance"?

Censorship

It is easy to understand that the Giver, as the sole repository of memory, is the only one in the community permitted to have history books, but why can't the rest of the community have access to other types of books? What about films, visual arts, theater, music, and other art forms?

Read *The Day They Came to Arrest the Book* (Hentoff). Does your community have to deal with issues of censorship?

Has *The Giver* been the object of censorship? Consult the American Library Association Web site at <http://www.ala.org/bbooksat> and related Web sites.

Write a rationale for why *The Giver* should not be banned.

COMMUNICATION

Language

What are the effects of how language is used and controlled in the community?

How is lying or deception related to word choice?

Contrast Jonas's and Asher's use of language.

At the Ceremony of Twelve, the Chief Elder says: "Jonas has not been assigned. Jonas has been *selected*." Is this distinction important? How?

What important words do we have in our language that are missing from theirs?

Trace the etymology of words such as *community*, *future*, and *utopia*.

THE GIVER BY LOIS LOWRY: A WEB OF POSSIBILITIES

Science and Technology

How are science and technology used in *The Giver*? Give some examples. Compare this with the ways technology is used in other futuristic novels.

Buckminster Fuller (Potter)
Fuller wanted to build a dome over Manhattan to control the climate. Do you think this would be a good idea? What are the pros and cons?

Living in Space (Kettelkamp)
What might happen to the world of the future if hunger were eliminated or if robots took over your school or if a nonpolluting, renewable fuel were discovered? Think through the impact of one such scientific advancement.

Making a Difference: Dreamers, Choosers, Changers, and Leaders

Once Jonas began to receive memories and to learn some of the terrible truths about his community, his vision of the community's future changed. He then took action to help realize his new vision. Has new information ever changed your view of how things should be? If so, what did you or can you do in response?

Read *A Swiftly Tilting Planet* (L'Engle) or *The Green Futures of Tycho* (Sleator). How did characters in these books change and affect change?

Study people in your own world who have made changes for the better.

Other Visions of the Future

Eva (Dickinson)
The Kindling (Armstrong and Butcher)
When the Hermit Thrush Sings (Butler)
The White Mountains (Christopher)
A Wind in the Door (L'Engle)
Z for Zachariah (O'Brien)
Make a comparison chart of these visions of the future.

Gathering Blue (Lowry)
Messenger (Lowry)
What are the parallels between *Gathering Blue*, *The Giver*, and *Messenger*?

Web prepared by Jennifer Madden O'Hear

Without Differences?

In Jonas's community there were no racial or ethnic differences. Is that desirable? What are the pros and cons? What about economic class differences?

Conformity

When Jonas asks, "What if we could hold up things that were bright red or bright yellow, and [Gabriel] could choose?" the Giver responds, "He might make wrong choices." What are the advantages and disadvantages of having choices? Have you ever made a wrong one? Have you ever regretted having to choose?

Jonas lives in a community that has turned to "Sameness." Are there times in your life when you choose sameness or conformity? What are they? When do you act independently?

Compare to issues of conformity in *A Wrinkle in Time* (L'Engle)

Family

Read *Families: A Celebration of Diversity, Commitment, and Love* (Jenness).

How do the contemporary families profiled in this book compare with Jonas's family? With your own family?

Compare how elderly people are treated in Jonas's community with the way they are treated in American society and in other countries.

Read *Families: Poems Celebrating the African American Experience* (Strickland and Strickland), and *Fathers, Mothers, Sisters, Brothers* (Hoberman).

What type of poetry might Jonas write about his family?

Division of Labor

In Jonas's community everyone who was able worked. There was no unemployment. How did they determine who would do which job? Were all the jobs equally desirable or equally respected in the community? Do you think this is a good system?

Ask adults in your family if they would like to be guaranteed a job for life. Would they like someone else to choose it for them?

How does Pattie's community handle these problems in *The Green Book* (Walsh)?

Government and Rules

Describe the government and the rules in *The Giver*.

How do they compare with those in our democratic system? With communism or totalitarianism? With other governments past or present that you've studied? Create a comparison chart.

If you could make the rules for a group of people, where would you start?

LIVING IN A COMMUNITY

Without Conflict?

Jonas's community appeared to be so isolated that it almost seemed to be surrounded by an invisible wall.

Read *Talking Walls* and *Talking Walls: The Story Continues* (Knight).

What have been the functions of walls throughout history and in the present? To separate, unite, protect, etc.? Are there walls in your vision of a perfect future world? If so, describe them.

Is it right to impose order by taking away choice?

Memory in Other Books by Lois Lowry

Memory is an important topic in Lowry's *Anastasia Krupnik* and *Autumn Street*.

Compare and contrast what these books suggest about the value of and the pain associated with memory.

Looking Back: A Book of Memories (Lowry)
How did memory influence the style of Lowry's memoir?

Lois Lowry's Memories

Read "On Writing *The Giver*" (Lowry) and "Newbery Award Acceptance Speech" (Lowry) for background information. How did Lowry's memories affect her writing of *The Giver*?

Discuss Lowry's reason for writing the novel's dedication. What are its implications?

MEMORY

Recall the memories that Jonas receives. How do they change him?

Personal and Familial Memory

The Giver's favorite memory is of "families, and holidays, and happiness." If you could give Jonas your favorite memory, what would it be? How is yours similar to and different from the Giver's?

Read such memoirs as *Family Pictures* (Garza) and *Homesick* (Fritz). Interview your grandparents and make a collection of family memories.

Community Memory

Record and preserve the memories of some of the older people in your community. Create a book of these memories and find an appropriate place for it in the community, such as the public library or the historical society.

at a medieval stage of development; the people still believe in magic and will reward anyone who can kill the "terrible dragon." The dragon, however, is really an earthmover with which the Imperialists intend to destroy forests and colonize the planet. Eventually the fourth son of an Andrecian woodcutter and Elana defeat the invaders with the values of love, faith, and sacrifice that transcend all levels of material development. The story helps readers see their own world in a different perspective, a function of all good literature. In a somewhat didactic sequel, *The Far Side of Evil*, Engdahl deals with the consequences of misusing nuclear power.

In Annette Klause's *Alien Secrets,* Robin Goodfellow, nicknamed "Puck," is a troubled 12-year-old expelled from her boarding school and traveling to join her parents on the distant planet of Shoon when she witnesses a murder. On board her spaceship she encounters an alien boy named Hush who has lost the Soo, a treasure of his people that he was entrusted with returning to them. It becomes apparent that, along with a few ghosts, the murderer is on board their spaceship, and the Soo is at the center of a devious plot. Puck risks her life to help Hush find the treasure, but the two make a great team. The mystery is solved, the villains unmasked, and the Soo restored to its rightful place. Both Puck and Hush find their strengths in adversity and also come to accept their faults. This is a thrilling story, interwoven with subtle political themes of oppression and colonization that raise the book far above the level of most outer space adventures. Similar themes drive Hilari Bell's suspenseful story, *A Matter of Profit.* Seventeen-year-old Ahvren is a soldier in the Emperor's Army who takes leave from the battlefield to visit T'Chin, where his father is governor of the conquered world. Sick of fighting, Ahvren dreams of a different way of life and makes a bargain with his father. If he can find the assassins who threaten the emperor's life, he can take a year to decide on his future path. He is caught up in a dangerous intrigue which also involves his beloved sister, Sabri, and a strange T'Chin scholar who becomes his mentor. Ahvren eventually solves the puzzle and discovers the inner strengths that he needs for his future.

Although outer space adventures have been popular since Jules Verne wrote *From the Earth to the Moon*, there is now a growing subgenre of science fiction set in cyberspace. In the hilarious *Lost in Cyberspace* by Richard Peck, Josh Lewis's friend Aaron figures out a way to use his laptop computer to travel through time. The two sixth graders then carry out the ultimate research paper and plan to present their findings at their school's Parents' Night. They continue their tinkering with cyberspace in *The Great Interactive Dream Machine.* In *Cyberstorm*, Gloria Skurzynski's 11-year-old heroine, Darcy, escapes into a virtual reality machine in the year 2015. Trying to save her dog, Chip, from the Animal Control Division, Darcy is sent back in time with Mrs. Galloway, an elderly woman who rented the machine to revisit her youth.

When the machine malfunctions, the two are caught in a terrifying world that might be real or surreal. The book has the type of fast-moving plot that appeals to middle-grade readers, but the characters also deal with more serious problems that confront families and cut across generations. Older readers will enjoy *Virtual War, The Clones,* and *The Revolt*, three titles in Skurzynski's Virtual War Chronologs where, following nuclear war and diseases that wipe out most of Earth's population, war is fought in cyberspace rather than in a real battleground.

Works like Orson Scott Card's *Ender's Game* and *Ender's Shadow,* two of the books in the Ender Wiggin Saga, although published for adult readers, have been discovered by adolescents who are devotees of computer games and steeped in the language of the computer. These readers might have the background to enjoy such young-adult titles as Vivian Vande Velde's *User Unfriendly* and Monica Hughes's *Invitation to the Game*, and they will certainly find Gillian Cross's *New World* accessible. Cross tells a gripping tale in which Miriam, Will, and Stuart, three 14-year-olds unknown to each other, are recruited by a computer company to test a prototype of a new virtual reality game. As each becomes more and more hooked on the game, one of them begins to suspect that there is something sinister behind the fun. In circumstances that become increasingly threatening, the youngsters are forced to face questions about their own identities and the nature of reality itself. In a thought-provoking and chilling scenario, Cross manages to address issues such as manipulation, greed, and the lengths to which young people will go for excitement.

Views of the Future

Science fiction of the highest level presents the reader with complex hypotheses about the future of humankind. Many novels raise questions about the organization of society or the nature of the world following a massive ecological disaster. Writers such as John Christopher and Madeleine L'Engle imagine other life-forms and their interactions with our world. William Sleator in *The Green Futures of Tycho* asks how present time can be altered to affect the future; in L'Engle's *A Swiftly Tilting Planet*, the past is altered to change the present and future. Throughout these novels of speculation runs the question of which human qualities and responsibilities will become—or remain—essential in time to come. The Web *"The Giver"* (see pp. 392–93) shows how these issues might be explored in Lois Lowry's Newbery Medal–winning novel.

A Wrinkle in Time suggests that love and individuality will continue to be important for the future. If there is a classic in the field of science fiction for children, it might be this Newbery Medal winner by Madeleine L'Engle. The exciting story concerns Charles Wallace, a 5-year-old brilliant beyond his age and time, and Meg, his 12-year-old sister, whose stubbornness later becomes an asset. With the help of Calvin O'Keefe, a 14-year-old

In her Newbery Medal–winning book *The Giver*, Lois Lowry raises fundamental questions about human nature and human society. Cover from *The Giver* by Lois Lowry. Copyright © 1993 by Lois Lowry. Reprinted by permission of Houghton Mifflin Company. All rights reserved.

situations and other creatures. The story concerns the fight to save Charles Wallace from a baffling illness. Meg, Calvin, and Mr. Jenkins, the cold, remote principal of the school, are led to a planet in galactic space where size does not exist. Here they are made small enough to enter Charles Wallace's body and help fight the attacking forces of evil, the Echthroi. Only when Meg names them with her own name does she overcome the Echthroi and save Charles. The story emphasizes the importance of every minuscule part of the universe in carrying out its purpose in living. *A Wind in the Door* is more complex than *A Wrinkle in Time,* but L'Engle is capable of conveying her message to perceptive children of 9 or 10 and up.

A Swiftly Tilting Planet completes L'Engle's Time Trilogy. Charles Wallace has been saved, first from the dehumanization of It, and second from a rare blood disease. Now, in this story, the reader discovers why Charles Wallace has been twice rescued, for his ultimate mission involves saving the world from total destruction. He must journey back in historical time to change some seemingly small part of past relationships so that a potential world war in the present can be averted. This is by far the most demanding of the three volumes, as there are many characters in several time frames to attend to. The Time Trilogy is a unique and wonderful combination of science fiction, modern fantasy, traditional lore, and religious symbolism by which L'Engle stretches the minds and the spirits of her readers.

In *Green Boy* Susan Cooper imagines a future for our earth that is devastated by pollution and unlimited industrial growth. The book begins in the present day as two brothers, the older Trey and his mute little brother Lou, set out to go fishing on Long Pond Cay near their Caribbean home. They love the natural beauty of the place and appreciate its delicate ecology, but it is threatened by developers who want to build a resort. As the boys explore the Cay they find themselves transported into Pangaia, a parallel world that is ruled by industrialists and inhabited by mutant monsters. There they find a group of renegades who believe that Lou is the Green Boy who holds the key to restoring the shattered natural balance of their planet. The solutions to the problems in both worlds are swift and devastating. Cooper's message is a bit heavy-handed at times, but the story moves swiftly and should captivate middle-grade readers.

The Ear, the Eye, and the Arm and *The House of the Scorpion* by Penelope Farmer are complex and gripping views of a post-apocalyptic earth. *The Ear, the Eye, and the Arm* is set in Zimbabwe in the year 2194. Thirteen-year-old Tendai and his younger brother and sister live in a protected enclave in a society that separates out the haves from the have-nots. Like children in other tales, however, they long for adventure, and when they venture out from behind the electrified fences one day, they get more than they bargained for. Kidnapped by the She Elephant's hooligans, they are taken to a toxic waste

on whose stability the two often rely, the children begin a frenzied search for their missing father, a scientist working for the government. They are aided in their search by three women who have supernatural powers—Mrs. Whatsit, Mrs. Who, and Mrs. Which. The children travel by means of a wrinkle in time, or a tesseract, to the evil planet Camazotz. The people of Camazotz, having given up their identities to "It," do everything in synchronization. When Charles Wallace attempts to resist It by reason, he, too, is captured. Though Meg is able to save her father, they must leave Charles Wallace behind. Exhausted and still under the evil influence of It, Meg is slowly nursed back to love and peace by another strange but loving creature, Aunt Beast. When Meg realizes that only she can save Charles Wallace, she returns to confront It with what she knows It does not have or understand—the power of love. This many-layered story can be read for the exciting plot alone or for the themes and the values it espouses.

A Wind in the Door, also by L'Engle, is a companion story involving many of the previous characters with new

dump where an evil old woman holds court. They escape to an idyllic village where technology is banned and the people live in pastoral splendor. But they find that the price for this peace is often death for those who are weak or won't conform. Close behind the three children in their escapades is an unusual trio of detectives—Ear, Eye, and Arm—who have unusual powers because of genetic mutation and have been hired by the children's parents to bring them home. As in all good cliffhangers, however, they discover the children's whereabouts just a fraction too late to rescue them, and the children, particularly Tendai, must take responsibility for themselves. Farmer weaves Shona mythology, science fiction, and a little Hollywood action thriller into a book that has many layers. In *The Ear, the Eye, and the Arm* she raises searching questions about social and political issues without neglecting issues that are closer to the heart of a young boy's coming of age, all in the context of a strapping good yarn. *The House of the Scorpion* is an equally thrilling story set in the country of Opium, somewhere between the United States and what used to be Mexico. Its hero is Matt, a clone of El Patron, a drug lord who rules over the poppy fields farmed by human beings with computer chips implanted in their heads. As in her other books, Farmer explores questions of what it means to be human and how it is that some children who grow up under the most awful of circumstances manage to hold on to some vestige of goodness and an innate sense of what is right.

Margaret Haddix explores the possible effects of overpopulation in her Shadow Children series. In the highly authoritarian world Haddix imagines, couples are limited to only two children. In *Among the Hidden* we are introduced to 12-year-old Luke, a third child who must stay out of sight, cooped up in his house with no friends, no school, no camping trips or visits to the mall. When a housing development is built next to his house, wiping out the forest that grew there, he finds that he is not the only hidden child. This thrilling series follows Luke out of his house and into boarding school where we meet additional characters whose peril-ridden adventures round out the series.

The White Mountains quartet by John Christopher describes a future world that has been reduced to a primitive society. However, people in this twenty-first-century world are controlled by machine creatures called Tripods. At age 14, each human being must be "capped," a ceremony in which a steel plate is inserted into the skull to make the wearer a servant of the state. Over the course of the four books, young Will leads the revolt that defeats the Tripods and leaves humans free to set up their own government. Christopher's second science-fiction series—*The Prince in Waiting, Beyond the Burning Lands,* and *The Sword of the Spirits*—deals with England in the twenty-first century following the "Disaster," a period of volcanic activity, earthquakes, and strong radiation from the sun that destroyed all of humanity's technical accomplishments. These books are much more violent than the White Mountains quartet, which is in

keeping with their imagined setting. However, the violence may be justified because it raises the ethical questions of whether violence impersonalized by distance and machine is any different from hand-to-hand violence and whether it is possible to keep "rules" in war. Mature readers who enjoy the Christopher books will want to read other titles about dystopian future worlds. Garth Nix's *Shade's Children* portrays a world where an alien race harvests the brains of children when they reach the age of 14. In Scott Westerfeld's *Uglies,* people's status is decided on the basis of appearance until a group of rebel Uglies decide to take matters into their own hands. M. T. Anderson's *Feed* imagines a world where infants are connected to the Internet through implants and people are consumed by material desires and the latest trends. Janet McNaughton's *The Secret Under My Skin* tells of a future world where technology has been outlawed and a totalitarian government holds sway. These books raise many questions among adolescents about the balance of progress and basic human dignity.

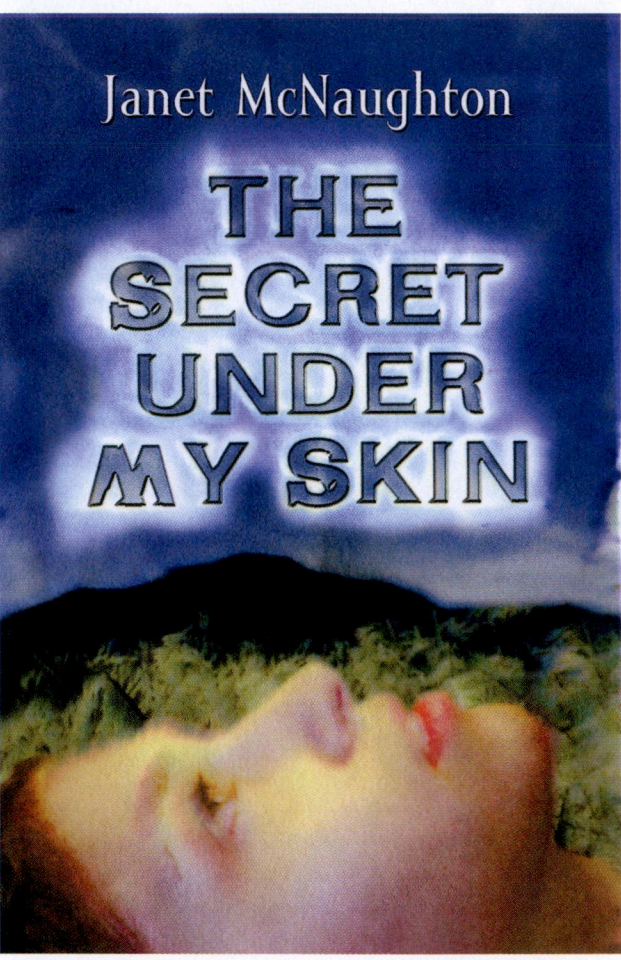

In Janet McNaughton's *The Secret Under My Skin,* an adolescent girl plays a key role in a world of the future where the environment is toxic and technology is illegal.
Jacket of *The Secret Under My Skin* by Janet McNaughton. Copyright © 2005. Used by permission of HarperCollins Children's Books, a division of HarperCollins Publishers, Inc.

Teenager Ann Burden in *Z for Zachariah* by Robert C. O'Brien thinks she is the last living person on Earth after a nuclear war. She begins to carve out a solitary life, accompanied only by the family dog, when she sees what appears to be smoke from a campfire on the horizon. She finds another survivor, John Loomis. But instead of providing Ann with hoped-for companionship, he becomes more and more possessive. At last she decides on a plan of escape and leaves the valley in hopes that she will find other survivors she has dreamed about. Written in the form of a diary kept by Ann, this story is rich in the details of her survival and growing resolve. Ann relates her doubt and anger about the many choices she must make, but the reader does not doubt that Ann will find the others for whom she searches.

In 1975 when *Z for Zachariah* was published, nuclear war was the worst disaster most writers could imagine. In the early twenty-first century disease seems to be the new threat to humanity's future. In their Fire-Us series Jennifer Armstrong and Nancy Butcher explore the outcomes of a terrible pandemic that has wiped out almost all the adults in the world as well as many children. In *The Kindling* we meet a group of surviving children who have banded together in a deserted house to try to hold on to what little they remember of their previous lives. Mommy is a nurturing adolescent who is also an agoraphobic. Teacher, the oldest, keeps a huge book of brochures and clippings and stays awake each night to write down the children's dream ravings in hopes of some revelation. Hunter is a nearsighted youth who scavenges their small Florida town for food and clothing. He also hides the remains of dead bodies that litter the streets so that the little ones, Action Figure, Teddy Bear, Baby, and Doll, won't be frightened. The older children are becoming more and more worried as their food supplies dwindle, when Angerman appears. He is a half-crazed adolescent who drags a plastic mannequin around on a rope, and he first cajoles and then forces them to set out on a journey to Washington, D.C. to find the President. Their journey continues in *The Keepers of the Flame* and *The Kiln*. The books are suspenseful and frightening cautionary tales. Armstrong and Butcher have created well-developed characters whose reactions to the disaster are wholly believable. Their eccentricities, their use of language, and their fears are what we would expect from children who have survived for so long without adult help or guidance. In *Hole in the Sky*, for more mature readers, Pete Hautman explores a similar scenario of a world sent mad by devastating disease.

The authors of the previously discussed books have drawn clear distinctions between the world of reality and the world of fantasy. There are several books, however, that could be considered as works of contemporary realism yet seem best discussed in this section because their authors, rather than focus just on family relationships or on the difficulties of growing up in today's world, also speculate about human actions and interactions that might lead to dramatic alterations in humanity's future.

In John Marsden's *Tomorrow When the War Began*, a group of teenagers return from a camping trip in a remote Australian canyon to find their town invaded by an unknown army. In this book and the following volumes in Marsden's Tomorrow series—*The Dead of Night, A Killing Frost, Darkness Be My Friend, Burning for Revenge, The Night Is for Hunting,* and *The Other Side of Dawn*—the teens face critical issues of right and wrong as they attempt to fight a guerrilla war against the totalitarian enemy. Meg Rosoff's Sibert Award winner *How I Live Now* also seems very contemporary. In this tale a 15-year-old American girl goes to visit relatives in rural England. At first she and her cousins share idyllic weeks, and Daisy finds herself falling in love with her cousin Edmond. Then a world war breaks out, and England is invaded by unnamed foreigners. Daisy and Edmund are separated, and Daisy must struggle to survive in an entirely new reality. All these books work beautifully as survival stories, but they also raise important moral and political questions that link them to contemporary conflicts in the wider world.

Lois Lowry's *The Giver* imagines a future that at first seems benign and idyllic. Pollution is gone, family life is tranquil, and communities are orderly and peaceful. In this world young Jonas approaches the Ceremony of Twelve with anticipation, for this is when he will be assigned to his life's work. He is stunned when his name is passed over during the ceremony, but then the Chief Elder announces that Jonas has been selected to be the next Receiver of Memory. This is the one person in the community who holds memories, not just of events, but of feelings. As he is instructed by the old Receiver, now the Giver, he comes to understand the fullness of human experience in all its color, joy, and pain. He also begins to see beneath the orderly surface of his existence and to understand the terrible price his people have paid for their serenity. Determined to change the course of the future, Jonas and the Giver plan for his escape. But at the last moment a terrible threat to Gabriel, a foster child about whom Jonas cares deeply, forces a change of plan, and Jonas sets out on a journey that might lead to his end or might bring him full circle to his humanity. *The Giver* is a richly rewarding fantasy, full of subtle clues, connections, and ideas. Lowry has given each reader the wonderful gift that Jonas's community lacked, the gift of choice. This is a book to be read, enjoyed, and understood on an intensely personal level. In her Newbery acceptance speech, Lowry remarked on the interpretation a young reader brought to the book.

> The child—as we all do—has brought her own life to a book. She has found a place, a place in the pages of a book, that shares her own frustrations and feelings. . . . Most of the young readers who have written to me have perceived the magic of the circular journey—the truth that

INTO THE CLASSROOM

Modern Fantasy

It may be hard to believe in the face of the Harry Potter craze, but some children do not like to read fantasy. Younger children go through a developmental phase where they try to sort out what is real from what is imagined (perhaps this is the time when they stop believing in Santa Claus and the tooth fairy). This is a time when they may reject works of fantasy. Other children seem to be very concrete and find it difficult to suspend disbelief when reading about elves, hobbits, and animals that talk. For these children teachers may want to find those works of fantasy that are grounded in the real world. Time-shift stories like David Wiseman's *Jeremy Visick* or science fiction such as Jennifer Armstrong and Nancy Butcher's *The Kindling* may serve as an invitation to other types of fantasy. A thorough understanding of traditional literature with its many motifs and archetypes may also provide an entrée into more complicated works of fantasy. The activities mentioned below are designed to bring children back into works of fantasy to live within the world of the book for a time.

1. **Mapmaking.** Make an illustrated map to show an extraordinary world or imaginary realm that you have discovered in a book. Make a key to locate events of the story. Visit T. A. Barron's Web site at <http://www.tabarron.com> to see some maps of extraordinary worlds.

2. **Symbols Key.** Make a display or a chart of the many symbols and their meaning found in *The Dark Is Rising* by Susan Cooper or *A Stranger Came Ashore* by Mollie Hunter.

3. **Magic Amulet.** Think of some family heirloom that might act as a magical amulet that would take you back to the time when your mother or father was 12 years old. How does the heirloom "work"? Where would you be? What might you witness?

4. **Imagining Scientific Advancement.** Ask yourself what might happen to the world of tomorrow if hunger were eliminated, or if robots took over your school, or if hydrogen fusion were made a workable source of energy. Think through the impact of one such scientific advancement.

 Go to the Online Learning Center at **www.mhhe.com/kiefer9e** or your Resources CD-ROM to find these additional classroom activities:

5. **Games**
6. **New Worlds**
7. **Book Talks**
8. **Genre Study**

---

we go out and come back, and that what we come back to is changed, and so are we.[21]

Lowry's *Gathering Blue* is not a sequel to *The Giver* but a good companion book in which Lowry imagines a future where there is little technology and little concern for kindness or compassion. Missing also is a plant that will give the color blue to dye the threads that Kira, the heroine of the story, needs for her marvelous embroidery. Kira has been lame from birth, and many in her village believe she should have been killed for her "defect." But she has come to the attention of the Guardians, the autocratic rulers of her village, because of her talents as an embroiderer. She is taken to live at the magnificent Council Edifice and set to repairing the robe of The Singer, who every year relays the history of her world at The Gathering. Eventually she will add new pictures to the robe: like Jonas in *The Giver*, Kira is charged with keeping the memories of her people. She meets two others in the Edifice, Thomas, a young Carver, and little Jo, who will become the next Singer. Kira gradually begins to realize, as Jonas did, that her safe life is really a prison. In the end,

she and the others escape to a world where other rejects from her village have created a truly humane society and where she can gather the color blue for her beautiful art. In Lowry's *Messenger* we learn, somewhat offhandedly, what happened to Jonas and meet a new character, a boy named Matty, who has secret powers that could prove destructive. Matty's village has long welcomed all newcomers, but as resources dwindle, greed turns neighbors into enemies. The Village decides to shut itself in behind a great wall. The characters from *The Giver*, *Gathering Blue*, and *Messenger* all come together in the subtle and beautifully written conclusion.

The ability to change lives is the power of such good writing. Fantasy for children needs no defense. Whether a modern fairy tale like *Many Moons* or *The Little Prince*, modern fantasy like *Charlotte's Web* or *The Dark Is Rising*, or the science fiction of *A Wrinkle in Time* or *The Giver*, these lasting books can speak for our time and the times to come. They stretch children's imaginations, present our own world in a new perspective, and ask readers to consider how present actions might affect Earth's ecological, political, and social future.

---

[21]Lois Lowry, "Newbery Medal Acceptance," *Horn Book Magazine* (July/August 1994): 420–21.

Chapter Review

Go to the Online Learning Center at **www.mhhe.com/kiefer9e** or your Resources CD-ROM to take chapter quizzes, practice with key terms, and review the chapter.

Explorations

1. Write a modern fairy tale, fable, or tall tale using the old forms, but with twenty-first-century content reflecting today's changing values. For example, you might want to consider reversing the stereotyped sex roles of the prince and princess.

2. Ask a group of your friends to list their ten favorite children's books. How many of these could be categorized as modern fantasy?

3. Compare the Chronicles of Narnia by C. S. Lewis with Lloyd Alexander's Prydain Chronicles; or compare two animal fantasies, such as E. B. White's *Charlotte's Web* and Dick King-Smith's *Pigs Might Fly.* In what ways are they alike? How are they different?

4. Choose a book of high fantasy or time fantasy, and identify motifs that seem derived from folklore, myth, or legend. Which of these motifs are common in other modern fantasies?

5. Choose a theme or topic found in works of fantasy, such as "transformations," "trickery," "small worlds," "castles and kingdoms," or "journeys." Search the Children's Literature database located on the Resources CD-ROM, and compile a list of titles from picture books, poetry, and traditional literature that you could use to introduce children to longer works of fantasy.

Web Links

Go to the Online Learning Center at **www.mhhe.com/kiefer9e** to find links to the following Children's Literature Web sites:

Artemis Fowl

Brian Jacques Home Page

Censorship, the Internet, Intellectual Freedom, and Youth

Cornelia Funke

David Almond

Digital Librarian

Elizabeth Winthrop Online: *The Castle in the Attic* and *The Battle for the Castle*

Garth Nix

Harry Potter

Lois Lowry

The Lost Land

Madeleine L'Engle

Mesa Library Fantasy Recommendations

Strongest Links: A Website for UK Librarians

T. A. Barron

Wonderful Wizard of Oz Web Site

Related Readings

Anderson, Douglas A. *The Annotated Hobbit.* Illustrated by J. R. R. Tolkien. New York: Houghton Mifflin, 1988.

This volume provides fascinating background information on Tolkien's sources for story, choices of names, scholarship, revisions, and illustrations, including many examples from foreign editions.

Campbell, Joseph. *The Hero with a Thousand Faces.* 2nd ed. Princeton, N.J.: Princeton University Press, 1968.

This standard scholarly work on the "monomyth," or the archetypal story of the hero, helps the serious student of high fantasy to see the protagonist of the quest in a universal perspective.

Cooper, Susan. *Wishes and Dreams: Essays on Writing for Children.* New York: McElderry, 1996.

> This collection of speeches made by Cooper over the years shows her growth as a writer for children and the inspirations, ideas, and events that have fed her fantasy writing.

Egoff, Sheila. *Worlds Within: Children's Fantasy from the Middle Ages to Today.* Chicago: American Library Association, 1988.

> Egoff studies the development of children's fantasy from its roots in ancient myth and legend to the intense and sometimes violent novels being written today.

Gose, Elliott. *Mere Creatures: A Study of Modern Fantasy Tales for Children.* Toronto: University of Toronto Press, 1988.

> In twelve thoughtful essays Gose focuses on creatures in fantasy, from the "real" rabbits of Watership Down to the toy animals in Winnie-the-Pooh to mythical creatures in The Hobbit, and finds psychological as well as literary underpinnings.

Mahy, Margaret. "A Dissolving Ghost: Possible Operations of Truth in Children's Books and the Lives of Children." In the ALA *Arbuthnot Lectures 1980–1989.* Chicago: American Library Association, 1990.

> Mahy's intriguing essay reveals the transformation of a real-life experience into a fantastic tale. See also Patricia Wrightson's essay "Stones in Pools," in the same volume, in which she discusses the continuity of story from ancient times and the wonder found in fantasy.

Children's Literature

 Go to the Children's Literature Database on your Resources CD-ROM for a searchable listing of these and other children's literature titles.

The books listed here are recommended, subject to the qualifications noted in the text. Original publication dates appear in square brackets. See Appendix C for publishers' complete addresses.

Adams, Richard. *Watership Down.* Macmillan, 1974.

Adlington, L. J. *The Diary of Pelly D.* Greenwillow, 2005.

Ahlberg, Allan. *The Giant Baby.* Illustrated by Fritz Wegner. Viking, 1994.

Aiken, Joan. *Black Hearts in Battersea.* Illustrated by Robin Jacques. Doubleday, 1964.

———. *Cold Shoulder Road.* Delacorte, 1996.

———. *Dangerous Games.* Delacorte, 1999.

———. *Is Underground.* Delacorte, 1995.

———. *Midwinter Nightingale.* Delacorte, 2003.

———. *Nightbirds on Nantucket.* Illustrated by Robin Jacques. Doubleday, 1966.

———. *The Witch of Clatteringshaws.* Delacorte, 2005.

———. *The Wolves of Willoughby Chase.* Illustrated by Pat Marriott. Doubleday, 1963.

Alexander, Lloyd. *The Arkadians.* Dutton, 1995.

———. *The Beggar Queen.* Dutton, 1984.

———. *The Black Cauldron.* Holt, 1965.

———. *The Book of Three.* Holt, 1964.

———. *The Castle of Llyr.* Holt, 1966.

———. *The Cat Who Wished to Be a Man.* Dutton, 1973.

———. *The Drackenburg Adventure.* Dutton, 1988.

———. *The El Dorado Adventure.* Dutton, 1987.

———. *The Gorgon and the Boy.* Dutton, 2001.

———. *Gypsy Rizka.* Dutton, 1999.

———. *The High King.* Holt, 1968.

———. *The Illyrian Adventure.* Dutton, 1986.

———. *The Iron Ring.* Dutton, 1997.

———. *The Jedera Adventure.* Dutton, 1989.

———. *The Kestrel.* Dutton, 1982.

———. *The Marvelous Misadventures of Sebastian.* Dutton, 1970.

———. *The Philadelphia Adventure.* Dutton, 1990.

———. *The Remarkable Journey of Prince Jen.* Dutton, 1991.

———. *The Rope Trick.* Dutton, 2002.

———. *Taran Wanderer.* Holt, 1967.

———. *Westmark.* Dutton, 1981.

———. *The Wizard in the Tree.* Illustrated by Laszlo Kubinyi. Dutton, 1975.

———. *The Xanadu Adventure.* Dutton, 2004.

Almond, David. *The Fire Eaters.* Delacorte, 2004.

———. *Kit's Wilderness.* Delacorte, 2000.

———. *Secret Heart.* Delacorte, 2002.

———. *Skellig.* Delacorte, 1999.

Andersen, Hans Christian. *The Emperor's New Clothes.* Illustrated by Virginia Lee Burton. Houghton, 1949.

———. *Hans Christian Andersen: The Complete Fairy Tales and Stories.* Translated by Erik Haugaard. Doubleday, 1974.

———. *The Little Match Girl.* Illustrated by Jerry Pinkney. Fogleman, 1999.

———. *The Nightingale.* Illustrated by Jerry Pinkney. Fogelman/Putnam, 2002.

———. *The Nightingale.* Illustrated by Lisbeth Zwerger. North-South, 1999.

———. *The Nightingale.* Retold by Stephen Mitchell. Illustrated by Bagram Ibatoulline. Candlewick, 2002.

———. *The Snow Queen.* Translated by Anthea Bell. Illustrated by Bernadette Watts. Picture Book Studio, 1985.

———. *The Steadfast Tin Soldier.* Retold by Tor Seidler. Illustrated by Fred Marcellino. HarperCollins, 1992.

————. *The Ugly Duckling.* Illustrated by Jerry Pinkney. Morrow, 1999.

————. *The Wild Swans.* Retold by Amy Ehrlich. Illustrated by Susan Jeffers. Dial, 1981.

Anderson, M. T. *The Clue of the Linoleum Lederhosen.* Thrilling Tales. Harcourt, 2006.

————. *Feed.* Candlewick, 2002.

————. *Whales on Stilts.* Thrilling Tales. Harcourt, 2005.

Armstrong, Alan. *Whittington.* Random, 2005.

Armstrong, Jennifer, and Nancy Butcher. *The Keepers of the Flame.* Fire-Us Trilogy. HarperCollins, 2002.

————. *The Kiln.* Fire-Us Trilogy. HarperCollins, 2003.

————. *The Kindling.* Fire-Us Trilogy. HarperCollins, 2002.

Asbjørnsen, Peter Christian, and Jorgen E. Moe. *East o'the Sun and West o'the Moon.* Translated by George Webbe Dasent. Dover, 1970 [1842–1843].

Atwater, Richard, and Florence Atwater. *Mr. Popper's Penguins.* Illustrated by Robert Lawson. Little, 1938.

Avi. *The Book without Words.* Hyperion, 2005

————. *Poppy.* Illustrated by Brian Floca. Orchard, 1995.

————. *Poppy's and Rye.* HarperCollins, 1999.

————. *Poppy's Return.* HarperCollins, 2005.

Babbitt, Natalie. *Kneeknock Rise.* Farrar, 1970.

————. *The Search for Delicious.* Farrar, 1969.

————. *Tuck Everlasting.* Farrar, 1975.

Bailey, Carolyn Sherwin. *Miss Hickory.* Illustrated by Ruth Gannett. Viking, 1962 [1946].

Banks, Lynne Reid. *The Indian in the Cupboard.* Illustrated by Brock Cole. Doubleday, 1981.

Barron, T. A. *The Fires of Merlin.* Philomel, 1998.

————. *The Great Tree of Avalon: Child of the Dark Prophecy.* Philomel, 2004.

————. *The Great Tree of Avalon: Shadows on the Stars.* Philomel, 2005.

————. *The Lost Years of Merlin.* Philomel, 1996.

————. *The Mirror of Merlin.* Philomel, 1999.

————. *The Seven Songs of Merlin.* Philomel, 1997.

————. *The Wings of Merlin.* Philomel, 2000.

Barry, Dave, and Ridley Pearson. *Peter and the Shadow Thieves.* Hyperion, 2006.

————. *Peter and the Star Catchers.* Hyperion, 2005.

Bass, L. G. *Sign of the Qin.* Hyperion, 2004.

Baum, L. Frank. *The Wizard of Oz.* World, 1972 [1900].

Bell, Hilari. *A Matter of Profit.* HarperCollins, 2001.

Bellairs, John. *The House with a Clock in Its Walls.* Dial, 1973.

Bernstein, Nina. *Magic by the Book.* Farrar, 2005.

Billingsley, Franny. *The Folk Keeper.* Atheneum, 1999.

————. *Well Wished.* Atheneum, 1997.

Bode, N. E. *The Anybodies.* HarperCollins, 2004.

————. *The Nobodies.* HarperCollins, 2005.

Bond, Michael. *A Bear Called Paddington.* Illustrated by Peggy Fortnum. Houghton, 1960.

Bond, Nancy. *A String in the Harp.* Atheneum, 1976.

Boston, L. M. *The Children of Green Knowe.* Illustrated by Peter Boston. Harcourt, 1955.

————. *An Enemy at Green Knowe.* Illustrated by Peter Boston. Harcourt, 1964.

————. *The River at Green Knowe.* Illustrated by Peter Boston. Harcourt, 1959.

————. *The Treasure of Green Knowe.* Illustrated by Peter Boston. Harcourt, 1958.

Brown, Marcia. *Stone Soup.* Scribner's, 1947.

Browne, Anthony. *The Tunnel.* Knopf, 1990.

Bruchac, Joseph. *The Dark Pond.* HarperCollins, 2004.

————. *Skeleton Man.* HarperCollins, 2001.

————. *Whisper in the Dark.* HarperCollins, 2005.

Butterworth, Oliver. *The Enormous Egg.* Illustrated by Louis Darling. Little, 1956.

Cameron, Eleanor. *The Court of the Stone Children.* Dutton, 1973.

————. *The Wonderful Flight to the Mushroom Planet.* Illustrated by Robert Henneberger. Little, 1954.

Card, Orson Scott. *Ender's Game.* Tor, 1985.

————. *Ender's Shadow.* Tor, 1999.

Carman, Patrick. *Beyond the Valley of the Thorns.* The Land of Elyon, Book 1. Scholastic, 2005.

————. *The Dark Hills Divide.* The Land of Elyon, Book 2. Scholastic, 2005.

Carroll, Lewis [Charles L. Dodgson]. *Alice's Adventures in Wonderland and Through the Looking Glass.* Illustrated by John Tenniel. Macmillan, 1963 [1865, 1872].

Catling, Patrick Skene. *The Chocolate Touch.* Illustrated by Margot Apple. Morrow, 1979 [1952].

Christopher, John. *Beyond the Burning Lands.* Macmillan, 1971.

————. *The City of Gold and Lead.* White Mountains Quartet. Macmillan, 1967.

————. *The Guardians.* Macmillan, 1968.

————. *The Pool of Fire.* White Mountains Quartet. Macmillan, 1968.

————. *The Prince in Waiting.* Macmillan, 1970.

————. *The Sword of the Spirits.* Macmillan, 1972.

————. *When the Tripods Came.* White Mountains Quartet. Dutton, 1988.

————. *The White Mountains.* White Mountains Quartet. Macmillan, 1967.

Cleary, Beverly. *The Mouse and the Motorcycle.* Illustrated by Louis Darling. Morrow, 1965.

————. *Ralph S. Mouse.* Illustrated by Paul O. Zelinsky. Morrow, 1982.

————. *Runaway Ralph.* Illustrated by Louis Darling. Morrow, 1970.

Clement-Davies, David. *Fire Bringer.* Dutton, 2001.

————. *The Sight.* Dutton, 2002.

Collins, Suzanne. *Gregor and the Curse of the Warmbloods.* Underland Chronicles. Scholastic, 2005.

———. *Gregor the Overlander.* Underland Chronicles. Scholastic, 2003.

———. *Gregor and the Prophecy of Bane.* Underland Chronicles. Scholastic, 2004.

Conly, Jane. *Racso and the Rats of NIMH.* Illustrated by Leonard Lubin. Harper, 1986.

———. *R-T, Margaret, and the Rats of NIMH.* Illustrated by Leonard Lubin. HarperCollins, 1990.

Conrad, Pam. *Stonewords.* HarperCollins, 1990.

Constable, Kate. *The Singer of All Songs.* Chanters of Tremaris Trilogy. Scholastic, 2004.

———. *The Tenth Power.* Chanters of Tremaris Trilogy. Scholastic, 2006.

———. *The Waterless Sea.* Chanters of Tremaris Trilogy. Scholastic, 2005.

Cooper, Susan. *The Boggart.* McElderry, 1993.

———. *The Boggart and the Monster.* McElderry, 1997.

———. *The Dark Is Rising.* Illustrated by Alan E. Cober. Atheneum, 1973.

———. *Green Boy.* McElderry, 2002.

———. *Greenwitch.* Atheneum, 1974.

———. *The Grey King.* Atheneum, 1975.

———. *King of Shadows.* McElderry, 1999.

———. *Over Sea, Under Stone.* Illustrated by Marjorie Gill. Harcourt, 1966.

———. *The Selkie Girl.* Illustrated by Warwick Hutton. Macmillan, 1986.

———. *Silver on the Tree.* Atheneum, 1977.

———. *Tam Lin.* Illustrated by Warwick Hutton. Macmillan, 1990.

Corbett, Scott. *The Lemonade Trick.* Illustrated by Paul Galdone. Little, 1972 [1960].

Cross, Gillian. *The Black Room.* The Dark Ground Trilogy. Dutton, 2006.

———. *The Dark Ground.* The Dark Ground Trilogy. Dutton, 2004.

———. *New World.* Holiday. 1995.

Crossley-Holland, Kevin. *At the Crossing Place.* Scholastic, 2002.

———. *King of the Middle March.* Scholastic, 2004.

———. *The Seeing Stone.* Scholastic/Levine, 2001.

Curry, Jane Louise. *The Black Canary.* Simon, 2005.

Dahl, Roald. *Charlie and the Chocolate Factory.* Illustrated by Joseph Schindelman. Knopf, 1972.

———. *Charlie and the Great Glass Elevator.* Illustrated by Joseph Schindelman. Knopf, 1972.

———. *James and the Giant Peach.* Illustrated by Nancy Ekholm Burkert. Knopf, 1961.

———. *The Minpins.* Illustrated by Patrick Benson. Viking, 1991.

Dale, Anna. *Whispering to Witches.* Bloomsbury, 2004.

de Beaumont, Mme. *Beauty and the Beast.* Illustrated by Jan Brett. Houghton, 1989.

Di Camillo, Kate. *The Miraculous Adventures of Edward Tulane.* Illustrated by Bagram Ibatoulline. Candlewick, 2006.

Dickinson, Peter. *Eva.* Delacorte, 1989.

———. *The Ropemaker.* Delacorte, 2001.

DiTerlizzi, Tony, and Holly Black. *The Field Guide: The Spiderwick Chronicles.* Simon, 2003.

———. *The Wrath of Mulgarath: The Spiderwick Chronicles.* Simon, 2004.

Divakaruni, Chitra Banerjee. *The Conch Bearer.* The Brotherhood of the Conch. Roaring Brook, 2004.

———. *The Mirror of Fire and Dreaming.* The Brotherhood of the Conch. Roaring Brook, 2005.

Doherty, Berlie. *Daughter of the Sea.* DK, 1997.

DuBois, William Pène. *The Twenty-One Balloons.* Viking, 1947.

DuPrau, Jeanne. *The City of Ember.* Random, 2003.

———. *The People of Sparks.* Random, 2004.

Dyer, Heather. *The Fish in Room 11.* Scholastic, 2004.

Eager, Edward. *Half Magic.* Illustrated by N. M. Bodecker. Harcourt, 1954.

———. *Seven-Day Magic.* Illustrated by N. M. Bodecker. Harcourt, 1962.

Edwards, Julie Andrews, and Emma Walton Hamilton. *The Great American Mousical.* HarperCollins, 2006.

Engdahl, Sylvia Louise. *Enchantress from the Stars.* Walker, 2001.

———. *The Far Side of Evil.* Walker, 2003.

Farmer, Nancy. *The Ear, the Eye, and the Arm.* Orchard, 1994.

———. *The House of the Scorpion.* Atheneum, 2002.

———. *The Sea of Trolls.* Atheneum, 2004.

———. *The Warm Place.* Orchard, 1995.

Fisher, Catherine. *The Oracle Betrayed: The Oracle Prophecies.* Greenwillow, 2004.

———. *Snow-Walker.* Greenwillow, 2005.

———. *The Sphere of Secrets: The Oracle Prophecies.* Greenwillow, 2005.

Flanagan, John. *Ranger's Apprentice: The Ruins of Gorlan.* Philomel, 2005.

Fleischman, Paul. *The Half-a-Moon Inn.* Illustrated by Kathy Jacobi. Harper, 1980.

Fleischman, Sid. *The Midnight Horse.* Illustrated by Peter Sis. Greenwillow, 1990.

———. *The Whipping Boy.* Illustrated by Peter Sis. Greenwillow, 1986.

Fletcher, Susan. *Shadow Spinner.* Atheneum, 1998.

Foon, Dennis. *The Dirt Eaters: The Longlight Legacy.* Firefly, 2004.

———. *Freewalker: The Longlight Legacy.* Firefly, 2004.

Fritz, Jean. *Homesick: My Story.* Putnam, 1982. (Biography)

Funke, Cornelia. *Dragon Rider.* Scholastic, 2004.

———. *Inkheart.* Scholastic, 2003.

———. *Inkspell.* Scholastic, 2005.

———. *The Thief Lord.* Scholastic, 2002.

Gaiman, Neil. *Coraline.* Illustrated by Dave McKean. HarperCollins, 2002.

Gardner, Sally. *I, Coriander*. Dial, 2005.

Garza, Karen Lomas. *Family Pictures*. Children's, 1990. (Picture book)

Gilmore, Kate. *The Exchange Student*. Houghton, 1999.

Gliori, Debi. *Pure Dead Brilliant*. Knopf, 2003.

———. *Pure Dead Magic*. Knopf, 2001.

———. *Pure Dead Trouble*. Knopf, 2005.

———. *Pure Dead Wicked*. Knopf, 2003.

Grahame, Kenneth. *The Reluctant Dragon*. Illustrated by Ernest H. Shepard. Holiday, 1938.

———. *The Wind in the Willows*. Illustrated by E. H. Shepard. Scribner's, 1940 [1908].

Grimm brothers. *The Frog Prince or Iron Henry*. Translated by Naomi Lewis. Illustrated by Binette Schroeder. North-South, 1998.

———. *Rumpelstiltskin*. Illustrated by Paul O. Zelinsky. Dutton, 1986.

Gruber, Michael. *The Witch's Boy*. Harper, 2005.

Haddix, Margaret. *Among the Barrons*. Simon, 2003.

———. *Among the Betrayed*. Simon, 2002.

———. *Among the Brave*. Simon, 2004.

———. *Among the Enemy*. Simon, 2005.

———. *Among the Free*. Simon, 2006.

———. *Among the Hidden*. Simon, 1999.

———. *Among the Imposters*. Simon, 2000.

Hahn, Mary Downing. *The Old Willis Place: A Ghost Story*. Clarion, 2004.

———. *Time for Andrew: A Ghost Story*. Clarion, 1994.

———. *Wait Till Helen Comes: A Ghost Story*. Houghton, 1986.

Hamilton, Virginia. *The Girl Who Spun Gold*. Illustrated by Leo and Diane Dillon. Scholastic, 2000.

———. *The Magical Adventures of Pretty Pearl*. Harper, 1983.

———. *Sweet Whispers, Brother Rush*. Philomel, 1982.

Haptie, Charlotte. *Otto and the Bird Charmers*. Holiday, 2005.

———. *Otto and the Flying Twins*. Holiday, 2004.

Hautman, Pete. *Hole in the Sky*. Simon, 2001.

Hearne, Betsy. *Wishes, Kisses, and Pigs*. McElderry, 2001.

Hentoff, Nat. *The Day They Came to Arrest the Book*. Dell, 1983. (Fiction)

Hesse, Karen. *Phoenix Rising*. Holt, 1994.

Hickman, Janet. *Ravine*. Greenwillow, 2002.

Hoban, Russell. *The Mouse and His Child*. Illustrated by Lillian Hoban. Harper, 1967.

Hoberman, Mary Ann. *Fathers, Mothers, Sisters, Brothers*. Viking, 1993. (Poetry)

Hodges, Margaret. *St. George and the Dragon*. Illustrated by Trina Schart Hyman. Little, 1984.

Hoffman, Mary. *Stravaganza: City of Flowers*. Bloomsbury, 2005.

———. *Stravaganza: City of Masks*. Bloomsbury, 2004.

———. *Stravaganza: City of Stars*. Bloomsbury, 2004.

Howe, Deborah, and James Howe. *Bunnicula*. Illustrated by Leslie Morrill. Atheneum, 1983.

Howe, James. *Bunnicula Strikes Again!* Atheneum, 1999.

———. *The Celery Stalks at Midnight*. Illustrated by Leslie Morrill. Atheneum, 1983.

———. *Howliday Inn*. Illustrated by Lynn Munsinger. Atheneum, 1982.

Hughes, Monica. *Invitation to the Game*. Simon, 1990.

Hunter, Mollie. *The Mermaid Summer*. Harper, 1988.

———. *A Stranger Came Ashore*. Harper, 1975.

Hurmence, Belinda. *A Girl Called Boy*. Clarion, 1982.

Ibbotson, Eva. *Dial a Ghost*. Illustrated by Kevin Hawkes. Dutton, 2001.

———. *The Great Ghost Rescue*. Illustrated by Kevin Hawkes. Dutton, 2002.

———. *Island of the Aunts*. Illustrated by Kevin Hawkes. Dutton, 2000.

———. *The Secret of Platform 13*. Dutton, 1998.

———. *Which Witch?* Dutton, 1999.

Jacques, Brian. *The Legend of Luke*. Philomel, 2000.

———. *Lord Brocktree*. Philomel, 2000.

———. *Mariel of Redwall*. Illustrated by Gary Chalk. Philomel, 1992.

———. *Martin the Warrior*. Philomel, 1994.

———. *Mattimeo*. Illustrated by Gary Chalk. Philomel, 1990.

———. *Mossflower*. Illustrated by Gary Chalk. Philomel, 1988.

———. *Redwall*. Illustrated by Gary Chalk. Philomel, 1987.

———. *Triss*. Philomel/Putnam, 2002.

Jarrell, Randall. *The Bat-Poet*. Illustrated by Maurice Sendak. Macmillan, 1964.

Jenness, Lynette. *Families: A Celebration of Diversity, Commitment, and Love*. Houghton, 1990. (Nonfiction)

Jones, Diana Wynne. *Charmed Life*. Greenwillow, 1989.

———. *Howl's Moving Castle*. Harper, 2001.

———. *The Lives of Christopher Chant*. Greenwillow, 1988.

Jordan, Sherryl. *The Hunting of the Last Dragon*. HarperCollins, 2002.

———. *The Raging Quiet*. Simon, 2004.

———. *Secret Sacrament*. HarperCollins, 2003.

Juster, Norton. *The Phantom Tollbooth*. Illustrated by Jules Feiffer. Random, 1961.

Kaaberbol, Lene. *Shamer's Daughter*. Holt, 2004.

Katz, Welwyn Wilton. *Time Ghost*. McElderry, 1995.

Keehn, Sally. *Gnat Stokes and the Foggy Bottom Swamp Queen*. Philomel, 2005.

Kendall, Carol. *The Gammage Cup*. Illustrated by Erik Blegvad. Harcourt, 1959.

Kettelkamp, Larry. *Living in Space*. Morrow, 1993. (Nonfiction)

Key, Alexander. *The Forgotten Door*. Westminster, 1965.

Kindl, Patricia. *Goose Chase*. Houghton, 2001.

———. *Owl in Love*. Houghton, 1993.

King-Smith, Dick. *Ace: The Very Important Pig*. Illustrated by Lynette Hemmant. Crown, 1990.

———. *Babe: The Gallant Pig.* Illustrated by Mary Rayner. Crown, 1985.

———. *The Fox Busters.* Illustrated by Jon Miller. Delacorte, 1988.

———. *Harriet's Hare.* Illustrated by Roger Roth. Crown, 1994.

———. *Pigs Might Fly.* Illustrated by Mary Rayner. Viking, 1982.

———. *Three Terrible Trins.* Illustrated by Mark Teague. Crown, 1994.

Klause, Annette Curtis. *Alien Secrets.* Delacorte, 1993.

Knight, Margery Burns. *Talking Walls.* Illustrated by Ann Sibley O'Brien. Tilbury, 1995. (Fiction)

———. *Talking Walls: The Story Continues.* Illustrated by Ann Sibley O'Brien. Tilbury, 1997. (Fiction)

Lally, Soinbhe. *A Hive for the Honeybee.* Illustrated by Patience Brewster. Scholastic, 1999.

Langrish, Katherine. *Troll Fell.* Harper, 2004.

Langton, Jane. *The Diamond in the Window.* Illustrated by Erik Blegvad. Harper, 1962.

———. *The Fledgling.* Harper, 1980.

Larbalestier, Justine. *Magic Lessons.* Magic or Madness Trilogy. Penguin, 2006.

———. *Magic or Madness.* Penguin, 2005.

Lawrence, Michael. *A Crack in the Line.* Greenwillow, 2004.

———. *Small Eternities.* Greenwillow, 2005.

Lawson, Robert. *Rabbit Hill.* Viking, 1944.

———. *The Tough Winter.* Viking, 1954.

Lee, Tanith. *Wolf Queen.* Claidi Journals. Dutton, 2002.

———. *Wolf Star.* Claidi Journals. Dutton, 2001.

———. *Wolf Tower.* Claidi Journals. Dutton, 2000.

Le Guin, Ursula K. *The Farthest Shore.* Illustrated by Gail Garraty. Atheneum, 1972.

———. *Gifts.* Harcourt, 2004.

———. *Tehanu: The Last Book of Earthsea.* Atheneum, 1990.

———. *The Tombs of Atuan.* Illustrated by Gail Garraty. Atheneum, 1971.

———. *A Wizard of Earthsea.* Illustrated by Ruth Robbins. Parnassus, 1968.

L'Engle, Madeleine. *A Swiftly Tilting Planet.* The Time Trilogy. Farrar, 1978.

———. *A Wind in the Door.* The Time Trilogy. Farrar, 1973.

———. *A Wrinkle in Time.* The Time Trilogy. Farrar, 1962.

Levine, Gail Carson. *Ella Enchanted.* HarperCollins, 1997.

———. *The Two Princesses of Bamarre.* HarperCollins, 2001.

Lewis, C. S. *The Horse and His Boy.* Illustrated by Pauline Baynes. Macmillan, 1962.

———. *The Last Battle.* Illustrated by Pauline Baynes. Macmillan, 1964.

———. *The Lion, the Witch, and the Wardrobe.* Illustrated by Pauline Baynes. Macmillan, 1961.

———. *The Magician's Nephew.* Illustrated by Pauline Baynes. Macmillan, 1964.

———. *Prince Caspian: The Return to Narnia.* Illustrated by Pauline Baynes. Macmillan, 1964.

———. *The Silver Chair.* Illustrated by Pauline Baynes. Macmillan, 1962.

———. *The Voyage of the "Dawn Treader."* Illustrated by Pauline Baynes. Macmillan, 1962.

Lindgren, Astrid. *Pippi Goes on Board.* Translated by Florence Lamborn. Illustrated by Louis S. Glanzman. Viking, 1957.

———. *Pippi in the South Seas.* Translated by Florence Lamborn. Illustrated by Louis S. Glanzman. Viking, 1959.

———. *Pippi Longstocking.* Illustrated by Louis S. Glanzman. Viking, 1950.

———. *Pippi on the Run.* Viking, 1976.

Lively, Penelope. *The Ghost of Thomas Kempe.* Illustrated by Anthony Maitland. Dutton, 1973.

Lowry, Lois. *Anastasia Krupnik.* Houghton, 1979. (Fiction)

———. *Autumn Street.* Houghton, 1980. (Fiction)

———. *Gathering Blue.* Houghton, 2000.

———. *The Giver.* Houghton, 1993.

———. *Looking Back: A Book of Memories.* Houghton, 1980. (Biography)

———. *Messenger.* Houghton, 2004.

———. "Newbery Award Acceptance Speech." *Horn Book Magazine* 70.4 (1994): 423–26.

———. "On Writing *The Giver.*" Book Links (May 1994).

Lunn, Janet. *The Root Cellar.* Scribner's, 1983.

MacDonald, George. *At the Back of the North Wind.* Garland, 1976 [1871].

———. *The Golden Key.* Illustrated by Maurice Sendak. Farrar, 1967 [1867].

———. *The Light Princess.* Illustrated by Maurice Sendak. Farrar, 1969.

Mahy, Margaret. *The Haunting.* Macmillan, 1982.

Marsden, John. *Burning for Revenge.* Houghton, 2000.

———. *Darkness Be My Friend.* Houghton, 1999.

———. *The Dead of Night.* Houghton, 1997.

———. *A Killing Frost.* Houghton, 1998.

———. *The Night Is for Hunting.* Houghton, 2002.

———. *The Other Side of Dawn.* Houghton, 2002.

———. *Tomorrow When the War Began.* Houghton, 1995.

Martin, Ann, and Laura Godwin. *The Doll People.* Illustrated by Brian Selznick. Hyperion, 2000.

———. *The Meanest Doll in the World.* Hyperion, 2003.

Martini, Clem. *The Mob.* Feather and Bone: The Crow Chronicles. Kids Can, 2005.

———. *The Plague.* Feather and Bone: The Crow Chronicles. Kids Can, 2005.

Mayne, William. *Earthfasts.* Dutton, 1967.

McCaffrey, Anne. *Dragondrums.* Illustrated by Fred Marcellino. Atheneum, 1979.

———. *The Dragonriders of Pern.* Ballantine, 1988.

———. *Dragonsinger.* Atheneum, 1977.

———. *Dragonsong.* Illustrated by Laura Lydecker. Atheneum, 1976.

McClure, Gillian. *Selkie*. Farrar, 1999.

McGraw, Eloise. *The Moorchild*. McElderry, 1996.

McKillip, Patricia. *The Forgotten Beast of Eld*. Harcourt, 1996.

McKinley, Robin. *Beauty: A Retelling of the Story of Beauty and the Beast*. Harper, 1978.

———. *The Blue Sword*. Greenwillow, 1982.

———. *The Hero and the Crown*. Greenwillow, 1985.

McNaughton, Janet. *The Secret Under My Skin*. HarperCollins, 2005.

Melling, O. R. *The Hunter's Moon*. The Chronicles of Faerie. Abrams, 2005.

———. *The Light-Bearer's Daughter*. The Chronicles of Faerie. Abrams, 2006.

———. *The Summer King*. The Chronicles of Faerie. Abrams, 2006.

Merrill, Jean. *The Pushcart War*. Illustrated by Ronni Solbert. Scott, 1964.

Milne, A. A. *The House at Pooh Corner*. Illustrated by Ernest H. Shepard. Dutton, 1928.

———. *Winnie the Pooh*. Illustrated by Ernest H. Shepard. Dutton, 1926.

Moore, Lilian. *I'll Meet You at the Cucumbers*. Illustrated by Sharon Wooding. Atheneum, 1988.

Morris, Gerald. *The Ballad of Sir Dinadin*. Houghton, 2003.

———. *The Lioness and Her Knight*. Houghton, 2005.

———. *Parsifal's Page*. Houghton, 2001.

———. *The Savage Damsel and the Dwarf*. Houghton, 2001.

———. *The Squire, His Knight and His Lady*. Houghton, 1999.

———. *The Squire's Tale*. Houghton, 1998.

Mosley, Walter. *47*. HarperCollins, 2005.

Napoli, Donna. *Beast*. Dutton, 2000.

———. *The Magic Circle*. Dutton, 1993.

———. *Spinners*. Dutton, 1999.

———. *Zel*. Dutton, 1996.

Nicholson, William. *Firesong*. The Wind on Fire Trilogy. Illustrated by Peter Sis. Hyperion, 2002.

———. *Seeker*. Noble Warriors Series, Book 1. Harcourt, 2006.

———. *Slaves of the Mastery*. The Wind on Fire Trilogy. Hyperion, 2001.

———. *The Wind Singer*. The Wind on Fire Trilogy. Hyperion, 2000.

Nix, Garth. *Abhorsen*. HarperCollins, 2003.

———. *Lirael*. HarperCollins, 2001.

———. *Sabriel*. Eos, 1996.

———. *Shade's Children*. HarperCollins, 1997.

Norton, Mary. *The Borrowers*. Illustrated by Beth and Joe Krush. Harcourt, 1953.

———. *The Borrowers Afield*. Illustrated by Beth and Joe Krush. Harcourt, 1955.

———. *The Borrowers Afloat*. Illustrated by Beth and Joe Krush. Harcourt, 1959.

———. *The Borrowers Aloft*. Illustrated by Beth and Joe Krush. Harcourt, 1961.

———. *The Borrowers Avenged*. Illustrated by Beth and Joe Krush. Harcourt, 1982.

O'Brien, Robert C. *Mrs. Frisby and the Rats of NIMH*. Illustrated by Zena Bernstein. Atheneum, 1971.

———. *Z for Zachariah*. Atheneum, 1975.

Oppel, Kenneth. *Airborn*. Harper, 2004.

———. *Firewing*. Simon, 2003.

———. *Silverwing*. Simon, 1997.

———. *Skybreaker*. Harper, 2005.

———. *Sunwing*. Simon, 2000.

Paolini, Christopher. *Eldest*. Knopf, 2005.

———. *Eragon*. Knopf, 2003.

Pattou, Edith. *East*. Harcourt, 2004.

Paver, Michelle. *Spirit Walker: The Chronicles of Ancient Darkness*. HarperCollins, 2005.

———. *Wolf Brother: The Chronicles of Ancient Darkness*. HarperCollins, 2005.

Pearce, Philippa. *Tom's Midnight Garden*. Illustrated by Susan Einzig. Lippincott, 1959.

Pearson, Kit. *A Handful of Time*. Viking Penguin, 1988.

Peck, Richard. *The Great Interactive Dream Machine*. Dial, 1996.

———. *Lost in Cyberspace*. Dial, 1995.

Peck, Sylvia. *Seal Child*. Illustrated by Robert Andrew Parker. Morrow, 1989.

Pierce, Meredith. *Birth of the Firebringer*. Atheneum, 1985.

———. *Dark Angel*. Magic Carpet, 1998.

———. *Treasure at the Heart of the Tanglewood*. Viking, 2001.

Pierce, Tamora. *Alanna, the First Adventure*. Song of the Lioness. Atheneum, 1982.

———. *Briar's Book*. Circle of Magic. Scholastic, 1999.

———. *Cold Fire*. The Circle Opens. Scholastic, 2002.

———. *Daja's Book*. Circle of Magic. Scholastic, 2000.

———. *Emperor Mage*. The Immortals. Simon, 1995.

———. *First Test*. Protector of the Small. Random, 2000.

———. *In the Hand of the Goddess*. Song of the Lioness. Atheneum, 1984.

———. *Lady Knight*. Protector of the Small. Random, 2002.

———. *Lioness Rampant*. Song of the Lioness. Atheneum, 1988.

———. *Magic Steps*. The Circle Opens. Scholastic, 2000.

———. *Page*. Protector of the Small. Random, 2000.

———. *The Realms of the Gods*. The Immortals. Random, 1997.

———. *Sandry's Book*. Circle of Magic, Book 1. Scholastic, 1997.

———. *Squire*. Protector of the Small. Random, 2001.

———. *Street Magic*. The Circle Opens. Scholastic, 2001.

———. *Terrier*. The Provost's Dog. Random, 2006.

———. *Wild Magic*. The Immortals. Atheneum, 1992.

———. *The Will of the Empress*. The Circle Reforged. Scholastic, 2005.

———. *Wolf-Speaker*. The Immortals. Atheneum, 1994.

———. *The Woman Who Rides Like a Man*. Song of the Lioness. Atheneum, 1986.

Pope, Elizabeth Marie. *The Perilous Gard*. Houghton, 2001.

Potter, Robert R. *Buckminster Fuller*. Silver Burdett, 1990. (Biography)

Pratchett, Terry. *The Bromeliad Trilogy: Truckers, Diggers and Wings*. Harper, 2003.

———. *A Hat Full of Sky: The Wee Free Men*. Harper, 2004.

Pullman, Philip. *The Amber Spyglass*. His Dark Materials. Knopf, 2000.

———. *Clockwork: Or All Wound Up*. Scholastic, 1998.

———. *The Firework-Maker's Daughter*. Illustrated by S. Saelig Gallagher. Levine, 1999.

———. *The Golden Compass*. His Dark Materials. Knopf, 1996.

———. *I Was a Rat*. Knopf, 2000.

———. *The Ruby in the Smoke*. Knopf, 1994.

———. *The Scarecrow and His Servant*. Knopf, 2005.

———. *The Subtle Knife*. His Dark Materials. Knopf, 1997.

Reeve, Philip. *Mortal Engines*. The Hungry City Chronicles. HarperCollins, 2003.

———. *Predator's Gold*. The Hungry City Chronicles. HarperCollins, 2003.

Riordan, Rick. *The Lightning Thief*. Percy Jackson and the Olympians. Hyperion, 2005.

———. *The Sea of Monsters*. Percy Jackson and the Olympians. Hyperion. 2006.

Roberts, Katherine. *Crystal Mask*. Chicken House, 2002.

———. *Dark Quetzal*. Chicken House, 2003.

———. *Song Quest*. Chicken House, 2000.

Robertson, M. P. *The Egg*. Fogelman, 2001.

Rodda, Emily. *Rowan and the Ice Creepers*. Greenwillow, 2003.

———. *Rowan and the Keeper of the Crystal*. Greenwillow, 2001.

———. *Rowan and the Travelers*. Greenwillow, 2001.

———. *Rowan and the Zebak*. Greenwillow, 2002.

———. *Rowan of Rin*. Greenwillow, 2001.

Rosoff, Meg. *How I Live Now*. Random, 2004.

Rowling, J. K. *Harry Potter and the Chamber of Secrets*. Scholastic, 1999.

———. *Harry Potter and the Half-Blood Prince*. Scholastic, 2005.

———. *Harry Potter and the Prisoner of Azkaban*. Scholastic, 1999.

———. *Harry Potter and the Sorcerer's Stone*. Scholastic, 1998.

Russon, Penni. *Undine*. Greenwillow, 2006.

Saint-Exupéry, Antoine de. *The Little Prince*. Translated by Katherine Woods. Harcourt, 1943.

Sauer, Julia. *Fog Magic*. Illustrated by Lynd Ward. Viking, 1943.

Schmidt, Gary D. *Straw into Gold*. Clarion, 2001.

Scieszka, Jon. *2095*. Illustrated by Lane Smith. Viking, 1995.

———. *Da Wild, Da Crazy, Da Vinci*. Viking, 2004.

———. *Hey Kid! Want to Buy a Bridge?* Illustrated by Adam McCauley. Viking, 2002.

———. *Knights of the Kitchen Table*. Illustrated by Lane Smith. Viking, 1991.

———. *Oh Say, I Can't See*. Viking, 2005.

———. *Sam Samuri*. Illustrated by Adam McCauley. Viking, 2001.

———. *See You Later, Gladiator*. Illustrated by Adam McCauley. Viking, 2000.

———. *Summer Reading Is Killing Me*. Illustrated by Lane Smith. Viking, 1998.

———. *Tut, Tut*. Illustrated by Lane Smith. Viking, 1996.

———. *Viking and Liking It*. Illustrated by Adam McCauley. Viking, 2002.

———. *Your Mother Was a Neanderthal*. Illustrated by Lane Smith. Viking, 1993.

Seidler, Tor. *Mean Margaret*. HarperCollins, 1997.

Selden, George. *Chester Cricket's Pigeon Ride*. Illustrated by Garth Williams. Farrar, 1981.

———. *The Cricket in Times Square*. Illustrated by Garth Williams. Farrar, 1960.

———. *Harry Cat's Pet Puppy*. Illustrated by Garth Williams. Farrar, 1974.

———. *Tucker's Countryside*. Illustrated by Garth Williams. Farrar, 1969.

Sendak, Maurice. *Higglety, Pigglety, Pop!* Harper, 1967.

Skurzynski, Gloria. *The Clones: Virtual War Chronologs*. Simon/Atheneum, 2002.

———. *Cyberstorm*. Macmillan, 1995.

———. *The Revolt*. The Virtual War Chronologs. Simon, 2005.

———. *Virtual War*. The Virtual War Chronologs. Simon, 1997.

Slade, Arthur. *Dust*. Knopf, 2003.

Sleator, William. *The Duplicate*. Dutton, 1988.

———. *The Green Futures of Tycho*. Dutton, 1981.

Slote, Alfred. *My Robot Buddy*. Lippincott, 1975.

Snicket, Lemony. *The Bad Beginning: A Series of Unfortunate Events*. HarperCollins, 1999.

———. *The Grim Grotto: A Series of Unfortunate Events*. HarperCollins, 2004.

Snyder, Zilpha Keatley. *Song of the Gargoyle*. Delacorte, 1991.

Springer, Nancy. *I Am Mordred: A Tale from Camelot*. Philomel, 1998.

———. *I Am Morgan le Fay*. Philomel, 2002.

Stanley, Diane. *Bella at Midnight: The Thimble, the Ring, and the Slippers of Glass*. Illustrated by Bagram Ibatoulline. Harper, 2006.

———. *The Mysterious Matter of I. M. Fine*. HarperCollins, 2001.

Steig, William. *Abel's Island*. Farrar, 1976.

Stewart, Paul. *Greeglader*. The Edge Chronicles. Random, 2006.

Stewart, Paul, and Chris Riddell. *The Last of the Sky Pirates*. The Edge Chronicles. Random, 2005.

———. *Stormchaser*. The Edge Chronicles. Random, 2004.

Stewig, John. *Stone Soup*. Illustrated by Margot Tomes. Holiday, 1991.

Stone, Jeff. *Tige: The Five Ancestors*. Random, 2005.

Strickland, Dorothy, and Michael Strickland. *Families: Poems Celebrating the African American Experience*. Illustrated by John Ward. Boyds-Mills, 1994. (Poetry)

Stroud, Jonathan. *The Amulet of Samarkand.* The Bartimaeus Trilogy, Book 1. Hyperion, 2003.

———. *The Golem's Eye.* The Bartimaeus Trilogy, Book 2. Hyperion, 2003.

———. *Ptolemy's Gate.* The Bartimaeus Trilogy. Hyperion, 2005.

Thurber, James. *Many Moons.* Illustrated by Marc Simont. Harcourt, 1990.

Tolkien, J. R. R. *The Fellowship of the Ring. The Two Towers. The Return of the King.* The Lord of the Rings trilogy. Houghton, 1965.

———. *The Hobbit.* Houghton, 1938.

Travers, P. L. *Mary Poppins.* Illustrated by Mary Shepard. Harcourt, 1934.

———. *Mary Poppins Comes Back.* Illustrated by Mary Shepard. Harcourt, 1935.

———. *Mary Poppins in the Park.* Illustrated by Mary Shepard. Harcourt, 1952.

———. *Mary Poppins Opens the Door.* Illustrated by Mary Shepard and Agnes Sims. Harcourt, 1943.

Vande Velde, Vivian. *User Unfriendly.* Harcourt, 1991.

Vinge, Joan D. *Psion.* Delacorte, 1982.

Wallace, Barbara Brooks. *Ghosts in the Gallery.* Atheneum, 2000.

Walsh, Jill Paton. *A Chance Child.* Farrar, 1978.

———. *The Green Book.* Illustrated by Lloyd Bloom. Farrar, 1982.

Waugh, Sylvia. *Earth Born.* Delacorte, 2002.

———. *The Mennyms.* Greenwillow, 1994.

———. *The Mennyms Alive.* Greenwillow, 1997.

———. *The Mennyms Alone.* Greenwillow, 1996.

———. *The Mennyms in the Wilderness.* Greenwillow, 1995.

———. *The Mennyms Under Siege.* Greenwillow, 1996.

———. *Space Race.* Delacorte, 2000.

———. *Who Goes Home?* Delacorte, 2004.

Westerfeld, Scott. *Uglies.* Simon, 2005.

White, E. B. *Charlotte's Web.* Illustrated by Garth Williams. Harper, 1952.

———. *Stuart Little.* Illustrated by Garth Williams. Harper, 1945.

———. *The Trumpet of the Swan.* Illustrated by Edward Frascino. Harper, 1970.

Wilde, Oscar. *The Happy Prince.* Illustrated by Ed Young. Simon, 1989.

———. *The Selfish Giant.* Illustrated by Lisbeth Zwerger. Picture Book Studios, 1984.

Williams, Jay. *Everyone Knows What a Dragon Looks Like.* Illustrated by Mercer Mayer. Four Winds, 1976.

Williams, Margery. *The Velveteen Rabbitt.* Illustrated by William Nicholson. Doubleday, 1969 [1922].

Winthrop, Elizabeth. *The Battle for the Castle.* Holiday, 1993.

———. *The Castle in the Attic.* Holiday, 1985.

Wiseman, David. *Jeremy Visick.* Houghton, 1981.

Wrede, Patricia C. *Calling on Dragons.* Harcourt, 1993.

———. *Dealing with Dragons.* Harcourt, 1990.

———. *Searching for Dragons.* Harcourt, 1991.

———. *Talking to Dragons.* Harcourt, 1993.

Wright, Betty Ren. *The Ghost Comes Calling.* Scholastic, 1994.

———. *Out of the Dark.* Scholastic, 1995.

Yep, Laurence. *The Dragon of the Lost Sea.* Harper, 1982.

———. *Tiger's Apprentice.* HarperCollins, 2004.

———. *Tiger's Blood.* HarperCollins, 2005.

Yolen, Jane. *Dove Isabeau.* Illustrated by Dennis Nolan. Harcourt, 1989.

———. *Dragon's Blood.* Delacorte, 1982.

———. *Heart's Blood.* Delacorte, 1984.

———. *A Sending of Dragons.* Delacorte, 1987.

Zemach, Harve. *Duffy and the Devil.* Illustrated by Margot Zemach. Farrar, 1986.

Chapter Eight

Poetry

Chapter Outline

Media Resources

A fifth-grade teacher finished reading aloud Katherine Paterson's *Bridge to Terabithia* to her class. This is the well-loved story of friendship between a highly imaginative girl, Leslie, and Jess—middle child in a rural family of five. It was Leslie's idea to create Terabithia, their secret kingdom in the woods that could be approached only by swinging across a stream on a rope. And it was this frayed rope that brought about the tragedy in the story.

Following the completion of the story, the group was silent for a moment thinking about Leslie's death and the legacy she had left Jess. Wisely, the teacher respected their silence, recognizing that this book had moved them deeply. They did not discuss it immediately but quietly began to do other work. That evening one of the girls in the class wrote this poem:

As the stubborn stream swirls and pulls out a song,

The hillside stands in the cold dark sky.

Over the hillside stands a lonely palace.

Before it shook with joy

But now its queen is dead

So the sour sweet wind blows the tassels of the weak rope,

And the tree mourns and scolds the rope,

Saying "Couldn't you have held on a little longer?"

—Cheri Taylor, Highland Park School,
Grove City, Ohio; Linda Charles, teacher

Poetry was as much a part of this classroom as prose was. The teacher shared some poetry every day, in addition to reading stories. Frequently she read a poem that reflected the same content or feeling as the novel she was reading. So it was natural for Cheri to write a poem in response to her feelings about *Bridge to Terabithia*.

Poetry is the language of emotions. It can encapsulate a deep response in a few words. For Cheri, poetry was the only way to capture her feelings about a book that had moved her as no other had ever done.

THE MEANING OF POETRY

There is an elusiveness about poetry that makes it defy precise definition. It is not so much what it is that is important, as how it makes us feel. In her *Poems for Children*, Eleanor Farjeon tells us that poetry is "not a rose, but the scent of the rose. . . . Not the sea, but the sound of the sea."[1] Fine poetry is this distillation of experience that captures the essence of an object, a feeling, or a thought. Such intensification requires a more highly structured patterning of words than prose does. Each word must be chosen with care for both sound and meaning, because poetry is language in its most connotative and concentrated form. Laurence Perrine defines poetry as "a kind of language that says more and says it more intensely than ordinary language."[2]

Poetry can both broaden and intensify experience, or it might present a range of experiences beyond the realm of personal possibility for the individual listener. It can also illuminate, clarify, and deepen an everyday occurrence in a way the reader never considered, making the reader see more and feel more than ever before. For poetry does more than mirror life; it reveals life in new dimensions. Robert Frost said that a poem goes from delight to wisdom. Poetry does delight children, but it also helps them develop new insights, new ways of sensing their world.

---

[1]*Poetry* originally appeared in *Sing for Your Supper*. Copyright © 1938 by Eleanor Farjeon; renewed 1966 by Gervase Farjeon. Used by permission of HarperCollins Publishers, New York, NY.

[2]Laurence Perrine, *Sound and Sense: An Introduction to Poetry*, 10th ed. (New York: Harcourt Brace Jovanovich, 2000), p. 3.

Poetry communicates experience by appealing to both the thoughts and the feelings of its reader. It has the power to evoke in its hearers rich sensory images and deep emotional responses. Poetry demands total response from the individual—all the intellect, senses, emotion, and imagination. It does not tell *about* an experience as much as it invites its hearers to *participate in* the experience. Poetry can happen only when the poem and the reader connect. Eleanor Farjeon says this about poetry:

Poetry

What is Poetry? Who Knows?
Not a rose but the scent of the rose;
Not the sky but the light in the sky;
Not the fly but the gleam of the fly;
Not the sea but the sound of the sea;
Not myself but what makes me
See, hear, and feel something that prose
Cannot, and what it is, who knows?

> —Eleanor Farjeon. "Poetry" (in Bobbye Goldstein, ed., *Inner Chimes*) "Poetry" from *Poems for Children* by Eleanor Farjeon. Copyright 1938 by Eleanor Farjeon. Copyright renewed 1966 by Gervase Farjeon. Reprinted by permission of Harold Ober Associates Incorporated.

Much of what poetry says is conveyed by suggestion, by indirection, by what is not said. As Carl Sandburg put it, "What can be explained is not poetry. . . . The poems that are obvious are like the puzzles that are already solved. They deny us the joy of seeking and creating."[3] A certain amount of ambiguity is characteristic of poetry, for more is hidden in it than in prose. The poet does not tell readers "all," but invites them to go beyond the literal level of the poem and discover its deeper meanings for themselves.

Robert Frost playfully suggested that poetry is what gets lost in translation—and translation of poetry into prose is as difficult as translation of poetry into another language. To paraphrase a poem is to destroy it. Would it be possible to reduce Frost's "Mending Wall" to prose? The scene, the situation, the contrast of the two men's thoughts about the wall they are repairing can be described, but the experience of the poem cannot be conveyed except by its own words.

Poetry for Children

Poetry for children differs little from poetry for adults, except that it comments on life in dimensions that are meaningful for children. Its language should be poetic and its content should appeal directly to children. Bobbi

Katz describes the feel of cat kisses in a way that appeals to children's sensory experiences and helps them think about a cat in a new, imaginative way.

Sandpaper kisses
on a cheek or a chin—
that is the way
for a day to begin!

Sandpaper kisses—
a cuddle, a purr
I have an alarm clock
that's covered with fur.

> —Bobbi Katz. "Cat Kisses." Copyright © 1974 by Bobbi Katz. Reprinted with permission of the author.

The comparison of the rough feel of a cat's tongue to sandpaper kisses and a cat's function as an alarm clock are both metaphors that will delight a child. These metaphors are childlike, but not "childish."

The emotional appeal of children's poetry should reflect the real emotions of childhood. Poetry that is cute, coy, nostalgic, or sarcastic might be *about* children, but it is not *for* them. Whittier's "The Barefoot Boy" looks back on childhood in a nostalgic fashion characteristic of adults, not children; "The Children's Hour" by Longfellow is an old man's reminiscences of his delight in his children (both poems can be found in Helen Ferris's *Favorite Poems Old and New*). Some poems patronize childhood as a period in life when children are "cute" or "naughty." Joan W. Anglund's poetry is as cute and sentimental as her pictures of "sweet little boys and girls."

Many poems are didactic and preachy. Unfortunately, some teachers will accept moralizing in poetry that they would never accept in prose. Sentimentality is another adult emotion that is seldom felt by children. The poem "Which Loved Best," frequently quoted before Mother's Day, drips with sentiment and morality. Poems that are *about* childhood or aim to instruct are usually disliked by children.

Yet children do feel deep emotions; they can be hurt, fearful, bewildered, sad, happy, expectant, satisfied. Almost all surveys show that adults believe children have a harder time growing up today than their parents did.[4] More and more modern poetry for children reflects the despair of struggling to grow up in America today. Some poets have been successful in capturing the real feelings of troubled children. For example, the adolescent narrator of Angela Johnson's *Running Back to Luddie* has been raised by her father and aunt after her mother deserted her. She's brave and strong-willed, determined not to be defeated by her loss. But sometimes her voice betrays her terrible sadness, as in this poem:

---

[3]Carl Sandburg, "Short Talk on Poetry," in *Early Moon* (New York: Harcourt Brace, 1930), p. 27.

[4]Kati Haycock, "Producing a Nation of Achievers," *Journal of Youth Services in Libraries* 4 (spring 1991): 237.

The Only One

Vicki has six brothers
and their house vibrates in the
evening
with radio sounds
and yelling from floor
to
floor.
I sit on their stairs
and drink the house in
between dinner with tons
of food and so much talk and
laughter it almost becomes
one loud food-filled yell.
And it isn't like home
where sometimes (if everybody is
working late)
I'm the only one
eating at our kitchen table,
and only the sound of the ceiling fan
spins against the quiet.

> —"The Only One," from *Running
> Back to Luddie* by Angela Johnson
> © 2001. Reprinted by permission
> of Scholastic Inc.

Marilyn Nelson's *A Wreath for Emmett Till* demonstrates the power of poetry to illuminate the past, present, and future.

Poets have many ways of speaking to the needs and interests of children.

The Elements of Poetry

A child responds to the total impact of a poem and should not be required to analyze it. However, teachers need to understand the language of poetry if they are to select the best to share with children. How, for example, can you differentiate between real poetry and mere verse? Mother Goose, jump-rope rhymes, tongue twisters, and the lyrics of some songs are not poetry; but they *can* serve as a springboard for diving into real poetry. Elizabeth Coatsworth, who has written much fine poetry and verse for children, refers to rhyme as "poetry in petticoats."[5] Such rhymes might have the sound of poetry, but they do not contain the quality of imagination or the depth of emotion that characterizes real poetry.

It is a difficult task to identify elements of poetry for today's children, for modern poets are breaking traditional molds in both content and form. Poetry speaks directly to the reader about all subjects. Frequently the words are spattered across pages in a random fashion, or they become poem-pictures, as in concrete poetry. Many authors are revisiting story in one of its earliest forms, the epic narrative poem. Writers for older children and young adults like Karen Hesse in *Out of the Dust* and Sharon Creech in *Love That Dog* and *Heartbeat*

are using poetry to redefine the form of the novel. Juan Felipe Herrera, a well-known Mexican American poet, has written *Downtown Boy*, a novel in verse about a young Mexican migrant worker who tries to hold his life together when his family moves to San Francisco. Marilyn Nelson chose the traditional fourteenth-century Petrarchan form called a heroic crown of sonnet to reflect upon life and death in *A Wreath for Emmett Till*. In *Carver: A Life in Poems*, Nelson created a biography in poems. As children become more sophisticated through their exposure to films and television, the dividing line between what is poetry for adults and what is poetry for children becomes fainter. It is, however, possible to identify those poems that contain the elements of fine poetry yet still speak to children.

Rhythm

The young child is naturally rhythmical. She beats on the tray of her high chair, kicks her foot against the table, and chants her vocabulary of one or two words in a singsong fashion. She delights in the sound of "Pat-a-cake, pat-a-cake, baker's man," or "Ride a cock-horse to Banbury Cross" before she understands the meaning of the words. She is responding to the monotonous rocking-horse

---

[5]Elizabeth Coatsworth, *The Sparrow Bush,* illustrated by Stefan Martin (New York: Norton, 1966), p. 8.

rhythm of Mother Goose. This response to a measured beat is as old as humans themselves. Primitive people had chants, hunting and working songs, dances, and crude musical instruments. Rhythm is a part of the daily beat of our lives—the steady pulse rate, regular breathing, and pattern of growth. The inevitability of night and day, the revolving seasons, birth and death provide a pattern for everyone's life. The very ebb and flow of the ocean, the sound of the rain on the window, and the pattern of rows of corn in a field reflect the rhythm of the world around us.

Poetry satisfies the child's natural response to rhythm. A poem has a kind of music of its own, and the child responds to it. The very young child enjoys the rocking rhythm of Mother Goose and expects it in all other poems. In the following poem from *The Llama Who Had No Pajama*, Mary Ann Hoberman explores other rhythms in the child's life as she links weather and seasonal patterns to the rhythm of a child's swinging:

> *Hello and good-by*
> *Hello and good-by*
> When I'm in a swing
> Swinging low and then high,
> Good-by to the ground
> Hello to the sky.
>
> Hello to the rain
> Good-by to the sun,
> Then hello again sun
> When the rain is all done.
>
> In blows the winter,
> Away the birds fly.
> *Good-by and hello*
> *Hello and good-by.*

> —"Hello and Good-by," from *The Llama Who Had No Pajama: 100 Favorite Poems* by Mary Ann Hoberman. Copyright © 1959 and renewed 1987 by Mary Ann Hoberman. Reprinted with permission of Harcourt, Inc.

This poem could be compared with Robert Louis Stevenson's well-known poem "The Swing" (in *Tomie dePaola's Book of Poems*), which suggests a different meter for the physical sensation of swinging.

In some poems, both the rhythm and the pattern of the lines are suggestive of the movement or mood of the poem. The arrangement of these poems forces the reader to emphasize a particular rhythm. For example, in Eleanor Farjeon's "Mrs. Peck-Pigeon" (in de Regnier et al., *Sing a Song of Popcorn*), "Mrs. Peck Pigeon is picking for bread, Bob-bob-bob goes her little round head"—the repetition of the hard sounds of *b* and *p* help create the bobbing rhythm of the pigeon herself.

A change of rhythm is indicative of a new element in the poem: a warning, a different speaker, a contrast in mood, for example. The following poem by Dennis Lee recalls the pounding rhythm of surf in the first two stan-

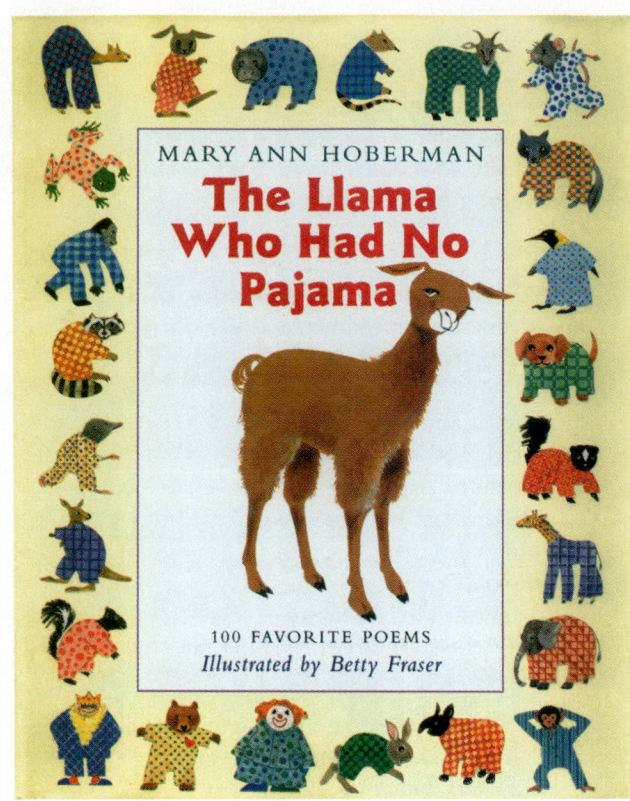

Collections such as Mary Ann Hoberman's *The Llama Who Had No Pajama* introduce children to the delights of poetry. Book cover from *The Llama Who Had No Pajama: 100 Favorite Poems*, by Mary Ann Hoberman, illustration copyright © 1998 by Betty Fraser, reprinted by permission of Harcourt, Inc.

zas, then switches to a gentler lapping beat in the third stanza before a return to the original meter in the last stanza. Here we find the sea in all its moods.

The Waves

> They're old, they're old, they're very old,
>   As old as ever more,
> The long blue slap and the sucking waves
>   That pound against the shore.
>
> And starfish and anemones
>   Go trundling to and fro,
> Like starfish and anemones
>   A million years ago.
>
> And the waves roll in, and the tides roll in,
>   And the sea rolls in each day.
> And people for a thousand years
>   Have heard the ocean say,
>
> We're old, we're old, we're very old,
>   As old as ever more,
> The long blue slap and the sucking waves
>   That pound against the shore.

> —Dennis Lee. "The Waves," from *Bubblegum Delicious* by Dennis Lee. Copyright © 2000 by Dennis Lee. Reprinted with permission of HarperCollins.

Rhyme and Sound

In addition to the rhythm of a poem, children respond to its rhyme—for rhyme helps to create the musical qualities of a poem, and children enjoy the "singingness of words." The Russian poet Kornei Chukovsky maintains that in the beginning of childhood we are all "versifiers," and that it is only later in life that we begin to speak in prose.[6] Chukovsky is referring to the young child's tendency to double all syllables, so that *mother* is first "mama" and *water* "wa-wa." This, plus the regular patterning of such words as *daddy, mommy, granny,* and so on, makes for a natural production of rhyme. The young child's enjoyment of Mother Goose is due almost entirely to the rhyme and rhythm of these verses. This poem by Eloise Greenfield captures the rhythm of the turning rope and the slapping sound of the rope itself:

> Get set, ready now, jump right in
> Bounce and kick and giggle and spin
> Listen to the rope when it hits the ground
> Listen to that clappedy-slappedy sound
> Jump right up when it tells you to
> Come back down, whatever you do
> Count to a hundred, count by ten
> Start to count all over again
> That's what jumping is all about
> Get set, ready now,
> Jump
>   right
>   out!

> —Eloise Greenfield. "Rope Rhyme," from *Honey, I Love and Other Poems* by Eloise Greenfield. Text copyright © 1978 by Eloise Greenfield. Used by permission of HarperCollins Publishers.

If children have not heard any poetry or do not know any Mother Goose rhymes, teachers may want to introduce poetry with street rhymes, jump-rope rhymes, or raps through such books as Judy Sierra's *Schoolyard Rhymes* or Veronica Chambers's *Double Dutch: A Celebration of Jump Rope Jive and Sisterhood.* But children need to be freed from the notion that all poetry must rhyme. They should be introduced to some poetry that doesn't rhyme, such as free verse or haiku, so that they begin to listen to the meaning of a poem as well as the sound of it.

Rhyme is only one aspect of sound; alliteration, or the repetition of initial consonant sounds, is another; assonance, or the repetition of particular vowel sounds, is still another. Jack Prelutsky frequently uses alliteration to create the humor in his verse. For example, read "The Grobbles" in his *The Snopp on the Sidewalk* (see p. 455) and listen to the repetition of the *gr* sounds. Younger children delight in the sounds of the mud that "splishes

Children have universally enjoyed the folklore of the playground found in Judy Sierra's lively *Schoolyard Rhymes.* "Illustrations" by Melissa Sweet, copyright © 2005 by Melissa Sweet from *Schoolyard Rhymes* by Judy Sierra and Melissa Sweet. Used by permission of Alfred A. Knopf, an imprint of Random House Children's Books, a division of Random House, Inc.

and sploshes" in Rhoda Bacmeister's well-known poem "Galoshes" (in *Tomie dePaola's Book of Poems*).

The quiet *s* sound and the repetition of the double *o* in *moon* and *shoon* suggest the mysterious beauty of the moon in Walter de la Mare's poem "Silver" (in Helen Ferris's *Favorite Poems Old and New*). The term *onomatopoeia* refers to the use of words that make a sound like the action represented by the word, such as *crack, hiss,* and *sputter.* Occasionally a poet will create an entire poem that resembles a particular sound. David McCord has successfully imitated the sound of a railroad train in "Song of the Train." That slightly irregular beat is reinforced by the poet's use of dashes and italics.

Song of the Train

Clickety-clack
Wheels on the track,
This is the way
They begin the attack:
Click-ety Clack,

---

[6]Kornei Chukovsky, *From Two to Five,* translated and edited by Miriam Morton (Berkeley: University of California Press, 1963), p. 64.

Click-ety clack,
Click-ety *clack*-ety
Click-ety
Clack.

Clickety-clack
Over the crack,
Faster and faster
The song of the track:
Clickety-clack,
Clickety, clack,
Clickety, clackety
Clackety
Clack.

Riding in front,
Riding in back,
*Every*one hears
The song of the track:
Clickety-clack,
Clickety-clack,
Clickety, *clickety*
Clackety
Clack.

—"Song of the Train," from *One at a Time* by David
McCord. Copyright 1965, 1966 by David McCord.
By permission of Little, Brown & Co.

Repetition is another way the poet creates particular sound effects in a poem. Certainly, David McCord employed repetition along with onomatopoeia to create "Song of the Train." Robert Frost frequently used repetition of particular lines or phrases to emphasize meaning in his poems. The repetition of the last line "miles to go before I sleep" in his famous "Stopping by Woods on a Snowy Evening" (in de Regniers et al., *Sing a Song of Popcorn*) adds to the mysterious element in that poem.

Children are intrigued with the sound of language and enjoy unusual and ridiculous combinations of words. The gay nonsense of Laura Richards's "Eletelephony" (also in the de Regniers et al. anthology) is as much in the sound of the ridiculous words as in the plight of the poor elephant who tried to use the "telephant." Children love to trip off the name "James James Morrison Morrison Weatherby George Dupree" in A. A. Milne's "Disobedience" (in *The World of Christopher Robin*). Poets use rhyme, rhythm, and the various devices of alliteration, assonance, repetition, and coined words to create the melody and sound of poetry loved by children.

Imagery

Poetry draws on many kinds of language magic. The imagery of a poem involves direct sensory images of sight, sound, touch, smell, or taste. This aspect of poetry has particular appeal for children, as it reflects one of the major ways they explore their world. The very young child grasps an object and immediately puts it in her mouth. Children love to squeeze warm, soft puppies, and they squeal with delight as a pet mouse scampers up their arms. Taste and smell are also highly developed in the young child.

In our modern society, children are increasingly deprived of natural sensory experiences. One of the first admonitions they hear is "Don't touch." On the endless pavements of our cities, how many children have an opportunity to roll in crunchy piles of leaves? Air pollution laws ensure that they will never enjoy the acrid autumn smell of burning bonfires (rightly so, but still a loss). Many also miss the warm, yeasty odor of homemade bread or the sweet joy of licking the bowl of brownie batter. Some of our newest schools are windowless, so children are even deprived of seeing the brilliant blue sky on a crisp, cold day or the growing darkness of a storm or the changing silhouette of an oak tree on the horizon.

Poetry can never be a substitute for actual sensory experience. A child can't develop a concept of texture by hearing a poem or seeing pictures of the rough bark of a tree; he must first touch the bark and compare the feel of a deeply furrowed oak with the smooth-surfaced trunk of a beech tree. Then the poet can call up these experiences and extend them or make the child see them in a new way.

Because children are visual minded, they respond readily to the picture-making quality of poetry. Lilian Moore's "Rain Pools" (from *Mural on Second Avenue*) sparkles with the reflected light of sun-mixed raindrops.

Rain Pools

The rain
litters
the street
with mirror splinters,
silver
brown.

Now
Each piece
glitters with

sky
cloud
tree
upside down.

—Lilian Moore. "Rain Pools," from *Mural
on Second Avenue* by Lilian Moore. Copyright
© 2005 by Lilian Moore. Candlewick.

Here, even the way the poem is shaped on the page reinforces the imagery of raindrops provided by the words.

In Tennyson's "The Eagle" (in Nancy Larrick's *Piping Down the Valleys Wide*), the description of the eagle is rich in the use of visual imagery. In the first verse the reader can see the eagle perched on the crest of a steep mountain, posed ready for his swift descent whenever he sights his quarry. But in the second verse the poet

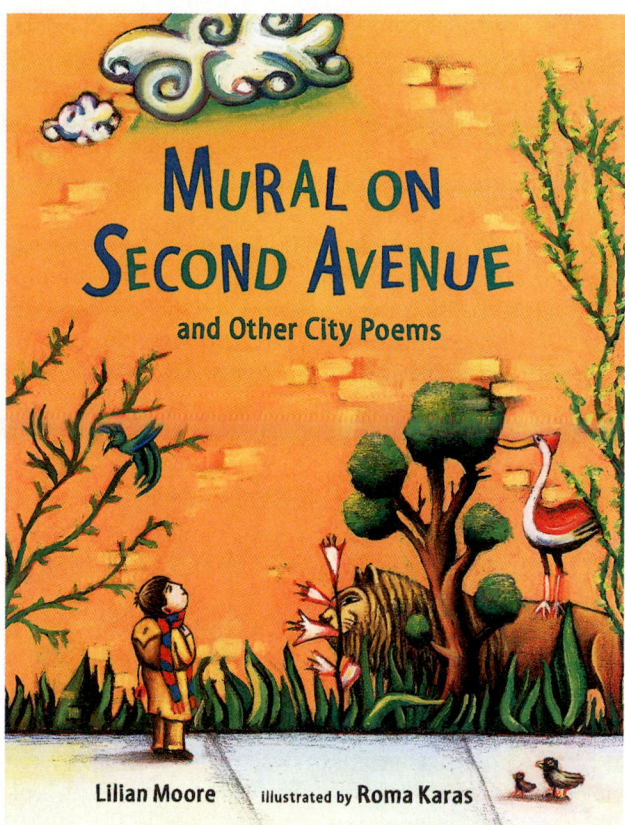

Lilian Moore's "Rain Pools," found in *Mural on Second Avenue and Other City Poems,* contains vivid images to delight young children. Poems by Lilian Moore. Illustrations copyright © 2004 Roma Karas. Reproduced by permission of the publisher Candlewick Press, Inc., Cambridge, MA.

"enters into" the eagle's world and describes it from the bird's point of view. Looking down from his lofty height, the might of the waves is reduced to wrinkles and the sea seems to crawl:

> He clasps the crag with crooked hands;
> Close to the sun in lonely lands,
> Ringed with the azure world, he stands.
>
> The wrinkled sea beneath him crawls;
> He watches from his mountain wall,
> And like a thunderbolt he falls.
>
> —Alfred Lord Tennyson. "The Eagle," in *Piping Down the Valleys Wild,* ed. Nancy Larrick.

The lonely, peaceful scene is shattered by the natural metaphor of the final line: "And like a thunderbolt he falls." In your mind's eye you can see, almost feel, the wind on your wings as you plunge down the face of the cliff.

Most poetry depends on visual and auditory imagery to evoke a mood or response, but imagery of touch, taste, and smell is also used. Valerie Worth's poem "Mud" makes fingers tingle with the feel of squishy earth:

> Mud mixed
> With a stick

> To the right
> Thickness,
> Not too stiff
> Nor too full
> of rain,
>
> Can then
> Be picked up
> In the hand,
> Soft, still cold
> As a stone,
> And squeezed
> Until it strains
>
> Out between the fingers—
> Warmed a bit,
> But still heavy
> With earth's
> Rich grit and grain.
>
> —Valerie Worth. "Mud," from *All the Small Poems and Fourteen More* by Valerie Worth. Copyright © 1987, 1994 by Valerie Worth. Reprinted by permission of Farrar, Straus and Giroux, LLC.

Psychologists tell us that some of children's earliest memories are sensory, recalling particularly the way things smell and taste. Most children have a delicate sense of taste that responds to the texture and smell of a particular food. In "Hard and Soft," in his *Eats: Poems,* Arnold Adoff contrasts the crunch of eating a carrot with the quiet sound of swallowing raisins. Rose Rauter captures both the feel of a fresh-picked peach and its delicious taste in this poem:

> Touch it to your cheek and it's soft
> as a velvet newborn mouse
> who has to strive
> to be alive.
> Bite in. Runny
> honey
> blooms on your tongue—
> as if you've bitten open
> a whole hive.
>
> —Rose Rauter. "Peach," from *Knock at a Star: A Child's Introduction to Poetry* by X. J. Kennedy and Dorothy M. Kennedy. Copyright © 1982 by X. J. Kennedy and Dorothy M. Kennedy. Reprinted by permission of Little, Brown & Company.

Figurative Language: Comparison and Contrast

Because the language of poetry is so compressed, every word must be made to convey the meaning of the poem. Poets do this by comparing two objects or ideas with each other in such a way that the connotation of one word gives added meaning to another.

In "Peach," Rose Rauter compared the soft fuzzy feel of a peach to a velvety newborn mouse; its sweet taste made her think of a whole hive of honey. Kristine O'Connell George makes the following observation about the surprise waiting on the branch of a winter tree,

Bud

A tiny velveteen satchel,
the color of pale cream,
Is perched on the tip
of this bare branch.

Snap open the clasp—
And you will find,
Inside this tiny valise,
One rolled and folded
neatly packed
leaf.

—"Bud," from *Old Elm Speaks* by Kristine O'Connell George. Text copyright © 1998 by Kristine O'Connell George. Reprinted by permission of Clarion Books, an imprint of Houghton Mifflin Company. All rights reserved.

BY VALERIE WORTH · PICTURES BY NATALIE BABBITT

peacock
and other poems

Natalie Babbitt created the lovely illustrations for Valerie Worth's *Peacock and Other Poems.* Reprinted by permission of Farrar, Straus and Giroux, LLC. Jacket design by Natalie Babbit from *Peacock and Other Poems* by Valerie Worth. Copyright © 2002 by Natalie Babbit.

When writers compare one thing with another, using such connecting words as *like* or *as*, they are using a *simile.* In a *metaphor* the poet speaks of an object or idea as if it *were* another object. In recent years we have paid little attention to the difference between these two techniques, referring to both as examples of metaphorical or figurative language.

It is not important that children know the difference between a simile and a metaphor. It is important that they know what is being compared and that the comparison is fresh and new and helps them view the idea or object in a different and unusual way. Two well-known poems containing metaphors that help children see their world afresh are Carl Sandburg's "Fog" and Vachel Lindsay's "The Moon's the North Wind's Cooky" (both in Jack Prelutsky's *The Random House Book of Poetry for Children*). Perhaps the reason these poems have endured is that they also reveal a true understanding of a child's point of view.

Some figurative language is so commonplace that it has lost its ability to evoke new images. Language and verse are filled with clichés like "it rained cats and dogs," "a blanket of snow," "quiet as a mouse," or "thin as a rail." Poet Eve Merriam described a cliché as what lazy people use in their writing. Good poetry helps look at the usual in unusual ways.

Valerie Worth received the National Council of Teachers of English Award for Excellence in Poetry for Children for her *Small Poems* books. These have been combined and added to her *All the Small Poems and Fourteen More* and *Peacock and Other Poems.* Her simple free verse contains vivid metaphors that describe ordinary objects like chairs, earthworms, safety pins, and umbrellas:

Umbrella

Slack wings
Folded, it
Hangs by a
Claw in
The closet.

Sleeping
Or moping
Or quietly
Hatching
A plot

To flap out
And escape
On the furious
Sweep of
The storm.

—Valerie Worth. "Umbrella," from *Peacock and Other Poems* by Valerie Worth. Copyright © 2002. Farrar, Straus and Giroux.

Some poets sustain a metaphor throughout the poem. Most children are intrigued with the subject of dinosaurs and readily respond to Charles Malam's poem that compares a steam shovel to those enormous beasts.

> The dinosaurs are not all dead.
> I saw one raise its iron head
> To watch me walking down the road
> Beyond our house today.
> Its jaws were dripping with a load
> Of earth and grass that it had cropped.
> It must have heard me where I stopped,
> Snorted white steam my way,
> And stretched its long neck out to see,
> And chewed, and grinned quite amiably.
>
> —"Steam Shovel," from *Upper Pastures: Poems* by Charles Malam. Copyright © 1930, 1958 by Charles Malam. Reprinted by permission of Henry Holt and Company, LLC.

Personification is a way of speaking about inanimate objects and animals as though they were persons. Human beings have always personified inanimate objects. Young children personify their toys; adolescents and adults name their computers, their cars, and boats. Poetry simply extends this process to a wider range of objects. In *Dirty Laundry Pile: Poems in Different Voices* Paul Janeczko has collected twenty-seven poems written in the voices of animals such as mosquitoes, cats, and turtles and objects like washing machines, scarecrows, and kites. Diane Siebert personifies the river in her book *Mississippi*, the desert in *Mojave*, and the Sierra Nevada Mountains in *Sierra*. Deborah Chandra sings winter's song with a mother's voice in this poem:

> The leaves are gone,
> The world is old,
> I hear a whisper from the sky—
> The dark is long,
> The ground's grown cold,
> I hear the snow's white lullaby.
> She breathes it softly
> Through the air,
> While with her gown of flakes she sweeps
> The sky, the trees, the ground grown cold,
> Singing hush
> Now hush.
>   Now hush,
>   Hush
>   Sleep.
>
> —Deborah Chandra. "Snowfall," from *Balloons and Other Poems* by Deborah Chandra. Copyright © 1990 by Deborah Chandra. Reprinted by permission of Farrar, Straus and Giroux, LLC.

Another way of strengthening an image is through contrast. Elizabeth Coatsworth employs this device in much of her poetry. Her well-known "Swift Things Are Beautiful" contrasts the beauty of swift things with that of those that are slow and steady.

Swift Things Are Beautiful

> Swift things are beautiful:
> Swallows and deer,
> And lightning that falls
> Bright-veined and clear,
> Rivers and meteors,
> Wind in the wheat,
> The strong-withered horse,
> The runner's sure feet.
>
> And slow things are beautiful:
> The closing of day,
> The pause of the wave
> That curves downward to spray,
> The embers that crumbles,
> The opening flower, and the ox that moves on
> In the quiet of power.
>
> —Elizabeth Coatsworth. "Swift Things Are Beautiful," in *Reflections on a Gift of Watermelon Pickle*, ed. Stephen Dunning et al. Copyright © 1966 Lothrop.

Shape

The first thing children notice about reading a poem is that it looks different from prose. And usually it does. Most poems begin with capital letters for each line and have one or more stanzas.

Increasingly, however, poets are using the shape of their poems to reinforce the image of the idea. In "The Grasshopper" (in his *One at a Time*) David McCord describes the plight of a grasshopper that fell down a deep well. As luck would have it, he discovers a rope and up he climbs one word at a time! The reader must read up the page to follow the grasshopper's ascent. Eve Merriam's "Windshield Wiper" (in *Knock at a Star*, ed. X. Kennedy and D. Kennedy) not only sounds like the even rhythm of a car's wiper but has the look of two wipers. Abram Bunn Ross writes about siblings sharing the same sleeping space in "Two in Bed" (in Simon James's *Days Like This*). The words form the shape of an arrowhead—or the sharp pain of a brother's knee poking into one's back.

Two in Bed

> When my brother Tommy
> Sleeps in bed with me
> He doubles up
> And makes
> himself
> exactly
> like
> a
> V
> And 'cause the bed is not so wide
> A part of him is on my side.
>
> —Abram Bunn Ross. "Two in Bed," in *Days Like This*, ed. Simon James. Copyright © 2000.

Children enjoy mounting their own poems on a piece of paper shaped in the image of their poem, such as a verse about a jack-o'-lantern on a pumpkin shape or a poem about a plane mounted on the silhouette of a plane. Later, the words themselves may form the shape of the content, as in concrete poetry.

Emotional Force

We have seen how sound, language, and the shape of a poem can all work together to create the total impact of the poem. Considered individually, the rhyme scheme, imagery, figurative language, and appearance of the poem are of little importance unless all of these inter-relate to create an emotional response in the reader. The craft of the poem is not the poem.

In the following poem, a modern poet writes of the way two children feel when caught in the vortex of their parents' quarrel:

> Listening to grownups quarreling,
> standing in the hall against the
> wall with my little brother, blown
> like leaves against the wall by their
> voices, my head like a pingpong ball
> between the paddles of their anger:
> I knew what it meant
> to tremble like a leaf.
>
> Cold with their wrath, I heard
> the claws of the rain
> pounce. Floods
> poured through the city,

> skies clapped over me,
> and I was shaken, shaken
> like a mouse
> between their jaws.

> —Ruth Whitman. "Listening to Grownups Quarreling," from *The Marriage Wig and Other Poems.* Copyright © 1968 and renewed 1996 by Ruth Whitman. Reprinted by permission of Harcourt, Inc.

A teacher could destroy the total impact of this poem for children by having them count the number of metaphors in it, looking at their increasing force and power. Children should have a chance to hear it, comment on it if they wish, or compare it with other similar poems. All elements of these poems work together to create the feeling of being overpowered by a quarrel between those you love most.

Good poetry has the power to make readers moan in despair, catch their breath in fear, gasp in awe, smile with delight, or sit back in wonder. For poetry heightens emotions and increases one's sensitivity to an idea or mood.

Teachers need to be able to identify the characteristics of good poetry in order to make wise selections to share with children. They need to know the various kinds of poetry and the range of content of poetry for children. Then they can select poetry that will gradually develop children's appreciation and sense of form. The questions listed in Evaluation Criteria: "Evaluating Poetry for Children" would not be appropriate to use for every

EVALUATION CRITERIA

Evaluating Poetry for Children

- How does the rhythm of the poem reinforce and create the meaning of the poem?
- If the poem rhymes, does it sound natural or contrived?
- How does the sound of the poem add to its meaning? Does the poem use alliteration? onomatopoeia? repetition?
- Does the poem create sensory images of sight, touch, smell, or taste?
- Are these images related to children's delight in their particular senses?
- What is the quality of imagination in the poem? Does the poem make the child see something in a fresh, new way, or does it rely on tired clichés?
- Is the figurative language appropriate to children's lives? Are the similes and metaphors ones that a child would appreciate and understand?

- What is the tone of the poem? Does it patronize childhood by looking down on it? Is it didactic and preachy? Does it see childhood in a sentimental or nostalgic way?
- Is the poem appropriate for children? Will it appeal to them, and will they like it?
- How has the poet created the emotional intensity of the poem? Does every word work to heighten the feelings conveyed?
- Does the shape of the poem—the placement of the words—contribute to the poem's meaning?
- What is the purpose of the poem? To amuse? To describe in a fresh way? To comment on humanity? To draw parallels in our lives? How well has the poet achieved this purpose?

poem. However, they can serve as a beginning way to look at poetry for children.

Forms of Poetry for Children

Children are more interested in the "idea" of a poem than in knowing about the various forms of poetry. However, teachers will want to expose children to various forms of poetry and note their reactions. Do these children like only narrative poems? Do they think all poetry must rhyme, or will they listen to some free verse? Are they ready for the seemingly simple, yet highly complex, form of haiku? Understanding of and appreciation for a wide variety of poetry grow gradually as children are exposed to different forms and types of poems. Paul Janeczko's *A Kick in the Head: An Everyday Guide to Poetic Forms* is a lively introduction to forms of poetry that will appeal to children. Each form is accompanied by poems of example and a brief explanation of structure. Janeczko's choice of poems and Chris Raschka's illustrations liven up what might otherwise be just a tedious list of definitions.

Ballads

Ballads are narrative poems that have been adapted for singing or that give the effect of a song. Originally, they were not made or sung for children but were the literature of all the people. Characteristics of the ballad form are the frequent use of dialogue in telling the story, repetition, marked rhythm and rhyme, and refrains that go back to the days when ballads were sung. Popular ballads have no known authors, as they were handed down from one generation to the next; the literary ballad, however, does have a known author. Ballads usually deal with heroic deeds and include stories of murder, unrequited love, feuds, and tragedies. American ballads frequently were popular songs, such as "On Top of Old Smoky" (in the Kennedys' *Knock at a Star*). Children in the middle grades enjoy the amusing story of the stubborn man and his equally stubborn wife in "Get Up and Bar the Door" (in *The Oxford Book of Poetry for Children*, ed. Edward Blishen). The Scottish ballad "Tamlane" has been retold in prose by Susan Cooper in *Tam Lin* (see Chapter 6).

Narrative Poems

The narrative poem relates a particular event or episode or tells a long tale. It may be a lyric, a sonnet, or free verse; its one requirement is that it must tell a story. Many of children's favorite poems are these so-called story poems. One of the best-known narrative poems is Robert Browning's *The Pied Piper of Hamelin*. First illustrated by Kate Greenaway in 1888, it continues to be published with new illustrators.

The most popular narrative poem in this country is Clement Moore's *The Night Before Christmas* (or *A Visit from St. Nicholas*). Every artist from Grandma Moses to Tasha Tudor to Ted Rand and Jan Brett has illustrated this Christmas story. Presently there are more than fifty editions of *The Night Before Christmas*.

A. A. Milne's narrative poems are favorites of many young children. They love his story of a lost mouse in "Missing" and the disappearing beetle in "Forgiven." Six-, 7-, and 8-year-olds delight in Milne's "The King's Breakfast" and "King John's Christmas," poems about petulant kings, one of whom wants a "bit of butter" for his bread and the other of whom wants a big red India-rubber ball (all of these poems are in *The World of Christopher Robin*). The long narrative tale "Custard the Dragon" by Ogden Nash, in *The Tale of Custard the Dragon*, has been illustrated by Lynn Munsinger.

Without a doubt the all-time favorite narrative poems of children today are the outrageously funny ones in Shel Silverstein's *Where the Sidewalk Ends*, *A Light in the Attic*, and *Falling Up*. Some of their favorite story verses include Shel Silverstein's "Sick," in which Peggy Ann McKay claims to have every known symptom of dreadful diseases until she realizes it is Saturday; the sad tale "Sarah Cynthia Sylvia Stout Who Would Not Take the Garbage Out"; and "Boa Constrictor," in which a man is slowly being swallowed alive (all are in Silverstein's *Where the Sidewalk Ends*).

Children also enjoy Jack Prelutsky's story verse, particularly his collection of poems about the bully Harvey and the children's ultimate revenge on him, *Rolling Harvey Down the Hill*. Middle graders delight in Prelutsky's macabre tales in *Nightmares* and *The Headless Horseman*, enriched by Arnold Lobel's grisly black-and-white illustrations.

Not all narrative poems for children are humorous. Older children will thrill to the novel-length epic of sea-going treachery and redemption in *The Voyage of the Arctic Tern* by Hugh Montgomery. They will also respond to the pathos of Eve Merriam's poem "To Meet Mr. Lincoln" (in *Sing a Song of Popcorn*, ed. de Regniers et al.) and to Robert Service's spooky *The Cremation of Sam McGee*. They are stirred by the galloping hoofbeats in Longfellow's *Paul Revere's Ride*, in versions illustrated by Ted Rand and Christopher Bing. A favorite romantic tale is the dramatic *Highwayman* by Alfred Noyes, which has been portrayed in a stunning picture book illustrated by Charles Keeping. English author Kevin Crossley-Holland has chosen fifteen narrative poems for *Once Upon a Poem: Favorite Poems That Tell Stories*. The collection includes poems such as Edward Lear's "The Owl and the Pussycat" and A. B. "Banjo" Paterson's "The Man from Snowy River" and is truly a book for all ages. Each of the poems has a brief introduction by a well-known modern author, and the collection is illustrated by four different English artists.

One of the best ways to capture children's interest in poetry is to present a variety of narrative poems. Teachers

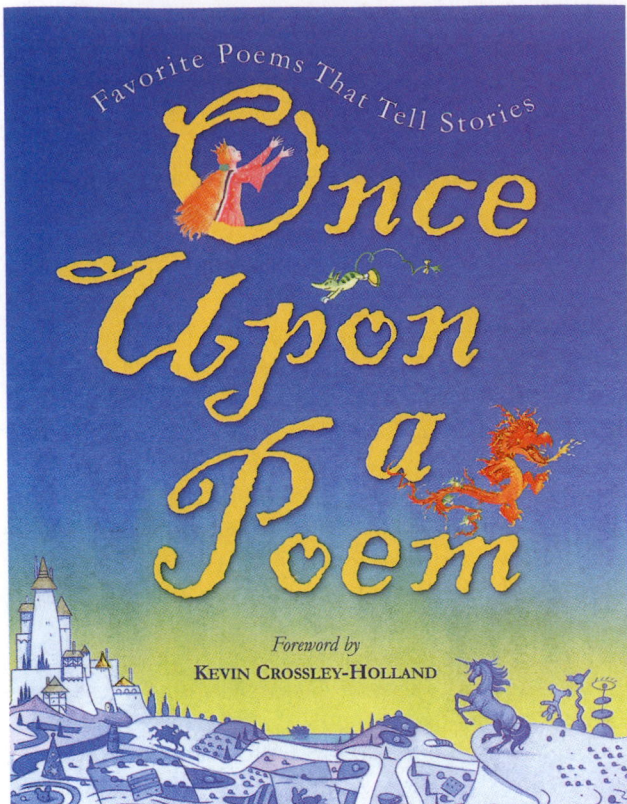

Once Upon a Poem, collected by Kevin Crossley-Holland, contains storytelling poems that are consistent favorites of children. Illustration by Chris Mewa from *Once Upon a Poem: Favorite Poems That Tell Stories.* Published by The Chicken House/Scholastic Inc. Cover illustration © 2004 by The Chicken House. Reprinted by permission.

will want to build a file of story poems appropriate to the interests of the children in their classes to use to introduce poetry to the children.

Lyrical Poetry

Most of the poetry written for children is lyrical. The term *lyrical* derives from the word *lyric* and means poetry that sings its way into the minds and memories of its listeners. It is usually personal or descriptive poetry, with no prescribed length or structure other than its melody.

Much of William Blake's poetry is lyrical, beginning with the opening lines of his introductory poem to *Songs of Innocence:* "Piping down the valleys wild / Piping songs of pleasant glee" (in *Piping Down the Valleys Wild,* ed. Nancy Larrick). Robert Louis Stevenson's poems have a singing quality that makes them unforgettable. Everyone knows his poems "The Swing" and "The Wind" (both in *A Child's Garden of Verses*). Equally popular is his mysterious "Windy Nights," which compares the sound of the wind to a galloping horseman:

> Whenever the moon and stars are set,
>   Whenever the wind is high,
> All night long in the dark and wet,
>   A man goes riding by.

Late in the night when the fires are out,
Why does he gallop and gallop about?

> Whenever the trees are crying aloud,
>   And ships are tossed at sea,
> By, on the highway, low and loud,
>   By at the gallop goes he.
> By at the gallop he goes, and then
> By he comes back at the gallop again.

> —Robert Louis Stevenson. "Windy Nights," in
> *Sing a Song of Popcorn,* ed. Beatrice Shenk de
> Regniers et al.

John Masefield's well-known poem "Sea Fever" (in *Favorite Poems Old and New,* ed. Helen Ferris) would be a good one to read after sharing *The True Confessions of Charlotte Doyle* by Avi. Children always respond to the sound of the internal rhyme in Irene Rutherford McLeod's "The Lone Dog" (in Ferris's *Favorite Poems Old and New*), which begins with "I'm a lean dog, a keen dog, a wild dog and lone." Lyrical poetry is characterized by this lilting use of words that gives children an exhilarating sense of melody.

Limericks

A nonsense form of verse that is particularly enjoyed by children is the limerick. This is a five-line verse in which the first and second lines rhyme, the third and fourth rhyme, and the fifth line rhymes with lines 1 and 2 and usually is a surprise or humorous statement. Freak spellings, oddities, and humorous twists characterize this form of poetry. David McCord, in his book *One at a Time,* suggests that "a limerick, to be lively and successful, *must* have *perfect* riming and *flawless* rhythm."

Other delightful collections of limericks have been produced by John Ciardi, Arnold Lobel, and Bill Grossman. Ciardi's collection *The Hopeful Trout and Other Limericks* offers limericks on a variety of themes from families to outer space. Arnold Lobel's *The Book of Pigericks* is a most humorous book of limericks, with verses about different pigs from various cities in the United States. His illustrations of humanized pigs are as funny as the limericks. Bill Grossman's *Timothy Tunny Swallowed a Bunny* is illustrated by Kevin Hawkes and provides a silly and smart collection of limericks that plays on words as well as rhythms.

Children in the middle grades enjoy writing limericks, whether based on nursery rhymes, pigs, or their own names. It is certainly a far easier form for them to write than the highly abstract haiku.

Free Verse

Free verse does not have to rhyme but depends on rhythm or cadence for its poetic form. It may use some rhyme, alliteration, and pattern. Though it frequently looks different on the printed page, it sounds very much like other poetry when read aloud. Children who have the opportunity to hear this form of poetry will be freed from thinking that all poetry must rhyme. Many of Valerie Worth's deceptively simple poems in *Small Poems* are written in free verse.

While much of Eve Merriam's poetry rhymes, she has also written free verse. Her well-known poem "How to Eat a Poem" (in *A Jar of Tiny Stars*, ed. Bernice E. Cullinan) is written in free verse. Langston Hughes's melodic "April Rain Song" (in *The Dream Keeper*) and Carl Sandburg's "Fog" (in *Rainbows Are Made*, ed. Lee Bennett Hopkins) are other examples of the effective use of free verse. Kristine O'Connell George's collections of poems, *Old Elm Speaks: Tree Poems, Little Dog Poems,* and *The Great Frog Race and Other Poems,* contain many examples of free verse that will appeal to children.

Haiku

Haiku is an ancient Japanese verse form that can be traced back to the thirteenth century. There are only seventeen syllables in the haiku; the first and third lines contain five syllables, the second line seven. Almost every haiku can be divided into two parts: first, a simple picture-making description that usually includes some reference, direct or indirect, to the season; and second, a statement of mood or feeling. A relationship between these two parts is implied—either a similarity or a telling difference.

The greatest of haiku writers, and the one who crystallized the form, was Basho. In his lifetime Basho produced more than eight hundred haiku. In the following poem the negative emotion expressed in the first line is reversed in the surprisingly pleasing image left by the last line. This image of black on white maintains the contrast of the two emotions that sustain the poem.

> Detestable crow!
> Today alone you please me—
> black against the snow.

Matthew Gollub includes some of the poems of Issa, another famous Haiku poet, in his biography *Cool Melons Turn to Frogs.* The poet's life story and Gollub's note at the book's end should help demystify this ancient form. G. Brian Karas's illustrations for *The Stars Are Whispering* lend great appeal to Issa's poems. In a real change from his usual humorous style Jack Prelutsky composes haiku in celebration of animals in *If Not for the Cat.* Elegant watercolors by Ted Rand capture the essence of Japanese scroll paintings. For *Stone Bench in an Empty Park* Paul Janeczko found poems that often break the traditional rules but never lose the essence of haiku. In addition, these poems are not about the rural scenes usually found in haiku poetry. Instead, the poems are set in cities where living things are seen reflected against the hard-edged urban landscape.

The meaning of haiku is not expected to be immediately apparent. The reader is invited to add his or her own associations and meanings to the words, thus completing the poem in the mind. Each time the poem is read, new understandings will develop. Haiku is deceiving in that the form appears simple yet it requires much

from its reader. Unless children have reached the Piagetian level of formal operations in their thinking, haiku might be too abstract a form of poetry for them to fully understand. The common practice of asking young children to write haiku suggests that teachers do not understand its complexity. In this case, short is not simple!

Concrete Poetry

Many poets today are writing picture poems that make the reader see what they are saying. The message of the poem is presented not only in the words (sometimes just letters or punctuation marks) but in the arrangement of the words. Meaning is reinforced, or even carried, by the shape of the poem.

Perhaps because today's children are so visually oriented, concrete poetry has become increasingly popular in the past few years, and there are some lively collections available. Chris Raschka's abstract illustrations are an interesting accompaniment to the concrete poems in Paul Janeczko's *A Poke in the I.* Joan Bransfield Graham has created attractive graphic forms for poems about water in *Splish Splash*, illustrated by Steve Scott, and poems about light in *Flicker Flash*, illustrated by Nancy Davis. Other recent collections of concrete poems include John Grandits's *Technically, It's Not My Fault,* Heidi Roemer's *Come to My Party and Other Shape Poems,* Brad Burg's *Outside the Lines: Poetry at Play,* and J. Patrick Lewis's *Doodle Dandies.*

Once children have been exposed to concrete poetry, they invariably want to try creating some of their own. However, some children become so involved in the picture-making process, they forget that the meaning of the poem is carried by both words and arrangement. If emphasis is placed on the meaning first, then the shaping of the words will grow naturally from the idea of the poem.

SELECTING POETRY FOR CHILDREN

Before they enter school, children seem to have a natural enthusiasm for the sounds and rhythms of language. Schoolteachers and librarians will want to select poems and poets that will build upon these inclinations and that appeal to children's interests. They will also want to find ways to extend and deepen children's initial preferences into a lifelong love of poetry.

Children's Poetry Preferences

Starting in the early 1920s, children's interest in poetry has been the subject of many research studies. The interesting fact about all these studies is the similarity of the findings and the stability of children's poetry preferences over the years. According to Ann Terry, these studies suggest the following:

1. Children are the best judges of their preferences.
2. Reading texts and courses of study often do not include the children's favorite poems.

Birthday Candles

Happy Day Happy Year

Like shooting stars that blaze the dark, you flame — then disappear. But when I look, I see your light in faces, circled near.

Art and words combine to create poems about light in Joan Graham's book of concrete poetry, *Flicker Flash*, with illustrations by Nancy Davis. "Happy Day, Happy Year" from *Flicker Flash*. Text copyright © 1999 by Joan Bransfield Graham. Illustrations copyright © 1999 by Nancy Davis. Reprinted by permission of Houghton Mifflin Company. All rights reserved.

3. Children's poetry choices are influenced by (1) the poetry form, (2) certain poetic elements, and (3) the content, with humor and familiar experience being particularly popular.

4. A poem enjoyed at one grade level may be enjoyed across several grade levels.

5. Children do not enjoy poems they do not understand.

6. Thoughtful, meditative poems are disliked by children.

7. Some poems appeal to one sex more than the other; girls enjoy poetry more than boys do.

8. New poems are preferred over older, more traditional ones.

9. Literary merit is not necessarily an indication that a poem will be liked.[7]

Terry also reported that in her study of children in grades 4 through 6, narrative poems, such as John Ciardi's

"Mummy Slept Late and Daddy Fixed Breakfast" (in *A Jar of Tiny Stars*, ed. Bernice E. Cullinan), and limericks, including both modern and traditional, were the children's favorite forms of poetry. Haiku was consistently disliked by all grade levels. Elements of rhyme, rhythm, and sound increased children's enjoyment of the poems, as evidenced by their preference for David McCord's "The Pickety Fence" (in *Every Time I Climb a Tree*) and "Lone Dog" (in *Favorite Poems Old and New*, ed. Helen Ferris). Poems that contained much figurative language or imagery were disliked. Children's favorite poems at all three grade levels contained humor or were about familiar experiences or animals. All children preferred contemporary poems containing modern content and today's language to the older, more traditional poems.

Carol Fisher and Margaret Natarella[8] found similar preferences among first, second, and third graders, as did Karen Kutiper[9] among seventh, eighth, and ninth graders. However, the younger children enjoyed poems about strange and fantastic events, such as Jack Prelutsky's "The Lurpp Is on the Loose" (in *The Snopp on the Sidewalk*) and Ogden Nash's "Adventures of Isabel" (in *The Adventures of Isabel*), while the older children opted for more realistic content. Younger children also appeared to like traditional poems more than the older children did. They insisted that poetry must rhyme, and all of the traditional poems did, so they could have been selecting on the basis of rhyme rather than content. However, one consistent finding of these studies was that adults cannot accurately predict which poems children will like.

How then can we most effectively select poetry for children? Certainly a teacher will want to consider children's needs and interests, their previous experience with poetry, and the types of poetry that appeal to them. A sound principle to follow is to begin where the children are. Teachers can share poems that have elements of rhyme, rhythm, and sound, such as Rhoda Bacmeister's "Galoshes" (in *Sing a Song of Popcorn*, ed. Beatrice de Regniers et al.) or David McCord's "Song of the Train" (in *One at a Time*) (see p. 413). They can read many narrative

---

[7]Ann Terry, *Children's Poetry Preferences: A National Survey of the Upper Elementary Grades* (Urbana, Ill.: National Council of Teachers of English, 1974), p. 10.

[8]Carol J. Fisher and Margaret A. Natarella, "Young Children's Preferences in Poetry: A National Survey of First, Second and Third Graders," *Research in the Teaching of English* 16 (December 1982): 339–53.

[9]Karen Sue Kutiper, "A Survey of the Adolescent Poetry Preferences of Seventh, Eighth and Ninth Graders" (Ed.D. dissertation, University of Houston, 1985).

verses and limericks and look for humorous poems and poems about familiar experiences and animals. They should share only those poems that they really like themselves; enthusiasm for poetry is contagious. However, teachers will not want to limit their sharing only to poems that they know children will like. For taste needs to be developed, too; children should go beyond their delight in humorous and narrative poetry to develop an appreciation for variety in both form and content. We want children to respond to more poetry and to find more to respond to in poetry.

It may well be that the consistency in children's poetry preferences over the years simply reflects the poverty of their experience with poetry. We tend to like the familiar. If teachers read only traditional narrative poems to children, then these children will like narrative poems. Or having had little or no exposure to fine imaginative poetry, children might not have gone beyond their natural intuitive liking for jump-rope rhymes or humorous limericks. In brief, the results of the studies of children's interests in poetry might be an indictment more of the quality of their literature program than of the quality of their preferences. We need to ascertain children's poetry preferences after they have experienced a rich, continuous exposure to poetry throughout the elementary-school years. Sharon Creech provides a wonderfully moving example of how this might be done in *Love That Dog*. This deceptively simple book is profound in its message that poetry of all kinds can give children a way of understanding and even changing themselves. Jack, Creech's young narrator, begins his journal by telling his teacher Miss Stretchberry that he won't write poetry because only girls do. A week later he complains, "I don't understand the poem about the red wheelbarrow and why so much depends upon them" (p. 3). The poem he refers to is William Carlos Williams's "The Red Wheelbarrow" (the least favorite poem of children in the Terry study). Over the course of the school year, however, by reading poetry by Williams, Robert Frost, Valerie Worth, Walter Dean Myers, and others and by gaining confidence in his own poetry writing, Jack comes to appreciate the power of poetry and to find relief for his personal grief. There could be no better guide for teachers who want to extend children's appreciation and love of poetry than Miss Stretchberry in *Love That Dog*. We have no doubt that like Jack, as children have increased experience with a wide range of quality poetry by various poets, they will grow in appreciation and understanding of the finer poems.

Poets and Their Books

Recent years have seen an increase in the number of writers of verse for children and the number of poetry books published for the juvenile market. Poetry itself has changed, becoming less formal, more spontaneous, and imitative of the child's own language patterns. The range of subject matter has expanded with the tremendous variation in children's interests. It is difficult to categorize a poet's work based on the content of his or her poems, for many poets interpret various areas of children's experience. However, an understanding of the general subject matter of the works of each poet will help the teacher select poems and make recommendations to children.

Humorous Verse

In every preference study that has been done, children prefer narrative rhyme and humorous verse. Today the popularity of the verse of Shel Silverstein and Jack Prelutsky attests to this. The use of imaginative symbols and vivid imagery and metaphor marks the difference between real poetry and verse. The versifiers provide instant gratification, but leave the reader with little to ponder. However, because children begin here in their enjoyment of poetry, it seems appropriate to start this section with writers of humorous verse.

Almost all poets have written some humorous verse, but only a few have become noted primarily for this form. In the nineteenth century the names of Edward Lear and Lewis Carroll became almost synonymous with humorous nonsense poems. Lear's limericks, alphabet rhymes, and narrative poems have been compiled into one book, *The Complete Nonsense Book.* Each absurd verse is illustrated by the poet's grotesque drawings, which add greatly to Lear's humor. Artist Valorie Fisher has given a more contemporary look to Lear's poetry in *Nonsense!* Jan Brett, Hilary Knight, and James Marshall have all produced distinctive illustrations for Lear's narrative poem "The Owl and the Pussycat."

Much of what children consider funny is frequently sadistic and ghoulish. Colin McNaughton's *Who's Been Sleeping in My Porridge?* and *Making Friends with Frankenstein* are collections that range from the stomach-turning "Cockroach Sandwich" to the mournful satire of "The Doom Merchant," with much pure silliness in between. McNaughton's bizarre illustrations add humor and clarify his wordplay, as in "Frankenstein's Monster Is Finally Dead." We see Frankenstein's feet, head, and other body parts sprouting angel wings ("may he rest in pieces"). Jack Prelutsky's macabre poems in *Nightmares* and *The Headless Horseman* and Arnold Lobel's black-and-white illustrations are splendidly terrifying. One seventh-grade teacher of children in the inner city maintained that this book got her through her first year of teaching! Prelutsky is also a master at creating such zany imaginary creatures as the "Wozzit," who is hiding in the closet, and the "Grobbles," who quietly wait to gobble someone up. Both of these poems are in *The Snopp on the Sidewalk*. He creates more appealing creatures in *The Baby Uggs Are Hatching*, including the "Sneezy-Snoozer," the "Dreary Dreeze," and the "Sneepies." *The Dragons Are Singing Tonight*, one of several collaborations with illustrator Peter Sis, includes a dragon whose cold is cured with a dose of turpentine and one whose fire is doused in a bout with a thunderstorm.

Peter Sis created the imaginative pictures for Jack Prelutsky's humorous collections *The Dragons Are Singing Tonight* and *Monday's Troll.* Illustration from *The Dragons Are Singing Tonight* by Jack Prelutsky, illustrated by Peter Sis. Illustration copyright © 1993 by Peter Sis. Used by permission of Greenwillow Books, an imprint of HarperCollins Publishers.

John Ciardi's light verse for children is enjoyed by girls and boys with enough sophistication to appreciate his tongue-in-cheek humor. His "Mummy Slept Late and Daddy Fixed Breakfast" (in *A Jar of Tiny Stars*, ed. Bernice E. Cullinan) was the most popular poem of the children in the fourth, fifth, and sixth grades in the Terry study (see p. 421). A former poetry editor for the *Saturday Review*, Ciardi could write serious verse as well as light verse. His "How to Tell the Top of the Hill" (in *The Reason for the Pelican*) and "The River Is a Piece of the Sky" (in Larrick's *Piping Down the Valleys Wild*) are both proof of this. X. J. Kennedy is a kindred spirit to Ciardi in his style and sense of humor. This teacher, anthologist, and poet has written some hilariously silly poems that can be found in *Exploding Gravy: Poems to Make You Laugh.* This volume includes poems about far-out families ("Great-Great-Grandma Don't Sleep in Your Tree House Tonight") and peculiar characters ("Stevie the Internet Addict"). Both Ciardi and Kennedy are winners of the NCTE Poetry Award.

All ages enjoy Jack Prelutsky's large collections (more than a hundred poems) titled *The New Kid on the Block, Something Big Has Been Here, It's Raining Pigs and Noodles,* and *A Pizza the Size of the Sun,* which include humorous realistic poems such as "I'm Disgusted with My Brother," "The Wumpaloons, Which Never Were," and "My Sister Is a Sissy," plus many funny characters and more zany creatures.

Prelutsky has written some lighthearted realistic verse for younger children about special holidays and seasons. Selections include some useful poems in *It's Halloween* and *It's Thanksgiving*. His books *Ride a Purple*

Many of Douglas Florian's rhymes in *Beast Feast* are reminiscent of Ogden Nash's animal sketches in their brevity and their sense of playfulness:

Just when you think you know the boa
There's moa and moa and moa and moa.

> —"The Boa," from *Beast Feast* by Douglas Florian.
> Copyright © 1994 by Douglas Florian. Reprinted
> by permission of Harcourt, Inc.

Florian's witty artwork adds to the delight in his other collections about the animal world, *Zoo's Who; Lizards, Frogs and Polliwogs; In the Swim; Insectlopedia; Mammalabilia; Bowwow, Meow Meow;* and *On the Wing. Bing Bang Bong* and *Laugh-eteria* are longer collections of rhymes that place Florian in the company of Shel Silverstein and Jack Prelutsky as a writer of nonsense poems that delight children. Florian can also be more serious, though no less delightful, in books such as *Handsprings, Winter Eyes, Autumnblings,* and *Summersaults.* Here he turns his talents to such topics as "Dog Day" and "Icicles." As in all his books, his charming watercolor paintings enliven his words.

Douglas Florian combines witty wordplay and droll illustrations in his many collections of poetry including *zoo's who: poems and paintings.* Illustration copyright © 2005 by Douglas Florian, reprinted with permission of Harcourt, Inc.

Pelican and *Beneath a Blue Umbrella* are filled with Mother Goose–type verses that appeal to preschoolers. Garth Williams has made large, handsome, colored illustrations for each of these joyous poems that play with place names—such as "Grandma Bear from Delaware" and "Cincinnati Patty" (both in *Ride a Purple Pelican*).

Fans of Douglas Florian and Jack Prelutsky will enjoy Tony Milton's *Plum,* a deliciously eclectic collection of twenty poems that should provide something for everyone's taste. Milton delivers shorter poems that include "My Hat!" and "Puzzled Pea" and longer pieces such as "The Snake and the Apple" and "Growing." Milton's "Mrs. Bhattacharya's Chapati Zap Machine" is a long and deliciously funny narrative poem. Mary GrandPré has contributed luscious paintings that really bring the poems to life.

Shel Silverstein's *Where the Sidewalk Ends* was on the *New York Times* best-sellers list for three years. It is the one poetry book that all teachers, children, and parents seem to know. Librarians complain that they can't keep the book on the shelf, no matter how many copies they have. Here you meet a boy who turns into a TV set, a king who eats only a "Peanut-Butter Sandwich," and those three characters "Ickle Me, Pickle Me, Tickle Me Too." Much of the humor of these poems is based on the sounds of words, the preposterous characters, and amusing situations. While some verses are slightly unsavory, others surprise you with their sensitivity, such as "Invitation," "Listen to the Mustn'ts," and the title poem, "Where the Sidewalk Ends." *A Light in the Attic* and *Falling Up* provide more of the same fun. *Runny Babbit: A Billy Sook,* published after Silverstein's death, is a collection some twenty years in the making, and its lighthearted silliness and inventive wordplay will not disappoint the poet's many fans.

Poetry is neglected in our schools today, but there is no dearth of humorous verse. Children take to it as they do to a hamburger, fries, and a shake. And like a fast-food meal, it is enjoyable but not the only food to include in a balanced diet.

Interpreters of the World of Childhood

Robert Louis Stevenson was the first poet to write of childhood from the child's point of view. *A Child's Garden of Verses,* published in 1885, continues to be popular today. Stevenson was himself a frail child and spent much of his early life in bed or confined indoors. His poetry reflects a solitary childhood, but a happy one. In "Land of Counterpane" and "Block City," he portrays a resourceful, inventive child who can create his own amusement. He found playmates in his shadow, in his dreams, and in his storybooks. The rhythm of Stevenson's "The Swing," "Where Go the Boats?" and "Windy Nights" appeals to children today as much as it did to the children of a century ago. In *Where Go the Boats?* Max Grover has illustrated four of Stevenson's poems with bright pictures that appeal to children. Penny Dale and

In *Where Go the Boats?* Max Grover's illustrations for four of Robert Louis Stevenson's poems for children show how some classics never go out of date. Cover from *Where Go the Boats? Play-Poems of Robert Louis Stevenson* by Max Grover, cover art copyright © 1998 by Max Grover, reproduced by permission of Browndeer Press, a division of Harcourt, Inc.

Monique Felix have each done illustrated volumes of Stevenson's *My Shadow,* expanding the meaning of this poem to incorporate children from all over the world. Stevenson's *Block City* has been illustrated by Ashley Wolff and Daniel Kirk. All these editions make a fine introduction to Stevenson's poems.

Perhaps the best loved of British children's poets is A. A. Milne. Some of his poems, such as "Halfway Down" and "Solitude," show perceptive insight into the child's mind. "Happiness" captures a child's joy in such delights as new waterproof boots, a raincoat, and a hat. Most of Milne's poems are delightfully funny. The poetry from both of Milne's poetry books has now been collected into one volume, titled *The World of Christopher Robin.* Illustrations by Ernest Shepard seem to belong with Milne's poetry as much as Pooh belongs with Christopher Robin; it is hard to imagine one without the other.

Mary Ann Hoberman, winner of the 2003 NCTE Poetry Award, writes lively rhythmical verse for young children. The poems in her collection *The Llama Who Had No Pajama* range from the delightful nonsense of the title poem to the swinging rhythm of "Hello and Good-by" (see p. 412). Hoberman's poem "Brother" (in *Sing a Song of Popcorn,* ed. Beatrice Schenk de Regniers et al.), about a boy who is a bit of a bother to everyone, is a favorite with children and could well be shared as an introduction to books on sibling rivalry. Primary children also enjoy the long, sustained poem in Hoberman's picture book *A House Is a House for Me*. In this book she plays with the concept of houses, including regular houses and animals' houses, and then looks at other possibilities, such as a glove becoming a house for a hand and a pocket as a house for pennies. All of Hoberman's poetry is distinguished by its fast-paced rhymes and marked rhythms.

Karla Kuskin also observes the world with the eyes of a child as she creates her well-known poems. Her book *Moon, Have You Met My Mother?* includes many of her best-known, such as "I Woke Up This Morning," which tells of a child who feels she/he hasn't done anything right since "quarter past seven." She can write mysterious poems, such as the haunting "Where Would You Be?" or play with the sounds of words, as in "The Bear Coat." Many of her poems contain both humor and wisdom, as in this quizzical one:

> People always say to me
> "What do you think you'd like to be
> When you grow up?"
> And I say "Why,
> I think I'd like to be the sky
> Or be a plane or train or mouse
> Or maybe a haunted house
> Or something furry, rough and wild . . .
> Or maybe I will stay a child."

> —Karla Kuskin. "The Question," from *The Middle of the Trees* by Karla Kuskin. Copyright © 1959, renewed 1986 by Karla Kuskin. Used by permission of Scott Treimel New York.

Kuskin's *Soap Soup and Other Verses* is a collection of easy-to-read poems. Karla Kuskin often illustrates her own poetry books with tiny, precise pen-and-ink drawings. She designed the artwork for the NCTE Poetry Award and then was the third recipient of that coveted prize. Another recent collection of her poems has been gathered together in *The Sky Is Always in the Sky*.

Multicultural Poetry

 Long before the experiences of African-Americans became recognized in literature, Pulitzer Prize winner Gwendolyn Brooks wrote poignant poetry about African American children living in the inner city. *Bronzeville Boys and Girls* contains thirty-four poems, each bearing the name, thoughts, and feelings of an individual child. There is "John, Who Is Poor"; "Michael," who is afraid of the storm; "Beulah," who has quiet thoughts at church; and "Luther and Breck," who have a make-believe dragon fight. Unfortunately, this poet has written only one volume of poetry for children.

Langston Hughes was the first African American to write poems of black protest and pride, such as "What Happens to a Dream Deferred?" *The Dream Keeper and Other Poems* is a handsome collection of his poems illustrated by Brian Pinkney. "Dreams" and "April Rain Song" and "Mother to Son" are among the sixty-six poems that show the full range of this poet's powerful voice. The title poem reflects the lyrical beauty of Hughes's imagination.

> Bring me all of your dreams,
> You dreamers
> Bring me all of your
> Heart melodies
> That I may wrap them
> In a blue cloud cloth
> Away from the too rough fingers
> Of the world.

> —Langston Hughes. "The Dream Keeper," from *Collected Poems* by Langston Hughes. Copyright © 1994 by the Estate of Langston Hughes. Reprinted by permission of Alfred A. Knopf, a Division of Random House Inc.

The poetry of two other important but long-neglected African American poets can be found in two recent collections for young people. Effie Lee Newsome was one of the first African American poets to write for an audience of children. Rudine Sims Bishop has selected many of her poems for the book *Wonders*. In *Jump Back, Honey* well-known African American illustrators have interpreted poems of the noted turn-of-the-century writer Paul Laurence Dunbar. The paintings of Ashley Bryan, Carol Byard, Jerry Pinkney, Brian Pinkney, Faith Ringgold, and Jan Spivey Gilchrist provide backdrops for the varied moods, topics, and language styles found in such poems as "Dawn," "Little Brown Baby," and "Rain-Songs." Both Newsome and Dunbar are important voices whose words still speak to children.

Today, we can find many wonderful African American poets represented in books for children. *Honey, I Love* is by Eloise Greenfield, who has a great capacity for speaking in the voice of a young African American child. This joyous little book of sixteen poems includes a chant, a jump-rope rhyme (see p. 413), and thoughtful observations on experiences like dressing up ("I look pretty") or thinking about a neighbor who left her a nickel before she died ("Keepsake"). Leo Dillon and Diane Dillon's illustrations are as sensitive as these poems that celebrate the rich content of a child's world. Greenfield has often teamed with artist Jan Spivey Gilchrist in books such as *Nathaniel Talking* and *Night on Neighborhood Street*. In *In the Land of Words: New and Selected Poems*, a collection that brings together many of Greenfield's poems, Gilchrist uses felt patchwork and stitchery to capture the shapes and rhythms of poems such as "Nathaniel's Rap" and "Two Poems." Greenfield has also written poems to go with Amos Ferguson's Bahamian folk-art paintings in *Under the Sunday Tree.* Greenfield is a recipient of the NCTE Award for Excellence in Poetry for Children.

Nikki Giovanni is well known for her adult poetry, but she has also written for children. *Spin a Soft Black Song* has been reissued with new illustrations. "Poem for Rodney" expresses both a child's point of view and an adult's. Rodney is tired of everyone asking him what he is going to do when he grows up; his reply is simply that he'd like to grow up. Noted artist and storyteller Ashley Bryan has illustrated a collection of thirteen of Giovanni's poems in *The Sun Is So Quiet.*

Sing to the Sun, by Ashley Bryan, is a collection of his own poems that are as vibrant as the paintings that decorate the book's pages. While there is poignancy in poems such as "Leaving," there are also strong rhythms and bright images that fulfill the promise of the sunny title and evoke the warmth of Caribbean culture. Bryan's special magic is present in "Storyteller," about a storyteller whose stories were pieced together with bird song, and in "Artist," about an artist who can transform sorrow. James Berry, a noted Jamaican poet, has several collections of poetry that celebrate the life of the Caribbean islands with a unique voice. *Everywhere Faces Everywhere* includes a variety of topics and poetic forms, and Berry weaves a sense of magic with both formal English and Caribbean patois.

Arnold Adoff writes strong poems about the inner thoughts and feelings of a girl born of a mixed-race marriage. In *All the Colors of the Race,* as in his other work, he shapes each poem to balance the semantic and rhythmic lines of force. He wants his words to sing as well as say. Adoff's poem "The way I see any hope for later" is one that everyone should read and heed. His story-poem *Black Is Brown Is Tan* describes a biracial family growing up happy in a house full of love:

> Black is brown is tan
> is girl   is boy
> is nose   is face
> is all the colors
> of the race
> is dark   is light
> singing songs
> in singing night
> kiss big woman   hug big man
> black   is brown   is tan

> —Arnold Adoff. *Black Is Brown Is Tan* by
> Arnold Adoff. Copyright © 1973 by Arnold Adoff.
> Used by permission of HarperCollins Publishers.

These poems not only reflect Arnold Adoff's love for his own family but also celebrate diversity and individuality. Adoff is also a 1988 recipient of the prestigious NCTE Award for Excellence in Poetry for Children.

Nikki Grimes is a versatile poet whose work ranges from novels in verse such as *Dark Sons, What Is Goodbye?* and *A Dime a Dozen,* to poems that explore the pleasure and pain of growing up, to *It's Raining Laughter,* about the everyday experiences of younger readers. *Danitra Brown, Class Clown; Meet Danitra Brown;* and *Danitra Brown Leaves Town* comprise a series of poems that portrays the friendship between two African American girls. In other books such as *Thanks a Million* and *A Pocketful of Poems,* Grimes plays inventively with poetry forms. Grimes has also built two fine novels, *Jazmin's Notebook* and *Bronx Masquerade,* around young characters whose lives are enriched by poetry (see Chapter 9).

Gary Soto's poetry collections for older students, *Canto Familiar* and *Neighborhood Odes,* capture the Latino experience and zero in on the heart of life experience. His *Neighborhood Odes* sings the praises of everything from tortillas to tennis shoes. In "Ode to Señor Leal's Goat" a goat amuses the chickens and shocks Señor Leal when he runs away with the man's smoking pipe. "Ode to My Library" touches upon the rich life in, and out of, books that the library provides a young dreamer. Soto's connected poems about adolescent friendship, found in *Worlds Apart: Traveling with Fernie and Me* and *Fearless*

Javaka Steptoe's collage constructions add depth to Nikki Grimes's imaginative collection of haiku and free verse, *A Pocketful of Poems.* Cover from *A Pocketful of Poems* by Nikki Grimes, illustrated by Javaka Steptoe. Jacket illustration copyright © 2001 by Javaka Steptoe. Reprinted by permission of Clarion Books/Houghton Mifflin Company. All rights reserved.

Fernie: Hanging Out with Fernie and Me, speak to universal concerns of children, especially boys on the cusp of adolescence. There is uncertainty and insecurity, exhilaration, and pure happiness neatly captured in these poems. Best of all there is "friends forever" embodied by the character of Fernie. Other notable collections by Latino poets can be found in books by Jane Medina (*My Name Is Jorge*), Pat Mora (*Confetti*), Francisco X. Alarcón (*Angels Ride Bikes* and *Iguanas in the Snow*), Jorge Argueta (*A Movie in My Pillow* and *Trees Are Hanging from the Sky*) and Lori Carlson (*Cool Salsa* and *Red Hot Salsa*).

Janet S. Wong, of Korean and Chinese descent, has several poetry collections that will appeal to adolescents: *A Suitcase of Seaweed and Other Poems, Good Luck and Other Poems,* and *The Rainbow Hand: Poems about Mothers and Daughters.* Her lovely *Night Garden* evokes the surrealistic world of dreams and will be appreciated by middle-grade children as well as those in middle school. *Night Garden* and *Knock on Wood: Poems about Superstitions* were both illustrated by Julie Paschkis. A versatile and talented writer, Wong also has published a novel in verse. *Minn and Jake,* for middle-grade readers, is about friendship, courage, and lizard catching. "The Ticket" (in *Behind the Wheel: Poems about Driving*), for older readers, is about a teenager who speeds and gets a traffic ticket.

In My Mother's House by Ann Nolan Clark was a breakthrough book when it was first published in 1941. Now reissued, it contains poems describing a close-knit farming community of Pueblo Indians. Based on stories told by Pueblo children, it was the first book to represent a Native American point of view. Velino Herrera did the beautifully clear pictures for this fine book of poems.

Noted Navajo poet Luci Tapahonso has published several collections for children. *Songs of Shiprock Fair,* illustrated by Anthony Chee Emerson, relates the experiences of Nezbah and her family at the parade and carnival held during the Shiprock Fair. *A Breeze Swept Through* is a collection of Tapahonso's poems that includes "Note to a Younger Brother" and "For Misty Starting School."

There are many multicultural voices that are beginning to be heard through some of the fine collections of poetry that are now being published. Many of these anthologies are discussed in the section "Specialized Collections" later in this chapter.

Poets of Nature

Like poets, children are very attuned to the world around them. They are fascinated by the constant changes in nature and enjoy poems that communicate their delight in the first snow, their sense of wonder when they touch a pussy willow or hear a foghorn or see a deer.

Aileen Fisher is adept at observing both nature and children. She views the natural world through the eyes of the child, preserving a remarkable sense of wonder, as in this poem:

Bluebird

In the woods a piece of sky
fell down, a piece of blue.
"It must have come from very high,"
I said. "It looks so new."

It landed on a leafy tree
and there it seemed to cling,
and when I squinted up to see,
I saw it had a *wing*
and then a *head*, and suddenly
I heard a bluebird sing!

> —Aileen Fisher. "Bluebird," from *In the Woods In the Meadow In the Sky* by Aileen Fisher. Copyright © 1965, 1993 by Aileen Fisher. Used by permission of Marian Riener.

Fisher's poems are simple and fresh, very much within the experience of the young child, yet very true to the realities of nature. *The Story Goes On,* for example, presents children with the wonder and drama inherent in the food cycle. *Know What I Saw?* reflects a child's delight at the things she sees on a trip into the country. Aileen Fisher was the second recipient of the NCTE Award for Excellence in Poetry for Children.

Lilian Moore describes the changing moods and seasons of both the city and the country in her short-line free verse. Her poems frequently appeal to the senses, as she talks about the moaning of foghorns or the "tree-talk" or "wind-swish" of the night. "Wind Song" (in *Sing a Song of Popcorn,* ed. Beatrice Schenk de Regniers et al.) describes the flapping and snapping noise the wind makes as it blows flags and ashcans, and "Until I Saw the Sea" (in Schenk de Regniers et al., *Sing a Song of Popcorn*) provides a fresh new image of the "wrinkled sea." A former teacher, reading specialist, and editor who lived in the city, Moore's most recent collection, *Mural on Second Avenue and Other City Poems,* reflects her close observations of her surroundings and a knowledge of what

Profile in Literature

Janet Wong

Janet Wong has had an unusual career path to writing for children. After graduating from Yale Law School, she returned to her native California and went to work as a corporate lawyer. But her spirit was not enriched by the work she was doing, and she stepped back to take stock of her life. A serendipitous visit to a children's book store revealed a new path, and she has been on it ever since. Go to the Online Learning Center at **www .mhhe.com/kiefer9e** or your Resources CD-ROM to learn more about Janet Wong.

Aileen Fisher focuses on the world of nature in her many poems, including *The Story Goes On*. Cover from *The Story Goes On* by Aileen Fisher. Illustrated by Mique Moriuchi. Copyright © 2005 by Mique Moriuchi. Reprinted by permission of Henry Holt and Company, LLC.

children enjoy. Moore is also a recipient of the NCTE Poetry Award.

Byrd Baylor writes story-length prose poems that reflect her appreciation for nature and the beauty of the landscape of the Southwest. In *The Other Way to Listen,* an older man tells a young girl how it's possible to hear wildflower seeds burst open or a rock murmuring or hills singing—of course, it takes practice! *Your Own Best Secret Place, Everybody Needs a Rock,* and *I'm in Charge of Celebrations* are fine poetry workshop starters, as they inspire children to describe their secret places or plan special celebrations. Peter Parnall makes the text part of his bold illustrations.

Constance Levy has written several volumes of poetry that make strong connections to children's experiences with nature. *When Whales Exhale* brings together poems about traveling, *A Crack in the Clouds* focuses on the wonders of the world in the backyard, and *Splash!* highlights the wonder of water. In *I'm Going to Pet a Worm Today,* Levy muses in "The Color Eater" about how night laps up the sunset. She wonders about bees in "The Busi-

ness of Bees" and about butterflies in "Questions to Ask a Butterfly."

Many poems by Robert Frost are both simple enough for a child to understand and complex enough for graduate study. Before his death, Frost selected some of his poems to be read to, or by, young people. Interestingly, the title of this collection, *You Come Too,* was taken from a line of "The Pasture," the first poem in this collection and the introductory poem of the very first book Frost ever published. Upon initial reading, this poem seems no more than a literal invitation to join someone as he cleans the pasture spring. However, the poem takes on more meaning when viewed in the context of its placement; the trip to the pasture to clean the spring might well be an invitation to the enjoyment of poetry itself— "you come too!" By reading *You Come Too,* children can enjoy "The Runaway," "Dust of Snow," "The Last Word of a Bluebird," and "The Pasture," poems on their level of understanding. Older children will begin to comprehend the deeper meanings in "Mending Wall," "The Road Not Taken," and "The Death of the Hired Man."

Versatile Poets

It is almost impossible to characterize the wide variety of poems produced by certain poets. David McCord's poetry, for example, ranges in subject matter from poems about everyday experiences to nature poems to verses about verse. McCord plays with sound in "The Pickety Fence" and "Song of the Train"; with form, including couplets, quatrains, limericks, and triolets, in "Write Me a Verse"; and with words and their meanings in many of his poems, including "Glowworm," "Ptarmigan," and "Goose, Moose and Spruce." He can write with a lively wit or quietly enter the serious inner world of the child. McCord's *Every Time I Climb a Tree* was one of the first poetry books to be illustrated by the well-known picture-book illustrator Caldecott Medal–winning Marc Simont. McCord was the first winner of the NCTE Award for Excellence in Poetry for Children.

Several other versatile poets and NCTE Poetry Award winners have had a lasting influence on children's poetry. Unfortunately, many of the books of Eve Merriam, Barbara Esbensen, and Myra Cohn Livingston are no longer in print, although their individual poems are represented in many fine anthologies such as *A Jar of Tiny Stars,* selected by Beatrice E. Cullinan. Livingston's work also survives in the works by her many students at UCLA including Deborah Chandra, Kristine O'Connell George, Tony Johnston, Alice Schertle, Janet Wong, Joan Bransfield Graham, and other well-known poets. A wonderful collection of poems written by those students was published after Livingston's death. Titled *I Am Writing a Poem About . . . A Game of Poetry,* the collection came about when Livingston challenged the students to write a poem in which one word, *rabbit,* appeared. She then went on to give them three words, *blanket, ring,* and *drum,* to incorporate in their poems. The group then agreed on a choice of six words, *hole, friend, candle, ocean, snake,* and either *bucket* or *scarecrow.* The results are truly delightful and illuminate the wonderful range of possibility that words offer the imagination.

Deborah Chandra, one of Livingston's students, has been awarded the International Reading Association/Lee Bennett Hopkins Promising Poet Award for *Balloons and Other Poems.* Many of her poems, such as "Snowfall," focus on the natural world. Other poems show her ability to uncover fresh images in the everyday concerns of children. In Chandra's "Bubble" (in *Balloons*) a child discovers

> my breath
> wrapped in a
> quivering skin
> . . . .
> so marble-round,
> and glistening. (p. 5)

> —Deborah Chandra. In "Bubble," from *Balloons and Other Poems* by Deborah Chandra. Copyright © 1990. Farrar, Straus & Giroux.

Kristine O'Connell George, another student of Livingston's, has produced a number of poetry collections that display her versatility. This fine writer has the ability to address the concerns of younger children in books like *Little Dog Poems* and *Little Dog and Duncan* and to capture the angst of adolescents in *Swimming Upstream: Middle School Poems.* She has focused her observations on the natural world with delicacy and wonder in *Hummingbird Nest* and *Old Elm Speaks.* The poems in *Toasting Marshmallows* and *Fold Me a Poem* demonstrate her ability to turn an imaginative eye to the most mundane of childhood objects and occupations. In "Night" (from *Fold Me a Poem*) a child's origami object becomes part of the large universe.

> Night
>
> Night
> unfolds
> softly.
> I'll
> add
> my own
> star.

> —"Night," from *Fold Me a Poem* by Kristine O'Connell George. Copyright © 2005 by Kristine O'Connell George, reprinted by permission of Harcourt.

Poet and former teacher J. Patrick Lewis has also demonstrated his inventiveness with different subjects and forms in all of his many books. His humorous outlook delights children in such books of riddle poems as *Riddle-icious* and *Arithme-tickle* but also invites them to think carefully. Lewis has explored different poetic forms in *Doodle Dandies* and curricular subjects in *A World of Wonders: Geographic Travels in Verse and Rhyme* and *Heroes and She-roes: Poems of Amazing and Everyday Heroes.* Lewis tackles more serious subjects in *Swan Song,* a tribute to vanishing species. The title poem in *Please Bury Me in the Library* surely expresses the passion that poetry readers come to feel for favorite authors like Lewis.

> Please bury me in the library
> In the clean, well lighted stacks
> Of Novels, History and Poetry
> Right next to the Paperbacks,
>
> Where the Kid's Books dance
> With True Romance
> And the Dictionary dozes.
> Please bury me in the library
> With a dozen long-stemmed proses.
>
> Way back by a rack of Magazines,
> I won't be sad too often,
> If they bury me in the library
> With Bookworms in my coffin.

> —"Please Bury Me in the Library," from *Please Bury Me in the Library* by J. Patrick Lewis. Copyright © 2005 by J. Patrick Lewis, reprinted by permission of Harcourt.

Anthologies of Poems for Children

Today poetry anthologies do not stay in print as long as they used to, because time limits are usually placed on permissions to use certain poems. This has meant the publication of fewer large anthologies and the proliferation of many specialized collections containing fewer than twenty poems.

Comprehensive Poetry Collections

Every family with children will want to own at least one excellent anthology of poetry for children. Teachers will want to have several, including some for their personal use and some for the children's use.

Sing a Song of Popcorn, edited by Beatrice Schenk de Regniers and others, is a stunning collection of poetry for all children. The poems were first selected for a popular paperback called *Poems Children Will Sit Still For* (now out of print, this Scholastic title sold more than a quarter of a million copies). The selection of poetry for *Sing a Song of Popcorn* has been updated and is now illustrated in full color by nine Caldecott Medal–winning artists. The volume contains 128 poems that had to meet the criterion of captivating children. The represented poets range from Mary Ann Hoberman to Emily Dickinson. Included are such well-known poems as "Galoshes," "Eletelephony," "Brother," and "Stopping by Woods on a Snowy Evening." If a teacher or parent could have only one collection, this would be the one to buy.

Tomie dePaola's Book of Poems is also a handsome anthology. Emily Dickinson's poem "There is no frigate like a book" is used to symbolically unite the cover, title page, introduction, and final page. These eighty-six well-chosen poems include classics like Stevenson's "Land of Counterpane" and contemporary poems like Myra Cohn Livingston's "Secret Door" and Eve Merriam's funny "Alligator on the Escalator." A unique addition is some poems in Spanish.

Many parents and teachers will be attracted to the large *Random House Book of Poetry for Children*, with its 572 poems selected by Jack Prelutsky and profusely illustrated with Arnold Lobel's lively pictures. For children who have known only Shel Silverstein's and Jack Prelutsky's humorous verse, this is a good place to begin. Though much of the book is dominated by humorous verse (including some 38 poems by Prelutsky himself), fine poems by Robert Frost, Eve Merriam, Eleanor Farjeon, Emily Dickinson, Myra Cohn Livingston, Dylan Thomas, and others are interspersed with them. Arnold Lobel's humorous full-color illustrations also draw children to this anthology. Prelutsky's *Twentieth Century Children's Poetry*, illustrated with the ethereal watercolors of Meilo So, is a shorter anthology but a bit more serious in tone. Taken together, Prelutsky's two anthologies provide a valuable classroom poetry resource.

David Booth's *Til All the Stars Have Fallen* is an exciting collection of over seventy poems for children ages 8 and up. These include poems by such well-known Canadian poets as Dennis Lee and Jean Little and some wonderful new voices such as Duke Redbird, A. M. Klein, Lois Simmie, and George Swede. Kady Denton has echoed the poetic imagery of many of these poems in her expressive watercolors and collage illustrations.

Knock at a Star: A Child's Introduction to Poetry, compiled by the well-known adult poet and anthologist X. J. Kennedy and his wife, Dorothy, is a memorable collection of poetry for children 8 years old and up. The poets represented range widely, from adult poets like James Stephens, Emily Dickinson, Robert Frost, and William Stafford to children's poets Aileen Fisher, David McCord, and Lillian Morrison. Many familiar poems are here, but most are new and fresh to children's collections. The three section headings in this book also are addressed to children and provide an understanding of how poetry does what it does: (1) "What Do Poems Do?" (make you laugh, tell stories, send messages, share feelings, start you wondering); (2) "What's Inside a Poem?" (images, word music, beats that repeat, likenesses); and (3) "Special Kinds of Poems." Teachers, librarians, and parents as well as children can learn from this wise book, which teaches at the same time as it develops enthusiasm for poetry.

X. J. Kennedy and Dorothy M. Kennedy's *Talking Like the Rain*, illustrated by Jane Dyer, contains a mixture of old and new poems that have the kind of sound and wordplay that is particularly appealing to younger children. *Talking Like the Rain* contains 123 poems, ranging from Robert Louis Stevenson's "The Swing" to Myra

Cohn Livingston's "Working with Mother." Michael Rosen's *Poems for the Very Young* have been chosen with special consideration for "the physical side of language," those sound elements that intrigue the youngest child. Rosen has not neglected more formal forms of poetry, and the collection includes Carl Sandburg's vivid "Portrait of a Motor Car" as well as the delightful doggerel of "If You Ever."

> If you ever ever ever ever ever
> If you ever ever ever meet a whale
> You must never never never never never
> You must never never never touch its tail:
> For if you ever ever ever ever ever
> If you ever ever ever touch its tail,
> You will never never never never never
> You will never never never meet another whale.
>
> —Anonymous. "If You Ever," in *Poems for the Very Young*, ed. Michael Rosen. Kingfisher, 2004.

Illustrations by Bob Graham will keep even the most jaded parents amused.

Paul Janeczko's *Seeing the Blue Between* and *The Place My Words Are Looking For* are two superb collections that

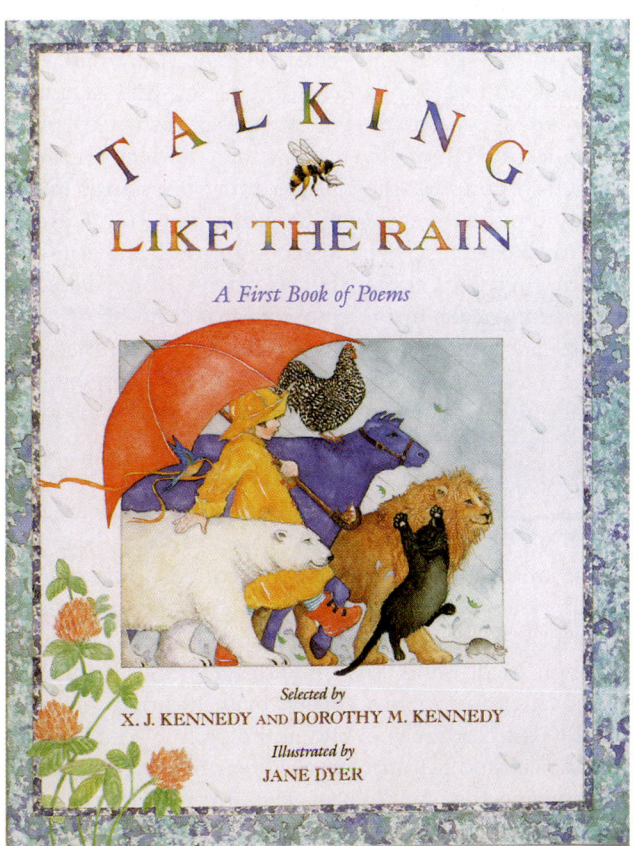

X. J. Kennedy and Dorothy M. Kennedy's poetry and Jane Dyer's illustrations provide an inviting introduction to poetry for young children in *Talking Like the Rain*. From the cover of *Talking Like the Rain: A First Book of Poems* by X. J. Kennedy and Dorothy M. Kennedy, illustrated by Jane Dyer. Illustrations copyright © 1992 by Jane Dyer. By permission of Little, Brown, and Company, Inc.

provide insight into how some poets work and how they feel about their poems. In *Seeing the Blue Between* 32 poets share advice for aspiring writers of poetry and then several of their poems that illustrate their advice. In *The Place My Words Are Looking For* Jack Prelutsky, X. J. Kennedy, Myra Cohn Livingston, and others talk about how they create their poetry, by providing personal comments and examples of their poems. Pictures of the poets accompany each section so that children can see what their favorite poet looks like. For example, Lillian Morrison comments on how she wrote "The Sidewalk Racer":

> Writing poems can be a way of pinning down a dream (almost); capturing a moment, a memory, a happening; and, at the same time, it's a way of sorting out your thoughts and feelings. Sometimes words tell you what you didn't know you knew.[10]

One of the most enduring current anthologies is *Reflections on a Gift of Watermelon Pickle and Other Modern Verses*, edited by Stephen Dunning and others. Illustrated with superb black-and-white photographs surrounded by much space, this anthology appeals to the eye as well as the ear of older students in middle school. They will take delight in "Sonic Boom" by John Updike, "Ancient History" by Arthur Guiterman, "Dreams" by Langston Hughes, and "How to Eat a Poem" by Eve Merriam. They will appreciate the honesty and realistic viewpoint of "Husbands and Wives," in which Miriam Hershenson tells of couples who ride the train from station to station without ever speaking to each other. Ruth Gordon and Liz Rosenberg have also contributed fine anthologies of poetry for adolescents. Gordon's *Pierced by a Ray of the Sun* speaks to the emotional roller coaster that is adolescence. In Rosenberg's *Roots and Flowers: Poets and Poems on Family*, forty poets, including Rosenberg herself, tell about their families and present poems that grew out of their family experiences.

 Several volumes of multicultural poetry for older children deserve to be considered among the "must-haves" in any home or classroom. Catherine Clinton has edited a fine anthology of poetry called *I, Too, Sing America: Three Centuries of African American Poetry*. Illustrated in muted tones by Stephen Alcorn, the book provides a chronological history of African American poetry by including poets from the 1700s to today. Poet and anthologist Naomi Shihab Nye has edited beautiful books that celebrate the arts of Mexico and the Middle East: *This Tree Is Older Than You Are: A Bilingual Gathering of Poems and Stories from Mexico* and *The Space between Our Footsteps: Poems and Paintings from the Middle East*. Nye has gathered poems, stories, and paintings from two widely separated and under-

represented peoples and provided important insights into their cultural, political, and social lives. In Nye's *This Same Sky: A Collection of Poems from around the World*, 129 poets from 68 countries look at the world in poems rich with images and feeling. This is an international collection with universal connections. We must also mention *19 Varieties of Gazelle: Poems of the Middle East*. These superb poems by Nye are based on her own experiences as an Arab-American. The book begins with an introduction and poem about the effects of September 11th on her and other Arab-Americans. Some poems speak passionately for peace while others, such as "My Father and the Figtree," are exquisite in their examination of everyday experience.

Specialized Collections

As mentioned earlier, as poetry permissions have become more expensive and more difficult to obtain for long lengths of time, anthologists have turned to making small, specialized collections. Most of these are organized for a particular age level or around certain subjects, such as dogs or seasons. Some are related to the ethnic origin of the poems, such as poetry of Native Americans or poems that celebrate the experiences of African-Americans. An increasing number of specialized collections contain stunning illustrations. Some of the best of these are noted in the text; others are listed in Teaching Resources: "Specialized Collections of Poetry."

Children will find imaginative connections to themes such as "time" or "animals" and to subjects as varied as American history, music, and science through many of these anthologies. Barbara Rogasky's collection *Winter Poems*, beautifully illustrated by Trina Schart Hyman, recreates a cycle of time from late autumn to the first buds of spring with poems like Elizabeth Coatsworth's "Cat on a Night of Snow" and Robert Frost's "A Patch of Old Snow." Hyman has also illustrated John Updike's *A Child's Calendar*, a lovely collection of year-round poems that won a Caldecott Honor Medal in 2000. Ralph Fletcher takes older readers from winter into spring in *Ordinary Things: Poems from a Walk in Early Spring*, and Rebecca Dotlich extends the journey into summer with *Lemonade Sun and Other Summer Poems*.

Alice Schertle continues to delight children with her many special collections of poetry. Cows have never been more appealing than in the fifteen poems in her *How Now, Brown Cow?* Schertle ruminates on various topics in "The Cow's Complaint" (the grass is always greener) and "The Bull" (the title character wonders if the cows can see him bellowing, blowing, and striking a pose). Schertle's imaginative *Advice for a Frog* is a collection of poems about animals found in the wild, including "Black Rhino," "Iguana," and "Secretary Bird."

---

[10]Lillian Morrison in Paul Janeczko, ed., *The Place My Words Are Looking For* (New York: Bradbury Press, 1990), p. 11.

Trina Schart Hyman has provided the details of a year's worth of family moments to accompany John Updike's *A Child's Calendar.* Illustration © 1999 by Trina Schart Hyman. All rights reserved. Reprinted from *A Child's Calendar,* written by John Updike, by permission of Holiday House, Inc.

TEACHING **RESOURCES**

Specialized Collections of Poetry

OLC Visit the Online Learning Center at **www.mhhe.com/kiefer9e** for a printable version of this list.

CHILDREN'S EVERYDAY EXPERIENCES

Compiler, Poet	Title	Age Level	Description
Arnold Adoff	*The Basket Counts*	8 and up	Adoff celebrates the game of basketball.
Arnold Adoff	*Eats*	6–12	These poems convey a passion for tasty treats, particularly sweets.
Arnold Adoff	*Street Music: City Poems*	6–12	These poems present the vigor of city life, its commotion and its vibrancy.
Karen English	*Speak to Me (And I Will Listen between the Lines)*	7–10	Six inner-city schoolchildren are portrayed as they journey through a school year.
Ralph Fletcher	*Have You Been to the Beach Lately?*	8–12	A boy entering adolescence spends a day at the beach.

(continued)

Specialized Collections of Poetry (*continued*)

CHILDREN'S EVERYDAY EXPERIENCES (*continued*)

Compiler, Poet	Title	Age Level	Description
Ralph Fletcher	*A Writing Kind of Day: Poems for Young Poets*	8–12	A fictional narrator composes poems about writing poetry.
Kristine O'Connell George	*Fold Me a Poem*	5–10	This collection of haiku poems celebrates children's experimentations with origami paper folding.
Kristine O'Connell George	*Swimming Upstream*	11–14	George turns her talents to poems about being in middle school.
Nikki Grimes	*A Dime a Dozen*	12 and up	Twenty-eight poems explore the pleasure and pain of growing up.
Nikki Grimes	*It's Raining Laughter*	6–8	Bright photographs illustrate this sunny collection of poetry about everyday experiences.
Georgia Heard	*This Place I Know: Poems of Comfort*	8–11	Eighteen poets address sorrow and grief in the aftermath of September 11.
Lee Bennett Hopkins	*Extra Innings*	10–12	These poems about baseball will invite fans of the sport as well as non-fans to enjoy the runs and the rhythms of the game.
Lee Bennett Hopkins	*Oh, No! Where Are My Pants and Other Disasters*	7–12	This collection focuses on events that often spell disaster for a child—some funny, some poignant.
Lee Bennett Hopkins	*Surprises* and *More Surprises*	6–8	With unerring taste for good poetry and what children enjoy, Hopkins has selected poems that children can read independently.
Simon James	*Days Like This: A Collection of Small Poems*	3–7	Short poems by well-known authors capture a young child's everyday joys and trials.
Paul Janeczko	*Very Best (Almost) Friends*	7–10	This short but lively collection portrays the ups and downs of friendships.
Bobbi Katz	*Pocket Poems*	5–9	These poems are meant to be shared each and every day.
Dennis Lee	*Bubblegum Delicious*	5–10	See text.
Myra Cohn Livingston	*I Like You, If You Like Me*	10 and up	This collection contains nearly a hundred poems that celebrate friends and comradeship. Some are funny, others are sad or lonesome.
Sally Mavor	*You and Me: Poems of Friendship*	6–8	Mavor's wonderful stitchery pictures illustrate these cheerful poems about friends.
Lilian Moore	*I'm Small and Other Verses*	2–5	Eighteen poems about being small make up this collection.

Specialized Collections of Poetry (continued)

CHILDREN'S EVERYDAY EXPERIENCES (continued)

Compiler, Poet	Title	Age Level	Description
Heidi Mordhorst	*Squeeze*	8 and up	This collection presents everyday childhood experiences in a humorous way.
Takayo Nado	*Dear World*	4–8	A child narrator describes the beauties of the everyday world in this series of brief poems.
Naomi Shihab Nye	*A Maze Me*	12 and up	Nye's poems reflect the inner life and concerns of adolescent girls.
Neil Philip	*The Fish Is Me: Bathtime Rhymes*	Preschool	This lively collection of poetry by well-known poets includes writing by Carl Sandburg and Aileen Fisher.
Charlotte Pomerantz	*Thunderboom!*	2–8	This is a delightful collection of new and familiar poems by an author with an eye to young children.
Betsy R. Rosenthal	*My House Is Singing*	6–8	Short poems pay homage to everyday objects and places around the house.
Cynthia Rylant	*God Went to Beauty School*	12 and up	These wonderful poems reflect on God's marvelous creations.
Gary Soto	*Fearless Fernie* and *Worlds Apart*	9–12	These two volumes contain sensitive, funny, and beautifully written poems about childhood friends.
April Halprin Wayland	*Girl Coming In for a Landing*	12 and up	This volume tells one adolescent girl's story over the course of a school year in poems.
Janet Wong	*Grump*	Birth to 5	This tired Mom with an energetic baby will be familiar to many.
Jane Breskin Zalben	*Let There Be Light: Poems and Prayers for Repairing the World*	4–8	This beautifully illustrated collection of poems and prayers represents cultures and faiths around the world.
Tracie Vaughn Zimmer	*Sketches from a Spy Tree*	8–12	Anne Marie observes her world from her hidden perch in the "Spy Tree."

FAMILIES

Compiler, Poet	Title	Age Level	Description
Arnold Adoff	*Love Letters*	7–12	Loving poems about family and friends fill this book.
Ralph Fletcher	*Relatively Speaking*	10–12	Fletcher's poems about family reflect his growing up in a large family.
Nikki Grimes	*Hopscotch Love*	9–12	Different characters experience love in different ways.

(continued)

Specialized Collections of Poetry *(continued)*

FAMILIES *(continued)*

Compiler, Poet	Title	Age Level	Description
Carol G. Hittleman and Daniel Hittleman	*A Grand Celebration: Grandparents in Poetry*	5–8	Various poets provide diverse and loving portraits of grandparents.
Angela Johnson	*Running Back to Luddie*	9–12	Poems circle a time in the life of an adolescent who hears from her long-absent mother.
Pat Mora	*Love to Mama: A Tribute to Mothers*	9–12	Poems honor mothers, grandmothers, and caregiving women.
Liz Rosenberg	*Roots and Flowers: Poets and Poems on Family*	12 and up	Forty poets tell about their families and present poems that grew out of their experiences.
Dorothy Strickland and Michael R. Strickland	*Families: Poems Celebrating the African American Experience*	5–8	Poems celebrating African American family life make up this volume.
Vera B. Williams	*Amber Was Brave, Essie Was Smart*	7–10	Two sisters support and comfort each other through good times and bad.
Janet Wong	*The Rainbow Hand: Poems about Mothers and Daughters*	12 and up	This sensitive collection reveals the complex relations that exist between mothers and daughters.

POETRY OF NATURE AND SEASONS

Compiler, Poet	Title	Age Level	Description
Arnold Adoff	*In for Winter, Out for Spring*	6–10	Poems of the changing seasons capture the joy of everything from the first snowflake in winter to pumpkins in late October.
Kurt Cyrus	*Hotel Deep: Light Verse from Deep Water*	7–12	A tiny sardine relays the drama of life in the deep ocean from its point of view.
Rebecca Kai Dotlich	*Lemonade Sun*	6–8	These sunny poems about the pleasures of summertime dazzle.
Ralph Fletcher	*Ordinary Things*	10 and up	These poems about a walk in the woods uncover the hidden treasures in ordinary things.
Douglas Florian	*Autumnblings, Hand-springs, Summersaults, and Winter Eyes*	5–10	Lovely watercolors illustrate these four volumes of poetry about the seasons.
Kristine O'Connell George	*Hummingbird Nest: A Journal of Poems*	7–12	The poet observes a hummingbird's nest through a season of building and birth.
Kristine O'Connell George	*Toasting Marshmallows: Camping Poems*	5–10	Simple and short, these poems capture the joys of camping outdoors.
James Hayford	*Knee-Deep in Blazing Snow*	10 and up	A noted poet reflects on his childhood winters in Vermont.

Specialized Collections of Poetry (*continued*)

POETRY OF NATURE AND SEASONS (*continued*)

Compiler, Poet	Title	Age Level	Description
Lee Bennett Hopkins	*Hoofbeats, Claws, and Rippled Fins*	8–12	Stephen Alcorn's beautiful woodcuts adorn these 14 poems about animals.
Susan Katz	*Looking for Jaguar*	7–12	This collection focuses on the flora and fauna of the rain forest.
Kate Kiesler	*Wings on the Wind: Bird Poems*	4–8	Kiesler's oil paintings illustrate 23 poems about birds.
J. Patrick Lewis	*Earth Verses and Water Rhymes*	9–12	Lewis begins with poems about the fall and progresses through the seasons. Among these poems' fresh images is his description of trees as "Earth umbrellas."
Charlotte F. Otten	*January Rides the Wind*	6–8	Otten uses poetic elements that young children will understand and enjoy in these short poems about each month of the year.
Paul Paolilli and Dan Brewer	*Silver Seeds*	5–8	These acrostic poems describe familiar sights and objects in the young child's world.
Barbara Rogasky	*Leaf by Leaf: Autumn Poems*	9–14	This fine collection by poets old and new celebrates fall.
Steven Schnur	*Winter: An Alphabet Acrostic*	6–10	This book completes Schnur's acrostic poems about the four seasons.
Joyce Sidman	*Song of the Water Boatman*	7–12	Poems in the voices of pond dwellers are accompanied by exquisite woodcut illustrations and convey factual information about pond ecology.
Marilyn Singer	*Central Heating* and *Footprints on the Roof*	7–12	These volumes reflect on the elements of earth and fire.
Jane Yolen	*Color Me a Rhyme* and *Wild Wings*	6–10	Yolen and her photographer son, Jason Stemple, collaborate on several volumes about the natural world.
Jane Yolen	*Once Upon Ice*	8–12	Seventeen poets composed poems inspired by Jason Stemple's exquisite photographs of icy settings.
Ed Young (illustrator)	*Birches* (Robert Frost)	10 and up	Young never pictures the swinger of birches but leaves that to the reader's imagination. He does portray lovely birches seen from various perspectives. The complete poem is given at the end.

(continued)

TEACHING RESOURCES

Specialized Collections of Poetry *(continued)*

ANIMAL POEMS

Compiler, Poet	Title	Age Level	Description
Diane Ackerman	*Animal Sense*	8–12	Poems illustrated by Peter Sis show how the five senses shape experience.
Kristine O'Connell George	*Little Dog Poems* and *Little Dog and Duncan*	3–8	These volumes chronicle the adventures of a small dog and a small boy.
Maya Gottfried	*Good Dog*	5–10	Each of sixteen dogs provides an amusing insight into its personality.
David Greenberg	*Bugs!*	5–8	This delicious menu of funny poems about insects comes from the subversive author of *Slugs*.
Lee Bennett Hopkins	*Dinosaurs*	8 and up	These 18 poems, including "The Last Dinosaur" and "How the End Might Have Been," are useful for discussion and dinosaur units.
Betsy Lewin	*Animal Snackers*	5–10	These brief, funny poems highlight animal habits.
Jeff Moss	*Bone Poems*	7–12	Dinosaur lovers will devour these 40 poems inspired by a visit to the American Museum of Natural History.
Susan Pearson	*Who Swallowed Harold?*	5–10	This collection of humorous poems focuses on children and their pets.
Jack Prelutsky, ed.	*The Beauty of the Beast*	7–12	Meilo So's exquisite watercolor paintings make these beasts truly beautiful. More than 200 poems celebrate the animal world.
Jack Prelutsky	*If Not for the Cat*	7–10	Different animals are the subject of these haiku poems.
Cynthia Rylant	*Boris*	12 and up	Beautifully written narrative poems muse about the author's life with her cat.
Judy Sierra	*Antarctic Antics*	4–8	Lively verses celebrate the emperor penguin (from the penguin's point of view).
Amy E. Sklansky	*From the Doghouse: Poems to Chew On*	4–8	Sklansky gives children a lighthearted and lively look at dogs.
Wade Zahares	*Big, Bad, and a Little Bit Scary: Poems That Bite Back!*	6–11	Zahares provides wonderful artistic interpretations of poems about scary animals.

HUMOROUS POETRY

Compiler, Poet	Title	Age Level	Description
William Cole	*Poem Stew*	6–12	Children love this hilarious feast of poems about food.

Specialized Collections of Poetry (*continued*)

HUMOROUS POETRY (*continued*)

Compiler, Poet	Title	Age Level	Description
Charley Hoce	*Beyond Old MacDonald*	5–10	These funny verses recount adventures down on the farm.
X. J. Kennedy	*Exploding Gravy: Poems to Make You Laugh*	9–12	Silly, over-the-top poems fill this book.
Dennis Lee	*Dinosaur Dinner (with a Slice of Alligator Pie)*	5–10	This master at delighting children has provided a wonderful collection of silly poems.
Colin McNaughton	*Making Friends with Frankenstein* and *Who's Been Sleeping in My Porridge?*	7–12	Wacky poems and pictures make up these two collections.
Colin McNaughton	*Wish You Were Here and I Wasn't: A Book of Poems and Pictures for Globe-Trotters*	9–12	McNaughton pokes fun at traveling and vacationing.
Jack Prelutsky	*Awful Ogre's Awful Day*	7–11	Eighteen poems tell the tale of an awful ogre's awful day.
Jack Prelutsky	*For Laughing Out Loud: Poems to Tickle Your Funnybone*	5–10	Lively colored illustrations by Marjorie Priceman add to the humor of more than 130 of the funniest poems.
Jack Prelutsky	*The Frogs Wore Red Suspenders*	3–9	Prelutsky provides a fresh collection of poetry and rhymes for younger listeners.
Jack Prelutsky	*It's Raining Pigs and Noodles*	5–10	Nonsense and humor mark another volume from the creators of *New Kid on the Block*.
Jack Prelutsky	*Poems by A. Nonny Mouse* and *A. Nonny Mouse Writes Again*	5–10	The first volume contains more than 70 of the silliest poems attributed by publishers to "anony-mous." The sequel contains some 50 more poems that are short, silly, and fun to recite.
Jack Prelutsky	*Scranimals*	6 and up	Peter Sis's illustrations are perfect for these poems about mixed-up and crossed-over animals.

MULTICULTURAL POETRY COLLECTIONS

Compiler, Poet	Title	Age Level	Description
Arnold Adoff	*I Am the Darker Brother: An Anthology of Modern Poems by Black Americans*	10 and up	This collection contains some of the best-known poetry of Langston Hughes, Gwendolyn Brooks, and Countee Cullen, as well as some modern poets.

(continued)

Specialized Collections of Poetry *(continued)*

MULTICULTURAL POETRY COLLECTIONS *(continued)*

Compiler, Poet	Title	Age Level	Description
Arnold Adoff	*My Black Me*	8 and up	This collection of contemporary poems mixes Black pride with power and protest. Brief biographical notes on each of the poets add interest.
John Agard and Grace Nichols	*Under the Moon and Over the Sea*	4–8	This fine collection of poems from the Caribbean is illustrated by various artists.
Francisco X. Alarcón	*Angels Ride Bikes, From the Bellybutton of the Moon, Iguanas in the Snow,* and *Laughing Tomatoes*	5–8	Four bilingual volumes celebrate the singular joys of each season.
Francisco X. Alarcón	*Poems to Dream Together*	5–8	Bilingual poems focus on children and their connections to family, friends, and community.
Jorge Argueta	*A Movie in My Pillow/ Una película en mi almohada*	10–14	Bilingual poems describe growing up in El Salvador and San Francisco.
James Berry	*A Nest Full of Stars*	8–12	Berry reflects on his youth in the Caribbean.
John Bierhorst	*On the Road of Stars*	5–8	Native American night poems and sleep charms comprise this book.
Tanya Bolden	*Rock of Ages*	5–8	Poems praise the power of Black churches.
Ashley Bryan	*Ashley Bryan's ABC of African American Poetry*	5–8	African American poets and their poems, from A to Z, are showcased and illustrated with Bryan's usual sunny style.
Lori Marie Carlson	*Cool Salsa* and *Red Hot Salsa*	12 and up	Two collections of bilingual poems describe growing up Latino.
Lori Marie Carlson	*Sol a Sol*	5–8	These vibrant poems follow a family from morning to sundown with poems in both English and Spanish.
Nikki Giovanni	*The Sun Is So Quiet*	4–8	Thirteen of Giovanni's sensitive poems are illustrated by Ashley Bryan.
Eloise Greenfield	*In the Land of Words*	5–8	New poems and old favorites make up this collection from noted poet Greenfield.
Eloise Greenfield	*Nathaniel Talking*	6–10	Nathaniel gives us his "philosophy" of life in 18 poems.
Eloise Greenfield	*Night on Neighborhood Street*	6–10	Poems tell about family, friends, and neighbors who live on Neighborhood Street.

Specialized Collections of Poetry *(continued)*

MULTICULTURAL POETRY COLLECTIONS *(continued)*

Compiler, Poet	Title	Age Level	Description
Nikki Grimes	*Is It Far to Zanzibar? Poems about Tanzania*	8 and up	Thirteen poems evoke life in Zanzibar.
Monica Gunning	*America, My New Home*	8–10	A Jamaican child reflects on her move to America.
Monica Gunning	*Not a Copper Penny in Me House*	4–8	Everyday life and special celebrations of the author's Jamaican childhood are related in these poems.
Minfong Ho	*Maples in the Mist*	7 and up	Lovely watercolor illustrations accompany these fine translations of Tang Dynasty poems.
Siyu Liu and Orel Protopopescu	*A Thousand Peaks: Poems from China*	11–14	Poems by Chinese poets span two millennia.
Michio Mado	*The Magic Pocket*	4–8	Mitsumasa Anno's illustrations add charm to this lovely collection of verses for young children by a Japanese author.
Kam Mak	*My Chinatown: One Year in Poems*	6–10	Exquisite paintings by Mak accompany poems of a childhood year in Chinatown.
Jane Medina	*My Name Is Jorge*	7–12	A Mexican immigrant struggles between two cultures in these bilingual poems.
Tony Medina	*Love to Langston*	6–12	Vignettes of Langston Hughes's life are captured in 14 poems.
Pat Mora	*Confetti*	4–8	Bright pictures by Enrique O. Sanchez enliven this warm collection of poems about a young girl's life in the Southwest.
Walter Dean Myers	*Here in Harlem: Poems in Many Voices*	12 and up	Poems in different voices and styles draw a picture of living in Harlem.
Marilyn Nelson	*Fortune's Bones: The Manumission Requiem*	12 and up	Poems honor the memory of a slave whose bones were preserved for use as an anatomy specimen.
Marilyn Nelson	*A Wreath for Emmett Till*	12 and up	A complex and moving elegy on the life and death of Emmett Till.
Cynthia Rylant	*Waiting to Waltz*	9–12	The poems in Rylant's book capture the essence of growing up in a small town in Appalachia.
Javaka Steptoe	*In Daddy's Arms I Am Tall*	6–9	Steptoe's stunning collages bring energy and warmth to this collection of poems about African American fathers.
Maria Testa	*Something about America*	12 and up	This novel in verse is based on a true account of a community that rallied around Somali immigrants.

(continued)

Specialized Collections of Poetry (continued)

MULTICULTURAL POETRY COLLECTIONS (continued)

Compiler, Poet	Title	Age Level	Description
Joyce Carol Thomas	*The Blacker the Berry* and *Gingerbread Days*	7–10	These collections celebrate African American identities.
Janet Wong	*Good Luck and Other Poems* and *A Suitcase of Seaweed and Other Poems*	12 and up	Wong's versatility as a poet is evident in these two collections.
Ed Young	*Beyond the Mountains*	8 and up	This elegant edition captures the majesty of Chinese art, writing, and poetry.

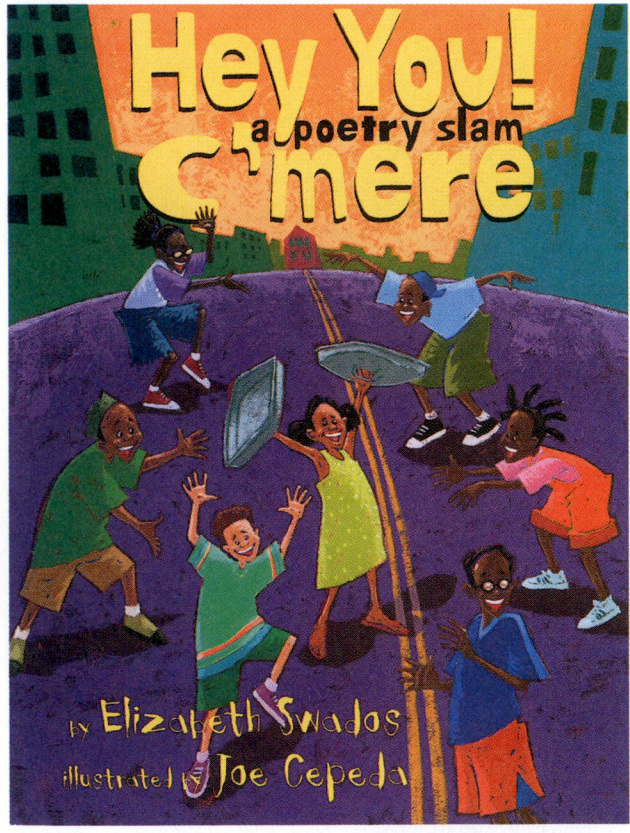

Joe Cepeda's intense paintings for Elizabeth Swados's *Hey You! C'Mere: A Poetry Slam* seem to dance right off the page. Illustration copyright © 2002 by Joe Cepeda from *Hey You! C'Mere, A Poetry Slam* by Elizabeth Swados. An Arthur A. Levine Book, published by Scholastic Press/Scholastic, Inc. Reprinted by permission.

Several books invite children to move to the beat and sing with the music of poetry. Michael R. Strickland has poems and songs about music and music makers, dancers and dance, in *My Own Song and Other Poems to Groove To* and *Poems That Sing to You*. Jamie Adoff's *Song Shoots out of My Mouth* begs older children to try poetry performance—to approach a microphone and sing out loud. Elizabeth Swados, a playwright and poet, has built on the enthusiasm for poetry slams and captured the exuberant rhythm of urban street kids in *Hey You! C'Mere: A Poetry Slam*. This book is a lively invitation to street theater and performance poetry, which seems to be gaining a following in the adult world.

Collected African American poetry can be found in such attractive illustrated editions as Tom Feelings's *Soul Looks Back in Wonder*, a winner of the Coretta Scott King Award for illustration. Feelings has chosen selections from thirteen poets that celebrate African American heritage and sing of African pride. Wade Hudson's collection *Pass It On*, illustrated by Floyd Cooper, is broader in scope. It includes poems like Nikki Giovanni's "Prickled Pickles Don't Smile" and Henry Dumas's "Peas," which are light in tone, as well as more serious reflections such as Lucille Clifton's "Listen, Children." All volumes include well-known poets and introduce newer voices.

Several collections of poetry represent Native American poets. Stephen Gammell illustrates *Dancing Teepees*, edited by Virginia Driving Hawk Sneve, with sensitive full-color watercolors. This is a handsome book of some twenty poems chosen from various tribes. John Bierhorst also emphasizes humanity's close relationship to nature in his anthology *In the Trail of the Wind: American Indian Poems and Ritual Orations.*

We can be grateful for the reissue of . . . *I Never Saw Another Butterfly*, edited by Hana Volavkova. This book contains poems and pictures created by children in the Terezin concentration camp from 1942 to 1944. These drawings and poems are all that are left of the fifteen thousand children who passed through this camp on their way to Auschwitz. They are an eloquent statement of their courage and optimism in the midst of despair.

Picture-Book Editions of Single Poems

It was inevitable that poetry should also follow the trend to single-poem editions already established by the many beautifully illustrated editions of single fairy tales and folk songs.

The first book of poetry to be presented with the Newbery Medal was *A Visit to William Blake's Inn* by Nancy Willard. In the same year, the illustrators for this book, Alice Provensen and Martin Provensen, received a Caldecott Honor Award. Inspired by Blake's work, Nancy Willard created a book of connected poems about life at an imaginary inn run by William Blake himself. Children ages 8 and up will be intrigued by the detailed pictures of the inn and its guests.

Susan Jeffers has illustrated two well-known poems in picture-book format. Her pictures for Robert Frost's *Stopping by Woods on a Snowy Evening* evoke the quiet stillness of the forest in contrast to the staid New England village. In *Hiawatha,* she pictures the romantic Indian in keeping with Henry Wadsworth Longfellow's poem and time. Lovely pictures of Nokomis and a growing Hiawatha hold children's interest. The artist is not always consistent in portraying the age of the Iroquois lad, however; he seems older, then younger, before he reaches manhood and leaves the tribe.

In some instances these stunning picture books may create new interest in a poem like Longfellow's *Hiawatha* or *Paul Revere's Ride*, or Ernest L. Thayer's *Casey at the Bat.* Loren Long's exquisite paintings for Walt Whitman's *When I Heard the Learn'd Astronomer* help children understand the irony of the poet's words. The inclusion of Long's children's pencil drawings also brings home the message that children see the true wonders of the universe more clearly than any scientist. It is generally a good idea to read the poem through once to children before sharing the pictures, because turning the pages to look at the illustrations interrupts the flow of the poem. Many of these picture/poetry books provide the text of the complete poem at the end of the book. Because po-etry is the most concentrated and connotative use of language, it needs to be shared several times anyway.

Contemporary poets are also represented in single-poem editions. Notozake Shange's poem "Mood Indigo," which recalls her childhood among the great figures of the Harlem Renaissance, has been illustrated by Kadir Nelson in *Ellington Was Not a Street.* The bold shapes and contrasting values of Nelson's art bring the wonder of this time alive for modern children. Chris Raschka's lively linear artistic style seems perfect for Nikki Giovanni's wonderfully hopeful poem *The Genie in the Jar* and bell hooks's *Happy to Be Nappy.* All of these books celebrate the uniqueness of African American culture yet speak joyfully to all children.

SHARING POETRY WITH CHILDREN

There can be no question that very young children respond spontaneously to the sensory-motor action of "Ride a Cock Horse" or "Peas porridge hot/Peas porridge cold." Children in the primary grades love to join in with the wacky words and rhythm of Jack Prelutsky's "Bleezer's Ice Cream Store" in *The New Kid on the Block.* Younger children naturally delight in the sound, rhythm, and language of poetry.

We have seen that sometime toward the end of the primary grades, children begin to lose interest in poetry. The poet William Jay Smith comments: "How natural and harmonious it all is at the beginning; and yet what happens along the way later to make poetry to many children the dullest and least enjoyable of literary expressions?"[11] There may be many reasons for this lessening of enthusiasm. Some studies suggest that teachers tend to read traditional poems or sentimental poems that are *about* childhood rather than contemporary poems that would be more suited to the modern child's maturity, experiences, and interests.[12] Poems that are too difficult, too abstract for children to understand, will also be rejected.

Other studies have indicated that teachers neglect poetry. Ann Terry found, for example, that more than 75 percent of the teachers in the middle grades read poetry to their children only once a month or less.[13] Children can hardly be expected to develop a love of poetry when they hear it fewer than nine times a year! It is also possible to hear too much poetry, particularly at one time. Teachers who read poetry for an hour or have every child read a poem on a Friday afternoon are contributing to children's dislike of poetry as much as those who simply neglect it. This also happens when we relegate poetry to

---

[11]Virginia Haviland and William Jay Smith, *Children and Poetry* (Washington, D.C.: Library of Congress, 1969), p. iv.

[12]Chow Loy Tom, "Paul Revere Rides Ahead: Poems Teachers Read to Pupils in the Middle Grades," *Library Quarterly* 43 (January 1973): 27–38.

[13]Ann Terry, *Children's Poetry Preferences*, p. 29.

a "Poetry Week" in the spring. Poetry needs to be shared naturally every day by a teacher who loves it.

Another way to create distaste for poetry is by requiring children to memorize certain poems, usually selected by the teacher. It is especially dull when everyone has to learn the same poem. Many children do enjoy memorizing favorite poems, provided they can do it voluntarily and can select the poem. But choosing to commit a certain poem to memory is quite different from being required to do so.

Too-detailed analysis of every poem is also detrimental to children's enjoyment of poetry. An appropriate question or comment to increase meaning is fine; but critical analysis of every word in a poem, every figure of speech, and every iambic verse is lethal to appreciation. Jean Little captures one student's reaction to too much analysis in this poem:

> I used to like "Stopping by Woods on a Snowy Evening,"
> I liked the coming darkness,
> The jingle of harness bells, breaking—and adding to—the stillness,
> The gentle drift of snow . . .
>
> But today, the teacher told us what everything stood for.
> The woods, the horse, the miles to go, the sleep—
> They all have "hidden meanings."
> It's grown so complicated now that,
> Next time I drive by,
> I don't think I'll bother to stop.
>
> —Jean Little. "After English Class," from *Hey World, Here I Am!* by Jean Little. Copyright © 1989. Reprinted by permission of Harper & Row.

Creating a Climate for Enjoyment

There have always been teachers who love poetry and who share their enthusiasm for poetry with students. There are teachers who make poetry a natural part of the daily program of living and learning. They realize that poetry should not be presented under the pressure of a tight time schedule, but should be enjoyed every day. Children should be able to relax and relish the humor and beauty that the sharing of poetry affords. The Web "In Praise of Poetry" describes some of the classroom experiences with poetry these teachers provide for their children.

Finding Time for Poetry

Teachers who would develop children's delight in poetry will find time to share poetry with them sometime each day and find ways to connect poetry to the experiences in children's lives. They know that anytime is a good time to read a poem to children, but they will especially want to capitalize on exciting experiences like the first snow, a birthday party, or the arrival of a classmate's new baby brother. Perhaps there has been a fight on the playground and someone is still grumbling and complaining—that might be a good time to share poetry about feelings. The teacher could read Karla Kuskin's "When I Woke Up This Morning" (in *Moon, Have You Met My Mother?*), and then everyone could laugh the bad feelings away. Poetry can also be thought of as a delicious snack to nibble on during transition times between going out to recess or the last few minutes of the day. Anytime is a good time for a poetry snack!

Inspiring teachers frequently read poetry cycles, three or four poems with the same theme. One teacher capitalized on children's interest in "special places." She shared Byrd Baylor's poetic story *Your Own Best Secret Place* and Dennis Lee's "The Secret Place" (in *Poetry by Heart*, comp. Liz Attenborough) with a group of third graders. Later the children wrote about their own secret places in both prose and poetry. Children also enjoy selecting a particular subject and creating their own poetry cycles from anthologies in the library or classroom.

One way to be sure to share poetry every day is to relate children's favorite prose stories to poetry. One teacher who keeps a card file of poems always slips one or two cards into the book that is to be read aloud that day. For example, after sharing *Whistle for Willie* by Ezra Jack Keats, Jack Prelutsky's "Whistling" (in *Read-Aloud Rhymes for the Very Young*) could be read. A fifth-grade teacher paired Gail Carson Levine's *Ella Enchanted* with Laura Whipple's *If the Shoe Fits: Voices from Cinderella*. Students then went on to read other novelizations of fairy tales and to write poems in the voices of the characters. Librarians and teachers will want to make their own poetry/prose connections. We hope that Teaching Resources: "Connections between Poetry and Prose" will get you started.

Other subjects and activities in the curriculum can be enriched with poetry. A "science discovery walk" could be preceded by reading Florence McNeil's "Squirrels in My Notebook" (in *Til All the Stars Have Fallen*, ed. David Booth), in which a child records his observations of a squirrel, including the fact that he couldn't repeat what the squirrel said to him! Older children would enjoy John Moffitt's well-known poem "To Look at Anything" (in *Reflections on a Gift of Watermelon Pickle*, ed. Stephen Dunning et al.). A math lesson might be introduced with one of the riddle-rhymes in *Arithme-tickle* by J. Patrick Lewis or by poems from Lee Bennett Hopkins's collection *Marvelous Math*. Many poems can enhance social studies. Geography need not be neglected with appealing collections such as Hopkins's *My America: A Poetry Atlas of the United States* and *Got Geography!*, as well as Lewis's *A World of Wonders: Geographic Travels in Verse and Rhyme*. American history is also well represented by collections such as Hopkins's *Lives: Poems about Famous Americans* and Susan Katz's *A Revolutionary Field Trip*. *Remember the Bridge: Poems of a People*, a collection of poems by Carole Boston Weatherford, is a fine introduction to Black History for adolescents. Bobbi Katz's *We the*

Wonderfully Exciting Books

Poetry Cycles
Find and read poems about similar themes.
Feelings—
   "Wrong Start" (Chute),
   "When I Woke Up This Morning"
   (Kuskin)
Weather—
   "Fog" (Sandburg),
   "Fog" (Chandra)

Poetry Celebrations
I'm in Charge of Celebrations (Baylor)
Find something simple and special to celebrate
   every day.
Compile a class list of special celebrations.
Hold a Poetry Celebration Day.
Invite parents and other special people to
   read or recite favorite poems.
Display class poetry collections.

Eats (Adoff)
Poem Stew (Cole)
"Rah, Rah Peas" (Levy)
"Spaghetti" (Silverstein)
Have a class feast, inspired by poems
   about food.

Poetry/Prose Connections
Find poems to match the mood, theme,
   etc., of favorite books.

"Mother to Son" (Hughes)/
Scorpions (Myers)
"Until I Saw the Sea" (Moore)/
Time of Wonder (McCloskey)

Poetry Models
A House Is a House for Me (Hoberman)
*I Am Writing a Poem About . . . A Game of
   Poetry* (Myra Cohn Livingston)
Poetry from A to Z (Janeczko)
Prayers from the Ark (Bernos de Gasztold)
Read a Rhyme, Write a Rhyme (Prelutsky)
Use poems as springboards to try
   your own forms.

Hailstones and Halibut Bones (O'Neill)
A Song of Colors (Hindley)
Think of a favorite color. Write color
   poems or color phrases.

Limericks
The Book of Pigericks (Lobel)
The Hopeful Trout and Other Limericks
   (Ciardi)
Make a class book of limericks on a theme
   or topic.

IN PRAISE OF POETRY

Poetry Corner
Everybody Needs a Rock (Baylor)
Hailstones and Halibut Bones (O'Neill)
"Seashell" (Worth) and "Shell" (Chandra)
Establish a rotating display around special topics
   such as "Small Things" or "Color."
Display poems, artwork, and artifacts that fit
   the theme.

Poetry and the Arts
Heart to Heart (Greenberg)
Paint Me a Poem (Rowden)
Talking to the Sun (Koch and Farrell)
Collect reproductions of paintings based
   on a theme and choose poems that
   match each painting.

Song Shoots out of My Mouth (Adoff)
Poems That Sing to You (Strickland)
Hey You! C'Mere (Swados)
Select poems about a topic. Choose music
   that matches the mood, rhythm, or
   theme of the poems. Put together a
   poetry reading to music.

Haiku
Stone Bench in an Empty Park (Janeczko)
Write haiku or tanka poems. Illustrate
   them with collage or prints.

Patterned Poems
Doodle Dandies (Lewis)
A Poke in the I (Janeczko)
Splish Splash (Graham)
Write a poem about a concrete object
   like trees, waterfalls, or popsicles.
   Change it into a visual art form.

Sensory Explorations
"Mud" (Worth)
"Peach" (Rauter)
Blindfold group members. Have them
   touch, taste, or smell objects. List
   words or phrases they use to describe
   their sensory impressions. Compare
   these to ways that poets have
   compared similar experiences.

Reading Aloud
"Harriet Tubman" (Greenfield)
Read poems together in one voice.

Wham! It's a Poetry Jam (Holbrook)
Read poems and create hand or body
   movements to accompany yourselves.

"The Grobbles" (Prelutsky)
"Song of the Train" (McCord)
Plan choral reading with single and many
   voices, loud and soft sounds, high and
   low pitch.

Big Talk (Fleischman)
I Am Phoenix (Fleischman)
Joyful Noise (Fleischman)
Read poems in two, three, or four voices.
   Write your own poems for several voices.

Connections between Poetry and Prose

 Visit the Online Learning Center at **www.mhhe.com/kiefer9e** for a printable version of this list.

Subject/Theme	Age Level	Poems	Prose
Bears	5–7	"The Bear Coat" by Karla Kuskin, in *Moon, Have You Met My Mother?*	*The Bear's Toothache* (David McPhail)
		Bear in Mind by Bobbye Goldstein	*Brown Bear, Brown Bear, What Do You See?* (Bill Martin, Jr.)
		"Grandpa Bear's Lullaby" by Jane Yolen, in *Sing a Song of Popcorn,* ed. Beatrice Schenk de Regniers et al.	*Corduroy* (Don Freeman)
			Goldilocks and the Three Bears (Jan Brett)
		"Koala" by Karla Kuskin, in *Moon, Have You Met My Mother?*	*Ira Sleeps Over* (Bernard Waber)
		"Oh, Teddy Bear" by Jack Prelutsky, in *The New Kid on the Block*	*Jamberry* (Bruce Degen)
			Koala Lou (Mem Fox)
		The Three Bears Holiday Rhyme Book by Jane Yolen	*Where's My Teddy?* (Jez Alborough)

Subject/Theme	Age Level	Poems	Prose
Family	5–7	"All Kinds of Grands" by Lucille Clifton, in *Sing a Song of Popcorn,* ed. Beatrice Schenk de Regniers et al.	*A Chair for My Mother* (Vera Williams)
			Dogger (Shirley Hughes)
		"Little" by Dorothy Aldis, in *Tomie dePaola's Book of Poems*	*Mr. Rabbit and the Lovely Present* (Charlotte Zolotow)
		"My Brother" by Marci Ridlon, in *The Random House Book of Poetry for Children,* ed. Jack Prelutsky	*The Stories Julian Tells* (Ann Cameron)
			The Whales' Song (Dyan Sheldon)

Subject/Theme	Age Level	Poems	Prose
Feelings	6–8	"I'm in a Rotten Mood" by Jack Prelutsky, in *The New Kid on the Block*	*Alexander and the Terrible, Horrible, No Good, Very Bad Day* (Judith Viorst)
		"A Small Discovery" by James Emannuel, in *Tomie dePaola's Book of Poems*	*The Hating Book* (Charlotte Zolotow)
			Lilly's Purple Plastic Purse (Kevin Henkes)
		"Sometimes I Feel This Way" by John Ciardi, in *A Jar of Tiny Stars,* ed. Bernice Cullinan	*Lost in the Museum* (Miriam Cohen)
			When Sophie Gets Angry—Really, Really Angry (Molly Bang)
		"When I Was Lost" by Dorothy Aldis, in *The Random House Book of Poetry for Children,* ed. Jack Prelutsky	*Will I Have a Friend?* (Miriam Cohen)
		"When I Woke Up This Morning" by Karla Kuskin, in *Moon, Have You Met My Mother?*	

Connections between Poetry and Prose *(continued)*

Subject/Theme	Age Level	Poems	Prose
Feelings *(continued)*		"Wrong Start" by Marchette Chute, in *The Random House Book of Poetry for Children,* ed. Jack Prelutsky	
Sibling rivalry	5–7	"Brother" by Mary Ann Hoberman, in *Tomie dePaola's Book of Poems*	*A Baby Sister for Frances* (Russell Hoban)
		"For Sale" by Shel Silverstein, in *A Light in the Attic*	*Julius, the Baby of the World* (Kevin Henkes)
		"I'm Disgusted with My Brother" by Jack Prelutsky, in *The New Kid on the Block*	*Noisy Nora* (Rosemary Wells)
			Peter's Chair (Ezra Jack Keats)
		"Moochie" by Eloise Greenfield, in *Honey, I Love*	*She Come Bringing Me That Little Baby Girl* (Eloise Greenfield)
			Titch (Pat Hutchins)
Death/loss	7–8	"Chelsea" by James Stevenson, in *Sing a Song of Popcorn,* ed. Beatrice Schenk de Regniers et al.	*The Accident* (Carol Carrick and Donald Carrick)
		"For a Dead Kitten" by Sara Henderson Hay, in *Reflections on a Gift of Watermelon Pickle,* ed. Stephen Dunning et al.	*The Best Cat in the World* (Lesléa Newman)
			Blow Me a Kiss, Miss Lily (Nancy W. Carlstrom)
		"Poem" by Langston Hughes, in *The Dream Keeper*	*The Tenth Good Thing about Barney* (Judith Viorst)
		"Skipper" by Gwendolyn Brooks, in *Bronzeville Boys and Girls*	*The Very Best of Friends* (Margaret Wild)
Folktales	7–8	"The Builders" by Sara Henderson Hay, in *Reflections on a Gift of Watermelon Pickle,* ed. Stephen Dunning et al.	*Cinderella* (Charles Perrault)
			The Frog Prince (Edith Tarcov)
			The Frog Prince Continued (Jon Scieszka)
		"The Gingerbread Man" by Rowena Bennett, in *Sing a Song of Popcorn,* ed. Beatrice Schenk de Regniers et al.	*The Gingerbread Boy* (Paul Galdone)
		"In Search of Cinderella" by Shel Silverstein, in *A Light in the Attic*	*Strega Nona* (Tomie dePaola)
			The Three Little Pigs (James Marshall)
		"Spaghetti" by Shel Silverstein, in *Where the Sidewalk Ends*	*The True Story of the 3 Little Pigs!* (Jon Scieszka)

(continued)

Connections between Poetry and Prose (*continued*)

Subject/Theme	Age Level	Poems	Prose
Secret places	7–8	"Hideout" by Aileen Fisher, in *Tomie dePaola's Book of Poems*	*Dawn* (Uri Shulevitz)
		"Tree House" by Shel Silverstein, in *Where the Sidewalk Ends*	*The Little Island* (Golden MacDonald)
		Your Own Best Secret Place, ed. Byrd Baylor	*When I Was Young in the Mountains* (Cynthia Rylant)
			Wild Boy (Mordicai Gerstein)

Subject/Theme	Age Level	Poems	Prose
Courage and pride	10–12	. . . *I Never Saw Another Butterfly,* ed. Hana Volavkova	*The Land I Lost: Adventures of a Boy in Vietnam* (Quang Nhuong Huynh)
		"I Too Sing America" by Langston Hughes, in *The Dream Keeper*	*Lyddie* (Katherine Paterson)
		It's a Woman's World, ed. Neil Philip	*The Most Beautiful Place in the World* (Ann Cameron)
		"Mother to Son" by Langston Hughes, in *The Dream Keeper*	*Number the Stars* (Lois Lowry)
		"Otto" by Gwendolyn Brooks, in *Bronzeville Boys and Girls*	*Roll of Thunder, Hear My Cry* (Mildred Taylor)
			Running the Road to ABC (Denizé Lauture)
			Sounder (William Armstrong)

Subject/Theme	Age Level	Poems	Prose
The environment	12–13	"Hurt No Living Thing" by Christina Rossetti, in *The Random House Book of Poetry for Children,* ed. Jack Prelutsky	*Ancient Ones* (Barbara Bash)
		Sierra, by Diane Siebert	*The Great Kapok Tree* (Lynne Cherry)
		"To Look at Anything" by John Moffit, in *Reflections on a Gift of Watermelon Pickle,* ed. Stephen Dunning et al.	*Hawk, I'm Your Brother* (Byrd Baylor)
			One Day in the Tropical Rain Forest (Jean George)
		"Tree Coming Up" by Constance Levy, in *I'm Going to Pet a Worm Today*	*On the Far Side of the Mountain* (Jean George)
			The Way to Start a Day (Byrd Baylor)
			Who Really Killed Cock Robin? (Jean George)
			Window (Jeannie Baker)
			The Year of the Panda (Miriam Schlein)

Subject/Theme	Age Level	Poems	Prose
Relationships	10–14	*Fearless Fernie* by Gary Soto	*Bridge to Terabithia* (Katherine Paterson)

Connections between Poetry and Prose *(continued)*

Subject/Theme	Age Level	Poems	Prose
Relationships *(continued)*		"Friendship" by Shel Silverstein, in *A Light in the Attic*	*Criss Cross* (Lynne Rae Perkins)
		Hey World, Here I Am! by Jean Little	*Last Summer with Maizon* (Jacqueline Woodson)
		I Like You, If You Like Me by Myra Cohn Livingston	*Lizzie Bright and the Buckminster Boy* (Gary D. Schmidt)
		Locomotion by Jacqueline Woodson	*Other Bells for Us to Ring* (Robert Cormier)
		"Poem" by Langston Hughes, in *The Dream Keeper*	*When Zachary Beaver Came to Town* (Kimberly Willis Holt)
		"Some People" by Charlotte Zolotow, in *Very Best (Almost) Friends,* ed. Paul Janeczko	

Subject/Theme	Age Level	Poems	Prose
Holocaust/war	11–14	"Earth" by John Hall Wheelock, in *Relections on a Gift of Watermelon Pickle,* ed. Stephen Dunning et al.	*Anne Frank: Diary of a Young Girl* (Anne Frank)
		"The House That Fear Built: Warsaw, 1943" by Jane Flanders, in *War and the Pity of War,* ed. Neil Philip	*Eyes of the Emperor* (Graham Salisbury)
		. . . I Never Saw Another Butterfly, ed. Hana Volavkova	*Hiroshima No Pika* (Toshi Maruki)
			The Man from the Other Side (Uri Orlev)
		"Inside" by Kim China, in *This Same Sky,* ed. Naomi Shihab Nye	*Number the Stars* (Lois Lowry)
			Rose Blanche (Christophe Gallaz and Roberto Innocenti)
		"War" by Dan Roth, in *Sing a Song of Popcorn,* ed. Beatrice Schenk de Regniers et al.	*The Wall* (Eve Bunting)
			Year of Impossible Goodbyes (Sook Nyul Choi)

People begins with "The First Americans" and takes us to the edge of the twenty-first century in "Imagine." In each poem Katz speaks through the voice of a person, real or imagined, who experienced important events in American history. In *Heroes and She-roes* J. Patrick Lewis pays tribute to men and women from around the world, some who are well known and others who may have gone unnamed.

Several volumes pair poetry and art in unique ways. Jan Greenberg, who with Sandra Jordan has written many books about twentieth-century art, invited forty-two poets to choose a work of twentieth-century art and write a poem about it. The result, *Heart to Heart,* is a de-light and a revelation. Greenberg thoughtfully divides the poems into four groups: Stories, Voices, Impressions, and Expressions. This helps readers understand that there are many ways to look at art and many more ways to respond to it. Some poets tell stories about a work, some speak from inside the work, others respond to the elements of the work, and still others reflect on the essence of the art. The poems, Greenberg's cogent introduction, the vivid reproductions of art, and the exquisite book design contribute to an enlightening experience with the art of word and image. In *Talking to the Sun* by Kenneth Koch and Kate Farrell and *Celebrate America* by Nora Panzer the editors have matched paintings with poems. Koch and Farrell found classic and little-known poems for many of the paintings in the various galleries of the Metropolitan Museum. Panzer's volume includes works and images that represent the many cultures in American life, both past and present. These are books that middle graders would enjoy looking at and reading over and over again. In addition, books like these might inspire children to make their own connections between art and poetry.

Children will also be delighted with excellent poetry books on sports, such as Robert Burleigh's *Goal* and *Hoops*, Lee Bennett Hopkins's *Extra Innings*, and *American Sports Poems* selected by R. R. Knudson and May Swenson. All areas of the curriculum can be enhanced with poetry; teachers should realize that there are poems on every subject, from dinosaurs to quasars and black holes. The Literature in Action box "Studying Poetry and Nature" shows how one teacher found connections between poetry and the natural world.

Reading Poetry to Children

Poetry should be read in a natural voice with a tone that fits the meaning of the poem. Generally, the appropriate pace for reading poetry is slower than for reading prose. It is usually recommended that a poem be read aloud a second time, perhaps to refresh children's memories, to clarify a point, or to savor a particular image. Most poetry, especially good poetry, is so concentrated and compact that few people can grasp its meaning in one exposure. Following the reading of a poem, discussion should be allowed to flow. In certain instances, discussion is unnecessary or superfluous. Spontaneous chuckles might follow the reading of Kaye Starbird's "Eat-It-All Elaine" (in *The Random House Book of Poetry for Children*, ed. Jack Prelutsky), while a thoughtful silence might be the response to Robert P. Tristram Coffin's "Forgive My Guilt" (in *Reflections on a Gift of Watermelon Pickle*, ed. Stephen Dunning et al.). It is not necessary to discuss or do something with each poem read, other than enjoy it. The most important thing you as a teacher or librarian

LITERATURE IN **ACTION**

Studying Poetry and Nature

Linda Woolard combines poetry and nature study with her fifth-grade class on their visits to the school's William E. Miller Land Lab in Newark, Ohio. The students explore the land lab's trails on a wooded hillside by the school. Each student has selected a favorite spot and returns there each season. They usually spend the first ten minutes in silence to better use all their senses. They observe the woods carefully, sketching and recording their observations. They may list their sightings using books to identify wildflowers, rocks, animals, or other special finds. Linda encourages them to record their thoughts and feelings also.

Before they visit the wooded area, Linda reads to them from books and poems, such as Jean George's *My Side of the Mountain*, Jim Arnosky's books on sketching nature in different seasons, John Moffitt's poem "To Look at Anything" (in *Reflections on a Gift of Watermelon Pickle*, ed. Stephen Dunning et al.), Marcie Han's "Fueled" (in the same anthology), Lew Sarrett's "Four Little Foxes" (in *Piping Down the Valleys Wild*, ed. Nancy Larrick), and many more.

The children bring back their notebooks; nature specimens, such as interesting fossils, leaf rubbings, and sketches; lists of bird sightings and wildflowers; and so on. These are placed on a special bulletin board. Poems are reread, reference books consulted, and pictures mounted. Many of the careful observations now become part of poems. Two that came from these trips follow:

The Woods Are So Still
Still
Still

The woods are very
Still;
Water dripping, dripping
Off the trees.
Nothing moves
It all stays very
Still.
　—*Katie Hopkins*

Eagle
Soaring high
　Soaring low
From mountain to hill
　And back
Wind whispering under his
magnificent wings
　gently falling
climbing
　falling
　　climbing
　　then he lands.
—*Brian Dove*

Linda writes poetry at the same time as her students do, and she is brave enough to ask them to make suggestions on how she can improve! Obviously, this is another classroom where a love of poetry is nurtured by much sharing of poetry, relating it to children's experiences, and modeling the joy of writing it by the teacher herself.

Linda Woolard, teacher
Miller Elementary School, Newark, Ohio

can do when you are reading poetry is share your enthusiasm for the poem.

Discussing Poetry with Children

After teachers or librarians have shared a poem with children, they may want to link it to other poems children have read, comparing and contrasting how the poet dealt with the concept. This could open up natural avenues for thoughtful discussion. Suppose a second-grade teacher reads the picture book *The Accident* by Carol Carrick and Donald Carrick to children. She or he may want to follow that book with Sarah Henderson Hay's "For a Dead Kitten" (in *Reflections on a Gift of Watermelon Pickle*, ed. Stephen Dunning et al.) or Myra Cohn Livingston's "For a Bird" (in *Poem Stew*, ed. William Cole). Children could then compare how those in the poems felt about the cat and the little bird. Were they as hurt by their loss as Christopher was when Bodger was struck by a truck? How much detail can an author and artist give? How much can a poet give? With many such discussions, children will eventually see how poetry has to capture the essence of a feeling in very few words and how important each of the words must be. Starting then with the content (children will want to tell of their experiences of losing pets—and they should have a chance to link these real-life experiences with literature), the teacher can gradually move into a discussion of the difference between prose and poetry. Discussion should center on meaning and feelings first. Only after providing much exposure to poetry does a teacher move into the various ways a poet can create meaning.

Children might help each other find meaning in a poem by meeting in small discussion groups, or the teacher might lead a whole-class discussion. In the following class discussion, the teacher had read aloud this short poem by Nikki Giovanni:

> Daddy says the world
> Is a drum
> Tight and hard
> And I told him
> I'm gonna beat out my own rhythm.
>
> —Nikki Giovanni. "The Drum," from *Spin a Soft Black Song*, rev. ed. by Nikki Giovanni. Copyright © 1971, 1985 by Nikki Giovanni. Reprinted by permission of Farrar, Straus and Giroux, LLC.

This fifth- and sixth-grade group of children had heard and discussed many poems, so they were eager to talk about the meaning of this one with their teacher, Sheryl, and offered the following opinions in answer to her question "What do you think about this poem?"

"Well, when Mike said about when the father was telling what the world was going to be like—he said the world is a tight drum. He said it is, not it will be," Aaron answered, seemingly intent on examining each word carefully so he understood the poet's message.

"Yes," agreed Sheryl. "Why did the father say the world is a drum, tight and hard? Why did he say it *is* instead of it *will be*?"

"Because it is right now," answered many voices.

"Because he is the one that has to pay all the taxes and make a living," said Stacie.

"Why does the father know that and the girl doesn't?" Sheryl asked again, intent on helping them delve as far into the poem as they could.

Many voices again responded: "Because he's out in the world." "He knows about life." "He's lived longer." And similar comments were offered. . . .

Carrie had an interesting observation. "This reminds me of that poem by . . . I forget . . . the one you read yesterday to us about the crystal stairs." She was referring to Langston Hughes's moving poem "Mother to Son," in which a black mother gives advice to her child about not giving up in the face of adversity. "The part . . . when he said the part about the drum, is tight," she continued, "that's the part that reminded me of the [Hughes] poem because it talks about nails and spots without any boards and no carpet. That sounded the same."

"That is an interesting connection because Langston Hughes and Nikki Giovanni could well have had similar experiences growing up," answered Sheryl. "Do people who heard 'Mother to Son' see any relationship between these poems?"

Jennifer had an idea. "They're both talking about how life is or was. Like the mother was talking about how hard hers was and the dad—he is talking about how hard his life was."

"It also seems like they're alive and it could happen," added Aaron.

"Like my dad," said Deon. "My mom and dad . . . he always says things like you can't get your own way—just like that poem."

"All right," responded Sheryl.

"I think that in both poems—that this one and the one we're comparing it to—that they're warning their children of what life will be and they should be ready for it," said Jennifer.

"And in 'The Drum,' how is the child responding to that?" Sheryl asked the group.

"She's gonna beat her own rhythm," answered Stacie and Deon together.

"Is it okay to do that?" Sheryl wanted to know. Many children shook their heads no. "If you didn't, what would you be like?"

"Boring," said Stacie, wrinkling up her nose in distaste.

A class poetry book includes third graders' poems that are expressed in both visual and verbal form. Greensview School, Upper Arlington Public Schools, Upper Arlington, Ohio. Susan Lee, teacher.

"You would be the same as everybody else," added Mike.

"Or at least the same as what?" asked Sheryl. "Do you think the father was telling her she *had* to live her life in a certain way?"

Her question was greeted by a strong chorus of "No."

"She chose to live that way," added Angela.

"But he is trying to warn her what life is going to be like. Nevertheless she is going to try—just like the mother in Langston Hughes's poem, she is going to climb her stairs," said Sheryl.[14]

Not only did the children understand the meaning of this poem, they connected it with their own lives and with another poem. Notice that the teacher did not tell them the meaning of the poem but let them discover the meaning for themselves. In the total discussion, she re-read the poem twice. By comparing this poem with the Langston Hughes poem "Mother to Son" (in his *The Dream Keeper*), the children extended their understanding of both poems. They also considered the idea of creating their own individual lives—beating their own rhythms.

Children Writing Poetry

Children need to hear much poetry and discuss it before attempting to write it themselves. Teachers can invite children to write poetry by providing them with poetry models and by developing a workshop approach to writing that helps children to understand that writing poetry takes time and effort.

Using Models from Literature

Children's early efforts at writing poetry are usually based on the false notion that all poetry must rhyme. Acting on this assumption, beginning efforts might be rhyme-driven and devoid of meaning. A third-grade teacher, in an effort to avoid the rhyming trap, read her children *Silver Seeds,* Paul Paolilli and Dan Brewer's book of acrostic poetry, and Joyce Sidman's "Aquatic Fashion" (in *Song of the Water Boatman*), which is shaped like the caddis fly it describes. One child created an acrostic "Winter Is" and another one did a shaped poem about a mouse. These were then included in a bound book of class poems for all to read. The mouse poem showed the

Talking Point

How do you feel about poetry?

Have your own experiences with poetry been positive or negative? Do you read poetry for your own pleasure?

Go to the Online Learning Center at **www.mhhe .com/kiefer9e** or your Resources CD-ROM to learn more.

---

[14]Amy A. McClure, Peggy Harrison, and Sheryl Reed, *Sunrises and Songs: Reading and Writing Poetry in an Elementary Classroom* (Portsmouth, N.H.: Heinemann Educational Books, 1990), pp. 61–62.

Aquatic Fashion

Smart
young
caddis worms
select only
the best to
dress them-
selves: strong
sticky silk,
pin-point
pebbles,
snips of
leaves, or
the tiny
whorled
eyelets of
snail shells,
edged in
sand. Who
cares if
each sleek
suit measures
less than
an inch?
First prize
gets
wings.

Poems from books such as *Song of the Water Boatman* by Joyce Sidman can serve as models for writing or springboards for curriculum studies. From *Song of the Water Boatman and Other Pond Poems* by Joyce Sidman, illustrated by Beckie Prange. Illustrations copyright © 2005 by Beckie Prange. Reprinted by permission of Houghton Mifflin Company. All rights reserved.

influence of hearing Mary O'Neill's well-loved poems about color in *Hailstones and Halibut Bones.* The first time children try to write their own takeoffs on these poems, they are apt to make a kind of grocery list of all the objects that are a particular color. By returning to the book they can begin to appreciate the craft of the poems, realizing that all lines do not begin in the same way. They see that the poems contain objects that are that color but also describe the way the color made the poet feel, smell, and taste. One sixth grader made several revisions of her poem before she was satisfied with it:

> My Red Mood
>
> Red is the heat from a hot blazing fire,
> A soft furry sweater awaiting a buyer.
> Red is the sweet smell of roses in the spring,
> Red are my cheeks that the winter winds sting.
> Red is a feeling that rings deep inside
> When I get angry and want to hide.
> Red is a sunset waving good-bye.
> Red is the sunrise shouting "Surprise!"
>
> —Treeva. Ridgemont Elementary School, Mt. Victory, Ohio. Sheryl Reed, Peggy Harrison, teachers.

Looking at the way other poets have described color can extend children's thinking. Examples are Christina Rossetti's well-known poem "What Is Pink?" (in *The Random House Book of Poetry for Children,* ed. Jack Prelutsky) or David McCord's "Yellow" (in his *One at a Time*).

Different forms of poetry can offer poetic structures to children and serve as models for creative poetry writing. We have seen how shaped poetry can get children started. Concrete poetry is another gateway. Using J. Patrick Lewis's *Doodle Dandies* or Joan Graham's *Splish, Splash,* children could try creating their own concrete poems. Again the emphasis should be on the meaning of the poem first, then its shape.

Poetry Workshop

Using models can be a way to get children started in writing poetry. It provides the opportunity to "write like a poet," and the given structures usually help the child produce an acceptable poem. This approach does not help a child *think* like a poet. That will happen only after much sustained writing and many revisions.

In a small rural school in Ohio, two teachers, Sheryl Reed and Peggy Harrison, began a year-long poetry program with their combined group of fifth and sixth graders. Amy McClure spent a year studying this poetry program and then writing an ethnographic research report on it.[15] Still later this study was rewritten into a fine book for teachers on how to include poetry in the classroom.[16]

These teachers begin their poetry workshop with reading poetry aloud several times a day. The classroom collection of over two hundred poetry books is extensive. Children read poetry for ten or fifteen minutes a day and keep poetry journals in which they write every day. They do not have to produce a poem a day—they

---

[15]Amy A. McClure, "Children's Responses to Poetry in a Supportive Literary Context" (Ph.D. dissertation, Ohio State University, Columbus, 1984).

[16]McClure, Harrison, and Reed, *Sunrises and Songs.*

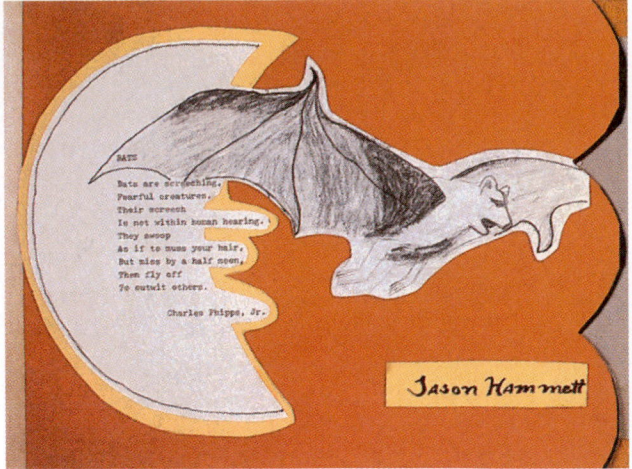

Two sixth graders worked together to create this book of poems titled *Bats and Owls*. Charles Phipps, Jr., created the poetry while his friend Jason Hammett drew the illustrations. Notice how the pages are scalloped like the wings of owls.

can list possibilities, revise a poem they have been working on, or invite one of their friends to critique a poem. Frequently, they illustrate one of their best poems, or they make anthologies of their own poetry or create personal anthologies of their favorite poems from various books. This requires that the child read a wide variety of poetry and then decide on the organizing feature. Is it to be a book of animal poems or, as one child titled his, "deep feeling poems"?

One student wrote over four hundred poems in the two years he was in this class. He created an anthology with all the poems he had written about bats and owls, an interest that developed from his teacher's reading of Randall Jarrell's story of *The Bat-Poet*. He then asked one of his friends in the class who was known for his artistic ability to illustrate it with detailed black-and-white pencil drawings. These pictures were mounted on black, tan, and gray pages cut with scalloped edges to imitate the shape of an owl's wing. Their finished book reflected the subject as well as the carefully crafted poems. Here is one of the poems from their book:

A Bat

A bat
Feeds lavishly
On moths
And beetles
Flies loops
And twirls
Catches bugs
From behind
When the sun

Rises faintly
The bat
Retires to rest

> —Charles Phipps, Jr., Ridgemont Elementary School, Mt. Victory, Ohio. Sheryl Reed, Peggy Harrison, teachers.

In New York City, Georgia Heard, a published poet herself, also encourages children to write what they know and what they feel when she conducts poetry workshops with all age groups. In conferring with children, she frequently asks them to close their eyes and visualize their topic. Jason had written a first draft of a poem about cats:

Cats are cats
Cats are great
Cats can't be beat

After reading Jason's poem, Georgia Heard wrote:

> The old me wants to evaluate Jason's poem. The researcher, the curious me, notices what Jason knows about poetry. There's some rhythm in his poem, repetition, and a little rhyme; it sounds like a chant or a cheer. He definitely knows the difference between a poem and a story. I tell him what I notice about his poem, but I also want to know why he chose cats as his subject.[17]

When she discovered that Jason owned a cat, Heard asked him to close his eyes again and visualize his cat. Slowly, he told her what he saw. She repeated his words back to him, and Jason wrote his poem again:

---

[17]Georgia Heard, *For the Good of the Earth and Sun: Teaching Poetry* (Portsmouth, N.H.: Heinemann Educational Books, 1989), pp. 40–41.

My Cat

My cat is black and white
I pretend he is my son
I love him.
His feet smell like popcorn.[18]

At another time, this child might want to play with the order of his lines. However, because he is just beginning to write poems, Georgia Heard wisely let his second draft stand. He has specifically described *his* cat and how he feels about him in this poem, a far cry from his first generic poem about all cats.

Children's poems do not have to be perfect. One of the reasons for having them write poetry is to increase their enjoyment of poetry; it is not necessary to produce poets. In critiquing children's poems, it is important to evaluate improvement. In Georgia Heard's evaluation conferences, she asks students to bring all of their poems to her, and then they spread them out on the floor. Here are some of the questions she offers as guidelines:

What things do you usually write about?

What kind of poems do you tend to write? Rhyming poems, long, short, narrative, lyric?

What kind of lines do you usually work with? Long or short?

What are you really good at? Titles, images, interesting words, repetition, rhyme?

What are you not so good at? How would you like to improve?

Do you revise? How do you do it? Do you change or add a word or overhaul the whole poem?

What is the hardest part of writing a poem for you? Where do you get stuck?

Are there any new things you'd like to learn?[19]

This process enables the child, rather than the teacher, to be the evaluator. It is a learning process for both of them, however. Children who hear poetry every day, who read poetry every day, and who write it every day develop a deep love for poetry. Writing honest poems that reflect their own thoughts and feelings helps children develop a real appreciation for poetry.

Choral Reading

The reading and sharing of poetry through choral speaking is another way to foster interest in poetry. Choral speaking or reading is the interpretation of poetry by several voices speaking as one. At first, young children *speak* it as they join in the refrains. Middle-grade children might prefer to *read* their poems. They are not always read in unison; in fact, this is one of the most difficult ways to present a poem.

Several types of choral speaking are particularly suited for use in the elementary school. In the "refrain" type, one person (teacher or child) reads the narrative and the rest of the class joins in on the refrain. The teacher might use the well-known folk poem that begins "In a dark, dark wood there was a dark dark house" and let children join in on the "dark darks." Eve Merriam's "Windshield Wiper" (in *Knock at a Star,* ed. X. Kennedy and D. Kennedy) and Sara Holbrook's "Copycat" (in *Wham! It's a Poetry Jam*) are good echo poems to try.

Another way to do a group reading, called antiphonal, is to divide the class into two groups and let the groups take turns reading each verse. An effective approach with young children is the "line-a-child" arrangement, where different children say, or read, individual lines, with the class joining in in unison at the beginning or end of the poem. "One, Two, Buckle My Shoe" is a good rhyme to introduce this type of choral reading. The dialogue of David McCord's "At the Garden Gate" (in his *One at a Time*) lends itself to this approach for children in the middle grades. A more difficult and formal version of this method is part speaking. Groups are divided according to the sound of their voices into high, middle, and low parts. The poem is then interpreted much as a song might be sung in parts. This is usually done with mature groups and is the method utilized by verse-speaking choirs. Another difficult method is to have children say the whole poem in unison, giving just one interpretation.

Many variations to these approaches will be used by creative teachers and children. A certain sound that complements both the rhythm and the meaning of the poem may be an accompaniment, such as "clickety clack" for David McCord's "Song of the Train" (see p. 413). One group might repeat this phrase as another group says the words of the poem.

Children could also plan how to read Jack Prelutsky's "The Grobbles" (in his *The Snopp on the Sidewalk*). One child can be the innocent soul walking through the woods, while others can each give a line describing the grobbles. Then the poem can grow with scary intensity as the person walks closer to the grobbles:

The grobbles are gruesome	(Child 1)
The grobbles are green	(Child 2)
The grobbles are nasty	(Child 3)
The grobbles are mean	(All)
The grobbles hide deep	(Child 4)
in a hollowy tree	
just waiting to gobble	(All)
whomever they see	

---

[18]Ibid., p. 41.

[19]Ibid., p. 53.

I walk through the woods   (Solo)
for I'm quite unaware
that the grobbles are waiting
to gobble me there
they suddenly spring   (Children 1–4)
from their hollowy tree
Oh goodness! the grobbles   (Solo)
are gobbling m . . .

> —Jack Prelutsky. "The Grobbles," from *The Snopp
> on the Sidewalk* by Jack Prelutsky. Text copyright
> © 1977 by Jack Prelutsky. Used by permission of
> HarperCollins Publishers.

This interpretation of how to read "The Grobbles" is only one of many that could be developed. After you have worked with children in choral reading, they will suggest different ways to interpret poems. Try these out and see which ones are the most pleasing to the ear and the most appropriate for the meaning of the poem. More serious poetry can also be read effectively by a group.

Several books come ready-made for multiple-voice readings. Younger children can get started on this technique with David Harrison's *Farmer's Dog Goes to the Forest: Rhymes for Two Voices*. Older children particularly enjoy practicing reading Paul Fleischman's poems for multiple voices found in his Newbery Medal book *Joyful Noise* and in his *I Am Phoenix*. All of the poems in *Joyful Noise* are about insects. In *I Am Phoenix* all of the poems are about birds. With two columns of words placed side by side, sometimes each reader reads alone, and at other times the readers are reading in unison or sometimes in opposition. The result is a wonderful image of each bird or insect that results as much from the sound of the reading as from the meaning of the words. In *Big Talk*, illustrated by Beppe Giacobbe, Fleischman provides four voices. The three long poems "The Quiet Evenings Here," "Seventh Grade Soap Opera," and "Ghost's Grace" are presented in horizontal bands of four different colors. An introduction provides helpful hints for reading aloud.

The values of children reading poetry together are many. They derive enjoyment from learning to respond as a group to the rhythm and melody of the poem. They learn much about the interpretation of poetry as they help plan various ways to read the poem. Shy children forget their fears when participating with the group, and all children learn to develop cooperation as they work together with a leader to present a poem. It is necessary to remember that the process of choral reading is much more important than the final product. Teachers must work for the enjoyment of poetry, not perfection of performance. Too frequently choral reading becomes a "stunt" or a quick way to entertain a PTA group. If teachers and children are pressured into a "production," interpretation of poetry will be exploited for unnatural ends.

Boys and girls should have many opportunities to share poetry in interesting and meaningful situations, if they are to develop appreciation for the deep satisfactions that poetry brings. Appreciation for poetry develops slowly. It is the result of long and loving experience with poetry over a period of years. Children who are fortunate enough to have developed a love of poetry will always be the richer for it.

INTO THE CLASSROOM

Poetry

We have found that many teachers find the teaching of poetry very threatening. Perhaps they have had bad experiences with poetry in their own school experience, or perhaps they feel that they have to be experts in poetry forms and analysis. In this chapter we have tried to stress the joys of poetry for children. We have included examples of poems that we love and shown how willingly children respond when teachers share poetry every day. The more poetry you read to children and the more types of poetry you read to children, the more rewarding you will find it. Along with the activities listed throughout the chapter, the activities below will help you begin to experience the delights of poetry for children.

1. **Reading and Responses.** Select three different kinds of poems and read them to a group of children. Record their responses. What poems had the greatest appeal? Why?
2. **Poetry Images and Developmental Stages.** Select one or two poems that contain figurative language. Share them with children at different developmental stages. When do children appear to understand the metaphors being used? One way to link into their understanding is to ask them to draw a picture of the images they see.
3. **Choral Presentation.** Work with a group of children or classmates in planning ways to present one

of several poems chorally. If possible, tape-record these interpretations.

4. **Poetry Self-Portrait.** Draw an outline of each child on a large piece of chart paper. Have the children find poems that they respond to in a personal way. Each child can then write or paste the poems inside their outline, creating a poetry self-portrait. A poem about food might be placed on the stomach, a sad or happy poem on the heart.
5. **Poetry Spiral.** Have one child choose a favorite poem and share it with a classmate. That child can choose a word or image from the poem and find another poem on that topic. Other children continue the connection, creating a poetry spiral.

 Go to the Online Learning Center at **www.mhhe.com/kiefer9e** or your Resources CD-ROM to find these additional classroom activities:

6. **Composing Music**
7. **Experimenting with Poetry**
8. **Reader's Theater Poetry**
9. **Publishing Poetry on the Web**
10. **Art as Inspiration for Poetry**
11. **Poetry Response as a Quick Write**

Chapter Review

 Go to the Online Learning Center at **www.mhhe.com/kiefer9e** or your Resources CD-ROM to take chapter quizzes, practice with key terms, and review the chapter.

Explorations

1. Begin a poetry collection for future use with children. Make your own filing system. What categories will you include? Indicate possible uses for some poems, possible connections with prose, ways to interpret poems.

2. Make a study of one poet. How would you characterize that poet's work in style and usual content? What can you find out about her or his background? How are these experiences reflected in the poetry?

3. Make a cycle of poems about one particular subject—for example, friends, secret places, the city, loneliness. Share these with the class.

4. Bring your favorite children's poem to present to the class or to tape-record. Invite class members to comment on both your selection and your presentation.

5. Find a poem to go with a passage in a book or with your favorite picture book.

6. Make a survey of the teachers in an elementary school to see how often they read poetry to their students, what their favorite poems are, what their favorite sources for poetry are. Make a visual presentation of your results.

7. Listen to some recordings of poetry read by authors and by interpreters. Contrast the presentations and appropriateness of the records for classroom use. Share these with children. Which ones do they prefer?

8. Try writing some poetry yourself. You may want to use some experimental verse forms, such as concrete poetry or found poetry.

9. Search the database using the term "poetry." Browse through the topics column of the entries you find and pick a topic like "school" or "animals." Make a list of titles you could use in a classroom text set.

Web Links

 Go to the Online Learning Center at **www.mhhe.com/kiefer9e** to find links to the following children's literature Web sites:

The Academy of American Poets

A Child's Garden of Verses

Edsitement Poetry Lesson Plans

Favorite Poem Project

Glossary of Poetic Terms

A Glossary of Rhetorical Terms with Examples

The Internet School Library Media Page for Children's Poetry

Kristine O'Connell George Children's Author

Mary Ann Hoberman

NCTE Award for Poetry

Nikki Giovanni

Ongoing Tales: Electronic Poetry for Children of All Ages

The Poetry Zone

Young People's Poetry Week

Related Readings

Chatton, Barbara. *Using Poetry across the Curriculum: A Whole Language Approach.* Phoenix: Oryx Press, 1993.

An indispensable classroom resource for any classroom teacher, this book will enable teachers to immerse children in poetry throughout the school day. Chapters include suggestions for making connections to all the content areas, including science, mathematics, and social studies. Also included are thematic units that are filled with poems, multicultural resources, and ideas for sharing poetry with children.

Chukovsky, Kornei. *From Two to Five.* Translated and edited by Miriam Morton. Berkeley: University of California Press, 1963.

> This is a classic review of the young child's delight in poetry. Written by a well-known Russian poet, it emphasizes that poetry is the natural language of little children.

Cullinan, Beatrice, Marilyn C. Scala, and Virginia C. Schroeder. *Three Voices: An Invitation to Poetry across the Curriculum.* York, Maine: Stenhouse, 1995.

> This practical book includes thirty-three detailed strategies for using poetry with children and provides three hundred additional brief suggestions. Teachers describe the classroom poetry activities in which their children were involved and include examples of student work.

Fletcher, Ralph. *Poetry Matters: Writing a Poem from the Inside Out.* New York: HarperCollins, 2002.

> Although this inviting book is written for children, it provides teachers with a nonthreatening guide to teaching poetry. The book is divided into two sections, "Lighting the Spark" and "Nurturing the Flame," and is written with a wry sense of humor and fun. The book is about reading poetry as well as writing it and includes interviews with poets and an annotated bibliography.

Heard, Georgia. *Awakening the Heart: Exploring Poetry in the Elementary and Middle School.* Portsmouth, N.H.: Heinemann Educational Books, 1999.

> A published poet provides marvelous ideas for engaging children with poetry. She shares ideas for introducing poetry to children and setting up poetry centers. Chapters also offer help for reading, writing, and discussing poetry.

Heard, Georgia. *For the Good of the Earth and Sun: Teaching Poetry.* Portsmouth, N.H.: Heinemann Educational Books, 1989.

> Heard describes her methods of teaching elementary children in New York City schools to enjoy poetry, to read poetry, and to write poetry. She describes the many poetry workshops she does with children from kindergarten through sixth grade. Filled with practical suggestions, this book offers the reader help and inspiration for ways to teach poetry to children.

Holbrook, Sara. *Practical Poetry: A Nonstandard Approach to Meeting Content Area Standards.* Portsmouth, N.H.: Heinemann Educational Books, 2005.

> In the introduction and rationale, poet and teacher Holbrook provides a compelling argument for immersing middle-school students in poetry. Then, in subsequent chapters she demonstrates how children's experiences with poetry meet the language arts, math, science, and social studies standards and benchmarks. The book includes detailed activities, examples of children's writing, and solid connections to standards. Holbrook also provides criteria for identifying children's poetry that reflects quality in both thinking and writing.

Hopkins, Lee Bennett. *Pass the Poetry, Please.* Rev. ed. New York: Harper & Row, 1998.

> This revised edition of a well-known book presents a wealth of ideas for making poetry come alive in the classroom. It contains suggestions for sparking children's interest in writing poetry. It also includes interviews with more than twenty contemporary poets.

Janeczko, Paul. *How to Write Poetry.* Scholastic, 1999.

———. *Poetry from A to Z: A Guide for Young Writers.* Bradbury Press, 1994.

> Both books are aimed at an audience of children and young adults, but teachers will enjoy them as resources. The first book addresses the finding of ideas, starting to write, and writing both rhyming poetry and free verse. In the second book Janeczko includes seventy-two poems that can serve as models and fourteen poetry-writing exercises that invite children to poetry in engaging, nonthreatening ways. The A-to-Z format is meant to show children that they can write poetry about anything. The exercises include patterns such as acrostics and haiku and themes such as prayer poems, memory poems, and opposites.

Livingston, Myra Cohn. *Poem-Making: Ways to Begin Writing Poetry.* New York: HarperCollins, 1991.

> Livingston provides positive help for middle-grade students or teachers who want to learn more about the form and elements of poem making. She clearly presents the process of writing poetry and gives many poems as examples. Teachers will find this a very useful book.

Children's Literature

 Go to the Children's Literature Database on your Resources CD-ROM for a searchable listing of these and other children's literature titles.

Poetry

Ackerman, Diane. *Animal Sense.* Illustrated by Peter Sis. Knopf, 2003.

Adoff, Arnold. *All the Colors of the Race.* Illustrated by John Steptoe. Lothrop, 1982.

———. *The Basket Counts.* Illustrated by Michael Weaver. Simon, 2000.

———. *Black Is Brown Is Tan.* Illustrated by Emily McCully. HarperCollins, 2002.

———. *Eats: Poems.* Illustrated by Susan Russo. Lothrop, 1979.

———, ed. *I Am the Darker Brother: An Anthology of Modern Poems by Black Americans.* Macmillan, 1970.

———. *In for Winter, Out for Spring.* Illustrated by Jerry Pinkney. Harcourt, 1991.

Adoff, Arnold. *Love Letters.* Illustrated by Lisa Desimini. Blue Sky, 1997.

———, ed. *My Black Me: A Beginning Book of Black Poetry.* Dutton, 1994 [1974].

———. *Street Music: City Poems.* Illustrated by Karen Barbour. HarperCollins, 1995.

Adoff, Jamie. *Song Shoots out of My Mouth: A Celebration of Music.* Illustrated by Martin French. Dutton, 2002.

Agard, John, and Grace Nichols, eds. *Under the Moon and Over the Sea: A Collection of Caribbean Poems.* Illustrated by Christopher Coor, Sara Fanelli, Cathie Felstead, Satoshi Kitamura, and Jane Ray. Candlewick, 2003.

Alarcón, Francisco X. *Angels Ride Bikes: And Other Fall Poems/ Los Angeles Andan En Cicicleta: Y Otros Poemas de Otono.* Children's, 2005.

———. *From the Bellybutton of the Moon and Other Summer Poems.* Illustrated by Maya Christina Gonzalez. Children's, 1998.

———. *Iguanas in the Snow and Other Winter Poems.* Illustrated by Maya Christina Gonzalez. Children's, 2001.

———. *Laughing Tomatoes: And Other Spring Poems/Jitomates Risueños: Y Otros Poemas de Primavera.* Children's, 2005.

———. *Poems to Dream Together/Poems Para Soñar Juntos.* Illustrated by Paula Barragán. Lee, 2005.

Argueta, Jorge. *A Movie in My Pillow/Una película en mi almohada.* Illustrated by Elizabeth Gómez. Children's, 2001.

———. *Trees Are Hanging from the Sky.* Illustrated by Rafael Yocktang. Groundwood, 2003.

Attenborough, Liz, comp. *Poetry by Heart: A Child's Book of Poems to Remember.* Scholastic, 2002.

Baylor, Byrd. *Everybody Needs a Rock.* Illustrated by Peter Parnall. Scribner's, 1974.

———. *I'm in Charge of Celebrations.* Illustrated by Peter Parnall. Scribner's, 1986.

———. *The Other Way to Listen.* Illustrated by Peter Parnall. Scribner's, 1978.

———. *Your Own Best Secret Place.* Illustrated by Peter Parnall. Scribner's, 1979.

Bernos de Gasztold, Carmen. *Prayers from the Ark.* Translated by Rumer Godden. Illustrated by Barry Moser. Viking, 1992.

Berry, James. *Everywhere Faces Everywhere.* Illustrated by Reynold Ruffins. Simon, 1997.

———. *A Nest Full of Stars.* Illustrated by Ashley Bryan. Greenwillow, 2004.

Bierhorst, John, ed. *In the Trail of the Wind: American Indian Poems and Ritual Orations.* Farrar, 1971.

———, ed. *On the Road of Stars: Native American Night Poems and Sleep Charms.* Illustrated by Judy Pedersen. Macmillan, 1994.

Blishen, Edward, ed. *The Oxford Book of Poetry for Children.* Illustrated by Brian Wildsmith. Bedrick, 1984 [1963].

Bolden, Tanya. *Rock of Ages.* Illustrated by R. Gregory Christie. Knopf, 2001.

Booth, David, ed. *Til All the Stars Have Fallen: Canadian Poems for Children.* Illustrated by Kady MacDonald Denton. Kids Can, 1989.

Brooks, Gwendolyn. *Bronzeville Boys and Girls.* Illustrated by Ronni Solbert. Harper, 1965.

Browning, Robert. *The Pied Piper of Hamelin.* Illustrated by Kate Greenaway. Random, 1993 [1889].

Bryan, Ashley, ed. *Ashley Bryan's ABC of African American Poetry.* Atheneum, 1997.

———. *Sing to the Sun.* HarperCollins, 1992.

Burg, Brad. *Outside the Lines: Poetry at Play.* Illustrated by Rebecca Gibbon. Putnam, 2002.

Burleigh, Robert. *Goal.* Illustrated by Stephen T. Johnson. Silver Whistle, 2001.

———. *Hoops.* Illustrated by Stephen T. Johnson. Silver Whistle, 1997.

Carlson, Lori M., ed. *Cool Salsa: Bilingual Poems on Growing Up Latino in the United States.* Holt, 1994.

———, ed. *Red Hot Salsa: Bilingual Poems on Being Young and Latino in the United States.* Holt, 2005.

———, ed. *Sol a Sol.* Illustrated by Emily Lisker. Holt, 1998.

Chambers, Veronica. *Double Dutch. A Celebration of Jump Rope, Rhyme, and Sisterhood.* Jump at the Sun/Hyperion, 2002.

Chandra, Deborah. *Balloons and Other Poems.* Illustrated by Leslie Bowman. Farrar, 1990.

———. "Fog." In *Balloons and Other Poems.* Illustrated by Leslie Bowman. Farrar, 1990.

———. "Shell." In *Balloons and Other Poems.* Illustrated by Leslie Bowman. Farrar, 1990.

Chute, Marchette. "Wrong Start." In *The Random House Book of Poetry for Children.* Edited by Jack Prelutsky. Illustrated by Arnold Lobel. Random, 1983.

Ciardi, John. *The Hopeful Trout and Other Limericks.* Illustrated by Susan Meddaugh. Houghton, 1992.

———. *The Reason for the Pelican.* Illustrated by Dominic Catalano. Boyds Mills, 1994.

Clark, Ann Nolan. *In My Mother's House.* Illustrated by Velino Herrera. Viking, 1991 [1941].

Clinton, Catherine. *I, Too, Sing America: Three Centuries of African American Poetry.* Illustrated by Stephen Alcorn. Houghton, 1998.

Cole, William, ed. *Poem Stew.* Illustrated by Karen Ann Weinhaus. Lippincott, 1981.

Creech, Sharon. *Heartbeat.* HarperCollins, 2004.

———. *Love That Dog.* HarperCollins, 2001.

Crossley-Holland, Kevin. *Once Upon a Poem: Favorite Poems That Tell Stories.* Chicken House/Scholastic, 2004.

Cullinan, Bernice E., ed. *I Heard a Bluebird Sing: Children Select Their Favorite Poems by Aileen Fisher.* Boyds Mills, 2002.

———, ed. *A Jar of Tiny Stars: Poems by NCTE Award-Winning Poets.* Boyds Mills, 1996.

Cyrus, Kurt. *Hotel Deep: Light Verse from Deep Water.* Harcourt, 2005.

dePaola, Tomie, ed. *Tomie dePaola's Book of Poems.* Putnam, 1988.

de Regniers, Beatrice Schenk, et al., eds. *Sing a Song of Popcorn.* Illustrated by nine Caldecott Medal artists. Scholastic, 1988.

Dotlich, Rebecca Kai. *Lemonade Sun: And Other Summer Poems.* Illustrated by Jan Spivey Gilchrist. Wordsong, 1998.

Dunbar, Paul Laurence. *Jump Back, Honey: The Poems of Paul Laurence Dunbar.* Hyperion, 1999.

Dunning, Stephen, Edward Lueders, and Hugh Smith. *Reflections on a Gift of Watermelon Pickle and Other Modern Verse.* Lothrop, 1966.

English, Karen. *Speak to Me (And I Will Listen between the Lines).* Illustrated by Amy June Bates. Farrar, 2004.

Feelings, Tom. *Soul Looks Back in Wonder.* Dial, 1993.

Ferris, Helen, ed. *Favorite Poems Old and New.* Illustrated by Leonard Weisgard. Doubleday, 1957.

Fisher, Aileen. *I Heard a Bluebird Sing: Children Select Their Favorite Poems by Aileen Fisher,* edited by Bernice E. Cullinan. Illustrated by Jennifer Emery. Wordsong/Boyds Mills, 2002.

———. *Know What I Saw?* Illustrated by Deborah Durland de Saix. Roaring Brook, 2006.

———. *The Story Goes On.* Illustrated by Mique Moriuchi. Roaring Brook, 2005.

Fleischman, Paul. *Big Talk: Poems for Four Voices.* Illustrated by Beppe Giacobbe. Candlewick, 2000.

———. *I Am Phoenix: Poems for Two Voices.* Illustrated by Ken Nutt. Harper, 1985.

———. *Joyful Noise: Poems for Two Voices.* Illustrated by Eric Beddows. Harper, 1988.

Fletcher, Ralph. *Have You Been to the Beach Lately?* Orchard, 2001.

———. *Ordinary Things: Poems from a Walk in Early Spring.* Illustrated by Walter Lyon Krudop. Atheneum, 1997.

———. *Relatively Speaking: Poems about Family.* Illustrated by Walter Lyon Krudop. Orchard, 1999.

———. *A Writing Kind of Day: Poems for Young Poets.* Boyds Mills, 2005.

Florian, Douglas. *Autumnblings.* Greenwillow, 2003.

———. *Beast Feast.* Harcourt, 1994.

———. *Bing Bang Bong.* Harcourt, 1994.

———. *Bowwow, Meow Meow.* Harcourt, 2003.

———. *Handsprings.* Greenwillow, 2006.

———. *Insectlopedia: Insect Poems and Paintings.* Harcourt, 1998.

———. *In the Swim: Poems and Paintings.* Harcourt, 1997.

———. *Laugh-eteria.* Harcourt, 1999.

———. *Lizards, Frogs and Polliwogs.* Harcourt, 2001.

———. *Mammalabilia.* Harcourt, 2000.

———. *On the Wing: Bird Poems and Paintings.* Harcourt, 1996.

———. *Summersaults.* Greenwillow, 2002.

———. *Winter Eyes.* Greenwillow, 1999.

———. *zoo's who.* Harcourt, 2005.

Frost, Robert. *Birches.* Illustrated by Ed Young. Holt, 1988.

———. *Stopping by Woods on a Snowy Evening.* Illustrated by Susan Jeffers. Dutton, 1978.

———. *You Come Too.* Illustrated by Thomas W. Nason. Holt, 1995 [1959].

George, Kristine O'Connell. *Fold Me a Poem.* Illustrated by Lauren String. Harcourt, 2005.

———. *The Great Frog Race and Other Poems.* Illustrated by Kate Kiesler. Clarion, 1997.

———. *Hummingbird Nest: A Journal of Poems.* Illustrated by Barry Moser, Harcourt, 2004.

———. *Little Dog and Duncan.* Illustrated by June Otani. Clarion, 2002.

———. *Little Dog Poems.* Illustrated by June Otani. Clarion, 1999.

———. *Old Elm Speaks: Tree Poems.* Illustrated by Kate Kiesler. Clarion, 1998.

———. *Swimming Upstream: Middle School Poems.* Illustrated by Debbie Tilley. Clarion, 2002.

———. *Toasting Marshmallows: Camping Poems.* Illustrated by Kate Kiesler. Clarion, 2001.

Giovanni, Nikki. *The Genie in the Jar.* Illustrated by Chris Raschka. Holt, 1996.

———. *Spin a Soft Black Song: Poems for Children.* Illustrated by George Martins. Hill & Wang, 1985 [1971].

———. *The Sun Is So Quiet.* Illustrated by Ashley Bryan. Holt, 1996.

Goldstein, Bobbye S. *Bear in Mind: A Book of Bear Poems.* Puffin, 1991.

———, ed. *Inner Chimes: Poems on Poetry.* Illustrated by Jane Breskin Zalben. Birdsong/Boyds Mills, 1992.

Gollub, Matthew. *Cool Melons Turn to Frogs: The Life and Poems of Issa.* Illustrated by Kazuko G. Stone. Lee, 1998.

Gordon, Ruth. *Pierced by a Ray of Sun: Poems about the Times We Feel Alone.* HarperCollins, 1995.

Gottfried, Maya. *Good Dog.* Illustrated by Robert Rahway Zakanitch. Knopf, 2005.

Graham, Joan Bransfield. *Flicker Flash.* Illustrated by Nancy Davis. Houghton, 1999.

———. *Splish, Splash.* Illustrated by Steve Scott. Ticknor & Fields, 1994.

Grandits, John. *Technically, It's Not My Fault: Concrete Poems.* Clarion, 2004.

Greenberg, David T. *Bugs!* Illustrated by Lynn Munsinger. Little, 1997.

———. *Octopi.* Illustrated by Lynn Munsinger. Little, 2003.

Greenberg, Jan, ed. *Heart to Heart: New Poems Inspired by Twentieth Century American Art.* Abrams, 2001.

Greenfield, Eloise. "Harriet Tubman." In *Honey I Love: And Other Poems.* Illustrated by Leo Dillon and Diane Dillon. Harper, 1978.

———. *Honey, I Love: And Other Poems.* Illustrated by Leo Dillon and Diane Dillon. Harper, 1978.

———. *In the Land of Words: New and Selected Poems.* Illustrated by Jan Spivey Gilchrist. Amistad, 2004.

———. *Nathaniel Talking.* Illustrated by Jan Spivey Gilchrist. Black Butterfly, 1988.

———. *Night on Neighborhood Street.* Illustrated by Jan Spivey Gilchrist. Dial, 1991.

———. *Under the Sunday Tree.* Illustrated by Amos Ferguson. Harper, 1988.

Grimes, Nikki. *Danitra Brown, Class Clown.* Illustrated by E. B. Lewis. HarperCollins, 2005.

———. *Dark Sons.* Hyperion, 2005.

———. *Danitra Brown Leaves Town*. Illustrated by Floyd Cooper. HarperCollins, 2001.

———. *A Dime a Dozen*. Illustrated by Angelo. Dial, 1998.

———. *Hopscotch Love: A Family Treasury of Love Poems*. Illustrated by Melodye Rosales. Lothrop, 1999.

———. *Is It Far to Zanzibar? Poems about Tanzania*. Illustrated by Betsy Lewin. HarperCollins, 2000.

———. *It's Raining Laughter*. Photographs by Myles C. Pinkney. Dial, 1997.

———. *Meet Danitra Brown*. Illustrated by Floyd Cooper. Lothrop, 1994.

———. *A Pocketful of Poems*. Illustrated by Javaka Steptoe. Clarion, 2001.

———. *Thanks a Million*. Illustrated by Cozbi Cabrera. Greenwillow, 2006.

———. *What Is Goodbye?* Hyperion, 2004.

Grossman, Bill. *Timothy Tunny Swallowed a Bunny*. Illustrated by Kevin Hawkes. HarperCollins, 2001.

Gunning, Monica. *America, My New Home*. Illustrated by Ken Condon. Wordsong/Boyds Mills, 2004.

———. *Not a Copper Penny in Me House: Poems from the Caribbean*. Illustrated by Frané Lessac. Wordsong, 1993.

Harrison, David L. *Farmer's Dog Goes to the Forest: Rhymes for Two Voices*. Wordsong/Boyds Mills, 2005.

Hayford, James. *Knee-Deep in Blazing Snow: Growing Up in Vermont*. Chosen by X. J. Kennedy and Dorothy M. Kennedy. Illustrated by Michael McCurdy. Wordsong/Boyds Mills, 2005.

Heard, Georgia. *This Place I Know: Poems of Comfort*. Illustrated by Peter Sis. Candlewick, 2002.

Herrera, Juan Felipe. *Downtown Boy*. Scholastic, 2005.

Hesse, Karen. *Out of the Dust*. Scholastic, 1997.

Hindley, Judy. *A Song of Colors*. Illustrated by Mike Bostock. Candlewick, 1998.

Hittleman, Carol G., and Daniel Hittleman. *A Grand Celebration: Grandparents in Poetry*. Illustrated by Kay Life. Wordsong/Boyds Mills, 2002.

Ho, Minfong. *Maples in the Mist: Children's Poems from the Tang Dynasty*. Illustrated by Jean Tseng and Mou-Sien Tseng. Lothrop, 1996.

Hoberman, Mary Ann. *A House Is a House for Me*. Illustrated by Betty Fraser. Penguin, 1982.

———. *The Llama Who Had No Pajama*. Illustrated by Betty Fraser. Harcourt, 1998.

Hoce, Charley. *Beyond Old MacDonald: Funny Poems from Down on the Farm*. Wordsong/Boyds Mills, 2005.

Holbrook, Sara. *Wham! It's a Poetry Jam: Discovering Performance Poetry*. Wordsong/Boyds Mills, 2002.

hooks, bell. *Happy to Be Nappy*. Illustrated by Chris Raschka. Hyperion, 1999.

Hopkins, Lee Bennett, ed. *Dinosaurs*. Illustrated by Murray Tinkelman. Harcourt, 1987.

———, ed. *Extra Innings: Baseball Poems*. Illustrated by Scott Medlock. Harcourt, 1993.

———. *Got Geography!* Illustrated by Phillip Stanton. Greenwillow, 2006.

———. *Hoofbeats, Claws and Rippled Fins*. Illustrated by Stephen Alcorn. HarperCollins, 2002.

———. *Lives: Poems about Famous Americans*. Illustrated by Leslie Staub. HarperCollins, 1999.

———, ed. *Marvelous Math*. Illustrated by Karen Barbour. Simon, 1997.

———, ed. *More Surprises*. Illustrated by Megan Lloyd. Harper, 1987.

———. *My America: A Poetry Atlas of the United States*. Illustrated by Stephen Alcorn. HarperCollins, 2000.

———. *Oh, No! Where Are My Pants and Other Disasters: Poems*. Illustrated by Wolf Erlbruch. Harper, 2005.

———, ed. *Rainbows Are Made: Poems by Carl Sandburg*. Illustrated by Fritz Eichenberg. Harcourt, 1984.

———, ed. *Surprises*. Illustrated by Megan Lloyd. Harper, 1984.

Hudson, Wade, ed. *Pass It On: African American Poetry for Children*. Illustrated by Floyd Cooper. Scholastic, 1993.

Hughes, Langston. "Mother to Son" in *The Dream Keeper and Other Poems*. Illustrated by Brian Pinkney. Knopf, 1994 [1932].

———. *The Dream Keeper and Other Poems*. Illustrated by Brian Pinkney. Knopf, 1994 [1932].

Issa. *See* Kobayashi, Issa.

James, Simon, selector. *Days Like This: A Collection of Small Poems*. Candlewick, 2000.

Janeczko, Paul B. *Dirty Laundry Pile: Poems in Different Voices*. Illustrated by Melissa Sweet. HarperCollins, 2001.

———. *A Kick in the Head: An Everyday Guide to Poetic Forms*. Illustrated by Chris Raschka. Candlewick, 2005.

———, ed. *The Place My Words Are Looking For*. Bradbury, 1990.

———, ed. *Poetry from A to Z*. Bradbury, 1994.

———, selector. *A Poke in the I: A Collection of Concrete Poems*. Illustrated by Chris Raschka. Candlewick, 2001.

———, selector. *Seeing the Blue Between: Advice and Inspiration for Young Poets*. Candlewick, 2001.

———. *Stone Bench in an Empty Park*. Orchard, 2000.

———. *Very Best (Almost) Friends*. Illustrated by Christine Davenier. Candlewick, 1999.

Johnson, Angela. *Running Back to Luddie*. Illustrated by Angelo. Orchard, 2001.

Katz, Bobbi. *Pocket Poems*. Illustrated by Marilyn Hafner. Dutton, 2004.

———. *We the People*. Illustrated by Nina Crews. Greenwillow, 2000.

Katz, Susan. *Looking for Jaguar and Other Rain Forest Poems*. Illustrated by Lee Christiansen. Greenwillow, 2005.

———. *A Revolutionary Field Trip: Poems of Colonial America*. Illustrated by R. W. Alley. Simon, 2004.

Kennedy, X. J. *Exploding Gravy: Poems to Make You Laugh*. Illustrated by Joy Allen. Little, 2002.

Kennedy, X. J., and Dorothy M. Kennedy, comp. *Knock at a Star: A Child's Introduction to Poetry*. Illustrated by Karen Ann Weinhaus. Little, 1999 [1982].

———, comp. *Talking Like the Rain*. Illustrated by Jane Dyer. Little, 1992.

Kiesler, Kate. *Wings on the Wind: Bird Poems.* Clarion, 2002.

Knight, Hilary. *Hilary Knight's The Owl and the Pussy-Cat.* Simon, 2001 [1983].

Knudson, R. R., and May Swenson. *American Sports Poems.* Orchard, 1988.

Kobayashi, Issa. *The Stars Are Whispering: A Haiku Journey with Poems.* Illustrated by G. Brian Karas. Scholastic, 2005.

Koch, Kenneth, and Kate Farrell. *Talking to the Sun: An Illustrated Anthology of Poems for Young People.* Holt, 1985.

Kuskin, Karla. *Moon, Have You Met My Mother?* Illustrated by Sergio Ruzzier. Harper, 2003.

———. *The Sky Is Always in the Sky.* Illustrated by Isabelle Dervaux. HarperCollins, 1997.

———. *Soap Soup and Other Verses.* HarperCollins, 1992.

Larrick, Nancy, ed. *Piping Down the Valleys Wild.* Illustrated by Ellen Raskin. Delacorte, 1985 [1968].

Lear, Edward. *The Complete Nonsense Book.* Dodd, 1946.

Lear, Edward. *Nonsense!* Illustrated by Valorie Fisher. Atheneum, 2004.

———. *The Owl and the Pussycat.* Illustrated by James Marshall. HarperCollins, 1998.

———. *The Owl and the Pussycat.* Illustrated by Jan Brett. Putnam, 1991.

Lee, Dennis. *Bubblegum Delicious.* Illustrated by David McPhail. HarperCollins, 2000.

———. *Dinosaur Dinner (with a Slice of Alligator Pie): Favorite Poems.* Selected by Jack Prelutsky. Illustrated by Debbie Tilley. Knopf, 1997.

Levy, Constance. *I'm Going to Pet a Worm Today and Other Poems.* Illustrated by Ron Himler. Macmillan, 1991.

———. "Rah, Rah Peas!" in *I'm Going to Pet a Worm Today and Other Poems.* Illustrated by Ron Himler. Macmillan, 1991.

———. *Splash!: Poems of Our World.* Illustrated by David Soman. Scholastic, 2000.

Lewin, Betsy. *Animal Snackers.* Holt, 2004.

Lewis, J. Patrick. *Arithme-tickle: An Even Number of Odd Riddle-Rhymes.* Illustrated by Frank Remkiewicz. Harcourt, 2002.

———. *Doodle Dandies.* Illustrated by Lisa Desimini. Atheneum, 1998.

———. *Earth Verses and Water Rhymes.* Illustrated by Robert Sabuda. Atheneum, 1991.

Lewis, J. Patrick. *Heroes and She-roes: Poems of Amazing and Everyday Heroes.* Illustrated by Jim Cooke. Dial, 2005.

———. *Please Bury Me in the Library.* Illustrated by Kyle M. Stone. Harcourt, 2005.

———. *Riddle-icious.* Illustrated by Debbie Tilley. Knopf, 1996.

———. *Riddle-lightful: Oodles of Little Riddle-Poems.* Illustrated by Debbie Tilley. Knopf, 1998.

———. *Swan Song: Poems of Extinction.* Illustrated by Christopher Wormell. Creative Editions, 2003.

———. *A World of Wonders: Geographic Travels in Verse and Rhyme.* Illustrated by Alison Jay. Dial, 2002.

Little, Jean. *Hey World, Here I Am!* Illustrated by Sue Truesdell. Harper, 1986.

Liu, Siyu, and Orel Protopopescu. *A Thousand Peaks: Poems from China.* Pacific View, 2002.

Livingston, Myra Cohn, ed. *I Am Writing a Poem About . . . A Game of Poetry.* McElderry, 1997.

———, ed. *I Like You, If You Like Me: Poems of Friendship.* McElderry, 1987.

Lobel, Arnold. *The Book of Pigericks.* Harper, 1983.

Longfellow, Henry Wadsworth. *Hiawatha.* Illustrated by Susan Jeffers. Dial, 1983.

———. *The Midnight Ride of Paul Revere.* Illustrated by Christopher Bing. Handprint, 2001.

———. *Paul Revere's Ride.* Illustrated by Ted Rand. Dutton, 1990.

Mado, Michio. *The Magic Pocket: Selected Poems.* Translated by Empress Michiko of Japan. Illustrated by Mitsumaso Anno. McElderry, 1998.

Mak, Kam. *My Chinatown: One Year in Poems.* HarperCollins, 2002.

Mavor, Sally. *You and Me: Poems of Friendship.* Orchard, 1997.

McCord, David. *Every Time I Climb a Tree.* Illustrated by Marc Simont. Little, 1967.

———. *One at a Time.* Illustrated by Henry B. Kane. Little, 1977.

———. "Song of the Train." In *One at a Time.* Illustrated by Henry B. Kane. Little, 1977.

McNaughton, Colin. *Making Friends with Frankenstein: A Book of Monstrous Poems and Pictures.* Candlewick, 1994.

———. *Who's Been Sleeping in My Porridge? A Book of Wacky Poems and Pictures.* Candlewick, 1998.

———. *Wish You Were Here and I Wasn't: A Book of Poems and Pictures for Globe-Trotters.* Candlewick, 2000.

Medina, Jane. *My Name Is Jorge: On Both Sides of the River.* Illustrated by Fabricio Vanden Broeck. Boyds Mills, 1999.

Medina, Tony. *Love to Langston.* Illustrated by R. Gregory Christie. Lee, 2002.

Milne, A. A. *The World of Christopher Robin.* Illustrated by E. H. Shepard. Dutton, 1958.

Milton, Tony. *Plum.* Illustrated by Mary GrandPré. Scholastic, 2003.

Montgomery, Hugh. *The Voyage of the Arctic Tern.* Candlewick, 2002.

Moore, Clement. *The Night Before Christmas.* Illustrated by Jan Brett. Putnam, 1998.

———. *The Night Before Christmas.* Illustrated by Grandma Moses. Random, 1962.

———. *The Night Before Christmas.* Illustrated by Ted Rand. North-South, 1995.

———. *The Night Before Christmas.* Illustrated by Tasha Tudor. Macmillan, 1975.

Moore, Lilian. *I'm Small and Other Verses.* Illustrated by Jill McElmurry. Candlewick, 2001.

———. *Mural on Second Avenue and Other City Poems.* Illustrated by Roma Karas. Candlewick, 2005.

———. "Until I Saw the Sea" in Beatrice Schenk de Regniers et al., eds. *Sing a Song of Popcorn.* Illustrated by nine Caldecott Medal artists. Scholastic, 1988.

Mora, Pat. *Confetti.* Illustrated by Enrique O. Sanchez. Lee, 1996.

———. *Love to Mama: A Tribute to Mothers.* Illustrated by Paula S. Barragán. Lee, 2001.

Mordhorst, Heidi. *Squeeze: Poems from a Juicy Universe.* Illustrated by Jesse Torrey. Boyds Mills, 2005.

Moss, Jeff. *Bone Poems.* Illustrated by Tom Leigh. Workman, 1997.

Myers, Walter Dean. *Here in Harlem: Poems in Many Voices.* Holiday, 2004.

Nado, Takayo. *Dear World.* Dial, 2003.

Nash, Ogden. *The Adventures of Isabel.* Illustrated by James Marshall. Little, 1991.

———. *The Tale of Custard the Dragon.* Illustrated by Lynn Munsinger. Little, 1995.

Nelson, Marilyn. *Carver: A Life in Poems.* Front St., 2001.

Nelson, Marilyn. *Fortune's Bones: The Manumission Requiem.* Houghton, 2004.

———. *A Wreath for Emmett Till.* Illustrated by Philippe Lardy. Houghton, 2005.

Newsome, Effie Lee. *Wonders: The Best Children's Poems of Effie Lee Newsome.* Selected by Rudine Sims Bishop. Boyds Mills, 1999.

Noyes, Alfred. *The Highwayman.* Illustrated by Charles Keeping. Oxford UP, 1981.

Nye, Naomi Shihab. *19 Varieties of Gazelle: Poems of the Middle East.* Greenwillow, 2002.

———. *A Maze Me: Poems for Girls.* Greenwillow, 2005.

———. *The Space between Our Footsteps: Poems and Paintings from the Middle East.* Simon, 1998.

———. *This Same Sky: A Collection of Poems from around the World.* Four Winds, 1992.

———. *This Tree Is Older Than You Are: A Bilingual Gathering of Poems and Stories from Mexico with Paintings by Mexican Artists.* Simon, 1995.

O'Neill, Mary. *Hailstones and Halibut Bones: Adventures in Color.* Illustrated by John Wallner. Philomel, 1989 [1961].

Otten, Charlotte F. *January Rides the Wind: A Book of Months.* Illustrated by Todd L. W. Doney. Lothrop, 1997.

Panzer, Nora, ed. *Celebrate America: In Poetry and Art.* Hyperion, 1994.

Paolilli, Paul, and Dan Brewer. *Silver Seeds: A Book of Nature Poems.* Illustrated by Steve Johnson and Lou Fancher. Viking, 2001.

Pearson, Susan. *Who Swallowed Harold?* Illustrated by David Slonim. Cavendish, 2005.

Philip, Neil. *The Fish Is Me: Bathtime Rhymes.* Illustrated by Claire Henley. Clarion, 2002.

———. *It's a Woman's World: A Century of Women's Voices in Poetry.* Dutton, 2000.

———. *War and the Pity of War.* Illustrated by Michael McCurdy. Clarion, 1998.

Pomerantz, Charlotte. *Thunderboom! Poems for Everybody.* Front St., 2006.

Prelutsky, Jack, ed. *A. Nonny Mouse Writes Again.* Illustrated by Marjorie Priceman. Knopf, 1993.

———. *Awful Ogre's Awful Day.* Illustrated by Paul O. Zelinsky. Greenwillow, 2001.

———. *The Baby Uggs Are Hatching.* Illustrated by James Stevenson. Greenwillow, 1982.

———. *The Beauty of the Beast: Poems from the Animal Kingdom.* Illustrated by Meilo So. Knopf, 1997.

———. *Beneath a Blue Umbrella.* Illustrated by Garth Williams. Greenwillow, 1990.

———. *The Dragons Are Singing Tonight.* Illustrated by Peter Sis. Greenwillow, 1993.

———. *For Laughing Out Loud: Poems to Tickle Your Funnybone.* Illustrated by Marjorie Priceman. Knopf, 1991.

———. *The Frogs Wore Red Suspenders.* Illustrated by Petra Mathers. Greenwillow, 2002.

———. "The Grobbles" in *The Snopp on the Sidewalk and Other Poems.* Illustrated by Byron Barton. Greenwillow, 1977.

———. *The Headless Horseman: More Poems to Trouble Your Sleep.* Illustrated by Arnold Lobel. Greenwillow, 1977.

———. *If Not for the Cat.* Illustrated by Ted Rand. Greenwillow, 2004.

———. *It's Halloween.* Illustrated by Marylin Hafner. Greenwillow, 1977.

———. *It's Raining Pigs and Noodles.* Illustrated by James Stevenson. Greenwillow, 2000.

———. *It's Thanksgiving.* Illustrated by Marylin Hafner. Greenwillow, 1982.

———. *Monday's Troll.* Illustrated by Peter Sis. Greenwillow, 1996.

———. *The New Kid on the Block.* Illustrated by James Stevenson. Greenwillow, 1984.

———. *Nightmares: Poems to Trouble Your Sleep.* Illustrated by Arnold Lobel. Greenwillow, 1976.

———. *A Pizza the Size of the Sun.* Illustrated by James Stevenson. Greenwillow, 1996.

———, ed. *Poems by A. Nonny Mouse.* Illustrated by Henrik Drescher. Knopf, 1989.

———, ed. *The Random House Book of Poetry for Children.* Illustrated by Arnold Lobel. Random, 1983.

———. *Read-Aloud Rhymes for the Very Young.* Illustrated by Marc Brown. Knopf, 1986.

———. *Read a Rhyme, Write a Rhyme.* Illustrated by Meilo So. Knopf, 2005.

———. *Ride a Purple Pelican.* Illustrated by Garth Williams. Greenwillow, 1986.

———. *Rolling Harvey Down the Hill.* Illustrated by Victoria Chess. Greenwillow, 1980.

———. *Scranimals.* Illustrated by Peter Sis. Greenwillow, 2002.

———. *The Snopp on the Sidewalk and Other Poems.* Illustrated by Byron Barton. Greenwillow, 1977.

———. *Something Big Has Been Here.* Illustrated by James Stevenson. Greenwillow, 1990.

———. *Twentieth Century Children's Poetry.* Illustrated by Meilo So. Greenwillow, 1999.

Rauter, Rose. "Peach." In *Knock at a Star: A Child's Introduction to Poetry,* compiled by X. J. Kennedy and Dorothy M. Kennedy, illustrated by Karen Ann Weinhaus. Little, 2000.

Roemer, Heidi. *Come to My Party and Other Shape Poems.* Illustrated by Hideko Takahashi. Holt, 2004.

Rogasky, Barbara. *Leaf by Leaf: Autumn Poems*. Photographs by Marc Tauss. Scholastic, 2001.

———. *Winter Poems*. Illustrated by Trina Schart Hyman. Scholastic, 1994.

Rosen, Michael. *Poems for the Very Young*. Illustrated by Bob Graham. Kingfisher, 2005 [1993].

Rosenberg, Liz. *Roots and Flowers: Poets and Poems on Family*. Martin, 2001.

Rosenthal, Betsy R. *My House Is Singing*. Illustrated by Margaret Chodos Irvine. Harcourt, 2004.

Rowden, Justine. *Paint Me a Poem: Poems Inspired by Masterpieces of Art*. Wordsong/Boyds Mills, 2005.

Rylant, Cynthia. *Boris*. Harcourt, 2005.

———. *God Went to Beauty School*. HarperCollins, 2003.

———. *Waiting to Waltz: A Childhood*. Illustrated by Stephen Gammell. Simon, 1984.

Sandburg, Carl. "Fog." In *The Random House Book of Poetry for Children*, edited by Jack Prelutsky, illustrated by Arnold Lobel. Random House, 1983.

Schertle, Alice. *Advice for a Frog*. Illustrated by Norman Green. Lothrop, 1995.

———. *How Now, Brown Cow?* Illustrated by Amanda Schaffer. Browndeer/Harcourt, 1994.

Schnur, Steven. *Winter: An Alphabet Acrostic*. Clarion, 2002.

Service, Robert. *The Cremation of Sam McGee*. Illustrated by Ted Harrison. Kids Can, 1992.

Shange, Ntozake. *Ellington Was Not a Street*. Illustrated by Kadir Nelson. Simon, 2004.

Sidman, Joyce. *Song of the Water Boatman: and Other Pond Poems*. Illustrated by Beckie Prange. Houghton, 2005.

Siebert, Diane. *Mississippi*. Illustrated by Greg Harlin. HarperCollins, 2001.

———. *Mojave*. Illustrated by Wendell Minor. Crowell, 1988.

———. *Sierra*. Illustrated by Wendell Minor. Crowell, 1991.

Sierra, Judy. *Antarctic Antics: A Book of Penguin Poems*. Illustrated by Jose Aruego and Ariane Dewey. Gulliver, 1998.

———. *Schoolyard Rhymes: Kids' Own Rhymes for Rope Skipping, Hand Clapping, Ball Bouncing, and Just Plain Fun*. Illustrated by Melissa Sweet. Knopf, 2005.

Silverstein, Shel. *Falling Up*. HarperCollins, 1996.

———. *A Light in the Attic*. Harper, 1981.

———. *Runny Babbit: A Billy Sook*. HarperCollins, 2005.

———. "Spaghetti" in *Where the Sidewalk Ends: Poems and Drawings*. Harper, 1974.

———. *Where the Sidewalk Ends: Poems and Drawings*. Harper, 1974.

Singer, Marilyn. *Central Heating: Poems about Fire and Warmth*. Illustrated by Meilo So. Knopf, 2005.

———. *Footprints on the Roof: Poems about the Earth*. Illustrated by Meilo So. Knopf, 2002.

Sklansky, Amy E. *From the Doghouse: Poems to Chew On*. Illustrated by Karla Firehammer, Karen Dismukes, Sandy Koeser, and Cathy McQuitty. Holt, 2002.

Sneve, Virginia Driving Hawk. *Dancing Teepees*. Illustrated by Stephen Gammell. Holiday, 1989.

Soto, Gary. *Canto Familiar*. Illustrated by Anneke Nelson. Harcourt, 1995.

———. *Fearless Fernie: Hanging Out with Fernie and Me*. Illustrated by Regan Dunnick. Putnam, 2002.

———. *Neighborhood Odes*. Illustrated by David Diaz. Harcourt, 1992.

———. *Worlds Apart: Traveling with Fernie and Me*. Putnam, 2005.

Steptoe, Javaka. *In Daddy's Arms I Am Tall: African Americans Celebrating Fathers*. Lee, 1997.

Stevenson, James. *Corn Chowder*. Greenwillow, 2003.

———. *Corn-Fed*. Greenwillow, 2002.

———. *Just Around the Corner*. Greenwillow, 2001.

———. *Popcorn*. Greenwillow, 1998.

Stevenson, Robert Louis. *Block City*. Illustrated by Ashley Wolff. Dutton, 1988.

———. *Block City*. Illustrated by Daniel Kirk. Simon, 2005.

———. *A Child's Garden of Verses*. Illustrated by Diane Goode. Morrow, 1998.

———. *A Child's Garden of Verses*. Illustrated by Tasha Tudor. Oxford UP, 1947 [1885].

———. *A Child's Garden of Verses*. Illustrated by Brian Wildsmith. Oxford UP, 1966 [1885].

———. *My Shadow*. Illustrated by Monique Felix. Creative Editions, 2002.

———. *My Shadow*. Illustrated by Penny Dale. Candlewick, 1999.

———. *Where Go the Boats?* Illustrated by Max Grover. Browndeer, 1998.

Strickland, Dorothy S., and Michael R. Strickland. *Families: Poems Celebrating the African American Experience*. Illustrated by John Ward. Boyds Mills/Wordsong, 1994.

Strickland, Michael R. *My Own Song: And Other Poems to Groove To*. Illustrated by Eric Sabee. Boyds Mills, 1997.

———. *Poems That Sing to You*. Illustrated by Alan Leiner. Boyds Mills/Wordsong, 1993.

Swados, Elizabeth. *Hey You! C'Mere: A Poetry Slam*. Illustrated by Joe Cepeda. Levine/Scholastic, 2002.

Tapahonso, Luci. *A Breeze Swept Through*. U New Mexico P, 1987.

———. *Songs of Shiprock Fair*. Illustrated by Anthony Chee Emerson. Kiva, 1999.

Testa, Maria. *Something about America*. Candlewick, 2005.

Thayer, Ernest L. *Casey at the Bat. A Ballad of the Republic Sung in the Year 1888*. Illustrated by Christopher Bing. Handprint, 2000.

Thomas, Joyce Carol. *The Blacker the Berry*. Illustrated by Floyd Cooper. HarperCollins, 2005.

———. *Gingerbread Days*. Illustrated by Floyd Cooper. HarperCollins, 1995.

Updike, John. *A Child's Calendar*. Illustrated by Trina Schart Hyman. Holiday, 1999.

Viorst, Judith. *If I Were in Charge of the World and Other Worries*. Illustrated by Lynne Cherry. Atheneum, 1982.

Volavkova, Hana, ed. *. . . I Never Saw Another Butterfly: Children's Drawings and Poems from Terezin Concentration Camp, 1942–1944*. Schocken, 1992.

Wayland, April Halprin. *Girl Coming In for a Landing: A Novel in Poems.* Knopf, 2002.

Weatherford, Carole Boston. *Remember the Bridge: Poems of a People.* Philomel, 2002.

Whipple, Laura. *If the Shoe Fits: Voices from Cinderella.* Illustrated by Laura Beingessner. McElderry, 2002.

Willard, Nancy A. *A Visit to William Blake's Inn.* Illustrated by Alice Provensen and Martin Provensen. Harcourt, 1981.

Williams, Vera B. *Amber Was Brave, Essie Was Smart.* Greenwillow, 2001.

Whitman, Walt. *When I Heard the Learn'd Astronomer.* Illustrated by Loren Long. Simon, 2004.

Wong, Janet. *Behind the Wheel: Poems about Driving.* McElderry, 1999.

———. *Good Luck and Other Poems.* McElderry, 1994.

———. *Grump.* Illustrated by John Wallace. McElderry, 2001.

———. *Knock on Wood: Poems about Superstitions.* Illustrated by Julie Paschkis. McElderry, 2003.

———. *Minn and Jake.* Foster/Farrar, 2003.

———. *Night Garden: Poems from the World of Dreams.* Illustrated by Julie Paschkis. McElderry, 2000.

———. *The Rainbow Hand: Poems about Mothers and Daughters.* McElderry, 1999.

———. *A Suitcase of Seaweed and Other Poems.* McElderry, 1996.

Woodson, Jacqueline. *Locomotion.* Putnam, 2003.

Worth, Valerie. *All the Small Poems and Fourteen More.* Illustrated by Natalie Babbitt. Farrar, 1994.

———. "Mud." In *All the Small Poems and Fourteen More,* illustrated by Natalie Babbitt. Farrar, 1994.

———. *Peacock and Other Poems.* Illustrated by Natalie Babbitt. Farrar, 2002.

———. "Seashell." In *All the Small Poems and Fourteen More.* Illustrated by Natalie Babbitt. Farrar, 1994.

———. *Small Poems.* Illustrated by Natalie Babbitt. Farrar, 1972.

Yolen, Jane. *Color Me a Rhyme: Nature Poems for Young People.* Photographs by Jason Stemple. Wordsong, 2000.

———. *Once Upon Ice: and Other Frozen Poems.* Illustrated by Jason Stemple. Wordsong, 1997.

———. *The Three Bears Holiday Rhyme Book.* Illustrated by Jane Dyer. Harcourt, 1995.

———. *Wild Wings: Poems for Young People.* Photographs by Jason Stemple. Wordsong, 2002.

Young, Ed. *Beyond the Mountains: A Visual Poem about China.* Charlesbridge, 2005.

Zahares, Wade. *Big, Bad, and a Little Bit Scary: Poems That Bite Back!* Viking, 2001.

Zalben, Jane Breskin. *Let There Be Light: Poems and Prayers for Repairing the World.* Dutton, 2002.

Zimmer, Tracie Vaughn. *Sketches from a Spy Tree.* Illustrated by Andrew Glass. Clarion, 2005.

Prose

Alborough, Jez. *Where's My Teddy?* Candlewick, 1992.

Armstrong, William H. *Sounder.* Illustrated by James Barkley. Harper, 1969.

Arnosky, Jim. *Sketching Outdoors in the Spring.* Morrow, 1997.

Avi. *The True Confessions of Charlotte Doyle.* Orchard, 1990.

Baker, Jennie. *Window.* Greenwillow, 1991.

Bang, Molly. *When Sophie Gets Angry—Really, Really Angry.* Scholastic, 1999.

Bash, Barbara. *Ancient Ones: The World of the Old Growth Firs.* Sierra Club, 1994.

Baylor, Byrd. *Hawk, I'm Your Brother.* Illustrated by Peter Parnall. Scribner's, 1976.

———. *The Way to Start a Day.* Illustrated by Peter Parnall. Scribner's, 1978.

Brett, Jan. *Goldilocks and the Three Bears.* Dodd, 1987.

Bunting, Eve. *The Wall.* Illustrated by Ronald Himler. Clarion, 1990.

Cameron, Ann. *The Most Beautiful Place in the World.* Illustrated by Thomas B. Allen. Knopf, 1988.

———. *The Stories Julian Tells.* Illustrated by Ann Strugnell. Knopf, 1981.

Carlstrom, Nancy W. *Blow Me a Kiss, Miss Lilly.* Illustrated by Amy Schwartz. HarperCollins, 1990.

Carrick, Carol, and Donald Carrick. *The Accident.* Seabury, 1976.

Cherry, Lynne. *The Great Kapok Tree.* Harcourt, 1990.

Choi, Sook Nyul. *Year of Impossible Goodbyes.* Houghton, 1991.

Cohen, Miriam. *Lost in the Museum.* Illustrated by Lillian Hoban. Dell, 1983.

———. *Will I Have a Friend?* Illustrated by Lillian Hoban. Aladdin, 1989.

Cormier, Robert. *Other Bells for Us to Ring.* Illustrated by Deborah Kogan Ray. Delacorte, 1990.

Degen, Bruce. *Jamberry.* Harper, 1983.

dePaola, Tomie. *Strega Nona.* Prentice-Hall, 1975.

Fox, Mem. *Koala Lou.* Illustrated by Donald A. Mackay. Bradbury, 1968.

Frank, Anne. *Anne Frank: Diary of a Young Girl.* Doubleday, 1952.

Freeman, Don. *Corduroy.* Viking, 1968.

Galdone, Paul. *The Gingerbread Boy.* Clarion, 1979.

Gallaz, Christophe, and Roberto Innocenti. *Rose Blanche.* Illustrated by Roberto Innocenti. Creative Education, 1985.

George, Jean Craighead. *My Side of the Mountain.* Dutton, 1988.

———. *One Day in the Tropical Rain Forest.* Illustrated by Gary Allen. Crowell, 1990.

———. *Who Really Killed Cock Robin?* HarperCollins, 1991 [1971].

Gerstein, Mordicai. *Wild Boy.* Farrar, 1998.

Greenfield, Eloise. *She Come Bringing Me That Little Baby Girl.* Illustrated by John Steptoe. Lippincott, 1974.

Grimes, Nikki. *Bronx Masquerade.* Putnam, 2002.

———. *Jazmin's Notebook.* Dial, 1998.

Henkes, Kevin. *Julius, the Baby of the World.* Greenwillow, 1990.

———. *Lilly's Purple Plastic Purse.* Greenwillow, 1996.

Hoban, Russell. *A Baby Sister for Frances.* Illustrated by Lillian Hoban. Harper, 1970.

Holt, Kimberly Willis. *When Zachary Beaver Came to Town.* Holt, 1999.

Hughes, Shirley. *Dogger.* Lothrop, 1988.

Hutchins, Pat. *Titch.* Macmillan, 1971.

Huynh, Quang Nhuong. *The Land I Lost: Adventures of a Boy in Vietnam.* Illustrated by Vo-Dinh Mai. Harper, 1982.

Jarrell, Randall. *The Bat-Poet.* Illustrated by Maurice Sendak. Macmillan, 1964.

Keats, Ezra Jack. *Peter's Chair.* Harper, 1967.

———. *Whistle for Willie.* Viking, 1964.

Lauture, Denizé. *Running the Road to ABC.* Illustrated by Reynold Ruffins. Simon, 1996.

Levine, Gail Carson. *Ella Enchanted.* HarperCollins, 1997.

Lowry, Lois. *Number the Stars.* Houghton, 1989.

MacDonald, Golden [Margaret Wise Brown]. *The Little Island.* Illustrated by Leonard Weisgard. Doubleday, 1946.

Marshall, James. *The Three Little Pigs.* Dial, 1989.

Martin, Bill, Jr. *Brown Bear, Brown Bear, What Do You See?* Illustrated by Eric Carle. Holt, 1983.

Maruki, Toshi. *Hiroshima No Pika* (The Flash of Hiroshima). Lothrop, 1980.

McCloskey, Robert. *Time of Wonder.* Viking, 1957.

McPhail, David. *The Bear's Toothache.* Little, 1972.

Myers, Walter Dean. *Scorpions.* Harper, 1988.

Newman, Lesléa. *The Best Cat in the World.* Illustrated by Ron Himler. Eerdmans, 2004.

Orlev, Uri. *The Man from the Other Side.* Translated by Hillel Ahlkin. Houghton, 1984.

Paterson, Katherine. *Bridge to Terabithia.* Illustrated by Donna Diamond. Crowell, HarperCollins, 1977.

———. *Lyddie.* Dutton, 1991.

Perkins, Lynne Rae. *Criss Cross.* Greenwillow, 2005.

Perrault, Charles. *Cinderella.* Retold by May Ehrlich. Illustrated by Susan Jeffers. Dial, 1985.

Rylant, Cynthia. *When I Was Young in the Mountains.* Illustrated by Diane Goode. Dutton, 1982.

Salisbury, Graham. *Eyes of the Emperor.* Random, 2005.

Schlein, Miriam. *The Year of the Panda.* Illustrated by Kam Mak. Crowell, 1990.

Schmidt, Gary D. *Lizzie Bright and the Buckminster Boy.* Clarion, 2004.

Scieszka, Jon. *The Frog Prince Continued.* Illustrated by Steve Johnson. Viking, 1991.

———. *The True Story of the 3 Little Pigs!* Illustrated by Lane Smith. Viking, 1989.

Sheldon, Dyan. *The Whales' Song.* Illustrated by Gary Blythe. Dial, 1991.

Shulevitz, Uri. *Dawn.* Farrar, 1974.

Tarcov, Edith H. *The Frog Prince.* Illustrated by James Marshall. Scholastic, 1987.

Taylor, Mildred. *Roll of Thunder, Hear My Cry.* Dial, 1976.

Viorst, Judith. *Alexander and the Terrible, Horrible, No Good, Very Bad Day.* Illustrated by Ray Cruz. Atheneum, 1972.

———. *The Tenth Good Thing about Barney.* Illustrated by Erik Blegvad. Atheneum, 1971.

Waber, Bernard. *Ira Sleeps Over.* Houghton, 1972.

Wells, Rosemary. *Noisy Nora.* Dial, 1973.

Wild, Margaret. *The Very Best of Friends.* Illustrated by Julie Vivas. Harcourt, 1990.

Williams, Vera B. *A Chair for My Mother.* Greenwillow, 1982.

Woodson, Jacqueline. *Last Summer with Maizon.* Putnam, 2002.

Zolotow, Charlotte. *The Hating Book.* Illustrated by Ben Shecter. Harper, 1969.

———. *Mr. Rabbit and the Lovely Present.* Illustrated by Maurice Sendak. Harper, 1962.

Chapter Nine

Contemporary Realistic Fiction

Media Resources

A small group of seventh graders read Katherine Paterson's *The Great Gilly Hopkins* in their in-depth reading group. One of their options when they finished the book was to write about ways they were like Gilly and different from Gilly. One student observed:

Gilly in Me

I think I am a lot like Gilly in some ways. One way is everything somebody says I can't do, I have to show them that I can do it or something like it. I think Gilly and I feel the same way about foster parents. If I had foster parents, I probably would feel that my mother would come and get me; but I wouldn't run away or steal money.

In school I don't act like she does, going to the principal or slipping notes in teacher's books. It seems she doesn't like to be with her friends. I like to be around with my friends. I don't like to be by myself. I think Gilly gets mad easy. I get mad easy like getting called names. I always have to call them a name back.

—Amy Kauffman, seventh grade
   Delaware Public Schools, Ohio
   Christy Slavik, teacher

Obviously, Amy had identified with the character Gilly Hopkins. By contrasting her perception of herself with her observations about Gilly, she learned more about Gilly and developed insight into her own personality.

The power of Gilly's story is likely to be reflected in the lives of many children besides Amy. We can see how this happens more clearly in M. J. Auch's *Wing Nut*, published in 2005. Here Gilly provides inspiration and support to a twelve-year-old, Grady, who has followed his mother from place to place for years following his father's death. He treasures a battered paperback copy of *The Great Gilly Hopkins* discarded by a kind librarian, and he rereads it over and over. For Grady,

It was comforting to find another kid who was worse off than him, even if she was only a made-up character. Gilly wanted to be with her real mother. Bad. No matter how many times Grady got moved and no matter where he got shuffled to, he always had his mom right there with him. So that made him better than Gilly. (pp. 15–16)

Books such as M. J. Auch's *Wing Nut* help children see their own concerns in the context of a wider human community. From *Wing Nut: A Novel* by M. J. Auch. Copyright © 2005 by M. J. Auch. Reprinted by permission of Henry Holt and Company, LLC.

A well-written contemporary story should do more than just mirror modern life. It should take children inside a character and help them understand the causes of behavior; at the same time, it should take them outside themselves to reflect on their own behavior. For Amy and for Auch's Grady, *The Great Gilly Hopkins* opened a window of understanding and let them view themselves and the world with slightly changed perception.

REALISM IN CONTEMPORARY CHILDREN'S LITERATURE

Realistic fiction may be defined as imaginative writing that accurately reflects life as it was lived in the past or could be lived today. Everything in such a story can conceivably happen to real people living in our natural physical world, in contrast to fantasy, where impossible happenings are made to appear quite plausible even though they are not possible. Historical fiction (see Chapter 10) portrays life as it may have been lived in the past; contemporary realism focuses on the problems and issues of living today. In this chapter we arbitrarily chose the 1950s as the dividing line between contemporary and historical fiction (perhaps because, for the authors, that period was contemporary).

Though other genres in children's literature, such as fantasy, are popular, children consistently are found to prefer realistic fiction. The books discussed in this chapter can be categorized as contemporary realistic fiction for children. Many are stories about growing up today and finding a place in the family, among peers, and in modern society. In addition, aspects of coping with the problems of the human condition may be found in contemporary literature for children. Books that are humorous or reflect special interests—such as animal or sports stories and mysteries—are also classified as realistic literature and so are included in this chapter.

The content of contemporary realism for children has changed dramatically in the past forty years. These changes have provoked controversy among writers, critics, librarians, teachers, and parents. For this reason we give attention to some of the values of contemporary realism for children and some of these issues.

The Value of Contemporary Fiction

Realistic fiction serves children in the process of understanding and coming to terms with themselves as they acquire "human-ness." Books that honestly portray the realities of life help children gain a fuller understanding of human problems and human relationships and, thus, a fuller understanding of themselves and their own potential. In describing her purpose in writing for children, Nina Bawden states:

> If a children's writer presents his characters honestly and is truthful about their thoughts and their feelings, he is giving his readers "a means to gain a hold on fate" by showing them that they can trust their thoughts and their feelings, that they can have faith in themselves. He can also show them a bit of the world, the beginning of the path they have to tread; but the most im-portant thing he has to offer is a little hope and courage for the journey.[1]

This is not a function unique to contemporary realism. Other types of books can show children a slice of the world. Some fantasy is nearer to truth than realism; biography and autobiography frequently provide readers with models of human beings who offer "hope and courage for the journey." The ability to maintain one's humanity and courage in the midst of deprivation is highlighted in *Number the Stars,* Lois Lowry's historical fiction about Danish efforts to save Jewish citizens in World War II. Personal bravery and responsible behavior under dire circumstances is also one of the themes of the high fantasy *A Wizard of Earthsea* by Ursula Le Guin. However, most children appear to identify more readily with characters in books of contemporary realism than with those of historical fiction or fantasy.

Realistic fiction helps children enlarge their frames of reference while seeing the world from another perspective. For example, human rights abuses in Haiti are memorably portrayed in Frances Temple's *Taste of Salt.* No one reading about the plight of these characters could think of them as "other." Instead, Temple places the reader directly in her characters' shoes. Children who are repelled or frightened by the problems of the elderly might come to understand the elderly as real people through M. J. Auch's *Wing Nut* or Kazumi Yumoto's *The Friends.* Stories like these help young people develop compassion for and an understanding of human experiences.

Realistic fiction also reassures young people that they are not the first in the world to have faced problems. In Hilary McKay's *Permanent Rose,* Kimberly Willis Holt's *When Zachary Beaver Came to Town,* and Marion Dane Bauer's *A Question of Trust,* they read of other children whose parents have separated or divorced. In Kevin Henkes's *The Birthday Room,* Lynne Rae Perkins's *Criss Cross,* and Joan Bauer's *Stand Tall,* they read about characters who are beginning to be concerned about relationships with the opposite sex. They gain some solace from recognizing the problems a low-income background poses for Jamal in Walter Dean Myers's *Scorpions,* Livy Two in Kerry Madden's *Gentle's Holler,* or Jazmin in Nikki Grimes's *Jazmin's Notebook.* This knowledge that they are not alone brings a kind of comfort to child readers. James Baldwin recognized the power of books to alleviate pain:

> You think your pain and your heartbreak are unprecedented in the history of the world, but then you read. It was books that taught me that the things that tormented me the most were the very things that connected me with all the people who were alive, or who had ever been alive.[2]

---

[1] Nina Bawden, "Emotional Realism in Books for Young People," *Horn Book Magazine* (February 1980): 33.

[2] James Baldwin, "Talk to Teachers," *Saturday Review* 21 (December 1963): 42–44, 60.

Realistic fiction can also illuminate experiences that children have not had. A child with loving parents whose only chore consists of making a bed may have a deeper need to read Katherine Paterson's *The Same Stuff as Stars* than a child of poverty whose life is more nearly reflected in the story. A child who takes school for granted might gain much from Ann Cameron's poignant *The Most Beautiful Place in the World*, about a Guatemalan who desperately wants an education. Realistic fiction can be a way of experiencing a world we do not know.

Some books also serve as a kind of preparation for living. Far better to have read Katherine Paterson's *Bridge to Terabithia* or Kimberly Willis Holt's *Keeper of the Night* than to experience firsthand at age 10 or 12 the death of your best friend or the suicide of your mother. For many years, death was a taboo subject in children's literature. Yet, as children face the honest realities of life in books, they are developing a kind of courage for facing problems in their own lives. Madeleine L'Engle, whose *Meet the Austins* was among the first works of modern children's literature to treat the subject of death, maintained that "to pretend there is no darkness is another way of extinguishing light."[3]

Realistic fiction for children does provide many possible models, both good and bad, for coping with problems of the human condition. As children experience these stories, they may begin to filter out some meaning for their own lives. This allows children to organize and shape their own thinking about life as they follow, through stories, the lives of others. The Web "Growing Up Is Hard to Do" suggests how contemporary realistic fiction can provide the foundation for a classroom exploration of problems and prospects facing the modern child.

Issues Relating to Realistic Fiction

More controversy surrounds the writing of contemporary realistic fiction for children than perhaps any other kind of literature. Everyone is a critic of realism, for everyone feels he or she is an expert on what is real in today's world. But realities clash, and the fact that "what is real for one might not be real for another" is a true and lively issue. Some of the questions that seem uniquely related to contemporary realism in writing for children need to be examined.

What Is Real?

The question of what is "real" or "true to life" is a significant one. C. S. Lewis, the British author of the well-known Narnia stories (see Chapter 7), described three types of realistic content:

But when we say, "The sort of thing that happens," do we mean the sort of thing that usually or often happens, the sort of thing that is typical of the human lot? Or do we mean "The sort of thing that might conceivably happen or that, by a thousandth chance, may have happened once?"[4]

Middle graders reading the Narnia series know that these stories are fantasy and couldn't happen in reality. However, middle graders might read stories like Vera Cleaver and Bill Cleaver's *Where the Lilies Bloom* or Gary Paulsen's *Hatchet* and believe that children can survive any hardship or crisis if only they possess determination. These well-written books cast believable characters in realistic settings facing real problems. But an adult reader might question whether this is the sort of thing that "by a thousandth chance, may have happened once."

Adding to the question of what is real is the recent trend toward magic realism in literature for children. In other cultures the belief that the spirit world is as real as the one we can see and touch is common. Increasingly, authors from the United States, Great Britain, Canada, and Australia feel no compunction in blending these worlds. We have dealt with some of these books in "Modern Fantasy" (Chapter 7). In this chapter we include others when we feel the thrust of the book speaks to contemporary real-life concerns. We suspect that as the twenty-first century moves forward the lines between traditional genres will become more and more blurred.

How Real May a Children's Book Be?

Controversy also centers on how much graphic detail may be included in a book for children. How much violence is too much? How explicit may an author be in describing bodily functions or sexual relations? These are questions that no one would have asked thirty-five years ago. But there are new freedoms today. Childhood is not the innocent time we like to think it is (and it probably never was). In addition, authors of young adult literature (defined in the American Library Association's Printz Award as ages 12–18) have been more willing to tackle issues for adolescents as frankly as they would in a book for adults. In this book we focus on children ages birth to 14. It is therefore often difficult to make decisions about what literature is appropriate for those adolescents in middle school. Basically, we have worked under the assumption that although these youth might not need protection, they do still need the perspective that good literature can give. A well-written book makes the reader aware of the human suffering resulting from inhumane acts by others, whereas television and films are more apt to concentrate on the acts themselves.

---

[3]Madeleine L'Engle, in a speech before the Florida Library Association, May 1965, Miami.

[4]C. S. Lewis, *An Experiment in Criticism* (Cambridge: Cambridge University Press, 1961), p. 57.

Wonderfully Exciting Books

Friendships
All Alone in the Universe (Perkins)
The Big Nothing (Fogelin)
Bluish (Hamilton)
Bridge to Terabithia (Paterson)
Crash (Spinelli)
Criss Cross (Perkins)
The Cybil War (Byars)
Donuthead (Stauffacher)
Friends of the Heart (Banks)
Libby on Wednesday (Snyder)
The Misfits (Howe)
The Schwa Was Here (Shusterman)
The Secret Language of Girls (Dowell)
Under the Watsons Porch (Shreve)
The View from Saturday (Konigsburg)
Share ideas about how a book's author
   makes a friendship seem real.
Learn to make friendship bracelets.
Write to pen pals.

Fears
Alice the Brave (Naylor)
Deliver Us from Normal (Klise)
Dog Friday (McKay)
The Fear Place (Naylor)
Jakarta Missing (Kurtz)
What were some of the fears you used to
   have? What helped you overcome them?
Create monster symbols for your fears; make
   them huge!

Memories
All the Places to Love (MacLachlan)
26 Fairmount Ave. (dePaola)
Write about your first or your most vivid
   memory.
Make a timeline or a pictorial map of
   highlights in your life; include future
   as well as past events.
Write your own memoir.

Trolls (Horvath)
Interview a relative about their memorable moments.

Peer Pressure
Here Today (Martin)
In the Night, on Lanvale Street (Conly)
Scorpions (Myers)
Some Friend (Bradby)
Wringer (Spinelli)
What types of pressure and bullying do you
   find in these books? What are the causes?
How does your school deal with these
   issues? Do you agree with its approach?
   Write an editorial for or against the
   policies.
Find out about conflict resolution programs
   and peer mediation. Role-play some of
   the situations in the books using these
   techniques. Put them into practice in
   real life.

Family Additions, Subtractions, Separations
Afternoon of the Elves (Lisle)
The Birthday Room (Henkes)
Donuthead (Stauffacher)
Fig Pudding (Fletcher)
Homecoming (Voigt)
The House of Wings (Byars)
Tadpole (White)
Words of Stone (Henkes)
Create Venn diagrams of families: girls and
   boys, hair color, eye color.
Invent variations of the family tree chart to
   show blended families.

GROWING UP IS HARD TO DO: A WEB OF POSSIBILITIES

Growing Up in Tough Situations
Fly Away Home (Bunting)
Home (Rosen)
Monkey Island (Fox)
Create a service project to help the homeless.
Establish a school-to-school partnership to allow
   children contacts with those of different ethnic
   or social backgrounds.
Make a file of news stories detailing problems
   children face.
Compare characters in two or more books; write
   letters from one character to another.

Living with Disabilities
Deaf Child Crossing (Matlin)
Joey Pigza Swallowed the Key (Gantos)
My Buddy (Osofsky)
My Name Is Brain Brian (Betancourt)
Rainy (Deans)
True Friends (Wallace)
Spend some time blindfolded or with your
   writing hand in your pocket; have a
   partner observe and take notes as you go
   about ordinary tasks.
Ask the school district special education
   specialist to visit your classroom and talk
   about helping children with special needs.

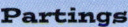

Partings

Alexander, Who's Not (Do You Hear Me? I Mean It!) Going to Move (Viorst)
Amber Brown Is Not a Crayon (Danziger)
The Ashwater Experiment (Koss)
Eagle Song (Bruchac)
Hey New Kid! (Duffy)
The Leaving Morning (A. Johnson)
My Name Is María Isabel (Ada)
Post a map of the United States and the world; have students mark where they have lived.
Survey the school to find out: How many people have moved? How many times?

Baby (MacLachlan)
Chicken Boy (Dowell)
Each Little Bird That Sings (Wiles)
Getting Near to Baby (Couloumbis)
Keeper of the Night (Holt)
Mick Harte Was Here (Park)
Missing May (Rylant)
Sun and Spoon (Henkes)
How has each of the characters in these books been affected by death?
How does each of them learn to say goodbye?
Learn more about the stages of grief.

Coping with School

Adam Canfield of the Slash (Winerip)
The Burning Questions of Bingo Brown (Byars)
Dear Mr. Henshaw (Cleary)
Flour Babies (Fine)
Flying Solo (Fletcher)
Hey World, Here I Am! (Little)
If You're Not Here, Please Raise Your Hand (Dakos)
The Landry News (Clements)
Write letters of advice to younger students.
Write (anonymously) what you expect from the next school year or of a specific year yet to come; read and discuss each other's ideas.
Identify common school problems and explore solutions through creative drama.

Rites of Passage

Becoming Naomi Leon (Ryan)
Cuba 15 (Osa)
Finding Miracles (Alvarez)
Kinaalda: A Navajo Girl Grows Up (Roessel)
The Red Rose Box (Woods)
Rites of Passage: Stories about Growing Up by Black Writers from around the World (Bolden)
Research rites of passage in other cultures.
Create a chart showing ages, ceremonies, etc. Find out what is expected of people of different ages in another culture.
Create your own rite of passage: What ceremony would you invent? Who would be invited? What would be the initiation?

Physical and Psychological Changes

Fit for Life (Parsons)
365 Foods Kids Love to Eat (Ellison)
How does food contribute to your body's changes? Plan and cook meals that promote healthy growth.

Are You There God? It's Me, Margaret (Blume)
Boy2Girl (Blacker)
It's So Amazing (Harris)
The Secret Blog of Raisin Rodriquez (Goldschmidt)
Then Again, Maybe I Won't (Blume)
Learn more about your body's physical changes.

Growing Up Beyond Your Borders

Against the Storm (Hiçyilmaz)
Colibrí (Cameron)
The Garbage King (Laird)
Journey to Jo'burg (Naidoo)
Little Soldier (Ashley)
Parvana's Journey (Ellis)
Secrets in the Fire (Mankell)
Zlata's Diary (Filipovic)
What are the most serious problems facing children around the world? What are the political, economic, social, and other factors that contribute to these problems?
Do any of these problems exist in your own country?
What are the United Nations' Rights of the Child? How are these rights being extended to children around the world? What can you do to help?

Entering the World of Work

A Day's Work (Bunting)
Love as Strong as Ginger (Look)
Interview an adult about his or her job.

Help Wanted: Stories about Young People Working (Silvey)
Ask a working teenager to come in and talk about work experiences.
Compare working wages of today with wages of 50 or 100 years ago.

The Day of Ahmed's Secret (Heide and Gilliland)
Free the Children (Kielburger)
Iqbal (D'Adamo)
Iqbal Masih and the Crusaders against Child Slavery (Kuklin)
Study working conditions for children around the world. What can you do to help?

Based on *The Web: Wonderfully Exciting Books,* ed. Janet Hickman and Rudine Sims Bishop
The Ohio State University, Vol. XVIII, 3 (Winter 1995)

Talking Point

How real should a children's book be?

Are children harmed or helped by reading about tragedy or violence? How would you respond to parents who object to books that deal with difficult issues?

Go to the Online Learning Center at **www.mhhe .com/kiefer9e** or the Resources CD-ROM to learn more.

The TV newscasts of the local Saturday-night killings or the body count in the latest "peacekeeping" effort seldom show the pain and anguish that each death causes. The rebuilding of human lives is too slow and tedious to portray in a half-hour newscast. Even video games are based on violence. The winner of the game is the one who can eliminate or destroy the "enemy." Reasons or motivations are never given, and the aftereffects of violence are not a part of the game.

By way of contrast to the media world, a well-written story provides perspective on the pain and suffering of humankind. In a literary story the author has time to develop the characters into fully rounded human beings. The reader knows the motives and pressures of each individual and can understand and empathize with the characters. If the author's tone is one of compassion for the characters, if others in the story show concern or horror for a brutal act, the reader gains perspective.

A story that makes violence understandable without condoning it is Suzanne Fisher Staples's *Shabanu, Daughter of the Wind*. In the Pakistani desert culture in which 12-year-old Shabanu lives, obedience to rules has enabled many tribes to live in peace in an environment that offers little material comfort. When Shabanu runs away to avoid an arranged marriage to a middle-aged man, she discovers her favorite camel has broken its leg. In choosing to remain with the camel, Shabanu tacitly agrees to the rules of her clan. Her father catches up with her and beats her severely. But she is soaked with his tears as he does what he must, and the reader realizes both are trapped in roles their society has defined for them.

James Giblin, a former children's book editor, suggests that a book can be realistic without being overly graphic.

> For instance, if the young detective in a mystery story was attacked by a gang of bullies, I wouldn't encourage an author to have them burn his arms with a cigarette to get him to talk (although that might conceivably happen in an adult mystery). However, I would accept a scene in which the gang *threatened* to do so: that would

convey the reality and danger of the situation without indulging in all the gory details.[5]

Giblin maintains that very few subjects are inappropriate in themselves; it is all in how the author treats them. The facts of a situation, ugly as they might be, can be presented with feeling and depth of emotion, which carry the reader beyond the particular subject.

The same criteria are appropriate for evaluating explicitness about sex and bodily functions in books for children. Betty Miles raises this issue in *Maudie and Me and the Dirty Book*. When seventh grader Kate Harris teams up with a classmate to read aloud to first graders, one of her choices—a story about a puppy being born—triggers a discussion among the 6-year-olds about human birth and conception. Although Kate handles the discussion with poise, a parent complaint eventually brings about a town meeting concerning what is appropriate in the elementary classroom curriculum. Miles treats the topics of conception, birth, and censorship in an open and forthright way. Chris Crutcher presents a similar situation regarding issues in *The Sledding Hill*. Here, a controversy is sparked by the reading of a young adult novel that includes a gay character. Crutcher's work is more heavy-handed in its message about censorship than is Miles's, but it will certainly prompt interesting discussions. Futhermore, the essence of the book is about friendship and healing rather than sexual orientation.

Bias and Stereotyping

Children's books have always reflected the general social and human values of a society, so it is not surprising that they are also scrutinized for implied attitudes or biases of that society. Contemporary realistic fiction is examined for racism, cultural inaccuracies, sexism, ageism, and treatment of people with physical or mental impairments. Because consciousness generally has been raised in the world of children's book publishing, there are now more books that present diverse populations positively and fairly.

The political and social activism of the 1960s contributed to an awareness of racism in children's books. At the beginning of the twenty-first century children have been able to find fully realized characters from diverse cultures in books such as Virginia Hamilton's *Cousins*, Linda Sue Park's *Project Mulberry*, Pam Muñoz Ryan's *Becoming Naomi Leon*, and Angela Johnson's *Heaven*. These characters exist in their own right and not so that a white main character can "find" herself or himself. Still, adults need to be alert to reissues of books from an earlier era—such as the 1945 Newbery Honor Book *The Silver Pencil*,[6] which contains many racist descriptions of people in Trinidad. Books like this help us recognize the gains of recent decades.

---

[5]James Cross Giblin, *Writing Books for Young People* (Boston: The Writer, 1990), p. 73.

[6]Alice Dalgliesh, *The Silver Pencil* (New York: Puffin, 1991 [1944]).

Marley, the main character in Angela Johnson's *Heaven*, struggles with questions of identity that are common to all children. Reprinted with the permission of Simon & Schuster Books for Young Readers, an imprint of Simon & Schuster Children's Publishing Division from the cover of *Heaven* by Angela Johnson. Illustrations copyright © 1998 by John Jude Palencar.

Because feminists in the 1970s made us more aware of the subtle ways in which literature has perpetuated stereotypes, contemporary realistic fiction now does a much better job of portraying women in a variety of roles. Capable working mothers; caring female role models outside of a child's family; characters who fight sexism; intelligent, independent, and strong girls and women; and romance as a consequence of strong friendship are all found in realistic fiction of the present decade.

Boys have also been subtly victimized by the stereotypes of the past. They have been consistently reminded that men and boys don't cry, for example. But more-modern realistic fiction shows that everyone may cry as they grieve, as do a boy and his father following the drowning of a friend in *On My Honor* by Marion Dane Bauer. Boys have also been frequently stereotyped in ani-

mal stories as having to kill an animal they have loved as an initiation rite. In Marjorie Kinnan Rawlings's *The Yearling,* for instance, Jody is ordered to shoot his pet deer because it is destroying the family crops: "He did not believe he should ever again love anything, man or woman or his own child, as he loved the Yearling. He would be lonely all his life. But a man took it for his share and went on" (p. 400). In Fred Gipson's *Old Yeller,* after the boy shoots his possibly rabid dog, his father tells him to try to forget and go on being a man. Stories such as these cause us to question the way some of our best literature conditions boys to be hard and unfeeling. The issue of presenting multiple role models in books for boys has led to a campaign by popular author Jon Scieszka. Scieszka's Web site, called Guys Read <www.guysread.com>, has suggestions for books and activities that will appeal to boys. Scieszka has also selected various male authors to contribute to *Guys Write for Guys Read,* a collection of short stories for boys.

People with mental or physical impairments have in the past been depicted as "handicapped" or "disabled." A more enlightened view suggests that the person is more important than the impairment; one can be differently abled without necessarily being disabled. Older people (and other adults) in children's literature have often been dismissed as irrelevant in a young person's life, as ineffectual in contrast to the vibrancy of young spirits, or as unable to do certain things because of their age. (See the section "Coping with Problems of the Human Condition" later in this chapter.) High-quality contemporary realistic fiction stories depict adults and older people in many ways—as mentors to young people, for instance, and as having their own romances, problems, and triumphs.

Children's books have made great gains in the depiction of our changing society. However, today's books need to continue to reflect the wide ranges of occupations, education, speech patterns, lifestyles, and futures that are possible for all, regardless of race, gender, age, ability, or belief.

The Author's Background

 Another controversy swirls around authors' racial backgrounds. Must an author be black to write about African Americans, or Native American to write about Native Americans? As Virginia Hamilton states:

> It happens that I know Black people better than any other people because I am one of them and I grew up knowing what it is we are about. . . . The writer uses the most comfortable milieu in which to tell a story, which is why my characters are Black. Often being Black is significant to the story; other times, it is not. The writer will always attempt to tell stories no one else can tell.[7]

---

[7]Virginia Hamilton, "Writing the Source: In Other Words," *Horn Book Magazine* (December 1978): 618.

As we discussed in Chapter 3, it has been generally accepted that an author should write about what he or she knows. But Ann Cameron, an Anglo-American author who has lived in Guatemala for many years, is the author of many books about children from diverse places and cultures, including *The Stories Julian Tells*, *Gloria Rising*, *The Most Beautiful Place in the World*, and *Colibrí*. Cameron maintains a different point view:

> It seems to me that the people who advise "write about what you know" drastically underestimate the human capacity for imagining what lies beyond our immediate knowledge and for understanding what is new to us. Equally, they overestimate the extent to which we know ourselves. A culture, like a person, has blind spots. . . . Often the writer who is an outsider—an African writing about the United States, an American writing about China—sees in a way that enriches him as an observer, the culture he observes, and the culture he comes from.[8]

Moreover, although it may be true that Cameron, and other writers who have spent years living and working in other countries (Elizabeth Laird, Jane Kurtz, and Nancy Farmer, for example) may not be able to give a culturally authentic picture of the characters they write about, they do Western children a great service by pointing out issues of social justice and human rights. As world cultures become more and more interdependent in the twenty-first century, that is surely a worthwhile goal.

The hallmark of fine writing is the quality of imagining it calls forth from us. Imagination is not the exclusive trait of any race or gender but is a universal quality of all fine writers. No authors or artists want to be limited to writing about or portraying only the experiences of persons of a single race or cultural background, nor should they be. We need to focus on two aspects of every book: (1) What is its literary merit? and (2) Will children enjoy it? For some additional criteria to keep in mind, see Evaluation Criteria: "Evaluating Contemporary Realistic Fiction."

Categorizing Literature

Reviewers, educators, and curriculum makers often categorize books according to their content. Categorizing serves textbook authors by allowing them to talk about several books as a group. It serves educators who hope to group books around a particular theme for classroom study. While one person might place Katherine Paterson's *Bridge to Terabithia* in a group of books about "making friends," it could just as easily be placed in other groups, such as books about "growing up" or "learning to accept death," or "well-written books." It is a disservice to both book and reader if, in labeling a book, we

Ann Cameron's life and work in Guatemala serve as a foundation for her writing about a Guatemalan girl's experiences in *Colibrí*. Cover of *Colibri* by Ann Cameron. Copyright © 2003 by Ann Cameron. Reprinted by permission of Farrar, Straus & Giroux, LLC.

imply that this is all the book is about. Readers with their own purposes and backgrounds will see many different aspects and strengths in a piece of literature. It is helpful to remember that our experiences with art occur at many different, unique, and personal levels. Even though teachers might wish to lead children to talk about a particular aspect of a book, they will not want to suggest that this is the only aspect worth pursuing. Author Jean Little argues that teachers need to trust children to find their own messages in books.

> Individual readers come to each story at a slightly different point in their life's journey. If nobody comes between them and the book, they may discover within it some insight they require, a rest they long for, a point of view that challenges their own, a friend they may cherish for life. If we, in the guise of mentor, have all

---

[8]Ann Cameron, "Write What You Care About," *School Library Journal* 35.10 (June 1989): 50.

EVALUATION **CRITERIA**

Evaluating Contemporary Realistic Fiction

- Does the book honestly portray the realities of life for today's children?
- Does the book illuminate problems and issues of growing up in today's world?
- Does the story transcend the contemporary setting and have universal implications?
- Are the characters convincing and credible to today's child?
- Are controversial topics such as sexuality dealt with in an open and forthright way?

- If violence or other negative behavior is part of the story, does the author provide motivations and show aftereffects?
- Does the author avoid stereotyping?
- Does the book truly represent the experience of the culture depicted?
- Does the book help children enlarge their personal points of view and develop appreciation for our ever-changing pluralistic society?

the good messages listed or discussed in small groups . . . the individual and vitally important meeting of child and story may never happen.[9]

A second issue in the categorizing of literature is age-appropriateness. Realistic fiction is often categorized as being for upper elementary or middle-grade and junior high or young-adult readers. Yet anyone who has spent time with 9- to 14-year-old readers has surely noticed the wide ranges of reading interests, abilities, and perceptions present. Betsy Byars's *The Pinballs* and Judy Blume's *Are You There, God? It's Me, Margaret* have challenged and entertained readers from fourth grade through high school. To suggest that these titles are only "for 10- to 12-year-old readers" would ignore the ages of half the readership of these popular authors.

In this chapter, books are arranged according to categories based on theme and content merely for the convenience of discussion. They could have been arranged in many other ways. The ages of main characters are noted, where appropriate, as a clue to potential readership. In some instances we have also noted, with references to actual classroom teachers' experiences, at which grade levels certain titles seem to have the greatest impact.

BECOMING ONE'S OWN PERSON

The story of every man and every woman is the story of growing up, of becoming a person, of struggling to become one's own person. The kind of person you become has its roots in your childhood experiences—how much you were loved, how little you were loved; the people who were significant to you, the ones who were not; the places you've been, and those you did not go to; the things you had, and the things you did not get. Yet a person is always more than the totality of these experiences;

the way a person organizes, understands, and relates to those experiences makes for individuality.

Childhood is not a waiting room for adulthood but the place where adulthood is shaped by one's family, peers, society, and, most important, the person one is becoming. The passage from childhood to adulthood is a significant journey for each person. It is no wonder that children's literature is filled with stories about growing up in our society today.

Living in a Family

The human personality is nurtured within the family; here the growing child learns of love and hate, fear and courage, joy and sorrow. The first "family life" stories tended to portray families without moments of anger and hurt, emphasizing only the happy or adventurous moments. Today the balance scale has tilted in the other direction, and it is often more difficult to find a family story with well-adjusted children and happily married parents than it is to find a story about family problems.

Children still enjoy series such as Eleanor Estes's pre-television-era books *The Moffats*, *The Middle Moffat*, and *Rufus M*, or Sydney Taylor's All-of-a-Kind Family series, which recreates family life in a Lower East Side Jewish home in the 1930s, and adults often point to them as evidence of the pleasures of a less fast-paced life. However, many young readers prefer stories about today's children, those they might meet in the neighborhood, the shopping center, a playground, or the classroom. Jeanne Birdsall's *The Penderwicks: A Summer Tale of Four Sisters, Two Rabbits, and a Very Interesting Boy* is a contemporary novel that recalls the straightforward innocence of these older stories. The four sisters, ages 4 through 12, are pretty much left on their own to have adventures when their widowed father rents a summer cottage on the grounds of a huge estate. And marvelous, funny escapades they

---

[9]Jean Little, "A Writer's Social Responsibility," *New Advocate* 3 (spring 1990): 83.

do have, including running away, a first crush, and a friendship with the misunderstood son of the mansion's snooty owner. The story is reminiscent of the more innocent stories of an earlier age, yet the characters are up-to-date in their personalities and behavior. It will not be surprising to find that Birdsall's characters will join those of Estes and Taylor in the genre of family stories that will be loved for many years.

Generally, most novels about present-day families include fully developed adults with both strengths and weaknesses and show children interacting with them, although formula stories might depict parents and adults as completely inept and unable to cope with or understand their children. If children are to see life wholly and gain some perspective from their reading, educators must help children balance their reading choices.

Family Relationships

Episodic stories centered comfortably in a warm family setting are often the first chapter-book stories younger children read independently. Young readers who more readily follow episodic rather than complicated plots find that Johanna Hurwitz's Russell and Elisa stories, Jessica Scott Kerrin's Martin Bridge series, and Katy Kelly's Lucy Rose series are all good examples of books with easy-to-follow plots. See Teaching Resources: "'To Be Continued': Popular Series Books for Children" on p. 518 for more suggestions.

Beverly Cleary's perennially popular and humorous stories about Ramona are enjoyed both by 7- to 9-year-olds who identify with Ramona's problems and by 10- and 11-year-olds who remember "how I used to be." Cleary's stories concern "the problems which are small to adults but which loom so large in the lives of children, the sort of problems children can solve themselves."[10] In *Ramona and Her Mother*, Ramona worries that her mother doesn't love her as much as she loves Beezus, Ramona's older sister. In *Ramona and Her Father*, Ramona is able to be with her father more often now that she returns from school to find him waiting for telephone calls about jobs he has applied for. In *Ramona's World*, Ramona is involved with her new baby sister and beginning to feel the first romantic stirrings for her old friend "Yard Ape." Now a fourth grader and a more mature, *older* sister, Ramona continues to be her irrepressible dramatic self. Ramona and her family are people worth knowing.

In Lois Lowry's *Anastasia Krupnik*, Anastasia is the only girl in fourth grade whose name will not fit on the front of a sweatshirt. To top off the list of "Things I Love/Things I Hate" that Anastasia keeps, one of the things she is sure she is going to hate is the arrival of a new baby brother. In an effort to appease her, Anastasia's parents let her choose the baby's name, and she considers the worst ones possible. But the death of her grandmother

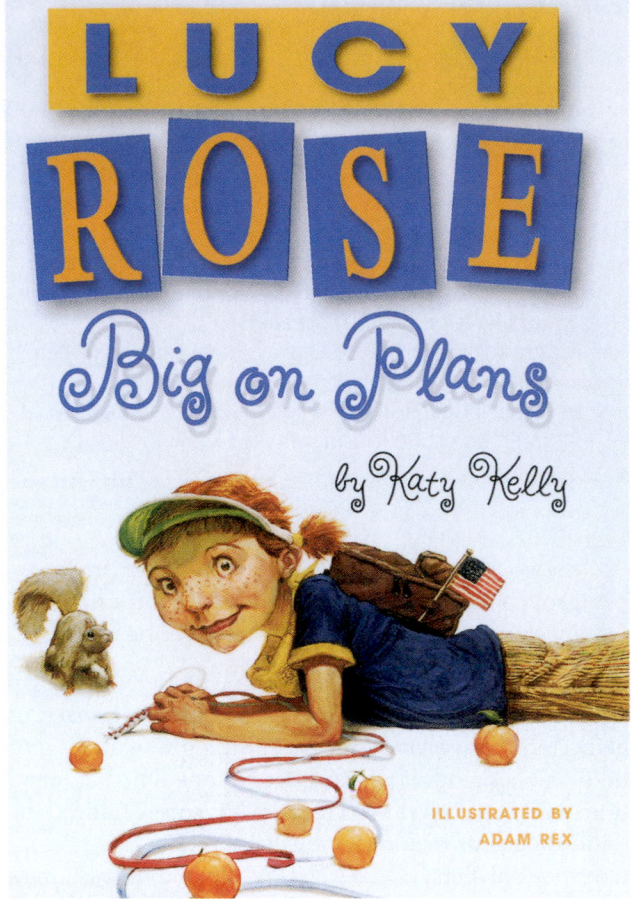

Children who are just moving into fluent reading seem to devour easy chapter books like Katy Kelly's *Lucy Rose: Big on Plans*. Jacket cover from *Lucy Rose: Big on Plans* by Katy Kelly. Used by permission of Random House Children's Books, a division of Random House, Inc., NY.

gives Anastasia some thoughts about the importance of family and of memories—and the new baby is named Sam after her grandfather, whom Anastasia knows only through the reminiscences of her grandmother. Sam's story is told in the hilarious *All about Sam*. Anastasia and Sam have both been featured in a succession of wonderful books. In each, the Krupnik parents treat Anastasia and Sam with openness, humor, and respect; they are both literate and concerned parents whose careers as artist and English teacher do not interfere with their interactions with Anastasia and Sam. Lowry has a gift for natural-sounding dialogue and situational humor, anchored by keen observations of human nature and family relationships.

Names play a key role in several family stories. In Jane Kurtz's *Jakarta Missing*, 12-year-old Dakar is the younger daughter of adventuresome parents who have traveled the world to study and provide aid to commu-

---

[10]Beverly Cleary, "The Laughter of Children," *Horn Book Magazine* (October 1982): 557.

nities experiencing disasters, such as cholera epidemics and earthquakes. Dakar and her sister were named for the places where they were born, and have grown up in Africa. When the family returns to North Dakota, it is a real jolt for Dakar, whose overly fearful outlook is in contrast to that of her father, who seems to thrive in dangerous situations. Dakar misses Kenya and, most of all, her sister, Jakarta, who remained at her boarding school in Kenya. When Jakarta is reported missing in a political disturbance, Dakar faces the fact that her "perfect" family is in a highly fragile state. Left on her own for a time, Dakar learns that she can't be so fixated with being safe that she forgets to be fully alive.

In both *Saffy's Angel* by Hilary McKay and *Dillon Dillon* by Kate Banks, children discover that they are adopted because of their unusual names. When she learns to read and can examine the color wheel in her artist-parents' kitchen, Saffron Casson discovers that she can find the names of sisters Cadmium and Rose and brother Indigo on the wheel, but not her own. When a bungling health visitor, there to check on sickly baby Rose, exclaims, "Doesn't she know?", Saffy's mother is forced to tell her the truth. She is the daughter of her mother's sister, killed in a car accident in Italy when Saffy was just a baby. Saffy suddenly feels like a stranger, despite the love and affection shown by her adopted family. When Saffy is 13, her maternal grandfather dies and leaves her an unusual legacy, "her angel in the garden." Saffy's search for the angel and for the answer to who she really is form the nucleus of this warm and funny family story. As in her other books, such as *The Exiles* and *Dog Friday*, McKay creates a wonderfully eccentric group of characters, but this story of the bond that holds together a family is very true. We get to know other members of the Casson family in two more wonderful books by McKay, *Indigo's Star* and *Permanent Rose*.

Like Saffy, Dillon Dillon has questions about his name. The summer he turns 10 his family travels to their cabin on Lake Waban in New Hampshire, and Dillon finally asks his parents, "Why did you name me Dillon Dillon?" They tell him, reluctantly, that his real parents, his father's sister and her husband, were killed in a car accident when he was a baby. He had been named Dillon McDermott, but they couldn't bear to change his first name when they adopted him. Devastated by this news, Dillon wonders if parents can love an adopted child as much as their "real" children, especially when one is as precious as his little sister, Daisy, or as talented as his older brother, Didion. The red rowboat he received for his birthday allows him to explore the lake at the same time he tries to explore his feelings. When he discovers a family of loons on a nearby island and a book about loons that his birth mother had owned, he is on the way to understanding that his family's love for him is uncondi-tional. Kate Banks, illustrator of many fine picture books, has created a vivid setting and memorable characters in this magical, beautiful story.

No book has revealed the complexities of sibling rivalry with as much depth as Katherine Paterson's challenging Newbery Medal–winning story *Jacob Have I Loved*. Louise is convinced that she lives in her twin sister's shadow. Caroline, her beautiful, blond, delicate sister, is the talented one, who leaves their island home of Rass each week to take piano lessons. Louise, or "Wheeze," the hated name Caroline has given her, believes her sister has stolen everything from her: her parents' affection, her friends Call and the Captain, and her chance for an education. Her half-crazed Bible-quoting grandmother recognizes her burning resentment of Caroline and taunts her with the quote "Jacob have I loved but Esau have I hated."

Paterson has skillfully woven the Bible story of Esau, firstborn, who was tricked into giving up his birthright to Jacob, the younger of the twin brothers, into this modern novel of sibling rivalry. Only maturity and a family of her own can help Louise to put her hatred and resentment of her sister to rest. The novel ends on a theme of reconciliation as Louise, now a midwife in a mountain community, fights to save the life of the weaker second-born baby of a pair of twins. In her Newbery acceptance speech for *Jacob Have I Loved*, the author, herself the middle child of five, said: "Among children who grow up together in a family there run depths of feeling that will permeate their souls for good and ill as long as they live."[11]

In *The Birthday Room*, Kevin Henkes deals with long-held grudges between grown siblings. Twelve-year-old Ben's mother has never forgiven her brother Ian for an accident that maimed Ben's hand. When Ian asks Ben to come for a visit to Oregon, Ben's mother reluctantly agrees to accompany him. There they find that Ian's new wife, Nina, is soon to give birth. Even though sister and sister-in-law form an immediate bond, the tension continues between sister and brother. Ben, caught in the middle, is distracted by his feelings for Lynnie, a neighbor girl. However, Ben's efforts to help Lynnie's younger twin siblings, Kale and Elke, with a special project result in a near tragedy when Kale falls out of a tree and breaks his arm and leg. Ben's feelings of guilt and remorse are mirrored by those of his Uncle Ian and his mother for their own culpability in Ben's accident years before. Unlike these two, however, Ben accepts responsibility for his role in the accident and sets about to make amends to Kale. At the book's end, perhaps influenced by Ben's example, his mother and Uncle Ian are reconciled. In a lovely reference to the book's title, Ben, pleased to have reestablished these family connections, makes room in his life for his new baby cousin.

---

[11]Katherine Paterson, "Newbery Medal Acceptance," in *Gates of Excellence* (New York: Elsevier/Nelson Books, 1981), p. 118.

Twelve-year-old Ben learns that the long-standing relationship between his mother and his uncle has an important effect on his own self-awareness. Jacket from *The Birthday Room* by Kevin Henkes. Jacket illustrations copyright © 1999 by Laura Dronzek. Used by permission of Greenwillow Books, a division of William Morrow Company/HarperCollins Publishers.

Mother-daughter conflict is the subject of Gennifer Choldenko's *Notes from a Liar and Her Dog*. Sixth grader Antonia (Ant) MacPherson is a middle child, so different from her seemingly perfect sisters that she is convinced she has been left with the MacPhersons by her real parents. She calls her mother Mrs. MacPherson and finds other ways to act out her anger. Her father's job as a consultant forces the family to move often, and Ant has trouble fitting in at school as well as in her family. She has only one eccentric friend, Harrison, and one tiny old dog, Pistachio, both of whom her mother dislikes. When their art teacher invites Ant and Harrison to become part of Zoo Teens, volunteers at the local zoo, their work there becomes a positive force in their lives. However, Pistachio becomes ill, and Ant's mother is reluctant to spend money on vet bills for the aging dog. Their conflict escalates, and Ant's lies get her into deeper trouble. Finally, convinced that her mother is going to have Pistachio put to sleep before the family moves again, Ant puts herself in real danger when she takes Pistachio along on her Saturday job, and he escapes into a lion's den. As a result,

she, Harrison, and her teacher are banished from the zoo. She finally realizes that her troublemaking has hurt other people in addition to herself. She and her mother have a confrontation that is both honest and painful, opening up the possibility of a better relationship in the future. Told in the first person, *Notes from a Liar and Her Dog* is both amusing and poignant, a believable story of adolescent angst and the misunderstandings that can arise between parent and child during these difficult years.

Extended Families

The extended family of grandparents, uncles, aunts, cousins, and so on, often plays a significant role in a child's developing perception of the world. Children's literature presents other adults, and sometimes even children, acting in the place of absent or incapacitated parents.

Patricia MacLachlan's *Journey* is the story of an 11-year-old boy named Journey who is devastated and angered when his mother leaves him with his grandparents. He cannot accept the fact that his mother is gone—not for the summer, but for good. His loving grandparents, a cat named Bloom, and his grandfather's photographs finally help him to accept the loss of his mother. His grandfather has told him that "sometimes pictures show us what is really there," and later his sister explains that the collection of photographs his grandfather has taken represent his grandfather's efforts to give him back everything that his mother took away. Journey understands then that his grandparents, unlike his mother, have given him the family he has longed for. MacLachlan's writing respects readers' intelligence and suggests that what is important or real is often at first difficult to see.

In Betsy Byars's *The House of Wings*, Sammy's parents leave him behind with his aged grandfather, a recluse in an old run-down house, while they go ahead to find a place to stay in Detroit. When Sammy refuses to believe his parents have left and tries to follow them, the old man runs after the furious boy. But in the midst of the chase his grandfather calls him to come and look at a wounded crane. Together the two of them catch the crane and care for it. Suddenly the boy desperately wants his grandfather to know him the way he knows birds:

> He wanted his grandfather to be able to pick him
> out of a thousand birds the way he could pick
> out the blackbird, the owls, the wild ducks. . . .
> He said, "My name's Sammy." (p. 141)

His grandfather looks at Sammy and then, instead of calling him "Boy," calls him "Sammy," and the relationship is sealed. *The House of Wings* is still one of Byars's best books. Her two characters are well drawn: the eccentric old man, more interested in birds than in his grandson; the boy Sammy, furious at being left, uncertain of himself, and desperately wanting to love and be loved.

Unlike Sammy, 9-year-old Rivers is perfectly happy with a replacement father in *Uncle Daddy* by Ralph Fletcher. His mother's uncle, "Uncle Daddy" has stepped in to take the place of the father who abandoned Rivers and his mother when Rivers was 3. Uncle Daddy is a gentle and nurturing man, and Rivers adores him. But their relationship is turned upside down when Rivers's real father shows up asking for forgiveness. It's hard for these three to open up their tight-knit family structure to someone who hurt them so badly. Then Uncle Daddy has a near-fatal heart attack, and Rivers's father pitches in to help convert their garage into an apartment where Uncle Daddy can recover. His earnest efforts and his honesty about why he left help Rivers and his mother begin to forgive him. The book ends with Uncle Daddy back home and the possibility of a renewed and stronger relationship among Rivers, his mother, and his father.

Fourteen-year-old Marley must come to terms with family secrets in Angela Johnson's *Heaven*. Raised in a loving family in an idyllic small town called Heaven, Marley is shocked to learn that her "parents" are really her aunt and uncle and that her real father is her itinerant uncle. She eventually comes to terms with her anger and feelings of betrayal, in large part because the members of the small community teach her that no family is perfect and that families are created by loving support rather than by genetics. Johnson's *The First Part Last*, the prequel to *Heaven*, tells the story of Marley's birth father and his struggle to keep his baby. This book won the Printz Award for Young Adult Literature but would still be appropriate reading for younger adolescents as well, especially for those who love Marley's story.

Cynthia Voigt's saga about the Tillerman family spans at least six novels as it fills in the events of several families' lives in a small Chesapeake Bay town. *Homecoming* introduces 13-year-old Dicey Tillerman, who, along with her two younger brothers and a younger sister, was abandoned in the parking lot of a Connecticut shopping mall by her mentally ill mother. Dicey decides the children must walk south along the Connecticut shoreline to Bridgeport to live with an aunt. But the aunt has died and her daughter, Cousin Eunice, wants to divide the family into foster homes. From Eunice, Dicey discovers that they have a grandmother living in Maryland. Determined to keep her family together, Dicey manages against all odds to reach her grandmother's home on the Chesapeake Bay, only to find an eccentric, independent, and angry old lady. The children try to keep up the huge rundown house and garden and quickly grow to love the place. But they are less sure about their prickly grandmother. This believable survival story ends with the formation of a tentative understanding between Gram and the children. In the sequel, *Dicey's Song*, Dicey must learn to let her family change, accept her own move toward maturity, and acknowledge her feelings for others. It is the growing warmth the Tillermans take on as they learn to be a family that lets the children, and the reader, accept their mother's death at the story's end. Other stories carry on the Tillerman saga, and two young-adult

novels, *The Runner* and *Seventeen against the Dealer*, conclude the story. In all of her novels about the Tillerman family, Voigt explores love in its many forms—love that can't be expressed, love achieved through learning, manipulative love, and family love.

Aunts or uncles replace absent parents in a number of recent books for children, including Polly Horvath's *The Vacation* and E. L. Konigsburg's *The Outcasts of 19 Schuyler Place*. Horvath's character Henry is left in the care of two very eccentric aunts when his parents go off to Africa. Aunt Magg and Aunt Pigg decide to take the highly anxious Henry on a road trip, which proceeds from one disaster to another. In the end the trio survives, and Henry learns to surrender himself (a bit) to the moment. In Konigsburg's *The Outcasts of 19 Schuyler Place* we meet Margaret Rose, a character like Konigsburg's memorable Claudia in *From the Mixed-Up Files of Mrs. Basil E. Frankweiler*. With her parents in Peru, Margaret Rose begins summer at the disastrous Camp Talequa until she is banished for her headstrong behavior. Her

Henry, a rather uptight young boy, learns to loosen up and enjoy life's ride in a road trip with two unconventional aunts in Polly Horvath's *The Vacation*. Cover of *The Vacation* by Polly Horvath. Copyright © 2005 by Polly Horvath. Reprinted by permission of Farrar, Straus & Giroux, LLC.

beloved great-uncles, Alexander and Morris, rescue her and take her to their home at 19 Schuyler Place. Here Margaret Rose finds herself in another battle of wills, this time over the three weird and wonderful clock towers her uncles have been building for years. When the city council declares that the towers must come down, Margaret Rose rises to the occasion.

Ruth Wallace-Brodeur's *Heron Cove* and Julie Schumacher's *Grass Angel* involve absent parents and eccentric aunts, but both are written on a more serious note. Wallace-Brodeur's book introduces Sage, a 12-year-old girl whose mother leaves her with her great-aunts in Maine while she attends a summer retreat. The long absence and then death of Sage's father has left Sage and her mother at odds. However, her Aunts Addie and Bea introduce Sage to a family history she has never known, and as the summer progresses Sage comes to better understand her mother's actions and her own place in the family story. In Schumacher's *Grass Angel* 11-year-old Frances is also angry and bitter over her father's death and with her undemonstrative mother's expectations of perfection. When her mother, who seems to be constantly searching for some kind of spiritual fulfillment, decides to head off to Oregon to a spiritual retreat, Frances refuses to go. While her mother and little brother head west, Frances is left behind with her mother's sister, Blue, a rather slovenly computer whiz who has long been at odds with her sister. Resentful and worried that her mother and brother are caught up in a cult, Frances manages to get herself into one scrap after another, including an incident of vandalism. However, Aunt Blue proves to be a true-blue friend and gradually helps Frances to realize that growing up means taking responsibility for one's actions. When Frances's little brother disappears from the Oregon camp, she is the one who takes thoughtful action to find him and to help bring her mother home.

Families in Transition

The 1998 U.S. census report found that 27 percent of American children live in single-parent families; although a majority of suburban children live with married parents, as many as two-thirds of city children do not. Nearly one out of every two marriages now ends in divorce. It is only natural, then, that books acknowledge children's attempts to deal with the disruption and confusion or pain and anger that often result from divorce, death, and other family upsets.

Beverly Cleary won the Newbery Medal for *Dear Mr. Henshaw*, the story of Leigh Botts, a child of divorce. The plot is skillfully revealed through a series of letters to an author, Mr. Henshaw. Sixth grader Leigh writes Mr. Henshaw and asks for an immediate answer to ten questions. Mr. Henshaw responds with ten questions of his own. In the process of answering these questions (his mother says he has to), Leigh reveals how much he misses his truck-driver father and Bandit, his dog, and his many other concerns. Though not as humorous as some of Beverly Cleary's other books, this one is more thoughtful and certainly presents an honest picture of a child living in a single-parent home. Cleary's ear for the way children think and speak is remarkably true. Cleary's *Strider*, a buoyant sequel, begins four years later when Leigh is in high school and his hurt over his father's abandonment has been lessened by new friends and his success in school.

Twelve-year-old "Tree," in Joan Bauer's *Stand Tall*, is so nicknamed because he has always been the tallest boy in his class. Now in seventh grade he is six feet three and a half inches tall and still growing. Yet the added inches do not mean added agility. He is hopeless at sports, especially basketball, a fact that is particularly difficult to accept in the shadow of the athletic abilities shown by his two older brothers. But worst of all for Tree is his parents' recent divorce and his difficulty in getting used to trading houses every week. Tree has some good things going for him, however. His beloved Grandpa, a Viet-

Each of the main characters in Ruth White's warmly affecting *Belle Prater's Boy* must deal with the loss of a parent. Jacket design by Elizabeth Sayles from *Belle Prater's Boy* by Ruth White. Jacket art copyright © 1996 by Elizabeth Sayles. Reprinted by permission of Farrar, Straus and Giroux, LLC.

nam vet whose lower leg has just been amputated due to an old war injury, has a lot to teach him about courage. An eighth-grade girl named Sophie has a lot to show him about confidence. And an aging dog named Bradley has a lot to show him about second chances. In *Stand Tall*, Bauer, as in her other books, writes with a finely honed sense of humor and develops unique yet believable characters who do their best to muddle through in a less than perfect world. In the end, of course, Tree accepts those imperfections in himself and others and finds that he has, indeed, learned to stand tall.

Ruth White's *Belle Prater's Boy* tells of Woodrow Prater, cousin to Gypsy Leemaster of Coal City, West Virginia. Although on the surface life seems "fresh and bright, pink and white" as Gypsy describes it, both cousins have secret pain that they hide and mysteries that they each need to solve. Woodrow's problems are out front for the world to see. Not only has his mother disappeared, leaving him with an alcoholic father who is unable to care for him, but his cross-eyed visage and hand-me-down clothes leave him open to pity as well as ridicule. Gypsy, who seems to have everything Woodrow lacks, suffers too—from strange nightmares and nameless fears. Her own family secret has been buried almost too deeply for her to acknowledge. As the story progresses, each cousin draws strength from the other, supported in their quest for truth about their family by a wonderfully quirky yet loving cast of characters. White's story is enriched by her intimate knowledge of small-town Appalachian life. She portrays this very human story with a sense of humor and warmth that seem to grow uniquely out of this setting. Woody and Gypsy return in *The Search for Belle Prater* and find a happy ending for Woody and Belle. Kerry Madden's *Gentle's Holler*, discussed in Chapter 1, also centers on the singular characters and relationships that exist in the Appalachian region. Madden follows the story of Livy Two told in *Gentle's Holler* with the points of view of two other siblings in *Louise's Palette* and *Jessie's Mountain*.

Living with a single parent often means living on the edge of security and lacking a consistent routine. Such is the case in Jacqueline Wilson's *The Illustrated Mum* and Michael de Guzman's *Beekman's Big Deal*. Funny and poignant, both books involve main characters who exist outside the norm, eccentric but loving single parents, and a supporting cast of caring adults and friends. In *The Illustrated Mum*, 10-year-old Dol must eventually leave her mother to find herself. In *Beekman's Big Deal*, 12-year-old Beekman learns to take charge of his own future and helps his wheeler-dealer father get a firmer grip on reality.

In Cynthia Rylant's Newbery Medal book *Missing May*, Summer has finally found a family only to lose its heart. Following her mother's death, Summer had been bounced around from one relative to another until her Aunt May and Uncle Ob had shown up and taken her

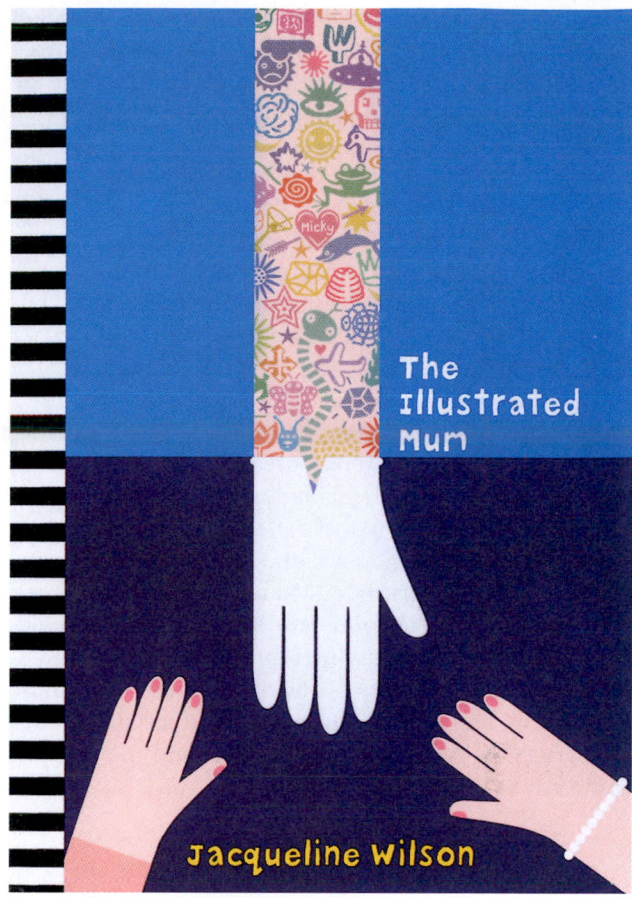

Jacqueline Wilson's main character fights a losing battle to stay with an unstable mother in *The Illustrated Mum*. Jacket cover of *The Illustrated Mum* by Jacqueline Wilson. Jacket illustration copyright © 2005 by Linda Davick. Used by permission of Random House Children's Books, a division of Random House, Inc.

home with them. Home was only a trailer in the West Virginia hills, but it was heaven to the little 6-year-old, and May was its center.

> May was the best person I ever knew. Even better than Ob. She was a big barrel of nothing but love and while Ob and me were off in our dreamy heads, May was there in this trailer seeing to it there was a good home for us when we were ready to land. She understood people and she let them be whatever way they needed to be. She had faith in every single person she ever met, and this never failed her, for nobody ever disappointed May. Seems people knew she saw the very best of them and they'd turn that side to her to give her a better look. (pp. 15–16)

Summer is 12 when May dies, and she and Ob cannot seem to find their way without her. *Missing May* is about the grieving that people need to do and the healing that comes with time, with love, and—in this case—with a little help from Summer's strange friend Cletus, a dead medium named Miriam Young, and perhaps a guardian angel named May. And while Summer, Ob, and Cletus set out on a real journey to cure their pain, it is the journey of the spirit that finally brings them home, ready to be a family to each other with May's memory at the center.

The words of a storyteller also prove healing in Sharon Creech's *Walk Two Moons.* Salamanca Tree Huddle has found it difficult to reconcile herself to the changes in her family's situation. Living in suburban Cleveland, she longs for the family's beautiful Kentucky farm, but most of all she desperately misses her mother, who went West to find herself following the death of her newborn baby. Sal is convinced that if she can only get to her mother in Idaho in time for her birthday, she can bring her home. Her grandparents agree to undertake the long journey, and in the car Salamanca regales them with stories of her friend Phoebe Winterbottom, Phoebe's mother's disappearance, a kidnapping, and an ax murder that the two girls set out to solve. Interwoven with this story and the ongoing story of their trip are Salamanca's memories of her mother and their life in Kentucky. Her grandparents, wonderfully warm and funny characters, give her the help she needs to accept the truth about her family. Sal comes to understand the purpose that these stories have served for her.

> It seems to me that we can't explain all the truly awful things in the world like war and murder and brain tumors, and we can't fix these things so we look at the frightening things that are closer to us and we magnify them until they burst open. Inside is something that we can manage, something that isn't as awful as it had at first seemed. (p. 277)

Betsy Byars frequently writes about children who live in single-parent families and are often left on their own. Even though adult intervention eventually helps allay a crisis, Byars's main characters generally work things out for themselves while realizing a "little moment of growth." *The Pinballs* deals with three children who have been placed in a foster home. Carlie is a tough, likable 12-year-old girl who has repeatedly been beaten up by her third stepfather. She endures her world by watching television and making caustic comments. Harvey comes to the Masons in a wheelchair because his alcoholic father accidentally ran him over and broke both his legs. The third child in this mismatched group is Thomas J., a boy who is 8 going on 80. Elderly twin spinsters had tried to raise him without notifying the authorities, so Thomas J. had never gone to school. Carlie maintains that they are all "just like pinballs. Somebody put in a dime and punched a button and out we come, ready or not, and settled in the same groove" (p. 29). By the end of the story,

Carlie has learned that life is determined not only by blind chance but also by initiative, for it is her creative planning that finally breaks through Harvey's depression and gives him some reason to live. Carlie's change, from being a defensive, self-centered person into becoming a compassionate human being, is gradual and believable, and she never loses her comical perspective on life. Middle-grade students enjoy hearing this story read aloud and meeting this fine cast of characters. A keen ear for dialogue and humor and an accurate eye for the memorable incidents of childhood typify novels by Betsy Byars.

In Katherine Paterson's *The Great Gilly Hopkins,* Gilly is not nearly the likable character that Carlie is. When Gilly arrives at her next foster home, she can't bear the huge, semiliterate Maime Trotter and her "retard" 7-year-old ward. So she sends a letter to her beautiful mother in California greatly exaggerating her situation. When she steals over a hundred dollars of Trotter's foster-care money and tries to buy a ticket to California, she is stopped by the police. Finally she understands the real love and trust that Trotter has for her as Trotter refuses to let the social worker move Gilly to yet another home. It is too late, however, as Gilly receives an answer to her letter in the form of a visit from her grandmother, whom she never knew existed. Desperately sad about leaving Trotter, Gilly learns then that one has to accept responsibility for one's own actions. One of the consistent themes in Paterson's writings is that main characters always get their wishes—but not in the way they expected.[12] This is also true for 11-year-old Angel in Paterson's *The Same Stuff as Stars.* Angel is not nearly as tough as Gilly, in spite of the fact that she has had to play the role of adult in her dysfunctional family. But her father is in jail and now, unable to face up to his responsibilities, her mother has taken off. She has left Angel and her 7-year-old brother Bernie with her father's old grandmother, a woman who can barely care for herself, much less two children. When her mother comes back to get Bernie only to run off again with a new boyfriend, Angel is distraught and contacts her father at the prison, hoping he can help. Instead, he breaks away from a work gang and shows up promising to take her to Florida. Unlike her father, Angel understands how impossible such a future would be. Her desperate wish, that her father would never leave her again, was just as unrealistic. This is a heartbreaking story about adults who have very few options in life and about the children who suffer for the wrong choices those adults often make. But Angel has a strong heart and is supported by two unlikely adults. Star Man is a mysterious recluse who teaches her to read the nighttime sky, and Miss Liza is an ancient librarian who feeds her need for words with books like Peter Sis's *Starry Messenger.* Angel learns through these adults that she is made of the same stuff

---

[12]Christy Richards Slavik, "The Novels of Katherine Paterson: Implications for the Middle School" (Ph.D. dissertation, Ohio State University, 1983).

as stars, and she finds that her brave spirit burns with just as strong a light.

Sara Moone, in Canadian author Julie Johnston's *Adam and Eve and Pinch-Me,* could be an older Gilly, an adolescent who has been passed around from one foster home to another. At 15, however, she'll soon be able to be on her own, and there is nothing this isolated teen wants more than to be left alone. Like the computer that she types her thoughts into, Sara is a cold machine, unable to show emotions to the outside world. And just as her computer is without a printer, she is without the ability to reveal her thoughts to anyone. Impinging on this isolation are the Huddlestons, her new foster parents, their two other foster children, and a mysterious stranger who is in town looking for her long-lost daughter. Their problems soon draw Sara into the middle of a suspenseful and somewhat complicated plot. The ending is not quite what Sara, or the reader, expected, but the "Queen of Cool" finds the warm and loving home she has needed all along and the courage to finally put her words into printed form.

Julie Johnston's *In Spite of Killer Bees* is a warm and funny story about three sisters who manage to create a somewhat unique family unit after their mother abandons them and their father, a reformed small-time thief, dies. When the grandfather they never knew also dies and names them in his will, they imagine they will receive millions. Instead, they receive the family home on a lake in Canada with the stipulation that an eccentric old aunt must agree to move in with them. The two older girls struggle to find jobs until they can pick up and leave for greener pastures. This is tough to do, however, in a town that knows their father's reputation and is suspicious of their eccentric ways. Aggie, the 14-year-old narrator who dresses in vintage clothing and views her life in terms of a screenplay, longs to stay and put down roots. Her efforts to create the stable family she never had means she has to face the real world and see some truths that she would rather ignore. Johnston's stories are highly original, and in all her books she is sensitive to the thoughts, feelings, and dreams of her adolescent characters.

The themes surrounding the need for a family unit and the love and acceptance that can be found within that unit have intrigued writers of literature for children for more than a century. In books such as *Heidi* by Johanna Spyri (1884) and *Anne of Green Gables* by Lucy Montgomery (1908), the circumstances of the orphaned child seemed mainly to thrust the plot forward to a happy ending. At the beginning of the twenty-first century, children on their own in books such as Martine Leavitt's *Heck Superhero,* Richard Peck's *Strays like Us,* and Heather Quarles's *A Door near Here* are presented with such realities as addictions, AIDS, and an overburdened welfare system. These characters don't always achieve success, happiness, and the perfect nuclear family. However, they do find a measure of self-understanding and self-respect over the course of these books, and their need to be part of a supportive and loving unit is as strong as it was in books written a century ago.

Living with Others

Three- and 4-year-olds show momentary concern for their sandbox companions, but it is usually only when children go to school that the peer group becomes important. By the time children approach the middle of elementary school, what other children think is often more significant than what parents, teachers, or other adults think. By the time children reach middle school or junior high school, the peer group and making friends are all-important.

Finding Peer Acceptance

A classic example of children's cruelty to others who are "different" is the well-known, somewhat didactic story *The Hundred Dresses* by Eleanor Estes, first published in 1944. Wanda, a poor Polish girl, attempts unsuccessfully to win a place in the group by telling of the hundred dresses she owns. It is only after she moves away, and the hundred dresses—all drawings—are displayed, that her peers understand that their cowardice in not befriending Wanda and their meanness have deprived them of both a friend and their own self-respect.

Louise Fitzhugh's *Harriet the Spy* has also achieved the status of a modern classic. It is the story of a precocious child who finds it difficult to relate to either her parents or her peers. Harriet tells her own story, interspersed with her notes about people she observes at school and after school. Her baby-sitter, Ole Golly, has been Harriet's consistent source of security, and when she leaves, Harriet's loneliness is compounded when her classmates find her journal. The underlying theme of this forty-plus-year-old story is still relevant today. It contains serious statements about how children respond to teachers, to cliques, and to each other.

It is clear that children's cruelty is not a new phenomenon. Indeed, it is of major concern to today's parents and educators. Several excellent contemporary novels deal directly with the topic of bullying and peer pressure. Ann Martin's *Here Today* is a nuanced story about a family breakup, but the outcome of bullying is a clear theme throughout. Doris Day Dingman, mother of 11-year-old Ellie and her younger siblings, Albert and Marie, is clearly caught up in her own dreams of celebrity and stardom in a small New York State town in the early 1960s. Ellie has pretty much assumed the role of mother, not just for her siblings but for the entire neighborhood that surrounds Witch Tree Lane. This tight community is made up of diverse families: Ellie's best friend, Holly, and her never-married mother, two older women who may or may not be lesbians, an observant Jewish family, and a family of French gypsies. These families have become the butt of teasing by the other children in Ellie's school, harassment that begins with words but soon escalates into vandalism and physical and psychological tortures. The heart of the story is about Ellie's acceptance of her mother's neglect and ultimate desertion and the new life that she, her father, and the community build together.

Deliver Us from Normal by Kate Klise also concerns a family who are seen as outcasts. In this case, the hero, Charles Harrisong, a seventh grader and the second child in a large, lower income Catholic family, is also highly neurotic and prays constantly for his family to be "normal," like the name of their Illinois town. As the book's narrator, he explains: "This, I believed was my secret gift: I could see and hear things—words, messages, hidden meanings—without my eyes and ears. I could feel things other people didn't feel" (p. 13). As a result Charles has become the sensitive loner in his new middle school, the boy who cried in class at the end of Majorie Rawlings's *The Yearling*, the kid who takes on his family's tragedies, real and imagined. His older sister, Clara; his parents; and several of his teachers seem to recognize that his mental problems may be serious, but the bullying and taunting he receives at school go unchecked. However, when Clara, a born optimist, becomes the butt of libel during her campaign for seventh-grade class president, the Harrisongs pick up and leave Normal. Dad has found an old houseboat for sale cheap, and the family reluctantly follow him to Alabama. The houseboat, named the "O'Migosh" by younger sister, Laura, proves to be a disaster at first, but as the family works to refinish and clean it, they draw together and Charles finds some measure of comfort. On their first voyage, however, the boat springs a terrible leak, and Charles and his father must try to fix it. This incident is almost the breaking of Charles. In his panic he imagines first that his father is trying to kill him and then that he must kill his father. But his father is a strong and resolute man and helps Charles through the crisis. Charles, a huge fan of choose-your-own-ending books, decides he is capable of choosing his own happy ending. Both Martin's *Here Today* and Klise's *Deliver Us from Normal* are fine coming-of-age stories at their centers. But both books also bring home the cruelty of bullying to their readers and make fine stepping-off places for discussion.

Amy Goldman Koss examines peer relationships from the point of view of the outsider in *The Ashwater Experiment*. Hillary has spent her life traveling from craft fair to craft fair with her hippie parents. She has never had a chance to form friendships and has learned to shut herself off from relationships. When her parents take on a long-term house-sitting job in Ashwater, California, Hillary decides to be more open to her classmates as an experiment, and this "exercise" allows her to be more vulnerable. She finds, to her surprise, that she is welcomed into the clique surrounding Serena, one of the most popular girls in the school, but she is also drawn to Cass, another loner. Hillary is able to maintain both friendships without being drawn in by the lure of the in-crowd. Although she must move away, in the end she has learned

In *Deliver Us from Normal* by Kate Klise a boy on the verge of a mental breakdown is supported by a loving if eccentric family. Cover illlustration copyright © 2005 by Joe Zeff from *Deliver Us from Normal* by Kate Klise. Published by Scholastic Pess/Scholastic Inc. Reprinted by permission.

that friendships are not a matter of place but of feelings. She is now confident that she will remain connected to the friends in Ashwater at the same time as she makes new friends in her new home.

Several books—among them, Jerry Spinelli's *Wringer*—examine the serious consequences of peer pressure. In Spinelli's *Wringer*, 9-year-old Palmer is pushed to be "one of the boys" by enduring physically painful rituals. In addition, he is pressured into taunting his one-time friend, Dorothy. Worst of all he is expected to be part of a rite of passage that requires 10-year-old boys to attend the community pigeon shoot to act as "wringers." These boys seek out the pigeons that have been wounded in the shoot and wring their necks, with a prize given to the boy who collects the most pigeons. Palmer is uncomfortable with the new role he is forced to play, but he is downright sickened by the thought of being a "wringer," especially after he makes a pet of a pigeon that has landed on his windowsill. Spinelli, with his usual wry sense of humor still in evidence, examines important issues of peer pressure and gender roles in a serious way.

Titles for middle-school students that deal with the effects of peer pressure, including gang violence, include Jane Leslie Conly's *In the Night, on Lanvale Street* and Walter Dean Myers's *Scorpions* and *Shooter*.

Making Friends

The theme of building friendships is often a part of realistic fiction. Stories about life in families commonly include one child's relationship with someone outside the home. Popular fiction traces the ups and downs of friendships in the classroom. Other stories, such as Lisa Yee's *Millicent Kwan, Girl Genius*, Frances O'Roark Dowell's *Where I'd Like to Be*, Kazumi Yumoto's *The Friends*, or Beverly Cleary's depiction of Ramona and her friends, have multiple themes besides the tentative ways boys and girls form important friendships. In Kimberly Willis Holt's *When Zachary Beaver Came to Town*, 13-year-old Toby must deal with his mother's absence from their small Texas town, his crush on a neighbor girl, and his longing for a brother like his best friend Cal's. The arrival in his small Texas town of Zachary Beaver, an immensely overweight boy who has been abandoned by his side-show manager, is the catalyst for the book's adventures and its many subthemes. But all these events center around friendships—the ups and downs of longtime friends and the forging of new friendships.

Two fifth-grade friendships are presented in Betsy Byars's *The Cybil War*; the first is a long-standing one between Simon Newton and Cybil Ackerman, and the other is a rocky one between Simon and his boastful, lying friend Tony Angott. While both boys vie for Cybil's attention, Tony tricks her into going out on a first date with him. However, his scheme backfires, for Cybil recognizes Tony's true nature. Simon's triumphant bicycle ride with Cybil provides a satisfying conclusion to this lighthearted tale of friendship.

Characters in Zilpha Keatley Snyder's books are often intelligent children from differing backgrounds who develop strong friendships. In *The Egypt Game*, six young children in a Berkeley, California, neighborhood set up in an abandoned storage yard an imaginary game based on their research into the ceremonies and culture of ancient Egypt. When one of the game players is attacked and another neighborhood child is murdered, the children's outdoor play is curtailed. In this mystery, Snyder leads readers to believe that a junk dealer/professor who owns the storage yard is the murderer. But he is instrumental in apprehending the criminal, which forces the children to reconsider their appraisal of him. The children continue their friendship, this time with a game based on gypsies.

Four highly unusual characters find friends in each other in E. L. Konigsburg's Newbery Medal–winning *The View from Saturday*. This richly layered story is woven around a middle-school academic bowl and is put in motion by Mrs. Olinsky, the teacher who has chosen Noah, Ethan, Julian, and Nadia to represent the sixth grade. As the story unfolds at the state finals, flashbacks reveal the personalities and vulnerabilities as well as the special talents that will make each character so important to winning the match. Better than a trophy, however, is what the four gain from each other's friendship. Gathered together for one of their Saturday teas at Sillington House, Julian's father's inn, Ethan reflects on the way his friendship with the other three has changed him.

> Something in Sillington House gave me permission to do things I had never done before. Never even thought of doing. Something there triggered the unfolding of those parts that had been incubating. Things that had lain inside me, curled up like the turtle hatchlings newly emerged from their eggs, taking time in the dark of their nest to unfurl themselves. (p. 93)

Indeed, all four are changed profoundly by the sense of acceptance and affection they glean from one another. Konigsburg's wonderful sense of humor is firmly in place here, but she also manages to create highly believable characters who are linked together by surprising connections.

Konigsburg explores the theme of friendship in a very different way in *Silent to the Bone*. In this story 13-year-old Connor cannot believe that his best friend, Branwell, has had anything to do with Bran's baby sister's near death. But Bran, the main suspect, can't or won't speak about what happened. Connor is left to puzzle out the facts by using a code he develops for Bran. He eventually works out the complex set of relationships that have developed among Bran, his family, and his sister's nanny. In *Up On Cloud Nine* Anne Fine also writes about friendship threatened by mental illness. Steady Ian and his likable parents have become a surrogate family for Stol, whose own celebrity parents just don't have time for him. Stol is quite a character, and his outrageous antics are a great contrast to Ian's steady and practical character. But Ian begins to realize that Stol's many "accidents" may really be a cry for attention, and when a fall from an upper story window leaves Stol in a coma, Ian reflects back on the important events in their friendship. He is forced to confront the fact that Stol may have jumped rather than fallen and is torn by whether to tell his parents of his suspicions. Both *Silent to the Bone* and *Up On Cloud Nine* are complex stories of love, loyalty, and the human psyche. Konigsburg and Fine raise important issues that middle-school readers will surely find worthy of much discussion.

In Katherine Paterson's Newbery Medal book *Bridge to Terabithia*, imaginary play is the basis for a friendship that develops between 10-year-old Jess Aarons, an artistic boy who is a misfit in his family, and Leslie Burke, a newcomer who is a misfit at school. Leslie's parents, both writers, have moved to rural Virginia in pursuit of a simpler lifestyle. These two lonely children invent an imaginary realm based on Leslie's image of Narnia and other

The longtime friendship between two boys is remembered when one of the boys is seriously injured in a fall that may not have been accidental, in Anne Fine's *Up On Cloud Nine*.
Jacket cover from *Up On Cloud Nine* by Anne Fine. Jacket illustration by Rafal Oblinski. Jacket illustration copyright © 2002 by Rafal Oblinski. Used by permission of Random House Children's Books, a division of Random House, Inc.

fantasy worlds in literature. Their "Terabithia" is a real place, however, a private hideout in the woods reached by swinging on a rope across a dry creek bed. On a day when spring rains turn the creek into a torrent, Leslie goes alone to their meeting place, falls off the rope swing, and drowns. As Jess works through his complex feelings of grief, he comes to see a more supportive side of his usually unsympathetic family and realizes that Leslie's gifts to him—a wider perspective and confidence in his own imaginative powers—are gifts that last and can be shared.

> Now it occurred to him that perhaps Terabithia was like a castle where you came to be knighted. After you stayed for a while and grew strong you had to move on. . . . Now it was time for him to move out. She wasn't there, so he must go for both of them. It was up to him to pay back

to the world in beauty and caring what Leslie loaned him in vision and strength. (p. 126)

With lumber given him by Leslie's father, Jess builds a bridge to Terabithia, a safe entry for his younger sister, May Belle, as he leads her into the shining realm with the unspoken hope that her world, like his own, will grow. By asking fourth and fifth graders if there are any other "bridges" in this story, teachers have allowed children to discuss the many emotional or metaphorical bridges portrayed in Paterson's beautifully written book.

The topic of cross-gender friendships and budding romance has proved to be fruitful material for children since Jess and Leslie first met. Linda Sue Park's delightful *Project Mulberry* deals with the friendship of two seventh graders, Korean American Julia Song and her neighbor Patrick. Park creates a story that takes readers beyond their strong friendship, however, to consider issues of identity, prejudice, sustainable farming, and the scientific method!

Lynne Rae Perkins's *Criss Cross* is a superb exploration of adolescents caught on the brink of discovering their identities largely through the intertwining relations of old friends. Perkins follows multiple characters—boys and girls—as they teeter on the cusp between childhood and adulthood, exploring friendships and first love. As one of the characters explains:

> "I think," he said, "that it's a good thing to get out of your usual, you know surroundings. Because you find things out about yourself that you didn't know or forgot. And then you go back to your regular life and you're changed, you're a little bit different because you take those new things with you. Like a Hindu except all in one life; you sort of get reincarnated depending on what happened and what you figure out. And any one place can make you go forward or backward, or neither but gradually you find all your pieces, your important pieces and they stay with you so that you're your whole self no matter where you go." (p. 267)

Loosely plotted, with each character's story weaving over and under the others', *Criss Cross* is nonetheless compelling for Perkins's thorough character development and exquisite language.

Virginia Hamilton presents an achingly tender story of friendship that revolves around questions of illness and death in *Bluish*. Dreenie, new to her Manhattan school, has been slow in making new friends. Her little sister and a wacky classmate, Tuli, occupy her time, but both are needy in different ways. They seem to demand more of Dreenie than they give back in the way of friendship. When Natalie Winburn arrives in their fifth-grade class in a wheelchair, her head covered by a knitted cap, Dreenie writes in her journal, "This girl is like moonlight. So pale you see the blue veins all over. You can tell though once she had some color." Dreenie and her classmates are fascinated and yet repelled by Natalie's strangeness. They "call her Bluish and grin and look at her hard." Eventually we find out that Natalie has leukemia and has endured the terrible pain of a bone marrow transplant. Her physical suffering and her desire not to seem different have made her angry and hard to know. But Dreenie reaches out to Bluish in small ways at first and then gets past her own fear of Bluish's illness to form a firm friendship. This lovely story unfolds in alternating chapters through the pages of Dreenie's journal and through a third-person voice. In this way we come to see the loving connections that are slowly built within the classroom community by Dreenie, two concerned teachers, and the other children. Eventually those bonds extend beyond the classroom to the families of Dreenie, Bluish, and Tuli. Bluish is not the passive recipient of friendship and compassion but has real contributions of her own to make to their lives. Although we do not know if Bluish will be one of the 85 to 90 percent who survive treatment, the story ends with a warmly hopeful scene in which Bluish reveals her profound trust in the girls by removing her knitted cap and revealing her newly growing hair.

> They jumped up and down. "You have hair!" Dreenie shouted. It had to be the shortest copper-red hair anybody'd ever seen.
>
> "Looks just like peach fuzz," Willie said.
>
> "No, it's shiny and curlier than fuzz. It's gonna be ringlets. It's cute!" Dreenie said. "Bluish!"
>
> "No Reddish!" They all yelled it at once. And the color of a new penny. Hollering and laughing until Dreenie's Mom knocked and opened the door, to see what in the world was going on. (p. 124)

The topic of making friends seldom focuses on broken friendships, but in reality two children who have shared years of closeness might suddenly grow apart. This process can be particularly painful to the friend who feels left behind or left out when a new person enters the relationship. Such is the case in Lynne Rae Perkins's poignant and funny *All Alone in the Universe*. Thirteen-year-olds Debbie and Maureen have been friends since third grade when Glenna enters the picture. Suddenly the other two girls have little secrets and rituals that leave Debbie out in the cold. "I'm just left by myself, like we were never friends, like I don't even exist," Debbie cries. She wants to blame Glenna for the rift, but eventually she comes to understand that it is Maureen who has left her all by herself with no urging from Glenna. Debbie's heartbreak is very real, but she has the warm support of family, neighbors, teachers, and other adults who help her to see that she is a good person capable of having friends. Her thirteenth year is painful, but she emerges

In Lynne Rae Perkins's *All Alone in the Universe* 13-year-old Debbie is devastated when Maureen, her longtime friend, finds a new best friend. From *All Alone in the Universe* by Lynne Rae Perkins. Copyright © 1999 by Lynne Rae Perkins. Used by permission of HarperCollins Publishers.

with new understandings about herself and others—and with a new best friend.

Growing toward Maturity

In building a concept of self, each person begins to answer questions like "What kind of person am I?" "How am I changing?" "What do others think of me?" "What are my roles in society?" Based on their experiences, children begin to see themselves as worthy and successful people who can give and receive love and respect.

As children move toward adulthood, they may experience brief moments of awareness of this growth process. A conversation, an event, or a literary experience might give a child the sudden realization that he or she has taken a step toward maturity. The step might be toward understanding complex human emotions, acknowledgment of sexuality, or acceptance of responsibility for one's actions. This process of becoming is never easy or painless. In modern realistic fiction, there are models of ordinary girls and boys who find the courage to grow and change, or to stand up for their beliefs.

Developing Sexuality

The first children's story to discuss menstruation, *The Long Secret* by Louise Fitzhugh, was published in 1965. In it, a girl explains menstruation to her friend in a matter-of-fact manner to correct misinformation the friend's grandmother had given her. Neither of the girls is pleased with the prospect, but they take some satisfaction in the fact that when they have their periods, they'll be able to skip gym. Judy Goldschmidt's *The Secret Blog of Raisin Rodriquez* certainly brings the topic of menstruation into sync with twenty-first-century mores, although more crudely than does the Fitzhugh book. Written in the form of a Web log to her two friends back home in Berkeley, Raisin's blog covers all aspects of her thirteen-year-old life, especially the traumas of her first period. Judy Blume's *Are You There God? It's Me, Margaret*, in print now for more than thirty-five years, is still one of the best books to deal with a girl's maturation. Margaret prays for her period because she doesn't want to be the last of her secret club to start menstruating. She regularly does exercises that she hopes will increase her 28-inch bust, and she practices wearing a sanitary napkin. Mixed with her desire for physical maturation is a search for a meaningful relationship with God. Adults find this book very funny and reminiscent of their own preadolescence, but it is extremely serious for 10- and 11-year-old girls who share Margaret's concern for their own physical maturation. Mavis Jukes's *Expecting the Unexpected: Sex Ed with Mrs. Gladys B. Furley R.N.* is aimed at middle-school students and is frank about matters of maturation, in keeping with its 1990s view of the world.

Judy Blume has also written a book about the physical and emotional maturing of a boy, *Then Again, Maybe I Won't*. One strand of the story concerns the sexual awakening of Tony, a 13-year-old boy who is embarrassed and concerned about erections and nocturnal emissions. The other concerns the conflicts that Tony feels about his family's sudden adoption of a new lifestyle when they move from a cramped two-family house in Jersey City to an acre of land on Long Island. The title conveys the same ambiguity as the direction of Tony's life. There is no doubt that Tony has achieved physical maturation, but will he be able to sustain his personal values in the difficult task of growing toward psychological and emotional maturity?

In Brock Cole's remarkable novel *The Goats*, a boy and girl are stripped of their clothes and left on an island in the night as a summer camp prank. Angry and humiliated, the two outcasts, or "goats," decide not to return to camp and instead to escape from the island. They begin an aimless journey, and as a friendship gradually develops between them, the two become awkwardly aware of each other and more self-aware. When they cleverly figure out a way to stay in a motel at someone else's expense, a suspicious cleaning woman accuses them of "spending the afternoon in the same bed." Ironically, it is the adult suspicion of sexual activity, rather than their thievery of clothes, food, or a motel room, that leads to the two fugitives being caught. The girl and boy, nameless to each other until the final chapter, are reunited with the girl's mother and other adults who will straighten things out. But Laura and Howie are different now: more self-reliant, able to form real friendships based on their own inner sense of themselves, and unlikely ever again to be gullible victims of peer cruelty or thoughtlessness. Emotionally gripping and thought-provoking, this story leads individual young-adult readers to consider what it means to be alienated from one's peers and what it means to have a trusted friend. Cole has written another book, *The Facts Speak for Themselves*, that provides a grim look at a young teenager. Thirteen-year-old Linda has been abused both emotionally and sexually by so many people in her short life that she refuses to look below the surface to accept the psychological trauma that she has suffered. This book is notable for its literary style and its level of honesty, but the callous treatment of sex requires a very mature reader.

Jacqueline Woodson's *I Hadn't Meant to Tell You This* is a powerfully moving story that deals with sexual abuse in the context of larger social issues. The town of Chauncey, Ohio, is divided along racial lines but in an unexpected way. Poor white families live on one side of town and prosperous middle-class African Americans on the other. Twelve-year-old Marie is from the latter group, a confident, popular black girl who is somehow drawn to the new white girl, Lena Bright, perhaps because they have both lost their mothers. Marie is isolated from her unemotional professor father, who seems even more distant since her mother left him. Marie wonders why he never touches her. Lena has the opposite problem—her father touches her in the wrong ways. She confides in Marie but exacts a promise that Marie will tell no one; caught in a social service system that has not served her well, Lena is afraid that if she reports the abuse she will be taken away from her younger sister again, the only loving connection she has had since her mother died. Marie must struggle with her own hurt at the same time as she desperately tries to protect Lena without violating her confidence. This is not a typical problem novel, nor is it a book that provides easy answers. Rather, Woodson raises critical questions about class, race, prejudice, and loyalty in the context of this beautifully realized friendship.

Books for younger adolescents continue to break ground in dealing with other formerly delicate topics regarding sexuality. Female genital mutilation (FGM) is appropriately introduced to a middle-grade audience in *Our Secret, Siri Aang* by Cristina Kessler and *No Laughter Here* by Rita Williams-Garcia. *Our Secret, Siri Aang*, set among the Masai in Kenya, is a highly descriptive look at Masai culture and rites of passage. (Kessler lived and worked in Africa as a Peace Corps worker.) FGM is implied as a rite of passage for Namelok, the main character, but only defined in a footnote at the end of the book. More direct mention is made of female circumcision in Williams-Garcia's *No Laughter Here.* Rather than focus on the graphic details of FGM, however, the story highlights the friendship of two African American girls, and the repercussions on their families and friendship when one returns from a visit to her grandmother in Nigeria having been circumcised. The terrible consequences of the AIDS crisis in Africa is made plain in *Chanda's Secrets* by Allan Stratton, a book for mature adolescents.

First published in 1969 and now out of print, John Donovan's sensitively told story *I'll Get There, It Better Be Worth the Trip* was the first book for younger readers to confront questions of homosexuality. Australian author Kate Walker's *Peter* is a gently beautiful book about a 15-year-old boy who is unmercifully teased by his male classmates because he does not conform to their macho image. Peter finds he is very much attracted to David, his brother's older gay friend. Distraught and confused, Peter begins to wonder if he is gay. Eventually the wise and understanding David helps Peter to understand that he is still in the process of becoming an adult and doesn't have to put a label on himself as his classmates have tried to do.

Writers for middle-grade audiences have generally approached the topic of gay and lesbian identities in books such as Jacqueline Woodson's *From the Notebooks of Melanin Sun* and George Ella Lyon's *Sonny's House of Spies* that deal with young people's relationships with gay parents or relatives. Young-adult authors have dealt more frankly with issues of homosexuality in books such as Francesca Lia Block's *Weetzie Bat,* M. E. Kerr's *Hello I Lied,* and Nancy Garden's *Annie on My Mind.* Perhaps because of groundbreaking books such as these, authors will now be able to incorporate sexuality and issues of sexual orientation into stories suitable for younger readers.

In the meantime, *Boy2Girl* by Terence Blacker is a wise and funny book about gender roles that will have to bridge the gap between middle-grade and high school audiences. In *Boy2Girl,* an American boy, 13-year-old Sam Lopez, has been the neglected child of a free-spirited Englishwoman living in California who dies in a car accident there. With his con man father, Crash, in prison, Sam's Aunt Mary brings him back to England to live and into his cousin Matthew's life. Sam is angry, bitter, and wild, and his early days in this rather staid, middle-class British home don't go well. Matt and his two friends, Jake and Tyrone, are outside the pale, at loose ends, and at war with Charley, Zia, and Elena, the three girls they've grown up with. When Matt finally has enough of Sam's rebellion, they determine to lock him out of their group. Sam, wise to the ways of the street, insists that to be included in their "gang," he will be glad to pass an initiation—jump a bridge, write graffiti, or perform some other lawless action. Instead, the boys come up with a foolproof scheme to be rid of Sam. Long-haired hippie Sam, who is slight and skinny, must dress up as a girl and pass at their school for a week. Needless to say, the scheme takes off in unexpected directions. Sam is a surprisingly believable girl. Over the course of the book, he finds that the role reversal has positive benefits, not the least the relief of his anger and grief. Matthew observes:

> At first I thought it was just a crazy novelty of the situation that had put a spring in his step, a new and unfamiliar smile on his face. Then it occurred to me that dressing up had done something else for Sam.
>
> Suddenly, he was no longer the tragic kid whose mother had died and whose life had turned upside down. Girl Sam was happier, more straightforward than Boy Sam, and had virtually none of his problems. (p. 109)

Sam's transformation has unexpected effects on all the participants, not just himself. Short, first-person narratives by the boys, girls, parents, and teachers (everyone but Sam) carry this funny and ultimately enlightening

Terence Blacker explores—and upsets—traditional adolescent gender roles in the delightfully funny *Boy2Girl.* Cover of *Boy2Girl* by Terence Blacker. Copyright © 2004 by Terence Blacker. Reprinted by permission of Farrar, Straus & Giroux, LLC.

book to its inevitable conclusion. It will certainly afford children in grades five through eight an engaging read. It should also provide a jumping-off place for some meaty discussions about gender identity.

Finding Oneself

Most of the stories about physical maturing also suggest a kind of emotional growth or coming to terms with oneself. The process of becoming a mature person is a lifelong task that begins in the later stages of childhood and continues for as long as a person lives. Many stories in children's literature chronicle the steps along the way to maturity.

A psychologically complex novel, *One-Eyed Cat* by Paula Fox, begins when 11-year-old Ned Willis receives from his favorite uncle an unexpected birthday present— an air rifle. But Ned's minister father banishes the gun to the attic until Ned is older. Longing to shoot just once, Ned steals into the attic at night, points the gun out the window, and fires toward something moving near a shed. He is immediately guilt-stricken. Was it an animal? As he broods on his disobedience, he begins to lie, and each lie "makes the secret bigger." He can't confide in his mother, who is wheelchair-bound by arthritis, or in his preoccupied father. Carrying his uncomfortable secret, Ned does odd jobs after school for an elderly neighbor, Mr. Scully. There he and the old man see a sickly one-eyed cat that they feed and observe during the winter. When Mr. Scully suffers a stroke, Ned is afraid he has lost both his friend and the cat. Finally, on a visit to the home where Mr. Scully, unable to speak, resides, Ned gathers enough courage to tell his guilty secret to his friend. This release brings a change in Ned and enables him to repair the pains of separation and assuage his guilt. Ned's rich interior monologues contrast with his own inability to talk to anyone; this motif of being unable to speak about some of life's most important moments recurs throughout the story. Fox's carefully chosen images, such as "people aging the way trees do, getting gnarled and dried out" or "the gun was a splinter in his mind," lend depth to this perceptive and well-written story. Although it is set in 1935, children are likely to see the book not as historical fiction but rather as a story of the moral dilemmas that result from Ned's disobedience and lying.

Readers know that Ned has made it through a difficult time; they are not so sure that 12-year-old Joel will be able to do the same in the powerful story *On My Honor* by Marion Dane Bauer. Goaded by his friend Tony, Joel asks his father if the two boys can ride their bicycles to the bluffs outside of town and is surprised when his father gives permission. Joel promises on his honor to be careful, but when the two boys come to a bridge across a swiftly moving river, they agree to stop for a swim. When they reach the fast current, Tony, who can't swim, is swept away and drowns. Joel, horrified, doesn't know what to do. When he reaches his home, he can't tell anyone what

has happened and withdraws to his bed. Finally, the arrival of the police at Tony's house and the anguish of the adults force Joel to tell his story. He angrily blames his father and himself. In a moving scene by Joel's bedside, his father says: "We all made choices today, Joel. You, me, Tony. Tony's the only one who doesn't have to live with his choice" (p. 88). His father's admission of partial responsibility frees Joel to cry and begin to grieve. Although for some children the book ends abruptly, it is not a story of dealing with the death of a friend. Instead, it is a story about facing the tragic consequences of your own actions with the help of a loving family. After reading this story, fifth graders are anxious to discuss honor, conscience, and parental obligations versus self-responsibility. They are also eager to predict a hopeful future for Joel.

Ricky Gordon, the 11-year-old hero of Sis Deans's *Racing the Past*, has been traumatized all his life by his abusive father. Even after his father is killed in an accident, Ricky, his younger brother Matt, and his mother find it difficult to escape the past, especially in the small town in Maine where everyone knows their business. Ricky is taunted at school by sixth grader Bugsie McCarthy, who tells him the best thing his father ever did for the family was to run "his truck off Dead Man's Curve." Ricky can't fight back anymore or his mother will be called into school, so he tries to stay away from Bugsie by walking home from school rather than taking the bus. Mocked by Bugsie and the other kids as the school bus rushes past, Ricky decides he'll try to beat the bus by running to and from school. Ricky, a gifted mathematician, begins to keep records of his times and to figure ways to improve. By the end of the book, of course, the goal of beating the bus doesn't matter to him much anymore. He has discovered that his running has helped him develop the self-confidence and sense of achievement that allows him to put his past behind him. This is a moving story of the terrible toll that abuse takes on members of a family. It is also an uplifting tale of neighbors, friends, and family members whose support can help those damaged by abuse.

His real name is Jeffrey Lionel Magee, but the kids of Two Mills call the homeless boy who became a legend "Maniac Magee." Jerry Spinelli's Newbery Medal book *Maniac Magee* is more a tale of a modern-day superman than it is realistic fiction. There is nothing Maniac can't do. He beats a kid called Mars Bar in a race running backward; he hits home runs and scores touchdowns; he teaches old Mr. Grayson to read and gets the famous McNab twins to go to school. Most important, he brings together the town, which is racially divided. Yet Maniac continues running. He finds many shelters for himself, but no home. He lives for a while with the Beals, a kind African American family, and later with the McNabs, who are racist whites. He is happiest with Mr. Grayson, a locker room attendant at the YMCA who lives with him under a band shell. But when Grayson dies, Maniac is running again. Only when Amanda Beal goes to the zoo where Maniac is now spending his nights and forces Maniac to listen does he finally know that someone is calling him home. Maniac is bigger than life, a legend in his own world. Spinelli seems to have a special insight into outsiders. In books such as *Loser* and *Stargirl* (for older readers) he continues to focus on the child who dances to the beat of a different drummer. Likable characters, short chapters, punchy dialogue, and nonstop action make Spinelli's books difficult to put down.

Told in blank verse, Robert Cormier's *Frenchtown Summer* takes place "in the days in which I knew my name but did not know who I was," young Eugene relates. During a brief summer, small everyday occurrences and larger tragedies shape Eugene's reflections about himself. His relationship with his father, whom he finds remote and unapproachable, is especially troubling to him. Yet as the summer progresses Eugene gleans unexpected insights from the members of his family and his larger community. These, in turn, help him shape a clearer understanding of his identity and the role his father has played in shaping that identity. Cormier's distilled writing is lyrical and subdued, but it evokes a powerful emotional response that lingers long after the book is closed.

In contrast to Eugene's experience, 13-year-old Mikey Donovan's journey to self-understanding depends much more on physical action than on inward reflection in Graham Salisbury's *Lord of the Deep.* Mikey idolizes his stepfather, Bill, the captain of a charter fishing boat in the Hawaiian Islands and the so-called Lord of the Deep. He badly wants to live up to Bill's expectations of him and become as good a charter captain as his stepfather. When two bored and boorish game fishermen hire the boat and treat Bill like an idiot, Mikey can't understand Bill's acceptance of their behavior. But when the men ask Bill to lie about who caught the record-breaking fish and Bill agrees, Mikey is stunned. Not only could the lie destroy Bill's career as a charter captain, but it threatens to destroy Mikey's belief in Bill. Mikey must decide whether to go along with the lie or stand up for his own beliefs. In light of his love for his stepfather, this is the most difficult decision of his young life and one that ultimately reflects his transition from childhood to adult responsibilities and burdens.

Joan Bauer has dealt with similar issues of identity with great insight and good humor in books like *Stand Tall,* discussed previously. In *Best Foot Forward, Squashed, Rules of the Road, Backwater,* and *Hope Was Here,* Bauer presents feisty female teen protagonists who remain outside the pale, nonconformists who for one reason or another don't fit in with the in-crowd. In *Hope Was Here* Bauer introduces Hope Yancy, who lives with her Aunt Addie, a superb cook. The have moved often to follow Addie's jobs, and the move from New York City to rural Wisconsin is especially difficult for the 16-year-old. But Hope and Addie find a warm reception at the Welcome Stairways Diner in the person of its owner, G. T., and a short-order

Thirteen-year-old Mikey must make a difficult decision that signals his coming of age in Graham Salisbury's *Lord of the Deep.* Jacket cover from *Lord of the Deep* by Graham Salisbury. Used by permission of Random House Children's Books, a division of Random House, Inc.

cook named Braverman. When G. T. develops leukemia, Hope, Addie, and Braverman take over his diner and his campaign for mayor. Over the course of this and other Bauer books, each likable heroine takes a personal journey that crystallizes her self-understanding and reaffirms her worth.

In Virginia Euwer Wolff's *Make Lemonade,* 14-year-old LaVaugn takes a job baby-sitting for a teenage mother, interested only in the extra money to put into her college account. But 17-year-old Jolly is as much a child as her two children, Jilly and Jeremy, and LaVaugn is soon so involved with this family that she begins to neglect her studies. As she tries desperately to give Jolly the kind of moral support that her own mother has given her, LaVaugn must also struggle with being a mother to the two children. With LaVaugn's help, Jolly begins to pull her life together. Each of these young women has learned to "make lemonade" from whatever lemons life hands her. Wolff tells the story in LaVaugn's voice, placing the words like poetry on the page in phrasing that rings of the rhythms of speech patterns. This lends a sense of immediacy to the telling and underscores the important truths in this coming-of-age story. *True Believer* follows LaVaugn into high school, where she is determined not to fall into Jolly's situation until her old friend Jody moves back to town—and she suddenly finds herself in the throws of first love.

In *Scorpions* by Walter Dean Myers, 12-year-old Jamal reluctantly takes his brother's place as leader of a Harlem gang, the Scorpions, after his brother is sent to prison. His best friend, Tito, constantly counsels him not to get involved with the gang, while his long-suffering mother and his sister, Sassy, fear that he might follow in his brother's footsteps. When Jamal is given the gang's gun, he briefly displays it to get away from a school bully. Then, in a nighttime encounter with two older boys in the gang, Jamal is beaten and Tito, who is holding the gun, shoots the assailants. Both boys are stunned by the incident, but Tito worries and finally goes to the police. Because he is a minor, he may return to Puerto Rico to avoid prosecution. The novel leaves readers to wonder if Jamal, who has lost his best friend and his innocence, is strong enough to follow his own conscience and resist becoming a "thrown-away guy" himself.

Survival Stories

Survival stories have powerful appeal to children in the middle grades. Numerous stories in all genres portray an individual child or a small group of children, without adults, in situations that call for ingenuity, quick thinking, mastery of tools and skills, and strength of character. Survivors return to civilization or their former lives knowing that they have changed as a result of their experiences. In primitive societies, surviving a hazardous experience often marked the transition from childhood to adulthood. Today, we have forms of this in "survival training" conducted in schools, camps, or juvenile homes. Children in the middle grades avidly read survival stories and wonder, "Could I do it? How? What would I do in this same situation?"

Armstrong Sperry's quintessential survival story *Call It Courage* begins and ends in the manner of a story told in the oral tradition:

> It happened many years ago, before the traders and the missionaries first came into the South Seas, while the Polynesians were still great in numbers and fierce of heart. But even today the people of Hikueru sing this story in their chants and tell it over the evening fires. It is the story of Mafatu, the Boy Who Was Afraid. (p. 7)

Taunted for his fears, Mafatu sets out to conquer his dread of the water by sailing to some other island, accompanied only by his pet albatross and his dog. On a distant island his character gradually develops as he proves his courage to himself: He defies a taboo, steals a much-needed spear from an idol, fights dangerous animals, and

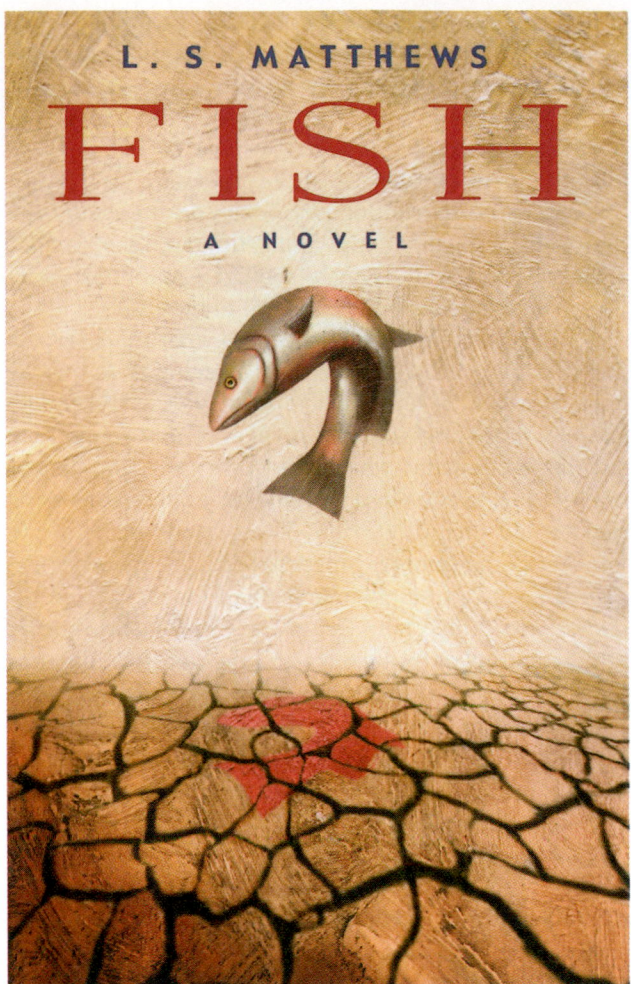

In L. S. Matthews's *Fish* a young boy whose own survival is at risk is determined to keep a rescued fish alive as he and his parents flee a war-torn African country. *Jacket cover from Fish: A Novel* by L. S. Matthews. Copyright © 2004. Used by permission of Random House Children's Books, a division of Random House, Inc.

escapes from cannibals. These heroic deeds, which represent the many faces of courage, build his self-esteem. As in so many survival stories, having proven to himself that he can carve out an existence, Mafatu is ready to return to his former life as a changed person who knows his own worth. The first paragraph of the book is repeated at the end—only the last sentence is left off.

L. S. Matthews's *Fish*, with its African locale, will be equally satisfying to middle-grade readers. Here the young boy is stranded with his aide-worker parents in the middle of a drought, a flood, and then a civil war. Tiger, who appears to be about seven or eight, and his parents have stayed with the villagers they served too long, and now the border is closed. They hire a local man and his donkey to get them to safety, but they face one terrible hurdle after another. Although adults are present in this story, it is Tiger's resilience and his efforts to bring a tiny fish found faltering in a drying water hole to safety that drives the story. His care for that fish becomes the metaphor for the caring and community that ultimately lead the group to safety. Reading Tiger's personal story should enlighten children's understanding of similar events in Africa and other areas of the world.

Nancy Farmer's *A Girl Named Disaster* centers on an 11-year-old Shona girl whose real name is Nhamo. Living as a poor relation with her dead mother's family, Nhamo's only source of support is her beloved grandmother. Because of her father's earlier misdeeds, she is blamed for an outbreak of cholera in her village, and a shaman insists that she marry a despicable man to appease the angry spirits. Her grandmother urges her to run away from their village and travel by river from Mozambique to Zimbabwe to find her father. Lost on the river, Nhamo faces terrible obstacles, including hunger, dangerous leopards, and marauding baboons. In mystical dream states she calls on companions from tribal lore to give her the strength to survive. Nhamo is eventually rescued and taken in by researchers in a tsetse fly station before she sets off to find her father. The book is long and complex, but Nhamo is a compelling heroine—and the book stands alongside such other survival stories as Jean George's *Julie of the Wolves* and Scott O'Dell's *Island of the Blue Dolphins*.

In George's Newbery Medal novel *Julie of the Wolves*, Miyax, the Eskimo heroine of this beautiful story, finds herself alone on the Alaskan tundra. She realizes that her salvation or her destruction depends on a nearby pack of wolves. Julie (Miyax is her Eskimo name) watches the wolves carefully and gradually learns to communicate with them by glance, movement, and caress until Amaroq, their leader, acknowledges her as a friend. Because of the wolves, Julie survives and finds her way back to civilization. But civilization kills Amaroq, as white hunters wantonly shoot him down from a plane for the "sport" of killing. Much of the story is based on research on wolves conducted at the Arctic Research Laboratory.[13] Children will want to read the sequels, *Julie* and *Julie's Wolf Pack*, and to keep up with the news of Alaska's legal return to aerial wolf shooting in 2004.

George's well-loved *My Side of the Mountain* is about a city boy who chooses to spend a solitary winter in the Catskills on family land. Armed with knowledge from reading, he makes a home in a hollow tree, tames a falcon, sews buckskin clothing, and lays up stores for the winter. In his journal, he records his observations as he goes about the business of living. When a reporter discovers him in the spring, Sam realizes he is ready to be found. Thirty years after the publication of this story, George wrote a bittersweet but worthy sequel, *On the Far Side of the Mountain*, which picks up the plot immediately following the first story. Sam allows his younger sister Alice to become his neighbor while he continues to enrich his environment and his life in the wild. But a criminal posing as a conservation officer steals Sam's falcon and his sister vanishes. In both books George expresses concern about our relationship to the natural world and our responsibility to preserve it.

Canadian author James Houston has based his survival story *Frozen Fire* on the actual survival experiences of a boy in the Canadian Arctic. Two boys, Matthew Morgan and his Inuit friend Kayak, set forth on a snowmobile to search for Matthew's prospector father, whose plane has been downed by a snowstorm. Carelessness in securing the cap of the gas can leaves them stranded seventy miles from Frobisher Bay. Kayak is able to use the skills taught him by his grandfather and helps both boys eventually walk out on the ice, where they are seen and rescued. They discover that Matthew's father has also been saved. Houston's crisp telling and cliffhanger chapter endings make this a fast-paced story. Whereas the strengths of George's books about wolves lie in her naturalist's knowledge of wolf behavior, Houston spent twelve years among the Inuit people and is able to weave aspects of a changing Eskimo culture and folk wisdom into the text.

Gary Paulsen's survival story *Hatchet* also begins with a crash of a bush plane. On his way to meet his father when the pilot suffers a heart attack, Brian Robeson manages to land the plane in a lake in the Canadian wilderness and swim to shore. Alone, 13-year-old Brian lets self-pity and anxiety over his parents' impending divorce distract him from the immediate needs of survival, and he is soon sick and frightened. But gradually he begins to act intelligently—building a shelter, finding ripe berries, fending off a bear, and discovering respect for a cow moose that nearly kills him. A hatchet his mother had given him as a parting gift becomes essential to his survival. When a huge storm disturbs the plane enough to raise its tail in the water, Brian ventures out to seek the survival kit all pilots carry with them. But his carelessness when he loses his hatchet in the water and his horror of what he might find when he dives to the cockpit nearly prevent him from retrieving the kit. Ironically, Brian is cooking a delicious meal of trail food in a real pot and has survived for over two months when he is finally spotted from the air by a mapping plane. In *Brian's Winter*, Paulsen speculates on what it might have been like had Brian been forced to spend the winter in the wilderness. In *The River*, Brian is once again pitted against the elements when he agrees to make a film to teach survival techniques to the military. But Derek, the man recording Brian's experiences, is struck by lightning and will die unless Brian can build a raft and navigate them downriver to a trading post. Brian's experiences finally lead to the realization that he belongs in the wilderness rather than the city, and he leaves his old life behind for a permanent home in *Brian's Return*. Other survival stories

---

[13]See Jean Craighead George's Newbery Medal acceptance speech in *Horn Book Magazine*, August 1973, pp. 337–47.

by Paulsen include *Dogsong,* which is partially based on the author's own experiences of training sled dogs for the Iditarod trail race, and *The Voyage of the Frog,* which reveals the courage of a boy who ventures out on the ocean to scatter his dead uncle's ashes and is caught unprepared in a sudden storm.

Bearstone by Will Hobbs tells the story of 14-year-old Cloyd Atcitty, a Ute Indian who has lived resentfully in a group home in Durango, Colorado, for much of his life. Cloyd is placed for the summer on a ranch where he will work for an old widower named Walter. Angry, Cloyd runs off after he is driven to the remote ranch in the Colorado/Utah mountain country. Taking refuge in a small cave, he discovers a small, carved stone bear, an animal important to Ute tribal beliefs. Adopting this bear as his totem, Cloyd decides to give Walter and ranch life a try. While Cloyd and Walter develop respect for each other, Cloyd finds respect for himself. More important, in this excellent coming-of-age story, Cloyd's knowledge of his people's ways finally gives him the power to control his own life. *Beardance* continues Cloyd's story. Middle-school readers who enjoy Hobbs's survival stories will also want to read and compare them to Ben Mikaelsen's *Touching Spirit Bear.*

Vera Cleaver and Bill Cleaver's *Where the Lilies Bloom* is a well-known survival story set in Appalachia. The torturous death of Roy Luther from "worms in the chest" puts the full responsibility for the survival of the family on Mary Call, his 14-year-old daughter. She and Romey, her younger brother, bury Roy secretly so the "county people" will not find out that they are orphaned and separate them. Then Mary Call strives to keep her "cloudy-headed" older sister, Devola, and her two younger siblings alive through the winter. Mary Call's fierce pride gives her fortitude to overcome a severe winter, a caved-in roof, and the constant pretense that Roy Luther still lives. At 14, Mary Call's strength and responsibility have made her mature beyond her years, but she pulls the family through the crisis:

> My name is Mary Call Luther, I thought, and someday I'm going to be a big shot. I've got the guts to be one. I'm not going to let this beat me. If it does, everything else will for the rest of my life. (p. 144)

Mary Call and her family do survive, through wildcrafting on the mountains, scheming, and pure grit. The authors have captured the beauty of the Smokies and of this memorable family who live in what an old hymn calls the land "Where the Lilies Bloom So Fair."

Thrilling survival stories for children are not limited to survival in the great outdoors. Donna Jo Napoli's *Three Days* is set in Italy where an 11-year-old American girl is kidnapped when her father has a heart attack at the wheel of their car. Jackie, who has been highly sheltered, is suddenly put in a situation where she does not speak the language and is desperately afraid for herself and her father. The story of her escape is both frightening and highly suspenseful. This story's tone stands in sharp contrast to that in E. L. Konigsburg's *From the Mixed-Up Files of Mrs. Basil E. Frankweiler,* in which two children decide to run away from home and live in comfort in the Metropolitan Museum of Art. Claudia, feeling unappreciated at home and bored with the sameness of her straight-A life, wants to do something that is different and exciting. She chooses her brother Jamie to go along with her because he has the money they need. Claudia is a good organizer, and the two of them take up residence in the museum. They take baths in the museum's fountain, eat meals from vending machines and the museum's cafeteria, and join tour groups for their education. Their adventure grows more exciting when Claudia becomes involved in the mystery surrounding the statue of a little angel. The children's research finally takes them to the home of Mrs. Basil E. Frankweiler, who arranges for Claudia to return home the way she had hoped she would—different in some aspect. Now she is different because she knows the secret of the angel. In return for this knowledge the two children tell Mrs. Frankweiler the details of their survival; she carefully records it and then writes their story. This story-within-a-story is a sophisticated and funny account of two very resourceful survivors.

Three other survival stories set in New York City take place in much grimmer circumstances. In Felice Holman's *Slake's Limbo,* Slake is a 13-year-old nearsighted orphan who lives with his aunt and thinks of himself as a worthless lump. Slake has no friends; his vision makes him a poor risk for any gang, and a severe reaction to smoke and drugs makes him useless in other ways. Hunted and hounded for sport, Slake takes refuge in the subway, staying for 121 days. He earns a little money reselling papers he picks up on the trains and makes his home in a hidden cave in the subway wall. One day when the subway repair crew comes through, Slake realizes that his "home" will be destroyed. He becomes ill and is taken to the hospital, where he is given nourishment and proper eyeglasses. Later he slips out of the hospital. His first reaction is to return to the subway, but when he hears a bird sing he looks up and decides he could perhaps exist on the roofs of some of the buildings: "He turned and started up the stairs and out of the subway. Slake did not know exactly where he was going but the general direction was up" (p. 117). Neil Shusterman's *Downsiders,* also set beneath the New York streets in the subway tunnels, is a survival tale that reads more like science fiction than realism, but Shusterman raises interesting questions about the fate of outsiders in today's world. The book makes compelling reading and serves as a good companion to Holman's story.

A more hopeful story is told in Paula Fox's *Monkey Island.* Eleven-year-old Clay Garrity is abandoned by his despondent and pregnant mother, and not wishing to let his neighbor in the New York welfare hotel report him to the social worker, Clay runs away. On the street, he manages to survive because two homeless men share with him their place in a park, a box where they sleep. Calvin and Buddy become his family, sharing their food and their life stories. Clay learns to wear all his clothes at once, where to find food, and how not to attract attention during the day. One terrifying November night, a street gang destroys the makeshift shelters of the homeless people living in the park, Calvin disappears, and Clay catches pneumonia. Realizing his friend needs help, Buddy makes the choice of taking him to a hospital even though it means Clay will lose his freedom. But in a hopeful conclusion, Clay, his mother, and his new baby sister are reunited. Fox's story prompts readers to consider the causes of homelessness and its results. Clay's dangerous journey is made at least partially bearable by the dog-eared copy of *Robinson Crusoe* he carries from the welfare hotel. Later, a copy of *David Copperfield,* the story of a life outside a lost family, lends Clay some courage. Fox creates memorable characters in an unsentimental but hopeful survival story in which the social services of a large city, as well as caring individuals who take action, are able to do well for at least one boy and one family.

There are intriguing patterns in stories of survival. Many deal with questions and themes basic to humankind. Some survival stories suggest that surviving with another person provides comforting benefits as well as difficulties. Questions readers might ask while comparing survival stories of all genres include these: What qualities make one able to survive? How does surviving an ordeal change a person's outlook? After basic wants are satisfied, what other needs do survivors seem to have? Which is more difficult, physical survival or emotional survival? What role does art or beauty play in the survivor's ability to endure?

COPING WITH PROBLEMS OF THE HUMAN CONDITION

People in all times and places must cope with problems of the human condition—birth, pain, and loneliness; poverty, illness, and death. Children do not escape these problems, but literature can give them windows for looking at different aspects of life, show them how some characters have faced personal crises, and help them ask and answer questions about the meaning of life.

In discussing the portrayal of emotionally significant themes in children's literature, Mollie Hunter points out:

A broken home, the death of a loved person, a divorce between parents—all these are highly charged emotional situations once considered unsuitable for children's reading, but which are nevertheless still part of some children's experience; and the writer's success in casting them in literary terms rests on the ability to create an emotional frame of reference to which children in general can relate.[14]

David Elkind, a psychologist, warns that we might nonetheless be overburdening our children with the ills of society before they have an opportunity to find themselves. He says:

This is the major stress of the literature of young children aimed at making them aware of the problems in the world about them before they have a chance to master the problems of childhood.[15]

Certainly teachers and librarians should balance the reading of "problem books" with those that emphasize joy in living.

Physical Disabilities

Good stories about people with physical disabilities serve two purposes. They provide positive images with which youngsters with disabilities can identify, and they can help children who do not have disabilities develop a more intelligent understanding of some of the problems that persons with disabilities face. In stories, disabilities should be neither exaggerated nor ignored, neither dramatized nor minimized, neither romanticized nor belittled.[16] It is particularly important that stories of people with disabilities be well written, not sentimental or maudlin. They should not evoke pity for what children with disabilities cannot do, but respect for what they *can* do. As in all well-written stories, characters should be multidimensional persons with real feelings and frustrations rather than serve as a foil for another character's good deeds. The author should be honest in portraying the condition and future possibilities for the character. Illustrations should also portray disabilities in an honest and straightforward manner.

Literary treatment of people with disabilities might rely on time-honored themes: a person with disabilities has special powers, grace, or a predetermined destiny; a person with a disability serves as a catalyst in the maturation of others; a disability is a metaphor for society's ills, such as a blind person who can "see" what others do not choose to acknowledge or are too insensitive to see. Occasionally, disabilities are somewhat misleadingly portrayed as something that can be overcome with

---

[14]Mollie Hunter, *Talent Is Not Enough* (New York: HarperCollins, 1990), p. 20.

[15]David Elkind, *The Hurried Child: Growing Up Too Fast Too Soon* (Reading, Mass.: Addison-Wesley, 1981), p. 84.

[16]Barbara H. Baskin and Karen H. Harris, *More Notes from a Different Drummer: A Guide to Juvenile Fiction Portraying the Disabled* (New York: Bowker, 1984).

determination, faith, and grit,[17] but in the hands of a fine writer, themes like these avoid becoming clichés and can present the reader with fresh insight into coping with the human condition.

In *Tiger's Fall* Molly Bang has written a short but affecting book about an 11-year-old girl paralyzed after a fall from a tree. Growing up in her Mexican village, Lupe is vigorous and fearless, traits which earn her the nickname of Tiger. Following her accident her parents must transport her by bus to a hospital far from home. Here a burned-out doctor bluntly tells her family that she will never walk again and insists that her hospital bill be paid before she can be released. Her father must sell most of their possessions, and Lupe returns to their almost empty house with an empty and despairing heart. When she develops a fever, the local healer discovers a badly infected pressure sore and encourages her family to take her to a center for disabled people in another village. When she arrives at the center, all Lupe wants to do is die. She is furious at the cheerful people at the center, all children and adults who also have disabilities. But they tend her carefully and lovingly. Lupe begins to respond to those around her, first with anger, then determination, and finally with hope. Bang based the story on PROJIMO, in English, the Project of Rehabilitation Organized by Disabled Youth of Western Mexico. *Tiger's Fall* is an uplifting story that fulfills all the criteria of good literature at the same time that it provides a frank and realistic look at people coping with physical disabilities.

Older stories have depicted children with cerebral palsy and families who deal courageously with this illness. The theme "what kind of help and how much" is evident in Jean Little's *Mine for Keeps.* When Sally, who has cerebral palsy, returns from a special school to live at home, she attends regular school and faces several problems. But a dog that may be hers "for keeps" helps her gain physical skill and the emotional courage to help another child who has been ill.

Ben Mikaelsen's moving *Petey* is based on the true story of a boy born with cerebral palsy but diagnosed as mentally retarded. Hospitalized in a state home for years, Petey is finally rediagnosed and released to a nursing home. Here he meets a young eighth grader whose own life is changed dramatically by his friendship with Petey. Although the book is long and somewhat sentimentalized, Petey's character is portrayed with great dignity. The message is clear that each of us deserves respect and the chance to realize our potential.

Stephen Roos's *The Gypsies Never Came* and Priscilla Cummings's *A Face First* both present characters who are physically challenged, one by a birth defect and the other by the burns that resulted from a car accident. In *The Gypsies Never Came* sixth grader Augie Knapp was born without a left hand. He uses a glove to hide his missing hand, but he can't cover up the fact that his father is also missing, having walked out after Augie's birth. Augie wants very much to fit in with the other kids in his rural school, and he is horrified when a newcomer, the extroverted and highly nonconforming Lydie Rose, claims that they are two of a kind. Lydie Rose insists that Augie will feel differently about himself when the gypsies come and affirm his special nature. The gypsies in the title remain something of a mystery, but by the end of the book Augie himself has realized his unique talents and is able to discard the glove as well as his prickly defenses. In Cummings's *A Face First* Kelly's physical disabilities are much more central to the story than are Augie's to *The Gypsies Never Came.* This is an emotionally powerful story that takes the reader along on Kelly's journey to recovery following a car accident. We live through Kelly's initial disorientation following her rescue from the burning car. We follow her through the terrible days of recovery in her hospital bed. We understand her withdrawal from her friends and family as she tries to recuperate from her burns. We celebrate her reconciliation with her mother, who was at fault in causing the accident. Finally we applaud her decision to put her face first and re-embrace life, scarred face and all.

Marlee Matlin, the first deaf actor to win an Academy Award, has written an agreeable, light story whose central character is deaf. Nine-year-old Megan is an outgoing child whose longing for a best friend is satisfied when the painfully shy Cindy moves into her neighborhood. The two quickly become best friends and Cindy studies sign language so that she can communicate better with Megan. Their friendship hits some bumps when Megan becomes friends with another deaf girl she meets at summer camp. Eventually both Megan and Cindy learn that friends must give each other a little space to take risks in their lives. The book is most notable for the fact that Matlin writes about a deaf character from inside the Deaf culture. Deaf children will find a character much like themselves in Megan, and all children will find a pleasing story about friendship in *Deaf Child Crossing.*

Developmental and Learning Disabilities

Betsy Byars won a Newbery Medal for her story about an adolescent girl and her retarded brother in *The Summer of the Swans.* Sara feels very much like the ugly duckling in her difficult fourteenth summer. She weeps over her big feet, her skinny legs, and her nose, even over her gross orange sneakers. But when her brother is lost in the woods, her tears vanish in the terror she feels for Charlie. In her anguish Sara turns to Joe Melby—whom she had despised the day before—and together they find Charlie. It is the longest day of the summer and Sara knows that she will never be the same again. Like the awkward flight

---

[17]Baskin and Harris, *More Notes from a Different Drummer,* chap. 2.

of the swans with their "great beating of wings and ruffling of feathers," Sara is going to land with a long, perfect glide. Sara's love for her brother and concern for his safety help her break through her shell of adolescent moodiness.

In *My Louisiana Sky* Kimberly Willis Holt's Tiger Ann Parker must cope with adults with developmental disabilities, her own parents. Raised by her grandmother, who also looks after her childlike mother and learning-disabled father, Tiger Ann is ashamed of her parents, especially when her classmates make fun of her family situation. She longs for the type of life her sophisticated Aunt Doreen can give her. However, when her beloved grandmother dies and her aunt takes her to Baton Rouge to live, Tiger Ann understands that there is a trade-off between big-city sophistication and her small but close-knit rural community. She begins to recognize that her parents have unusual talents, and she reaches out to grasp the role that she can play in this loving if eccentric family.

Sue Ellen Bridgers portrays an important summer in 12-year-old Casey Flanagan's life in *All Together Now*. Casey has come to spend the summer with her grandparents in a small southern town. There she meets Dwayne Pickens, a retarded man who is her father's age. Dwayne has the mind of a 12-year-old and a passion for baseball. Their friendship grows when Dwayne, who dislikes girls but mistakes Casey for a boy, includes her in his endless baseball sessions. Casey contracts what might be polio, and her anxious family sits with her through several terrible August days. Dwayne faithfully visits during the long convalescence that follows and keeps her spirits up. By summer's end, Casey has grown in awareness of herself and the nature of friendship.

Joey Pigza has problems of a different sort in Jack Gantos's stories about a boy with attention-deficit/hyperactivity disorder (ADHD). In *Joey Pigza Swallowed the Key*, in addition to an abusive grandmother and an absent father, Joey's ADHD is out of control. Despite medication, Joey cannot seem to stop his impulsive behavior. He sticks his finger in a pencil sharpener, swallows his house key, and drives his classmates to distraction. When his impetuous actions injure another student, he is sent to a special education program in another school. Here Joey finds a knowledgeable teacher who has the time to help him learn how to deal with his behavior. A physical evaluation identifies a medication that is more suitable for him, and eventually he is able to return to his original school. In *Joey Pigza Loses Control* Joey's progress is threatened when his father returns and tries to convince Joey he doesn't need his medication. In *What Would Joey Do?* Joey seems to have his own problems under control and is convinced he can help solve the problems of those around him, including his warring mother and father and the blind girl he has been partnered with at school.

In *Rainy* Sis Deans presents a different perspective on ADHD. Based on her own experiences as a child, Deans writes with firsthand knowledge of the struggles of children with the disorder and the lack of knowledge about medication to treat it. Ten-year-old Rainy Tucker is well aware that she is different from other children, and her parents and her older sister, Jewel, have struggled to help her bring some sort of order to her life. When Jewel wants to take a summer job instead of babysitting for Rainey, Camp Megunticook is offered as an alternative. Rainy struggles through the activities and altercations typical of summer camp and is barely managing to get by when a letter from her sister gives away the secret that her beloved dog, Max, has been killed. Rainy comes close to losing any gains she has made over the summer. She steals off from camp on a pilgrimage that is both reckless and yet, for her, highly organized in its planning. She rows across the lake and climbs a mountain where 12-year-old Eleanora French had fallen to her death in 1864. At the edge of the cliff Rainy leaves Max's ball, to comfort both herself and Eleanora. This incident results in expulsion from the camp, but Rainy returns home with new confidence in herself. Like Joey Pigza,

The title character of Sis Deans's *Rainy* is a 10-year-old girl who struggles to control her ADHD while away from her supportive family at summer camp. From *Rainy* by Sis Deans. Copyright © 2005 by Sis Deans. Reprinted by permission of Henry Holt and Company, LLC.

Rainy is a highly likable character. Both Gantos and Deans do a fine job of letting us inside the heads of children with ADHD. These sympathetic portraits of different children will resonate with all youngsters.

Mental Illness

Few stories in which the protagonist suffers from mental illness have been written for the elementary school child, but several well-written books for adolescents and young adults feature characters who are struggling with mental illness. In a demanding and serious book, *3 NBs of Julian Drew* by James Deem, 15-year-old Julian has been traumatized and abused both physically and mentally. Writing in a code he has invented as a way of escaping his pain, he keeps a series of notebooks, which this book is named after. Deem has told the story through this cryptic code, mirroring Julian's mental state in a way conventional spelling could not. Thus the book is for mature and accomplished readers who will be intrigued by the device and moved by Julian's struggle to escape the tyranny of his home and the prison of his disturbed mind.

Thirteen-year-old Carrie Stokes, in Zibby Oneal's *The Language of Goldfish*, does not like what is happening to her. She wishes her family could return to the days when they lived in a cramped Chicago apartment rather than in an affluent suburb. If only things hadn't changed, she would still be close to her sister, Moira, and they would share all that they had as children. Instead, Carrie is under pressure from her mother and sister to wear more appropriate and stylish clothes, to go to school dances, and, somehow, be someone Carrie feels she is not. When she attempts suicide by overdosing on pills, her mother still avoids dealing with the real Carrie. Gradually, as Carrie mends, she is better able to understand her mother's denial. She is helped in this by a therapist, a trusted art teacher, and a new friend, a neighbor boy. Finally she learns to accept changes in others and herself while those closest to her display various ways in which they, too, cope with mental illness.

While there are few books about mentally ill children, there are several that present a child or children dealing with a mentally ill sibling or adult. In a moving story about mental illness, Ann Martin's *A Corner of the Universe* tells the story of 12-year-old Hattie. Hattie is a shy, introspective child, whose worldview is dramatically changed when her previously unknown Uncle Adam is discharged from his mental hospital and returns home. This event is of great consternation to Hattie's proper and snobbish grandmother, and it introduces unexpected turmoil into her sheltered, small-town life. Ruth White's *Memories of Summer* presents a heartbreaking view of schizophrenia, which gradually overtakes 13-year-old Lyric's older sister in this story. Cynthia Voigt's *Homecoming* and *Dicey's Song* portray the aftereffects of a depressed mother's abandonment of her children. Paula Fox's *The Village by the Sea* concerns a girl's two-

The summer she turns 12, Hattie Owens's life is changed when her mentally ill Uncle Adam comes back to live in her small town in Ann Martin's *A Corner of the Universe*. Cover from *A Corner of the Universe* by Ann M. Martin. Copyright © 2002 by Ann M. Martin. Used by permisssion of Scholastic Press, a division of Scholastic Inc. Photograph: Michael Prince/Corbis.

week stay with a mentally ill aunt. Bruce Brooks, in *The Moves Make the Man*, shows through the eyes of a compassionate and articulate boy narrator how the mental breakdown of his friend's mother nearly brings about the breakdown of the friend as well.

In Kristine L. Franklin's *Eclipse*, sixth grader Trina must deal with the changes in her father's mental state following an accident that disabled him. As she looks forward to the birth of a sibling the family has wanted for years, her normally outgoing father either sleeps all the time or lashes out irrationally at Trina. Trina is troubled by his behavior and the fear that the new baby could be born retarded because of her mother's age. Her mother tries to protect her from the truth but finally admits to Trina that her father has attempted suicide. When the baby is born prematurely, her father cannot seem to cope and, refusing to take his medication, falls further into depression. On the night of a lunar eclipse, in a tremendously tense and painful conclusion, he takes a rifle into their barn and a shot rings out just as Trina and her mother realize what his calm goodnight must have meant. The consequences of mental illness to families are painfully clear in this moving yet ultimately hopeful story.

Aging and Death

In the early part of the twentieth century the aging and death of loved ones were accepted as a natural part of a child's firsthand knowledge. However, most modern children are removed from any such knowledge of senility and death. Few grandparents live with their families anymore, and many relocate to apartments or retirement communities. When older relatives become ill, they are shunted off to hospitals and nursing homes. Few people die at home today, and many children have never attended a funeral. Seldom is death discussed with children. Contemporary authors realize that there is enough genuine mystery about death, without hiding it under this false cloak of secrecy.

Today, realistic fiction for children reflects society's concern for honesty about aging and dying. We have moved from a time when the subject of death was one of the taboos of children's literature to a time when it is being discussed openly and frankly.

Aging

Many recent picture books have portrayed young people learning to accept older people as they are or to recall them fondly as they were (see Chapter 5). Realistic fiction portrays older people in all their rich variety, as treasured grandparents, as activists or as passive observers, as senile or vitally involved in events around them, and as still-valuable contributors to a society they have helped to build.

The Hundred Penny Box, written by Sharon Bell Mathis and illustrated by Leo Dillon and Diane Dillon, tells of the love between Great-Great-Aunt Dew, an aged African American woman, and Michael, a young boy. Aunt Dew is 100 years old and she keeps a box full of pennies, one for each year of her life. Michael loves to count them out while Aunt Dew tells him the story behind each one, relating it to life and historical events. Michael's mother wants to give the old box away, but Michael plans a special hiding place for it. This story is remarkable for presenting perspectives on aging from the viewpoints of three different persons: Aunt Dew, who is content to sing her long song and recall the past with her pennies; Michael's mother, who has to take care of her; and Michael, who loves her but in his childlike way also wants to be entertained by her storytelling.

There are also books that portray older people as active, lively, and engaging. In Kimberly Willis Holt's *Dancing in the Cadillac Light* Jaynelle Lambert's Grandpap is wonderfully alert, if a bit forgetful and somewhat

eccentric, until his death from a heart attack. Eleven-year-old Jaynelle relishes his antics and internalizes his spirit even after he is gone from their rural community of Moon, Texas. In Deborah Wiles's *Love, Ruby Lavender* 9-year-old Ruby adores her grandmother. Miss Eula, having recently lost her husband, decides to travel from their small town in Mississippi to visit her son and new grandbaby in Hawaii. Ruby is convinced that her grandmother will want to stay in Hawaii. In order to lure her home, Ruby writes not-so-subtle letters that relay the events happening at home in Halleluia and that tell how much Ruby misses her. Both these books are as much about friends, family, and community, but the relationship with a beloved grandparent provides the impetus that drives each story forward. Holt and Wiles each do a wonderful job of capturing life in the rural south in the not-too-distant past. Eccentric characters, lively dialogue, and warmhearted outcomes will prove highly attractive to middle-grade readers.

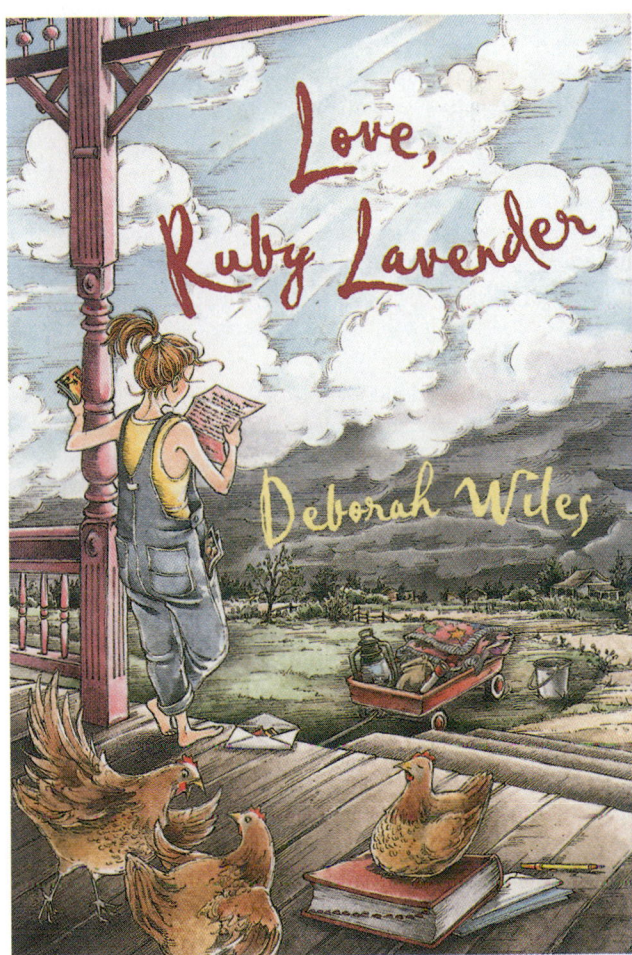

Nine-year-old Ruby's comfortable world is shaken by her grandfather's death and her beloved grandmother Miss Eula's departure for Hawaii in *Love, Ruby Lavender* by Deborah Wiles. Book cover from *Love, Ruby Lavender*, copyright © 2001 by Deborah Wiles. Reproduced by permission of Harcourt, Inc.

British author Nina Bawden portrays vital and energetic older people in many of her books. In the humorous *Granny the Pag* Catriona Brooke's beloved Granny is a psychiatrist who tools around town on her Harley-Davidson motorcycle. In *The Friends* by Kazumi Yumoto, three boys have a horrified fascination with death and begin to spy on a reclusive old neighbor, hoping to observe the process firsthand. But the old man turns out to be a vital if somewhat curmudgeonly character, and the boys find themselves taken in by his personality and his needs.

Another book that suggests that different generations have much to offer each other is Angela Johnson's *Toning the Sweep.* Fourteen-year-old Emily and her mother have traveled to the desert Southwest to bring her sick grandmother back to Cleveland. Grandma Ola has built a rich life for herself in this desert land she loves so much, and the summer visit is the opportunity for Emily to discover her grandmother's present and her own past. She undertakes a video project and interviews Ola, her mother, and the people who make up her grandmother's community. The story that emerges includes the awful facts about her grandfather's death in Alabama and the painful truth that her grandmother is coming home to die. But this story is not about dying. Rather, it is a celebration of a remarkable woman who has lived a full, if unconventional, life. Emily's project becomes a fitting way to "tone the sweep" for her grandmother, the opportunity to ring her soul to heaven as her ancestors in South Carolina might have done in previous generations.

Death and Dying

A child's first experience with death is frequently the loss of a pet. While picture books for younger children portray this experience with younger protagonists, several longer books have depicted slightly older children dealing with the death of a pet.

Other children's first experience with death is the loss of a grandparent. Two warmly illustrated short stories show a child coping with the death of one grandparent while continuing a rewarding relationship with the remaining one. In Mavis Jukes's *Blackberries in the Dark,* Austin spends the summer on the farm with Grandma and everywhere around him are reminders of his grandfather: the tire swing he built, his fishing reel hanging in the barn, and his treasured old fishing knife now strangely out of place in the dining room cupboard. Grandpa had promised to teach him how to fish this summer, and with him gone, there's no one to teach him or to help him pick blackberries at night. After Grandma and Austin recall the past summer, however, Austin starts out to pick blackberries on his own, only to have his grandmother follow, complete with her husband's fishing gear, so the two of them can teach each other to fish. Readers can almost feel the two resolve to move on from grief to new challenges, and the decision is neatly punc-

tuated by Grandma's gift of Grandpa's fishing knife to Austin. Thomas B. Allen's black-and-white soft-pencil illustrations capture poignancy, accept the pleasant loneliness of the farm, and depict the humor of Austin's story.

For Comfort Snowberger, in *Each Little Bird That Sings* by Deborah Wiles, the routine of death is more familiar. Her family runs a funeral home in Snapfinger, Mississippi. But when Comfort's Great-Uncle Edisto dies and several months later she loses her Great-Great-Aunt Florentine, Comfort is faced with a new reality. The last straw occurs when the familiar funeral routine is interrupted by the disgraceful behavior of her cousin Peach. Comfort is angry, distraught, and downright mean. Eventually a crisis occurs where Comfort has to make a crucial choice, and the result for her is a mixture of sorrow and catharsis. Told in Wiles's lively, colloquial prose, *Each Little Bird That Sings* provides children with an enjoyable story and a fine introduction to the rituals of loss and grieving.

A Taste of Blackberries by Doris Smith is a believable story of the sudden death of a young boy. Jamie and his friends are catching Japanese beetles for Mrs. House when Jamie shoves a slim willow limb down a bee hole. The bees swarm out and Jamie is stung. Allergic to bee stings, Jamie screams and gasps and falls to the ground. His best friend thinks Jamie is just showing off, until the ambulance arrives. Jamie is dead by the time he arrives at the hospital. His friend goes to the funeral, and the author graphically describes his reaction to seeing Jamie:

> There was Jamie. He was out straight with one hand crossed over his chest. He didn't look like he was asleep to me. Jamie slept all bunched up. Jamie looked dead. (p. 34)

After the funeral Jamie's friend picks blackberries because the two of them had planned to do so together. He shares the berries with Jamie's mother, who is very loving toward him. Because the story is told in the first person, the reader views death through a child's eyes. Simple, yet direct, this story seems very real. Katherine Paterson's *Bridge to Terabithia* and Marion Dane Bauer's *On My Honor,* which were discussed earlier in this chapter, are each about a child who suffers after the death of a friend.

Several other stories deal with the process of grieving the death of a brother or sister. Ruth Wallace-Brodeur's *Blue Eyes Better* focuses on the guilt felt by a surviving sister who blames herself for her older brother's death in a car accident. Tessa also feels abandoned by her mother, whose grief at losing her best-loved, blue-eyed boy causes her to abandon the family. Barbara Park's *Mick Harte Was Here* also deals with guilt felt by the survivors left behind when a child dies. The book begins after the bike accident that killed 13-year-old Phoebe's younger brother, Mick. As she remembers this lively boy and deals with her guilt at the petty quarrels they had, Phoebe learns that her mother and father are struggling under the burden of their own guilt. The family members finally acknowledge the "if onlys" each of them has carried silently. When Phoebe cries, "If only I had ridden his bike home Mick would still be here" (p. 84), her father sits her down and makes a list of all the other "if onlys" the family has used to blame themselves. Bringing these out into the open signals a new and healthier stage in their grieving. *Beat the Turtle Drum* by Constance Greene is narrated by 13-year-old Kate and tells of the summer when Joss saved her money, rented a horse, and finally, in an accidental fall from a tree, was killed. Readers who have come to know the two sisters feel, along with Kate and her parents, the tragedy of Joss's death. *A Summer to Die* by Lois Lowry presents two sisters who quarrel constantly until the older one contracts leukemia. Although Lowry juxtaposes the celebration of birth with the sadness of a death, and Meg moves through the stages of dealing with her sister's death, the other two stories seem more compelling.

Getting Near to Baby by Audrey Couloumbis reveals the heartbreaking aftereffects of the death of a baby sister on a family. Little Sister has stopped talking, and Mother has fallen apart in her effort to overcome her guilt and grief. Willa Jo, the 13-year-old eldest sister, tries to carry the burden of care for her family. The story concerns the conflict between Willa Jo and Aunt Patty, Willa Jo's mother's oldest sister. When Aunt Patty and Uncle Hob insist that the two girls come to stay with them, Willa Jo resents her aunt's interference and her fussy, class-conscious ways. The book begins as Willa Jo crawls out on the roof of the house one morning to watch the sun rise. Joined by Little Sister, she decides to just stay on the roof, to the consternation of Aunt Patty and the bemusement of Uncle Hob and the neighbors. Gradually, in between episodes on the roof, the story of Baby's death and the resulting events is revealed in flashbacks. Through these finely interwoven strands of story the terrible burden of sadness that each of the characters carries is revealed. We also come to see the complex personalities of Willa Jo and Aunt Patty, both of them more alike than they want to admit. In the end they find that all of them have had something important to contribute to the healing process that has occurred.

In Janet Taylor Lisle's *The Lost Flower Children* we also find two sisters who have been traumatized by a death. After their mother dies, Olivia and her younger sister, Nellie, are sent to live with their Great-Aunt Minty. This circumstance appalls 9-year-old Olivia, who takes the move as a betrayal by her father. Olivia, who is fiercely protective of her demanding and explosive younger sister, focuses all her energy on caring for Nellie, perhaps as a way of vanquishing her own pain. Olivia views Aunt Minty's spinsterish, old-lady habits with disdain, and Aunt Minty seems to be at a loss to know how to care for the two girls. Her efforts at entertaining them and finding friends for them seem to end in disaster. But when she unearths a little china cup in her overgrown garden,

the two girls are curious despite themselves. When Olivia finds an old storybook hidden in Aunt Minty's vast library, the meaning of the tiny tea cup is revealed. The children are soon captivated by the task of finding the other pieces of the tea set, which they believe will release a party of children transformed into flowers by a spell of enchantment. The search for the lost tea set becomes the focal point of their lives and the unconscious channel into which they pour their grief. Gradually the girls bloom just as Aunt Minty's garden is revived. One of Lisle's great strengths as a writer is her ability to create magic and enchantments that seem absolutely real. Whether this is a work of fantasy or realism will be up to individual children to decide. Whether the characters have been enriched and healed by giving free reign to their imagination is not in dispute.

The untimely death of a parent can have long-lasting effects on a child's life. In *The Tiger Rising* by Kate DiCamillo 12-year-old Rob Horton has developed a terrible rash, likely an outward result of keeping his feelings about his mother's death locked up inside. Following a move to Florida with his father, who is also emotionally damaged, Rob finds a caged tiger in the woods behind the Kentucky Star Motel where the two are staying. The tiger becomes a metaphor for Rob's frozen emotions and for the release that follows when he and his friend Sistine attempt to free the tiger. In Nancy Hope Wilson's *Mountain Pose* 12-year-old Ellie is still affected by her mother's death that occurred seven years earlier. The pain of loss is brought alive once more when her maternal grandmother, estranged from the family for many years, dies and leaves Ellie the family home in Vermont, along with instructions for Ellie to read diaries left behind by her female ancestors. Ellie's sculptor father is violently opposed to reopening any connection to his dead wife's mother. But Ellie perseveres and learns much about the family secrets that led to her mother's relationship with her grandmother. Ellie also finds the family roots that she has craved for so long in the reconciliation and acceptance of her history.

Keeper of the Night by Kimberly Willis Holt and *The Letters* by Kazumi Yumoto both deal with the heartbreaking aftermath of a parent's suicide. Holt's *Keeper of the Night* is 13-year-old Isabel Moreno. Following her mother's suicide, Isabel tries to assume the responsibility of caring for her family in her mother's place. Each night she covers her father's sleeping body, as he falls asleep on the bedroom floor because he cannot bear to return to an empty bed. She watches over her younger sister, Olivia, who has begun having nightmares and wetting the bed. She worries over younger brother Frank who, night after night, carves "I hate you" on his bedroom wall with a knife. But Isabel's best efforts are not enough to banish the pain and grief that no one will talk about. The family members slide further and further into disrepair until Frank's act of self-mutilation brings the help and healing that the family members have needed.

Brief chapters told in Isabel's voice provide everyday details of life with extended family and friends on their island home of Guam. The clipped passages seem innocuous at first, but over the course of the book we come to realize how they symbolize Isabel's pain, too tightly clutched inside her heart and head. Holt has written a masterful and moving story of the terrible psychological damage that follows a parent's suicide. Yumoto's *The Letters* is set in Japan and concerns the long-lasting legacy left by the death of 6-year-old Chiaki's father. Chiaki becomes physically ill after she and her mother move into a small block of flats owned by the eccentric Mrs. Yanagi. The gruff old landlady promises Chiaki that she has a drawer full of letters that she will take to those beyond the grave when she dies. As Chiaki learns to write she begins to address letters to her father and entrust them to Mrs. Yanagi. It is only when Chiaki is an adult and Mrs. Yanagi dies that Chiaki discovers that her mother also entrusted Mrs. Yanagi with letters to her dead husband. Given permission to read those letters, Chiaki is stunned by the anguish in her mother's written outpouring of grief and guilt at his suicide. Chiaki comes to accept that, in keeping the secret for so long, her mother has given her the time she needed to accept her father's death. Chiaki is also able to see her own suicidal depression in a different light and realizes that she can choose life even as her father chose death. Author Yumoto opens and closes the book with Chiaki's adult voice and thus identifies an audience of mature readers. However, she focuses most of the scenes through the eyes of a young child—the faces of neighbors, a poplar tree as it changes through the seasons, the smell of sweet potatoes roasting in a pile of burning autumn leaves, and the pain of those left behind when someone dies.

Crescent Dragonwagon's *Winter Holding Spring* is a simple poetic story with complex ideas about death, time, hope, and love. It begins as 11-year-old Sarah and her father can tomatoes just as her mother used to before she died. Both adult and child find it difficult to talk about their feelings, but they observe, as a yellow leaf falls, that the season of summer holds fall. As the seasons progress, the two go about the daily chores of living, and Sarah uses the idea of a future embedded in the present to give herself hope and courage.

Previously discussed books deal with a child who recovers from the death of a friend, sibling, parent, or grandparent. *Hang Tough, Paul Mather* tells a memorable story of a boy who is anticipating his own death. Alfred Slote writes of Paul, a Little Leaguer who develops leukemia. The family moves from California to Michigan to be close to the university hospital where Paul will have special treatments. He is not supposed to play baseball, but the neighborhood team needs a pitcher for their big game. Paul slips out without his parents' knowledge, forges the permission slip, and pitches a great game. However, he injures himself and endures a long stay in the hospital. There, a young doctor becomes his friend.

Their discussion of death is one of the most honest in children's literature. Paul leaves the hospital in his wheelchair, at least long enough to watch and help win another game. While Paul sounds hopeful at the end of the story, he is back in the hospital and his condition has worsened.

A powerful story that asserts that coming to terms with death can be an affirmation of life and hope is Madeleine L'Engle's *A Ring of Endless Light*. Vicky Austin, whom readers met in *Meet the Austins*, begins her sixteenth summer at graveside services for a family friend who has suffered a heart attack after rescuing a spoiled teenager from an attempted suicide. While Vicky is already grieving for the impending death of her beloved grandfather, she tries to understand what mortality and immortality mean. She also deals with the attentions of three different young men. Zachary, the boy who attempted suicide, is rich, impulsive, and exciting; Leo, whose father had tried to save Zachary, is plain and awkward but reliable and candid; and Adam, a marine biologist studying dolphin communication, is warm, kind, and intensely eager to involve Vicky in his research after he sees her natural ability to communicate with dolphins. When the death of a child numbs Vicky, it is her experience with the dolphins that brings her back to an emotional present. Throughout the story shines the "ring of endless light" that her grandfather has been leading her to see. He tells Vicky, in the depths of her grief and denial:

> You have to give the darkness permission. It cannot take over otherwise. . . . Vicky, do not add to the darkness. . . . This is my charge to you. You are to be a light-bearer. You are to choose the light. (p. 318)

Not all serious illnesses end with death, but the trauma of such an illness can have particularly damaging outcomes. Virginia Hamilton's *Bluish* and Valerie Hobbs's *Defiance* focus on children dealing with the aftermath of cancer treatments and recovery. The effects of a parent's illness are sensitively dealt with in Katherine Hannigan's *Ida B . . . and Her Plans to Maximize Fun*. Ida B is, at the outset of the book, an imaginative, happy child. Schooled at home, she sets about planning one creative adventure after another, and she is most at home roaming the orchard behind her house—and talking to her beloved apple trees. Then her mother develops cancer, and her world falls apart. She is sent to public school, her father is preoccupied, and her normally attentive mother is absent in mind, if not body. Worst of all perhaps, the family has to sell the orchard to developers to help pay the medical costs. Ida shuts down, angry and afraid. The steadfast love of her parents and the support of her fourth-grade teacher help Ida through her worst crisis, a mean-spirited confrontation with the people who have built on her orchard. The first step to her recovery starts with an apology, what Ida B refers to as "spring clean-

Katherine Hannigan's *Ida B . . . and Her Plans to Maximize Fun* follow a formerly carefree character through the crisis of her mother's serious illness. Copyright © 2004 by Katherine Hannigan. Used by permission of HarperCollins Children's Books, a division of HarperCollins Publishers.

ing." Once she gets started, she realizes, she can't stop with one room. Someone is telling her:

> Keep going, You're almost done, No quitting allowed.
>
> Then all of a sudden you are done. It was an awful terrible time, and you never want to have to do it again in your whole life. But it is kind of nice seeing everything clean and looking just right. (p. 223)

For Ida B things won't be the same, but things can get better—a hopeful message for all children to remember.

The friendship between Tut (James) Tuttle, a longtime resident of a Maine fishing village, and Alex, daughter of a New Age flibbertigibbet, in *The Last Codfish* by J. D. McNeill is an unlikely one. Devastated by his mother's death in a boat accident, Tut has become an isolated loner, while his father copes with his grief and guilt through alcohol. The result for the two is poverty of both body and spirit. Alex, on the other hand, has her every material want satisfied but has been emotionally neglected

by her self-centered mother. As a result of his trauma Tut has become mute, whereas Alex talks all the time. When the two are drawn together, a strange chemistry emerges that serves as a catalyst for both to begin their recoveries.

The end of life need not be the end of everything, as several recent books for adolescent readers show us. Chris Crutcher's *The Sledding Hill* and Adele Griffin's *Where I Want to Be* are both told by dead narrators. *The Sledding Hill* is a book about friendship and grieving. *Where I Want to Be* explores the relationships of siblings and their reactions to death. *Elsewhere* by Gabrielle Zevin, a poignant and beautifully told story, focuses most directly on the meaning of the cycle of life and death. The heroine, 15-year-old Liz, wakes up aboard the SS *Egypt* en route to Elsewhere, a place where life takes on a reverse cycle. All who die come there and age backwards until they are babies who are released back to Earth to assume another existence. From the moment of her waking, Liz goes through the stages of grief for her own life and for the people she left behind, but she is helped in her ultimate acceptance of Elsewhere by a wonderful cast of characters, including a grandmother she had never met. Although none of these books fits neatly into a category of realistic fiction, they seem more fittingly discussed in this chapter than in Chapter 7: "Modern Fantasy." Their characters and themes are firmly grounded in the problems and issues of adolescents in the contemporary world. Their explorations of death and life give readers many opportunities for reflection and discussion.

LIVING IN A DIVERSE WORLD

 In a true pluralistic society it is essential that we learn to respect and appreciate cultural diversity. Books can never substitute for firsthand contact with other people, but they can deepen our understanding of different cultures. Rather than falsely pretend that differences do not exist, children need to discover what is unique to each group of persons and universal to the experience of being human.

African American Experiences in Books for Children

 In the past decades many fine books have been published that reflect the social and cultural traditions associated with growing up as an African American child in America. This "culturally conscious fiction," says Rudine Sims Bishop, has certain recurring features that offer all children, but especially African American children, a unique perspective in fiction. Culturally conscious fiction often contains references to distinctive language patterns and vocabulary; relationships between a young person and a much older one; extended or three-generational families; descriptions of skin shades, including positive comparisons, such as "dark as a pole of Ceylon ebony"; and acknowledgment

of African American historical, religious, and cultural traditions.[18]

Today, the number of chapter books for younger readers is still small. A chapter book that children aged 7 or 8 can read easily is Lucille Clifton's *The Lucky Stone*. In four short chapters Clifton traces the path of a black stone with a letter scratched on it as it is passed from generation to generation of African-Americans, from slave times to now. Mildred Pitts Walter's *Justin and the Best Biscuits in the World* draws on information about African American cowboys on the American frontier in the late 1800s while telling a contemporary story. Tired of his family of sisters and his mother, 10-year-old Justin is relieved when his grandfather invites him to stay at his Missouri ranch. From Grandpa, Justin learns family history and how to clean fish, keep his room in order, and cook. When he goes home, Justin has developed self-confidence, and his family is more appreciative of his talents. Walter's digressions about African-Americans in the old West, under the guise of books read by Justin, might send some children to the library for further research. Walter's *Suitcase* is about a sixth grader whose height seems ideal for a basketball player. His physical ability is more suited to drawing than to dribbling, however, and this artistic talent both puzzles and disappoints his father. *Have a Happy . . .* , also by Walter, traces an 11-year-old boy's feelings as he tries to earn money to help out his family during the Christmas season. His participation in the events of Kwanza is presented so that even readers unfamiliar with this modern African American holiday can visualize the celebration and understand its significance. The same audience that enjoys Walter's books will want to read Alice Mead's Junebug series about Junebug, a likable and resourceful 10-year-old boy who has lived most of his life in the New Haven projects, until his mother is able to move the family to an apartment building that houses the elderly patients she looks after.

A winner of the Coretta Scott King and Michael L. Printz awards, Walter Dean Myers sets many of his stories in Harlem, but he portrays a less grim, and even humorous, city existence in some of his stories. *The Mouse Rap*, which alternates between poetry and prose, is written in the vernacular of jive-talking, rapping, 14-year-old Mouse Douglas, boy "hoop" player. Myers also relies on the keen observations of an intelligent boy narrator in his *Fast Sam, Cool Clyde, and Stuff*, a story of the interdependence of a group of basketball-playing boys who inadvertently become involved with drugs while trying to help a former addict. The author's lighter books also show boys coping successfully with urban life.

Nikki Grimes also chooses an urban setting to provide a glimpse of the pressures and problems faced by an adolescent girl living in Harlem in the 1960s in *Jazmin's Notebook*. Jazmin's problems, not the least of which are a dead father and an alcoholic mother, would seem almost stereotypical, but her response to them is not. Jazmin keeps a notebook to record her observations of life and to write her poetry. Her strong character, her dreams of college, and her determination to succeed are revealed within its pages. Eventually, the stable home she finds with an older sister and the support of the other caring adults she meets promise Jazmin a positive future. Jazmin, perhaps like author Grimes, finds strength in her love of poetry. In *Bronx Masquerade* Grimes further celebrates the power of poetry. Here, a high school English teacher invites his students to an open mike Friday, encouraging them to read their poems out loud. The students, many from the inner-city projects, are skeptical at first. Grimes lets us inside the head of each character to glimpse the thoughts, fears, and dreams of each member of the diverse group. Then she presents the poem that each has composed. By the end of the year each teen has been changed for the better by the experience with poetry.

In 1975, Virginia Hamilton became the first African American to win the Newbery Medal, with *M. C. Higgins, the Great*. It is set in southern Ohio where 13-year-old Cornelius Higgins and his family live on old family property just beneath a slagheap created by strip miners. M. C. dreams of moving his family away from the slow-moving heap that threatens to engulf their home. His place of refuge from which he surveys the world is a 40-foot steel pole. From there M. C. sees a "dude" who he imagines will make his mother a singing star and enable them to move. Another outsider, Lurhetta, who is hiking through this section of Appalachia, awakens M. C.'s initiative and makes him see that he is never going to solve his problems by daydreaming about them. M. C. is finally moved to a small but symbolic action.

Among Hamilton's many books are those that draw on her family experiences as part of the fifth generation of free African Americans to have lived in southern Ohio. On one level, *Cousins* is the story of 10-year-old Cammy, who is consumed with jealousy for her beautiful and probably bulimic cousin, Patty Ann. During a summer camp outing, Patty Ann disappears in a sinkhole of a fast-moving river after saving another cousin from drowning, and Cammy is convinced the death is her fault for having hated this perfect cousin so much. In *Second Cousins*, set a year later, Cammy is still trying to deal with the effects of the drowning. A family reunion brings new relatives and new family secrets out into the open, yet these events threaten Cammy's recovery. Both stories, told with Hamilton's unsurpassed style, reveal how interconnected tensions, complex relationships, and surpris-

---

[18]Rudine Sims Bishop, *Shadow and Substance: Afro-American Experience in Contemporary Children's Fiction* (Urbana, Ill.: National Council of Teachers of English, 1982), pp. 49–77.

ing discoveries can nurture and sustain each member of an extended family. Hamilton's *Zeely,* another story set in Ohio, concerns 11-year-old Geeder Perry's need to make a Watusi queen out of Zeely Taber, a herder of pigs. It is Zeely who convinces Geeder that real beauty comes from accepting yourself and others for what they are. Published posthumously, Hamilton's *Time Pieces: The Book of Times* is semi-autobiographical. The book centers on Valena, a young African American girl growing up in a small town in Ohio with loving parents and siblings. Valena's experiences, both joyful and fearful, over the course of a summer are interwoven with "reckons." This is the term Valena's mother gives to stories of the past that preserve the memories of forebearers who left no written accounts of their journeys to freedom. These "reckons" give Valena a sense of who she is and what she may become. In her previous books, Virginia Hamilton left a legacy of stories to generations to come. In *Time Pieces* she has given us a final gift, a lovely tapestry of past, present, and future that is truly timeless and universal in its appeal.

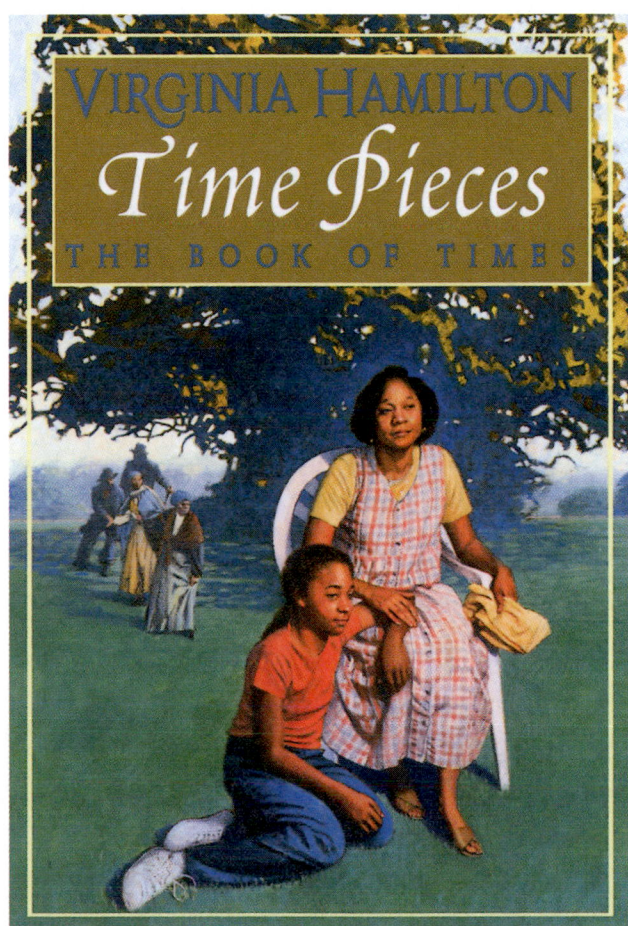

Virginia Hamilton's *Time Pieces* provides glimpses of the lives of several generations of an African American family. Cover illustration by John Thompson from *Time Pieces: The Book of Times* by Virginia Hamilton. Published by The Blue Sky Press/Scholastic, Inc. Illustration copyright © 2002 by Scholastic, Inc. Reprinted by permission.

Several books look at middle-class African-Americans and the special pressures they face as they try to succeed in an often-hostile white world. Jacqueline Woodson's *Margaret and Maizon* are best friends growing up in Brooklyn when Maizon wins a scholarship to a mostly white private school. Her struggles to fit into a world that is alien and alienating are detailed in *Maizon at Blue Hill.* Margaret's own year apart from Maizon is related in *Last Summer with Maizon.* The two are reunited in *Between Madison and Palmetto* when Maizon drops out of Blue Hill and returns home to Madison Street. In all these books the girls confront difficult issues of race and class, but first and foremost these are stories about real young people whose friendship is strengthened through a variety of trials.

Woodson tackles a different and more serious topic in *Hush.* In this powerful story Toswiah/Evie, the 12-year-old protagonist, must watch her normal middle-class family fall apart when they are forced to move and assume new identities after their policeman father testifies against white cops accused of killing a black teenager. Many of Woodson's other fine books, such as *Behind You* and *If You Come Softly,* are addressed to an older teen audience, but her fine writing and strong characters would be appropriate for mature middle-school readers. Other fine authors who deal authentically with the African American experience for older readers are Jamie Adoff (*Jimi and Me*), Sharon Draper (*Forged by Fire*), Sharon Flake (*Bang*), Joyce Hansen (*One True Friend*), Janet McDonald (*Brother Hood*), and Brenda Woods (*Emako Blue*).

Books That Extend Understanding of Diversity

 For some years the quality and range in novels about African-Americans have been far better than for other ethnic or racial groups. Informational books, folktales, biographies, and picture books have done a much better job of reflecting the multicultural society in which we now live than has fiction. In older books about Hispanic Americans, for instance, forced stories and thin characterizations tended to perpetuate stereotypes rather than dispel them. Other titles, such as *Felita* by Nicholasa Mohr, suggested that "stick

Janet McDonald's *Brother Hood* portrays the struggle for identity of a young African American boy from Harlem who attends a prestigious prep school. Cover of *Brother Hood* by Janet McDonald. Copyright © 2004 by Janet McDonald. Reprinted by permission of Farrar, Straus & Giroux, LLC.

to your own kind" was the only way 9-year-old Felita and her family could cope with prejudice from their new neighbors. They return to the ghetto rather than stay in an apartment building where they have no friends. In *Going Home,* Felita, now a sixth grader, spends a summer in Puerto Rico and recognizes the universality of prejudice when her friendliness and artistic talents cause jealousy from her Puerto Rican peers.

In striking contrast, more-recent publications provide honest and memorable portrayals of many aspects of Latino and Hispanic culture. Nicholasa Mohr's *El Bronx Remembered,* Viola Canales's *The Tequila Worm,* and Judith Ortiz Cofer's *An Island like You* and *The Hunger of Birds* include excellent short stories for older adolescents. Gary Soto's *Baseball in April and Other Stories, Local News, Help Wanted,* and *Petty Crimes* are inspired collections of short stories that depict a variety of Hispanic children and adolescents in daily life. In *Baseball in April* Fausto longs for a guitar, but his scheme to raise the money to buy one makes him feel so guilty that he fi-

nally gives the money to a church. His honorable behavior is amply rewarded when he becomes the owner of his grandfather's *guitarron.* In other stories one girl becomes marbles champ while another learns that it can be more painful to stay home when your family goes on vacation than it is to endure their company. *Local News* includes the wonderfully funny "School Play" and the sweetly gentle "New Year's Eve." In *Petty Crimes* Soto takes a more serious tone in several of the stories, depicting adolescents who struggle with poverty and gang violence. Soto's portrayal of these central-California youngsters, through description and dialogue, reflects sympathy for the universal experiences of growing up.

Soto's fine novels explore these experiences further. In *Taking Sides,* Lincoln Mendoza finds that he has divided loyalties when he moves from a barrio school to a suburban junior high school and competes in basketball against his former teammates. In *Pacific Crossing,* Lincoln and his friend Tony travel to Japan for a summer exchange program and find a further mixture of culture. *Crazy Weekend* and *Summer on Wheels* follow the adventures of Hector and Mando, two teenage friends, and in *Boys at Work* and *The Pool Party* 10-year-old Rudy Herrera is the main character. Soto adds a female protagonist, Miata Ramirez, to his extended family of books in *The Skirt* and *Off and Running.* In the latter, Miata runs against Rudy Herrera for school president. In all his books Soto writes gentle stories of family and friends that are infused with the rhythms and images of Mexican American culture. Glossaries in the books help those readers who cannot use context to translate the Spanish words and phrases that flow naturally through the story.

Francisco Jimenez has built two notable books around his memories as a child of migrant workers in 1940s California. *The Circuit* and *Breaking Through* chronicle his personal journey from his Mexican village to the fields of California's farms. He provides a moving portrait of migrant families and a message of hope to all children in his eventual triumph over adversity. An older story of a boy of Spanish descent is Joseph Krumgold's *. . . And Now Miguel.* Miguel is the middle brother of a Hispanic family living on a New Mexico sheep ranch. Pedro, the younger brother, seems satisfied with what he has, but Miguel thinks his 19-year-old brother, Gabriel, not only can do everything but also has everything. Miguel has one all-consuming desire, and that is to be able to go with the men when they take the sheep to the Sangre de Cristo Mountains. His prayers are answered, but not as Miguel wished. Because Hispanics are one of the fastest-growing groups of immigrants to the United States, we still urgently need more contemporary realistic fiction that reflects Hispanic culture.

Asian Americans are among the most rapidly growing groups in North America. Many of the excellent stories set in this country that include children from countries in Asia are historical fiction titles such as Yoshiko Uchida's books that build on her experiences in the 1930s and in relocation camps for Japanese Americans in World War II. Bette Bao Lord's *In the Year of the Boar and Jackie Robinson* is also set in the past.

Notable exceptions are Laurence Yep's fine contemporary novels. *Child of the Owl* is the story of a Chinese American girl who finds herself and her roots when she goes to live with Paw Paw, her grandmother, in San Francisco's Chinatown. At first Casey doesn't like the narrow streets and alleys or the Chinese schools. But Paw Paw tells her about Jeanie, the mother Casey never knew, about her true Chinese name, and the story of the family's owl charm. Gradually she comes to appreciate it all and to realize that this place that has been home to Paw Paw, Jeanie, and Casey's father, Barney, is her home, too. *Child of the Owl* is as contemporary as the rock music that Paw Paw enjoys and as traditional as the owl charm, but Casey and Paw Paw are true originals. *Thief of Hearts* follows Casey's daughter Stacy on her own journey to understanding. Set in contemporary suburbia south of San Francisco, the book explores more subtle issues of prejudice and belonging. A mixed-race child, Stacy has her father's blond hair and her mother's Chinese eyes. She is a confident adolescent, at home in her multiethnic middle school, until her mother urges a new friend upon her. Hong Ch'un and her family are newly arrived from China and the girl is aloof and critical of American society. She and Stacy do not hit it off at all. When Hong Ch'un is accused of theft, however, Stacy stands up for her and finds that friends whom she has trusted hold her mixed-race status against her. Suddenly she sees her world in a different light.

> All my life I thought I had lived in a safe warm secure world where I was just like everyone else, but it had only been my little fantasy. I looked too Chinese. And yet, even if I learned Chinese and the culture, I looked too American. (p. 45)

Fortunately, Paw Paw is there to set things right. Now called Tai-Paw, Stacy's great-grandmother, the wonderful old woman has moved in with the family. She, too, has lost her familiar world, and this becomes even clearer when she and Stacy return to Chinatown to solve the mystery regarding Hong Ch'un. The Chinatown that existed when she raised Stacy's mother is almost unrecognizable, and many of her old friends are dead. But the old woman is as wise as ever, and she helps heal some of Stacy's hurt at the same time as she smooths a growing rift between Stacy and her mom. Well written, with fully developed, likable characters and a wonderful story, *Thief of Hearts* is a worthy sequel to *Child of the Owl*.

Yep has written many other titles for the middle-grade child. Although they are not as richly textured as *Child of the Owl*, they still provide satisfying stories and offer insights into Chinese American culture. Among these books are the warmly funny *Cockroach Cooties*, *Later, Gator*, and mysteries such as *The Case of the Firecrackers*, which features a young protagonist and her great-aunt

as a crime-solving duo in San Francisco's Chinatown. In *The Amah, Angelfish, The Cook's Family,* and *Ribbons*, Yep presents Stephanie Chin, a young girl determined to be a ballet dancer despite the many setbacks that beset her family.

Lensey Namioka addresses a younger audience in *Yang the Youngest and His Terrible Ear.* Nine-year-old Yingtao Yang would rather play baseball than practice the violin with his musical siblings. His American friend Matthew has the opposite problem. Unlike Yingtao, he has quite an ear for music and would love to have violin lessons. With the help of Third Sister everyone gets to play the instrument of his or her choice. The stories of other irrepressible family members are continued in *Yang the Third and Her Impossible Family, Yang the Second and Her Secret Admirers,* and *Yang the Eldest and His Odd Jobs.* All of these warm, amusing books tell of a Chinese immigrant family and their attempts to fit in with the people and customs of their new country. Younger readers will also enjoy Carolyn Marsden's *The Gold Threaded Dress* about Oy, a Thai-American fourth grader. Oy, renamed Olivia by her teacher, feels out of place in her predominately Mexican American school, and she longs to be part of the special club of girls. In order to impress the girls, Oy smuggles her special Thai dress, a gift from her grandmother, to school. When the girls treat it roughly the dress is damaged and Oy must face the consequences.

More contemporary stories featuring youngsters from the Indian culture have flourished in the past several years. Almost all of these feature female protagonists, and some, such as Narinder Dhami's *Bollywood Babes* and *Bindy Babes,* are lighthearted romps that feature characters comfortable in their home culture as well as their country. On the other hand, in Anjali Banerjee's *Maya Running* Maya Muherjee has spent most of her life in Manitoba, Canada, the only "browned skinned" girl in her middle school. Like many children in this situation, Maya doesn't know where she fits in. The visit of her exotic cousin Pinky from India becomes the catalyst for Maya's deeper understanding of herself, her family, and her culture. Kashmira Sheth's *Blue Jasmine* presents fine insights into life in India and the sometimes-painful, sometimes-joyful transitions that occur when a young person must move between cultures. Twelve-year-old Seema is perfectly happy living with her large extended family in their small town in India. She does well in school and has found a particular friend in her cousin Raju, whom she considers her brother. When Seema's father is invited to join his mentor at a university in Iowa, her serenity is shattered. Raju is angry that she would consider going to America, and her relatives fear that she will lose her Indian values if she moves. She cannot bear to be away from her immediate family, however, and so Seema makes the long journey to America with them. The huge changes in lifestyle and her difficulty with English are setbacks for Seema, but she finds a sympathetic teacher and a group of American friends

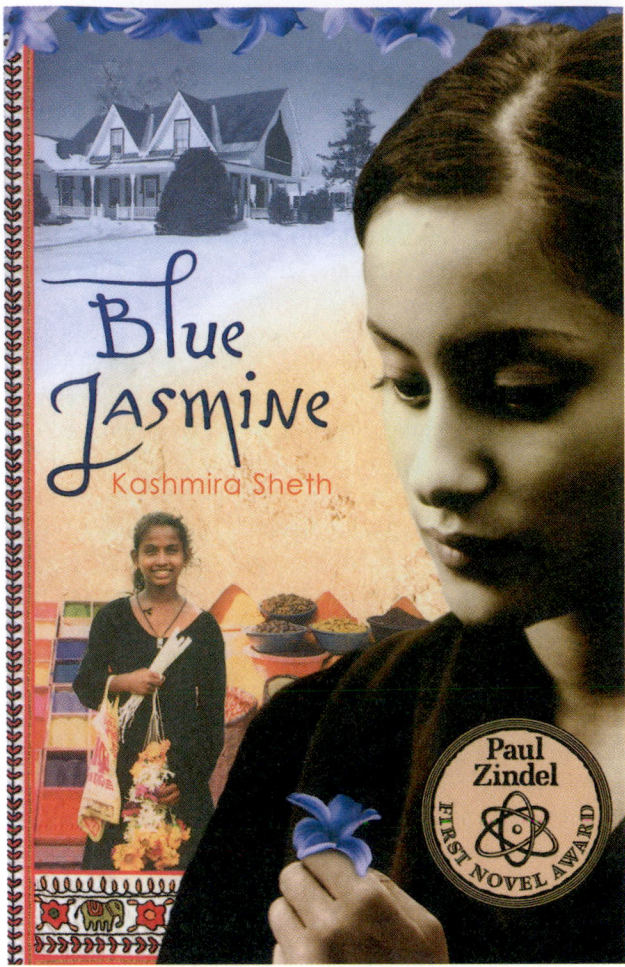

In Kashmira Sheth's *Blue Jasmine* a 12-year-old girl from India is confronted with the cultural dissonance between her two worlds when her family moves to Iowa. Cover from *Blue Jasmine* by Kashmira Sheth. Copyright © 2004 by Kashmira Sheth. Reprinted by permission of Hyperion Books for Children.

person, too, and he decides that although he will be American, he will also keep his Vietnamese name. Gilson allows Tuan to reveal parts of his harrowing boat escape from Vietnam, and a classmate's current-events report fills in other details. Himelblau's *The Trouble Begins* relates a Vietnamese immigrant's story from his point of view. Like Tuan, Du Nguyen has trouble fitting in, but in this case Du has finally joined his real family, who had moved to the United States ten years before, leaving Du with his grandmother in the Philippines. Du must accommodate not only to a new culture but also to a family who seem like strangers to him. Fortunately he has his grandmother to help ease the transition and help him find the "dragon" inside him.

A Step from Heaven by An Na is a much more serious story about the wrenching effects of changing countries and cultures. Born in Korea, Young Ju and her family move to America when she is four. They are sure they will find a better life there, and Young Ju even imagines that the plane is taking her to heaven where she will

In *A Step from Heaven* by An Na, when Young Ju and her family emigrate from Korea to the United States, they find that the adjustment to a new country and culture is more difficult than they had imagined. Cover from *A Step from Heaven* by An Na. Copyright © 2001 by An Na. Used by permission of Front Street Books.

who ease her way. A sudden return visit to India after a year in Iowa helps her find the best parts of both cultures that will serve to solidify her identity.

Children caught between two places and two cultures are the subject of other fine books such as Alice Mead's *Swimming to America,* about Albanian immigrants; Uma Krishnaswami's *Naming Maya,* about a thoroughly Americanized Indian girl who visits India with her mother; and Barbara Cohen's brief story about Russian immigrants, *Molly's Pilgrim.* The result of the Vietnam War and the often-difficult relocation of so many Vietnamese is the topic of two books, Jamie Gilson's *Hello, My Name Is Scrambled Eggs* and Linda Himelblau's *The Trouble Begins. Hello, My Name Is Scrambled Eggs* takes its name from the stick-on labels Harvey Trumble uses to teach Vietnamese refugee Tuan Nguyen to speak English while Tuan, his father, and his grandmother are staying with Harvey until their own home is ready. But 12-year-old Tuan, eager to please, is nonetheless his own

be reunited with her grandparents. But the reality of life in the United States proves very different—"a step from heaven," her American uncle warns. As the years pass Young Ju struggles to find the right fit for her Korean and American selves. Her younger brother grows more remote and hostile, and her father becomes increasingly depressed, taking out his unhappiness by beating his wife. The book ends on a positive note as Young Ju prepares to leave for college. Her mother has left her father, and brother Joon has straightened himself out, but the difficulties faced by newcomers to America are made painfully clear. An emotionally powerful work, *A Step from Heaven* won the Printz award for outstanding youngadult fiction.

Novels about Native Americans told with an authentic view of culture are hard to find. Joseph Bruchac, best known perhaps for his retellings of Native American folktales, has written two works of contemporary fiction that feature Native American characters. In *Eagle Song*, Danny Bigtree is a young Mohawk whose family moves to Brooklyn where his ironworker father can find work. In *The Heart of a Chief* Chris Nicola, a Penacook Indian, lives on a reservation where his people face multiple issues including the opening of a gambling casino. Both books provide details of the warm family relationships that sustain each protagonist as he deals with problems that, though they might be particular to his culture, speak to universal issues facing children growing up in today's world. Bruchac's *Hidden Roots* is a brief novel set in the 1960s that is based on real events in fairly recent Abenaki history. In the 1930s Vermont, along with many other states, passed a law allowing the state to sterilize people whom it considered social misfits. People of the Abenaki were singled out as "gypsies" and more than two hundred of them were officially sterilized over a twenty-year period. As a result, many Abenaki rejected their culture and went underground, trying their best to pass as French Canadians or Anglos. In *Hidden Roots* Bruchac imagines what the effect of that suppression might have been like on a young boy and his family.

Other books about Native Americans have geographically diverse settings but depict young people involved in survival who must draw on their Native American heritage in various ways. In Kirkpatrick Hill's well-crafted survival story *Toughboy and Sister*, the title characters are suddenly on their own at the family summer fish camp in Canada's Yukon Territory after their widowed father, an alcoholic, literally drinks himself to death. Eleven-year-old Toughboy, an Athabascan Indian, and his sister expect to be rescued in a few days, because their father's boat with his corpse in it will float downriver by their village. But when no one comes, the two must work together to cook, fish, make bread, deal with a pesky bear, and keep their clothes and cabin clean. The trials of these two resourceful children don't compare to those in many other stories in the survival genre, which usually feature greater dangers and deprivations.

Joseph Bruchac's warm and realistic *Eagle Song* is one of the few books for children that feature a Native American character in a contemporary setting. Cover from *Eagle Song* by Joseph Bruchac, illustrated by Dan Andreasen, copyright © 1997 by Dan Andreasen. Used by permission of Dial Books for Young Readers, a division of Penguin Putnam, Inc.

However, this story does provide fourth- and fifth-grade readers with a sympathetic glimpse into the life of two self-reliant and strong Native American children. Hill's *The Year of Miss Agnes* is much lighter in tone, a wonderful book for third- and fourth-grade readers. This is the story of a dedicated teacher who changes the lives of her pupils in a remote Athabascan village in the late 1940s. Unlike their previous teachers, Miss Agnes appreciates the children's culture and enriches their learning with art, wonderful literature, and lessons about their own heritage. Hill, a teacher of thirty years, many of them in schools in Alaska bush country, dedicates the book to master teacher Sylvia Ashton-Warner, whose book *Teacher* must have served as the guidebook for Miss Agnes.

Understanding Various World Cultures

 Despite the increasing number of fine books of nonfiction and folklore and picture books from and about other countries, there are fewer novels that attempt to portray the lives of modern children and their families living in other places. Yet, it is critical that children also be made aware of the stories

that reveal the feelings of people in those countries. Children will find descriptions of Australian culture in books by such fine writers as Ivan Southall, Colin Thiele, Patricia Wrightson, Ruth Park, and Robin Klein. In addition, the American Library Association annually gives the Batchelder Award to the publisher of the most outstanding book of that year originally published in a foreign language in a foreign country. These books are excellent firsthand accounts of life in other countries (see Appendix A). However, children might need to be reminded that no single book can convey a complete picture of a country and its people. To make this point clear, one might ask students to consider what book, if any, they would like to have sent to other countries as representative of life in the United States.

The First Person Fiction series from Orchard Books is a fine way to build a bridge from America to other world cultures. In books such as *Behind the Mountains* by Edwidge Danticat, authors provide first-person accounts of life growing up in another country and then detail their characters' journeys to new homes in America. Danticat writes in the persona of 13-year-old Celiane Espérance, a child who lives in the mountains of Haiti with her mother and brother while they wait to join their father in New York. At first Celiane's life seems almost idyllic. She writes vividly about her rural mountain home, her school, her friend Thérèse, her beloved family, and her longing to see her father again. But when she and her mother are almost killed in a political bombing on a visit to her Aunt Rose in Port-au-Prince, efforts are made to get the family out of Haiti and they are soon on their way to New York. Here the adjustment to a new climate and culture are difficult for everyone, but eventually the family pulls together. Celiane writes, "We had faced mountains of obstacles, but with the help from family and friends seem to have conquered them, at least for now" (p. 159). Other books in the series include *Gathering the Dew* by Minfong Ho, *Flight to Freedom* by Ana Veciana-Suarez, *Call Me Maria* by Judith Ortiz Cofer, and *Finding My Hat* by John Son.

One of the few books for younger children that reflect urban life in a Central American country is Ann Cameron's *The Most Beautiful Place in the World*, which tells of 7-year-old Juan, who lives in Guatemala. His young mother has remarried, but her new husband can't support Juan, so Juan moves in with his grandmother, who puts him to work helping her in the marketplace each day. As he waits for customers, Juan practices reading on scraps of newspaper, produce signs, and other print that comes his way. When Juan asks to go to school, his grandmother tries to enroll him, but they are nearly turned away until Juan shows that he has learned to read. When his grandmother explains why she never went to school, Juan realizes how important an education could have been to her. He might live in the "most beautiful place in the world," as the travel poster says, but he knows that truly the best place is where there is someone like his grandmother who loves him. Third- or fourth-grade children who read this story will learn something of the geography of Guatemala, the distant volcanoes and the cornfields, the customary stroll through the streets in the evening, and what a marketplace is like. They will learn nothing, however, about the political realities of the pervasive military influence in this country. The same cannot be said of Cameron's *Colibrí*, a book for more mature readers. This is a tightly plotted and moving story about a Mayan Guatemalan girl who is kidnapped as a young child and used as a shill for her "Uncle's" shady schemes. "Uncle" has convinced Colibrí (for "Hummingbird"; Tzunún in her native Ixil) that her parents abandoned her, and she is too afraid of being entirely alone to think about any other life—until, that is, she finds the personal courage to reunite her "divided heart." *Colibrí* is a frank look at an all-too-frequent occurrence in the world, the merciless exploitation of children. In addition to telling a difficult but ultimately satisfying story, Cameron paints a vivid picture of life in the mountains and small towns of Guatemala and of the massacres that took place during the long civil war.

Readers who are moved by *Colibrí* will want to read other books about social justice and children's rights. Many such books focus on recent events in Africa such as Elizabeth Laird's *The Garbage King*, set in Ethiopia; Henning Mankell's *Secrets in the Fire*, set in Mozambique; and Bernard Ashley's *Little Soldier*, set in Lasai, Africa. *Iqbal* by Francesco D'Adamo is a fictionalized and heartbreaking account of the life and death of Iqbal Masih, a young Pakistani boy who campaigned against the bondage of children in Pakistani carpet factories.

In Beverley Naidoo's *Journey to Jo'burg*, 13-year-old Naledi is forced to face the terrible realities of apartheid when she must journey from her sheltered village to Johannesburg. On the way, Naledi contrasts her own family's values and lifestyle with those of the white families and begins to question the political system that divided South Africa. In a sequel for older readers, *Chain of Fire*, Naledi learns that the people of her village are to be relocated to a "homeland." A peaceful student demonstration is violently terminated by police, some of Naledi's neighbors betray their own people, and homes are bulldozed. The move will eventually transpire, but not before Naledi and others unify to fight injustice. Naidoo's *The Other Side of Truth* reveals the consequences of political repression in Nigeria. When 12-year-old Sade's journalist father attempts to reveal corruption in the government, her mother is killed. Sade and her brother leave Nigeria for England, but the woman who smuggles them into the country abandons the two. Sade is desperate to contact her father but afraid to reveal the truth to authorities in London. Eventually she and her brother are reunited with her father, but he is detained as an illegal immigrant. The book details the day-to-day problems

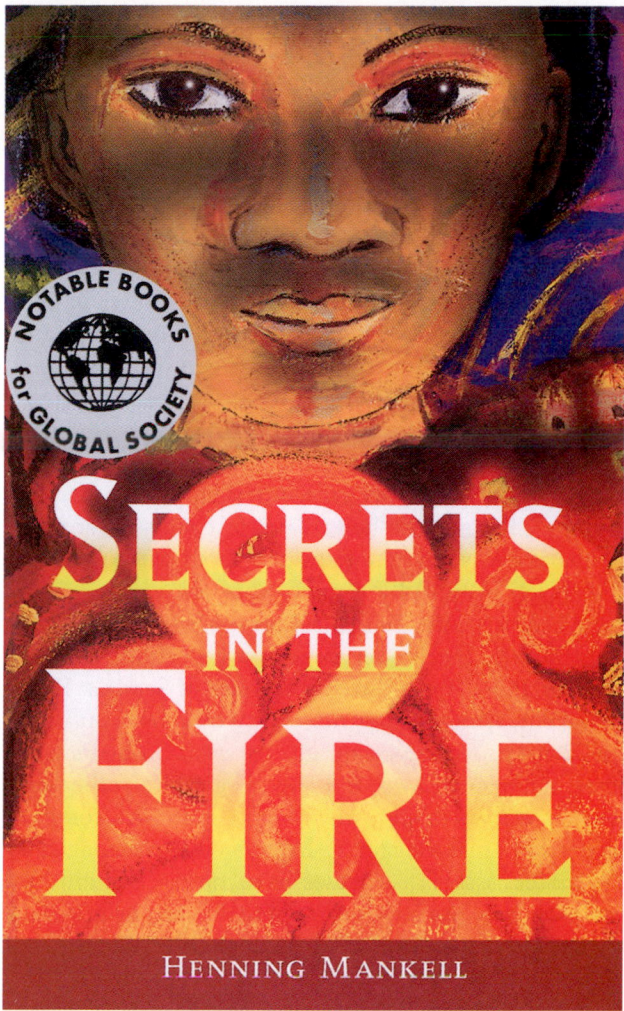

Henning Mankell's moving *Secrets in the Fire,* the story of a young girl caught in the civil war in Mozambique, is based on the experiences of a real person. Cover from *Secrets in the Fire* by Henning Mankell. Copyright © 2003. Annick Press, Ltd.

Such issues are still very much at the center of many countries in the world, and several excellent novels for middle-school readers provide a powerful glimpse of what it is like to live in poverty and fear. Lynn Joseph and Julia Alvarez have written about life in the Dominican Republic during the reign of dictator Rafael Trujillo. Joseph's *The Color of My Words* is a brief book for middle-grade readers that focuses more directly on 12-year-old Ana's life in her beautiful village—her family, her friends, and her love for writing. However, when the government decides to move the villagers out to make way for a hotel complex, Ana's brother Guario is appointed spokesperson for the resistance movement that the villagers have organized. A peaceful demonstration turns into a riot and Guario is killed. The government eventually backs off its plans, but life will never be the same for Ana and her family. Alvarez's *Before We Were Free,* for older readers, is a more direct portrait of the political history of the Dominican Republic in the early 1960s. Seen through the eyes of Anita, a 12-year-old girl, the plot to assassinate Trujillo and the consequences to her family are particularly horrific.

Several authors have explored the more recent history of Haiti in powerful and deeply moving stories. In Frances Temple's *Taste of Salt,* two voices retell events in Haitian history as Djo, one of Father Jean-Bertrand Aristide's street boys, lies near death from a fire bombing by Aristide's enemies. Jeremie, a Haitian girl, has been sent to record Djo's story and perhaps to give him reason to live. At first Djo's voice, full of the rhythms of the native Creole, remembers his childhood in the streets and alleys of Port-au-Prince, the harshness of his life, and the political realities of Haiti. When Djo slips into a coma, Jeremie's distinctive voice takes up the narrative. Born into poverty like Djo, she has been fortunate to fall under the protection of Catholic nuns and to be educated at the same time as she has been sheltered from important truths. As she reflects on her own and Djo's stories, she is faced with difficult choices about the future. The title *Taste of Salt* comes from the books that one of the priests is using to teach Djo and others to read. The term is taken from the belief that giving a zombie a taste of salt will open his true eyes and he will become free of his master. It is a powerful hope to give an oppressed people.

The story of a young Haitian girl, Paulie, and a small group of refugees desperately trying to escape to the United States is told in Temple's *Tonight, by Sea,* while Temple's *Grab Hands and Run* follows the journey of a family from El Salvador who must flee government soldiers after the father disappears. Their journey on a modern-day underground railroad to freedom in Canada is full of danger, despair, and betrayal. Temple's books give vivid and compelling accounts of the human yearning for freedom and security, and the terrible price that some must pay to obtain the rights too many of us take for granted.

of fitting into a new culture but also relays the horrific obstacles faced by those who struggle against repressive regimes.

Sheila Gordon's *The Middle of Somewhere* depicts the effects on two families of relocating their village. Nine-year-old Rebecca's family refuses to leave, and when Rebecca's father is arrested in a demonstration, the family must struggle to survive without him. Outside observers at his trial help gain his release at the time when Nelson Mandela is also released. This story of a family helping itself through difficult times is written for a younger reader than Gordon's earlier *Waiting for the Rain,* which also captures a feel for the geography, the people, and the language of South Africa. Happily, these books can now be read as historical fiction, but they give young readers a powerful glimpse of human rights abuses that continue in other parts of the world.

Jaira Placide's *Fresh Girl* could easily be the sequel to Temple's *Tonight, by Sea* as it explores life in the United States for another Haitian refugee. Told in the first person by Mardi, a 14-year-old girl, much of the book focuses on Mardi's attempts to fit into her new country, her conflicts with her overprotective mother, and her relationships with her new schoolmates. But there are occasional flashbacks to her life in Haiti, and eventually we learn the worst: Mardi was raped during the bloody coup in 1991. For mature readers, *Fresh Girl* is a moving story of courage in the face of the often-unimaginable obstacles faced by many of America's newcomers.

While these books give young people a glimpse of political and economic realities that children face in other countries, Joan Abelove's *Go and Come Back* provides insights into cultural realities and points of view. Mature readers will be fascinated by this view of another culture, although in this case it is their own. Told by Alicia, a Peruvian teenager, the story centers on her experiences with two American anthropologists who come to "study" her people. Alicia is a critical and astute observer of the habits and attitudes of the American women, whom she finds amusing, stingy, and ignorant. Alicia's descriptions of her people's customs and concerns are set against the women's attempts at fitting in with the life in this Amazon region and their struggles to remain objective observers. In this thought-provoking story, Abelove, an anthropologist herself, reveals that the worldview that one person holds can, in effect, be very different from the reality experienced by someone else.

Several excellent books about countries in the Middle East provide young people with insights into social and political issues at the same time as they involve readers with compelling characters in exciting stories. Elizabeth Laird's *Kiss the Dust* follows the journey of 13-year-old Tara and her family of middle-class Kurds. They have a comfortable home in Iraq, but because the father has been involved with the Kurdish resistance movement, the family is forced to flee. They journey first to the mountains of northern Iraq, where they experience rural Kurdish culture, and then they are forced into a refugee camp in Iran. Finally they are able to immigrate to England, but their lives are drastically altered by the events that have taken place. In Gaye Hiçyilmaz's *Against the Storm*, 12-year-old Mehmet and his family try to escape the circumstances of poverty. When they leave their beautiful country village to move to Ankara, their previously close family is torn apart by the crowded and dehumanizing conditions of the city. Only Mehmet seems to have the energy to fight against this storm and seek a better life. Vedat Dalokay's view of Turkey is more benign in *Sister Shako and Kolo the Goat*. Suitable for a younger audience, this evocative memoir centers on an old woman whose family has been killed in a vendetta and who moves into a deserted stable on the narrator's father's land. Kolo is the unusual and somewhat miraculous goat

who appears at Sister Shako's door one day. This "Guest of God," as Sister calls her, becomes the leader of the village flock and the perpetrator of some funny and strangely supernatural incidents. The book is memorable not so much for its facts about Turkish life but for its sense of a Turkish culture, which is conveyed through the cadences of the prose and the images in the writing.

Three books provide a Palestinian point of view of recent history in Israel. In Naomi Shihab Nye's *Habibi* Liyana Abboud is a 14-year-old who has grown up in St. Louis. Her father, a doctor, decides to move his family back to his native Jerusalem, and the main focus of the story is on Liyana's attempts to fit into her new home and to find her true identity. But these events are set within Arab-Israeli conflict, the effects of the conflict on Liyana's family, and her growing friendship with a Jewish boy. The purpose here is not to champion any one point of view but to raise questions about the roots of conflict. Nye's beautifully written story also raises prayers for a lasting peace. Daniella Carmi's *Samir and Yonatan* won the 2000 Batchelder award for best children's book in translation. It is a moving account of Samir, a Palestinian boy, who must spend several months in an Israeli hospital, recovering from an operation on a shattered knee. He is suspicious and frightened of the other children on the ward, all Jewish, but he gradually comes to understand that they are as frightened and damaged by the conflict as he is. As he begins to interact with the others, especially the strange Yonatan, he also reflects back on recent events in his enclave, his father's depression at being unemployed, and his beloved brother's death from an Israeli bullet. Like *Habibi, Samir and Yonatan* ends in reconciliation for this small group of children, and provides, perhaps, a small glimmer of hope for peace in this continuing conflict. A less hopeful look at the Israeli-Palestinian conflict can be found in Cathryn Clinton's *A Stone in My Hand*. Set in Gaza in the late 1980s, the story is told by 11-year-old Malaak, a Palestinian girl whose family is pulled apart and nearly destroyed when they are caught in the conflict. Malaak's father, an out-of-work mechanic, is killed when he stops to help a bus driver repair a breakdown and a suicide bomber attacks the bus. Her brother Hamid is increasingly attracted by the rhetoric of the radical Palestinians, and when he and a friend throw rocks at an Israeli soldier, Hamid is shot and nearly killed. Malaak, her mother, and her older sister must find the courage to live amidst this destruction. *A Stone in My Hand* is a moving portrayal of an ordinary family and the ways in which war and hate can destroy both lives and dreams.

Other books give readers a glimpse of the environments and cultures of Asian and South Asian countries. In *The Year of the Panda* by Miriam Schlein, Lu Yi rescues a starving baby panda against his father's wishes and names it Su Lin. The pandas are moving down from the high ground, where their food source, bamboo, has died

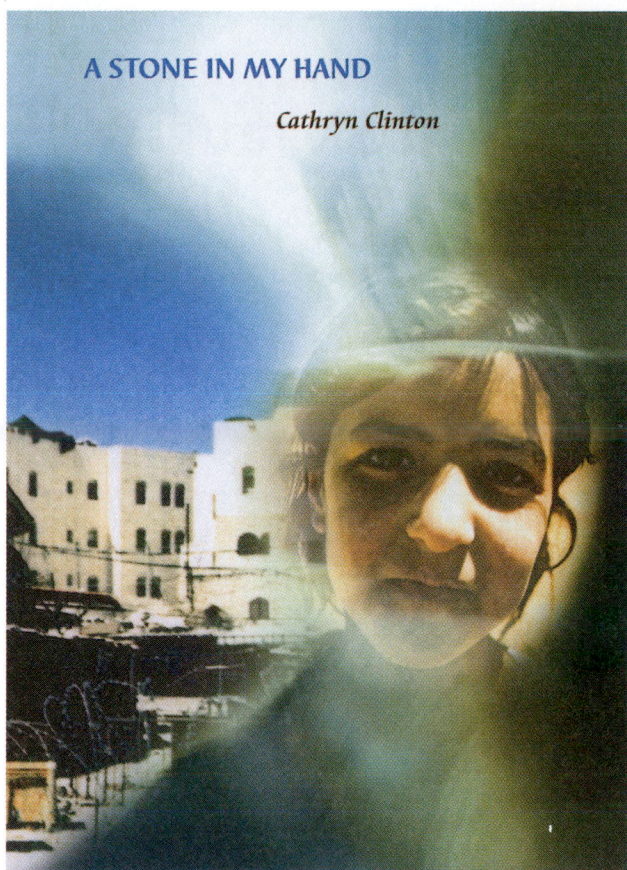

Cathryn Clinton shows the human cost of the Israeli-Palestinian conflict in *A Stone in My Hand*. Cover from *A Stone in My Hand*. Copyright © 2002 by Cathryn Clinton. Cover background photograph copyright © 2002 by Paul Gent. Cover photograph of feather copyright © 2004 by Ralph Mercer/Getty Images. Reproduced by permission of Candlewick Press, Cambridge, MA.

out as it does every seventy years. Their needs conflict with those of the people in Lu Yi's village, and the government urges the villagers to relocate so that their land can be made into a refuge for wild pandas. His family refuses to move, and Lu Yi agrees to accompany his pet by helicopter to a panda rescue center. There he witnesses what American and Chinese scientists are doing to save the giant pandas. Other books focus more directly on political policies in contemporary China, including Gloria Whelan's *Chu Ju's House*, about the effects of population control policies in rural China. Ji-Li Jiang's memoir, *Red Scarf Girl*, and *Little Green*, a novel in verse by Chun Yu, provide readers with important understandings about the consequences of China's Cultural Revolution.

Southeast Asia is presented in two books for middle-grade readers, *The Land I Lost* by Quang Nhuong Huynh and *Silk Umbrellas* by Carolyn Marsden. *The Land I Lost* is a series of portraits remembered from the author's home village in the central highlands of Vietnam. Although it is "endless years of fighting" that make his homeland lost, his reminiscences barely mention war. Instead, his stories focus on people: farmers, hunters, bandits, his karate-expert grandmother, and his older cousin who could capture pythons and train birds to sing popular tunes. Each episode is sparely told, often humorous, and infused with elusive meanings of folklore. Marsden's *Silk Umbrellas* tells of the changes modernization brings to a family and gives readers a glimpse of life in contemporary Thailand.

Two moving books for children are rich in details of many aspects of Indian culture. In Gloria Whelan's *Homeless Bird* Koli, daughter of an impoverished village family, is married early and just as soon widowed when her young husband dies before the marriage is ever consummated. Unable by custom to return to her own family, she is abused and mistreated by her mother-in-law. When her father-in-law dies her mother-in-law abandons Koli in Vrindavan, "the city of widows." At first Koli joins the hundreds of homeless widows who struggle for survival while living on the streets, but with the help of Raji, a young rickshaw driver, Koli eventually finds shelter at a refuge for widows. Here Koli's talent for embroidery and her growing love for Raji open up a future of promise. Koli's strong character, her need for friends and family, and her perseverance in the face of so many obstacles will resonate with children of any culture.

Suzanne Fisher Staples's *Shiva's Fire* is a magical work of fiction that is also set in India. The book's main character, Parvati, is born in the middle of a devastating cyclone that kills her father and almost wipes out her village in Southern India. From the moment of her birth she seems to burn with a need to dance just as the Hindu God Shiva dances in flames on the little wooden statue carved by her late father. Parvati's unearthly talents and uncanny vision isolate her from the other villagers and she grows up a reserved, introverted child fiercely protected by her loving mother. When a famous Indian guru and dance teacher offers her a place at his school she is torn at the thought that she will be separated from her mother but thrilled at the chance to become a devadasi, a dancer whose life and art are devoted to the gods. *Shiva's Fire* is a fascinating look at a world that will be unfamiliar to most Western children. Although Parvati may be unusual in her single-minded determination to dance and in her willingness to sacrifice so much for her art, she is also achingly familiar in her need for human connections.

The Cholistan desert area of modern Pakistan is the setting for the coming-of-age story *Shabanu, Daughter of the Wind*, also by Suzanne Fisher Staples. Staples, a former UPI correspondent, was based in India and Pakistan and spent three years participating in a study of women in the deserts of Pakistan. *Shabanu*, based on some of her experiences living among these women, is a riveting portrait of a young girl in a family of nomadic camel herders. Shabanu, nearly 12, knows that she must accept an arranged marriage in the next year following the wedding of her older sister, Phulan. However, as the time of Phulan's marriage draws near, the two girls are accosted by a rich landowner's hunting guests, who threaten to abduct and rape the pair. In seeking revenge, Phulan's intended husband is killed. Phulan is quickly married to her sister's betrothed, and Shabanu is promised against her will to an older man as his fourth wife. Shabanu struggles to reconcile her own independent spirit with her loyalty to her family. An aunt offers support, saying, "Keep your wits about you. Trust yourself. Keep your inner reserves hidden." Shabanu chooses to run away, but when a much-loved camel she has raised breaks his leg in the desert, she decides to stay with him and accept the beating she knows will follow when her father finds her. She will accept her marriage, too, but she vows to herself that no one can ever unlock the secrets of her heart. Telling her compelling story in present tense, Shabanu faces giving up her life as a camel herder, discovers and accepts her sexuality, and finds a place in the adult world. Vivid details of camel behavior, camel-trading fairs, feasts and celebrations, the differing roles of men and women, and the ever-changing desert are brilliantly evoked for older readers. It is difficult for Western readers to imagine that this story takes place in the modern world. Reading *Shabanu* and its sequel, *Haveli,* would certainly lead readers to discuss women's roles in other countries as well as in their own.

Canadian author Deborah Ellis has provided an equally moving glimpse of life in war-torn Afghanistan in *The Breadwinner* and *Parvana's Journey.* These two books follow Parvana, an Afghani girl, through several years under Taliban rule. In *The Breadwinner* Parvana must masquerade as a boy in order to support her family when her foreign-educated father is imprisoned. *Parvana's Journey* finds her on her own after her father dies, and she sets out to find her mother, sisters, and brother. Still disguised as a boy, she picks up several stragglers on her journey, a toddler she finds next to the body of his mother in a bombed-out building, a boy with one leg hiding in a cave, and a little girl who she soon calls sister. The group faces appalling conditions, danger, and starvation until they finally arrive at a teeming refugee camp. The tragedy at the book's ending does not preclude a reunion between Parvana and the rest of her family, and the ending hints at the dissolution of the Taliban. Ellis based the book on stories told to her by Afghani women in refugee camps in Pakistan. She does not attempt to deal with the religious aspects of the events there, but paints a grim portrait of the oppression of women and the terrible effects of decades of war on the Afghani people. Suzanne Fisher Staples covers similar territory for older readers in *Under the Persimmon Tree.* This story alternates between two points of view. The first is that of Najmah, a rural Afghani girl whose mother and baby brother die in American attacks on the Taliban following 9/11. Because her father and brother have been kidnapped by Taliban soldiers, leaving her homeless, Najmah decides to try to get to the refugee camps in Pakistan disguised as a boy. In one

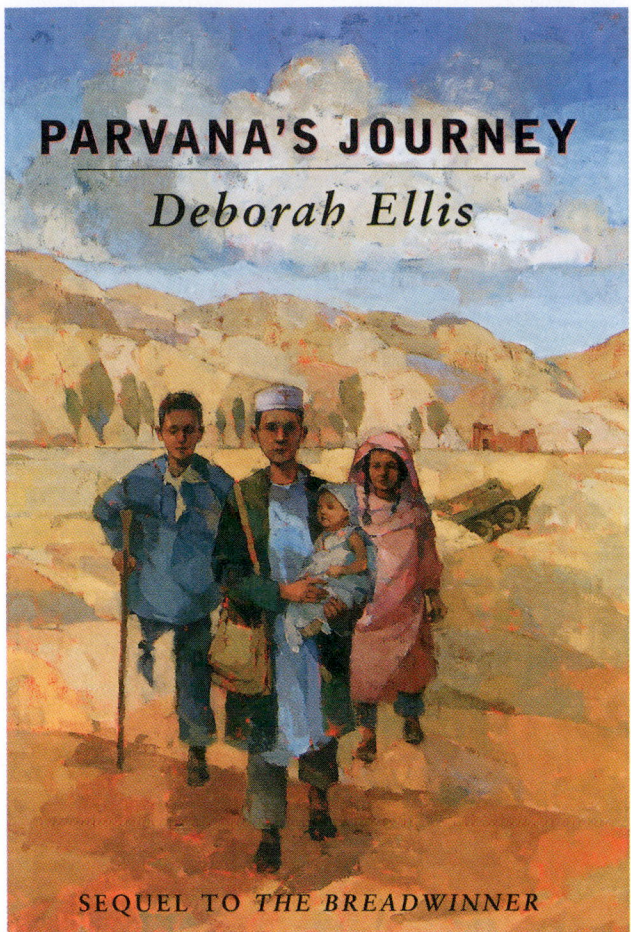

Parvana's Journey by Deborah Ellis chronicles the incredible difficulties endured by children living in Afghanistan during and just after the Taliban regime. Cover illustration from *Parvana's Journey.* Text copyright © 2002 by Deborah Ellis. Illustrated by Pascal Milelli. First published in Canada by Groundwood Books/Douglas & McIntyre. Reprinted by permission of the publisher.

of the camps in Pakistan an American woman works as a teacher while she anxiously awaits word from her Afghani husband, who has gone to volunteer in one of the medical clinics in his native country. Only when the two finally meet can either face the truth about their past and move toward a new, perhaps more hopeful, future.

Many other young-adult novels deal with the contemporary lives of children from many cultures. Tanuja Desai Hidier's *Born Confused* provides a lighthearted look at an Indian American family. *The Return* by Sonia Levitin is a survival story of Ethiopian Jews trying to escape to Jerusalem. Minfong Ho's *Rice without Rain* presents the class struggles for land reform in Thailand in the 1970s as seen by 17-year-old Jinda. Some middle schoolers will be ready for the complex political and emotional scopes of young-adult novels such as those discussed here, but teachers should first read any of these titles before introducing them into the classroom.

All children deserve a chance to read about the lives of children in other lands. As modern technology reduces

Teachers Discuss Literature by and about Parallel Cultures

Three curriculum specialists in the Fairfax County Schools in northern Virginia were concerned that teachers were not incorporating books by and about parallel cultures into their classroom reading programs. With a significant and growing multicultural population, the school system needed to modify its choices of assigned reading. The specialists noted that although they provided annually updated book lists and library media specialists added multicultural titles to school collections, these titles did not then become a part of classroom study. They concluded that teachers would not work recent books into their curriculum unless they had read and discussed the books. Providing book lists was not enough to change teacher behaviors.

A modest sum of grant money was available for programs designed to "improve minority achievement." So the specialists invited teachers in grades 4 through 12 to hold book discussion groups. Groups of at least three teachers agreed to discuss one book per month for a three-, four-, or five-month period. In-service credits could be earned for time spent in discussion. The specialists supplied a list of paperback books (purchased with grant and other money) that could be checked out from a central office location and were available in multiple copies. Titles included Gary Soto's *Baseball in April, El Chino* by Allen Say, *The Talking Earth* by Jean Craighead George, Virginia Hamilton's *Cousins,* Diana Kidd's *Onion Tears,* and Mildred Taylor's *The Friendship.*

The specialists were overwhelmed by the response. More than three hundred administrators and teachers in all subject areas formed groups in 35 of the 37 schools in their area. The three facilitators drew up charts of which schools needed which books and shipped them via interoffice mail. The facilitators' advice to discussion leaders was to talk about the book. "Talk about whatever you want. Did you like it? Was it good? And save the inevitable question of how you would use it in the classroom for the very last." The groups began to meet.

As a result of these discussions, teachers discovered many books that were new to them and also read beyond the book list to find additional titles to add to it. Their book evaluation skills increased. They became risk takers as they ventured opinions and discovered how others' responses meshed with, illuminated, or conflicted with their own. In fact, in evaluating the program, teachers indicated that what was most important to them was the experience of discussing books with their peers. Many of the books are now in children's hands. A grant provided some extra funding so that participating schools could purchase multicultural literature. The discussion groups are still meeting and continuing to add new books to their classroom reading plans.

This could happen anywhere, couldn't it? What it takes is some planning, some seed money to purchase multiple paperbacks of selected titles, and the belief that teachers are willing to change if given support.

This program was designed and carried out by Joan Lewis, Shirley Bealor, and Patricia M. Williams, Curriculum Specialists in Area II
Fairfax County Public Schools, Virginia

---

the distances between cultures, books such as these contribute to a deeper, richer, more sympathetic and enduring communication between people.

Literature in Action: "Teachers Discuss Literature by and about Parallel Cultures" shows how three teachers began an effort to introduce their district to some of the many books that represent the cultures of their community and the children of the world.

POPULAR TYPES OF REALISTIC FICTION

Certain categories of realistic fiction are so popular that children ask for them by name. They want a good animal story, usually about a dog or horse; a sports book; a "funny" book; or a good mystery. Each decade seems to have a popular series, as well, that lingers on the bookshelves. From Gertrude Chandler Warner's Boxcar Children to Ann Martin's Baby-Sitters Club series, from Nancy Drew and the Hardy Boys to Patricia Reilly Giff's Kids of Polk Street School series, children read one volume of a series and demand the next. Many of these books are not high-quality literature, and we would hope that children would not read these titles to the exclusion of other books. Yet many of these stories do serve the useful function of getting children hooked on books so that they will move on to better literature.[19] Children also develop fluency and reading speed as they quickly read through popular books or a series. Teachers and librarians need to identify and evaluate these popular books. Knowing and honoring the books children like increases an adult adviser's credibility, while also allowing him or

---

[19]See Margaret Mackey's "Filling the Gaps: *The Baby-Sitters Club,* the Series Book, and the Learning Reader," *Language Arts* 67.5 (September 1990): 484–89; and *Bookbird* 33.3/4, special issue "Bad Books, Good Reading" (fall/winter 1995–1996).

her to recommend other titles that can broaden children's reading choices. Teaching Resources "'To Be Continued': Popular Series Books for Children" lists some popular series for children.

Humorous Stories

Children like to laugh. The humorous verses of contemporary poets like Shel Silverstein and Jack Prelutsky are some of children's favorite poetry (see Chapter 8). Collections of jokes and riddles circulate at all levels of the elementary school. Humorous realistic fiction often presents characters involved in amusing or exaggerated predicaments that are solved in clever or unique ways. Funny books such as Judy Blume's *Tales of a Fourth Grade Nothing,* Thomas Rockwell's *How to Eat Fried Worms,* Barbara Robinson's *The Best Christmas Pageant Ever,* and Barbara Park's *Skinnybones* have become classics, as have favorite comic characters such as Beverly Cleary's Henry and Ramona and Betsy Byars's Bingo Brown. Contemporary authors such as Polly Horvath, Paula Danziger, Louise Rennison, and Chris Lynch can be relied on for their zany humor and witty characters. Sometimes these stories are part of a continuing series, like Rennison's Georgia Nicholson stories or Lynch's Elvin Bishop series. Others, such as Horvath's *Everything on a Waffle* and Danziger's *The United Tates of America,* carry subtle messages beneath the funny surface.

The opening chapter of Barbara Park's *Skinnybones* is also hilarious. The self-acclaimed funniest person in the sixth grade is telling his story about trying to enter a cat food commercial contest. In addition, Alex (also known as "Skinnybones") has been a size "small" in Little League for six years, never is able to catch the ball or make a hit, and is the butt of the class bully's jokes. The bully wins the baseball trophy, but Alex wins, too, in this story of a wisecracker with a knack for getting into trouble.

My Life as a Fifth Grade Comedian by Elizabeth Levy has its wildly funny moments but also makes a serious attempt to portray the personal pain that is sometimes masked by a class clown. Bobby Garrick has always been a champion jokester, but life doesn't seem so funny as his once-close relationships with his father and brother fall apart when his father kicks his brother out of the house. Bobby's clowning in school masks his unhappiness but also leads to poor grades and constant visits to the principal's office. When a sympathetic teacher helps him channel his energies into a school comedy contest, he finds an outlet for his energies and the self-esteem he needs to change his behavior.

Peter Hatcher's endless problems with his brother begin in Judy Blume's *Tales of a Fourth Grade Nothing.* In this story, 2-year-old Fudge, whose real name is Farley Drexel Hatcher, eats Peter's pet turtle but the long-suffering Peter earns a pet dog. In *Superfudge,* Peter narrates further complications in his life—his new baby sister Tootsie, new school, and new friends—when his family moves to New Jersey. Fudge begins kindergarten much to Peter's embarrassment and dismay. *Double Fudge* continues the hilarious adventures. Dialogue and plot unfold like television situation comedies in these entertaining stories appealing to children in second through fifth grades.

How to Eat Fried Worms by Thomas Rockwell begins with a dare and a fifty-dollar bet. To win it, Billy plans to eat fifteen worms in fifteen days. They are fried, boiled, and smothered with catsup, horseradish, and other toppings. Each ingestion becomes more bizarre the closer Billy comes to winning his bet. The brief chapters, extensive and amusing dialogue, and plot make this a favorite story of less-able middle-grade readers.

In *The Exiles,* a funny novel by British writer Hilary McKay, the four Conroy sisters, Ruth, Naomi, Rachel, and Phoebe, ranging in age from 6 to 13, don't mean to be difficult, they just gravitate to trouble the way rain ends up in puddles. They hold races with their father's fishing maggots. They collect cast-off school projects and attract disorder and disaster. Their parents are driven by frustration and the happy circumstance of a house-remodeling job to send the girls to imposing Big Grandma's house in the country for the summer, and

TEACHING RESOURCES

"To Be Continued": Popular Series Books for Children

 Visit the Online Learning Center at www.mhhe.com/kiefer9e for a printable version of this list.

Author	Titles	Description	Grade level
David A. Adler	*Cam Jansen and the New Girl Mystery* and others	An easy-to-read series about a young girl and her talent in solving mysteries	1–3
Betsy Byars	*Death's Door, King of Murder,* and others	Mysteries starring Herculeah Jones and her friend Meat	4–6

"To Be Continued": Popular Series Books for Children (*continued*)

Author	Titles	Description	Grade level
Betsy Byars	*Bingo Brown, Gypsy Lover,* and others	A funny look at a young adolescent boy's problems as he grows up	4–8
Betsy Byars	*Wanted . . . Mud Blossom* and others	The continuing adventures of the wacky Blossom family	3–6
Ann Cameron	*The Stories Julian Tells, The Stories Huey Tells,* and others	Easy-reading adventures of two young African American boys	1–4
Lauren Child	*Clarice Bean Spells Trouble* and others	The reappearance of this irrepressible picture-book heroine in chapter books for middle-grade readers	3–6
Matt Christopher	*The Captain Contest, Stealing Home,* and others	Sports stories for younger readers	2–4
Matt Christopher	*Spike It!* and others	A long list of titles by Christopher that center on the thrill of the play and action of a sport	3–7
Paula Danziger	*Amber Brown Goes Fourth* and others	A feisty heroine's appealing first-person account of her trials and tribulations	2–4
Judy Delton	*Angel Bites the Bullet* and others	A series of warmly funny stories that center on Angel and her extended family	2–4
Walter Farley	*The Black Stallion* and others	Popular horse and dog adventures	4–7
Jack Gantos	*Jack on the Tracks* and others	Hilarious misadventures of an adolescent boy, told in episodic hard-to-put-down chapters	3–6
Patricia Reilly Giff	*The Beast in Ms. Rooney's Room* and others	Adventures of the Kids of Polk Street School through second grade	1–3
Jamie Gilson	*Hobie Hanson, Greatest Hero of the Mall* and others	A fourth grader's antics in and out of school	2–4
Stephanie Greene	*Owen Foote, Mighty Scientist* and others	Beginning chapter books about an irresponsible middle grader	2–4
Carolyn Haywood	*"B" Is for Betsy* and others	A classic series about Betsy and Eddie that provides a safe, predictable experience for fledgling readers	1–3
Marguerite Henry	*Misty of Chincoteague* and others	Well-researched, well-written, and well-loved horse stories	3–6
James Howe	*Dew Drop Dead* and others	Sebastian Barth mysteries, which develop situations and characters to a depth seldom found in a mystery series	4–6
Johanna Hurwitz	*Busybody Nora* and others	Episodic family stories featuring Elisa, Russell, Nora, and her brother Teddy, who all live in the same apartment building	1–3

(continued)

"To Be Continued": Popular Series Books for Children (*continued*)

Author	Titles	Description	Grade level
Johanna Hurwitz	*Aldo Applesauce* and others	Humorous stories featuring fifth grader Aldo and his friend DeDe	2–5
Katie Kelly	*Lucy Rose, Big on Plans* and others	A first-person account of day-to-day living by a funny and clever 9-year-old	2–5
Jessica Scott Kerrin	*Martin Bridge: Ready for Takeoff!* and others	Episodic events from the life of a funny third grader	2–4
Suzy Kline	*Orp Goes to the Hoop* and others	Sports stories with a middle-school hero	5–8
Maggie Lewis	*Morgy, Coast to Coast* and others	Coping with school, a move, and hobbies	3–5
Janet Taylor Lisle	*The Gold Dust Letters* and others	Well-written books featuring "Investigators of the Unknown," friends who solve mysteries that might or might not involve the supernatural	2–4
Lenore Look	*Ruby Lu, Brave and True* and others	The adventures of a high-energy and highly funny Chinese American girl	1–3
Maude Hart Lovelace	*Betsy-Tacy* and others	A popular series, originally published in the 1940s, that details the adventures of two best friends	2–5
Lois Lowry	*Anastasia Krupnik* and others	Sensitive, funny, and well-written books with a strong-minded heroine	4–7
Lois Lowry	*All about Sam* and others	Anastasia's younger genius brother has a unique viewpoint on growing up	2–5
Chris Lynch	*Me, Dead Dad and Alcatraz* and others	Tales of Elvin Bishop, a highly amusing, somewhat overweight teen, and his misadventures	7 and up
Megan McDonald	*Judy Moody Declares Independence* and others	The continuing adventures of a funny, feisty, and mercurial third grader	2–4
Megan McDonald	*Stink, the Incredible Shrinking Kid* and others	New adventures of Judy Moody's younger brother, Stink	2-4
Claudia Mills	*Dynamite Dinah* and others	A well-written series that follows an intrepid middle grader through the trials and tribulations of childhood	4–8
Claudia Mills	*Gus and Grandpa and Show-and-Tell* and others	Continuing stories of a young boy and his grandfather in an easy-to-read format	1–3
Marisa Montes	*Mystery Neighbors: Get Ready for Gabi* and others	The continuing adventures of a likable third-grade Latina who is of Puerto Rican and Argentinian heritage	2–4
Marissa Moss	*Amelia Works It Out* and others	A series of journal entries and drawings about Amelia's experiences	3–5

"To Be Continued": Popular Series Books for Children *(continued)*

Author	Titles	Description	Grade level
Phyllis Reynolds Naylor	*Alice Alone, Alice on Her Way,* and others	Growing up female in an all-male household	4–8
Phyllis Reynolds Naylor	*Starting with Alice* and others	Stories of Naylor's well-loved character Alice in books for younger readers	3–6
Barbara Park	*Junie B.: Toothless Wonder* and others	A series of hilarious adventures starring an irrepressible primary grader	1–3
Peggy Parish	*Amelia Bedelia* and others	A longtime favorite, easy-to-read series that features the literal-minded maid of the Rogers family	1–3
Robert Newton Peck	*Soup* and others	The antics of Soup and friends, which boys especially enjoy	4–8
Louise Rennison	*Knocked Out by My Nunga-Nungas* and others	A hip teen's diary about her experiences, in the mode of Bridget Jones	6–10
Cynthia Rylant	*Henry and Mudge* and others	An easy-to-read series about likable Henry and his lovable dog	1–3
Louis Sachar	*Marvin Redpost: Why Pick on Me?* and others	Hilarious misadventures of Marvin and his classmates in an easy-to-read format	1–4
Louis Sachar	*Wayside School Gets a Little Stranger* and others	Crazy misadventures at the thirty-story Wayside School	2–5
Marilyn Sachs	*JoJo and Winnie Again: More Sister Stories* and others	Enjoyable stories about a 10-year-old girl and her younger sister	2–4
Marjorie Wiseman Sharmat	*Nate the Great*	Entertaining detective stories for beginning readers	1–4
Janice Lee Smith	*Serious Science* and other Adam Joshua stories	A funny series that follows Adam Joshua and his friends through the trials and tribulations of elementary school	1–4
Zilpha Keatly Snyder	*Libby on Wednesday* and others	A gifted child's adventures in middle school	4–8
Eileen Spinelli	*Lizzie Logan, Second Banana* and others	Lizzie and her best friend, Heather, deal with friends and family	2–4
Wendelin Van Draanen	*Sammy Keyes and the Art of Deception* and others	A middle-grade girl detective who solves crime at the same time as she deals with life's problems	4–6
Carol Weston	*Melanie in Manhattan* and others	A series in diary form	9–12
Lisa Yee	*Millicent Min, Girl Genius* and others	Stories of Millicent Min and other feisty Chinese-Americans and friends	9–12

they become "the exiles." Big Grandma looks on their visit as an opportunity to instill discipline, fresh air and exercise, and a little hard work. Moreover, Big Grandma thinks they read too much, so she hides all her books away in a locked room. The girls, starved for reading materials, discover adventures outside the covers of books (some that Big Grandma wishes they hadn't). The outcome of this family conflict is poetic *and* hilarious. There are lessons to be learned by everyone and more than one surprise in store for all concerned, including the reader. Their adventures continue in *The Exiles at Home* and *Exiles in Love*. McKay has also written several warmly humorous stories featuring 10-year-old Robie Brogan and his uninhibited next-door neighbors, the Robinson family. *Dog Friday, The Amber Cat,* and *Dolphin Luck* are more poignant stories than are the Exiles books, but in all three books McKay writes with warm good humor and a keen eye to events and people that capture the imagination of middle-grade readers.

Louis Sachar, well loved for his humorous Wayside School and Marvin Redpost series, has written a highly original comedy in the Newbery Award–winning *Holes*. Because of an implausible circumstance with a sneaker, the totally unassuming, somewhat overweight Stanley Yelnats is introduced to Camp Green Lake, a Texas camp that is really a reform school, on a lake that is really as dry and brown as yesterday's leftover toast. The setting is as wild as the host of ludicrous characters, both past and present, who populate the story. At first, each wacky character seems unconnected to the events that unfold, yet they all are interrelated in surprising and satisfying ways. In the end, Stanley Yelnats, Victim, becomes Stanley Yelnats, Hero; and the curse that shaped the destiny of Stanley and his family is finally put to rest. This highly entertaining comedy might stretch the definition of realistic contemporary fiction, but part of the fun of the book is believing that all these coincidences might really have happened.

The popularity and huge success of *Holes* seems to have spawned a new subgenre in humorous fiction, the "caper" story. Like their Hollywood counterparts, these books hinge on exaggerated plots. They also feature less-than-lawful adults engaged in less-than-legal activities, sometimes with a bit of help from the child characters and sometimes in spite of them. Readers attracted to this kind of over-the-top story will love books such as Colin Bateman's Gang with No Name series, which includes *Bring Me the Head of Oliver Plunkett* and *Running with the Reservoir Pups*. Christopher Paul Curtis's *Mr. Chickee's Funny Money* and *Bucking the Sarge,* Carolyn Coman's *The Big House,* Michael de Guzman's *The Bamboozlers,* and Frank Boyce's *Millions* are also fast moving and highly comical stories that also treat the dilemmas facing contemporary children with respect.

There are certainly many other books in which humor plays a part. The fantasies of Roald Dahl and Daniel

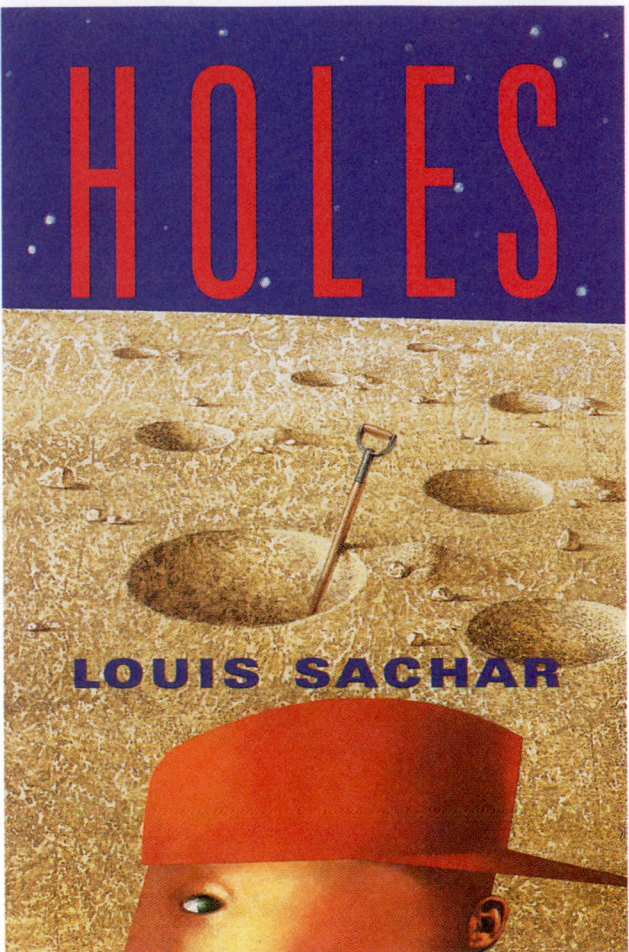

Understated humor, unique characters, and a finely constructed plot provide the winning elements for Louis Sachar's Newbery Award–winning *Holes. Jacket design by Vladimir Radunsky from* Holes *by Louis Sachar. Jacket art copyright © 1998 by Vladimir Radunsky. Reprinted by permission of Farrar, Straus and Giroux, LLC.*

Pinkwater, for instance, often portray absurd situations that children find funny. The animal antics in stories by Farley Mowat or Nina Bawden cause readers to laugh out loud. The snappy retorts of Carlie in Betsy Byars's *The Pinballs* or the accurate and humorous observations about everyday school situations in *The Burning Questions of Bingo Brown* give readers a smile of recognition. The Magic School Bus series by Joanna Cole and Bruce Degen is an example of nonfiction packaged in child-appealing humorous asides and funny conversation balloons. Humorous books need no justification other than that they provide pure enjoyment. They are a healthy contrast to a reading diet that might be overburdened with contemporary social problems. Funny stories also beg to be shared with other readers in the classroom and are powerful reading catalysts. Children who laugh with books are building a love of reading in which enjoyment is the foundation.

Animal Stories

Stories about animals provide children with the vicarious experience of giving love to and receiving devotion and loyalty from an animal. Frequently these animal tales are really stories of the maturing of their major characters. For example, Sterling North's *Rascal: A Memoir of a Better Era* presents a boy who shares happy outings with his father, worries about his older brother serving in World War I, builds a canoe in the living room, and raises a crow and a raccoon as pets. But Sterling gradually and painfully realizes that his beloved companion raccoon, Rascal, will survive only in the wild. As mentioned earlier, Jean Craighead George draws on her own experiences with animals to imbue her many stories with fascinating insights into animal behavior and to provide fascinating information.

The horse stories of Walter Farley and Marguerite Henry have long been popular with middle-grade readers. More recently Australian author and illustrator Alison Lester has written two fine horse stories for this age group, *The Quicksand Pony* and *The Snow Pony*. *The Quicksand Pony* adds a mystery and a survival tale to the story of a girl and her beloved pony. Ten-year-old Biddy is finally allowed to go on the family muster that rounds up the cattle that have been grazing wild in the Australian back country. Just after the trip begins, Biddy's pony, Bella, is caught in the quicksand that dots the shoreline. Biddy is inconsolable when she is forced to leave the horse to its fate. When she returns to the spot the next day, however, she finds that Bella has escaped, and she notices small human footprints in the sand. As she sets off to find Bella, Biddy begins to uncover the mystery of a disappearance that had affected her family years before. This gentle, warmly satisfying story unfolds through Biddy's experiences in the present as well as through past events that lead up to her discovery of her long-lost cousin. Canadian author Natale Ghent has written a fine contemporary horse story in *No Small Thing*, about three siblings who volunteer to take a free pony only to find that the responsibilities of caring for it are almost more than this faltering family can handle.

Dogs respond to human affection and return it warmly. This bond of love is one of the themes in Theodore Taylor's *The Trouble with Tuck*, based on a true story. Helen lacked self-confidence until she became involved in raising Tuck, a beautiful golden Labrador retriever given to her by her parents. Tuck once saved Helen from drowning and is devoted to her. By the time Helen reaches 13, Tuck has grown totally blind. Rejecting the advice of the veterinarian to give Tuck to the university for research or have him put to sleep, Helen finds an alternative—she obtains a seeing-eye dog for Tuck. Jealous and confused, Tuck refuses to accept this stranger until Helen's patient and innovative training methods teach Tuck to follow the guide dog. As the two dogs parade before Helen and her proud family, the reader rejoices in

Horse stories like *no small thing* by Natale Ghent demonstrate how children grow in responsibility through their contacts with animals. From *no small thing* by Natale Ghent. Copyright © 2005 by Natale Ghent. Reprinted by permission of Henry Holt and Company, LLC.

both canine and human triumphs. In a sequel, *Tuck Triumphant*, the focus shifts from Tuck to a Korean boy the family adopts.

Dog training is also the focus of Jessie Haas's *Shaper*, but this book weaves in more complex themes of coming of age and family reconciliation. Fourteen-year-old Chad Holloway is furiously angry with his grandfather and sister, whom he blames for the death of his beloved dog. His adolescent anger extends to other members of his eccentric family and the world at large, and he will have nothing to do with Queenie, the new family dog. When David Burton, an animal trainer, moves in next door, he offers Chad a job as his "subject," a novice to whom he can teach his techniques so that he can write a book he has under contract. Chad takes the job to be near David's beautiful daughter, but he soon finds himself intrigued by David's technique of using a clicker to modify behavior. Working with the ill-behaved Queenie,

Chad soon realizes that his own negative behavior has reinforced his anger and caught him in a vicious cycle of blame. He grows to accept Queenie and to better appreciate the uniqueness of his family.

In Jane Resh Thomas's *The Comeback Dog,* Daniel must decide if he is once again going to risk his love on a dog that has already rejected him. While 9-year-old Daniel is still grieving for the loss of his old dog, Captain, he discovers a starving and nearly drowned English setter in the culvert near his family's Michigan farm. He brings the dog home, names her Lady, and nurses her back to health, assuming that she will return his love in the same way Captain did. But Lady, who has been mistreated, cringes at Daniel's touch and refuses to wag her tail for him. One day, in anger at her lack of affection, Daniel releases Lady from her chain, and she bounds away over the fields. She is gone, only to return a week later bristling with porcupine quills. Sympathetic parents who show their love finally help Daniel show his. Troy Howell's frequent illustrations, the believable dialogue, and short chapters make this book easily approachable by independent 8- and 9-year-old readers.

The same age group will enjoy Karen Hesse's *Sable,* which is also about a stray dog. Tate is determined to keep Sable when she turns up one day in the family's yard, even though Tate's mother is afraid of dogs. An uneasy compromise is arrived at, and Sable is allowed to stay on the property. But the dog keeps roaming and causing trouble with the neighbors. When Sable is given to a family friend, Tate is heartbroken but determined to prove she is responsible enough to take care of a dog. After much reading and planning, she builds a fence to keep Sable out of trouble, but when she goes to bring Sable home she finds that the dog has run away. Her parents are impressed with her hard work and softened by her devotion to the dog, so that when Sable finally turns up weeks later, skinny and torn, they accept the fact that they have a dog in the family.

A stray dog is also featured in Kate DiCamillo's *Because of Winn-Dixie.* On a trip to the grocery store in her new Florida town, 10-year-old India Opal Buloni finds a dog that looks like a "piece of old brown carpet left out in the rain" (p. 11). When the mutt smiles at her, his fate is sealed, and instead of groceries, India goes home with a dog. Winn-Dixie, named after the grocery store where he was found, proves to be just what Opal needs. She is at a difficult time in her life. India and her preacher father have just moved, and she is also trying to come to terms with her mother's abandonment. The dog serves as the key that opens the door to friends and neighbors and also allows India and her father to face up to their loss. Quirky characters, a loving community, and one very special dog make *Because of Winn-Dixie* a winning book.

Colby Rodowsky's short chapter book *Not My Dog* presents a different sort of dilemma. Eight-year-old Ellie has been dreaming of having a puppy of her own for years, but her parents insist that she wait until she is 9 and old enough to take care of it. Then her great-aunt Margaret must move into an apartment that doesn't allow dogs and she asks Ellie's family to take her dog, Preston. Ellie is horrified. This "square brown dog with sort of sticking up ears and a skinny tail" is not at all what she imagined her puppy would be like, and Ellie exclaims to her family that Preston is "not *my* dog." Not hers, that is, until Preston begins to work his wiles on her. She is gradually won over by Preston's intelligence, his obvious preference for her company, and his ability to get her home when she gets lost. When her teacher asks Ellie to write about someone important in her life, she writes about Preston, and realizes that he has indeed become *her* dog. Rodowsky's Sara Barker in *The Next-Door Dogs* is also a character struggling with dog problems, but in her case it is an irrational fear of dogs. Nine-year-old Sara is forced to face those fears when her elderly neighbor, owner of the "next-door dogs," falls and breaks her leg.

The plight of homeless dogs is portrayed in two fine books, Meindert DeJong's *Hurry Home, Candy* and Ann Martin's *A Dog's Life,* both of which provide the dog's point of view. DeJong's classic story tells of one dog's search for love and security. Candy had first been owned by two children and punished with a broom by their impatient mother. In a storm Candy is separated from the family, and fear of a broom across the ditch prevents him from crossing to them. Alone, hungry, lost, and sorrowful, he at last finds shelter with a lonely old man, a retired captain turned artist. The captain discovers the source of the dog's fear; at the same time, he gains understanding of his own. The big man tosses the broom aside, and the dog edges his way to food, to love, and to home. Martin's *A Dog's Life* is narrated by the homeless dog Squirrel and therefore might be classified as fantasy. But it is a true "dog story" in every other sense of the word. As with Candy, we feel Squirrel's suffering firsthand, first as she struggles to survive as a young puppy and then as she bounces from one bad situation to another. Like Candy, Squirrel eventually finds a caring adult who looks past her neurotic mannerisms and difficult behavior to give her a chance at a loving home.

In Phyllis Reynolds Naylor's Newbery Medal–winning *Shiloh,* Marty Preston befriends a cringing stray beagle that surrounds the boy with joy. The dog, however, belongs to a neighbor known for abusing his animals; Marty, obedient to his father, reluctantly returns the puppy. When the half-starved dog later slinks back to the field by the Preston home, Marty decides to hide the dog in the woods of his West Virginia mountain hollow. He deceives his family until a crisis forces him to fight for his principles and confront the owner of the dog, whom he has named Shiloh. Well-drawn characters, a strongly realized setting, and a quick-paced plot are woven into the first-person narrative that continues in *The Shiloh Season* and *Saving Shiloh.*

Marion Dane Bauer's *A Question of Trust* raises similar problems for Brad and his brother, who are hurt and angered by their parents' divorce. Although their father, with whom they are living, forbids them to have any pets, Brad comes across a stray mother cat and her two newborn kittens. He is determined to care for them even though he risks losing his father's trust. However, he finds that he is in over his head when things go dreadfully wrong with one of the kittens. Like Bauer's *On My Honor,* these two stories ask upper elementary students to think about what constitutes honorable and responsible behavior when rebelling against parents and their beliefs.

Heroic dogs who overcome obstacles are the subject of popular animal stories for children. Sheila Burnford's *The Incredible Journey* recounts the odyssey of courage and endurance of three runaway pets, a young Labrador retriever, an old bull terrier, and a Siamese cat. Left with a friend of their owner, the animals try to reach their home more than 250 miles away. Hunger, storms, dangerous river crossings, and fights are the nearly insurmountable problems these three animals face. Their survival and care for each other make a remarkable story.

A sled dog named Searchlight and his owner, little Willy, are the heroes of John Reynolds Gardiner's well-loved *Stone Fox.* Little Willy needs five hundred dollars to pay off the back taxes on his grandfather's farm or it will be taken from them. So Willy and Searchlight enter a dogsled race. But among the contestants is the legendary Indian Stone Fox with his five Samoyed sled dogs. Willy nearly wins the race, but Searchlight's heart gives out in a final burst of speed just before the finish line. In the moving conclusion, Stone Fox and his team halt just short of the finish while Willy carries his dog across the line to win the race and save his farm. This short story, an excellent read-aloud choice, causes fourth- and fifth-grade readers to ask for tissues and more animal stories.

Where the Red Fern Grows by Wilson Rawls is a heartwarming sentimental tale of the love between two hound dogs and their master. Young Billy trains his two dogs, Old Dan and Little Ann, to be the finest hunting team in the Cherokee country of the Ozarks in northeastern Oklahoma. Twenty-five sets of hounds are entered in the big coon hunt. After five nights of hunting, catching raccoons, skinning them, and turning in the hides, Billy's hounds win three hundred dollars and the first-place cup. During the hunt, Old Dan and Little Ann nearly freeze to death after getting lost during an unexpected blizzard. When the family decides to move, Billy plans to remain behind with his beloved grandfather and the two dogs. But when the dogs die, one defending Billy against a mountain lion attack and one pining away, he regretfully departs with his family. Billy's decision is reaffirmed when a legendary red fern springs up at the dogs' gravesite. This story is memorable to 10-, 11-, and 12-year-olds because of its warmth and its strong portrayal of devotion between humans and animals.

Occasionally books intended for an adult audience become part of the reading of older children. Jack London's *The Call of the Wild* was written for adults but is read by some gifted middle-grade students. The men in the story are ruthless, and the dog Buck returns to the wildness of nature just as the men revert to force and cruelty to survive. Jim Kjelgaard communicates a love of wilderness through exciting dog stories like *Big Red,* the tale of an Irish setter groomed for championship showing who, along with his 17-year-old trainer, faces the bear Old Majesty. Farley Mowat's *The Dog Who Wouldn't Be* tells of his boyhood on the Saskatchewan prairie in the company of his Prince Albert retriever, Mutt, and a score of other animal pets. In his shorter novel *Owls in the Family,* Mowat recounts in hilarious detail his adventures in acquiring and training two pet great horned owls, the intrepid Wol and his timid companion, Weeps.

Sports Stories

Sports fiction for children reflects their energetic participation and interest in a variety of individual and team sports. Recent fiction includes books about team sports, like baseball, football, soccer, and basketball, and popular individual sports like tennis, running, gymnastics, dirt-bike racing, skateboarding, and swimming. Fiction, biography, and informational books about sports extend and enrich the personal experiences of the child who participates in or observes sports.

It is sometimes difficult to find well-written sports stories. In many books the characters are flat and one-dimensional. The dialogue tends to be stilted, and the plots predictable. Nevertheless, children continue to select these stories because they are so personally involved and interested in the activities. Matt Christopher's series and the Rookies series, by various authors, cater to sports fans. Bruce Brooks, noted author of young-adult fiction, has created an appealing sports story for younger readers in *Throwing Smoke.* The story about a Little League team with a long losing streak verges on fantasy but is grounded in Brooks's obvious love of the game of baseball.

Even though there are now many more stories that feature girls in sports, there are still few female athletes in formula sports fiction. The same clichés—making the team through hard work or overcoming fear and triumphing over pain—are prevalent in both stories for boys and stories for girls. One important change, however, is that girls on boys' sports teams are no longer greeted with disbelief and protest. Futhermore, readers will find more girl characters involved in sports in more nuanced, well-written fiction for children. Recent titles include Carolyn Marsden's *Moon Runner,* about a fourth grader who finds success, friendship, and her identity on a track team; Kristi Roberts's *My 13th Season,* about the only girl on a boys' softball team; and Elizabeth Levy's funny *Tackling Dad,* about a girl's relationship with her

Kristi Roberts

Being the only girl on a boys' baseball team serves as the catalyst for Fran to resolve her other problems in Kristi Roberts's *My 13th Season. From My 13th Season* by Kristi Roberts. Copyright © 2005 by Kristi Roberts. Reprinted by permission of Henry Holt and Company, LLC.

former-football-star father and her own attempts to play the game.

A serious story that portrays characters of real depth and understanding is *Thank You, Jackie Robinson* by Barbara Cohen. Though the story takes place in 1947–1948, it is written in the first person and told as a reminiscence to a contemporary child. Sam Green is the only son of a Jewish widow who runs an inn in New Jersey. He doesn't care much about sandlot ball, but he can recite the batting order and play-by-play for every Dodgers game since the time he became a fan. Sam's best friend is the inn's African American cook, Davy, who takes Sam to his first Dodgers game. The two see other games together, and the hero of all the games for both of them is Jackie Robinson. In mid-season Davy has a heart attack. Sam gathers his courage, buys a baseball, and goes alone to a Dodgers game, where he asks Jackie Robinson to autograph the ball for Davy. Then Davy's son-in-law, Elliott, helps Sam sneak into the hospital in a laundry cart so that he can personally present the ball to Davy. This book succeeds at

many levels: as a warm and understanding consideration of friendship across ages and races, as a realistic presentation of death, and as a retrospective look at Jackie Robinson and the Brooklyn Dodgers during the height of their baseball fame. Chris Lynch also uses the game of baseball to delve into racial issues in *Gold Dust.* Set in Boston in 1975, when mandatory school busing begins, the story focuses on the friendship and baseball dreams of two seventh graders, one from a white working-class family and the other the son of a professor of Caribbean literature, newly arrived from the Dominican Republic.

Another book that succeeds on many levels is Alfred Slote's *The Trading Game.* Andy Harris, who loves to play baseball and collect baseball cards, receives the cards his deceased father had bequeathed to him. Among them is a precious 1953 Mickey Mantle card worth over two thousand dollars. But the card Andy truly wants is Ace 459, the card of his grandfather, a former major league player, whom he idolizes. Greedy Tubby Watson owns the card and won't part with it unless Andy will trade the Mickey Mantle card. When Grampa comes to visit, it is clear to Andy that the cards his father collected are of no importance to the old man and that Grampa has not reconciled himself to his son's death. Andy eventually realizes that friendships and the memories the cards represent are more important than winning and the money the cards are worth. Slote's books, many of which are told in the first person, capture the emotions, actions, and conversation of typical fifth- and sixth-grade boys.

Upper elementary school students have laughed at the antics of Orp, or Orville Rudemeyer Pygenski, Jr. In one story in the series by Suzy Kline, *Orp Goes to the Hoop,* the seventh grader is trying to make the basketball team of his Connecticut middle school. With a mother who was a free-throw champion and a father with a terrific layup, Orp receives great advice. Even though Orp's story is one of near-continuous successes both on the court and in the social arena, readers will appreciate Orp's long pass to a teammate for the winning basket.

Middle schoolers ready to move into more complex novels that use sports to explore other subjects might be guided to Scott Johnson's *Safe at Second,* Bruce Brooks's *The Moves Make the Man,* Robert Lipsyte's *The Contender,* Virginia Euwer Wolff's *The Mozart Season,* or Chris Crutcher's *Stotan!* Sports fiction at its best provides readers with the vicarious satisfactions of playing the sport as well as struggling with the problems and issues that arise in practice, in play, and at home.

School Stories

Stories that take place in school offer children the solace of the familiar. All schoolchildren recognize settings furnished with desks and lockers; characters like the friendly custodian or principal, the class bully, the understanding teacher, the hatchet-faced teacher, the cheating student; and situations such as the looming deadline for a project or paper, misunderstandings between friends, and seasonal celebrations. Books like these do not always encourage readers to stretch their abilities, but they do provide a kind of support for horizontal growth as children learn to read faster with more satisfaction. Unfortunately (or fortunately for the readers), many of these stories are part of a numbered series and children want to read them in order. This challenges teachers and parents to help children find other books while they are "waiting for number 7 of the series."

Beverly Cleary, Jamie Gilson, and Johanna Hurwitz make use of the humor of school situations for third and fourth graders. In Cleary's *Ramona Quimby, Age 8,* Ramona arrives in third grade, where she enjoys her teacher's "Dear" (Drop Everything and Read) time. She also stages a hilarious parody of a cat food commercial for her book report, makes a friend of "Yard Ape," and realizes that her teacher likes her. In *Class Clown,* Hurwitz introduces Lucas Cott, the most obstreperous boy his third-grade teacher has ever seen. Lucas finally settles down when he stands in for a sick classmate to become the ringmaster of the class circus. Gilson's *4-B Goes Wild* and *Thirteen Ways to Sink a Sub* and her Hobie Hansen books are also popular school tales. Gilson's stories are fast moving and full of pranks and funny dialogue, with reasonable adults who remain very much in the background.

Andrew Clements explores the relationships between students and teachers in several books including *The School Story, Lunch Money,* and *A Week in the Woods.* In Clements's *Frindle,* Nick Allen is a clever smart aleck who loves to outwit his teachers. When Mrs. Granger, the veteran fifth-grade teacher who loves vocabulary lessons, asks him to do a report on the origin of words, Nick's somewhat devious mind goes to work. Steeped in etymological knowledge as a result of a study of word origins, Nick decides to coin a new word for "pen," frindle. Neither Nick nor Mrs. Granger has any idea of how this incident will build into a war of wits and words that will have unexpected results for Nick, Mrs. Granger, and the children of the Westfield school district. Cara Landry is another bright fifth grader whose editorial for *The Landry News* has unexpected consequences for herself and her teacher. Cara finds herself in the middle of a controversy about freedom of speech and responsible reporting.

School newspapers provide the catalyst for change in several other fine books for children. In Walter Dean Myers's *Darnell Rock Reporting,* Darnell is a normal underachieving middle-school student who spends as much time in the principal's office as he does in a classroom. To get the principal off his back, Darnell mentions that he is thinking of joining the school newspaper—this is the delaying tactic he needs to keep his parents ignorant of his little problems. As he attends newspaper staff meetings, Darnell's interest is piqued and he begins to get involved. When he interviews Seebie, a homeless man, he begins to see the man as a human being and takes on his cause. At the same time, Darnell's success at writing

begins to have an effect on the way he sees himself. Darnell realizes that being on the newspaper has changed how he sees himself and also made people look at him differently. Believing that a garden is a way of helping Seebie and other homeless people in the area become self-sufficient, he asks that they be given the same chance he was. Myers writes with a keen understanding of adolescent concerns and creates funny, likable characters. In this case he shapes to perfection a picture of an underachieving middle-class boy, and mirrors a segment of the population that doesn't often see itself reflected in books.

Adam, in Michael Winerip's *Adam Canfield of the Slash,* is the polar opposite of Darnell Rock, an overprogrammed, middle-class kid who seems to be holding his life together with duct tape. When he agrees to co-edit the school paper with his African American classmate Jennifer, sixth grader Adam thinks he's in for smooth sailing. He doesn't count on an intrepid third grader determined to be a star investigative reporter, an out-of-control principal, or school standards and standardized

Michael Winerip's amusing *Adam Canfield of the Slash* pits investigative reporters for a school newspaper against the educational establishment. *Adam Canfield of the Slash.* Written by Michael Winerip. Jacket photo copyright © 2005 by Image Source Photography/Veer. Reproduced by permission of the publisher Candlewick Press, Inc., Cambridge, MA.

testing preparation to get in his way. When Adam and Jennifer uncover a school scandal, they are faced with a moral dilemma. Should they report both sides of a story they know the principal will kill? Or should they leak the facts to avoid responsibility? In addition to writing a winning story, Winerip presents important ideas for young people to consider. First, he shows tremendous empathy for today's overprogrammed, time-deprived adolescents. There's also a clear message that in the current educational climate good teaching and critical learning are being pushed aside in favor of standardized lesson plans, standardized curriculum, and standardized testing. Even more important, however, are the understandings about what journalists owe to their subjects and their audiences. All this is interwoven with likable characters, humorous style, and a fast-moving plot. If there were a Junior Pulitzer, Winerip's Adam would win in a flash.

Avi develops a student-teacher conflict in *Nothing but the Truth.* Ninth grader Philip Malloy has dreams about being a track star, but a D in English has kept him off the school track team. When Philip challenges a school rule for silence during the singing of the national anthem, Mrs. Narwin, the English teacher who has given him the poor grade, sends him to the principal's office. This begins a chain of events that spirals out of control for both student and teacher. Philip is eventually suspended, and his story attracts media attention. A variety of administrators, community leaders, and media mavens enter the fray, and Philip and Mrs. Narwin become the pawns of people with their own personal and political agendas. Eventually Mrs. Narwin, a dedicated and caring teacher, resigns. Philip is forced to change schools and to give up his dreams of being a running legend. His new school can't afford to support a track team. Avi composes this powerful story through dialogue, journal entries, letters, memos, and other primary source materials and invites readers to a deeper understanding about the meaning of truth. The manipulation of truth by those in positions of power has critical importance in today's world.

Anne Fine zeroes in on a group of young teens in her very funny, but ultimately very poignant, *Flour Babies.* Room 8 at St. Boniface's School is a teacher's nightmare, the classroom where the "Sads and the Bads" end up. It is time for the school science fair, and in an effort to avoid repeating previous disasters, Mr. Cassidy presents the boys with some pretty tame choices. In a glorious misunderstanding, Simon Martin, a "clumsy young giant," convinces his classmates to choose the child development experiment, eighteen days of caring for flour sacks as if they were babies. Simon believes that the boys will be allowed to explode the sacks at the end of the experiment. But before this end occurs, Simon finds he has grown quite attached to his sack. He paints eyes on it and confides his innermost thoughts to it. Not only does the experiment teach the boys the weighty responsibilities of parenting, but it also gives Simon, whose own father skipped out when he was 6 weeks old, some important insights about fathering. Simon gets his explosive ending, but he also ends up knowing that "if keeping what you care for close and safe counts for any thing" (p. 127), he'll make a better father than most.

Ralph Fletcher, whose *Fig Pudding* provides a warm and insightful story of family life, has written a thought-provoking school story in *Flying Solo.* When Mr. Fabiano calls in sick and the substitute fails to show up, the kids take over the class. The tension builds as readers try to anticipate the outcome—Will they be discovered? Will anarchy reign? Surprisingly, these sixth graders are, for the most part, mature, thoughtful adolescents. As the day proceeds, they manage to hide their lack of adult supervision, conduct and complete class business, discuss a host of ethical questions that their experiment raises, and come to grips with some of their individual problems and heartaches. There are consequences for their actions in the end, but *Flying Solo* is a well-written, realistic story that will raise smiles of recognition as well as important questions of responsibility in the middle-grade audience.

Other authors also set their stories within the cozy confines of a school. Kate Klise presents *Trial by Journal* as the actual journal kept by sixth grader Lily Watson when she's called to serve on jury duty. In Gordon Korman's *No More Dead Dogs* eighth grader Wallace Wallace, tired of reading books where the dog character dies, ends up kicked off the football team when he refuses to read "Old Shep, My Pal" for his English class. Older readers also enjoy Korman's private school, Macdonald Hall, which has been the setting for many of his slapstick stories.

Mysteries

Most children enjoy mystery stories during some period in their lives. James Howe, author of the popular Sebastian Barth mysteries, has said that in adult mysteries "Who done it?" is the question to be answered but in children's mysteries the question is more likely to be "What's going on here?"[20] Children enjoy figuring out the "rules of the game" in a mystery, and they are proud to be masterful solvers of the problem. They enjoy the order of a mystery's universe, where loose ends are tied up, everything is explained, and evil is punished. They like escapist reading just as much as adult mystery fans do.

Even first- and second-grade readers demand mysteries. Whole series, such as the Something Queer books by Elizabeth Levy, Crosby Bonsall's mystery stories, Patricia Reilly Giff's Polka Dot Private Eye books, and

---

[20]James Howe, "Writing Mysteries for Children," *Horn Book Magazine* (March/April 1990): 178–83.

David A. Adler's Young Cam Jansen and Jeffrey Bone series, satisfy a child's need to keep reading.

Slightly older children usually become enmeshed in the Nancy Drew or Hardy Boys series. These formula books have predictable plots, one-dimensional characters, stilted dialogue, and cliché-ridden prose. Although most librarians and teachers do not order these books, they continue to sell well. Rather than discount mystery stories in general because of popular series, teachers and librarians should look for better-written mysteries and other books that contain the elements of mystery, such as "suspense and supernatural fantasy" (see Chapter 7), to expand children's interests.

Two popular mystery series give the reader a chance to match wits with clever boys. Both boys and girls enjoy the Encyclopedia Brown stories by Donald Sobol. In *Encyclopedia Brown Takes a Case*, Mr. Brown, chief of police of Idaville, brings home all the cases his detectives cannot solve. At dinner he describes them to his son, Encyclopedia Brown, who usually solves them before it is time for dessert. Each Encyclopedia Brown book presents ten cases whose solutions are included in the back of the book. Seymour Simon, author of many nonfiction titles, also features short mysteries in his Einstein Anderson series. In *Einstein Anderson Lights Up the Sky,* the brainy Einstein applies his knowledge of science to show that mysterious UFOs are really spotlights reflected off low nighttime clouds, and he "solves" another nine problems. While each series features both a consistent format and a continuing cast of characters, Einstein's incidental jokes, puns, and riddles and the scientific observations give this series extra appeal and depth.

The House of Dies Drear by Virginia Hamilton is a compelling story of the weird and terrifying happenings that threaten and mystify an African American professor and his family when they rent a house that was formerly an Underground Railway station. The brooding old house holds many secrets for Thomas Small and his family, who are threatened by dangers from outside as well as inside the house. The treasure of fleeing slaves that is discovered by Thomas in this title becomes one of the problems in a sequel, *The Mystery of Drear House.* Now the Small family must help determine the fate of the abolitionist's house and the disposal of the goods. Hamilton's finely crafted plot, elegant prose, and well-developed characters provide gripping reading.

Carl Hiaasen, a best-selling author of adult mysteries, turns his talents to writing for a middle-grade audience in the funny ecological mysteries *Hoot* and *Flush.* In *Hoot* Hiaasen pits his 12-year-old hero, Roy Eberhardt, against the corporate executives of Mother Paula's All-American Pancake House, who want to destroy the habitat of burrowing owls in order to put up their latest restaurant. In *Flush* young Noah is determined to help his dad prove that a casino boat is dumping raw sewage at the local beach. Quirky characters, outlandish events, and a vivid south Florida setting add up to two winning mysteries.

Joan Lowery Nixon's riveting story *The Other Side of Dark* won the Edgar Allan Poe Mystery Writer's Award for its distinctive portrayal of a girl who, after witnessing the murder of her mother and being shot herself, loses her memory for four years. At 17, Stacy McAdams regains some of her memory and is adjusting to being an adolescent. When publicity suggests that she might remember the face of the killer, Stacy is again in danger—and she attempts to identify the killer before he kills her. The plot is complicated when it appears that new friends might not be what they seem. Stacy's first-person narrative reveals her desire for revenge, her confusion over who she is, and her growth toward adulthood in this thriller. Older readers enjoy Nixon's compelling mysteries for their skilled combination of human emotions, suspense, romance, and terror, with fast-moving plots and cliffhanger chapters.

Although mysteries are one of the most popular subgenres of fiction for children, several authors have proven that they can also serve as the impetus for fine writing. In Ellen Raskin's classic *The Westing Game*, millionaire Sam Westing cut out the words to the song "America the Beautiful" and distributed them among his heirs as clues to his murderer.[21] At the reading of his will, the sixteen characters are presented with a directive to discover the identity of his murderer and other clues cleverly hidden within the will. The characters, all with their own physical, moral, or emotional imperfections, play in pairs. They include a judge, a Chinese restaurateur, a dressmaker, a track star, a 15-year-old boy with cerebral palsy, a reluctant bride-to-be, and a 13-year-old terror, Turtle Wexler. It is Turtle who begins to link clues and discover patterns as she and readers piece together Westing's amazing game. In a tightly constructed story divided into many short sections, Raskin piles detail upon detail; rereading shows that what appears to be insignificant always proves otherwise. Warmly realized characters interrelate and grow in this Newbery Medal winner, but it is Turtle who, unbeknownst to any of the other players, quietly solves the puzzle and bikes up to the Westing house to receive her prize in the satisfying ending.

Contemporary authors have also found the mystery to be a successful format for creating complex and thought-provoking books. Mathematical and historical puzzles are woven into *Chasing Vermeer* by Blue Balliett and *Shakespeare's Secret* by Elise Broach. Tim Wynne-Jones explores powerful psychological ideas in *The Boy in the Burning House* and *A Thief in the House of Memory.* In *The Boy in the Burning House* 14-year-old Jim Hawkins is

---

[21]See Ellen Raskin, "Newbery Medal Acceptance," *Horn Book Magazine* (August 1979): 385–91.

Author Tim Wynne-Jones establishes an aura of menacing suspense in the fast-paced mystery *The Boy in the Burning House.* Jacket design by Jennifer Browne from *The Boy in the Burning House* by Tim Wynne-Jones. Jacket design copyright © 2001 by Jennifer Browne. Jacket art copyright © 2001 by Cliff Nielsen. Reprinted by permission of Farrar, Straus & Giroux, LLC.

determined to discover what happened to his father, who disappeared from their small Ontario farm two years earlier. Most people in the area believe Hub Hawkins committed suicide, but Ruth Rose, a teenager with a reputation for craziness, insists her minister stepfather killed him. An absent parent is also the focus of the mystery in Wynne-Jones's *A Thief in the House of Memory.* In this case Declan Steeple's mother has disappeared, and Declan begins to suspect that his father has killed her. In both books, Wynne-Jones creates richly textured and nuanced stories that are impossible to put down.

Popular fiction should be evaluated with the same criteria used to consider all fiction, with the recognition that its major appeals are fast action, contemporary characters in familiar settings, straightforward plot development, humor, and suspense. Children develop the skills of rapid reading, vocabulary building, prediction, and the ability to notice relevant details when they read popular fiction. They develop a love of reading with popular novels, and skillful teachers can extend and diversify readers' choices with all that realistic fiction has to offer. Contemporary realistic fiction is diverse. It has moved away from the problem novels of the 1960s and 1970s to serious fiction balanced with characters less prone to despair.

Contemporary novels encompass diverse themes and writing styles. Although paperback series and popular novels continue to attract readers, these selections are now counterbalanced by many well-written and compelling stories. The diverse cultures of the United States and many other world cultures are represented in literature for children, and the number of titles available continues to grow. Contemporary realistic fiction, the most popular genre among child readers, continues to thrive in this new century.

INTO THE CLASSROOM

Contemporary Realistic Fiction

Realistic fiction is a highly popular genre with children. Teachers and librarians who hope to encourage life-long reading may want to introduce children to some of the more popular fiction first, providing them with some of the good series books that will give them plenty of practice as readers. Reading aloud and discussing the more complex works of realistic fiction should encourage children to move beyond easy books and to relish the challenges and rewards provided in the best works of fiction. Below are some suggestions for deepening children's appreciation of well-written works of contemporary realistic fiction.

1. **The Influence of Characters.** Discuss with a small group of children a novel such as M. J. Auch's *Wing Nut,* Virginia Hamilton's *Bluish,* Valerie Hobbs's *Defiance,* or Ann M. Martin's *Here Today.* How is the main character influenced by other characters in the book? When the child character becomes an adult, which of these other characters might he or she want to thank? Why?

2. **Comparing Relationships.** Compare the relationships of parents and children in several titles discussed in the section of this chapter titled "Living in a Family."

3. **Comparing Survival Stories.** Compare several survival stories discussed in this chapter. After basic wants are satisfied, what else does the surviving person seem to need? What qualities does each person possess or develop in order to survive? How does (or might) surviving change a person?

4. **Comparing Humorous Stories.** Compare several humorous stories. Where does the humor lie? (slapstick? exaggeration? puns or wordplay? situations? satire?) How would you rank these titles from lesser to greater sophistication?

 Go to the Online Learning Center at **www.mhhe.com/kiefer9e** or your Resources CD-ROM to find these additional classroom activities:

5. **Comparison Charts**
6. **Diaries and Letters**
7. **Read-Alouds to Build Comprehension**
8. **Studying the Author's Craft**

Chapter Review

Go to the Online Learning Center at **www.mhhe.com/kiefer9e** or your Resources CD-ROM to take chapter quizzes, practice with key terms, and review the chapter.

Explorations

1. Find books about a specific culture. Look for poetry, biography, fiction, picture storybooks, nonfiction, and Web sites that would deepen understanding of these books in a classroom. What kinds of books were the easiest to find, and which were the most difficult to find?

2. Select a current subject in realistic fiction, such as single-parent families, foster children, immigration, or disability, and create an annotated bibliography. Find some nonfiction that can be grouped with the fiction.

3. Compare the treatment of a topic, such as the death of a pet, a child, or a grandparent, in a picture book, a novel, poetry, and informational books. Select several books from various decades that portray a particular culture. Do you find stereotypes? What themes prevail?

4. Select a contemporary problem that is relevant to children of today (death and dying, human rights, peer pressure). Search the database for a list of titles. Make a list of titles you could use in a class study for grades 4–8. In addition to works of contemporary fiction, try to find titles in other genres.

Web Links

Go to the Online Learning Center at **www.mhhe.com/kiefer9e** to find links to the following children's literature Web sites:

Betsy Byars Home Page

Fifty Multicultural Books Every Child Should Know

Guys Read

Juvenile Series and Sequels

Kids Read

Multicultural Literature in the Elementary Classroom

Multicultural Pavilion

Multicultural Resources for Children

9/11 and Children

The Official Gary Paulsen Website

Sharon Creech

Virginia Hamilton, Welcome to My World

Related Readings

Bishop, Rudine Sims. *Presenting Walter Dean Myers.* New York: Twayne, 1990.

This discussion and criticism of Myers's books about young urban African Americans includes an analysis of humor, theme, characterization, and other patterns found in Myers's work. Other titles in this critical series discuss works by authors such as Sue Ellen Bridgers, Robert Cormier, Richard Peck, and Judy Blume.

Day, Frances. *Multicultural Voices in Contemporary Literature.* Portsmouth, N.H.: Heinemann, 1999.

This updated and revised edition of an earlier work serves as a highly useful classroom resource. Day provides a wealth of information on more than forty multicultural authors and includes classroom activities and reviews of more than 120 of their books to help teachers thoroughly explore the books and authors. Appendixes include lesson plans, additional activities, and lists of resources.

Lehr, Susan, ed. *Battling Dragons: Issues and Controversy in Children's Literature.* Portsmouth, N.H.: Heinemann, 1995, and *Beauty, Brains, and Brawn: The Construction of Gender in Children's Literature.* Portsmouth, N.H.: Heinemann, 2001.

These two volumes offer essays on timely issues in children's books by scholars, teachers, and children's book authors and illustrators. Unique and important perspectives are provided on topics of concern to adults who work with children's literature.

Stan, Susan. *The World through Children's Books.* Latham, MD: Scarecrow Press, 2002, and Tomlinson, Carl M. ed. *Children's Books from Other Countries.* Latham, MD: Scarecrow Press, 1998.

These valuable resources provide a history of the publishing of children's books outside the United States and make suggestions for incorporating international books into classroom studies. Over 1,400 titles published in English or translated into English are annotated and evaluated in the two volumes.

Children's Literature

 Go to the Children's Literature Database on your Resources CD-ROM for a searchable listing of these and other children's literature titles.

The books listed here are recommended, subject to the qualifications noted in this chapter. See Appendix C for publishers' complete addresses. References to books of genres other than realism are noted in parentheses. Original publication dates are in square brackets.

Abelove, Joan. *Go and Come Back.* DK Ink, 1998.

Ada, Alma Flor. *My Name Is María Isabel.* Atheneum, 1993.

Adler, David A. *Cam Jansen and the Birthday Mystery.* Illustrated by Susanna Natti. Viking, 2000.

———. *Young Cam Jansen and the New Girl Mystery.* Viking, 2005.

Adoff, Jamie. *Jimi and Me.* Hyperion, 2005.

Alvarez, Julia. *Before We Were Free.* Knopf, 2002.

———. *Finding Miracles.* Knopf, 2004.

An, Na. *A Step from Heaven.* Front St., 2001.

Ashley, Bernard. *Little Soldier: A Novel.* Scholastic, 2002.

Auch, M. J. *Wing Nut.* Holt, 2005.

Avi. *Nothing but the Truth.* Orchard, 1991.

Balliett, Blue. *Chasing Vermeer.* Scholastic, 2004.

Banerjee, Anjali. *Maya Running.* Random, 2005.

Bang, Molly. *Tiger's Fall.* Holt, 2001.

Banks, Kate. *Dillon Dillon.* Farrar, 2002.

———. *Friends of the Heart: Amici del Cuore.* Farrar, 2005.

Bateman, Colin. *Bring Me the Head of Oliver Plunkett.* Delacorte, 2005.

———. *Running with the Reservoir Pups.* Delacorte, 2005.

Bauer, Joan. *Backwater.* Putnam, 1999.

———. *Best Foot Forward.* Putnam, 2005.

———. *Hope Was Here.* Putnam, 2000.

———. *Rules of the Road.* Putnam, 1998.

———. *Squashed.* Delacorte, 1992.

———. *Stand Tall.* Putnam, 2002.

Bauer, Marion Dane. *On My Honor.* Houghton, 1986.

———. *A Question of Trust.* Houghton, 1994.

Bawden, Nina. *Granny the Pag.* Clarion, 1996.

Betancourt, Jeanne. *My Name Is Brain Brian.* Scholastic, 1993.

Birdsall, Jeanne. *The Penderwicks; A Summer Tale of Four Sisters, Two Rabbits, and a Very Interesting Boy.* Knopf, 2005.

Blacker, Terence. *Boy2Girl.* Farrar, 2005.

Block, Francesca Lia. *Weetzie Bat.* Harper, 1999.

Blume, Judy. *Are You There God? It's Me, Margaret.* Bradbury, 1970.

———. *Double Fudge.* Dutton, 2002.

———. *Superfudge.* Dutton, 1980.

———. *Tales of a Fourth Grade Nothing.* Illustrated by Roy Doty. Dutton, 1972.

———. *Then Again, Maybe I Won't.* Bradbury, 1971.

Bolden, Tonya, ed. *Rites of Passage: Stories about Growing Up by Black Writers from around the World.* Hyperion, 1994.

Boyce, Frank. *Millions.* HarperCollins, 2004.

Bradby, Marie. *Some Friend.* Atheneum, 2004.

Bridgers, Sue Ellen. *All Together Now.* Knopf, 1979.

Broach, Elise. *Shakespeare's Secret.* Holt, 2005.

Brooks, Bruce. *The Moves Make the Man.* Harper, 1984.

———. *Throwing Smoke.* HarperCollins, 2000.

Bruchac, Joseph. *Eagle Song.* Dial, 1997.

———. *The Heart of a Chief.* Dial, 1998.

———. *Hidden Roots.* Scholastic, 2004.

Bunting, Eve. *A Day's Work.* Illustrated by Ron Himler. Clarion, 1991.

———. *Fly Away Home.* Illustrated by Ron Himler. Clarion, 1991.

Burnford, Sheila. *The Incredible Journey.* Illustrated by Carl Burger. Little, 1961.

Byars, Betsy. *Bingo Brown, Gypsy Lover.* Viking, 1990.

———. *The Burning Questions of Bingo Brown.* Viking, 1988.

———. *The Cybil War.* Illustrated by Gail Owens. Viking, 1981.

———. *Death's Door: A Herculeah Jones Mystery.* Viking, 1998.

———. *The House of Wings.* Illustrated by Daniel Schwartz. Viking, 1972.

———. *King of Murder.* Sleuth/Viking, 2006.

———. *The Pinballs.* Harper, 1977.

———. *The Summer of the Swans.* Illustrated by Ted CoConis. Viking, 1970.

———. *Wanted . . . Mud Blossom.* Delacorte, 1991.

Cameron, Ann. *Colibri.* Farrar, 2003.

———. *Gloria Rising.* Illustrated by Lis Toth. Farrar, 2002.

Cameron, Ann. *The Most Beautiful Place in the World.* Illustrated by Thomas B. Allen. Knopf, 1988.

———. *The Stories Huey Tells.* Illustrated by Roberta Smith. Knopf, 1995.

———. *The Stories Julian Tells.* Illustrated by Ann Strugnell. Knopf, 1981.

Canales, Viola. *The Tequila Worm.* Random, 2005.

Carmi, Daniella. *Samir and Yonatan.* Levine/Scholastic, 2000.

Child, Lauren. *Clarice Bean Spells Trouble.* Candlewick, 2005.

Choldenko, Gennifer. *Notes from a Liar and Her Dog.* Putnam, 2001.

Christopher, Matt. *The Captain Contest.* Illustrated by Daniel Vasconcellos. Little, 1999.

———. *Spike It!* Little, 1999.

———. *Stealing Home.* Little, 2004.

Cleary, Beverly. *Dear Mr. Henshaw.* Illustrated by Paul O. Zelinsky. Morrow, 1983.

———. *Ramona and Her Father.* Illustrated by Alan Tiegreen. Morrow, 1977.

———. *Ramona and Her Mother.* Illustrated by Alan Tiegreen. Morrow, 1979.

———. *Ramona Quimby, Age 8.* Illustrated by Alan Tiegreen. Morrow, 1981.

———. *Ramona's World.* Illustrated by Alan Tiegreen. Morrow, 1999.

———. *Strider.* Illustrated by Paul O. Zelinsky. Morrow, 1991.

Cleaver, Vera, and Bill Cleaver. *Where the Lilies Bloom.* Illustrated by James Spanfeller. Lippincott, 1969.

Clements, Andrew. *Frindle.* Simon, 1996.

———. *The Landry News.* Simon, 1996.

———. *Lunch Money.* Simon, 2005.

———. *The School Story.* Illustrated by Brian Selznick. Simon, 2001.

———. *A Week in the Woods.* Simon, 2002.

Clifton, Lucille. *The Lucky Stone.* Illustrated by Dale Payson. Delacorte, 1979.

Clinton, Cathryn. *A Stone in My Hand.* Candlewick, 2002.

Cofer, Judith Ortiz. *See* Ortiz Cofer, Judith.

Cohen, Barbara. *Molly's Pilgrim.* Illustrated by Michael J. Deraney. Lothrop, 1983. (Historical fiction)

———. *Thank You, Jackie Robinson.* Illustrated by Richard Cuffari. Lothrop, 1974.

Cole, Brock. *The Facts Speak for Themselves.* Front St., 1997.

———. *The Goats.* Farrar, 1987.

Coman, Carolyn. *The Big House.* Boyds Mills, 2004.

Conly, Jane Leslie. *In the Night, on Lanvale Street.* Holt, 2005.

Cormier, Robert. *Frenchtown Summer.* Delacorte, 1999.

Couloumbis, Audrey. *Getting Near to Baby.* Putnam, 1999.

Creech, Sharon. *Walk Two Moons.* HarperCollins, 1994.

Crutcher, Chris. *The Sledding Hill.* Greenwillow, 2005.

———. *Stotan!* Greenwillow, 1986.

Cummings, Priscilla. *A Face First.* Dutton, 2001.

Curtis, Christopher Paul. *Mr. Chickee's Funny Money.* Lamb/Random, 2005.

———. *Bucking the Sarge.* Lamb/Random, 2004.

Dakos, Kalli. *If You're Not Here, Please Raise Your Hand: Poems about School.* Illustrated by G. Brian Karas. Four Winds, 1990.

Dalokay, Vedat. *Sister Shako and Kolo the Goat.* Translated by Güner Ener. Lothrop, 1994.

D'Adamo, Francesco. *Iqbal.* Atheneum, 2003.

Danticat, Edwidge. *Behind the Mountains.* Orchard, 2002.

Danziger, Paula. *Amber Brown Goes Fourth.* Illustrated by Tony Ross. Putnam, 1995.

———. *Amber Brown Is Not a Crayon.* Putnam, 1994.

———. *The United Tates of America.* Scholastic, 2002.

Deans, Sis. *Racing the Past.* Holt, 2001.

———. *Rainy.* Holt, 2005.

Deem, James. *3 NBs of Julian Drew.* Houghton, 1994.

de Guzman, Michael. *The Bamboozlers.* Farrar, 2005.

———. *Beekman's Big Deal.* Farrar, 2004.

DeJong, Meindert. *Hurry Home, Candy.* Illustrated by Maurice Sendak. Harper, 1953.

Delton, Judy. *Angel Bites the Bullet.* Houghton, 2000.

dePaola, Tomie. *26 Fairmount Ave.* Putnam, 1999.

Dhami, Narinder. *Bindy Babes.* Delacorte, 2004.

———. *Bollywood Babes.* Delacorte, 2005.

DiCamillo, Kate. *Because of Winn-Dixie.* Candlewick, 2000.

———. *The Tiger Rising.* Candlewick, 2001.

Dowell, Frances O'Roark. *Chicken Boy.* Atheneum, 2005.

———. *The Secret Language of Girls.* Atheneum, 2004.

———. *Where I'd Like to Be.* Simon, 2003.

Dragonwagon, Crescent. *Winter Holding Spring.* Illustrated by Ronald Himler. Macmillan, 1990.

Draper, Sharon. *Forged by Fire.* Atheneum, 1997.

Duffy, Betsy. *Hey New Kid!* Viking, 1996.

Ellis, Deborah. *The Breadwinner.* Groundwood, 2001.

———. *Parvana's Journey.* Groundwood, 2002.

Ellison, Sarah. *365 Foods Kids Love to Eat.* Sourcebooks, 1995.

Estes, Eleanor. *The Hundred Dresses.* Illustrated by Louis Slobodkin. Harcourt, 1944.

———. *The Middle Moffat.* Illustrated by Louis Slobodkin. Harcourt, 1942.

———. *The Moffats.* Illustrated by Louis Slobodkin. Harcourt, 1941.

———. *Rufus M.* Illustrated by Louis Slobodkin. Harcourt, 1943.

Farley, Walter. *The Black Stallion.* Illustrated by Keith Ward. Random, 1944.

Farmer, Nancy. *A Girl Named Disaster.* Orchard, 1996.

Filipovic, Zlata. *Zlata's Diary.* Viking, 1994.

Fine, Anne. *Flour Babies.* Little, 1994.

———. *Up On Cloud Nine.* Delacorte, 2002.

Fitzhugh, Louise. *Harriet the Spy.* Harper, 1964.

————. *The Long Secret*. Harper, 1965.

Flake, Sharon. *Bang*. Hyperion, 2005.

Fletcher, Ralph. *Fig Pudding*. Clarion, 1995.

————. *Flying Solo*. Clarion, 1999.

————. *Uncle Daddy*. Holt, 2001.

Fogelin, Adrian. *The Big Nothing*. Peachtree, 2004.

Fox, Paula. *Monkey Island*. Orchard, 1991.

————. *One-Eyed Cat*. Bradbury, 1984.

————. *The Village by the Sea*. Orchard, 1988.

Franklin, Kristine L. *Eclipse*. Candlewick, 1995.

Gantos, Jack. *Jack on the Tracks: Four Seasons of Fifth Grade*. Farrar, 1999.

————. *Joey Pigza Loses Control*. Farrar, 2000.

————. *Joey Pigza Swallowed the Key*. Farrar, 1998.

————. *What Would Joey Do?* Farrar, 2002.

Garden, Nancy. *Annie on My Mind*. Farrar, 1992.

Gardiner, John Reynolds. *Stone Fox*. Illustrated by Marcia Sewall. Crowell, 1980.

George, Jean Craighead. *Julie*. Illustrated by Wendell Minor. HarperCollins, 1994.

————. *Julie of the Wolves*. Illustrated by John Schoenherr. Harper, 1972.

————. *Julie's Wolfpack*. HarperCollins, 1997.

————. *My Side of the Mountain*. Dutton, 1959.

————. *On the Far Side of the Mountain*. Dutton, 1990.

————. *The Talking Earth*. Harper, 1983.

Ghent, Natale. *No Small Thing*. Candlewick, 2005.

Giff, Patricia Reilly. *The Beast in Ms. Rooney's Room*. Dell, 1985.

Gilson, Jamie. *4-B Goes Wild*. Illustrated by Linda S. Edwards. Lothrop, 1983.

————. *Hello, My Name Is Scrambled Eggs*. Illustrated by John Wallner. Lothrop, 1985.

————. *Hobie Hanson, Greatest Hero of the Mall*. Illustrated by Anita Riggio. Lothrop, 1989.

————. *Hobie Hanson, You're Weird*. Illustrated by Elise Primavera. Lothrop, 1987.

————. *Thirteen Ways to Sink a Sub*. Illustrated by Linda S. Edwards. Lothrop, 1982.

Gipson, Fred. *Old Yeller*. Illustrated by Carl Burger. Harper, 1956.

Goldschmidt, Judy. *The Secret Blog of Raisin Rodriguez*. Penguin, 2005.

Gordon, Sheila. *The Middle of Somewhere: A Story of South Africa*. Orchard, 1990.

————. *Waiting for the Rain*. Orchard, 1987.

Greene, Constance C. *Beat the Turtle Drum*. Illustrated by Donna Diamond. Viking, 1976.

Greene, Stephanie. *Owen Foote, Mighty Scientist*. Clarion, 2004.

Griffin, Adele. *Where I Want to Be*. Putnam, 2005.

Grimes, Nikki. *Bronx Masquerade*. Putnam, 2002.

————. *Jazmin's Notebook*. Dial, 1998.

Haas, Jessie. *Shaper*. Greenwillow, 2002.

Hamilton, Virginia. *Bluish*. Scholastic, 1999.

————. *Cousins*. Philomel, 1990.

————. *The House of Dies Drear*. Illustrated by Eros Keith. Macmillan, 1968.

————. *M. C. Higgins, the Great*. Macmillan, 1974.

————. *The Mystery of Drear House*. Greenwillow, 1987.

————. *Second Cousins*. Scholastic, 1998.

————. *Time Pieces: The Book of Times*. Scholastic, 2002.

————. *Zeely*. Illustrated by Symeon Shimin. Macmillan, 1967.

Hannigan, Katherine. *Ida B . . . and Her Plans to Maximize Fun, Avoid Disaster, and (Possibly) Save the World*. Greenwillow, 2004.

Hansen, Joyce. *One True Friend*. Clarion, 2001.

Harris, Robie H. *It's So Amazing: A Book about Eggs, Sperm, Birth, Babies and Families*. Illustrated by Michael Emberley. Candlewick, 1999.

Haywood, Carolyn. *"B" Is for Betsy*. Harcourt, 1956.

Heide, Florence Parry, and Judith Heide Gilliland. *The Day of Ahmed's Secret*. Illustrated by Ted Lewin. Lothrop, 1990.

Henkes, Kevin. *The Birthday Room*. Greenwillow, 1999.

————. *Sun and Spoon*. Greenwillow, 1997.

————. *Words of Stone*. Greenwillow, 1992.

Henry, Marguerite. *Misty of Chincoteague*. Illustrated by Wesley Dennis. Macmillan, 1947.

Hesse, Karen. *Sable*. Illustrated by Marcia Sewall. Holt, 1994.

Hiaasen, Carl. *Flush*. Knopf, 2005.

————. *Hoot*. Knopf, 2002.

Hiçyilmaz, Gaye. *Against the Storm*. Joy St., 1990.

Hidier, Tanuja Desai. *Born Confused*. Scholastic, 2002.

Hill, Kirkpatrick. *Toughboy and Sister*. McElderry, 1990.

————. *The Year of Miss Agnes*. McElderry, 2000.

Himelblau, Linda. *The Trouble Begins*. Delacorte, 2005.

Ho, Minfong. *Gathering the Dew*. Orchard, 2003.

————. *Rice without Rain*. Lothrop, 1988.

Hobbs, Valerie. *Defiance*. Farrar, 2005.

Hobbs, Will. *Beardance*. Atheneum, 1993.

————. *Bearstone*. Atheneum, 1989.

Holman, Felice. *Slake's Limbo*. Scribner's, 1974.

Holt, Kimberly Willis. *Dancing in the Cadillac Light*. Putnam, 2001.

————. *Keeper of the Night*. Holt, 2003.

————. *My Louisiana Sky*. Holt, 1998.

————. *When Zachary Beaver Came to Town*. Holt, 1999.

Horvath, Polly. *Everything on a Waffle*. Farrar, 2001.

————. *The Pepins and Their Problems*. Farrar, 2004.

————. *Trolls*. Farrar, 1999.

————. *The Vacation*. Farrar, 2005.

Houston, James. *Frozen Fire*. Atheneum, 1977.

Howe, James. *Dew Drop Dead: A Sebastian Barth Mystery*. Atheneum, 1990.

———. *The Misfits.* Simon, 2001.

Hurwitz, Johanna. *Aldo Applesauce.* Illustrated by John Wallner. Morrow, 1979.

———. *Busybody Nora.* Illustrated by Susan Jeschke. Morrow, 1976.

———. *Class Clown.* Illustrated by Sheila Hamanaka. Morrow, 1987.

———. *Russell and Elisa.* Illustrated by Lillian Hoban. Morrow, 1989.

Huynh, Quang Nhuong. *The Land I Lost: Adventures of a Boy in Vietnam.* Illustrated by Vo-Dinh Mai. Harper, 1982.

Jiang, Ji-Li. *Red Scarf Girl: A Memoir of the Cultural Revolution.* HarperCollins, 1997.

Jimenez, Francisco. *Breaking Through.* Houghton, 2001.

———. *The Circuit: Stories from the Life of a Migrant Child.* Houghton, 2001.

Johnson, Angela. *The First Part Last.* Simon, 2003.

———. *Heaven.* Simon, 1998.

———. *The Leaving Morning.* Illustrated by David Soman. Orchard, 1992.

———. *Toning the Sweep.* Orchard, 1993.

Johnson, Scott. *Safe at Second.* Philomel, 1999.

Johnston, Julie. *Adam and Eve and Pinch-Me.* Little, 1994.

———. *In Spite of Killer Bees.* Tundra, 2001.

Joseph, Lynn. *The Color of My Words.* HarperCollins, 2000.

Jukes, Mavis. *Blackberries in the Dark.* Illustrated by Thomas B. Allen. Knopf, 1985.

———. *Expecting the Unexpected: Sex Ed with Mrs. Gladys B. Furley R.N.* Delacorte, 1996.

Kelly, Katy. *Lucy Rose: Big on Plans.* Illustrated by Adam Rex. Delacorte, 2005.

———. *Lucy Rose: Here's the Thing about Me.* Illustrated by Adam Rex. Delacorte, 2004.

Kerr, M. E. *Hello I Lied.* Harper, 1997.

Kerrin, Jessica Scott. *Martin Bridge: On the Lookout!* Illustrated by Joseph Kelly. Kids Can, 2005.

———. *Martin Bridge: Ready for Takeoff!* Illustrated by Joseph Kelly. Kids Can, 2005.

Kessler, Cristina. *Our Secret, Siri Aang.* Putnam, 2004.

Kidd, Diana. *Onion Tears.* Illustrated by Lucy Montgomery. Orchard, 1991.

Kielburger, Craig. *Free the Children: A Young Man's Personal Crusade against Child Labor.* HarperCollins, 1999.

Kjelgaard, Jim. *Big Red.* Illustrated by Bob Kuhn. Holiday, 1956.

Kline, Suzy. *Orp.* Putnam, 1989.

———. *Orp Goes to the Hoop.* Putnam, 1991.

Klise, Kate. *Deliver Us from Normal.* Scholastic, 2005.

———. *Trial by Journal.* HarperCollins, 2001.

Konigsburg, E. L. *From the Mixed-Up Files of Mrs. Basil E. Frankweiler.* Atheneum, 1967.

———. *The Outcasts of 10 Schuyler Place.* Atheneum, 2004.

———. *Silent to the Bone.* Atheneum, 2000.

———. *The View from Saturday.* Atheneum, 1996.

Korman, Gordon. *This Can't Be Happening at Macdonald Hall.* Scholastic, 1978.

———. *No More Dead Dogs.* Hyperion, 2001.

Koss, Amy Goldman. *The Ashwater Experiment.* Dial, 1999.

Krishnaswami, Uma. *Naming Maya.* Farrar, 2004.

Krumgold, Joseph. *. . . And Now Miguel.* Illustrated by Jean Charlot. Crowell, 1953.

Kuklin, Susan. *Iqbal Masih and the Crusaders against Child Slavery.* Holt, 1998.

Kurtz, Jane. *Jakarta Missing.* HarperCollins, 2001.

Laird, Elizabeth. *The Garbage King.* Barrons, 2003.

———. *Kiss the Dust.* Dutton, 1992.

Leavitt, Martine. *Heck Superhero.* Front St., 2004.

Le Guin, Ursula K. *A Wizard of Earthsea.* Illustrated by Ruth Robbins. Houghton, 1968. (Fantasy)

L'Engle, Madeleine. *Meet the Austins.* Dell, 1981 [1960].

———. *A Ring of Endless Light.* Farrar, 1980.

Lester, Alison. *The Quicksand Pony.* Houghton, 1998.

———. *The Snow Pony.* Houghton/Lorraine, 2003.

Levitin, Sonia. *The Return.* Atheneum, 1987.

Levy, Elizabeth. *My Life as a Fifth Grade Comedian.* HarperCollins, 1997.

———. *Tackling Dad.* HarperCollins, 2005.

Lewis, Maggie. *Morgie, Coast to Coast.* Illustrated by Michael Chesworth. Houghton, 2005.

Lipsyte, Robert. *The Contender.* Harper, 1967.

Lisle, Janet Taylor. *Afternoon of the Elves.* Orchard, 1989.

———. *The Gold Dust Letters.* Orchard, 1994.

———. *The Lost Flower Children.* Philomel, 1999.

Little, Jean. *Hey World, Here I Am!* Illustrated by Sue Truesdell. Harper, 1989.

———. *Mine for Keeps.* Viking, 1995.

London, Jack. *The Call of the Wild.* Illustrated by Charles Pickard. Dutton, 1968 [1903].

Look, Lenore. *Love as Strong as Ginger.* Illustrated by Stephen T. Johnson. Atheneum, 1999.

———. *Ruby Lu, Brave and True.* Illustrated by Ann Wilsdorf. Simon, 2004.

Lord, Bette Bao. *In the Year of the Boar and Jackie Robinson.* Illustrated by Marc Simont. Harper, 1984. (Historical fiction)

Lovelace, Maude Hart. *Betsy-Tacy.* Illustrated by Lois Lensky. Harper, 1940.

Lowry, Lois. *All about Sam.* Houghton, 1988.

———. *Anastasia Krupnik.* Houghton, 1979.

———. *Number the Stars.* Houghton, 1989. (Historical fiction)

———. *A Summer to Die.* Illustrated by Jenni Oliver. Houghton, 1977.

Lynch, Chris. *Gold Dust.* HarperCollins, 2000.

———. *Me, Dead Dad and Alcatraz.* HarperCollins, 2005.

Lyon, George Ella. *Sonny's House of Spies.* Simon, 2004.

MacLachlan, Patricia. *All the Places to Love.* Illustrated by Mike Wimmer. HarperCollins, 1994.

———. *Baby.* Delacorte, 1993.

———. *Journey.* Delacorte, 1991.

Madden, Kerry. *Gentle's Holler.* Viking, 2005.

———. *Jessie's Mountain.* Viking, 2008.

———. *Louise's Palette.* Viking, 2007.

Mankell, Henning. *Secrets in the Fire.* Annick, 2003.

Marsden, Carolyn. *The Gold Threaded Dress.* Candlewick, 2002.

———. *Moon Runner.* Candlewick, 2005.

———. *Silk Umbrellas.* Candlewick, 2004.

Martin, Ann M. *A Corner of the Universe.* Scholastic, 2002.

———. *A Dog's Life: The Autobiography of a Stray.* Scholastic, 2005.

———. *Here Today.* Scholastic, 2004.

Mathis, Sharon Bell. *The Hundred Penny Box.* Illustrated by Leo Dillon and Diane Dillon. Viking, 1975.

Matlin, Marlee. *Deaf Child Crossing.* Simon, 2002.

Matthews, L. S. *Fish.* Delacorte, 2004.

McDonald, Janet. *Brother Hood.* Farrar, 2004.

McDonald, Megan. *Judy Moody Declares Independence!* Candlewick, 2005.

———. *Judy Moody Predicts the Future!!* Illustrated by Peter Reynolds. Candlewick, 2003.

———. *Stink, the Incredible Shrinking Kid.* Candlewick, 2005.

McKay, Hilary. *The Amber Cat.* Simon, 1998.

———. *Dog Friday.* Simon, 1995.

———. *Dolphin Luck.* Simon, 1999.

———. *The Exiles.* McElderry, 1992.

———. *The Exiles at Home.* McElderry, 1994.

———. *Exiles in Love.* McElderry, 1998.

———. *Indigo's Star.* Simon, 2004.

———. *Permanent Rose.* Simon, 2005.

———. *Saffy's Angel.* Simon/McElderry, 2002.

McNeill, J. D. *The Last Codfish.* Holt, 2005.

Mead, Alice. *Junebug in Trouble.* Farrar, 2002.

———. *Swimming to America.* Farrar, 2005.

Mikaelsen, Ben. *Petey.* Hyperion, 1998.

———. *Touching Spirit Bear.* HarperCollins, 2001.

Miles, Betty. *Maudie and Me and the Dirty Book.* Knopf, 1980.

Mills, Claudia. *Dynamite Dinah.* Simon, 1992.

———. *Gus and Grandpa and Show-and-Tell.* Illustrated by Catherine Stock. Farrar, 2002.

Mohr, Nicholasa. *El Bronx Remembered: A Novella and Stories.* HarperCollins, 1988.

———. *Felita.* Illustrated by Ray Cruz. Dial, 1979.

———. *Going Home.* Dial, 1986.

Montes, Marisa. *Mystery Neighbors: Get Ready for Gabí.* Scholastic, 2003.

Montgomery, L. M. *Anne of Green Gables.* Bantam, 1976 [1908].

Moss, Marissa. *Amelia Works It Out.* Pleasant, 2000.

Mowat, Farley. *The Dog Who Wouldn't Be.* Little, 1957.

———. *Owls in the Family.* Little, 1961.

Myers, Walter Dean. *Darnell Rock Reporting.* Delacorte, 1994.

———. *Fast Sam, Cool Clyde, and Stuff.* Viking, 1975.

———. *The Mouse Rap.* HarperCollins, 1990.

———. *Scorpions.* Harper, 1988.

———. *Shooter.* Amistad/HarperCollins, 2004.

Naidoo, Beverley. *Chain of Fire.* Illustrated by Eric Velasquez. Lippincott, 1990.

———. *Journey to Jo'burg.* Illustrated by Eric Velasquez. Lippincott, 1986.

———. *The Other Side of Truth.* HarperCollins, 2001.

Namioka, Lensey. *Yang the Eldest and His Odd Jobs.* Little, 2000.

———. *Yang the Second and Her Secret Admirers.* Little, 1998.

———. *Yang the Third and Her Impossible Family.* Illustrated by Kees de Kiefte. Little, 1995.

———. *Yang the Youngest and His Terrible Ear.* Illustrated by Kees de Kiefte. Little, 1992.

Napoli, Donna Jo. *Three Days.* Dutton, 2001.

Naylor, Phyllis Reynolds. *The Agony of Alice.* Atheneum, 1985.

———. *Alice Alone.* Atheneum, 2001.

———. *Alice the Brave.* Atheneum, 1995.

———. *Alice on Her Way.* Atheneum, 2005.

———. *The Fear Place.* Atheneum, 1994.

———. *Saving Shiloh.* Atheneum, 1997.

———. *Shiloh.* Atheneum, 1991.

———. *The Shiloh Season.* Atheneum, 1996.

———. *Starting with Alice.* Atheneum, 2002.

Nixon, Joan Lowery. *The Other Side of Dark.* Delacorte, 1986.

North, Sterling. *Rascal: A Memoir of a Better Era.* Illustrated by John Schoenherr. Dutton, 1963.

Nye, Naomi Shihab. *Habibi.* Simon, 1997.

O'Dell, Scott. *Island of the Blue Dolphins.* Houghton, 1960.

Oneal, Zibby. *The Language of Goldfish.* Viking, 1980.

Ortiz Cofer, Judith. *Call Me Maria.* Orchard, 2004.

———. *The Hunger of Birds.* Farrar, 2005.

———. *An Island like You: Stories of the Barrio.* Orchard, 1995.

Osa, Nancy. *Cuba 15.* Delacorte, 2003.

Osofsky, Audrey. *My Buddy.* Illustrated by Ted Rand. Holt, 1992.

Parish, Peggy. *Amelia Bedelia.* Illustrated by Fritz Siebel. Harper, 1963.

Park, Barbara. *Junie B. First Grader: Toothless Wonder.* Random, 2002.

———. *Mick Harte Was Here.* Apple Soup, 1995.

———. *Skinnybones.* Knopf, 1982.

Park, Linda Sue. *Project Mulberry.* Clarion, 2005.

Parsons, Alexandra. *Fit for Life.* Watts, 1996.

Paterson, Katherine. *Bridge to Terabithia.* Illustrated by Donna Diamond. Crowell, 1977.

———. *The Great Gilly Hopkins.* Crowell, 1978.

———. *Jacob Have I Loved.* Harper, 1980.

———. *The Same Stuff as Stars.* Clarion, 2002.

Paulsen, Gary. *Brian's Return.* Delacorte, 1999.

———. *Brian's Winter.* Delacorte, 1996.

———. *Dogsong.* Bradbury, 1985.

———. *Hatchet.* Bradbury, 1987.

———. *The River.* Delacorte, 1991.

———. *The Voyage of the Frog.* Bradbury, 1989.

Peck, Richard. *Strays like Us.* Dial, 1998.

Peck, Robert Newton. *Soup.* Illustrated by Charles Gehm. Knopf, 1974.

Perkins, Lynne Rae. *All Alone in the Universe.* Greenwillow, 1999.

———. *Criss Cross.* Greenwillow, 2005.

Placide, Jaira. *Fresh Girl.* Random House, 2002.

Quarles, Heather. *A Door near Here.* Delacorte, 1998.

Raskin, Ellen. *The Westing Game.* Dutton, 1978.

Rawlings, Marjorie Kinnan. *The Yearling.* Illustrated by Edward Shenton. Scribner's, 1938.

Rawls, Wilson. *Where the Red Fern Grows.* Doubleday, 1961.

Rennison, Louise. *Knocked Out by My Nunga-Nungas.* HarperCollins, 2002.

Roberts, Kristi. *My 13th Season.* Holt, 2005.

Robinson, Barbara. *The Best Christmas Pageant Ever.* Illustrated by Judith Gwyn Brown. Harper, 1972.

Rockwell, Thomas. *How to Eat Fried Worms.* Watts, 1973.

Rodowsky, Colby. *The Next-Door Dogs.* Illustrated by Amy June Bates. Farrar, 2005.

———. *Not My Dog.* Farrar, 1999.

Roessel, Monty. *Kinaalda: A Navajo Girl Grows Up.* Lerner, 1993.

Roos, Stephen. *The Gypsies Never Came.* Simon, 2001.

Rosen, Michael. *Home: A Collaboration of Thirty Distinguished Authors and Illustrators of Children's Books to Aid the Homeless.* HarperCollins, 1992.

Ryan, Pam Muñoz. *Becoming Naomi Leon.* Scholastic, 2004.

Rylant, Cynthia. *Henry and Mudge: The First Book of Their Adventures.* Illustrated by Suçie Stevenson. Bradbury, 1987.

———. *Missing May.* Orchard, 1992.

Sachar, Louis. *Holes.* Farrar, 1998.

———. *Marvin Redpost: Why Pick on Me?* Illustrated by Neal Hughes. Random, 1993.

———. *Wayside School Gets a Little Stranger.* Illustrated by Joel Schick. Morrow, 1995.

Sachs, Marilyn. *JoJo and Winnie Again: More Sister Stories.* Illustrated by Meredith Johnson. Dutton, 2000.

Salisbury, Graham. *Lord of the Deep.* Delacorte, 2001.

Say, Allen. *El Chino.* Houghton, 1996.

Schlein, Miriam. *The Year of the Panda.* Harper, 1992.

Schumacher, Julie. *Grass Angel.* Delacorte, 2004.

Scieszka, Jon. *Guys Write for Guys Read: Boys' Favorite Authors Write about Being Boys.* Viking, 2005.

Sharmat, Marjorie Wiseman. *Nate the Great.* Illustrated by Marc Simont. Putnam, 1986.

Sheth, Kashmira. *Blue Jasmine.* Hyperion, 2004.

Shreve, Susan. *Under the Watsons' Porch.* Knopf, 2004.

Shusterman, Neal. *Downsiders.* Simon, 1999.

———. *The Schwa Was Here.* Dutton, 2004.

Silvey, Anita. *Help Wanted: Stories about Young People Working.* Little, 1997.

Simon, Seymour. *Einstein Anderson Lights Up the Sky.* Illustrated by Fred Winkowski. Viking, 1982.

Sis, Peter. *Starry Messenger.* Farrar, 1996.

Slote, Alfred. *Hang Tough, Paul Mather.* Lippincott, 1973.

———. *The Trading Game.* Lippincott, 1990.

Smith, Doris Buchanan. *A Taste of Blackberries.* Illustrated by Charles Robinson. Crowell, 1973.

Smith, Janice Lee. *Serious Science: An Adam Joshua Story.* Illustrated by Dick Gackenbach. HarperCollins, 1993.

Snyder, Zilpha K. *The Egypt Game.* Illustrated by Alton Raible. Atheneum, 1967.

———. *Libby on Wednesday.* Delacorte, 1990.

Sobol, Donald. *Encyclopedia Brown Takes a Case.* Illustrated by Leonard Shortall. Nelson, 1973.

Son, John. *Finding My Hat.* Orchard, 2003.

Soto, Gary. *Baseball in April and Other Stories.* Harcourt, 1990.

———. *Boys at Work.* Delacorte, 1995.

———. *Crazy Weekend.* Scholastic, 1995.

———. *Help Wanted: Stories.* Harcourt, 2005.

———. *Local News.* Harcourt, 1993.

———. *Off and Running.* Delacorte, 1996.

———. *Pacific Crossing.* Harcourt, 1992.

———. *Petty Crimes.* Harcourt, 1998.

———. *The Pool Party.* Delacorte, 1993.

———. *The Skirt.* Delacorte, 1992.

———. *Summer on Wheels.* Scholastic, 1995.

———. *Taking Sides.* Harcourt, 1991.

Sperry, Armstrong. *Call It Courage.* Macmillan, 1968.

Spinelli, Eileen. *Lizzy Logan, Second Banana.* Simon, 1998.

Spinelli, Jerry. *Crash.* Knopf, 1996.

———. *Loser.* HarperCollins, 2002.

———. *Maniac Magee.* Little, 1990.

———. *Stargirl.* Knopf, 2000.

———. *Wringer.* HarperCollins, 1997.

Spyri, Johanna. *Heidi.* Illustrated by Troy Howell. Messner, 1982 [1884].

Staples, Suzanne Fisher. *Haveli.* Knopf, 1993.

———. *Shabanu: Daughter of the Wind.* Knopf, 1989.

———. *Shiva's Fire.* Farrar, 2000.

———. *Under the Persimmon Tree.* Farrar, 2005.

Stauffacher, Sue. *Donuthead.* Knopf, 2004.

Stratton, Allan. *Chanda's Secrets.* Annick, 2004.

Taylor, Mildred. *The Friendship.* Illustrated by Max Ginsburg. Dial, 1987. (Historical fiction)

Taylor, Sydney. *More All-of-a-Kind Family.* Illustrated by Mary Stevens. Follett, 1954.

Taylor, Theodore. *The Trouble with Tuck.* Doubleday, 1981.

———. *Tuck Triumphant.* Doubleday, 1991.

Temple, Frances. *Grab Hands and Run.* Orchard, 1993.

———. *Taste of Salt.* Orchard, 1992.

———. *Tonight, by Sea.* Orchard, 1995.

Thomas, Jane Resh. *The Comeback Dog.* Illustrated by Troy Howell. Houghton, 1981.

Van Draanen, Wendelin. *Sammy Keyes and the Art of Deception.* Knopf, 2003.

Veciana-Suarez, Ana. *Flight to Freedom.* Scholastic, 2002.

Viorst, Judith. *Alexander, Who's Not (Do Your Hear Me? I Mean It!) Going to Move.* Illustrated by Robin Price Glasser. Atheneum, 1995.

Voigt, Cynthia. *Dicey's Song.* Atheneum, 1983.

———. *Homecoming.* Atheneum, 1981.

———. *The Runner.* Atheneum, 1985.

———. *Seventeen against the Dealer.* Atheneum, 1985.

Walker, Kate. *Peter.* Houghton, 2001.

Wallace, Bill. *True Friends.* Holiday, 1994.

Wallace-Brodeur, Ruth. *Blue Eyes Better.* Dutton, 2002.

———. Ruth. *Heron Cove.* Dutton, 2005.

Walter, Mildred Pitts. *Have a Happy. . . .* Lothrop, 1989.

———. *Justin and the Best Biscuits in the World.* Illustrated by Catherine Stock. Knopf, 1986.

———. *Suitcase.* Lothrop, 1999.

Weston, Carol. *Melanie in Manhattan.* Knopf, 2005.

Whelan, Gloria. *Chu Ju's House.* HarperCollins, 2004.

———. *Homeless Bird.* HarperCollins 2000.

White, Ruth. *Belle Prater's Boy.* Farrar, 1996.

———. *Memories of Summer.* Farrar, 2000.

———. *The Search for Belle Prater.* Farrar, 2005.

———. *Tadpole.* Farrar, 2003.

Wiles, Deborah. *Each Little Bird That Sings.* Harcourt, 2005.

———. *Love, Ruby Lavender.* Harcourt, 2001.

Williams-Garcia, Rita. *No Laughter Here.* Amistad/HarperCollins, 2004.

Wilson, Jacqueline. *The Illustrated Mum.* Delacorte, 2005.

Wilson, Nancy Hope. *Mountain Pose.* Farrar, 2001.

Winerip, Michael. *Adam Canfield of the Slash.* Candlewick, 2005.

Wolff, Virginia Euwer. *Make Lemonade.* Holt, 1993.

———. *The Mozart Season.* Holt, 1991.

———. *True Believer.* Atheneum, 2001.

Woodson, Jacqueline. *Between Madison and Palmetto.* Delacorte, 1993.

———. *Hush.* Putnam, 2002.

———. *I Hadn't Meant to Tell You This.* Delacorte, 1994.

———. *Last Summer with Maizon.* Delacorte, 1990.

———. *Maizon at Blue Hill.* Delacorte, 1992.

Wynne-Jones, Tim. *The Boy in the Burning House.* Farrar, 2001.

———. *A Thief in the House of Memory.* Farrar, 2005.

Woods, Brenda. *Emako Blue.* Knopf, 2004.

———. *The Red Rose Box.* Knopf, 2004.

Woodson, Jacqueline. *Behind You.* Putnam, 2004.

———. *From the Notebooks of Melanin Sun.* Scholastic, 1999.

———. *If You Come Softly.* Putnam, 1998.

Yee, Lisa. *Millicent Min, Girl Genius.* Scholastic, 2003.

Yep, Laurence. *The Amah.* Putnam, 1999.

———. *Angelfish.* Putnam, 2001.

———. *The Case of the Firecrackers.* HarperCollins, 1999.

———. *Child of the Owl.* Harper, 1977.

———. *Cockroach Cooties.* Hyperion, 2001.

———. *The Cook's Family.* Putnam, 1998.

———. *Later, Gator.* Hyperion, 1995.

———. *Ribbons.* Putnam, 1998.

———. *Thief of Hearts.* HarperCollins, 1995.

Yu, Chun. *Little Green: Growing Up during the Chinese Revolution.* Simon, 2005.

Yumoto, Kazumi. *The Friends.* Translated by Cathy Hirano. Farrar, 1996.

———. *The Letters.* Translated by Cathy Hirano. Farrar, 2002.

Zevin, Gabrielle. *Elsewhere.* Farrar, 2005.

Chapter Ten

Historical Fiction

Media Resources

The author of an historical novel visited a public library's after-school program to meet with a group of children. In her talk she described the research she had done to establish an authentic Civil War background for her book. To make these efforts more concrete for the children, she had brought along many examples of source material: maps, reproductions of nineteenth-century photographs, books and pamphlets, and a three-ring binder bulging with notes. One 10-year-old girl regarded this display with a troubled expression; when the time came for questions, she quickly raised her hand.

"You found out a lot of things that you didn't put in the book, didn't you?" she asked. The author agreed, and the girl smiled. "Good!" she said. "If you had put all *that* stuff in, there wouldn't have been any room for the imagining!"

This child intuitively knew that historical fiction must draw on two sources, fact and imagination—the author's information about the past and her or his power to speculate about how it was to live in that time.

Biography for children also draws on both sources (see Chapter 12). Although biography is by definition a nonfiction genre, its success depends as much on its imaginative presentation of facts as on accuracy. Both historical fiction and biography have narrative appeal. By personalizing the past and making it live in the mind of the reader, such books can help children understand both the public events that we usually label "history" and the private struggles that have characterized the human condition across the centuries.

HISTORICAL FICTION FOR TODAY'S CHILD

Historical fiction is not as popular with readers today as it was a generation or two ago. Today's children generally select realistic fiction, the so-called "I" stories with modern-day characters and settings. Even so, children have more historical fiction available now than in the 1980s.

Publishers have capitalized on children's interest in series books by developing collectible sets of historical fiction titles. The American Girl books, published by the Pleasant Company, offer six different series, each chronicling the adventures of a girl in a particular time. These books, along with the expensive dolls and period costumes that go with them, have been phenomenally successful. The same company also publishes The American Girl History Mysteries (with titles such as *Betrayal at Cross Creek* by Kathleen Ernst and *Mystery on Skull Island* by Elizabeth McDavid Jones) and the Girls of Many Lands series (which includes *Saba:*

Under the Hyena's Foot by Jane Kurtz and *Spring Pearl: The Last Flower* by Laurence Yep). Other publishers have also targeted the 7-to-11 age range. Viking's Once Upon America books, written by many different authors, vary widely in quality. However, they offer an unusually wide range of settings, such as the Oklahoma land rush (*Beautiful Land* by Nancy Antle) and the polio epidemic of 1952 (*Close to Home* by Lydia Weaver). In 1996, Scholastic introduced the Dear America series of fictional journals by young girls, which provide "eyewitness" accounts of events in American history. All the books are written by well-known authors, though with mixed results. Joyce Hansen's *I Thought My Soul Would Rise and Fly* received a Coretta Scott King Honor medal in 1998; other titles have been severely criticized.[1] Perhaps most disturbing is the series's attempt to look like authentic diaries rather than like fiction. No author's name is given on the cover or spine. Following the diary entries is an epilogue describing what happened to the character following the accounts in the diary. An historical note

---

[1]See Marlene Atleo et al., "A Critical Review of Ann Rinaldi's *My Heart Is on the Ground*," and Beverly Slapin's "A Critical Review of Ann Turner's *The Girl Who Chased Away Sorrow*," available on the World Wide Web at <www.oyate.org>.

and archival photographs follow. Buried at the back of the book is a brief "About the Author" section, and the dedication, acknowledgments, and CIP information are given on the final page. It is no wonder that many children and teachers believe these stories are real accounts. The popularity of the series has spawned three others that use a similar format. The My America series is for a younger audience and has a continuing series of books narrated by the same fictional character. The My Name Is America series features fictional boys' reports of significant happenings in American history, and the Royal Diaries series provides fictional chronicles of famous young women such as Elizabeth I and Cleopatra. Teachers who want to share these books with children will want to select titles carefully and ensure that children read them with a critical eye.

Another noticeable trend in historical fiction is the number of picture storybooks that portray the life of a particular period. For example, children can experience the terror of slaves traveling on the Underground Railroad in Deborah Hopkinson's *Under the Quilt of Night* with James Ransome's vivid oil paintings to illuminate the fearful journey. In Eve Bunting's *Dandelions* they can travel across the prairie, or they can greet the arrival of Lewis and Clark from a Native American perspective in Virginia Driving Hawk Sneve's *Bad River Boys*. They can experience the detention of a young Chinese immigrant newly arrived in San Francisco in Katrina Saltonstall Currier's *Kai's Journey to Gold Mountain*. They can walk among the tenements of an immigrant community in New York City in Elisa Bartone's *Peppe the Lamplighter* or experience the horrors of World War II and the Holocaust

in books such as *The Cats in Krasinski Square* by Karen Hesse, *Rose Blanche* by Christophe Gallaz and Roberto Innocenti, or *Hiroshima No Pika* by Toshi Maruki. "Easy-to-read" books about historical events are also readily available, including Louise Borden's *Sleds on Boston Commons* and Patricia Lee Gauch's *Aaron and the Green Mountain Boys*, both about the American Revolution.

The increased use of books across the curriculum has created a demand for more historical fiction and biography in the social studies curriculum. Many books that were written in the 1950s—such as Eloise McGraw's *Moccasin Trail* and William Steele's *Winter Danger* and *The Buffalo Knife*—have been reissued in paperback. These are still exciting, well-written stories of frontier living and will capture children's interest. Based on a true story, *On to Oregon!* by Honoré Morrow is an almost unbelievable tale of the courage of the six Sager children, who, after their parents' deaths, walked more than a thousand miles by themselves through the wilderness until they reached the Whitman missionary station. First published in 1926, then again in 1946 and 1954, and then in paperback in the 1990s, this novel proves the lasting quality of a true survival story.

While many books of American historical fiction are being reissued, many fine books, such as Rosemary Sutcliff's books about early Britain, have been allowed to go out of print in the United States. Except for an increase in the number of titles about the Holocaust, we have fewer books of historical fiction about other lands. This is a loss, indeed, in a world in which we are all becoming increasingly interdependent. We need to know our history *and* the history of other countries. One way for teachers to overcome this problem is to seek out some of these important titles through Internet bookstores. These give teachers access to titles published in the United Kingdom that were heretofore almost impossible to find in the United States. Those we discuss here are well worth the time it takes to locate them.

The Value of Historical Fiction

Historical novels for children help a child to experience the past—to enter into the conflicts, the suffering, the joys, and the despair of those who lived before us. There is no way children can feel the jolt of a covered wagon, the tediousness of the daily trek in the broiling sun, or the constant threat of danger unless they take an imaginative journey in books like Jean Van Leeuwen's *Bound for Oregon* or *A Heart for Any Fate* by Linda Crew. Well-written historical fiction offers young people the vicarious experience of participating in the life of the past.

Greg Shed's illustration represents the isolation of life on the prairie in Eve Bunting's *Dandelions*. Illustration from *Dandelions* by Eve Bunting, illustrations copyright © 1995 by Greg Shed, reproduced by permission of Harcourt, Inc.

Bill Farnsworth's illustrations for Virginia Driving Hawk Sneve's *Bad River Boys* help provide a Native American perspective on the journey of Lewis and Clark. Illustration copyright © 2005 by Bill Farnsworth. All rights reserved. Reprinted from *Bad River Boys: A Meeting of the Lakota Sioux with Lewis and Clark*, written by Virginia Driving Hawk Sneve, by permission of Holiday House.

Historical fiction encourages children to think as well as feel. Every book set in the past invites a comparison with the present. In addition, opportunities for critical thinking and judgment are built into the many novels that provide conflicting views on an issue and force characters to make hard choices. Readers of *My Brother Sam Is Dead* by James L. Collier and Christopher Collier can weigh Sam's Patriot fervor against his father's Tory practicality as young Tim tries to decide which one is right. Readers will question Will Page's dislike of his uncle because he refused to fight the Yankees in Carolyn Reeder's *Shades of Gray*. And yet there have been conscientious objectors to every war this nation has participated in. Mary Downing Hahn deals with the same issue in *Stepping on the Cracks*, a story set during World War II.

An historical perspective also helps children see and judge the mistakes of the past more clearly. They can read such books as *Day of Tears* by Julius Lester, *Nory Ryan's Song* by Patricia Reilly Giff, or *Under the Blood-Red Sun* by Graham Salisbury and realize the cruelty people are capable of inflicting on each other, whether by slavery,

persecution, or the internment of Japanese-Americans in "relocation centers." Such books will quicken children's sensibilities and bring them to a fuller understanding of human problems and human relationships. We hope that our children will learn not to repeat the injustices of the past. Many years ago George Santayana cautioned: "Those who cannot remember the past are condemned to repeat it."

Stories of the past help children see that times change, nations rise and fall, but universal human needs have remained relatively unchanged. All people need and want respect, belonging, love, freedom, and security, regardless of whether they lived during the period of the Vikings or the pioneers or are alive today. The pain of moving from home to home and place to place is present in Laura Ingalls Wilder's series and Louise Erdrich's *The Birchbark House* and *The Game of Silence*. But the solace drawn from loving families is what gives all the characters hope. Children today living in tenements, trailers, or suburban homes seek the same feeling of warmth and family solidarity that Wilder and Erdrich portray so effectively in their books.

Historical fiction also enables children to see human interdependence. We are all interconnected and interrelated. We need others as much as Christopher needed Asha-po in Kathleen Karr's *Worlds Apart* or Ellen Rosen needed Annemarie Johansen's family in order to escape the Nazis in Lois Lowry's award-winning book *Number the Stars*. Such books also dramatize the courage and integrity of the thousands of "common folk" who willingly take a stand for what they believe. History does not record their names, but their stories are frequently the source of inspiration for books of historical fiction.

Children's perceptions of chronology are inexact and develop slowly. Even so, stories about the past can develop a feeling for the continuity of life and help children to see themselves and their present place in time as part of a larger picture. Books such as Bonnie Pryor's *The House on Maple Street* provide this sense for younger elementary students. In Pryor's book, lost objects from early times are unearthed in a contemporary child's yard. Paintings by Beth Peck link past and present, showing changes that came to that specific setting over the intervening centuries. Reading historical fiction is one way children can develop this sense of history and begin to understand their place in the sweep of human destiny.

Types of Historical Fiction

The term *historical fiction* can be used to designate all realistic stories that are set in the past. Even though children tend to see these in one undifferentiated category (because all the action happened "in the olden days" before they were born), students of literature will want to keep in mind that various distinctions can be made on the basis of the author's purpose and the nature of the research and writing tasks required. Teachers and librarians should help children differentiate between the fictionalized aspects and the factual aspects in all types of historical fiction.

In the most obvious type of historical fiction, an author weaves a fictional story around actual events and people of the past. *Johnny Tremain* by Esther Forbes, the story of a fictional apprentice to Paul Revere, is a novel of this sort. The author had previously written a definitive adult biography of Revere and had collected painstakingly accurate details about life in Boston just before the Revolutionary War: the duties of apprentices, the activities of the Committee for Public Safety, and much, much more. Johnny Tremain's personal story, his development from an embittered boy into a courageous and idealistic young man, is inextricably connected with the political history and way of life of his place and time. It is not uncommon in recent books of historical fiction to find that the author has added an author's note and bibliography of sources at the end of the book.

In other stories of the past, fictional lives are lived with little or no reference to recorded historical events or real persons. However, the facts of social history dictate the background for how the characters live and make their living; what they wear, eat, study, or play; and what conflicts they must resolve. Australian writer Sonya Hartnett's *Thursday's Child* is of this type. Written about a family struggling to cope with their circumstances during the Great Depression in the Australian outback, this superb book is a moving examination of a family torn apart by circumstances beyond their control. The rural Midwest and western America provide the setting for several books whose main thrust is humor rather than historical detail. Richard Peck's books *The Teacher's Funeral, A Year Down Yonder,* and *A Long Way from Chicago* are set in rural Illinois in the nineteenth and middle-twentieth centuries. Their main focus is on wonderfully eccentric characters and amusing plot lines. These same qualities make David Ives's *Scrib,* about a 16-year-old boy who makes a precarious living writing letters for "ill-literates" in the "wild" West of the 1860s, so appealing.

More often in this type of historical fiction the historical setting simply provides the background for ripping good adventure stories that rely on the structures of Robert Louis Stevenson's *Treasure Island* or Johann David Wyss's *The Swiss Family Robinson.* Stories that fall into this category would include Eva Ibbotson's *The Star of Kazan,* about a young girl involved in mystery and intrigue in early-twentieth-century Vienna. *Operation Red Jericho* by Joshua Mowll is a 1920s adventure that blends aspects of Jules Verne and Indiana Jones. The book, whose shape and cover mimic an old journal, is purportedly told by the very person who has inherited and researched the archives of a secret society. Mowll includes maps, diagrams, and photographs found in the archives as well as excerpts from teenage heroine Becca's diary and her brother Doug's sketchbook. Other historical series, all set in the nineteenth century, that follow this high-adventure model include Eleanor Updale's Mont-

morency series and Iain Lawrence's High Seas Trilogy and his *Convicts* and *Cannibals* set on a prison ship bound for Australia. Kathleen Karr's *Skullduggery* and *Bone Dry* take place in 1830s Europe and Egypt. Traditional female roles have been turned upside down in Avi's *The True Confessions of Charlotte Doyle* and Louis A. Meyer's stories about Mary "Jacky" Faber, such as *Bloody Jack, Curse of the Blue Tattoo,* and *Under the Jolly Roger.* In all these stories the heroines assume the roles of able sailor lads and prove their grit when trouble strikes their ships. Often such historical adventure stories rely on circumstances that border on the fantastic, although the settings are built on historical sources.

In a third type of historical fiction, authors recreate, largely from memory, their own personal experiences of a time that is "history" to their child audience. The Little House books, for example, are all based on actual childhood experiences in the life of their author, Laura Ingalls Wilder, or her husband. Such books require searching one's memory for details and then sorting and imagina-

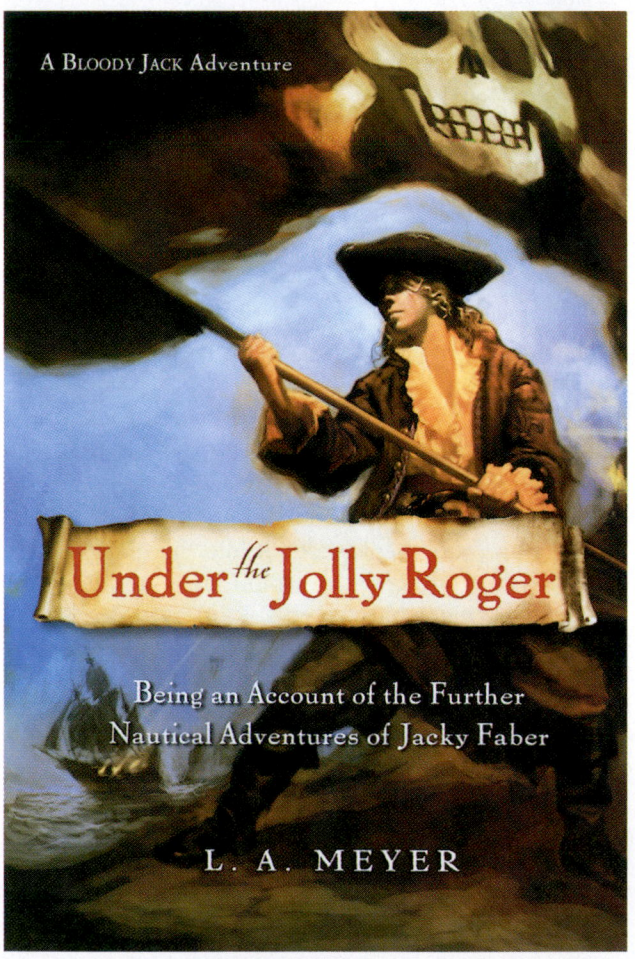

Jacky Faber, better known aboard ship as Bloody Jack, is the intrepid heroine of Louis A. Meyer's *Under the Jolly Roger,* one of a series of high adventures set in an historical period. Cover art from *Under the Jolly Roger: Being an Account of the Further Nautical Adventures of Jacky Faber* by L. A. Meyer, copyright © 2005 by L. A. Meyer, reprinted with permission of Harcourt, Inc.

tively retelling significant events, but extensive research is seldom done.

In other instances, a purely contemporary story about a significant event might endure until it acquires historical significance. *Snow Treasure* by Marie McSwigan is the exciting story of Norwegian children who heroically strapped gold bullion under their sleds and slid downhill to the port past the watchful Nazi commandant. Written as realism in 1942, this book is read by children today as historical fiction. We must also realize that Katherine Paterson's *Park's Quest* and other books about the Vietnam War might be read as historical fiction by today's child, despite the fact that for many of us these events were lived first hand.

Some historical stories defy commonly accepted classifications. Walter Mosley's graphically moving *47* vividly portrays the experiences of slavery in 1832 Georgia. The story's narrator is named only Number Forty-Seven, following the practice of dehumanization that was common to slave owners in the South. However, Forty-Seven is looking back on his life from the ripe old age of 180. Furthermore, the other major character in the story is a runaway slave named Tall John, whom many on the plantation suspect of being the legendary African hero High John the Conqueror. Instead of being this mythical African, however, Tall John is actually an alien from another planet. Clearly, Mosley has broken the format of traditional historical fiction for children. But the book presents such an accurate and brutal picture of slavery that it will provide important historical insights to mature readers.

A few authors tell stories of the past in the guise of another genre to draw the hesitant reader in more quickly. Jane Yolen's devastating story of the Holocaust, *The Devil's Arithmetic*, begins in the present when Hannah, bored with all the remembering of the Passover Seder, opens the door to welcome symbolically the prophet Elijah and finds herself in the unfamiliar world of a Polish village in the 1940s. In Lois Ruby's *Steal Away Home* and its companion book *Soon Be Free*, 12-year-old Dana Shannon finds a skeleton in a closet after her family moves into an old house in Kansas. A small black diary found with the skeleton helps Dana discover that the skeleton is that of Lizbeth Charles, who had died 130 years earlier. In addition, alternate chapters take the reader back to the 1850s, when the house was owned by a Quaker family and was part of the Underground Railroad. Other devices are used to transport the main character (and the reader) from the present day to a carefully researched past in books like Janet Lunn's *The Root Cellar* (see Chapter 7).

Cynthia DeFelice's *Lostman's River* is an exciting adventure set in the Florida Everglades in the early 1900s. Children will learn more about the fragile ecology of the Everglades than they will about historical details, but

Talking Point

To what standards should writers of historical fiction adhere?

Should authors of historical fiction include a note about their research and a list of sources? How faithful should an author be to the attitudes and language of the times? Do authors need to provide a balanced point of view when writing about conflict? How will you deal with these issues in your classroom?

Go to the Online Learning Center at **www.mhhe/kiefer9e** or to your Resources CD-ROM to learn more.

the story is based on real events—particularly the murder of an Audubon Society game warden hired to protect the rookeries of birds who were being wiped out for their feathers. E. L. Konigsburg's unique story of Eleanor of Aquitaine, *A Proud Taste for Scarlet and Miniver*, combines fantasy, historical fiction, and biography. Categorizing books like these is far less important than bringing them to the attention of children, for they all tell good stories and make their subjects memorable.

No type of historical story is intrinsically better than another. However, the type of story might influence a teacher's selection process when choosing books for specific classroom purposes. And in applying the criteria for evaluating historical fiction, which are described in the following section, standards of authenticity must be applied most rigorously to stories that give a prominent place to real people and real events.

Criteria for Historical Fiction

Books of historical fiction must first of all tell a story that is interesting in its own right. The second, and unique, requirement is balancing fact with fiction. Margery Fisher maintains that a good story should not be overwhelmed by facts:

> For the more fact he [the author] has to deal with, the more imagination he will need to carry it off. It is not enough to be a scholar, essential though this is. Without imagination and enthusiasm, the most learned and well-documented story will leave the young reader cold, where it should set him on fire.[2]

Historical fiction *does* have to be accurate and authentic. However, the research should be thoroughly digested, making details appear as an essential part of the story, not tacked on for effect. Mollie Hunter, a well-known Scottish writer of fine historical fiction for children, maintains that an author should be so steeped in

---

[2]Margery Fisher, *Intent upon Reading: A Critical Appraisal of Modern Fiction for Children* (New York: Watts, 1962), p. 225.

the historical period of the book that "you could walk undetected in the past. You'd wake up in the morning and know the kind of bed you'd be sleeping in, . . . even to the change you'd have in your pocket!"[3] The purpose of research, she said, is

> to be able to think and feel in terms of a period so that the people within it are real and three-dimensional, close enough to hear the sound of their voices, to feel their body-warmth, to see the expression in their eyes.[4]

This obligation applies not only to details of person, place, and time but also to the values and norms of the culture or cultures depicted. To provide a faithful representation of a culture, an author needs to grasp the language, emotions, thoughts, concerns, and experiences of her character rather than shape that character to fit a mainstream point of view. In Ann Rinaldi's *My Heart Is on the Ground: The Diary of Nannie Little Rose, a Sioux Girl,* in addition to many factually inaccurate details, there are cultural miscues as well. For example, Lakota (Sioux) children are taught to be deferential and respectful to their elders and would be unlikely to criticize their mothers. Yet Nannie's disdain for her mother is a thread that runs throughout the book. Her continuing disapproval of her brother's actions also conflicts with the special bond that existed between Lakota brother and sister, one that even exceeded the bond between husband and wife.[5] Comparing these relationships with those of the Ojibwa family in Louise Erdrich's *The Birchbark House* and *The Game of Silence* can reveal the importance of accurate depiction of culture in historical fiction for children. To fail in this regard is, at the very least, insensitive to children who are members of that culture. Such a failure also does a disservice to children from outside that culture whose worldview and understanding could be enriched by exposure to the attitudes, values, and goals of another group.

Although fictional characters and invented turns of plot are accepted in historical novels, nothing should be included that contradicts the actual record of history. If President Lincoln was busy reviewing Union troops in Virginia on a given day in 1863, an author must not "borrow" him for a scene played in New York City, no matter how great the potential dramatic impact. It breaks the unwritten contract between author and child reader to offer misinformation in any form.

Stories must accurately reflect the spirit and values of the time, as well as the events. Historical fiction can't be made to conform to today's more enlightened point of view concerning medical knowledge, women's rights, or civil rights. George Washington can't be saved with a shot of penicillin. Although in Carol Ryrie Brink's *Caddie Woodlawn,* Caddie's father allows her to be a tomboy while she is growing up in the Wisconsin backwoods, it is highly unlikely that girls raised in the Victorian era could refuse to assume the persona of a "proper lady" in adulthood. Many African-Americans may have suffered the indignity of racism in silence as the family in William Armstrong's *Sounder* did. But there were also women and people of many cultures in our history who fought against the roles that society dictated for them. Authors of historical fiction can inspire us with their stories in books based on real characters such as Kirkpatrick Hill's *Dancing at the Odinochka,* Sheila P. Moses's *The Legend of Buddy Bush* and *The Return of Buddy Bush,* and Liza Ketchum's *Where the Great Hawk Flies.*

The historian Christopher Collier, who has collaborated with his brother James Lincoln Collier on several novels set during the era of the American Revolution, maintains that authors should pay careful attention to historiography, "that is, the way that professional historians have approached and interpreted the central episode of the story."[6] Collier believes that authors should weigh opposing views on the causes or meaning of a conflict and decide which should be predominant in the story, but also find a way to include the other significant interpretations. One way is to have different characters espouse different points of view. In *Bull Run,* Paul Fleischman deals with this reality by telling the story of this early battle of the Civil War through the voices of sixteen different characters—northerners and southerners, male and female, civilian and military, slave and free. However, fiction that draws the reader into the thoughts and feelings of a central character cannot be truly impartial. In the middle of a massacre scene, a bleeding settler who cries "But the Indians are only fighting for what is theirs!" will sacrifice the story's credibility. Many fine books, like K. M. Grant's *Blood Red Horse,* Carolyn Reeder's *Shades of Gray,* and Avi's *The Fighting Ground,* do let the reader feel more than one side of an issue. But for a more inclusive viewpoint, teachers and librarians will want to provide a variety of books, each with its own point of view and approach to the topic.

The authenticity of language in historical fiction should be given careful attention. We have no recordings of the speech of people from much earlier times, but the spoken word in a book with an historical background should give the flavor of the period. However, too many *prithee*s and *thou*s will seem artificial and might discourage children's further reading. Some archaic words can be used if they are explained in the content. For example, the book *The Cabin Faced West* notes

---

[3]Mollie Hunter, lecture, the Ohio State University, Columbus, Ohio, November 1968.

[4]Mollie Hunter, "Shoulder the Sky," in *Talent Is Not Enough* (New York: Harper, 1976), pp. 43–44.

[5]Atleo et al., "A Critical Review of Ann Rinaldi's *My Heart Is on the Ground.*"

[6]Christopher Collier, "Criteria for Historical Fiction," *School Library Journal* 28 (August 1982): 32.

that George Washington "bated" at the Hamiltons. The author, Jean Fritz, makes it very clear by the action in the story that "bated" means "stopped by for dinner."

Some words commonly used in earlier times are offensive by today's standards. Authors must consider whether it would be misleading to omit such terms entirely and how necessary such language is for establishing a character. In Graham Salisbury's *Under the Blood-Red Sun,* "haoles," or white Hawaiians, refer to the Japanese as "Japs." The word "nigger" is used by African American authors Julius Lester in *Day of Tears,* Sheila P. Moses in *The Legend of Buddy Bush,* and Walter Mosley in *47.* It would have defeated the purpose and softened the brutality of the times of these stories to have these characters use more acceptable language. Walter Mosley explains *47's* use of the phrase "a nigger like me" in a footnote: "That was before I met Tall John and he taught me about the word 'nigger' and how wrong it was for me to use such a term" (p. 7). Authors' notes about the reasons for choices they have made regarding language are useful to both students and teachers. Explaining the dilemma she faced in *Crooked River,* a story about the clash of Anglo and Native Americans in Ohio in 1812, Shelley Pearsall remarks:

> Sadly, the language of the past also reflected the prejudices and hatreds of the past. Some of the characters in *Crooked River* use words such as *savages, half-breeds,* and *beasts* to describe the Native American people. It was with a heavy heart that I put those words into the story. They were used on the frontier and found in the historical documents I read. Appallingly, even the governor of Ohio used this language in an 1812 address to the Ohio Legislature where he called the Indians "hordes of barbarians." As a historical writer I could not ignore the language of the past, but I hope that it causes readers to reflect upon the destructive power that words of hate can wield. (p. 239)

Pearsall also counteracts the sting of such language by her sensitive shaping of the character of John Mic, an Ojibwa Indian who is accused of the murder of a white man. In the chapters narrated by John, Pearsall chose to use story poems, which she felt best expressed "the powerful, descriptive language" of the Ojibwa.

Teachers should try to be aware of the reasoning behind authors' decisions and should be prepared to discuss controversial issues that arise in books like these with students and their parents.

Well-written historical fiction also makes use of figurative language that is appropriate for the times and characters in the story. For example, in Katherine Paterson's powerful story *Lyddie,* about a farm girl who goes to work in the fabric mills of Lowell, Massachusetts, in the 1840s, all allusions and metaphors are those of an uneducated rural girl. In the very beginning of the story a bear

The cover of Katherine Paterson's *Lyddie* introduces a main character whose fortitude is written on her face. From *Lyddie* by Katherine Paterson, jacket illustration by Debbie Chabrian, copyright © 1991 by Katherine Paterson. Used by permission of Lodestar Books, an affiliate of Dutton Children's Books, a division of Penguin Putnam, Inc.

gets into their farm cabin and Lyddie stares him down while the other children climb the ladder to the loft. Finally she herself backs up to the ladder, climbs it, and pulls it up behind her. Throughout the book Lyddie alludes to "staring down the bears." She thinks of the huge machines as "roaring clattering beasts . . . great clumsy bears" (p. 97). And when she throws a water bucket at the overseer to get him to let go of a young girl, she laughs as she imagines she hears the sound of an angry bear crashing the oatmeal bucket in the cabin. Everything about this book works together to capture Lyddie's view of the world. At the same time, the long thirteen hours a day of factory work, life in the dormitories, the frequency of tuberculosis, and the treatment of women all reflect the spirit and the values of the times. More important than the authenticity of the writing is the fast-paced story and Lyddie's grit, determination, and personal growth.

A book of historical fiction should do even more than relate a good story of the past authentically and imaginatively. It should illuminate today's problems by examining those of other times. The themes of many historical

Evaluating Historical Fiction

- Does the book tell a good story?
- Is fact blended with fiction in such a way that the background is subordinate to the story?
- Is the story as accurate and authentic as possible?
- Does the author provide background information in an afterword or author's note that will help readers distinguish between what is fact and what has been fictionalized?
- Does the story accurately reflect the values and norms of the culture depicted?
- Does the author avoid any contradiction or distortion of the known events of history?

- Are background details authentic, in keeping with accurate information about the period?
- Does the story accurately reflect the values and spirit of the time?
- Are different points of view on the issues of the time presented or acknowledged?
- Does the dialogue convey a feeling of the period without seeming artificial? Does it reflect character as well as setting?
- Is the language of the narrative appropriate to the time, drawing figures of speech from the setting?
- Does the theme provide insight and understanding for today's problems as well as those of the past?

books are basic ones about the meaning of freedom, loyalty and treachery, love and hate, acceptance of new ways, closed minds versus questioning ones, and, always, the age-old struggle between good and evil. Many tales of the past echo recent experience. Books like *Catherine, Called Birdy* by Karen Cushman, *Lyddie* by Katherine Paterson, and *Prairie Songs* by Pam Conrad could well be used in a discussion of the history of women's roles. All these books can shed light and understanding on today's problems.

To summarize, historical fiction must first meet the requirements of good writing, but it demands special criteria beyond that. In evaluating historical fiction the reader will want to consider whether the story meets these specialized needs.

Historical fiction can dramatize and humanize facts of history that can seem sterile in so many textbooks. It can give children a sense of participation in the past and an appreciation for their historical heritage. It should enable the child to see that today's way of life is a result of what people did in the past and that the present will influence the way people live in the future. For some of the most important criteria to keep in mind, see Evaluation Criteria: "Evaluating Historical Fiction."

One way to approach historical fiction is to look at common topics or themes as they are presented in different settings across the centuries; Teaching Resources: "Recurring Themes in Historical Fiction" groups titles by such themes. Another approach is to discuss books chronologically, according to the periods and settings they represent; the following sections are organized in this fashion.

STORIES OF PREHISTORIC TIMES

Anthropologists and geologists are slowly uncovering scientific data that make it possible to imagine what life in prehistoric times might have been like. Authors and

their readers have been fascinated with trying to reconstruct the minds and feelings of primitive people. How did they discover that there were others living in the world? Were all the tribes at the same level of development, or did different groups mature ahead of others? What happened when two groups met? These and other questions have provided the stimulus for several fine stories, many of which center on a character who is an outsider and independent thinker.

T. A. Dyer's *A Way of His Own* deals with early people of North America, a small band of hunters and gatherers on an inland prairie. According to their way, they abandon young Shutok because he cannot keep up and because they believe his "crippled" back houses an evil spirit responsible for all their misfortunes. But Shutok, a well-developed character with great determination, does not die as expected. He is joined by the escaped slave girl Uita, and together the two outcasts kill the fearsome jaguar that invades their cave, struggle against bitter cold and hunger, and live to reclaim a position of worth with Shutok's people. The story is fast-paced, with lively dialogue. Justin Denzel's *Boy of the Painted Cave* and its sequel *Return to the Painted Cave* also center on a hero with disabilities. Tao, a young adolescent, is rejected by his tribe because of a "lame" foot until his wall paintings are believed to bring luck to his tribe. Both stories are strongly plotted, with believable details of Stone Age life.

STORIES OF THE EASTERN HEMISPHERE

Children in the United States are often more interested in stories of the American frontier, the Civil War, or World War II than they are in fiction about ancient or medieval days. However, there is some fine historical fiction that portrays ancient times in vivid and exciting terms.

Recurring Themes in Historical Fiction

 Visit the Online Learning Center at www.mhhe.com/kiefer9e for a printable version of this list.

Theme	Title (Author)	Setting
The clash of cultures	*The Arrow over the Door* (Bruchac)	American Revolution, 1777
	Crooked River (Pearsall)	Ohio, 1812
	The Lantern Bearers (Sutcliff)	Fifth-century England
	The Man from the Other Side (Orlev)	Poland, World War II
	The Sign of the Beaver (Speare)	Maine Territory, 1760s
	Walk across the Sea (Fletcher)	California, 1886
	Where the Great Hawk Flies (Ketchum)	Post–Revolutionary War Vermont
	Witness (Hesse)	Vermont, 1924
	Worlds Apart (Karr)	South Carolina, 1600s
	Year of Impossible Goodbyes (Choi)	North Korea, 1940s
The human cost of war	*The Eternal Spring of Mr. Ito* (Garrigue)	Canada, World War I
	Lord of the Nutcracker Men (I. Lawrence)	Britain, World War II
	My Brother Sam Is Dead (Collier and Collier)	American Revolution
	Private Peaceful (Morpurgo)	World War I
	The Slopes of War (Perez)	U.S. Civil War
In quest of freedom	*Black Storm Comin'* (Wilson)	Pre–Civil War Nevada and California
	The Captive (Hansen)	United States, 1840s
	The Clay Marble (Ho)	Cambodia, 1980s
	Jump Ship to Freedom (Collier and Collier)	United States, 1780s
	North to Freedom (Holm)	Europe, 1940s
Overcoming handicaps	*All the Way Home* (Giff)	United States, 1940s
	Apple Is My Sign (Riskind)	United States, early 1900s
	The Door in the Wall (de Angeli)	Medieval England
	The King's Shadow (Alder)	Medieval England
	A Way of His Own (Dyer)	Prehistoric America
	Wintering Well (Wait)	Maine, 1820s

Ancient Times

The ancient world of Egypt with all of its political intrigue provides a rich background for Eloise McGraw's *Mara, Daughter of the Nile*. Mara, the mistreated slave of a wealthy jewel trader, is bought by a mysterious man who offers her luxury in return for her services as a spy for the queen. On a Nile riverboat Mara meets Lord Sheftu, who employs her as a spy for the king. In this exciting and sinister story of espionage and counterespionage, the transformation of Mara from a selfish, deceitful slave into a loyal and courageous young woman is made slowly and believably. McGraw has written another exciting, complex story of this period of ancient history titled *The Golden Goblet*, which has been reissued in paperback. Julius Lester's *Pharaoh's Daughter* is the story of Batya, who saved the baby Moses, and of Moses, himself, during his teenage years as he struggles to sort out his identity as well as his spiritual beliefs. Jill Rubalcaba's *A Place in the Sun* is a shorter but highly readable adventure set in thirteenth-century Egypt. Senmut, the young hero, is exiled to work in the gold mines in Nubia after he accidentally kills a sacred dove. This is a fate worse than death except that his talent for stone carving comes to the attention of Ramses II and he is eventually freed.

The Roman Empire is well represented in a highly readable mystery series by Caroline Lawrence, *The Thieves of Ostia*, *The Secrets of Vesuvius*, *The Enemies of Jupiter*, *The Gladiators from Capua*, and *The Pirates of Pompeii*. *The Thieves of Ostia*, set in first-century Italy, introduces four lively characters: Flavia, daughter of a Roman merchant; Jonathon, son of a Jewish doctor who lives next door; Nubia, an African slave girl, bought and freed by Flavia; and Lupus, a mute beggar boy. These four become fast friends and wily detectives, solving one mystery after another using their wits and their adolescent energy. Lawrence, who has a degree in classical archaeology, has written highly appealing mysteries, but the setting is so well detailed and described that the books will be valuable additions to the social studies curriculum.

In Elizabeth George Speare's *The Bronze Bow*, Daniel Bar Jamin has one all-consuming purpose in life, to avenge the cruel death of his father and mother by driving the Romans out of his land, Israel. First with an outlaw band, and then with a group of boy guerrillas, Daniel nurses his hatred and waits for the hour to strike. He takes comfort in the verse 2 Samuel 22:35: "He trains my hands for war, so that my arms can bend a bow of bronze." A bronze bow is a symbol for what no one can do. *The Bronze Bow* is the story of Daniel's tormented journey from blind hatred to his acceptance and understanding of love. Only after he has nearly sacrificed his friends and driven his sister, Leah, deeper into mental darkness does he seek the help of Simon's friend, Jesus. The healing strength of Jesus cures Leah, and at that moment Daniel can forgive the Romans. He understands at last that only love can bend the bow of bronze.

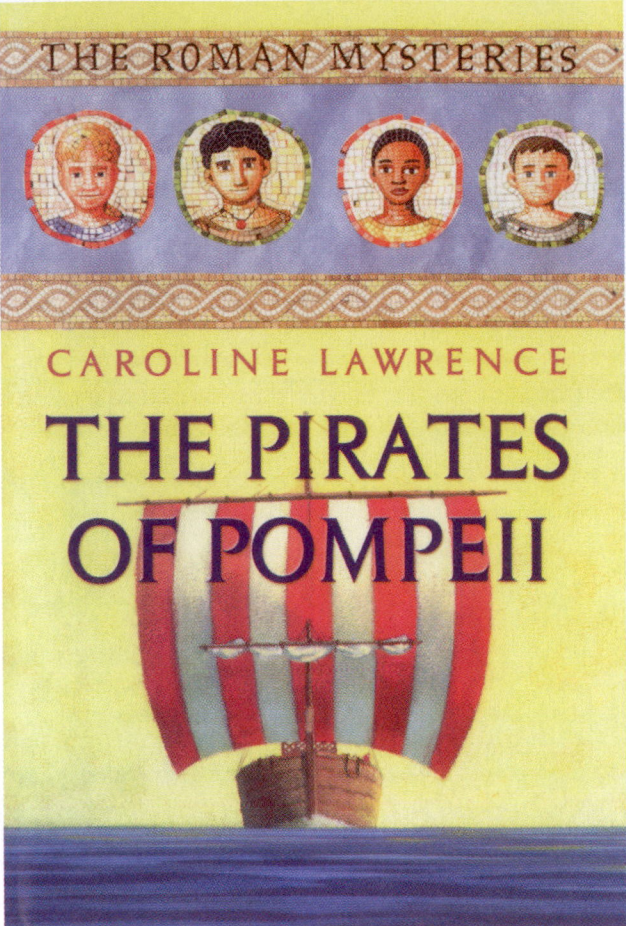

Caroline Lawrence's books, including *The Pirates of Pompeii*, are set during the Roman Empire and involve four young friends whose use of logic and cunning helps them solve a variety of mysteries. *The Pirates of Pompeii: Roman Mystery, Book III.* Copyright © 2002 by Caroline Lawrence. Illustrations by Peter Sutton and Fred van Deelen. Permission granted by Orion Children's Books, an imprint of The Orion Publishing Group.

Each character stands out in this startling story of conflict between good and evil.

Tales of Early Britain

No one has surpassed Rosemary Sutcliff in her ability to recreate the life and times of early Britain. In books such as *Sun Horse, Moon Horse* and *Warrior Scarlet*, she vividly portrays the Iron and Bronze Age peoples of Britain, of whom there is no written record. Equally remarkable, she writes of the native peoples of Britain and of the Roman occupation forces with equal skill and sympathy. Sutcliff's *The Eagle of the Ninth*, *The Silver Branch*, and *The Lantern Bearers* form a trilogy that describes the period when Britain was ruled by Romans. In the third book, the last of the Roman auxiliaries sets sail in its galleys and abandons Britain to internal strife and the menace of invasion by Saxons. At the final moment, one Roman officer decides that his loyalties lie with Britain rather than with the legions. Aquila returns to his family villa, only to see all that he loves destroyed by the Saxons. His father is killed, his sister is captured, and he is enslaved by a band of invaders. Three years later he escapes his thralldom, but it is many years before he can rid himself of the black bitterness of his sister's marriage to a Saxon.

In *The Shining Company* Sutcliff tells of the king's betrayal of his war host of three hundred young men sent to fight the invading Saxons. Among them is his own son, Gorthyn, and his shieldbearer, Prosper. Set in A.D. 600, the story is based on *The Gododdin,* the earliest surviving North British poem. It is a story of adventure and heroism, loyalty and betrayal. Sutcliff's *Sword Song* is a fine coming-of-age story that focuses on the Viking occupation of Britain and on Bjarni Sigurdson, a young Viking warrior who is banished from his village in Northern Scotland for accidentally killing a man.

Rebecca Tingle turns to Southwest England in the late 800s to tell the story of Æthelflæd, the oldest daughter of the legendary King Alfred, in *The Edge on the Sword* and *Far Traveler. The Edge on the Sword* begins as 15-year-old Æthelflæd, or Flæd, is reluctantly betrothed to Ethelred of Mercia. She has never met this older man, but their marriage represents an important alliance for the Anglo-Saxon people. When Flæd, already an accomplished scholar, is threatened by men who seek to destroy the alliance, her bodyguard, Red, is allowed to educate her in the skills of combat. These skills will save her life when, on her journey to Ethelred's stronghold, she and her escorts are attacked by their enemies. Tingle has written an exciting and suspenseful story about the early years of a remarkable woman. Strong-willed, courageous, and intelligent, Flæd represents one of the greatest heroines of early Britain, one who would be called the "most renowned queen of the Saxons" in written records of the time.

The Later Middle Ages

In the Middle Ages, the chivalrous deeds of the knights were a window to the light. Young children of 7 and 8 are intrigued with stories of the days of knighthood. Some of them will be able to read Clyde Bulla's *The Sword in the Tree,* the story of a boy who saved his father and their castle by bravely going to King Arthur for help. Younger readers will also enjoy reading or listening to Newbery Medal winners *Adam of the Road* by Elizabeth Janet Gray and *The Door in the Wall* by Marguerite de Angeli. *Adam of the Road* is the story of Adam; his minstrel father, Roger; and Adam's devoted dog, Nick; who travel the roads of thirteenth-century England. *The Door in the Wall,* set in fourteenth-century England, recounts the dramatic story of Robin, who is set to become a page to Sir Peter de Lindsay until an illness robs him of the ability to walk. Robin's rebellion, final acceptance, and then challenge to live a rich life with his disability should provide inspiration for children today.

English-speaking children know little of the Crusades that took place in the Middle East beginning in 1096 and lasting for more than two centuries. These wars between members of the two major religions of the time have immediate relevance for conflicts in today's world, but for many years they have been touched on only lightly in books for children. More recently, however, three notable series have appeared that will give children a more thorough picture of the Crusades. Although a work of fantasy, Kevin Crossley-Holland's Arthur Trilogy, which ends with *King of the Middle March,* is centered in the Fourth Crusade, which took place in the early thirteenth century (see Chapter 7). Australian writer Catherine Jinks has created a highly entertaining series about Pagan, a wisecracking orphan who reluctantly becomes a squire to the saintly Templar knight Lord Roland Roucy de Bram. *Pagan's Crusade,* the first in the series, provides a balanced look at the conflict between Christian and Muslim and would make an engaging lure for adolescents who may otherwise be reluctant to pick up historical fiction. *Blood Red Horse,* Book 1 of the de Granville Trilogy by K. M. Grant, is perhaps the best of the new books about the Crusades. Featuring brothers Gavin and Will

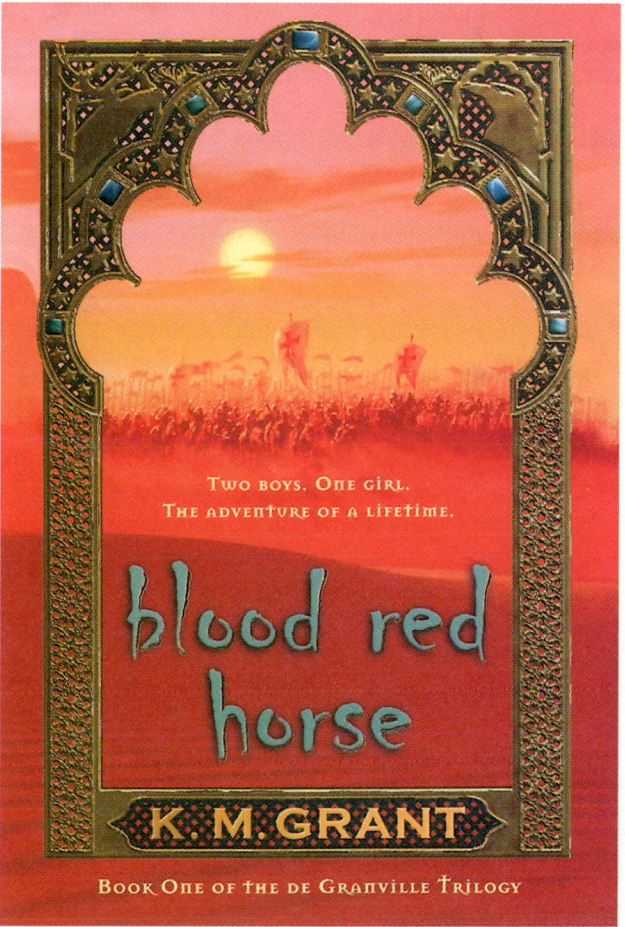

Appealing characters, grand adventures, and Christian and Muslim perspectives on the Crusades are present in K. M. Grant's thrilling *blood red horse. blood red horse: Two Boys. One Girl. The Adventure of a Lifetime.* Written by K. M. Grant. Illustrations copyright © 2004 K. M. Grant. Reproduced by permission of Walker Books, Ltd., London.

de Granville, their cousin Eleanor, and an exceptional horse named Hosanna, the story has a fast-moving plot, highly engaging characters, and worthy themes. Grant places these in a solid foundation of details about the time period. In addition, she introduces the point of view of Kamil, a Muslim youth who has become the trusted aide of the great Muslim leader Saladin. During the course of the story, Grant provides a balanced look at the atrocities committed by both sides in the First Crusade, and we see the human cost of the war to individuals on both sides of the conflict. Middle-grade and middle-school readers will be captivated by this wonderful story. They should also be helped to see the parallels in modern-day conflicts.

Frances Temple's *The Ramsey Scallop* centers upon Eleanor and Thomas, two youngsters who have been betrothed by their families but have grown up with little knowledge of one another. Fourteen-year-old Eleanor is frightened of marriage and the burdens that will be placed upon her as an adult woman. Thomas, just returned from the Crusades, is sick at heart and in spirit, and he doesn't think much of marriage either. Father Gregory, their village priest, proposes a pilgrimage of penance to the shrine of Saint James in Spain. The journey of these two young people (who promise chastity as part of their penance) takes them from England to France and Spain, and gives Temple the opportunity for rich descriptions of life in the Middle Ages. At the same time, however, she never loses sight of Eleanor and Thomas, and she skillfully tells the story of their coming of age and their gaining of faith. Their pilgrimage successfully accomplished, they return home committed to each other and to the future of their community. A companion book, *The Beduins' Gazelle,* follows Etienne, one of the characters Eleanor and Thomas met on their pilgrimage, to the Middle East. Here the young scholar becomes involved with a young Beduin couple and aids in a daring rescue.

Author Karen Cushman has given us two memorable heroines whose experiences provide insights into women's roles in the Middle Ages. The title character of *Catherine, Called Birdy* is the daughter of a minor baron whose schemes to marry her off to one appalling husband after another form the center of the plot. Catherine, called "Birdy" because of the birds she keeps as pets, wishes desperately for the freedom to move about the countryside and beyond the limitations placed upon her. The birds' cages represent her own constraints, and although she escapes from confinement long enough to have an adventure with a dancing bear, she must return to her cage like this performing animal and step into the role she has been given. The outcome is not tragic, however, for Catherine escapes marriage with the worst of her ancient suitors and ends up with a husband who can match her wit and independent spirit. Told in the form of Catherine's journal, the book is earthy and funny. The wonderfully descriptive and often obscure Saints Days that mark each diary entry, as well as her descriptions of

the more vulgar aspects of medieval life, lend Catherine's voice an unusual ring of truth that will appeal especially to middle-school readers.

Cushman's *The Midwife's Apprentice* strikingly contrasts the lot of a midwife's apprentice with Catherine's more privileged life. In fact, this young girl cannot get much farther from a castle keep than the midden heap into which she crawls for warmth at the book's beginning. She has little memory of her origins, and none of her name, and so she is called "Brat" by the urchins who tease and torment her, "Dung Beetle" by the sharp-tongued midwife who takes her in, and "Midwife's Apprentice" by the people in the community to which she has come. As she finds companionship with a stray cat and kindness from some of the people she meets, she also begins to discover her identity. At St. Swithin's Day Fair, she is given a comb, a wink, and a compliment and then is mistaken for a woman named Alyce who knows how to read. These experiences lead her to stop and examine her reflection in a horse trough as she heads for home.

> "And this is me Beetle." She stopped. Beetle was no name for a person, no name for someone who looked like she could read.
>
> Frowning she thought a minute, and then her face shone as though a torch were fired inside her. "Alyce," she breathed. Alyce sounded clean and friendly and smart. You could love someone named Alyce. She looked back at the face in the water. "This then is me Alyce." It was right. (pp. 31–32)

This incident does not end Alyce's story but begins the real tempering-through-adversity that is at the heart of a good book. This Newbery Medal–winning story is almost heartbreakingly beautiful in its portrait of a child who comes to a full understanding of her true self.

The hero of Avi's *Crispin: The Cross of Lead* has no name but "Asta's son," much like the heroine of *The Midwife's Apprentice.* When Asta dies, however, the young man learns that his name is Crispin and that his real identity puts him in terrible danger. Hounded as a less than human "wolf's head" by the evil bailiff Aycliffe, Crispin is aided by Bear, a wandering entertainer, who is secretly working to improve working conditions in fourteenth-century England. Led into one close escape after another, Crispin discovers the reason for Aycliffe's villainy and the true calling of his real name.

In *The King's Shadow* by Elizabeth Alder, it is the year 1053 and Evyn, a young Welsh boy, loses rather than finds his name. He must also give up his dreams of being a "storiawr" (storyteller) when, in revenge for his uncle's misdeed, his tongue is cut out and he is sold into slavery to Lady Ealdgyth, the consort of the Saxon leader Harold Godwinson. Evyn is called "Shadow" because of his black hair, and his bitterness at his fate is just as dark. Yet Lady Ealdgyth is kind to him, and when he breaks his arm she sends him to Lewys, a Welsh monk, who teaches him how to read and write. This ability opens up new doors for him. When he finally accepts the identity fate has handed him, he finds a greater destiny than he had ever imagined. Shadow eventually becomes the squire and then the foster son of Harold Godwinson and witnesses events leading up to the Battle of Hastings. When Harold is defeated and killed by William the Conqueror, Shadow is rescued at the point of death. Nursed back to health by Lewys, he spends his remaining days writing his eyewitness account of these momentous events, an account that will become part of the Anglo-Saxon Chronicle.

Henrietta Branford provides an unusual perspective on the Middle Ages in *Fire, Bed and Bone*. Branford unfolds the events leading up to the Peasant's Revolt in the England of 1381 through the eyes of an old farm dog. The author remains faithful to her character's canine characteristics and perceptions, focusing on sights and smells of the time and revealing the human suffering that abounded. The book is highly believable, a moving account of a period of history on the cusp of consequential social change.

In *The King's Swift Rider* Mollie Hunter has woven an exciting story around the fourteenth-century Scottish hero Robert the Bruce. Young Martin Crawford, the story's narrator, wants to be a scholar rather than a soldier but when he encounters the fugitive Bruce their lives are entwined. Martin becomes the king's swift rider, a spy who passes information about the English army. Over the course of seven years Martin is witness to the brilliant tactics of a man whose forces are outnumbered by the merciless English yet who finally wins Scottish freedom at the battle of Bannockburn. Hunter writes with passion and insight about a crowning moment in Scottish history but never neglects the human relationships and desires that bring good historical fiction to life.

Authors Jane Yolen and Robert J. Harris have built two novels around the lives of royal women of Scotland. *Girl in a Cage* is the story of Marjorie Bruce, daughter of Robert Bruce. Marjorie is held hostage by Edward of England when her father declares himself King of Scotland. Kept in a cage like a wild animal and displayed in a village square, Marjorie exhibits the same courage as her famous father, showing a strong will to survive in the face of the most terrible psychological and physical torture. *The Queen's Own Fool,* also by Yolen and Harris, takes readers into Renaissance Scotland and tells the story of Mary Queen of Scots through the eyes of her fool, Nicola Ambruzzi. Nicola is a performer at the French court when she comes to the attention of Mary. She becomes Mary's trusted companion and is thus in a position to provide an account of Mary's tragic life up to the time of her imprisonment by Elizabeth I. Both books, for older readers, provide a wealth of detail about historical events and life in fourteenth- and sixteenth-century Scotland.

Fifteenth-century Eastern Europe is vividly portrayed as the background of Eric Kelly's Newbery Medal winner *The Trumpeter of Krakow*. This is a complex tale of the quest for the shimmering Great Tarnov Crystal, coveted by a Tartar chieftain for its supposed magical powers and zealously guarded by the ancestral oath of a Ukrainian family.

The Emergence of the Modern World

 The Renaissance and the centuries that followed were particularly remarkable for the flowering of art and architecture that occurred in Europe. Several books have given us glimpses of what life might have been like for the young people who inhabited the world of the great masters. In *The Second Mrs. Giaconda*, E. L. Konigsburg hypothesizes the true identity of the Mona Lisa through the point of view of a young apprentice to Leonardo da Vinci. Set in a later time period, Elizabeth Borton de Trevino's *I, Juan de Pareja* is the fictionalized account of the real apprentice of Spanish master Diego Velázquez. Pilar Molina Llorente's *The Apprentice*, winner of the Batchelder Award, is the story of a Florentine boy whose greatest wish is to become a painter. His father, who is one of the finest tailors in the city, is against this, but he agrees to give Arduino one chance at success in the workshop of Cosimo di Forli. Arduino discovers that the life of an apprentice is tedious at best and that his new master is mean-spirited and worse. Jealous of the talents of Donato, his head assistant, Cosimo has imprisoned him in an attic room. Arduino discovers this secret and befriends Donato, sneaking to his prison late at night, where Donato gives him drawing lessons and talks about painting. When di Forli falls ill and cannot complete a commission, Arduino convinces him to give Donato the chance. Although somewhat melodramatic, the story provides a vivid picture of a time in history that is not often addressed in children's books.

Donna Jo Napoli's *Daughter of Venice,* although not directly concerned with the Italian art world, provides fascinating details of life in Venice in 1592. Fourteen-year-old Donata, the sheltered daughter of a wealthy family, is hungry for the knowledge and adventure denied her because she is a woman. She disguises herself as a boy in order to explore the city and meets a young boy from the Jewish ghetto who helps her get a job as a copyist. An action she takes on behalf of her friends almost brings dishonor on her family, but her parents appreciate her courage and her strong sense of justice, and they eventually give her permission to study at the university, her life-long dream. Napoli based the story of Donata on Elena Lucrezia Cornaro Piscopia, who was the first woman ever to earn a doctoral degree (although almost a century after this book's setting).

The flourishing world of Renaissance theater is portrayed in several excellent works of historical fiction, Gary Blackwood's exciting *The Shakespeare Stealer* and its sequel *Shakespeare's Scribe* and J. B. Cheaney's *The Playmaker* and *The True Prince. The Shakespeare Stealer* begins the story of 14-year-old Widge, a young orphan who has been taught a system of shorthand by an unscrupulous clergyman. Apprenticed to the mysterious Simon Bass, Widge is ordered to attend performances of Will Shakespeare's *Hamlet* in order to copy down the script, a common custom in a time before copyright laws. Instead, he ends up employed at the Globe theater and befriended by many members of the acting company. Widge soon learns for the first time what it means to belong to a "family," and he is torn between his loyalty to the company and his fear of reprisal at the hands of his master. Blackwood does a fine job of portraying Shakespeare's world, yet the fascinating details never overwhelm the exciting story or detract from the engaging characters. Cheaney's hero is Richard Mallory, who becomes an apprentice in Shakespeare's company after the death of Mallory's mother. In *The Playmaker* Richard is involved in uncovering a plot against Queen Elizabeth. *The True Prince* sees Richard involved in another conspiracy, this time involving the company. Sharply plotted and well-written, these books, along with Susan Cooper's *King of Shadows* (discussed in Chapter 7), provide a wonderful context for understanding Shakespeare's plays and the world in which he lived.

Stories in English about life in China, Korea, and Japan during this period are less numerous than those depicting life in Europe, but those that are available give children a fascinating glimpse of life in Asia as well as a satisfying tale. These include Katherine Paterson's masterful stories of feudal Japan: *The Sign of the Chrysanthemum, Of Nightingales That Weep,* and *The Master Puppeteer.* Lensey Namioka has set three exciting stories, *Den of the White Fox, The Coming of the Bear,* and *Island of Ogres,* in the same time period with young samurai warriors as heroes. Dorothy Hoobler and Thomas Hoobler's *The Ghost in the Tokaido Inn, In Darkness, Death,* and *The Demon in the Teahouse* are fast-paced mystery stories set in eighteenth-century Japan. Geraldine McCaughrean's *The Kite Rider* is set in thirteenth-century China and tells the fascinating and swiftly paced story of 12-year-old Haoyou, whose talent for making kites leads him to the court of Kublai Khan. Malcolm Bosse's *The Examination* looks at life in China during the late sixteenth century. Meant for older readers, this book follows two brothers who set out for Beijing, where the older boy hopes to take exams that will ensure his future and restore his family's honor.

Linda Sue Park, a Korean-American, has written several fine books set in Korea's past. Her first book, *Seesaw Girl,* is set in the seventeenth century and tells the story of Jade Blossom, whose desire for knowledge and whose adventuresome spirit provide a nice parallel to Donna Jo Napoli's Donata in *Daughter of Venice,* set half a world away. In *The Kite Fighters,* set in the fifteenth century, two brothers build and fly marvelous kites for the young king of Korea. Park's Newbery Medal–winning *A Single Shard,* set in the twelfth century, tells the fascinating story of Tree-Ear, a young orphan boy who grows up to create the Thousand Cranes vase, a famous masterwork of celadon pottery. At the outset of the story, 12-year-old Tree-Ear's

Linda Sue Park won the Newbery Medal for *A Single Shard,* the story of a young orphan, Tree-Ear, who becomes a master potter of Korea's fabled celadon ware. From the cover of *A Single Shard* by Linda Sue Park. Copyright © 2001 by Linda Sue Park. Reprinted by permission of Clarion Books/Houghton Mifflin Company. All rights reserved.

main concern is to forage for enough food for himself and his old guardian, Crane-Man, but he is fascinated with the work of the potters who live in the village of Ch'ul'po, especially master potter Min. When he accidentally breaks a piece of Min's pottery, the gruff old man grudgingly allows him to work off the cost. Tree-Ear, who had dreamed of working with clay, is set to menial tasks instead. Gradually he gains some measure of Min's confidence and is entrusted with the difficult task of delivering a pot to the King's Emissary at Songdo. His journey is marked by disaster, but his courage is rewarded in a way he never expected. All of Park's books provide fascinating details about the arts, history, and culture of Korea but never at the expense of her stories. She crafts compelling plots and develops likable characters who face their problems with pluck and determination.

Three stories of exploration and adventure round out this time period and lead us into stories set in the Western Hemisphere. Henry Garfield's *The Lost Voyage of John Cabot* alternates between the letters of 14-year-

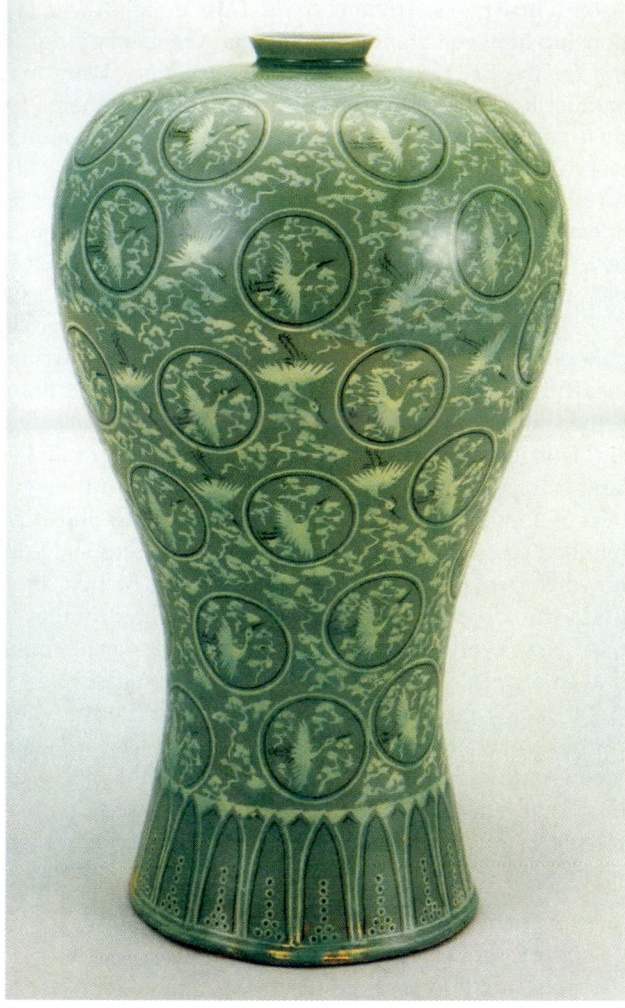

Linda Sue Park wove *A Single Shard* around "The Thousand Cranes Vase," a treasured work of celadon created by an unknown potter who might just have been Tree-Ear. Kansong Museum of Art, South Korea.

takes him around the world. In Karen Hesse's *Stowaway*, 11-year-old Nicholas Young is a stowaway who also sails around the world, almost 150 years later. Nicholas's journey with Captain James Cook and naturalist Joseph Banks is filled with fascinating details based on the diaries of Cook and Banks. Hesse also describes the superior attitudes and the cruelty exhibited by Europeans toward the peoples they encountered. Primarily, however, *Stowaway* is an exciting tale of survival and a young boy's coming of age.

STORIES OF THE WESTERN HEMISPHERE

 Although recorded history in the Americas is relatively brief in comparison to European and Asian chronicles, the years from the fifteenth century to the present have been of interest to many writers of historical fiction. Many of these books show how the past has shaped present events in the United States and in the world.

Native Americans

 Too often in historical fiction, Native Americans have been portrayed as cruel, bloodthirsty savages attacking small groups of helpless settlers. The provocations for the attacks are seldom explained. Thus, in Walter Edmonds's story *The Matchlock Gun*, the reader can only guess the Indians' reasons for wounding Edward's mother and burning their cabin. In Rachel Field's *Calico Bush*, the Indians seem equally cruel as they burn the settler's house.

More recently, several Native American authors have written fine works of historical fiction that begin to balance the picture of Native American cultures that children have seen in earlier books. In *The Birchbark House* and *The Game of Silence*, Louise Erdrich has created a moving and significant counterpart to Laura Ingalls Wilder's Little House books. In both books Omakayas (Little Frog), an Ojibwa girl living on an island in Lake Superior, relates her experiences over the course of a single year, recounting details of family and tribal life and customs and the tragedies that almost overcame her people. Erdrich's exquisite writing lends great power to the story. Although Omakaya's voice is more sophisticated than we would expect from a child of 7 and then 9, her emotions and reactions to events seem authentic, and young readers will have no trouble identifying with Omakayas just as they do with Laura Ingalls. The books would make a fine read-aloud for children in the middle grades and, shared with Wilder's *Little House in the Big Woods*, would provide many opportunities for comparison and discussion.[7] The Web "The Birchbark House" on pages 558–59

old Sancio, a member of Cabot's crew on his mysterious second voyage, and the story of Cabot's youngest son, Sebastian, who has resentfully remained behind in England. Garfield provides a fact-filled but fascinating narrative for an historical period that appears dry in many textbooks. Michelle Torrey's *To the Edge of the World* provides the details that will allow children to understand the obstacles faced by the early explorers of the fifteenth and sixteenth centuries. A thrilling survival tale, this book focuses on the voyage of Ferdinand Magellan. At the outset, Mateo, a 14-year-old Spanish boy, has been orphaned by the plague. When Gonzalo de Espinosa offers him the job of cabin boy on one of the ships about to set sail on a voyage to the Spice Islands, Mateo has no good reason to refuse. He sets out on what will be the greatest adventure of his life, a three-year journey that

---

[7]See Michael Dorris, "Trusting the Words," *Booklist* 89.1 and 89.15 (June 1993): 1820–22, for the perspective of a Native American parent on the Little House books.

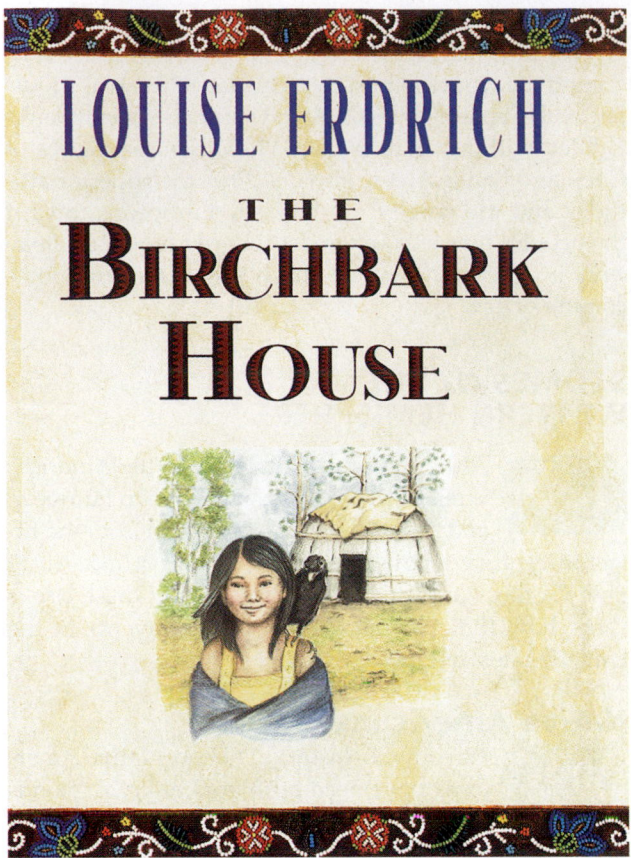

In *The Birchbark House* Louise Erdrich provides a moving account of Native American life in the mid-nineteenth century through the eyes of a 7-year-old Ojibwa girl. *The Birchbark House* by Louise Erdrich. Copyright © 1999. Louise Erdrich. Reprinted by permission of Hyperion Books for Children.

suggests opportunities for study of this book and connections teachers might make to other books and other events in American history.

Joseph Bruchac, well known for his many picture books and collections of legends and Native lore, has written several fine works of historical fiction that focus on the peoples of the northeastern woodlands. Bruchac's *Dawn Land,* set during the Ice Age, is a richly detailed novel for older readers that weaves together Native American folklore and spiritual values with an exciting coming-of-age story. *Children of the Longhouse* is set in the late 1400s, before European contact, and tells an exciting story of Ohkwa'ri', a young Mohawk boy who overhears plans by young warriors in his village to raid a neighboring village. Such an act would violate the terms of the Great League of Peace, which bound the Iroquois nations. Ohkwa'ri' prevents the raid but earns the enmity of the older boys. Their conflict is played out in a game of Tekwaarathon (which later became lacrosse). *The Winter People* tells of 14-year-old Saxso, whose Abenaki village in Canada is attacked by British soldiers during the French and Indian War in 1759. Saxso sets out to track down the raiders and rescue his mother and two younger

sisters. Bruchac's *Arrow over the Door* details the relationship between Stands Straight, an Abenaki boy fighting for the British during the Revolutionary War, and Samuel Russell, a Quaker lad whose family adheres to their pacifist principles. This is a readable and engaging story of the clash between Abenaki and European cultures that is a good companion story to Elizabeth George Speare's *Sign of the Beaver* (discussed later in the chapter). Bruchac has also written two excellent fictionalized biographies, of *Sacajawea* and *Geronimo*.

Author Michael Dorris wrote three books that evoke generalities of a Native American way of life, drawing his reader emotionally close to his characters rather than providing specific details of time and place. In *Morning Girl* Dorris gives us an almost ethereal portrait of an island culture and two children who are the central members of a loving family unit. Morning Girl and Star Boy tell their stories in alternate chapters, providing insights into their own personalities as well as details of their day-to-day life on the island. A terrible storm, their mother's miscarriage, and Star Boy's running away are events that emerge in a circular pattern characteristic of Native American storytelling. One day, curious to know what people see when they look at her, Morning Girl asks her mother and her brother, but their answers do not satisfy her. Finally her father motions her to stand beside him. He kneels down beside Morning Girl and tells her to look into his eyes. She explains,

> I leaned forward, stared into the dark brown circles, and it was like diving into the deepest pools. Suddenly I saw two tiny girls looking back. Their faces were clear, their brows straight as canoes, and their chins as narrow and clean as lemons. As I watched their mouths grew wide. They were pretty.
>
> "Who are they?" I couldn't take my eyes off those strange new faces. "Who are these pretty girls who live inside your head?"
>
> "They are the answer to your question," Father said. "And they are always here when you need to find them." (p. 36)

It is through such evocative reflecting, rather than through the relating of particular facts, that we learn the most about these people. The ending, an excerpt from Christopher Columbus's journal describing Morning Girl's people, is all the more powerful because we have come to know them with such intimacy.

Dorris's *Guests* and *Sees Behind Trees* offer additional perspectives on Native American cultures. In *Guests* Dorris enlarges our understanding of the American Thanksgiving holiday, an event that has long been portrayed from a European point of view. *Guests* begins as an unnamed people are preparing to share their yearly harvest meal with some strange outsiders. These people are never named, nor is Moss's tribe identified, but children are likely to make the connection to Pilgrim and Pawtuxet. Young Moss is angered that this special time will be ruined by ignorant people who don't know how to behave properly. He runs off into the forest, hoping to learn his true identity during a special coming-of-age event, but he really discovers that the world is much more complicated than he had first considered. "Sees Behind Trees" is the name eventually earned by young Walnut, a boy who cannot live up to tribal expectations for males because of his poor eyesight. Walnut learns to compensate for his near-sightedness by increasing his sensitivity to his surroundings through other senses. Then through a series of events he truly discovers his identity and earns his new name. In all his books Dorris's skill with characterization lends emotional power to our reading.

Another fine book that relates historical events about Native Americans, although it might lack nuances of cultural details, is Scott O'Dell's *Sing Down the Moon*. O'Dell's title takes on tragic significance when compared to the southwestern Indians' creation myths that tell of "singing up the mountains." His book describes the Long Walk, the disastrous three-hundred-mile march the Navajo were forced to make from their canyon homes to Fort Sumter. One of the most popular stories about Native Americans is O'Dell's Newbery Medal book *Island of the Blue Dolphins*. Based on fact, the story concerns Karana, an Indian girl who lived alone on an island off the coast of California for some eighteen years. Following an attack by Aleuts who had come to kill otters, all of Karana's people leave their island home by boat. When Karana realizes that her younger brother has been left on the island, she jumps overboard and returns to him. Within a few hours the boy is killed by wild dogs, and memories of the tribe are all Karana has left. Despite her despair when she realizes the boat will not return, Karana creates a life for herself. She makes a house and utensils and fashions weapons, although in so doing she violates a tribal taboo against women making weapons. Eventually she makes friends with the leader of the dog pack, and thereafter enjoys his protection and companionship. When Spanish priests "rescue" Karana, she leaves in sadness. The reader may question whether she will find as much happiness at the mission with human companionship as she had known alone on the island. The question is answered in a sequel, *Zia*, in which Karana's last days are witnessed through the eyes of her niece.

Several books are based on accounts of Indians' capture of white settlers. *Calico Captive* by Elizabeth George Speare is for more mature readers. Based on real people and events, this is a fictionalized account of the experiences of young Miriam Willard, who had just been to her first dance when she was captured by Indians. Her sister, brother-in-law, three children, and a neighbor are captured with her, taken to Montreal, and sold as slaves. Their hardships and ordeals are taken from a diary kept by a real captive in 1754. Speare tells this story with her usual fine characterizations and attention to authentic detail. Often white settlers captured by Indians, espe-

cially young children, found it difficult to return to their former lives. In *Moccasin Trail* by Eloise McGraw, Jim Heath is rescued from a grizzly bear by Crow Indians and brought up to think and feel like an Indian. Eventually reunited with his younger sister and brothers, Jim longs for the sensible Indian ways. *Jenny of the Tetons* by Kristiana Gregory is the fictionalized account of an Englishman called Beaver Dick and his Shoshone wife, Jenny. When an Indian attack leaves Carrie Hill wounded and alone, she decides to join Beaver Dick and help care for his family. She is horrified when she finds that he is married to a Native American, but she gradually learns to respect this gentle person who carefully tends her wound. This is a moving story of changing relationships.

Two books, *Crossing the Panther's Path* by Elizabeth Alder and *Crooked River* by Shelley Pearsall, provide a glimpse of the years following the Revolutionary War when the great Western expansion began. Alder based her characterization on the real Billy Calder, the 15-year-old son of a Mohawk mother and an Irish father, who witnessed the events that led to the War of 1812 from his unique cross-cultural perspective. In this well-written and engrossing story Billy, well-educated and fluent in several European and Indian tongues, is appalled at the American settlers' treatment of the Indians as they push westward toward the Mississippi. He joins the entourage of the great Shawnee chief Tecumseh and is witness to Tecumseh's struggle to unite the Indian tribes against the Americans. Rebecca Carver, the heroine of *Crooked River*, is the daughter of white settlers who returns to her Ohio home in 1812 to find that her father is holding Amik, an Ojibwa, to be tried for murder. Also based on a true story, *Crooked River* depicts Rebecca's struggle between her community's xenophobic outlook and her own sense of right and wrong. Added to Rebecca's voice is that of the gentle Amik and his own attempts to understand the justice of the white man.

Several books based on the experiences of real indigenous peoples are set in the more recent past. Kirkpatrick Hill's *Dancing at the Odinochka* is a highly enjoyable if ultimately sad story of Russian Alaska in the late 1800s and the cross-cultural blending that occurred between Russian traders and Native peoples. Hill, who has lived most of her life in rural Alaska, has told a story that rivals Louise Erdrich's books in its mischievous heroine, Erinia, and in its details of everyday life.

Peter Lerangis's *Smiler's Bones* is the heartbreaking story of Minik, one of the six natives of Greenland to be coerced into following explorer Robert Peary to New York City. Once there, they were literally put on exhibit at the Museum of Natural History and then virtually abandoned by Peary. When Minik's father, Qisuk, dies, his body is boiled and his skeleton used as a research exhibit. Minik, who at first seems to have become comfortable with his new life, finally finds out that his father has not been given the proper burial demanded by his

Wonderfully Exciting Books

Childhood vs. Adulthood

Growing Up

What are the events in Omakayas's life that contribute to her maturity? Make a time line of these events.

Omakayas longs to grow up so that she may experience various privileges. She learns, however, that with growth comes both privilege and responsibility. Think about the privileges that you have gained as you have grown. Which would you rather be, adult or child? Why? Think about the common English saying, "The grass is always greener on the other side." How might this saying apply to desires to grow up?

Play

Native American children of Omakayas's time obviously did not have video games or televisions with which to entertain themselves. What toys, games, or hobbies were used as entertainment by the Ojibwa children?

Go to a park or a place outdoors. Use natural materials to make your own toy or game.

Education

Oral Tradition

What do Omakayas and her siblings learn from oral stories? Make a mural depicting these stories and the lessons learned.

Read and listen to more Ojibwa stories. Memorize one story and tell it aloud.

Grandmother's Gift: Stories from the Anishinabeg (Dunn)
When Beaver Was Very Great (Dunn)
Winter Thunder (Dunn)

Is the oral tradition of storytelling still alive today? If so, what role does it play? Ask a parent or grandparent about a story that has been passed down from generation to generation in your family or cultural groups. Make an audio or visual recording of this story to share with generations to come.

Missionary Schools vs. Ojibwa Education

Compare and contrast these two approaches to education. What types of things were taught in each? Who did the teaching? Create a Venn diagram to show differences and similarities.

THE BIRCHBARK HOUSE BY LOUISE ERDRICH: A WEB OF POSSIBILITIES

Clothing

When making clothing, the Ojibwa people paid attention to both comfort and style. What materials did they use for clothing and how did they add style? Find passages where the clothing is described and draw the members of the family as you imagine they would look from the descriptions. Read *Shannon: An Ojibwa Dancer* (King) for a closer look.

Learn more about Ojibwa beadwork. Design your own Ojibwa dress shirt or moccasins.

Shelter

The Ojibwa people used the materials available to them to make their summer and winter homes. Make a sketch or model of each, pointing out the similarities and differences.

Economics

The Objiwa people traded for goods with others. Write receipts for what was given and what was gained in various trades in the books. Can you figure out the hierarchy? What goods were most and least valuable? Why?

Survival

Food

Make a list of various types of food Omakayas's family eats. In a time before supermarkets and convenience stores, the accumulation of food was the responsibility of the entire community. Make a web showing the division of labor among the family.

Read *Ininatig's Gift of Sugar* (Wittstock) and *Four Seasons of Corn* (Hunter). Create an Ojibwa cookbook and have an Ojibwa feast.

Hardships

Omakayas watches as her entire family falls ill with smallpox. Keep a diary in Omakayas's voice. What kinds of thoughts would she have written down during this period of her life?

When Neewo dies Omakayas grieves. Eventually she begins to enjoy life again. Choreograph and perform an interpretive dance illustrating Omakayas's cycle of emotions during this period.

European settlers brought many diseases with them, as well as plant and animal life, that the Native Americans and the local ecosystems were not equipped to handle. What modern-day issues of this sort does the United States face? Find out about Asian longhorn beetles or other pests that have been introduced to the Western Hemisphere. Write an informational brochure that could be made available to the public.

Literary Elements

Characterizations

How does the author's use of descriptive language contribute to the reader's visual image of various characters? Make a list of some of the adjectives and phrases that you find.

What personality traits do Old Tallow, Deydey, Little Pinch, and Omakayas represent? Create character portraits for one of these characters.

Point of View

This story is told from the third-person point of view. What are the pros and cons of writing from this perspective? Retell a chapter of your choice from the point of view of Old Tallow, Deydey, Little Pinch, Omakayas, or even one of the animals.

The Shape of the Novel

What shape does the novel take? Make a visual representation of the novel's main events.

The last chapter is titled "Full Circle." How does Erdrich establish a pattern of circles in this book? What other patterns can you find in the writing?

The Author

How is Louise Erdrich personally connected to this novel? Read her biography at <www.voices.cla.umn .edu/authors/LouiseErdrich.html>.

Humans and Nature

Omakayas comes into contact with various birds and mammals. Make a list of wildlife she encounters. Use a field guide to find out more about the habitats, physicality, and behaviors of some of these creatures. Are there any creatures that are now extinct or endangered? If so, what are the causes? How would Omakayas feel about such a loss?

The Ojibwa people use vegetation and wildlife for survival purposes. They take only what they need (as with birchbark, p. 7) and use all of what they kill. What other evidence can you find of this practice? Read *Spirit of the White Bison* (Culleton) and compare the Ojibwa ethic with the ethics of the white settlers of the time. Look at your own life. Make a list of the types of waste you see around you.

Nakomis states, "We're very small . . . just human." (p.101). The Ojibwa do not view humans as the greatest of all living things. Rather, they see themselves as just a small part of the larger universe. This is partially evidenced by their prayer to animal spirits. Modern American culture views human life as the most important. How do you think today's view of human beings affects the environment? Quality of life? Write an editorial arguing for or against the Ojibwa worldview.

Relationships

Family and Friends

Old Tallow is a very frightening figure at the beginning of the book. How does Omakayas's relationship with Old Tallow change?

Can you think of any other books that have a similar relationship between an older character and a young one?

Omakayas has some pretty exciting encounters with animals. How do the animals change her? Look back at Omakayas's encounters with Andeg and the bear cubs. Make a plot graph of these events from the novel. First put events in order from beginning to end. Then rank them according to how exciting they are.

On pages 10 and 11 the author begins to describe the very different relationships that Omakayas has with each of her three siblings. The relationship between Omakayas and each of these siblings evolves over time. What are the steps in the evolution? Do any of her relationships with a sibling remind you of one you have?

Compare the role of the elderly in Ojibwa society in the book and the roles of the elderly in your culture and present community. Draw a Venn diagram showing likenesses and differences.

White Settlers and the Ojibwa People

"LaPointe was becoming more Chimookoman every day, and there was talk of sending the Anishinabeg to the west" (p. 77). Many white settlers believed that it was the divine right of the white man to move into and occupy what is now the western United States. Thousands of native peoples were forced off their lands. Find out more about these forced relocations. Divide into groups to study the experiences of different tribes. See *Children of the Wild West* (Freedman) for further background information.

Check out original maps of the growing U.S. territories. Fishtail tells Angeline and Omakayas, "I went to the priest's school. To learn to read the Chimookoman's tracks. That way they can't cheat us with treaties" (p. 112). Examine an old treaty at <www.ohiokids.org/ohc/history/h_indian/treaties/mr1817.html>. What are the pros and cons to this treaty? If you were a settler or native of that time, what kind of treaty would you make? Write your own treaty. Be sure to be able to defend your reasoning for the agreements in a debate.

The Erie Canal made passage westward through Ojibwa/Chippewa territory easier. How did technology and construction affect life in the 1800s for natives? Settlers? Compare this construction with modern-day prospects of drilling for oil in the Arctic National Refuge. What are the positive and negative consequences?

After reading *The Birchbark House*, read *The Little House in the Big Woods* (Wilder), *Prairie Songs* (Conrad), and *The Game of Silence* (Erdrich). Construct a comparison chart showing likenesses and differences among the books. How might the groups in these books have reconciled their differences? Create a play where the main characters come together to talk about their experiences with each other's culture.

How important is it to experience multiple points of view of historical and current events? What examples can you find of culture clashes occurring in today's world? Make a bulletin board of news clippings, and suggest solutions. Find and read other books that provide multiple viewpoints of events in history.

Web prepared by Alison Coviello

people. He spends most of the rest of his sad life trying to right this terrible wrong.

Mature readers will also enjoy the highly fictionalized biography *Ishi, Last of His Tribe* by Theodora Kroeber. Most of the Yahi Indians of California had been killed or driven from their homes by the invading gold seekers and settlers during the early 1900s, but a small band resisted their fate by living in concealment. Ishi is the last survivor of this tribe, and hungry and ill, he allows himself to be found. Haltingly, he tells his story to an anthropologist, who takes him to live at the University of California's museum. Here he dwells happily for five years, helping to record the language and ways of the Yahi world.

Colonial America

The varied settings and conflicts of colonial America have inspired an unusually large number of books about this period. *A Lion to Guard Us* by Clyde Bulla tells of three motherless London children who sail to Jamestown in hopes of finding their father, who has gone ahead to the new colony. The carefully limited historical detail and simple writing style make this book accessible to readers as young as 8 or 9. Several fine picture books also bring this time period alive for younger readers. *The Thanksgiving Story* by Alice Dalgliesh details the life of one family on the *Mayflower,* including their hardships on the voyage and during their first winter. It tells, too, of joy in the arrival of their new baby, of spring in their new home, of planting, harvest, and giving thanks. *The Pilgrims of Plimoth,* written and illustrated with full-color illustrations by Marcia Sewall, provides a descriptive text that discusses the travels of the Pilgrims and their way of life at the settlement. Using George Ancona's black-and-white photographs of the reconstructed settlement at Plymouth Plantation, Joan Anderson presents her concept of the first Thanksgiving in *The First Thanksgiving Feast.* The text includes dialogue based on historical accounts from the era. All these picture books are appropriate for children in grades 2 and up. They can serve to celebrate Thanksgiving or as an introduction to a serious study of the Pilgrims. Older readers can find a more detailed account of the difficulties of these early voyages in Katherine Kirkpatrick's *Escape Across the Wide Sea.* This book focuses on the less well known plight of persecuted French Huguenots in 1686 and also touches on the horrors of the slave trade.

Younger children will enjoy *The Cabin Faced West* by Jean Fritz, the poignant story of lonely 10-year-old Ann Hamilton, who was the only girl in the wilderness of early eastern Pennsylvania. Although the story takes place more than 150 years later than that of the Pilgrims, Ann Hamilton's longing for the books and other niceties she formerly owned is a familiar theme. Ann's father urges the family to look forward, or westward, toward their new life. At last, a special occasion arises when George Washington stops at the Hamilton cabin for dinner. Ann wears ribbons in her hair and sets the table in the way she has longed to do. This final episode is based

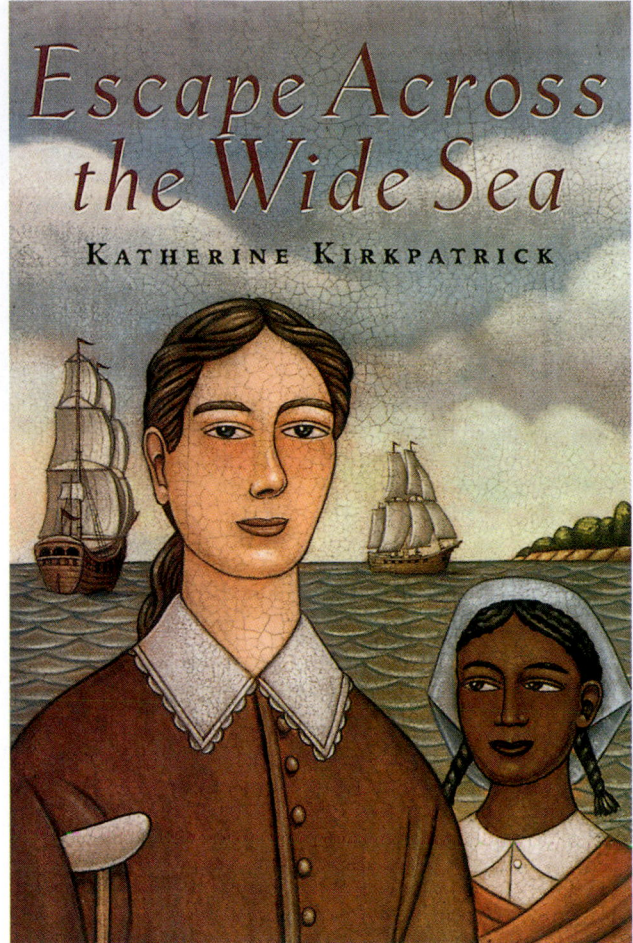

In Katherine Kirkpatrick's *Escape Across the Wide Sea* a Huguenot boy and his family end up on a slave ship to Africa when they attempt to escape persecution in France. Cover of *Escape Across the Wide Sea* © 2004 by Long Gao and Katherine Anne Kirkpatrick. Illustration by Marc Burckhardt © 2004. All rights reserved. Reprinted from *A Child's Calendar,* written by John Updike, by permission of Holiday House, Inc.

on fact and really happened to Ann Hamilton, who was the author's great-great-grandmother.

A study of the Pilgrims might begin with Patricia Clapp's *Constance: A Story of Early Plymouth,* which is written in the form of a diary and details the story of Constance Hopkins, a young girl who sailed on the *Mayflower.* Constance describes the grim first winter at Plymouth— the fear of Indians, the deaths of many of the colonists, and difficulties with the English backers of the settlement. The device of a diary allows the author to use first-person narrative, which promotes the reader's immediate identification with Constance. An excellent romance, the book is all the more fascinating for being the story of real people.

The Puritans soon forgot their struggle for religious freedom as they persecuted others who did not follow their beliefs or ways. Older students will thoroughly enjoy the superb story *The Witch of Blackbird Pond* by Elizabeth George Speare. Flamboyant, high-spirited Kit Tyler is a misfit in the Puritan household of her aunt and stern-faced uncle. The only place where Kit feels any peace or freedom is in the meadows near Blackbird Pond. Here she meets the lonely, bent figure of Quaker Hannah, regarded as a witch by the colonists. Here, too, Kit meets Nathaniel Eaton, the sea captain's son, with his mocking smile and clear blue eyes. Little Prudence, a village child, also comes to the sanctuary in the meadows. One by one, outraged townspeople draw the wrong conclusions, and the result is a terrifying witch hunt and trial. The story is fast-paced and the characters are drawn in sharp relief against a bleak New England background. *Tituba of Salem Village* by Ann Petry focuses on the witch-hunting frenzy that occurred in Salem, Massachusetts, in 1692. The fact that Tituba is both a slave and black makes her particularly vulnerable to suspicion and attack from the obsessed witch hunters in Salem. A sense of foreboding, mounting terror, and hysteria fill this story of great evil done in the name of God.

In Paul Fleishman's *Saturnalia,* 14-year-old William has survived a vicious attack by the Massachusetts Militia that took place during King Phillip's War, a Native American uprising that occurred in Massachusetts in 1675. William is apprenticed to a printer, who has the boy taught Greek and Latin and the Bible and treats him as a member of his family. Fleishman weaves the complex stories of good and evil characters back and forth like a musical fugue. Only William is a part of all the worlds depicted here: night and day, servant and family,

Indian and colonial, educated and nonliterate. His is the melody that holds this many-layered novel together.

Kathleen Karr's *Worlds Apart* relates a moving story of the first Europeans to arrive in South Carolina and the members of the Sewee tribe who had settled there after being driven from their homes in the West by warring tribes. Christopher West is the son of the acting governor when the shipload of settlers arrive in the spring of 1670. They are welcomed by the Native Americans, among them a young man named Asha-po. Asha-po and Christopher become friends and soon learn each other's language. Asha-po and his people teach the new settlers techniques of survival, and Christopher comes to admire their way of life and their beliefs. He is also aware of the tragic conflict that exists in views of land ownership that ultimately drives the Sewees to seek redress in England. The tragic result of the conflict of cultures is similar in *The Sign of the Beaver* by Elizabeth George Speare. Set in the territory of Maine, just prior to the Revolutionary War, the story features two boys, Matt, who is left to tend the new cabin while his father goest back to Massachusetts for the rest of the family, and Attean, grandson of the chief of the Beaver clan. The story explores their growing friendship, their changing attitudes, and the shifting balance between their two cultures.

The Sign of the Beaver, although presenting detailed portraits of the lives of the white settlers, has been criticized for its inaccurate portrayal of Native Americans.

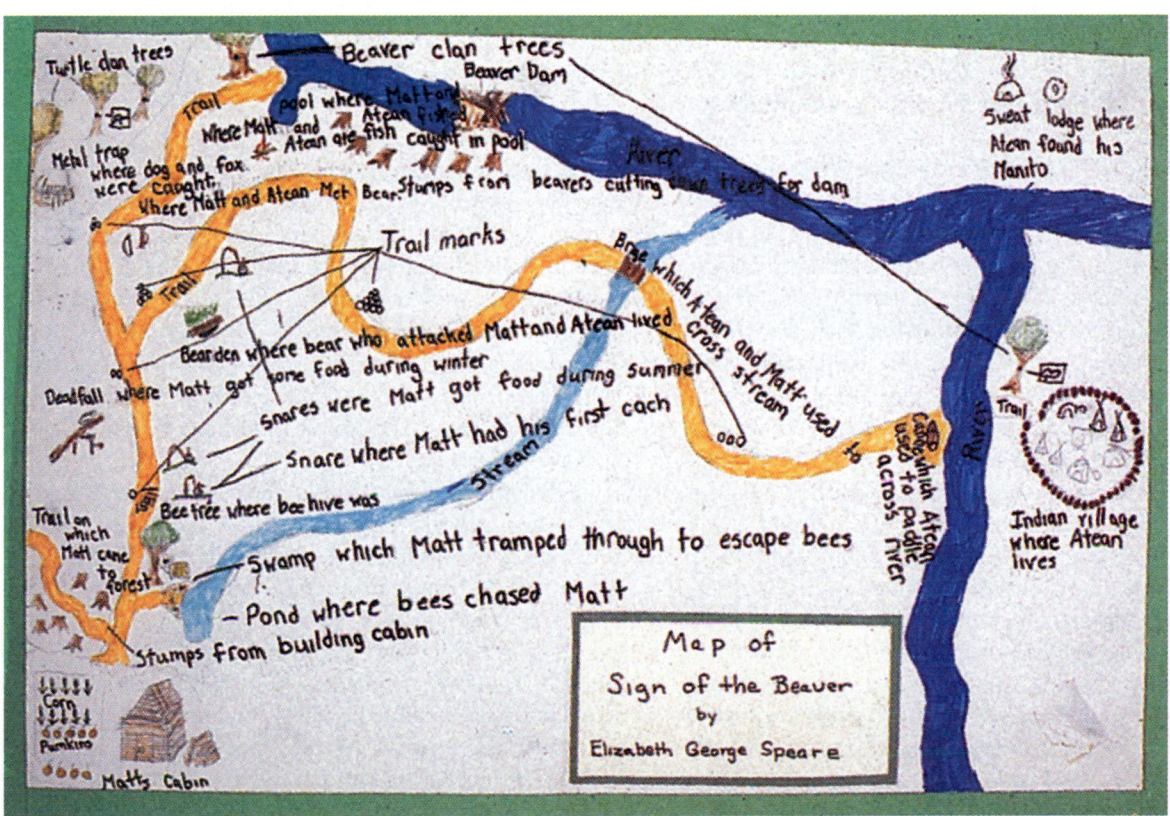

One of the projects that grew out of an in-depth study of Elizabeth George Speare's *The Sign of the Beaver* was this imaginary map of the places in the story. Barrington Road School, Upper Arlington, Ohio. Marlene Harbert, teacher.

Teachers who choose to include it as part of their social studies will want to ask children to apply a critical lens in their reading of the book. They might ask children to compare *The Sign of the Beaver* with Karr's *Worlds Apart* and Joseph Bruchac's *The Arrow over the Door,* which establishes a similar relationship between Stands Straight, an Abenaki boy fighting for the British during the Revolutionary War, and Samuel Russell, a Quaker lad whose family adheres to their pacifist principles. Although Bruchac's book is set in a later period than *The Sign of the Beaver,* it presents a Native American point of view and would promote critical discussion.

The Revolutionary Era

One of the best-known stories of the American Revolution for children is *Johnny Tremain* by Esther Forbes. Johnny Tremain is a silversmith's apprentice, a conceited, cocky young lad who is good at his trade and knows it. The other apprentices are resentful of his overbearing manner and are determined to get even with him. Their practical joke has disastrous results, and Johnny's hand is maimed for life. Out of a job and embittered, Johnny joins his new friend Rab and becomes involved in pre-Revolutionary activities. As a dispatch rider for the Committee of Public Safety he meets such men as Paul Revere, John Hancock, and Samuel Adams. Slowly, Johnny regains his self-confidence and overcomes his bitterness. Rab is killed in the first skirmish of the Revolution, and Johnny is crushed but not defeated. Somehow, this greatest of blows makes him a man of fortitude and courage, a new man of a new nation.

For Johnny Tremain, the decision to join the Patriot cause was clear. In many other books, because the Loyalist tradition and point of view are presented in a more compelling way, the characters are perceived to have a more difficult choice. In *Early Thunder* by Jean Fritz, 14-year-old Daniel adopts his father's loyalty to the king. Daniel hates the rowdy Liberty Boys who creep up on Tory porches and distribute their "Liberty Gifts" of manure, but he becomes equally disillusioned by the British attitudes. Daniel's struggle to sort out his loyalties will help children see that issues in war are seldom clear-cut.

My Brother Sam Is Dead by James Lincoln Collier and Christopher Collier tells of conflicting loyalties within a family and the injustices that are always inflicted on the innocent in time of war. Sam is the only member of his Connecticut family who is fighting for the rebel cause. Ironically, Sam is falsely accused of stealing his own cattle and is executed as an example of General Putnam's discipline. No one will believe the real facts of the case, for despite Sam's excellent war record, his family are Tories. This story takes on special poignancy because it is told by the younger brother, Tim, who loves and admires Sam.

Some of the same dreams of glory that drew Sam into the Patriot army plague 13-year-old Jonathan in *The Fighting Ground* by Avi. In 1778, near Trenton, Jonathan desperately wants to be in on the "cannons and flags and drums and dress parades." When he is caught up in a real battle and captured by Hessians who seem no worse than the Patriots, Jonathan does not know which way to turn. The action takes place in little more than one day, with the text divided into many short segments labeled by the hour and minute. This makes the book look simpler than it is, for although the print is not dense on the page, the story makes strong emotional demands on the reader.

The title character in Scott O'Dell's *Sarah Bishop* hates war, and with good reason. Her father, a British Loyalist, dies after being tarred and feathered by Patriot sympathizers. Her brother dies on a British prison ship, and Sarah herself is arrested on a false pretense. She escapes and flees to the Connecticut wilderness, where she struggles against the elements instead of soldiers. Her biggest battle is with herself, however, as she brings herself to face the world of towns and people once again. This story is based on the experiences of a real Sarah Bishop during the Revolutionary period. *Just Jane* by William Lavender tells the story of a British girl caught in very different circumstances than Sarah. Jane is Lady Jane Prentice who, following her father's death in England, comes to live with her Uncle Robert, in Charleston, South Carolina, in the early part of 1776. Robert Prentice is a firmly loyal British supporter but other extended family members are not, and Jane is soon caught among the types of conflicts that faced so many families in America at the time. This book is better read as light romance than as serious fiction, but it does present a different view of the Revolutionary War and a setting that is less often explored in children's fiction.

Another little-known story of the American Revolution is that of a spunky young girl named Tempe Wick, who hid her horse in her bedroom for three days to save it from Revolutionary soldiers looting the countryside around their New Jersey camp. Finally, when a soldier demanded to search the house, the feisty Tempe threw him out in the snow. This humorous legend of the Revolutionary War is told by Patricia Lee Gauch in a brief book, *This Time, Tempe Wick?* A fuller characterization of this heroine is given in Ann Rinaldi's novel for older readers, *A Ride into Morning.*

Few stories are available about the role of African Americans prior to and during the Revolutionary era. Older readers will enjoy the extensive period details in Ann Rinaldi's *Hang a Thousand Trees with Ribbons,* the tragic story of Phillis Wheatley, an African American poet whose talents were largely unrecognized during her short lifetime. The Collier brothers have featured black characters in several books, however, including a trilogy that deals with the wartime problems of blacks in the northern colonies and their futile hope for a guarantee of liberty under the new government. In *Jump Ship to Freedom,* the memory of the late Jack Arabus, who had won his freedom in the courts as a result of his service in the Continental army, serves as inspiration for his son Dan. The boy's first problem is keeping the soldiers' notes earned by Jack to buy his family's freedom. Even if the notes can be saved, they might be worth nothing under the terms of the new Constitution just being written. Exciting action brings Dan as a messenger to the site of the Constitutional Convention. Because he is bringing important word about the slavery compromise (which will, ironically, set up a fugitive slave law), he gets to meet George Washington, Alexander Hamilton, and other statesmen. A strong theme of this book is Dan's growing belief in himself and his abilities. The other titles in this trilogy are *War Comes to Willy Freeman* and *Who Is Carrie?* Each features a young African American woman as the central character.

Novels about Revolutionary America offer an intriguing variety of viewpoints. Individual books will help children feel the intense emotions of the time, but the impact of several read for comparison and contrast will be much greater. Children can also increase their knowledge of details about a time period in this way. Knowing more background each time, they will read each succeeding book with greater ease.

The American Frontier

No other period in U.S. history has been more dramatized in films and television than that of the westward movement of the American pioneers. Because civilization grows with a ragged edge, nineteenth-century frontier stories are set in widely scattered locations. Some settlers moved with the wilderness, like Pa Ingalls in the Little House books by Laura Ingalls Wilder. These stories describe the growing up of the Ingalls girls and the Wilder boys. In the first book of the series, *Little House in the Big Woods*, Laura is only 6 years old; the final two books—*Little Town on the Prairie* and *These Happy Golden Years*—tell of Laura's teaching career and her courtship. Based on the author's own life, these books portray the hardships and difficulties of pioneer life in the 1870s and 1880s and describe the fun and excitement that were also a part of daily living in those days. Throughout the stories the warmth and security of family love run like a golden thread that binds the books to the hearts of their readers. The family faces many hardships but there are wonderful moments as well. Best of all are the long winter evenings of firelight and the clear singing of Pa's fiddle. These mean love and security, whether the home is in Wisconsin, in the wild Kansas country as described in *Little House on the Prairie*, in the Minnesota of *On the Banks of Plum Creek*, or in Dakota Territory as in *By the Shores of Silver Lake*.

Another favorite book of pioneer days is *Caddie Woodlawn* by Carol Ryrie Brink. This story takes place in the Wisconsin wilderness of the 1860s, but it is primarily the story of the growing up of tomboy Caddie. Caddie had been a frail baby, and so her father persuaded her mother to allow her to be reared more freely than her older sis-

ter, Clara, who was restricted by the rules of decorum for young ladies. Caddie was free to run about the half-wild Wisconsin frontier with her two brothers. Their escapades and adventures read like a feminine *Tom Sawyer*. Caddie is a self-willed, independent spirit who is assured a memorable place in children's literature.

Like Caddie, May Amelia in Jennifer L. Holm's *Our Only May Amelia* is an independent female somewhat limited by the strictures of her day. She is the only girl in a family of seven brothers, and even worse, the only girl born into her rural Finnish American community. Expected to work on her family's farm as well as take on more traditional female roles, May Amelia has a hard time conforming to the role of "Proper Young Lady." She dreams of growing up to sail the world like her sea captain uncle but in the meantime has some marvelously funny adventures chasing sheep, fishing for salmon, running from bears, and encountering ghosts. This warm and lighthearted account of growing up in early-twentieth-century Washington state is told in May Amelia's appealingly fresh voice. This Newbery Honor story was inspired by the author's grandaunt's diary. Holm's 16-year-old Jane Peck is another heroine in the mold of Caddie and May Amelia and perhaps represents the young woman either might have become. In *Boston Jane: An Adventure*, the first book of a trilogy, Jane appears in three personas. She is first just Jane, the motherless daughter of a Philadelphia doctor who spends her pre-adolescent years roaming the streets with her best friend Jebediah or accompanying her father on his rounds. As a young adolescent, however, she develops a crush on her father's assistant William, who convinces her that girls can only become proper young ladies through careful tutoring. She thus enrolls in Miss Hepplewhite's Young Ladies Academy and endeavors to become the perfect woman as recommended by *The Young Ladies Confidante*, a book she consults as regularly as the Bible. Now, in 1854, she wishes to be addressed as the proper *Miss* Jane Peck. When a long correspondence with William, who has moved to the Pacific Northwest to make his fortune, results in a proposal of marriage, her terminally ill father reluctantly agrees to let her go. But in Washington territory Jane, who is called Boston Jane by the settlers and Chinook Indians she meets, finds that her former outspoken and independent ways are much better suited to survival than the knowledge of how to pour a proper cup of tea or which pair of gloves to wear. Older readers will find Jane's adventures, continued in *Boston Jane, Wilderness Days*, and *Boston Jane: The Claim*, particularly engaging.

Black Storm Comin' by Diane Lee Wilson is a thrilling tale about a young rider on the Pony Express. Colton Westcote is 12 when his mother convinces his father to leave Missouri for California in 1860. Missouri is a dangerous place for people of color, even free ones. Although Colton's father is white and Colton is light-skinned, his mother and sisters feel threatened by the

In the mid-1800s a biracial adolescent boy joins the Pony Express to support his family in Diane Lee Wilson's exciting *Black Storm Comin'*. Reprinted with the permission of Margaret K. McElderry Books, an imprint of Simon & Schuster Children's Publishing Division from *Black Storm Comin'* by Diane Lee Wilson. Copyright © 2005 Diane Lee Wilson.

possibility of capture by slave hunters. Colton's Pa has never been much of a provider, and his bumbling behavior on the wagon train, as well as the family's racial mix, leave all the Westcotes open to censure. When Pa accidentally shoots Colton, he abandons the family out of guilt and they have to struggle on without him. They make it as far as Carson City, Nevada, and are stuck there with a broken wagon and wasting oxen. Even worse, Ma is suffering from childbirth fever following her baby son's birth and death. Colton, who is determined to support his family, applies to be a Pony Express rider. When he proves his skill at handling a half-wild horse, Mr. Robert, the division superintendent, reluctantly takes him on despite his youth. For the first time in his life, Colton feels free and takes avidly to the life despite its hardships. His encounters with terrible terrain, terrible weather, and a terrible villain are compounded by his fear that his mixed blood will be revealed and he will lose his job. Colton's ultimate success serves as a turning point for the boy to examine his own identity and his own heart.

Black Storm Comin' is one of the better books about the American frontier in some years.

By the mid-nineteenth century, the far western frontier was in California and Oregon. In *Daughter of the Madrugada* Frances M. Wood provides a refreshing perspective on California history and reminds readers that Europeans were not the only ones to carve out a place in the state's history. Thirteen-year-old Cesa de Haro is the daughter of a wealthy Mexican family living on their huge ranch in the 1840s. When Mexico loses the war with the United States and gold is discovered, Cesa's life is dramatically changed. Cesa's first-person account of these events is a fine coming-of-age story that also reveals the stereotypes that different groups create of one another. The book also raises important questions about what it means to be an American. A similar story about the clash of cultures is Susan Fletcher's *Walk across the Sea.* Set in Crescent City, California, the book is based on true accounts of the racist attacks on Chinese immigrants carried out throughout the West during the late 1800s. It is narrated by Eliza, a 15-year-old girl who befriends Wah Chung, a Chinese boy, when he saves her from drowning. The terrible events that occur when the white townspeople of Crescent City expel the Chinese community and the consequences to Eliza's family when she tries to save Wah Chung make compelling reading.

Karen Cushman's *The Ballad of Lucy Whipple* is, for the most part, a much more lighthearted account of the California gold rush as seen through the eyes of an 11-year-old girl. Lucy feels highly put out when her widowed mother decides to run a boarding house for miners and drags her and her two siblings from their comfortable home in Massachusetts to the rough-hewn and roughhouse life of a mining camp. Lucy does everything in her power to get back home, yet when she is finally given the chance she turns it down to remain as the town librarian. Cushman's *Rodzina* is the story of a young Polish immigrant girl who finds herself orphaned in the mid-1850s in Chicago. Rodzina survives on the street for a time but is eventually one of the children rounded up and sent west on the orphan trains. Although Cushman writes with her customary sense of humor and attention to historical details, *Rodzina* is much more serious in tone than *The Ballad of Lucy Whipple.* Rodzina, who witnesses the callous treatment of the orphans, who are viewed as chattel by the adults who take them in, manages to escape from the train; but she has to learn a whole new set of survival skills as she faces life on the frontier.

The hardships encountered on the Oregon Trail and the records kept by many travelers have sparked the imagination of many authors who write for children. In *Trouble for Lucy,* Carla Stevens uses information from first-person accounts of a journey in 1843 to set the scene for each of the brief chapters. Appropriate for 8- and 9-year-old readers, the story focuses on Lucy's efforts to keep her fox terrier puppy from being a nuisance to the oxen and drivers and the adventures that ensue. There is no pretending here that the pioneers' way was easy, yet the story is more concerned with the universal feelings of childhood than it is with hardship. *On to Oregon!* by Honoré Morrow and Jean Van Leeuwen's *Bound for Oregon* are based on accounts of real people who braved the Oregon Trail, and they make fascinating reading for middle graders. Older readers will admire the courage of 17-year-old Lovisa King in Linda Crews's *A Heart for Any Fate* as she, her parents, and eleven of her siblings and their families set out for Oregon.

Another vivid story for older readers is *Prairie Songs* by Pam Conrad. It contrasts two points of view of homesteading in the new lands, that of the Downing family, who had settled in a "soddy," and that of the beautiful, cultured wife of the new doctor in Howard County, Nebraska, who has come to live in the next soddy. The story is told by young Louisa Downing and reflects her wonder at the back-East world of wealth and learning that Mrs. Emmeline Berryman represents. Never able to adjust to her life on the prairie, Mrs. Berryman is terrified out of all reason one winter day by the visit of two Indians, and she flees. She is finally found sitting in the snow, frozen to death. Louisa's narration is vivid, and her casual acceptance of life in a soddy points up the irony of Mrs. Berryman's inability to cope. The woman Louisa had admired could not match her own mother in strength of spirit or the special kind of beauty that made Louisa feel good inside.

Moving westward and settling the frontier was a major force in the lives of many Americans throughout the nineteenth century. Farming the vast mid-American prairies put special demands on families. In *Sarah, Plain and Tall,* a beautifully written short novel by Patricia MacLachlan, motherless Anna and Caleb are delighted when Papa's advertisement for a mail-order bride brings Sarah to their prairie home. Sarah comes from the coast of Maine, with mementos of the sea she loves, her gray cat Seal, a moon shell for Caleb, and a round sea stone for Anna. She has agreed only to a month's visit, and the children, who quickly learn to love her lively, independent ways, are afraid that they will lose her. On the day Sarah goes to town for colored pencils to add the blue, gray, and green of the ocean to the picture she has drawn of the prairie, they realize that she will stay. She misses the sea, she tells them, but she would miss them more. The rhythm and lyrical simplicity of the writing are especially effective when read aloud. MacLachlan continues the story in *Skylark,* an equally well-written sequel. In *Three Names,* a slice-of-life picture book that would make a good companion piece for the two books, MacLachlan tells of her great-grandfather when he went to a one-room schoolhouse on the prairie with his dog, Three Names. Alexander Pertzoff's lovely watercolors show the beauty and spaciousness of the wide-open prairie.

Not all stories of this period take place in the West, however. Liza Ketchum's *Where the Great Hawk Flies* takes place soon after the end of the Revolutionary War in rural Vermont. In this story Daniel, son of an Englishman and a Pequot woman, and Hiram, whose family is staunchly Yankee, find themselves neighbors. Both families were terrorized by a Caughnawaga raid instigated by the British during the war. For Hiram and his mother, the presence of Daniel on the next farm stirs vicious hatreds, and the two boys become bitter enemies. A visit from Daniel's Pequot grandfather and the birth of Hiram's twin siblings serve as catalysts for their eventual reconciliation, but not before tragedy strikes both families. Lea Wait's sensitively told *Wintering Well* begins in rural Maine as it achieves statehood in 1820. Told in the alternating voices of an omniscient narrator and the journal of 11-year-old Cassie Ames, the story centers on Cassie and her older brother Will, two members of a large farming family. Will wants nothing more than to be a farmer until a tragic accident results in amputation of his leg. His father feels he's a hopeless "cripple" who will be a burden on the family for the rest of his life. Cassie, who nurses him through his illness and recovery, is fiercely determined to help him make a new life for himself. The story of how they both find their identities—Cassie through helping the doctor who saved Will, and Will through his skill at wood carving—lies at the core of this compelling story.

Although *Wintering Well* touches on the state of medical treatment in the early 1800s, Cynthia DeFelice has focused more intensely on the topic in *The Apprenticeship of Lucas Whitaker.* Lucas's family has been decimated by tuberculosis, and after a period of homeless wandering, he is taken in as an apprentice to the local doctor. The local townspeople want to exhume the bodies of tuberculosis victims in order to burn their hearts and breathe the smoke, believing that this can cure the illness. Lucas is torn between science and superstition as he struggles with his loyalty to Dr. Beecher and his desire to find a cure for the awful disease.

Although set in the early 1900s, Mary Riskind's *Apple Is My Sign* is less an historical novel than a story of a 10-year-old deaf child learning to live among the hearing with his disability. Harry Berger, called "Apple" because of his family's orchards, is sent to a school for the deaf in Philadelphia. His whole family is deaf, but Harry is the first one to leave home, and his early days at the school are difficult and lonely. Harry tells his family that he thinks he'd like to be a teacher, but a family friend signs "Hearing best teacher." His mother, however, reassures Harry: "I-f you want teach deaf, must try. That's-all. Never know, i-f never try. In head must think can. Brave" (p. 119). Riskind conveys the rapidity of signed talk by approximating its actual meanings, eliminating the little words or word endings, as signers do, and spelling out meanings for which there are no signs. Through Harry's story, readers may come to realize that opportunities for people with disabilities have changed over the years.

Author Janet Hickman focuses on a largely unexamined episode in American history through themes of

Janet Hickman

Janet Hickman is the author of many books for children, as well as a respected scholar of children's literature. Although Hickman is equally at home with contemporary fiction and fantasy, writing historical fiction and the research it entails has always been her main passion. Go to the Online Learning Center at www.mhhe.com/kiefer9e or to your Resources CD-ROM to learn more about Janet Hickman.

family ties and conflicted loyalties. In the beautifully written *Susannah,* Hickman explores the topic of families broken apart by tenets of religion rather than by the finality of death. In 1810, following the death of her mother, Susannah's father brings her into a Shaker community in southern Ohio. In keeping with Shaker beliefs, 14-year-old Susannah is separated from her father and must live with the other children in the community. She longs for the remembered warmth of her mother's love and wants desperately to leave the community. However, she finds it difficult to leave a 6-year-old girl she has come to care for. Like Lucas Whitaker, Susannah must deal with the loss of her family and the difficult choices that ensue between self-satisfaction and self-sacrifice. Hickman provides fascinating details of Shaker life, but her greatest strength is her ability to deal with universal human problems.

The Civil War Era

Attention to American history in the nineteenth century often seems to be centered on the Civil War. The events leading up to the war and those that followed also need to be considered if children are to have an accurate picture of this volatile period.

Resistance to Slavery

The country was involved and concerned with the issue of slavery long before the Civil War. *Nettie's Trip South* by Ann Turner is a picture book based on the real diary of the author's great-grandmother. When Nettie is 10 years old, she goes with her older brother, a reporter, and her 14-year-old sister on a trip from Albany, New York, to Richmond, Virginia. As Nettie writes to her friend Addie, she remembers all of the things she saw in that prewar city, including Tabitha, a black slave, in the hotel, who had no last name, and the slave auction where two children clasping hands were bought by different masters. Ronald Himler illustrated this moving account of a young girl's horror at her first exposure to slavery.

That cruelty is viewed from a variety of perspectives in several fine books for older children. In smoky tones of gray and black Tom Feelings's powerful *The Middle Passage* presents vivid images of the slaves' jour-

ney across the Atlantic. The pictures are preceded by a lengthy introduction that provides background about Feelings's work and details about the slave trade. The artwork is presented without words, however, because no written text could express the horror that these pictures convey.

Two fine novels, Joyce Hansen's *The Captive* and James Berry's *Ajeemah and His Son,* give readers an understanding of the lives their characters lived in Africa prior to their enslavement. At the beginning of Hansen's *The Captive,* Kofi, the 12-year-old son of an Ashanti chief, is attending a ceremony honoring Ashanti kings. When Kofi's father is murdered in a plot to weaken the Ashanti tribes, Kofi is captured and eventually placed aboard a "water house" bound for Boston. Kofi is sold to a white merchant and must adjust to his master's cruelties and the terrible bleakness of New England winters, but he never gives up his dreams of returning home. When he runs away, he is helped by Paul Cuffe, a free black merchant sea captain. Because the importing of slaves is illegal in Massachusetts, a judge declares that Kofi cannot be held as a slave and he is given into Paul Cuffe's custody. In Cuffe's caring home Kofi comes of age and eventually joins Cuffe in fighting slavery. In Berry's *Ajeemah and His Son,* Ajeemah and his son, Atu, are on their way to present the dowry for Atu's bride when they are captured and sent aboard a slaver to Jamaica. There the two are separated, and parallel chapters portray their experences of slavery in moving detail. Atu is killed in an escape attempt, but Ajeemah is freed in 1838 when the British outlaw slavery. Although he creates a new family for himself, Ajeemah forever misses Atu and the loved ones he left behind in Africa.

Andrea Davis Pinkney also provides two points of view of life as a slave in the highly readable *Silent Thunder.* Eleven-year-old Summer and her older brother Roscoe have grown up on the Parnell plantation in Virginia. In 1862, as events of the Civil War envelop them, they are old enough to rebel against their circumstances and long to choose their own futures. Summer's heart's desire is to learn to read; Roscoe longs to run away and join the Union army. As the story evolves we see how both of them manage to achieve their goals. Pinkney, although mistakenly placing the Battle of Vicksburg in 1862 instead of 1863, does a fine job of depicting the terrible injustice of slavery. Her real strength lies in her portrayal of complex personalities and relationships and in her ability to show the courage and determination of people filled with silent thunder.

Several books do not stint on conveying the dehumanization and the suffering that slaves experienced. Walter Mosley's *47,* mentioned earlier, is a blend of fantasy and historical fiction that gives us a first-person narrative from 47, a slave identified by number rather than name, as were the other slaves on Master Tobias's plantation. Orphaned as a baby and raised by a loving house slave named Big Mama Flore, 47 finds his relatively easy

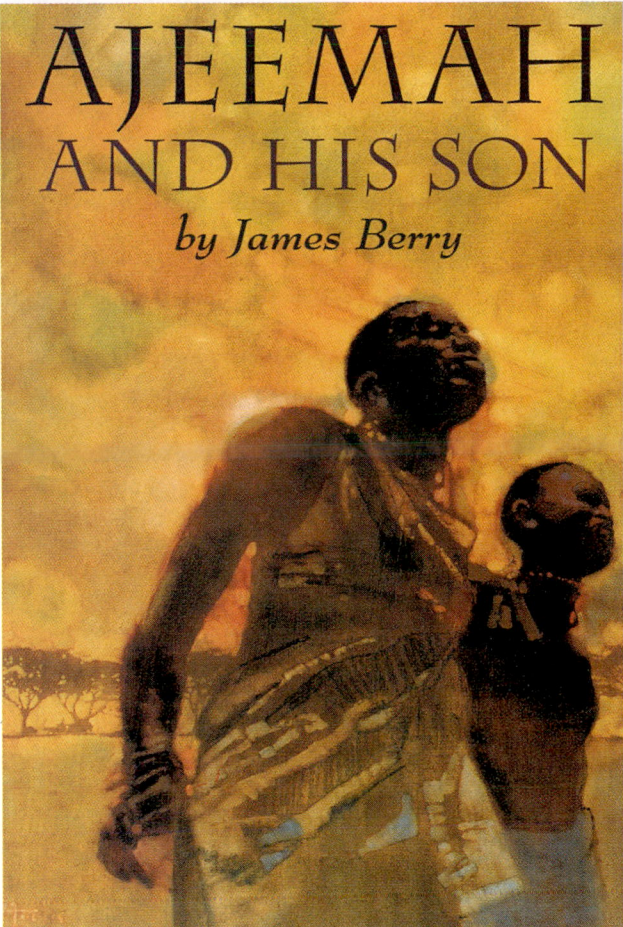

Ajeemah and His Son, by James Berry, shows how one family was affected by the brutality of the slave trade. Cover from *Ajeemah and His Son* by James Berry. Cover art copyright © 1991 by Bernie Fuchs. Jacket copyright © 1991 by HarperCollins Publishers. Used by permission of HarperCollins Publishers.

early life shattered when he is sent to work in the cotton fields. We see firsthand the brutality the slaves experienced. We also see the effect of this treatment on their sense of identity. When a mysterious runaway named Tall John shows up on the plantation, however, things start to change. Tall John provides the impetus for 47 to reexamine his position and reluctantly accept Tall John's assurance that he is meant to be the savior of his people. Told by an elderly 47 (at approximately 180 years of age), the story takes place in Georgia in 1832. The tantalizing ending predicts sequels that will take 47 through the history of African American struggles into the present day. Julius Lester relates the painful betrayals of slavery in *Day of Tears*, a multiple-perspective novel that tells of the repercussions that follow when a white southern plantation owner must sell his slaves to pay his gambling debts. Based on the details of the largest slave auction ever held, in 1859 in Georgia, Lester looks at the events of the two-day auction from the perspectives of both freeborn and slave, male and female—and again from these observers' old age. Gary Paulsen's *Nightjohn* is another graphic

and emotionally wrenching account of the cruelties of slavery. Sarny, a young slave on the Waller plantation, narrates the story of Nightjohn, who is brought to the plantation in a most inhumane way by owner Clel Waller. Although he has been brutally used, that night in the slave quarters Nightjohn offers Sarny the gift of literacy. When Waller discovers Sarny writing a letter in the dirt, Nightjohn pays a terrible price. In *Sarny* Paulsen continues the girl's story into adulthood and the end of the Civil War, when Sarny sets off for New Orleans to find her two young children.

Mary Lyons's *Letters from a Slave Girl* is a fictionalized account of Harriet Jacob's early life as a slave in North Carolina. The letters, addressed to her dead or absent relatives, provide a moving account of her growing-up years, her longing for freedom, and her love for her family. Although not as horrifying as those in Paulsen's book, Harriet's experiences also portray the dehumanizing effects of slavery, particularly for women. After hiding for seven years in an attic storeroom, Harriet escapes, and later her memoir becomes important to the abolitionist movement.

Elisa Lynn Carbonne's *Stealing Freedom* is also based on a real person, Ann Maria Weems. Ann Maria is the daughter of a free father and a slave mother in Maryland in the 1850s. When her brothers are sold South, her father seeks help from abolitionists, who raise funds to buy Ann Marie, her mother, and her sister. Her master refuses to sell Ann, and she determines to run away. Traveling on the Underground Railroad, she hides in Baltimore for some months and finally reaches relatives in Canada. Carbonne does not stint on details of slave life, but this is really a book about the importance of family ties and the terrible pain of families torn apart by this cruel institution. *Trouble Don't Last* is the story of two fictional travelers on the Underground Railroad, but author Shelley Pearsall did extensive research on the Kentucky and Ohio sites and on the people who aided slaves escaping to Canada on this particular route. Like Carbonne, Pearsall details some of the horrors of life as a slave. But these do not overwhelm the exciting story told by 11-year-old Samuel about his harrowing journey to freedom with his foster father Harrison, the old slave who accompanies him.

In Sandra Forrester's *Sound the Jubilee* Maddie bears witness to the cruelties of human bondage on her North Carolina plantation. When the Civil War breaks out, she and her family manage to escape to Roanoke Island, where the Union army provides sanctuary for runaway slaves. Forrester shows that mistreatment of African-Americans was not limited to southerners, however, as Union promises of land and education are withdrawn with the end of the war.

Another eyewitness account of slavery is provided in *The Slave Dancer* by Paula Fox. Jessie Bollier is a 13-year-old white boy who is shanghaied in New Orleans and made to join the crew of a slave ship. In this grim story,

Reading Historical Fiction with Early Fluent Readers

After teacher Isaac Brooks introduced book talk groups to his fourth graders in early February, several of the children at the Manhattan School for Children in New York City chose to read *Nightjohn* by Gary Paulsen. The book appeared slim and the language accessible for these six students who were just moving into fluent reading. However, these children had never really had to deal with some of the difficult issues in America's history, and they weren't quite ready for the graphic depictions of a Southern white master's idea of disciplining his black slaves. Isaac had supplied vocabulary words and brought in pictures of enslaved Africans to support this heterogeneous group of readers. A few read independently, but the majority read in pairs out loud and put Post-its where they had questions. The brevity of the chapters made rereading less onerous. Among the jobs shared by the members of Isaac's book group on a rotating basis, the word finder assumed crucial importance. Students read the book out loud together and quizzed one another. "Do you get it? Do you understand?" Isaac decided to help them through the book by providing them a chapter by chapter explanation of plantation life from the point of view of the enslaved.

When their reading was done, just seven brief chapters later, the group found itself wanting to know more. "How did they get to be slaves?" the group wondered. "What brought them there?" Isaac decided to introduce a follow-up book choice, *The Slave Dancer* by Paula Fox. The two books couldn't have been more opposite. *Nightjohn* took the point of view of an almost-14-year-old slave girl named Sarny. The language reflected the extent of Sarny's literacy and fit well with the collective abilities of the book talk group as a whole. *The Slave Dancer* was more complex and was written in more formal prose. The group found many more words they couldn't understand, even when using context to sort them out.

Isaac wondered if he had made a mistake by asking this group of readers to attempt such a challenging book. However, they were motivated by their intense interest in the subject. They also found that some of the habits engendered in their reading of *Nightjohn* helped them with the material in *Slave Dancer,* and they were more successful in moving through the text. To help them further, Isaac decided to read a big portion of each assigned reading out loud.

A parent of one of the girls in the group invited the others to come to her home on the weekend. She rented *The Amistad* and *The House of Dies Drear* and showed excerpts from each having to do with the Middle Passage and the Underground Railroad. The videos helped give the children even more of a context for understanding *The Slave Dancer.* The children read the week's assigned chapters together and talked about it over refreshments.

The focus of the group gradually shifted from efforts at decoding and making meaning to exploring questions about the themes of the book. They raised questions about treating people as cargo and the conflicted motives of the sailors aboard the ship. Briana said that the book "explained more of the things we didn't know about [after they had read *Nightjohn*]. Like how they 'stored' slaves below deck and how they handled feeding them and exercise." Asia found that the book reaffirmed for her the fact that "people weren't always free." Jonathan said that the group cared about the main character and that they hoped he'd get away from being kidnapped. All of the members of the book talk group agreed that talking about the book made them want to read more.

Isaac was pleased that he had decided to continue with the reading of *The Slave Dancer,* despite his early misgivings. He realized that he could ask early fluent readers to read other complex works of literature by giving them lots of support in the form of reading strategies, discussions, and plenty of background information.

Isaac B. Brooks
Manhattan School for Children, New York City

Jessie is forced to play his fife and "dance the slaves" so that their muscles will remain strong and they will bring a higher price on the slave market. Jessie is young, innocent, and still capable of feeling shock. Everyone else on board the ship is so hardened that they have become indifferent to human suffering. And this is the real message of the story—the utter degradation that eventually engulfs everyone connected with slavery, including the captain, the black Portuguese broker, the depraved Ben Stout, and even Jessie himself. In one of the most compelling and symbolic scenes in the book, Jessie is forced into the hold of the ship to look for his fife. Here he must touch, literally step on, the bodies of the captives, who are so crowded together that there is no room to walk. Jessie's descent into that hold somehow represents the descent of the whole of humankind.

Many stories of the pre–Civil War period relate to slavery and the activities of the Underground Railroad, when people faced the moral issue of breaking laws out of compassion for other human beings. F. N. Monjo titled his easy-reading book *The Drinking Gourd* after the "code song" that the slaves sang. The song was used to point the direction for escape by following the North Star, using the Big Dipper as a guide. The words to the song are included in this short story of how a young mischievous boy helps a family on their way to freedom.

In *Brady,* Jean Fritz tells the story of a very believable boy who discovers that his father is an agent for the Underground Railroad. His parents had not told him of their forbidden activities, for Brady just cannot keep a secret. However, Brady discovers the secret for himself when his father suffers a broken leg during a fire in the barn and Brady must carry out the plan for moving a fugitive slave.

A fugitive slave whom Catherine never meets brings changes to her life in *A Gathering of Days: A New England Girl's Journal, 1830–32* by Joan Blos. Catherine and her friend Cassie agonize over a plea for help slipped into her writing book when she leaves it in the woods. They have heard about slavery and the abolitionist movement from their teacher, yet their activities are circumscribed by strict but loving families. Finally compassion and a sense of justice outweigh their respect for authority, and they leave food and a quilt where the fugitive will be sure to find them. Much later a packet arrives from Canada with a cryptic message and two bits of lace as a thankyou; the runaway is safe and free.

Paul Fleischman tells the moving story of Georgina Lott's life in *The Borning Room.* In one of the episodes, Georgina recalls hiding a runaway slave in the barn loft. Later, when her mother is giving birth and they cannot get the midwife, Georgina goes out to the barn and brings in Cora to help her mother. When her father comes home that night, he drives Cora by moonlight to the home of Mr. Reedy, a Quaker. Georgina's mother says:

> It's been a day of deliverance, . . . Cora brought Zeb here out of the womb. And we helped deliver her from slavery. . . . We must continue with that work, Georgina. (p. 33)

In *Jip: His Story* Katherine Paterson relates the story of a young boy who is affected by the long arm of slavery in rural Vermont in 1855. Jip is a foundling who has been raised in a charity orphanage. This American Oliver Twist is just as independent as Dickens's hero and involved with some equally memorable characters. Jip's dream of a real home turns into a nightmare when a mysterious stranger claims him as his son. Caught in a tug of war between abolitionists and slave hunters, Jip finally breaks free and finds a place where he belongs.

Patricia Beatty's *Jayhawker* is the story of Lije Tulley, a Kansas 12-year-old who joins in his family's abolitionist activities. Lije rides in his dead father's place in raids to free slaves across the border in Missouri. As war begins, he becomes a spy to serve the cause, posing as a supporter of the South while working on a Missouri farm. Courage, loneliness, and conflicting loyalties are highlighted in this well-crafted story with a dramatic conclusion.

The Civil War

There are many fine stories for children about the Civil War itself. Most of these describe the war in terms of human issues and suffering, rather than political issues. Two books focus on very different adventures of young drummer boys in the Civil War. *Charley Skedaddle,* written by Patricia Beatty, tells the story of 13-year-old Charley Quinn, a tough kid from the New York Bowery who, after his older brother is killed at Gettysburg, enlists in the Union army as a drummer boy. When the horrors of war become a reality to him, he runs away to the Blue Ridge Mountains. Here he must prove his courage in a different way. Charley's gradual change from a boy filled with bravado into one who shows real bravery is made very believable in this fast-paced story.

Ransom Powell is not as lucky as Charley Skedaddle, for two years after joining the Tenth West Virginia Regiment as a drummer boy for the Union army, he is captured with eighteen others and sent to Andersonville Prison. Well loved by his company for his humor, helpfulness, and red cap, Powell beat taps on his drum for every member of his group. G. Clifton Wisler has told Ransom Powell's story in *Red Cap,* based on authentic records and other men's reminiscences. This is the only Civil War story for children that details the horrors of Andersonville Prison.

In *Thunder at Gettysburg,* Patricia Lee Gauch tells the story of Tillie Pierce, a little girl caught in the midst of battle. She had gone out to a farm for safety and to help a neighbor with her children. The farm was right by Little Round Top, and for three days battle roared around them. Tillie carried water and helped with the wounded. The high drama of this three-day battle is also the focus of a story for older readers, *The Slopes of War* by N. A. Perez. Buck Summerhill returns to Gettysburg, his home town, as a soldier in the Army of the Potomac and loses his leg in the fight for Little Round Top. His sister Bekah cares for a wounded Union officer, Captain Waite, upstairs in the family's home while injured rebels are taken into the parlor. *The Slopes of War* is packed with authentic information about real officers and battle strategies, as well as several threads of fictional story line.

Rifles for Watie by Harold Keith tells of the life of a Union soldier and spy engaged in fighting the western campaign of the Civil War. Jefferson Davis Bussey, a young farm boy from Kansas, joins the Union forces and becomes a scout and, quite accidentally, a member of Stand Watie's Cherokee Rebels. Jeff is probably one of the few soldiers in the West to see the Civil War from both sides. This vibrant novel is rich in detail, with fine characterizations.

With Every Drop of Blood by James Collier and Christopher Collier is the first-person narrative of 14-year-old Johnny. After his father is killed fighting for the Confederate army, Johnny is desperately worried that he will not be able to keep his family alive. He is lured into transporting food for Confederate troops despite his promise to his family to stay out of the fighting. He is captured by Cush, an African American Union soldier, but as the war disintegrates into chaos, the two find that their dependence on each other overrides their enmity. Their bond of friendship grows as their questions about the war and its savagery deepen. At the war's end, the two have survived, but they wonder about the future in a world that is so full of meanness and hate. Patricia Polacco's *Pink and Say* is a moving picture book that deals with a similar friendship, this one between two Union soldiers (see Chapter 5).

Soldiers were not the only ones who suffered during the Civil War. Family relationships were also torn apart over its long course. The effect of the war on a frontier family in Illinois has been told by Irene Hunt in the fine historical novel *Across Five Aprils*. Jethro Creighton is only 9 years old at the outbreak of a war that at first seems exciting and wonderful. As the war continues, though, Jethro learns that it is not glorious and exciting, but heartbreaking and disruptive to all kinds of relationships. This book makes difficult reading because the device of letter writing is used to carry the action of the story to different places and provide historical detail, but it is beautifully written and thought provoking.

Blame fuels the anger of 12-year-old Hamp Cravey in *Trembling Earth* by Kim Siegelson. Hamp has grown up exploring the far reaches of the Okefenokee Swamp and is an experienced swamp rat. Hamp hates the Yankees for taking his father's leg in a Civil War battle, but he also blames his father for enlisting and making their family's hardscrabble life even more difficult. When he finds out that there is a 500-gold piece reward for an escaped slave named Duff, Hamp is determined to use his tracking skills to capture him. He does not count on a family of runaways he encounters or on the sympathies of his mother and younger sister toward the slave's plight. When Duff turns the tables on Hamp and forces Hamp to lead him to safety in Florida, Hamp must make a difficult choice. The experience proves to be his coming of age, and he begins to understand his own complex identity as well as that of his father.

In *How I Found the Strong*, Margaret McMullan focuses on the anger and resentments of 10-year-old Frank Russell, a young boy left behind in Mississippi when his father and brother join the Rebel army. When his grandparents die, Frank is left with his pregnant mother and the family's slave, Buck, to care for the family farm. As battles rage nearby and a drought reduces the family to near-starvation, Frank tries to make sense of the war and the sacrifices his family is asked to make. His growing love and admiration for Buck, who refuses to run off, challenges the core of all he has believed in. When his brother is killed in battle and his father returns minus his hand, Frank is forced to make a difficult choice.

In Patricia Beatty's *Turn Homeward, Hannalee*, the story of 12-year-old Hannalee Reed from Roswell, Georgia, Hannalee, her little brother Jem, and hundreds of other young millworkers in Yankee-occupied Georgia are branded as traitors for making cloth and rope for the Confederacy. They are sent north by Sherman's soldiers

How I Found the Strong by Margaret McMullan focuses on the struggles of a relatively poor southern family and the young boy who is left to support them during the Civil War.
Cover of *How I Found the Strong: A Novel of the Civil War* by Margaret McMullen, copyright © 2004. Reprinted by permission of Houghton Mifflin Company, Inc.

to work in mills in Kentucky and Indiana or hired out as servants to northern families. This book emphasizes the point that few southerners were slaveholders, and it forces readers to consider the war's effects on the common people of the South—a good balance to the many books that present northerners' views. The sequel to this story, *Be Ever Hopeful, Hannalee*, tells of the family's struggle to survive the aftermath of the war.

Shades of Gray by Carolyn Reeder is also a story about the aftermath of the Civil War. Twelve-year-old Will Page blames the Yankees for the loss of his entire family. He is sent to live with his aunt and uncle out in the Virginia Piedmont. He can endure living in the country, but he finds it hard to accept the hospitality of his uncle, who had refused to fight the Yankees because he did not believe in war. It is even more difficult for Will to hang on to his resentment because his uncle is so fair and kind and can do everything well. Gradually, Will begins to understand the courage it took for his uncle to stand up for his beliefs. When his uncle shelters a wounded Yankee on his way home to Pennsylvania, Will learns that there were good men fighting on both sides of the war. Well plotted, this is an exciting story that will make readers think of the many "shades of gray" that surround all prejudices.

The Age of Economic Revolution

Although a runaway slave is part of the many-layered *Lyddie* by Katherine Paterson, the main focus of the story is on the rights of child laborers in the eighteenth and early nineteenth centuries. When Lyddie's mother abandoned their farm, she hired out 13-year-old Lyddie to a hotel for fifty cents a week. Determined to find a better job in order to buy back her beloved farm, Lyddie travels to Lowell, Massachusetts, to work in the textile mills. Lyddie must adjust to the long hours and miserable conditions of nineteenth-century mills, but her indomitable spirit as well as the friendships she forms allow her to survive. On a visit home, Lyddie finds a runaway slave hidden next door and is tempted to turn him in for the reward. But the more she talks with Ezekiel, the more she sees a parallel with her own life. In the end she gives him all the money she has and wishes him a safe journey. He in turn hopes she will find her freedom. This is something Lyddie thinks about frequently, as she realizes she is no more than a slave at the textile mills that enslave young women to provide cheap labor for cruel industrialists.

M. J. Auch also highlights the appalling working conditions that extended into the twentieth century in *Ashes of Roses*, the story of a young Irish immigrant girl who is left to support herself after her parents are forced to return to Ireland with their sick son. She is able to find work at the Triangle Shirt Factory, where she is caught up in one of the worst industrial disasters in American history.

Younger readers will enjoy Ellen Howard's lovely story *The Gate in the Wall*, set in late-nineteenth-century England. Ten-year-old Emma is an orphan who works ten hours a day in the spinning mills to help support her older sister, her brutal brother-in-law, and their sickly baby. Shut out of the mill for being late one day, Emma is afraid to go home. She discovers an old gate that leads her to a nearby canal and a beautiful boat filled with a cargo of potatoes. Seeing no one around, she hungrily takes some of the potatoes but is discovered by the boat's owner, Mrs. Minshull, who offers her work instead of turning her in to the law for stealing. As she and Mrs. Minshull travel the canals with their various cargoes, Emma finds that she has a job that makes the most of her talents rather than victimizes her. However, her loyalty and anxiety for her sister hang over her head, and she temporarily deserts Mrs. Minshull to return home. Her sister recognizes that Emma's future lies with Mrs. Minshull and a home that nourishes both her body and her spirit, and she sends Emma back to the canal boat.

Other viewpoints on the effects of an industrialized society, particularly on children, can be found in fine books such as Jill Paton Walsh's *A Chance Child* and David Wiseman's *Jeremy Visick*, time fantasies discussed

Ellen Howard's warmly engaging *The Gate in the Wall* provides a view of the effects of industrialization on the children of mid-nineteenth-century England. Illustration copyright © 1999 by Robin Moore from *The Gate in the Wall* by Ellen Howard, illustrated by Robin Moore. Used with permission of the illustrator and BookStop Literary Agency. All rights reserved.

in Chapter 7. These books look largely at the negative side of industrialization, but there is also a positive side to the economic revolution that began in the 1700s. The innovations and inventions that accompanied industrialization are highlighted in Richard Peck's *Fair Weather*, about the 1893 World's Columbian Exposition held in Chicago. Peck provides a wonderful collection of characters in the Beckett family: 13-year-old Rosie, older sister Lottie, younger brother Buster, Mama, and Granddad. Invited to visit their rich Aunt Euterpe in Chicago, the children and Granddad travel by train from their rural Illinois farm to the dazzling city of Chicago and the even more spectacular Exposition. They are amazed by the exhibits, the huge buildings, and the giant ferris wheel. Even better, they meet Buffalo Bill Cody and Lillian Russell. Archival photographs are included throughout the book, but it is Peck's witty writing that brings this event to life and helps us to experience it with the same sense of wonder as the Becketts.

Immigrants

 Immigrants who came to North America in the nineteenth and early twentieth centuries had many different origins and destinations. Still, like the immigrants who came before them in previous centuries, they shared common dreams of a better life and faced similar difficulties in making a place for themselves in a new country.

These themes are universal and seem to resonate with children of all ages. For that reason the stories of immigrants seem an appropriate place to introduce young children to their own family roots through many fine picture books such as *Immigrant Girl* by Brett Harvey, *When Jesse Came across the Sea* by Amy Hest, *The Memory Coat* by Elvira Woodruff, and *Coolies* by Yin. Early middle-grade readers will find accessible books by Joan Lowery Nixon such as *Land of Hope* and books in the Dear America series such as *Dreams in the Golden Country* by Kathryn Lasky.

In *Esperanza Rising* Pam Muñoz Ryan breaks some of the stereotypes about Mexican immigrants. At the beginning of the story 13-year-old Esperanza Ortega lives on a beautiful ranch in Mexico as the pampered daughter of a wealthy landowner. When her father dies and her mother is threatened by a forced marriage, they flee to the United States. As a child of privilege Esperanza finds life in Depression-era California horrendous, and she complains bitterly about her living and working conditions. When her mother falls ill, she is forced to grow up quickly, but she finds the courage for hard work she needs in order to survive. With the help of friends Esperanza succeeds in gaining some measure of independence and security for herself and her mother.

Patricia Reilly Giff's moving *Nory Ryan's Song* provides the ghastly background for understanding the huge wave of Irish emigration that took place during the Great Hunger of 1845–52. Twelve-year-old Nory's family just scrapes by on their small holding in rural Ireland. Mam has died giving birth to baby Patch, and Da must travel far to find work to feed the family. Those remaining—Nory, her older sisters Maggie and Celia, Granda, and Patch—have to forage for food to round out their meager diet of potatoes. It seems things could not be much worse, but then one beautiful fall day Maggie awakes to a strange smell in the air—the first sign of a potato blight that will utterly destroy their staple crop and threaten their very lives. Nory's struggle to stay alive and to keep her family together is heartbreaking and real. *Maggie's Door*, the ultimately happier, though no less harrowing, sequel, follows Nory, her Granda, and Patch on their journey to America to join Maggie. Giff's books, based on the experiences of some of her own family members, are ultimately uplifting, and her portrayals of one girl's brave efforts are almost unbearably moving. Giff has turned to the other side of her family history for the book *A House of Tailors*. This story begins in Germany and follows the exuberant, sometimes stubborn, Dina to America to live with her stern uncle's family in Brooklyn. Dina is determined that she will never become a tailor like her mother, and when Uncle Lucas insists she take on odd tailoring jobs, she is determined to earn enough money to get back to Germany. She doesn't count on her own talents as a dress designer and milliner, nor does she realize how much she has come to love her aunt, her baby cousin, and a certain young man named Johann. It takes a family tragedy to open her eyes to the fact that home is the place where people love you.

Donna Jo Napoli has based the story of *The King of Mulberry Street* on family stories about the experiences of her Italian Jewish grandfather, who emigrated from Italy in the late 1800s. In the book, Dom is the illegitimate son of an educated but poverty-stricken woman. When her plans for passage to America fall through, she sneaks him aboard a freighter bound for New York. Dom is devastated when he realizes she has abandoned him, and on his arrival he narrowly escapes being caught and taken in by a padrone who operates an illegal labor ring

Author Patricia Reilly Giff had delved into her own family's history to tell the story of Dina, a German immigrant girl, in *A House of Tailors*. Jacket cover of *A House of Tailors* by Patricia Reilly Giff. Jacket illustration copyright © 2004 by Sheldon Greenberg. Used by permission of Random House Children's Books, a division of Random House, Inc.

of orphan boys. The saving grace for Dom is a pair of new shoes his mother gave him before he left. The authorities think he must be the child of middle-class parents because he has such nice shoes and he escapes the clutches of the padrone. Dom still faces a hard life on the streets, but he eventually finds friends, and his cleverness earns him a living selling sandwiches from a street cart. His heartache over the loss of his mother does not fade, but he begins to feel at home in America.

Readers will be captivated by Laurence Yep's Golden Mountain Chronicles, books based on the many generations of the Young family of Three Willows Village. *Dragon's Gate*, which received a Newberry Honor medal, begins in China when young Otter, whose father and uncle have gone to America to find work, is held responsible for the death of a Manchu soldier. His family decides he must be sent to America to escape punishment. Otter arrives in the Sierra Nevada in February of one of the worst winters on record, and he finds the Chinese engaged in a brutal battle to tunnel through mountains that seem made of iron. The story of how they accomplish this, their tremendous contributions to the building of the transcontinental railroad, and the unfairness of their treatment by the white bosses is told in the remainder of the book, with Otter, his father, and his uncle as the central characters. Yep weaves fascinating cultural and historical details into all his stories, which include *The Serpent's Children, Mountain Light, Dragonwings,* and *The Traitor* (Golden Mountain Chronicles) and *The Star Fisher* and *Dream Soul* (set in West Virginia in the 1920s).

INTO THE TWENTIETH CENTURY

The twentieth century was a period of new hopes for many people and of broken dreams for others. As we look back on this century from the new millennium, we can see how many different stories have shaped our world.

The Struggle for Civil Rights

The history of civil rights has centered on the struggles of African Americans from the late 1800s through the twentieth century. This is a bitter record of high hopes brought low by others' prejudice, hatred, and greed. The books we will discuss in this section examine issues and situations that are still sensitive today. They also present memorable characters facing the uncertain future common to African Americans in the South during the first half of the twentieth century. These stories are worth sharing with children in a classroom context where careful reflection and discussion about these issues and events are encouraged.

Mildred Taylor, one of the first African American authors to win a Newbery Medal, has written with understanding about the experiences of African Americans in rural Mississippi during the 1930s. *Roll of Thunder, Hear My Cry* is the story of the Logan family, their pride in the land they have owned since Reconstruction, and

their determination not to let injustice go unchallenged. The crucial action in the narrative is the conflict that 9-year-old Cassie observes in the adult world around her: night riders who terrorize the black community; her mother's teaching job gone as a result of her efforts to organize a boycott of the store whose white owners are among those night riders; and her father's dramatic part in rescuing a black teenager, T. J., from a lynch mob. The grim nature of the events is offset by the portrayal of the family caught up in them, the warmth of their concern for one another, the strength of their pride, and their courage. A prequel, *The Land,* takes place during Reconstruction and tells the heartbreaking story of how Cassie's grandfather, Paul, built the family's property. A sequel, *Let the Circle Be Unbroken,* follows the tragic trial of T. J. and carries Cassie's family saga into 1935. Taylor has written several shorter stories of the Logan family including *Mississippi Bridge* and *The Well.* Both books portray the terrible effects of prejudice and the fear that was a daily part of life in rural Mississippi in the 1930s.

Sheila P. Moses turns to real events of 1947 to frame *The Legend of Buddy Bush.* The story of how a group of white men attempted to lynch Buddy is told by 12-year-old Patti Mae, a family friend who idolizes Buddy for his urbane ways and dreams of following him to Harlem, where she would live with her sister BarJean. When Buddy returns to North Carolina for a visit, he sets events in motion that have repercussions for Patti Mae's family and the nation. In *The Return of Buddy Bush* Patti Mae gets her wish to go to Harlem, where she searches for the escaped Buddy and soaks in the atmosphere of the Harlem Renaissance. Both books are steeped in African American history, but at their heart they are stories of an irresistible heroine and her wonderful extended family.

David L. Dudley and Karen English have created two equally likable characters in *The Bicycle Man* and *Francie.* Dudley's *The Bicycle Man* introduces 12-year-old Carissa, who struggles with her widowed mother in rural Georgia of the late 1920s. The appearance of an elderly man on a blue bicycle serves as the mechanism for change, for both Cassie's future and her understanding of who she is. The title character of English's *Francie* has a strong sense of self and a strong role model in her mother. Her father, a Pullman porter, has moved to Chicago and has promised to send for the family as soon as he is able. While the family waits, Francie takes an awful risk in helping a young black man accused of attacking a white employer. All these stories present strong and likable characters, young adolescents whose intelligence and courage serve them well as they experience the everyday humiliations and injustices of the Jim Crow South.

Racism was not limited to the southern states in the twentieth century, as we see in Gary D. Schmidt's *Lizzie Bright and the Buckminster Boy.* Set in Maine in 1910 the story focuses on Turner Buckminster, the son of a preacher who brings his family to a new church in Phippsburg, Maine, in the early 1900s. Turner is the butt of teasing by

Sheila Moses's *The Return of Buddy Bush* and its prequel, *The Legend of Buddy Bush,* are based on an historical incident but center on the character of an African American girl growing up in the late 1940s. Reprinted with the permission of Margaret K. McElderry Books, an imprint of Simon & Schuster Children's Publishing Division from *The Return of Buddy Bush* by Shelia P. Moses. Copyright © 2005 Shelia P. Moses.

the other boys in town but soon becomes friends with Lizzie Bright, an African American girl, who teaches him about baseball and about the game of life. Based on the true account of an entire African American community forcibly removed from their island property for the benefit of white businessmen, *Lizzie Bright and the Buckminster Boy* is a powerful story of injustice, friendship, and coming of age.

The Great Depression

In the past decade the Great Depression has served as a rich source for writers to explore important human themes. Karen Hesse's Newbery Medal winner *Out of the Dust* is the emotionally wrenching story of a young girl's grim existence in the dust bowl of the Oklahoma panhandle. In the midst of the terrible external presence of dust, wind, and dying crops, Billie Jo must cope with her inner pain—her complicity in her mother's terrible death by fire and her anger at her father's helpless sur-

render to grief. Her one solace, playing the piano, is no longer available because of the burns she sustained in trying to help her mother. Hesse's narrative, written in free verse, magnifies Billie Jo's anguish and brings the red Oklahoma dust off the printed page and into the reader's heart.

Titles such as Marian Hale's *The Truth about Sparrows,* Cynthia DeFelice's *Nowhere to Call Home,* and Tracey Porter's *Treasures in the Dust* also feature strong girl characters. In Hale's *The Truth about Sparrows,* 12-year-old Sadie Wynn and her family are forced to leave their home in drought-stricken Missouri. Arriving in Texas, the family must live with other squatters at the edge of a seawall in Aransas Pass. Sadie is determined not to make friends, sure the family will go back to Missouri. But her father, whose polio-stricken legs don't slow him down one bit, is just as determined to make a better life for his family. In *Nowhere to Call Home* DeFelice's heroine, 12-year-old Frances, finds herself riding the rails with other victims of the Great Depression after her father commits suicide. Porter's *Treasures in the Dust* is told in alternating chapters by two friends separated by events of the 1930s. Annie stays in Oklahoma as her family struggles to hold onto their farm. Violet travels to California with her family and tells of her own experiences with prejudice and mistreatment. *Treasures in the Dust* would make a good companion book to Zilpha Keatley Snyder's *Cat Running.* Cat's family lives comfortably in California, and Cat's challenges have more to do with conflicts with her father and her own struggle to break away from gender stereotypes than with economic realities. However, her encounters with a family of "Okies" changes her attitude about her own family and gives her courage to find her own way.

Christopher Paul Curtis's Newbery Medal book *Bud, Not Buddy* is set in the mid-1930s in Michigan. Although the main character lives in a world where African-Americans must face the results of strong prejudice in addition to the effects of the Great Depression, his main struggle lies in finding his own identity and a place to call home. Raised in orphanages and foster homes following the death of his mother, 10-year-old Bud is a feisty, street-smart kid. His decision to head to Grand Rapids from Flint, to find his father, leads him on a journey to self-discovery that has an unexpected but satisfying outcome. The setting is rich with detail about African American life in the North during this time, especially the world of jazz. Bud is a highly engaging character, and Curtis, as he did in *The Watsons Go to Birmingham—1963,* draws us into the story with wonderfully humorous episodes only to unexpectedly seize our hearts with an emotionally wrenching climax.

The World at War

Unfortunately, much of the history of the twentieth century is the story of a world at war. Many books for young people chroni-

In Depression-era Michigan, 10-year-old Bud undertakes a journey to find his father in Christopher Paul Curtis's Newbery Award–winning *Bud, Not Buddy.* Jacket cover from *Bud, Not Buddy* by Christopher Paul Curtis. Used by permission of Random House Children's Books, a division of Random House, Inc.

cle its horrors. In these stories the common enemy is war itself. Though most of them depict people's inhumanity to each other, they also show many individual acts of humanity and extreme courage.

Oddly enough, very few books about World War I for children have been published. Iain Lawrence's *Lord of the Nutcracker Men* is set in England in the early years of the war. We see the war through the eyes of 10-year-old Johnny, whose toy soldiers, the nutcracker men of the title, are his greatest treasures. When his father is sent to the front, he writes letters back to Johnny, and Johnny loves acting out the battles with his toy soldiers. As the war progresses his father's letters become more horrific, and suddenly Johnny is torn between his love of the game of war and what he begins to see are the real consequences of this Great War. *After the Dancing Days* by Margaret I. Rostkowski is a moving story of the aftermath of that war for those who were wounded. Annie, who accompanies her physician father on visits to the veterans' hospitals, meets Andrew, a bitter, withdrawn young veteran with a disfigured face. In time Annie no longer sees his face as horrible and begins to draw him out of his shell. At the end of the summer Andrew is beginning to heal both physically and psychologically, and Annie has matured while confronting the ironies of war. Michael Morpurgo's *Private Peaceful* is one of the few books for mature readers to address the terrible battles of World War I and the consequences of prolonged and sometimes pointless warfare on young soldiers. When Charley Peaceful is forced to enlist in the British Army, his younger brother Tom insists on going also, to keep him out of the "nasty scrapes" he's always getting into. On the front in France Charley's attitude doesn't change, and a brutal sergeant seems to follow them through the awful battles like an evil harbinger of death. When Charley refuses to leave his wounded brother to launch a suicidal attack, the sergeant accuses him of treason, a charge that could result in execution. Morpurgo's book draws a parallel between the tight bonds of family and the bonds of comradeship. He also clearly depicts the heartbreaking contrast between life at home and life in the trenches, showing us in the process the ultimate futility of war.

The horrors that affected individuals and families in World War I are reflected in Michael Morpurgo's moving *Private Peaceful*. Illustration copyright © 2003 by The Imperial War Museum/ HarperCollins, Ltd. from *Private Peaceful* by Michael Morpurgo. Published by Scholastic Press/Scholastic Inc. Reprinted by permission.

The majority of war stories for children are about World War II and the Holocaust. Joseph Bruchac's excellent *Code Talkers* provides a gripping account of the Navajo Marines who were instrumental in winning the war on the Pacific front by using their native language to create an unbreakable code. The story of the code talkers was unknown for many years, supposedly for security reasons, but we are shown the thrilling story of these heroes through the character of 16-year-old Ned Begay. Bruchac provides a look at the training and service of Ned and his fellow code talkers as they entered into the heart of the battles on Iwo Jima and other hard-fought islands in the Pacific. *Code Talkers* also goes beyond the war itself to relate a brief history of the Navajo people, their forced march on the Long Walk, and their ill-treatment following their return to the Four Corners area. This is an important history that will surely appeal to young adolescents.

Escape and Resistance

Some of the most popular war stories are about families who escaped to freedom or endured long years of hiding from the Nazis. *Journey to America* by Sonia Levitin tells of a German Jewish family who become refugees when Hitler comes to power. *When Hitler Stole Pink Rabbit* by Judith Kerr is the story of another family's escape to Switzerland and their trials in trying to earn a living there, then in France, and finally in England. Both of these are prewar stories taking place in the 1930s.

Others made their escape by hiding for the duration of the war. *The Upstairs Room* by Johanna Reiss is a moving account based on the author's own experiences when she and her sister were hidden by a farm family, the Oostervelds. In *Hide and Seek* Ida Vos tells the story of one Jewish family in the Netherlands after the arrival of the German army. Uri Orlev's *The Island on Bird Street* takes the reader into an almost deserted Polish ghetto where Alex, not yet 12, has an ingenious hiding place high in the ruins of building No. 78, where he waits for his father's return. As the months pass, Alex proves to be a clever and courageous survivor, avoiding detection even when German soldiers come to blast open a secret bunker under the cellar. The story ends as Alex and his father, now part of the Underground, are miraculously reunited. The author's confident tone comes from experience; he spent two years hiding in the Warsaw ghetto as a child. Warsaw is also the setting for two thrilling survival stories, Orlev's *Run, Boy, Run,* based on a survivor's account, and Jerry Spinelli's *Milkweed,* about a young orphaned gypsy boy who follows his Jewish friends into the ghetto but is one of the few to survive.

Orlev's *The Man from the Other Side* is a Batchelder Award–winning book about Marek, a young Polish boy, who must help his stepfather smuggle food into the Warsaw ghetto for monetary rather than altruistic reasons. These activities give him access to the ghetto through the sewers and bring him into the middle of the ghetto uprising. When he finds out that his real father was Jewish, he reflects on his own attitude toward the Jews and begins to examine the anti-Semitism that is so prevalent in Polish society. Based on the experiences of a Polish journalist, this is an exciting story that raises important questions about community attitudes and the terrible consequences of prejudice.

In David Chotjewitz's *Daniel Half Human and the Good Nazi,* Daniel Kraushaar is a half-Jewish boy growing up in Hamburg during Hitler's rise to power. He and his best friend, Armin Hillman, are at first enamored by Hitler's Brown Shirts and want to join the Hitler Youth organization. But things begin to go amiss when Daniel's Jewish background is questioned. The story takes us from 1922 through the events of Kristallnacht in 1938 by way of flashbacks from Daniel's return to Hamburg after the war. Like Hans Peter Richter's classic *Friedrich,* Chotjewitz's *Daniel* is the story of the limits of friendship and the betrayals that can occur when fear overcomes human decency.

One of the best survival stories is *The Endless Steppe* by Esther Hautzig, the author's own account of growing up in a slave labor camp in Siberia. The Rudomins, a wealthy Jewish family, live in Vilna, a city in Poland. The Russians occupy Vilna and confiscate the family business; then one day they arrest the whole family as "capitalists and therefore enemies of the people." The Rudomins are shipped in filthy, stiflingly hot cattle cars across Siberia—the barren flat land that is to be their home for five endless years. Despite poverty and privation, Esther manages to satisfy her adolescent needs and find hope in a hopeless situation. During the time the Rudomins are in Siberia, the Nazis enter Poland and kill all their Jewish relatives and friends; in retrospect they consider themselves supremely lucky to have been deported to "the endless steppe." The ending of this story is less grim than that of Anne Frank, but both stories are a tribute to the courage of the human spirit.

Many refugees were helped to flee or hide from authorities by common folk who did what they could to resist the Nazis. Many stories relate the roles that children played in helping these resisters. Two stories of enduring popularity with young readers are Claire Bishop's *Twenty and Ten,* in which French orphans manage to hide ten Jewish children during a Nazi investigation, and Marie McSwigan's *Snow Treasure,* which tells how a brave group of Norwegian children helped smuggle gold out of the country to keep it from the Nazis. Lois Lowry tells the dramatic story of the Danish Resistance as they successfully smuggled nearly seven thousand Jews across the sea to Sweden. In *Number the Stars,* she details the story of how one family saved the lives of the Rosens, their friends. Perhaps the most exciting scene is when the German soldiers come to the house where Ellen Rosen is staying and pretending to be a member of the family. She still wears her Star of David necklace, and Annemarie hisses to her to take it off. She is unable to get it unclasped, so Annemarie yanks it off just before the Nazis enter the room. When they leave,

Annemarie relaxed the clenched fingers of her right hand, which still clutched Ellen's necklace. She looked down, and saw that she had imprinted the Star of David into her palm. (p. 49)

Only through the cooperation and extraordinary bravery of the common people were the Danes able to save most of their Jewish population. This theme of community responsibility is explored in Carol Matas's moving *Greater Than Angels*. Older readers will enjoy this story of the French citizens of Le Chambon-sur-Lignon, who risked their lives to shelter Jews who had taken refuge in the town. Another story of a dramatic rescue of Jewish children by a whole French town is told in *Waiting for Anya* by Michael Morpurgo.

Some of the most dramatic stories about young people who lived through the conflict in Europe are autobiographical. However, they employ many of the techniques of fiction, including the creation of dialogue. Anita Lobel's *No Pretty Pictures: A Child of War* is a moving account of the artist's fearful childhood during and after World War II in Poland, where she moved from hiding to concentration camp to refugee camp. Aranka Siegal's own story of her Hungarian childhood, *Upon the Head of the Goat,* is filled with dread, for the Davidowitz family is Jewish. The final scene is emotionally shattering, as Piri and her mother, brother, and two sisters are forced to board a train for a destination with a name that is unfamiliar to them—Auschwitz.

Books like these are really for adolescents, but they require maturity of their readers, whatever their age level. Children in Asia also suffered during the war years. Sook Nyul Choi writes a poignant story of her childhood in northern Korea in the 1940s in *Year of Impossible Goodbyes.* As the war rages, 10-year-old Sookan, her mother, her brother, and Aunt Tiger endure the cruelties of the Japanese occupation. Her father is a resistance fighter in Manchuria, and her brothers have been taken to Japanese labor camps. When the war is over in 1945, the Koreans hope for a permanent peace, but then communist Russian troops come. By now Sookan and her family have lost everything dear to them. They decide to escape to the Americans at the 38th parallel, but their guide double-crosses them and their mother is taken into custody. Left alone, Sookan and her little brother escape after a terrifying dash through barbed wire. The two children finally make it to the Red Cross center and are later reunited with their parents. This story emphasizes that the so-called victors of a war always make the people of a country their victims. Again it relates the uncommon courage of the common people. Linda Sue Park's *When My Name Was Keoko* is also based on family accounts of the years under Japanese occupation. The story, told in alternating chapters by Sun-hee (forced by the Japanese to assume the name Keoko) and her brother Tae-yul (Nobuo), takes place over a longer time period and provides a more detailed account of the resistance undertaken by Koreans to Japanese occupation.

Set in a similar time period, *So Far from the Bamboo Grove* by Yoko Kawashima Watkins is another true story that tells of a Japanese family living in northern Korea at the close of the war. Fleeing from the Korean communists, 11-year-old Yoko, her older sister Ko, and her mother head south, hoping their brother, Hideyo, and their father will catch up with them on their journey. Their nightmarish trip is described in harrowing detail, and when they reach Japan they find a country devastated by war and all their relatives killed. Their mother places the two girls in school, but when she dies suddenly, they must struggle to survive, selling cloth toys, shining shoes, and picking food from garbage cans. Eventually Hideyo finds them in Kyoto and this unforgettable story ends on a note of hope. Watkins continues their story in the equally moving *My Brother, My Sister, and I.*

The Impact of World War II on the Home Front

 Thousands of American families lost parents, husbands, wives, children, brothers, sisters, friends, and relatives in World War II, but we never endured the physical horror of war in North America. For this reason, perhaps, we have fewer stories about the impact of the war in North America.

One story tells of the English children who were sent to Canada for the duration of the war. In *The Sky Is Falling* by Kit Pearson, Norah and her younger brother, Gavin, are sent to live with a rich woman and her sister in Toronto. This story details the children's difficult adjustment, particularly because "Aunt Florence" obviously prefers Gavin to Norah. This well-written story tells a believable tale of the gradual change in the relationship between 10-year-old Norah and her sponsor.

The Summer of My German Soldier by Bette Greene is the story of 12-year-old Patty Bergen, who is Jewish and the awkward elder daughter of a small-town Arkansas department store owner. Except for the real love of Ruth, the Bergens' African American cook, Patty lives in a loveless situation. Perhaps this explains her compassion for a handsome, well-educated German prisoner of war named Anton who lives in a prison camp near town and comes to her father's store. Patty begins to think of him as her friend, and later, when she sees him running down the railroad tracks, she offers him the safety of her special hideout room over the garage. Only after Anton has gotten away and is captured elsewhere is Patty's role in his escape uncovered. She is arrested and sent to a reform school, clinging to the knowledge that one day she will be free to leave her family and become a "person of value," a term Anton had used.

The painful family separations that were the effect of the war can be seen in several books that are as pertinent to today's child as they are true to the time period. Patricia Reilly Giff's *Lily's Crossing* and *Willow Run* follow two friends through the war years. *Lily's Crossing* concerns a lonely 10-year-old girl who is frustrated and angry at the way the war has changed her life, separating her from her father and her best friend, Maggie. She spends much of her time making up fantasies that turn more and more destructive. Only when she befriends a Hungarian refugee boy does she come to realize the real consequences of the war and those of her own behavior. *Willow Run* recounts Maggie's story and her own loneliness in her new home in Michigan. As she struggles to adjust, Maggie worries about the prejudice shown her German grandfather and her older brother's survival overseas.

The main character in Carolyn Reeder's *Foster's War* is an 11-year-old boy who has lost his older brother to the army and his best friend to the Japanese internment camps. When the family learns that the brother, Mel, who enlisted to get away from their abusive father, has been killed in action, they come close to falling apart. *Foster's War* is a moving portrayal of the everyday sacrifices and the devastating losses the war inflicted on families.

Citizens of the United States and Canada can take no pride in the treatment of Japanese Americans during the war against Japan. In *Journey to Topaz,* Yoshiko Uchida has given a fictionalized account of her family's evacuation and internment in a relocation camp. Yuki's father, a businessman, is taken away from his family on the day of the attack on Pearl Harbor. Taken first to a temporary center at an old racetrack, Yuki and her mother and older brother eventually end up in the "permanent" camp in Topaz, Utah. The author writes the story with restraint and no bitterness. The quiet courage, dignity, and loyalty with which this Japanese family endures their unjust internment makes its own statement to the reader.

Several other books vividly recreate the paranoia that occurred following the attack on Pearl Harbor. In Graham Salisbury's *Under the Blood-Red Sun,* until the bombing Tomi was a typical eighth grader in Hawaii, more interested in baseball than in his studies, and eager to help out on his father's fishing boat. But the attack turns his world upside down. His father's boat is scuttled and his father imprisoned. Tomi is further torn between his need to fit in with his "haoli" (white) friends and his loyalty to his grandfather, who cannot give up his Japanese identity.

Citizens of Japanese descent in Canada were subjected to similar treatment. Sheila Garrigue's *The Eternal Spring of Mr. Ito* helps its readers experience the passionate anti-Japanese feeling along the Pacific Coast even as it demonstrates the blamelessness of those who were shunned, jeered, vandalized, and interned. J. B. Cheaney's *My Friend the Enemy* is set in a rural Oregon community where all the Japanese citizens have supposedly been relocated. Twelve-year-old Hazel Anderson is an avid defender of U.S. security, and her active imagination has her constantly on the lookout for Japanese spies and saboteurs. When she discovers Sogoji, a young Japanese orphan boy, hidden on the farm nearby, she is sure he is the enemy helping to plan a sneak attack. Her resolution to turn him over to the authorities is stopped when she

The lives of two friends are unalterably affected by the bombing of Pearl Harbor in Graham Salisbury's *Under the Blood-Red Sun.* Cover from *Under the Blood-Red Sun* by Graham Salisbury, copyright © 1994 by Graham Salisbury. Reprinted by permission of Random House Children's Books, a division of Random House, Inc.

discovers that Jed, her sister's fiancé and her own beloved friend, is the one who urged his parents to hide Sogoji. Her conceptions of "the enemy" and her own worldview begin to change as she gets to know Sogoji as a real flesh-and-blood person. On the surface of Virginia Euwer Wolff's *Bat 6* is a book about a girl's baseball league set in a small Oregon community in 1949. However, Wolff uses the framework of the game as the setting for the playing out of rivalries and hatreds not unlike those that led to World War II in the first place. The people in this rural community have all been affected by Japanese internment as well as other tragedies of war. In multiple points of view, the twenty-one girls who make up two opposing baseball teams reveal the events of the war on the home front and its effects on the community. Moreover, they find that when left unexamined, the aftereffects linger on, with results just as tragic as those on the battlefield.

War Continues
Unfortunately war did not end with World War II but has continued in other conflicts, such as those in Vietnam, Iraq, and the Balkans.

The Clay Marble by Minfong Ho tells of 12-year-old Dara and her family, who are among the thousands forced to flee from their villages in war-torn Cambodia during the early 1980s. In the refugee camp, there is peace and plenty of food, and Dara makes a new friend, Jantu. Then the shells and bombs start falling again, this time in the middle of camp. In the chaos, Dara is separated from her family and from Jantu. Alone, she must find the strength to reunite her family. When she finally finds them, her brother wants to enlist in the army rather than go home to help them plant their rice crop. Listening to the propaganda over the loudspeaker, Jantu says:

> They all say the same thing. They seem to think it's a game. . . . They take sides, they switch sides, they play against each other. Who wins, who loses, whose turn it is to kick next—it's like an elaborate soccer game. Except they don't use soccer balls. They use us. (p. 141)

The author grew up in Thailand and worked as a nutritionist with an international relief organization on the Thai-Cambodian border in 1980. Dara and Jantu's story is the story of every child in that refugee camp.

Well-written historical fiction like that reviewed in this chapter can enable children to see the continuity of life and their own places in this vast sweep of history. The power of good historical fiction can give children a feeling for a living past. History can become an extension of their own personal experiences, rather than a sterile subject assigned to be studied in school. Such books can offer children new perspectives by which they come to realize that people make and shape their destinies through their own decisions and actions. As we have seen in many of the books discussed in the section "Understanding Various World Cultures" in Chapter 9 (pp. 511–17), events that are happening today do become the history of tomorrow.

INTO THE **CLASSROOM**

Historical Fiction

Reading books about the past demands a willingness to step back into another time and another place. Some children are eager to do so, while others may require some convincing. Teachers wanting to undertake chronological studies of history could introduce a special period through the many picture books we have mentioned throughout this chapter. Another entry point to historical fiction might be the easier-to-read series books that are available. A third option is to study historical fiction through themes that cut across time periods such as "the clash of cultures" or "in quest of freedom." Sometimes it is easier to show children how such themes are relevant to their own lives. However one approaches historical fiction, it is important to help children be critical readers of this genre by helping them to ask questions such as these: "What really happened and what is made up?" "What research did the author do?" "Is there an author's note and bibliography included?" "What else can I find out about this story through primary and secondary sources?"

1. **Period Portfolio Making.** Prepare a decorated portfolio or box of materials of a particular event or period of time to help children build a background for selected books of historical fiction. You might want to include copies of newspaper clippings, artifacts, an annotated bibliography, copies of appropriate paperback books, and examples of art, music, and handicrafts. Plan activity cards for children's use and extension of these materials. (See the description of jackdaws in Chapter 13.)

2. **Role-Playing.** Work with classmates or middle-grade students in role-playing dramatic confrontations in

historical fiction. Some possible choices would be the witch trial of Kit Tyler in *The Witch of Blackbird Pond* by Elizabeth George Speare or Sam Meeker's argument with his father about going to war in *My Brother Sam Is Dead* by James Lincoln Collier and Christopher Collier.

3. **Comparing Values and Attitudes.** Compare the values and attitudes of the heroine of *Lyddie* by Katherine Paterson with those of a young heroine in a contemporary novel, such as Dicey in *Dicey's Song* by Cynthia Voigt. What are their hopes and expectations? How do they express themselves? How are their priorities different or alike?

4. **Comparing Genres.** Compare a picture storybook such as *Rose Blanche* by Christophe Gallaz and Roberto Innocenti, a fantasy such as *The Devil's Arithmetic* by Jane Yolen, and a realistic adventure like *Hide and Seek* by Ida Vos. What does each genre do that is unique? How much information do you receive from each? Chart the differences and similarities.

 Go to the Online Learning Center at **www .mhhe.com/kiefer9e** or your Resources CD-ROM to find these additional classroom activities:

5. **Cooking**
6. **Quiltmaking**
7. **Newspapers and Newscasting**
8. **Reenactment**

Chapter Review

Go to the Online Learning Center at **www.mhhe.com/kiefer9e** or your Resources CD-ROM to take chapter quizzes, practice with key terms, and review the chapter.

Explorations

1. Read four or five books about one particular period or place, and chart the references to kinds of food, clothing, houses, transportation, language, and so on. Which books give the most authentic picture?

2. Collect examples of dialogue and descriptive language from several books of historical fiction. You might want to include something by Patricia Beatty, Paul Fleischman, or Rosemary Sutcliff in this sample. What techniques do the authors use to indicate the setting?

3. Analyze a work of historical fiction for accuracy of facts as well as literary qualities.

4. Search the database and make a list of text sets on a historical theme or time period. Include works of fiction, nonfiction, poetry, and picture books. Then search the Internet to find additional primary source materials that support exploration of your theme.

Web Links

Go to the Online Learning Center at **www .mhhe.com/kiefer9e** to find links to the following children's literature Web sites:

Author Spotlight: Karen Cushman

Avi

Historical Fiction for Children

Historical Fiction for Hipsters

Historical Fiction for Young Adults

Katherine Paterson

Little House in the Big Woods

Notable Trade books for Young People

The Scott O'Dell Historical Fiction Award

Sign of the Beaver

Top Ten Favorites: Children's Historical Fiction

Traveling Through American History

Related Readings

Collier, Christopher. "Johnny and Sam: Old and New Approaches to the American Revolution." *Horn Book Magazine,* April 1976, pp. 132–38.

One of the co-authors of popular novels about the American Revolution discusses three historiographic interpretations of that conflict and contends that modern historical fiction should not present historical events in simple or one-sided terms.

Collier, Christopher, ed. *Brother Sam and All That: Historical Context and Literary Analysis of the Novels of James and Christopher Collier.* Clearwater, Fl.: Clearwater Press, 1999.

This highly useful resource offers essays about many of the Colliers' books, background information and photographs of many of their settings, and classroom activities including dramatizations of The Clock *and* My Brother Sam Is Dead.

Collins, Fiona M., and Judith Graham, eds. *Historical Fiction for Children: Capturing the Past.* London: David Fulton Publishers, 2001.

Although focused on historical fiction published in the United Kingdom, this collection of essays will be of interest to a broad international audience of teachers and librarians. Sections such as "Exploring the Narrative Past," "Writing about the Narrative Past," and "Teaching the Narrative Past" provide an overview of the field; consideration of important writers; discussion of issues, themes, and topics in historical fiction; and descriptions of classroom practice.

Haugaard, Erik Christian. "'Before I Was Born': History and the Child." *Horn Book Magazine,* October 1979, pp. 514–21.

> The author writes of the relationship between history and truth and makes an eloquent case for the value of history in showing that people always have choices.

Levstik, Linda S., and Keith C. Barton. *Doing History: Investigating with Children in the Elementary and Middle Schools.* Mahwah, N.J.: Erlbaum, 2005.

> This superb book's content builds strong connections from historical study to the broader fields of social studies, reading, science, mathematics, and the arts with children's literature at the center of the curriculum. The book, grounded in sound learning theory filtered through the voices of teachers and children engaged in critical inquiries, provides a framework for extending such studies into all classrooms.

Segel, Elizabeth. "Laura Ingalls Wilder's America: An Unflinching Assessment." *Children's Literature in Education* 25 (summer 1977): 63–70.

> Segel examines the values portrayed in the Little House series, particularly *Little House on the Prairie,* and points out that Wilder, through the character of Laura, not only presented the attitudes and beliefs of nineteenth-century America but also questioned them.

Children's Literature

 Go to the Children's Literature Database on your Resources CD-ROM for a searchable listing of these and other children's literature titles.

Alder, Elizabeth. *Crossing the Panther's Path.* Farrar, 2002.

———. *The King's Shadow.* Farrar, 1995.

Anderson, Joan. *The First Thanksgiving Feast.* Photographs by George Ancona. Clarion, 1983.

Antle, Nancy. *Beautiful Land: A Story of the Oklahoma Land Rush.* Illustrated by John Gampert. Viking, 1994.

Armstrong, William H. *Sounder.* Illustrated by James Barkley. Harper, 1969.

Auch, M. J. *Ashes of Roses.* Holt, 2002.

Avi [Avi Wortis]. *Crispin: The Cross of Lead.* Hyperion, 2002.

———. *The Fighting Ground.* Lippincott, 1984.

———. *The True Confessions of Charlotte Doyle.* Orchard, 1990.

Bartone, Elisa. *Peppe the Lamplighter.* Illustrated by Ted Lewin. Lothrop, 1993.

Beatty, Patricia. *Be Ever Hopeful, Hannalee.* Morrow, 1988.

———. *Charley Skedaddle.* Morrow, 1987.

———. *Jayhawker.* Morrow, 1991.

———. *Turn Homeward, Hannalee.* Morrow, 1984.

Berry, James. *Ajeemah and His Son.* HarperCollins, 1992.

Bishop, Claire Huchet. *Twenty and Ten.* As told by Janet Jolly. Illustrated by William Pène DuBois. Viking, 1964.

Blackwood, Gary. *The Shakespeare Stealer.* Dutton, 1998.

———. *Shakespeare's Scribe.* Dutton, 2000.

Blos, Joan W. *A Gathering of Days: A New England Girl's Journal, 1830–32.* Scribner's, 1979.

Borden, Louise. *Sleds on Boston Common: A Story from the American Revolution.* Illustrated by Robert Andrew Parker. McElderry, 2000.

Bosse, Malcolm. *The Examination.* Farrar, 1994.

Branford, Henrietta. *Fire, Bed and Bone.* Candlewick, 1998.

Brink, Carol Ryrie. *Caddie Woodlawn.* Illustrated by Trina Schart Hyman. Macmillan, 1973.

———. *Caddie Woodlawn.* Illustrated by Kate Seredy. Macmillan, 1936.

Bruchac, Joseph. *The Arrow over the Door.* Dial, 1998.

———. *Children of the Longhouse.* Dial, 1996.

———. *Code Talker.* Scholastic, 2005.

———. *Geronimo.* Dial, 2006.

———. *Sacajawea.* Silver Whistle/Harcourt, 2000.

———. *The Winter People.* Dial, 2002.

Bulla, Clyde Robert. *A Lion to Guard Us.* Illustrated by Michelle Chessare. Harper Trophy, 1990 [1981].

———. *The Sword in the Tree.* Illustrated by Paul Galdone. Crowell, 1956.

Bunting, Eve. *Dandelions.* Illustrated by Greg Shed. Harcourt, 1995.

Carbonne, Elisa Lynn. *Stealing Freedom.* Knopf, 1999.

Cheaney, J. B. *My Friend the Enemy.* Knopf, 2005.

———. *The Playmaker.* Knopf, 2002.

———. *The True Prince.* Knopf, 2002.

Choi, Sook Nyul. *Year of Impossible Goodbyes.* Houghton, 1991.

Chotjewitz, David. *Daniel Half Human and the Good Nazi.* Translated by Doris Orgel. Atheneum, 2004.

Clapp, Patricia. *Constance: A Story of Early Plymouth.* Lothrop, 1968.

Collier, James Lincoln, and Christopher Collier. *Jump Ship to Freedom.* Delacorte, 1981.

———. *My Brother Sam Is Dead.* Four Winds, 1974.

———. *War Comes to Willy Freeman.* Delacorte, 1983.

———. *Who Is Carrie?* Delacorte, 1984.

———. *With Every Drop of Blood.* Delacorte, 1994.

Conrad, Pam. *Prairie Songs.* Illustrated by Darryl Zudeck. Harper, 1985.

Crew, Linda. *A Heart for Any Fate: Westward to Oregon, 1845.* Oregon Historical Society, 2005.

Crossley-Holland, Kevin. *King of the Middle March.* Arthur Trilogy. Scholastic, 2004.

Culleton, Beatrice. *Spirit of the White Bison.* Illustrated by Robert Kakaygeesick. Book Pub., 1989.

Currier, Katrina Saltonstall. *Kai's Journey to Gold Mountain.* Illustrated by Gabor Utomo. Angel Island, 2005.

Curtis, Christopher Paul. *Bud, Not Buddy.* Delacorte, 1999.

———. *The Watsons Go to Birmingham—1963.* Delacorte, 1995.

Cushman, Karen. *The Ballad of Lucy Whipple.* Clarion, 1996.

———. *Catherine, Called Birdy.* Clarion, 1994.

———. *The Midwife's Apprentice.* Clarion, 1995.

———. *Rodzina.* Clarion, 2003.

Dalgliesh, Alice. *The Thanksgiving Story.* Illustrated by Helen Sewell. Scribner's, 1954.

de Angeli, Marguerite. *The Door in the Wall.* Doubleday, 1949.

DeFelice, Cynthia C. *The Apprenticeship of Lucas Whitaker.* Farrar, 1996.

———. *Lostman's River.* Macmillan, 1994.

———. *Nowhere to Call Home.* Farrar, 1999.

Denzel, Justin. *Boy of the Painted Cave.* Philomel, 1988.

———. *Return to the Painted Cave.* Philomel, 1997.

de Trevino, Elizabeth Borton. *I, Juan de Pareja.* Farrar, 1965.

Dorris, Michael. *Guests.* Hyperion, 1994.

———. *Morning Girl.* Hyperion, 1992.

———. *Sees Behind Trees.* Hyperion, 1996.

Dudley, David L. *The Bicycle Man.* Clarion, 2005.

Dunn, Anne M. *Grandmother's Gift: Stories from the Anishinabeg.* Holy Cow, 1997.

———. *When Beaver Was Very Great: Stories to Live By.* Holy Cow, 1995.

———. *Winter Thunder: Retold Tales.* Holy Cow, 2001.

Dyer, T. A. *A Way of His Own.* Houghton, 1981.

Edmonds, Walter D. *The Matchlock Gun.* Putnam, 1989.

English, Karen. *Francie.* Farrar, 1999.

Erdrich, Louise. *The Birchbark House.* Hyperion, 1999.

———. *The Game of Silence.* HarperCollins, 2005.

Ernst, Kathleen. *Betrayal at Cross Creek.* American Girl, 2004.

Feelings, Tom. *The Middle Passage: White Ships/Black Cargo.* Introduction by Dr. John Henrik Clarke. Dial, 1995.

Field, Rachel. *Calico Bush.* Illustrated by Allen Lewis. Macmillan, 1931.

Fleischman, Paul. *The Borning Room.* HarperCollins, 1991.

———. *Bull Run.* HarperCollins, 1993.

———. *Saturnalia.* HarperCollins, 1990.

Fletcher, Susan. *Walk across the Sea.* Atheneum, 2001.

Forbes, Esther. *Johnny Tremain.* Illustrated by Lynd Ward. Houghton, 1946.

Forrester, Sandra. *Sound the Jubilee.* Lodestar, 1995.

———. *Storm Warriors.* Knopf, 2001.

Fox, Paula. *The Slave Dancer.* Illustrated by Eros Keith. Bradbury, 1973.

Freedman, Russell. *Children of the Wild West.* Clarion, 1983.

Fritz, Jean. *Brady.* Illustrated by Lynd Ward. Coward-McCann/Penguin, 1987 [1960].

———. *The Cabin Faced West.* Illustrated by Feodor Rojankovsky. Coward-McCann, 1958.

———. *Early Thunder.* Illustrated by Lynd Ward. Coward-McCann, 1967.

Gallaz, Christophe, and Roberto Innocenti. *Rose Blanche.* Illustrated by Roberto Innocenti. Creative Education, 1985.

Garfield, Henry. *The Lost Voyage of John Cabot.* Atheneum, 2004.

Garrigue, Sheila. *The Eternal Spring of Mr. Ito.* Bradbury, 1985.

Gauch, Patricia Lee. *Aaron and the Green Mountain Boys.* Boyds Mills, 2005.

———. *This Time, Tempe Wick?* Illustrated by Margot Tomes. Putnam, 1974.

———. *Thunder at Gettysburg.* Illustrated by Stephen Gammell. Putnam, 1990 [1975].

Giff, Patricia Reilly. *All the Way Home.* Delacorte, 2001.

———. *A House of Tailors.* Random, 2004.

———. *Lily's Crossing.* Delacorte, 1997.

———. *Maggie's Door.* Random, 2003.

———. *Nory Ryan's Song.* Delacorte, 2000.

———. *Willow Run.* Random, 2005.

Grant, K. M. *Blaze of Silver.* de Granville Trilogy. Walker, 2006.

———. *blood red horse.* de Granville Trilogy. Walker, 2005.

———. *Green Jasper.* de Granville Trilogy. Walker, 2006.

Gray, Elizabeth Janet. *Adam of the Road.* Illustrated by Robert Lawson. Viking, 1942.

Greene, Bette. *The Summer of My German Soldier.* Bantam, 1984 [1973].

Gregory, Kristiana. *Jenny of the Tetons.* Harcourt, 1989.

Hahn, Mary Downing. *Stepping on the Cracks.* Clarion, 1991.

Hale, Marian. *The Truth about Sparrows.* Holt, 2004.

Hansen, Joyce. *The Captive.* Scholastic, 1994.

———. *I Thought My Soul Would Rise and Fly: The Diary of Patsy a Freed Girl.* Scholastic, 1997.

Hartnett, Sonya. *Thursday's Child.* Candlewick, 2002.

Harvey, Brett. *Immigrant Girl: Becky of Eldridge Street.* Illustrated by Deborah K. Ray. Holiday, 1987.

Hautzig, Esther. *The Endless Steppe: Growing Up in Siberia.* Crowell, 1968.

Hesse, Karen. *The Cats in Krasinski Square.* Illustrated by Wendy Watson. Scholastic, 2004.

———. *Out of the Dust.* Scholastic, 1997.

———. *Stowaway.* McElderry, 2000.

———. *Witness.* Scholastic, 2001.

Hest, Amy. *When Jessie Came across the Sea.* Illustrated by P. J. Lynch. Candlewick, 1997.

Hickman, Janet. *Susannah.* Greenwillow, 1998.

Hill, Kirkpatrick. *Dancing at the Odinochka.* McElderry, 2005.

Ho, Minfong. *The Clay Marble.* Farrar, 1991.

Holm, Anne. *North to Freedom.* Translated by L. W. Kingsland. Harcourt, 1965.

Holm, Jennifer L. *Boston Jane: An Adventure.* HarperCollins, 2001.

———. *Boston Jane: The Claim.* HarperCollins, 2004.

———. *Boston Jane: Wilderness Days.* HarperCollins, 2001.

———. *Our Only May Amelia.* HarperCollins, 1999.

Hoobler, Dorothy, and Thomas Hoobler. *The Demon in the Teahouse.* Philomel, 2001.

———. *The Ghost in the Tokaido Inn.* Philomel, 1999.

———. *In Darkness, Death.* Philomel, 2005.

Hopkinson, Deborah. *Under the Quilt of Night.* Illustrated by James E. Ransome. Simon, 2001.

Howard, Ellen. *The Gate in the Wall.* Atheneum, 1999.

Hunt, Irene. *Across Five Aprils.* Follett, 1964.

Hunter, Mollie. *The King's Swift Rider: A Novel of Robert the Bruce.* HarperCollins, 1998.

Hunter, Sally M. *Four Seasons of Corn: A Winnebago Tradition.* Illustrated by Joe Allen. Lerner, 1996.

Ibbotson, Eva. *The Star of Kazan.* Illustrated by Kevin Hawkes. Dutton, 2004.

Ives, David. *Scrib.* HarperCollins, 2005.

Jinks, Catherine. *Pagan's Crusade.* Candlewick, 2003.

———. *Pagan's Exile.* Candlewick, 2004.

———. *Pagan's Scribe.* Candlewick, 2004.

———. *Pagan's Vows.* Candlewick, 2004.

Jones, Elizabeth McDavid. *Mystery on Skull Island.* Pleasant, 2002.

Karr, Kathleen. *Bone Dry.* Hyperion, 2000.

———. *Skullduggery.* Hyperion, 2002.

———. *Worlds Apart.* Cavendish, 2005.

Keith, Harold. *Rifles for Watie.* Crowell, 1957.

Kelly, Eric P. *The Trumpeter of Krakow.* Rev. ed. Illustrated by Janina Domanska. Macmillan, 1966 [1928].

Kerr, Judith. *When Hitler Stole Pink Rabbit.* Coward-McCann, 1972.

Ketchum, Liza. *Where the Great Hawk Flies.* Clarion, 2005.

King, Sandra. *Shannon: An Ojibway Dancer.* Photographs by Catherine Whipple. Lerner, 1993.

Kirkpatrick, Katherine. *Escape across the Wide Sea.* Holiday, 2004.

Konigsburg, E. L. *A Proud Taste for Scarlet and Miniver.* Atheneum, 1973.

———. *The Second Mrs. Giaconda.* Macmillan, 1978.

Kroeber, Theodora. *Ishi, Last of His Tribe.* Illustrated by Ruth Robbins. Parnassus, 1964.

Kurtz, Jane. *Saba: Under the Hyena's Foot.* American Girl, 2003.

Lasky, Kathryn. *Dreams in the Golden Country: The Diary of Zipporah Feldman, a Jewish Immigrant Girl, New York City, 1903.* Scholastic, 1998.

Lavender, William. *Just Jane: A Daughter of England Caught in the Struggle of the American Revolution.* Harcourt, 2002.

Lawrence, Caroline. *The Enemies of Jupiter.* Roaring Brook, 2005.

———. *The Gladiators from Capua.* Roaring Brook, 2005.

———. *The Pirates of Pompeii.* Roaring Brook, 2003.

———. *The Secrets of Vesuvius.* Roaring Brook, 2002.

———. *The Thieves of Ostia.* Roaring Brook, 2002.

Lawrence, Iain. *The Buccaneers.* Delacorte, 2000.

———. *The Cannibals.* Delacorte, 2005.

———. *The Convicts.* Delacort, 2005.

———. *Lord of the Nutcracker Men.* Delacorte, 2001.

———. *The Smugglers.* Delacorte, 2000.

———. *The Wreckers.* Delacorte, 2000.

Lerangis, Peter. *Smiler's Bones.* Scholastic, 2005.

Lester, Julius. *Day of Tears: A Novel in Dialogue.* Hyperion, 2005.

———. *Pharaoh's Daughter: A Novel of Ancient Egypt.* Harcourt, 2000.

Levitin, Sonia. *Journey to America.* Illustrated by Charles Robinson. Atheneum, 1970.

Llorente, Pilar Molina. *The Apprentice.* Translated by Robin Longshaw. Illustrated by Juan Ramón Alonso. Farrar, 1993.

Lobel, Anita. *No Pretty Pictures: A Child of War.* Greenwillow, 1998.

Lowry, Lois. *Number the Stars.* Houghton, 1989.

Lunn, Janet. *The Root Cellar.* Macmillan, 1983.

Lyons, Mary E. *Letters from a Slave Girl: The Story of Harriet Jacobs.* Scribner's, 1992.

MacLachlan, Patricia. *Sarah, Plain and Tall.* Harper, 1985.

———. *Skylark.* HarperCollins, 1994.

———. *Three Names.* Illustrated by Alexander Pertzoff. HarperCollins, 1991.

Maruki, Toshi. *Hiroshima No Pika* (The Flash of Hiroshima). Lothrop, 1980.

Matas, Carol. *Greater Than Angels.* Simon, 1998.

McCaughrean, Geraldine. *The Kite Rider.* HarperCollins, 2002.

McGraw, Eloise Jarvis. *The Golden Goblet.* Viking Penguin, 1986 [1961].

———. *Mara, Daughter of the Nile.* Viking Penguin, 1985 [1953].

———. *Moccasin Trail.* Viking Penguin, 1986 [1952].

McMullan, Margaret. *How I Found the Strong.* Houghton, 2005.

McSwigan, Marie. *Snow Treasure.* Illustrated by Alexander Pertzoff. HarperCollins, 1991.

Meyer, Louis A. *Bloody Jack: Being an Account of the Curious Adventures of Mary "Jacky" Faber, Ship's Boy.* Bloody Jack Adventures. Harcourt, 2004.

———. *Curse of the Blue Tattoo: Being an Account of the Misadventures of Jack Faber, Midshipman and Fine Lady.* Bloody Jack Adventures. Harcourt, 2005.

———. *Under the Jolly Roger: Being an Account of the Further Nautical Adventures of Jacky Faber.* Bloody Jack Adventures. Harcourt, 2005.

Monjo, F. N. *The Drinking Gourd.* Illustrated by Fred Brenner. Harper, 1970.

Morpurgo, Michael. *Private Peaceful.* Scholastic, 2004.

———. *Waiting for Anya.* Viking, 1990.

Morrow, Honoré. *On to Oregon!* Beech Tree, 1991 [1946].

Moses, Sheila. *The Legend of Buddy Bush.* McElderry, 2004.

———. *The Return of Buddy Bush.* McElderry, 2005.

Mosley, Walter. *47*. Little, 2005.

Mowll, Joshua. *Operation Red Jericho*. Candlewick, 2005.

Namioka, Lensey. *The Coming of the Bear*. HarperCollins, 1992.

———. *Den of the White Fox*. Harcourt, 1997.

———. *Island of Ogres*. Harper, 1989.

Napoli, Donna Jo. *Daughter of Venice*. Random, 2002.

———. *The King of Mulberry Street*. Random, 2005.

Nixon, Joan Lowery. *Land of Hope*. Bantam, 1992.

O'Dell, Scott. *Island of the Blue Dolphins*. Houghton, 1960.

———. *Sarah Bishop*. Houghton, 1980.

———. *Sing Down the Moon*. Houghton, 1970.

———. *Zia*. Illustrated by Ted Lewin. Houghton, 1976.

Orlev, Uri. *The Island on Bird Street*. Translated from the Hebrew by Hillel Halkin. Houghton, 1984.

———. *The Man from the Other Side*. Translated by Hillel Halkin. Houghton, 1991.

———. *Run, Boy, Run*. Translated by Hillel Halkin. Houghton, 2003.

Park, Linda Sue. *The Kite Fighters*. Clarion, 2000.

———. *Seesaw Girl*. Clarion, 1999.

———. *A Single Shard*. Clarion, 2001.

———. *When My Name Was Keoko*. Clarion, 2002.

Paterson, Katherine. *Jip: His Story*. Lodestar, 1996.

———. *Lyddie*. Lodestar, 1988.

———. *The Master Puppeteer*. Harper, 1975.

———. *Of Nightingales That Weep*. Harper, 1974.

———. *Park's Quest*. Dutton, 1991.

———. *The Sign of the Chrysanthemum*. Harper, 1973.

Paulsen, Gary. *Nightjohn*. Delacorte, 1993.

———. *Sarny*. Delacorte, 1997.

Pearsall, Shelley. *Crooked River*. Knopf, 2005.

———. *Trouble Don't Last*. Knopf, 2002.

Pearson, Kit. *The Sky Is Falling*. Viking, 1989.

Peck, Richard. *Fair Weather*. Dial, 2001.

———. *A Long Way from Chicago*. Dial, 1999.

———. *The Teacher's Funeral: A Comedy in Three Parts*. Dial, 2004.

———. *A Year Down Yonder*. Dial, 2000.

Perez, N. A. *The Slopes of War*. Houghton, 1984.

Petry, Ann. *Tituba of Salem Village*. Crowell, 1964.

Pinkney, Andrea Davis. *Silent Thunder*. Hyperion, 1999.

Polacco, Patricia. *Pink and Say*. Philomel, 1994.

Porter, Tracey. *Treasures in the Dust*. HarperCollins, 1997.

Pryor, Bonnie. *The House on Maple Street*. Illustrated by Beth Peck. Morrow, 1987.

Reeder, Carolyn. *Foster's War*. Scholastic, 1998.

———. *Shades of Gray*. Macmillan, 1989.

Reiss, Johanna. *The Upstairs Room*. Crowell, 1972.

Richter, Hans Peter. *Friedrich*. Translated by Edite Kroll. Puffin, 1987.

Rinaldi, Ann. *Hang a Thousand Trees with Ribbons*. Harcourt, 1996.

———. *My Heart Is on the Ground: The Diary of Nannie Little Rose, a Sioux Girl (Dear America)*. Scholastic, 1999.

———. *A Ride into Morning: The Story of Tempe Wick*. Gulliver, 1991.

Riskind, Mary. *Apple Is My Sign*. Houghton, 1981.

Rostkowski, Margaret I. *After the Dancing Days*. Harper, 1986.

Rubalcaba, Jill. *A Place in the Sun*. Clarion, 1997.

Ruby, Lois. *Soon Be Free*. Simon, 2000.

———. *Steal Away Home*. Macmillan, 1994.

Ryan, Pam Muñoz. *Esperanza Rising*. Scholastic, 2000.

Salisbury, Graham. *Under the Blood-Red Sun*. Delacorte, 1994.

Schmidt, Gary D. *Lizzie Bright and the Buckminster Boy*. Clarion, 2004.

Sewall, Marcia. *The Pilgrims of Plimoth*. Atheneum, 1986.

Siegal, Aranka. *Upon the Head of the Goat: A Childhood in Hungary, 1939–1944*. Farrar, 1981.

Siegelson, Kim. *Trembling Earth*. Philomel, 2004.

Sneve, Virginia Driving Hawk. *Bad River Boys: A Meeting of the Lakota Sioux with Lewis and Clark*. Illustrated by Bill Farnsworth. Holiday, 2005.

Snyder, Zilpha Keatley. *Cat Running*. Delacorte, 1994.

Speare, Elizabeth George. *The Bronze Bow*. Houghton, 1961.

———. *Calico Captive*. Illustrated by W. T. Mars. Houghton, 1957.

———. *The Sign of the Beaver*. Houghton, 1983.

———. *The Witch of Blackbird Pond*. Houghton, 1958.

Spinelli, Jerry. *Milkweed*. Knopf, 2003.

Steele, William O. *The Buffalo Knife*. Illustrated by Paul Galdone. Harcourt, 1952.

———. *Winter Danger*. Illustrated by Paul Galdone. Harcourt, 1954.

Stevens, Carla. *Trouble for Lucy*. Illustrated by Ronald Himler. Clarion, 1979.

Stevenson, Robert Louis. *Treasure Island*. Scribner's, 1981 [1883].

Sutcliff, Rosemary. *The Eagle of the Ninth*. Illustrated by C. W. Hodges. Walck, 1954.

———. *The Lantern Bearers*. Illustrated by Charles Keeping. Walck, 1959.

———. *The Shining Company*. Farrar, 1990.

———. *The Silver Branch*. Illustrated by Charles Keeping. Walck, 1959.

———. *Sun Horse, Moon Horse*. Dutton, 1978.

———. *Sword Song*. Farrar, 1998.

———. *Warrior Scarlet*. Walck, 1958.

Taylor, Mildred. *The Land*. Fogelman, 2001.

———. *Let the Circle Be Unbroken*. Dial, 1981.

———. *Mississippi Bridge*. Illustrated by Max Ginsburg. Dial, 1990.

———. *Roll of Thunder, Hear My Cry*. Illustrated by Jerry Pinkney. Dial, 1976.

———. *The Well*. Dial, 1995.

Temple, Frances. *The Beduins' Gazelle*. Orchard, 1996.

———. *The Ramsey Scallop*. Orchard, 1994.

Tingle, Rebecca. *The Edge on the Sword.* Putnam, 2001.

———. *Far Traveler.* Putnam, 2005.

Torrey, Michelle. *To the Edge of the World.* Knopf, 2003.

Turner, Ann. *Nettie's Trip South.* Illustrated by Ronald Himler. Macmillan, 1987.

Uchida, Yoshiko. *Journey to Topaz.* Illustrated by Donald Carrick. Scribner's, 1971.

Updale, Eleanor. *Montmorency.* Scholastic, 2004

———. *Montmorency and the Assassins.* Scholastic, 2006.

———. *Monmorency on the Rocks.* Scholastic, 2005.

Van Leeuwen, Jean. *Bound for Oregon.* Illustrated by James Watling. Dial, 1994.

Vos, Ida. *Hide and Seek.* Translated by Terese Edelstein and Inez Smidt. Houghton, 1991.

Wait, Lea. *Wintering Well.* McElderry, 2004.

Walsh, Jill Paton. *A Chance Child.* Farrar, 1978.

Watkins, Yoko Kawashima. *My Brother, My Sister, and I.* Bradbury, 1994.

———. *So Far from the Bamboo Grove.* Lothrop, 1986.

Weaver, Lydia. *Close to Home: A Story of the Polio Epidemic.* Illustrated by Aileen Arrington. Viking, 1993.

Wilder, Laura Ingalls. *By the Shores of Silver Lake.* Illustrated by Garth Williams. Harper, 1953 [1939].

———. *Little House in the Big Woods.* Illustrated by Garth Williams. Harper, 1953 [1932].

———. *Little House on the Prairie.* Illustrated by Garth Williams. Harper, 1953 [1935].

———. *Little Town on the Prairie.* Illustrated by Garth Williams. Harper, 1953 [1932].

———. *On the Banks of Plum Creek.* Illustrated by Garth Williams. Harper, 1953 [1937].

———. *These Happy Golden Years.* Illustrated by Garth Williams. Harper, 1953 [1943].

Wilson, Diane Lee. *Black Storm Comin'.* McElderry, 2005.

Wiseman, David. *Jeremy Visick.* Houghton, 1981.

Wisler, G. Clifton. *Red Cap.* Dutton, 1991.

Wittstock, Laura W. *Ininatig's Gift of Sugar: Traditional Native Sugar Making.* Photographs by Dale Kakkak. Lerner, 1993.

Wolff, Virginia Euwer. *Bat 6.* Scholastic, 1998.

Wood, Frances M. *Daughter of Madrugada.* Delacorte, 2002.

Woodruff, Elvira. *The Memory Coat.* Illustrated by Michael Dooling. Scholastic, 1999.

Wyss, Johann David. *The Swiss Family Robinson.* Sharon, 1981 [1814].

Yep, Laurence. *Dragon's Gate.* HarperCollins, 1993.

———. *Dragonwings.* Harper, 1977.

———. *Dream Soul.* HarperCollins, 2000.

———. *Mountain Light.* Harper, 1985.

———. *The Serpent's Children.* Harper, 1984.

———. *Spring Pearl: The Last Flower.* Pleasant, 2002.

———. *The Star Fisher.* Morrow, 1991.

———. *The Traitor.* HarperCollins, 2003.

Yin. *Coolies.* Illustrated by Chris Soentpiet. Philomel, 2001.

Yolen, Jane. *The Devil's Arithmetic.* Viking Penguin, 1990.

Yolen, Jane, and Robert Harris. *Girl in a Cage.* Philomel, 2002.

———. *The Queen's Own Fool: A Novel of Mary Queen of Scots.* Philomel, 2000.

Chapter Eleven

Nonfiction Books

Chapter Outline

Media Resources

We know a 6-year-old who loves to go to the school library because there he can choose any book he wants. At story time he listens eagerly to picture storybooks and other fiction, but the books he chooses to check out, to keep for a time and to pore over at home, are nonfiction.

His favorites are about airplanes, rockets, space travel, and complex machinery. He often chooses books far above his level of understanding (once it was an encyclopedia of space facts so big that he could barely carry it by himself). Part of his fun is looking at the illustrations over and over again, but he also wants an adult to "read" these difficult books to him. In this case he means reading the picture captions and talking through main ideas or intriguing details in response to his many questions. He joins in the reading by looking for words he knows or can figure out in the boldface headings or diagram labels.

We call attention to this common scenario because it demonstrates so much about the special role of nonfiction literature in children's lives. The audience for nonfiction books is broad, including young children as well as older students, girls as well as boys. Adult ideas about what is appropriate for a given age level are often less important than a child's desire to know about a particular topic. A reader's approach to a nonfiction book might not always be to read pages in order from first to last, as fiction demands. In this type of reading, illustration plays a vital part by focusing interest and clarifying or extending information. Most of all, our example shows how nonfiction literature can provide powerful motivation to read and to enjoy experiences with books. Children are curious about the world and how it works, and they develop passionate attachments to the right books at the right time. They deserve teachers and librarians who can help them discover this particular kind of satisfaction in reading.

TRENDS IN NONFICTION BOOKS

For many years children's literature scholars have used the term *informational* books rather than *nonfiction* books to designate literature for children that is based in the actual rather than the imagined. One recent trend in children's literature is the movement to the term *nonfiction* rather than *informational*. Author Penny Colman argues that the term *informational* tends to make people think of encyclopedias and textbooks.

> The term does not readily trigger associations with the variety of nonfiction books—biographies, history, true adventures, science, sports, photographic essays, memoirs, etc.—that are available and accessible for children and young adults and that can be just as compelling, engaging and beautifully written as good fiction.[1]

In this chapter and in Chapter 12, "Biography," we will most often use the term *nonfiction* rather than *informational* to refer to this body of literature, as is common with adult literature.

New worlds and new interests lie waiting for children between the covers of nonfiction books. The secrets of a water droplet, the fascinating world of entomologists, or the search for the legendary pink dolphin have all been revealed in attractive and inviting formats. For proof, have a look at Walter Wick's *A Drop of Water*, Donna M. Jackson's *The Bug Scientists*, or Sy Montgomery's *Encantado: Pink Dolphin of the Amazon*. Nonfiction books also offer children new perspectives on familiar topics, as can be found in Patricia Lauber's *What You Never Knew about Tubs, Toilets, and Showers* or Alexandra Siy and Dennis Kunkel's *Mosquito Bite*. Some nonfiction books, like Jane Goodall's *The Chimpanzees I Love* or Stephen Kramer's *Hidden*

---

[1] Penny Colman, "Nonfiction Is Literature Too," *New Advocate* 12.3 (summer 1999): 217.

Worlds: Looking through a Scientist's Microscope, have tremendous eye appeal and invite browsing. Others are designed to reward sustained attention, like Susan Campbell Bartoletti's *Black Potatoes: The Story of the Great Irish Famine, 1845–1850* or James Cross Giblin's explanation of the unraveling of an ancient mystery in *The Riddle of the Rosetta Stone.*

Nonfiction books for children are more numerous, more various, and more appealing than ever. Only recently have they begun to receive the critical recognition and classroom attention that they have long deserved. We begin here by looking briefly at some of the current trends in nonfiction books for today's child. In many ways these trends mirror recent changes in the larger world of children's books. The following overview covers the more obvious developments of recent years.

Increase in Quantity and Quality

Today, trade book publishers are producing many attractive, well-written works of nonfiction books, more than ever before. Frequently these titles are edited, designed, and produced with the same care that was once reserved for picture books. Jean Fritz's *Leonardo's Horse,* illustrated by Hudson Talbot, is one example. This fascinating story of the modern-day casting of Leonardo da Vinci's design for a bronze horse begins with beautiful bronzed endpapers, and the book has an unusual domed shape that echoes the arching neck of Leonardo's horse and the domes of Renaissance Florence. Talbott's richly executed oil paintings add artistic veracity to the information presented and show how attention to details of a book's visual design can add to the child's understanding of facts.

A Focus on the Very Young

Part of the increased production of nonfiction books can be attributed to a growing awareness of a new market for younger children. In keeping with the emphasis on the importance of early childhood education, there is a new focus on the preschool and early primary audience for nonfiction books. Concept books and identification books that provide the names of objects have long been a popular type of nonfiction picture book for young children (see Chapter 4), and for many years HarperCollins has published books for primary grade children in its Let's Read and Find Out series. Recently the publisher has updated many of those titles and extended its list to include preschool readers. Currently many types of nonfiction formats can be found for the very young. Candlewick's Read and Wonder series, which includes titles such as *Gentle Giant Octopus* by Karen Wallace, provides beautifully illustrated and well-written books for preschoolers. Books in the See How They Grow series, published by DK, use clear photos and minimal text to show how baby animals change in the first few weeks of life. Angela Royston's *Insects and Crawly Creatures,* a book in the Eye-Openers series, focuses on naming and identification

Jean Fritz's *Leonardo's Horse,* illustrated by Hudson Talbott, is an example of elegant book design. From *Leonardo's Horse* by Jean Fritz, illustrated by Hudson Talbott, illustrations copyright © 2001 by Hudson Talbott, illustrations. Used by permission of G. P. Putnam's Sons, a division of Penguin Putnam Group for Young Readers, a member of Penguin Group (USA) Inc., 345 Hudson St., New York, NY 10014. All rights reserved.

but adds information about each insect and close-up drawings of significant details. Both series are printed on extra-heavy stock to allow for hard wear by preschoolers. Both also originate in England and share some of the visual characteristics of the popular Eyewitness Books series for older readers (published by DK).

The photo essay is another format sometimes directed now to a very young audience, as in Ron Hirschi's gentle commentaries on the seasons in *Spring, Summer, Fall,* and *Winter.* Even experiment books, usually the province of older students, can be appropriate for younger classes if they are as simple and inviting as Cindy Blobaum's *Insectigations.* Although nonfiction series for young children account for many of the new titles, some authors and illustrators do produce fine nonfiction picture books that are one of a kind. Lola M. Schaefer's *Pick, Pull, Snap! Where Once a Flower Bloomed,* illustrated by Lindsay Barrett George; Steve Jenkins and Robin Page's *Move;* and Byron Barton's *I Want to Be an Astronaut* fit this category.

In the orchard, a honeybee buzzes from tree to tree, flying in and out of blossoms.

Its legs brush pollen inside a fragrant, pink flower.

Deep inside the flower, a small, green fruit grows around one seed.

The petals fade and drop to the ground.

Weeks pass, and the fruit, large and sweet, hangs low near passing eyes.

On a late summer day, twist . . .

Lift-the-flap pages and clear, detailed illustrations by Lindsay Barrett George in *Pick, Pull, Snap! Where Once a Flower Bloomed* by Lola M. Schaefer will appeal to younger readers. Text copyright © 2003 by Lola Schaefer. Illustrations copyright © 2003 by Lindsay Barrett George. Reprinted by permission of HarperCollins Publishers.

A Focus on the Visual

Another feature of nonfiction books that has changed in recent years is the increased reliance on visuals, especially photography. In our media-conscious society, both children and adults have become more visually oriented, more likely to expect pictures in magazines, newspapers, and other print materials. At the same time, technological improvements in making and reproducing pictures have made it possible to satisfy the demand for color, close-ups, and novel perspectives.

Nonfiction books for all ages often sell themselves, and their topic, on the basis of sophisticated photography or ingenious illustration. In *A Drop of Water*, Walter Wick's exquisite photographs of different states of water bring a sense of wonder to something that we take for granted most of the time. Stephen Biesty's Spectacular Cross-Section books, such as *Egypt: In Spectacular Cross-Section* with text by Stewart Ross and *Rome: In Spectacular Cross-Section* with text by Andrew Solway, are full of facts, but the real fascination of these books lies in Biesty's intricate illustrations.

Unconventional Formats and Approaches

A related trend in nonfiction books today is enthusiasm for unconventional approaches, including experimental formats and combinations of fact and fiction. Among the most spectacular examples are Robert Sabuda and Matthew Reinhart's pop-up books, *Encyclopedia Prehistorica: Dinosaurs* and *Encyclopedia Prehistorica: Sharks and*

Other Beasts of the Sea. The breathtaking paper engineering of these two works provides children with an unprecedented look at the creatures of the Mesozoic age. Scholastic's First Discovery books, such as Pascale de Bourgoing's *Weather*, have clear plastic overlays that help children visualize important concepts. Dorling Kindersley's Eyewitness 3D series includes a mirror device that provides a three-dimensional look at books like *Insects* by Theresa Greenaway. This is the next best thing to holding the little bugs in your hand. The text of Sheila Hamanaka's distinguished book *The Journey: Japanese Americans, Racism, and Renewal* is organized around a mural painted by the author; each segment of text accompanies and describes one or two details of the larger painting.

Other books that look like conventional picture books might be innovative in the ways they deliver information, often using a fictitious story as the vehicle or at least borrowing from the techniques of fiction. Claudia Logan's *The 5,000-Year-Old Puzzle* provides details of an expedition to Giza in 1924 and is classified as fiction. As the book's foreword explains, however, only the narrator, Will, and his family are "fictitious, the rest of the information about Giza 7000X is true" (p. 1). Will's narrative provides factual material on how scientist George Reisner developed a systematic approach to site excavation and how he and other archaeologists formed theories about their discoveries. Reproductions of postage stamps, money, and photographs from the expedition and a diagram of the dig provide visual reality to the truth behind this fictional narrative. *The Magic School Bus*

inside the Earth and the 2005 addition to the Magic School Bus series, *Ms. Frizzle's Adventures: Imperial China* by Joanna Cole and Bruce Degen, could also be classified as fantasy picture books with their miniaturized school bus and impossible field trips led by the intrepid teacher, Ms. Frizzle. Yet, as in *The 5,000-Year-Old Puzzle,* the books are clearly designed to present information, both in the details of each journey and in the notes on every page.

Specialized Topics

During the past decade, more nonfiction books have been published about highly specialized topics. There have always been specialized books, but today more and more books reflect very specific interests. They might report personalized perspectives, give detailed information about a narrowly defined topic, or cut across subject matter in a new way. There are books about special topics like dust (April Pulley Sayre's *Stars beneath Your Bed*), adjectives (Ruth Heller's *Many Luscious Lollipops*), and dragonflies (Laurence Pringle's *A Dragon in the Sky*). Although students might not identify these topics as something they want or need to read about, the books frequently create interest in the topics.

Recognition and Awards

Many of the trends we have looked at here indicate that nonfiction books are innovative and creative. They carry the unique perspective of individual authors and of artists free to experiment with formats and media. It is not surprising, then, that nonfiction books for children are finally being recognized for their aesthetic qualities as literature. In the past, nonfiction books have not earned their fair share of critical attention and recognition. In 1981, author Betty Bacon pointed out that nonfiction books had won the Newbery Medal only six times in fifty-eight years, and those winners were from history or biography, in which the chronological narrative form is very much like fiction.[2] This is quite a contrast to literature for adults, where authors like John McPhee and

Tracy Kidder regularly win critical acclaim for their work, and nonfiction frequently dominates the best-sellers lists. As a result of this imbalance, in 1990 the National Council of Teachers of English established the Orbis Pictus Award for Outstanding Nonfiction for Children. Its name commemorates what is thought to be the first book of facts produced for children, dating back to the seventeenth century. Recent winners include Jennifer Armstrong's *Shipwreck at the Bottom of the World: The Extraordinary True Story of Shackleton and the Endurance,* Jerry Stanley's *Hurry Freedom: African Americans in Gold Rush California,* and Jim Murphy's *An American Plague,* also a Sibert Award winner.

In 2000, the Association of Library Services to Children established the Robert F. Sibert Informational Book Award. This award is meant to honor an author whose work of nonfiction has made a significant contribution to the field of children's literature in a given year. Susan Campbell Bartoletti's *Black Potatoes: The Story of the Great Irish Famine, 1845–1850,* Sophie Webb's *My Season with Penguins: An Antarctic Journal,* and James Cross Giblin's *Secrets of the Sphinx* are among those titles named as Sibert Award winners or honor books.

The Boston Globe-Horn Book Awards have included a nonfiction category for many years. Some of the books recognized in this category have been Natalie S. Bober's *Abigail Adams: Witness to a Revolution,* Robie H. Harris's *It's Perfectly Normal: A Book about Changing Bodies, Growing Up, Sex, and Sexual Health,* Steve Jenkins's *The Top of the World: Climbing Mount Everest,* and Phillip Hoose's *The Race to Save the Lord God Bird.*

With the Boston Globe-Horn Book recognition and other prestigious awards, there are now many more opportunities for all kinds of nonfiction books to receive the acclaim they deserve.

CRITERIA FOR EVALUATING NONFICTION BOOKS

One critic who has given close attention to nonfiction books for children is Jo Carr.[3] Teachers and librarians who want to choose the very best books available can be guided by her view that a nonfiction writer is first a teacher, then an artist, and should be concerned with feeling as well as thinking, passion as well as clarity. Specific criteria can be used to help identify this level of achievement. Being familiar with these criteria and with the types of books in which information is presented will make it easier to choose the best books at the right time. The individual reviewer must judge the relative value of the various criteria in terms of particular books. Sometimes a book's strengths in one or two categories may far out-

---

[2]Betty Bacon, "The Art of Nonfiction," *Children's Literature in Education* 12 (spring 1981): 3.

[3]Jo Carr, "Writing the Literature of Fact," in *Beyond Fact: Nonfiction for Children and Young People* (Chicago: American Library Association, 1982), pp. 3–12.

Evaluating Nonfiction Books

ACCURACY AND AUTHENTICITY

- Is the author qualified to write about this topic? Has the manuscript been checked by authorities in the field?
- Are the facts accurate according to other sources?
- Is the information up-to-date?
- Are all the significant facts included?
- Do text and illustrations reveal diversity and avoid stereotypes?
- Are generalizations supported by facts?
- Is there a clear distinction between fact and theory?
- Are the text and illustrations free of anthropomorphism and teleological explanations?

CONTENT AND PERSPECTIVE

- For what purpose was the book designed?
- Is the book within the comprehension and interest range of its intended audience?
- Is the subject adequately covered? Are different viewpoints presented?
- Does the book lead to an understanding of the scientific method? Does it foster the spirit of inquiry?
- Does the book show interrelationships? If it is a science book, does it indicate related social issues?

STYLE

- Is information presented clearly and directly?
- Is the text appropriate for the intended audience?
- Does the style create the feeling of reader involvement?
- Is the language vivid and interesting?

ORGANIZATION

- Is the information structured clearly, with appropriate subheadings?
- Does the book have reference aids that are clear and easy to use, such as table of contents, index, bibliography, glossary, appendix?

ILLUSTRATIONS AND FORMAT

- Do illustrations clarify and extend the text or speak plainly for themselves?
- Are size relationships made clear?
- Are media suitable to the purposes for which they are used?
- Are illustrations explained by captions or labels where needed?
- Does the total format contribute to the clarity and attractiveness of the book?

---

weigh its weakness in others. See Evaluation Criteria: "Evaluating Nonfiction Books" for an overview of these criteria.

Accuracy and Authenticity

Accuracy is of primary importance in nonfiction books for children. No one wants inaccurate information, no matter how well it is presented, especially because many children believe that anything printed in a book is true. The author's qualifications, the way in which the author presents facts and generalizations, the correctness of the illustrations, and many other factors need to be considered in evaluating a book's accuracy and authenticity.

The Author's Qualifications

Nonfiction books are written by people who are authorities in their fields, such as astronaut Sally Ride, or they are written by writers who study a subject, interview specialists, and compile the data. A few, like naturalist Jean Craighead George, are both specialists and writers. It is always a good idea to check the book's jacket copy, title page, introduction, or "About the Author" page at the back for information about the author's special qualifications, often expressed in terms of professional title or affiliation. Expertise in one field does not necessarily indicate competency in another, however, so we expect

a high degree of authenticity only if the author has limited the book to what appears to be his or her specialty.

If a book is written by a "writer," not by an expert in the field, facts can be checked by authorities and the authorities cited. For example, Donna M. Jackson is an insect enthusiast but is not a trained scientist. In *The Bug Scientists*, however, she acknowledges and names a long list of experts she interviewed and consulted, and photo credits show that the illustrations were furnished by individuals and universities with an established expertise. The record of sources and research provided here gives assurance that the book is accurate.

A number of authors have earned the reputation of writing dependably good nonfiction books. When in doubt, teachers and librarians are likely to turn first to writers who have proved their integrity with facts—Penny Colman, Patricia Lauber, James Cross Giblin, Russell Freedman, Milton Meltzer, Laurence Pringle, Seymour Simon, and Helen Roney Sattler, among others. But authorship, while it may be a valuable rule of thumb, is a dangerous final criterion. Each book must be evaluated on its own merits.

Factual Accuracy

Fortunately, many of the errors of fact in children's nonfiction books are minor. Children who have access to a variety of books on one topic should be encouraged to notice discrepancies and pursue the correct answer, a valuable exercise in critical reading.

Errors that teachers and children recognize are less distressing than those that pass for fact because the topic is unfamiliar or highly specialized; then the reader must depend on a competent reviewer to identify inaccuracies. Ideally, a book with technical information should be reviewed by someone with expertise in that field. *Appraisal: Science Books for Young Readers* is a periodical that offers paired reviews, one by a science professional and one by a teacher or librarian. *Science Books and Films* includes reviews by specialists in the field. *Horn Book Magazine* singles out science books for special reviewing efforts, although other nonfiction is included. The *School Library Journal* often provides helpful criticism. *Social Education* and *Science and Children* magazines also give some attention to appropriate books, and both publish a list of outstanding books in their respective fields each year. Both of these lists can be accessed through the Children's Book Council Web site at <www.cbcbooks.org>. Generally speaking, science books are more likely to be challenged by experts than are those about history or other topics in the humanities.

Up-to-Dateness

Some books that are free of errors at the time of writing become inaccurate with the passage of time, as new discoveries are made in the sciences or as changes occur in world politics. Books that focus on the past are less likely to be rapidly outdated, although new discoveries in archaeology or new theories in history and anthropology call for a reevaluation of these materials also.

Kathleen Weidner Zoehfeld's *Dinosaur Parents, Dinosaur Young* details the mistakes that, for many years, led scientists to believe that dinosaur parents did not care for their young. She then describes how scientists Michael Novacek and Mark Norell were able to deduce that the oviraptor actually sat on its nest and incubated its eggs. This type of information helps children to understand how what we know about an extinct species changes as scientists continue to ask questions. Books that focus on subjects on which vigorous research and experimentation are being done, such as viruses and disease or space technology, are even more quickly outdated. It is worth noting, however, that the latest trade books are almost always more up-to-date than the latest textbooks or encyclopedias.

It is also difficult, but important, to provide children with current information about other countries where national governments are emerging or where future political developments are uncertain. Current events that generate an interest in books about a particular country

also call attention to the fact that those books might be out-of-date. Internet sites would be an excellent way to keep track of current events, although these too require critical evaluation. The American Library Association lists more than 700 Great Sites for Children at <www.ala.org/parentspage/greatsites/amazing.html>. Teachers will want to make note of other sites vetted by professional organizations, such as the Web site for the National Council for the Social Studies <www.ncss.org> and the Web site for the National Science Teachers Association <www.nsta.org>.

Books about minority cultures also need to include material on contemporary experience, as well as heritage. Books like *Celebrating Ramadan* and *Potlatch: A Tsimshian Celebration,* both by Diane Hoyt-Goldsmith, show families who take pride in continuing their traditions but who also are clearly people of today's world. Being up-to-date is one of the ways that books of this kind can combat stereotypes.

Inclusion of All the Significant Facts

Although the material presented in a book might be current and technically correct, the book cannot be totally accurate if it omits significant facts. Forty years ago science books that dealt with animal reproduction frequently glossed over the specifics of mating or birth. In Robert McClung's *Possum,* the process was explained like this: "All night long the two of them wandered through the woods together. But at dawn each went his own way again. Possum's babies were born just twelve days later."[4] Fortunately, the changing social mores that struck down taboos in children's fiction have also encouraged a new frankness in nonfiction books. For instance, close-up photographs and forthright text in *My Puppy Is Born* and *How You Were Born* by Joanna Cole mark these as straightforward books about animal and human reproduction and birth. *Egg to Chick* by Millicent Selsam pictures the mating of a rooster and a hen. Gail Saltz's *Amazing You* is a frank and engaging look at male and female sexual organs.

Human reproduction and sexuality have so often been distorted by omissions that books with accurate terminology and explicit information are particularly welcome. Older children and adolescents will find that Robie H. Harris's *It's So Amazing: A Book about Eggs, Sperm, Birth, Babies, and Families* or *It's Perfectly Normal: A Book about Changing Bodies, Growing Up, Sex, and Sexual Health* are thorough and frank guides to adolescent and adult sexuality. In both books Michael Emberley's detailed illustrations add a wonderful touch of humor to what is often a touchy subject for this age group.

The honest presentation of all information necessary for understanding a topic is just as important in

---

[4]Robert McClung, *Possum* (New York: Morrow, 1963), p. 41.

Careful research by Catherine O'Neill Grace and Margaret M. Bruchac for *1621: A New Look at Thanksgiving* helps undo many of the stereotypes about the first "Thanksgiving" feast. Photograph from *1621: A New Look at Thanksgiving* by Catherine O'Neill Grace and Margaret M. Bruchac with Plimoth Plantation. Published by the National Geographic Society. Photography copyright © 2001 by Sisse Brimberg and Cotton Coulson.

historical or cultural accounts as in the sciences. This may be difficult to achieve because social issues are complex, and writing for a young audience requires that the author be brief. Judging whether a book includes all the significant facts can also be difficult, for deciding what really counts is a matter of interpretation, often dependent on the book's intended audience.

For many years, myths surrounding the first Thanksgiving went unchallenged. In *1621: A New Look at Thanksgiving* Catherine O'Neill Grace and Margaret M. Bruchac, in cooperation with the staff of Plimoth Plantation, show how those myths evolved and present new information. They state:

> In 1947, the founders of Plimoth Plantation created a museum to honor the 17th-century English colonists who would come to be known

to the world as the Pilgrims. In doing so, the founders left out the perspective of the Wampanoag people who had lived on the land for thousands of years. At Plimoth Plantation today, we ask questions about what really happened in the past. We draw from the new research of scholars who study documents, artifacts, home sites, culture, and formerly untapped sources such as the Wampanoag people themselves. (p. 7)

This fascinating account includes photographs taken at the museum site and shows children what the harvest festival was probably like. The book also provides an important lesson about historical research and the need to include many sources and many points of view when interpreting historical events.

Avoidance of Stereotypes

A book that omits significant facts tells only part of the truth; a book that presents stereotypes pretends, wrongly, to have told the truth. One very common sort of stereotyping is by omission. If we never see women or minorities in science books, for instance, we are left with the incorrect impression that all scientists must be white males. In recent years, fortunately, more authors, illustrators, and publishers have made conscious efforts to represent the great variety of roles that women and minorities play in science and the world of work. Harlow Rockwell's *My Doctor* was a leader in portraying a woman physician in a book for the very young, and Gail Gibbons has made many similar contributions, including a woman surveyor on the work crew of *New Road!* George Ancona's lively photographs in *Let's Dance!* include boys and men and a woman dancing in a wheelchair. Susan Kuklin's *Families*, which includes photographs and voices of children describing their families, surveys the many groupings of loving adults and children who make up today's families. This no-fanfare approach helps combat stereotypes because it encourages children to understand the contributions of people as a matter of course.

Books about countries around the world and those that describe life in a minority culture are the most likely to include stereotypes. Children can be taught to watch for sweeping general statements and for unwarranted claims about what "everybody" thinks or does. However, all readers need to realize that it is almost impossible to portray a country or region completely in *all* its diversity of people, terrain, industry, lifestyles, and the like. When the region is large and the book is limited in length, it is good if the author deliberately highlights differences rather than generalizing too freely. In *Chidi Only Likes Blue: An African Book of Colors,* Ifeoma Onyefulu provides lovely pictures of the colors found in a child's village in Nigeria. From the title, however, one might generalize these images to all of Africa. Only a map on the end pages indicates that this is a small country on a large continent. In Onyefulu's *Saying Goodbye: A Special Farewell to Mama Nkwelle* an author's note and a map of Africa showing Nigeria are provided at the outset of the story, giving readers the background they need to understand the pictures and information that follow.

Another way authors try to avoid stereotyping is by relating the story of one individual within a community. Diane Hoyt-Goldsmith's books about Native Americans focus on one tribe and then on a particular child's family, school, and community experiences. Readers associate the facts in these books with specific persons and places. Consequently, they should be less likely to assume that this description of Native American life represents the way *all* people of Native American heritage live.

Use of Facts to Support Generalizations

To be distinguished from stereotype or simple opinion, a proper generalization needs facts for support. Phillip

In *The Race to Save the Lord God Bird* author Phillip Hoose shows readers how scientists have attempted to find out about the existence or extinction of the ivory-billed woodpecker. Cover of *The Race to Save the Lord God Bird* by Phillip Hoose. Copyright © 2004. Reprinted by permission of Farrar, Straus & Giroux, LLC.

Hoose provides such support throughout *The Race to Save the Lord God Bird.* Hoose is careful to make sure his readers understand that scientists are not sure if the ivory-billed woodpecker (nicknamed the Lord God Bird for its magnificent plumage) is extinct or not. Instead, Hoose takes readers through the tantalizing mystery of the bird's existence with facts about the sightings and search for the elusive bird. He also provides extensive notes of his sources in an afterword. Laurence Pringle builds a convincing case that global warming is indeed underway in *Global Warming: The Threat of Earth's Changing Climate* through fourteen short chapters that begin with the facts about global warming and end with a call to action to address the challenges of the future. Critical readers need to be aware of generalizations and judge for themselves whether adequate facts are provided to support them.

Distinction between Fact and Theory

Careful writers make careful distinctions between fact and theory; but even so, children need guidance in learning to recognize the difference. Often the distinction depends on key words or phrases—such as *scientists believe, so far as we know,* or *perhaps.* Consider the importance of the simple phrase *may have* in this description of a prehistoric reptile: "Pterodactyls lived near the shores of prehistoric seas and may have slept hanging from tree branches by their feet, like bats."[5] Some discussion of different kinds of possible evidence might be in order to help children see that one-half of this statement is presented as fact, the other as theory.

Books about the disappearance of the dinosaurs make good material for helping children sort out the difference between fact and theory, because the problem is dramatic and the evidence provides for legitimate disagreement among scientists. Franklin Branley's *What Happened to the Dinosaurs?* does a particularly good job of helping primary-age children understand what a theory is.

Although it is important to distinguish between fact and theory in all of the sciences, including the social sciences, the matter receives most attention in books dealing with evolution and human origins. In some communities this is a very sensitive topic, but it would seem that children everywhere have a right to information about scientists' discoveries and theories regarding our origins. David Peters's *From the Beginning: The Story of Human Evolution* fails to acknowledge the process by which ideas about evolution have become accepted in the scientific community. On the other hand, Steve Jenkins and Robin Page as well as Christopher Sloan have provided scientifically valid explanations. Jenkins and Page's *Life on Earth: The Story of Evolution* is an excellent and visually appealing introduction for younger readers. Sloan's *The Human Story: Our Evolution from Prehistoric Ancestors to Today* is aimed at older children and adolescents and concentrates on the scientific process that built our present-day understanding. It is reassuring to note that balanced coverage of this important topic is available in nonfiction books at a time when many school districts are reluctant to include the topic in their curricula.

Avoidance of Anthropomorphism

In poetry and fiction, the assignment of human feelings and behavior to animals, plants, or inanimate objects is called *personification*—an accepted literary device that can be used with great effect. In science, however, this device is unacceptable and is known as *anthropomorphism*. Science writer Millicent Selsam addressed the problem of interpreting what animals do in one of her early books on animal behavior:

> It is hard to keep remembering that animals live in a different kind of world from our own. They see, hear, smell, and taste things differently. And they do not have human intelligence or emotions, so we must avoid interpreting their behavior in terms of our own feelings and thoughts.

For example, it looks to us as though parent birds are devoted to their young in the same way that human parents are devoted to theirs. But only experimental work can show whether this interpretation is true.[6]

Many books with these anthropomorphic touches are still in print. In *Antarctica,* an otherwise lovely book about the animal life on this great continent, Helen Cowcher tries to convey the negative impact of human intrusion on the animal life. She states, "Out at sea anxious songs ring out from the depths. Weddell seals call to their friends under the ice."[7] The words *anxious* and *friends* attribute human emotions and human relationships to the seals and may lead children to the types of interpretation that Selsam cautions against. Sandra Markle's *A Mother's Journey* is also an emotionally gripping book about the Antarctic and its emperor penguins, but Markle and illustrator Alan Marks achieve that response through good writing and fine illustration.

Closely related to anthropomorphism is another error called teleological explanation of phenomena. Briefly, *teleology* attempts to account for natural phenomena by assigning a purpose to the plants, animals, or forces involved. Science books should not suggest that leaves turn toward the light in order to bask in the sun or that "Mother Nature," capitalized and personified, is at work carving the walls of canyons. Such a description has a certain poetic effect, but it also conveys a basically unscientific attitude.

Content and Perspective

Consideration of the purpose of a book, its intended audience, and the objectivity of its author can help readers evaluate a nonfiction book's content and perspective. A good nonfiction book should also foster reflective inquiry in children and enable them to see relationships across disciplines.

Purpose

It is futile to try to pass judgment on the content of a nonfiction book without first determining the purpose for which the book was designed. Identifying the scope of the book lets us know what we can reasonably expect. A quick look at James Buckley, Jr.'s *The Visual Dictionary of Baseball* reveals a fascinating collection of facts for browsing, whereas both the title and the appearance of Martin Redfern's *The Kingfisher Young People's Book of Space* indicate a comprehensive treatment of the topic. Titles can be misleading, particularly those that promise to tell "all about" a subject but offer limited coverage instead. At best, titles indicate the scope of the book's

---

[5]David C. Knight, *Dinosaurs That Swam and Flew,* illus. Lee J. Ames (Englewood Cliffs, N.J.: Prentice Hall, 1985), p. 39.

[6]Millicent Selsam, *Animals as Parents,* illus. John Kaufmann (New York: 1965), p. 16.

[7]Helen Cowcher, *Antarctica* (New York: Farrar, Straus & Giroux, 1990), unpaged.

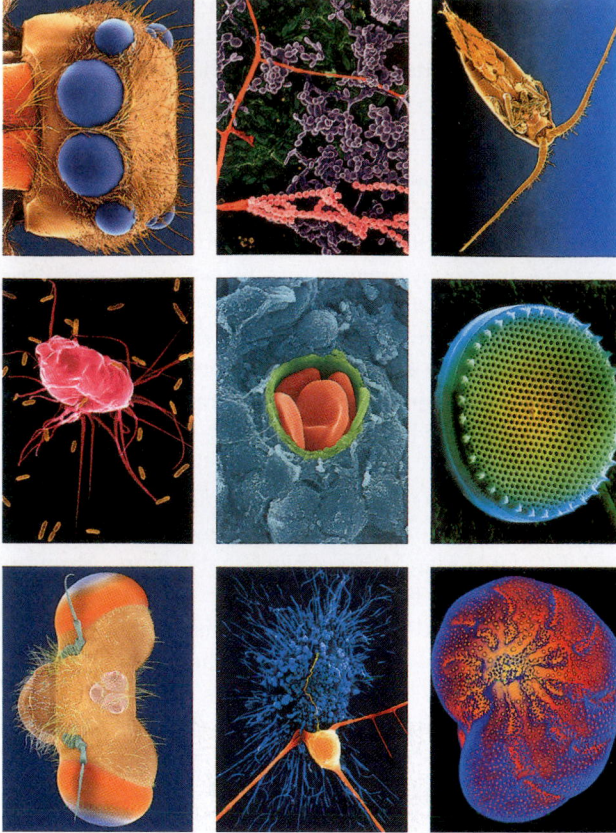

Eye-catching photographs and an appealing title will invite children to pick up *Hidden Worlds: Looking through a Scientist's Microscope* by Stephen Kramer. Photographs from *Hidden Worlds: Looking through a Scientist's Microscope* by Stephen Kramer, photographs by Dennis Kunkel. Photographs copyright © 2001 by Dennis Kunkel. Reprinted by permission of Houghton Mifflin Company. All rights reserved.

content and pique the reader's curiosity, as do titles such as *Secrets from the Rocks: Dinosaur Hunting with Roy Chapman Andrews* by Albert Marrin and *Hidden Worlds: Looking through a Scientist's Microscope* by Stephen Kramer. More about the scope and purpose of nonfiction books can be found in the section "Types of Nonfiction Books" later in this chapter.

Intended Audience

Before evaluating content, we have to know not just for what the book was intended, but for whom. Book jackets and book reviews often indicate an age range according to reading level or interest. It is difficult to know whether one or both of these factors are reflected in the age recommendation. Generally, a book's reading level is not as important as its content in relation to the reader's actual interest in a subject. Older students and adults might turn to children's nonfiction books for introduc-

tory material on an unfamiliar topic. In using nonfiction books, children will read "beyond their abilities" when reading for particular facts. Children will frequently turn to difficult books if they contain many pictures or useful diagrams. At the same time, vocabulary, sentence length, size of type, and the book's organization are factors to be considered. Children might reject a book that contains useful information if they see crowded pages, relatively small type, and few pictures.

The choice of topic, then, is an important factor in determining whether a book will be suitable for its intended audience. Books for young children most often reflect their basic egocentric concerns and their curiosity about themselves and other living things; it is a mistake to assume that they will not be interested in other subjects, however. Many early primary children enjoy browsing through the widely diverse titles of the Eyewitness series, such as Andrée Grau's *Dance*, Theresa Greenaway's *Jungle*, or *Pyramid* by Jane McIntosh, even though these books are designed for an older audience. On the other hand, books that look like picture books are frequently aimed at upper-grade children. Some of these may require readers to keep track of some complex concepts while they follow the ins and outs of the visual and verbal narrative.

Examples chosen by an author to clarify concepts are related to the level of cognitive ability needed to get the most out of a book. In *Samuel Eaton's Day* and *Sarah Morton's Day*, Kate Waters caters to a young child's need to approach historical understanding through concrete details. Double-page spreads of sequenced color photos show Sarah and Samuel, the Pilgrim children, getting dressed in their overgarments. For Sarah, first comes the petticoat, then stockings, garters, two more petticoats, a waistcoat, coif, apron, "pocket," and shoes. For Samuel, stockings, garters, breeches, doublet, shoes, "points," and hat—a clear contrast to sweatsuits and sneakers!

Adequacy of Coverage

Recognizing the purpose of a book and its intended level, the reader has a basis for deciding if the author has said too much about the topic or too little. Jim Murphy's many fine books, such as *The Great Fire* and *An American Plague*, are close to two hundred pages. The focus of the topic is limited, but the treatment is detailed.

Broader topics, like the history or culture of a nation, might require many pages in order to give even brief attention to all the significant material. History textbooks have earned particularly harsh criticism for faulty coverage,[8] and good trade books help fill in perspectives that the textbooks omit. A generation ago, Gerald Johnson expressed the need for careful writing in the introduction to his book *America Is Born*:

---

[8]See Frances FitzGerald, *America Revised* (Boston: Atlantic/Little, Brown, 1979).

Part of the story is very fine, and other parts are very bad, but they all belong to it, and if you leave out the bad parts you never understand it all. (pp. viii–ix)[9]

Authors who fail to acknowledge more than one viewpoint or theory fail to help children learn to examine issues. Even young children should know that authorities do not always agree, though the context might be simple. It is far more common, though, and certainly more necessary, for books about complex issues to deal with varying points of view.

Demonstration of the Scientific Method

Because we are concerned about *how* as well as *what* children learn, it is important to note what kind of thinking a book encourages, as well as the body of facts it presents. Nonfiction books should illustrate the process of inquiry, the excitement of discovery. James Cross Giblin's *The Mystery of the Mammoth Bones: And How It Was Solved* and Johann Reinhard's *Discovering the Inca Ice Maiden* give readers a good idea of the problems scientists try to solve and the kind of day-to-day work that is involved.

While these are fine accounts of the scientific method at work, the reader's involvement is still vicarious. Some books are designed to give children more-direct experience with the skills of inquiry. Millicent Selsam's *How to Be a Nature Detective* encourages children to ask "What happened, who was here, and where did he go?" in order to learn how to read animal tracks. At each step of the process, Marlene Donnelly's illustrations help children follow this sequence as if they were actually outdoors tracking various animals. Sandra Markle's guides for observing ants in *Exploring Autumn* provide simple directions (no pictures needed), ask questions that direct attention to important features like the relation between the size of an ant's burden to its body, and give background information that helps children interpret what they see.

The photographs in Patricia Lauber's *Dinosaurs Walked Here and Other Stories Fossils Tell* are chosen and placed to help children make their own observations about the fossil record. A photo of a present-day horseshoe crab beside the fossil print of its 140-million-year-old ancestor allows readers to conclude that these creatures have scarcely changed over time; a companion picture lets us discover how beavers have shrunk in the past fifteen thousand years. All of Lauber's books demonstrate this commitment to presenting scientific evidence in such a way that children can confirm some conclusions for themselves.

The scientific method applies to the social sciences, too. Jean Fritz has illustrated techniques of historical research in a fictionalized account that children like very much—*George Washington's Breakfast*. The story illustrates the role of perseverance and good luck in problem solving. After young George, who is trying to find out what George Washington customarily ate for breakfast, has asked questions, exhausted library resources, and gone on a futile fact-finding trip to Mt. Vernon, he happens to find the answer in an old book written during Washington's lifetime, about to be discarded from his own attic. When he finds the answer to his question, he has discovered the usefulness of primary source materials. Intermediate children can also find out about using primary sources for studying personal history in *The Great Ancestor Hunt* by Lila Perl. *The Riddle of the Rosetta Stone: Key to Ancient Egypt* by James Cross Giblin and Kathy Pelta's *Discovering Christopher Columbus: How History Is Invented* demonstrate how historians study evidence and develop hypotheses.

Interrelationships and Implications

A list of facts is fine for an almanac, but nonfiction books should be expected to put facts into some sort of perspective. After all, linking facts in one way or another transforms information into knowledge. Thomas Locker's *Sky Tree* shows how the same tree changes through the seasons and how it interacts with the animals, the earth, and the sky around it throughout the year. *Come Back Salmon* by Molly Cone intersperses information about coho salmon, the watershed, and water pollution in a story about a class of fifth graders who cleaned up a dead stream near their school and saw the salmon return to spawn there.

Interrelationships of a different sort are pointed out in Barbara Brenner's *If You Were There in 1492*. This book helps readers see the cultural context in which a major event, Columbus's first voyage, took place. The author describes the world as it would have been known to ordinary people in Spain in terms of food, clothing, education, books, the arts, crime, ships, and many other aspects. The vivid presentations of the 1492 expulsion of Jews from Spain and the everyday life of the Lucayan people on the island where Columbus would land are especially good for prompting discussion about the relationship of one culture to another.

Intertwining science and technology with modern culture has become crucial, and many recent nonfiction books have taken this issue as a focus. *A Home by the Sea: Protecting Coastal Wildlife* by Kenneth Mallory discusses effects of commercial and residential development on coastal wildlife in New Zealand and the efforts being made to protect wildlife species. Even books not specifically designed to call attention to the related social

---

[9]Gerald White Johnson, *America Is Born*, illus. Leonard Everett Fisher (New York: William Morrow, 1959).

It is the remembered smell of its home stream that tells a salmon when its journey is over. Its nostrils quiver as it recognizes the smell. Its body quickens. At last it is home again. Where it finally comes to a stop may be only yards from its birthplace, or, in the case of the Jackson School salmon, from the spot where it was released into the creek.

But not all salmon migrating from stream to ocean will return.

Many smolt-size salmon are gobbled up almost as soon as they enter the sea. Water birds such as mergansers, kingfishers, sea gulls, and great blue herons feed on the tiny fish. Whales, seals, and sea lions eat larger salmon, as do eagles and

GROWING UP IN THE OCEAN

All species of Pacific salmon leave their home streams to feed and to grow to maturity in the salty waters of the Pacific Ocean. But different species of Pacific salmon stay in the ocean for different lengths of time. A Coho, or "Silver," usually lives in the ocean for about one and a half to two years before returning to its home stream to spawn. However, some early-maturing Cohos, known as "Jacks," return from the ocean after less than a year.

The Pacific salmon that stays in the ocean the longest is the Chinook. This "king of salmons" sometimes grows to more than a hundred pounds (while a fully grown Coho usually weighs no more than twelve pounds). No other species grows as big. The Chinook may take four years or more of feeding in the ocean to reach its immense size.

During their life in the ocean, Chinook and Coho salmon may journey as far north as Baranof Island, Alaska, and as far south as the coast of northern California. Pacific salmon generally travel in a counterclockwise direction until the time comes for them to begin their race toward their home streams.

ALASKAN BROWN BEARS ARE EXPERTS AT FISHING.

Molly Cone's *Come Back Salmon* provides facts about Pacific salmon alongside the story of fifth graders who restored salmon spawning grounds.
From *Come Back Salmon* by Molly Cone, text copyright © 1992 by Molly Cone. Photo copyright © 1992 by Jim Nilsen. Used by permission of Sierra Club Books for Children.

problems of science and technology ought to acknowledge that such problems exist. Where the uses of science have serious implications for society, the relationships should be made clear. (See the discussion of the study theme "Stewards of the Earth" in Chapter 13 for more about this issue.)

Style

The style of a nonfiction book can be crucial in attracting children to the book and in helping them understand the concepts presented there. The clarity of presentation and the appropriateness of the language for its intended audience are important matters to consider in evaluating a book's style. In addition, the writing should involve readers in the topic and provide them with an absorbing and vivid learning experience. Author Penny Colman suggests that in evaluating nonfiction writing we should ask how authors effect transitions, craft the ending, "establish a point of view, create a sense of time, use adjectives, adverbs, metaphors, or varied sentence lengths."[10] These qualities of style are just as important in nonfiction as they are in fiction.

Clarity and Directness

It is difficult to list all of the criteria that influence clarity. The use of precise language and specific detail is one important factor. Nothing is vague in Miriam Schlein's description of a vampire bat's dinner in *Billions of Bats*. She names the animals that are likely prey ("a horse, a cow, a donkey, or even a chicken"), describes the approach and the bite ("only about a tenth of an inch long"), and goes on to explain how the bat curves its tongue into a funnel shape and sucks in blood ("for about a half hour"). The language is simple and direct, giving the reader a clear picture of the process.

Before 1990 or so we could say with some certainty that information presented in the guise of fiction was confusing and ought to be avoided. More recent books, however, have offered skillful combinations of fact and fiction in which information is clearly presented. Patricia McKissack and Frederick McKissack contrast the lives of white and African American families prior to the Civil War in *Christmas in the Big House, Christmas in the Quarters.* By placing the facts about life on a plantation in the context of two imaginary families, the contrast between the two cultures and between free whites and enslaved blacks is given greater impact. The story element in books like this can help children understand facts that might otherwise seem too distant. On the other hand, not every author is this successful in making the combination; some fail to do a very good job of both entertaining and informing. When a picture book is only loosely based in fact, as in Emily Arnold McCully's *The Bobbin Girl* or Pam Conrad's *Call Me Ahnighito,* we cannot call it nonfiction (perhaps *informational fiction* or *faction*[11] would be good terms)—and we

Profile in Literature

[10]Colman, "Nonfiction Is Literature Too," p. 220.

[11]See Carol Avery, "Nonfiction Books: Naturals for the Primary Level," in *Making Facts Come Alive: Choosing Quality Nonfiction for Children,* ed. Rosemary Banford and Janice Kristo (Norwood, Mass.: Christopher Gordon, 1998).

need to make sure children understand the difference. Each book must be judged on its own merits.

Level of Difficulty

Although the vocabulary does have to be within the child's range, books for primary-grade children need not be restricted to a narrow list of words. New terms can be explained in context. In *Follow the Water from Brook to Ocean*, Arthur Dorros provides a two-paragraph description of the effects of moving water before introducing the word *erosion*. He also gives helpful context through examples and illustrations for the words *meanders* and *reservoir*. Context does not serve to explain everything, however; a writer aware of the background of the intended audience takes pains to make new words clear.

Words that look unpronounceable are another stumbling block for most children. A glossary is helpful, but youngsters who are intent on a book's content might not take time to look in the back. In some cases, authors provide pronunciation guides in parentheses for daunting words. Such is the case in Caroline Arnold's *Pterosaurs* and Cathy Camper's *Bugs before Time: Prehistoric Insects and Their Relatives*.

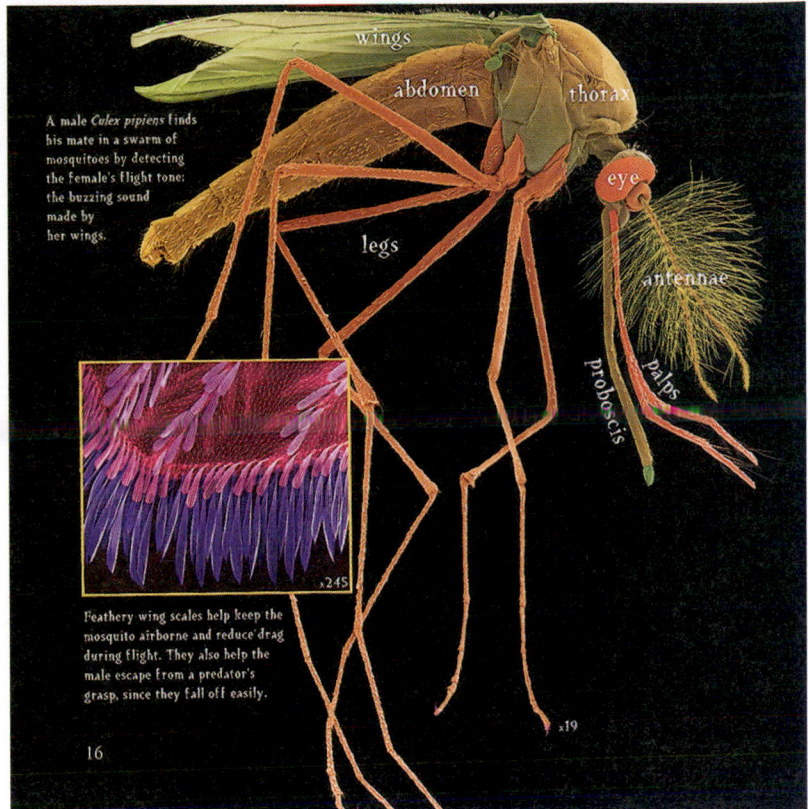

In *Mosquito Bite* Alexandra Siy tantalizes readers with a suspenseful text and black-and-white photographs that soon give way to stunning full-color photographs of the villain lurking in the backyard. Text and black-and-white photographs copyright © 2005 by Alexandra Siy. Photomicrographs copyright © 2005 by Dennis Kunkel. Used with permission by Charlesbridge Publishing, Inc. All rights reserved.

Reader Involvement

Authors use many different techniques to engage their readers' attention and help them stay involved with a book's subject matter. Alexandra Siy begins *Mosquito Bite* with black-and-white photographs of a girl and a boy playing a backyard game of hide-and-seek. As the boy peeks from behind a tree, the tantalizing text reads like the introduction to a horror film:

> He listens. He hears the girl's footsteps near the garden, or the driveway, now by the flowers along the walk.
>
> She's getting closer.
>
> Suddenly there's another sound. A droning buzz.
>
> The boy's hand flutters across his face and brushes the back of this neck.
>
> Something else is looking for the boy. (p. 5)

Siy and photographer Dennis Kunkel then go on to describe the life cycle of the *Culex pipiens* mosquito using stunning colorized electron micrographs.

Nonfiction authors also use direct address—sentences that speak to the reader as "you." Sometimes an author asks direct questions to claim a bond of communication with the reader. Paul Showers hooks the primary-grade audience for *How Many Teeth?* with a variety of rhymes interspersed throughout the text to ask "How many teeth have you?"

One technique that lends itself to nonfiction for children is called "creative nonfiction." Such writers of adult nonfiction as Annie Dillard and Frank Conroy have long used this approach to invigorate their topics.[12] Author Penny Colman explains that in writing creative nonfiction, "I adhere to the basic tenets of nonfiction writing as well as use stylistic and narrative strategies traditionally found in fiction."[13] Colman begins *Corpses, Coffins and Crypts: A History of Burial* with her own reflection about spending the day with her uncle's dead body, and in subsequent chapters she relays the real-life experiences of many others to cover subjects such as autopsies, embalming and cremation, and burial customs. These real-life experiences and personal reflections add zest to her explanations, yet her meticulous research and attention to detail are evident not only in her writing but also in her extensive use of archival material and site visits.

---

[12]Lee Gutkind, "From the Editor: The 5R's of Creative Nonfiction," *Creative Nonfiction* 6 (1996): 1–16.

[13]Colman, "Nonfiction Is Literature Too," p. 219.

The results are highly engaging books like *Corpses, Coffins and Crypts; Rosie the Riveter: Women Working on the Home Front in World War II; Girls: A History of Growing Up Female in America;* and *Where the Action Was: Women War Correspondents in World War II.*

Vividness of Language

The writer of nonfiction books uses the same techniques as the writer of fiction to bring a book to life, although the words must be accurate as well as attractive. Imagery is used to appeal to the senses, as in Barbara Bash's *Ancient Ones: The World of the Old-Growth Douglas Fir:*

> Walking into an old-growth forest, you enter a strangely silent world. The Earth feels moist and springy underfoot, and the air is thick with the fragrance of decomposing needles. (p. 7)

This quiet beginning in Jim Murphy's *Gone A-Whaling* provides a sense of anticipation:

> The water in the bay was calm. Mewing gulls soared and dipped feverishly, searching for fish, before gliding off toward the rocky shore. For a few seconds, all was quiet. (p. 9)

When a forty-ton whale erupts out of the sea, the reader's emotional leap is all the more exciting.

Children probably will not be able to describe an author's style, but they certainly will respond to it. They know that a well-written nonfiction book somehow does not sound the same as an encyclopedia essay, and they enjoy the difference.

Organization

Even if a book is vividly written, accurate, and in command of its topic, children will not find it very useful unless it also furnishes a clear arrangement of information. The way a book's content is structured and the reference aids it includes should help readers find and then understand key concepts and facts.

Structure

Every author must choose a structure, or organizing principle, as a basis for presenting facts. Sometimes an author uses a very obvious principle, such as organizing a collection of facts alphabetically. This format allows Jonathan Chester to introduce readers to interesting details about mountain climbing in *The Young Adventurer's Guide to Everest: From Avalanche to Zopkio.* In this book, as in others, the alphabet device makes a good format for browsing and is easily understood by children, although it pays less attention to the relationship among facts.

The question-and-answer approach has become more widely used in recent years. For very young children, questions and pictured answers can change a concept book into an engaging guessing game. Several of Margaret Miller's books, such as *Guess Who?*, repeat a question and suggest four silly answers; turn the page and discover a word or phrase and the photographs of the correct answer. Melvin Berger and Gilda Berger's Question and Answer series includes hard-to-resist titles such as *How Do Frogs Swallow with Their Eyes?*, *Where Did the Butterfly Get Its Name?*, and *Why Do Volcanoes Blow Their Tops?* These books, meant for middle graders, begin with a brief, one-page overview followed by such questions as "How hot is it inside the earth?", "Does all rock melt?", and "What makes a volcano erupt?"

Another structure closely related to questions and answers is the true/false approach that states common myths or misconceptions and then offers corrected or updated information. One of the best of these books is Seymour Simon's *Animal Fact/Animal Fable.* On each right-hand page Diane de Groat has a lively illustration to highlight statements such as "bats are blind," "[an] owl is a wise bird," and "some fish can climb trees." When the page is turned, Simon provides the information that explains whether the statement is fact or fable. Another fine example of this approach is Patricia Lauber's *The News about Dinosaurs,* with its meticulous but not too technical updates on the scientific interpretations of information about the dinosaurs.

A common and sensible arrangement for many books, especially about history or biological processes, is based on chronology. Kate Waters's *Samuel Eaton's Day* and *Sarah Morton's Day* allow modern-day children to compare their own morning-to-nighttime activities to those of children who lived almost four hundred years ago. *Cactus Hotel* by Brenda Guiberson reveals both history and science in its account of the two-hundred-year growth of a giant saguaro cactus.

Regardless of its topic, a general-survey type of book should have a system of headings that helps the reader get an overview of the content, unless the book is very brief and has pictures that serve as graphic guides for skimming. The longer the book and the more complex its topic, the greater the need for manageable division. Subheadings are helpful as indicators of structure, especially for less-practiced readers.

Reference Aids

With the exception of certain simple and special types, factual books should offer help at both front and back for the reader who needs to locate information quickly. It is important for children to develop reference skills early, so a table of contents and an index should be included in any book whose structure warrants it. Two of Ann Morris's concept books for younger children, *Weddings* and *Shoes, Shoes, Shoes,* provide visual indexes with additional information about each of the countries that she has visited in photographs in the books. A map identifies each of the countries shown in the pictures. This is a good way to introduce younger readers to indexes and other reference aids. For older children an index will be truly useful only if it is complete and has necessary cross-references. It is difficult to think of all the possible words children might use to look up a topic or to answer a question, yet writers should consider as many possibilities as seem reasonable.

Other helpful additions to a book are glossaries, bibliographies, suggestions for further reading, and nonfiction appendixes. Picture glossaries are on the increase with the growing number of nonfiction picture books. Nancy Winslow Parker and Joan Richards Wright include illustrated glossaries that summarize growth patterns and add detail about anatomy in their joint productions *Bugs* and *Frogs, Toads, Lizards, and Salamanders.* Either book would be good for demonstrating to children the use of reference aids, because both have touches of humor that add appeal as well as a full range of devices for locating and extending information.

If children are to understand methods of inquiry, they need to learn that a writer uses many sources of information. Penny Colman's *Corpses, Coffins and Crypts* has five pages of references. In an author's note Colman provides information about the people whose experiences she related, and she lists the sources that were particularly helpful to her. Photo credits that include many of her own photographs show how thorough and wide-ranging her research was.

Appendixes are used to extend information in lists, charts, or tabulations of data that would seem cumbersome in the text itself. *Commodore Perry in the Land of the Shogun,* Rhoda Blumberg's award-winning account of the opening of Japanese harbors to American ships, seems all the more credible because of the documents and lists presented in the appendixes. Having read that lavish gifts were exchanged during the negotiations, children can discover in an appendix that the emperor was offered more than thirty items, including two telegraph sets, a copper lifeboat, champagne, tea, muskets, swords, and two mailbags with padlocks.

Illustrations and Format

In our visually oriented culture, readers of all ages demand that a book's illustrations make it more interesting and attractive. In a nonfiction book, the illustrations and design must do that, and much more.

Clarification and Extension of Text

One of the basic functions of illustrations is to clarify and extend the text. *Our Patchwork Planet* by Helen Roney Sattler has photographs of Earth taken from space, photos of nature features on Earth, and computer-generated images that show Earth's shifting surface. It also has drawings and diagrams by Guilio Maestro that help make complicated ideas about plate tectonics more

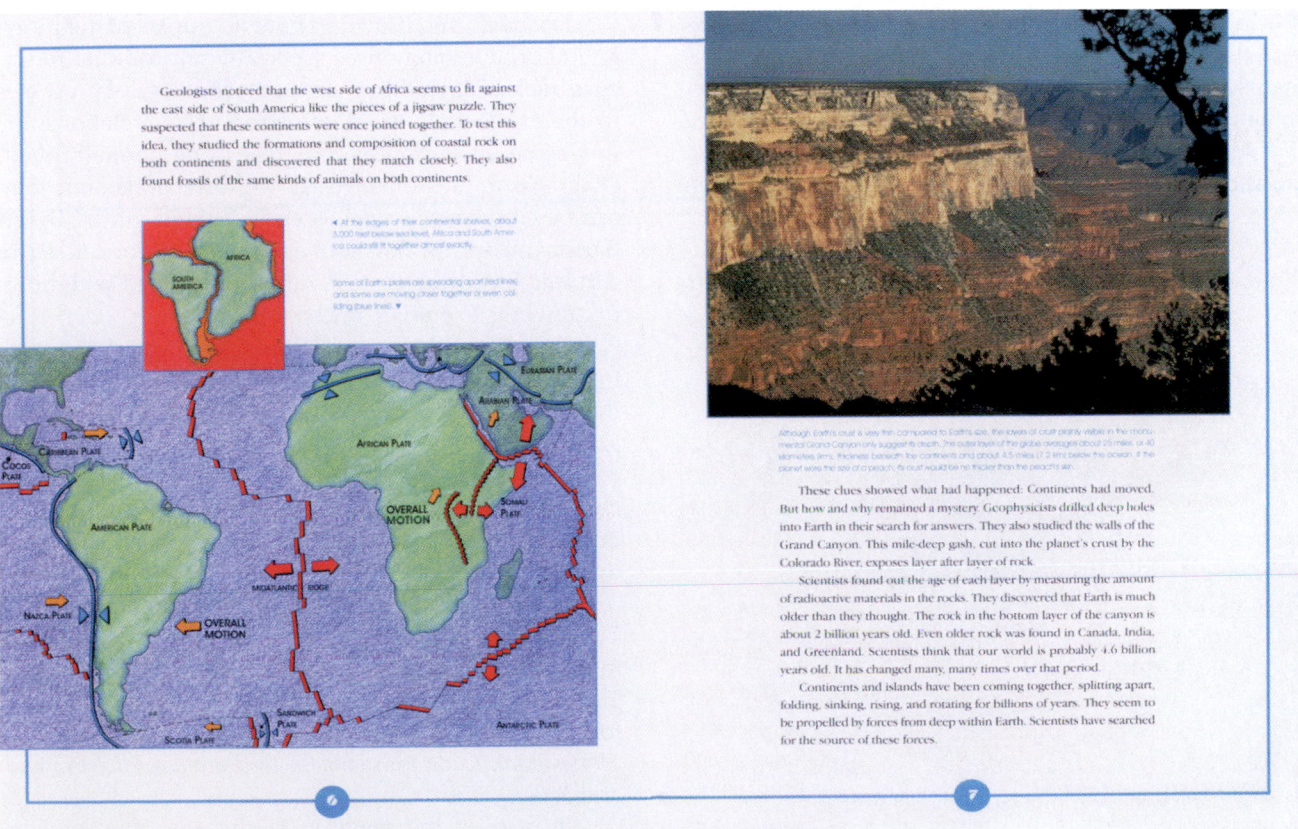

The photographs and computer-generated images in Helen Roney Sattler's *Our Patchwork Planet* help children understand the concept of plate tectonics. From *Our Patchwork Planet* by Helen Roney Sattler. Text copyright © 1995 Helen Roney Sattler. Illustration copyright © 1995 by Guilio Maestro. Used by permission of HarperCollins Publishers, Inc.

understandable. Cutaway views and clear labeling are other good features of the pictures in this book.

The more abstract the topic, the more important it is that pictures help children "see" explanations. Latitude, longitude, and other mapping concepts, for instance, are often hard for children to grasp, so it is especially important that they be illustrated clearly, as Harriet Barton has done for Jack Knowlton's introductory book *Maps and Globes.* These big, bright pictures use color to focus attention on the equator, contour lines, and other specific aspects of simplified maps.

Illustrations are especially important in clarifying size relationships. Paul Facklam's illustrations for Margery Facklam's *The Big Bug Book* show the actual size of really big bugs and then place them with familiar objects to help children visualize just how large they really are. Illustrator Steve Jenkins has delighted younger children with his *Actual Size* and *Prehistoric Actual Size,* both of which make use of an extra-large trim size, double-page spreads, and foldouts to give children a sense of their own size in relation to different animals. For example, only the teeth of the great white shark are shown on a twelve-inch by twenty-inch double-page spread. Not many topics lend themselves to life-size portrayals, of course, and that makes it important for artists to find other ways to be clear. Photographs and drawings often show magnified parts or wholes, and often some information about actual size is needed.

In many books the illustrations add detail and extend the information of the text; in others the illustrations themselves provide the bulk of the information, or become the subject of the text. In Walter Wick's *A Drop of Water,* the amazing photographs invite the reader to ask questions about such things as how a straight pin can indent the surface of water in a glass or how a huge bubble can rest on a metal frame. The text functions here to clarify and extend the pictures rather than the other way around. When illustrations are this important to a book, they need to have substantive content, high-quality reproduction, and a logical presentation or layout. For other good examples of effective presentation, look at Seymour Simon's books about the planets or Patricia Lauber's *Volcano: The Eruption and Healing of Mt. St. Helen's.*

Suitability of Media

Both illustrations and photographs can be clear and accurate, but one medium might be more suitable than another for a given purpose. Paul Carrick and Bruce Shillinglaw's paintings in *Dinosaur Parents, Dinosaur Young: Uncovering the Mystery of Dinosaur Families* by Kathleen Weidner Zoehfeld are important in allowing the reader to visualize the circumstances that may have led to the creation of the oviraptor fossils. On the other hand, painting would not create the sense of wonder that photographs do in *Hidden Worlds: Looking through a Scientist's Microscope* by Stephen Kramer. It is important for teachers to help children consider the reasons for the choices of media for nonfiction books. One first-grade teacher was astonished to learn that her students were categorizing books as nonfiction if they had photographs and as fiction if they had illustrations!

Diagrams and drawings have an impact of their own and also have many uses especially appropriate to science books. Diagrams can reduce technological processes to their essentials or show astronomical relationships that represent distances too great to be photographed. Diagrams are also fine for giving directions, and they can be charming as well as clear. This is true of Byron Barton's work for Seymour Simon's popular *The Paper Airplane Book,* where scenes are interspersed with how-to drawings to enliven the text.

Sometimes the perception of a graphic artist is vital to the purpose of a book. David Macaulay's *Ship* traces the modern-day discovery of a sixteenth-century wreck and then takes the reader back in time to watch its construction. Using various color schemes to indicate changes in time and place, Macaulay intersperses realistic drawings with sketches, diagrams, letters, and other documents to show how archaeologists painstakingly research and reconstruct the Spanish caravel *Magdelena.* Then through a "newly" discovered diary from archives in Seville he reveals how the ship was built and launched. The same standard of excellence, attention to detail, and touches of humor can be found in Macaulay's *The Way Things Work, Cathedral, City, Castle, Pyramid, Underground,* and *Mill.*

In spite of the range of media available for nonfiction books, the medium of choice is now photography. Photographs help establish credibility for real-life stories like Diane Hoyt-Goldsmith's *Las Posadas: An Hispanic*

Paul Facklam's drawing of a Goliath beetle shows its size in relation to familiar objects in Margery Facklam's *The Big Bug Book.* From *The Big Bug Book* by Margery Facklam. Copyright © 1994 by Margery Facklam (text); copyright © 1994 by Paul Facklam (illustrations). By permission of Little, Brown and Company, Inc.

Christmas Celebration and add to the fascination of such topics as bog people in James M. Deem's *Bodies from the Ash*. Photographs reveal the natural world in its astonishing variety, recording minute detail in an instant. The photos by Nic Bishop for Joy Cowley's *Chameleon, Chameleon* and *Red-Eyed Tree Frog* (see p. 606) reveal marvels of skin textures, colors, and patterns that would be difficult to reproduce with complete accuracy in a painting.

Photographs in nonfiction books furnish more than technical accuracy, however. Photographers can be artists as well as recorders of information. Sometimes artistry results not from a single photographer's work but from the careful choice of pictures to accompany a nonfiction text. The photographs that illustrate Seymour Simon's many books come from a variety of sources, but their effect is breathtaking in such books as *Guts, Horses, Galaxies,* and *Crocodiles and Alligators*.

Captions

Children need to be able to look at an illustration and know what they are seeing, and that requires a wise use of captions and labels. Many writers use the text itself, if it is brief, to explain the pictures, eliminating the need for additional captions. The short paragraphs in much of Kathryn Lasky's *Interrupted Journey: Saving Endangered Sea Turtles* are clearly situated next to Christopher G. Knight's photographs. The arrangement of the text on the page and clear references to details in each picture help readers get maximum information about the rescue efforts of Kemp's ridley turtles by the staff of the New England Aquarium.

Sometimes it is helpful to have labels or other text printed within the illustration itself. In *Maps: Getting from Here to There* by Harvey Weiss, many drawings and diagrams include labels and arrows to show specifically where items like "a south latitude" or "an east longitude" are represented on the globe. Explanation within the pictures also helps identify contour lines and the features of a marine chart. Only occasionally does Weiss use a conventional caption to refer to an entire illustration. However an author chooses to use captions, they should be clear.

Format

The total look of a book is its *format,* involving type size, leading, margins, placement of text and pictures, and arrangement of front and back matter—these include title and copyright pages in the front and indexes, bibliographies, and other aids at the back. *Mummies Made in Egypt* by Aliki incorporates hieroglyphic writing on the dedication and half-title pages, and many of the illustrations are arranged like the friezes that decorated the tombs of antiquity. This author frequently arranges sequences of pictures on the page in a comic strip or storyboard variation.

There are no absolute rules for format; the look of a book should be responsive to its purpose and its content. The broad coverage of topic intended in the Eyewitness

In spring, she'll take them hunting, and for two years she'll protect and feed them, until they've learnt, like her, to hunt ... alone.

Polar bear mums usually have two cubs at a time, but sometimes they have one or, very rarely, triplets.

The simple text by Nicola Davies and lovely illustrations by Gary Blythe in *Ice Bear* are fine examples of nonfiction writing and illustration for younger children. *Ice Bear: In the Steps of the Polar Bear.* Written by Nicola Davies. Illustrations copyright © 2005 Gary Blythe. Reproduced by permission of the publisher Candlewick Press, Inc., Cambridge, MA, on behalf of Walker Books, Ltd., London.

series published by DK makes the busy layout of its pages seem rich rather than crowded. Nicola Davies's *Ice Bear* is aimed at younger audiences and has uncluttered page layouts and simple captions that give the book an attractive and inviting look.

Even a book that is sparingly illustrated can be notable for its overall design. Spacious margins and tastefully ornamented headings can make a long text seem less forbidding. The format of a nonfiction book is an asset if it contributes to clarity or if it makes the book more appealing to its audience.

TYPES OF NONFICTION BOOKS

Anyone who chooses nonfiction books for children soon notices several subgenres or recognizable types with common characteristics. Knowing about these types helps the teacher and librarian provide balanced and rich resources for learning as they choose particular books for particular purposes.

Concept Books

Concept books explore the characteristics of a class of objects or of an abstract idea. Most of the nonfiction books intended for very young children are of this type. Typically they cover such concepts as size, color, shape, spatial relationships, self, and family. Concept books for this age are discussed at length in Chapter 4. For school-age children, concept books begin with what is already familiar and move toward the unfamiliar, some by showing new ways to consider well-known materials, others by furnishing new and different examples or perspectives. Such books are often useful as idea sources for classroom experiences and discussion.

One good book for discussion is Peter Spier's *People,* an oversize picture book that appeals to many different ages as it celebrates the possibilities for variation among the several billion human beings who live on Earth. Spier's drawings include many shapes and colors of ears, eyes, and noses; costumes, shelters, and pastimes from around the world; architecture, alphabets, and foods. Although the author emphasizes the uniqueness of individual appearances and preferences, the concept of cultural differences is implicit in the book. Concept books about culture always raise the issue of stereotyping. Help children think about the author's choice of representative images for this book. Students might compare Spier's drawings with the photographs in *In Your Face* by Donna M. Jackson.

Nonfiction Picture Books

As earlier sections of this chapter show, more and more nonfiction books look more and more like picture storybooks—that is, they are lavishly illustrated or published in picture-book format. Books such as Jean Fritz's *Leonardo's Horse* or Lynn Curlee's *Parthenon* present information through conventional, well-written expository text, but the beautiful illustrations and elegant design of these books add to our aesthetic pleasure as well as to our understanding of the topics they present. Other books, such as *When Bugs Were Big, Plants Were Strange, and Tetrapods Stalked the Earth* by Hannah Bonner, present information in less conventional ways.

One of the first modern picture storybooks, *Pelle's New Suit* by Elsa Beskow, came to this country from Sweden more than seventy-five years ago. This story shows a little boy getting wool from his pet lamb, then having it carded, spun, dyed, woven, and finally taken to the tailor to be made into a new suit. Compare this classic with *"Charlie Needs a Cloak"* by Tomie dePaola, which also presents, as a story, basic information about making wool into cloth. The saga of Charlie's cloak is enhanced by humor, and the illustrations serve to emphasize the steps in the cloth-making process. dePaola was a leader in combining narrative, humor, and attractive pictures to make books that are both good stories and nonfiction resources.

The most popular nonfiction picture books of recent years are the Magic School Bus stories by Joanna Cole and Bruce Degen. *The Magic School Bus inside the Earth* was followed by other popular titles. All of these fantastic field trips are presided over by Ms. Frizzle, a memorable teacher, and endured by a group of children who develop recognizable personalities. A new format was introduced in *Ms. Frizzle's Adventures: Ancient Egypt* and *Imperial China.* Leaving the school bus behind, the indomitable Ms. Frizzle dons a parachute to travel to ancient Egypt and rides a cloth dragon to China. Just as the School Bus books explore science concepts, Ms. Frizzle's new adventures are meant to convey social studies concepts.

In *Nobody Particular* Molly Bang provides the narrative voice for Diane Wilson, a real-life crusader against pollution. In this innovative picture book Bang places black-and-white drawings against vivid painted backgrounds that effectively relate and dramatize Wilson's struggles. In addition to the first-person narrative, Bang uses speech bubbles and hand-written footnotes to provide the backdrop for Wilson's fight to stop chemical companies from dumping PCBs into East Texas bays. This is an exemplary use of the picture-book format to present information.

Judith St. George has authored several excellent picture books on American history topics. *So You Want to Be President?* is a brief and highly engaging look at the characters of each of the U.S. presidents. Illustrated by David Small, the book won the Caldecott Medal in 2001 and was updated in 2004. *The Journey of the One and Only Declaration of Independence,* illustrated by Will Hillenbrand, is a lively overview of this vital document and its role throughout U.S. history. Although brief, these books could easily introduce or substitute for drier textbooks on American history.

Many nonfiction picture books for older readers tell good stories about places or things, although they might

Molly Bang's artwork for *Nobody Particular* shows how illustration can enhance nonfiction. From *Nobody Particular: One Woman's Fight to Save the Bays* by Molly Bang. Copyright © 2001 by Molly Bang. Used by permission of Henry Holt & Company.

not have the central human characters that bring warmth to fiction. Books like David Macaulay's *Ship* and William Kurelek's *Lumberjack* are examples of this type. Nadia Wheatley and Donna Rawlin's *My Place* visits the same neighborhood in Australia back through many decades to a time before the Europeans arrived. On each double-page spread a new child narrator draws a map of the place and describes life in the neighborhood that is "my place." The book ends in 1788 as a child explains, "My name is Barangaroo. I belong to this place." Cultural, sociological, and environmental concepts in books like these are particularly good springboards for discussion with older children who have some prior knowledge of history and can explore similar issues in their own communities.

Photographic Essays

With the increased use of photography in children's books today, the photo essay is an increasingly popular form. However, only some of the books that use photographs are photographic essays. Although the books by Dorothy Hinshaw Patent (such as *Animals on the Trail with Lewis and Clark*) depend on photographs by William Muñoz on almost every page, they are not photographic essays. The essay relies on the camera in different ways: to particularize general information, to document emotion, to assure the reader of truth in an essentially journalistic fashion.

A sensitive and vital photo essay can contribute to children's appreciation of cultural and religious diversity. Photographs by George Ancona illuminate Latino life and traditions in books such as *Fiesta U.S.A.* and *Mi Casa: My House*. A long-standing collaboration between author Diane Hoyt-Goldsmith and photographer Lawrence Migdale has produced many fine photo essays about American cultures in books such as *Celebrating Ramadan* and *Potlatch: A Tsimshian Celebration*.

Other books about American cultures and history often gain entry to these cultures through physical structures, as in Raymond Bial's *Cajun Home, One Room School*, and *Tenement: Immigrant Life on the Lower East Side*. By focusing his camera on buildings and the everyday objects within, Bial illuminates much about the people who lived or worked there. In *One Good Apple: Growing Our Food for the Sake of the Earth* Catherine Paladino provides vivid evidence of the effects of pesticides on the environment and lucid illustrations of the efforts people around the country are making to counteract those effects.

Identification Books

In its simplest form, an identification book is a naming book, and this may well be the first sort of book that a very young child sees. *Tool Book* by Gail Gibbons shows simple drawings of common tools in bright colors, with appropriate labels. A phrase or two describes the common function of all the tools displayed on a double spread. This is information for the youngest child. But just as children grow in their ability to discriminate and classify, so do identification books become more detailed, precise, and complex.

When a child brings a stone or a leaf to school and asks, "What kind is it?" the teacher or librarian has a built-in opportunity to introduce books to help that child discover the answer. Millicent Selsam and Joyce Hunt's First Look At series is useful for teaching younger children how to examine a specimen and pick out the features that will be important in making an identification. The National Audubon Society and Scholastic have created a series of First Field Guides for children. Among those titles are *Rocks and Minerals* by Edward Ricciuti and *Trees* by Brian Cassie. National Geographic has also produced a series of identification books in its My First Pocket Guide series. These include *Great Mammals* by Carolinda Hill, *Stars and Planets* by John O'Byrne, and *Garden Birds* by Terence Lindsey.

Life-Cycle Books

A fascination with animals is one of the most general and durable of children's interests, beginning very early and often continuing through adolescence into adulthood. There is always an audience for factual books that describe how animals live, with an emphasis on the inherent story element. These books cover all or some part of the cycle of life, from the birth of one animal to the birth of its progeny, or the events of one year in the animal's life, or the development of one animal throughout its lifetime. Gail Gibbons has written and illustrated several books that focus on the life cycle of birds, *Owls, Chickens!, Penguins!,* and *Soaring with the Wind: The Bald Eagle.*

An account of authentic behavior often produces the effect of characterization; thus children frequently read nonfiction books as "stories" rather than as reference books. Holling C. Holling's beautifully illustrated classics *Minn of the Mississippi* and *Pagoo,* which trace the life histories of a turtle and a crawfish, are unique survival stories. More recently Laurence Pringle and illustrator Bob Marstall have provided similar fascinating accounts in *A Dragon in the Sky: The Story of a Green Darner Dragonfly* and *An Extraordinary Life: The Story of the Monarch Butterfly.* These longer life-cycle stories are often stories of survival against the elements and enemies in the environment and read with all the same drama of a fictional adventure story.

Charles Micucci's attractively designed and thorough books about apples, ants, peanuts, and honeybees are every bit as intriguing as these life-cycle stories about animals. *The Life and Times of the Apple* details the growth of apples, how they are cross-fertilized and grafted, and how they are harvested and marketed. Micucci also includes information about types of apples, their history, and the legend of Johnny Appleseed. *The Life and Times of the Ant, The Life and Times of the Peanut,* and *The Life and Times of the Honeybee* are equally informative.

Experiment and Activity Books

To some children the word *science* is synonymous with *experiment,* and certainly experience is basic to scientific understandings. Many basic nonfiction books suggest a few activities to clarify concepts; in contrast, experiment books take the activities themselves as content. The appearance of a supplementary experiment or activity, frequently as a final note in a book, is quite common today. For instance, Gail Gibbons includes numbered and illustrated directions for a project on raising bean plants at the end of her *From Seed to Plant,* for primary-age readers.

Many experiment books for older children also focus on one subject or one material. Modern reproduction techniques allow full-color photography and sophisticated layouts that make the steps in experiments easy to follow. Chicago Review Press has developed many tempting experiment books on a variety of topics. Among the science areas covered are *Insectigations: 40 Hands-on Activities to Explore the Insect*

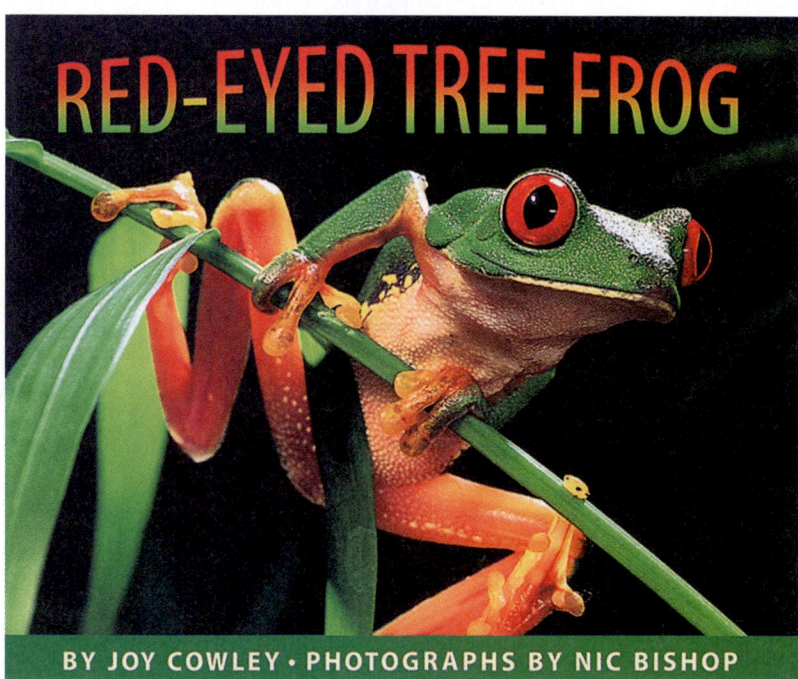

Nic Bishop has provided amazingly vivid close-up photographs for Joy Cowley's *Red-Eyed Tree Frog.* Illustration copyright © 1999 by Nic Bishop from *Red-Eyed Tree Frog* by Joy Cowley. Published by Scholastic Press/Scholastic, Inc. Reprinted by permission.

World by Cindy Blobaum and *Darwin and Evolution for Kids with 21 Activities* by Kristen Lawson. Joe Rhatigan has written a number of appealing activity books, including *Out-of-This-World Astronomy: 50 Amazing Activities and Projects, Prize-Winning Science Fair Projects for Curious Kids*, and *The Kids' Guide to Nature Adventures: 80 Great Activities for Exploring the Outdoors*, the first two in collaboration with Rain Newcomb.

Some of the most engaging books of science experiments are those by Vicki Cobb. Her *I Fall Down, I Get Wet,* and *I See Myself* are discovery books about gravity, water, and light directed at preschoolers. An interesting approach to chemistry is found in Cobb's *More Science Experiments You Can Eat*, a book that is fun for children old enough to handle various cooking procedures safely. *See for Yourself: More Than 100 Experiments for Science Fairs and Projects* includes experiments inspired by toy stores and supermarkets but covers concepts from the traditional sciences. *Chemically Active! Experiments You Can Do at Home* is arranged so that one experiment leads directly to the next. All the books by Cobb are designed with a commentary to link the experiments so that they can be read straight through for information as well as used to guide the actual procedures.

Some books that suggest experiments also include experiences of other kinds, along with collections of interesting facts, anecdotes, or other material. Books like these that encourage children to explore a topic through a broad range of activities have gained popularity in recent years. *Good for Me! All about Food in 32 Bites* by Marilyn Burns is a compilation of facts, learning activities, experiments, and questions that can lead to further investigation. This is one of many titles from the Brown Paper School Books series, published by Little, Brown, which consistently use this format.

Books like these make good browsing and are a source of possible projects for individual study or for activities that might be tried and discussed in class. Teachers as well as students appreciate the variety and creativity of the ideas. However, it is important to remember that activity books are not designed for reference. There is seldom an index, and headings might have more entertainment value than clarity. For easy access to specific information, other types of books are required.

Documents and Journals

An important contribution to literature for children in recent years has been the publication of books based on sketchbooks, journals, and original documents. Betsy Lewin and Ted Lewin, well-known authors and illustrators in their own right, have teamed up to travel the world and chart their experiences in several fine sketchbook/journals, including *Top to Bottom, Down Under* and *Elephant Quest.* Sophie Webb and Jennifer Owings Dewey have both created lively books based on their own sketchbook journals. Webb's *Looking for Seabirds: Journal from an Alaskan Voyage* and *My Season with Penguins: An Antarctic Journal* focus on her stays in these remote areas, and her first-person narratives are illustrated with her paintings, sketches, and hand-written notes. Dewey spent four months in Antarctica on a grant from the National Science Foundation, and her *Antarctic Journal: Four Months*

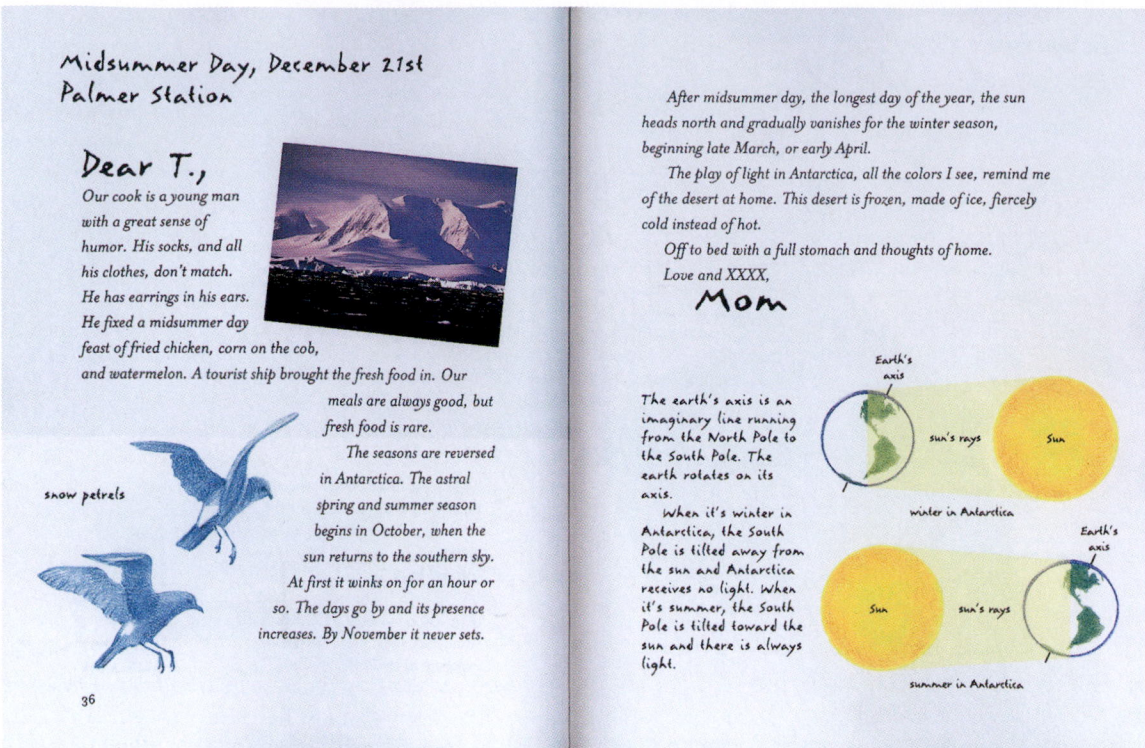

at the Bottom of the World was the result. Dewey's text begins, "Depart from home in the early morning, to be gone four months to Antarctica, a part of the planet as remote as the moon in its own way" (p. 6). The immediacy and informality of her voice provide added excitement to an account that includes letters, sketches, drawings, and photographs. Virginia Wright-Frierson uses a similar format to describe different ecosystems in *A Desert Scrapbook, An Island Scrapbook,* and *A North American Rainforest Scrapbook*. All these books provide children with excellent models for observing their own world through words and pictures.

Milton Meltzer uses letters and other primary sources in such fine books as *Voices from the Civil War*. Julius Lester's extraordinary *To Be a Slave,* a Newbery Honor Book in 1969, provides reproductions of primary sources as a background for the study of African American history. The author combines the verbatim testimony of former slaves with his own strong commentary:

> To be a slave was to be a human being under conditions in which that humanity was denied. They were not slaves. They were people. Their condition was slavery. (p. 28)

More recent works that focus on a broader sweep of history are *We Were There, Too! Young People in U.S. History* by Phillip Hoose, Tanya Bolden's *Tell All the Children Our Story: Memories and Mementos of Being Young and Black in America, We Shall Overcome: A Living History of the Civil Rights Struggle* by Herb Boyd, Diane McWhorter's *A Dream of Freedom*, and *Now Is Your Time! The African American Struggle for Freedom* by Walter Dean Myers. The authors use primary sources, period photographs, and reproductions of lists and documents that lend compelling evidence to critical moments in America's history.

Firsthand accounts are also the base for Jim Murphy's *The Boys' War: Confederate and Union Soldiers Talk About the Civil War*. On both sides, many soldiers were underage boys who had gone off to war looking for something more adventuresome than routine farm chores. The author quotes a Wisconsin boy who wrote of his experiences at Shiloh:

> I want to say, as we lay there and the shells were flying over us, my thoughts went back to my home, and I thought what a foolish boy I was to run away and get into such a mess as I was in. I would have been glad to have seen my father coming after me. (p. 33)

Books like this lend authenticity to the picture of conflict that students get in historical fiction such as Patricia Beatty's *Charley Skedaddle*.

Russell Freedman frequently uses photographs from archival sources to document his historical books as well as his biographies. *Immigrant Kids* includes reproductions of photos of passengers on the steerage deck of an immigrant liner in 1893, street scenes from New York City's Lower East Side in 1898, and school scenes. In *Kids at Work* Freedman uses photographs by Lewis Hine, who worked to reform child labor laws in the United States in the early part of the twentieth century. Freedman's *Children of the Great Depression* documents the effects of this era on children. *Children of the Wild West* furnishes photographs from a time and place where cameras were scarce. Children interested in the westward movement in the United States can study the pictures as well as the text of this book for information. Photos of families with their covered wagons clearly show modes of dress and meager possessions. Log cabins, sod houses, and school-rooms can be compared and described. The pictures of Native American children in tribal dress and at govern-ment boarding schools are particularly interesting.

Survey Books

The purpose of a survey book is to give an overall view of a substantial topic and to furnish a representative sampling of facts, principles, or issues. Such a book em-phasizes balance and breadth of coverage, rather than depth. The National Geographic Society has developed an exceptional list of such books with titles like *National Geographic Dinosaurs* by Paul Barrett, *National Geographic Prehistoric Mammals* by Alan Turner, *Bury the Dead: Tombs, Corpses, Mummies, Skeletons and Rituals* by Christopher Sloan, and *Insects* by Robin Bernard. Books by this pub-lisher can be relied on to present good science in broad overviews of topics that fascinate children.

Seymour Simon's fine books such as *Dogs, Cats, Horses, Sharks,* and *Crocodiles and Alligators* are excellent examples of survey books that will entice children to learn more about animal subjects. Even the endpapers are embossed with a pattern that mirrors crocodilian skin. *Raptors* by Bobbie Kalman offers a general introduction to raptors with information about physical character-istics, habitats, nesting habits, and survival techniques. Headings make information easy to find, and there are many captioned close-up photographs. A child looking for in-depth information on a specific genus might need to go on to sources such as Karen Dudley's *Alligators and Crocodiles* or *Bald Eagles.* The survey book furnishes an authoritative introduction to a topic but not necessarily all the information a student could want.

A few books attempt to give children a survey of the important people, places, and events in the history of the world. Hendrik Van Loon's *The Story of Mankind* was the first book to interpret world history to children in an interesting and nonfiction fashion. This book, a pioneer in the field and the winner of the first Newbery Medal, in 1922, is now available in a revised edition.

Historical surveys today are more likely to adopt a particular perspective, an "angle" on history that makes wide-ranging content more manageable. Bruce Kosciel-niak's *About Time* focuses on the concept of time and timekeeping over the ages. Elspeth Leacock and Susan Buckley's *Journeys in Time: A New Atlas of American His-tory* and *Places in Time: A New Atlas of American History* provide a credible overview of American history and geography through the lenses of time and place. In *Food* and *Clothing,* Italian artist Piero Ventura looks at history through these familiar lenses that also convey concepts about basic human needs.

Survey books are available at many different levels of complexity and reading difficulty. A teacher or librarian

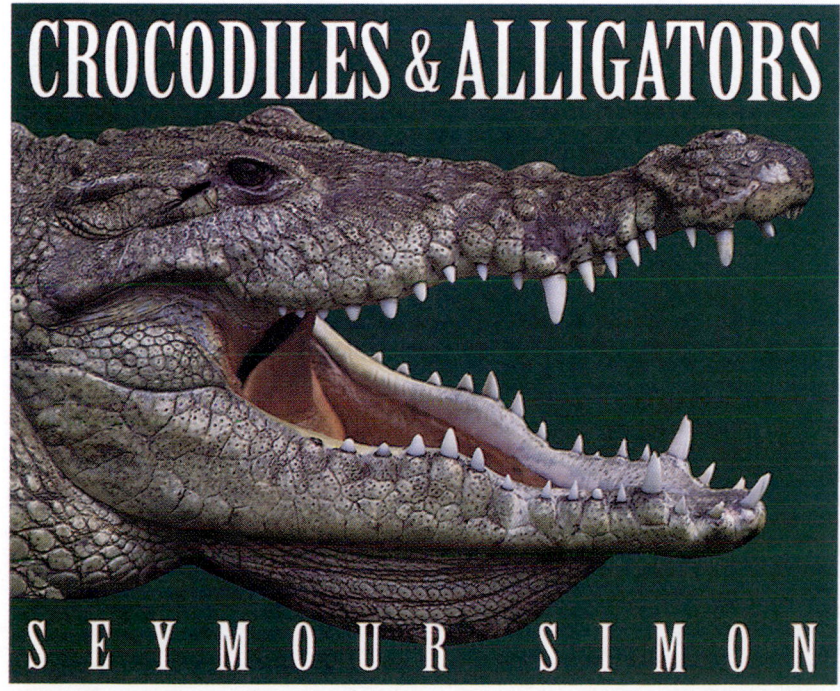

Seymour Simon chooses photographs that never fail to invite the reader's attention in such books as *Crocodiles & Alligators.* Cover from *Crocodiles & Alligators* by Seymour Simon. Jacket photograph © Tom McHugh/Photo Researchers, Inc. From *Crocodiles & Alligators,* copyright © 1999. Used by permission of HarperCollins Publishers, Inc.

may need to help children skim to find those that are most appropriate for their use.

Specialized Books

Specialized books are designed to give specific information about a relatively limited topic. These books satisfy particular interests; they are more likely to be used intensively than extensively, on a one-time basis rather than as a frequent reference. James Giblin's many books, such as *When Plague Strikes, The Truth about Unicorns, Good Brother, Bad Brother,* and *The Mystery of the Mammoth Bones,* illustrate how thorough research and good writing can illuminate the most mundane of topics. With their vivid language and highly involving organization, Jim Murphy's books read like suspense novels and are every bit as hard to put down. *Gone A-Whaling* is a history of the whaling industry that focuses on the young boys who signed aboard the whalers. Murphy's other specialized books include *An American Plague,* about the yellow fever epidemic that struck Philadelphia in 1793; *Inside the Alamo,* about the war for Texas and the siege of the Alamo; *Blizzard! The Storm That Changed America,* about the great storm that struck the New England states in 1888; *Across America on an Emigrant Train,* the story of Robert Louis Stevenson's trip across the con-

tinent in 1879; and *The Great Fire,* about the Chicago fire of 1871.

Many specialized books extend content areas that are frequently part of the elementary social studies curriculum. Michael Cooper's *Dust to Eat: Drought and Depression in the 1930s* makes use of archival photographs, letters, and firsthand accounts to describe the tragedy of the drought that devastated so many states. Jerry Stanley's *Children of the Dust Bowl* tells how educator Leo Hart started a special school for children of migrant workers who had come to California from drought-stricken Oklahoma in the 1930s. The book also provides information about the climatic and the economic changes that caused this great migration. A mass migration to America was caused by the potato famine in Ireland in the nineteenth century. Although several recent books focus on this event, none bring the tragedy to life more vividly than Susan Campbell Bartoletti's *Black Potatoes: The Story of the Great Irish Famine, 1845–1850.* Read alongside such works of historical fiction as Patricia Reilly Giff's *Nory Ryan's Song* and even Paula Fox's *The Slave Dancer,* this book raises important questions about acts of genocide that have continued to haunt the human race.

Many specialized books are geared to the personal interests of children. There is certainly something about

Jim Murphy's exhaustive research and engaging writing style take readers *Inside the Alamo.* Cover from *Inside the Alamo* by Jim Murphy © 2003. Used by permission of Delacorte Press, an imprint of Random House Children's Books, a division of Random House, Inc.

mud that attracts many children. Jennifer Owings Dewey has thoroughly investigated the topic in *Mud Matters*. Dewey's own illustrations and photographs by Stephen Trimble highlight the coverage of such topics as "Ritual Mud," "Building Mud," "Magic Mud," and "Mud Between Your Toes."

Teachers and librarians have noted that today's specialized books are more specialized than ever, covering narrow topics and unique interests. Some of these involve children's curiosity about medical treatment and disease, including such books as *Guinea Pig Scientists: Bold Self-Experimenters in Science and Medicine* by Leslie Dendy and Mel Boring, *Invisible Enemies: Stories of Infectious Disease* by Jeanette Farrell, and *ER Vets: Life in an Animal Emergency Room* by Donna M. Jackson. Many of these books have intriguing, impossible-to-resist titles, such as *The Race to Save the Lord God Bird* by Phillip Hoose or *The Man-Eating Tigers of the Sundarbans* by Sy Montgomery. But other excellent books, such as *The Cod's Tale* by

Mark Kurlansky, might not be discovered on the library shelf unless they are introduced. Readers do not deliberately seek a book on a topic that they do not know exists. For that reason, an adult might need to make a special effort to point out these special books.

Craft and How-To Books

A fascinating array of craft and activity books give directions for making and doing. Kids Can Press has a series of large, clearly illustrated craft and activity books that includes *The Jumbo Book of Needlecrafts* by Judy Ann Sadler and *The Jumbo Book of Drama* by Deborah Dunleavy. Bobbe Needham's *Ecology Crafts for Kids: 50 Great Ways to Make Friends with Planet Earth* offers directions for more than fifty projects all made from recycled materials and information about environmental issues as well. Janis Herbert's *Leonardo da Vinci for Kids: His Life and Ideas* is part biography and part activity book. The suggested projects include active ones like making

Ellen B. Senisi shows children how to make colors from natural substances in *Berry Smudges and Leaf Prints*. From *Berry Smudges and Leaf Prints: Finding and Making Colors from Nature* by Ellen B. Senisi, copyright © 2001 by Ellen B. Senisi. Used by permission of Dutton Children's Books, a division of Penguin Young Readers Group, a Member of Penguin World (USA), 345 Hudson St., New York, NY 10014. All rights reserved.

a catapult or a map and cooking Leonardo's favorite minestrone soup, and more cerebral ones like memory exercises. Other books in this appealing series include *Marco Polo for Kids* by Janis Herbert and *Monet and the Impressionists for Kids* by Carol Sabbeth. Ellen B. Senisi's *Berry Smudges and Leaf Prints: Finding and Making Colors from Nature* engages children with artistic experiments and the natural world. Here vivid photographs of natural objects like ferns and frogs introduce pictures of children engaged in various projects such as Great Green Leaf Prints and Spinach Ink. The book is a wonderful melding of art and science.

Directions are usually clearer if appropriately illustrated. *The Children's Book of Yoga* by Thia Luby provides clear photographs demonstrating various yoga positions and includes pictures of animals, plants, and objects that children can imitate in their poses. Rebecca Whitford's *Little Yoga* provides simple illustrations by Martina Selway to introduce preschoolers to yoga postures. Line drawings effectively demonstrate the steps in *How to Make Pop-Ups* and *How to Make Super Pop-Ups* by Joan Irvine. These books have a high success rate with students; they are able to make quite complex-looking paper designs in three dimensions with a minimum of adult help. Older readers who have been captivated by the Irvine books will find that *The Elements of Pop-Up* by David A. Carter and James Diaz provides more advanced activities and does this by showing actual pop-up and pull-tab forms.

Some craft books deal so specifically with approaches and techniques common to the activity-centered classroom that it is likely they will be used as much by teachers as by individual children. Helen Roney Sattler's *Recipes for Art and Craft Materials* will prove indispensable to teachers. Included are recipes for a variety of basic substances that children can make for their own use—such as paste, modeling and casting compounds, papier-mâché, inks, and dried-flower preservatives.

Cookbooks for children ought to have sparkling, clear directions and adequate warnings about the safe use of tools and equipment. *Emeril's There's a Chef in My Soup: Recipes for the Kid in Everyone*, written by celebrity chef Emeril Lagasse, certainly meets these criteria. Even better, however, are the appealing recipes for a host of simple dishes such as 1-2-3 Lasagne or Cheesy Star Snacks. The list includes standard kid favorites like pizza and chocolate chip cookies, but there are plenty of appealing vegetable recipes as well. Although the book is clearly directed at children, the title aptly describes the book—this is one that cooks of all ages will want to add to their cookbook shelves. A popular character who has inspired a cookbook is Peter Rabbit. *The Peter Rabbit and Friends Cookbook* offers recipes and vignettes from Beatrix Potter's popular books. Another literature-based recipe collection is Barbara Walker's *The Little House Cookbook: Frontier Foods from Laura Ingalls Wilder's Classic Stories.*

USING LITERATURE ACROSS THE CURRICULUM

One of the important components of a literature program (see Chapter 13) is using literature across the curriculum. If children are to become real readers, they should meet good books, not only at reading time, but also as they study history, science, the arts—all subject areas. Outstanding nonfiction books, those that might qualify as what author John McPhee calls "the literature of fact," are the most obvious places to begin in choosing titles to use in the content areas.

Nonfiction Books in the Classroom

Like books of any other genre, the best nonfiction books should be appreciated for their artistry. Good writing, fine illustration, and high-quality bookmaking all have intrinsic aesthetic value. And like fiction, nonfiction books can provide satisfaction and delight for interested readers. Nonfiction books are a bit different, however. They also fulfill special teaching functions that need to be considered in planning classroom materials and activities.

The information in trade books is a major content resource for the curriculum. Elementary school textbooks are frequently overgeneralized or oversimplified in the attempt to keep them reasonably short and readable. A selection of nonfiction books can provide the depth and richness of detail not possible in textbook coverage of the same topic. The latest nonfiction books are also likely to be more up-to-date than textbooks, since the process of producing and choosing textbooks can take many months or even years. The adopted series then might not be revised, or replaced, for quite some time. However, new trade books on popular or timely topics appear every year.

Many teachers would use an up-to-date nonfiction book like Ellen Jackson's *Looking for Life in the Universe* or Gloria Skurzynski's *Are We Alone? Scientists Search for Life in Space* to supplement the science textbook. Others might completely bypass the textbook and assemble many books about space and the solar system (probably including such titles as Franklyn Branley's *Mission to Mars* and *The International Space Station*, Alvin Jenkins's *Next Stop Neptune*, Sally Ride's *Exploring Our Solar System*, David Getz's *Life on Mars*, Seymour Simon's *Destination Mars*, and Patricia Lauber's *Journey to the Planets*) to provide information much richer than the text could offer.

Making several nonfiction books available on a single topic is important for teachers to consider because this presents ready-made opportunities to encourage critical reading. When children's information all comes from one source, they are likely to accept the author's selection and interpretation of facts without question. The use of two or more books prompts comparison. Younger children could compare April Pulley Sayre's *The Bumblebee Queen* with Sara van Dyck's *Bumblebees*. Middle graders might compare and contrast James Cross Giblin's *When Plague Strikes: Black Death, Smallpox, AIDS* with Bryn Barnard's *Outbreak: Plagues That Changed History* and Jim Murphy's *An American Plague: The True and Terrifying Story of the Yellow Fever Epidemic of 1793* in terms of style of writing and treatment of content. Encouraging children to ask themselves questions about these differences helps them make practical and critical judgments about what they are reading.

At the prereading level, children can compare books read aloud by the teacher, look critically at the illustrations, and decide which ones give them needed information. A kindergarten teacher who shared several books about tools with her children asked them to decide which book's pictures did the best job of showing how the tools worked. To check their judgment, they took turns at the classroom workbench and, under adult supervision, tried out the tools.

Most teachers or librarians who encourage the critical comparison of books find that helping children construct a chart of similarities and differences is an aid to clear thinking. As older children are introduced to techniques of inquiry, such as using a table of contents, finding information in indexes, and conducting a library search, they can also be encouraged to develop a list of criteria that they would apply to nonfiction books. Such activities help children become more critical readers of nonfiction books and more careful writers of their own materials. Literature in Action: "Helping Children Evaluate Nonfiction Books" shows how a school librarian and a group of fourth graders developed a list of questions that helped them evaluate nonfiction books.

Authors of fine nonfiction books approach their material in interesting ways that can easily be adapted for the classroom. Although it's more usual to find good books that support a lesson, it's also possible for a good book to suggest a lesson or an entire unit of study. The Web "The World beneath Your Feet" on pages 614–15, aimed at middle graders, was developed around the book *Hidden under the Ground: The World beneath Your Feet* by Peter Kent. It was planned in keeping with the National Science Education Standards, particularly those for critical thinking and inquiry. The Web shows how standards might be covered using good nonfiction and also demonstrates how fiction and nonfiction can be connected.

A unit on "Family History" might begin with Lila Perl's *The Great Ancestor Hunt,* which offers good suggestions for collecting family folklore at holiday get-togethers as well as tips for using public records. Investigations begun with Perl's book could be extended through books like David Weitzman's *My Backyard History Book* and lead to a class study of "Immigration" or "Difficult Journeys."

For young children, concept books often lead to ideas for good classification activities. Steve Jenkins and Robin Page have collaborated on many excellent books for younger children that introduce a variety of science topics. In *I See a Kookaburra!* they present concepts about climate and ecosystems in an appealing "I spy" format.

LITERATURE IN **ACTION**

Helping Children Evaluate Nonfiction Books

When Rebecca Thomas, a school librarian in Shaker Heights, Ohio, introduced *Storms* by Seymour Simon to a group of fourth graders, she covered up most of the front jacket. With only the title visible, she asked them to think what might be included in a book about storms. Their first response was to name the kinds of storms they knew—thunderstorms, snowstorms, tornadoes, and hurricanes. They also suggested other topics that could be in such a book: winds, thunder and lightning, the damage storms can cause, and how scientists know about storms. They decided that a book about storms should be illustrated with high-quality photographs that really picture storms and their actions.

With the librarian's help, they then began to develop some questions they would use to decide if the book was a good one:

Does the book cover the subject?
How good are the pictures?
Who will be able to understand the book?
How much actual information is included?
Does it set information straight (correct mistaken ideas)?

By the time this brief discussion was finished, the children were eager to see if Seymour Simon's book met their expectations, and of course they registered immediate approval when the librarian showed them the front jacket. As she read aloud, she encouraged students to note whether their questions had been answered. She stopped frequently so they could discuss particular pictures and the clarity of the writing based on their question "Who will be able to understand the book?"

These students used the criteria they had developed in question form to measure the success not only of *Storms* but also of other titles on the same topic as they completed a classroom unit on weather. The librarian's introduction engaged the children's interest in one book as it set the stage for their reading of other nonfiction titles. Helping children focus on the possibilities and strengths of specific books encourages them to develop understandings about genre and the broader world of literature.

Rebecca Thomas, Librarian
Fernway School, Shaker Heights, Ohio

Wonderfully Exciting Books

Underneath the City

Underground (Macaulay)
The Magic School Bus at the Waterworks (Cole)
Choose one underground system and make a
  study of it. Include diagrams of how it is built
  and explain how it works in your report.

The New York City Subway System (McNeese)
"The New York City Subway System" (www)
Plan a trip on the subway. What places do you
  want to visit? How much will it cost you? How
  many miles could you travel on one fare?

Living Underground

Slake's Limbo (Holman)
Downsiders (Shusterman)
The City of Ember (DuPrau)
Compare the problems the characters face
  in these three books. How does their life
  underground affect them?

"Coober Pedy: Opal Capital of Australia's
  Outback" (Moore)
Find out about people who have built
  underground homes in places like
  Coober Pedy in Australia or missile silos
  in Nebraska.
Design your own underground home.

Treasure beneath Your Feet

The Search for Riches (Langley)
The Children's Atlas of Lost Treasures (Reid)
How to Hunt for Buried Treasure (Deem)
Hide your own treasure and make a map showing
  where it is.

Wind Catcher (Avi)
The Treasure Bird (Griffin)
The Treasure of Bessledorf Hill (Naylor)
Treasure Island (Stevenson)
Choose one of these titles to read with a group.
  Meet regularly to discuss your reactions.
  How does buried treasure drive the book's plot?
  Characters?
Plan a reader's theater presentation of the most
  exciting part.

*Buried Blueprints: Maps and Sketches of Lost Worlds
  and Mysterious Places* (Lorenz)
Make a map of one of the settings in the novels.

Animals Underground

Animals under the Ground (Fowler)
The Burrow (Orr)
Prairie Dogs (Bernhard)
Prairie Dogs (Patent)
The Prairie Dog (Crewe)
Dig, Wait, Listen: A Desert Toad s Tale (Sayre)
Thinking About Ants (Brenner)
Ant (Stetoff)
Inside an Ant Colony (Fowler)
Ant Cities (Dorros)
Exploring Underground Habitats (Phinney)
"Worms" (www)
What conditions affect animals living
  underground? How are they adapted
  for this type of life?
What environmental changes could affect
  underground creatures?
Find out about other underground animals
  and write your own nonfiction book.
What are the advantages of living
  underground?

LIFE UNDERGROUND

THE WORLD BENEATH YOUR FEET: A WEB OF POSSIBILITIES

Working Underground

Roads and Tunnels (Pollard)
The World of Caves, Mines, and Tunnels (Hoare)
What problems confront builders underground?
Write a journal entry as one of these workers.

Growing Up in Coal Country (Bartoletti)
Jeremy Visick (Wiseman)
"The Navigator" (VHS)
How do underground conditions affect human
  beings? What dangers do they face?
What other professionals work underground?

What's under the Surface?

Hidden World: Under the Ground (Delafosse)
Our Patchwork Planet: The Story of Plate Tectonics (Sattler)
Planet Earth: Inside Out (Gibbons)
Shaping the Earth (Patent)
"Great Archaeological Sites" (www)
How is the earth constructed?
Name the earth's layers.

How to Dig a Hole to the Other Side of the World (McNulty)
The Magic School Bus inside the Earth (Cole)
Read these two books. What is fact and what is fantasy in each? How do the authors separate the two?

A Handful of Dirt (Bial)
What types of scientists study things beneath the surface? Interview an archaeologist, paleontologist, geologist, etc.

DIGGING BENEATH THE SURFACE

Under the Ice

Discovering the Inca Ice Maiden (Reinhard)
Frozen Girl (Getz)
Frozen Man (Getz)
Secrets of the Iceman (Patent)
Discovering the Iceman (Tanaka)
What conditions preserved the bodies in bogs and ice? How do scientists study them? What can they find out by studying them?

Rocks and Fossils

Everybody Needs a Rock (Baylor)
If You find a Rock (Christian)
Rocks in His Head (Hurst)
Make up rules for owning a rock.
Find a special rock and sketch it.
Write a description.
Can others find your rock by reading your description?
Find poems about rocks and create a display.
Write a poem about your rock.

Stories in Stone: The World of Animal Fossils (Kittinger)
Fossils and Bones (Pirotta)
Digging Up Dinosaurs (Aliki)
Fossils Tell of Long Ago (Aliki)
Fossil (Taylor)
Where are fossils found? How are they formed?

A Look at Rocks: From Coal to Kimberlite (Kittinger)
A Look at Minerals: From Galena to Gold (Kittinger)
Rocks and Minerals (Oldershaw; Parker; Ricciuti; Symes)
In small groups, study different nonfiction books on the same topic. List your criteria. Meet with members of other groups and present an award to the best book.

"Smithsonian Gem and Mineral Collection" (www)
Where are the oldest rocks found? What type are they?
Study classifications of rocks.
Make your own collection and create a rock museum.

Buried beneath Your Feet

Graveyards of the Dinosaurs (Tanaka)
Mummies Made in Egypt (Aliki)
Bodies from the Ash (Deem)
Bury the Dead (Sloan)
Tales Mummies Tell (Lauber)
Mummies, Tombs, and Treasure (Perl)
Mummy (Putnam)
Egyptian Mummies: People from the Past (Pemberton)
Secrets of the Mummies (Tanaka)
Corpses, Coffins and Crypts (Colman)
"Mummies Unwrapped" (VHS, National Geographic)
"At the Tomb of Tutankhamen" (www)
Do all cultures bury their dead?
How are bodies preserved? What natural conditions affect the preservation of bodies?

Movement beneath Your Feet

On Shifting Ground (Kidd)
Geysers: When the Earth Roars (Gallant)
How Mountains Are Made (Zoehfeld)
Earth: The Making of a Planet (Gallant)
Dance of the Continents (Gallant)
Earthquakes (Branley; George; Morris; Pope; Simon)
"National Earthquake Information" Center (www)
Volcanoes (Branley; Morris; Simon; Sipiera)
"Volcano" (VHS, National Geographic)
"Volcano World" (www)
What different conditions cause earthquakes, geysers, and volcanoes? What do they have in common?
Make a map of the world showing current volcanic activity.

Underground Chambers

Limestone Cave (Davis)
Limestone Caves (Gallant)
Cave (Siebert; Silver)
Caves and Caverns (Gibbons)
Hidden Worlds: Caves (Delafosse)
"Mysteries Underground" (VHS, National Geographic)
How are caves formed? How do spelunkers feel about caving? What special dangers do they face?

Painters of the Caves (Lauber)
Visit caves at Lascaux and Chauvet (www).
Write a story about how the cave paintings were created.
Find out about other cave art.

Earthfasts (Mayne)
Harry Potter and the Chamber of Secrets (Rowling)
Gregor the Overlander (Rowling)
How do the authors develop a setting around underground chambers? Compare use of language, style, and mood in the settings.
Arrange a TV talk show interview with the characters from the books.

In the jungle I see . . .

This jungle, or rain forest, is in the Amazon River basin of South America.

Steve Jenkins and Robin Page's lively *I See a Kookaburra!* effectively presents concepts about animal habitats to younger children. Illustration from *I See a Kookaburra!* by Steve Jenkins and Robin Page. Illustrations copyright © 2005 by Steve Jenkins. Reprinted by permission of Houghton Mifflin Company. All rights reserved.

Other exceptional concept books by Steve Jenkins include *Move!* (with Robin Page); *Life on Earth: The Story of Evolution; Slap, Squeak and Scatter; What Do You Do with a Tail Like This?*; and *Animals in Flight* (both with Robin Page).

Regardless of the topic to be studied, teachers might need to consider common purposes and the functions of nonfiction books so that their choices will represent a wide range of possibilities. The following checklist can be used as a reminder of what to look for:

- Books to attract attention to the topic
- Books for browsing and exploring content
- Books with read-aloud possibilities
- Books for independent reading at varying levels of difficulty
- Basic reference books
- Books with enough information for in-depth study
- Books with a limited focus for very specific interests
- Books to guide activities and experiments
- Books that can be readily compared
- Books that introduce new perspectives or connections
- Books to accommodate new and extended interests

A selection of quality nonfiction books representing the categories discussed in the preceding sections supports children's growth in reading and appreciation for good writing as well as their development of understandings within the content area.

Integrating Fact and Fiction

Using literature across the curriculum can begin with nonfiction books, but it certainly does not have to end there. Many picture books, poems, traditional stories, novels, and biographies are natural choices for extending children's interest or knowledge base in a subject area. However, literature should never be distorted to fulfill the purposes of a lesson. One student participant from a university read Taro Yashima's *Crow Boy* to a class of 9- and 10-year-olds. When she finished the book, she told the children that the story took place in Japan and asked them if they knew where Japan was. There was a mad dash for the globe to see who could be the first to locate Japan. Then the participant went on to ask what Japan was, finally eliciting the answer she wanted—"an island." Next she asked what appeared to be a very unrelated question: "Why did Chibi have a rice ball wrapped in a radish leaf for his lunch instead of a hamburger?" The children were baffled. Finally, the participant gave them a brief but erroneous geography lesson in which she told them that because Japan was an island, it was very wet and flat, so the Japanese people could only raise rice, not beef for hamburgers! The student's university supervisor finally stepped in to save the day by helping the children talk about the real strengths of the book, Chibi's loneliness and the artist's use of space and visual symbols.

Scholar Louise Rosenblatt[14] warns against this way of "using" fiction, saying that teachers have a responsi-

---

[14]Louise Rosenblatt, "Literature—S.O.S.!" *Language Arts* 68 (October 1991): 444–48.

bility not to confuse children about the predominant stance or attitude appropriate for a particular reading purpose. The purpose we most want to encourage for works of *fiction* is reading for pleasure and insight (what Rosenblatt calls "aesthetic" reading). The carrying away of factual material ("efferent" reading) is more appropriate to the reading of nonfiction books, although certainly pleasure and insight are also important outcomes of reading nonfiction.

Using literature across the curriculum does not mean forcing connections between fact and fiction, as the student in our example attempted to do. Nor does it mean reading a nature poem for literal information about a bird's habitat or using sentences from a favorite story as the basis for language drill or diagramming sentences. It does mean recognizing that some pieces of literature have a strong background of fact and provide a unique human perspective on historical, scientific, and technological subjects. Works like Jean George's *Julie*, Lois Lowry's *Number the Stars,* and Eve Bunting's *Dandelions* give readers a perspective that allows them to know facts in another way. It is especially important for children to confirm what they are learning from nonfiction sources by meeting similar ideas in the more human frame of fiction.

Pulling together fiction and nonfiction selections that work well together is an ongoing process for most teach-ers. A record of titles should be kept so that these books can be shelved or displayed together when appropriate. A few sample groupings are shown in Teaching Resources: "Fact and Fiction."

Combining fact and fiction resources on a large scale can lead to the creation of an integrated theme unit encompassing learning in many subjects. As in "The World beneath Your Feet" Web on pages 614–15 the focus topic might be taken from the sciences, or it might begin with history or social studies (colonial life or houses), or language and the arts (signs and symbols). The topic must be broad enough to allow students to develop in many skill areas as they work through a wide range of interrelated content, using trade books and other materials. Textbooks are used as reference resources, if at all. This challenging but satisfying way of teaching requires a thorough knowledge of children's literature. (See Chapter 13 for more information about planning units of study.)

Fine nonfiction books and related books of fiction are important to the curriculum, whether they serve as the major resource or as supplements to formal instructional materials. Enthusiastic teachers who have learned to recognize the best and to choose wisely for a variety of purposes will put children in touch with an exciting and satisfying way to learn.

TEACHING **RESOURCES**

Fact and Fiction: Books to Use Together

 Visit the Online Learning Center at **www.mhhe.com/kiefer9e** for a printable version of this list.

EGGS (GRADES K–2)

Egg (Burton) Nonfiction	*The Extraordinary Egg* (Lionni) Picture Book
A Nestful of Eggs (P. Jenkins) Nonfiction	*Just Plain Fancy* (Polacco) Picture Book
Where Do Chicks Come From? (Sklansky) Nonfiction	*When Chickens Grow Teeth* (de Maupassant) Picture Book
From Chick to Chicken (Powell) Nonfiction	*Cook-a-Doodle-Doo!* (Stevens and Stevens) Picture Book
The Talking Eggs (San Souci) Traditional	*Big Fat Hen* (Baker) Counting Book
Chicken Man (Edwards) Picture Book	*Daniel's Mystery Egg* (Ada) Easy Picture Book
Hilda Hen's Search (Wormell) Picture Book	

BUGS (GRADES 2–3)

Bugs (Parker and Wright) Nonfiction	*Monarch Butterfly* (Gibbons) Nonfiction
Ladybug (Bernhard) Nonfiction	*The Big Bug Book* (Facklam) Nonfiction

(continued)

Fact and Fiction: Books to Use Together (continued)

BUGS (GRADES 2–3) (continued)

The Tarantula Scientist (Montgomery) Nonfiction

Big Bugs (Simon) Nonfiction

Honey in a Hive (Rockwell) Nonfiction

What's That Bug? (Froman) Nonfiction

Bugs Are Insects (Rockwell) Nonfiction

Flit, Flutter, Fly (Hopkins) Poetry

Joyful Noise (Fleischman) Poetry

Little Buggers (Lewis) Poetry

Bugs! (Greenberg) Poetry

James and the Giant Peach (Dahl) Fantasy

WET WEATHER (GRADES 1–3)

Down Comes the Rain (Branley) Nonfiction

A Rainy Day (Markle) Nonfiction

Flash, Crash, Rumble and Roll (Branley) Nonfiction

Thunderstorms (Sipiera and Sipiera) Nonfiction

Storms (Simon) Nonfiction

Weather! Watch How Weather Works (Rupp) Nonfiction

The Tree That Rains (Bernhard and Bernhard) Traditional

The Magic Bean Tree (Van Laan) Traditional

Come a Tide (Lyon) Picture Book

Peter Spier's Rain (Spier) Picture Book

Hurricane! (London) Picture Book

Twister (Beard) Picture Book

In the Rain with Baby Duck (Hest) Picture Book

Where Does the Butterfly Go When It Rains? (Garelick) Picture Book

Rain Talk (Serfozo) Picture Book

NATIVE AMERICANS ON THE PLAINS (GRADES 3–5)

An Indian Winter (Freedman) Nonfiction

Indian Chiefs (Freedman) Nonfiction

Children of the Wild West (Freedman) Nonfiction

. . . If You Lived with the Sioux Indians (McGovern) Nonfiction

Buffalo Hunt (Freedman) Nonfiction

The First Americans: The Story of Where They Came From and Who They Became (Nelson) Nonfiction

Follow the Stars (Rodanas) Traditional

The Lost Children (Goble) Traditional

Shingebiss, An Ojibwa Legend (Van Laan) Traditional

Sootface: An Ojibwa Cinderella (San Souci) Traditional

Dancing with the Indians (Medearis) Picture Book

Bad River Boys (Sneve) Picture Book

What Is the Most Beautiful Thing You Know about Horses? (Van Camp) Picture Book

Geronimo (Bruchac) Historical Fiction.

The Game of Silence (Erdrich) Historical Fiction

The Birchbark House (Erdrich) Historical Fiction

ONCE UPON THE PRAIRIE (GRADES 3–6)

Sod Houses on the Prairie (Rounds) Nonfiction

Children of the Wild West (Freedman) Nonfiction

Prairies (Patent) Nonfiction

The Prairie Builders (Collard) Nonfiction

On the Trail of Sacagawea (Lourie) Nonfiction

Prairie Willow (Trottier) Picture Book

Fact and Fiction: Books to Use Together *(continued)*

ONCE UPON THE PRAIRIE (GRADES 3–6) *(CONTINUED)*

Pioneer Girl: Growing Up on the Prairie (Warren) Biography

Dandelions (Bunting) Picture Book

Dakota Dugout (Turner) Picture Book

Three Names (MacLachlan) Picture Book

My Prairie Christmas (Harvey) Picture Book

Sarah, Plain and Tall (MacLachlan) Historical Fiction

Prairie Songs (Conrad) Historical Fiction

My Daniel (Conrad) Historical Fiction

Calling Me Home (Hermes) Historical Fiction

Worth (LaFaye) Fiction

SLAVERY AND FREEDOM (GRADES 4–6)

Escape from Slavery (Rappaport) Nonfiction

To Be a Slave (Lester) Nonfiction

Christmas in the Big House, Christmas in the Quarters (McKissack and McKissack) Nonfiction

Amistad Rising: The Story of Freedom (Chambers) Nonfiction

From Slave Ship to Freedom Road (Lester) Nonfiction

The Underground Railroad for Kids (Carson) Nonfiction

Days of Jubilee (McKissack and McKissack) Nonfiction

Lincoln: A Photobiography (Freedman) Biography

Harriet Beecher Stowe and the Beecher Preachers (Fritz) Biography

Anthony Burns: The Defeat and Triumph of a Fugitive Slave (Hamilton) Biography

Nettie's Trip South (Turner) Picture Book

The Middle Passage (Feelings) Picture Book

Sky Sash So Blue (Hawthorne) Picture Book

In the Time of the Drums (Siegelson) Picture Book

Pink and Say (Polacco) Picture Book

The Captive (Hansen) Historical Fiction

Honey Bea (Siegelson) Fantasy

Steal Away Home (Ruby) Historical Fiction

Letters from a Slave Girl (Lyons) Historical Fiction

Jip: His Story (Paterson) Historical Fiction

I Thought My Soul Would Rise and Fly (Hansen) Historical Fiction

Sarny (Paulsen) Historical Fiction

Steal Away Home (Carbonne) Historical Fiction

Nightjohn (Paulsen) Historical Fiction

Silent Thunder (Pinkney) Historical Fiction

Jayhawker (Beatty) Historical Fiction

With Every Drop of Blood (Collier and Collier) Historical Fiction

Forty Acres and Maybe a Mule (Robinett) Historical Fiction

North by Night: A Story of the Underground Railroad (Ayres) Historical Fiction

Ajeemah and His Son (Berry) Historical Fiction

Alec's Primer (Walter) Historical Fiction

The House of Dies Drear (Hamilton) Fiction

Days of Tears (Lester) Historical Fiction

47 (Mosley) Fantasy

I, Too, Sing America: Three Centuries of African American Poetry (Clinton) Poetry

(continued)

Fact and Fiction: Books to Use Together (*continued*)

DIFFICULT JOURNEYS (GRADES 5–8)

World War II, Asian American
I Am an American (Stanley) Nonfiction

Baseball Saved Us (Mochizuki) Picture Book

The Bracelet (Uchida) Picture Book

Journey to Topaz (Uchida) Historical Fiction

Under the Blood-Red Sun (Salisbury) Historical Fiction

My Friend the Enemy (Cheaney) Historical Fiction

Eyes of the Emperor (Salisbury) Historical Fiction

World War II, Europe and Asia
Remember World War II: Kids Who Survived Tell Their Stories (Nicholson) Nonfiction

The Hidden Children (Greenfeld) Nonfiction

Rescue (Meltzer) Nonfiction

One More Border: The True Story of One Family's Escape from War-Torn Europe (Kaplan) Nonfiction

Hitler Youth: Growing Up in Hitler's Shadow (Bartoletti) Nonfiction

Shadow Life: A Portrait of Anne Frank and Her Family (Deneberg) Nonfiction

Memories of Survival (Krinitz) Nonfiction

The Journey That Saved Curious George (Borden) Nonfiction

Surviving Hitler: A Boy in the Nazi Camps (Warren) Nonfiction

Daniel Half Human and the Good Nazi (Chotjewitz) Historical Fiction

No Pretty Picture: A Child of War (Lobel) Memoir

Anne Frank (Poole) Picture Book; Biography

The Cats in Krasinski Square (Hesse) Picture Book

Hidden Child (Millman) Picture Book

Always Remember Me: How One Family Survived World War II (Russo) Picture Book

Rose Blanche (Gallaz and Innocenti) Picture Book

The Lily Cupboard (Oppenheim) Picture Book

Milkweed (Spinelli) Historical Fiction

Number the Stars (Lowry) Historical Fiction

The Man from the Other Side (Orlev) Historical Fiction

Greater Than Angels (Matas) Historical Fiction

My Freedom Trip (Park and Park) Historical Fiction

The Endless Steppe (Hautzig) Historical Fiction

Year of Impossible Goodbyes (Choi) Historical Fiction

So Far from the Bamboo Grove (Watkins) Historical Fiction

War and the Pity of War (Philip) Poetry

When My Name Was Keoko (Park) Fiction

Modern-Day Refugees
Escape from Saigon (Warren) Nonfiction

A Haitian Family (Greenberg) Nonfiction

A Nicaraguan Family (Malone) Nonfiction

The Lost Boys of Natinga: A School for Sudan's Young Refugees (Walgren) Nonfiction

On the Wings of Eagles: An Ethiopian Boy's Story (Schrier) Picture Book

How Many Days to America? (Bunting) Picture Book

My Name Is María Isabel (Ada) Fiction

Kiss the Dust (Laird) Fiction

Tonight, by Sea (Temple) Fiction

Grab Hands and Run (Temple) Fiction

Goodbye Vietnam (Whelan) Fiction

Secrets in the Fire (Mankell) Fiction

Under the Persimmon Tree (Staples) Fiction

TEACHING RESOURCES

Fact and Fiction: Books to Use Together *(continued)*

DIFFICULT JOURNEYS (GRADES 5–8) *(CONTINUED)*

The Frozen Waterfall (Hiçyilmaz) Fiction

Behind the Mountains (Danticat) Fiction

Flight to Freedom (Veciana-Suarez) Fiction

Gathering the Dew (Ho) Fiction

Colibrí (Cameron) Fiction

The Garbage King (Laird) Fiction

The Trouble Begins (Himelblau) Fiction

INTO THE CLASSROOM

Nonfiction Books

The genre of nonfiction includes all those books "written and illustrated to present, organize, and interpret documentable factual material for children."[1] We often associate nonfiction with an expository style of writing. That is, we expect a nonfiction book about bears to contain statements like "Bears are carnivorous animals" or "Bears hibernate in winter" rather than "Once upon a time there was a bear named Clarence who ate meat and hibernated all winter." In children's literature many authors go beyond a strictly expository style to increase the appeal of their presentation. They may present facts in the context of a narrative or in a question-and-answer format. The diversity of presentation may sometimes make it hard for children to identify nonfiction through format or style of writing alone. In addition, children in the elementary grades take a long time sorting out what is fact and fiction, real or imaginary. Even older adolescents and adults have trouble distinguishing fact from opinion or recognizing generalizations that are not supported by facts. Therefore, teachers and librarians will need to give children guidance as they read nonfiction. Adults can help children use the same criteria in reading nonfiction that they themselves use in purchasing it (see Evaluation Criteria: "Evaluating Nonfiction Books" on page 591). By using fiction and nonfiction across the curriculum, teachers can also present children with many opportunities to apply criteria and to compare fiction with fact. Asking children to conduct research using primary and secondary sources and then write nonfiction should also help children to become critical readers of nonfiction books.

1. **What Is a Nonfiction Book?** Librarians who use the Dewey Decimal cataloging system will often shelve folktales, folklore, and poetry in with books about factual topics. Visit the library with a small group of

children. Ask them to show you the nonfiction section. Interview them about how they tell if a book is presenting factual or imaginary material. If you find misunderstandings, help them determine a way to clarify their understanding of what is a nonfiction book. Have children make a poster or develop guidelines to help other children choose nonfiction books.

2. **Nonfiction Books and Hobbies.** Talk to a group of children to find what special interests or hobbies they have. Make a survey of nonfiction to see what nonfiction books might enrich these interests. Plan a display of some of these books for a classroom or library interest center.

3. **Activity Directions.** Working with one child or a small group of children, select a craft or activity book that seems suited to their age level. Watch carefully as children follow the directions given. What difficulties do they have? What questions do they ask? Could you make the directions clearer, safer, or more imaginative?

4. **Writing a Nonfiction Book.** Work with a group of children in writing a nonfiction book modeled after one of the documentary accounts or a photo essay using their own snapshots. What kinds of research and choices are involved in following the form?

Go to the Online Learning Center at **www.mhhe.com/kiefer9e** or your Resources CD-ROM to find these additional classroom activities:

5. **Nonfiction's Influence on Report Writing**
6. **Directions, Explanations, and Surveys**
7. **Nonfiction Magazines for Children**

---

[1]According to the guidelines for the Robert F. Sibert Award given by the Association of Library Services to Children <www.ala.org/ala/alsc/awardsscholarships/literaryawards/sibertmedal/sibertterms/sibertmedalterms.htm>.

Chapter Review

Go to the Online Learning Center at **www.mhhe.com/kiefer9e** or your Resources CD-ROM to take chapter quizzes, practice with key terms, and review the chapter.

Explorations

1. Select several nonfiction books on one topic—such as ecology, the solar system, or China. Evaluate them, using the criteria in this chapter. Plan activity cards or questions that would interest children in the books and help them use the books more effectively.

2. Working with a small group of your peers, locate nonfiction books published within a single year. Review and discuss these to select one or more "award winners." What criteria would you use? What categories would you establish? What issues arise as you discuss what makes a high-quality nonfiction book?

3. Choose one nonfiction book with potential for interconnections in many subject areas, such as Aliki's *Mummies Made in Egypt*. Plan questions and activities; choose other literature to help children explore some related topics, such as building the pyramids, writing with hieroglyphics, using preservatives, or the art of ancient Egypt.

4. Develop and use with children a learning activity that will encourage critical reading of nonfiction books. Focus on identifying authors' points of view, comparing authenticity of sources, verifying facts, and the like.

5. Begin a file of book combinations that could be used in science, social studies, the arts, or language study. Consider the different perspectives that children will draw from each.

6. Visit the Web site for the National Council for Social Studies at <www.socialstudies.org/resources/notable/> or the National Science Teachers Association at <www.nsta.org/ostbc>. Read through their lists of notable books. Put together a reading list of nonfiction books on a single topic, such as women's history or the environment.

7. Search the database for a topic that pertains to your science, math, or social studies standards. Make a list of titles for nonfiction and other genres for that topic.

Web Links

Go to the Online Learning Center at **www.mhhe.com/kiefer9e** to find links to the following children's literature Web sites.

Boston Globe–Horn Book Awards
Great Web Sites for Kids

NCTE News: Orbis Pictus Award Winners
Nonfiction for Children and Young Adults
Notable Trade Books for Young Children
Outstanding Science Trade Books
Robert F. Sibert Informational Book Medal

Related Readings

Ansberry, Karen Rohrich, and Emily Morgan. *Picture-Perfect Science Lessons: Using Children's Books to Guide Inquiry.* Arlington, Va.: NSTA Press, 2005.

> This excellent book presents fifteen inquiry-based lessons for grades 3–6 that begin with a children's book and are based on the 5E Instructional Model—Engage, Explore, Explain, Elaborate, Evaluate—developed by the Biological Sciences Curriculum Study Group.

Bamford, Rosemary, and Janice Kristo, eds. *Making Facts Come Alive: Choosing Quality Nonfiction for Children.* 2nd ed. Norwood, Mass.: Christopher Gordon, 2003.

> In this fine collection of essays about nonfiction books, chapters provide an overview of types of nonfiction as well as information about integrating nonfiction books across the curriculum.

Freeman, Evelyn B., and Diane Goetz Person. *Using Nonfiction Trade Books in the Elementary Classroom.* Urbana, Ill.: National Council of Teachers of English, 1992.

> This collection of essays includes a section by authorities such as Russell Freedman and James Cross Giblin that extends understandings about trends and issues in nonfiction books. Subsequent chapters provide many practical suggestions for

integrating nonfiction books throughout the curriculum in primary through middle-school classrooms.

Graves, Donald H. *Investigate Nonfiction.* Portsmouth, N.H.: Heinemann, 1989.

Through its insights into children's efforts to create nonfiction, this slim volume provides new ways of thinking about and teaching about the genre.

Harvey, Stephanie. Nonfiction Matters: Reading, Writing, and Research in Grades 3–8. York, Me.: Stenhouse, 1998.

This is an excellent book about using nonfiction to develop inquiry projects. In addition to useful information about nonfiction books, the author includes sections on choosing topics, making observations and collecting information, and finding different ways of presenting the results of the inquiry. Appendixes include forms and facsimiles as well as selected nonfiction titles on various topics.

Jobe, Ron, and Mary Dayton-Sakari. *Info-Kids: How to Use Nonfiction to Turn Reluctant Readers into Enthusiasts.* Ontario, Canada: Pembroke and distributed in Portland, Me.: Stenhouse, 2002.

This engaging book is aimed at reluctant readers—those who will listen to nonfiction read aloud but don't want to read it. It includes ideas for classroom studies that are designed to engage the "non-engaged" reader. Even better, it is also an excellent book for all readers, including those who may not care to read nonfiction. Each chapter, with titles such as "Info-Kids Who Are Hands-On" or "Info-Kids Who Gravitate to Gross Facts," focuses on a different hypothetical "reluctant-reader" and includes a teaching focus, an extensive bibliography, as well as details about teaching reading comprehension and research project skills.

Kobrin, Beverly. *Eyeopeners II: Children's Books to Answer Children's Questions about the World around Them.* New York: Viking, 1995.

Enthusiastic and practical, this review of more than five hundred nonfiction books offers teaching tips for "parents, grandparents, and other educators." The emphasis on linking specific books and activities and an easy-to-read format combine to make a handy classroom reference.

Pappas, Christine C., Barbara Z. Kiefer, and Linda S. Levstik. *An Integrated Language Perspective in the Elementary School: Theory into Action.* 4th ed. White Plains, N.Y.: Longman, 2006.

The approaches described in this comprehensive text show literature as one of the aspects of language to be integrated throughout the content areas. The specific examples of teaching strategies and of solving problems of classroom logistics are especially helpful.

Web sites

www.ala.org/parentspage/greatsites/amazing.html General listing of recommended sites

www.culture.gouv.fr/culture/arcnat/en/ Great Archaeological sites

www.nationalgeographic.com/kids/ National Geographic

www.nationalgeographic.com/egypt/ At the Tomb of Tutankhamen

galaxy.einet.net/images/gems/gems-icons.html Smithsonian Gem and Mineral Collection

volcano.und.nodak.edu/ Volcano World

www.primordialsoup.com/ Primordial Soup

www.nycsubway.org/ New York City Subway

www.nj.com/yucky/worm/ Worm World

www.neic.cr.usgs.gov/neis/eqlists/10maps.html National Earthquake Information Center

Children's Literature

 Go to the Children's Literature Database on your Resources CD-ROM for a searchable listing of these and other children's literature titles.

Nonfiction Books

Aliki [Aliki Brandenberg]. *Digging Up Dinosaurs.* Crowell, 1988.

———. *Fossils Tell of Long Ago.* HarperCollins, 1990.

———. *Mummies Made in Egypt.* Crowell, 1979.

Ancona, George. *Fiesta U.S.A.* Lodestar, 1995.

———. *Let's Dance!* Morrow, 1998.

———. *Mi Casa: My House.* Scholastic, 2005.

Armstrong, Jennifer. *Shipwreck at the Bottom of the World: The Extraordinary True Story of Shackleton and the Endurance.* Crown, 1988.

Arnold, Caroline. *Pterosaurs: Rulers of the Skies in the Dinosaur Age.* Illustrated by Laurie Caple. Clarion, 2004.

Bang, Molly. *Nobody Particular: One Woman's Fight to Save the Bays.* Holt, 2001.

Barnard, Bryn. *Outbreak: Plagues That Changed History.* Crown, 2005.

Barrett, Paul. *National Geographic Dinosaurs.* Illustrated by Raul Martin. National Geographic, 2001.

Bartoletti, Susan Campbell. *Black Potatoes: The Story of the Great Irish Famine, 1845–1850.* Houghton, 2001.

———. *Growing Up in Coal Country.* Houghton, 1996.

———. *Hitler Youth: Growing Up in Hitler's Shadow.* Scholastic, 2005.

Barton, Byron. *I Want to Be an Astronaut.* Crowell, 1988.

Bash, Barbara. *Ancient Ones: The World of the Old-Growth Douglas Fir.* Sierra Club, 1994.

Berger, Melvin, and Gilda Berger. *How Do Frogs Swallow with Their Eyes?* Illustrated by Karen Carr. Scholastic, 2003.

———. *Where Did the Butterfly Get Its Name? Questions and Answers about Butterflies and Moths.* Scholastic, 2005.

———. *Why Do Volcanoes Blow Their Tops?* Illustrated by Higgins Boyd. Scholastic, 2002.

Bernard, Robin. *Insects.* National Geographic, 2001.

Bernhard, Emery. *Ladybug.* Illustrated by Durga Bernhard. Holiday, 1992.

———. *Prairie Dogs.* Illustrated by Durga Bernhard. Harcourt, 1997.

Beskow, Elsa. *Pelle's New Suit.* Harper, 1929.

Bial, Raymond. *Cajun Home.* Houghton, 1998.

———. *A Handful of Dirt.* Walker, 2000.

———. *One Room School.* Houghton, 1999.

———. *Tenement: Immigrant Life on the Lower East Side.* Houghton, 2002.

Biesty, Stephen. *Egypt: In Spectacular Cross-Section.* With text by Stewart Ross. Scholastic, 2005.

———. *Rome: In Spectacular Cross-Section.* With text by Andrew Solway. Scholastic, 2003.

Blobaum, Cindy. *Insectigations: 40 Hands-on Activities to Explore the Insect World.* Chicago Review, 2005.

Blumberg, Rhoda. *Commodore Perry in the Land of the Shogun.* Lothrop, 1985.

Bober, Natalie S. *Abigail Adams: Witness to a Revolution.* Atheneum, 1995.

Bolden, Tanya. *Tell All the Children Our Story: Memories and Mementos of Being Young and Black in America.* Abrams, 2002.

Bonner, Hannah. *When Bugs Were Big, Plants Were Strange, and Tetrapods Stalked the Earth: A Cartoon Prehistory of Life before Dinosaurs.* National Geographic, 2004.

Borden, Louise. *The Journey That Saved Curious George: The True Wartime Escape of Margaret and H. A. Ray.* Illustrated by Allan Drummond. Houghton, 2005.

Bourgoing, Pascale De. *Weather.* First Discovery Books. Scholastic, 1991.

Boyd, Herb. *We Shall Overcome: A Living History of the Civil Rights Struggle Told in Words, Pictures, and the Voices of Participants.* Sourcebooks Mediafusion, 2004.

Branley, Franklyn M. *Down Comes the Rain.* Illustrated by James Graham Hale. HarperCollins, 1997.

———. *Earthquakes.* Illustrated by Richard Rosenblum. HarperCollins, 1994.

———. *Flash, Crash, Rumble and Roll.* Illustrated by Barbara and Ed Emberley. Rev. ed. Crowell, 1985.

———. *The International Space Station.* Illustrated by True Kelley. HarperCollins, 2002.

———. *Mission to Mars.* Illustrated by True Kelley. HarperCollins, 2002.

———. *Volcanoes.* Illustrated by Marc Simont. HarperCollins, 1985.

———. *What Happened to the Dinosaurs?* Illustrated by Marc Simont. Crowell, 1989.

Brenner, Barbara. *If You Were There in 1492.* Bradbury, 1991.

———. *Thinking About Ants.* Illustrated by Carol Schwartz. Mondo, 1997.

Buckley, James, Jr. *The Visual Dictionary of Baseball.* DK, 2001.

Burns, Marilyn. *Good for Me! All about Food in 32 Bites.* Little, 1978.

Burton, Robert. *Egg.* Photographed by Jane Burton and Kim Taylor. Kindersley, 1994.

Camper, Cathy. *Bugs before Time: Prehistoric Insects and Their Relatives.* Illustrated by Steve Kirk. Simon, 2002.

Carson, Mary Kay. *The Underground Railroad for Kids: From Slavery to Freedom with 21 Activities.* Chicago Review, 2005.

Carter, David A., and James Diaz. *The Elements of Pop-Up.* Simon, 1999.

Cassie, Brian. *Trees.* Scholastic, 1999.

Chambers, Veronica. *Amistad Rising: The Story of Freedom.* Illustrated by Paul Lee. Harcourt, 1998.

Chester, Jonathan. *The Young Adventurer's Guide to Everest: From Avalanche to Zopkio.* Tricycle, 2002.

Cobb, Vicki. *Chemically Active! Experiments You Can Do at Home.* Illustrated by Theo Cobb. Lippincott, 1985.

———. *I Fall Down.* Illustrated by Julia Gorton. HarperCollins, 2004.

———. *I Get Wet.* Illustrated by Julia Gorton. HarperCollins, 2002.

———. *I See Myself.* Illustrated by Julia Gorton. HarperCollins, 2002.

———. *More Science Experiments You Can Eat.* Illustrated by Peter Lippman. Lippincott, 1972.

———. *See for Yourself: More Than 100 Experiments for Science Fairs and Projects.* Illustrated by Dave Klug. Scholastic, 2001.

Cole, Joanna. *How You Were Born.* Photographs by Margaret Miller. HarperCollins, 1994.

———. *The Magic School Bus at the Waterworks.* Illustrated by Bruce Degen. Scholastic, 1988.

———. *The Magic School Bus inside the Earth.* Illustrated by Bruce Degen. Scholastic, 1987.

———. *Ms. Frizzle's Adventures: Ancient Egypt.* Illustrated by Bruce Degen. Scholastic, 2001.

———. *Ms. Frizzle's Adventures: Imperial China.* Illustrated by Bruce Degen. Scholastic, 2005.

———. *My Puppy Is Born.* Photographs by Margaret Miller. Mulberry, 1991.

Collard, Sneed B, III. *The Prairie Builders: Reconstructing America's Grasslands.* Houghton, 2005.

Colman, Penny. *Corpses, Coffins and Crypts: A History of Burial.* Holt, 1997.

———. *Girls: A History of Growing Up Female in America.* Scholastic, 2000.

———. *Rosie the Riveter: Women Working on the Home Front in World War II.* Crown, 1994.

———. *Where the Action Was: Women War Correspondents in World War II.* Crown, 2002.

Cone, Molly. *Come Back Salmon.* Photographs by Sidnee Wheelwright. Sierra Club, 1992.

Cooper, Michael L. *Dust to Eat: Drought and Depression in the 1930s.* Clarion, 2004.

Cowcher, Helen. *Antarctica.* Farrar, 1990.

Cowley, Joy. *Chameleon, Chameleon.* Photographs by Nic Bishop. Scholastic, 2005.

———. *Red-Eyed Tree Frog.* Photographs by Nic Bishop. Scholastic, 1999.

Crewe, Sabrina. *The Prairie Dog.* Illustrated by Graham Allen. Raintree, 1996.

Curlee, Lynn. *Parthenon.* Simon, 2004.

Davies, Nicola. *Ice Bear: In the Steps of the Polar Bear.* Illustrated by Gary Blythe. Candlewick, 2005.

Davis, Wendy. *Limestone Cave.* Children's Press, 1997.

Deem, James. *Bodies from the Ash: Life and Death in Ancient Pompeii.* Houghton, 2005.

———. *How to Hunt for Buried Treasure.* Illustrated by True Kelley. Houghton, 1992.

Delafosse, Claude. *Hidden World: Caves.* Illustrated by Pierre De Hugo. Scholastic, 2000.

———. *Hidden World: Under the Ground.* Illustrated by Daniel Moignot. First Discovery Books. Scholastic, 1999.

Dendy, Leslie, and Mel Boring. *Guinea Pig Scientists: Bold Self-Experimenters in Science and Medicine.* Holt, 2005.

Deneberg, Barry, *Shadow Life: A Portrait of Anne Frank and Her Family.* Scholastic, 2005.

dePaola, Tomie. *Charlie Needs a Cloak.* Simon, 1974.

Dewey, Jennifer Owings. *Antarctic Journal: Four Months at the Bottom of the World.* HarperCollins, 2001.

———. *Mud Matters.* Photographs by Stephen Trimble. Cavendish, 1998.

Dorros, Arthur. *Ant Cities.* Crowell, 1987.

———. *Follow the Water from Brook to Ocean.* HarperCollins, 1991.

Dudley, Karen. *Alligators and Crocodiles.* Raintree, 1998.

———. *Bald Eagles.* Raintree, 1997.

Dunleavy, Deborah. *The Jumbo Book of Drama.* Kids Can, 2004.

Facklam, Margery. *The Big Bug Book.* Illustrated by Paul Facklam. Little, 1994.

Farrell, Jeanette. *Invisible Enemies: Stories of Infectious Disease.* Farrar, 2005.

Fowler, Allan. *Animals under the Ground.* Scholastic, 1998.

———. *Inside an Ant Colony.* Children's Press, 1998.

Freedman, Russell. *Buffalo Hunt.* Holiday, 1988.

———. *Children of the Great Depression.* Clarion, 2005.

———. *Children of the Wild West.* Clarion, 1983.

———. *Immigrant Kids.* Dutton, 1980.

———. *Indian Chiefs.* Holiday, 1987.

———. *An Indian Winter.* Holiday, 1992.

———. *Kids at Work: Lewis Hine and the Crusade against Child Labor.* Clarion, 1994.

———. *Lincoln: A Photobiography.* Clarion, 1987.

Fritz, Jean. *George Washington's Breakfast.* Illustrated by Tomie dePaola. Paper Star, 1998.

———. *Harriet Beecher Stowe and the Beecher Preachers.* Putnam, 1994.

———. *Leonardo's Horse.* Illustrated by Hudson Talbot. Putnam, 2001.

Froman, Nan. *What's That Bug?* Illustrated by Julian Mulock. Madison, 2001.

Gallant, Roy A. *Dance of the Continents.* Benchmark, 1999.

———. *Earth: The Making of a Planet.* Illustrated by Christopher Schuberth. Cavendish, 1998.

———. *Geysers: When the Earth Roars.* Watts, 1997.

———. *Limestone Caves.* Watts, 1998.

George, Michael. *Earthquakes.* Creative Education, 1997.

Getz, David. *Frozen Girl.* Illustrated by Peter McCarty. Holt, 1998.

———. *Frozen Man.* Illustrated by Peter McCarty. Holt, 1994.

———. *Life on Mars.* Holt, 2005 [1997].

Gibbons, Gail. *Caves and Caverns.* Harcourt, 1993.

———. *Chickens!* Holiday, 2003.

———. *From Seed to Plant.* Holiday, 1991.

———. *Monarch Butterfly.* Holiday, 1989.

———. *New Road!* Crowell, 1983.

———. *Owls.* Holiday, 2005.

———. *Penguins!* Holiday, 1998.

———. *Planet Earth: Inside Out.* Morrow, 1995.

———. *Soaring with the Wind: The Bald Eagle.* Morrow, 1998.

———. *Tool Book.* Holiday, 1982.

Giblin, James Cross. *Good Brother, Bad Brother: The Story of Edwin Booth and John Wilkes Booth.* Clarion, 2005.

———. *The Mystery of the Mammoth Bones: And How It Was Solved.* HarperCollins, 1999.

———. *The Riddle of the Rosetta Stone: Key to Ancient Egypt.* Crowell, 1990.

———. *Secrets of the Sphinx.* Illustrated by Bagram Ibatoulline. Clarion, 2005.

———. *The Truth about Unicorns.* HarperCollins, 1991.

———. *When Plague Strikes: The Black Death, Smallpox, AIDS.* Illustrated by David Frampton. HarperCollins, 1995.

Goodall, Jane. *The Chimpanzees I Love: Saving Their World and Ours.* Scholastic, 2001.

Grace, Catherine O'Neill, and Margaret M. Bruchac. *1621: A New Look at Thanksgiving.* Photographs By Sisse Brimberg and Cotton Coulson. National Geographic, 2001.

Grau, Andrée. *Dance.* Kindersley, 1998.

Greenaway, Theresa. *Insects.* Kindersley, 1998.

———. *Jungle.* Photographs by Geoff Dann. DK, 2004.

Greenberg, Keith Elliott. *A Haitian Family.* Lerner, 1998.

Greenfeld, Howard. *The Hidden Children.* Ticknor, 1993.

Guiberson, Brenda Z. *Cactus Hotel.* Illustrated by Megan Lloyd. Holt, 1991.

Hamanaka, Sheila. *The Journey: Japanese Americans, Racism, and Renewal.* Orchard, 1990.

Hamilton, Virginia. *Anthony Burns: The Defeat and Triumph of a Fugitive Slave.* Knopf, 1988.

Harris, Robie H. *It's Perfectly Normal: A Book about Changing Bodies, Growing Up, Sex, and Sexual Health.* Illustrated by Michael Emberley. Candlewick, 1994.

————. *It's So Amazing: A Book about Eggs, Sperm, Birth, Babies, and Families.* Illustrated by Michael Emberley. Candlewick, 1999.

Heller, Ruth. *Many Luscious Lollipops: A Book about Adjectives.* Grosset, 1989.

Herbert, Janis. *Leonardo da Vinci for Kids: His Life and Ideas.* Chicago Review, 1998.

————. *Marco Polo for Kids: His Marvelous Journey to China.* Chicago Review, 2001.

Hill, Carolinda. *My First Pocket Guide: Great Mammals.* National Geographic, 2001.

Hirschi, Ron. *Fall.* Photographs by Thomas D. Mangelsen. Cobblehill/Dutton, 1991.

————. *Spring.* Photographs by Thomas D. Mangelsen. Cobblehill/Dutton, 1990.

————. *Summer.* Photographs by Thomas D. Mangelsen. Cobblehill/Dutton, 1991.

————. *Winter.* Photographs by Thomas D. Mangelsen. Cobblehill/Dutton, 1990.

Hoare, Stephen. *The World of Caves, Mines, and Tunnels.* Illustrated by Bruce Hogarth. Bedrick, 1999.

Holling, Holling C. *Minn of the Mississippi.* Houghton, 1951.

————. *Pagoo.* Houghton, 1957.

Hoose, Phillip. *The Race to Save the Lord God Bird.* Farrar, 2004.

————. *We Were There, Too! Young People in U.S. History.* Farrar/Kroupa, 2001.

Hoyt-Goldsmith, Diane. *Celebrating Ramadan.* Photographs by Lawrence Migdale. Holiday, 2001.

————. *Las Posadas: An Hispanic Christmas Celebration.* Photographs by Lawrence Migdale. Holiday, 1997.

————. *Potlatch: A Tsimshian Celebration.* Photographs by Lawrence Migdale. Holiday, 1997.

Irvine, Joan. *How to Make Pop-Ups.* Illustrated by Barbara Reid. Morrow, 1988.

————. *How to Make Super Pop-Ups.* Illustrated by Linda Hendry. Morrow, 1992.

Jackson, Donna M. *The Bug Scientists.* Houghton, 2002.

————. *ER Vets: Life in an Animal Emergency Room.* Houghton, 2005.

————. *In Your Face: The Facts about Your Face.* Viking, 2004.

Jackson, Ellen. *Looking for Life in the Universe.* Photographs by Nic Bishop. Houghton, 2002.

Jenkins, Alvin. *Next Stop Neptune.* Illustrated by Steve Jenkins. Houghton, 2004.

Jenkins, Priscilla Belz. *A Nestful of Eggs.* Illustrated by Lizzy Rockwell. HarperCollins, 1995.

Jenkins, Steve. *Actual Size.* Houghton, 2004.

————. *Prehistoric Actual Size.* Houghton, 2005.

————. *Slap, Squeak and Scatter.* Houghton, 2001.

————. *The Top of the World: Climbing Mount Everest.* Houghton, 1999.

Jenkins, Steve, and Robin Page. *Animals in Flight.* Houghton, 2001.

————. *I See a Kookaburra!* Houghton, 2005.

————. *Life on Earth: The Story of Evolution.* Houghton, 2002.

————. *Move!* Houghton, 2006.

————. *What Do You Do with a Tail Like This?* Houghton, 2003.

Kalman, Bobbie. *Raptors.* Crabtree, 1998.

Kaplan, William. *One More Border: The True Story of One Family's Escape from War-Torn Europe.* Illustrated by Shelley Tanaka. Groundwood, 1998.

Kent, Peter. *Hidden under the Ground: The World beneath Your Feet.* Dutton, 1998.

Kidd, J. S., and Renee A. Kidd. *On Shifting Ground: The Story of the Continental Drift.* Facts on File, 1997.

Kittinger, Jo S. *A Look at Minerals: From Galena to Gold.* Watts, 1998.

————. *A Look at Rocks: From Coal to Kimberlite.* Watts, 1998.

————. *Stories in Stone: The World of Animal Fossils.* Watts, 1998.

Knowlton, Jack. *Maps and Globes.* Illustrated by Harriett Barton. Crowell, 1985.

Koscielniak, Bruce. *About Time: A First Look at Time and Clocks.* Houghton, 2004.

Kramer, Stephen. *Hidden Worlds: Looking through a Scientist's Microscope.* Photographs by Dennis Kunkel. Houghton, 2001.

Krinitz, Esther Nisenthal, and Bernice Steinhardt. *Memories of Survival.* Hyperion, 2005.

Kuklin, Susan. *Families.* Hyperion, 2006.

Kurelek, William. *Lumberjack.* Houghton, 1974.

Kurlansky, Mark. *The Cod's Tale.* Illustrated by S. D. Schindler. Penguin Putnam, 2001.

Lagasse, Emeril. *Emeril's There's a Chef in My Soup: Recipes for the Kid in Everyone.* HarperCollins, 2002.

Langley, Andrew. *The Search for Riches.* Remarkable World series. Raintree Steck-Vaughn, 1997.

Lasky, Kathryn. *Interrupted Journey: Saving Endangered Sea Turtles.* Photographs by Christopher G. Knight. Candlewick, 2001.

Lauber, Patricia. *Dinosaurs Walked Here and Other Stories Fossils Tell.* Bradbury, 1987.

————. *Journey to the Planets.* Crown, 1993 [1982].

————. *The News about Dinosaurs.* Bradbury, 1989.

————. *Painters of the Caves.* National Geographic, 1998.

————. *Tales Mummies Tell.* Crowell, 1985.

————. *Volcano: The Eruption and Healing of Mt. St. Helens.* Bradbury, 1986.

————. *What You Never Knew about Tubs, Toilets, and Showers.* Illustrated by John Manders. Simon, 2001.

Lawson, Kristen. *Darwin and Evolution for Kids with 21 Activities.* Chicago Review, 2003.

Leacock, Elspeth, and Susan Buckley. *Journeys in Time: A New Atlas of American History.* Illustrated by Randy Jones. Houghton, 2001.

————. *Places in Time: A New Atlas of American History.* Illustrated by Randy Jones. Houghton, 2001.

Lester, Julius. *From Slave Ship to Freedom Road.* Illustrated by Rod Brown. Dial, 1998.

————. *To Be a Slave.* Illustrated by Tom Feelings. Dial, 1968.

Lewin, Ted, and Betsy Lewin. *Elephant Quest.* HarperCollins, 2000.

————. *Top to Bottom, Down Under.* HarperCollins, 2005.

Lindsey, Terence. *My First Pocket Guide: Garden Birds.* National Geographic, 2001.

Lobel, Anita. *No Pretty Picture: A Child of War.* Greenwillow, 1998.

Locker, Thomas, with Candace Christiansen. *Sky Tree.* HarperCollins, 1995.

Logan, Claudia. *The 5,000-Year-Old Puzzle: Solving a Mystery of Ancient Egypt.* Illustrated by Melissa Sweet. Farrar, 2002.

Lorenz, Albert. *Buried Blueprints: Maps and Sketches of Lost Worlds and Mysterious Places.* Abrams, 1999.

Lourie, Peter. *On the Trail of Sacagawea.* Boyds Mills, 2001.

Luby, Thia. *The Children's Book of Yoga.* Clear Light, 1998.

Macaulay, David. *Castle.* Houghton, 1977.

———. *Cathedral: The Story of Its Construction.* Houghton, 1973.

———. *City: The Story of Roman Planning and Construction.* Houghton, 1974.

———. *Mill.* Houghton, 1983.

———. *Pyramid.* Houghton, 1975.

———. *Ship.* Houghton, 1993.

———. *Underground.* Houghton, 1976.

———. *The Way Things Work.* Houghton, 1988.

Malone, Michael. R. *A Nicaraguan Family.* Lerner, 1998.

Mallory, Kenneth. *A Home by the Sea: Protecting Coastal Wildlife.* Gulliver, 1998.

Markle, Sandra. *Exploring Autumn.* Atheneum, 1984.

———. *A Mother's Journey.* Illustrated by Alan Marks. Charlesbridge, 2005.

———. *A Rainy Day.* Illustrated by Cathy Johnson. Orchard, 1993.

Marrin, Albert. *Secrets from the Rocks: Dinosaur Hunting with Roy Chapman Andrews.* Dutton, 2002.

McClung, Robert. *Possum.* Morrow, 1963.

McGovern, Ann. . . . *If You Lived with the Sioux Indians.* Scholastic, 1976.

McIntosh, Jane. *Pyramid.* Photographs by Geoff Brighting. Knopf, 1994.

McKissack, Patricia C., and Frederick McKissack. *Christmas in the Big House, Christmas in the Quarters.* Illustrated by John Thompson. Scholastic, 1994.

———. *Days of Jubilee: The End of Slavery in the United States.* Scholastic, 2003.

McNulty, Faith. *How to Dig a Hole to the Other Side of the World.* Illustrated by Marc Simont. HarperCollins, 1979.

McWhorter, Diane. *A Dream of Freedom: The Civil Rights Movement from 1954–1968.* Scholastic, 2004.

Meltzer, Milton. *Rescue: The Story of How Gentiles Saved Jews in the Holocaust.* Harper, 1988.

———. *Voices from the Civil War: A Documentary History of the Great American Conflict.* Harper, 1989.

Micucci, Charles. *The Life and Times of the Ant.* Houghton, 2003.

———. *The Life and Times of the Apple.* Orchard, 1992.

———. *The Life and Times of the Honeybee.* Ticknor, 1994.

———. *The Life and Times of the Peanut.* Houghton, 2000.

Miller, Margaret. *Guess Who?* Greenwillow, 1994.

Montgomery, Sy. *Encantado: Pink Dolphin of the Amazon.* Photographs by Diane Taylor Snow. Illustrated by Liddy Hubbell. Houghton, 2002.

———. *The Man-Eating Tigers of Sundarbans.* Photographs by Eleanor Briggs. Houghton, 2001.

———. *The Tarantula Scientist.* Photography by Nic Bishop. Houghton, 2004.

Moore, Kenny. "Coober Pedy: Opal Capital of Australia's Outback." *National Geographic* (November 1976): 560–71.

Morris, Ann. *Shoes, Shoes, Shoes.* Lothrop, 1995.

———. *Weddings.* Lothrop, 1995.

Morris, Neil. *Earthquakes.* Crabtree, 1998.

———. *Volcanoes.* Crabtree, 1995.

Murphy, Jim. *Across America on an Emigrant Train.* Clarion, 1993.

———. *An American Plague: The True and Terrifying Story of the Yellow Fever Epidemic of 1793.* Houghton, 2003.

———. *Blizzard! The Storm That Changed America.* Scholastic, 2000.

———. *The Boys' War: Confederate and Union Soldiers Talk About the Civil War.* Clarion, 1990.

———. *Gone A-Whaling: The Lure of the Sea and the Hunt for the Great Whale.* Clarion, 1998.

———. *The Great Fire.* Scholastic, 1995.

———. *Inside the Alamo.* Knopf, 2003.

Myers, Walter Dean. *Now Is Your Time! The African American Struggle for Freedom.* HarperCollins, 1991.

Needham, Bobbe. *Ecology Crafts for Kids: 50 Great Ways to Make Friends with Planet Earth.* Sterling, 1998.

Nelson, S. D. *The First Americans: The Story of Where They Came From and Who They Became.* Illustrated by Anthony Aveni. Scholastic, 2005.

Nicholson, Dorinda Makanaōnalani. *Remember World War II: Kids Who Survived Tell Their Stories.* National Geographic, 2005.

O'Byrne, John. *My First Pocket Guide: Stars and Planets.* National Geographic, 2002.

Oldershaw, Cally. *Rocks and Minerals.* Kindersley, 1999.

Onyefulu, Ifeoma. *Chidi Only Likes Blue: An African Book of Colors.* Dutton, 1997.

———. *Saying Goodbye: A Special Farewell to Mama Nkwelle.* Millbrook, 2001.

Orr, Richard. *The Burrow.* Photographs by Shaila Awan. Kindersley, 1997.

Paladino, Catherine. *One Good Apple: Growing Our Food for the Sake of the Earth.* Houghton, 1999.

Parker, Nancy Winslow, and Joan Richards Wright. *Bugs.* Illustrated by Nancy Winslow Parker. Greenwillow, 1987.

———. *Frogs, Toads, Lizards, and Salamanders.* Illustrated by Nancy Winslow Parker. Greenwillow, 1990.

Parker, Steve. *Rocks and Minerals.* Kindersley, 1997.

Patent, Dorothy Hinshaw. *Animals on the Trail with Lewis and Clark.* Photographs by William Muñoz. Clarion, 2002.

———. *Prairie Dogs.* Photographs by William Muñoz. Clarion, 1993.

———. *Prairies.* Holiday, 1996.

———. *Secrets of the Ice Man (Frozen in Time).* Cavendish, 1998.

———. *Shaping the Earth.* Photographs by William Muñoz. Clarion, 2000.

Pelta, Kathy. *Discovering Christopher Columbus: How History Is Invented.* Lerner, 1991.

Pemberton, Delia. *Egyptian Mummies: People from the Past.* Harcourt, 2001.

Perl, Lila. *The Great Ancestor Hunt: The Fun of Finding Out Who You Are.* Clarion, 1989.

———. *Mummies, Tombs, and Treasure: Secrets of Ancient Egypt.* Illustrated by Erika Weihs. Houghton, 1987.

Peters, David. *From the Beginning: The Story of Human Evolution.* Morrow, 1991.

Phinney, Margaret Y. *Exploring Underground Habitats.* Illustrated by Stephen Petruccio. Mondo, 1999.

Pirotta, Saviour. *Fossils and Bones.* Raintree, 1997.

Pollard, Michael. *Roads and Tunnels.* Raintree, 1996.

Poole, Josephine. *Anne Frank.* Illustrated by Angela Barrett. Knopf, 2005.

Pope, Joyce. *Earthquakes.* Illustrated by Ian Moores. Copper Beech, 1998.

Potter, Beatrix. *The Peter Rabbit and Friends Cookbook.* Warne, 1994.

Powell, Jillian. *From Chick to Chicken.* Raintree, 2001.

Pringle, Laurence. *A Dragon in the Sky: The Story of a Green Darner Dragonfly.* Illustrated by Bob Marstall. Scholastic, 2001.

———. *An Extraordinary Life: The Story of the Monarch Butterfly.* Illustrated by Bob Marstall. Orchard, 1997.

———. *Global Warming: The Threat of Earth's Changing Climate.* SeaStar, 2001.

Putnam, Jim. *Mummy.* Photographs by Peter Hayman. Knopf, 1993.

Rappaport, Doreen. *Escape from Slavery: Five Journeys to Freedom.* Illustrated by Charles Lilly. HarperCollins, 1991.

Redfern, Martin. *The Kingfisher Young People's Book of Space.* Kingfisher, 1998.

Reid, Struan. *The Children's Atlas of Lost Treasures.* Millbrook, 1997.

Reinhard, Johann. *Discovering the Inca Ice Maiden: My Adventure on Ampato.* National Geographic, 1998.

Rhatigan, Joe. *The Kids' Guide to Nature Adventures: 80 Great Activities for Exploring the Outdoors.* Lark, 2003.

Rhatigan, Joe, and Rain Newcomb. *Out-of-This-World Astronomy: 50 Amazing Activities and Projects.* Lark, 2004.

———. *Prize-Winning Science Fair Projects for Curious Kids.* Lark, 2006.

Ricciuti, Edward. *Rocks and Minerals.* Scholastic, 1998.

Ride, Sally, and Tam O'Shaughnessy. *Exploring Our Solar System.* Crown, 2003.

Rockwell, Anne. *Bugs Are Insects.* Illustrated by Steve Jenkins. HarperCollins, 2001.

———. *Honey in a Hive.* Illustrated by S. D. Schindler. HarperCollins, 2005.

Rockwell, Harlow. *My Doctor.* Macmillan, 1973.

Rounds, Glen. *Sod Houses on the Prairie.* Holiday, 1995.

Royston, Angela. *Insects and Crawly Creatures.* Photographs by Jerry Young. Illustrations by Jane Cradock-Watson and Dave Hopkins. Aladdin/Simon, 1992.

Rupp, Rebecca. *Weather! Watch How Weather Works.* Storey Kids, 2003.

Russo, Marisbina. *Always Remember Me: How One Family Survived World War II.* Atheneum, 2005.

Sabbeth, Carol. *Monet and the Impressionists for Kids.* Chicago Review, 2002.

Sabuda, Robert, and Matthew Reinhart. *Encyclopedia Prehistorica: Dinosaurs.* Candlewick, 2006.

———. *Encyclopedia Prehistorica: Sharks and Other Beasts of the Sea.* Candlewick, 2006.

Sadler, Judy Ann. *The Jumbo Book of Needlecrafts.* Kids Can, 2005.

Saltz, Gail. *Amazing You: Getting Smart about Your Private Parts.* Illustrated by Lynne Cravath. Dutton, 2005.

Sattler, Helen Roney. *Our Patchwork Planet: The Story of Plate Tectonics.* Illustrated by Guilio Maestro. Lothrop, 1995.

———. *Recipes for Art and Craft Materials.* Lothrop, 1987 [1973].

Sayre, April Pulley. *The Bumblebee Queen.* Illustrated by Patricia Wynne. Charlesbridge, 2005.

———. *Dig, Wait, Listen: A Desert Toad's Tale.* Illustrated by Barbara Bash. Greenwillow, 2001.

———. *Stars beneath Your Bed: The Surprising Story of Dust.* Illustrated by Ann Jonas. Greenwillow, 2005.

Schaefer, Lola. *Pick, Pull, Snap! Where Once a Flower Bloomed.* Illustrated by Lindsay Barrett George. Greenwillow, 2003.

Schlein, Miriam. *Billions of Bats.* Illustrated by Walter Kessle. HarperCollins, 1982.

Selsam, Millicent. *Egg to Chick.* Illustrated by Barbara Wolff. Harper Trophy, 1987.

———. *How to Be a Nature Detective.* Illustrated by Marlene Hill Donnelly. HarperCollins, 1995 [1958].

Selsam, Millicent, and Joyce Hunt. *A First Look at Bats.* Illustrated by Harriet Springer. Walker, 1991.

Senisi, Ellen B. *Berry Smudges and Leaf Prints. Finding and Making Colors from Nature.* Dutton, 2001.

Showers, Paul. *How Many Teeth?* Illustrated by True Kelley. HarperCollins, 1991.

Siebert, Diane. *Cave.* Illustrated by Wayne McLoughlin. HarperCollins, 2000.

Silver, Donald M. *Cave.* Illustrated by Patricia J. Wynne. McGraw-Hill, 1997.

Simon, Seymour. *Animal Fact/Animal Fable.* Illustrated by Diane de Groat. Crown, 1987.

———. *Big Bugs.* Chronicle, 2005.

———. *Cats.* HarperCollins, 2004.

———. *Comets, Meteors, and Asteroids.* Morrow, 1994.

———. *Crocodiles and Alligators.* HarperCollins, 1999.

———. *Destination Mars.* HarperCollins, 2000.

———. *Dogs.* HarperCollins, 2004.

———. *Earthquakes.* Morrow, 1991.

————. *Galaxies*. Morrow, 1988.

————. *Guts*. HarperCollins, 2005.

————. *Horses*. HarperCollins, 2006.

————. *The Paper Airplane Book*. Illustrated by Byron Barton. Viking, 1971.

————. *Sharks*. HarperCollins, 1995.

————. *Storms*. Morrow, 1989.

————. *Volcanoes*. Morrow, 1995.

Sipiera, Paul P., and Diane M. Sipiera. *Thunderstorms*. Children's Press, 1998.

————. *Volcanoes*. Children's Press, 1998.

Siy, Alexandra, and Dennis Kunkel. *Mosquito Bite*. Charlesbridge, 2005.

Sklansky, Amy E. *Where Do Chicks Come From?* Illustrated by Pam Paparone, Harper, 2005.

Skurzynski, Gloria. *Are We Alone? Scientists Search for Life in Space*. National Geographic, 2004.

Sloan, Christopher. *Bury the Dead: Tombs, Corpses, Mummies, Skeletons and Rituals*. National Geographic, 2002.

————. *The Human Story: Our Evolution from Prehistoric Ancestors to Today*. National Geographic, 2004.

Sneve, Virginia Driving Hawk. *Bad River Boys: A Meeting of the Lakota Sioux with Lewis and Clark*. Illustrated by Bill Farnsworth. Holiday, 2005.

Spier, Peter. *People*. Doubleday, 1980.

Stanley, Jerry. *Children of the Dust Bowl: The True Story of the School at Weedpatch Camp*. Crown, 1992.

————. *Hurry Freedom: African Americans in Gold Rush California*. Crown, 2000.

————. *I Am an American: A True Story of the Japanese Internment*. Crown, 1994.

Stetoff, Rebecca. *Ant*. Benchmark, 1998.

St. George, Judith. *So You Want to Be President?* Illustrated by David Small. Philomel, 2004. [2000].

————. *The Journey of the One and Only Declaration of Independence*. Illustrated by Will Hillenbrand. Philomel, 2005.

Symes, R. F. *Rocks and Minerals*. Photographs by Colin Ketes. Knopf, 1988.

Tanaka, Shelley. *Discovering the Iceman: What Was It Like to Find a 5,300-Year-Old Mummy?* Illustrated by Laurie McGaw. Hyperion, 1997.

————. *Graveyards of the Dinosaurs: What It's Like to Discover Prehistoric Creatures*. I Was There series. Hyperion, 1998.

————. *Secrets of the Mummies: Uncovering the Bodies of Ancient Egyptians*. Illustrated by Greg Ruhl. Hyperion, 1999.

Taylor, Paul D. *Fossil*. DK, 1998.

Turner, Alan. *National Geographic Prehistoric Mammals*. Illustrated by Mauricio Antón. National Geographic, 2004.

Van Dyck, Sara. *Bumblebees*. Lerner, 2005.

Van Loon, Hendrik W. *The Story of Mankind*. Illustrated by John M. Merriam. Rev. ed. Liveright, 1998 [1921].

Ventura, Piero. *Clothing*. Houghton, 1994.

————. *Food*. Houghton, 1994.

Walgren, Judy. *The Lost Boys of Natinga: A School for Sudan's Young Refugees*. Houghton, 1998.

Walker, Barbara M. *The Little House Cookbook: Frontier Foods from Laura Ingalls Wilder's Classic Stories*. Illustrated by Garth Williams. Harper, 1979.

Wallace, Karen. *Gentle Giant Octopus*. Illustrated by Mike Bostock. Candlewick, 1998.

Warren, Andrea. *Escape from Saigon: How a Vietnam War Orphan Became an American*. Farrar, 2004.

————. *Pioneer Girl: Growing Up on the Prairie*. Morrow, 1998.

————. *Surviving Hitler: A Boy in the Nazi Death Camps*. HarperCollins, 2001.

Waters, Kate. *Samuel Eaton's Day: A Day in the Life of a Pilgrim Boy*. Photographs by Russ Kendall. Scholastic, 1993.

————. *Sarah Morton's Day: A Day in the Life of a Pilgrim Girl*. Photographs by Russ Kendall. Scholastic, 1989.

Webb, Sophie. *Looking for Seabirds: Journal from an Alaskan Voyage*. Houghton, 2004.

————. *My Season with Penguins: An Antarctic Journal*. Houghton, 2000.

Weiss, Harvey. *Maps: Getting from Here to There*. Houghton, 1991.

Weitzman, David. *My Backyard History Book*. Illustrated by James Robertson. Little, 1975.

Wheatley, Nadia, and Donna Rawlins. *My Place*. Kane/Miller, 1992.

Whitford, Rebecca. *Little Yoga: A Toddler's First Book of Yoga*. Illustrated by Martina Selway. Holt, 2005.

Wick, Walter. *A Drop of Water*. Scholastic, 1997.

Wright-Frierson, Virginia. *A Desert Scrapbook: Dusk to Dawn in the Sonoran Desert*. Simon, 1996.

————. *An Island Scrapbook: Dust to Dawn on a Barrier Island*. Simon, 1998.

————. *A North American Rainforest Scrapbook*. Walker, 1999.

Zoehfeld, Kathleen Weidner. *Dinosaur Parents, Dinosaur Young: Uncovering the Mystery of Dinosaur Families*. Illustrated by Paul Carrick and Bruce Shillinglaw. Clarion, 2001.

Other References

Ada, Alma Flor. *Daniel's Mystery Egg*. Illustrated by G. Brian Karas. Harcourt, 2001.

————. *My Name Is Maria Isabel*. Atheneum, 1993.

Avi. *Wind Catcher*. Simon, 1991.

Ayres, Kathryn. *North by Night: A Story of the Underground Railroad*. Delacorte, 1998.

Baker, Keith. *Big Fat Hen*. Harcourt, 1994.

Baylor, Byrd. *Everybody Needs a Rock*. Scribner's, 1987.

Beard, Carleen Bailey. *Twister*. Illustrated by Nancy Carpenter. Farrar, 1999.

Beatty, Patricia. *Charley Skedaddle*. Morrow, 1987.

————. *Jayhawker*. Morrow, 1991.

Bernhard, Emery, and Durga Bernhard. *The Tree That Rains: The Flood Myth of the Huichol Indians of Mexico*. Holiday, 1994.

Berry, James. *Ajeemah and His Son*. HarperCollins, 1992.

Bruchac, Joseph. *Geronimo*. Dial, 2006.

Bunting, Eve. *Dandelions*. Illustrated by Greg Shed. Harcourt, 1995.

———. *How Many Days to America? A Thanksgiving Story.* Illustrated by Beth Peck. Ticknor, 1988.

Cameron, Ann. *Colibrí.* Farrar, 2003.

Carbonne, Elisa Lynn. *Steal Away Home.* Knopf, 1999.

Cheaney, J. B. *My Friend the Enemy.* Knopf, 2005.

Choi, Sook Nyul. *Year of Impossible Goodbyes.* Houghton, 1991.

Chotjewitz, David. *Daniel Half Human and the Good Nazi.* Translated by Doris Orgel. Atheneum. 2004.

Christian, Peggy. *If You Find a Rock.* Illustrated by Barbara Hirsch Lember. Harcourt, 2000.

Clinton, Catherine. *I, Too, Sing America: Three Centuries of African American Poetry.* Illustrated by Stephen Alcorn. Houghton, 1998.

Collier, James Lincoln, and Christopher Collier. *With Every Drop of Blood.* Delacorte, 1994.

Collins, Suzanne. *Gregor the Overlander.* Scholastic, 2003.

Conrad, Pam. *Call Me Ahnighito.* Illustrated by Richard Egielski. HarperCollins, 1995.

———. *My Daniel.* Harper, 1989.

———. *Prairie Songs.* Illustrated by Darryl Zudeck. Harper, 1985.

Dahl, Roald. *James and the Giant Peach.* Illustrated by Nancy Burkert. Knopf, 1962.

Danticat, Edwidge. *Behind the Mountains.* Orchard, 2002.

de Maupassant, Guy. *When Chickens Grow Teeth.* Illustrated by Wendy Anderson Halperin. Orchard, 1996.

DuPrau, Jeanne. *The City of Ember.* Random, 2003.

Edwards, Michelle. *Chicken Man.* Lothrop, 1991.

Erdrich, Louise. *The Birchbark House.* Hyperion, 1999.

———. *The Game of Silence.* HarperCollins, 2005.

Feelings, Tom. *The Middle Passage: White Ships/Black Cargo.* Introduction by Dr. John Henrik Clarke. Dial, 1995.

Fleischman, Paul. *Joyful Noise: Poems for Two Voices.* Illustrated by Eric Beddows. Harper, 1988.

Fox, Paula. *The Slave Dancer.* Bradbury, 1973.

Gallaz, Christophe, and Roberto Innocenti. *Rose Blanche.* Illustrated by Roberto Innocenti. Creative Education, 1985.

Garelick, May. *Where Does the Butterfly Go When It Rains?* Illustrated by Nicholas Wilton. Mondo, 1997.

George, Jean Craighead. *Julie.* HarperCollins, 1995.

Giff, Patricia Reilly. *Nory Ryan's Song.* Knopf, 2000.

Goble, Paul. *The Lost Children.* Bradbury, 1993.

Greenberg, David T. *Bugs!* Illustrated by Lynn Munsinger. Little, 1997.

Griffin, Peni R. *The Treasure Bird.* McElderry, 1992.

Hamilton, Virginia. *The House of Dies Drear.* Illustrated by Eros Keith. Macmillan, 1968.

Hansen, Joyce. *The Captive.* Scholastic, 1994.

———. *I Thought My Soul Would Rise and Fly: The Diary of Patsy a Freed Girl.* Scholastic, 1997.

Harvey, Brett. *My Prairie Christmas.* Illustrated by Deborah Kogan Ray. Holiday, 1990.

Hautzig, Esther. *The Endless Steppe: Growing Up in Siberia.* Crowell, 1968.

Hawthorn, Libby. *Sky Sash So Blue.* Illustrated by Benny Andrews. Simon, 1998.

Hermes, Patricia. *Calling Me Home.* Avon, 1998.

Hesse, Karen. *The Cats in Krasinski Square.* Illustrated by Wendy Watson. Scholastic, 2004.

Hest, Amy. *In the Rain with Baby Duck.* Illustrated by Jill Barton. Candlewick, 1995.

Hiçyilmaz, Gaye. *The Frozen Waterfall.* Farrar, 1994.

Himelblau, Linda. *The Trouble Begins.* Delacorte, 2005.

Ho, Minfong. *Gathering the Dew.* Scholastic, 2003.

Holman, Felice. *Slake's Limbo.* Atheneum, 1974.

Hopkins, Lee Bennett. *Flit, Flutter, Fly: Poems about Bugs and Other Crawly Creatures.* Illustrated by Peter Palagonia. Doubleday, 1992.

Hurst, Carol Otis. *Rocks in His Head.* Illustrated by James Stevenson. Greenwillow, 2001.

LaFaye, Alexandria. *Worth.* Simon, 2004.

Laird, Elizabeth. *The Garbage King.* Barrons, 2003.

———. *Kiss the Dust.* Dutton, 1992.

Lester, Julius. *Days of Tears: A Novel in Dialogue.* Hyperion, 2005.

Lewis, J. Patrick. *Little Buggers: Insect and Spider Poems.* Illustrated by Victoria Chess. Dial, 1998.

Lionni, Leo. *The Extraordinary Egg.* Knopf, 1994.

Logan, Claudia. *The 5,000-Year-Old Puzzle.* Illustrated by Melissa Sweet. Farrar, 2002.

London, Jonathan. *Hurricane!* Illustrated by Henri Sorensen. Lothrop, 1998.

Lowry, Lois. *Number the Stars.* Houghton, 1989.

Lyon, George Ella. *Come a Tide.* Illustrated by Stephen Gammell. Orchard, 1990.

Lyons, Mary E. *Letters from a Slave Girl: The Story of Harriet Jacobs.* Scribner's, 1992.

MacLachlan, Patricia. *Sarah, Plain and Tall.* Harper, 1985.

———. *Three Names.* Illustrated by Alexander Pertzoff. HarperCollins, 1991.

Mankell, Henning. *Secrets in the Fire.* Annick, 2003.

Matas, Carol. *Greater Than Angels.* Simon, 1998.

Mayne, William. *Earthfasts.* Smith, 1989.

McCully, Emily Arnold. *The Bobbin Girl.* Dial, 1996.

Medearis, Angela Shelf. *Dancing with the Indians.* Illustrated by Samuel Byrd. Holiday, 1991.

Millman, Isaac. *Hidden Child.* Farrar, 2005.

Mochizuki, Ken. *Baseball Saved Us.* Illustrated by Dom Lee. Lee, 1993.

Mosley, Walter. *47.* Little, 2005.

Naylor, Phyllis Reynolds. *The Treasure of Bessledorf Hill.* Simon, 1998.

Oppenheim, Shulamith Levy. *The Lily Cupboard: A Story of the Holocaust.* Illustrated by Ronald Himler. HarperCollins, 1992.

Orlev, Uri. *The Man from the Other Side.* Houghton, 1991.

Park, Frances, and Ginger Park. *My Freedom Trip.* Illustrated by Debra Reid Jenkins. Boyds Mills, 1998.

Park, Linda Sue. *When My Name Was Keoko.* Clarion, 2002.

Paterson, Katherine. *Jip: His Story.* Lodestar, 1996.

Paulsen, Gary. *Nightjohn.* Delacorte, 1993.

———. *Sarny.* Delacorte, 1997.

Philip, Neil. *War and the Pity of War.* Illustrated by Michael McCurdy. Clarion, 1998.

Pinkney, Andrea Davis. *Silent Thunder.* Hyperion, 1999.

Polacco, Patricia. *Just Plain Fancy.* Bantam/Doubleday, 1990.

———. *Pink and Say.* Philomel, 1994.

Robinett, Harriette Gillem. *Forty Acres and Maybe a Mule.* Atheneum, 1998.

Rodanas, Kristina. *Follow the Stars.* Cavendish, 1998.

Rowling, J. K. *Harry Potter and the Chamber of Secrets.* Scholastic, 1999.

Ruby, Lois. *Steal Away Home.* Macmillan, 1994.

Salisbury, Graham. *Eyes of the Emperor.* Random, 2005.

———. *Under the Blood-Red Sun.* Delacorte, 1994.

San Souci, Robert D. *Sootface: An Ojibwa Cinderella.* Illustrated by Daniel San Souci. Doubleday, 1994.

———. *The Talking Eggs.* Illustrated by Jerry Pinkney. Dial, 1989.

Schrier, Jeffrey. *On the Wings of Eagles: An Ethiopian Boy's Story.* Millbrook, 1998.

Serfozo, Mary. *Rain Talk.* Illustrated by Keiko Narahashi. McElderry, 1990.

Shusterman, Neil. *Downsiders.* Simon, 1999.

Siegelson, Kim L. *Honey Bea.* Hyperion, 2005.

———. *In the Time of the Drums.* Illustrated by Brian Pinkney. Hyperion, 1999.

Spier, Peter. *Peter Spier's Rain.* Doubleday, 1982.

Spinelli, Jerry. *Milkweed.* Knopf, 2003.

Staples, Suzanne Fisher. *Under the Persimmon Tree.* Farrar, 2005.

Stevens, Janet, and Susan Crummel Stevens. *Cook-a-Doodle-Doo!* Harcourt, 1999.

Stevenson, Robert Louis. *Treasure Island.* Scribner's, 1981.

Temple, Frances. *Grab Hands and Run.* Orchard, 1993.

———. *Tonight, by Sea.* Orchard, 1995.

Trottier, Maxine. *Prairie Willow.* Illustrated by Laura Fernandez and Rick Jacobson. Stoddart, 1998.

Turner, Ann. *Dakota Dugout.* Illustrated by Ronald Himler. Macmillan, 1985.

———. *Nettie's Trip South.* Illustrated by Ronald Himler. Macmillan, 1987.

Uchida, Yoshiko. *The Bracelet.* Illustrated by Joanna Yardley. Philomel, 1993.

———. *Journey to Topaz.* Illustrated by Donald Carrick. Scribner's, 1971.

Van Camp, Richard. *What Is the Most Beautiful Thing You Know about Horses?* Illustrated by George Littlechild. Children's, 2003.

Van Laan, Nancy. *The Magic Bean Tree.* Illustrated by Beatriz Vidal. Houghton, 1998.

———. *Shingebiss, an Ojibwe Legend.* Illustrated by Betsy Bowen. Houghton, 1997.

Veciana-Suarez, Ana. *Flight to Freedom.* Scholastic, 2002.

Walter, Mildred Pitts. *Alec's Primer.* Illustrated by Larry Johnson. Vermont Folklife Center, 2004.

Watkins, Yoko Kawashima. *So Far from the Bamboo Grove.* Lothrop, 1986.

Whelan, Gloria. *Goodbye Vietnam.* Knopf, 1992.

Wiseman, David. *Jeremy Visick.* Houghton, 1981.

Wormell, Mary. *Hilda Hen's Search.* Harcourt, 1994.

Yashima, Taro. *Crow Boy.* Viking, 1955.

Chapter Twelve

Biography

Media Resources

Following

a classroom study of biographies, a fourth-grade teacher asked her students to reflect on their experiences in their response journals. Nicholas, age 10, wrote:

Reading about the lives of other people could be very interesting. Each person has his unique life experiences. You can learn about when and where he was born, how he was raised, what kind of family did he come from. You can also learn about where he went to school and what kind of student he was when he went to school. Most of all, you can learn about his dreams and how he fulfilled his dreams. For example if I happened to be reading a book about Michael Jordan, I would be very interested to know how he trained himself to be a great basketball star. Also why did he all of a sudden switch his career as basketball player to become a baseball player. I would want to know who was his role model when he was young like me.

How did he become interested in basketball games? What kind of advice would he give to young people who have the same kind of dream to become a basketball star?

—Nicholas Lee, fourth grade, PS 124, Manhattan
Mary S. Gallivan, teacher

Elementary and middle-school students are in the process of becoming themselves, and reading about real people can provide glimpses of the kinds of lives they might choose to live. Biographies can answer questions that are important to young readers like Nicholas and raise questions about how their futures might unfold.

BIOGRAPHY FOR TODAY'S CHILD

In children's literature, biography often bridges the gap between historical fiction and nonfiction books. A life story might read like fiction, but, like other types of nonfiction, it will center on facts and events that can be documented. In the past, writers of biography for children have been allowed more freedom in the use of fictional techniques than have those who write for adults. As a result, children's biographies over the years have shown a wide range of factual orientations, from strict authenticity to liberal fictionalization. The trend today, however, is clearly toward authenticity.

Authentic biography follows many of the same rules as serious scholarly works written for adults. A book of this type is a well-documented, carefully researched account of a person's life. Only statements that are known to have been made by the subject are included as dialogue. Jean Fritz was one of the first authors to demonstrate that biographies for children could be authentic as well as lively and readable. Her writing helped set a new standard. Her books about famous figures of the American Revolution—including *And Then What Happened, Paul Revere?* and *Will You Sign Here, John Hancock?*—are based on detailed research. Natalie S. Bober's *Abigail Adams: Witness to a Revolution,*

Russell Freedman's *The Voice That Challenged a Nation,* Jan Greenberg and Sandra Jordan's *Vincent van Gogh: Portrait of an Artist,* and Rhoda Blumberg's *York's Adventures with Lewis and Clark* are among many other excellent examples of authentic biography.

Fictionalized biography is grounded in thorough research, but the author dramatizes certain events and personalizes the subject. In contrast to those who write authentic biography, authors of fictionalized biography may invent dialogue and even ascribe unspoken thoughts to the subject. These conversations might be based on facts taken from diaries, journals, or other period sources, but it is important for teachers to help children distinguish between fictionalized and authentic biographies in addition to picture books and novels that fit into the category of historical fiction.

Several picture books that were published to celebrate the two hundredth anniversary of the birth of Mary Anning use the technique of fictionalized biography. Mary was a young English girl who discovered a dinosaur fossil in Lyme Regis in the late 1700s. *Stone Girl, Bone Girl* by Laurence Anholt, *Mary Anning and the Sea Dragons* by Jeannine Atkins, *Rare Treasure: Mary Anning and Her Remarkable Discoveries* by Don Brown, and *The Fossil Girl: Mary Anning's Dinosaur Discovery* by Catherine Brighton all relate incidents from Mary's

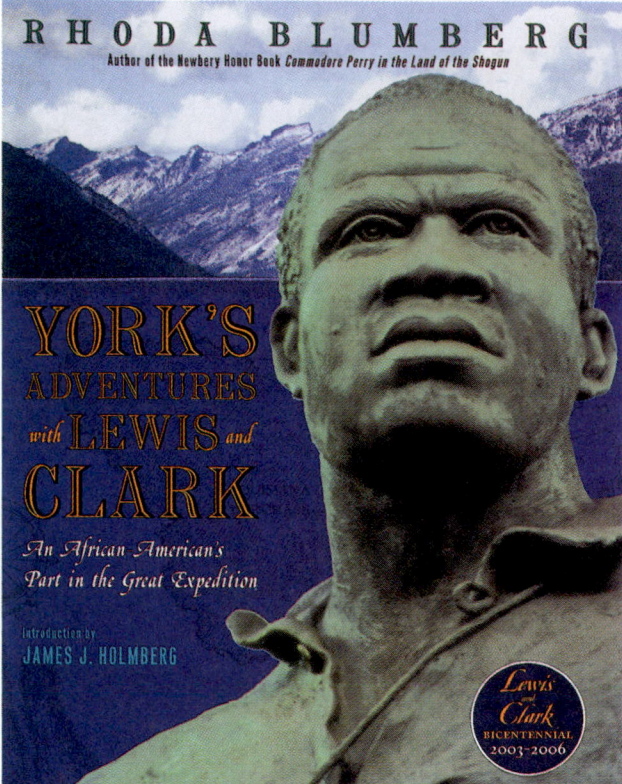

York's Adventures with Lewis and Clark by Rhoda Blumberg, about the African American slave who accompanied and supported the extraordinary expedition, is an example of excellence in biography for children. Copyright © 2004 by Rhoda Blumberg. Used by permission of HarperCollins Children's Books, a division of HarperCollins Publishers.

life. These are fictionalized biographies, however; the factual details are essentially true, but their presentation is imagined.

Not everyone agrees where to draw the line between fictionalized biography or memoirs and historical fiction. When Jean Fritz wrote about her childhood in China and her much-longed-for trip to the United States in *Homesick: My Own Story,* she found that her "memory came out in lumps," and she finally chose not to worry about exact sequence. She telescoped events of all her childhood into a two-year span. The library cataloging information in the front of this book designates it as fiction, but many readers will think of it as the autobiography of Jean Fritz. The inclusion of a section of family photographs from their days in China strengthens the book's claim to authenticity. Fritz's humor, her depth of feeling, and her vivid portrayal of the turmoil in China during the 1920s make *Homesick* worth reading, regardless of the label that is put on it. Older readers and adults might enjoy a sequel, *China Homecoming,* that is clearly nonfiction.

Publishers of biography for children have been quick to capitalize on trends in the social studies curriculum as well as shifts in children's interests. In the mid 1970s, many biographies about leaders in the American Revo-

lution appeared in connection with the bicentennial. Likewise, dozens of new books about Lewis and Clark came out in time for the bicentennial that began in 2003. As attention to multicultural education has grown, more stories about women, African-Americans, and other underrepresented groups have also been written.

Biographies of popular-culture celebrities and other contemporary figures continue to feed children's tremendous interest in sports and entertainment personalities. Although such books tend to be objective and almost journalistic in their approach, many are superficial in scholarship and poorly written. A great number of these and other biographies are published as parts of series, and the result is often life stories that are tailored to fit certain format specifications rather than explored in all their uniqueness.

A rekindled interest in the lives of historical figures, the appearance of many autobiographies by children's authors, and the growing use of photographs and picture-book formats have all had significant impact on the genre of biography. It is true that many mediocre biographies are still being published, but the number of high-quality books continues to grow. Biographies have received several prestigious awards in the past two decades. Russell Freedman won the Newbery Medal in 1988 for *Lincoln: A Photobiography* and Newbery Honor designations for *The Wright Brothers: How They Invented the Airplane* in 1992 and *Eleanor Roosevelt: A Life of Discovery* in 1993. Jean Fritz's *The Great Little Madison* was the first-ever winner of the Orbis Pictus Award for nonfiction, and Diane Stanley's *Leonardo da Vinci* won in 1997. Caldecott Honor Medals were awarded to *Bill Peet: An Autobiography* in 1990 and to Barbara Kerley's *The Dinosaurs of Waterhouse Hawkins* in 2002. Not all good books win awards, of course. Teachers and librarians need to be able to decide for themselves which biographies are distinctive and deserving of attention. The Web "Life Stories" on pages 636–37 shows how a classroom study for middle graders that begins with the genre of biography can extend to other types of life stories.

Talking Point

How should authors choose subjects for biographies for children?

Biographies for children no longer glorify their subjects as they often did in the past. We know that human beings are not perfect and believe that biographers should try to present balanced views of their subjects. Are there some subjects whose deeds are so negative or lives so complex that they might not be appropriate in biographies for children?

Go to the Online Learning Center at **www.mhhe.com/kiefer9e** or to your Resources CD-ROM to learn more.

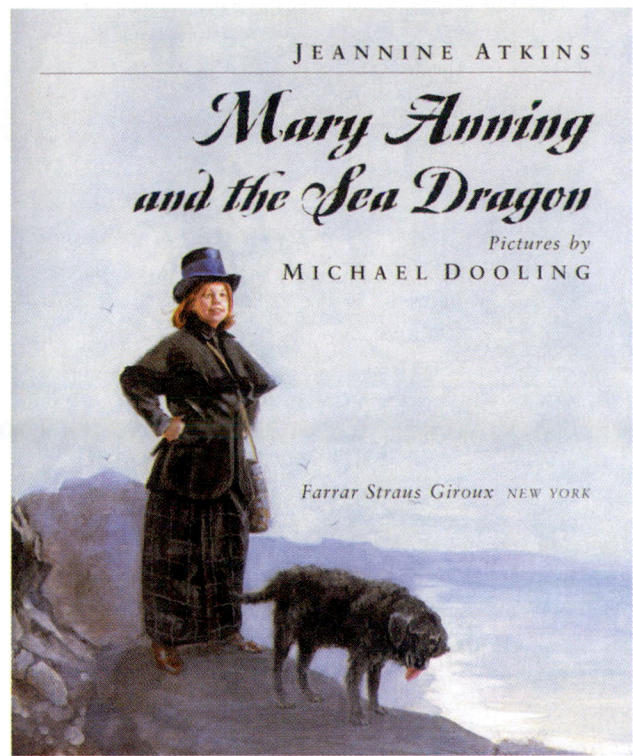

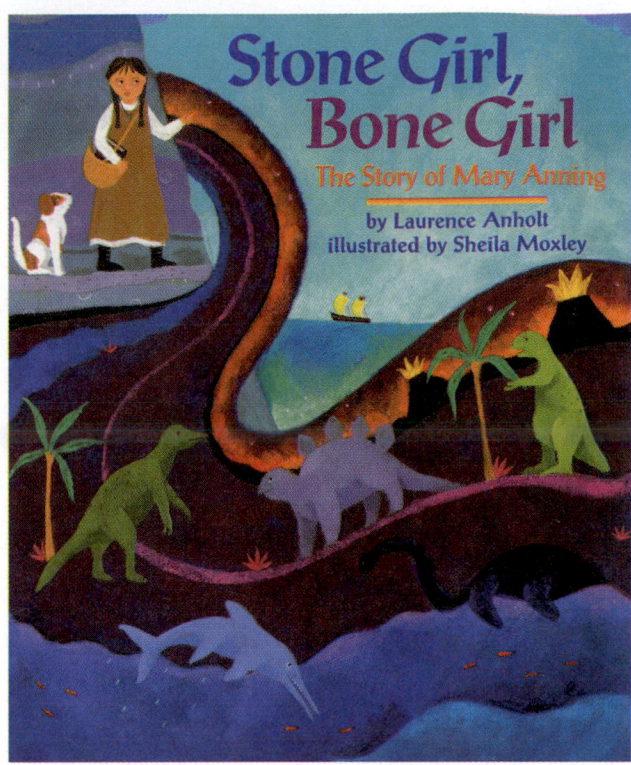

Multiple biographies of the same person, such as Jeannine Atkins's *Mary Anning and the Sea Dragon*, illustrated by Michael Dooling, and Laurence Anholt's *Stone Girl, Bone Girl*, illustrated by Sheila Moxley, can invite children's critical comparison. *Left:* Jacket design by Michael Dooling from *Mary Anning and the Sea Dragon* by Jeannine Atkins. Jacket art copyright © 1999 by Michael Dooling. Reprinted by permission of Farrar, Straus and Giroux, LLC. *Right:* Cover illustration copyright © 1998 by Sheila Moxley from *Stone Girl, Bone Girl* by Laurence Anholt. Published by Orchard Books/Scholastic Inc. Reprinted by permission.

CRITERIA FOR JUVENILE BIOGRAPHY

The criteria for evaluating biographies for children differ somewhat from those established for juvenile fiction. They also diverge somewhat from generally accepted patterns for adult biography. Children read biography as they read fiction—for the story, or *plot*. Children demand a fast-moving narrative. In biography, events and actions become even more exciting because "they really happened." Thus, children like biography written as a story with continuity; they do not want just a collection of facts and dates. An encyclopedia gives them facts in a well-organized fashion. Biography, to do more than this, must help them *know* the person as a living human being.

Choice of Subject

Formerly, most biographies for children were about familiar figures of the past in the United States, particularly those whose lives offered the readiest action material, such as Daniel Boone or Abraham Lincoln. Now the range of subjects is much broader, including artists and intellectuals as well as soldiers and presidents, plus world figures whose presence suggests the widened concerns of our pluralistic society. Biographies of contemporary figures in the worlds of sports and entertainment continue to reflect the influence of the mass media.

Diane Stanley's picture-book biographies such as *Leonardo da Vinci* include attention to historically accurate visual details as well as to factual information. Copyright © 1996 by Diane Stanley. Used by permission of HarperCollins Publishers.

Wonderfully Exciting Books

Stories of Childhood

The Boy on Fairfield Street (Krull)
Coming Home: From the Life of Langston Hughes (F. Cooper)
Eleanor (Cooney)
Escape from Slavery: The Boyhood of Frederick Douglass in His Own Words (McCurdy)
Jack: The Early Years of John F. Kennedy (I. Cooper)
Jackie Robinson and the Big Game (Gutman)
Mozart: Scenes from the Childhood of the Great Composer (Brighton)
Richard Wright and the Library Card (Miller)
Tomas and the Library Lady (Mora)
The Young Hans Christian Andersen (Hesse)
Young Thomas Edison (Dooling)
Zora Hurston and the Chinaberry Tree (Miller)
What obstacles did each of these people have to overcome as children?
How did their childhood experiences influence their future lives?
Find out more about them as adults.

Catching the Moon (Hubbard)
Facing the Lion (Lemasolai-Lekuton)
Maritcha: A Nineteenth Century American Girl (Bolden)
Sixteen Seconds in Sixteen Years: The Sammy Lee Story (Yoo)
How did these authors reconstruct the biographies of these children? What artifacts and materials could you contribute to a biography of yourself or someone you know?

Living for the Same Cause

Anthony Burns: The Defeat and Triumph of a Fugitive Slave (Hamilton)
The Bus Ride That Changed History (Edwards)
César: ¡Sí, Se Puede! Yes, We Can! (Bernier-Grand)
The Forbidden Schoolhouse (Jermain)
Frederick Douglass: The Last Days of Slavery (Miller)
Harriet Tubman, Conductor on the Underground Railroad (Petry)
Ida B. Wells: Mother of the Civil Rights Movement (Fradin and Fradin)
Mary McLeod Bethune (Greenfield)
Nelson Mandela (Kramer)
Rosa (Giovanni)
Sojourner Truth: Ain't I a Woman? (McKissack and McKissack)
The Voice That Challenged a Nation (Freedman)
How were these people alike and different?
Plan and write a script for a play that depicts these characters meeting together and sharing experiences.

Personal Stories

My Back Yard History Book (Weitzman)
Through the Eyes of Your Ancestors (Taylor)
Visit an oral history Web site. Collect an oral history of someone in your family.

Amelia's Notebook (Moss)
Scooter (Williams)
Find other fiction books written in the style of a memoir. Use this format to record or write about events in your own life.

Life Cycles

A Dragon in the Sky (Pringle)
The Life and Times of the Apple (Micucci)
The Life and Times of the Honeybee (Micucci)
Minn of the Mississippi (Holling)
Owls (Gibbons)
Pagoo (Holling)
Penguins (Gibbons)
Soaring with the Wind: The Bald Eagle (Gibbons)
Tree: A Life Story (Suzuki and Grady)
Keep an illustrated notebook of observations of one living thing over time.

LIFE STORIES: A WEB OF POSSIBILITIE

One Life, Several Points of View

Stone Girl, Bone Girl (Anholt)
Mary Anning and the Sea Dragon (Atkins)
The Fossil Girl: Mary Anning's Dinosaur Discovery (Brighton)
Rare Treasure: Mary Anning and Her Remarkable Discoveries (Brown)
How do each of these authors and artists represent Mary Anning? Check their stories against other sources. How accurate are they?
Explore other biographies about a single character. Make a comparison chart.

Odd Boy Out: Young Albert Einstein (Brown)
Genius: A Photobiography of Albert Einstein (Delano)
The Seuss, the Whole Seuss, and Nothing but the Seuss (Cohen)
The Boy on Fairfield Street (Krull)
Young Thomas Edison (Dooling)
Who Was Thomas Alva Edison? (Frith)
Compare picture-book biographies to complete biographies. What decisions do these authors make about what to leave out and what to include?

Unsung Heroes and Heroine

Bicycle Rider (Scioscia)
Bottle Houses (Slaymaker)
Leon's Story (Tillage)
Mr. Williams (Barbour)
Orphan Train Rider: One Boy's True Story (Warren)
Pick and Shovel Poet (Murphy)
Pioneer Girl: Growing Up on the Prairie (Warren)
The Way West: Journal of a Pioneer Woman (Knight)
Yankee Doodle Boy (J. Martin)
What makes a person a hero or heroine?
Find an unsung hero or heroine in your community. Write a biography celebrat his or her accomplishments.

Places Have Stories

Cathedral: The Story of Its Construction (Macaulay)
City: The Story of Roman Planning and Construction (Macaulay)
Mosque (Macaulay)
My Place (Wheatley and Rawlins)
The Story of a Farm (Goodall)
The Story of a Main Street (Goodall)
William Shakespeare and the Globe (Aliki)
Categorize the types of changes that have occurred in these places over time.
Trace the life story of your own house, neighborhood, or town.

Living during the Same Period in History

And Then What Happened, Paul Revere? (Fritz)
Can't You Make Them Behave, King George? (Fritz)
What's the Big Idea, Ben Franklin? (Fritz)
Why Don't You Get a Horse, Sam Adams? (Fritz)
Will You Sign Here, John Hancock? (Fritz)
How does Jean Fritz make her subjects come alive? Find out about her research methods.

The Revolutionary John Adams (Harness)
Ben Franklin's Almanac (Fleming)
The Remarkable Ben Franklin (Harness)
George Washington: An Illustrated Biography (Adler)
George Washington, Spymaster (Allen)
Choose a period in history. Research and create a class book of biographies from that time period.

Autobiographies and Memoirs

26 Fairmont Avenue (dePaola)
The Abracadabra Kid: A Writer's Life (Fleischman)
Bowman's Store: A Journey to Myself (Bruchac)
Boy: Tales of Childhood (Dahl)
Don't Tell the Girls: A Family Memoir (Giff)
A Girl from Yamhill: A Memoir (Cleary)
Hidden Child (Millman)
I Plant You a Lilac Tree (Hillman)
Looking Back: A Book of Memories (Lowry)
Memories of Survival (Krinitz and Steinhardt)
Reaching for the Moon (Aldrin)
Red Land, Yellow River (Zhang)
War Boy: A Country Childhood (Foreman)
How has each author "remembered" their lives?
How have they chosen to present their memories?

Life in the Arts

Alvin Ailey (Pinkney)
Andy Warhol: Prince of Pop (Greenberg and Jordan)
Celia Cruz, Queen of Salsa (Chambers)
Dickens (Rosen)
Duke Ellington: The Piano Prince and His Orchestra (Pinkney)
In Search of the Spirit: The Living National Treasures of Japan (Hamanaka and Ohmi)
Martha Graham: A Dancer's Life (Freedman)
Michelangelo (D. Stanley)
My Name Is Georgia: A Portrait (Winter)
On the Frontier with Mr. Audubon (Brenner)
Painting Dreams: Minnie Evans, Visionary Artist (Lyons)
Sebastian: A Book about Bach (Winter)
Seurat and La Grande Jatte (Burleigh)
Sholom's Treasure (Silverman)
Starting Home: The Story of Horace Pippin (Lyons)
Talking with Tebé: Clementine Hunter, Memory Artist (Lyons)
Toulouse-Lautrec (Burleigh)
Walt Whitman: Words for America (Kerley)
When Marian Sang (Ryan)
Choose one artist, musician, or dancer to research. Present your findings in the medium that the artist worked in.

Remarkable Women

Abigail Adams: Witness to a Revolution (Bober)
Adventurous Women (Colman)
African Princesses (Hansen)
Amelia to Zora (Chin-Lee)
Babe Didrikson Zaharias (Freedman)
Charlotte Forten: A Black Teacher in the Civil War (Burchard)
Cleopatra (D. Stanley and Vennema)
Eleanor Roosevelt: A Life of Discovery (Freedman)
Our Eleanor (Fleming)
Susan B. Anthony (Hopkinson)
Ten Queens: Portraits of Women of Power (Meltzer)
A Woman for President (Krull)
You Want Women to Vote, Lizzie Stanton? (Fritz)
What characteristics do these women share?
What difficulties did they face because of their gender?
How did they surmount these obstacles?

How Do We Find Out about Ancient Lives?

Archaeologists Dig for Clues (Duke)
Christopher Columbus: The Great Adventure and How We Know About It (West)
Fossils Tell of Long Ago (Aliki)
Find out how scientists learn about the past. If scientists from another planet visited your home, what might they conclude about your life?

Based on *The Web: Wonderfully Exciting Books*, ed. Charlotte Huck and Janet Hickman, The Ohio State University, Vol. III 4 (fall 1978).

For many years biography for children was limited to subjects whose lives were considered worthy of emulation. This is no longer true. There are books about people remembered for their misdeeds, like *Traitor: The Case of Benedict Arnold* by Jean Fritz. Controversial persons like Hitler, Fidel Castro, Ho Chi Minh, and Lenin have all been subjects of juvenile biographies. As long as the biographies are objective and recognize the various points of view concerning the subjects, these books can serve a useful purpose in presenting a worldview to boys and girls.

Biographies of less well-known figures or subjects whose accomplishments are highly specialized also have value for children. Mary Anning, who was little known a decade ago, had inspired over ten biographies by the end of the twentieth century. Diane Stanley's picture-book biography, *The True Adventures of Daniel Hall*, is the story of a young New England boy who sailed aboard a whaling ship in 1856 and jumped ship off the coast of Siberia. With the help of some local villagers, he managed to survive the awful Siberian winter until he was rescued the following June. Rhoda Blumberg tells an equally fascinating survival story in *Shipwrecked!: The True Adventures of a Japanese Boy*. Shipwrecked on an island off the coast of isolationist Japan in 1841, young Manjiro had no hope of returning home. Rigid Japanese laws mandated death to anyone who left the country. Rescued by the crew of an American whaleboat, Manjiro traveled to America, the first Japanese citizen to do so. He lived an amazing life, eventually returning home to Japan despite the risk of execution. The story of another little-known immigrant to America is told in Jim Murphy's *Pick and Shovel Poet: The Journeys of Pascal D'Angelo*. Pascal endured a lifetime of poverty and hardship, both in Italy and in his new home, but he never gave up his dream of writing, and his story is both heartbreaking and inspiring. Marshall Taylor, a champion cyclist at the end of the nineteenth century when bicycle racing was a popular sport, was the first black person to ride in integrated races. Mary Scioscia's *Bicycle Rider* tells the story of his first victory, focusing on family values and pride of accomplishment. *El Chino* by Allen Say introduces readers to Bong Way "Billy" Wong, a Chinese-American who longed to be a great athlete and found his niche as a bullfighter.

A sense of discovery is added to the satisfaction of a good story when children read about intriguing but little-known lives. Children have a right to read biographies about a wide range of subjects—famous persons, great human beings who were not famous, and even antiheroes.

Accuracy and Authenticity

Accuracy is the hallmark of good biographical writing, whether it is for adults or for children. More and more writers of juvenile biography are acknowledging primary sources for their materials in either an introductory note or an appended bibliography. Conscientious authors of well-written children's biographies frequently travel to the locale of the story in order to get a "feeling" for the place. They visit museums to study actual objects that were used by their subjects; they spend hours poring over original letters and documents. Much of this research might not be used in the actual biography, but its effect will be evident in the author's true insight into the character of the subject and in the accuracy of the historical detail.

The same kind of careful research should be reflected in the accuracy of the illustrations that convey the time, place, and setting. The dress of the period, the interiors of the houses, the very utensils that are used must be authentic representations. Many books, such as Susanna Reich's *Clara Schumann: Piano Virtuoso*, Dorothy Hinshaw Patent's *Charles Darwin: The Life of a Revolutionary Thinker*, and Candace Fleming's *Ben Franklin's Almanac: Being a True Account of the Good Gentleman's Life* make use of reproductions of maps, letters, and artwork of the period to authenticate the subject matter.

But most difficult of all, perhaps, is the actual portrayal of the subject. There are many drawings and paintings of most historical figures, but an accurate likeness is problematical, particularly for subjects who lived before the advent of photography. In their book *Christopher Columbus: The Great Adventure and How We Know About It*, Delno West and Jean West point out:

> There are hundreds of paintings, engravings, woodcuts, and statues of Christopher Columbus, but they were all made after he died by people who never saw him. (p. 13)

Several of these competing portraits are reproduced in their book. They also quote Columbus's son, Ferdinand, who described his father's long face, light eyes, big nose, and red hair, so that readers have a basis for reacting to the illustrations.

Photographs provide authentic illustrations for many biographical accounts of recent subjects, such as Russell Freedman's highly acclaimed photobiographies, Elizabeth Partridge's *Restless Spirit: The Life and Work of Dorothea Lange*, Ruud van der Rol and Rian Verhoeven's *Anne Frank beyond the Diary*, Kathi Appelt and Jeanne Schmitzer's *Down Cut Shin Creek: The Pack Horse Librarians of Kentucky*, and Marfe Ferguson Delano's *Genius: A Photobiography of Albert Einstein*.

An authentic biography must be true in every detail. A fictionalized biography must also be true to the factual record, and any invented dialogue or background detail must be plausible and true to the times. Yet the truth of what is included in a biography does not quite answer the entire question of its accuracy. Sometimes what is left out is just as important as what goes in.

Formerly, authors of biographies for children avoided writing about certain aspects of the lives of their subjects. Serious criticism has been leveled at biographies of Washington and Jefferson that did not include the fact that they owned many slaves. More-recent biographies,

Elizabeth Partridge's *This Land Was Made for You and Me: The Life and Songs of Woody Guthrie* is a frank and intense biography for older children. "Jacket illustration" by Lane Smith, copyright © 2002 by Lane Smith, jacket illustration from *This Land Was Made for You and Me: The Life and Songs of Woody Guthrie* by Elizabeth Partridge. Used by permission of Viking Penguin, a division of Penguin Young Readers Group, a Member of Penguin Group (USA) Inc., 345 Hudson St., New York, NY 10014. All rights reserved.

even those for younger children, do include this information. In *Thomas Jefferson* James Cross Giblin approaches his subject with the same meticulous research he applies to his many nonfiction books (see Chapter 11) and writes of Jefferson's ambivalence about slavery. In her biography for older readers, *This Land Was Made for You and Me: The Life and Songs of Woody Guthrie*, Elizabeth Partridge writes honestly about Guthrie's irresponsible and often reckless behavior as well as his passionate regard for the plight of the working classes.

When writing for younger children, certain biographers might present only a portion of a person's life. In planning their picture book *Abraham Lincoln*, Ingri d'Aulaire and Edgar Parin d'Aulaire deliberately omitted his assassination and closed the book with the end of the Civil War. The authors' purpose was to present the greatness of the man as he lived, for too frequently, they believed, children remember only the manner of Lincoln's death. There is a danger, however, that omissions might oversimplify and thereby distort the truth about a person's life. The critic Jo Carr has argued that it is better not to offer biography to young children at all than to present them with unbalanced portraits distorted by flagrant omissions.[1]

For many years it was thought that children were interested only in reading about the childhoods of great men and women and not about the complexities of their adult activities. For this reason many earlier biographies focused primarily on childhood pranks and legends that suggested future accomplishments, but neglected or rushed through the real achievements of later life. The current emphasis on authentic biography has reversed this trend, since it is much more difficult to find primary source material about a subject's childhood than about her or his adult life. Increasingly, the best authors respect children's right to read honest, objective biographies that tell more of the truth and document their writing with source notes or a bibliography. Literature in Action: "Thinking Critically about Biographies" shows how one teacher asked his students to compare biographies of the same subject in order to help them think more critically about authors' objectivity and accuracy.

Style

The author's language is especially important to biography because it bears the burden of making the subject seem alive and sound real. Documented quotes should be woven smoothly into the narrative. When dialogue is invented, it should have the natural rhythms of speech, regardless of the period it represents, because stilted writing makes characters seem wooden.

In today's authentic biography, the author's way with words makes all the difference between a dull and a lively book. Amy Cohn and Suzy Schmidt begin their picture-book biography, *Abraham Lincoln*, with this folksy, directly personal address:

> See that tall thin man in the tall black hat? Know who he is? That's right, he's the man on the penny—Abraham Lincoln, sixteenth president of the U.S.
>
> Was he always that way, straight as an arrow, tall as a tree, serious as can be?
>
> Let's go back, Let's go back a ways, and see. (p. 6)

Rhoda Blumberg's *Shipwrecked!: The True Adventures of a Japanese Boy* begins with this amazing statement, "Head of the family at the age of nine! When his father died in 1836 Manjiro had to support his mother, three younger sisters, one younger brother, and an invalid older brother who was too weak to work" (p. 9).

---

[1]Jo Carr, "What Do We Do about Bad Biographies?" in *Beyond Fact: Nonfiction for Children and Young People* (Chicago: American Library Association, 1982), pp. 119–29.

Thinking Critically about Biographies

At Hilltonia Middle School in Columbus, Ohio, Richard Roth put his students in groups of four to consider which of two biographies was the better book. Some groups read about Abraham Lincoln, using *Lincoln: A Photobiography* by Russell Freedman and *True Stories about Abraham Lincoln* by Ruth Belov Gross. Other groups read *Bully for You, Teddy Roosevelt!* by Jean Fritz and a second biography of Roosevelt. Still others read two selections about Leonardo da Vinci.

First, students read the books individually and noted their reactions to the cover, chapter titles, pictures, and content (facts, bias, writing style), and rated their usefulness. Groups needed only two copies of each book, because each student could read one title and then trade with a partner. Sharing copies also encouraged students to take good notes, including page numbers for reference.

When the students had read both books, the teacher gave each student a blank chart with space for rating each book on the same items, with the following directions: "Rate the categories for each book from 1 to 10: 10 is excellent, 5, average, and 1, poor. As a group, decide what score each book deserves for each category. Then total the scores and determine which book the group thought best overall." The final step was to work as a group to compose a recommendation of their top book for other students to read.

Although not all the groups chose the book that the teacher (or critics) would have chosen, the students gained valuable experience in exercising their own judgment. The teacher planned this study because he wanted all his students to have the opportunity to take stock of their own responses and share them with classmates. He also knew that his students would participate more fully in discussion if they first had a chance to formulate their ideas and write them down. In retrospect, he reported that this process really did encourage critical thinking. There were meaningful group discussions with healthy disagreements about which book was superior. Moreover, students were able to rethink their own first impressions and make comparisons in the interest of fairness and accuracy. In the class discussion that followed the completion of the small-group work, the teacher gave the students still more to think about by encouraging them to share their own perspectives on the books they had read.

As in most middle schools, this teacher has many students and a limited time with them each day. One of the advantages of this biography study was that it gave Roth new insight into their responses and the factors that contribute to their reading interests. It also confirmed his thinking that it is important for students to work through their own responses as they develop ways to appreciate literature.

Richard Roth
Hilltonia Middle School, Columbus City Schools, Ohio

The narrator's tone always pervades the presentation, but a dispassionate point of view usually is used for authentic biography. Whatever the form or viewpoint, the background materials should be integrated into the narrative with smoothness and proportion. The judicious use of quotes from letters or journals may support the authenticity of the biography, but it should not detract from the absorbing account of the life of the subject. Children enjoy a style that is clear and vigorous. The research must be there, but it should be a natural part of the presentation.

The choice of narrator, or point of view, is also an important consideration in the style of a biography. Writers of biography most often use the third person. But some authors take a more intimate point of view. Mary E. Lyons chose to tell the life story of African American artist Clementine Hunter in the first person. In *Talking with Tebé*, Lyons explains that despite the fact that over eighty articles were written about Hunter, many critics still did not consider her a real artist.

These notions convinced me that it was time Hunter spoke for herself. Most of the text in *Talk-*

ing with Tebé is written in her own words. I gathered quotations from magazines, newspapers, and twenty-two taped interviews made by Hunter's friend Mildred Bailey, in 1978. A few quotations are from newspaper columns by François Mignon. (p. 6)

Hearing Hunter's story in her own dignified voice lends the book immediacy and impact.

Characterization

The characterization of the subject of a biography must be true to life, neither adulatory nor demeaning in tone. The reader should have the opportunity to know the person as a real human being with both shortcomings and virtues. To emphasize the worthiness of their subjects, juvenile biographers sometimes portray them as too good to be true.

Jean Fritz is one author who manages to create vivid portraits of great figures without according them pseudo-sainthood. She has presented Paul Revere as a busy and sometimes forgetful human being in her humorous yet authentic picture-book biography *And Then What Hap-*

Mary Lyons presents the life of Clementine Hunter through the artist's own words in *Talking with Tebé: Clementine Hunter, Memory Artist.* Cover of *Talking with Tebé: Clementine Hunter, Memory Artist* by Mary E. Lyons, editor, © 1998. Reprinted by permission of Houghton Mifflin Company, Inc.

pened, Paul Revere?* He didn't always meet his deadlines, once producing a hymnbook some eighteen months after he had promised it! A dreamer, he even left one page in his "Day Book" simply for doodling. The author does not debunk her character; she simply makes him come alive by admitting his foibles, as well as describing his accomplishments.

Comparing two or more biographies of the same subject is one way of understanding the importance of characterization. Doris Faber's *Eleanor Roosevelt, First Lady of the World* and Maryann Weidt's *Stateswoman to the World: A Story about Eleanor Roosevelt* are similar in length and coverage. Both are generally suitable for grades 3 to 5. Both books emphasize the young Eleanor's growing desire for independence, but they provide somewhat different views of the childhood experiences that helped shape her determination and sense of duty.

Biography must not degenerate into mere eulogy; reexamining should not become debunking. The background of subjects' lives, their conversations, their thoughts, and their actions should be presented as faithfully to the facts as possible. The subject should also be seen in relation to her or his times, for no person can be "read" in isolation.

Theme

Underlying the characterization in all biography— whether it be authentic or fictionalized—is the author's interpretation of the subject. No matter how impartial an author might be, a life story cannot be written without some interpretation. An author's selection of facts can limit the dimensions of the portraiture or highlight certain features. In this context every author walks a thin line between theme and bias. Time usually lends perspective and objectivity, but contemporary biography might tend more toward bias. Teachers and librarians need to help children realize that all biographies have a point of view determined by their authors. Again, a comparison of several biographies of the same person written in different time periods would help children discover this fact.

Frequently in juvenile biography the theme will be identified in the title, as in Suzanne Jurmain's *The Forbidden Schoolhouse: The True and Dramatic Story of Prudence Crandall and Her Students, Martin Luther King: The Peaceful Warrior* by Ed Clayton, or Julie Cummins's *Tomboy of the Air: Daredevil Blanche Stuart Scott.* These titles name their subjects and point up the theme of the books.

In picture-book biographies, illustrations as well as the story title reveal the theme. Author/illustrator Peter Sis offers an artist's interpretation of Christopher Columbus in *Follow the Dream: The Story of Christopher Columbus.* Sis grew up in Czechoslovakia, a country surrounded by a political "wall" known as the Iron Curtain. He relates his background to Columbus's by emphasizing the many forces that walled Columbus in. A wall motif appears consistently throughout the book, always countered by an opening or archway through which Columbus can follow his dream. Although this book ends with Columbus's arrival in the New World in 1492 and says nothing about his character as a leader or his later cruelty to the native people, the theme of breaking down the wall surrounding the Old World is a fresh insight. James Rumford's illustrations for *Sequoyah: The Cherokee Man Who Gave His People Writing* pay homage to the woodblock prints of such Japanese artists of the nineteenth century as Hokusai and Hiroshige. They evoke the contrast between Eastern and Western art styles and subtly emphasize the two cultures Sequoyah represented and brought together through his invention of a Cherokee alphabet. Demi pays reverent attention to customs of Islam in her biography of *Muhammad,* never representing his human form but showing only a silhouette of Muhammad in gold leaf. The style of her illustrations, resembling the miniatures of ancient Persia, also conveys the wonder and piety of the life of this holy prophet.

There is a danger in oversimplifying and forcing all facts to fit a single mold. An author must not re-create and interpret a life history in terms of one fixed picture, particularly in a biography that covers the full scope of a subject's life. Ordinary people have several facets to their personalities; the great are likely to be multidimensional. The perceptive biographer concentrates on those items from a full life that helped mold and form that personality. It is this selection and focus that create the theme of the biography. The Evaluation Criteria box "Evaluating

The picture-book biography *Sequoyah* by James Rumford evokes important cultural themes and information through both pictures and words. *Illustration from* Sequoyah: The Cherokee Man Who Gave His People Writing *by James Rumford. Copyright © 2004 by James Rumford. Reprinted by permission of Houghton Mifflin Company. All rights reserved.*

Juvenile Biography" summarizes the criteria we have discussed in this section.

TYPES OF PRESENTATION AND COVERAGE

Writers of adult biography are by definition bound to try to re-create the subject's life as fully as possible, with complete detail and careful documentation. Writers of children's biography, however, may use one of several approaches. The resulting types of biography need individual consideration, for each offers to children a different perspective and a different appeal. Keep in mind, however, that a single book might fit into more than one of the following categories.

Picture-Book Biographies

A biography cast in a picture-book form might span the subject's lifetime or a part of it; it might be directed to a very young audience or to a somewhat older one; it might be authentic or fictionalized. Whatever the case, it remains for the pictures to carry a substantial part of the interpretation, as Leonard Marcus points out:

> Illustrations, then, contribute more to a picture book biography than occasional picture-equivalents of the author's words. They traffic to some degree in unnamable objects, states and feelings. . . . Along with what it tells us about the values, temperament and concerns of a biography's central character, fine illustration also puts us in contact with an individuality—and a form of praise—that is esthetic.[2]

This sense of heightened perception accompanies Bryan Collier's edgy sepia collages for Doreen Rappaport's biographies of Martin Luther King (*Martin's Big Words*) and John Lennon (*John's Secret Dreams*). Collier also collaborated with poet Nikki Giovanni on *Rosa*, the story of Rosa Parks. Collier's work captures the essence of these figures and sets a dignified, somewhat somber mood that marks the struggles these figures endured. Alice Provensen and Martin Provensen's illustrations for *The Glorious Flight: Across the Channel with Louis Blériot, July 25, 1909* also take this biography beyond the scope of mere words. Blériot carries himself with intrepid grace in his unsuccessful attempts to fly, and the pictures that show him above the Channel use contrast and perspective to convey the elation and danger of flight. Historical and background details also appear in the pictures, inviting speculation, inferences, and discussion.

The mood, or tone, of a biography can be quickly established by its pictures. The Illustrations for Jean Fritz's biographies immediately set an inviting, lighthearted tone for readers. In *What's the Big Idea, Ben Franklin?* the droll pictures by Margot Tomes emphasize a particular side of Franklin's character—his ingenuity. Trina Schart Hyman's illustrations for *Why Don't You Get a Horse, Sam Adams?* and *Will You Sign Here, John Hancock?* serve up American history with a lively twist. Tomie dePaola's pictures for *Can't You Make Them Behave, King George?* emphasize Fritz's humor as she helps readers think of the unpopular English monarch in a new way. On the

---

[2]Leonard S. Marcus, "Life Drawings: Some Notes on Children's Picture Book Biographies," *The Lion and the Unicorn* 4 (summer 1980): 17.

EVALUATION CRITERIA

Evaluating Juvenile Biography

CHOICE OF SUBJECT

- Does the subject's life offer interest and meaning for today's child?
- Will knowing this historical or contemporary figure help children understand the past or the present?
- Can the subject's experiences widen children's views on the possibilities for their own lives?

ACCURACY AND AUTHENTICITY

- Do the text and illustrations reflect careful research and consistency in presentation?
- Does the author provide notes about original source material, a bibliography, or other evidence of documentation?
- Are there discrepancies of fact in comparison with other books?
- Are there significant omissions that result in a distorted picture of the subject's life?

STYLE

- Are quotations or dialogue used in a way that brings the subject to life?
- For a fictionalized biography, does the choice of narrator's point of view add to the story?
- Is the author's style clear and readable, with background material included naturally?

CHARACTERIZATION

- Is the subject presented as a believable, multidimensional character, with both strengths and weaknesses?
- Does the author avoid both eulogizing and debunking?

THEME

- Does the author's interpretation of the subject represent a fair and balanced approach?
- Does the author avoid oversimplifying or manipulating the facts to fit the chosen theme?

other hand, Rocco Baviera's richly textured oil paintings provide a dark and brooding underpinning to Joseph Bruchac's *A Boy Called Slow: The True Story of Sitting Bull*. Brian Zelznick's muted drawings capture the physical essence and the inner dignity of Marian Anderson's life in *When Marian Sang* by Pam Muñoz Ryan. Brian Pinkney's scratchboard pictures add a sense of vigorous movement to Andrea Davis Pinkney's many biographies of African American figures such as Benjamin Banneker, Alvin Ailey, Bill Picket, Ella Fitzgerald, and Duke Ellington.

This ability to lend emotional power to biography can also be seen in Angela Barrett's illustrations for Josephine Poole's *Anne Frank* or in Max Ginsburg's pictures for Robert San Souci's *Kate Shelley: Bound for Legend*. Comparing illustrations in picture-book biographies can help children see how an artist's point of view can alter their own understanding of a subject. Gregory Christie's paintings for Anne Rockwell's biography of Sojourner Truth, *Only Passing Through*, provide an up-to-date viewpoint that links Sojourner's fight against slavery to modern-day struggles for human rights. On the other hand, Gershom Griffith's illustrations in *A Picture Book of Sojourner Truth* by David Adler convey a more direct sense of the historical time period.

Visual interpretations of the young fossil discoverer Mary Anning can give rise to interesting discussions among children as they compare four different picture-book biographies. Catherine Brighton's watercolors for *The Fossil Girl* are solidly realistic, but the illustrations are set in comic-book format and conversations are carried in speech balloons. Sheila Moxley's bright, flat colors in *Stone Girl, Bone Girl* by Lawrence Anholt give

a primitive folk-art appeal to the pictures. Michael Dooling's illustrations for *Mary Anning and the Sea Dragon* by Jeannine Atkins are representational oil paintings, whereas Don Brown's impressionistic watercolor pictures in *Rare Treasure* are lighter in tone and mood.

Michael Dooling has done the illustrations for his own biography of *Young Thomas Edison* and for James Cross Giblin's biographies of Americans such as Thomas Jefferson and Benjamin Franklin. Don Brown has contributed other fine picture-book biographies, such as *Odd Boy Out: Young Albert Einstein; Across a Dark and Wide Sea*, the story of Columcille, who was responsible for establishing the monastery on Iona in the sixth century; and biographies of two unusual women travelers, *Far Beyond the Garden Gate: Alexandra David-Neel's Journey to Lhasa* and *Uncommon Traveler: Mary Kingsley in Africa*.

Many picture-book biographies are available about people from cultures around the world, and throughout history, who have made noteworthy contributions of many kinds. Many of these books, such as *Mother Teresa* by Demi and *César* by Carmen Bernier-Grand, feature contemporary figures.

Other authors look further back into history for their subjects. In *The Travels of Benjamin of Tudela* Uri Shulevitz tells the story of a Spanish Jew who, in 1159, set out on a journey through the Middle East that lasted fourteen years. Two hundred years later, in 1325, a young Moroccan boy began a journey that would eventually cover 75,000 miles across the known world of Africa, India, and China. James Rumford tells his story in *Traveling Man: The Journey of Ibn Battuta, 1325–1354*. Kathryn Lasky has written fictionalized picture-book biographies about two

Angela Barrett's illustrations for *Anne Frank* by Josephine Poole convey an overall mood of tragedy throughout this moving picture-book biography. From *Anne Frank* by Josephine Poole and Angela Barrett, illustrator, copyright © 2005 by Josephine Poole Illustrations. Copyright © 2005 by Angela Barrett. Used by permission of Alfred A. Knopf, Inc., an imprint of Random House Children's Books, a division of Random House, Inc.

men who contributed to our understanding of latitude and longitude and thus helped open the world to exploration. *The Librarian Who Measured the Earth* was the Greek Eratosthenes, who became head of the library in Alexandria but also devised a method for measuring the circumference of the earth. *The Man Who Made Time Travel* is about John Harrison, the clock maker who discovered a way to measure longitude. Both books are illustrated by Kevin Hawkes, who also illustrated M. T. Anderson's lively *Handel, Who Knew What He Liked.*

Children will also find many biographies of people in the arts. Deborah Kogan Ray's *Hokusai: The Man Who Painted a Mountain* is the story of the well-known Japanese printmaker whose work influenced many nineteenth-century European artists. *The Pot That Juan Built* by Nancy Andrews-Goebel is a charming story about Juan Quezada, the premier Mexican potter who transformed the village of Mata Ortiz with his inventive techniques. Juan's life is told partially through a rhyme built on the "House That Jack Built" format. It is illustrated by David Diaz with bright, airbrushed paintings that resemble the glazes of Mexican pottery. Jeanette Winter's paintings, in her many biographies such as *My Name Is Georgia: A Portrait, Sebastian: A Book about Bach, Cowboy Charlie: The Story of Charles M. Russell,* and *Diego,* written by Jonah Winter, bring rich color and meaning to these brief books. In *Diego* we learn about the life of the famous Mexican artist Diego Rivera. The small pictures construct scenes from his early years, full of a magical sense of celebrations and play, as well as times of turmoil that were reflected in the huge murals Rivera painted as an

adult. Jonah Winter's *Frida,* about Diego Rivera's even more famous wife Frieda Kahlo, makes a fine companion book. Ana Juan's illustrations convey a wonderful sense of this artist's style without directly copying it.

Diane Stanley is known for biographies in picture-book format with exquisitely detailed paintings. Her *Saladin: Noble Prince of Islam,* illustrated with jewellike paintings in the style of Persian miniatures, tells the story of the twelfth-century sultan of Egypt and Syria who united the Islamic world against the armies of the First Crusade. Stanley's *Leonardo da Vinci* was a winner of the Orbis Pictus Award in 1997, and her *Michelangelo* is an equally fine portrait of a Renaissance artist. In both books, Stanley incorporates reproductions of the artists' work into her illustrations. Stanley's *Joan of Arc* is based on Joan's own words, taken from the transcripts of her trial. The illustrations, which include maps and close-ups of fifteenth-century artifacts, recall the illuminated books of such masters as the Limbourg Brothers. In Stanley's *Cleopatra* (written in collaboration with husband Peter Vennema) the mosaic portrait of Cleopatra on the cover suggests this Egyptian queen's Greek ancestry, and motifs of Greek art are found throughout the book. No book as brief as this can do full justice to a complex subject, but Stanley and Vennema do succeed in portraying Cleopatra's strengths as a leader and in providing an intriguing invitation to further study.

In addition to *Cleopatra,* Stanley and Vennema collaborated in writing *Shaka: King of the Zulus, Good Queen Bess: The Story of Elizabeth I of England, Charles Dickens: The Man Who Had Great Expectations,* and *Bard of Avon: The*

Story of William Shakespeare. Diane Stanley both wrote and illustrated *Peter the Great*. Fay Stanley, Diane Stanley's mother, wrote *The Last Princess: The Story of Princess Ka'iulani of Hawai'i*. Clear, almost primitive paintings by Diane Stanley help to tell the poignant story of the betrayal of Hawaii by Americans and the sad death of Hawaii's last princess at age 23.

In *William Shakespeare and the Globe* Aliki sets the few known facts about Shakespeare in dramatic form and in five acts manages to convey a wealth of information about Shakespeare, his time, and the story of the reconstruction of the Globe Theater, which was finished in 1997. The book is a fine example of the integration of pictures and text. The imaginative form, the lively verbal narrative, the quotes from Shakespeare's works, and the pictures, diagrams, maps, and overall visual design convey an understanding of Shakespeare's life that is much more than the sum of anecdotes and facts. Aliki always includes details that intrigue children, but in so doing also provides insight into the way her subjects lived.

Milton Meltzer reminds us that biography is more than the personal history of one person:

> If biography is well done, it is also social history. [As a biographer] I must tell the story of my subject's time and of the people who lived through that time.[3]

This approach usually calls for a complete biography of the subject. In the case of picture-book biographies, it suggests that the sharing of several titles with different points of view would be a good way to help younger children to develop an understanding of both author point-of-view and author research techniques. For older children, picture-book biographies can be a fine introduction to the more extensive biographies that may be available.

Simplified Biographies

Not all children who have an interest in biographical information are in full command of the skills of reading. Some of these children are beginning readers; some read independently but are not ready for a long or complex text; some are older children with specialized interests but low skill levels. Various kinds of simplified biographies, usually short and with many illustrations, have been published in response to the needs of these children.

Many picture-book biographies, of course, are written in simple language that many primary-grade readers can handle on their own. David Adler's *A Picture Book of Thomas Jefferson* and *A Picture Book of Benjamin Franklin* provide straightforward accounts of highlights from the lives of these two founding fathers. Companion books are available about George Washington, Abraham Lincoln, and John F. Kennedy as well as other well-known

figures, such as Lewis and Clark, Harriet Beecher Stowe, Martin Luther King, Jackie Robinson, and Rosa Parks. The advantage of these books is their readability and the support provided by their illustrations. The disadvantage is that, to increase readability, the author had to leave out many of the complexities of character and accomplishment that make these subjects memorable.

Aliki also writes and illustrates easy-vocabulary picture biographies. In *The Story of Johnny Appleseed*, she has captured the humor and simplicity of the legendary pioneer. Similar in simplicity is *A Weed Is a Flower: The Life of George Washington Carver*. Again, Aliki has made meaningful for the youngest reader the inspiring story of a man who was born a slave but lived to become one of the greatest research scientists in the United States.

Many simplified biographies are not just for beginning readers but are directed toward an older audience. One account that is simply told but difficult to put down is Ann McGovern's *The Secret Soldier: The Story of Deborah Sampson*. Dressed as a man, Deborah Sampson fought in the American Revolution, managing to escape detection for more than a year. Newly proficient readers will appreciate the detail about Deborah's childhood as well as the format that breaks the text into manageable parts.

Publishers who produce series of easy-to-read books now include some biography and other nonfiction along with their many fiction titles. Grosset's All-Aboard Reading series includes biographies such as *Sacajawea* and *Pocahontas*, both by Joyce Milton. Milton's books provide responsible, if not detailed, introductions to the lives of these two Native American women. The same publisher has created a series of brief Who Was? biographies including Margaret Frith's *Who Was Thomas Alva Edison?* and Deborah Hopkinson's *Who Was Charles Darwin?* HarperCollins has also published several biographies directed at 7- to 10-year-olds that emphasize contemporary figures and those from minority populations. These include *Mary McLeod Bethune* by Eloise Greenfield and *Malcolm X* by Arnold Adoff. In *Rosa Parks*, Eloise Greenfield tells the story of the African American woman whose refusal to move to the back of the bus in Montgomery, Alabama, triggered events that grew into the civil rights movement. These books are characterized by brief text enhanced by many pictures.

Laura Driscoll's *Sammy Sosa*, illustrated by Ken Call, and Andrew Gutelle's *Tiger Woods* are among the simplified biographies that fall into the high-interest/low-reading-level category, where the most popular subjects seem to be from the sports and entertainment worlds. The text in these books might be very brief, and illustrations or photographs might be used very liberally. In short, the books are designed to catch and keep the eye of the reluctant or less-able older reader. Unfortunately, the writing in some of these books is heavily influenced

---

[3]Milton Meltzer, "Selective Forgetfulness: Christopher Columbus Reconsidered," *New Advocate* 5 (winter 1992): 1.

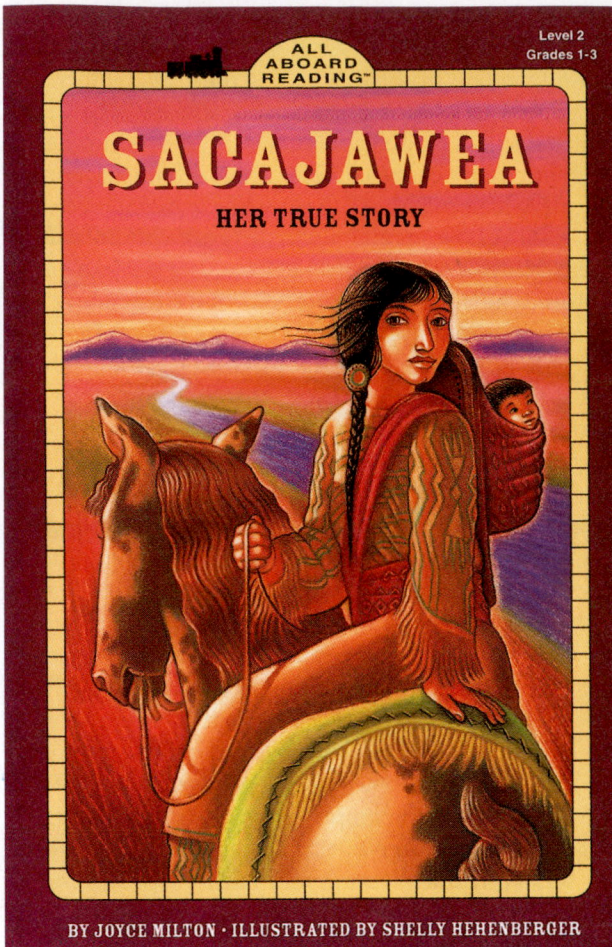

Sacajawea by Joyce Milton is an example of an easy-to-read biography for younger readers. From *Sacajawea: Her True Story* (All Aboard Reading Level 3) by Joyce Milton, illustrated by Shelly Hehenberger, copyright © 2001 by Shelly Hehenberger, illustrations. Used by permission of Grosset & Dunlap, a division of Penguin Young Readers Group, a Member of Penguin Group (USA) Inc., 345 Hudson St., New York, NY 10014. All rights reserved.

by the tendency to "hype" a subject. Even though children have a great appetite for personal close-ups of celebrities, it is difficult to find books of this type that are written with perspective and produced with care.

Some biographies can be considered simplified not because of their easy-to-read format but because they tend to be shorter than complete biographies and are accompanied by many illustrations and photographs. Julie Cummins's lively biography *Tomboy of the Air: Daredevil Blanche Stuart Scott* falls into this category. In eighty pages, with a large typeface and plenty of white space, the book tells the story of a singular character whose love for speed led her to become the first woman automobile salesperson, the first woman to drive a car across the country, and the first woman to fly a plane in public. Mary Lyons's fine series on African American artists would also fit into the category of simplified biography. In addition to her life of Clementine Hunter (*Talk-*

ing with Tebé, discussed on p. 640), Lyons's biographies include books on painters Minnie Evans, Bill Traylor, and Horace Pippin, quiltmaker Harriet Powers, blacksmith Philip Simmons, and woodworker and carpenter Tom Day. Through words and pictures Lyons gives readers glimpses of social history, fascinating details about the lives of these fine artists, and information about the links each of them had to their African heritage. Cheryl Harness has written several fine simplified biographies for National Geographic including *The Remarkable Ben Franklin* and *The Revolutionary John Adams*. *Sojourner Truth* by Peter Roop and Connie Roop and *The Wright Brothers* by George Sullivan are among the titles found in a series of biographies from Scholastic called In Their Own Words. Each book has just over one hundred pages; large, easy-to-read type; and many illustrations. Most notable is the authors' use of primary source materials to ground their stories. Each book contains a clear introduction that helps children understand the difference between primary and secondary sources and why primary sources are preferred when writing biography.

Partial Biographies

One of the liberties allowed writers of biographies for juveniles is the freedom to write about only part of the subject's life. Authors are able to focus, if they wish, on a time of high drama, and let the demands of constructing a good story help set the time frame for the book. Ilene Cooper's *Jack: The Early Years of John F. Kennedy* is a fine portrayal of Kennedy's youth and adolescence. William Miller has chosen the picture-book format to recount critical moments in the lives of two African-Americans. In *Frederick Douglass: The Last Days of Slavery* Miller tells of Douglass's childhood experiences that led to his rebellion against slavery. Miller's *Zora Hurston and the Chinaberry Tree* highlights Hurston's important relationship with her mother and her fascination with the folklore and songs of her African American heritage. By highlighting these events, Miller shows how these experiences became influential in the life's work of Douglass and Hurston.

David Kherdian deals with only a portion of the life of Veron Dumehjian, his mother, in *The Road from Home: The Story of an Armenian Girl*. What is central to the story is her family's suffering in the massacre and dispersal of Armenians by the Turks. If those events had been related as only a small part of her life experiences, their impact and historical significance might have been less perceptible. Kherdian chose to assume his mother's first-person point of view, which adds passion and immediacy to this fictionalized biography.

Some partial biographies do furnish information about the subject's entire life but focus on a few incidents that are particularly memorable. Virginia Hamilton has written a complex story in *Anthony Burns: The Defeat and Triumph of a Fugitive Slave*. By creating a fictional narrative about Burns's early life from documents about his later life, Hamilton interweaves historical fiction with true biography. Born a slave in Virginia, Anthony Burns was 20 when he escaped to Boston. For a few short months he lived as a free man, until his former owner came to Boston and invoked the Fugitive Slave Act, demanding him back. Thousands of abolitionists rioted and Richard Dana defended him without charge. Yet it was to no avail. Burns was sent back to Virginia, where he was shackled and imprisoned in a tiny room for the next four months. Finally news of his whereabouts reached two ministers in Boston, who raised money to purchase him. He was freed and sent to Canada, where he became a minister. He died when he was only 28 years old, from the dreadful treatment he had received while in jail. Students in middle school interested in pursuing the meaning of the Fugitive Slave Act could do no better than to read this compelling story of the last slave ever seized on Massachusetts soil.

Other biographies are incomplete for the simple reason that a full treatment of the subject's complex life would make a book too long and unwieldy for young readers. There have been several such biographies of Abraham Lincoln, for instance. Carl Sandburg wrote a partial biography for children titled *Abe Lincoln Grows Up*. It was made from the first twenty-seven chapters of the first volume of the longest and most definitive biography of Lincoln for adults, Sandburg's *Abraham Lincoln: The Prairie Years*. For his juvenile biography Sandburg included Lincoln's birth and boyhood until he was 19 and "grown up." In singing prose that begs to be read aloud, the author describes Lincoln's desire for knowledge:

> And some of what he wanted so much, so deep down, seemed to be in books. Maybe in books he would find the answers to dark questions pushing around in the pools of his thoughts, and the drifts of his mind. (p. 135)

Many authors of partial biographies have focused on the childhood years of their subjects. Karen Hesse and Erik Blegvad have collaborated on the early years of the Danish storyteller and writer in *The Young Hans Christian Andersen*. Composed of brief, partly imagined episodes from Hans's early life to age 14, the book includes an author's note and a bibliography of sources on Andersen's life. Danish artist Blegvad's lovely watercolor and pen-and-ink illustrations lend a whimsical mood to Andersen's less than happy childhood.

In *Maritcha: A Nineteenth Century American Girl*, a biography of a young African-American, Tonya Bolden has scrupulously uncovered archival materials about Maritcha Lyons, a middle-class child growing up in New York City in the mid-1800s. Bolden began her research with Maritcha's memoir, finished in 1928. This handsome biography includes photographs, maps, paintings, and other materials Bolden found in her research and presents a fascinating picture of girlhood and culture seldom explored before, in either fact or fiction.

Nineteenth-century historical records, photographs, and artifacts bring fascinating life to the story of an ordinary middle-class African American girl in *Maritcha* by Tonya Bolden. Cover of *Maritcha: A Nineteenth-Century American Girl* by Tonya Bolden, copyright © 2005. Reprinted by permission of Harry N. Abrams, Inc.

Andrea Warren has focused on the childhood years of two unfamiliar figures. In *Orphan Train Rider: One Boy's True Story,* winner of the 1996 Boston Globe–Horn Book Award for nonfiction, Warren relates the story of the Children's Aid Society's efforts to resettle orphaned city children in the Midwest beginning in the 1850s and ending in 1929. This information is grounded in the story of one boy, Lee Nailling, who experienced two difficult placements before he finally found a loving home with his third. His efforts to stay with his younger brother and to find his other siblings are heartbreaking. Lee's story makes the information about the orphan trains all the more poignant and compelling. Warren's *We Rode the Orphan Trains* extends Lee Nailling's perspective through interviews with eight adults about their childhood experiences and the long-lasting results of being sent on the orphan trains. Warren's *Pioneer Girl: Growing Up on the Prairie* tells the story of Grace McCance Synder, who grew up in Nebraska in the late 1800s. Warren based the story on Snyder's memoirs, and added information on settler life from additional sources. The book makes a wonderful companion to Laura Ingalls Wilder's Little House books and to William Anderson's *Laura Ingalls Wilder: A Biography*, and *Laura's Album: A Remembrance Scrapbook of Laura Ingalls Wilder*.

Biographical works about real young people in history can provide a limited but interesting view of famous figures who were close to them. Barbara Brenner's *On* the Frontier with Mr. Audubon is technically a partial biography of apprentice painter Joseph Mason. As a young teenager he accompanied John James Audubon on an expedition down the Mississippi River to collect and make life drawings of birds. Mason painted some of the backgrounds for Audubon's *Birds of America*, although his name did not appear on the finished paintings. Brenner used Audubon's diary to reconstruct the activities of their trip, then recreated the story as a journal that the apprentice might have kept, focusing on Audubon's obsession with his work.

Ruud van der Rol and Rian Verhoeven have produced an unusual form of biography in *Anne Frank beyond the Diary: A Photographic Remembrance*. The authors, both staff members of the Anne Frank House in Amsterdam, have gathered together a variety of materials including photographs from Otto Frank's widow, Elfriede, and Miep Gies, the woman who helped hide the Frank family. In this powerful photobiography, captioned photographs provide a brief introduction to Anne's childhood before the war and events surrounding Hitler's rise, but the book concentrates mainly on the days following Anne's thirteenth birthday and the gift of her diary. Interspersed with explanatory narrative, the family photographs, maps, diagrams, journal excerpts, and interviews broaden the context for Anne's diary and help readers visualize the setting for her brief life. This documentation helps deepen the power of Anne's words and further strengthens her memory.

Complete Biographies

Complete biography spans the subject's lifetime. It can be relatively simple or difficult, authentic or fictionalized, but the reader should expect a view that has some depth, some balance, some sense of perspective. Among types of biographies, this category has traditionally been the largest, although in recent years trends have favored other kinds of presentations.

Russell Freedman's many books are excellent examples of biographies that are complete and authentic. In Freedman's *Franklin Delano Roosevelt* the inherent drama of the subject, the clarity of the writing, and the generous use of photographs all contribute to the book's appeal for readers age 10 and up. This fine biography sketches out Roosevelt's major achievements as a politician and statesman, but its real strength lies in the detailed information it provides about his personal life. Freedman probes the façade of a man who managed to be a very private person in spite of having the very public job of being president of the United States. Students are fascinated by the lengths to which Roosevelt went in order to camouflage his paralysis. He was hardly ever photographed in a wheelchair, but Freedman does provide one such picture. Freedman's *Eleanor Roosevelt* is a wonderful companion book. By highlighting Eleanor's insecurities, as well as her great accomplishments, Freedman presents

an inspiring portrait for children awash in modern-day media blitzes that seem to worship glamour and triviality over courage and inner strength. Freedman's *Lincoln: A Photobiography* was groundbreaking in the use of archival photographs not just to break up and decorate the text but to seriously extend the reader's understanding of the subject. Yet the text stands as an accomplishment in its own right as a comprehensive, insightful, and readable account of a complex person living in a complicated time. It is very difficult to bring fresh perspective, as Freedman has done, to a story that has been told so often.

Some of Jean Fritz's picture-book biographies could be classified as complete because they deal with the subject's entire life span, but she has also written longer books about American figures, such as James Madison in *The Great Little Madison*, Theodore Roosevelt in *Bully for You, Teddy Roosevelt!* and General Thomas J. Jackson in *Stonewall*. All three books deal with complex characters in an evenhanded way. In *Stonewall*, for instance, Fritz contrasts the general's heroic Civil War battlefield behavior against his personal idiosyncrasies. The man who kept his line "standing like a stone wall" at Manassas prescribed unusual diets for himself (stale bread and lean meat, or lemons to suck) and lived by arbitrary, self-imposed rules for posture, prayer, and every other form of human conduct. In *Harriet Beecher Stowe and the Beecher Preachers* and *You Want Women to Vote, Lizzie Stanton?* Fritz turns her talents to two important female subjects. Both of these women were born into ages that expected little of them, and both rose above these limitations to contribute to the fight for human rights and women's rights. In all her books Fritz gives us authentic narrative enlivened by personal observations and quotes from contemporaries. Her lists of sources and bibliographies demonstrate her high standards for careful scholarship as well as vivid writing.

The increased interest in biographies of women can be seen in many other fine books. Polly Schoyer Brooks's *Cleopatra* is a well-written and vivid biography of one of the most famous women of the ancient world. Here Cleopatra's fascinating life story is presented in the context of the Roman conquest for control of Egypt and the Mediterranean region. Russell Freedman has turned his talented pen to many female subjects in such books as *Eleanor Roosevelt, Martha Graham: A Dancer's Life,* and *Babe Didrikson Zaharias*. Patricia McKissack and Frederick McKissack's *Sojourner Truth* is a wonderfully complete addition to the many picture-book biographies of this courageous crusader against slavery and prejudice. Dennis Brindell Fradin and Judith Bloom Fradin tell the story of a less well-known worker for civil rights in *Ida B. Wells: Mother of the Civil Rights Movement.* Doris Faber's *Calamity Jane* and Sue Macy's *Bull's Eye: A Photobiography of Annie Oakley* provide a look at two legendary women of the nineteenth-century West. Elaine Landau's *Heroine of the Titanic: The Real Unsinkable Molly Brown* extends beyond the well-known story of Molly's heroic actions aboard the *Titanic* to describe her humble beginnings and her life-long dedication to social issues. Two books about Helen Keller, Joan Dash's *The World at her Fingertips* and Laurie Lawlor's *Helen Keller: Rebellious Spirit*, provide in-depth portraits of Helen that will take readers beyond the usual idealization of Keller's life. In all these books, through scrupulous research and captivating narration, the authors manage to tackle larger-than-life heroines and turn them into real people without diminishing the significance of their achievements.

Natalie S. Bober's *Abigail Adams: Witness to a Revolution* is as fascinating for its inside look at a critical period of American history as it is for its portrait of an intelligent and independent woman who took very seriously her role as loving wife and mother. Using Adams's letters as her main source (over a thousand of them remain), Bober creates a compelling voice for this extraordinary woman and brings the years of America's beginnings to life. Becoming immersed in this thorough biography is like being a long-term guest in Abigail's home. Rather than being put off by its length, older children will close the book and return to their own time only with the greatest reluctance. Set in the same time period, *The Ingenious Mr. Peale: Patriot, Painter, and Man of Science* by Janet Wilson is a wonderful companion book. Both volumes paint a vivid portrait of eighteenth-century life and men and women who were actively involved with a wide range of interests and issues.

Elizabeth Partridge has written two compelling biographies about important artists whose work brought the world's attention to the suffering of poor Americans during the Great Depression. Partridge's excellent *Restless Spirit: The Life and Work of Dorothea Lange* is made all the more fascinating by the author's personal memories of Lange; her father, Ron Partridge, was Lange's assistant, and Lange was a close family friend until her death. This photobiography is also a history of major social issues of the first half of the twentieth century as we follow Lange from the migrant camps in the Depression to the Jim Crow South, to the Japanese internment camps, and to California shipbuilding factories staffed mainly by women during World War II. Lange's commitment to people rather than to pretty pictures is as evident through her moving photographs as through Partridge's words. Partridge continues her exploration of these episodes in America's past in *This Land Was Made for You and Me: The Life and Songs of Woody Guthrie*. Woody Guthrie was certainly never as disciplined as Lange nor as well educated, but his life story could be that of one of the Okies that Lange photographed. Born into a hardscrabble Oklahoma family, his young life was marked by calamity and tragedy. Even before he was born, his mother Nora had begun to act strangely, her behavior the early signs of Huntington's disease, which was largely unknown at the time. His parents' first house was destroyed in a fire that townspeople suspected was set by Nora, and when Woody was seven, his older sister Clara died in a fire that Nora may have set. In 1927 Nora did pour kerosene on Woody's father, Charley, and set him ablaze. Charley survived, but in terrible condition, and Nora was committed to an asylum. These early tragedies would come full circle when Woody's beloved first daughter, Cathie, died in a fire, and he, too, was diagnosed with Huntington's disease. Partridge's book is about far more than these dreadful events, however. Guthrie's continuing misfortunes as well as his illness may help explain his problems with alcohol, his arrests for vagrancy, and his irresponsible behavior toward his own family. But Woody's life is also recalled and celebrated here for his achievements as a self-taught musician who became the spokesperson for millions of the disenfranchised, the workers, the jobless, and the homeless who needed his songs to persevere during a dark time in America's history. Partridge's frank *John Lennon: All I Want Is the Truth* is for mature readers, but like her other biographies, it is as fascinating a portrait of an American era as it is of an individual.

Historian Albert Marrin has chosen well-known figures and documents their times as well as their lives. In *The Sea King* Marrin explores the world of Sir Francis Drake and provides a highly readable account of a significant historical period and a man who was a central figure in critically important events. Marrin weaves the same attention to detail and good storytelling into other books such as *George Washington and the Founding of a Nation*, *Unconditional Surrender: U. S. Grant and the Civil War*, and *Terror of the Spanish Main: Henry Morgan and His Buccaneers*. These books are illustrated with maps and reproductions of primary source materials and include footnotes and a list of additional readings.

Children, particularly those who are avid readers or writers, will enjoy reading about well-known creators of favorite books. Beverly Gherman, who has written fine biographies of Agnes DeMille and Georgia O'Keeffe for older readers, uncovers the essence of the gentle and shy creator of *Charlotte's Web* in *E. B. White: Some Writer*.

Charles D. Cohen has written a delightful biography of Dr. Seuss (Theodore Geisel) in *The Seuss, the Whole Seuss, and Nothing but the Seuss.* Cohen, a collector of Seuss memorabilia, has provided unmatched visual material that takes readers far beyond Seuss's children's books to provide an understanding of the cultural and historical background underlying Seuss's life. In *Ezra Jack Keats: A Biography with Illustrations,* Dean Engel and Florence B. Freedman have used interviews with Ezra Jack Keats and Keats's essays to form the basis of their loving portrait of this children's author and illustrator, who overcame a variety of obstacles to create a world of pleasure for children. Many of Keats's own drawings are used to illustrate his life and to make the connections between his own experiences and those of his characters. Barbara Elleman, former editor of *Book Links* magazine, has written two wonderful biographies of picture-book illustrators, *Tomie dePaola: His Art and His Stories* and *Virginia Lee Burton: A Life in Art.* Although both books were aimed at adult audiences, Elleman's lively style of writing, the elegant book design, and the copious reproductions of each artist's work will certainly appeal to older children, too.

In Audrey Osofsky's *Free to Dream: The Making of a Poet: Langston Hughes* we come to know this gentle man through excerpts from his poems and wonderful photographs as well as through Osofsky's writing. Older readers familiar with Walt Whitman's poetry will enjoy Catherine Reef's *Walt Whitman,* an honest portrayal of this great American poet. The biography includes mention of his homosexuality and focuses on Whitman's generous spirit and his democratic idealism. Accounts of his life, particularly his involvement in the Civil War as a battlefield nurse, are interspersed with quotes from his poetry and enlivened by photographs of Whitman's times and his works. This same audience will also benefit from the broad perspective presented in Clinton Cox's *Mark Twain.* The subtitle of this book is, appropriately, *America's Humorist, Dreamer, Prophet.* Told in lively prose, Cox's biography is filled with quotes from Twain's writing. In addition we come to see him not merely as a fine storyteller but also as someone haunted by the injustices of racism and committed to the rights of the common people.

Jan Greenberg and Sandra Jordan have contributed many books that illuminate the world of twentieth-century art, including the picture-book biography of Jackson Pollock, *Action Jackson,* and photobiographies of Frank O. Gehry, Andy Warhol, and Chuck Close. In *Vincent van Gogh: Portrait of an Artist* Greenberg and Jordan turn to the late nineteenth century and provide a complete biography of this fragile and frustrating man. This longer work, with an inset of full-color reproductions of van Gogh's work, is a moving portrayal of the troubled genius's life. Vincent's unpredictability, his difficulties with relationships, and his disregard for convention are frankly discussed. However, Vincent's passion for painting and his musings on his work are also detailed, providing remarkable insights into the mind of this great

artist. The book was named a 2002 Honor book by the Robert F. Sibert Informational Book Award committee. Frequently biographers choose subjects who are credited with unique achievements, whatever their field. Kathleen Krull, who has written many notable picture-book biographies for children, has created a lively look at the life of *Leonardo da Vinci* with illustrations by Boris Kulikov. Unlike authors of many of the other books about Leonardo, Krull focuses on Leonardo's contributions to scientific thinking and experimentation. Other great thinkers of the past are profiled by M. D. Usher in *Wise Guy: The Life and Philosophy of Socrates* and by Philip Steele in *Galileo: The Genius Who Faced the Inquisition.* Most authors would be dubious about writing an interesting biography for children about a mathematician, but Jean Lee Latham was challenged. She studied mathematics, astronomy, oceanography, and seamanship. Then she went to Boston and Salem to talk with descendants of Nathaniel Bowditch and to do research on the geographical and maritime backgrounds of her story. The result of all this

Leonardo da Vinci by Kathleen Krull focuses on this genius's contributions to scientific thinking and experimentation.
"Jacket illustration" copyright © 2005 by Boris Kulikov from *Leonardo da Vinci* by Kathleen Krull. Used by permission of Viking Penguin, a division of Penguin Young Readers Group, a Member of Penguin Group (USA) Inc., 345 Hudson St., New York, NY 10014. All rights reserved.

painstaking preparation was the Newbery Medal winner *Carry On, Mr. Bowditch,* the amazing story of Nat Bowditch, who had little chance for schooling but mastered the secrets of navigation and wrote a textbook that was used for more than a hundred years.

Collective Biographies

Many children looking for biographical information want brief material about specific people or about specific endeavors. Many collective biographies have been published to meet this need. In scope and difficulty they run the gamut—some have one-paragraph sketches of many subjects, others have long essays on just a few. Like other books, collective biographies must be judged on more than title and appearance.

Russell Freedman's *The Wright Brothers: How They Invented the Airplane* is an outstanding biography of two people whose lives and work were so closely intertwined that it would be difficult to choose just one to write about. Using archival photographs as he has done in other books, Freedman reconstructs the engrossing story that led to Kitty Hawk and many years of achievement thereafter. In the process he illuminates the character and commitment of Wilbur Wright and Orville Wright.

Collective biographies are an ideal format for highlighting the contributions of more ordinary people whose lives might not bring with them the documentation that lends itself to the writing of a full biography. Penny Colman's *Adventurous Women: Eight True Stories about Women Who Made a Difference* looks at eight women from diverse cultures, some whose names will be familiar and some who will be less well known to readers. Colman explains,

> Adventures are about being bold, about defying ways of thinking and behaving, about taking risks, going beyond the boundaries, the limitations, about overcoming the obstacles, about daring to be different. (Author's note)

In choosing such women as Louise Boyd, who braved physical challenges, and Mary McLeod Bethune, whose challenges were more cerebral, Colman shows that there are many ways "to live a passionate and productive and adventurous life."

Collective biographies seldom deal with subjects whose stories can be woven together as smoothly as *Adventurous Women* or *The Wright Brothers.* Most have many brief entries about individuals whose interests or accomplishments are similar. Women have not been slighted in such collections and books. Andrea Davis Pinkney received a Coretta Scott King Honor award for her collective biography of ten outstanding African American women in *Let It Shine: Stories of Black Women Freedom Fighters.* Illustrated with glowing paintings by Stephen Alcorn, the book covers historical figures such as Sojourner Truth and twentieth-century heroines such as Shirley Chisholm and Rosa Parks. Cynthia Chin-Lee's

Amelia to Zora: Twenty-Six Women Who Changed the World is an international look at women who have made contributions to their cultures and to the wider world. Presenting her subjects in an ABC format, Chin-Lee includes Quah Ah, a Puebla Indian painter who defied tradition in the 1930s, and Chen Xiefen, who supported women's education in early-twentieth-century China. *Visions: Stories about Women Artists* and *In Real Life: Six Women Photographers,* both by Leslie Sills, are excellent introductions to the stories of women who excelled in the arts. These books feature names that many children will recognize, but they also highlight the achievements of less well-known figures from diverse cultures. These include artists Mary Frank and Betye Saar and photographers Imogene Cunningham and Lola Alvarez Bravo.

In Search of the Spirit, by Sheila Hamanaka and Ayano Ohmi, is a beautifully presented photo essay about six Japanese artisans designated as living national treasures for their work. A brief life history is given for each artist, and clear photographs show how each of the men works. The book also provides directions for silk painting, bamboo weaving, Noh movements, and pottery making. Kathleen Krull and Kathryn Hewitt have collaborated on highly entertaining collections of anecdotes about famous politicians, athletes, artists, writers, and musicians. In *Lives of the Artists: Masterpieces, Messes (and What the Neighbors Thought)* Kathe Kollwitz is shown as a passionate antiwar activist who cared little about her appearance. Artist Marcel Duchamp had a wonderful sense of humor, ate spaghetti with butter and cheese for dinner every night, and let his apartment accumulate several inches of dust to use in his paintings. Although these aren't necessarily the facts found in the usual reference books, they help to highlight the uniqueness of the artist. These books also prove to children that heroes and heroines are not always perfect and sometimes are perfectly awful. The visual portraits by Kathryn Hewitt provide summaries of each artist's work and life.

Pat Cummings has provided similar insights into the lives of illustrators of children's books in three volumes of *Talking with Artists.* Illustrators such as Peter Sis, Paul O. Zelinsky, Floyd Cooper, Lois Ehlert, Denise Fleming, Brian Pinkney, and Vera B. Williams respond to Cummings's questions and reflect upon their current work as well as their childhood memories. Each profile is accompanied by examples of the artist's childhood art and recent work. In her *Talking with Adventurers,* Cummings interviews such risk takers as ethologist Jane Goodall, underwater photographer David Doubilet, and rainforest ecologist Christina Allen. Leonard Marcus provides profiles of children's book authors and illustrators in several engaging volumes, among them, *Ways of Telling: Conversations on the Art of the Picture Book* and *Side by Side: Five Favorite Picture-Book Teams Go to Work.* Marcus's interviews are less biographical than they are sketches of authors and illustrators and of how they approach their work. Marcus's keen understanding of the field of children's literature allows him to draw out wonderful insights from his subjects.

In *Americans Who Tell the Truth* artist Robert Shetterly takes an unusual approach to collective biography. Shetterly has created fifty portraits of Americans of many cultures, past and present, male and female, old and young, who exemplify the qualities of a decent, just, and caring society. Each portrait is accompanied by a quote from the subject, and brief biographical information on each can be found at the end of the book.

AUTOBIOGRAPHIES AND MEMOIRS

Life stories are often recalled and written down by the subjects themselves, as autobiographies or memoirs. Some children's books based on autobiographical material have been discussed earlier in Chapter 10 as historical fiction. Autobiography has advantages and disadvantages similar to those of nonfiction books of eyewitness history—the warmth and immediacy of personal detail, but a necessarily limited perspective. The criterion of objectivity is reversed here; it is the very subjectivity of this sort of biography that has value. But children do need to be aware of the inherent bias in autobiographies, and they can be encouraged to look to other sources for balance.

Four stories of deprivation and courage are especially powerful for being told in the first person. *Anne Frank: The Diary of a Young Girl* is the classic story of hiding from the Nazis. This is a candid and open account of the changes wrought upon eight people who hid for two years in a secret annex of an office building in Amsterdam and were ultimately found and imprisoned by the Nazis. Anne's diary reveals the thoughts of a sensitive adolescent growing up under extraordinary conditions. No one who lived in the annex survived the war except Anne's father. He returned to their hiding place and found Anne's diary. When it was published, it became an immediate best-seller and was translated into many languages. Its popularity continues today, an appropriate tribute to Anne Frank's amazing spirit.

Several Holocaust survivors have written moving memoirs, including Anita Lobel's story of her childhood in Nazi-occupied Poland, *No Pretty Pictures: A Child of War* (which was discussed in Chapter 10). Laura Hillman has written a vivid and painful book for older adolescents, *I Plant You a Lilac Tree: A Memoir of a Schindler's List Survivor*. Here Hillman, born Hannalore, relates her experiences in Nazi concentration camps. In her fifties, Esther Nisenthal Krintiz, also a survivor of the Holocaust in Poland, stitched thirty-six pieces of fabric art as a way of remembering her experiences. After her death, her daughter Bernice Steinhardt collected the tapestries and wrote her own versions of her mother's stories to accompany them. The result is the beautiful *Memories of Sur-*

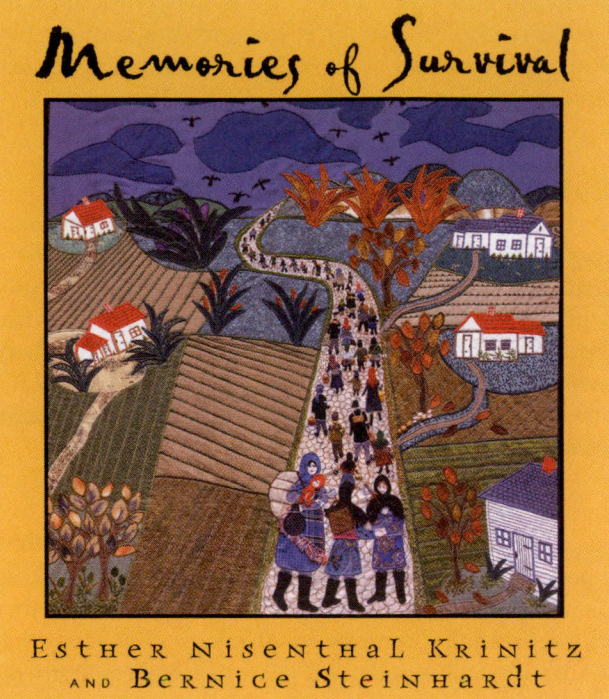

Esther Nisenthal Krinitz created beautiful fabric art to honor the Holocaust victims and remember her own experiences in *Memories of Survival. Cover of Memories of Survival* by Esther Nisenthal Krinitz and Bernice Steinhardt. Copyright © 2005 by Esther Nisenthal Krinitz and Bernice Steinhardt. Reprinted by permission of Hyperion Books for Children.

vival. Isaac Millman, who has written and illustrated such books as *Moses Goes to a Concert,* was finally able to face his own painful childhood memories of World War II in *Hidden Child.* Millman's illustrations, watercolor-and-pencil collages, convey a unique and painful vision of one child's journey through the nightmare of the Holocaust.

Mexican poet Juan Felipe Herrera has written two lovely bilingual picture-book memoirs about growing up as the child of migrant farm workers in California. *Calling the Doves/El canto de las palomas,* illustrated by Elly Simmons, concentrates on his first eight years traveling with his parents around the state. *The Upside Down Boy/ El niño de cabeza,* illustrated by Elizabeth Gómez, recalls his first days in school. Both books are written in lyrical prose and celebrate the love of family and the sensitivity to his surroundings that must have contributed to Herrera's success as a poet. *Leon's Story,* by Leon Tillage, is a moving memoir told by an African American man who grew up as a sharecropper's son in the Jim Crow South. Tillage's bravery in the face of lynchings and other horrific occurrences makes this an extraordinary story of courage and endurance. *Red Scarf Girl* is Ji-li Jiang's memoir of growing up in China during the Cultural Revolution. In it she relates the powerful story of her coming of age, as well as her coming of understanding. As the Red

Guards gain momentum and members of her family are accused of being reactionaries and worse, we see her change from a fervent believer in the dogma of Chairman Mao to a revolutionary of a different sort. She writes:

> Once my life had been defined by my goals, to be a dadui-zhang [student chairman of her elementary school], to participate in the exhibition, to be a Red Guard. Now my life was defined by my responsibilities. I had promised to take care of my family, and I would renew that promise everyday. I could not give up or withdraw, no matter how hard life became. I would hide my tears and my fear for Mom and Grandma's sake. It was my turn to take care of them. (p. 263)

These are noble sentiments coming from any young person. They are a remarkable tribute to the human spirit coming from a 14-year-old who had endured three years of a terror campaign. Two books provide interesting points of comparison to *Red Scarf Girl*. Ange Zhang's *Red Land, Yellow River* is a striking picture-book memoir of his experiences during the Cultural Revolution. Chun Yu's *Little Green: Growing Up during the Cultural Revolution* is a novel in verse that details her years living with her grandmother after both her parents were sent away for re-education.

Autobiographies by creators of children's books provide an easy introduction to this specialized form of writing. The fine photobiographies in the Meet the Author series, published by Richard C. Owen, show each author at home with family and pets; clear maps locate where they live. Each author tells something about his or her childhood and provides personal insights into the writing process. Included in the series are Laura J. Numeroff's *If You Give an Author a Pencil*, Eve Bunting's *Once Upon a Time*, Lee Bennett Hopkins's *The Writing Bug*, Margaret Mahy's *My Mysterious World*, Rafe Martin's *A Storyteller's Story*, and Cynthia Rylant's *Best Wishes*.

Other popular writers provide longer life stories. In *The Abracadabra Kid: A Writer's Life*, Sid Fleischman recalls his desire to be a magician, his service in World War II, and his successful career as a Hollywood screenwriter before he found that his real talent and passion were for writing children's books. In Lois Lowry's *Looking Back: A Book of Memories* the author recalls everyday incidents and important milestones in her life. Each chapter is introduced by a photograph. Reading the book is like having an intimate chat with Lowry over the pages of a photo album. Roald Dahl in *Boy: Tales of Childhood* recounts stories of his early family life and incidents from his boarding school days, including one that became a scene in one of his own novels. Some authors focus on their work, explaining the process of writing a book and adding advice for students who dream of writing for publication. *How I Came to Be a Writer* by Phyllis Reynolds Naylor reveals the same wit as her realistic novels.

Beverly Cleary's memoir *A Girl from Yamhill: A Memoir* speaks to adults who have read her books, as well as to older students. Careful readers will catch many glimpses of her popular character Ramona Quimby in Cleary's own childhood. The portrayal of her difficult relationship with her mother is particularly good for generating discussion. Cleary's story of her college years and her adult life is told in *My Own Two Feet*.

As we saw with Jean Fritz's *Homesick*, discussed on page 634, some autobiographies or memoirs might be classified as fictionalized. Tomie dePaola's wonderful series of books such as *26 Fairmont Avenue, What a Year!* and *Things Will Never Be the Same* are based on his childhood but are told in the manner of good fiction. Each episodic chapter is characterized by the same lively and humorous style of storytelling we find in dePaola's many picture storybooks.

Teaching Resources: "Author Autobiographies" lists the titles of a few of the memoirs by authors for children. Most of the books for primary grades are not complete autobiographies but are based on a single incident.

Other memoirs in the form of personal journals and letters can bring the voices of times past vividly to life. Milton Meltzer has based several fine nonfiction books, such as *The American Revolutionaries: A History in Their Own Words*, on such primary sources. In *Lincoln: In His Own Words* Meltzer uses a similar technique, framing selections from Lincoln's writings and speeches with commentary that explains the progression of his ideas in the context of his time. Stephen Alcorn's handsome linocut illustrations capture Lincoln's life through compelling visual symbols. Scratchboard illustrations by Michael McCurdy frame a short version of Frederick Douglass's words in *Escape from Slavery: The Boyhood of Frederick Douglass in His Own Words*. McCurdy's illustrations also lend dignity to Lillian Schisse's adaptation of Amelia Knight's *The Way West: Journal of a Pioneer Woman*. Joseph Plumb Martin's *Yankee Doodle Boy*, edited by George Scheer, is the lively firsthand account of a 15-year-old Connecticut farmer who served with Washington's Continental army. Though the somewhat archaic speech patterns of previous centuries require some editing, these memoirs do not lose their powerful effect for modern audiences under the skillful handling of Meltzer, Schisse, and Scheer.

Biographies of all types give children a glimpse into other lives, other places, other times. The best of them combine accurate information and fine writing in a context that children enjoy—the story that really happened. Good biographies serve to put facts into a frame of human feeling. Children can come to know about historical events or contemporary figures from textbooks, but literature that touches this content will bring them a different quality of knowing—more intimate and more memorable. All children deserve to have such books as part of their experience.

Author Autobiographies

 Visit the Online Learning Center at **www.mhhe.com/kiefer9e** for a printable version of this list.

Author	Title	Grade Level
Alma Flor Ada	*Under the Royal Palms: A Childhood in Cuba*	3–6
	Where the Flame Tree Blooms	
Stan and Jan Berenstain	*Down a Sunny Dirt Road: An Autobiography*	4 and up
Beverly Cleary	*A Girl from Yamhill: A Memoir*	5 and up
Donald Crews	*Bigmama's*	1–4
Roald Dahl	*Boy: Tales of Childhood*	5 and up
Tomie dePaola	*26 Fairmont Avenue*	1–4
Sid Fleischman	*The Abracadabra Kid: A Writer's Life*	5 and up
Ralph Fletcher	*Mansfield Dreams*	4–6
Michael Foreman	*War Boy: A Country Childhood*	4–6
Jean Fritz	*Homesick: My Own Story*	5 and up
Patricia Reilly Giff	*Don't Tell the Girls: A Family Memoir*	4–6
Juan Felipe Herrera	*The Upside Down Boy/El niño de cabeza*	1–4
Dick King-Smith	*Chewing the Cud*	5 and up
Helen Lester	*Author: A True Story*	1–4
Jean Little	*Little by Little: A Writer's Education*	5 and up
Walter Dean Myers	*Bad Boy*	6 and up
Phyllis Reynolds Naylor	*How I Came to Be a Writer*	5 and up
Gary Paulsen	*Woodsong*	5 and up
Bill Peet	*Bill Peet: An Autobiography*	3 and up
Jerry Spinelli	*Knots in My Yo-Yo String*	4–7
James Stevenson	*Higher on the Door*	2–5
	When I Was Nine	2–5
Laurence Yep	*The Lost Garden*	5 and up

Biography

Reading biography presents children with challenges that are similar to those of reading nonfiction. To become critical readers of biography they must ask questions of the text, such as "Are all the facts about this person's life presented? Does this person seem impossibly good or talented or is the subject presented as a complex human being?" Because there are many fictionalized biographies available, children should be encouraged to think about what is really factual in a book and what is made up and to ask questions like "Does the author provide notes that help readers to know what is true?" Comparing biographies of the same person can be a useful exercise in critical reading. Such an activity can also help children focus on the style of each writer (and illustrator) and how the writing and illustrations affect their own understanding and enjoyment of the biography.

1. **Examining Biography Illustrations.** Gather several picture-book biographies or simplified biographies with many illustrations. What information appears in the pictures but not the text? How do the illustrations help create focus and characterization?
2. **Evaluating Biographies through Comparison.** Compare picture-book biographies about an histori-

cal figure such as Christopher Columbus or Mary Anning. What events and details from the person's life does each author include? How can you evaluate the accuracy of the information given? Do you find any contradictions across books?

3. **Comparing Biographies.** Select several biographies of one subject, such as Eleanor Roosevelt. Make a chart to compare information, omissions, author's point of view, and the extent of documentation. Consider the ways a broader range of information makes you a more discriminating reader.
4. **Writing a Biography.** Choose someone from your own life and write that person's biography. Try to use a variety of sources including interviews, letters and photographs, maps, and newspaper archives.

Go to the Online Learning Center at **www .mhhe.com/kiefer9e** or your Resources CD-ROM to find these additional classroom activities:

5. **Videos and Computers**
6. **Author Studies**
7. **Conversations with the Past and Present**

Chapter Review

 Go to the Online Learning Center at **www.mhhe.com/kiefer9e** or your Resources CD-ROM to take chapter quizzes, practice with key terms, and review the chapter.

Explorations

1. Ask children to list the people they would like to read about. How many of their selections are contemporary living figures, and how many are historical? How do their preferences match library holdings?

2. Search the database for biographies. Make a checklist of how many biographies are about men, how many about women. What people have been the subject of many biographies? few biographies? one biography? What contemporary figures are presented in these biographies?

Web Links

 Go to the Online Learning Center at **www .mhhe.com/kiefer9e** to find links to the following children's literature Web sites:

The Biographical Dictionary

Biographies

Distinguished Women Past and Present

Kay Vandergrift's Author Biography and Autobiography Page

On-Lion for Kids: People and Places

The Public Broadcasting Service's History Page

White House Kids

Related Readings

Fritz, Jean. "The Very Truth." In *Celebrating Children's Books,* ed. Betsy Hearne and Marilyn Kaye, pp. 81–86. New York: Lothrop, Lee & Shepard, 1981.

> One of the very best writers of juvenile biography addresses the issue of censorship and discusses the necessity for telling all the truth.

The Lion and the Unicorn 4, no. 1 (summer 1980).

> This entire issue is devoted to biography for young people. Of special interest are Elizabeth Segel's article about a biography of Beatrix Potter, Leonard Marcus's comments on picture-book biographies for children, and an interview with Milton Meltzer by Geraldine DeLuca and Roni Natov.

Meltzer, Milton. "Selective Forgetfulness: Christopher Columbus Reconsidered." *New Advocate* 5 (winter 1992): 1–9.

> A writer of fine complete biographies discusses the dark side of the story of Columbus, namely, his treatment of Indians. He quotes letters and Columbus's own journal as documentation. These are included in his biography Columbus and the World Around Him (Franklin Watts, 1990).

Children's Literature

 Go to the Children's Literature Database on your Resources CD-ROM for a searchable listing of these and other children's literature titles.

Ada, Alma Flor. *Under Royal Palms: A Childhood in Cuba.* Atheneum, 1998.

———. *Where the Flame Tree Blooms.* Atheneum, 1994.

Adler, David A. *George Washington: An Illustrated Biography.* Holiday, 2004.

———. *A Picture Book of Sojourner Truth.* Illustrated by Gershom Griffith. Holiday, 1994.

Adoff, Arnold. *Malcolm X.* Illustrated by John Wilson. Harper Trophy, 1988 [1970].

Aldrin, Buzz. *Reaching for the Moon*. Illustrated by Wendell Minor. HarperCollins, 2005.

Aliki [Aliki Brandenberg]. *Fossils Tell of Long Ago*. HarperCollins, 1990.

———. *William Shakespeare and the Globe*. HarperCollins, 1999.

Allen, Thomas B. *George Washington, Spymaster: How the Americans Outspied the British and Won the Revolutionary War*. National Geographic, 2004.

Anderson, M. T. *Handel, Who Knew What He Liked*. Illustrated by Kevin Hawkes. Candlewick, 2001.

Anderson, William. *Laura Ingalls Wilder: A Biography*. HarperCollins, 1992.

———. *Laura's Album: A Remembrance Scrapbook of Laura Ingalls Wilder*. HarperCollins, 1998.

Andrews-Goebel, Nancy. *The Pot That Juan Built*. Illustrated by David Diaz. Lee, 2002.

Anholt, Laurence. *Stone Girl, Bone Girl*. Illustrated by Sheila Moxley. Orchard, 1999.

Appelt, Kathi, and Jeanne Cannella Schmitzer. *Down Cut Shin Creek: The Pack Horse Librarians of Kentucky*. HarperCollins, 2001.

Atkins, Jeannine. *Mary Anning and the Sea Dragon*. Illustrated by Michael Dooling. Farrar, 1999.

Barbour, Karen. *Mr. Williams*. Holt, 2005.

Berenstain, Stan, and Jan Berenstain. *Down a Sunny Dirt Road: An Autobiography*. Random, 2002.

Bernier-Grand, Carmen T. *César: ¡Sí, Se Puede! Yes, We Can!* Illustrated by David Diaz. Cavendish, 2005.

Blumberg, Rhoda. *Shipwrecked!: The True Adventures of a Japanese Boy*. HarperCollins, 2001.

———. *York's Adventures with Lewis and Clark: An African American's Part in the Great Expedition*. HarperCollins, 2004.

Bober, Natalie S. *Abigail Adams: Witness to a Revolution*. Atheneum, 1995.

Bolden, Tonya. *Maritcha: A Nineteenth Century American Girl*. Abrams, 2005.

Brenner, Barbara. *On the Frontier with Mr. Audubon*. Coward, 1977.

Brighton, Catherine. *The Fossil Girl: Mary Anning's Dinosaur Discovery*. Millbrook, 1999.

———. *Mozart: Scenes from the Childhood of the Great Composer*. Doubleday, 1990.

Brooks, Polly Schoyer. *Cleopatra*. HarperCollins, 1995.

Brown, Don. *Across a Dark and Wide Sea*. Houghton, 2002.

———. *Far Beyond the Garden Gate: Alexandra David-Neel's Journey to Lhasa*. Houghton, 2002.

———. *Odd Boy Out: Young Albert Einstein*. Houghton, 2004.

———. *Rare Treasure: Mary Anning and Her Remarkable Discoveries*. Houghton, 1999.

———. *Uncommon Traveler: Mary Kingsley in Africa*. Houghton, 2000.

Bruchac, Joseph. *Bowman's Store: A Journey to Myself*. Dial, 1997.

———. *A Boy Called Slow: The True Story of Sitting Bull*. Illustrated by Rocco Baviera. Philomel, 1995.

Bunting, Eve. *Once Upon a Time*. Owen, 1995.

Burchard, Peter. *Charlotte Forten: A Black Teacher in the Civil War*. Crown, 1995.

Burleigh, Robert. *Seurat and La Grande Jatte: Connecting the Dots*. Abrams, 2005.

———. *Toulouse-Lautrec: The Moulin Rouge and the City of Light*. Abrams, 2005.

Chambers, Veronica. *Celia Cruz, Queen of Salsa*. Illustrated by Julie Maren. Dial, 2005.

Chin-Lee, Cynthia. *Amelia to Zora: Twenty-Six Women Who Changed the World*. Charlesbridge, 2005.

Clayton, Ed. *Martin Luther King: The Peaceful Warrior*. Illustrated by David Hodges. Minstrel, 1986 [1968].

Cleary, Beverly. *A Girl from Yamhill: A Memoir*. Morrow, 1988.

———. *My Own Two Feet: A Memoir*. Morrow, 1995.

Cohen, Charles D. *The Seuss, the Whole Seuss, and Nothing but the Seuss*. Random, 2004.

Cohn, Amy L., and Suzy Schmidt. *Abraham Lincoln*. Illustrated by David Johnston. Scholastic, 2002.

Colman, Penny. *Adventurous Women: Eight True Stories about Women Who Made a Difference*. Holt, 2006.

Cooney, Barbara. *Eleanor*. Viking, 1996.

Cooper, Floyd. *Coming Home: From the Life of Langston Hughes*. Philomel, 1994.

Cooper, Ilene. *Jack: The Early Years of John F. Kennedy*. Dutton, 2003.

Cox, Clinton. *Mark Twain: America's Humorist, Dreamer, Prophet*. Scholastic, 1995.

Crews, Donald. *Bigmama's*. Greenwillow, 1991.

Cummings, Pat, ed. *Talking with Adventurers*. National Geographic, 1998.

———. *Talking with Artists*. Vol. 1. Bradbury, 1992.

———. *Talking with Artists*. Vol. 2. Simon, 1995.

———. *Talking with Artists*. Vol. 3. Bradbury, 1999.

Cummins, Julie. *Tomboy of the Air: Daredevil Blanche Stuart Scott*. HarperCollins, 2001.

Dahl, Roald. *Boy: Tales of Childhood*. Farrar, 1984.

Dash, Joan. *The World at Her Fingertips: The Story of Helen Keller*. Scholastic, 2001.

d'Aulaire, Ingri, and Edgar Parin d'Aulaire. *Abraham Lincoln*. Rev. ed. Doubleday, 1957.

Delano, Marfe Ferguson. *Genius: A Photobiography of Albert Einstein*. National Geographic, 2005.

Demi. *Mother Teresa*. Simon, 2004.

———. *Muhammad*. Simon, 2003.

dePaola, Tomie. *26 Fairmont Avenue*. Putnam, 1999.

———. *Things Will Never Be the Same*. Putnam, 2003.

———. *What a Year!* Putnam, 2002.

Dooling, Michael. *Young Thomas Edison*. Holiday, 2005.

Driscoll, Laura. *Sammy Sosa: He's the Man*. Illustrated by Ken Call. Grosset, 1999.

Duke, Kate. *Archaeologists Dig for Clues*. HarperCollins, 1997.

Edwards, Pamela Duncan. *The Bus Ride That Changed History: The Story of Rosa Parks*. Illustrated by Danny Shanahan. Houghton, 2005.

Elleman, Barbara. *Tomie dePaola: His Art and His Stories*. Putnam, 1999.

——. *Virginia Lee Burton: A Life in Art*. Houghton, 2002.

Engel, Dean, and Florence B. Freedman. *Ezra Jack Keats: A Biography with Illustrations*. Silver Moon, 1995.

Faber, Doris. *Calamity Jane: Her Life and Legend*. Houghton, 1992.

——. *Eleanor Roosevelt, First Lady of the World*. Illustrated by Donna Ruff. Viking, 1985.

Fleischman, Sid. *The Abracadabra Kid: A Writer's Life*. Greenwillow, 1996.

Fleming, Candace. *Ben Franklin's Almanac: Being a True Account of the Good Gentleman's Life*. Simon, 2003.

——. *Our Eleanor: A Scrapbook Look at Eleanor Roosevelt's Remarkable Life*. Simon, 2005.

Fletcher, Ralph. *Mansfield Dreams*. Holt, 2005.

Foreman, Michael. *War Boy: A Country Childhood*. Arcade, 1990.

Fradin, Dennis Brindell, and Judith Bloom Fradin. *Ida B. Wells: Mother of the Civil Rights Movement*. Clarion, 2000.

Frank, Anne. *Anne Frank: The Diary of a Young Girl*. Rev. ed. Translated by B. M. Mooyart. Introduction by Eleanor Roosevelt. Doubleday, 1967.

Freedman, Russell. *Babe Didrikson Zaharias*. Clarion, 1999.

——. *Eleanor Roosevelt: A Life of Discovery*. Clarion, 1993.

——. *Franklin Delano Roosevelt*. Clarion, 1990.

——. *Lincoln: A Photobiography*. Clarion, 1987.

——. *Martha Graham: A Dancer's Life*. Clarion, 1998.

——. *The Voice That Challenged a Nation: Marion Anderson and the Struggle for Equal Rights*. Clarion, 2004.

——. *The Wright Brothers: How They Invented the Airplane*. Holiday, 1991.

Frith, Margaret. *Who Was Thomas Alva Edison?* Illustrated by John O'Brien. Grosset, 2005.

Fritz, Jean. *And Then What Happened, Paul Revere?* Illustrated by Margot Tomes. Coward, 1973.

——. *Bully for You, Teddy Roosevelt!* Illustrated by Mike Wimmer. Putnam, 1991.

——. *Can't You Make Them Behave, King George?* Illustrated by Tomie dePaola. Coward, 1982.

——. *China Homecoming*. Putnam, 1985.

——. *The Great Little Madison*. Putnam, 1989.

——. *Harriet Beecher Stowe and the Beecher Preachers*. Putnam, 1994.

——. *Homesick: My Own Story*. Illustrated by Margot Tomes. Putnam, 1982.

——. *Stonewall*. Illustrated by Stephen Gammell. Putnam, 1979.

——. *Traitor: The Case of Benedict Arnold*. Putnam, 1981.

——. *What's the Big Idea, Ben Franklin?* Illustrated by Margot Tomes. Coward, 1982.

——. *Why Don't You Get a Horse, Sam Adams?* Illustrated by Trina Schart Hyman. Coward, 1982.

——. *Will You Sign Here, John Hancock?* Illustrated by Trina Schart Hyman. Coward, 1982.

——. *You Want Women to Vote, Lizzie Stanton?* Putnam, 1995.

Gherman, Beverly. *Agnes DeMille, Dancing Off the Earth*. Atheneum, 1990.

——. *E. B. White: Some Writer*. Atheneum, 1992.

——. *Georgia O' Keeffe: The "Wideness and Wonder" of Her World*. Atheneum, 1988.

Gibbons, Gail. *Owls*. Holiday, 2005.

——. *Penguins*. Holiday, 1998.

——. *Soaring with the Wind: The Bald Eagle*. Morrow, 1998.

Giblin, James Cross. *The Amazing Life of Benjamin Franklin*. Illustrated by Michael Dooling. Scholastic, 2000.

——. *Thomas Jefferson*. Illustrated by Michael Dooling. Scholastic, 1994.

Giff, Patricia Reilly. *Don't Tell the Girls: A Family Memoir*. Holiday, 2005.

Giovanni, Nikki. *Rosa*. Illustrated by Bryan Collier. Holt, 2005.

Goodall, John. *The Story of a Farm*. McElderry, 1989.

——. *The Story of a Main Street*. McElderry, 1987.

Greenberg, Jan, and Sandra Jordan. *Action Jackson*. Illustrated by Robert Andrew Parker. Roaring Brook, 2002.

——. *Andy Warhol: Prince of Pop*. Delacorte, 2004.

——. *Chuck Close, Up Close*. Delacorte, 1998.

——. *Frank O. Gehry: Outside In*. DK, 2000.

——. *Vincent van Gogh: Portrait of an Artist*. Delacorte, 2001.

Greenfield, Eloise. *Mary McLeod Bethune*. Illustrated by Jerry Pinkney. Crowell, 1993 [1977].

——. *Rosa Parks*. Illustrated by Gill Ashby. HarperCollins, 1995 [1973].

Gross, Ruth Belov. *True Stories about Abraham Lincoln*. Illustrated by Jill Kastner. Lothrop, 1989.

Gutelle, Andrew. *Tiger Woods*. Grosset, 2002.

Gutman, Dan. *Jackie Robinson and the Big Game*. Illustrated by Elaine Garvin. Simon, 2006.

Hamanaka, Sheila, and Ayano Ohmi. *In Search of the Spirit: The Living National Treasures of Japan*. Morrow, 1999.

Hamilton, Virginia. *Anthony Burns: The Defeat and Triumph of a Fugitive Slave*. Knopf, 1988.

Hansen, Joyce. *African Princesses: The Amazing Life of Africa's Royal Women*. Illustrated by Laurie McGraw. Hyperion, 2004.

Harness, Cheryl. *The Remarkable Ben Franklin*. National Geographic, 2005.

——. *The Revolutionary John Adams*. National Geographic, 2006.

Herrera, Juan Felipe. *Calling the Doves/El canto de las palomas*. Illustrated by Elly Simmons. Children's, 1995.

——. *The Upside Down Boy/El niño de cabeza*. Illustrated by Elizabeth Gómez. Children's, 2000.

Hesse, Karen. *The Young Hans Christian Andersen*. Illustrated by Erik Blegvad. Scholastic, 2005.

Hillman, Laura. *I Plant You a Lilac Tree: A Memoir of a Schindler's List Survivor*. Simon, 2005.

Holling, Holling C. *Minn of the Mississippi*. Houghton, 1951.

———. *Pagoo*. Houghton Mifflin, 1957.

Hopkins, Lee Bennett. *The Writing Bug*. Owen, 1992.

Hopkinson, Deborah. *Susan B. Anthony: Fighter for Women's Rights*. Illustrated by Amy June Bates. Simon, 2005.

———. *Who Was Charles Darwin?* Illustrated by Nancy Harrison. Grosset, 2005.

Hubbard, Crystal. *Catching the Moon*. Illustrated by Randy Deburke. Lee, 2005.

Jiang, Ji-li. *Red Scarf Girl: A Memoir of the Cultural Revolution*. HarperCollins, 1997.

Jurmain, Suzanne. *The Forbidden Schoolhouse: The True and Dramatic Story of Prudence Crandall and Her Students*. Houghton, 2005.

Kerley, Barbara. *The Dinosaurs of Waterhouse Hawkins*. Illustrated by Brian Selznick. Scholastic, 2001.

———. *Walt Whitman: Words for America*. Illustrated by Brian Selznick. Scholastic, 2004.

Kherdian, David. *The Road from Home: The Story of an Armenian Girl*. Greenwillow, 1979.

King-Smith, Dick. *Chewing the Cud*. Knopf, 2002.

Knight, Amelia. *The Way West: Journal of a Pioneer Woman*. Adapted by Lillian Schisse. Illustrated by Michael McCurdy. Simon, 1993.

Kramer, Ann. *Nelson Mandela: The Tribal Prince Who Grew Up to Be President*. National Geographic, 2005.

Krinitz, Esther Nisenthal, and Bernice Steinhardt. *Memories of Survival*. Hyperion, 2005.

Krull, Kathleen. *The Boy on Fairfield Street: How Ted Geisel Grew Up to Be Dr. Seuss*. Illustrated by Steve Johnson and Lou Fancher. Random, 2004.

———. *Leonardo da Vinci*. Illustrated by Boris Kulikov. Viking, 2005.

———. *Lives of the Artists: Masterpieces, Messes (and What the Neighbors Thought)*. Illustrated by Kathryn Hewitt. Harcourt, 1995.

———. *Lives of the Athletes: Thrills, Spills (and What the Neighbors Thought)*. Illustrated by Kathryn Hewitt. Harcourt, 1997.

———. *Lives of Extraordinary Women: Rulers, Rebels (and What the Neighbors Thought)*. Illustrated by Kathryn Hewitt. Harcourt, 2000.

———. *Lives of the Musicians: Good Times, Bad Times (and What the Neighbors Thought)*. Illustrated by Kathryn Hewitt. Harcourt, 1993.

———. *Lives of the Presidents: Fame, Shame (and What the Neighbors Thought)*. Illustrated by Kathryn Hewitt. Harcourt, 1998.

———. *Lives of the Writers: Comedies, Tragedies (and What the Neighbors Thought)*. Illustrated by Kathryn Hewitt. Harcourt, 1993.

———. *A Woman for President: The Story of Victoria Woodhull*. Illustrated by Jane Dyer. Walker, 2004.

Landau, Elaine. *Heroine of the Titanic: The Real Unsinkable Molly Brown*. Clarion, 2001.

Lasky, Kathryn. *The Librarian Who Measured the Earth*. Illustrated by Kevin Hawkes. Farrar, 2003.

———. *The Man Who Made Time Travel*. Illustrated by Kevin Hawkes. Kroupa/Farrar, 1994.

Latham, Jean Lee. *Carry On, Mr. Bowditch*. Illustrated by John O'Hara Cosgrave II. Houghton, 1955.

Lawlor, Laurie. *Helen Keller: Rebellious Spirit*. Holiday, 2001.

Lemasolai-Lekuton, Joseph. *Facing the Lion: Growing Up Maasai on the African Savanna*. National Geographic, 2005.

Lester, Helen. *Author: A True Story*. Houghton, 1998.

Little, Jean. *Little by Little: A Writer's Education*. Penguin, 1988.

Lobel, Anita. *No Pretty Pictures: A Child of War*. Greenwillow, 1998.

Lowry, Lois. *Looking Back: A Book of Memories*. Houghton, 1998.

Lyons, Mary E. *Catching Fire: Philip Simmons, Blacksmith*. Illustrated by Mannie Garcia. Houghton, 1997.

———. *Deep Blues: Bill Traylor, Self-Taught Artist*. Scribner's, 1994.

———. *Master of Mahogany: Tom Day, Free Black Cabinetmaker*. Scribner's, 1994.

———. *Painting Dreams: Minnie Evans, Visionary Artist*. Houghton, 1996.

———. *Starting Home: The Story of Horace Pippin*. Scribner's, 1993.

———. *Stitching Stars: The Story Quilts of Harriet Powers*. Scribner's, 1993.

———. *Talking with Tebé: Clementine Hunter, Memory Artist*. Houghton, 1998.

Macaulay, David. *Cathedral: The Story of Its Construction*. Houghton, 1973.

———. *City: The Story of Roman Planning and Construction*. Houghton, 1974.

———. *Mosque*. Houghton, 2003.

Macy, Sue. *Bull's Eye: A Photobiography of Annie Oakley*. National Geographic, 2001.

Mahy, Margaret. *My Mysterious World*. Owen, 1995.

Marcus, Leonard S. *Side by Side: Five Favorite Picture-Book Teams Go to Work*. Walker, 2001.

———. *Ways of Telling: Conversations on the Art of the Picture Book*. Dutton, 2002.

Marrin, Albert. *George Washington and the Founding of a Nation*. Dutton, 2001.

———. *The Sea King: Sir Francis Drake and His Times*. Atheneum, 1995.

———. *Terror of the Spanish Main: Henry Morgan and His Buccaneers*. Dutton, 1999.

———. *Unconditional Surrender: U. S. Grant and the Civil War*. Atheneum, 1994.

Martin, Joseph Plumb. *Yankee Doodle Boy*. Edited by George Scheer. Illustrated by Victor Mays. Holiday, 1995 [1964].

Martin, Rafe. *A Storyteller's Story*. Photos by Jill Krementz. Owen, 1992.

McCurdy, Michael, ed. *Escape from Slavery: The Boyhood of Frederick Douglass in His Own Words*. Knopf, 1994.

McGovern, Ann. *The Secret Soldier: The Story of Deborah Sampson*. Illustrated by Ann Grifalconi. Four Winds, 1987 [1975].

McKissack, Patricia C., and Frederick McKissack. *Sojourner Truth: Ain't I a Woman?* Scholastic, 1992.

Meltzer, Milton. *The American Revolutionaries: A History in Their Own Words*. Crowell, 1987.

——. *Lincoln: In His Own Words*. Illustrated by Stephen Alcorn. Harcourt, 1994.

——. *Ten Queens: Portraits of Women of Power*. Dutton, 1998.

Micucci, Charles. *The Life and Times of the Apple*. Orchard, 1992.

——. *The Life and Times of the Honeybee*. Ticknor, 1994.

Miller, William. *Frederick Douglass: The Last Days of Slavery*. Illustrated by Cedric Lucas. Lee, 1995.

——. *Richard Wright and the Library Card*. Illustrated by Christie Gregory. Lee, 1997.

——. *Zora Hurston and the Chinaberry Tree*. Illustrated by Cornelius Van Wright and Ying-hwa Hu. Lee, 1994.

Millman, Isaac. *Hidden Child*. Farrar, 2005.

——. *Moses Goes to a Concert*. Farrar, 2002.

Milton, Joyce. *Pochahontas: An American Princess*. Illustrated by Shelley Hehenberger. Putnam, 2000.

——. *Sacajawea: Her True Story*. Illustrated by Shelley Hehenberger. Putnam, 2001.

Mora, Pat. *Tomas and the Library Lady*. Illustrated by Raúl Colón. Knopf, 1997.

Moss, Marissa. *Amelia's Notebook*. Pleasant, 1999.

Murphy, Jim. *Pick and Shovel Poet: The Journeys of Pascal D'Angelo*. Clarion, 2000.

Myers, Walter Dean. *Bad Boy: A Memoir*. HarperCollins, 2001.

Naylor, Phyllis Reynolds. *How I Came to Be a Writer*. Aladdin, 1987 [1978].

Numeroff, Laura J. *If You Give an Author a Pencil*. Owen, 2002.

Osofsky, Audrey. *Free to Dream: The Making of a Poet: Langston Hughes*. Lothrop, 1996.

Partridge, Elizabeth. *John Lennon: All I Want Is the Truth*. Viking, 2005.

——. *Restless Spirit: The Life and Work of Dorothea Lange*. Viking, 1998.

——. *This Land Was Made for You and Me: The Life and Songs of Woody Guthrie*. Viking, 2002.

Patent, Dorothy Hinshaw. *Charles Darwin: The Life of a Revolutionary Thinker*. Holiday, 2001.

Paulsen, Gary. *Woodsong*. Bradbury, 1990.

Peet, Bill. *Bill Peet: An Autobiography*. Houghton, 1989.

Petry, Ann. *Harriet Tubman, Conductor on the Underground Railroad*. HarperCollins, 1996.

Pinkney, Andrea Davis. *Alvin Ailey*. Illustrated by Brian Pinkney. Hyperion, 1993.

——. *Bill Picket: Rodeo Ridin' Cowboy*. Illustrated by Brian Pinkney. Hyperion, 1996.

——. *Dear Benjamin Banneker*. Illustrated by Brian Pinkney. Gulliver, 1994.

——. *Duke Ellington: The Piano Prince and His Orchestra*. Illustrated by Brian Pinkney. Hyperion, 1998.

——. *Ella Fitzgerald: The Tale of a Vocal Virtuosa*. Illustrated by Brian Pinkney. Hyperion, 2002.

——. *Let It Shine: Stories of Black Women Freedom Fighters*. Illustrated by Stephen Alcorn. Harcourt/Gulliver, 2000.

Poole, Josephine. *Anne Frank*. Illustrated by Angela Barrett. Knopf, 2005.

Pringle, Laurence. *A Dragon in the Sky: The Story of a Green Darner Dragonfly*. Illustrated by Bob Marstall. Scholastic, 2001.

Provensen, Alice, and Martin Provensen. *The Glorious Flight: Across the Channel with Louis Blériot, July 25, 1909*. Viking, 1983.

Rappaport, Doreen. *John's Secret Dreams: The Life of John Lennon*. Illustrated by Bryan Collier. Hyperion, 2004.

——. *Martin's Big Words*. Illustrated by Bryan Collier. Hyperion/Jump at the Sun, 2001.

Ray, Deborah Kogan. *Hokusai: The Man Who Painted a Mountain*. Farrar, 2001.

Reef, Catherine. *Walt Whitman*. Clarion, 1995.

Reich, Susanna. *Clara Schumann: Piano Virtuoso*. Clarion, 1999.

Rockwell, Anne. *Only Passing Through: The Story of Sojourner Truth*. Illustrated by Gregory Christie. Knopf, 2000.

Roop, Peter, and Connie Roop. *Sojourner Truth*. Scholastic, 2003.

Rosen, Michael. *Dickens: His World and Work*. Illustrated by Robert Ingpen. Candlewick, 2005.

Rumford, James. *Sequoyah: The Cherokee Man Who Gave His People Writing*. Translated into Cherokee by Anna Sixkiller Huckaby. Houghton, 2004.

——. *Traveling Man: The Journey of Ibn Battuta, 1325–1354*. Houghton, 2001.

Ryan, Pam Muñoz. *When Marian Sang: The True Recital of Marian Anderson: The Voice of a Century*. Illustrated by Brian Selznick. Scholastic, 2002.

Rylant, Cynthia. *Best Wishes*. Photos by Carlo Ontal. Owen, 1992.

San Souci, Robert D. *Kate Shelley: Bound for Legend*. Illustrated by Max Ginsburg. Dial, 1995.

Sandburg, Carl. *Abe Lincoln Grows Up*. Illustrated by James Daugherty. Harcourt, 1975 [1926].

Say, Allen. *El Chino*. Houghton, 1990.

Scioscia, Mary. *Bicycle Rider*. Illustrated by Ed Young. Harper, 1983.

Shulevitz, Uri. *The Travels of Benjamin of Tudela: Through Three Continents in the Twelfth Century*. Farrar, 2005.

Shetterly, Robert. *Americans Who Tell the Truth*. Dutton, 2005.

Sills, Leslie. *In Real Life: Six Women Photographers*. Holiday, 2000.

——. *Visions: Stories about Women Artists*. Edited by Leslie Sills and Abby Levine. Whitman, 1993.

Silverman, Erica. *Sholom's Treasure: How Sholom Aleichem Became a Writer*. Illustrated by Mordicai Gerstein. Farrar, 2005.

Sis, Peter. *Follow the Dream: The Story of Christopher Columbus*. Knopf, 1991.

Slaymaker, Melissa Eskridge. *Bottle Houses: The Creative World of Grandma Prisby*. Holt, 2004.

Spinelli, Jerry. *Knots in My Yo-Yo String*. Knopf, 1998.

Stanley, Diane. *Joan of Arc*. Morrow, 1998.

——. *Leonardo da Vinci*. Morrow, 1996.

——. *Michelangelo*. HarperCollins, 2000.

——. *Peter the Great*. Four Winds, 1986.

——. *Saladin: Noble Prince of Islam*. HarperCollins, 2000.

——. *The True Adventures of Daniel Hall*. Dial, 1995.

Stanley, Diane, and Peter Vennema. *Bard of Avon: The Story of William Shakespeare*. Illustrated by Diane Stanley. Morrow, 1992.

———. *Charles Dickens: The Man Who Had Great Expectations*. Illustrated by Diane Stanley. Morrow, 1993.

———. *Cleopatra*. Illustrated by Diane Stanley. Morrow, 1994.

———. *Good Queen Bess: The Story of Elizabeth I of England*. Illustrated by Diane Stanley. Four Winds, 1990.

———. *Shaka: King of the Zulus*. Illustrated by Diane Stanley. Morrow, 1988.

Stanley, Fay. *The Last Princess: The Story of Princess Ka'iulani of Hawai'i*. Illustrated by Diane Stanley. Four Winds, 1991.

Steele, Philip. *Galileo: The Genius Who Faced the Inquisition*. National Geographic, 2005.

Stevenson, James. *Higher on the Door*. Greenwillow, 1987.

———. *When I Was Nine*. Greenwillow, 1986.

Sullivan, George. *The Wright Brothers*. Scholastic, 2003.

Suzuki, David, and Wayne Grady. *Tree: A Life Story*. Illustrated by Robert Bateman. Greystone, 2004.

Taylor, Maureen. *Through the Eyes of Your Ancestors*. Houghton, 1999.

Tillage, Leon. *Leon's Story*. Illustrated by Susan Roth. Farrar, 1997.

Usher, M. D. *Wise Guy: The Life and Philosophy of Socrates*. Illustrated by William Branhall. Farrar, 2005.

van der Rol, Ruud, and Rian Verhoeven. *Anne Frank beyond the Diary: A Photographic Remembrance*. Translated by Tony Langham and Plym Peters. Viking, 1993.

Warren, Andrea. *Orphan Train Rider: One Boy's True Story*. Houghton, 1996.

———. *Pioneer Girl: Growing Up on the Prairie*. Morrow, 1998.

———. *We Rode the Orphan Trains*. Houghton, 2001.

Weidt, Maryann N. *Stateswoman to the World: A Story about Eleanor Roosevelt*. Illustrated by Lydia M. Anderson. Carolrhoda, 1991.

Weitzman, David L. *My Back Yard History Book*. Little, 1975.

West, Delno, and Jean West. *Christopher Columbus: The Great Adventure and How We Know About It*. Atheneum, 1991.

Wheatley, Nadia, and Donna Rawlins. *My Place*. Kane/Miller, 1992.

Williams, Vera B. *Scooter*. Greenwillow, 1993.

Wilson, Janet. *The Ingenious Mr. Peale: Patriot, Painter, and Man of Science*. Atheneum, 1996.

Winter, Jeanette. *Cowboy Charlie: The Story of Charles M. Russell*. Harcourt, 1995.

———. *My Name Is Georgia: A Portrait*. Silver Whistle, 1998.

———. *Sebastian: A Book about Bach*. Browndeer, 1999.

Winter, Jonah. *Diego*. Illustrated by Jeannette Winter. Translation by Amy Prince. Knopf, 1991.

———. *Frida*. Illustrated by Ana Juan. Scholastic, 2002.

Yep, Laurence. *The Lost Garden*. Smith, 1999.

Yoo, Paula. *Sixteen Seconds in Sixteen Years: The Sammy Lee Story*. Illustrated by Dom Lee. Lee, 2005.

Yu, Chun. *Little Green: Growing Up during the Cultural Revolution*. Simon, 2005.

Zhang, Ange. *Red Land, Yellow River: A Story from the Cultural Revolution*. Douglas/Groundwood, 2004.

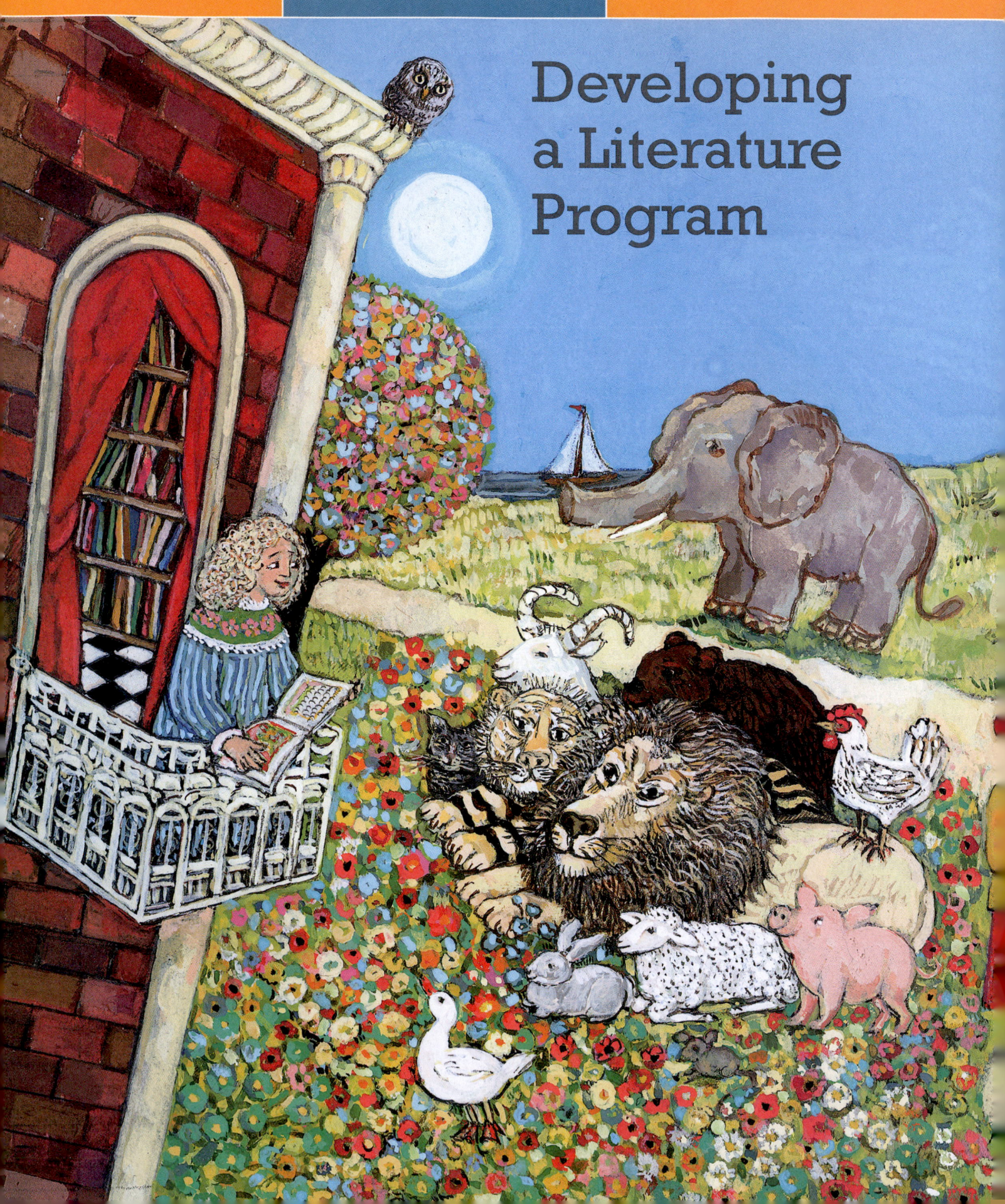

Part Three

Developing a Literature Program

Planning the Literature Program

Students

in a fifth- and sixth-grade class unanimously agreed that *The Pinballs* by Betsy Byars was their favorite book. Their teacher then asked them to discuss the book, telling what it was that made them like it so much. Part of their discussion follows:

Lenny says, "This is the best book I've ever read. I'd like to know Harvey because I'd like to cheer him up." He decides that "he shows real courage because he has two broken legs." Barb adds, "All the kids do because they have to go to a foster home." "So does Thomas J. because the twins are going to die and he has to go to the hospital to see them," says Will.

Jack talks about Carlie, saying, "She's really funny because she's so rude." The teacher suggests that a book that is "basically serious can have funny elements." Tom says, "You know that Carlie is really tough."

Then Tom goes on to explain the title by saying, "Carlie thinks they're pinballs because they are always being thrown around like pinballs."

By April of that year, eighteen of the class had read *The Pinballs*. They also were reading other Betsy Byars books; thirteen had read *The Summer of the Swans*, eight *Good-bye, Chicken Little*.[1]

Individual children had read many books (from 24 to 122 over the year), yet they singled out *The Pinballs* as their favorite. Though it is still difficult for them to articulate why they like the story, they have moved beyond the usual circular kind of statement, "I liked it because it was good." They are beginning to recognize the importance of character development and readily identify with Carlie and Harvey. Lenny, who was not a particularly good reader and had read few books, empathizes with Harvey to the point of wanting to comfort him. These students have extended their horizons to imagine the courage it would require to live in a foster home away from their family and to have to visit people who are dying in the hospital. Tom attempts a rough statement of the meaning of the title without any prompting.

In this class, book discussions occurred every day during the last fifteen minutes of an hour-long period for sustained silent reading. The children readily supported each other in their selection of books and in their evaluations; they exemplify what we have referred to as a "community of readers." It is obvious from their discussion that they were gaining a greater sense of form and were beginning to see more in books than just story.

It takes time for reading and literature to grow in a classroom. The children in this classroom had, for the most part, been exposed to good literature throughout their school attendance. The teacher had been working on a literature-based reading program over a period of several years. Her major goal was to develop children who could read and who loved reading. From this base she added a growing appreciation for and understanding of good literature.

---

[1]Based on children's comments recorded by Susan Hepler in "Patterns of Response to Literature: A One-Year Study of a Fifth and Sixth Grade Classroom" (Ph.D. dissertation, Ohio State University, 1982).

PURPOSES OF THE LITERATURE PROGRAM

Each school staff will want to develop its own literature program in terms of the background and abilities of the children it serves. Teachers and librarians need to know both their children and the potential of their material and have an understanding of the structure of literature; then they will be free to make the right match between child and book. This chapter can suggest guidelines and give examples, but it cannot prescribe *the* literature program that will work with all children.

One of the major purposes of any literature program is to provide children with the opportunity to experience literature, to enter into and become involved in a book. The goal of all reading programs should be not only to teach children to learn to read but to help them learn to love reading, to discover joy in reading. Their every activity, every assignment, should pass this test: "Will this increase children's desire to read? Will it make them want to continue reading?" A literature program must get children excited about reading, turned on to books, tuned in to literature.

Another important purpose for using real books in a reading program is to help children connect literature with their own lives. As teachers and librarians, we want to encourage children to discover personal meaning in books so that they can better understand their lives and extend their perceptions of others' lives. Kindergarten children listen to *Ira Sleeps Over* by Bernard Waber and

Two first graders share the reading of a picture book and exchange reading strategies. PS 116, New York, New York. Ilana Dubin-Spiegel, teacher.

Two fourth-grade girls reveal their delight in literature by sharing some "book talk." PS 124, New York, New York. Mary S. Gallivan, teacher.

talk about their own bears and the decisions they had to make about taking them on vacations or overnights. A fifth grader, when asked why Jean George's *My Side of the Mountain* was his favorite book, replied, "I just always thought I could do what Sam Gribley did." As children search for meaning in books, they naturally connect what they are reading to their own lives.

A school literature program should also help children develop literary awareness and appreciation. We want children to develop an understanding of literary genres and to recognize the unique qualities and criteria of many types of literature. We want to introduce children to literary classics and to the authors and illustrators who create the books that they love. We expect that over time children will become familiar with the many components of literature, such as the traditional constants of plot, characterization, theme, style, setting, and author's point of view. However, their knowledge about literature should be secondary to their wide experiencing of literature. Too frequently, we have substituted the study of literary criticism for the experience of literature itself. Attention to content should precede consideration of form.

Teachers need to know something of the structure of literature in order to provide children with a frame of reference to direct their insights. Knowledge of the structure of a discipline frees a teacher in her approach to teaching. Knowing literature, she may tune in to where the children are and extend their thinking and understandings. The teacher does not have to rely on the questions in a teacher's manual; she is free to ask questions directly related to the needs of the children in the class.

A framework for thinking about literature develops gradually as children consider what kinds of stories they particularly like or what kinds of information they need for a particular purpose. When teachers consistently nurture children's enjoyment of literature by reading aloud exciting, well-selected books, and by giving children time

Children need opportunities to respond to books in a variety of ways. These two first graders are busy creating art following the reading of favorite books. PS 116, New York, New York. Ilana Dubin-Spiegel, teacher.

to read and discuss books in literature groups, the children's appreciation for quality literature will grow. One major goal of the literature program should be this development of discriminating critical readers.

LITERATURE-BASED PROGRAMS

For a good part of the twentieth century, reading instruction was delivered through the medium of basal readers, "a series of sequential, all inclusive instructional materials."[2] Basal reading programs are still widely used in American schools, but the number of teachers reporting the exclusive use of basals has dropped over the years.[3] Over the past thirty-five years, we have witnessed an expansion of the role of trade books in the schools. The accumulated weight of evidence from many studies, insights from professional educators, the success of many teachers who are making literature central to the curriculum, and the enthusiastic responses of children to reading real books are some of the reasons behind the growth of a literature-based curriculum. The current emphasis on standards and testing and government support for "research-based" reading programs does not in

any way preclude teachers from using literature as the core of the curriculum. In fact, the research conducted over the past forty-five years continues to show that knowledgeable, reflective, and flexible teachers are the most important factor in children's success.[4] In the following section we suggest the type of literature-based program that is used by just such teachers.

Literature Programs Using Trade Books

Programs in which trade books are used for all aspects of reading instruction and for integrating traditional areas of the curriculum are an accepted alternative to skills-oriented, textbook-based programs.[5] In a literature-based program, classrooms are flooded with books. Funds usually appropriated for the purchase of basal readers and workbooks are used for obtaining large classroom libraries of 400 to 500 books. There are books in an attractive reading corner, sets of paperback books for in-depth study, and a changing collection of books obtained from the school library and public libraries on whatever unit focus is in progress. Books are displayed along with the children's work. Children's interpretations of books, book surveys, and big books are seen throughout the room. Few commercial charts or pictures are seen, only quantities of children's work with captions, labels, or writing on it.

Knowing the research on the importance of reading aloud in developing concepts about print, a sense of story, prediction of plot, and understanding of characters, teachers read aloud to children three or four times a day. They frequently reread favorite stories until children almost know them by heart. Parent aides are encouraged to read aloud to small groups of children. Frequently teachers establish a "buddy system" in which older children read with one or two younger ones.

Rather than work on worksheets or workbook activities, children do a variety of things. Some may be seen reading from the big books, some are working on picture sorts or word sorts with an aide, others may be reading individually with the teacher, while still others may be busy reading or writing stories of their own or writing in

[2]Kenneth Goodman, Patrick Shannon, Yvonne Freeman, and Sharon Murphy, *Report Card on Basal Readers* (Katonah, N.Y.: Richard C. Owen, 1988), p. 1.

[3]Linda B. Gambrell, "Elementary School Literacy Instruction: Changes and Challenges," in *Elementary School Literacy: Critical Issues*, ed. M. J. Dreher and W. H. Slater (Portsmouth, N.H.: Heinemann, 1992), pp. 227–39.

[4]Curt Dudley-Marling, "At Last: The Complex Relationship between Reading Research and Classroom Practice," *Research in the Teaching of English* 40 (August, 2005): 127–30.

[5]Sarah J. McCarthy, James V. Hoffman, and Lee Galda, "Readers in Elementary Classrooms: Learning Goals and Instructional Principles That Can Inform Practice," in *Engaged Reading: Processes, Practices, and Policy Implications*, ed. John T. Guthrie and Donna E. Alvermann (New York: Teachers College Press, 1999), pp. 46–80. Leslie M. Morrow and Linda B. Gambrell, "Literature-Based Reading Instruction," in *Handbook of Reading Research, Vol. III*, ed. M. L. Kamil, P. B. Mosenthal, P. D. Pearson, and R. Barr (Mahwah, N.J.: Lawrence Erlbaum, 2000), pp. 563–86. Douglas Fisher, James Flood, and Diane Lapp, "Material Matters: Using Children's Literature to Charm Readers," in *Best Practices in Literacy Instruction*, ed. Lesley Mandel Morrow, Linda B. Gambrell, and Michael Pressley (New York: Guilford Press, 2003), pp. 167–86.

A story map of "The Story of the Three Little Pigs" helped first-grade children to retell the story. Columbus Public Schools, Columbus, Ohio. Connie Compton, teacher.

their literature response journals. Many of the literature extension activities described later in this chapter are done during this work time. Quiet talk about books flows as children create murals or map the action of a story.

An independent reading time is provided every day. Frequently, however, children read quietly in pairs. Time for discussion of books almost always follows these periods.

The in-depth study of the books of one author, a genre of books, or one book begins as early as kindergarten. With older children, sets of paperbacks like *Number the Stars* by Lois Lowry, *Roll of Thunder, Hear My Cry* by Mildred Taylor, *Lizzie Bright and the Buckminster Boy* by Gary D. Schmidt, and *Tuck Everlasting* by Natalie Babbitt are used for literature study. All children are involved in groups for in-depth reading, but the groups are not formed on the basis of ability. Rather, children choose to join a reading group based on their interest in the book or a topic, and these groups change as the focus of a study changes.

Literature and Content-Area Learning

Reading and writing across the curriculum are characteristic of this integrated program. Children do research in informational books on the particular class unit. Units and projects that cut across traditional subject-matter areas might be chosen by a class or a small group of children to study. For example, over the period of a year, one second- and third-grade class studied the topics "Fairy Tales," "Plumbing and Water Sources," and "Immigration to the United States." They also had mini-units on "Books by Pat Hutchins," "Grandparents," and "Dinosaurs."

Children learn research skills in the process of using many books and reference books for projects, along with electronic sources. The library is open all day long for

children to use as they research particular topics. Parent assistants may help children in one part of the room to find their materials if the librarian is reading a story or working with others.

Children learn strategies for reading many different types of texts through real reading and inquiry. When teachers do direct teaching of such strategies, the strategies are related to children's needs and not isolated drills. No worksheets or workbooks are used. Rather, children write in their response journals, do purposeful reading, and create their own books and group projects.

Teachers and children keep records of children's reading. Each child has a portfolio containing samples of his or her story writing, artwork, and research reports from the beginning of school. These are shared with par-

A teacher shares her enthusiasm for books with one or two children as well as the class. Idyllwild Elementary School, Idyllwild, California. Sharon Schmidt, teacher. Photo by Larry Rose.

ents during individual conference times. Book reports are not required, because children are sharing books in a variety of ways. Teachers know what children are reading because they are reacting to their reading in their reading journals each week. All children know what others are reading because they discuss their books every day. Children frequently recommend books to others, as they know each other's reading interests. These children become a community of readers as they discuss and recommend particular titles. Books are an essential part of their lives.

Basal readers are not likely to disappear from classrooms any time soon. A 1994 survey of teachers in eight states found that only 18% of the teachers used literature exclusively.[6] However, 80% used a combination of literature and basal readers. Clearly a large majority of teachers recognize the importance of literature in their students' lives. In the current climate of strict standards and high-stakes testing, teachers can feel confident that a heavy emphasis on the use of literature can have significantly positive effects on reading proficiency.[7] Literature-based programs that use real books offer a challenge to teachers. They require an in-depth knowledge of children and children's literature. Only when a teacher knows the potential of a child and a book and is willing to trust the interaction between the two does learning really occur.

COMPONENTS OF A LITERATURE PROGRAM

The day-to-day routines in classrooms centered around children's literature may vary greatly according to the age of the students, the needs of the community, and the dictates of local and state curriculum. But children in all literature-based classrooms need to be surrounded by enthusiastic, book-loving adults and many, many good books.

The most important aspect of the classroom environment is the teacher. She or he creates the climate of the classroom and arranges the learning environment. If the teacher loves books, shares them with children, and provides time for children to read and a place for them to read, children will become enthusiastic readers. The teacher who reads to the children every day, talks about books and characters in books as if they were good friends, and knows poems and stories to tell is serving the class as an adult model of a person who enjoys books. One teacher regularly used to read a new children's book while her class was reading. She would keep the book in an old beat-up briefcase that she delighted in carrying. A kind of game she played with her 7- and 8-year-old

Every classroom should have an inviting corner where children can choose and read favorite books. PS 116, New York, New York. Ilana Dubin-Spiegel, teacher.

students was to keep the book hidden from them. Their delight was to find out what book she was reading, so they could read the same one. Of course they always found out, which was what she had in mind in the first place. Enthusiasm for books is contagious; if the teacher has it, so will the children.

If we want children to become readers, we will want to surround them with books of all kinds. We know that wide reading is directly related to accessibility; the more books available and the more time for reading, the more children will read and the better readers they will become.

Books should be a natural part of the classroom environment. There should be no argument about whether to have a classroom collection of books or a library media center; both are necessary. Children should have immediate access to books whenever they need them. The books in the classroom collection will vary from those in the library media center. Many classrooms have an extensive paperback collection (400 to 500 titles). Frequently, there are five or six copies of the same title, so several children can read the same book and have an in-depth discussion of it.

The classroom teacher will also want to provide for a changing collection of books depending on the themes or units the children are studying. The librarian might provide a rolling cart of materials that will enhance children's study of bugs or folktales or the Civil War or

[6]Donald Strickland et al., *School Book Clubs and Literacy Development: A Descriptive Study* (Rep. No. 222) (Albany: State University of New York, National Research Center on Literature Teaching and Learning, 1994).

[7]Lesley M. Morrow, "The Impact of a Literature-Based Program on Literacy Achievement, Use of Literature, and Attitudes of Children from Minority Backgrounds," *Reading Research Quarterly* 27 (1992): 251–75.

explorers. It is important that teachers be thoroughly acquainted with the content of these books so they can help their students use them. If the library media center does not have particular books that the children or the teacher needs, they might be obtained from local public libraries or from a bookmobile. Some state libraries will send boxes of books to teachers in communities that are not serviced by public libraries. An increasing number of teachers are demanding and receiving their share of monies allocated for instructional materials. Teachers using real books as the heart of their curriculum should receive the same amount of money as those using basal readers, workbooks, social studies, science, and other textbooks. We admire the number of teachers who spend their own money to buy trade books for their classrooms, but at the same time we question the practice. Real books are essential to the making of a fluent reader and should be an unquestioned item of every school budget.

SHARING LITERATURE WITH CHILDREN

From the time of the earliest primitive fire circle to the Middle Ages—when minnesingers and troubadours sang their ballads—to the modern age of television, people have found delight in hearing stories and poems. Because literature serves many educational purposes in addition to entertainment and enjoyment, teachers should place a high priority on sharing literature with children. Boys and girls of all ages should have the opportunity to hear good literature every day.

Reading to Children

One of the best ways to interest children in books is to read to them frequently from the time they are first able to listen. Preschoolers and kindergartners should have an opportunity to listen to stories three or four times a day. Parent or grandparent volunteers, high school students, college participants—all can be encouraged to read to small groups of children throughout the day. Children should have a chance to hear their favorite stories over and over again at a listening center. A child from a book-loving family might have heard over a thousand bedtime stories before she ever comes to kindergarten; some children might never have heard one.

Teachers accept the idea of reading at least twice a day to the primary-grade child. The daily story time is advocated by almost all authorities in reading. The research reported in Chapters 1 and 4 emphasizes the importance of reading aloud to all children, not only for enjoyment but also for their growth in reading skills. Reading to children improves children's reading. Rereading favorite stories is as important as the initial reading.

Unfortunately, daily story times are not as common in the middle grades and middle school as in the primary grades, yet we know that they are just as essential

Primary children need to hear many stories read several times a day by an enthusiastic teacher. Highland Park Elementary School, South-Western City Schools, Grove City, Ohio. Kristen Kerstetter, teacher.

there. Reading comprehension is improved as students listen to and discuss events, characters, and motivation. They learn to predict what will happen in exciting tales like Mollie Hunter's *A Stranger Came Ashore* or Louis Sachar's *Holes*. Their vocabulary increases as they hear fine texts such as Donald Hall's *Ox-Cart Man* or Jane Yolen's poetic *Owl Moon*. Older students can discuss homelessness and prejudice as they hear Paula Fox's *Monkey Island* or Leon Tillage's *Leon's Story*. They can add to their knowledge of Abraham Lincoln's presidency by reading Russell Freedman's remarkable photobiography *Lincoln*. Teachers can take advantage of this time to introduce various genres, such as fantasy, biography, or poetry, that students might not be reading on their own.

Primarily, however, the read-aloud time will cause children to want to read. Once children have heard a good book read aloud, they can hardly wait to savor it again. Reading aloud thus generates further interest in books. Good oral reading should develop a taste for fine literature.

Selecting Books to Read Aloud

Teachers and librarians will want to select read-aloud books in terms of the children's interests and background in literature and the quality of writing. Usually teachers will not select books that children in the group are reading avidly on their own. This is the time to stretch their imaginations, to extend interests, and to develop appreciation of fine writing. If children have not had much experience in listening to stories, begin where they are. Appreciation for literature appears to be developmental and sequential. Six- and 7-year-olds who have had little exposure to literature still need to hear many traditional fairy tales, including "Hansel and Gretel," "Sleeping Beauty," and *Ananse and the Lizard* by Pat Cum-

Profile in Literature

Diane Driessen

Diane Driessen has been a school media specialist in Upper Arlington, Ohio, for the past nineteen years. Diane plays a multifaceted role at Wickliffe, working closely with both teachers and students to promote literature and information literacy and to foster the love of libraries and reading. Her goal is to provide authentic and integrated experiences for her patrons. Some of her activities include organizing author and illustrator visits and participating in a traveling program that brings literature alive to the elementary schools in Upper Arlington. She has been involved with developing a Web site and video of Ohio's authors and illustrators. Go to the Online Learning Center at **www.mhhe.com/kiefer9e** or your Resources CD-ROM to learn more about Diane Driessen.

mins. They delight in such favorite picture storybooks as Jan Ormerod's *When an Elephant Comes to School,* Patricia C. McKissack's *Flossie and the Fox,* and Karma Wilson's *Bear Wants More.* Other children of the same age who have had much exposure to literature might demand longer chapter books like *Ramona Forever* by Beverly Cleary, *James and the Giant Peach* by Roald Dahl, or *The Pepins and Their Problems* by Polly Horvath.

Picture storybooks are no longer just for "little kids." There is a real place for sharing some of the beautiful picture books with older children as well as younger ones. *Dawn* by Uri Shulevitz creates the same feeling visually as one of Emily Dickinson's clear, rarefied poems. It is a literary experience for all ages, but particularly for anyone who has felt "at-oneness" with the world before the sunrise. Older students particularly enjoy Jon Scieszka's *Seen Art?* and Kevin O'Malley's rip-roaring *Captain Raptor and the Moon Mystery.*

The teacher should strive for balance in what is read aloud to children. Children tend to like what they know. Introducing a variety of types of books will broaden their base of appreciation. If 11- and 12-year-olds are all reading contemporary fiction, the teacher might read Brian Jacques's powerful fantasy of the fight to save an ancient stone abbey in *Redwall* or introduce them to Katherine Paterson's indomitable *Lyddie,* the story of a girl who struggles against the unbearable working conditions of factory girls in the Lowell, Massachusetts, mills of the 1840s. The finely honed writing of Patricia MacLachlan's *Sarah, Plain and Tall,* the story of a mail-order bride and the family who longed for a new mother, could be shared with children as young as third grade and as old as fifth. Most of these books are too good for children to miss and should be read aloud to them.

Primary-grade teachers will read many picture books to their children, certainly a minimum of three to four a day. Middle-grade teachers might present parts of many books to their students during book talks or as teasers to interest children in reading the books. But how many entire books will a teacher read in the course of one school year? An educated guess might be that starting with 8-year-olds—when teachers begin to read longer, continuous stories to boys and girls—an average of some six to ten books are read aloud during the year. This means that for the next four years, when children are reaching the peak of their interest in reading, they might hear no more than forty or so books read by their teachers!

Today when there are thousands of children's books in print, read-aloud choices must be selected with care in terms of their relevance for students and the quality of their writing. A list of suggested books to read aloud is included on the endpapers of this book to serve as a beginning guide. Notice that the overlapping of age groups is deliberate. There is no such thing as a book for 5-year-olds or 10-year-olds. Very popular books, such as those by Dr. Seuss or poems by Shel Silverstein, do not appear on our read-aloud lists because most children will have read them on their own. Only a teacher who knows the children, their interests, and their background of experience can truly select appropriate books for a particular class.

We note with concern the increasing number of teachers who want to read such complex stories as *Tuck Everlasting* by Natalie Babbitt, *A Wrinkle in Time* by Madeleine L'Engle, or *The Giver* by Lois Lowry to 6- and 7-year-olds. Children this age might become involved in the plots of these well-written stories, but they will certainly miss many of the deeper meanings reflected in their themes. Read at the appropriate developmental levels, these books could provide the basis for serious in-depth discussion and study. The number of years when children read literature suited to their age appears to have decreased, as more and more 12- and 13-year-olds begin to read best-sellers and other books written for adults. The inappropriate selection of books for reading aloud by both parents and teachers may contribute to this erosion of childhood.

There is a difference, however, between what parents might choose for family reading and what is appropriate for classroom sharing. Parents have the advantage of knowing all the books that children have enjoyed at home. In a family sharing E. B. White's *Charlotte's Web,* the 5-year-old enjoys the humor of these talking barnyard animals while an 8-year-old might weep at Charlotte's death. The closeness of a family unit helps all members to find enjoyment in a read-aloud story regardless of age level. The teacher, on the other hand, has to consider children's backgrounds in literature, or lack of background, as he or she selects appropriate books to capture their attention.

A read-aloud program should be planned. What books are too good to miss? These should be included in the overall plan. Teachers should keep a record of the books that they have shared with the children they teach and a brief notation of the class's reaction to each title. This enables teachers to see what kind of balance is being achieved and what the particular favorites of the class are. Such a record provides the children's future teachers with information on the likes and dislikes of the class and their exposure to literature. It also might prevent the situation that was discovered by a survey of one school in which every teacher in the school, with the exception of the kindergarten and the second-grade teachers, had read *Charlotte's Web* aloud to the class! *Charlotte's Web* is a great book, but not for every class. Perhaps teachers in a school need to agree on what is the most appropriate time for reading particular favorites. Teachers and librarians should be encouraged to try reading new books to children, instead of always reading the same ones. But some self-indulgence should be allowed every teacher who truly loves a particular book, because that enthusiasm can't help but rub off on children.

Effective oral reading is an important factor in capturing children's interest. Some teachers can make almost any story sound exciting; others plod dully through. The storyteller's voice, timing, and intonation patterns should communicate the meanings and mood of the story. To read effectively, the teacher should be familiar with the story and communicate his or her enthusiasm for the book. Teaching Resources: "Effective Practices for Reading Aloud" might prove useful. Check the list before selecting and reading a story to a whole class.

Storytelling

A 5-year-old said to his teacher: "Tell the story from your face." His preference for the story *told* by the teacher or librarian instead of the story read directly from the book is echoed by boys and girls everywhere. The art of storytelling is frequently neglected in the elementary school today. There are so many beautiful books to share with children, we rationalize, and our harried life allows little time for learning stories. Yet children should not be denied the opportunity to hear well-told stories. Through storytelling, the teacher helps transmit the literary heritage.

Storytelling provides for intimate contact and rapport with the children. No book separates the teacher from the audience. The story may be modified to fit group needs. A difficult word or phrase can be explained in context. Stories can be personalized for very young children

TEACHING **RESOURCES**

Effective Practices for Reading Aloud

 Visit the Online Learning Center at **www.mhhe.com/kiefer9e** for a printable version of this list.

1. Select a story appropriate to the developmental age of the children and their previous exposure to literature.
2. Determine whether you will share the book with the whole class, a small group, or an individual child.
3. Select books that will stretch children's imaginations, extend their interests, and expose them to fine art and writing.
4. Read a variety of types of books to capture the interests of all.
5. Remember that favorite stories should be reread at the primary level.
6. Plan to read aloud several times a day.
7. Select a story that you like so that you can communicate your enthusiasm.
8. Choose a story or chapter that can be read in one session.
9. Read the book first so that you are familiar with the content.
10. Seat the children close to you so that all can see the pictures.
11. Hold the book so that children can see the pictures at their eye level.
12. Communicate the mood and meaning of the story and characters with your voice.
13. Introduce books in various ways:
    Through a display
    Through a brief discussion about the author or illustrator
    By asking children to predict what the story will be about through looking at the cover and interpreting the title
    By linking the theme, author, or illustrator to other books children know
14. Encourage older children to discuss the progress of the story or predict the outcome at the end of the chapter.
15. Help children to link the story with their own experiences or other literature.
16. Keep a list of the books read aloud to the whole class that can be passed on to their next teachers.

For further assistance, see Caroline Feller Bauer's *New Handbook for Storytellers* (Chicago: American Library Association, 1993).

by substituting their names for those of the characters. Such a phrase as "and, David, if you had been there you would have seen the biggest Billy Goat Gruff . . ." will redirect the child whose interest has wandered. The pace of the story can be adapted to the children's interests and age levels.

Stories that are to be told should be selected with care. Stories worth the telling have special characteristics, including a quick beginning, action, a definite climax, natural dialogue, and a satisfying conclusion. It is best to select stories with only three or four speaking characters so that listeners can keep the characters straight. Finally, stories with rich literary language, such as Rudyard Kipling's *The Elephant's Child,* are best read aloud rather than told. Instead, select stories for telling that provide the immediacy of the storyteller's voice.

Folktales like "The Three Billy Goats Gruff," "The Little Red Hen," and "Cinderella" are particular favorites of younger children. The repetitive pattern of these tales makes them easy to tell. Originally passed down from generation to generation by word of mouth, these tales were polished and embellished with each retelling.

Six-, 7-, and 8-year-olds enjoy hearing longer folktales such as Ashley Bryan's *The Cat's Purr.* They also enjoy some of the tall tales about American folk heroes such as Paul Bunyan, Pecos Bill, and John Henry. Incidents from biographies and chapters from longer books may be told as a way of interesting children in reading them.

Book Talks

Librarians and teachers frequently use a book talk to introduce books to children. The primary purpose of a book talk is to interest children in reading the book themselves. Rather than reveal the whole story, the book talk tells just enough about the book to entice others to read it. A book talk may be about one title; it may be about several unrelated books that would have wide appeal; or it may revolve around several books with a similar theme, such as "getting along in the family" or "courage" or "survival stories."

The book talk should begin with the recounting of an amusing episode or exciting moment in the book. The narrator might want to assume the role of a character in a book, such as Julie in *Julie of the Wolves* by Jean George, and tell of her experience of being lost without food or a compass on the North Slope of Alaska. The speaker should stop before the crisis is over or the mystery is solved. Details should be specific. It is better to let the story stand on its own than to characterize it as a "terribly funny" story or the "most exciting" book you've ever read. The speaker's enthusiasm for the book will convey itself. This is one reason why book talks should be given only about stories the speaker genuinely likes. Children will then come to trust this evaluation. It is best if the book is on hand as it is discussed, so that the children can check it out as soon as the book talk is finished.

Fourth graders enjoy reading their books during SSR, or independent reading time. PS 124, New York, New York. Mary S. Gallivan, teacher.

PROVIDING TIME TO READ BOOKS

One of the primary purposes of giving book talks, telling stories, and reading aloud to children is to motivate them to read. A major goal of every school should be to develop children who *can* read but also *do* read—who love reading and will become lifetime readers.

To become fluent readers, children need to practice reading from real books that capture their interest and imagination. No one could become a competent swimmer or tennis player by practicing four minutes a day. Schools have little influence on the out-of-school life of their students, but they do control the curriculum in school. If we want children to become readers, we must reorder our priorities and provide time for children to read books of their own choosing every day.

Recognizing this need, many teachers have initiated a sustained silent reading (SSR) time. Teachers have used other names, such as "recreational reading," "free reading," or even the acronym *DEAR* (Drop Everything and Read) used by the teacher in *Ramona Quimby, Age 8* by

Small groups of children need time to discuss books together and time to plan responses to their books. PS 124, New York, New York. Mary S. Gallivan, teacher.

Beverly Cleary. Whatever the name, however, this is a time when everyone in the class (in some instances, the entire school) reads, including the teacher. SSR times have been successfully established in kindergarten through middle schools. Usually, the reading period is lengthened gradually from 10 minutes a day to 20, 30, or, in some upper-grade classes, 45 minutes per day. Recognizing the importance of social interaction among readers, teachers often allow children to read in pairs.

In classrooms that use real books for teaching reading and studying themes that cut across the curriculum, children are reading and writing throughout the day. Teachers still have a special time each day for children to read the books they have chosen to read for pleasure.

PROVIDING TIME TO TALK ABOUT BOOKS

Equally important as time for wide reading is time to talk about the books children are reading. When adults discuss books, we have good conversations about the ones we like, but we seldom quiz each other about character development, themes, or setting of the story. As teachers, we want to show this same respect for children as they share their thoughts about books.

A good time for informal talk about books is after children have had time to read by themselves. In pairs, small groups, or as a class, children may be invited to tell something about a book, show a picture and tell what is happening, read an interesting or powerful paragraph, and so forth. In such discussions, teachers can learn much about what children are reading and how they talk about

books. Margaret Meek observes this about talk in the classroom:

> Left to comment on their own, without the stimulus of a question, children often choose to talk about quite other aspects of a tale than those that preoccupy their elders. . . . They create a tissue of collaborative understandings for each other in a way that no single question from an adult makes possible.[8]

Maryann Eeds and Deborah Wells showed how well fifth and sixth graders explored the meaning of novels they were reading through nondirective response groups.[9] The literature discussion groups met two days a week, thirty minutes a day, for four to five weeks. The leaders were undergraduate education students who were instructed to let meaning emerge from the group rather than solicit it. The results of this study showed that the groups collaborated and built meaning that was deeper and richer than what they attained in their solitary reading. The authors concluded, "Talk helps to confirm, extend, and modify individual interpretations and creates a better understanding of the text."

As teachers listen carefully to children's responses in book discussion groups, they can identify teaching possibilities, plan future conversations, or make use of a teachable moment to make a point. When the teacher is an active participant rather than the director of a group, children more readily collaborate to fill their own gaps in understanding and make meaning together.

More structured discussion may occur with the books a teacher chooses to read aloud or to read with small

---

[8]Margaret Meek, "What Counts as Evidence in Theories of Children's Literature?" *Theory into Practice* 21.4 (1982): 289.

[9]Maryann Eeds and Deborah Wells, "Grand Conversations: An Exploration of Meaning Construction in Literature Study Groups," *Research in the Teaching of English* 23.1 (1989): 4–29.

A third- and fourth-grade group heard Byrd Baylor's story *I'm in Charge of Celebrations* and wrote about special days they wanted to remember. Mangere Bridge School, Auckland, New Zealand. Colleen Fleming, teacher.

groups. The teacher can play an important role in engendering fruitful discussions by demonstrating the types of responses she hopes children will make. When the teacher introduces the story, she might invite children to recognize the author or illustrator, to notice the dedication, or to speculate on the book's content as they look at the cover. As she gives children time to look at the illustrations in picture books, she asks, "How do these pictures make you feel?" "What are you thinking about as you look at these illustrations?" As she reads a chapter book, she asks what might happen next or why a character acts as he does. She might introduce Mollie Hunter's *A Stranger Came Ashore* by reading Susan Cooper's *Selkie Girl* and discussing selkie lore with the class. She might pause at a chapter's end and ask children how Hunter makes the reader feel that something dreadful is about to happen. She might ask what clues suggest that Finn Learson is not who he pretends to be. She might introduce the term *foreshadowing* and ask the children to listen for other examples as she reads. At first the teacher calls attention to aspects such as a well-written passage, an apt chapter heading, or a key moment when a character faces a choice. Later, children will begin noticing the kinds of things the teacher has brought out in these discussions. In this way a teacher models reader behaviors that mature readers practice.[10]

PROVIDING TIME FOR THE IN-DEPTH STUDY OF BOOKS

If children are to have an opportunity to read and discuss widely, this activity should be balanced with a time for studying books deeply. When children work with books in ways that are meaningful to them—through talk, art

making, writing, or drama and music—many things happen. Children have greater satisfaction with, and clarify personal meanings about, what they have read. These activities allow many books to be visible in the classroom. One child's work with a book can dramatically influence another child's willingness to read it. Children working on projects use various skills, exercise more choices, develop planning abilities, and experiment with a variety of learning experiences. In addition, these activities can allow children the opportunity to think more deeply about books and to return to them to explore responses in ways that deepen their understandings.

Teachers who know the children in their classes well recognize the diversity of learning styles this sort of active learning accommodates. They plan diverse activities that enhance children's delight in books, make them want to continue reading more and better books, and cause them to think both more widely and more specifically about what they have read. They know that many options should be open to children and do not expect all children to choose the same book or have the same type of response to a book. They consult with children about possibilities for projects and do not assign all children to do the same project; neither do they expect children to do an activity for every book that they read. The activities suggested here are planned to increase children's enjoyment and understanding of books. Other suggestions for extending books can be found in the "Framework for Webbing" on page 690.

Children's Writing and Children's Books

Children's written work should grow out of their own rich experiences, whether with people, places, and things;

---

[10]See Taffy E. Raphael and Susan I. McMahon, "Book Club: An Alternative Framework for Reading Instruction," *Reading Teacher* 48.2 (1994): 102–16 for another approach to discussion groups.

After a class study of alphabet books, a fifth grader created "An Occupied Alphabet," showing various occupations.
Allison Fraser, grade 5. George Mason Elementary School, Alexandria City Public Schools, Alexandria, Virginia. Susan Steinberg, teacher.

research and observation; or literature. Children's writing about books can take many forms. Children should have many opportunities to write about the books they are reading. They should also be encouraged to use books as models for their own writing.

Real possibilities for writing are all around us in the classroom; however, it is literature that gives children a sense of how the written word sounds and looks. Frank Smith suggests that the role of literature in the writing program is central:

> Reading seems to me to be the essential fundamental source of knowledge about writing, from the conventions of transcription to the subtle differences of register and discourse structures in various genres.[11]

Literature has made a tremendous impact on reading programs, and so too has the writing process approach. Few teachers would consider teaching reading without including writing, because learning in one area means learning in the other. Literature informs both processes. As children become authors, they look at professional authors to see how a book works and sounds. They borrow and improvise on the language, patterns, and format of published books.[12] Young children rewrite their favorite stories (see Chapter 4), particularly when they can use invented spellings and do not have to produce a "correct" copy. Writing and reading go on all day in a classroom where language arts and reading are intertwined and literature is at the heart of the curriculum.

Helping Children Write about Books

In most schools children are no longer required to write book reports, a particularly inert kind of writing. However, many teachers ask children to write about their reading in other ways. This writing resembles talk, in that a child shares ideas and someone responds to those ideas. Teachers find this is a time-saving idea and can set aside a weekly or biweekly time to react in writing to children's written responses. Some teachers demonstrate supportive responses and let pairs of children react to each other's written work as well. There are various ways a teacher can help children write about their reading.

A *reading log* is a simple record of the title and author of each book a child has read. Needless to say, this is a burden for young children, but it is a source of pride for second graders and older children who like to recall their

---

[11]Frank Smith, *Writing and the Writer* (New York: Holt, 1982), p. 177.

[12]See Frederick R. Burton, "Writing What They Read: Reflections on Literature and Child Writers," in *Stories to Grow On*, ed. Julie M. Jensen (Portsmouth, N.H.: Heinemann, 1989), pp. 97–105.

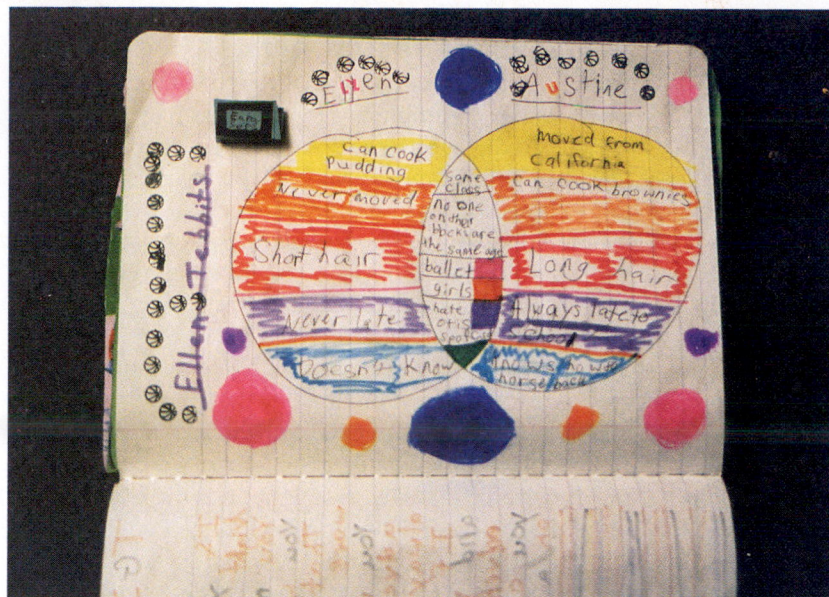

Fifth graders were invited to record their responses to books in sketchbook journals. Beginning with Children School, Brooklyn, New York. Carmen Gordillo, teacher. Photo by Barbara Z. Kiefer.

reading and measure their progress. Teachers might give children six-by-eight-inch cards and let them fill in one side. Then the teacher and child can use these records for generalizing as they talk together about a child's reading. If a child takes her most recent card to the library, librarians might better help her find a book by seeing what she has enjoyed so far.

In a *response journal* children record their comments as they read a novel. Children respond freely as they think about their reading and write about the things that concern or interest them. A *double-entry draft* is a two-sided journal entry in which the reader copies or paraphrases a quote from the book on the left half of the paper. On the right, the reader comments on the quote. Teachers react to both of these journals and engage in a written dialogue with the reader (thereby creating a *dialogue journal*). Whatever we call them, children's written responses to the books they read provide teachers with another window into understanding how readers teach themselves to read.

Writing about books in the same way every day becomes tedious. Teachers may want to vary the way children can respond. They might invite children to keep a *sketchbook/journal*, where visual art serves as a preface to writing.[13] A single dialogue journal might be kept by a group reading the same book and children can take turns responding. Children might ask their own questions and consider which ones are more interesting to write about. Media-savvy children might be motivated to keep journal entries in the form of a blog[14] or to submit commentary on books to bulletin boards or sites such as Amazon.com or Barnesandnoble.com.

Teachers might also ask children to address in their journals a particular question about their wide reading or about a class study book. They might write a journal entry from the point of view of a character in the book they are reading, for instance. During the group reading of a novel, a teacher might ask children to write about some issue prior to a class discussion as a way of rehearsing an idea. A small group who have just read the first ten pages of David Almond's *Skellig* might be asked to speculate on the identity of the creature Michael has found. After finishing this novel, children might discuss how and why Michael and Mina changed in the story, or what the story made them think about. They might consider how this book is like others they have read, thus making links between books.

What teachers need to avoid, however, is overusing written response or using a journal as a place in which children answer numbers of questions posed by the teacher. The primary power of journals is that the child owns the ideas, not the teacher. The child is director of the reading, and the child reflects on matters of interest to herself. When children write about their reading, they follow certain patterns, such as retelling, questioning particular words, clarifying meanings, reacting with like or dislike to a particular part of the story, relating a part of the story to their own lives, or otherwise reflecting.

Books and Children's Writing

When children have a chance to become writers themselves, they begin to notice how other authors work. Literature suggests the many forms that stories, information,

---

[13]See Karen Ernst, *Picturing Learning* (Portsmouth, N.H.: Heinemann, 1994).

[14]See Blog-City <www.blog-city.com/bc/> and Blog*Spot <www.blogger.com/start>.

or poetry can take; as children experiment with the model, they begin to develop a sensitivity to the conventions of the form. This awareness in turn allows them to bring a wider frame of reference to the reading and writing that follow.

Children in elementary classrooms should have an opportunity to experience a variety of well-written fiction, poetry, and nonfiction. At the same time, they can be encouraged to develop an appreciation of language and form through writing. In this way, children develop a sensitivity to language, an increasing control over the power of words, and a diverse writing repertoire.

Ideas for writing can come from the child's own life and from the classroom curriculum. They can also be inspired by books. Teachers can read aloud and then display individual books that serve as springboards or provocative formats for children's writing. Virginia Wright-Frierson's *A North American Rain Forest Scrapbook,* Margaret Wise Brown's *The Important Book,* or Vera B. Williams's *Three Days on a River in a Red Canoe* could serve as possible models for children to use. Many reading and writing connections have been explored in previous chapters. Teaching Resources: "Books That Serve as Writing Models" suggests stories that teachers might share as examples and incentives for children's own writing.

Exploring Literature through the Visual Arts

Young children communicate through visual symbols as easily as they communicate through language, yet by the middle grades many children feel very insecure about making art. Children of *all* ages who have the opportunity to transform their responses to books through visual means are learning to be confident creators. In addition, their familiarity with art can increase their visual literacy and their aesthetic understanding.

Too often children are given a box of crayons and a small space at the top of some lined newsprint paper and told to "make a picture" of the story. How much better it is to work with children who are "filled to overflowing" with knowledge about a book or theme. How much more lively artwork might be if the teacher provided many materials from which to choose instead of the usual crayons and thin newsprint. Chalk, paints, markers, colored tissue papers, yarn, steel wool, cotton, material scraps, wires—anything that might be useful in depicting characters and scenes should be readily accessible. Teachers might provide more interesting paper such as wallpaper samples, construction paper, hand-painted papers, and remainders from printers. Then when children are asked to make pictures of their favorite part of

After interviewing each other, fifth graders painted pictures and wrote biographical sketches following the pattern of *The Important Book* by Margaret Wise Brown, illustrated by Leonard Weisgard. Esther L. Walter Elementary School, Anaheim Public Schools, Anaheim, California. Janine Batzle, teacher.

Books That Serve as Writing Models

 Visit the Online Learning Center at **www.mhhe.com/kiefer9e** for a printable version of this list.

Title	Author	Grade Level	Type of Writing
The Jolly Postman, or Other People's Letters	Ahlberg and Ahlberg	1 and up	Letters from one folktale character to another
Gilda Joyce, Psychic Investigator	Allison	4–7	Letters, stories, journal entries
The Nutty News	Barrett	All ages	Parody of tabloid newspaper
A Gathering of Days: A New England Girl's Journal, 1830–1832	Blos	5 and up	Historical fiction in journal form
The Burning Questions of Bingo Brown	Byars	5–8	Journal of interesting questions
Dear Annie	Caseley	1–4	Letters between a girl and her grandfather
Dear Mr. Henshaw	Cleary	5–7	Story told in letters and journal entries
Strider	Cleary	6 and up	Journal entries
Catherine Called Birdy	Cushman	5 and up	Journal entries
Anne Frank: The Diary of a Young Girl	Frank	5 and up	Historical World War II diary
My Side of the Mountain	George	4–7	Diary
The Secret Blog of Raisin Rodriguez	Goldschmidt	6 and up	Blog entries
Jazmine's Notebook	Grimes	5–8	Notebook entries and poems
The Private Notebook of Katie Roberts, Age 11	Hest	4–6	Diary and letters
Onion Tears	Kidd	3–6	Story partially revealed in letters
Trial by Journal	Klise	5–7	Journal and scrapbook
Hey World, Here I Am!	Little	4–7	Poetry and journal entries from Kate, also a character in Little's books
Anastasia Krupnik	Lowry	3–6	Lists and poetry
Operation Red Jericho	Mowll	6 and up	Letters, maps, diagrams, photographs, and other supporting materials
Autobiography of My Dead Brother	Myers	6 and up	Sketches, comic strips, and text
TTYL	Myracle	6 and up	Instant messaging (IM) transcripts

(continued)

Books That Serve as Writing Models (*continued*)

Title	Author	Grade Level	Type of Writing
Z for Zachariah	O'Brien	4–6	Novel in diary form
Call Me María	Ortiz Cofer	6 and up	Poems, letters, and prose
Libby on Wednesday	Snyder	5–8	Writing group
Cherries and Cherry Pits	Williams	1 and up	Pictures that serve as prewriting for a child's story
Stringbean's Trip to the Shining Sea	Williams	2 and up	Story in postcard form
Three Days on a River in a Red Canoe	Williams	2–5	Journal in words and pictures
You Have to Write	Wong	2–5	A poem about developing writing ideas
An Island Scrapbook: Dawn to Dusk on a Barrier Island	Wright-Frierson	1–5	Naturalist's sketchbook/diary

A fourth grader made a stunning collage of Gerald McDermott's *Anansi the Spider* using colored tissue paper, yarn, and felt. Martin Luther King, Jr., Laboratory School, Evanston Public Schools, Evanston, Illinois. Barbara Friedberg, teacher.

a story, of a character doing something in the book they have read, or illustrations for their own stories, the results are more exciting.

Paintings, murals, sculptures, crafts, constructions, assemblages, collages, mobiles and stabiles, stitchery and multimedia creations are among the possibilities for visual expression in the classroom. Children's work should mirror the same range of artistic expression found in the world of visual art outside the classroom. The teacher's role is to design a rich environment for creativity by providing materials, challenging children's thinking, and honoring children's work.

Displays of children's responses can be assembled and mounted carefully. They can be placed alongside a book or books that inspired the work or arranged as a summary of a thematic study. Often a study of a book or genre is extensive enough to warrant a museum exhibit. Explanations written by children help clarify for parents and other classroom observers how the work was created.

Media Exploration

A teacher can also make use of a child's desire to replicate an illustrator's way of working by encouraging children to explore various media. Kindergarten children saved their finger-painting pictures, cut them up, and used them to create their own story illustrated in the col-

lage style of four of Eric Carle's stories, *The Very Hungry Caterpillar, The Very Busy Spider, The Very Clumsy Click Beetle*, and *The Very Quiet Cricket*. (See Literature in Action: "Creating Big Books with Emergent Readers" in Chapter 4.) Older children used dampened rice paper, ink, and watercolor to try to capture the look of traditional Japanese artwork used by Meilo So in *Tasty Baby Belly Buttons* by Judy Sierra. These children were answering for themselves the question "How did the illustrator make the pictures?"

Techniques that easily translate to the elementary classroom include collage, scratchboard, marbleized paper, many varieties of painting and printing, and stencil prints. By making these materials and processes readily available for children, teachers can extend the ways in which they visualize their world as well as their appreciation for illustrators' works. Teaching Resources: "Exploring Artists' Media" provides an overview of illustrators who work in some of these media and a list of materials that will allow children to explore these techniques.

Creating Graphic Organizers

A graphic organizer is a visual representation of an idea. Semantic maps, attribute Webs, or word Webs often are used to help children group similar ideas into categories following a brainstorming session and display them

After reading Kathy Jakobsen's *My New York,* fourth graders created a map of the city that showed their own favorite places in the city. PS 124, New York, New York. Mary S. Gallivan, teacher.

Exploring Artists' Media

 Visit the Online Learning Center at **www.mhhe.com/kiefer9e** for a printable version of this list.

MEDIUM: PRINTMAKING

Materials Needed
Styrofoam trays

Ballpoint pen or other blunt instrument

Soft rubber cutting blocks (available from art supply houses)

Linoleum block cutters

Potatoes

Water-based printing inks or acrylic paints in tubes

Books That Use Similar Techniques
My Beastie Book of ABC by David Frampton

Why the Sky Is Far Away by Mary-Joan Gerson, illustrated by Carla Golembe

At Jerusalem's Gate by Nikki Grimes, illustrated by David Frampton

Snowflake Bentley by Jaqueline Briggs Martin, illustrated by Mary Azarian

One Potato: A Counting Book of Potato Prints by Diana Pomeroy

MEDIUM: AIRBRUSH TECHNIQUE AND STENCILS

Materials Needed
Old file folders or stencil paper
Pastel chalks

Paint

Sponges, bristle brush, toothbrush

Books That Use Similar Techniques
Why Mosquitoes Buzz in People's Ears by Verna Aardema, illustrated by Leo Dillon and Diane Dillon

The Pot That Juan Built by Nancy Andrews-Goebel, illustrated by David Diaz

Sail Away by Donald Crews

All of You Was Singing by Richard Lewis, illustrated by Ed Young

MEDIUM: SCRATCHBOARD AND CRAYON RESIST

Materials Needed
Construction paper or poster board

Crayons

Black tempera paint or India ink

Incising tools or blunt instrument

Commercial scratchboard and tools

Books That Use Similar Techniques
Giants in the Land by Diana Appelbaum, illustrated by Michael McCurdy

A Creepy Countdown by Charlotte Huck, illustrated by Jos. A. Smith

The Hidden Folk by Lise Lunge-Larsen, illustrated by Beth Krommes

In the Time of the Drums by Kim Siegelson, illustrated by Brian Pinkney

Mammoths on the Move by Lisa Wheeler, illustrated by Kurt Cyrus

MEDIUM: COLLAGE AND CUT PAPER

Materials Needed
Wallpapers, wrapping papers, string, marbleized papers,

Books That Use Similar Techniques
To Be a Drum by Evelyn Coleman, illustrated by Aminah Brenda Lynne Robinson

Exploring Artists' Media (continued)

MEDIUM: COLLAGE AND CUT PAPER (continued)

Materials Needed	**Books That Use Similar Techniques**
construction paper, painted papers, paste papers	*Leaf Man* by Lois Ehlert
	The Top of the World: Climbing Mount Everest by Steve Jenkins
	One Horse Waiting for Me by Patricia Mullins
	Kogi's Mysterious Journey by Elizabeth Partridge, illustrated by Aki Sogabe
	The Subway Mouse by Barbara Reid
	Pumpkin Day by Nancy Elizabeth Wallace
	The Sons of the Dragon King by Ed Young

to others. In these graphic organizers, a word or idea is placed at the center of a chart with spokes radiating toward related words, attributes, or other examples. One group listed "Outsiders in Literature" at the center of a semantic map and drew lines out to the various characters from novels who seem different from their peers. At the chart's center were clustered words describing insiders. Word Webs or semantic maps are also useful synthesizing aids for children who are organizing material from a variety of books and sources prior to writing a report. The Webs that have been used throughout this book are examples of a kind of semantic mapping.

Venn diagrams and comparison charts have been used as tools for organizing talk and thought, too. One teacher asked a group of children who had read many novels by Betsy Byars to discuss how they are similar. Midway through the conversation children had raised such points as "The parents are never around," "The main character is usually about our age," and "Some big problem is always there." The teacher then helped children generate a chart with the titles of Byars's books, such as *The Night Swimmers, Cracker Jackson,* and *The Pinballs,* placed top-to-bottom on the left side of a large sheet of paper. Across the top of the chart, the children generated categories, such as "Where the Parents Are,"

A fourth grader carefully examined Suekichi Akaba's illustrations for *The Crane Wife* by Sumiko Yagawa before trying out his own watercolor response. Barrington Elementary School, Upper Arlington, Ohio. Marlene Harbert, teacher.

"About the Main Character," "Big Problems," and "Who Helps and How." Now that the conversation was well under way, the graphic organizer helped children focus and continue the discussion while they filled in the grid they had created on the chart. Later, other Byars books were added, such as *The Summer of the Swans* and *The House of Wings,* which children also read to see how they fit the pattern. Children created artwork that represented some of the categories and wrote about how the books were alike and different. These were matted and hung

Fifth and sixth graders made a type of sociogram to identify the "outsiders" in various stories. Personality traits that would make you an "insider" were written in the inner circle. Ridgemont Elementary School, Mt. Victory, Ohio. Sheryl Reed and Peggy Harrison, teachers.

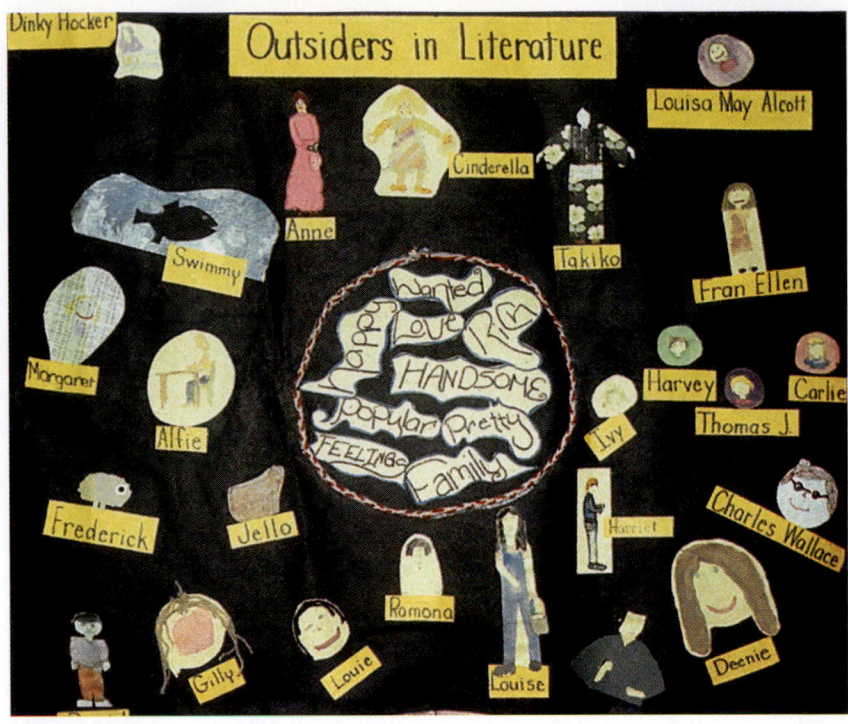

A group of primary children read five folktales and constructed a comparison chart to show similarities and differences among the stories. Wickliffe Alternative School, Upper Arlington, Ohio. Photo by Barbara Z. Kiefer.

next to the comparison chart. This activity helped the children analyze particular stories, synthesize several stories, and evaluate later readings. From the chart, they were able to generalize about books by one author, a sophisticated skill for 10- and 11-year-olds.

Music and Movement in the Classroom

Children often enjoy singing to picture-book versions of well-known songs. They can also interpret literature by composing music or creating a dance. These activities help them think more carefully about the mood of a story or poem and consider their emotional responses to books more thoroughly.

In recent years, there have been numerous fine picture-book interpretations of well-known songs, including *Yankee Doodle* by Mary Ann Hoberman, *The Farmer in the Dell* by Alexandra Wallner, and *A-Hunting We Will Go* by Steven Kellogg. To children who already know the song, the text of these books presents easy and enjoyable reading.

Many familiar folk songs have been researched and presented in authentic historic detail by such authors as Peter Spier and Woody Guthrie. Spier presents *The Star-Spangled Banner* with historical background so that the songs almost become an informational book, too. These various editions are a good way to make American history come alive as children are introduced to many folk songs that are a part of the American folk tradition.

In addition to the classroom extensions suggested, children might enjoy making their own book versions of other traditional songs like "Home on the Range," "Where Have All the Flowers Gone," or "Old Dan Tucker." Scott R. Sanders has invented details and told his own stories for twenty folk songs in *Hear the Wind Blow: American Folk Songs Retold*. Some of these long and often funny stories would inspire fifth and sixth graders' imaginations.

A group of 7-year-olds dance "The Wild Rumpus" after hearing Maurice Sendak's *Where the Wild Things Are.* West LaFayette Public Schools, Indiana. Nancy Sawrey, teacher.

Matching Music and Literature

The process of identifying appropriate music to accompany prose and poetry selections helps children appreciate mood and tone in both literature and music. Second graders discussed the kind of music that could accompany the action of Maurice Sendak's *Where the Wild Things Are.* They recognized and created music with increasing tempo and volume, followed by a quiet conclusion of the story. Older children might enjoy reading one of Jack Prelutsky's *Nightmares* poems to music of their own choosing. A teacher might let children listen to Edvard Grieg's "In the Hall of the Mountain King" or Richard Wagner's "Valkyries' Ride" and ask children which of Prelutsky's poems best suit these pieces.

Many themes of subjects featured in literature have counterparts in music. For instance, the quiet awakening of the day in *Dawn* by Uri Shulevitz might be compared to the "Sunrise" movement from the *Grand Canyon Suite* by Ferde Grofé or to Cat Stevens's rendition of Eleanor Farjeon's poem "Morning Has Broken." Teachers can encourage older students to develop their sensitivity to recurring themes in art by juxtaposing literature and music.

Composing Music

Poetry can be set to music as children create melody and identify the rhythmical elements. One group of talented 7-year-olds composed music to accompany their own sad tale of a princess who was captured during a battle and taken from her palace. Her knight-in-arms wandered the lonely countryside in search of her, while the poor princess grieved for him in her prison tower. The children made up a musical theme for each of the main characters, which they repeated during the various movements of their composition. The story was first told to

their classmates, and then the song was played on the autoharp and glockenspiel. Older students composed a three-movement rhythmical symphony for Ged in Ursula K. Le Guin's *A Wizard of Earthsea.* A recorder repeated Ged's theme in appropriate places in this percussion piece. When literature provides the inspiration for children's musical compositions, children's appreciation for both literature and music will be enriched. Computer programs such as Apple's GarageBand not only make the creation of musical compositions to interpret literature and accompany projects possible but also motivate children to undertake such activities.[15]

Movement and Literature

Increasing attention has been given to children's control of their own body movements. The relationship between thought and movement has received much attention, particularly in England. Basic rhythmical movements might be introduced through Mother Goose rhymes. For example, children could walk to "Tommy Snooks and Bessie Brooks," gallop to "Ride a Cock Horse," jump to "Jack Be Nimble," and run to "Wee Willie Winkie." Nursery rhymes could also motivate dramatic action with such verses as "Hickory Dickory Dock," "Three Blind Mice," and "Jack and Jill."

A favorite poem for young children to move to is "Holding Hands" by Lenore M. Link, which describes the ponderous way in which elephants walk. By way of contrast, Evelyn Beyer's poem "Jump or Jiggle" details the walk of frogs, caterpillars, worms, bugs, rabbits, and horses. It provides a wonderful opportunity for children to develop diverse movements. Both poems can be found in Jack Prelutsky's *Read-Aloud Rhymes for the Very Young.* In Jean Marzollo's *Pretend You're a Cat,* a longer poem that Jerry Pinkney illustrates as a picture book,

---

[15]For more information, go to <www.apple.com/education/garageband/lesson_plans/>.

Pinkney's watercolors portray twelve animals and, on the facing pages, children pretending to walk, wiggle, or jump like those particular animals. Children also enjoy making the hand motions and sounds for *We're Going on a Bear Hunt* by Michael Rosen, as the adventurous family goes through a river, "Splash, splosh."

As children learn basic movements, they can use them in different areas of space, at different levels, and at different tempos. Swinging, bending, stretching, twisting, bouncing, and shaking are the kinds of body movements that can be made by standing tall, at a middle position, or by stooping low. For example, "A Swing Song" by William Allingham could be interpreted by swinging, pushing motions that vary in speed according to the words in the poem. Other poetry that suggests movement includes "Stop, Go" by Dorothy Baruch, "The African Dance" by Langston Hughes, and "The Potatoes' Dance" by Vachel Lindsay. All of these poems can be found in *Favorite Poems Old and New,* compiled by Helen Ferris.

Children who have had this kind of experience are ready to create rhythmical interpretations of a longer story. *May I Bring a Friend?* by Beatrice Schenk de Regniers, *Where the Wild Things Are* by Maurice Sendak, and *Koala Lou* by Mem Fox are examples of stories that lend themselves to rhythmical interpretations.

Extending Literature through Drama

Books become more real to children as they identify with the characters through creative drama. Young children begin this identification with others through *dramatic play*. A 5-year-old engaged in impromptu play might become an airplane zooming to an airport built of blocks; another assumes the role of mother in the playhouse. Sometimes children of this age will play a very familiar story without adult direction. For example, "The Three Billy Goats Gruff" and "The Three Bears" are often favorites. Dramatic play represents this free response of children as they interpret experience.

In schools, this type of natural response can find an outlet in activities that are part of a creative drama program. Creative drama is structured and cooperatively planned playmaking, an approach to learning that focuses on processes rather than production. While occasionally a play developed creatively will be shared with others, the value of creative drama lies in the process of playing and does not require an audience. Creative drama activities exist on a continuum from interpretation to improvisation and can include pantomime, story dramatization, improvisation, readers' theater, and puppetry. All of these activities provide important ways for children to reenter the world of a book, to consider the characters, events, problems, and themes that are central in good literature. Such engagement brings children joy and zest in learning and living while broadening their understandings of both literature and life.

Dramatizing Stories

Very young children aged 3 through 5 will become involved in dramatic play, but they usually do not have the sustained attention to act out a complete story. They might play a part of a favorite folktale (for example, crossing the bridge as in "The Three Billy Goats Gruff"), but they seldom will complete a whole story. And no one should expect them to.

Primary-grade children enjoy playing simple stories such as the funny tale *Nine-in-One Grr! Grr!* by Blia Xiong or *The Little Red Hen* by Harriet Ziefert. Folktales are also a rich source of dramatization. They are usually short and have plenty of action, a quick plot, and interesting characters.

Stories from myths, such as "Pandora's Box" or "King Midas' Touch," are fine material for 9- to 11-year-olds to dramatize. Middle-grade children also enjoy presenting parts of books to each other in the form of debates, interviews, or discussions or television talk shows. A group of students played the roles of various characters in Natalie Babbitt's *Tuck Everlasting* and were interviewed by another student who took the role of a television talk-show host. They told about their own roles in the events that had taken place and voiced advantages and disadvantages of Winnie's living forever if she chose to drink water from a magic spring. Teachers can help children focus on important and complex issues that characters face in literature by providing these opportunities to explore ideas. This exploration is often a precursor of children's developing the ability to discover themes in literature or factors that influence characters to change.

Readers' Theater

Teachers who are hesitant to try drama in their classroom might well begin with *readers' theater,* which involves a group of children in reading a play, a story, or a poem. Children are assigned to read particular parts. After reading through their parts silently, children read the text orally.

Children thoroughly enjoy participating in readers' theater; even though they do not create the dialogue, as they do in improvisation or drama, they do interpret the character's personalities and the mood of the story. They also interact with each other in a kind of play form. The story provides the script, which makes it easy to try in the classroom.

In adapting a story for readers' theater, teachers or students must edit the text to omit phrases like *he said* and *she replied*. A child narrator needs to read the connecting prose between dialogue. Older children can write their own introductions and decide whether to leave out long descriptive passages or summarize them. Many teachers have found it useful to duplicate the parts of the story that children will read. This way, children can highlight their own parts and cross out unnecessary words.

The most effective readers' theater selections contain a lot of dialogue. Folktales are easily adapted for

With the help of their teacher a group of fifth graders create a readers' theater performance for their classmates. Beginning with Children School, Brooklyn, New York. Carmen Gordillo, teacher. Photo by Barbara Z. Kiefer.

primary children. Some good choices would be Steven Kellogg's *Chicken Little,* Paul Galdone's *The Little Red Hen,* or Carol Jones's *The Gingerbread Man.* At first the teacher might read the narrator's part and let children take the different roles. When children become more capable readers and have had practice with readers' theater, they can take over the role of narrator.

A variant of readers' theater best suited to younger children is a form of pantomime called *story theater.* Here a narrator reads a story aloud while children take the role of characters and act out the unfolding tale. Books that have a lot of action or emotional reaction make the best candidates for story theater. The teacher or librarian might read aloud Aleksei Tolstoy's *The Gigantic Turnip* while six children pantomime being the old man, the old woman, the little granddaughter, the dog, the calico cat, and the mouse. As the children gain confidence with this kind of drama, the teacher can stop at appropriate points when the old man calls to his wife and invite the designated child to create the dialogue. Moving from pantomime to extemporaneous dialogue is an easy transition to more complex forms of story reenactment.

Puppetry

Many children will lose themselves in the characterization of a puppet while hidden behind a puppet stage even though they might hesitate to express ideas and feelings in front of the class. Through puppetry, children learn to project their voices and develop facility in varying their voice quality to portray different characters. For example, a rather quiet, shy child might use a booming voice as he becomes the giant in "Jack and the Beanstalk." Puppetry also facilitates the development of skills in arts and crafts. Problems of stage construction, backdrops for scenery, and the modeling of characters provide opportunities for the development of creative thinking. A well-played puppet show extends children's appreciation and interpretation of stories and makes literature a more memorable experience for them.

Beginning in kindergarten with the construction of paper-bag or simple stick figures, children can gain pleasure from their involvement with puppetry. Materials and types of puppets will range from the simple to the complex, depending on age and the child.

The teaching techniques used in creative drama should be followed, as puppet plays are created cooperatively by children and teachers. It is highly recommended that children "play out" stories before using their puppets. Written scripts are not necessary and can prove very limiting. Playing the story creatively allows the child to identify with the characters before becoming involved with the creation and mechanical manipulation of the puppet.

CONNECTING LITERATURE AND LIFE

Children sometimes have difficulty picturing life in other times or places or understanding historical time. They can experience books more completely through making maps and time lines and by compiling special collections. Children who thus ask questions about the details and events in literature are also introduced to methods of inquiry and research.

Artifacts and Collections

Items or artifacts mentioned in books often seem strange to children, even if explained in context. A child who reads that Ma Ingalls cooked prairie dinners in a spider would be puzzled until she could see this three-legged pan in a reference such as *Colonial Life* by Bobbie Kalman. Hefting a modern-day cast-iron replica would give a child a sense of the endurance of these utensils. This object, although a small part of the story, nonetheless connects reader experience with a part of the real world.

A class collection could involve children in assembling book-related artifacts on a large scale. Second graders studying pioneers, for example, made and collected items that pioneers might have taken west with them:

such as a wooden spoon, a cornhusk doll, a flour sack, and a wagon wheel. As the teacher read aloud *Trouble for Lucy* by Carla Stevens, children added to the display their facsimiles of the wagon master's log, a bouquet of wildflowers gathered by those who walked beside the moving wagons, and a "letter" from Marcus Whitman detailing his experiences with the wagon train. Labels were made for each article as it was added to the display.

Maps and Time Lines

Often authors of books with historical settings include a geographical map to help the reader locate the story setting. In *Araminta's Paint Box* by Karen Ackerman, a map shows two routes—the route a pioneer girl took to California, and the route her paint box took after she lost it. Other stories make sufficient reference to actual places so that children can infer a story location by carefully comparing the story and a contemporary map. One group of fourth graders found on a road map the probable route Ann Hamilton took in the 1780s when she walked across Pennsylvania in Jean Fritz's *The Cabin Faced West.* The movement of the Wilder family in the Little House books by Laura Ingalls Wilder can be followed on a map. Many fictional and biographical accounts of immigrants can be traced on world maps.

As with many of the previous activities or projects in this chapter, maps, too, can help children look across a genre. The sources of folktales might be identified on a world map. The domains of tall-tale heroes and monsters might be located on a U.S. map. African folktales, fiction, and nonfiction might be located on a map of Africa as a way of differentiating features and regions of that continent. Children need many encounters with maps and their working parts (key, symbols, scale, direction) before they become skilled users of all that a map can reveal.

Older children often enjoy making detailed maps of imaginary "countries of the mind," such as that in Lloyd Alexander's *The Remarkable Journey of Prince Jen* or his Prydain in *The Book of Three,* Ursula K. Le Guin's archipelagos in *A Wizard of Earthsea,* or Brian Jacques's Mossflower Woods surrounding *Redwall.* While fantasy provides ample opportunities for children to design their own maps imaginatively, other genres of books can be mapped as well.

The concept of time is difficult for children to grasp until sometime near the end of the concrete operational stage of thinking or the beginning of formal operations (ages 11 to 12). Prior to this period, time lines may help students organize events in a person's life as represented in a book. Time lines also allow children to represent a synthesis of events in several books. A time line from Jean Fritz's *And Then What Happened, Paul Revere?* might include the date of Paul Revere's birth, the date he took over his father's business, the summer he spent in the army, his famous ride, and his death in 1818. Events in the lives of Revere's contemporaries, such as Benjamin

Franklin or George Washington, might be more easily compared if they were placed on a time line of the same scale as Revere's.

Placing book events in the world's time challenges even sophisticated readers to select relevant events in both the book and human history. A three-strand time line allows children to separate groups or types of events from others. While *Friedrich,* Hans Peter Richter's story of a Jewish boy caught in pre–World War II Germany, contains a "chronology" of dates in a reference at the back of the book, students might represent selected governmental decrees on one stratum of a time line. A second stratum might represent the number of Jews living in the Third Reich according to yearly censuses. A third stratum might list important events in Friedrich's life. In this way children could see more clearly the political events against which Friedrich's tragic life was played out.

In making time lines, children need to agree on a scale so that events can be clearly shown—by year or by decade, for instance. Time lines can be made of string from which markers for events and years are hung. If children make time lines on a long roll of paper, entries can be written on cards or Post-it notes and placed temporarily along the line. In this way, corrections or realignments can be made easily.

Jackdaws

The term *jackdaw* comes from the British name for a relative of the crow that picks up brightly colored objects and carries them off to its nest. Commercially prepared jackdaw collections are sometimes available from museums and historical sites. These collections, based on an

This jackdaw was assembled to help children understand the many themes and historical events in Graham Salisbury's *Under the Blood-Red Sun.*

A group of fourth graders studying New York City made a display of their responses to the books they had read. PS 124, New York, New York. Mary S. Gallivan, teacher.

historical event or period, often include facsimile copies of diaries, letters, newspaper articles, advertisements, and other evidence from the time.

Teachers of elementary school children have modified this concept to suit activities and discussion with younger children. These teacher-made collections assemble resource materials that the teacher and children can handle in discussion, in display, or in actual construction and use. A jackdaw for Yoshiko Uchida's *Journey to Topaz,* for example, might include maps of the western United States on which children could locate the camps in which this Japanese American family was imprisoned in World War II. The jackdaw might also include photocopies of newspaper headlines of the time, relevant articles from that period from magazines such as *Time* and *Colliers,* a facsimile copy of one of the exclu-

sion orders families were handed, and information about the author. Articles and documents that could accompany Laurence Yep's *Dragonwings* include reproductions of photographs of turn-of-the-century San Francisco's Chinatown, photographs of contemporary newspaper accounts of Chinese-built airplanes, a kite like the one Moon Shadow flew, and some green tea. Often sources for the factual material on which an historical fiction title is based are given in an author's note. Some jackdaws can then include copies of these actual source materials, or "facsimiles" can be created by the children. All materials can be placed in an appropriately decorated portfolio or box. Literature in Action: "Making a Jackdaw" suggests some of the items that might be included in a jackdaw. Individual book titles will suggest other artifacts that children could include.

LITERATURE IN **ACTION**

Making a Jackdaw

Each book will suggest its own specific items or references to collect. Here is a general list of things that might be included.

- Recipes from the book's time (a typical dinner, a menu for a celebration)
- Price lists of commonly purchased goods then and now (milk, shoes, a dozen eggs, a car)
- A time line of the book's events
- A time line of the period surrounding the book's events
- A map, actual or imagined, of the setting
- A letter, diary, log, or news article that could have been written by or about a book character

- A photocopy of a book-related news article or document
- Artwork from the period (painting, architecture, sculpture)
- Songs, music, or dances from the book's setting (sheet music or lyrics, tapes)
- Clothes of characters of the period (paper dolls, catalog format, collage)
- Something about the author of the book
- A list of other fiction or nonfiction references

Helping children make connections between literature and their own experiences is an important teacher role. However, teachers need to recognize when enough is enough. After a six-week study of Laura Ingalls Wilder's *Farmer Boy*, one fifth grader said, "I hate this book." If teachers' first priority is to foster children's love of reading, they will be less likely to overburden children with factual inquiry. Teachers who appreciate the child's desire to know as a prior condition of learning can appreciate Louise Rosenblatt's criterion for the usefulness of background information: "It will have value only when the student feels the need of it and when it is assimilated into the student's experience of particular literary works."[16]

CONNECTING BOOKS ACROSS THE CURRICULUM

The long-term goal of any literature program is the development of a lifetime pattern of preference for reading quality literature. James Britton maintained that in a quality reading/literature program "a student should read *more books* with satisfaction . . . [and] he should read books with *more satisfaction*."[17] This emphasis on both wide reading and in-depth reading is characteristic of a literature program that develops fluency and appreciation. It also requires that children make many connections among books and across the curriculum.

Teachers can plan in-depth studies of a single book; books by an author or illustrator; a part of a genre, such as dragon folktales or historical fiction that portrays the colonial period; or a theme that cuts across the curriculum but begins with a subject area such as science.

Using Webbing to Plan Curriculum

One way to begin planning curriculum is to make a Web of the many possibilities inherent as the class studies a book, a genre, an author, or a theme. Creating a Web is a way of brainstorming and outlining over a period of time. The goal is to get as many ideas and books as possible committed to paper before you shape their use in the classroom.

"A Framework for Webbing" (p. 691) is really a Web on the process of Webbing. For this reason, it does not contain any specific book titles, only general activities for children to do that might help you in your planning. For example, you could place any title of a book, a genre, a topic, or an author/illustrator that the class wants to study in the center of this Web and quickly see if there are ideas you could use. Webs are based on the strengths of the books and/or topics and the needs of your students.

They present a visual overview of possibilities to be explored, just a beginning plan, rather than a lesson plan set in stone.

Once you have thought of the many possibilities, you need to choose the ones that would be the most useful to try in your class. If your primary students have not done surveys, then you might decide to highlight that particular activity. If you like the idea of putting students in small groups to compare variants of a tale, you might choose that section. Then you can plan a tentative time line: How to begin the unit? What books will you use to introduce the topic? What activities will get the children intrigued to learn more?

Examples of Webs that explore a book, a genre, or an author can be found in previous chapters. The Webs for Lois Lowry's *The Giver* in Chapter 7 and Louise Erdrich's *The Birchbark House* in Chapter 10 showed the possibilities inherent in studying a book. The Webs "Learning to Read Naturally" in Chapter 4, "Exploring Folktales" in Chapter 6, and "In Praise of Poetry" in Chapter 8 showed the many different ways children could explore a genre; the Web "Brian Pinkney" in Chapter 5 pointed out various ways children might study an author or illustrator. The Webs "Growing Up Is Hard to Do," "The World beneath Your Feet," and "Life Stories" in Chapters 9, 11, and 12 link genres with broader curricular topics. The Web "Stewards of the Earth" in this chapter also details a unit designed to integrate many areas of the curriculum. It could be used across grade levels, but it is particularly aimed at fifth and sixth graders.

Studying a Theme: Stewards of the Earth—Ecology

A thematic unit such as one based on ecology contains many possibilities and provides many opportunities for reflective disciplined inquiry.[18] With a theme as large as "Stewards of the Earth," it is possible for a whole school to embark on a study of ecology. The Web "Stewards of the Earth" (pp. 692–93) begins to focus on what aspects of the earth are endangered, why this is so, and what people are doing about it. Some books feature the action of individuals; others show how groups of people form to improve a small part of our ecosystem. Both points are worth making in a study of this magnitude: Think globally but act locally; one person can make a difference.

Certain authors are well known for their activist stands on saving the earth. Jean Craighead George, in her novels as well as her nonfiction titles, always addresses interdependence among the living things on the planet. Ron Hirschi, Gail Gibbons, Laurence Pringle, and Helen

---

[16]Louise Rosenblatt, *Literature as Exploration* (New York: Noble & Noble, 1976), p. 123.

[17]James Britton, "The Nature of the Reader's Satisfaction," in *The Cool Web: The Pattern of Children's Reading,* ed. Margaret Meek, Aidan Warlow, and Griselda Barton (New York: Atheneum, 1978), p. 110.

[18]See Chapter 2, "The Theory behind Disciplined Inquiry" in Linda Levstik and Keith Barton, *Doing History: Investigating with Children in Elementary and Middle School* (Mahwah, N.J.: Lawrence Erlbaum Associates, 2005), pp. 9–25.

Wonderfully Exciting Books

Writing from Books

Parts of a Book
Dedication page
Title page
Prologue
Epilogue
Jacket flap
Table of contents
Index

Books as Models
Content
Style
Format
Further adventures
Diaries
Journals
Letters
Newspapers

Making a Book
Bookbinding
Parts of a book
Endpapers
Cover
Library call numbers

Questions: Elements of Literature

Fiction
Setting
Characters
Plot
Theme
Style
Point of view

Nonfiction
Authenticity
Accuracy
Content
Perspective
Style
Organization
Illustrations
Format

Picture Books
Style of art
Choice of medium
Size of book
Use of color, line, space
Perspective
Symbolism

Talk about Books

Taking Surveys
Favorite tales
Most-liked characters
Most-disliked characters
Favorite poems
Favorite authors

Book Discussions
Whole group
Small group
Interview author
Interview a character
Compare with other books

Telling Stories
Retelling story
Retell from a different point of view
Make a feltboard story
Create story boxes

A FRAMEWORK FOR WEBBING: BOOK, THEME, GENRE, AND UNIT

Building a Frame of Reference

Experiences
Field trips
Resource persons
Experiments
Research

Additional Readings
Same author
Same theme
Same topic
Sequels
Informational books
Poetry
Created books

Studying Authors or Illustrators
Style and type of writing
Style of illustrating
Medium of illustrating
Corresponding with author/illustrators
Telephone interview
Author or illustrator visit

Extending Books

Creating Displays
Museums
Character displays
Something-about-the-author display
Display artifacts
Make catalogs
Related books

Art Interpretations
Create a mural
Create a mobile
Create a diorama
Map the action
Make a comparison chart
Make a roller movie

Cooking
Book fare party
Cook something of the Era
Cook from the book

Drama and Movement
Become a character—tell your story
Dramatize a scene from a book
Move to a poem
Create a "what if" situation
Puppetry
Readers' theater

Sewing
Wall hanging
Quilt of favorite books
Character dolls

Music
Find appropriate accompaniment
Compose original music
Listen to music of the historical period

Games and Maps
Create a board game
Make a card game modeled on pairs or fours
Map the action
Make a sociogram of relationships

Wonderfully Exciting Books

Caring for the Animals

Aardvarks Disembark (Jonas)
And Then There Was One: The Mysteries of Extinction (Facklam)
Search for the Golden Moon Bear (Montgomery)
The Year of the Panda (Schlein)
The Maze (Hobbs)
Which animals are endangered? Why?
What animals are now extinct? Why?
Make a chart of endangered animals; tell why each is endangered; find out what people are doing to help save each animal.

The Chimpanzees I Love: Saving Their World and Ours (Goodall)
Interrupted Journey: Saving Endangered Sea Turtles (Lasky)
What are the threats to wildlife? How has this affected conservation policies?
Find out if there is a program to protect endangered animals in your area and get involved.

Cleaning Up after Ourselves

Recycle: A Handbook for Kids (Gibbons)
Waste, Recycling, and Re-use (Parker)
Form a playground or neighborhood trash pickup. Survey the trash to discover patterns.
What is the major source of trash? Who is responsible? How might you begin an anti-litter campaign?
Make a "life-cycle" map of a piece of trash.
Show where a soda can or cigarette butt starts out and where it might end up. Write about your map.

Do Animals Communicate?

Koko's Kitten (Patterson)
Prairie Dogs Kiss and Lobsters Wave: How Animals Say Hello (Singer)
How do animals communicate? Make a list of the types of languages animals use.

Dolphin Adventure (Grover)
How do people communicate with animals? Why is this exciting?
What good is it to communicate with other species?
Observe a family pet or other animal for several days. Write an informational booklet on how this animal communicates. What do its noises mean? Body movements? Expressions?

STEWARDS OF THE EARTH: ECOLOGY

Interconnections

Hoot (Hiaasen)
Flush (Hiaasen)
Who Really Killed Cock Robin? (George)
Tree Castle Island (George)
The Fire Bug Connection (George)
The Missing Gator of Gumbo Limbo (George)
Make a chart of causes and effects for these mysteries.

Weird Friends (Aruego and Dewey)
There's a Zoo on You (Darling)
What are symbiotic relationships?
Can you name other connected groups?
How do members depend on each other?

What are ecosystems? How are interactions among species vital to the environment?
How are they put out of balance?
The Talking Earth (George)
Everglades (George)
The Story of Rosie Dock (Baker)
What ideas about the earth are expressed?
Do you agree?

All God's Critters Got a Place in the Choir (Staines)
This Land Is Your Land (Guthrie)
Sing the songs. How do they represent what you've learned?

Caring for the Birds

Bird (Burnie)
Find feathers. Determine whether they are wing, pin, down, or some other kind of feather. Mount your collection.

Make a tree to feed birds, or a feeding station. Observe what comes there.
What birds are endangered? Why?
How can people help birds? Why should we?

Hawk, I'm Your Brother (Baylor)
Saving the Peregrine Falcon (Arnold)
Make a tree on which drawings of local birds are placed. Let different people count birds at different sites. How many birds can you count in a half hour?
Which site has the fewest/most birds? Why?

Pigeons (Schlein)
How have pigeons helped humankind?
Follow a pigeon. Try to describe its movements.
Debate: Are pigeons "rats with wings"?

Protecting the Water

What endangers our water? How can we help?
The Magic School Bus at the Waterworks (Cole)
Waterman's Boy (Sharpe)
Everglades (George)
One Less Fish (Toft and Sheather)
Write a news account of the capture of the
  polluters.
What are the consequences of water pollution?

Saving the Forests

What kinds of actions damage forests?
List individual actions that might help save trees.
Find out what kinds of paper can be recycled.
Start a recycling spot for school waste paper.

Where Once There Was a Wood (Fleming)
The Lorax (Seuss)

How does nature maintain a balanced ecology?
Should controlled fires be set to keep forests in balance?
Summer of Fire: Yellowstone, 1988 (Lauber)

Deep Dream of the Rain Forest (Bosse)
Garden of the Spirit Bear: Life in the Great Northern Rainforest
  (Patent)
Locate rain-forest areas on a map. Make a mural of a rain
  forest from canopy to forest floor. Show typical animals
  found in each zone.

One Day in the Tropical Rainforest (George)
The Great Kapok Tree (Cherry)
Rain Forest (Cowcher)
Where the Forest Meets the Sea (Baker)
Rain Forest Secrets (Dorros)
Make a collage of articles that come from rain forests.
  What is yet to be discovered in rain forests?

Developing Respect and a Sense of Wonder

What kinds of experiences fill us with wonder?
Pretend you are a person in one of these stories.
Tell or write about your moment of wonder:
Dawn (Shulevitz)
Salt Hands (Aragon)
The Lady and the Spider (McNulty)
Owl Moon (Yolen)
The Journey (Rylant)
Find examples of language that evokes the
  senses. Write your own earth poems.

Heartland; Mojave; Sierra (Siebert)
I Wonder If I'll See a Whale (Weller)
Whales' Song (Sheldon)
The Way to Start a Day (Baylor)
Make up your own way to greet a day.
Write a story of how your perfect day in nature
  might begin.

The Other Way to Listen (Baylor)
The Listening Walk (Showers)
Take a listening walk. What nature sounds can
  you hear?

Imagine Other Futures, Other Worlds

Green Boy (Cooper)
Just a Dream (Van Allsburg)
Z for Zachariah (O'Brien)
The Exchange Student (Gilmore)
When the Tripods Came (Christopher)
Eva (Dickinson)
The Monster Garden (Alcock)
The Ear, the Eye and the Arm (Farmer)
Time Ghost (Katz)
The City of Ember (DuPrau)
The Secret under My Skin (McNaughton)
How does each author see our future?
What kind of world are humans inhabiting?
  What has disappeared? Why?

The Lampfish of Twill (Lisle)
How do authors' imagined worlds
  incorporate environmental messages? How
  factually based are they?

Taking Action

How can individual people help? How do
  groups help?
A River Ran Wild (Cherry)
Come Back Salmon (Cone)
Miss Rumphius (Cooney)
Seedfolks (Fleischman)
Jackson Jones and the Puddle of Thorns
  (Quattlebaum)
Nobody Particular (Bang)
*Panda Rescue: Changing the Future for
  Endangered Animals* (Bortolotti)
*Gorilla Doctors: Saving Endangered Great
  Apes* (Turner)
The Missing Manatee (DeFelice)
Take a field trip to a trash-burning power
  plant, a recycling center. Report what
  you have found using a "Magic School
  Bus" format.
Interview city council members to find out
  what long-range plans they have for
  areas such as landfills, recycling, creation
  of parks, protection of water, etc.
Plant something and watch it grow.
Beautify the grounds and entrance of your
  school. Take care of the plants.

Then and Now: Changes

Make a "then and now" chart for one book.
Pretend you are older and looking back on a
  special place. Write about your memories and
  feelings for this place that has changed.
Debate: Is change good or bad?
Letting Swift River Go (Yolen)
Window (Baker)
My Place (Wheatley)
Find old photographs of your city or
  neighborhood. Find out what has changed
  since those pictures were taken.
Invite a longtime resident to the classroom to
  talk about changes he or she has seen in the
  place where you live.

Roney Sattler are only a few of the many authors of nonfiction who have raised concerns about the environment. Teachers of middle-school children might start with futuristic science fiction, such as the titles listed in the Web under "Imagine Other Futures," and raise this question: "How did humankind become what it is depicted as being in this imagined future?" Teachers of fifth or sixth graders might anchor this study with a core novel such as Jean Craighead George's *The Talking Earth*, Miriam Schlein's narrative of Chinese and American efforts to save the endangered panda in *The Year of the Panda*, Susan Sharpe's fictional account of a boy's discovery of who was dumping toxic waste in the Chesapeake Bay told in *Waterman's Boy*, or Mary Quattlebaum's story of a boy who becomes involved in a community garden in *Jackson Jones and the Puddle of Thorns*. Other classes might start with endangered birds, creatures of the sea, the way places change and why, or observances of nature.

In the "Stewards of the Earth" Web, activities that begin a topic are suggested as useful overarching concerns developed within the section that follows. Other activities might follow a particular book or culminate that section's content. There are many community resources that should be tapped in a study such as this, such as classroom visits by park rangers and city planners, field trips to preserves or recycling centers, newspapers and newspaper archives, or interviews with a longtime resident. Books are not the only way to bring the world to the classroom.

Developing a concern for the environment is a lasting topic, and there will always be new problems, new books, and new ways to approach it in the classroom. Even primary children can become interested in the preservation of Earth's natural diversity and the interdependence of all things on Earth.

ASSESSMENT AND EVALUATION

Assessment and evaluation of children's growth in any area of learning must be consistent with the goals and purposes of the program. As teachers move toward literature-based curricula that use real books, it makes little sense to evaluate children with tests that are geared to basal readers and hours of workbook practice of fill-in-the-blank, multiple-choice, and short-answer questions. Timed multiple-choice tests following the reading of short paragraphs hardly define what a child has learned as a result of all he or she encounters in the course of reading many books. Information gained by these tests does little to help the classroom teacher plan programs that lead students to become more satisfied, more widely adept readers. Evaluation of children's reading should begin with some knowledge of where individual children are

Displaying the results of thematic studies can invite other students to become interested in the topic. Wickliffe Alternative School, Upper Arlington, Ohio.

starting; observation and evidence of the child's understandings and abilities as revealed by discussion, classroom interactions, solicited and unsolicited responses to books; and evidence of changes, or growth, in that child's knowledge, appreciation, understandings, and abilities in reading. Informal tests such as Marie Clay's Concepts of Print or Kenneth Goodman's Modified Miscue Analysis give important information about children's reading abilities.[19] These and other methods of assessment demand that teachers constantly sharpen their observational skills, develop some means of record keeping, and be able to recognize important signs of insight and growth in the learners they teach.

Begin where children are. This maxim applies to literature as well as any other area. In planning a literature program, the staff or teacher must first consider what the children's previous experiences with literature have been. Are they fortunate enough to come from homes

---

[19]See Marie Clay, *The Early Detection of Reading Difficulties*, 3rd ed. (Portsmouth, N.H.: Heinemann, 1985); and *Reading Miscue Inventory: Alternative Procedures*, ed. Yetta Goodman et al. (Katonah, N.Y.: Richard C. Owens, 1987).

where reading is valued, where there are many books? Have they been read to regularly? Or is school their first introduction to books? What have previous teachers read aloud to these children? What common experiences, such as author or illustrator studies or thematic groupings in literature, have these children had?

Record Keeping

As a school year begins, it is important to have some record-keeping systems already in place that are simple and consume as little completion time as possible. In this way, records from the very first days of school can be compared as a child progresses, and the teacher will be better able to plan future curriculum.

One of the best kinds of assessment of children's growth is the notes teachers write as they observe children reading. Many teachers keep a tablet of sticky notes or sheets of gummed labels on their desk or in other parts of the room where reading is likely to occur. As they observe something significant about a child, they can quickly jot it down. Later the piece of paper can be transferred to a notebook under the child's name or into the child's individual folder.

A kindergarten teacher recorded when Jamie wrote his first complete sentence. Another teacher recorded a child's written definition of a story as "a mindfull of life." A fifth-grade teacher recorded one girl's generalizations about the many animal stories she had read during the year. A sixth-grade teacher noted the first time one boy uncharacteristically read for twenty minutes without looking up from his book.

Each day becomes more exciting as the teacher looks for and records typical moments and peak experiences in a child's reading life. These anecdotes make parent conferences rich with positive comments and evidence of growth that the parent recognizes as real. Each observation should be dated so that a teacher can see the ongoing growth of a student over the course of the school year.

Most teachers want children to keep their work together. In a classroom where the room is divided into work areas, generally each child has a writing folder or a work folder, and perhaps a reading log or response journal. Because teachers look at and respond to these, they must be easily accessible to both the children and the teacher. Clearly designated boxes, shelves, or bookcases should be reserved for the classroom's record-keeping folders.

At designated times in the year, teachers may ask children to go through their writing and art folders to select their best examples to include in their assessment portfolio. A portfolio of this sort is a year-long collection of a child's work that may be used in various ways by the teacher and child. A child can select from a month of writings the one that should go in the file, for instance. A teacher might honor a child's work by suggesting that it would be a fine addition to her special portfolio. If a student has worked cooperatively with another child—

A teacher listens attentively as a first grader reads *The Three Billy Goats Gruff*. She is taking a running record of his oral reading. Columbus Public Schools, Columbus, Ohio. Connie Compton, teacher.

for instance, to produce a research report—copies can be made of their project and placed in each child's portfolio. Photographs as well as written work might be included in the collection. As teachers and children confer about the work in the portfolio, the teacher can ask each child why she or he chose this work and record the child's reasons on a sticky note. Together they can build criteria for what constitutes good work. In this way, children know what is expected of them because they have helped to establish the standards.

Student and Parent Conferences

To help their students become part of a community of readers, teachers will want to plan time to communicate with them regularly about their reading. Parents, too, are an integral part of this community, and they will appreciate being informed about the literacy program and their child's progress. Most schools establish time for parent conferences several times a year, when teachers can share the work the child has accomplished or is presently working on. Emphasis should always be placed on what the child knows and is learning.

Talking with individual children in a conference takes time. Yet in conferences children frequently reveal their growing edges. Teachers will want to have frequent conferences with children about their reading. It helps if a child brings her reading log or response journal and a current book she is reading to such a conference. Teachers can chat with a child about patterns in her reading selections as evidenced by the log. They can recommend another book that fits the pattern, or suggest a sequel or another book by the child's favorite author. They might ask the child to read aloud from his current SSR book or from a title his small group is reading together. It is helpful to remember that a book conversation with a child may be simply a recounting of plot. Teachers can assist children's thinking by asking such questions as "Could there be any other bridges in Katherine Paterson's *Bridge to Terabithia?*" "Now that you've read three books by Gary Paulsen, how could you recognize one he wrote even if you couldn't see the author and title?" "Since you've read so many mysteries, can you say what makes a book a good mystery?"

In many classrooms, children never have a chance to talk alone with the teacher except in disciplinary situations. Conferences can be exceptionally rewarding to both participants.

Evaluating Children's Literary Understandings

Evaluation of a child's understandings must be seen in light of developmental patterns, as we discussed in Chapter 2. In addition, the teacher must consider a child's understandings as revealed in discussion with the group, in creating products such as murals or imaginary diaries discussed previously, and in some linear sort of way. What did the child start with? What does he know now? What will the child remember long after this moment has passed?

Though the following list of understandings is by no means exhaustive, it suggests how teachers might look at what children know following a study, for example, of the books of Ezra Jack Keats. Do they notice these things:

- Many books feature a character named Peter. Other characters overlap, too.
- Stories are set in the city, in apartment buildings, in the street.
- Illustrations are often collage, using materials, newspaper, wallpaper, marbleized paper, and some paint.
- There are some ideas here. "Giving up things that you've outgrown is part of growing up" from *Peter's Chair;* "There are many things to do outside when it snows, but you can't save snowballs!" from *The Snowy Day.*

In addition, would children be able to pick out a Keats illustration from ones by Vera B. Williams or Pat Hutchins? Would they remember Keats's name? Insights such as these would not be easily revealed in a multiple-choice test. But as children discuss their choices for materials they used in making a picture "like Ezra Jack Keats did," a teacher will see what children had noticed and remembered. When children go to the media center, a teacher might observe whether they ask the librarian for Keats's books by title or by author. Later a teacher might hear a child say about another book, "That's just like *Peter's Chair.* She gave her little sister something she had outgrown."

Third graders who studied folktales might be expected to recognize the following:

Children's products also reveal understandings and growth. Children created a board game with rules based on the plot of *Big Anthony and the Magic Ring* by Tomie dePaola. Highland Park Elementary School, South-Western City Schools, Grove City, Ohio.

- Some common tales
- Typical characters and settings
- Typical traits of characters
- That there are formal beginnings, endings, refrains, and other characteristics of folktale language
- Basic themes such as "Good is always rewarded" or "Little but honest wins over big," although they may not be able to state them succinctly
- That popular tales such as "Cinderella" exist in many versions and variants
- That some commonly recurring patterns, or motifs, such as magical objects, trickery, or wishes, are in many tales

Later, in fourth or fifth grade, when they hear such tales as Susan Cooper's *The Boggart,* Sid Fleischman's *The Whipping Boy,* or Mollie Hunter's *The Mermaid Summer,* can they recognize the folktale elements in these more complex tales?

Children's products also reveal understandings and growth. Did the "story map" of "The Gingerbread Boy" include all the important incidents? Could a child maintain Amos's point of view in his diary from *Amos and Boris* by William Steig? Did the child's version of *The Way to Start a Day* suggest a sensitivity to Byrd Baylor's use and arrangement of words? How did the student's two-part diorama reflect the contrasting settings of seashore and prairies in Patricia MacLachlan's *Sarah, Plain and Tall?* What teachers choose to evaluate depends on what they are hoping to have children understand after reading a book or pursuing a thematic study. It is helpful to list some goals and understandings, based on the evaluative criteria for a particular genre or the particular strengths and content of the theme, before evaluating children's literary understandings.

EVALUATION **CRITERIA**

Evaluating Children's Growth as Readers

- Does the child love one book, many books, reading in general?
- Does the child become easily involved or easily distracted in reading a book?
- Does the child predict, question, and confirm his way through a book?
- Does the child prefer one genre, author, or illustrator over others? Is she aware of her preference? Can she recognize characteristics of genre, author, or illustrator?
- Is the child a flexible reader who reads easily in several genres, who reads often and quickly?
- Can the child select books that satisfy him? Is he open to suggestions from other readers?
- What kinds of understandings and awareness do the child's products reveal?
- Does the child visualize, identify with, become involved with, or understand the motives of characters?
- Does the child visualize settings?

- What connections does the child make between a particular book and others by the same illustrator or author? of the same genre? with the same theme? What patterns does she see?
- What kind of thematic statements does the child make? Can he see a book title as a metaphor for a larger idea?
- What connection does the child make between literature and life?
- What questions does the child's reading raise for her?
- What literary elements, such as prologues, unique dedications, interesting chapter titles, language use, or narrative style, does the child notice?
- How are these reading patterns changing as the school years progress?
- Is the child voluntarily reading more at school? at home?
- Is the child responding to a greater range and complexity of work?

Evaluating Children's Growth as Readers

Throughout this text, we have suggested that children's learning accrues, reorganizes, and reformulates based on their own growth both as children and as readers. While observation and evaluation are daily tasks for teachers, the long-range goal of creating enthusiastic, versatile, and skillful readers should be the teacher's focus. By becoming documenters of children's encounters with literature, we become better observers. Observations of change, then, provide us with clues to a child's growth. Evaluation Criteria: "Evaluating Children's Growth as Readers" provides a beginning set of questions to guide observations. The most important questions we can ask are often not the easiest to answer: What is a child building? What kind of framework is the child creating based on his or her experiences? How is this sense of literature changing?

THE SCHOOL AND THE COMMUNITY

To be successful, a classroom literature program needs an enthusiastic teacher, a good book collection, and students who are eager to read. However, to create a true community of readers, each teacher must also involve other teachers, students, administrators, librarians, and parents in discovering the delights of good books.

The Whole-School Program

Children learn what they live. Increasingly, educators are concerned that the quality of living in a school be equal to the quality of learning in that school. The physical environment of the school provides the context of that learning, but it is only one aspect of it. What teachers really believe in and want for their students will usually be taught.

All teachers and librarians must have a strong commitment to literature. Few children discover books by themselves; in most instances, a parent, teacher, or librarian has served as the catalyst for bringing books and children together. As children grow up seeing significant adults as readers, they become readers. Find a teacher who is enthusiastic about children's books, and you will find a class of children who enjoy reading. Invariably, the teacher who reads, who knows books, and who shares this enthusiasm with students will inspire a love of reading. Many schools have made the development of readers their top priority. As a total school faculty they have met and planned certain activities to promote children's interest in reading.

Buddy reading involves students from older grades reading with partners in the kindergarten or first grade. Younger children proudly share a book that they can read with their buddies, and the older children then read a book to their partners. Younger children look forward to their buddy time (which is usually once a week), and the older students take a special interest in the progress of their special child. Buddy reading requires cooperation among teachers to establish schedules. Older students must be taught how to select appropriate books to read aloud and the importance of being supportive of

Sixth graders enjoy reading with their kindergarten and first-grade buddies. Mission School, Redlands Public Schools, Redlands, California. Nancy Anderson, teacher.

the younger reader's efforts to read or tell a story. Teachers who have tried such programs speak of their value for both sets of readers.

One school planned a whole-school unit on traditional literature. Children from kindergarten through sixth grade studied fairy tales, traditional folktales, fables, and myths. They created a Fairy Tale Museum with such objects as "the very pea that disturbed the princess's sleep" and the golden ball that the Frog Prince retrieved for the spoiled princess. Their *Fairy Tale Newspaper* included interviews with Cinderella and the Pied Piper; classified lost-and-found ads, including an ad for a found glass slipper; a society column; and a sports page describing the race of the Hare and the Tortoise. Older children created their own mythological characters and stories. Different groups dramatized traditional tales like "The Three Billy Goats Gruff" and "Little Red Riding Hood." This whole-school emphasis created a unity among the children and an appreciation for their traditional literary heritage.

Another school offered many minicourses in literature during Book Week. Children made puppets in one course, created a flannel story in another. Many children wrote their own stories in one course. Then, in another, they were introduced to the use of collage, marbleized papers, and ink prints made from Styrofoam. Another course offered bookbinding, and the children ended the week with their own bound and illustrated books. Teachers volunteered to offer the various courses. Some gave minicourses on particular genres of books, like folktales or poetry. Others offered drama and choral speaking. In this particular school, children have an opportunity to do these things frequently. However, the minicourses given near the beginning of school focused attention on bookmaking and provided children with skills they used throughout the year.

Involving Administrators

No literature program can be successful without the support of the principal. More and more principals and curriculum coordinators are taking time to read aloud to children. One curriculum coordinator makes it a point to read aloud in one of the classrooms in his school district every day.[20] Children look forward to his coming, and he anticipates their response to his choice of books. Another principal has developed a two-tiered reading

---

[20]James Mitchell, "Sound Bytes, Hamburgers and Billy Joel: Celebrating the Year of the Lifetime Reader," *Reading Today* 9 (August/September 1991): 29.

program called The Principal's Reading Club. Children from kindergarten through second grade make appointments to read with the principal for fifteen minutes from a book of their choice. Students in grades 3 to 6 select a book from a provided list and after three weeks return to discuss it with the principal. The participants receive a reading certificate, button, and pencil that has "I Read to the Principal" on it. More important, children see the principal as someone interested in them and their reading, and it's a wonderful way for the principal to get to know children and their reading abilities and preferences.

The School Library Media Center

Every school needs a trained librarian and a school library media center. While the name has changed over the years to reflect the inclusion of such nonprint materials as films, videos, tapes, slides, computers, and software as well as books, the purpose of the center is to provide the best services and materials to facilitate learning for children.

The library media center should be open all day, every day, to serve students in its unique way. Flexible scheduling of story hours or lessons on library research may be directed by the librarian in a special area, leaving the rest of the resources free for others to use. Children can learn without the constant presence of a teacher or librarian. A trained aide can help children find relevant books, films, videos, and records. Parents have served most effectively as volunteers in the school media center. Children increase in their ability to do independent study by using a variety of sources. An abundance of materials should be readily and freely available.

Increasingly, new school library media centers have become the focal point of many schools, with classrooms radiating out from them. The space should be as flexible and fluid as possible to allow for growth and change. The environment should encourage free access to materials at all times. Children flow in and out, doing projects, finding resources, making their own books, producing films. As the library media center becomes more closely identified with the total instructional program, it becomes more integrated into the total school environment.

The Library Media Specialist

The library media specialist plays a very important role in the quality of learning and living that takes place in the library media center, the school, and the community.[21] Serving as a full-time contributing faculty member, the librarian works with children, teachers, parents, and volunteer and professional aides. Specialized training provides background knowledge of children's books and all media for instruction, library media procedures, knowledge of children's development and behavior, under-

Involving parents in the literature program helps create a sense of community. In this classroom a parent helped children make pasta from the magic pasta pot in Tomie dePaola's *Strega Nona.* Highland Park Elementary School, South-Western City Schools, Grove City, Ohio. Photo by Barbara Peterson.

standing of various teaching methods, and knowledge of school curriculum needs and organization. Increasingly, the library media specialist is called on to give leadership, not only in providing the materials for instruction, but in shaping the curriculum itself. The library media program should be an integral part of the total school program. Working with teachers, the media specialist needs to be responsive to the curricular and instructional needs of the school. What units of study are the teachers planning to initiate this year? Books, films, and tapes on these subjects should be gathered together for the teachers' and children's use. Bibliographies of print and nonprint materials based on units of work should be developed cooperatively with teachers. Book lists and curriculum resources should be shared. The function of the school library media center is to provide an information-rich environment where teachers and students become effective users of print and nonprint materials.

In one school, the fifth grade was studying the rather abstract theme of famous "crossings." The children and teacher had webbed possibilities, and then the teacher had made an appointment with the librarian. The two of them filled a rolling cart full of books, films, and videos on such subjects as Columbus, the Pilgrims, the slave trade, crossing the Western Divide, and Hannibal crossing the Alps. There were many more topics, but the abstract concept allowed the children to study many time

---

[21]The terms *library media specialist* and *librarian* are used interchangeably to denote the person who is responsible for directing the school library media program. It is assumed that such a director would have had training as a school librarian and as a media specialist and in many instances would also have a teaching certificate.

periods and many famous events. Students chose what aspect of the topic they wished to study and then met in their study groups. The librarian worked with each group to find appropriate materials and Web sites. The children used the library's electronic database and the table of contents and index of each book to see what topics were covered. They checked the dates of publications and looked at the authors' qualifications. All of these research skills were taught in the context of a study in which the children wanted to obtain information, rather than an isolated library skills lesson.

Teachers and library media specialists become partners as they work together to help students learn to use information, to be critical of what they read and see, to make judgments about what is authentic and accurate, and to discover meaning. As students share their findings, they learn to question, compare, and combine information. Only such educated students can become contributing citizens to a democratic society.

Selecting Materials

Our children are growing up faster today than twenty years ago. In the limited time children have to be children, we want to give them the very best books available. The adage "The right book at the right time" still holds true. Most children's books have to be read at the appropriate age and developmental stage or they *will never be read.* The 8-year-old does not read Beatrix Potter's *The Tale of Peter Rabbit;* the 12-year-old doesn't want to be seen reading Beverly Cleary's *Ramona Quimby, Age 8;* and the 16-year-old has outgrown Elizabeth George Speare's *The Sign of the Beaver.* Introduced at the right time, each of these books would have provided a rich, satisfying experience of literature.

The number of books that any one child can read is limited, also. Assuming that a child reads one book every two weeks from the time he is 7 (when independent reading might begin) until he is 13 or 14 (when many young people start reading adult books), he will read about 25 books a year, or some 200 books. Given the number and variety of children's books in print, it is possible that a child could read widely *yet never read a significant book.* Under these circumstances, the need for good book selection becomes even more imperative.

With the increase of both numbers of books published and objections to the selection of certain books, it is essential that schools develop a selection policy. All professional library groups, and other professional organizations like the International Reading Association and the National Council of Teachers of English, strongly recommend that each school district develop a written statement that governs its selection of material. This policy statement should be approved by the school board and subsequently supported by its members if challenged. Factors to be considered in such a policy would include the following: who selects the materials, the quality of materials, appropriate content, needs and interests of special children, school curriculum needs, providing for balance in the collection, and procedures to follow for censorship and challenged material.

Because the subject matter of contemporary children's books is changing, the need for written criteria of selection has increased. Realism in children's books and young-adult novels reflects the same range of topics that can be seen on TV, at the movies, and in current bestsellers. It makes no sense to "protect" children from well-written or well-presented materials on such controversial subjects as abortion, narcotics, or sexual orientation when they see stories on the same subjects on TV. Increased sensitivity to sexism, racism, and bias in books and nonbook materials is another area of recent concern that points up the need for a clear statement on selection policies. Here are some general guidelines to consider when developing policies for book selection:

1. **Who Selects the Materials?**
   Teachers, students, and parents might recommend particular titles, but the final selection of materials for the school library should be determined by professionally trained personnel. Reliable reviews of children's books play an important part in the selection of books. Four well-known review journals are *Booklist,* the *Bulletin of the Center for Children's Books, Horn Book Magazine,* and the *School Library Journal.* Other sources for reviews are listed in Appendix B.

2. **Quality of Materials**
   Criteria for evaluation and selection of all types of instructional materials should be established and should be available in written form. Books for the collection should meet the criteria of good literature described in preceding chapters. There may need to be a balance between popular demand and quality literature, but this is a decision that must be made by individual librarians, based on their knowledge of the reading abilities and interests of the children they serve and their own basic philosophy of book selection. A written policy statement of the criteria to be used when purchasing books will help solve this dilemma.

3. **Appropriate Content**
   The content of the materials to be selected should be evaluated in terms of the quality of the writing or presentation. Almost any subject can be written about for children, depending on the honesty and sensitivity of its treatment by the author. We should not deliberately shock or frighten children before they have developed the maturity and inner strength to face the tragedies of life. However, literature is one way to experience life, if only vicariously. In the process, a reader can be fortified and educated.

4. **Children's Needs and Interests**
   Materials should be purchased with the children who will be using them in mind. This includes materials for children with special needs and books that

represent a wide diversity of multicultural experiences. Children from a particular culture should have opportunities to see themselves reflected in books. In a pluralistic society, however, all children should have an opportunity to read about children of different racial, religious, and ethnic backgrounds. Regardless of a child's background, a good selection policy should give children books that provide insight into their own lives but also take them out of those lives to help them see the world in its many dimensions.

5. **School Curriculum Needs**

   Librarians should consider the particular needs of the school curriculum when ordering materials. Particular units in social studies or intensive study of the local region will require additional copies of books about the particular state, industries, and people of the region. The function of the school library media center is to provide a wide range of materials specially chosen to meet the demands of the school curriculum.

6. **Balance in the Collection**

   Every school library needs to maintain a balanced collection. Keeping in mind the total needs of the school, the librarian should consider the following balances: book and nonbook material (including videotapes, tapes, records, films, discs, filmstrips, and other materials), hardback and paperback books, reference books, and trade books, fiction and non-

fiction, poetry and prose, classics (both old and "new"), realistic and fanciful stories, books for younger and older children, books for poor and superior readers at each grade level, books for teachers to read to students and use for enrichment purposes, and professional books for teachers and parents.

Selection versus Censorship

There is a fine line between careful selection of books for children and censorship. The goal of selection is to *include* a book on the basis of its quality of writing and total impact; the goal of censorship is to *exclude* a book in which the content (or even one part) is considered objectionable. Selection policies recommend a balanced collection representative of the various beliefs held by a pluralistic society; censors would impose their privately held beliefs on all.

The American Library Association's "Library Bill of Rights" was adopted in 1948 and amended in 1967, 1969, and 1980 and reaffirmed in 1996. This statement contains six policies relating to censorship of books and the right of free access to the library for all individuals or groups. This statement has been endorsed by the American Association of School Librarians. To read this statement, see Teaching Resources: "The Library Bill of Rights."

Almost every school and each children's librarian in a public library has faced some criticism of the books in the children's collection. Criticism is not necessarily

TEACHING **RESOURCES**

The Library Bill of Rights

Visit the Online Learning Center at **www.mhhe.com/kiefer9e** for a printable version of this list.

The American Library Association affirms that all libraries are forums for information and ideas, and that the following basic policies should guide their services.

1. Books and other library resources should be provided for the interest, information, and enlightenment of all people of the community the library serves. Materials should not be excluded because of the origin, background, or views of those contributing to their creation.
2. Libraries should provide materials and information presenting all points of view on current and historical issues. Materials should not be proscribed or removed because of partisan or doctrinal disapproval.
3. Libraries should challenge censorship in the fulfillment of their responsibility to provide information and enlightenment.
4. Libraries should cooperate with all persons and groups concerned with resisting abridgment of free expression and free access to ideas.
5. A person's right to use a library should not be denied or abridged because of origin, age, background, or views.
6. Libraries which make exhibit spaces and meeting rooms available to the public they serve should make such facilities available on an equitable basis, regardless of the beliefs or affiliations of individuals or groups requesting their use.

Source: *Information Power: Guidelines for School Library Media Programs* (Chicago: American Library Association, 1998) or <www.ala.org/work/freedom/lbr.html>.

censorship, however. Parents, other faculty members, and citizens have a right to discuss the reasons for the selection of a particular book and to make their own feelings known. Only when they seek to have the book banned, removed from the shelves, restricted in use, or altered are they assuming the role of censors.

In the past decade, censorship increased dramatically throughout the country. Individuals and groups from both the right and left, like the Christian Coalition, religious fundamentalists, members of the feminist movement, and the Council on Interracial Books for Children, have all demanded the removal of certain children's books from libraries for various reasons. Targets of the censor generally include profanity of any kind; sex, sexuality, nudity, obscenity; the "isms," including sexism, racism, ageism; and the portrayal of witchcraft, magic, religion, and drugs.

Award books are objects of censorship as readily as other books. The Caldecott Medal book *Sylvester and the Magic Pebble* by William Steig was objected to by law enforcement groups because it portrays police as pigs. It made no difference that all the characters in the book are animals, that Sylvester and his family are donkeys, and that other characters besides police are also shown as pigs.

Madeleine L'Engle's Newbery Medal book *A Wrinkle in Time* has been attacked as being non-Christian because of its references to the Happy Medium and Mrs. Who, Mrs. Whatsit, and Mrs. Which, supernatural beings that some have labeled "witches." Madeleine L'Engle is well known for her adult writings on Christianity; ironically, religious literalists have paid no attention to the total message of good overcoming evil in this well-written fantasy, but have seen only "witches." *The Great Gilly Hopkins*, a National Book Award winner written by Katherine Paterson, a minister's wife and twice the winner of the Newbery Medal for excellence in writing, was criticized because Gilly utters an occasional "damn." Yet surely a foster child who has been in three homes in three years is not likely to be a model of refinement. What is noteworthy about this book is the gradual and believable *change* in Gilly's behavior and character. In Jean Fritz's well-received picture-book biography *And Then What Happened, Paul Revere?* an English Redcoat swears as he apprehends Paul Revere riding to rouse Concord. Fritz was criticized for using *damn,* even though the utterance is a matter of historical record.

Contemporary fiction for older children has come under increasing attack as these books have begun to show the influence of the new freedom allowed in books and films for adults. Such titles as Alvin Schwartz's *Scary Stories to Tell in the Dark,* which recounts tales of horror

well known in folklore, or Judy Blume's *Deenie,* which includes several references to masturbation, have been targets of criticism and censorship attempts.

A more subtle and frightening kind of censorship is the kind practiced voluntarily by librarians and teachers. If a book has come under negative scrutiny in a nearby town, it might be carefully placed under the librarian's desk until the controversy dies down. Or perhaps the librarians and the teachers just do not order controversial books. "Why stir up trouble when there are so many other good books available?" they falsely reason. In-house censorship or closet censorship is difficult to identify. Selection is a positive process; books are added to a collection for their excellence, to meet a curriculum need, to bring balance to the curriculum. Censorship is negative. Whenever books are rejected for nonliterary reasons, for fear of outside criticism, for example, librarians and teachers need to ask themselves whether they are practicing selection or censorship.

Dealing with Censorship

If there is a demand for censorship, how should it be handled? The first rule is to recognize that anyone has the right to question specific selections. The second rule is to be prepared—have an accepted response process. A written selection policy statement should contain a standardized procedure to follow when materials are challenged and should be part of district policy. The Evaluation Criteria: "Dealing with a Demand for Censorship" might be useful.

Several "Reconsideration of Materials" forms are available upon request. The National Council of Teachers of English provides one in its booklet *The Students' Right to Know.*[22] The American Library Association suggests two items to include: (1) "What brought this title to your attention?" (2) "Please comment on the resource as a whole, as well as being specific about those matters that concern you."[23] The major consideration, then, is to have a form available when you need it and to make it specific to the book itself and simple enough to fill out.

Generally, if parents or other citizens feel their voices have been heard and that they have been dealt with fairly, they will abide by the decision of the book selection committee. If, however, they represent a group that is determined to impose its values on the schools, they will continue their pressure. This is why it is essential that every library have a selection policy supported by the board and administration. Librarians and teachers also need to be aware of the support they can obtain from organizations like the Office for Intellectual Freedom of the American Library Association, the Freedom to Read Foundation of ALA, the National Council of

---

[22]*The Students' Right to Know* (Urbana, Ill.: National Council of Teachers of English, 1982). <www.ncte.org/censorship>

[23]"Statement of Concern about Library/Media Center Resources," in *Intellectual Freedom Manual,* rev. ed. (Chicago: American Library Association, 1996), p. 167. <www.ala.org/alaorg/oif>

Dealing with a Demand for Censorship

1. Do not discuss the issue until you are prepared. Give the person who is seeking to censor a book a form for "reconsideration of a book" and make an appointment to discuss the book.
2. Write out a rationale for choosing and using this book with children if you have not already done so.
3. Make copies of reviews of the questioned book from professional reviewing journals.
4. Notify your principal of the expressed concern. Give her or him copies of the reviews and of your rationale.
5. At your conference, explain the school's selection policy and present copies of the reviews of the book and the rationale explaining your reasons for selecting it.
6. Listen to the stated concern as objectively as possible.
7. Inform the person that the material will be reconsidered by the selection committee if he or she wishes it to be.
8. Submit the reconsideration form to the book selection committee of librarians, teachers, and parent representatives for their discussion and decision.
9. Inform the person expressing the concern what the committee decided and why.

Teachers of English, the International Reading Association, the American Civil Liberties Union, and People for the American Way.

Any challenge to a book is a matter to be taken seriously. Ultimately, what is involved is the freedom to learn and freedom of information, both of which are essential to American rights based on our democratic heritage and principles.

Working with Parents and the Community

Many schools have found that by informing and involving parents in school programs and plans, problems such as censorship are headed off or resolved before they can develop into serious discord. Even more important, parent volunteers can be a particularly rich resource for teachers and librarians. Sometimes these volunteers can be parents of students, sometimes they might be volunteers from a senior citizen center. One kindergarten/first-grade teacher has "grandmothers" from a senior citizen center who come once a week for the whole morning. They read stories to small groups of children, even individuals. They help make big books that the teacher

uses. Whatever is needed, there is an extra pair of hands to do it.

Parents can also serve as resource persons, depending upon their background of experience. One parent who is an Egyptologist became a tremendous resource for third-grade children who were studying mummies. In preparation for this parent's visit, the teacher read aloud *Mummies Made in Egypt* by Aliki, and the children prepared questions to ask him. He brought Egyptian artifacts and pictures to share with them. Another group of first-grade students were studying about families. They wanted to interview the oldest member of their family about his or her childhood. One grandfather was invited to the class, and children learned how to conduct an interview with him. Wherever possible teachers should draw on the expertise of the community.

To help their students become part of a community of readers, teachers will want to plan time to communicate with them regularly about their reading. Parents, too, are an integral part of this community, and they will appreciate being informed about the literacy program and their child's progress.

Students can also reciprocate by contributing to the community themselves. Junior high school students in the Bronx so loved Katherine Paterson's *Bridge to Terabithia* that they wanted to share it with others. A literature group went out to the local senior citizens' residence and read it aloud to these new friends. Those seniors were invited to keep reading logs and join in the book discussions.

In one school the parents and children created the Book Nook, a tiny paperback bookstore literally made from a broom closet. They decorated it with Maurice Sendak posters and a charming hanging lamp and even turned the old sink into a "trading pot" where children could place a "used" paperback and exchange it for another. The whole school takes justifiable pride in this paperback bookstore. In another school the parents made

Talking Point

To what entities or groups should teachers be responsible? What are teachers' responsibilities to teaching good literature and addressing young people's needs and interests versus their responsibility to the community in which they teach when it comes to choosing what books to teach? to include in book discussion groups? to include in classroom libraries? to include in school libraries?

Go to the Online Learning Center at **www.mhhe .com/kiefer9e** or the Resources CD-ROM to learn more.

a large wooden case on wheels that can be opened to create a bookstore anywhere in the building. Closed, it can be pushed flat against a wall. Parents will need help in getting such bookstores started and assuming responsibility for their operation. The librarian, a teacher who knows books, parents, and one or two children could serve as the selection committee to order new books. If teachers and parents support the store in the beginning, it will sustain itself once children know its regular hours and can find the books they want to buy and read.

During Book Week one school had someone scheduled to read aloud every hour of the day in the library. The librarian helped the mayor, the police officer, the superintendent, and others select appropriate books for their story time. Different grades were scheduled to hear stories every day that week.

With good planning the community can be a wonderful resource for schools. The more a community participates, the more the people in that community will begin to take ownership and pride in their schools.

Working with the Public Library

The school librarian should work closely with the children's librarian of the public library. At the beginning of the year, she might send him a list of the possible study units the school will be undertaking. It is not fair to suddenly deluge public librarians with requests for books about building houses when they have had no warning that the entire third grade would study this topic that year.

Most public librarians are very helpful to teachers who want to supplement their classroom library with particular books. In turn, teachers must see to it that these books are handled carefully and returned to the library on time.

Many public libraries are serving their communities in unique ways. Realizing the importance of reading aloud to young children, they might have a story hour three or four times a week. These are scheduled at various times convenient for working parents. Many libraries hold "pajama" story hours at 8 P.M. on nights when they are open. All the children come in their pajamas, hear several stories, and go home to bed.

Increasingly, public libraries are giving outreach service to the many children who do not come to the library. Some librarians are holding story hours in soup kitchens for homeless children; others are going to churches and day schools and holding story hours for the unserved children of the community whose parents never bring them to the library.

Some visionary public librarians are sending a welcome kit to each newborn infant in the community. These kits, funded by a local business, include a brief pamphlet on the importance of reading aloud to the young child. A recommended list of books is part of the kit along with the notation that all titles are available in the library. Two books are included, such as *Goodnight Moon*

by Margaret Wise Brown and *Red, Blue, Yellow Shoe* by Tana Hoban (see Chapter 4). Along with the books are coupons for two more that may be obtained at the library. These forward-looking librarians know how important it is to read to babies and to develop the library habit early. They know that the future of libraries depends on the development of library users; these are apt to be the very youngsters who learned to love the library at an early age.

When teachers, librarians, and parents concentrate on plans to foster a love of reading in each child, communities become caring, literate places to live in. Only when every child has a library card and uses it, when every preschool group hears stories three or four times a day, when all teachers read aloud, when children have substantial time to read books of their own choosing, when all schools have trained librarians and information-rich media centers—only then will we begin to develop a nation of readers.

Evaluating the Literature Program

It is as easy to identify a school in which literature is an integral part of the curriculum as it is to recognize a home where books are loved and valued. Because we have not recommended any body of content that all children must learn, but rather have suggested that each school should plan its own literature program to include certain categories of experiences with literature, the Evaluation Criteria: "Evaluating a Literature Program" could serve in two ways. First, they suggest to schools in the planning stages of a literature program what experiences ought to be offered to children. Second, they suggest measures for assessing a literature program already in place in an elementary or middle school.

The first goal of all literature programs should be to develop lifetime readers. Since we know children are reading less and less in their free time at home, the school becomes their last best hope, not only for learning how to read, but also for *becoming readers.* Everything we do with books in schools should be measured against these criteria: Will this help children enjoy books? Will this help children become lifetime readers?

We know that children's reading for pleasure drops off when they are faced with the added homework and demands of middle school and high school. But if children have learned to love reading before that time, they will continue to read and increase their reading once they leave college. If they have not discovered the joys of reading before high school, they probably never will.

One 12-year-old wrote to her former fifth-grade teacher two years after moving away to tell her of a wonderful book she had just read. Here is her letter:

Dear Miss Woolard:

I just finished the book *A Ring of Endless Light* and I was so excited about it that I just had to write and tell you about it. (It's by Madeleine

EVALUATION CRITERIA

Evaluating a Literature Program

AVAILABILITY OF BOOKS AND OTHER MEDIA
- Is there a school library media center in each elementary school building? Does it meet American Library Association standards for books and other media?
- Is there a professionally trained librarian and adequate support staff in each building?
- Does every classroom contain several hundred paperbacks and a changing collection of hardbacks?
- Are reference books easily accessible to each classroom?
- May children purchase books in a school-run paperback bookstore?
- Do teachers encourage children to order books through various school book clubs?
- May children take books home?
- Are children made aware of the programs of the public library?

TIME FOR LITERATURE
- Do all children have time to read books of their own choosing every day?
- Do all teachers read to the children once or twice a day?
- Do children have time to discuss their books with an interested adult or with other children every day?
- Are children allowed time to interpret books through art, drama, music, or writing?
- Do children seem attentive and involved as they listen to stories? Do they ask to have favorites reread?
- Is literature a part of all areas, across the curriculum?

MOTIVATING INTEREST
- Do teachers show their enthusiasm for books by sharing new ones with children, reading parts of their favorite children's books, discussing them, and so on?
- Do classroom and library displays call attention to particular books?
- Are children encouraged to set up book displays in the media center, the halls, and their classrooms?
- Does the media specialist plan special events—such as story hours, book talks, sharing films, working with book clubs?
- Do teachers and librarians work with parents to stimulate children's reading?
- Are special bibliographies prepared by the librarians or groups of children on topics of special interest— mysteries, animal stories, science fiction, fantasy, and so on?
- Are opportunities planned for contacts with authors and illustrators to kindle interest and enthusiasm for reading?

BALANCE IN THE CURRICULUM
- Do teachers and librarians try to introduce children to a wide variety of genres and to different authors when reading aloud?

- Do teachers share poetry as frequently as prose?
- Do children read both fiction and nonfiction?
- Are children exposed to new books and contemporary poems as frequently as some of the old favorites of both prose and poetry?
- Do children have a balance of wide reading experiences with small-group, in-depth discussion of books?

EVALUATING CHILDREN'S GROWTH AS READERS
- Do children keep reading logs or records of their free reading?
- Do older students (grade 3 and up) keep a response journal of their reading?
- Do teachers record examples of children's growth and understanding of literature as revealed in their play, talk, art, or writing?
- Do students and teachers together create an assessment portfolio with samples of children's best work?
- Are children allowed to respond to books in a variety of ways (art, drama, writing), rather than by required book reports?
- Is depth of understanding emphasized, rather than the number of books read?
- Are children responding to a greater range and complexity of work?
- What percentage of the children can be described as active readers? Has this percentage increased?
- Are some children beginning to see literature as a source of lifelong pleasure?

EVALUATING TEACHERS' PROFESSIONAL GROWTH
- Are teachers increasing their knowledge of children's literature?
- What percentage of the staff have taken a course in children's literature in the past five years?
- Are some staff meetings devoted to ways of improving the use of literature in the curriculum?
- Do teachers attend professional meetings that feature programs on children's literature?
- Are in-service programs in literature made available on a regular basis?
- Are in-service programs, such as administering the running record or the Miscue Analysis, given regularly?
- Are such professional journals as *New Advocate, Horn Book Magazine, Book Links,* and *School Library Journal* available to teachers and librarians?
- Are professional books on children's literature available?
- Have the teachers and librarians had a share in planning their literature programs?
- Do teachers feel responsible not only for teaching children to read but also for helping children find joy in reading?

L'Engle.) She writes with such description that sometimes the book made me smile, and when the characters were hurt or sad, I was also. On page 308 I wanted to scream along with the characters.

This is by far the *best* book I have ever read. I discovered it at just the right time; it made me enjoy life more. The book really made me think about life, death, happiness, sadness, self-pity, and what kind of person I want to be. If you have not read this book, I suggest you do. Here are some of my favorite passages from the book [she quotes several]. I have a lot more passages that I like but these two were my favorites. I have no other news, bye, Love, Amber[24]

There is no doubt that Amber will be a lifetime reader, discovering just the right book at "just the right time." And because all readers want to share their love of a fine book, Amber will continue to do this. Here, she chose to share her reactions with her former fifth-grade teacher, who loves books and shared her enthusiasm with her students.

A fourth-grade girl chose to reflect on her reading for a 4-H speech contest. Here is the speech she delivered:

I know what you're thinking. You're thinking: Uh-oh, another fourth grader about to give another dull speech about another stupid subject that's so boring that you won't be able to stay awake for another five minutes.

And, ordinarily, that's what happens. And I'm a pretty ordinary kid. I'm in fourth grade; I have blond hair. I weigh about 68 pounds; I'm about four and a half feet tall. I have a hamster and two hermit crabs that I'm crazy about and I have a brother I'm not so crazy about. But am I ordinary? You decide while you listen to some of the experiences I've had.

For instance, one time I moved to the beach because my dad was fired. My sisters and I found out that our cousin had a boyfriend her parents didn't know about. My mom and dad were going through some hard times. I found out that my mom was going to have a baby. But, in the end, it turned out all right. Am I ordinary?

Another experience I had was when I moved into a boxcar with three other kids to hide from our grandfather. We found stuff to cook with and eat on in a junk pile. The oldest kid in our group got a job. After living like this for awhile, we met our grandfather and found out that he was actually very nice. Am I ordinary?

Another time I got a plastic Indian from my best friend and a cupboard from my brother. That night I put my Indian in the cupboard and the next morning I heard rapping sounds coming from the cupboard. It was the Indian! The cupboard had turned the Indian into a real human being! I found out that the cupboard turned any plastic object into the real thing. I turned a few other objects real. Do I still sound ordinary?

How would an ordinary kid like me have these experiences? Easy . . . I read. I love to read. I had these experiences in the books *The Jellyfish Season* [Hahn], *The Boxcar Children* [Warner], and *The Indian in the Cupboard* [Banks]. You're probably thinking, she just read them. But when I'm sitting in front of the fire with my dog on my lap and reading those books, I really am having those experiences. So I guess you were right. I am a pretty ordinary kid, but reading gives me extraordinary experiences. And I suggest it to you, if you are tired of being ordinary.

Susan Komoroske, grade 4
George Mason Elementary School
Alexandria City Public School, Virginia
Susan Steinberg, teacher

It lies within the power of every teacher and librarian to give children a rich experience with literature, to share our enthusiasms for fine books, and to develop readers like Amber and Susan who will find a lifetime of pleasure in the reading of good books.

---

[24]Letter written to Linda Woolard, Wm. E. Miller Elementary School, by Amber. Reprinted by permission of Linda Woolard, Wm. E. Miller Elementary School, Newark, Ohio.

INTO THE **CLASSROOM**

Planning the Literature Program

1. **Art Project.** Select a book or poem and ask children to extend it through one of the art activities suggested in this chapter. Have them write something to go with their piece. Mount and display their work and writing.

2. **Reading Log.** Ask at least five children to keep a log of titles and authors of books they have read in a month. What do you observe? What does this suggest to you about these children? about your next steps as a teacher?

3. **Literature Inventory.** Give a literature inventory to a group of children and draw some conclusions about their previous exposure to literature. Plan what you think might be a rich literature program for them.

4. **Creative Drama Activities.** Ask small groups of children to plan creative drama activities (interviews, debates, imaginary conversations, and so forth) in response to a book. Which activities required the children to think most deeply about their book?

Go to the Online Learning Center at **www.mhhe.com/kiefer9e** or your Resources CD-ROM to find these additional classroom activities:

5. **Developing Sensitivity to Language**
6. **Single Books as Springboards**
7. **Expanded Classroom Dramatics Suggestions**
8. **Literature Discussion Groups**

Chapter Review

Go to the Online Learning Center at **www.mhhe.com/kiefer9e** or your Resources CD-ROM to take chapter quizzes, practice with key terms, and review the chapter.

Explorations

1. Visit an elementary school and focus on the provisions for a literature program. Does the teacher read to the children? What is read? What are the children reading? What books are available for them to read? How often are these books changed?

2. Spend a day in a school library media center. What does the librarian do? Is she caught up in meeting schedules, or does the center have flexible scheduling? Interview the media specialist and ask to see the current selection policy statement. Ask if the library has had censorship problems and what was done about them.

3. Draw a floor plan of a classroom you would hope to have as a teacher. Plan the reading areas and list what you would have in them.

4. Examine basal readers, sample kits of literature, and published units on literature. Note the purposes, content, plans of organization, and activities. Analyze the types of questions that have been prepared.

5. Using the "Framework for Webbing" (p. 691), choose a book, genre, or unit to web for a particular age level.

6. Working in a small group, choose a chapter book or a picture book and suggest a variety of activities that would extend children's understanding and appreciation of the book. Be prepared to explain how each activity might extend children's thinking or enjoyment.

7. Visit the Banned Books Week Web site at <ala.org/bbooks/index.html>. Write a rationale for a frequently challenged book.

8. Using the Evaluation Criteria: "Evaluating a Literature Program" (see p. 705), visit an elementary school and evaluate its program. Certain members of the class could be responsible for finding the answers to different sections of the guide. Combine your findings in a report and make recommendations concerning the literature program of that school.

9. Visit the Online Learning Center, and find directions for exploring an artist's medium, such as airbrush techniques (also see Teaching Resources: "Exploring Artists' Media," p. 682). Share books by suggested illustrators, and ask students to use the illustrator's technique to respond to one of the books.

Web Links

Go to the Online Learning Center at **www.mhhe.com/kiefer9e** to find links to the following children's literature Web sites:

Awesome Library

Children's Book Council Web Site

Children's Literature Navigator

Children's Literature Web Ring

CyberGuide

Doucette Index: K–12 Literature-Based Teaching Ideas

Fifty Multicultural Books Every Child Should Know

KidPub

Language Arts Mini-Lessons

Librarian's Guide to Cyberspace for Parents and Kids

Merriam-Webster Word Central

Readers' Theater

Reading Rainbow

Wacky Web Tales

Related Readings

Bauer, Caroline Feller. *New Handbook for Storytellers.* Chicago: American Library Association, 1993.

> This is one of the most thorough resources on storytelling available. It includes suggestions for choosing and telling stories, and ideas for using film, music, crafts, puppetry, and other story media. Information on storytelling festivals throughout the United States is included.

Harwayne, Shelley. *Going Public: Priorities and Practice at the Manhattan New School.* Portsmouth, N.H.: Heinemann, 1999, *and Lifetime Guarantees: Toward Ambitious Literacy Teaching.* Portsmouth, N.H.: Heinemann, 1999.

> Harwayne has served in a variety of capacities in elementary schools—teacher, consultant, principal, and assistant superintendent. These books are based on her experiences as principal of the Manhattan New School, an alternative school in New York City. They provide a blueprint for successful school programs and include information about the role of principal, building a positive school community, planning for parental involvement, dealing with curriculum and assessment, developing literature-centered curriculum, and providing for the professional development of teachers.

McCaslin, Nellie. *Creative Drama in the Classroom and Beyond.* 7th ed. New York: Longman, 1999.

> A well-known drama specialist provides both the theory and the practical help teachers need to initiate a drama program. She includes many suggestions for dramatizing stories and poems, a long section on puppets, and a new one on masks and their importance in drama. A fine revision of a respected book.

Pappas, Christine C., Barbara Z. Kiefer, and Linda S. Levstik. *An Integrated Language Perspective in the Elementary School.* 4th ed. White Plains, N.Y.: Longman, 2006.

> This excellent text provides integrated language theory and a wealth of examples from the classroom. Eight detailed units for grades K–6 are featured, along with webs to show their development. Chapters on observation and assessment techniques are also included. Literature is shown as central to the curriculum.

Peterson, Ralph, and Maryann Eeds. *Grand Conversations: Literature Groups in Action.* New York: Scholastic, 1990.

> Both theoretical and practical, this fine discussion of teaching with real books differentiates between extensive, or wide, reading, where children just read for enjoyment, and intensive reading, where students read and study a book in depth. Highly recommended for any teachers involved in a literature-based reading program.

Roser, Nancy L., and Miriam Martinez, eds. *Book Talk and Beyond: Children and Teachers Respond to Literature.* Newark, Del.: International Reading Association, 1995.

> This volume contains detailed ideas and examples from classrooms where children's talk about literature leads to deepening understanding and appreciation. Sections focus on what teachers need to understand about talk and literature, creating classroom contexts that invite talk, guiding talk, extending talk to dialogue journals, and other responses.

Routman, Regie. *Conversations: Strategies for Teaching, Learning, and Evaluating.* Portsmouth, N.H.: Heinemann, 2000.

> This extensive compendium of ways to organize and manage a whole-language, literature-based reading and writing program discusses journal writing, planning guides, teaching strategies, mini-lessons, evaluation, publishing, and a host of other topics and illuminates each with classroom examples. Helpful bibliographies, both of children's books and of professional references, further extend teachers' thinking.

Short, Kathy Gnagey, and Kathryn Mitchell Pierce, eds. *Talking About Books: Creating Literate Communities.* Portsmouth, N.H.: Heinemann, 1998.

> Teachers and educators focus on the kinds of learning communities that support readers as they read and interact with others, particularly as they discuss literature. Emphasis is placed on collaborative learning from kindergarten through high school. Practical suggestions are provided about ways to organize the classroom to encourage talk about literature.

Simmons, John S., and Eliza T. Dresang, eds. *School Censorship in the 21st Century: A Guide for Teachers and Library Media Specialists.* Newark, Del.: International Reading Association, 2001.

> Chapters detail examples of censorship in elementary and secondary schools and methods used by censors. Practical information includes how to write rationales for literature selections and ways for teachers, librarians, and administrators to respond to censorship.

Tierney, Robert, Mark A. Carter, and Laura E. Desai. *Portfolio Assessment in the Reading-Writing Classroom.* Norwood, Mass.: Christopher-Gordon, 1991.

> This lucid and thorough discussion of the theory and use of portfolios of children's work in the classroom includes examples using elementary and high school students' portfolios, self-assessment by students, and the use of portfolios in parent conferences.

Watson-Ellam, Linda. *Start with a Story: Literature and Learning in Your Classroom.* Portsmouth, N.H.: Heinemann, 1991.

> Written by a Canadian professor who works extensively with teachers, this useful book contains strategies and activities to help make literature come alive in the classroom with drama, music, art, writing, and bookmaking.

Wilhelm, Jeffrey D. *"You Gotta BE the Book": Teaching Engaged and Reflective Reading with Adolescents.* New York: Teachers College Press, 1997.

> Wilhelm, an experienced high school English teacher, found his confidence and his beliefs about teaching and learning called into question when he was assigned to teach middle school and three sections of remedial reading. Confronted with adolescents who told him there was "no way" they were going to read, Wilhelm eventually found that extending books through creative drama and visual art proved to be a motivator for reading for most of his students. This book details his struggles and his methods.

Children's Literature

 Go to the Children's Literature Database on your Resources CD-ROM for a searchable listing of these and other children's literature titles.

Aardema, Verna. *Why Mosquitoes Buzz in People's Ears.* Illustrated by Leo Dillon and Diane Dillon. Dial, 1975.

Ackerman, Karen. *Araminta's Paint Box.* Illustrated by Betsy Lewin. Atheneum, 1990.

Ahlberg, Janet, and Allan Ahlberg. *The Jolly Postman, or Other People's Letters.* Little, 1986.

Alcock, Vivien. *The Monster Garden.* Delacorte, 1988.

Alexander, Lloyd. *The Book of Three.* Holt, 1964.

———. *The Remarkable Journey of Prince Jen.* Dutton, 1991.

Aliki [Aliki Brandenberg]. *Mummies Made in Egypt.* Harper, 1985.

Allison, Jennifer. *Gilda Joyce, Psychic Investigator.* Dutton, 2005.

Almond, David. *Skellig.* Delacorte, 1999.

Andrews-Goebel, Nancy. *The Pot That Juan Built.* Illustrated by David Diaz. Lee, 2002.

Appelbaum, Diana. *Giants in the Land.* Illustrated by Michael Mc-Curdy. Houghton, 1993.

Aragon, Jane. *Salt Hands.* Illustrated by Ted Rand. Dutton, 1989.

Arnold, Caroline. *Saving the Peregrine Falcon.* Photographs by Richard R. Hewett. Carolrhoda, 1985.

Aruego, Jose, and Ariane Dewey. *Weird Friends: Unlikely Allies in the Animal Kingdom.* Harcourt, 2002.

Babbitt, Natalie. *Tuck Everlasting.* Farrar, 1975.

Baker, Jeannie. *The Story of Rosie Dock.* Greenwillow, 1995.

———. *Where the Forest Meets the Sea.* Greenwillow, 1988.

———. *Window.* Greenwillow, 1991.

Bang, Molly. *Nobody Particular: One Woman's Fight to Save the Bays.* Holt, 2001.

Banks, Lynne Reid. *The Indian in the Cupboard.* Illustrated by Brock Cole. Doubleday, 1985.

Barrett, Ron. *The Nutty News.* Knopf, 2005.

Baylor, Byrd. *Hawk, I'm Your Brother.* Illustrated by Peter Parnall. Macmillan, 1976.

———. *I'm in Charge of Celebrations.* Illustrated by Peter Parnall. Macmillan, 1986.

———. *The Other Way to Listen.* Illustrated by Peter Parnall. Macmillan, 1978.

———. *The Way to Start a Day.* Illustrated by Peter Parnall. Macmillan, 1978.

Blos, Joan. *A Gathering of Days: A New England Girl's Journal, 1830–1832.* Scribner's, 1979.

Blume, Judy. *Deenie.* Bradbury, 1973.

Bortolotti, Dan. *Panda Rescue: Changing the Future for Endangered Animals.* Firefly, 2003.

Bosse, Malcolm. *Deep Dream of the Rain Forest.* Farrar, 1993.

Brown, Margaret Wise. *Goodnight Moon.* Illustrated by Clement Hurd. Harper, 1947.

———. *The Important Book.* Illustrated by Leonard Weisgard. Harper, 1949.

Bryan, Ashley. *The Cat's Purr.* Atheneum, 1985.

Burnie, David. *Bird.* Knopf, 1988.

Byars, Betsy. *The Burning Questions of Bingo Brown.* Viking Penguin, 1988.

———. *Cracker Jackson.* Viking, 1985.

———. *Goodbye, Chicken Little.* Harper, 1979.

———. *The House of Wings.* Viking, 1972.

———. *The Night Swimmers.* Delacorte, 1980.

———. *The Pinballs.* Harper, 1977.

———. *The Summer of the Swans.* Viking, 1970.

Carle, Eric. *The Very Busy Spider.* Philomel, 1984.

———. *The Very Clumsy Click Beetle.* Philomel, 1999.

———. *The Very Hungry Caterpillar.* Putnam, 1989 [1969].

———. *The Very Quiet Cricket.* Philomel, 1990.

Caseley, Judith. *Dear Annie.* Greenwillow, 1991.

Cherry, Lynne. *The Great Kapok Tree: A Tale of the Amazon Rain Forest.* Harcourt, 1990.

———. *A River Ran Wild: An Environmental History.* Gulliver, 1992.

Christopher, John. *When the Tripods Came.* Dutton, 1988.

Cleary, Beverly. *Dear Mr. Henshaw.* Morrow, 1983.

———. *Ramona Forever.* Illustrated by Alan Tiegreen. Morrow, 1984.

———. *Ramona Quimby, Age 8.* Illustrated by Alan Tiegreen. Morrow, 1981.

———. *Strider.* Illustrated by Paul O. Zelinsky. Morrow, 1991.

Cofer, Judith Ortiz. *See* Ortiz Cofer, Judith.

Cole, Joanna. *The Magic School Bus at the Waterworks.* Illustrated by Bruce Degen. Scholastic, 1986.

Coleman, Evelyn. *To Be a Drum.* Illustrated by Aminah Brenda Lynne Robinson. Walker, 2000.

Cone, Molly. *Come Back Salmon.* Photographs by Sidnee Wheelwright. Little, 1992.

Cooney, Barbara. *Miss Rumphius.* Penguin, 1982.

Cooper, Susan. *The Boggart.* McElderry, 1993.

———. *Green Boy.* McElderry, 2002.

———. *The Selkie Girl.* Illustrated by Warwick Hutton. McElderry, 1986.

Cowcher, Helen. *Rain Forest.* Farrar, 1988.

Crews, Donald. *Sail Away.* Greenwillow, 1995.

Cummins, Pat. *Ananse and the Lizard: A West African Tale.* Holt, 2002.

Cushman, Karen. *Catherine Called Birdy.* Clarion, 1994.

Dahl, Roald. *James and the Giant Peach.* Illustrated by Nancy Ekholm Burkert. Knopf, 1961.

Darling, Kathy. *There's a Zoo on You.* Millbrook, 2000.

DeFelice, Cynthia. *The Missing Manatee.* Farrar, 2005.

dePaola, Tomie. *Big Anthony and the Magic Ring.* Harcourt, 1979.

———. *Strega Nona.* Prentice-Hall, 1975.

de Regniers, Beatrice Schenk. *May I Bring a Friend?* Illustrated by Beni Montresor. Atheneum, 1964.

Dickinson, Peter. *Eva.* Delacorte, 1989.

Dorros, Arthur. *Rain Forest Secrets.* Scholastic, 1990.

DuPrau, Jeanne. *The City of Ember.* Random, 2004.

Ehlert, Lois. *Leaf Man.* Harcourt, 2005.

Facklam, Margery. *And Then There Was One: The Mysteries of Extinction.* Illustrated by Pamela Johnson. Sierra Club/Little, 1990.

Farmer, Nancy. *The Ear, the Eye and the Arm: A Novel.* Orchard, 1994.

Ferris, Helen, comp. *Favorite Poems Old and New.* Illustrated by Leonard Weisgard. Doubleday, 1957.

Fleischman, Paul. *Seedfolks.* HarperCollins, 1997.

Fleischman, Sid. *The Whipping Boy.* Illustrated by Peter Sis. Greenwillow, 1987.

Fox, Mem. *Koala Lou.* Illustrated by Pamela Lofts. Harcourt, 1989.

Fox, Paula. *Monkey Island.* Orchard, 1991.

Frampton, David. *My Beastie Book of ABC.* HarperCollins, 2002.

Frank, Anne. *Anne Frank: The Diary of a Young Girl.* Doubleday, 1952.

Freedman, Russell. *Lincoln: A Photobiography.* Clarion, 1987.

Fritz, Jean. *And Then What Happened, Paul Revere?* Illustrated by Margo Tomes. Coward-McCann, 1973.

———. *The Cabin Faced West.* Putnam, 1958.

Galdone, Paul. *The Little Red Hen.* Houghton, 1979 [1973].

George, Jean Craighead. *Everglades.* Illustrated by Wendell Minor. HarperCollins, 1995.

———. *The Fire Bug Connection: An Ecological Mystery.* HarperCollins, 1993.

———. *Julie of the Wolves.* Harper, 1972.

———. *The Missing Gator of Gumbo Limbo: An Ecological Mystery.* HarperCollins, 1992.

———. *My Side of the Mountain.* Dutton, 1988 [1959].

———. *One Day in the Tropical Rainforest.* Illustrated by Gary Allen. HarperCollins, 1990.

———. *The Talking Earth.* Harper, 1983.

———. *Who Really Killed Cock Robin? An Ecological Mystery.* HarperCollins, 1991 [1971].

Gerson, Mary-Joan. *Why the Sky Is Far Away: A Nigerian Folktale.* Illustrated by Carla Golembe. Little, 1992.

Gibbons, Gail. *Recycle: A Handbook for Kids.* Little, 1996.

Gilmore, Kate. *The Exchange Student.* Houghton, 1999.

Goldschmidt, Judy. *The Secret Blog of Raisin Rodriguez.* Penguin, 2005.

Goodall, Jane. *The Chimpanzees I Love: Saving Their World and Ours.* Scholastic, 2001.

Grimes, Nikki. *At Jerusalem's Gate.* Illustrated by David Frampton. Eerdmans, 2005.

———. *Jazmine's Notebook.* Dial, 1998.

Grimm brothers. *Hansel and Gretel.* Illustrated by Anthony Browne. Knopf, 1988 [1981].

Grover, Wayne. *Dolphin Adventure: True Story.* Illustrated by Jim Fowler. Greenwillow, 1990.

Guthrie, Woody. *This Land Is Your Land.* Illustrated by Kathy Jakobsen. Little, 1998.

Hahn, Mary Downing. *The Jellyfish Season.* Clarion, 1985.

Hall, Donald. *Ox-Cart Man.* Illustrated by Barbara Cooney. Viking, 1979.

Hest, Amy. *The Private Notebook of Katie Roberts, Age 11.* Candlewick, 1995.

Hiaasen, Carl. *Flush.* Knopf, 2005

———. *Hoot.* HarperCollins, 2002.

Hoban, Tana. *Red, Blue, Yellow Shoe.* Greenwillow, 1986.

Hobbs, Will. *The Maze.* Morrow, 1998.

Hoberman, Mary Ann. *Yankee Doodle.* Illustrated by Nadine Bernard Westcott. Little, 2004.

Horvath, Polly. *The Pepins and Their Problems.* Farrar, 2004.

Huck, Charlotte. *A Creepy Countdown.* Illustrated by Jos. A. Smith. Greenwillow, 1998.

Hunter, Mollie. *The Mermaid Summer.* Harper, 1988.

———. *A Stranger Came Ashore.* Harper, 1975.

Jacques, Brian. *Redwall.* Philomel, 1986.

Jakobsen, Kathy. *My New York.* Little, 1993.

Jenkins, Steve. *The Top of the World: Climbing Mount Everest.* Houghton, 1999.

Jonas, Ann. *Aardvarks Disembark.* Greenwillow, 1990.

Jones, Carol. *The Gingerbread Man.* Houghton, 2002.

Kalman, Bobbie. *Colonial Life.* Crabtree, 1992.

Katz, Welwyn Wilton. *Time Ghost.* McElderry, 1995.

Keats, Ezra Jack. *Peter's Chair.* Harper, 1967.

———. *The Snowy Day.* Viking, 1962.

Kellogg, Steven. *A-Hunting We Will Go.* Morrow, 1998.

——. *Chicken Little.* Morrow, 1985.

Kidd, Diana. *Onion Tears.* Illustrated by Lucy Montgomery. Orchard, 1991.

Kipling, Rudyard. *The Elephant's Child.* Illustrated by Lorinda Bryan Cauley. Harcourt, 1983.

Klise, Kate. *Trial by Journal.* HarperCollins, 2001.

Lasky, Kathryn. *Interrupted Journey: Saving Endangered Sea Turtles.* Photographs by Christopher G. Knight. Candlewick, 2001.

Lauber, Patricia. *Summer of Fire: Yellowstone, 1988.* Orchard, 1990.

Le Guin, Ursula K. *A Wizard of Earthsea.* Illustrated by Ruth Robbins. Parnassus, 1968.

L'Engle, Madeleine. *A Ring of Endless Light.* Farrar, 1980.

——. *A Wrinkle in Time.* Farrar, 1962.

Lewis, Richard. *All of You Was Singing.* Illustrated by Ed Young. Macmillan, 1991.

Lisle, Janet Taylor. *The Lampfish of Twill.* Orchard, 1991.

Little, Jean. *Hey World, Here I Am!* Illustrated by Sue Truesdell. Harper, 1989.

Lowry, Lois. *Anastasia Krupnik.* Houghton, 1979.

——. *The Giver.* Houghton, 1993.

——. *Number the Stars.* Houghton, 1989.

Lunge-Larsen, Lise. *The Hidden Folk: Stories of Dwarves, Selkies and Other Secret Beings.* Illustrated by Beth Krommes. Houghton, 2004.

MacLachlan, Patricia. *Sarah, Plain and Tall.* HarperCollins, 1985.

Martin, Jaqueline Briggs. *Snowflake Bentley.* Illustrated by Mary Azarian. Houghton, 1998.

Marzollo, Jean. *Pretend You're a Cat.* Illustrated by Jerry Pinkney. Dial, 1990.

McDermott, Gerald. *Anansi the Spider: A Tale from the Ashanti.* Holt, 1972.

McKissack, Patricia C. *Flossie and the Fox.* Illustrated by Rachel Isadora. Dial, 1986.

McNaughton, Janet. *The Secret under My Skin.* HarperCollins. 2005.

McNulty, Faith. *The Lady and the Spider.* Illustrated by Bob Marstall. Harper, 1986.

Montgomery, Sy. *Search for the Golden Moon Bear: Science and Adventures in the Asian Tropics.* Houghton, 2004.

Mowll, Joshua. *Operation Red Jericho.* Candlewick, 2005.

Mullins, Patricia. *One Horse Waiting for Me.* Simon, 1998.

Myers, Walter Dean. *Autobiography of My Dead Brother.* Illustrated by Christopher Meyers. HarperCollins, 2005.

Myracle, Lauren. *TTYL.* Abrams, 2005.

O'Brien, Robert C. *Z for Zachariah.* Macmillan, 1987 [1975].

O'Malley, Kevin. *Captain Raptor and the Moon Mystery.* Walker, 2005.

Ormerod. Jan. *When an Elephant Comes to School.* Orchard, 2005.

Ortiz Cofer, Judith. *Call Me María.* Orchard, 2004.

Parker, John. *Waste, Recycling, and Re-use.* Raintree, 1998.

Partridge, Elizabeth. *Kogi's Mysterious Journey.* Illustrated by Aki Sogabe. Dutton, 2003.

Patent, Dorothy Hinshaw. *Garden of the Spirit Bear: Life in the Great Northern Rainforest.* Illustrated by Deborah Milton. Clarion, 2004.

Paterson, Katherine. *Bridge to Terabithia.* Illustrated by Donna Diamond. Crowell, 1977.

——. *The Great Gilly Hopkins.* Crowell, 1978.

——. *Lyddie.* Lodestar/Dutton, 1991.

Patterson, Francine. *Koko's Kitten.* Photographs by Ronald H. Cohn. Scholastic, 1985.

Pomeroy, Diana. *One Potato: A Counting Book of Potato Prints.* Harcourt, 1996.

Potter, Beatrix. *The Tale of Peter Rabbit.* Warne, 1902.

Prelutsky, Jack. *Nightmares: Poems to Trouble Your Sleep.* Illustrated by Arnold Lobel. Greenwillow, 1976.

——, ed. *Read-Aloud Rhymes for the Very Young.* Illustrated by Marc Simont. Knopf, 1986.

Quattlebaum, Mary. *Jackson Jones and the Puddle of Thorns.* Delacorte, 1994.

Reid, Barbara. *The Subway Mouse.* Scholastic, 2005.

Richter, Hans Peter. *Friedrich.* Holt, 1970.

Rosen, Michael. *We're Going on a Bear Hunt.* Illustrated by Helen Oxenbury. Macmillan, 1989.

Rylant, Cynthia. *The Journey: Stories of Migration.* Illustrated by Lambert Davis. Scholastic, 2006.

Sachar, Louis. *Holes.* Farrar, 1998.

Salisbury, Graham. *Under the Blood-Red Sun.* Delacorte, 1994.

Sanders, Scott R. *Hear the Wind Blow: American Folk Songs Retold.* Atheneum, 1985.

Schlein, Miriam. *Pigeons.* Photographs by Margaret Miller. Crowell, 1989.

——. *The Year of the Panda.* Illustrated by Kam Mak. Crowell, 1990.

Schmidt, Gary D. *Lizzie Bright and the Buckminster Boy.* Clarion, 2004.

Schwartz, Alvin. *Scary Stories to Tell in the Dark.* Illustrated by Stephen Gammell. Harper, 1981.

Scieszka, Jon. *Seen Art?* Illustrated by Lane Smith. Viking, 2005.

Sendak, Maurice. *Where the Wild Things Are.* Harper, 1963.

Seuss, Dr. [Theodore S. Geisel]. *The Lorax.* Random House, 1981.

Sharpe, Susan. *Waterman's Boy.* Bradbury, 1990.

Sheldon, Dyan. *Whales' Song.* Illustrated by Gary Blythe. Dial, 1991.

Showers, Paul. *The Listening Walk.* Illustrated by Aliki. HarperCollins, 1991.

Shulevitz, Uri. *Dawn.* Farrar, 1974.

Siebert, Diane. *Heartland.* Illustrated by Wendell Minor. Crowell, 1989.

——. *Mojave.* Illustrated by Wendell Minor. Crowell, 1988.

——. *Sierra.* Illustrated by Wendell Minor. Crowell, 1991.

Siegelson, Kim L. *In the Time of the Drums.* Illustrated by Brian Pinkney. Hyperion, 1999.

Sierra, Judy. *Tasty Baby Belly Buttons.* Illustrated by Meilo So. Knopf, 1999.

Singer, Marilyn. *Prairie Dogs Kiss and Lobsters Wave: How Animals Say Hello.* Illustrated by Normand Chartier. Holt, 1998.

Snyder, Zilpha Keatley. *Libby on Wednesday.* Delacorte, 1990.

Speare, Elizabeth George. *The Sign of the Beaver.* Houghton, 1983.

Spier, Peter. *The Star-Spangled Banner.* Doubleday, 1973.

Staines, Bill. *All God's Critters Got a Place in the Choir.* Illustrated by Margot Zemach. Dutton, 1989.

Steig, William. *Amos and Boris.* Farrar, 1971.

———. *Sylvester and the Magic Pebble.* Simon, 1969.

Stevens, Carla. *Trouble for Lucy,* Illustrated by Ronald Himler. Clarion, 1979.

Taylor, Mildred. *Roll of Thunder, Hear My Cry.* Illustrated by Jerry Pinkney. Dell, 1976.

Tillage, Leon. *Leon's Story.* Illustrated by Barbara Roth. Farrar, 1997.

Toft, Kim Michelle, and Allan Sheather. *One Less Fish.* Charlesbridge, 2005.

Tolstoy, Aleksei. *The Gigantic Turnip.* Illustrated by Niamh Sharkey. Barefoot, 1999.

Turner, Pamela S. *Gorilla Doctors: Saving Endangered Great Apes.* Houghton, 2005.

Uchida, Yoshiko. *Journey to Topaz.* Illustrated by Donald Carrick. Creative Arts, 1985 [1971].

Van Allsburg, Chris. *Just a Dream.* Houghton, 1990.

Waber, Bernard. *Ira Sleeps Over.* Houghton, 1975.

Wallace, Nancy Elizabeth. *Pumpkin Day.* Cavendish, 2002.

Wallner, Alexandra. *The Farmer in the Dell.* Holiday, 1998.

Warner, Gertrude Chandler. *The Boxcar Children #1.* Whitman, 1990 [1924].

Weller, Frances. *I Wonder If I'll See a Whale.* Illustrated by Ted Lewin. Philomel, 1991.

Wheatley, Nadia. *My Place.* Illustrated by Donna Rawlings. Kane/Miller, 1993.

Wheeler, Lisa. *Mammoths on the Move.* Illustrated by Kurt Cyrus. Harcourt, 2006.

White, E. B. *Charlotte's Web.* Harper, 1952.

Wilder, Laura Ingalls. *Farmer Boy.* Illustrated by Garth Williams. Harper, 1973.

Williams, Vera B. *Cherries and Cherry Pits.* Greenwillow, 1986.

———. *Stringbean's Trip to the Shining Sea.* Illustrated by Vera B. Williams and Jennifer Williams. Greenwillow, 1988.

———. *Three Days on a River in a Red Canoe.* Greenwillow, 1981.

Wilson, Karma. *Bear Wants More.* Illustrated by Jane Chapman. McElderry, 2003.

Wong, Janet. *You Have to Write.* Illustrated by Teresa Falvin. McElderry, 2002.

Wright-Frierson, Virginia. *An Island Scrapbook: Dawn to Dusk on a Barrier Island.* Simon, 1998.

———. *A North American Rain Forest Scrapbook.* Walker, 1999.

Xiong, Blia. *Nine-in-One Grr! Grr!* Adapted by Cathy Spagnoli. Illustrated by Nancy Hom. Children's, 1989.

Yagawa, Sumiko. *The Crane Wife.* Translated by Katherine Paterson. Illustrated by Suekichi Akaba. Morrow, 1981.

Yep, Laurence. *Dragonwings.* Harper, 1977.

Yolen, Jane. *Letting Swift River Go.* Illustrated by Barbara Cooney. Little, 1992.

———. *Owl Moon.* Illustrated by John Schoenherr. Philomel, 1987.

Young, Ed. *The Sons of the Dragon King.* Atheneum, 2004.

Ziefert, Harriet. *The Little Red Hen.* Illustrated by Emily Bolam. Viking, 1995.

Appendixes

Children's Book Awards

JOHN NEWBERY MEDAL

The John Newbery Medal is named in honor of John Newbery, a British publisher and bookseller of the eighteenth century. He has frequently been called the father of children's literature because he was the first to conceive the idea of publishing books expressly for children.

The award is presented each year to "the author of the most distinguished contribution to American literature for children." Only books published in the preceding year are eligible, and the author must be an American citizen or a permanent resident of the United States. The selection of the winner is made by a committee of the Association for Library Service to Children (ALSC) of the American Library Association. There are now fifteen members on this committee. The winning author is presented with a bronze medal designed by René Paul Chambellan and donated by Frederick G. Melcher. The announcement is made in January or early February. Later, at the summer conference of the American Library Association, a banquet is given in honor of the award winners.

In the following list, for each year the Medal winner is listed first (in boldface italic type), followed by the Honor Books for that year. The date is the year in which the award was conferred. All books were published the preceding year.

1922   ***The Story of Mankind*** by Hendrik Willem van Loon. Liveright.

The Great Quest by Charles Boardman Hawes. Little.

Cedric the Forester by Bernard G. Marshall. Appleton.

The Old Tobacco Shop by William Bowen. Macmillan.

The Golden Fleece by Padraic Colum. Macmillan.

The Windy Hill by Cornelia Meigs. Macmillan.

1923   ***The Voyages of Doctor Dolittle*** by Hugh Lofting. Lippincott.

(No record of the Honor Books)

1924   ***The Dark Frigate*** by Charles Boardman Hawes. Little.

(No record of the Honor Books)

1925   ***Tales from Silver Lands*** by Charles J. Finger. Illustrated by Paul Honoré. Doubleday.

Nicholas by Anne Carroll Moore. Putnam.

The Dream Coach by Anne Parrish and Dillwyn Parrish. Macmillan.

1926   ***Shen of the Sea*** by Arthur Bowie Chrisman. Illustrated by Else Hasselriis. Dutton.

The Voyagers by Padraic Colum. Macmillan.

1927   ***Smoky, the Cowhorse*** by Will James. Scribner's.

(No record of the Honor Books)

1928   ***Gay Neck, The Story of a Pigeon*** by Dhan Gopal Mukerji. Illustrated by Boris Artzybasheff. Dutton.

The Wonder Smith and His Son by Ella Young. Longmans.

Downright Dencey by Caroline Dale Snedeker. Doubleday.

1929   ***Trumpeter of Krakow*** by Eric P. Kelly. Illustrated by Angela Pruszynska. Macmillan.

Pigtail of Ah Lee Ben Loo by John Bennett. Longmans.

Millions of Cats by Wanda Gág. Coward-McCann.

The Boy Who Was by Grace T. Hallock. Dutton.

Clearing Weather by Cornelia Meigs. Little.

Runaway Papoose by Grace P. Moon. Doubleday.

Tod of the Fens by Eleanor Whitney. Macmillan.

1930   ***Hitty, Her First Hundred Years*** by Rachel Field. Illustrated by Dorothy P. Lathrop. Macmillan.

Pran of Albania by Elizabeth C. Miller. Doubleday.

The Jumping-Off Place by Miran Hurd McNeely. Longmans.

A Daughter of the Seine by Jeanette Eaton. Harper.

1931   ***The Cat Who Went to Heaven*** by Elizabeth Coatsworth. Illustrated by Lynd Ward. Macmillan.

Floating Island by Anne Parrish. Harper.

The Dark Star of Itza by Alida Malkus. Harcourt.

Queer Person by Ralph Hubbard. Doubleday.

Mountains Are Free by Julia Davis Adams. Dutton.

Spice and the Devil's Cave by Agnes D. Hewes. Knopf.

Meggy McIntosh by Elizabeth Janet Gray. Doubleday.

1932   ***Waterless Mountain*** by Laura Adams Armer. Illustrated by Sidney Armer and the author. Longmans.

The Fairy Circus by Dorothy P. Lathrop. Macmillan.

Calico Bush by Rachel Field. Macmillan.

Boy of the South Seas by Eunice Tietjens. Coward-McCann.

Out of the Flame by Eloise Lownsbery. Longmans.

Jane's Island by Marjorie Hill Allee. Houghton.

Truce of the Wolf by Mary Gould Davis. Harcourt.

1933   ***Young Fu of the Upper Yangtze*** by Elizabeth Foreman Lewis. Illustrated by Kurt Wiese. Winston.

Swift Rivers by Cornelia Meigs. Little.

The Railroad to Freedom by Hildegarde Swift. Harcourt.

Children of the Soil by Nora Burglon. Doubleday.

1934   ***Invincible Louisa*** by Cornelia Meigs. Little.

The Forgotten Daughter by Caroline Dale Snedeker. Doubleday.

Swords of Steel by Elsie Singmaster. Houghton.

ABC Bunny by Wanda Gág. Coward-McCann.

Winged Girl of Knossos by Erick Berry. Appleton.

New Land by Sarah L. Schmidt. McBride.

Apprentices of Florence by Anne Kyle. Houghton.

1935 **Dobry** by Monica Shannon. Illustrated by Atanas Katchamakoff. Viking.

Pageant of Chinese History by Elizabeth Seeger. Longmans.

Davy Crockett by Constance Rourke. Harcourt.

Day on Skates by Hilda Von Stockum. Harper.

1936 **Caddie Woodlawn** by Carol Ryrie Brink. Illustrated by Kate Seredy. Macmillan.

Honk the Moose by Phil Stong. Dodd.

The Good Master by Kate Seredy. Viking.

Young Walter Scott by Elizabeth Janet Gray. Viking.

All Sail Set by Armstrong Sperry. Winston.

1937 **Roller Skates** by Ruth Sawyer. Illustrated by Valenti Angelo. Viking.

Phoebe Fairchild: Her Book by Lois Lenski. Lippincott.

Whistler's Van by Idwal Jones. Viking.

The Golden Basket by Ludwig Bemelmans. Viking.

Winterbound by Margery Bianco. Viking.

Audubon by Constance Rourke. Harcourt.

The Codfish Musket by Agnes D. Hewes. Doubleday.

1938 **The White Stag** by Kate Seredy. Viking.

Bright Island by Mabel L. Robinson. Random.

Pecos Bill by James Cloyd Bowman. Little.

On the Banks of Plum Creek by Laura Ingalls Wilder. Harper.

1939 **Thimble Summer** by Elizabeth Enright. Farrar.

Leader by Destiny by Jeanette Eaton. Harcourt.

Penn by Elizabeth Janet Gray. Viking.

Nino by Valenti Angelo. Viking.

"Hello, the Boat!" by Phyllis Crawford. Holt.

Mr. Popper's Penguins by Richard Atwater and Florence Atwater. Little.

1940 **Daniel Boone** by James H. Daugherty. Viking.

The Singing Tree by Kate Seredy. Viking.

Runner of the Mountain Tops by Mabel L. Robinson. Random.

By the Shores of Silver Lake by Laura Ingalls Wilder. Harper.

Boy with a Pack by Stephen W. Meader. Harcourt.

1941 **Call It Courage** by Armstrong Sperry. Macmillan.

Blue Willow by Doris Gates. Viking.

Young Mac of Fort Vancouver by Mary Jane Carr. Crowell.

The Long Winter by Laura Ingalls Wilder. Harper.

Nansen by Anna Gertrude Hall. Viking.

1942 **The Matchlock Gun** by Walter D. Edmonds. Illustrated by Paul Lantz. Dodd.

Little Town on the Prairie by Laura Ingalls Wilder. Harper.

George Washington's World by Genevieve Foster. Scribner's.

Indian Captive by Lois Lenski. Lippincott.

Down Ryton Water by E. R. Gaggin. Viking.

1943 **Adam of the Road** by Elizabeth Janet Gray. Illustrated by Robert Lawson. Viking.

The Middle Moffat by Eleanor Estes. Harcourt.

"Have You Seen Tom Thumb?" by Mabel Leigh Hunt. Lippincott.

1944 **Johnny Tremain** by Esther Forbes. Illustrated by Lynd Ward. Houghton.

These Happy Golden Years by Laura Ingalls Wilder. Harper.

Fog Magic by Julia L. Sauer. Viking.

Rufus M. by Eleanor Estes. Harcourt.

Mountain Born by Elizabeth Yates. Coward-McCann.

1945 **Rabbit Hill** by Robert Lawson. Viking.

The Hundred Dresses by Eleanor Estes. Harcourt.

The Silver Pencil by Alice Dalgliesh. Scribner's.

Abraham Lincoln's World by Genevieve Foster. Scribner's.

Lone Journey by Jeanette Eaton. Harcourt.

1946 **Strawberry Girl** by Lois Lenski. Lippincott.

Justin Morgan Had a Horse by Marguerite Henry. Rand McNally.

The Moved-Outers by Florence Crannell Means. Houghton.

Bhimsa, the Dancing Bear by Christine Weston. Scribner's.

New Found World by Katherine B. Shippen. Viking.

1947 **Miss Hickory** by Carolyn Sherwin Bailey. Illustrated by Ruth Gannett. Viking.

Wonderful Year by Nancy Barnes. Messner.

Big Tree by Mary Buff and Conrad Buff. Viking.

The Heavenly Tenants by William Maxwell. Harper.

The Avion My Uncle Flew by Cyrus Fisher. Appleton.

The Hidden Treasure of Glaston by Eleanore M. Jewett. Viking.

1948 **The Twenty-One Balloons** by William Pène du Bois. Viking.

Pancakes-Paris by Claire Huchet Bishop. Viking.

Li Lun, Lad of Courage by Carolyn Treffinger. Abingdon-Cokesbury.

The Quaint and Curious Quest of Johnny Longfoot by Catherine Besterman. Bobbs-Merrill.

The Cow-Tail Switch and Other West African Stories by Harold Courlander and George Herzog. Holt.

Misty of Chincoteague by Marguerite Henry. Rand McNally.

1949 **King of the Wind** by Marguerite Henry. Illustrated by Wesley Dennis. Rand McNally.

Seabird by Holling Clancy Holling. Houghton.

Daughter of the Mountains by Louise Rankin. Viking.

My Father's Dragon by Ruth S. Gannett. Random.

Story of the Negro by Arna Bontemps. Knopf.

1950 **The Door in the Wall** by Marguerite de Angeli. Doubleday.

Tree of Freedom by Rebecca Caudill. Viking.

The Blue Cat of Castle Town by Catherine Coblentz. Longmans.

Kildee House by Rutherford Montgomery. Doubleday.

George Washington by Genevieve Foster. Scribner's.

Song of the Pines by Walter Havighurst and Marion Havighurst. Winston.

1951 **Amos Fortune, Free Man** by Elizabeth Yates. Illustrated by Nora Unwin. Dutton.

Better Known as Johnny Appleseed by Mabel Leigh Hunt. Lippincott.

Gandhi, Fighter without a Sword by Jeanette Eaton. Morrow.

Abraham Lincoln, Friend of the People by Clara I. Judson. Wilcox & Follett.

The Story of Appleby Capple by Anne Parrish. Harper.

1952 **Ginger Pye** by Eleanor Estes. Harcourt.

Americans before Columbus by Elizabeth Baity. Viking.

Minn of the Mississippi by Holling Clancy Holling. Houghton.

The Defender by Nicholas Kalashnikoff. Scribner's.

The Light at Tern Rock by Julia L. Sauer. Viking.

The Apple and the Arrow by Mary Buff and Conrad Buff. Houghton.

1953 **Secret of the Andes** by Ann Nolan Clark. Illustrated by Jean Charlot. Viking.

Charlotte's Web by E. B. White. Harper.

Moccasin Trail by Eloise J. McGraw. Coward-McCann.

Red Sails for Capri by Ann Weil. Viking.

The Bears on Hemlock Mountain by Alice Dalgliesh. Scribner's.

Birthdays of Freedom by Genevieve Foster. Scribner's.

1954 **And Now Miguel** by Joseph Krumgold. Illustrated by Jean Charlot. Crowell.

All Alone by Clarie Huchet Bishop. Viking.

Shadrach by Meindert DeJong. Harper.

Hurry Home, Candy by Meindert DeJong. Harper.

Theodore Roosevelt, Fighting Patriot by Clara I. Judson. Follett.

Magic Maize by Mary Buff and Conrad Buff. Houghton.

1955 **The Wheel on the School** by Meindert DeJong. Illustrated by Maurice Sendak. Harper.

Courage of Sarah Noble by Alice Dalgliesh. Scribner's.

Banner in the Sky by James Ramsey Ullman. Lippincott.

1956 **Carry On, Mr. Bowditch** by Jean Lee Latham. Houghton.

The Golden Name Day by Jennie D. Lindquist. Harper.

The Secret River by Marjorie Kinnan Rawlings. Scribner's.

Men, Microscopes and Living Things by Katherine B. Shippen. Viking.

1957 **Miracles on Maple Hill** by Virginia Sorensen. Illustrated by Beth Krush and Joe Krush. Harcourt.

Old Yeller by Fred Gipson. Harper.

The House of Sixty Fathers by Meindert DeJong. Harper.

Mr. Justice Holmes by Clara I. Judson. Follett.

The Corn Grows Ripe by Dorothy Rhoads. Viking.

Black Fox of Lorne by Marguerite de Angeli. Doubleday.

1958 **Rifles for Watie** by Harold Keith. Illustrated by Peter Burchard. Crowell.

The Horsecatcher by Mari Sandoz. Westminster.

Gone-Away Lake by Elizabeth Enright. Harcourt.

The Great Wheel by Robert Lawson. Viking.

Tom Paine, Freedom's Apostle by Leo Gurko. Crowell.

1959 **The Witch of Blackbird Pond** by Elizabeth George Speare. Houghton.

The Family under the Bridge by Natalie S. Carlson. Harper.

Along Came a Dog by Meindert DeJong. Harper.

Chucaro by Francis Kalnay. Harcourt.

The Perilous Road by William O. Steele. Harcourt.

1960 **Onion John** by Joseph Krumgold. Illustrated by Symeon Shimin. Crowell.

My Side of the Mountain by Jean Craighead George. Dutton.

America Is Born by Gerald W. Johnson. Morrow.

The Gammage Cup by Carol Kendall. Harcourt.

1961 **Island of the Blue Dolphins** by Scott O'Dell. Houghton.

America Moves Forward by Gerald W. Johnson. Morrow.

Old Ramon by Jack Schaefer. Houghton.

The Cricket in Times Square by George Selden. Farrar.

1962 **The Bronze Bow** by Elizabeth George Speare. Houghton.

Frontier Living by Edwin Tunis. World.

The Golden Goblet by Eloise J. McGraw. Coward-McCann.

Belling the Tiger by Mary Stolz. Harper.

1963 **A Wrinkle in Time** by Madeleine L'Engle. Farrar.

Thistle and Thyme by Sorche Nic Leodhas. Holt.

Men of Athens by Olivia Coolidge. Houghton.

1964 **It's Like This, Cat** by Emily Neville. Illustrated by Emil Weiss. Harper.

Rascal by Sterling North. Dutton.

The Loner by Ester Wier. McKay.

1965 **Shadow of a Bull** by Maia Wojciechowska. Illustrated by Alvin Smith. Atheneum.

Across Five Aprils by Irene Hunt. Follett.

1966   *I, Juan de Pareja* by Elizabeth Borten de Treviño. Farrar.

The Black Cauldron by Lloyd Alexander. Holt.

The Animal Family by Randall Jarrell. Pantheon.

The Noonday Friends by Mary Stolz. Harper.

1967   *Up a Road Slowly* by Irene Hunt. Follett.

The King's Fifth by Scott O'Dell. Houghton.

Zlateh the Goat and Other Stories by Isaac Bashevis Singer. Harper.

The Jazz Man by Mary Hays Weik. Atheneum.

1968   *From the Mixed-Up Files of Mrs. Basil E. Frankweiler* by E. L. Konigsburg. Atheneum.

Jennifer, Hecate, Macbeth, William McKinley, and Me, Elizabeth by E. L. Konigsburg. Atheneum.

The Black Pearl by Scott O'Dell. Houghton.

The Fearsome Inn by Isaac Bashevis Singer. Scribner's.

The Egypt Game by Zilpha Keatley Snyder. Atheneum.

1969   *The High King* by Lloyd Alexander. Holt.

To Be a Slave by Julius Lester. Dial.

When Shlemiel Went to Warsaw and Other Stories by Isaac Bashevis Singer. Farrar.

1970   *Sounder* by William H. Armstrong. Harper.

Our Eddie by Sulamith Isk-Kishor. Pantheon.

The Many Ways of Seeing: An Introduction to the Pleasures of Art by Janet Gaylord Moore. World.

Journey Outside by Mary Q. Steele. Viking.

1971   *Summer of the Swans* by Betsy Byars. Viking.

Kneeknock Rise by Natalie Babbitt. Farrar.

Enchantress from the Stars by Sylvia Louise Engdahl. Atheneum.

Sing Down the Moon by Scott O'Dell. Houghton.

1972   *Mrs. Frisby and the Rats of NIMH* by Robert C. O'Brien. Atheneum.

Incident at Hawk's Hill by Allan W. Eckert. Little.

The Planet of Junior Brown by Virginia Hamilton. Macmillan.

The Tombs of Atuan by Ursula K. Le Guin. Atheneum.

Annie and the Old One by Miska Miles. Little.

The Headless Cupid by Zilpha Keatley Snyder. Atheneum.

1973   *Julie of the Wolves* by Jean Craighead George. Harper.

Frog and Toad Together by Arnold Lobel. Harper.

The Upstairs Room by Johanna Reiss. Crowell.

The Witches of Worm by Zilpha Keatley Snyder. Atheneum.

1974   *The Slave Dancer* by Paula Fox. Bradbury.

The Dark Is Rising by Susan Cooper. McElderry/ Atheneum.

1975   *M. C. Higgins the Great* by Virginia Hamilton. Macmillan.

My Brother Sam Is Dead by James Lincoln Collier and Christopher Collier. Four Winds.

Philip Hall Likes Me, I Reckon Maybe by Bette Greene. Dial.

The Perilous Gard by Elizabeth Marie Pope. Houghton.

Figgs and Phantoms by Ellen Raskin. Dutton.

1976   *The Grey King* by Susan Cooper. Atheneum.

Dragonwings by Laurence Yep. Harper.

The Hundred Penny Box by Sharon Mathis. Viking.

1977   *Roll of Thunder, Hear My Cry* by Mildred D. Taylor. Dial.

Abel's Island by William Steig. Farrar.

A String in the Harp by Nancy Bond. Atheneum.

1978   *Bridge to Terabithia* by Katherine Paterson. Crowell.

Anpao: An American Indian Odyssey by Jamake Highwater. Lippincott.

Ramona and Her Father by Beverly Cleary. Morrow.

1979   *The Westing Game* by Ellen Raskin. Dutton.

The Great Gilly Hopkins by Katherine Paterson. Crowell.

1980   *A Gathering of Days: A New England Girl's Journal, 1830–1832* by Joan W. Blos. Scribner's.

The Road from Home: The Story of an Armenian Girl by David Kherdian. Greenwillow.

1981   *Jacob Have I Loved* by Katherine Paterson. Crowell.

The Fledgling by Jane Langton. Harper.

Ring of Endless Light by Madeleine L'Engle. Farrar.

1982   *A Visit to William Blake's Inn: Poems for Innocent and Experienced Travelers* by Nancy Willard. Illustrated by Alice Provensen and Martin Provensen. Harcourt.

Ramona Quimby, Age 8 by Beverly Cleary. Morrow.

Upon the Head of the Goat: A Childhood in Hungary, 1939–1944 by Aranka Siegal. Farrar.

1983   *Dicey's Song* by Cynthia Voigt. Atheneum.

The Blue Sword by Robin McKinley. Greenwillow.

Doctor De Soto by William Steig. Farrar.

Graven Images by Paul Fleischman. Harper.

Homesick: My Own Story by Jean Fritz. Putnam.

Sweet Whispers, Brother Rush by Virginia Hamilton. Philomel.

1984   *Dear Mr. Henshaw* by Beverly Cleary. Morrow.

The Wish-Giver by Bill Brittain. Harper.

A Solitary Blue by Cynthia Voigt. Atheneum.

The Sign of the Beaver by Elizabeth George Speare. Houghton.

Sugaring Time by Kathryn Lasky. Photographs by Christopher Knight. Macmillan.

1985   *The Hero and the Crown* by Robin McKinley. Greenwillow.

The Moves Make the Man by Bruce Brooks. Harper.

One-Eyed Cat by Paula Fox. Bradbury.

Like Jake and Me by Marvis Jukes. Illustrated by Lloyd Bloom. Knopf.

1986 **Sarah, Plain and Tall** by Patricia MacLachlan. Harper.

Commodore Perry in the Land of the Shogun by Rhoda Blumberg. Lothrop.

Dogsong by Gary Paulsen. Bradbury.

1987 **The Whipping Boy** by Sid Fleischman. Greenwillow.

A Fine White Dust by Cynthia Rylant. Bradbury.

On My Honor by Marion Dane Bauer. Clarion.

Volcano by Patricia Lauber. Bradbury.

1988 **Lincoln: A Photobiography** by Russell Freedman. Clarion.

After the Rain by Norma Fox Mazer. Morrow.

Hatchet by Gary Paulsen. Bradbury.

1989 **Joyful Noise: Poems for Two Voices** by Paul Fleischman. Harper.

In the Beginning: Creation Stories from around the World by Virginia Hamilton. Harcourt.

Scorpions by Walter Dean Myers. Harper.

1990 **Number the Stars** by Lois Lowry. Houghton.

Afternoon of the Elves by Janet Taylor Lisle. Jackson/Orchard.

Shabanu: Daughter of the Wind by Suzanne Fisher Staples. Knopf.

The Winter Room by Gary Paulsen. Jackson/Orchard.

1991 **Maniac Magee** by Jerry Spinelli. Little.

The True Confessions of Charlotte Doyle by Avi. Jackson/Orchard.

1992 **Shiloh** by Phyllis Reynolds Naylor. Atheneum.

Nothing but the Truth by Avi. Jackson/Orchard.

The Wright Brothers by Russell Freedman. Holiday.

1993 **Missing May** by Cynthia Rylant. Jackson/Orchard.

The Dark-Thirty: Southern Tales of the Supernatural by Patricia C. McKissack. Knopf.

Somewhere in the Darkness by Walter Dean Myers. Scholastic.

What Hearts by Bruce Brooks. HarperCollins.

1994 **The Giver** by Lois Lowry. Houghton.

Crazy Lady by Jane Leslie Conly. HarperCollins.

Dragon's Gate by Laurence Yep. HarperCollins.

Eleanor Roosevelt: A Life of Discovery by Russell Freedman. Clarion.

1995 **Walk Two Moons** by Sharon Creech. HarperCollins.

Catherine, Called Birdy by Karen Cushman. Clarion.

The Ear, the Eye, and the Arm by Nancy Farmer. Jackson/Orchard.

1996 **The Midwife's Apprentice** by Karen Cushman. Clarion.

What Jamie Saw by Carolyn Coman. Front Street.

The Watsons Go to Birmingham: 1963 by Christopher Paul Curtis. Delacorte.

Yolonda's Genius by Carol Fenner. McElderry.

The Great Fire by Jim Murphy. Scholastic.

1997 **The View from Saturday** by E. L. Konigsburg. Atheneum.

A Girl Named Disaster by Nancy Farmer. Jackson/Orchard.

The Moorchild by Eloise McGraw. Simon.

The Thief by Megan Whalen Turner. Greenwillow.

Belle Prater's Boy by Ruth White. Farrar.

1998 **Out of the Dust** by Karen Hesse. Scholastic.

Ella Enchanted by Gail Carson Levine. HarperCollins.

Lily's Crossing by Patricia Reilly Giff. Delacorte.

Wringer by Jerry Spinelli. HarperCollins.

1999 **Holes** by Louis Sachar. Foster.

A Long Way from Chicago by Richard Peck. Dial.

2000 **Bud, Not Buddy** by Christopher Paul Curtis. Delacorte.

Getting Near to Baby by Audrey Couloumbis. Putnam.

Our Only May Amelia by Jennifer L. Holm. HarperCollins.

26 Fairmount Avenue by Tomie dePaola. Putnam.

2001 **A Year Down Yonder** by Richard Peck. Dial.

Because of Winn-Dixie by Kate DiCamillo. Candlewick.

Hope Was Here by Joan Bauer. Putnam.

Joey Pigza Loses Control by Jack Gantos. Farrar.

The Wanderer by Sharon Creech. HarperCollins.

2002 **A Single Shard** by Linda Sue Park. Clarion/Houghton.

Everything on a Waffle by Polly Horvath. Farrar.

Carver: A Life in Poems by Marilyn Nelson. Front Street.

2003 **Crispin: The Cross of Lead** by Avi. Hyperion.

The House of the Scorpion by Nancy Farmer. Atheneum.

Pictures of Hollis Woods by Patricia Reilly Giff. Random.

Hoot by Carl Hiaasen. Knopf.

A Corner of the Universe by Ann M. Martin. Scholastic.

Surviving the Applewhites by Stephanie S. Tolan. HarperCollins.

2004 **The Tale of Despereaux: Being the Story of a Mouse, a Princess, Some Soup, and a Spool of Thread** by Kate DiCamillo. Illustrated by Timothy Basil Ering. Candlewick.

Olive's Ocean by Kevin Henkes. Greenwillow.

An American Plague: The True and Terrifying Story of the Yellow Fever Epidemic of 1793 by Jim Murphy. Clarion.

2005 **Kira-Kira** by Cynthia Kadohata. Atheneum/Simon.

Al Capone Does My Shirts by Gennifer Choldenko. Putnam.

The Voice That Challenged a Nation: Marian Anderson and the Struggle for Equal Rights by Russell Freedman. Clarion/Houghton.

Lizzie Bright and the Buckminster Boy by Gary D. Schmidt. Clarion/Houghton.

2006 **Criss Cross** by Lynne Rae Perkins. Greenwillow.

Whittington by Alan Armstrong. Illustrated by S. D. Schindler. Random.

Hitler Youth: Growing Up in Hitler's Shadow by Susan Campbell Bartoletti. Scholastic.

Princess Academy by Shannon Hale. Bloomsbury.

Show Way by Jacqueline Woodson. Illustrated by Hudson Talbott. Putnam.

CALDECOTT MEDAL

The Caldecott Medal is named in honor of Randolph Caldecott, a prominent English illustrator of children's books during the nineteenth century. This award, presented each year by an awards committee of the Association for Library Service to Children (ALSC) of the American Library Association, is given to "the artist of the most distinguished American picture book for children." In the following list, for each year the Medal winner is listed first (in boldface italic type), followed by the Honor Books for that year. If an illustrator's name is not cited, the author illustrated the book.

1938   ***Animals of the Bible, A Picture Book.*** Text selected from the King James Bible by Helen Dean Fish. Illustrated by Dorothy P. Lathrop. Lippincott.

Seven Simeons: A Russian Tale by Boris Artzybasheff. Viking.

Four and Twenty Blackbirds compiled by Helen Dean Fish. Illustrated by Robert Lawson. Lippincott.

1939   ***Mei Li*** by Thomas Handforth. Doubleday.

The Forest Pool by Laura Adams Armer. Longmans.

Wee Gillis by Munro Leaf. Illustrated by Robert Lawson. Viking.

Snow White and the Seven Dwarfs. Translated and illustrated by Wanda Gág. Coward-McCann.

Barkis by Clare Turlay Newberry. Harper.

Andy and the Lion by James Daugherty. Viking.

1940   ***Abraham Lincoln*** by Ingri d'Aulaire and Edgar Parin d'Aulaire. Doubleday.

Cock-a-Doodle-Doo by Berta Hader and Elmer Hader. Macmillan.

Madeline by Ludwig Bemelmans. Viking.

The Ageless Story by Lauren Ford. Dodd.

1941   ***They Were Strong and Good*** by Robert Lawson. Viking.

April's Kittens by Clare Turlay Newberry. Harper.

1942   ***Make Way for Ducklings*** by Robert McCloskey. Viking.

An American ABC by Maud Petersham and Miska Petersham. Macmillan.

In My Mother's House by Ann Nolan Clark. Illustrated by Velino Herrera. Viking.

Paddle-to-the-Sea by Holling Clancy. Houghton.

Nothing at All by Wanda Gág. Coward-McCann.

1943   ***The Little House*** by Virginia Lee Burton. Houghton.

Dash and Dart by Mary Buff and Conrad Buff. Viking.

Marshmallow by Clare Turlay Newberry. Harper.

1944   ***Many Moons*** by James Thurber. Illustrated by Louis Slobodkin. Harcourt.

Small Rain. Text arranged from the Bible by Jessie Orton Jones. Illustrated by Elizabeth Orton Jones. Viking.

Pierre Pidgeon by Lee Kingman. Illustrated by Arnold Edwin Bare. Houghton.

Good-Luck Horse by Chih-Yi Chan. Illustrated by Plato Chan. Whittlesey.

Mighty Hunter by Berta Hader and Elmer Hader. Macmillan.

A Child's Good Night Book by Golden MacDonald [Margaret Wise Brown]. Illustrated by Jean Charlot. W. R. Scott.

1945   ***Prayer for a Child*** by Rachel Field. Pictures by Elizabeth Orton Jones. Macmillan.

Mother Goose. Compiled and illustrated by Tasha Tudor. Oxford UP.

In the Forest by Marie Hall Ets. Viking.

Yonie Wondernose by Marguerite de Angeli. Doubleday.

The Christmas Anna Angel by Ruth Sawyer. Illustrated by Kate Seredy. Viking.

1946   ***The Rooster Crows*** by Maud Petersham and Miska Petersham. Macmillan.

Little Lost Lamb by Golden MacDonald [Margaret Wise Brown]. Illustrated by Leonard Weisgard. Doubleday.

Sing Mother Goose. Music by Opal Wheeler. Illustrated by Marjorie Torrey. Dutton.

My Mother Is the Most Beautiful Woman in the World by Becky Reyher. Illustrated by Ruth C. Gannett. Lothrop.

You Can Write Chinese by Kurt Wiese. Viking.

1947   ***The Little Island*** by Golden MacDonald [Margaret Wise Brown]. Illustrated by Leonard Weisgard. Doubleday.

Rain Drop Splash by Alvin R. Tesselt. Illustrated by Leonard Weisgard. Lothrop.

Boats on the River by Marjorie Flack. Illustrated by Jay Hyde Barnum. Viking.

Timothy Turtle by Al Graham. Illustrated by Tony Palazzo. Welch.

Pedro, the Angel of Olvera Street by Leo Politi. Scribner's.

Sing in Praise by Opal Wheeler. Illustrated by Marjorie Torrey. Dutton.

1948   ***White Snow, Bright Snow*** by Alvin Tresselt. Illustrated by Roger Duvoisin. Lothrop.

Stone Soup. Told and illustrated by Marcia Brown. Scribner's.

McElligot's Pool by Theodor S. Geisel [Dr. Seuss]. Random.

Bambino the Clown by George Schreiber. Viking.

Roger and the Fox by Lavinia R. Davis. Illustrated by Hildegard Woodward. Doubleday.

Song of Robin Hood. Edited by Anne Malcolmson. Illustrated by Virginia Lee Burton. Houghton.

1949   ***The Big Snow*** by Berta Hader and Elmer Hader. Macmillan.

Blueberries for Sal by Robert McCloskey. Viking.

All around the Town by Phyllis McGinley. Illustrated by Helen Stone. Lippincott.

Juanita by Leo Politi. Scribner's.

Fish in the Air by Kurt Wiese. Viking.

1950 **Song of the Swallows** by Leo Politi. Scribner's.

America's Ethan Allen by Stewart Holbrook. Illustrated by Lynd Ward. Houghton.

The Wild Birthday Cake by Lavinia R. Davis. Illustrated by Hildegard Woodward. Doubleday.

The Happy Day by Ruth Krauss. Illustrated by Marc Simont. Harper.

Henry Fisherman by Marcia Brown. Scribner's.

Bartholomew and the Oobleck by Theodor S. Geisel [Dr. Seuss]. Random.

1951 **The Egg Tree** by Katherine Milhous. Scribner's.

Dick Whittington and His Cat. Told and illustrated by Marcia Brown. Scribner's.

The Two Reds by Will [William Lipkind]. Illustrated by Nicolas [Mordvinoff]. Harcourt.

If I Ran the Zoo by Theodor S. Geisel [Dr. Seuss]. Random.

T-Bone, the Baby-Sitter by Clare Turlay Newberry. Harper.

The Most Wonderful Doll in the World by Phyllis McGinley. Illustrated by Helen Stone. Lippincott.

1952 **Finders Keepers** by Will [William Lipkind]. Illustrated by Nicolas [Mordvinoff]. Harcourt.

Mr. T. W. Anthony Woo by Marie Hall Ets. Viking.

Skipper John's Cook by Marcia Brown. Scribner's.

All Falling Down by Gene Zion. Illustrated by Margaret Bloy Graham. Harper.

Bear Party by William Pène du Bois. Viking.

Feather Mountain by Elizabeth Olds. Houghton.

1953 **The Biggest Bear** by Lynd Ward. Houghton.

Puss in Boots. Told and illustrated by Marcia Brown. Scribner's.

One Morning in Maine by Robert McCloskey. Viking.

Ape in a Cape by Fritz Eichenberg. Harcourt.

The Storm Book by Charlotte Zolotow. Illustrated by Margaret Bloy Graham. Harper.

Five Little Monkeys by Juliet Kepes. Houghton.

1954 **Madeline's Rescue** by Ludwig Bemelmans. Viking.

Journey Cake, Ho! by Ruth Sawyer. Illustrated by Robert McCloskey. Viking.

When Will the World Be Mine? by Miriam Schlein. Illustrated by Jean Charlot. W. R. Scott.

The Steadfast Tin Soldier. Translated by M. R. James. Adapted from Hans Christian Andersen. Illustrated by Marcia Brown. Scribner's.

A Very Special House by Ruth Krauss. Illustrated by Maurice Sendak. Harper.

Green Eyes by Abe Birnbaum. Capitol.

1955 **Cinderella, or The Little Glass Slipper** by Charles Perrault. Illustrated by Marcia Brown. Scribner's.

Book of Nursery and Mother Goose Rhymes. Compiled and illustrated by Marguerite de Angeli. Doubleday.

Wheel on the Chimney by Margaret Wise Brown. Illustrated by Tibor Gergely. Lippincott.

The Thanksgiving Story by Alice Dalgliesh. Illustrated by Helen Sewall. Scribner's.

1956 **Frog Went A-Courtin'** by John Langstaff. Illustrated by Feodor Rojankovsky. Harcourt.

Play with Me by Marie Hall Ets. Viking.

Crow Boy by Taro Yashima. Viking.

1957 **A Tree Is Nice** by Janice May Udry. Illustrated by Marc Simont. Harper.

Mr. Penny's Race Horse by Marie Hall Ets. Viking.

1 Is One by Tasha Tudor. Walck.

Anatole by Eve Titus. Illustrated by Paul Galdone. McGraw-Hill.

Gillespie and the Guards by Benjamin Elkin. Illustrated by James Daugherty. Viking.

Lion by William Pène du Bois. Viking.

1958 **Time of Wonder** by Robert McCloskey. Viking.

Fly High, Fly Low by Don Freeman. Viking.

Anatole and the Cat by Eve Titus. Illustrated by Paul Galdone. McGraw-Hill.

1959 **Chanticleer and the Fox.** Edited and illustrated by Barbara Cooney. Crowell.

The House That Jack Built: La maison que Jacques a bâtie by Antonio Frasconi. Harcourt.

What Do You Say, Dear? by Sesyle Joslin. Illustrated by Maurice Sendak. W. R. Scott.

Umbrella by Taro Yashima. Viking.

1960 **Nine Days to Christmas** by Marie Hall Ets and Aurora Labastida. Viking.

Houses from the Sea by Alice E. Goudey. Illustrated by Adrienne Adams. Scribner's.

The Moon Jumpers by Janice May Udry. Illustrated by Maurice Sendak. Harper.

1961 **Baboushka and the Three Kings** by Ruth Robbins. Illustrated by Nicolas Sidjakov. Parnassus.

Inch by Inch by Leo Lionni. Obolensky.

1962 **Once a Mouse** by Marcia Brown. Scribner's.

Fox Went Out on a Chilly Night by Peter Spier. Doubleday.

Little Bear's Visit by Else H. Minarik. Illustrated by Maurice Sendak. Harper.

The Day We Saw the Sun Come Up by Alice Goudey. Illustrated by Adrienne Adams. Scribner's.

1963 **The Snowy Day** by Ezra Jack Keats. Viking.

The Sun Is a Golden Earring by Natalia M. Belting. Illustrated by Bernarda Bryson. Holt.

Mr. Rabbit and the Lovely Present by Charlotte Zolotow. Illustrated by Maurice Sendak. Harper.

1964 **Where the Wild Things Are** by Maurice Sendak. Harper.

Swimmy by Leo Lionni. Pantheon.

All in the Morning Early by Sorche Nic Leodhas [Leclaire Alger]. Illustrated by Evaline Ness. Holt.

Mother Goose and Nursery Rhymes by Philip Reed. Atheneum.

1965 **May I Bring a Friend?** by Beatrice Schenk de Regniers. Illustrated by Beni Montresor. Atheneum.

Rain Makes Applesauce by Julian Scheer. Illustrated by Marvin Bileck. Holiday.

The Wave by Margaret Hodges. Illustrated by Blair Lent. Houghton.

A Pocketful of Cricket by Rebecca Caudill. Illustrated by Evaline Ness. Holt.

1966 **Always Room for One More** by Sorche Nic Leodhas [Leclaire Alger]. Illustrated by Nonny Hogrogian. Holt.

Hide and Seek Fog by Alvin Tresselt. Illustrated by Roger Duvoisin. Lothrop.

Just Me by Marie Hall Ets. Viking.

Tom Tit Tot. Retold and illustrated by Evaline Ness. Scribner's.

1967 **Sam, Bangs and Moonshine** by Evaline Ness. Holt.

One Wide River to Cross by Barbara Emberley. Illustrated by Ed Emberley. Prentice-Hall.

1968 **Drummer Hoff** by Barbara Emberley. Illustrated by Ed Emberley. Prentice-Hall.

Frederick by Leo Lionni. Pantheon.

Seashore Story by Taro Yashima. Viking.

The Emperor and the Kite by Jane Yolen. Illustrated by Ed Young. World.

1969 **The Fool of the World and the Flying Ship** by Arthur Ransome. Illustrated by Uri Shulevitz. Farrar.

Why the Sun and the Moon Live in the Sky by Elphinstone Dayrell. Illustrated by Blair Lent. Houghton.

1970 **Sylvester and the Magic Pebble** by William Steig. Windmill/Simon.

Goggles by Ezra Jack Keats. Macmillan.

Alexander and the Wind-Up Mouse by Leo Lionni. Pantheon.

Pop Corn and Ma Goodness by Edna Mitchell Preston. Illustrated by Robert Andrew Parker. Viking.

Thy Friend, Obadiah by Brinton Turkle. Viking.

The Judge: An Untrue Tale by Harve Zemach. Illustrated by Margot Zemach. Farrar.

1971 **A Story, A Story** by Gail E. Haley. Atheneum.

The Angry Moon by William Sleator. Illustrated by Blair Lent. Little.

Frog and Toad Are Friends by Arnold Lobel. Harper.

In the Night Kitchen by Maurice Sendak. Harper.

1972 **One Fine Day** by Nonny Hogrogian. Macmillan.

If All the Seas Were One Sea by Janina Domanska. Macmillan.

Moja Means One: Swahili Counting Book by Muriel Feelings. Illustrated by Tom Feelings. Dial.

Hildilid's Night by Cheli Durán Ryan. Illustrated by Arnold Lobel. Macmillan.

1973 **The Funny Little Woman** by Arlene Mosel. Illustrated by Blair Lent. Dutton.

Hosie's Alphabet by Hosea Baskin, Tobias Baskin, and Lisa Baskin. Illustrated by Leonard Baskin. Viking.

When Clay Sings by Byrd Baylor. Illustrated by Tom Bahti. Scribner's.

Snow White and the Seven Dwarfs by the Brothers Grimm. Translated by Randall Jarrell. Illustrated by Nancy Ekholm Burkert. Farrar.

Anansi the Spider by Gerald McDermott. Holt.

1974 **Duffy and the Devil** by Harve Zemach. Illustrated by Margot Zemach. Farrar.

The Three Jovial Huntsmen by Susan Jeffers. Bradbury.

Cathedral by David Macaulay. Houghton.

1975 **Arrow to the Sun.** Adapted and illustrated by Gerald McDermott. Viking.

Jambo Means Hello: A Swahili Alphabet Book by Muriel Feelings. Illustrated by Tom Feelings. Dial.

1976 **Why Mosquitos Buzz in People's Ears** by Verna Aardema. Illustrated by Leo Dillon and Diane Dillon. Dial.

The Desert Is Theirs by Byrd Baylor. Illustrated by Peter Parnell. Scribner's.

Strega Nona. Retold and illustrated by Tomie dePaola. Prentice-Hall.

1977 **Ashanti to Zulu: African Traditions** by Margaret Musgrove. Illustrated by Leo Dillon and Diane Dillon. Dial.

The Amazing Bone by William Steig. Farrar.

The Contest by Nonny Hogrogian. Greenwillow.

Fish for Supper by M. B. Goffstein. Dial.

The Golem: A Jewish Legend by Beverly Brodsky McDermott. Lippincott.

Hawk, I'm Your Brother by Byrd Baylor. Illustrated by Peter Parnall. Scribner's.

1978 **Noah's Ark** by Peter Spier. Doubleday.

Castle by David Macaulay. Houghton.

It Could Always Be Worse by Margot Zemach. Farrar.

1979 **The Girl Who Loved Wild Horses** by Paul Goble. Bradbury.

Freight Train by Donald Crews. Greenwillow.

The Way to Start a Day by Byrd Baylor. Illustrated by Peter Parnall. Scribner's.

1980 **Ox-Cart Man** by Donald Hall. Illustrated by Barbara Cooney. Viking.

Ben's Trumpet by Rachel Isadora. Greenwillow.

The Treasure by Uri Shulevitz. Farrar.

The Garden of Abdul Gasazi by Chris Van Allsburg. Houghton.

1981 **Fables** by Arnold Lobel. Harper.

The Bremen-Town Musicians by Ilse Plume. Doubleday.

The Grey Lady and the Strawberry Snatcher by Molly Bang. Four Winds.

Mice Twice by Joseph Low. McElderry/Atheneum.

Truck by Donald Crews. Greenwillow.

1982 **Jumanji** by Chris Van Allsburg. Houghton.

A Visit to William Blake's Inn: Poems for Innocent and Experienced Travelers by Nancy Willard. Illustrated by Alice Provensen and Martin Provensen. Harcourt.

Where the Buffaloes Begin by Olaf Baker. Illustrated by Stephen Gammell. Warne.

On Market Street by Arnold Lobel. Illustrated by Anita Lobel. Greenwillow.

Outside over There by Maurice Sendak. Harper.

1983 **Shadow** by Blaise Cendrars. Illustrated by Marcia Brown. Scribner's.

When I Was Young in the Mountains by Cynthia Rylant. Illustrated by Diane Goode. Dutton.

A Chair for My Mother by Vera B. Williams. Greenwillow.

1984 **The Glorious Flight: Across the Channel with Louis Blériot, July 25, 1909** by Alice Provensen and Martin Provensen. Viking.

Ten, Nine, Eight by Molly Bang. Greenwillow.

Little Red Riding Hood by Trina Schart Hyman. Holiday.

1985 **Saint George and the Dragon** adapted by Margaret Hodges. Illustrated by Trina Schart Hyman. Little.

Hansel and Gretel by Rika Lesser. Illustrated by Paul O. Zelinsky. Dodd.

The Story of Jumping Mouse by John Steptoe. Lothrop.

Have You Seen My Duckling? by Nancy Tafuri. Greenwillow.

1986 **The Polar Express** by Chris Van Allsburg. Houghton.

The Relatives Came by Cynthia Rylant. Illustrated by Stephen Gammell. Bradbury.

King Bidgood's in the Bathtub by Audrey Wood. Illustrated by Don Wood. Harcourt.

1987 **Hey, Al** by Arthur Yorinks. Illustrated by Richard Egielski. Farrar.

Alphabatics by Suse MacDonald. Bradbury.

Rumpelstiltskin by Paul O. Zelinsky. Dutton.

The Village of Round and Square Houses by Ann Grifalconi. Little.

1988 **Owl Moon** by Jane Yolen. Illustrated by John Schoenherr. Philomel.

Mufaro's Beautiful Daughters: An African Story. Adapted and illustrated by John Steptoe. Lothrop.

1989 **Song and Dance Man** by Karen Ackerman. Illustrated by Stephen Gammell. Knopf.

The Boy of the Three-Year Nap by Dianne Snyder. Illustrated by Allen Say. Houghton.

Free Fall by David Wiesner. Lothrop.

Goldilocks and the Three Bears. Adapted and illustrated by James Marshall. Dial.

Mirandy and Brother Wind by Patricia McKissack. Illustrated by Jerry Pinkney. Knopf.

1990 **Lon Po Po: A Red-Riding Hood Story from China.** Adapted and illustrated by Ed Young. Philomel.

Bill Peet: An Autobiography by Bill Peet. Houghton.

Color Zoo by Lois Ehlert. Lippincott.

Herschel and the Hanukkah Goblins by Eric Kimmel. Illustrated by Trina Schart Hyman. Holiday.

The Talking Eggs by Robert D. San Souci. Illustrated by Jerry Pinkney. Dial.

1991 **Black and White** by David Macaulay. Houghton.

Puss in Boots by Charles Perrault. Translated by Malcolm Arthur. Illustrated by Fred Marcelino. di Capua / Farrar.

"More More More," Said the Baby by Vera B. Williams. Greenwillow.

1992 **Tuesday** by David Wiesner. Clarion.

Tar Beach by Faith Ringgold. Crown.

1993 **Mirette on the High Wire** by Emily Arnold McCully. Putnam.

Seven Blind Mice by Ed Young. Philomel.

The Stinky Cheese Man and Other Fairly Stupid Tales by Jon Scieszka. Illustrated by Lane Smith. Viking.

Working Cotton by Sherley Anne Williams. Illustrated by Carole Byard. Harcourt.

1994 **Grandfather's Journey** by Allen Say. Houghton.

Peppe the Lamplighter by Elisa Bartone. Illustrated by Ted Lewin. Lothrop.

In the Small, Small Pond by Denise Fleming. Holt.

Owen by Kevin Henkes. Greenwillow.

Raven: A Trickster Tale from the Pacific Northwest by Gerald McDermott. Harcourt.

Yo! Yes? by Chris Raschka. Jackson / Orchard.

1995 **Smoky Night** by Eve Bunting. Illustrated by David Diaz. Harcourt.

Swamp Angel by Paul O. Zelinsky. Dutton.

John Henry by Julius Lester. Illustrated by Jerry Pinkney. Dial.

Time Flies by Eric Rohmann. Crown.

1996 **Officer Buckle and Gloria** by Peggy Rathman. Putnam.

Alphabet City by Stephen T. Johnson. Viking.

Zin! Zin! Zin! a Violin by Lloyd Moss. Illustrated by Marjorie Priceman. Simon.

The Faithful Friend by Robert D. San Souci. Illustrated by Brian Pinkney. Simon.

Tops and Bottoms by Janet Stephens. Harcourt.

1997 **Golem** by David Wisniewski. Clarion.

Hush! A Thai Lullaby by by Minfong Ho. Illustrated by Holly Meade. Kroupa/Orchard.

The Graphic Alphabet by David Pelletier. Orchard.

The Paperboy by Dav Pilkey. Orchard.

Starry Messenger by Peter Sis. Foster/Farrar.

1998 **Rapunzel** by Paul O. Zelinsky. Dutton.

The Gardener by Sarah Stewart. Illustrated by David Small. Farrar.

Harlem by Walter Dean Myers. Illustrated by Christopher Myers. Scholastic.

There Was an Old Lady Who Swallowed a Fly by Simms Taback. Viking.

1999   *Snowflake Bentley* by Jacqueline Briggs Martin. Illustrated by Mary Azarian. Houghton.

Duke Ellington: The Piano Prince and His Orchestra by Andrea Pinkney. Illustrated by Brian Pinkney. Hyperion.

No, David! by David Shannon. Scholastic.

Snow by Uri Shulevitz. Farrar.

Tibet through the Red Box by Peter Sis. Foster.

2000   *Joseph Had a Little Overcoat* by Simms Taback. Viking.

A Child's Calendar by John Updike. Illustrated by Trina Schart Hyman. Holiday.

Sector 7 by David Wiesner. Clarion.

The Ugly Duckling by Hans Christian Andersen. Illustrated by Jerry Pinkney. Morrow.

When Sophie Gets Angry—Really, Really Angry . . . . by Molly Bang. Scholastic.

2001   *So You Want To Be President?* by Judith St. George. Illustrated by David Small. Philomel.

Casey at the Bat by Earnest Lawrence Thayer. Illustrated by Christopher Bing. Handprint.

Click, Clack, Moo: Cows That Type by Doreen Cronin. Illustrated by Betsy Lewin. Simon.

Olivia by Ian Falconer. Atheneum.

2002   *The Three Pigs* by David Wiesner. Clarion.

The Dinosaurs of Waterhouse Hawkins by Barbara Kerley. Illustrated by Brian Selznick. Scholastic.

Martin's Big Words by Doreen Rappaport. Illustrated by Brian Collier. Hyperion.

The Stray Dog by Marc Simont. HarperCollins.

2003   *My Friend Rabbit* by Eric Rohman. Roaring Brook.

The Spider and the Fly by Mary Howitt. Illustrated by Tony DiTerlizzi. Simon.

Hondo and Fabian by Peter McCarty. Holt.

Noah's Ark by Jerry Pinkney. Sea Star.

2004   *The Man Who Walked between the Towers* by Mordicai Gerstein. Roaring Brook.

Ella Sarah Gets Dressed by Margaret Chodos-Irvine. Harcourt.

What Do You Do with a Tail like This? by Steve Jenkins and Robin Page. Houghton.

Don't Let the Pigeon Drive the Bus by Mo Willems. Hyperion.

2005   *Kitten's First Full Moon* by Kevin Henkes. Greenwillow.

The Red Book by Barbara Lehman. Houghton.

Coming on Home Soon by Jacqueline Woodson. Illustrated by E. B. Lewis. Putnam.

Knuffle Bunny: A Cautionary Tale by Mo Willems. Hyperion.

2006   *The Hello, Goodbye Window* by Norton Juster. Illustrated by Chris Raschka. di Capua/Hyperion.

Rosa by Nikki Giovanni. Illustrated by Bryan Collier. Holt.

Zen Shorts by Jon J. Muth. Scholastic.

Hot Air: The (Mostly) True Story of the First Hot-Air Balloon Ride by Marjorie Priceman. Schwartz/Atheneum/Simon.

Song of the Water Boatman and Other Pond Poems by Joyce Sidman. Illustrated by Beckie Prange. Houghton.

BATCHELDER AWARD

The Batchelder Award, established in 1966, is given by the Association of Library Service to Children (ALSC) of the American Library Association to the publisher of the most outstanding book of the year that is a translation, published in the United States, of a book that was first published in another country. In 1990, Honor Books were added to this award. The original country of publication is given in parentheses.

1968   *The Little Man* by Erich Kästner, translated by James Kirkup. Illustrated by Rick Schreiter. Knopf. (Germany)

1969   *Don't Take Teddy* by Babbis Friis-Baastad, translated by Lise Sømme McKinnon. Scribner's. (Norway)

1970   *Wildcat under Glass* by Alki Zei, translated by Edward Fenton. Holt. (Greece)

1971   *In the Land of Ur, The Discovery of Ancient Mesopotamia* by Hans Baumann, translated by Stella Humphries. Pantheon. (Germany)

1972   *Friedrich* by Hans Peter Richter, translated by Edite Kroll. Holt. (Germany)

1973   *Pulga* by S. R. Van Iterson, translated by Alison Gode and Alexander Gode. Morrow. (Netherlands)

1974   *Petros' War* by Alki Zei, translated by Edward Fenton. Dutton. (Greece)

1975   *An Old Tale Carved out of Stone* by A. Linevskii, translated by Maria Polushkin. Crown. (Russia)

1976   *The Cat and Mouse Who Shared a House* by Ruth Hürlimann, translated by Anthea Bell. Illustrated by the author. Walck. (Germany)

1977   *The Leopard* by Cecil Bødker, translated by Gunnar Poulsen. Atheneum. (Denmark)

1978   No award

1979   Two awards given

Konrad by Christine Nöstlinger, translated by Anthea Bell. Illustrated by Carol Nicklaus. Watts. (Germany)

Rabbit Island by Jörg Steiner, translated by Ann Conrad Lammers. Illustrated by Jörg Müller. Harcourt. (Germany)

1980   *The Sound of the Dragon's Feet* by Alki Zei, translated by Edward Fenton. Dutton. (Greece)

1981   *The Winter When Time Was Frozen* by Els Pelgrom, translated by Maryka Rudnik and Rafael Rudnik. Morrow. (Netherlands)

1982   *The Battle Horse* by Harry Kullman, translated by George Blecher and Lone Thygesen-Blecher. Bradbury. (Sweden)

1983   *Hiroshima No Pika* by Toshi Maruki, translated by the Kurita Bando Agency. Lothrop. (Japan)

1984 *Ronia the Robber's Daughter* by Astrid Lindgren, translated by Patricia Crampton. Viking. (Sweden)

1985 *The Island on Bird Street* by Uri Orlev, translated by Hillel Halkin. Houghton. (Israel)

1986 *Rose Blanche* by Christophe Gallaz and Roberto Innocenti, translated by Martha Coventry and Richard Graglia. Creative Education. (Italy)

1987 *No Hero for the Kaiser* by Rudolf Frank, translated by Patricia Crampton. Lothrop. (Germany)

1988 *If You Didn't Have Me* by Ulf Nilsson, translated by Lone Tygesen-Blecher and George Blecher. Illustrated by Eva Eriksson. McElderry. (Sweden)

1989 *Crutches* by Peter Hätling, translated by Elizabeth D. Crawford. Lothrop. (Germany)

1990 *Buster's World* by Bjarne Reuter, translated by Anthea Bell. Dutton. (Denmark)

1991 *A Hand Full of Stars* by Rafik Schami, translated by Rika Lesser. Dutton. (Germany)

1992 *The Man from the Other Side* by Uri Orlev, translated by Hillel Halkin. Houghton. (Israel)

1993 No award

1994 *The Apprentice* by Molina Llorente, translated by Robin Longshaw. Farrar. (Spain)

1995 *The Boys from St. Petri* by Bjarne Reuter, translated by Anthea Bell. Dutton. (Denmark)

1996 *The Lady with the Hat* by Uri Orlev, translated by Hillel Halkin. Houghton. (Israel)

1997 *The Friends* by Kazumi Yumoto, translated by Cathy Hirano. Farrar. (Japan)

1998 *The Robber and Me* by Josef Holub, translated by Elizabeth C. Crawford. Holt. (Germany)

1999 *Thanks to My Mother* by Schoschana Rabinovici, translated by James Skofield. Dial. (Germany)

2000 *The Baboon King* by Anton Quintana, translated by John Nieuwenhuizen. Walker. (Netherlands)

2001 *Samir and Yonatan* by Daniella Carmi, translated by Yael Lotan. Scholastic. (Israel)

2002 *How I Became an American* by Karin Gündisch, translated by James Skofield. Cricket. (Germany)

2003 *The Thief Lord* by Cornelia Funke. Translated by Oliver Latsch. Scholastic. (Germany)

2004 *Run, Boy, Run* by Uri Orlev, translated by Hillel Halkin. Lorraine. (Israel)

2005 *The Shadows of Ghadames* by Joëlle Stolz, translated by Catherine Temerson. Delacorte/Random. (France)

2006 *An Innocent Soldier* by Josef Holub, translated by Michael Hofmann. Levine/Scholastic. (Germany)

LAURA INGALLS WILDER AWARD

The Laura Ingalls Wilder Award is given to an author or illustrator whose books (published in the United States) have made a substantial and lasting contribution to literature for children. Established in 1954, this medal was given every five years through 1980. As of 1983, it is given every three years by the Association of Library Service to Children (ALSC) of the American Library Association. The following are the award winners thus far.

1954 Laura Ingalls Wilder
1960 Clara Ingram Judson
1965 Ruth Sawyer
1970 E. B. White
1975 Beverly Cleary
1980 Theodor S. Geisel [Dr. Seuss]
1983 Maurice Sendak
1986 Jean Fritz
1989 Elizabeth George Speare
1992 Marcia Brown
1995 Virginia Hamilton
1998 Russell Freedman
2001 Milton Meltzer
2003 Eric Carle
2005 Laurence Yep

HANS CHRISTIAN ANDERSEN PRIZE

The Hans Christian Andersen prize, the first international children's book award, was established in 1956 by the International Board on Books for Young People. Given every two years, the award was expanded in 1966 to honor an illustrator as well as an author. A committee composed of members from different countries judges the selections recommended by the board or library associations in each country. The following have won the Hans Christian Andersen Prize.

1956 Eleanor Farjeon. Great Britian.
1958 Astrid Lindgren. Sweden.
1960 Eric Kästner. Germany.
1962 Meindert DeJong. United States.
1964 René Guillot. France.
1966 Tove Jansson (author). Finland.
    Alois Carigiet (illustrator). Switzerland.
1968 James Krüss (author). Germany.
    Jose Maria Sanchez-Silva (author). Spain.
    Jiri Trnka (illustrator). Czechoslovakia.
1970 Gianni Rodari (author). Italy.
    Maurice Sendak (illustrator). United States.
1972 Scott O'Dell (author). United States.
    Ib Spang Olsen (illustrator). Denmark.
1974 Maria Gripe (author). Sweden.
    Farshid Mesghali (illustrator). Iran.
1976 Cecil Bødker (author). Denmark.
    Tatjana Mawrina (illustrator). U.S.S.R.
1978 Paula Fox (author). United States.
    Svend Otto S. [Sørensen] (illustrator). Denmark.
1980 Bohumil Riha (author). Czechoslovakia.
    Suekichi Akaba (illustrator). Japan.
1982 Lygia Bojunga Nunes (author). Brazil.
    Zibigniew Rychlicki (illustrator). Poland.

1984	Christine Nöstlinger (author). Austria.
	Mitsumasa Anno (illustrator). Japan.
1986	Patricia Wrightson (author). Australia.
	Robert Ingpen (illustrator). Australia.
1988	Annie M. G. Schmidt (author). Netherlands.
	Dusan Kállay (illustrator). Yugoslavia.
1990	Tormod Haugen (author). Norway.
	Lisbeth Zwerger (illustrator). Austria.
1992	Virginia Hamilton (author). United States.
	Kveta Pacovská (illustrator). Czechoslovakia.
1994	Michio Mado (author). Japan.
	Jörg Müller (illustrator). Switzerland.
1996	Uri Orlev (author). Israel.
	Klaus Ensikat (illustrator). Germany.
1998	Katherine Paterson (author). United States.
	Tomi Ungerer (illustrator). France.
2000	Anna Maria Machado (author). Brazil.
	Anthony Browne (illustrator). United Kingdom.
2002	Aidan Chambers (author). United Kingdom.
	Quentin Blake (illustrator). United Kingdom.
2004	Martin Waddell (author). Ireland.
	Max Velthuijs (illustrator). Netherlands.

GENERAL AWARDS

Boston Globe–Horn Book Awards *Horn Book Magazine,* 11 Beacon St., Boston, MA 02108. Currently given for outstanding fiction or poetry, outstanding nonfiction, and outstanding illustration.

Golden Kite Award Society of Children's Book Writers, 8271 Beverly Blvd., Los Angeles, CA 90048. <www.scbwi.org>. Presented annually by the Society of Children's Book Writers to members whose books of fiction, nonfiction, and picture illustration best exhibit excellence and genuinely appeal to interests and concerns of children.

International Reading Association Children's Book Award International Reading Association, 800 Barksdale Rd., Newark, DE 19711. An annual award for a first or second book to an author from any country who shows unusual promise in the children's book field. Since 1987, the award has been presented to both a picture book and a novel.

New York Times Choice of Best Illustrated Children's Books of the Year *New York Times,* 229 W. 43rd St., New York, NY 10036. Books are selected for excellence in illustration by a panel of judges.

AWARDS BASED ON SPECIAL CONTENT

Jane Addams Book Award Jane Addams Peace Association, 777 United Nations Plaza, New York, NY 10017. For a book with literary merit stressing themes of dignity, equality, peace, and social justice.

Association of Jewish Libraries Awards National Foundation for Jewish Culture, 122 E. 42nd St., Room 1512, New York, NY 10168. Given to one or two titles that have made the most outstanding contribution to the field of Jewish literature for children and young people. The Sydney Taylor Body of Work Award, established in 1981, is given for an author's body of work.

Catholic Book Awards Catholic Press Association of the United States and Canada, 119 N. Park Ave., Rockville Centre, NY 11570. Honors selected in five categories and awarded to books with sound Christian and psychological values.

Child Study Children's Book Committee at Bank Street College Award Bank Street College of Education, 610 W. 112th St., New York, NY 10025. For a distinguished book for children or young people that deals honestly and courageously with problems in the world.

Christopher Awards The Christophers, 12 E. 48th St., New York, NY 10017. Given to works of artistic excellence affirming the highest values of the human spirit.

Eva L. Gordon Award for Children's Science Literature Helen Ross Russell, Chairman of Publications Committee, ANSS, 44 College Dr., Jersey City, NJ 07305. Given by the American Nature Study Society to an author or illustrator whose body of work in science trade books is accurate, inviting, and timely.

Jefferson Cup Award Children's and Young Adult Roundtable of the Virginia Library Association, P.O. Box 298, Alexandria, VA 22313. Presented for a distinguished book in American history, historical fiction, or biography.

Ezra Jack Keats Awards Given biennially to a promising new artist and a promising writer. The recipients receive a monetary award and a medallion from the Ezra Jack Keats Foundation.

Coretta Scott King Awards Social Responsibilities Round Table of the American Library Association, 50 E. Huron St., Chicago, IL 60611. Given to an African American author and an African American illustrator for outstanding inspirational and educational contributions to literature for children.

National Council of Teachers of English Award for Excellence in Poetry for Children National Council of Teachers of English, 1111 Kenyon Rd., Urbana, IL 61801. Given formerly annually and presently every three years to a living American poet for total body of work for children ages 3 to 13.

National Jewish Book Awards JWB Jewish Book Council, 15 E. 26th St., New York, NY 10010. Various awards are given for work or body of work that makes a contribution to Jewish juvenile literature.

New York Academy of Sciences Children's Science Books Awards The New York Academy of Sciences, 2 E. 63rd St., New York, NY 10021. For books of high quality in the field of science for children; three awards are given: Younger Children, Older Children, and the Montroll Award for a book that provides unusual historical data or background on a scientific subject.

Scott O'Dell Award for Historical Fiction Zena Sutherland, 1418 E. 57th St., Chicago, IL 60637. Honors a distinguished work of historical fiction set in the New World.

Orbis Pictus Award for Outstanding Nonfiction for Children Presented annually by the National Council of Teachers of English to the outstanding nonfiction book of the previous year.

Phoenix Award Given to the author of a book published for children twenty years before that has not received a major children's book award. Sponsored by the Children's Literature Association.

Edgar Allan Poe Awards Mystery Writers of America, 1950 Fifth Ave., New York, NY 10011. For best juvenile mystery.

Michael J. Prinz Award Given to a book that exemplifies literary excellence in young-adult literature. Sponsored by the Young Adult Library Services Association of the American Library Association.

Robert F. Sibert Informational Book Award Honors the author whose work of nonfiction has made a significant contribution to the field of children's literature in a given year. Sponsored by Association of Library Services to Children.

Washington Post/Children's Book Guild Nonfiction Award Washington Post, 1150 15th St. NW, Washington, DC 20071. Given to an author or illustrator for a body of work in juvenile informational books.

Western Writers of America Spur Award Western Writers of America, Inc., 508 Senter Pl., Selah, WA 98942. For the best western juvenile work in two categories, fiction and nonfiction.

Carter G. Woodson Book Award National Council for the Social Studies, 3501 Newark St. NW, Washington, DC 20016. Presented to outstanding social science books for young readers that treat sensitively and accurately topics related to ethnic minorities.

AWARDS FOR LASTING CONTRIBUTIONS OR SERVICE TO CHILDREN'S LITERATURE

Arbuthnot Award International Reading Association, 800 Barksdale Rd., Newark, DE 19714. Named after May Hill Arbuthnot, an authority on literature for children, this award is given annually to an outstanding teacher of children's literature.

Arbuthnot Honor Lecture The Association of Library Service to Children (ALSC) of the American Library Association, 50 E. Huron St., Chicago, IL 60611. This free public lecture is presented annually by a distinguished author, critic, librarian, historian, or teacher of children's literature. Both the lecturer and the site for the lecture are chosen by an ALSC committee.

Grolier Foundation Award American Library Association Awards Committee, 50 E. Huron St., Chicago, IL 60611. Given to a community librarian or a school librarian who has made an unusual contribution to the stimulation and guidance of reading by children and young people.

Landau Award Salt Lake County Library System, 2197 E. 7000 St., Salt Lake City, UT 84121. Co-sponsored by the Department of Education of the University of Utah and Salt Lake County Library System. The award is given biennially to a teacher of children's literature who has most inspired students to pursue a knowledge of the field.

Lucile Micheels Pannell Award Awards in the "general store" category and in the "children's specialty bookstore" category are presented annually by the Women's National Book Association to the owners of two bookstores whose innovative programs encourage children's reading.

Regina Medal Catholic Library Association, 461 West Lancaster Ave., Haverford, PA 19041. For "continued distinguished contribution to children's literature."

University of Southern Mississippi Children's Collection Medallion University of Southern Mississippi Book Festival, USM Library, Hattiesburg, MS 39401. For a writer or an illustrator who has made an "outstanding contribution to the field of children's literature."

For more information about these and other awards, including lists of all prize winners, see *Children's Books: Awards & Prizes*, published and revised periodically by the Children's Book Council, 568 Broadway, New York, NY 10012. Beginning in 1990, each year's *Books in Print* also publishes a listing of the current winners of various prizes.

Book Selection Aids

Note: Publishers' addresses may change. For complete and up-to-date information, see the current edition of *Literary Market Place* or *Children's Books in Print.*

COMPREHENSIVE LISTS AND DIRECTORIES

Children's Books in Print. **Greenwood Publishing Group, 88 Post Rd. W., Westport, CT 06881. Annual. $225.00.** A comprehensive listing of children's books currently in print. Includes titles for grades K–12. Titles are arranged alphabetically by author, title, and illustrator. A list of publisher addresses is provided. Also includes children's book awards for the previous ten years.

Children's Media Market Place, **4th ed. Barbara Stein. Neal-Schuman Publishers, 23 Leonard St., New York, NY 10013. 1995. 275 pp. $65.00, paper.** Annotated list of publishers of books and producers and distributors of nonprint materials, indexed by format, subject, and special interest. Includes a directory of wholesalers, bookstores, book clubs, and children's television sources.

Educational Media and Technology Yearbook. **Libraries Unlimited, P.O. Box 6633, Englewood, CO 80155. Annual. $80.00.** Includes articles, surveys, and research on various aspects of media administration, creation, and use. Lists organizations, foundations, and funding agencies for media as well as information on graduate programs. Includes an annotated mediography of basic resources for library media specialists.

Guide to Reference Books for School Media Centers, **5th ed. Barbara Ripp Safford. Libraries Unlimited, P.O. Box 6633, Englewood, CO 80155. 1998, 407 pp. $47.00.** Includes annotations and evaluations for 2,000 useful reference tools for school media centers. Materials are arranged in order by subject. Also includes a list of sources and selection aids for print and nonprint materials.

Magazines for Children: A Guide for Parents, Teachers, and Librarians, **2nd ed. Selma K. Richardson. American Library Association, 50 E. Huron St., Chicago, IL 60611. 1991. 139 pp. $25.00, paper.** An annotated list of magazines designed especially for children ages 2–14; includes descriptions of the publications, age levels of users, and evaluative comments.

Magazines for Young People, **2nd ed. Bill Katz and Kinda Sternberg Katz. Greenwood Publishing Group, 88 Post Rd. W., Westport, CT 06881. 2001. 250 pp. $49.95.** Evaluates over 1,000 magazines, journals, and newsletters for children and teachers in 60 subject areas.

Reference Books for Children. **Carolyn Sue Peterson and Ann D. Fenton. Scarecrow Press, 4501 Forbes Blvd., Lanham, MD 20706. 1992. 414 pp. $49.50.** Contains annotated entries over a broad range of curriculum areas, collection needs, interests, and reading levels of children. Books are classified by subject. Annotations provide some guidance in making selections for school collections.

Subject Guide to Children's Books in Print. **Greenwood Publishing Group, 88 Post Rd. W., Westport, CT 06881. Annual.** **$225.00.** A companion volume to *Children's Books in Print.* Arranges all children's titles currently in print using over 6,000 subject headings. Particularly useful for finding and ordering titles on specific subjects; however, titles are not annotated.

GENERAL SELECTION AIDS

Adventuring with Books: A Booklist for Pre-K–Grade 6, **13th ed. Amy McClure and Jan Kristo, eds. National Council of Teachers of English, 1111 Kenyon Rd., Urbana, IL 61601. 2002. 536 pp. $39.95, paper.** Annotates about 1,800 children's titles published from 1996 to 1998. Annotations include summary, age, and interest levels. Contents are arranged by genre, broad subject, and theme. Author, title, and subject indexes.

Award-Winning Books for Children and Young Adults. **Betty L. Criscoe. Scarecrow Press, 4501 Forbes Blvd., Lanham, MD 20706. Annual. $45.00.** Lists books that won awards during the previous year. Includes descriptions of the awards, criteria used for selection, plot synopses of winners, grade levels, and genres.

Best Books for Children: Pre-school through Grade 6. **John T. Gillespie. Greenwood Publishing Group, 88 Post Rd. W., Westport, CT 06881. 2005. 1,500 pp. $80.00.**

Best Books for Middle School and Junior High Readers: Grades 6–9. **John T. Gillespie and Catherine Barr. Greenwood Publishing Group, 88 Post Rd. W., Westport, CT 06881. 2004. 1,192 pp. $75.00.** Annotated listings of books that are selected to satisfy recreational needs, curricular needs, and interests of school children through grade 9. Books are arranged by broad age groups, subdivided by types of books. Each contains author, title, illustrator, and subject indexes.

Children's Books from Other Countries. **Carl M. Tomlinson, ed. Scarecrow Press, 4501 Forbes Blvd., Lanham, MD 20706. 1998. 304 pp. $29.95.** Sponsored by the United States Board on Books for Young People, which also awards the Hans Christian Andersen Medal, the book lists 724 titles published in English, with some translated into English, between 1950 and 1995. Twenty-nine countries are represented. Each book is annotated, and age range and country of origin are given.

Children's Catalog, **18th ed. H. W. Wilson Co., 950 University Ave., Bronx, NY 10452. 2005. 1,346 pp. $145.00.** A classified (Dewey Decimal System) catalog of about 6,000 recent "best" children's books, including publishing information, grade level, and a brief summary of each title. Also includes alphabetical author, title, subject, and analytical indexes. Contains a list of publishers with addresses. A new edition is issued every five years, with annual supplements in other years.

Choosing Books for Children. **Betsy Hearne. University of Illinois Press, 1325 S. Oak St., Champaign, IL 61820. 2000. 250 pp. $14.95, paper.** Contains general selection advice for parents, teachers, and librarians, combined with bibliographies.

The Elementary School Library Collection: A Guide to Books and Other Media, **21st ed. Linda L. Holms, ed. Brodart Co., 500 Arch St., Williamsport, PA 17705. 1998. 1,150 pp. $99.95.** A basic bibliography of materials, both print and nonprint, for elementary school media center collections. Materials are interfiled and arranged by subject classification (Dewey Decimal System). All entries include bibliographic information, age level, and a brief annotation. Contains author, title, and subject indexes.

Fiction for Youth: A Guide to Recommended Books. **Lillian L. Shapiro. Neal-Schuman Publishers, 23 Leonard St., New York, NY 10013. 1992. 300 pp. $35.00.** Provides a core collection of titles designed to encourage reading by young people who can read but don't choose to do so.

The Horn Book Guide to Children's and Young Adult Books. **Horn Book, Inc., 56 Roland St., Suite 200, Boston, MA 02129. Semi-annual. $35 per year.** Provides short reviews of children's and young-adult books published in the United States during the prior publishing season with references to longer reviews in *Horn Book Magazine.* Books are given a numerical evaluation from 1 to 6.

New York Times Parents' Guide to the Best Books for Children. **Eden Ross Lipson. Times Books/Random House, 201 E. 50th St., New York, NY 10022. 1988. 421 pp. $12.95.** Indexes books by age appropriateness, listening level, author, title, illustrator, and subject. Books are arranged in broad categories, such as wordless books and picture storybooks.

The World through Children's Books. **Susan Stans, ed. Scarecrow Press, 4501 Forbes Blvd., Lanham, MD 20706. 2002. 324 pp. $27.95, paper.** Companion volume to Children's Books in Other Countries, this book annotates nearly 700 titles written in, or translated into, English and representing approximately 70 countries.

BOOKLISTS FOR VARIOUS LEVELS OF READERS

Beyond Picture Books: A Guide to First Readers. **Barbara Barstow and Judith Riggle. Greenwood Publishing Group, 88 Post Rd. W., Westport, CT 06881. 1995. 501 pp. $49.95.** Annotates over 1,600 first readers for ages 4–7, with a plot summary, brief evaluation, and bibliographic information. Indexes by title, illustrator, readability, series, and subject.

Books for the Gifted Child. **Paula Hauser and Gail Nelson. 1988. 244 pp. $39.95. Greenwood Publishing Group, 88 Post Rd. W., Westport, CT 06881.** This volume critically annotates about 150 titles that would be useful in working with gifted children, ages preschool through 12. They are arranged in alphabetical order with bibliographic information and reading level included. Several chapters on the gifted child are included in the book.

Choices: A Core Collection for Young Reluctant Readers, Vol. 5. **Beverley Fahey and Maureen Whalen, eds. John Gordon Burke, Publisher, P.O. Box 1492, Evanston, IL 60204-1492. 2001. 272 pp. $45.00.** Annotates books for second through sixth graders reading below grade level, published between 1983 and 1988, with plot summary, interest level, and reading level. Contains author and subject indexes.

Gifted Books, Gifted Readers. **Nancy Polette. Libraries Unlimited, P.O. Box 6633, Englewood, CO 80155. 2000. 282 pp. $19.00.** Provides suggested units with activities and lists of books for four primary elements of literature (style, theme, character, setting). Books that stress these elements, or can be used to motivate thinking about them, are included in the lists.

More Rip-Roaring Reads for Reluctant Teen Readers. **Bette D. Ammon and Gale W. Sherman. Libraries Unlimited, P.O. Box 6633, Englewood, CO 80155. 1998. 161 pp. $26.50, paper.** Lists books of high literary quality for reluctant readers in grades 3–12. Has brief annotations, reading and interest levels, and popular subject headings.

BOOKLISTS AND INDEXES FOR PARTICULAR SUBJECTS

PICTURE BOOKS AND CONCEPT BOOKS

A to Zoo: Subject Access to Children's Picture Books, 6th ed. **Carolyn W. Lima. Greenwood Publishing Group, 88 Post Rd. W., Westport, CT 06881. 2005. 1,800 pp. $80.00.** Provides subject access to over 8,000 picture books through 600 subject headings with cross-references and full bibliographic citations. Most titles are useful for children from preschool through second grade. Includes author, illustrator, and title lists.

Alphabet: A Handbook of ABC Books and Book Extensions for the Elementary Classroom, 2nd ed. **Patricia L. Roberts. Scarecrow Press, 4501 Forbes Blvd., Lanham, MD 20706. 1994. 278 pp. $36.00.** Reviews over 200 alphabet books and provides about 80 activities to use with children from preschool to grade 6.

Alphabet Books as a Key to Language Patterns: An Annotated Action Bibliography. **Patricia L. Roberts. Shoe String Press, 2 Linsley St., North Haven, CT 06473. 1987. 263 pp. $36.00.** Lists over 500 alphabet books that can be used in aiding language development under categories such as alliteration, rhymes and verses, and wordless books.

Counting Books Are More Than Numbers: An Annotated Action Bibliography. **Patricia L. Roberts. Shoe String Press, 2 Linsley St., North Haven, CT 06473. 1990. 264 pp. $32.50.** Describes 350 books for preschool through second grade that can be used to encourage early understanding of mathematical concepts.

Informational Picture Books for Children. **Patricia Jean Cianciolo. American Library Association, 50 E. Huron St., Chicago, IL 60611. 1999. 205 pp. $38.00, paper.** An annotated listing of nonfiction books, divided into major subject areas such as "The Natural World" and "Numbers and Arithmetic." Annotations include age levels and brief synopses.

Picture Books for Children, 4th ed. **Patricia Jean Cianciolo. American Library Association, 50 E. Huron St., Chicago, IL 60611. 1997. 288 pp. $40.00, paper.** An annotated listing of picture books, divided into major subject areas such as "Me and My Family" and "The Imaginative World." Annotations include descriptions of media, age levels, and brief synopses of plot. Material is largely new to this edition, so older editions remain useful.

Popular Series Fiction for K–6 Readers. **Rebecca Thomas and Catherine Barr. Greenwood Publishing Group, 88 Post Rd. W., Westport, CT 06881. 2004. 816 pp. $60.00.** This annotated guide is organized alphabetically by series titles and includes information about the author, genre, and appropriate audience. Appendixes include series books for reluctant readers and ESL students.

FOLKLORE, STORYTELLING, AND READING ALOUD

Caroline Feller Bauer's New Handbook for Storytellers. **Caroline Feller Bauer. American Library Association, 50 E. Huron St., Chicago, IL 60611. 1993. 550 pp. $45.00, paper.** A thorough guide to telling stories, this book includes ideas for creating puppets, story media, and using music and film in storytelling.

Index to Fairy Tales, 1987–1992: Including 310 Collections of Fairytales, Folklore, Legends and Myths, 6th supp. Joseph W. Sprug, comp. Scarecrow Press, 4501 Forbes Blvd., Lanham, MD 20706. 1994. 602 pp. $70.00. Indexes a broad range of collections of folktales and other folk literature by author, compiler, subject of tale (including characters, countries, and so on), and titles of tale. Various editions cover different collections, so the total coverage is quite broad.

More Books Kids Will Sit Still For: The Complete Read-Aloud Guide, 2nd ed. Judy Freeman. Greenwood Publishing Group, 88 Post Rd. W., Westport, CT 06881. 1995. 869 pp. $49.95. Lists over 2,000 titles recommended for reading aloud, and includes plot summaries, extension ideas, and related titles.

The Read-Aloud Handbook, 5th. ed. Jim Trelease. Penguin Books, 375 Hudson St., New York, NY 10014. 2001. 387 pp. $12.95, paper. Contains a rationale for reading aloud, tips for good presentations, and an annotated list of books recommended for reading aloud.

Stories: A List of Stories to Tell and Read Aloud, 3rd ed. Marilyn B. Iarusso, ed. New York Public Library Publications Office, Fifth Ave. and 42nd St., New York, NY 10018. 1990. 104 pp. $6.00. Suggests proven stories to tell and read aloud to children. Includes poetry. Entries are briefly annotated.

Storyteller's Sourcebook. 1983–1999. Margaret Read MacDonald, ed. Gale Research, 835 Penobscot Bldg., Detroit, MI 48226-4094. 2001. 712 pp. $135.00. Provides access to folktales and folk literature in 700 collections. Tales are indexed by subject, motif, and title. Index is particularly useful in locating variants of tales.

Storytelling with Puppets, 2nd ed. Connie Champlin. American Library Association, 50 E. Huron St., Chicago, IL 60611. 1997. 264 pp. $35.00. Techniques for storytelling to younger audiences include open box theater, sound and action stories, and story aprons. Attention is given to multicultural themes and literature-based instruction.

The Storytime Sourcebook: A Compendium of Ideas and Resources for Storytellers. Carolyn M. Cullum. Neal-Schuman Publishers, 23 Leonard St., New York, NY 10013. 1999. 325 pp. $45.00. Arranged by themes, lists plans for story-hour programs including books, films, filmstrips, videocassettes, and toys. Includes activities for 3- to 7-year-olds. Print and nonprint indexes.

HISTORICAL FICTION, HISTORY, AND BIOGRAPHY

From Biography to History: Best Books for Children's Entertainment and Education. Catherine Barr. Greenwood Publishing Group, 88 Post Rd. W., Westport, CT 06881. 1998. 550 pp. $59.95. Indexes biographies in collections by individuals' names and by subject. Biographies are suitable for elementary school through junior high school.

Literature Connections to World History: K–6 Resources to Enhance and Entice. Lynda G. Adamson. Libraries Unlimited, P.O. Box 263, Littleton, CO 80160. 1998. 326 pp. $30.00. Lists and annotates books and media for younger readers about world history by time period and subject. Includes fiction and nonfiction.

Literature Connections to World History: 7–12 Resources to Enhance and Entice. Lynda G. Adamson. Libraries Unlimited, P.O. Box 263, Littleton, CO 80160. 1998. 326 pp. $32.50. Lists and annotates books and media for adolescents about world history by time period and subject. Includes fiction and nonfiction.

Peoples of the American West: Historical Perspectives through Children's Literature. Mary Hurlbut Cordier. Scarecrow Press, 4501 Forbes Blvd., Lanham, MD 20706. 1989. 230 pp. $35.00. Contains an analysis of historical fiction of the West as a genre and an annotated list of 100 books separated into grades K–3 and 4–9.

Historical Fiction for Children and Young Adults. Lynda G. Adamson. Greenwood Publishing Group, 88 Post Rd. W., P.O. Box 5007, Westport, CT 06881. 1994. 520 pp. $64.95. Authors, titles, main characters, and historical events are listed in dictionary format with longer entries under authors that describe their works. Appendixes list books by periods and events and by readability level.

CULTURAL AND SEXUAL IDENTITY

Against Borders: Promoting Books for a Multicultural World. Hazel Rochman. American Library Association, 50 E. Huron St., Chicago, IL 60611. 1993. 288 pp. $25.00, paper. Essays and annotated book lists focus on specific ethnic groups and issues that tie world cultures together through themes.

American Indian Reference Books for Children and Young Adults. Barbara J. Kuipers. Libraries Unlimited, P.O. Box 263, Littleton, CO 80160. 1995. 260 pp. $27.50. Lists over 200 nonfiction sources of material on Native Americans for grades 3–12. Includes strengths and weaknesses of each book as well as curriculum uses. A section of the book deals with general selection criteria to use for these subjects.

Basic Collection of Children's Books in Spanish. Isabel Schon. Scarecrow Press, 4501 Forbes Blvd., Lanham, MD 20706. 2001. 376 pp. $45.00. More than 500 titles for preschool through grade 6 are arranged in Dewey order, with access through author, title, and subject indexes. A list of Spanish-language distributors is included.

The Black American in Books for Children: Readings in Racism, 2nd ed. Donnarae MacCann and Gloria Woodard. Scarecrow Press, 4501 Forbes Blvd., Lanham, MD 20706. 1985. 310 pp. $31.00. Collections of articles in which the issue of racism in children's books is considered from a variety of points of view. Includes many citations to books of both good and poor quality that reflect positive and negative values.

Books in Spanish for Children and Young Adults: An Annotated Guide, series 3. Isabel Schon. Scarecrow Press, 4501 Forbes Blvd., Lanham, MD 20706. 1993. 305 pp. $45.00. Contains listings of books for preschool through high school that have been published since 1982. The listed books represent diverse Hispanic cultures, including Mexico and Central and South America.

Connecting Cultures: A Guide to Multicultural Literature for Children. Rebecca L. Thomas. Greenwood Publishing Group, 88 Post Rd. W., Westport, CT 06881. 1996. 689 pp. $40.00. Annotated lists for grades K–6 include fiction, folktales, poetry, and songbooks about diverse cultural groups.

The Coretta Scott King Awards: 1970–2004. Henrietta M. Smith. American Library Association, 50 E. Huron St., Chicago, IL 60611. 2004. 115 pp. $32.00. Lists and annotates award winners and honor books.

A Guide to Non-Sexist Children's Books: Volume 2, 1976–1985. Denise Wilms and Ilene Cooper, eds. Academy Publisher, 213 W. Institute Pl., Chicago, IL 60610. 1987. 240 pp. $17.95; $8.95, paper. Lists over 600 books in sections by grade level, through twelfth grade, subdivided into fiction and nonfiction. Indexes by author, title, fiction, and nonfiction subjects. Volume 1, which covered books up to 1976, is also available.

A Latino Heritage: A Guide to Juvenile Books about Latino Peoples and Cultures, **Volume 5. Isabel Schon. Scarecrow Press, 4501 Forbes Blvd., Lanham, MD 20706. 1995. 210 pp. $34.50.** An annotated subject bibliography of works about the people, history, culture, and politics in the Latino countries as well as works about Latino people in the United States. The author indicates in the annotations the passages in which cultural bias and stereotyping might appear. Covers grades K–12. Volumes 2 (1985) and 3 (1988) are also available.

Kaleidoscope—A Multicultural Booklist for Grades K–8, **4th ed. Nancy Hansen-Krening, ed. National Council of Teachers of English, 1111 W. Kenyon Road, Urbana, IL 61801-1096. 2001. 248 pp. $30.95.** Celebrating cultural diversity with annotations of nearly 400 books, covers a range from poetry to arts to biographies, folktales, and picture books, focusing especially on people of color.

OTHER SOCIAL ISSUES

The Bookfinder, Volume 5: When Kids Need Books. **Sharon Spredemann Dreyer. American Guidance Service, Publishers' Building, 4201 Woodland Rd., Circle Pines, MN 55014-1796. 1994. 519 pp. $64.95; $29.95, paper.** Subject, author, and title indexes are provided on the top half of the publication, and lengthy reviews that include subject cross-references, age levels, and specific information about the content of the book are on the bottom half. Both fiction and nonfiction are included. The books focus on problems children may experience, feelings, and relationships.

Books to Help Children to Cope with Separation and Loss, **4th ed. Masha K. Rudman, comp. Greenwood Publishing Group, 88 Post Rd. W., Westport, CT 06881. 1994. 514 pp. $55.00.** Includes several chapters on bibliotherapy plus annotated lists of titles in such categories as death, divorce, adoption, and foster children, and loss of mental or physical functions. About 600 books are arranged by topic with an annotation, evaluation, and recommendations for use with children. Age levels from 3 to 16, interest, and reading level are included in each annotation.

Portraying Persons with Disabilities: An Annotated Bibliography of Fiction for Children. **Debra Robertson. Greenwood Publishing Group, 88 Post Rd. W., Westport, CT 06881. 1992. 482 pp. $39.95.** Updates *Notes from a Different Drummer* and *More Notes from a Different Drummer,* books that provide annotated lists of titles that portray those with disabilities in fiction. Includes titles that promote better understanding and acceptance of the disabled.

Portraying Persons with Disabilities: An Annotated Bibliography of Nonfiction for Children. **Joan Brest Friedberg, June B. Mullins, and Adelaide Weir Sukiennik. Greenwood Publishing Group, 88 Post Rd. W., Westport, CT 06881. 1992. 400 pp. $39.50.** Updates *Accept Me as I Am,* listing over 350 nonfiction titles about those with disabilities. Includes introductory essays about the portrayal of disabilities in literature for children.

CURRICULUM AREAS AND GENRES OF LITERATURE

Anatomy of Wonder: A Critical Guide to Science Fiction. **Neil Barron, ed. Greenwood Publishing Group, 88 Post Rd. W., Westport, CT 06881. 2004. 1,016 pp. $80.00.** Includes a chapter that annotates titles for children and young adults, as well as 3,000 additional titles that would appeal to readers of the genre. Includes discussion of sci-fi poetry, film connections, and a chapter on classroom aids.

Celebrations: Read-Aloud Holiday and Theme Book Programs. **Caroline Feller Bauer. H. W. Wilson Co., 950 University Ave., Bronx, NY 10452. 1985. 301 pp. $60.00.** Includes readings and plans for holiday activities for both well-known and Bauer's invented holiday occasions.

Fantasy Literature for Children and Young Adults: An Annotated Bibliography, **4th ed. Ruth Nadelman Lyn. Greenwood Publishing Group, 88 Post Rd. W., Westport, CT 06881. 2005. 1,208 pp. $65.00.** Annotates about 4,800 fantasy novels for 8- to 17-year-olds in ten chapters arranged by topics. Includes specific subject indexes.

Index to Children's Songs: A Title, First Line, and Subject Index. **Carolyn Sue Peterson and Ann D. Fento. H. W. Wilson Co., 950 University Ave., Bronx, NY 10452. 1979. 318 pp. $55.00.** Indexes over 5,000 songs in 298 children's songbooks, both single titles and collections. Songs are indexed by title and first line as well as by 1,000 subject headings and cross-references.

Index to Poetry for Children and Young People, 1993–1997. **G. Meredith Blackburn, et al. H. W. Wilson Co., 950 University Ave., Bronx, NY 10452. 1999. 400 pp. $90.00.** The latest in a series of volumes that index collections of poetry by author, title, first line, and subject. Different collections are indexed in each volume. Classifies poems under a wide variety of subjects, making for easy access to poems by their topics.

It's the Story That Counts: More Children's Books for Mathematical Learning, K–6. **David J. Whitin and Sandra Wilde. 1995. 224 pp. $21.50, paper. Heinemann Books, 361 Hanover St., Portsmouth, NH 03801.** Discusses basic concepts in mathematics, such as place value, classification, and geometry, and suggests ways to explore these concepts with children's books.

The Literature of Delight: A Critical Guide to Humorous Books for Children. **Kimberly Olson Fakih. Greenwood Publishing Group, 88 Post Rd. W., Westport, CT 06881. 1993. 269 pp. $40.00.** Lists 1,000 fiction and nonfiction books with humorous presentations. Chapters include books of nonsense, books of satire and parody, poetry, and so on.

INFORMATION ABOUT AUTHORS AND ILLUSTRATORS

Bookpeople: A Second Album. **1990. 200 pp. $20.00, paper.**

Bookpeople: A Multicultural Album. **1992. 170 pp. $23.50, paper. Both by Sharon L. McElmeel. Libraries Unlimited, P.O. Box 263, Littleton, CO 80160.** Each volume introduces authors and illustrators of picture books for grades 3–9. Brief biographies include highlights of life and career and selected bibliographies of their work.

Children's Book Illustration and Design II. **Julie Cummins, ed. PBC International, One School St., Glen Cove, NY 11542. 1997. 240 pp. $55.00, hardcover.** This beautifully designed and printed volume includes a sample of picturebook illustrators, brief biographies, and information about the illustrators' media and techniques.

Children's Books and Their Creators. **Anita Silvey, ed. Houghton Mifflin, 222 Berkeley St., Boston, MA 02116. 1995. 800 pp. $40.00.** This handsomely designed book includes biographical descriptions of and first-person reflections by important twentieth-century authors and illustrators and critical essays on a range of topics central to the study of children's literature.

The Illustrator's Notebook. **Lee Kingman, ed. Horn Book, 11 Beacon St., Boston, MA 02108. 1978. 168 pp. $28.95.** Contains excerpts from articles by artists and illustrators that have appeared in the *Horn Book Magazine.* Articles discuss philosophy of illustration, history, illustration's place in the arts, and illustrators' experiences with various techniques of illustration.

Illustrators of Children's Books 1967–1976. **Lee Kingman, Grace Allen Hogarth, and Harriet Quimbly, eds. Horn Book, 11 Beacon St., Boston, MA 02108. 1978. 290 pp. $35.95.** Contains brief biographical and career sketches of artists and illustrators for children who were actively at work in this field during the period. Articles discuss techniques, philosophy, and trends in illustration during the period. Bibliographies are included for each illustrator, as are selected bibliographies covering art and illustration of the period.

The Marble in the Water: Essays on Contemporary Writers of Fiction for Children and Young Adults. **David Rees. Horn Book, 11 Beacon St., Boston, MA 02108. 1980. 224 pp. $9.95, paper.** Essays on 18 British and American authors, including Beverly Cleary, Paula Fox, Judy Blume, and Paul Zindel.

Meet the Authors and Illustrators: 60 Creators of Favorite Children's Books Talk About Their Work. **Vol. 2. Deborah Kovacs and James Preller. Scholastic Inc., 730 Broadway, New York, NY 10003. 1993. 142 pp. $19.95.** Two children's book authors have collected information on favorite authors and illustrators from around the world. Each two-page highlight includes information about the author or illustrator, selected titles, pictures, and a "do-it-yourself" activity suggested for children.

Newbery Medal Books: 1922–1955. **Bertha Mahoney Miller and Elinor Whitney Field, eds. 1955. 458 pp. $22.95.**

Caldecott Medal Books: 1938–1957. **Bertha Mahoney Miller and Elinor Whitney Field, eds. 1957. 239 pp. $22.95.**

Newbery and Caldecott Medal Books: 1956–1965. **Lee Kingman, ed. 1965. 300 pp. $22.95.**

Newbery and Caldecott Medal Books: 1966–1975. **Lee Kingman, ed. 1975. 321 pp. $22.95.**

Newbery and Caldecott Medal Books: 1976–1985. **Lee Kingman, ed. 1986. 321 pp. $24.95. All published by Horn Book, 11 Beacon St., Boston, MA 02108.** Each volume contains biographical sketches and texts of the award winners' acceptance speeches as well as general observations of trends in the awards.

Ninth Book of Junior Authors and Illustrators. **Connie Rockman, ed. 2005. 600 pp. $110.00. Latest in a series published by H. W. Wilson Co., 950 University Ave., Bronx, NY 10452.** These volumes provide readable biographies of popular authors for young people that include, generally, a biographical statement by the author or illustrator, a photograph, a brief biography, and a list of that person's works.

Pauses: Autobiographical Reflections of 101 Creators of Children's Books. **Lee Bennett Hopkins. HarperCollins, 10 E. 53rd St., New York, NY 10022. 1995. 233 pp. $23.00.** A collection of personal reflections taken from interviews with noted authors and illustrators.

A Sense of Story: Essays on Contemporary Writers for Children. **John Rowe Townsend. Horn Book, 56 Roland St., Ste. 200, Beacon St., Boston, MA 02129. 1973. 216 pp. $6.95.** Includes essays on 19 English-language authors for children, including brief biographies, notes on their books, critical remarks, and lists of their books. Essays reflect the critical position of the author.

Something about the Author. **Anne Commaire. Gale Research, 835 Penobscot Bldg., Detroit, MI 48226-4094. There are over 108 volumes in print, added to periodically. $153.25.** Clear and sizable essays on contemporary authors and illustrators.

Updating allows more-recent authors to be included. Contains photographs as well as reproductions from works of the illustrators. Suitable for middle-grade children to use for gathering biographical information.

A Sounding of Storytellers: New and Revised Essays on Contemporary Writers for Children. **John Rowe Townsend. Harper & Row, 10 E. 53rd St., New York, NY 10022. 1979. 218 pp. $15.25.** Townsend reevaluates seven of the authors included in his earlier *A Sense of Story,* including the new ground they have covered in more-recent works. Several American authors are included in the new selections, including Vera Cleaver and Bill Cleaver, Virginia Hamilton, and E. L. Konigsburg.

PERIODICALS

Appraisal: Science Books for Young People. **Children's Science Book Review Committee, Northeastern University, 54 Lake Hall, Boston, MA 02115. Quarterly. $46.00.** Each issue contains reviews of about 75 children's and young-adult science and technology books. Gives age levels and ratings of quality.

Bookbird. **IBBY, The International Board on Books for Young People, University of Toronto Press, 5201 Dufferin St., North York, Ontario M3H 5T8, Canada. Quarterly. $40.00.** This excellent journal reflects the international character of children's literature through articles and profiles of authors and illustrators from member countries. Themed issues have included "Children's Poetry," "Southeast Asia," "Girls and Women," and "Philosophy for Children."

Book Links. **American Library Association, 50 E. Huron St., Chicago, IL 60611. Six times/year. $28.95.** This publication connects books, libraries, and classrooms. Special features include "book strategies" or guides for teaching a particular book, interviews with authors and illustrators to discover their personal story behind the book, book themes, poetry, and "just for fun," books for children to read and enjoy.

Booklist. **American Library Association, 50 E. Huron St., Chicago, IL 60611. Twice/month. $89.95.** Reviews both adult and children's titles, including both print and nonprint materials. Reviews are annotated and graded by age levels and grades. Includes reviews of new selection tools. Often contains subject lists of good books in particular fields. Lists prize-winning books annually.

Book Review Digest. **H. W. Wilson Co., 950 University Ave., Bronx, NY 10452. Ten times/year. Service basis rates quoted on request.** Evaluates about 4,000 adult and children's books per year. For those books included, provides citations from several reviews that have appeared in other review periodicals.

Book World. **c/o Washington Post, 1150 15th St. NW, Washington, DC 20071. Weekly. $26.00.** A weekly supplement to the *Post* and several other newspapers. Reviews children's books regularly. Issues large special children's book editions in fall and spring.

The Bulletin of the Center for Children's Books. **Johns Hopkins University Press, 2715 N. Charles St., Baltimore, MD 21218. 11 issues. $50.00.** Reviews about 75 current children's books in each issue with negative as well as favorable reviews. Each entry is graded. Annotations stress curricular use, values, and literary merit.

Canadian Children's Literature. **CC Press, P.O. Box 335, University of Guelph, Guelph, Ontario N1G ZW1, Canada. Quarterly. US $39.00.** Literary analysis, criticism, and reviews of Canadian children's literature. A thematic approach for each issue. Predominantly written in English, but some articles are in French or in French and English.

CBC Magazine. **Children's Book Council, 12 W. 37th St., New York, NY 10018. <www.cbcbooks.org/cbcmagazine>.** A Web site about children's books, including information about special events, free and inexpensive materials from publishers, and lists of prize-winners, as well as discussion of new books.

Childhood Education. **Association for Childhood Education International, 17904 Georgia Ave., Suite 215, Olney, MD 20902. Six times/year. $65.00.** Includes a column on children's books that contains annotated reviews on about 25 books.

Children and Libraries. **Association for Library Services to Children and Young Adult Services Division, American Library Association, 50 E. Huron St., Chicago, IL 60611. Quarterly. $40.00.** Provides articles on issues in children's literature and children's librarianship, international news, texts of speeches, and lists of upcoming events of interest in the field. Articles are often annotated bibliographies on subjects of current interest.

Children's Literature in Education. **c/o Agathon Press, 233 Spring St., New York, NY 10013. Quarterly. $29.00.** Publishes longer articles on English and American children's literature, including criticism, history, and biographical essays.

Cricket Magazine. **Marianne Carus, ed. Carus Corp., 315 Fifth St., Box 300, Peru, IL 61354. Monthly. $32.95.** A literary magazine for children of elementary school age. Includes new stories and poems by well-known children's authors as well as excerpts and serializations of older pieces of literature. Includes children's reviews of books, interviews with authors, and children's writing.

Five Owls. **Five Owls, 2000 Aldrich Ave. S., Minneapolis, MN 55405. Four issues/year. $35.00.** Each online issue provides an article on a theme or topic and bibliographies that enhance or support it. Includes a signed review section.

Horn Book Magazine. **Horn Book, Inc., 56 Roland St., Ste. 200, Boston, MA 02129. Bimonthly. $34.95. <www.hbook.com/>** Includes detailed reviews of children's books judged by the editorial staff to be the best in children's literature. Contains articles about the literature, interviews with authors, and text of important speeches in the field of literature (Newbery and Caldecott acceptance speeches are published in the August issue each year). October issue lists the outstanding books of the previous year.

Journal of Children's Literature. **Children's Literature Assembly of the National Council of Teachers of English. <www.childrensliteratureassembly.org>. Two issues/year. $20.00.** The journal comes with membership in the Children's Literature Assembly and features articles, book reviews, and classroom ideas that focus on children's literature.

Knowledge Quest (formerly *School Library Media Quarterly*). **American Association of School Librarians, American Library Association, 50 E. Huron St., Chicago, IL 60611. Quarterly. $40.00.** Official journal of the AASL. Includes articles on book evaluations, censorship, library services, standards of service, and so on.

Language Arts. **National Council of Teachers of English, 1111 Kenyon Rd., Urbana, IL 61801. Monthly September to May. $40.00.** "Books for Children" section features regular reviews of new books. Several issues focus on literature and reading, containing articles on authors, using literature in the classroom, and so on.

The Lion and the Unicorn. **Johns Hopkins University Press, P.O. Box 19966, Baltimore, MD 21211. Three issues/year. $31.00.** Literary criticism, book reviews, and interviews with authors of children's literature. Each issue presents a particular theme or genre around which articles are centered.

The New York Times Book Review. **New York Times Co., 229 W. 43rd St., New York, NY 10036. Weekly. $52.00.** Weekly column entitled "For Younger Readers" reviews a few children's books. Two issues in fall and spring are devoted to children's books exclusively. Before Christmas, a list of outstanding books is included.

Publisher's Weekly. **R.R. Bowker, 121 Chanlon Rd., New Providence, NJ 07974. Weekly. $225.00.** Twice a year, in spring and fall, a "Children's Book Number" is published that includes new titles from all major publishers, as well as reviews. Negative reviews are included. Occasionally includes feature articles on children's books and publishing for children.

School Library Journal. **P.O. Box 16388, North Hollywood, CA 91615. Monthly. $124.00.** Reviews most children's books, using librarians, teachers, and critics from around the country as reviewers. Includes both positive and negative reviews. Categorizes reviews by age levels. Also includes feature articles on children's literature, children's library services, technology, and nonprint materials. December issue includes a "Best Books" section.

Science Books and Films. **American Association for the Advancement of Science, 1200 New York Ave. NW., Washington, DC 20005. Bimonthly. $45.00.** Reviews trade, text, and reference books for students in all grades in both pure and applied sciences. Includes nonprint materials. Indicates level of expertise required to use a piece of material. Books are reviewed by specialists in the field.

Science and Children. **National Science Teachers Association, 1840 Wilson Blvd., Arlington, VA 22201. Eight times/year. $72.00.** Includes a monthly column that reviews books and nonprint materials.

Signal: Approaches to Children's Books. **Thimble Press, Lockwood Station Rd., South Woodchester, Stroud Glos. GL5 5EQ, England. Three times/year. $27.00.** Articles of criticism on history of children's literature and on theory and practice of classroom use. The literature considered is largely British.

Teaching and Learning Literature with Children and Young Adults. **Essmont Publishing, P.O. Box 186, Brandon, VT 05733. Five times/year. $34.95.** This journal includes thoughtful essays and critiques on a range of topics and genres in children's literature. Each issue includes a "Workshop" feature, ideas for deepening children's responses to and understandings of books.

Wilson Library Bulletin. **The H. W. Wilson Co., 950 University Ave., Bronx, NY 10452. Monthly September to June. $52.00.** Includes discussions and reviews of all types of books and materials. Features a monthly column of reviews of children's books, plus articles about authors, a list of awards, and so on. The October issue is devoted to children's books.

SELECTED PROFESSIONAL WEB SITES

American Association of School Librarians
www.ala.org/aasl
The American Association of School Librarians is a division of the American Library Association responsible for planning, improving, and extending library media services for children and young people. Its Web site offers Kids Connect, a question

answering and referral service to help K–12 students with research or personal interests.

Association of Library Services to Children
www.ala.org/alsc/
The Association of Library Services to Children is the division of the American Library Association that oversees the Caldecott and Newbery awards and provides many other activities relating to children and books.

Children's Book Council
www.cbcbooks.org/
The Children's Book Council is the trade association of U.S. publishers of children's books. The Council promotes the use and enjoyment of trade books and related materials for young people and disseminates information about children's trade book publishing. This site provides links to author Web sites and provides bibliographies such as Notable Social Studies Trade Books for Children and Outstanding Science Books for Children.

Cooperative Children's Book Center (CCBC)
www.soemadison.wisc.edu/ccbc/index.htm
The Cooperative Children's Book Center at the University of Wisconsin is a noncirculating examination study and research library for adults with an interest in children's and young-adult literature. CCBC-Net is an electronic forum to discuss books for children and young adults.

International Reading Association
www.reading.org/
The International Reading Association seeks to promote literacy by improving the quality of reading instruction, serving as a clearinghouse for reading research, and promoting life-long reading habits.

National Council of Teachers of English
www.ncte.org/
NCTE is a professional organization of educators in English Studies, Literacy, and the Language Arts. NCTE-talk provides a monthly forum on special interests such as assessment.

Young Adult Library Services Association of the American Library Association
www.ala.org/yalsa/
The Young Adult Library Services Association is the division of the American Library Association that oversees the Printz Award and provides many other activities relating to young adults.

Publishers' Addresses

BOOK PUBLISHERS

Note: Publishers' addresses may change. For complete and up-to-date information, see the current edition of *Literary Market Place* or *Children's Books in Print*.

Abrams, 100 Fifth Ave., New York, NY 10010. www.abramsbooks.com

Addison-Wesley, 200 Old Tappan Way, Old Tappan, NJ 07675. www.aw.com

Aladdin Books, see Simon & Schuster.

Annick Press, 15 Patricia Ave., Toronto, Ontario M2M 1H9, Canada. www.annickpress.com

Apple Soup, see Random House Inc.

Arcade Publishing, 141 Fifth Ave., New York, NY 10010.

Astor-Honor, 16 E. 40th St., 3rd Flr., New York, NY 10016.

Atheneum Publishers, see Simon & Schuster.

Atlantic Monthly Press, see Grove/Atlantic.

August House Publishers, P.O. Box 3223, Little Rock, AR 72203. www.augusthouse.com

Avon Books, see HarperCollins.

Bantam Doubleday Dell, see Random House Inc.

Barefoot Books, 2067 Massachusetts Ave., 5th Flr., Cambridge, MA 02140. www.barefoot-books.com

Black Butterfly Children's Books, see Writers and Readers Publishing.

Bloomsbury, 175 Fifth Ave., Suite 300, New York, NY 10010. www.bloomsburyusa.com

Blue Apple Books, 515 Valley St., Maplewood, NJ 07040. www.blueapplebooks.com

Blue Sky, see Scholastic.

Book Pub Co., P.O. Box 99, Summertown, TN 38483.

Boyds Mills Press, 815 Church St., Honesdale, PA 18431. www.boydsmillspress.com

Bradbury Press, see Simon & Schuster.

Browndeer Press, see Harcourt.

Camelot, see HarperCollins.

Candlewick Press, 2067 Massachusetts Ave., Cambridge, MA 02140. www.candlewick.com

Carolrhoda Books, Inc., see Lerner Publications Co.

Carus Publishing, 322 South Michigan Ave., Suite 1100, Chicago, IL 60604.

Charlesbridge Publishing, 85 Main St., Watertown, MA 02472. www.charlesbridge.com

Children's Book Press, 246 First St., Ste. 101, San Francisco, CA 94105. www.cbookpress.org

Children's Press, see Grolier.

Chronicle Books, 85 Second St., 6th Floor, San Francisco, CA 94105. www.chroniclekids.com

Cinco Puntos Press, 701 Texas Ave., El Paso, TX 79901. www.cincopuntos.com

Clarion Books, 215 Park Ave., New York, NY 10003. www.houghtonmifflinbooks.com

Cobblehill Books, see Penguin Putnam Inc.

Collier, see Simon & Schuster.

Creative Arts Books, 833 Bancroft Way, Berkeley, CA 94710. www.creativeartsbooks.com

Creative Education Inc., 123 S. Broad, Mankato, MN 56001.

Crestwood House, 1633 Broadway, New York, NY 10019.

Cricket Books, see Carus Publishing.

Thomas Y. Crowell, see HarperCollins.

Crown Publishers, see Random House Inc.

Delacorte Press, see Random House Inc.

Dell Publishing, see Random House Inc.

Dial, see Penguin Putnam Inc.

Disney Press, 114 Fifth Ave., 12th Floor, New York, NY 10011. www.disneybooks.com

DK Publishing, Inc. (formerly Dorling Kindersley Publishing, Inc.), 95 Madison Ave., 10th Floor, New York, NY 10016. www.dk.com

Doubleday, see Random House Inc.

Dover Publications, Inc., 180 Varick St., New York, NY 10014.

Dutton Children's Books, see Penguin Putnam Inc.

Farrar, Straus & Giroux, Inc., 19 Union Square West, New York, NY 10003. www.fsgbooks.com/fsg.htm

Fitzhenry and Whiteside, 195 Allstate Parkway, Markam, Ontario L3R 4T8, Canada. www.fitzhenry.ca

Phyllis Fogelman Books, see Penguin Putnam Inc.

Four Winds Press, see Simon & Schuster.

David R. Godine, Publishers, Inc., 9 Hamilton Place, Boston, MA 02108-4715. www.godine.com

Golden Books, see Random House Inc. www.randomhouse.com/golden/

Green Tiger Press, 435 E. Carmel St., San Marcos, CA 92069.

Greenwillow Books, see HarperCollins.

Grolier Children's Publishing, 90 Sherman Turnpike, Danbury, CT 06816. www.grolier.com/

Grosset & Dunlap, Inc., see Penguin Putnam Inc.

Groundwood Books, 720 Bathurst St., Toronto, Ontario M5S 2R4, Canada. www.groundwoodbooks.com

Grove/Atlantic, 841 Broadway, 4th Floor, New York, NY 10003.

Gulliver Books, see Harcourt.

Handprint, 413 Sixth Ave., Brooklyn, NY 11215. www.handprintbooks.com

Harcourt Children's Books, 525 B St., Suite 1900, San Diego, CA 92101-4495. www.harcourtbooks.com

HarperCollins Children's Books, 1350 Avenue of the Americas, New York, NY 10019. www.harperchildrens.com

Harper Trophy Paperbacks, see HarperCollins.

Holiday House, 425 Madison Ave., New York, NY 10017. www.holidayhouse.com

Henry Holt and Company, Inc., 115 West 18th St., New York, NY 10011. www.henryholt.com

Holy Cow! Press, P.O. Box 3170, Duluth, MN 55803.

Houghton Mifflin, 222 Berkley St., Boston, MA 02116. www.houghtonmifflinbooks.com

Hyperion Books, see Disney Press. hyperionbooks.go.com

Jewish Publication Society, 60 East 42nd St., Suite 1339, New York, NY 10165. www.jewishpub.org

Joy Street Books, see Little, Brown.

Jump at the Sun, see Disney Press.

Kane/Miller Book Publishers, P.O. Box 8515, La Jolla, CA 92038. www.kanemiller.com

Kids Can Press, 2250 Military Rd., Tonawanda, NY 14150. www.kidscanpress.com

Alfred A. Knopf, see Random House, Inc.

Lee & Low Books Inc., 95 Madison Ave., New York, NY 10016. www.leeandlow.com

Lerner Publications Company, 241 First Ave., North, Minneapolis, MN 55401. www.lernerbooks.com

Frances Lincoln, 4 Torriano Mews, Torriano Ave., London NW5 2RZ, England. www.franceslincoln.com

Lippincott Junior Books, see HarperCollins.

Little, Brown & Co., 3 Center Plaza, Boston, MA 02108. www.twbookmark.com

Little Simon, see Simon & Schuster.

Lodestar Books, see Penguin Putnam Inc.

Lothrop, Lee & Shepard Books, see HarperCollins.

Macmillan Publishing Co., see Simon & Schuster.

Margaret K. McElderry Books, see Simon & Schuster.

Marshall Cavendish, 99 White Plains Rd. B 2001, Tarrytown, NY 10591. www.marshallcavendish.com

The Millbrook Press, Inc., 2 Old New Milford Rd., Brookfield, CT 06804. www.millbrookpress.com

Mondo, 980 Sixth Ave., New York, NY 10018. www.mondpub.com

Morrow Junior Books, see HarperCollins.

Mulberry Books, see HarperCollins.

National Geographic Press, 1147 17th St. NW, Washington, DC 20036. www.nationalgeographic.com

North-South Books, 1123 Broadway, Suite 1016, New York, NY 10010.

Orchard Books, see Scholastic.

Richard C. Owen, Publishers, Inc., P.O. Box 585, Katonah, NY 10536. www.rcowen.com

Oxford University Press, 198 Madison Ave., New York, NY 10016. www.oup-usa.org

Pantheon, see Random House Inc.

Paper Star, see Penguin Putnam Inc.

Parents Magazine Press, 685 Third Ave., New York, NY 10017.

Parnassus Press, see Houghton Mifflin.

Peachtree Publishers, 1700 Chattahoochee Ave., Atlanta, GA 30318. www.peachtree-online.com

Penguin Putnam Inc., 375 Hudson St., New York, NY 10014. www.penguinputnam.com/yreaders

Philomel Books, see Penguin Putnam Inc.

Picture Book Studio, 2 Center Plaza, Boston, MA 02108.

Pleasant Company, 8400 Fairway Place, P.O. Box 998, Middleton, WI 53562. www.americangirl.com

Puffin Books, see Penguin Putnam Inc.

G. P. Putnam's Sons, see Penguin Putnam Inc.

Raintree Steck-Vaughn Publishers, P. O. Box 26015, Austin, TX 78755. www.steck-vaughn.com

Rand McNally, P.O. Box 7600, Chicago, IL 60680. www.randmcnally.com

Random House Inc., 1540 Broadway, New York, NY 10036. www.randomhouse.com

Rising Moon–Luna Rising Books, 2900 N. Fort Valley Rd., Flagstaff, AZ 86001. www.northlandbooks.com

Rizzoli International Publications, Inc., 300 Park Ave., South, New York, NY 10010.

Roaring Brook, 143 West St., New Milford, CT 06776.

Running Press Book Publishers, 2300 Chestnut Ave., Suite 200, Philadelphia, PA 19103. www.perseusbooks.com

Sagebrush Press, 2846 Anteres St., Las Vegas, NV 89117. www.sagebrushpress.com

Scholastic Inc., 555 Broadway, New York, NY 10012. www.scholastic.com

Charles Scribner's Sons, see Simon & Schuster.

Sea Star, see Chronicle Books.

Sierra Club Books for Children, 100 Bush St., San Francisco, CA 94104. www.sierraclub.org/books

Silver Moon Press, 126 Fifth Ave., Suite 803, New York, NY 10011. www.silvermoonpress.com

Silver Whistle, see Harcourt.

Simon & Schuster Books for Young Readers, 1230 Avenue of the Americas, New York, NY 10020. www.SimonSaysKids.com

Sleeping Bear Press, 310 N. Main St., Suite 300, Chelsea, MI 48118. www.sleepingbearpress.com

St. Martin's Press, 175 5th Ave., S., New York, NY 10010. www.stmartins.com

Star Bright Books, The Star Building, 42–46 28th St., Suite 2B, Long Island City, NY 11101. www.starbrightbooks.com

Sterling, 819 Fulton Ave., Falls Church, VA 22046.

Stewart, Tabori & Chang, Inc., 575 Broadway, New York, NY 10012.

Tambourine Books, see HarperCollins.

Ticknor & Fields, see Clarion Books.

Tricycle/Ten Speed Press, P.O. Box 7123, Berkeley, CA 94707. **www.tenspeedpress.com**

Troll Associates, 100 Corporate Dr., Mahwah, NJ 07430. **www.troll.com**

Tundra Books, 481 University Ave., #802, Toronto, Ontario M5G 2E9, Canada.

Viking, see Penguin Putnam Inc.

Walker & Co., 435 Hudson St., New York, NY 10014.

Frederick Warne & Co., Inc., see Penguin Putnam Inc.

Franklin Watts, Inc., see Scholastic.

Western, see Random House Inc.

Albert Whitman & Co., 6340 Oakton St., Morton Grove, IL 60053. **www.awhitmanco.com**

Writers and Readers Publishing, Inc., 625 Broadway, New York, NY 10012. **www.writersandreaders.com**

PAPERBACK BOOK CLUBS

The Scholastic Book Clubs [Firefly: Preschool–K; See Saw: K–1; Lucky: 2–3; Arrow: 4–6]: Scholastic, Inc., 730 Broadway, New York, NY 10003. **teacher.scholastic.com/bookclubs/catalog/catalogs.htm**

The TrollCarnival Book Club: TrollCarnival Book Clubs, P. O. Box 3730, Jefferson City, MO 65102. **www.trollcarnival.com/index.shtml**

Hot Off the Press

Since its first edition, *Charlotte Huck's Children's Literature* has profiled not only the classics in children's literature, but also the very latest publications to incorporate into a children's reading program. Following is a quick guide to the new publications featured in this edition, as well as exciting new publications that are scheduled to publish after this text has gone to press.

For more of the very latest releases, visit **www.mhhe.com/kiefer9e** to access the Children's Literature database.

NEW ADDITIONS TO THIS TEXT

The following recent publications are visually represented in the text.

NEW PUBLICATIONS TO LOOK FOR

Searching the Internet will provide you with a wealth of the very latest titles to consider using. Make sure you follow and apply the appropriate evaluation criteria provided throughout this text when looking online and in the library.

Following is a sampling of titles that will be available after this book has gone to press. Contact the publishers for more information (see Appendix C for contact information). Many are shown on the following pages.

Picture Books

Chodos-Irving, Margaret. *Best Best Friends*. Harcourt, 2006.

Cronin, Doreen. *Dooby Dooby Moo*. Illustrated by Betsy Lewin. Atheneum, 2006.

Cunnane, Kelly. *For You Are a Kenyan Child*. Illustrated by Ana Juan. Simon, 2006.

Diakité, Penda. *I Lost My Tooth in Africa*. Illustrated by Baba Wagué Diakité. Scholastic, 2006.

Elya, Susan Middleton. *Bebé Goes Shopping*. Illustrated by Steven Salerno. Harcourt, 2006.

Henkes, Kevin. *Lilly's Big Day*. Greenwillow, 2006.

Look, Lenore. *Uncle Peter's Amazing Chinese Wedding*. Illustrated by Yumi Heo. Atheneum (Simon), 2006.

Wiesner, David. *Flotsam*. Clarion, 2006.

Willems, Mo. *Edwina, the Dinosaur Who Didn't Know She Was Extinct*. Hyperion, 2006.

Poetry

Katz, Bobbi, *Once around the Sun*. Illustrated by LeUyen Pham. Harcourt, 2006.

Lewis, J. Patrick. *Once upon a Tomb: Gravely Humorous Poems*. Illustrated by Simon Bartram. Candlewick, 2006.

Myers, Walter Dean. *Jazz*. Illustrated by Christopher Myers. Holiday House, 2006.

Nonfiction

Brown, Don. *Bright Path: Young Jim Thorpe*. Roaring Brook, 2006.

Colman, Penny. *Adventurous Women*. Holt, 2006.

Freedman, Russell. *The Adventures of Marco Polo*. Scholastic, 2006.

Jenkins, Steve, and Robin Page. *Move!* Houghton Mifflin, 2006.

Oppenheim, Joanne. *Dear Miss Breed*. Scholastic, 2006.

Fiction

Anderson, M. T. *The Clue of the Linoleum Lederhosen*. Harcourt, 2006.

Bruchac, Joseph. *Geronimo: A Novel*. Scholastic, 2006.

Draper, Sharon. *Copper Sun.* Atheneum (Simon), 2006.

Holt, Kimberly Willis. *Part of Me.* Holt, 2006.

Lowry, Lois. *Gossamer.* Houghton Mifflin, 2006.

MacLachlan, Patricia. *Grandfather's Dance.* HarperCollins, 2006.

Park, Linda Sue. *Archer's Quest.* Clarion, 2006.

Paterson, Katherine. *Bread and Roses, Too.* Clarion, 2006.

Tolan, Stephanie. *Listen!* HarperCollins, 2006.

Turner, Megan Whalen. *The King of Attolia.* HarperCollins, 2006.

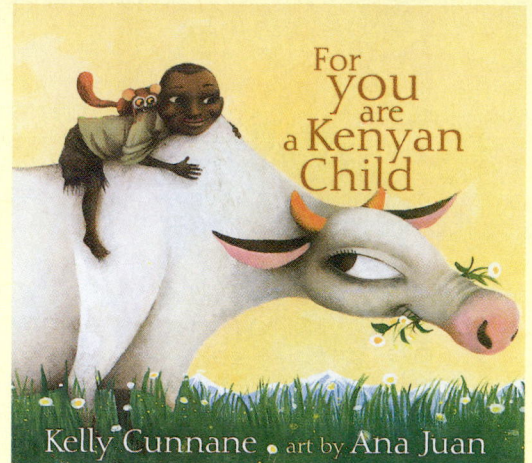

Cunnane, Kelly. *For You Are a Kenyan Child.* Illustrated by Ana Juan. Simon & Schuster, 2006. Reprinted with the permission of Atheneum Books for Young Readers, an imprint of Simon & Schuster Children's Publishing Division from *For You Are a Kenyan Child* by Kelly Cunnane, pictures by Ana Juan. Illustrations copyright © 2006 Ana Juan.

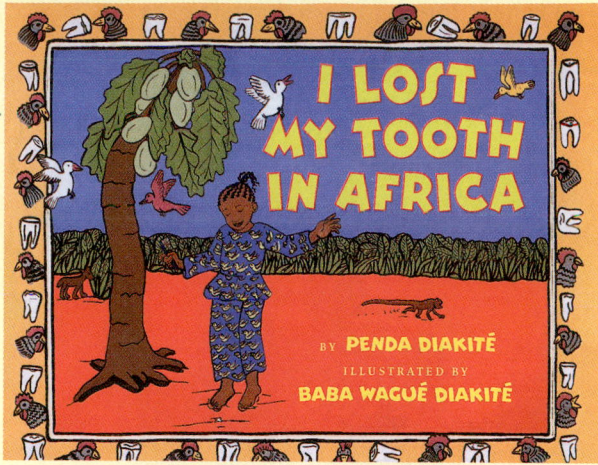

Diakité, Penda. *I Lost My Tooth in Africa.* Illustrated by Baba Wagué Diakité. Scholastic, 2006. Illustration copyright © 2006 by Baba Wagué Diakité from *I Lost My Tooth in Africa* by Penda Diakité. Published by Scholastic Press/Scholastic, Inc. Reprinted by permission.

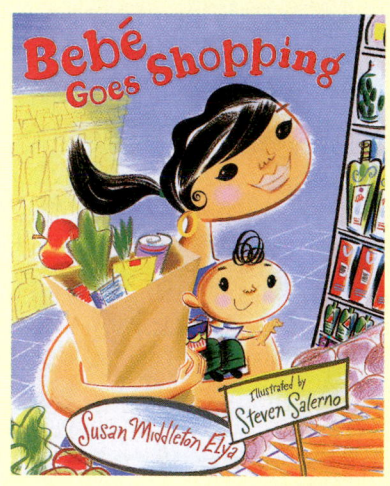

Elya, Susan Middleton. *Bebé Goes Shopping.* Illustrated by Steven Salerno. Harcourt, 2006. Cover from *Bebé Goes Shopping* by Susan Middleton Elya. Illustration copyright © 2006 by Steven Salerno, reproduced with permission of Harcourt, Inc.

Look, Lenore. *Uncle Peter's Amazing Chinese Wedding.* Illustrated by Yumi Heo. Atheneum, 2006. Reprinted with the permission of Atheneum Books for Young Readers, an imprint of Simon & Schuster Children's Publishing Division from *Uncle Peter's Amazing Chinese Wedding* by Lenore Look, pictures by Yumi Heo. Illustrations copyright © 2006 Yumi Heo.

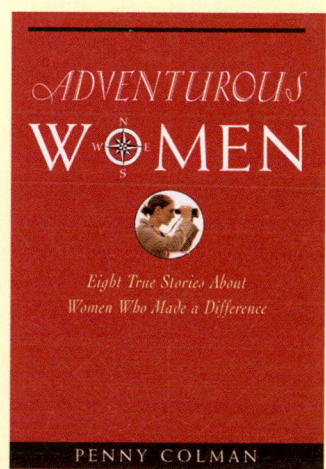

Colman, Penny. *Adventurous Women: Eight True Stories About Women Who Made a Difference.* Holt, 2006. From *Adventurous Women: Eight True Stories About Women Who Made a Difference* by Penny Colman. Copyright © 2006 by Penny Colman. Reprinted by permission of Henry Holt and Company, LLC.

Oppenheim, Joanne. *Dear Miss Breed.* Scholastic, 2006. Copyright © 2006 by Joanne Oppenheim from *Dear Miss Breed* by Joanne Oppenheim. Published by Scholastic Nonfiction/Scholastic, Inc. Reprinted by permission.

Bruchac, Joseph. *Geronimo: A Novel.* Scholastic, 2006.
Copyright © 2006 by Joseph Bruchac from *Geronimo* by Joseph Bruchac.
Published by Scholastic Press/Scholastic, Inc. Reprinted by permission.

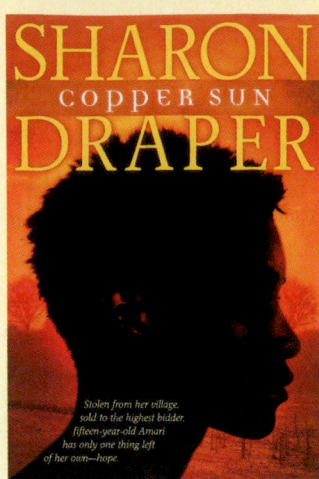

Draper, Sharon. *Copper Sun.* Atheneum, 2006. Reprinted with
the permission of Atheneum Books for Young Readers, an imprint of
Simon & Schuster Children's Publishing Division from *Copper Sun* by
Sharon M. Draper, pictures by Kamil Vojnar & Polly Kanevsky. Illustrations
copyright © 2006 Kamil Vojnar & Polly Kanevsky.

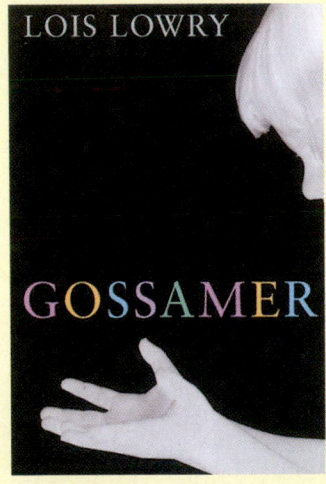

Lowry, Lois. *Gossamer.* Houghton Mifflin, 2006. Cover from
Gossamer by Lois Lowry. Copyright © 2006 by Lois Lowry. Reprinted by
permission of Houghton Mifflin Company. All rights reserved.

Park, Linda Sue. *Archer's Quest.* Clarion, 2006. Cover from
Archer's Quest by Linda Sue Park. Copyright © 2004 by Linda Sue Park.
Reprinted by permission of Clarion Books, an imprint of Houghton
Mifflin Company. All rights reserved.

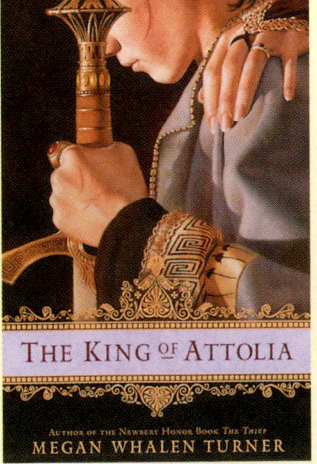

Turner, Megan Whalen. *The King of Attolia.* HarperCollins,
2006. Copyright © 2006 by Megan Whalen Turner. Used by permission
of HarperCollins Publishers.

Short, Kathy G., 109n37
Shotwell, Louisa, 104
Showers, Paula, 599
Shulevitz, Uri, 202, 206, 212, 298, 335, 671, 685
Shusterman, Neil, 496
"Shut My Mouth Wide Open: Realistic Fiction and Social Action," 96n20
Shy Charles, 146
Sian-tek, Lim, 99
Sibley, Brian, 385n16
"Sick," 419
"The Sidewalk Racer," 432
Sidjakov, Nicolas, 224, 225n8
Sidman, Joyce, 452
Sidney, Margaret, 87
Siebert, Diane, 417
Siegal, Aranka, 577
Siegelson, Kim, 210, 570
Sierra, 417
Sierra, Judy, 147, 246, 413, 681
The Sight, 361
The Sign of the Beaver, 556, 561, 561f, 562, 700
The Sign of the Chrysanthemum, 554
Silent Thunder, 566
Silent to the Bone, 487
Silk Umbrellas, 515
Silva, Simón, 157
"Silver," 413
The Silver Branch, 550
The Silver Cow, 294
Silver on the Tree, 385
The Silver Pencil, 474, 474n6
Silver Seeds, 452
The Silver Treasure, 325
Silverman, Erica, 242
Silverstein, Shel, 33, 36, 58, 90, 419, 423, 424, 425, 431, 671
Silverwing, 355, 357
Simmie, Lois, 431
Simmons, Jane, 173, 207
Simon, Seymour, 591, 600, 602, 603, 609, 612
Simont, Marc, 221, 429
Sinbad in the Land of Giants, 301
"Sinbad the Sailor," 83
Sinclair, Catherine, 86
Sing a Song of Popcorn, 412, 414, 419, 420, 422, 425, 428, 430
Sing a Song of Sixpence, 91, 92, 150
Sing Down the Moon, 557
Sing for Your Supper, 409n1
Sing Song, 90
Sing to the Sun, 427
Singer, Isaac Bashevis, 5, 281, 285, 299, 300
Singer, Marilyn, 218
A Single Shard, 554, 554f
A Sip of Aesop, 324
Sis, Peter, 423, 484
Sister Shako and Kolo the Goat, 514
"The Six Swans," 352
1621: A New Look at Thanksgiving, 593, 593f
Siy, Alexandra, 124, 587, 599
Skeleton Man, 376
Skellig, 21, 21n42, 56, 377, 677
Skin Again, 205
Skinnybones, 518

The Skirt, 508
Skullduggery, 544
Skurzynski, Gloria, 394, 612
The Sky Is Always in the Sky, 426
The Sky Is Falling, 577
Sky Tree, 213, 597
Skylark, 565
Slade, Arthur, 374
Slake's Limbo, 496
Slap, Squeak and Scatter, 616
Slapin, Beverly, 541n1
The Slave Dancer, 102, 567, 609
Slaves of Mastery, 383
Slavik, Christy Richards, 484n12
Sleator, William, 390, 394
The Sledding Hill, 124, 474, 505
Sleds on Boston Commons, 542
Sleeping Beauty, 83, 284, 297, 670
Sleepy Cadillac, 177
Sloan, Christopher, 595, 609
Sloat, Teri, 153
Slobodkina, Esphyr, 147, 306
The Slopes of War, 569
Slote, Alfred, 390, 504, 526
Small, David, 212, 604
Small Poems, 420
Smedley, Constance, 99
Smiler's Bones, 557
Smith, Doris Buchanan, 59, 502
Smith, E. Boyd, 97
Smith, Elva S., 81n11
Smith, Frank, 12, 12n29, 676n11
Smith, Jessie Wilcox, 92
Smith, Lane, 244
Smith, William Jay, 443, 443n11
The Smithsonian Book of Books, 81n10
Smoky Mountain Rose, 316
Smoky Night, 216
Smolkin, Laura B., 97n21
"The Snake and the Apple," 425
"Sneepies," 423
"Sneezy-Snoozer," 423
Sneve, Virginia Driving Hawk, 104, 442, 542
The Snopp on the Sidewalk, 413, 422, 423, 455, 456
Snow, 206
The Snow Pony, 523
The Snow Queen, 352
Snow Treasure, 545, 576
Snow White and the Seven Dwarfs, 88, 204, 278, 280, 288, 294
"Snowfall," 417
Snowflake Bentley, 26, 209, 209f
The Snowman, 171, 172
The Snowy Day, 204, 210, 229
Snyder, Diane, 288, 304
Snyder, Zilpha Keatley, 487, 574
So Far from the Bamboo Grove, 577
So, Meilo, 302, 431, 681
So Say the Little Monkeys, 322
So You Want to Be President, 604
Soap Soup and Other Verses, 426
Soaring with the Wind: The Bald Eagle, 606
Sobin, Dan I., 41n25
Sobol, Donald, 529
Social Education, 592
Soentpiet, Chris, 212
Sogabe, Aki, 211, 324
Solider and Tsar in the Forest, 298

"Solitude," 425
Solway, Andrew, 589
Some Smug Slug, 41
Something Big Has Been Here, 424
Something from Nothing, 300
Something Queer series, 528
Something Special for Me, 229
Son, John, 512
The Song of el Coqui and Other Tales of Puerto Rico, 318
The Song of Frances and the Animals, 209
"Song of the Train," 413, 414, 422, 429, 455
Song of the Water Boatman, 452, 453f
Song Quest, 381
Song Shoots out of My Mouth, 442
Songs of Childhood, 101
Songs of Innocence, 85, 420
Songs of Shiprock Fair, 428
"Sonic Boom," 432
Sonny's House of Spies, 491
The Sons of the Dragon, 214
Sons of the Dragon King, 303
Soon Be Free, 545
Sophie's Window, 9
Soto, Gary, 216, 427, 508
Souhami, Jessica, 294, 332
Soul Looks Back in Wonder, 442
Sound and Sense: An Introduction to Poetry, 409n2
"Sound Bytes, Hamburgers and Billy Joel: Celebrating the Year of the Lifetime Reader," 698n20
Sound the Jubilee, 567
Sounder, 102, 546
Southall, Ivan, 512
The Space between Our Footsteps: Poems and Paintings from the Middle East, 432
Space Race, 391
The Sparrow Bush, 411n5
Speak, 122
Speare, Elizabeth, 26, 550, 556, 557, 560, 561, 700
Spectacular Cross-Section books (series), 589
Sperry, Armstrong, 23, 494
Spiegelman, Art, 122
Spier, Peter, 171, 335, 604, 684
Spin a Soft Black Song, 427, 451
Spinelli, Jerry, 8, 486, 492, 493, 576
Spinners, 351
Spirin, Gennady, 298, 299
Spirit Child, 336
Spiritual Milk for Boston Babes in Either England, Drawn from the Breasts of Both Testaments for Their Souls' Nourishment, 82
Splash!, 166, 429
A Splendid Friend, Indeed, 205, 206f
Splish Splash, 421, 453
Spot Goes to School, 146
Spring, 588
Spring Pearl: The Last Flower, 541
Springer, Nancy, 351, 382
Spyri, Johanna, 87, 485

Squashed, 493
Squashed in the Middle, 228
Squids Will Be Squids, 245
The Squire, His Knight and His Lady, 351–352, 382
The Squire's Tale, 351, 382
"Squirrels in My Notebook," 444
St. Nicholas Magazine, 90
Stafford, Kim, 211
Stafford, William, 211, 431
Stamaty, Mark Alan, 122
Stand Tall, 6, 470, 482, 483, 493
Stanley, Diane, 100, 374, 381
Stanley, Jerry, 590, 609
Stanley Mows the Lawn, 212
Stanovich, Keith E., 11n24
Staples, Suzanne Fisher, 474, 515, 516
Star Boy, 310
The Star Fisher, 287, 573
The Star of Kazan, 6, 6, 544
The Star-Bearer, 325
Starbird, Kaye, 450
Stargirl, 493
Starry Messenger, 484
Stars and Planets, 606
The Stars Are Whispering, 421
Stars Beneath Your Bed, 590
Stars for Sam, 97
The Steadfast Tin Soldier, 352
Steal Away Home, 545
Stealing Freedom, 16, 567
"Steam Shovel," 417
Steamboat Annie and the Thousand Pound Catfish, 318
Steele, William, 542
Steichen, Edward, 98
Steig, William, 26, 41, 219, 224, 225, 325, 359, 696, 702
A Step from Heaven, 510, 510f, 511
Stephens, James, 431
Stepping on the Cracks, 543
Steptoe, Javaka, 73, 143, 210
Steptoe, John, 95, 100, 107, 205, 288, 306, 307
Sterling, Dorothy, 103
Stevens, Carla, 564, 688
Stevens, Cat, 685
Stevenson, James, 219
Stevenson, Robert Louis, 24, 87, 90, 412, 420, 425, 431, 544
Stevie, 95, 96, 96, 107, 205
"Stevie the Internet Addict," 424
Stewart, Sarah, 212
Stewig, John, 298
"The Sticks of Truth," 302
The Stinky Cheese Man, 244
Stock, Catherine, 229
Stockings of Buttermilk, 308
Stolen Thunder, 330
Stolz, Joelle, 109
Stone Bench in an Empty Park, 421
Stone Fox, 6, 525
A Stone in My Hand, 514, 515f
Stone Soup, 99, 288, 298, 351
The Stonecutter, 288
Stonewords, 376
"Stop, Go," 686
"Stopping by Woods on a Snowy Evening," 414, 430–431, 443
The Stories Julian Tells, 476

A

ABC books. *See* alphabet books
abilities, intellectual, 41
accuracy
    in biographies, 638
    in historical fiction, 546
    in nonfiction, 191–192, 591
acrylic paints, 213
action, 34
activity books, 606–607
ADHD. *See* attention-deficit-
    hyperactivity disorder
administrators, 698–699
adventure, 34. *See also* survival
        stories
    books, 87
    in high fantasy, 386–389
aesthetic stance, 56
Afghanistan, 516
Africa. *See also* African Americans
    apartheid in, 512
    folktales of, 305–307
    stories of, 512–513
African Americans, 95, 104,
        505–507. *See also* slavery
    in American Revolution,
        562–563
    folktales of, 316–317
    middle class, 507
    poetry of, 426–427
age stereotypes, 227
age-appropriateness, of
        literature, 477
aging, 501–502
ALA. *See* American Library
        Association
alcoholism, 104
Aldhelm, 80
aliens, 391
alliteration, 413
alphabet books, 41, 81, 154–157,
        676
    as picture books, 200
alphabet verses, 83
American Association of School
        Librarians, 701
American Booksellers
        Association, 93
American Civil Liberties Union,
        703
American frontier, 563–566
American Library Association
        (ALA), 26, 93, 593, 701, 702
American Revolution, 12
    historical fiction about,
        562–563
Amistad, 107
animals, 34, 35, 87, 100. *See also*
        anthropomorphism

in contemporary realistic
        fiction, 523–525
    in fantasy, 356
    as people, 232–243
    personification by, 306
    talking of, 280
    villains as, 360
Anselm, 80
anthologies
    comprehensive, 430–431
    of poetry, 430
    specialized, 431–443
anthropomorphism, 246
    avoidance of, 595
antiphonal, 455
anti-Semitism, 96
apartheid, 512
appendixes, 601
archetypes, 352
art. *See also* illustrations
    cartoon, 218
    computer-generated, 212, 225
    expressionistic, 216
    folk, 217
    impressionistic, 215
    naïve, 217
    representational, 214
    surrealistic, 216
arté popular, 219
Arté Publico, 107
Arthur, King, 385–386
artistic conventions, 214
Asia. *See also* Asian Americans;
        China; India; Japan; Korea;
        Pakistan
    folktales of, 302–305
    historical fiction of, 554
    stories of, 514–517
Asian Americans, 508–511
Asian Pacific Award for
        Literature, 107
assessment, of reading program,
        694–695
Association for Library Service
        to Children, 26, 109, 590
attention-deficit-hyperactivity
        disorder (ADHD), 499–500
Australia
    authors from, 383
    mythology of, 326
    stories of, 512
authentic biographies, 633, 638
authors
    from Australia, 383
    autobiographies of, 653
    backgrounds of, 475–476
    of biographies, 638, 649–650
    of contemporary realistic
        fiction, 475–476
    experience of, 22
    impartiality of, 641

from New Zealand, 383
    qualifications of, 591
autobiographies, 470, 633
    of authors, 653
    subjectivity of, 652
Award for Excellence in Poetry
        for Children, 26, 102
awards. *See* book awards

B

ballads, 418
basal reading programs, 667, 669
baseball, 526
Batchelder Award. *See* Mildred
        L. Batchelder Award
Battledore, 81
Beach, Richard, 55
beast tales, 280
BIA. *See* Bureau of Indian Affairs
BIB. *See* Biennale of Illustrations
        in Bratislava,
        Czechoslovakia
Bible stories
    collections of, 334–335
    as literature, 334–336
    morals of, 80
    picture books, 80
    single, 335–336
bibliographies, 601
Biennale of Illustrations in
        Bratislava, Czechoslovakia
        (BIB), 110
big books
    by children, 185
    expense of, 186
bilingual books, 227
binding, 22–23
biographies, 11, 35, 98, 470. *See*
        also autobiographies;
        historical fiction
    accuracy in, 638
    of artists, 644
    authentic, 633, 638
    of authors, 638, 649–650
    characters in, 640–641
    children in, 647
    of Civil War, 639
    collective, 651–652
    complete, 648–651
    as easy-reading books, 645
    entertainers, 635
    evaluation of, 635
    exclusions from, 638–639
    fictionalized, 633, 638
    as historical fiction, 541, 542
    illustrations in, 638, 641,
        642–645
    of illustrators, 651–652
    juvenile, 635

language in, 639–640
    narrators in, 640
    partial, 646–648
    photography in, 638, 648
    picture book, 642–645
    plot in, 635
    point of view in, 640
    research for, 638
    simplified, 645–646
    sports, 635
    as stories, 635
    theme in, 641
    of women, 648–649
birthdays, 229
Black Butterfly Press, 107
book(s). *See also* concept books;
        contemporary realistic
        fiction; fantasy; historical
        fiction; nonfiction; picture
        books; poetry; science
        fiction
    ABC, 41, 81, 154–157, 200, *676*
    activity, 606–607
    adventure, 87
    age-appropriate, *700*
    alphabet, 41, 81, 154–157, 200,
        676
    big, 185–186
    bilingual, 227
    chapter, 506
    clubs, 93
    cooking, 612
    counting, 157–167, 200
    craft, 611–612
    design, 22
    discussions about, 674–675
    easy-reading, 181–184, 645
    experiment, 606–607
    first, 143, 200
    format, 220–225, 603
    how-to, 611–612
    identification, 605–606
    informational, 587
    life-cycle, 606
    naming, 143, 605
    pop-up, 588
    predictable, 178–181
    problem, 497
    for reading programs,
        669–670
    reports, 669
    series, 34
    sketchbooks in, 677
    specialized, 590, 610, 611
    survey, 609
    talks, 673
    textbooks, 587, 612
    toy, 91, 146, 147
    trade, 667–668
    wordless, 170–172
book awards, 24–27

elderly. *See also* aging;
  grandparents; stereotypes
  in contemporary realistic
  fiction, 475
Elementary and Secondary
  Education Act of 1965, 93,
  107
Elkind, David, 39
Elucidarium, 80
emotion, in poetry, 410, 418–419
encyclopedias, 587
endpapers, 221–224
engravings, 209
enlightenment, 84
environment
  in picture books, 247–258
  in reading programs, 690–694
  in science fiction, 395
epics, 330–334
  of India, 331–332
Erikson, Erik, 43
Eskimos, 308
  mythology of, 326
etching, 209
evaluation
  of biographies, 635
  of counting books, 157
  of fantasy, 355
  of fiction, 13–15
  of nonfiction, 590
  of reading programs, 696
evil *vs.* good. *See also* didacticism
  in high fantasy, 385–386
experience
  of authors, 22
  of children, 4–5
  universality of, 8–9
  vicarious, 8
experiment books, 606–607
expository text, 10
expressionistic art, 216
extended families, 480–482
extra-terrestrials. *See* aliens

F

fables, 322
  characteristics of, 324
  editions of, 324–325
fact *vs.* fiction, 616–617
fact *vs.* theory, 594–595
faction, 598
fairy tales, 6, 38, 83, 87–88. *See
  also* fantasy
  modern, 352
  religious themes of, 354
families, 477–478. *See also*
  grandparents; parents;
  sibling rivalry
  conflicts in, 480
  extended, 480–482
  picture books for, 228
  single-parent, 482–485
  stories, 228
  in transition, 482–485
fantasy, 34, 87–88, 100–101. *See
  also* high fantasy; science
  fiction; tall tales
  animals and, 356
  consistency in, 355
  diversity of, 351

dolls in, 361
eccentric in, 363–366
endurance of, 350
evaluation of, 355
extraordinary worlds in,
  366–372
ghosts in, 376
human psyche and, 352
imaginary realms in, 380–384
imagination and, 350
insights from, 350
magic in, 372–373
metaphor and, 355
modern, 355
mysteries in, 378–379
occult and, 349
in picture books, 246–247
poetry and, 357
preposterous in, 363–366
psyche in, 352
realism of, 470
Scandinavian, 382
science fiction and, 389
self-understanding from, 379
supernatural in, 373–377
suspense in, 373–377
time-shift in, 377–380
toys in, 361
traditional lore in, 351
urban themes in, 359
female genital mutilation (FGM),
  490–491
feminism, 475
FGM. *See* female genital
  mutilation
fiction, 11, 12. *See also*
  contemporary realistic
  fiction; historical fiction
  characters in, 14, 17–18
  evaluation of, 13–15
  vs. fact, 616–617
  factories, 103
  plot in, 14, 15–16
  point of view in, 14, 20–22
  setting in, 14, 16
  style in, 14, 19–20
  theme in, 14, 16–17
fictionalized biographies, 633,
  638
finger plays, 83, 147–149
first books, 143, 200
First Words in Print, 125
folk art, 217
folktales, 5, 10, 11, 98–100. *See
  also* fairy tales
  for adults, 277
  of Africa, 305–307
  of African Americans, 316–317
  of Asia, 302–305
  beast, 280
  of Canada, 307–308
  of Caribbean, 318–322
  characters in, 284
  of China, 303–304
  cumulative, 279
  of France, 296
  functions in, 277
  of Germany, 294–295
  of Great Britain, 291–294
  of India, 300–302
  of Japan, 304
  of Jews, 299–300

of Korea, 304–305
of Mexico, 319–322
of Middle East, 300–302
modern, 243–245
of Native Americans, 107,
  308–316
oral history of, 278
origin of, 275
plot structures of, 281–284
pourquoi, 279
realistic, 281
of Russia, 277, 298–299
of Scandinavia, 295–296
of South America, 318–322
of United States, 307–308
wonder, 280–281
foreshadowing, 675
formal operations, 39
format
  components of, 603
  of picture books, 220–225
foster homes, 484–485
France, 296
Frankfurt Book Fair, 110
free verse, 420–421
Freedom to Read Foundation,
  702
Freud, Sigmund, 276
friendships
  among adolescents, 488
  broken, 489
  building of, 487–489
  cross-gender, 488
future, 394–398

G

gangs, 491, 494
Gardner, Howard, 41
gay themes, 22
gender
  girls *vs.* boys, 34–36
  stereotypes, 227
generalizations, 594
Germany, 294–295
ghosts, 376
Gilligan, Carol, 42
girls
  vs. boys, 34–36
  in sports stories, 525–526
glossaries, 601
good *vs.* evil, 385–386
gouache, 213
grandparents, 228
graphic organizers, 681–683
Great Britain
  characters from, 294
  folktales of, 291–294
Great Depression, 574
Greek mythology, 278, 327–329,
  331
Greenfield Review Press, 107
Guatemala, 512
Guttenberg, 81
Guys Read, 475

H

haiku, 421
Haiti, 513–514

Hans Christian Andersen Medal,
  26, 109
happy endings, 5
Harlem Renaissance, 106
harlequinades, 89
HarperCollins, 107
Henry VIII, 81
heroes. *See also* superheroes
  of legend, 330–334
  of Middle Ages, 332–334
  mythology of, 326–327
heterosexism, 96
hierarchy of needs, 43
high fantasy, 101
  adventures in, 386–389
  audience of, 384–385
  evil *vs.* good in, 385–386
  imaginary realms in, 384
  King Arthur in, 385–386
  quests in, 386–389
  sequels and, 384
Hispanic Americans, 507–508
historical fiction, 102, 471
  about American frontier,
    563–566
  about American Revolution,
    562–563
  about ancient times, 550
  about Cambodia, 579
  about China, 554
  about civil rights, 573
  about Civil War, 566–571
  about colonial America,
    560–562
  about Crusades, 551
  about early Asia, 554
  about early Britain, 550–551
  about economic revolution,
    571–573
  about Egypt, 550
  about Great Depression, 574
  about immigrants, 572–573
  about Japanese Americans,
    578
  about Middle Ages, 551–553
  about Native Americans,
    555–560
  about prehistoric times, 548
  about Renaissance, 553
  about Roman Empire, 550
  about war, 574–579
  accuracy in, 546
  biographies as, 541
  criteria for, 545–548
  language in, 546–547
  picture books of, 542
  popularity of, 541
  series books of, 541–542
  types of, 543–545
  value of, 542–543
historiography, 546
history, 35
Holocaust, 3, 542
  in picture books, 259
homosexuality, 104, 491. *See also*
  gay themes; lesbian themes
Honor Books, 25
Hornbooks, 81
horse stories, 523
how-to books, 611–612
Hudson River School, 213
Hume, David, 84

Grades 2–4

Burnett, Francis Hodgson. *The Secret Garden.* Illustrated by Tasha Tudor. Harper, 1987.

Byars, Betsy. *Keeper of the Doves.* Viking, 2002.

Creech, Sharon. *Ruby Holler.* HarperCollins, 2002.

de Regniers, Beatrice Schenk, ed. *Sing a Song of Popcorn.* Scholastic, 1988.

DiCamillo, Kate. *Mercy Watson to the Rescue.* Candlewick, 2005.

English, Karen. *Francie.* Farrar, 1999.

Fleischman, Paul. *Weslandia.* Illustrated by Kevin Hawkes. Candlewick, 1999.

Fleischman, Sid. *The Whipping Boy.* Illustrated by Peter Sis. Greenwillow, 1986.

Fritz, Jean. *Where Do You think You're Going, Christopher Columbus?* Illustrated by Margot Tomes. Putnam, 1980.

Giblin, James Cross. *The Mystery of the Mammoth Bones: And How It Was Solved.* HarperCollins, 1999.

Greenfield, Eloise. *Honey I Love and Other Poems.* Illustrated by Leo Dillon and Diane Dillon. Crowell, 1978.

Hamilton, Virginia. *Wee Winnie Witch's Skinny: An African American Scare Tale.* Illustrated by Barry Moser. Scholastic, 2003.

Hesse, Karen. *Just Juice.* Scholastic, 1998.

Hill, Kirkpatrick. *The Year of Miss Agnes.* McElderry, 2000.

Horvath, Polly. *The Pepins and Their Problems.* Farrar, 2004.

Lester, Julius. *The Old African.* Illustrated by Jerry Pinkney. Dial, 2005.

———. *The Tales of Uncle Remus: The Adventures of Brer Rabbit.* Illustrated by Jerry Pinkney. Dial, 1987.

Lewis, C. S. *The Lion, the Witch, and the Wardrobe.* Illustrated by Pauline Baynes. Macmillan, 1961.

Lisle, Janet Taylor. *The Lost Flower Children.* Philomel, 1999.

MacLachlan, Patricia. *Sarah, Plain and Tall.* Harper, 1985.

Matthews, L. S. *Fish.* Delacorte, 2004.

McKay, Hilary. *Saffie's Angel.* McElderry, 2002.

Meddaugh, Susan. *Cinderella's Rat.* Houghton, 2002.

Melmed, Laura Kraus. *Capital! Washington from A to Z.* Illustrated by Frané Lessac. HarperCollins, 2003.

Millman, Isaac. *Hidden Child.* Farrar, 2005.

O'Malley, Kevin. *Captain Raptor and the Moon Mystery.* Walker, 2005.

Philip, Neal. *Stockings of Buttermilk: American Folktales.* Illustrated by Jacqueline Marr. Clarion, 1999.

Pullman, Philip. *I Was A Rat.* Knopf, 2000.

Rathman, Peggy. *Officer Buckle and Gloria.* Putnam, 1995.

Simon, Seymour. *Crocodiles and Alligators.* HarperCollins, 1999.

Spinelli, Jerry. *Loser.* HarperCollins, 2002.

Stanley, Diane. *Saladin: Noble Prince of Islam.* HarperCollins, 2002.

Tchana, Katrin. *Sense Pass King: A Story from Cameroon.* Trina Schart Hyman. Holiday, 2002.

Weatherford, Carole Boston. *Freedom on the Menu: The Greensboro Sit-ins.* Illustrated by Jerome Lagarrigue. Dial, 2004.

Winthrop, Elizabeth. *Squashed in the Middle.* Illustrated by Pat Cummings. Holt, 2005.

Grades 4–6

Allison, Jennifer. *Gilda Joyce, Psychic Investigator.* Dutton, 2005.

Arnold, Louise. *Golden and Grey.* McElderry 2005.

Babbitt, Natalie. *Tuck Everlasting.* Farrar, 1975.

Bartoletti, Susan. *Kids On Strike.* Houghton, 1999.

Birdsall, Jeanne. *The Penderwicks; A Summer Tale of Four Sisters, Two Rabbits, and a Very Interesting Boy.* Knopf, 2005.

Blumberg, Rhoda. *Shipwrecked! The True Adventures of a Japanese Boy.* HarperCollins, 2001.

Boyce, Frank. *Millions.* HarperCollins, 2004.

Broach, Elise. *Shakespeare's Secret.* Holt, 2005.

Bruchac, Joseph. *The Winter People.* Dial, 2002.

Curtis, Christopher Paul. *Bud, Not Buddy.* Delacorte, 1999.

Erdrich, Louise. *The Game of Silence.* HarperCollins, 2005.

Fine, Anne. *Up On Cloud Nine.* Delacorte, 2002.

Fletcher, Ralph. *A Writing Kind of Day: Poems for Young Poets.* Boyds Mills, 2005.

Freedman, Russell. *Lincoln: A Photobiography.* Clarion, 1987.